D1613488

On the Trail
of the
Buffalo Soldier II

Thomas Elzey Polk was born to free parents in Upper Trappe, Maryland, on June 11, 1860, and lived eighty years. He was a farmer, sailor, and soldier and learned to read and write in the Army. He was one of three men named Thomas Polk in the Ninth Cavalry. His son, Everett Polk, helped found the Thomas Elzey Polk Chapter of the 9th and 10th (Horse) Cavalry Association. *Picture Courtesy of Ulysses and Velmar Polk Reunion Committee*

On the Trail
of the
Buffalo Soldier II

New and Revised
Biographies of African Americans
in the U.S. Army, 1866–1917

Compiled and Edited by
Irene Schubert
Frank N. Schubert

AN SR BOOK

THE SCARECROW PRESS, INC.
Lanham, Maryland • Toronto • Oxford
2004

An SR Book

SCARECROW PRESS, INC.

Published in the United States of America
by Scarecrow Press, Inc.
A wholly owned subsidiary of The Rowman & Littlefield Publishing Group, Inc.
4501 Forbes Boulevard, Suite 200, Lanham, Maryland 20706
www.scarecrowpress.com

PO Box 317
Oxford
OX2 9RU, UK

British Library Cataloguing in Publication Information Available

Library of Congress Cataloging-in-Publication Data

On the trail of the buffalo soldier II: new and revised biographies of African Americans in the U.S. Army, 1866–1917 / compiled and edited by Irene Schubert, Frank N. Schubert.
    p. cm.
  Includes bibliographical references and index.
  ISBN 0-8420-5079-5 (cloth : alk. paper)
  1. African American soldiers—Biography. 2. United States Army—Biography. 3. African American soldiers—History—20th century. 4. African American soldiers—History—19th century. I. Schubert, Irene, 1939– II. Schubert, Frank N.
U52 .O5 2004
355'.0092'396073—dc22   2003023427

In memory of

Aune Hermanson Kettunen (1912–1985)

and

Aina Hermanson (1914–1997)

IRENE SCHUBERT earned a Master of Library Science degree from the University of Denver. After more than ten years as a reference librarian in academic libraries, she joined the Congressional Research Service at the Library of Congress. During her twenty-two-year career at the Library, she also managed the Newspaper and Current Periodical Reading Room for four years and served for seven years as chief of the Preservation Reformatting Division in the Preservation Directorate. She retired in 2002.

FRANK SCHUBERT is the author and editor of four books on buffalo soldiers, including the original volume of *On the Trail of the Buffalo Soldier* (1995) and *Black Valor: Buffalo Soldiers and the Medal of Honor, 1870–1898* (1997). His most recent book is *Voices of the Buffalo Soldier: Records, Reports, and Recollections of Military Life and Service in the West* (2003). He retired in 2003 after twenty-seven years as a historian in the U.S. Department of Defense. Dr. Schubert is a graduate of Howard University and a Vietnam veteran. He holds a doctorate in history from the University of Toledo.

Contents

Acknowledgments

Like the original volume, this one would not have been possible without the help and support of friends, colleagues, and fellow buffalo soldier enthusiasts. We would like to thank Patrick Bowmaster, Booker T. Brooks, Thomas R. Buecker, Tony Burroughs, Lee N. Coffee, Roger Cunningham, Sandy Dickerson, Dr. William A. Dobak, Karla Dotson-Leger, Patricia Erickson, Gloria Haley, Mike Kaliski, Judith B. Lang, Margaret A. Lewis, Erwin D. Polk, Eva Slezak, George Sorenson, and Fachon A. Walker for sharing their research and their knowledge. We would also like to thank our friends at Scholarly Resources, with whom it is always a pleasure to work: Richard M. Hopper, Linda Pote Musumeci, James L. Preston, and Carolyn Travers. (Editor's note: Scholarly Resources, Inc., has been acquired by The Rowman & Littlefield Publishing Group, Inc.)

Introduction

SINCE THE PUBLICATION OF *On the Trail of the Buffalo Soldier* in 1995, a wide variety of new material on the African American men who served in the Army between the Civil War and World War I has continued to become available. New books appear frequently, new data bases are posted on the World Wide Web, and descendants of soldiers have reacted to the original volume by contacting us and sharing information. This book represents our efforts to compile this supplemental material into a single source and expand still further our knowledge of this fascinating group of soldiers and their families. It also corrects some errors in the earlier volume.

In addition to more than 2,000 new entries and about 1,000 revised ones, this volume offers two significant lists in the Appendix. One table contains the names of the sixty-one soldiers who were awarded the Certificate of Merit for valor or bravery, along with the dates and places of the action recognized. The other identifies 168 armed clashes, ranging from small skirmishes to major battles, in which black soldiers fought Indians. A Bibliography of the sources of new biographical information is also included.

Overall, the entries follow the same format used in the original volume. They start with the name, last rank attained, and military organization, then proceed with summaries of data and the sources of the information. Rather than divide the data in two, entries in the original book to which new details have been added have been carried over into this volume. In many cases, the new information may be as limited as the addition of another source or a change in a date. Old material in these entries is preceded by ‡.

In the entries themselves, personal names are spelled as they appear in the sources cited. For main entries, we have chosen the version that seems most accurate, based on frequency, source, and version used in the 1995 edition of *On the Trail of the Buffalo Soldier*. Variations are cross-referenced to entries that may appear in either volume. Full names have been provided whenever possible, even when the cited sources give only title or rank and last name. For some of the entries, gathered about twenty-five years ago, sources were not documented; therefore, a few of the entries lack citations.

Standard state abbreviations are used for all U.S. place names at first mention under a soldier's name to facilitate locating sites, including forts. Place names may also appear in the entries as they did in the original sources. Variations are cross-referenced in the Index at the end of this volume. We have listed the sources consulted to verify place names in the introduction to the Index.

Abbreviations

AAAG	Acting Assistant Adjutant General	LS	Letters Sent
AAG	Assistant Adjutant General	LTC	Lieutenant Colonel
ACP	Appointment, commission, and personal	Mass Inf	Massachusetts Infantry
		MG	Major General
Adj	Adjutant	MHI	Military History Institute
AG	Adjutant General	Misc	Miscellaneous
AGO	Adjutant General's Office	NCO	Noncommissioned Officer
Ala Inf	Alabama Infantry	NCS	Noncommissioned Staff
ANJ	*Army and Navy Journal*	NSHS	Nebraska State Historical Society
ANR	*Army and Navy Register*	Ord Sgt	Ordnance Sergeant
AR	*Annual Report*	OTT	*On the Trail of the Buffalo Soldier* (1995)
Bde	Brigade		
Bks	Barracks	PFC	Private First Class
Bn	Battalion	PI	Philippine Islands
Cav	Cavalry	PMG	Paymaster General
CG	Commanding General	Pvt 1st Cl	Private First Class
CO	Commanding Officer	QM	Quartermaster
Comsy Sgt	Commissary Sergeant	QM Sgt	Quartermaster Sergeant
DeptColo	Department of Colorado	RBHL	Rutherford B. Hayes Library
DeptMo	Department of the Missouri	Regt	Regiment
DeptPlatte	Department of the Platte	RO	Regimental Order
Det	Detachment	SD	Special Duty
DivMo	Division of the Missouri	SecWar	Secretary of War
DivPI	Division of the Philippines	SG	Surgeon General
DP	Department of the Platte	Sgt Maj	Sergeant Major
ES	Endorsements Sent	SO	Special Order
Ft	Fort	Sqdn	Squadron
GC	General Correspondence	Sup Sgt	Supply Sergeant
GCM	General Court Martial	Tech Sgt	Technical Sergeant
GCMO	General Court Martial Order	TRP	Troop
GO	General Order	TS	Telegrams Sent
HQ	Headquarters	USA	United States Army
Ill Inf	Illinois Infantry	USCT	United States Colored Troops [Civil War]
Inf	Infantry		
IT	Indian Territory	USMA	United States Military Academy
Kans Inf	Kansas Infantry	USV	United States Volunteers
KSHS	Kansas State Historical Society	VA	Veterans Administration
LR	Letters Received	Vol	Volunteer

I lost my health on account of my company being without water
half of the time as we could only find water in the mountains and
would have to make dry camp and travel all day in the hot sun
and dust without any water to drink either for ourselves or our horses.
—Sergeant John Casey, recalling the Geronimo campaign of 1886,
VA Pension File SC 138442

You lynch, you torture, and you burn negroes in the south, but we swear
by all that is good and holy that you shall not outrage us and our people
right here under the shadow of "Old Glory," while we have shot and shell,
and if you persist we will repeat the horrors of San Domingo—we will reduce your houses
and firesides to ashes and send your guilty souls to hell. "Who would be free
must themselves strike the blows." We have spoken and
we call upon the gods to witness that we are in earnest.
—Ninth Cavalry Broadside, "500 Men with the Bullet or the Torch,"
Fort Robinson, Nebraska, 1893

I said to the conductor so that everyone could hear,
that I ride only with the two leading races
of this country through Texas—
the white man and the Negro.
I do not ride with greasy Mexicans.
—Chaplain George Prioleau, *Cleveland Gazette*, August 19, 1899

A

ABBOTT, James W.; Ord Sgt; U.S. Army. ‡Born in Hendricks County, KY, 1860; occupation soldier; regimental clerk, 24 Mar 1884; discharged 29 Jul 1886; character excellent; Ht 5'8", complexion brown; reenlisted and joined regiment at Ft Sill, Indian Territory, 2 Aug 1886; marksman, 1883–87; made corporal, E/24th Infantry, 9 Dec 1886; reduced to ranks at own request, 6 Feb 1888; promoted to regimental sergeant major, 17 Feb 1889; extra duty as schoolteacher, Ft Bayard, NM, 13 Jun 1886–17 Feb 1889; detached service with Band/24th Infantry, Deming, NM, 18–22 Apr 1891, to receive president of the United States; discharged from Ft Bayard, 1 Aug 1891, character good; single; additional pay $2 per month, retained $60, clothing $7.19, deduction for subsistence stores $16.83. SOURCE: Descriptive Book, 24 Inf NCS & Band.

‡Mentioned as schoolteacher, Ft Bayard, temporarily reassigned from San Carlos, AZ, 1888. SOURCE: Billington, *New Mexico's Buffalo Soldiers*, 162.

‡Enlisted and joined regiment, Ft Bayard, 7 Aug 1891; on detached service, Washington, DC, conducting insane soldier to asylum, 4–19 Apr 1893; detached service, Trinidad, CO, with four companies and regiment headquarters protecting railroads from strikers; discharged from Ft Bayard, 6 Aug 1896, character excellent; single; additional pay $3 per month, retained $55.30, clothing $7.43. SOURCE: Descriptive Book, 24 Inf NCS & Band.

‡Author of neat roster of noncommissioned officers, correct to Apr 1890. SOURCE: *ANJ* 27 (3 May 1890): 679.

Lewis Hendricks, 24th Infantry, died Ft Bayard, Aug 1890; resolution of respect signed by James W. Abbott, Goodson M. Newlands, and John E. Green, of Noah's Ark Lodge, No. 3207, Grand Union of Odd Fellows, Ft Bayard. SOURCE: Cleveland *Gazette*, 30 Aug 1890.

‡Mentioned, at Ft Bayard, 1892. SOURCE: *ANJ* 29 (26 Mar 1892): 537.

Sergeant, 24th Infantry, stationed at Ft Bayard, Jan 1894, one of three managers of masquerade ball given by company. SOURCE: Schubert, *Voices of the Buffalo Soldier*, 198.

Appointed ordnance sergeant, 22 Jun 1897, from regimental sergeant major, 24th Infantry. SOURCE: Dobak, "Staff Noncommissioned Officers."

‡Appointed ordnance sergeant; with 24th Infantry since initial enlistment on 29 Jul 1881; now at Ft Douglas, UT. SOURCE: *ANJ* 34 (7 Aug 1897): 907.

ABBOTT, Winney; Private; K/25th Inf. Born in Maryland; Ht 5'6", black complexion; occupation laborer; enlisted in A/39th Infantry for three years on 16 Oct 1867, age 22, at New Orleans, LA; confined fifteen days under sentence; transferred to K/25th Infantry at Jackson Bks, LA, 20 Apr 1869. SOURCE: Descriptive Roll of A/39th Inf.

ACKFORTH, William; Private; G/9th Cav. Received Philippine Campaign Badge number 11819 for service as private in G/25th Infantry, 16 Oct 1901–11 Jul 1902; private in 9th Cavalry, Ft Leavenworth, KS, Mar 1905. SOURCE: Philippine Campaign Badge Recipients; Philippine Campaign Badge list, 29 May 1905.

ADAMS, Alexander; Corporal; H/10th Cav. ‡Pvt. Alex Adams, 10th Cavalry, not yet received at Ft Leavenworth, KS, from Jefferson Barracks, MO. SOURCE: Adj, Ft Leavenworth, to HQ, Jefferson Bks, 9 Oct 1866.

Cpl. Alexander Adams, H/10th Cavalry, died 6 Apr 1869 in hospital at Ft Wallace, KS. SOURCE: Regimental Returns, 10th Cavalry, 1869.

ADAMS, David; Private; C/10th Cav. Acquitted by military court of mutiny, 1871. SOURCE: Dobak and Phillips, *The Black Regulars*, 324–25.

ADAMS, Henry; Sergeant; 39th Inf. In 1880 told congressional committee investigating black life in the South that he was an experienced faith healer. SOURCE: Dobak and Phillips, *The Black Regulars*, 140.

ADAMS, Howard; Private; 9th Cav. Received Philippine Campaign Badge number 11758 for service as private in F/9th Cavalry; in 9th Cavalry, Ft Leavenworth, KS, Mar 1905. SOURCE: Philippine Campaign Badge list, 29 May 1905.

‡Cook, F/9th Cavalry, at Ft D. A. Russell, WY, in 1910; resident of Macon, GA. SOURCE: *Illustrated Review: Ninth Cavalry*, with picture.

ADAMS, John; Private; G/9th Cav. Received Philippine Campaign Badge number 11820 for service as private, 3 Mar 1902–16 Sep 1902; private in G/9th Cavalry, Ft Leavenworth, KS, Mar 1905. SOURCE: Philippine Campaign Badge Recipients; Philippine Campaign Badge list, 29 May 1905.

ADAMS, John D.; Private; D/9th Cav. With Captain Dodge at battle at Milk River, CO, 2–10 Oct 1879. SOURCE: Miller, *Hollow Victory,* 167, 206–7.

ADAMS, John Q.; Private; C/9th Cav. Cited for bravery against Apaches in the Florida Mountains, NM, in 24 Jan 1877 by Lt. Henry Wright; served in D/10th Cavalry against Utes in October 1878. SOURCE: Schubert, *Black Valor,* 46, 63; Leckie, *The Buffalo Soldiers,* 179.

ADAMS, King; Private; H/10th Cav. Born in Jackson, MS, 1862; enlisted San Antonio, TX; occupation laborer; Ht 5'10"; black complexion, hair, and eyes; served 28 Nov 1883–1 Feb 1886; at Ft Davis, TX, spring 1884.

Sentenced to six months hard labor, fined $10 per month for six months, Ft Grant, AZ, 21 Dec 1885, for failure to guard prisoner Pvt. Houston Robinson properly; sentenced to dishonorable discharge and one year at Alcatraz Island, CA, early 1886. SOURCE: Sayre, *Warriors of Color,* 1–4.

ADAMS, Walter; D/25th Inf. Died at Ft McIntosh, TX, 8 Mar 1907; buried at Fort Sam Houston National Cemetery, Section PE, number 411. SOURCE: Buffalo Soldiers Interred in Fort Sam Houston National Cemetery.

AGUIRRE, Martiriano; Private; U.S. Army. Seminole Negro Scout, served 1878–81. SOURCE: Schubert, Consolidated List of Seminole Negro Scouts.

Born in Mexico; Mexican parents; first enlisted for one year 8 Apr 1878, Ft Clark, TX; age 22, Ht 5'5", hair black, eyes brown, copper complexion; enlisted three additional times, one year each, at Ft Clark; last discharged at Ft. Clark, 14 May 1882; 1880 Census lists wife Marcebia, age 18. SOURCE: Swanson, 1.

AIKEN, John H.; Private; L/10th Cav. ‡Original member of 10th Cavalry; in troop when organized, Ft Riley, KS, 21 Sep 1867. SOURCE: McMiller, "Buffalo Soldiers," 78.

Died 28 Apr 1870 of disease at Ft Arbuckle, OK. SOURCE: Regimental Returns, 10th Cavalry, 1870.

ALEXANDER, Alfred; QM Sgt; D/9th Cav. At Ringgold Barracks, TX, 1899; warned by residents that it was unsafe to go to town of Rio Grande City, TX, after payday. SOURCE: Leiker, *Racial Borders,* 126.

ALEXANDER, Benjamin A.; Private; 25th Inf. Served in 49th U.S. Volunteer Infantry; discharged 22 Dec 1913; died 20 Jul 1921; buried in plot A 97 at San Francisco National Cemetery. SOURCE: San Francisco National Cemetery.

ALEXANDER, James H.; Sergeant; 10th Cav. ‡A pair of his gloves was stolen by Pvt. Charles Waters, when both were in L/10th Cavalry, Ft Bayard, NM, 1889. SOURCE: Billington, *New Mexico's Buffalo Soldiers,* 168.

‡At Ft Apache, AZ, 1890, sergeant, D/10th Cavalry, subscribed $.50 to testimonial to General Grierson. SOURCE: List of subscriptions, 23 Apr 1890, 10th Cavalry papers, MHI.

‡An excellent noncommissioned officer who should command, according to John E. Lewis, H/10th Cavalry, in letter, Lakeland, FL, 5 Jun 1898. SOURCE: Gatewood, *"Smoked Yankees,"* 36.

‡Served in 10th Cavalry, 1898; remained in U.S. during war with Spain. SOURCE: Cashin, *Under Fire with the Tenth Cavalry,* 346.

‡Was visited at Thanksgiving 1898, Camp Forse, AL, by his wife and family from Ft Assiniboine, MT. SOURCE: Richmond *Planet,* 3 Dec 1898.

‡Promoted from corporal. SOURCE: *ANJ* 35 (22 Jan 1898): 382.

Died 1 Oct 1906, buried in plot A W 21 at Ft Bayard, NM. SOURCE: "Fort Bayard National Cemetery, NM, Records of Burials"; Burials at Fort Bayard National Cemetery, NM.

In H/10th Cavalry; buried 1 Oct 1906, section A, row W, plot 21, at Ft Bayard, NM. SOURCE: Erickson, Burials at Fort Bayard National Cemetery, NM.

ALEXANDER, John Hanks; 2nd Lt; 9th Cav. ‡Born in Helena, AR, 6 Jan 1864; father had purchased mother and first three children from slavery by 1850; John H. was the fourth of seven; father was dry-goods merchant, first black justice of the peace in Arkansas, in state legislature from Phillips Co., died 1871. Went to Helena High School for blacks, was only graduate before abolition, worked selling papers, riding mail, other odd jobs; fall 1880 attended Oberlin after six months as teacher in Mississippi; worked summer in Cleveland hotel. Other United States Military Academy cadets were "very gentlemanly, friendly, and kind. The boys in my class treat me as well as could be desired, even some of them from the South acting very good-naturedly toward me. Today one of the gentlemen of the Senior class came home and expressed himself as glad to have me here. He gave me some good advice, and told me he would always be ready to help me if I needed assistance." SOURCE: Cleveland *Gazette,* 29 Nov 1884.

Ohio fourteenth congressional district alternate candidate for admission to West Point; admitted to U.S. Military

Academy, West Point, 1883; second African American graduate of West Point; lieutenant, 9th Cavalry, 1887–94; assigned to M/9th Cavalry, Ft Washakie, WY, Mar 1888–Oct 1891; transferred to I/9th Cavalry, Ft Robinson, NE, early 1892; received orders for transfer to Wilberforce University, Xenia, OH, for academic tour of duty 26 Jan 1894; died 26 Mar 1894. SOURCE: Kenner, *Buffalo Soldiers and Officers of the Ninth Cavalry*, 293–99.

‡Second black officer in regular Army, graduated from United States Military Academy in 1897; was "an inconspicuous second lieutenant for seven years with the Ninth Cavalry," and died in 1894 of natural causes. SOURCE: Thompson, "The Negro Regiments."

‡Recent graduate of USMA. SOURCE: Cleveland *Gazette*, 18 Jun 1887, with picture

‡Arrived at Ft Niobrara, NE, and tentatively assigned to A/9th Cavalry, according to Omaha *Excelsior*, 4 Aug 1887. SOURCE: *ANJ* 25 (6 Aug 1887): 23.

‡Reported for duty at Ft Robinson today: he is "quite small but very bright and pleasant." SOURCE: Corliss diary, vol. 2, entry for 1 Oct 1887, DPL.

‡Relieved from duty at Ft Robinson; to go to Ft Washakie for duty with M/9th Cavalry. SOURCE: *ANJ* 26 (24 Mar 1888): 694.

‡Mentioned. SOURCE: *ANJ* 27 (16 Nov 1889): 229; *ANJ* 27 (18 Jan 1890): 402.

‡To conduct horses and men transferred from C/9th Cavalry, Ft DuChesne, UT, to Ft Washakie. SOURCE: *ANJ* 28 (30 Aug 1890): 5.

‡Mentioned as first black officer at Ft DuChesne. SOURCE: Clark, "Twenty-fourth Infantry," 12.

‡To visit camp of Charlotte Light Infantry at Raleigh, NC, as instructor, 2–7 Nov 1891. SOURCE: Cleveland *Gazette*, 31 Oct 1891.

‡Acting adjutant, Ft Robinson, in absence of Lt. Grote Hutcheson. SOURCE: Cleveland *Gazette*, 18 Feb 1893.

‡Recently passed examination for first lieutenant at Ft Leavenworth, KS. SOURCE: Cleveland *Gazette*, 11 Nov 1893.

‡Died of apoplexy, in barbershop, Springfield, OH, 11 A.M., 26 Mar 1894. SOURCE: Cleveland *Gazette*, 31 Mar 1894.

‡When died, serving as military instructor, Wilberforce University. SOURCE: Work, *The Negro Year Book, 1912*, 76.

Appreciation and obituary by Ft Robinson post trader, W. E. Annin, published in Nebraska newspapers, reprinted. SOURCE: Schubert, *Voices of the Buffalo Soldier*, 200–203.

‡Orders 20, 9th Cavalry, Ft Robinson, 30 Mar 1894, mourned him and praised his "ability and energy" and his appreciation of "the delicate distinctions of social intercourse." SOURCE: Cleveland *Gazette*, 7 Apr 1894.

‡Drawing. SOURCE: Lynk, *The Black Troopers*, 145.

‡Camp Alexander, Newport News, VA, named for him. SOURCE: Cleveland *Gazette*, 26 Oct 1918.

‡Mentioned as United States Military Academy graduate. SOURCE: Billington, *New Mexico's Buffalo Soldiers*, 190.

ALEXANDER, Lewis; M/9th Cav. Born in Louisiana; black complexion; cannot read or write, age 26, Jul 1870, at Ft McKavett, TX. SOURCE: Bierschwale, *Fort McKavett*, 100.

ALEXANDER, Samuel H.; 1st Sgt; E/10th Cav. ‡Sergeant, F/10th Cavalry; served in 10th Cavalry in Cuba, 1898. SOURCE: Cashin, *Under Fire with the Tenth Cavalry*, 343.

‡Sergeant, B/10th Cavalry, on furlough at Cook's Ranch, NE, starting 22 Jul 1904, from Ft Robinson, NE. SOURCE: Regt Returns, 10 Cav, Jul 1904.

‡As first sergeant, E/10th Cavalry, participated in 9 Jan 1918 fight against Yaquis, Atasco Canyon, AZ. SOURCE: Wharfield, *10th Cavalry and Border Fights*, 7.

Born in Kentucky; died 23 Sep 1927; buried at Ft Huachuca Cemetery. SOURCE: Sage, Ft. Huachuca Cemetery.

ALEXANDER, Will; Private; 25th Inf. ‡Died of diarrhea, Maslinoc, Luzon, Philippines, 9 Jun 1901. SOURCE: *ANJ* 38 (3 Aug 1901): 1187.

Private, E/25th Infantry, died 9 Jan 1902; buried in plot A 911 at San Francisco National Cemetery. SOURCE: San Francisco National Cemetery.

ALLEN, Aberham E.; Private; G/24th Inf. Honorable discharge, 23 Feb 1891; died 27 Nov 1940; buried in plot E-WES542 at San Francisco National Cemetery. SOURCE: San Francisco National Cemetery.

ALLEN, Frank; Private; G/9th Cav. Private; issued Indian Wars Campaign Badge no. 1523 on 18 Oct 1909. SOURCE: Carroll, *Indian Wars Campaign Badge*, 44.

‡Veteran of Indian wars, Spanish-American War, and Philippine Insurrection; at Ft D. A. Russell, WY, in 1910. SOURCE: *Illustrated Review: Ninth Cavalry*.

ALLEN, Henry; Sergeant; H/10th Cav. ‡Born in Virginia; private, F/20th U.S. Colored Troops, 15 Oct 1864–7 Oct 1865; private and sergeant, H/10th Cavalry, 24 Aug 1869; private, D/10th Cavalry, 23 Aug 1882; corporal, 12 October 1892; sergeant, 15 Apr 1893; stationed at Ft Assiniboine, MT, in 1897. SOURCE: Baker, Roster.

Served at Ft Davis, TX, 1885. SOURCE: Sayre, *Warriors of Color*, 15.

‡Retired from Ft Assiniboine. SOURCE: *ANJ* 35 (30 Oct 1897): 156.

‡Retired from Ft Assiniboine, residing in Helena, MT, "and is doing well." SOURCE: Indianapolis *Freeman*, 11 Dec 1897.

ALLEN, Kendrick; Sergeant; C/9th Cav. ‡Sergeant, C/9th Cavalry, since 4 Aug 1883. SOURCE: Roster, 9 Cav, 1893.

Appointed sergeant 4 Aug 1883; in C/9th Cavalry at Ft Robinson, NE, Jan 1897. SOURCE: Ninth Cavalry, Roster of NCOs, 1897.

‡Retired from Ft Robinson. SOURCE: *ANJ* 35 (20 Nov 1897): 213; SO 267, AGO, 13 Nov 1897.

ALLEN, Samuel; Sergeant; A/38th Inf. ‡At Ft Cummings, NM, autumn 1867; acquitted of involvement in revolt but convicted of stealing greatcoat belonging to Pvt. John Hughes, A/38th Infantry, reduced to ranks, and fined $8 per month for three months. SOURCE: Billington, *New Mexico's Buffalo Soldiers*, 39, 41.

One of seven 38th Infantrymen acquitted by military court of mutiny, New Mexico, 1868. SOURCE: Dobak and Phillips, *The Black Regulars*, 324.

ALLEN, Walter; Private; A/9th Cav. Died 12 Sep 1902 on U.S. Army Transport *Sherman*; buried Nov 1902 in plot NEW A1190 at San Francisco National Cemetery. SOURCE: San Francisco National Cemetery.

ALLEN, William; Private; 25th Inf. Born in Barnwell, SC; Ht 5'7", black hair and eyes, dark complexion; occupation laborer, enlisted at age 22, Charleston, SC, 17 May 1881; left recruit depot, David's Island, NY, 2 Jul 1881, arrived Ft Randall, SD, 7 Jul 1881. SOURCE: Descriptive & Assignment Rolls of Recruits, 25 Inf.

ALLEN, William; Private; H/10th Cav. Born near Manchester, KY, 29 Jan 1856 (?); enlisted 17 Jan 1882 Cincinnati, OH; occupation shoemaker; Ht. 5'7", mulatto complexion, black hair and eyes; served in H/10th Cavalry; on a march to Eagle Springs, TX, in fall of 1882, returned to Ft Davis, TX, Dec 1882; at Fort Davis, April, Dec 1884, Jan 1885; appointed farrier, reduced to private 1 Feb 1885; at Ft Grant, AZ, May 1885; discharged 18 Jul 1885 on certificate of disability, Ft Grant, for gunshot wound, Ft Davis, Jan 1885, caused by bullet from pistol which fell out of his pocket, struck a table, and discharged; resided at Lebanon, OH, occupation minister, age 36 on 29 Nov 1897; married to Fannie Clouds, 21 Apr 1902; no children; died 10 Mar 1910; buried at #2 Cemetery, Eastern Kentucky Asylum, Lexington, KY. SOURCE: Sayre, *Warriors of Color*, 5–22, 360.

See **CASEY**, John F., First Sergeant, H/10th Cavalry

ALLEN, Willie; Private; 9th Cav. ‡Private in M/49th Infantry, engaged against enemy, Tuao, Cagayan, Philippines, 18 Oct 1900. SOURCE: *ANJ* 38 (11 May 1901): 901.

Received Philippine Campaign Badge number 11715 for service as private in E/9th Cavalry; in 9th Cavalry at Ft Leavenworth, KS, Mar 1905. SOURCE: Philippine Campaign Badge list, 29 May 1905.

ALLENSWORTH, Allen; Chaplain; 24th Inf. ‡Born 1842; escaped slavery to fight with Union in Civil War and stayed in Army; founder of black community in San Joaquin Valley, CA, called Allensworth, halfway between San Francisco and Los Angeles, 1908. SOURCE: *New York Times*, 22 Oct 1972.

Born in Kentucky; learned to read and write; sold several times; freed when Union army entered Louisville, KY; Civil War veteran; served in Army as male nurse; served on river gunboat in Navy; after discharge operated two restaurants in St Louis, MO, with brother, William; funded college education with sale of restaurants; teacher and missionary; attended theological seminary; injured in carriage accident in Manila, Philippines, while chaplain in 24th Infantry; after discharge settled with family in Los Angeles; with four others formed California Colony and Home Promotion Association to purchase 20 acres in Tulare County; founded colony in 1908; town grew to 80 acres and included school, library, post office, hotel, stores, livery stable, train station; town had girls' glee club, orchestra, brass band and Women's Improvement Club; Allensworth lived in Allensworth, CA, for six years until he died in 1914. SOURCE: *P G & E Progress*, Apr 1974, 8. Photocopy in authors' file.

Life and service to civilian believers as well as to soldiers, as teacher as well as clergyman, described. SOURCE: Dobak and Phillips, *The Black Regulars*, 116–18, 120, 123, 132–33.

‡His predecessor as teacher in Hopkinsville, KY, was Charles Spencer Smith, later African Methodist Episcopal bishop and doctor of divinity, who worked there Nov 1869–Jun 1870. SOURCE: Wright, *Centennial Encyclopedia of the AME Church*, 205.

‡Honorary Master's degree from Roger Williams University; superintendent of Sunday Schools, Kentucky State Baptist Convention and missionary, American Baptist Publication Society, for four years before taking Cincinnati congregation. SOURCE: Simmons, *Men of Mark*, 843–46.

‡"Mr. President: The bearer hereof, Rev. Mr. Allensworth, a Baptist Minister of Kentucky, desires to pay his respects to you, and if your time will permit, hold some conversation in reference to his people. I take pleasure in presenting him to you. Yr. obt servt, John M. Harlan." SOURCE: Harlan to Rutherford B. Hayes, Washington, DC, 31 Jan 1881, Hayes papers, RBHL.

‡Appointed chaplain, 24th Infantry, from Mound Street Church, Cincinnati, at $1,800 per year. SOURCE: Cleveland *Gazette*, 24 Apr 1886.

‡Reported for duty as chaplain, Ft Supply, Indian Territory, 2 Jul 1886, vice retired J. C. Laverty; Baptist ex-slave and Navy veteran; former teacher with Freedmen's Bureau; endorsed on application for chaplaincy by former owner, Mrs. A. P. Starbird. SOURCE: Fowler, *The Black Infantry*, 104–5.

‡Stationed at Ft Supply; during leave in Louisville, interviewed by Louisville *Commercial*, to which he spoke very highly of Army men: "There are several colored commissioned officers now in the Army—Chaplain Plummer, 9th Cav.; Lieut. Alexander, 9th Cav.; and myself and one cadet at West Point. As to how I am treated by the white officers, prudence suggests that I have not been in the service long enough to determine my status, from the fact that an officer's social status is governed by the time it takes him to become identified with his regiment or post. However, my social relations so far have been pleasant and considerate. This is one of the things I patiently allow to take its natural course." SOURCE: *ANJ* 25 (13 Aug 1887): 39.

‡Began in 1888 to train selected enlisted men as teachers; when War Department made elementary education compulsory for enlisted men, he was staffed and ready for influx of students; 118 men enrolled in his Ft Bayard, NM, school, 1889. SOURCE: Fowler, *The Black Infantry*, 105.

‡Supervised schoolchildren's viewing of amusements and fireworks, Ft Bayard, 4 Jul 1888. SOURCE: Cleveland *Gazette*, 14 Jul 1888.

‡"The pioneer colored chaplain of the army" spent week hunting in mountains and is reported as good there as he is as evangelist, "which is saying not a little." SOURCE: *ANJ* 26 (8 Dec 1888): 287.

‡His booklet *Outline of Course of Study and the Rules Governing Post Schools of Ft Bayard, N.M.* (Mar 1889) detailed graded levels of his program and reviewed content of each subject taught at every level. SOURCE: Fowler, *The Black Infantry*, 105.

‡Sponsored Literary and Debating Society, which met weekly in Ft Bayard school after duty hours, 1890. SOURCE: Fowler, *The Black Infantry*, 85.

‡His letter to Army chaplains, Ft Bayard, 18 Apr 1890, calls attention to National Education Association meeting in St. Paul, MN; chaplains should attend; could fill need for chaplains to convene; will show our interest in educational work and help overcome stereotype as placemen without concern for our men. SOURCE: *ANJ* 27 (3 May 1890): 680.

‡Recently delivered address in St. Paul on temperance in Army and spoke highly of canteen system; thought whole moral tone of Army was advancing and ascribed it to wise policy of War Department, aided by efforts of chaplains and line officers. SOURCE: *ANJ* 27 (9 Aug 1890): 922.

‡Asked by National Education Association to prepare paper on "The History and Progress of Education in the U.S. Army"; "The reverend gentleman is, to our knowledge, fully capable of handling the matter satisfactorily." SOURCE: *ANJ* 28 (25 Apr 1891): 590.

‡"The efficient superintendent of post schools" at Ft Bayard was asked by president of National Education Association to read paper on education at Toronto convention, 14–17 Jul; War Department refused his request to be ordered there. SOURCE: *ANJ* 28 (30 May 1891): 674.

‡Took leave to attend Toronto meeting of National Education Association and deliver paper on "Education in the United States Army." SOURCE: Fowler, *The Black Infantry*, 106.

‡Expects to leave Ft Bayard this week to spend until next Aug on leave. SOURCE: *ANJ* 28 (20 Jun 1891): 730.

‡Mentioned as second Afro-American chaplain. SOURCE: Cleveland *Gazette*, 29 Aug 1891.

‡Conducted public installation and dedication of Soldiers Home Lodge No. 3491, Grand United Order of Odd Fellows, Ft Grant, AZ, 4 Mar 1892; gave "very intelligent and interesting sermon" 6 Mar, then returned to post at Ft Bayard, 7 Mar. SOURCE: Cleveland *Gazette*, 19 Mar 1892.

‡Rejoined regiment at Ft Bayard after leave. SOURCE: *ANJ* 29 (12 Mar 1892): 502.

‡Detailed for duty pertaining to World's Columbian Exposition, Chicago. SOURCE: *ANJ* 30 (18 Feb 1893): 427.

‡Has opened cooking school at Ft Bayard, where chemistry of food is explained and cooking taught as science and art; kitchen of his quarters fitted up as model kitchen, where instructions are practically demonstrated. SOURCE: *ANJ* 31 (26 May 1894): 676.

‡Will be on leave from Ft Bayard for the summer "for the benefit of his health." SOURCE: *ANJ* 32 (11 May 1895): 604.

‡Daughter Eva at Ft Bayard appointed notary public by governor of New Mexico, according to St. Paul *Appeal*. SOURCE: Cleveland *Gazette*, 10 Oct 1896.

‡Post school, Ft Douglas, UT, "in a flourishing condition" under him, with 120 students and classes in grammar, arithmetic, history, printing, telegraphy, clerkship, signaling; graduates in clerkship readily detailed as clerks to commander, adjutant, quartermaster, and commissary. "There are few schools in the Army that are run on the plan of the one at Fort Douglas, at least if there is they are very seldom heard of. A school of this kind is very useful, and should be encouraged on every post of the United States." SOURCE: *ANJ* 34 (6 Feb 1897): 409.

‡His efforts as teacher discussed. SOURCE: Billington, *New Mexico's Buffalo Soldiers*, 161–63, with picture at 160.

‡Arrived at Ft Douglas with 24th Infantry in 1896. SOURCE: Clark, "Twenty-fourth Infantry," 58–60.

‡Quoted in Salt Lake City *Broadax* as saying that preachers should not hold political office. SOURCE: Cleveland *Gazette*, 13 Feb 1897.

‡At Ft Douglas, hosted Salt Lake City Ministers Association; doing remarkable job with post garden, with ten acres under cultivation and "great variety of vegetables." SOURCE: *ANJ* 34 (19 Jun 1897): 776.

‡Successfully recruited college graduates for 24th Infantry. SOURCE: Clark, "Twenty-fourth Infantry," 83.

‡His attitude regarding vice mentioned. SOURCE: Clark, "Twenty-fourth Infantry," 63.

‡His relations with Mormon leaders while at Ft Douglas mentioned. SOURCE: Clark, "Twenty-fourth Infantry," 65.

‡Daughter Nella spoke on "Confidence" to 24th Infantry's Christian Endeavor Society, Ft Douglas, Mar 1897. SOURCE: Clark, "Twenty-fourth Infantry," 68.

‡Went to Ogden, UT, from Ft Douglas on 27 Nov 1897 to deliver three lectures on 28 Nov 1897. SOURCE: *ANJ* 35 (4 Dec 1897): 253.

‡View of Spanish-American War. SOURCE: Stover, *Up from Handymen*, 109–10.

‡Authorized five-day leave on 26 Aug 1898. SOURCE: *ANJ* 36 (3 Sep 1898): 11.

‡With his wife at Presidio of San Francisco, entertained Rev. and Mrs. J. Ford of Los Angeles. SOURCE: *ANJ* 36 (17 Jun 1899): 1004.

‡"The Misses Allensworth" are visiting in Oakland from the Presidio. SOURCE: *ANJ* 36 (15 Jul 1899): 1100.

‡"The Misses Maryatt" of Oakland are guests of "The Misses Allensworth" at the Presidio. SOURCE: *ANJ* 36 (29 Jul 1899): 1148.

‡On Thursday, 24 Aug 1899, 6:30 P.M. at Soldiers Institute, Manila, Allensworth will give "Scoptoconical Projection"; "in simple language this is a new up to date limelight magic lantern with lots of slides"; all invited. SOURCE: Manila *Times*, 23 Aug 1899.

‡To preach on Sunday at 9:30 A.M. at Soldiers Institute, and marry Filipino couple. SOURCE: Manila *Times*, 2 Dec 1899.

‡Will deliver his humorous lecture "Humbugs" this evening at 6:30, Soldiers Institute. SOURCE: Manila *Times*, 8 Feb 1900.

‡To deliver his lecture on "Gems from the Life of Napoleon" tonight at YMCA, 7 P.M.; all invited. SOURCE: Manila *Times*, 16 Feb 1900.

‡"Chaplain Allensworth's lecture at the YMCA last night was given to a crowded room and proved not only interesting but amusing. The lecture presented certain phases of the life of the Famous General and Emperor . . . which he held up as examples to the American soldier." SOURCE: Manila *Times*, 17 Feb 1900.

‡Tomorrow to give sermon at YMCA, 10 A.M. SOURCE: Manila *Times*, 24 Feb 1900.

‡Lectured at Soldiers Institute, Manila, 28 Apr 1900, on "Rise and Fall of the Kiss"; "it might be suggested that it would be difficult to select a subject better fitted to develop homesickness in men thousands of miles from their home." SOURCE: *ANJ* 37 (16 Jun 1900): 985.

‡Experience in the Philippines discussed. SOURCE: Stover, *Up from Handymen*, 127–28.

‡His letter from Ft Harrison, MT, dated 4 Oct 1902, discusses accomplishments of 24th Infantry band and possibilities for men in it to advance and develop; praises regimental Sgt. Maj. Walter B. Williams, "one of the most efficient sergeant-majors of the Army." SOURCE: Indianapolis *Freeman*, 18 Oct 1902.

‡Promoted to major, 14 Jun 1904; one of four promoted out of fourteen who were eligible. SOURCE: Stover, *Up from Handymen*, 151.

‡Conducted church service for 174 men, Sunday, 10 Jul 1904, at Ft Robinson, NE; he "has a powerful influence among the enlisted men." SOURCE: Monthly Report, Chaplain Anderson, 1 Aug 1904, AGO File 53910.

‡Daughter Nella performed solo "Estella" at Christian Endeavor Society program, Ft Harrison, Nov 1904. SOURCE: Indianapolis *Freeman*, 17 Dec 1904.

‡At Ft Harrison, with his wife, entertained at dinner Mr. and Mrs. Clark of Helena, now "in the East on business." SOURCE: Indianapolis *Freeman*, 17 Dec 1904.

‡Relieved from duty with regiment and ordered home to retire. SOURCE: *ANR* 38 (1 Jul 1905): 21.

‡Reassigned to Los Angeles, CA, where he and his family will go on 17 Jul; address there at 1851 30th Place. SOURCE: Indianapolis *Freeman*, 15 Jul 1905.

‡Senior Army chaplain, now stationed in Los Angeles. SOURCE: Indianapolis *Freeman*, 19 Aug 1905.

‡Resignation offers opportunity for some aspiring young minister; place "is very desirable." SOURCE: Cleveland *Gazette*, 4 Oct 1905.

‡Retires as lieutenant colonel. SOURCE: Indianapolis *Freeman*, 14 Apr 1906.

‡Retires as lieutenant colonel, "the highest honor ever given an Afro-American in the army." SOURCE: Cleveland *Gazette*, 21 Apr 1906.

‡Lives in Los Angeles; replaced by Rev. Washington E. Gladden, Baptist minister of Denver. SOURCE: Cleveland *Gazette*, 12 May 1906, with picture of Allensworth.

‡"Lieutenant Colonel Allensworth, U.S.A., colored, has a movement on foot for the establishment of a Negro commonwealth in the United States. (It would be the worst mistake that the race could make.)" SOURCE: Washington *Bee*, 2 Nov 1907.

Enrolled in elementary school at age of 25 to learn to read; town of Allensworth, CA, founded by Allensworth and William Payne, thrived from 1908 to 1918 with 300 families; settlers purchased land parcels for about $300 an acre from Pacific Farming Co.; had an elected town council, Chamber of Commerce and post office; built a school and became a voting precinct in 1912 and later a judicial district with state's first black judge, Oscar Overr; water shortages and discovery of arsenic in drinking water in 1966 finished off the township; Allensworth home restored in Colonel Allensworth State Historic Park near Bakersfield, CA. SOURCE: *The Hanford Sentinel*, 11 May 1988, p 13. Photocopy in authors' files.

‡Mentioned. SOURCE: Work, *The Negro Year Book, 1912*, 76.

‡Mrs. Payne of Allensworth was guest of her uncle W. B. Wright of West 85th St. for some weeks, also visited her former home in Rendville, OH. SOURCE: Cleveland *Gazette*, 7 Sep 1912.

‡"Citizens of Allensworth, Cal., the Race town founded in the San Joaquin Valley by Col. Allensworth, backed by the Pacific Farming Co., is having its time, and the courts have been called upon to settle differences between the colonists and the Pacific Farming Co. The citizens have organized, raised funds, have a legal committee and have retained an irrigation attorney to force the farming co. to give what they declare due them.—Los Angeles (Cal.) *Liberator*." SOURCE: Cleveland *Gazette*, 16 Aug 1913.

‡Resided in Los Angeles; retired lieutenant colonel; killed in motorcycle accident, 1914. SOURCE: *Crisis* 9 (Nov 1914): 8.

‡Funeral 18 Sep 1914 was "much curtailed and simple" out of respect for wishes of his widow and daughters; memorial service conducted 27 Sep 1914 "when due tribute to our beloved leader was paid." SOURCE: Cleveland *Gazette*, 3 Oct 1914.

‡Mentioned as retired and deceased. SOURCE: Work, *The Negro Yearbook, 1918–1919*, 228.

‡Picture, "Col. Allen Allensworth, Reg'tal Chaplain, Died September 14, 1914." SOURCE: Muller, *The Twenty Fourth Infantry*, 285.

‡2nd Lt. Oscar Overr, 23rd Kansas Volunteer Infantry, resided in Allensworth. SOURCE: Beasley, *Negro Trailblazers*, 285.

‡Daughters Eva (Mrs. Harrie Skanks) and Nella (Mrs. L. M. Blodgett) "genuine gentlewomen of the old school of aristocracy." SOURCE: Beasley, *Negro Trailblazers*, 226.

‡Organized company for colonization of Negroes in California; subscription and purchase of lots; town site named for him. SOURCE: Beasley, *Negro Trailblazers*, 287.

‡Born a slave; educated at Baptist Roger Williams University, Nashville; appointed by American Baptist Association to travel and lecture to children; in Civil War, Spanish-American War, and Philippine Insurrection; retired to Los Angeles as lieutenant colonel. SOURCE: Beasley, *Negro Trailblazers*, 287.

‡Tragically died at hands of careless motorcyclist on streets of Monrovia, CA, near Los Angeles, Sunday morn-

ing, Sep 1914; while en route to preach at small Monrovia church, was run over when he stepped from Pacific Electric streetcar; "loved and respected by all who knew him." SOURCE: Beasley, *Negro Trailblazers*, 288.

‡Mrs. Josephine Leavell Allensworth stayed in San Francisco while he was in the Philippines and acted as treasurer for men of 24th Infantry; received their money and distributed it to their wives. When he retired, men of 24th presented him and his daughters with "handsome carved silver tray" and candelabra. She organized "Women's Improvement Club" of Allensworth, which established children's playground and other improvements; established public reading room named for her mother, Mary Dickson; was president of School Board. "A sincere club worker." SOURCE: Beasley, *Negro Trailblazers*, 226, 287.

‡Biography. SOURCE: Charles Alexander, *Battles and Victories of Allen Allensworth* (Boston, 1914), 435 pp.

‡Biographical sketches. SOURCE: Logan and Winston, eds., *Dictionary of American Negro Biography*, 13–14; Stover, *Up from Handymen*, 53–57.

‡Biographical sketch of Josephine L. Allensworth. SOURCE: Hine, ed., *Black Women in America*, 22–23.

Through the efforts of Cornelius Pope, draftsman for California Department of Parks and Recreation, California legislature determined town of Allensworth worthy of state park status; plans to develop Colonel Allensworth State Historic Park approved 14 May 1969. SOURCE: "Old Time Jubilee," 16 May 1987. Pamphlet in authors' files.

ALLENSWORTH, James; Private; B/24th Inf. Died 20 Mar 1912 at Camp Jossman, PI; originally buried at Military Cemetery, Augur Barracks, PI; buried in plot W SID934 at San Francisco National Cemetery. SOURCE: San Francisco National Cemetery.

ALLISON, Walter; Private; B/48th Inf. ‡Died of tuberculosis in the Philippines, 5 Jun 1900. SOURCE: *ANJ* 37 (6 Jun 1900): 999.

Died 5 Jun 1900 at San Fernando, Philippines; buried in plot NEW A 912 at San Francisco National Cemetery. SOURCE: San Francisco National Cemetery.

ALLMOND, Howard; Corporal; K/25th Inf. Born in Philadelphia, PA; Ht 5'4", light mulatto complexion; occupation soldier; enlisted in A/39th Infantry for three years on 10 Jun 1867, age 23, at Philadelphia; promoted to corporal 1 Nov 1868; transferred to K/25th Infantry at Jackson Bks, LA, 20 Apr 1869. SOURCE: Descriptive Roll of A/39th Inf.

ALSIE, Ross; Private; C/9th Cav. Praised for gallantry in action against Lipan Apaches, near Fort Davis, TX, Sep 1868. SOURCE: Kenner, *Buffalo Soldiers and Officers of the Ninth Cavalry*, 53.

ALSTON, Douglas; Private; C/49th Inf. ‡Died in the Philippines, 17 Oct 1900. SOURCE: *ANJ* 38 (3 Nov 1900): 235.

Died 17 Oct 1900; originally buried at San Fernando, PI; buried June 1907 in plot NEW A 936 at San Francisco National Cemetery. SOURCE: San Francisco National Cemetery.

ALSTON, Felix V.; Private; C/25th Inf. Died 12 Sep 1916; buried in plot WEST 1092-A at San Francisco National Cemetery. SOURCE: San Francisco National Cemetery.

ANDERSON, Amos; Private; 25th Inf. Died 1873, Ft Quitman, TX, as result of abdominal razor wound incurred in drunken brawl. SOURCE: Dobak and Phillips, *The Black Regulars*, 200.

ANDERSON, George; Private; K/10th Cav. Died 5 Feb 1875 of pneumonia at Ft Sill, OK. SOURCE: Regimental Returns, 10th Cavalry, 1875.

ANDERSON, Henry; F/9th Cav. Born in Kentucky; black complexion; cannot read or write, age 22, Jul 1870, at Ft McKavett, TX. SOURCE: Bierschwale, *Fort McKavett*, 96.

ANDERSON, Isaac; Farrier; G/9th Cav. ‡Farrier, Ft Robinson, NE, 1893.

‡Witness for defense in Barney McKay court martial, Ft Robinson, 1893; heard Pvt. Mathew Wyatt threaten to get McKay. SOURCE: Court Martial Records, McKay.

‡Private, relieved from extra duty with Quartermaster Department, Ft Robinson, as laborer. SOURCE: SO 86, Ft Robinson, 8 Aug 1896, Post Orders, Ft Robinson.

‡Authorized to reenlist as married soldier. SOURCE: Letter, AGO, 19 Aug 1896.

‡Family resides at Ft Robinson, claims indigence, dependent on charity of garrison for subsistence. SOURCE: CO, Ft Robinson, to CO, 9 Cav, 25 Jul 1898, LS, Ft Robinson.

Received Cuban Campaign Badge for service as private in B/24th Infantry, 22 Jun 1898–13 Aug 1898. SOURCE: Cuban Campaign Badge Recipients.

Received Philippine Campaign Badge number 11814 for service as farrier, 16 Sep 1900–16 Sep 1902; farrier in G/9th Cavalry, Ft Leavenworth, KS, Mar 1905. SOURCE: Philippine Campaign Badge Recipients; Philippine Campaign Badge list, 29 May 1905.

ANDERSON, James; Private; F/10th Cav. ‡Original member of 10th Cavalry; in troop when organized, Ft Leavenworth, KS, 21 Jun 1867. SOURCE: McMiller, "Buffalo Soldiers," 73.

Wounded by gunshot in left thigh in action against Indians, near Beaver Creek, KS, 21 Aug 1867. SOURCE: LR, DeptMo, 1867; Armes, *Ups and Downs*, 247; Schubert, *Voices of the Buffalo Soldier*, 20.

ANDERSON, James; Corporal; M/10th Cav. ‡Original member of 10th Cavalry; in troop when organized, Ft Leavenworth, KS, 15 Oct 1867. SOURCE: McMiller, "Buffalo Soldiers," 79.

Died 10 Sep 1869 in hospital at Ft Sill, OK. SOURCE: Regimental Returns, 10th Cavalry, 1869.

‡Commanding officer, M/10th Cavalry, reports in Dec 1869 that his company records are incomplete so he cannot furnish final statements regarding casualties Sergeant Jefferson and Corporal Anderson. SOURCE: ES, 10 Cav, 1866–77.

Died 10 Sep 1869, buried at Camp Douglas, UT. SOURCE: Record Book of Interments, Post Cemetery, 252.

ANDERSON, Jenon; Private; 9th Cav. Received Philippine Campaign Badge number 11873 for service as private in H/9th Cavalry; in 9th Cavalry at Ft Leavenworth, KS, Mar 1905. SOURCE: Philippine Campaign Badge list, 29 May 1905.

ANDERSON, John; Private; 9th Cav. Wounded himself in the leg while trying to stuff a pistol into his boot. SOURCE: Dobak and Phillips, *The Black Regulars*, 200.

ANDERSON, John B.; Private; B/25th Inf. Mustered in 14 July 1898, mustered out as private E/23rd Kansas Volunteer Infantry 10 Apr 1899; reenlisted 17 Jun 1899, discharged 16 Jun 1902, character excellent; reenlisted 17 Jun 1902, discharged 16 Jun 1905, character excellent; reenlisted 20 Jun 1905, discharged without honor 22 Nov 1906, Brownsville, TX. SOURCE: Powell, "Military Record of the Enlisted Men Who Were Discharged Without Honor."

‡Dishonorable discharge, Brownsville. SOURCE: SO 266, AGO, 9 Nov 1906.

ANDERSON, John H.; 1st Lt; D/48th Inf. ‡Private, A/9th Cavalry, and schoolteacher although not teaching, Ft Robinson, NE, 1 Nov 1893–30 Apr 1894. SOURCE: Reports of Schools, Ft Robinson, 1892–96.

‡On extra duty as schoolteacher, Ft Robinson. SOURCE: Order 8, 29 Jan 1894, Post Orders, Ft Robinson.

‡Appointed saddler sergeant, 9th Cavalry, Ft Robinson, 2 May 1896. SOURCE: *ANJ* 33 (9 May 1896): 652.

Appointed saddler sergeant 2 May 1896; in 9th Cavalry at Ft Robinson, Jan 1897. SOURCE: Ninth Cavalry, Roster of NCOs, 1897.

‡Promoted to sergeant major, 9th Cavalry, Ft Robinson, 6 Jul 1897, vice Jeremiah Jones, promoted to ordnance sergeant. SOURCE: *ANJ* 34 (17 Jul 1897): 854.

‡Sent to Hemingford, NE, to conduct deserter Frank H. Bosley, 8th Cavalry, to Ft Robinson. SOURCE: SO 42, 9 Mar 1898, Post Orders, Ft Robinson.

‡Served in Cuba as regimental sergeant major; commissioned second lieutenant, 10th Volunteer Infantry, 1898;

first lieutenant, 10th U.S. Volunteer Infantry, 1898; second lieutenant, 48th U.S. Volunteer Infantry, 1899. SOURCE: Cashin, *Under Fire with the Tenth Cavalry*, 360.

‡Served as squadron sergeant major, 9th Cavalry. SOURCE: *ANJ* 37 (9 Dec 1899): 344.

‡Mentioned as first lieutenant, D/48th Infantry. SOURCE: Beasley, *Negro Trailblazers*, 284.

ANDERSON, Levi; Private; D/10th Cav. Born in Williamsburg, SC; resided at enlistment in Allegheny, PA; awarded Distinguished Service Medal in lieu of certificate of merit for risking life in rescue of drowning comrade, 6 Jul 1911, Mallets Bay, near Ft Ethan Allen, VT. SOURCE: *Decorations, U.S. Army. Supplement I*, 35; AGO, Bulletin 9, 1912; Gleim, *The Certificate of Merit*, 61.

‡Served as officer, 368th Infantry, World War I; retired as private, D/10th Cavalry. SOURCE: *Crisis* 42 (Oct 1931): 346.

ANDERSON, Richard; Comsy Sgt; U.S. Army. From Missouri; veteran of 65th U.S. Colored Infantry; enlisted in B/9th Cavalry, at Baton Rouge, LA, 1866, became sergeant; after one enlistment, discharged, returned to St. Louis for nearly one year; reenlisted in regiment, became first sergeant. SOURCE: Dobak and Phillips, *The Black Regulars*, 82–83.

‡Sergeant, H/9th Cavalry, displayed extraordinary leadership against Nana, Gavilan Canyon, NM, Aug 1881. SOURCE: Billington, *New Mexico's Buffalo Soldiers*, 106–7; Kenner, *Buffalo Soldiers and Officers of the Ninth Cavalry*, 230.

Appointed post quartermaster sergeant 30 Jan 1885, from quartermaster sergeant, 9th Cavalry. SOURCE: Dobak, "Staff Noncommissioned Officers."

‡Appointed post quartermaster sergeant from regimental quartermaster sergeant, 9th Cavalry, 5 Feb 1885. SOURCE: Roster, 9 Cav, 1893.

‡Retired as commissary sergeant; narrates Victorio campaign. SOURCE: Steward, *The Colored Regulars*, 318–20.

ANDERSON, Robert; Lance Sgt; Band/10th Cav. ‡Private, Band/10th Cavalry, mentioned Mar 1874, as playing bass drum and cymbals. SOURCE: ES, 10 Cav.

‡Deposited $30 with paymaster, Ft Concho, TX, 29 Jan 1877. SOURCE: Adj, 10 Cav, to PMG, 30 Jan 1877, LS, 10 Cav, 1873–83.

‡Deposited $25 with paymaster, Ft Concho, 12 Mar 1877. SOURCE: Adj, 10 Cav, to PMG, 12 Mar 1877, LS, 10 Cav, 1873–83.

‡Deposited $80 with paymaster, Ft Concho, 7 May 1877. SOURCE: Adj, 10 Cav, to PMG, 7 May 1877, LS, 10 Cav, 1873–83.

‡At Ft Concho in 1877; "a gay darkey" who lived in tent on grounds of Colonel Grierson's quarters to look af-

ter his carriage and livestock. SOURCE: Miles, "Fort Concho in 1877," 31.

Lance sergeant, Band/10th Cavalry served at Ft Davis, TX, Oct 1884. SOURCE: Sayre, *Warriors of Color*, 83.

See **CASEY**, John F., First Sergeant, H/10th Cavalry

ANDERSON, Sandy; Private; Band/24th Inf. Died at Camp Eagle Pass, TX, on 3 Nov 1874; buried at San Antonio National Cemetery, Section F, number 1136. SOURCE: San Antonio National Cemetery Locator.

ANDERSON, William; Private; E/10th Cav. In Troop E/10th Cavalry stationed at Bonita Cañon Camp, AZ, 28 Feb 1886. SOURCE: Tagg, *The Camp at Bonita Cañon*, 231.

ANDERSON, William; Private; 9th Cav. Received Philippine Campaign Badge number 11874 for service as private in Company A, 24th Infantry and Troop H, 9th Infantry; in 9th Cavalry at Ft Leavenworth, KS, Mar 1905. SOURCE: Philippine Campaign Badge list, 29 May 1905.

ANDERSON, William; Musician; B/25th Inf. Enlisted 12 Aug 1905, discharged without honor as a musician 22 Nov 1906, Brownsville, TX. SOURCE: Powell, "Military Record of the Enlisted Men Who Were Discharged Without Honor."

ANDERSON, William; Sergeant; G/10th Cav. Sergeant when issued Indian Wars Campaign Badge number 1446 on 7 Sep 1909. SOURCE: Carroll, *Indian Wars Campaign Badge*, 42.

ANDERSON, William H.; C/25th Inf. Born in Maryland; black complexion; can read and write, age 26, 5 Sep 1870, at Ft McKavett, TX. SOURCE: Bierschwale, *Fort McKavett*, 109.

ANDERSON, William T.; Chaplain; 10th Cav. ‡Born a slave; mother led him to escape to Galveston, TX, to father, who was prominent merchant; worked five years as messenger for railroad and superintended African Methodist Episcopal Sunday School, Galveston; Texas Conference of African Methodist Episcopal Church sent him to Wilberforce University for three years, after which he supported himself with odd jobs; Mr. and Mrs. Stephen Watson (vice president, London Exchange Bank, Madison Co., OH) sent him to Howard University, where he graduated with honors, then to Homeopathic Medical College, Cleveland, OH, 1885; graduated 12 Mar 1888 with honors; superintendent, St. John's AME Sabbath School, Cleveland, going to Washington, DC, to practice medicine. SOURCE: Cleveland *Gazette*, 31 Mar 1888.

First black chaplain of 10th Cavalry, reported for duty in 1897. SOURCE: Dobak and Phillips, *The Black Regulars*, 117.

‡Born in Saguin, TX, 20 Aug 1859. SOURCE: Cashin, *Under Fire with the Tenth Cavalry*, 290.

‡Educated at Wilberforce, Howard, Cleveland Homeopathic Medical College; AME minister; chaplain since 1897 with 10th Cavalry, Ft Assiniboine, MT; major, Aug 1907; commander, U.S. Morgue, Manila, and chaplain, Ft William McKinley, 1909. SOURCE: *Colored American Magazine* 16 (Apr 1909): 223.

‡Arrived with bride at Urbana, OH. SOURCE: Cleveland *Gazette*, 28 Jul 1890.

‡Appointed to African Methodist Episcopal Church, Lima, OH. SOURCE: Cleveland *Gazette*, 13 Oct 1893.

‡Pastor, St. John's African Methodist Episcopal Church, Cleveland, May 1896–May 1897. SOURCE: *Encyclopedia of African Methodism* (1947), 357.

‡Ordered to duty by 1 Nov 1897, Ft Assiniboine. SOURCE: *ANJ* 35 (9 Oct 1897): 96.

‡Orders directing him to report amended to 11 Nov 1897. SOURCE: *ANJ* 35 (16 Oct 1897): 116.

‡Confirmed as chaplain by Senate, 16 Dec 1897. SOURCE: *ANJ* 35 (25 Dec 1897): 311.

‡Left Cleveland for 10th Cavalry and Ft Assiniboine, as new chaplain; reception in his honor at Forest City National Guard Armory, Forest Street. SOURCE: Cleveland *Gazette*, 6 Nov 1897.

‡En route to Ft Assiniboine 11 Nov and has conducted services twice per week since. SOURCE: Indianapolis *Freeman*, 11 Dec 1897.

‡Chastened for saying that he prefers the chaplaincy to "the best church in the country." SOURCE: Cleveland *Gazette*, 15 Jan 1898.

‡Defended as competent against attacks in *Gazette*; Mrs. Anderson "a lady of rare accomplishments" who plays organ and sings at his well-attended services. SOURCE: Indianapolis *Freeman*, 12 Feb 1898.

‡10th Cavalry to depart, with Chaplain Anderson staying at Ft Assiniboine as post commander. SOURCE: *ANJ* 35 (23 Apr 1898): 648.

‡As commander of Ft Assiniboine, first black officer to command military post. SOURCE: Stover, *Up from Handymen*, 111.

‡On arrival of Maj. Joseph M. Kelley at Ft Assiniboine, Anderson is to join his regiment. SOURCE: *ANJ* 35 (4 Jun 1898): 792.

‡In Cuba with regiment; physician by profession; commander Ft Assiniboine, 19 Apr–28 Jun 1898; at Ft MacIntosh, TX, 1899. SOURCE: Cashin, *Under Fire with the Tenth Cavalry*, 105, 290–91, picture on 290.

‡As one of several authors of *Under Fire with the Tenth Cavalry*. SOURCE: Cashin, *Under Fire with the Tenth Cavalry*.

‡Only black chaplain to serve with regiment in Cuba during war with Spain, 1898. SOURCE: Stover, *Up from Handymen*, 111.

‡On duty with regiment in Cuba, transferred from Gibara to Manzanillo. SOURCE: *ANJ* 36 (1 Jul 1899): 1047.

‡Anderson's letter from Manzanillo, 30 Jul 1899, gives biography of Signal Sgt. James A. Richards. SOURCE: Cleveland *Gazette*, 28 Oct 1899.

‡Post treasurer, Manzanillo, 12 Jan 1900; sanitary officer, 25 Jan 1900; exchange officer, 18 Jul 1901; on detached service at Holguin, Cuba, 20–30 Apr 1901; inspector of schools, Municipality of Manzanillo, May 1901–Apr 1902; two months' sick leave, from 22 Apr 1902; joined regiment at Ft Robinson, NE, 7 Jul 1902; post treasurer and in charge of library, 8 Jul 1902; on detached service on post, with regiment on practice march, 6–16 Sep 1902; in charge of post schools, 23 Sep 1903; on detached service on post, while regiment at Ft Riley, KS, 4 Oct–11 Nov 1903; absent with leave hunting 17–22 Oct 1904; left U.S. with regiment 3 Apr 1907 and took station at Ft William McKinley, Philippines; in charge of schools, 22 May 1907; post treasurer, 7 Aug 1907. SOURCE: Descriptive Book, 10 Cav Officers & NCOs.

‡His monthly reports from Ft Robinson, 1902–1906. SOURCE: AGO File 53910.

‡Played large part in development and success of 10th Cavalry YMCA. SOURCE: Indianapolis *Freeman*, 19 Jul 1902.

‡Ordered before retiring board: "President Taft seems determined to oust from office every Negro holding a decent position with the federal service. This is in accordance with his infamous 'new Southern policy.' " SOURCE: Cleveland *Gazette*, 7 Aug 1901.

‡Letter, Ft Robinson, 17 Jan 1903, to commander, Ft Robinson, asks that railroads of department grant furloughed soldiers half-rates; forwarded to Adjutant, Department of the Missouri, and returned, not approved by railroads. Letter to commander, Ft Robinson, 29 May 1903, reports departure on leave and address, "Finlay, Ohio." SOURCE: Register, LR, Ft Robinson, 1903.

‡Will preach at Congregational Church, Crawford, NE, next Sunday morning: "Be sure to hear him." SOURCE: Crawford *Bulletin*, 23 Oct 1903.

‡On Thanksgiving, Ft Robinson, 1904, sang duet "In Thy Love" with his wife at church service. SOURCE: Indianapolis *Freeman*, 3 Dec 1904.

‡Will preach at Crawford Methodist Church, Sunday, 12 Feb 1905. SOURCE: Crawford *Tribune*, 10 Feb 1905.

‡Biography with picture: a permanent trustee, Wilberforce University, and delegate to last General Conference, African Methodist Episcopal Church. SOURCE: Talbert, *The Sons of Allen*, 240.

‡"Among the many [Wilberforce graduates] who have reached eminence." SOURCE: Hartshorn, *An Era of Progress and Promise*, 281.

‡Promoted to major. SOURCE: Cleveland *Gazette*, 21 Sep 1907.

‡Sent Auditor Ralph W. Tyler "a handsome leather-trimmed Morris chair," of Philippine mahogany with brass fixtures and plate for engraving. SOURCE: Washington *Bee*, 25 Jun 1908.

‡Visited here ten days. SOURCE: Cleveland *Gazette*, 12 Jun 1909.

‡Granted leave until 16 Dec, date to be retired. SOURCE: Cleveland *Gazette*, 4 Dec 1909.

‡Retired with physical disability and replaced by white Roman Catholic priest, Rev. Joseph Kennedy, from Oregon; regiment practically all Protestant. SOURCE: Cleveland *Gazette*, 18 Dec 1909.

‡Retired for disability 10 Jan 1910, after treatment at Walter Reed Army Medical Center and at Hot Springs, AR, for "tropical fever" contracted in Cuba. SOURCE: Cleveland *Gazette*, 25 Aug 1934.

‡Lectured on travels in Palestine, Egypt, Japan at Northern District of Northern Ohio Conference, AME meeting at Sandusky. SOURCE: Cleveland *Gazette*, 27 May 1911.

‡Mrs. George Myers and daughter of Cleveland as guests of "Ex-chaplain and Mrs. W. T. Anderson" of Wilberforce. SOURCE: Cleveland *Gazette*, 8 Jul 1911.

‡Ex-chaplain Anderson, former pastor of St. John's, preached excellent sermon there on Sunday; now lives on "Bishop Arnett" homestead, which he bought and beautified; left here Tuesday for annual AME conference, Youngstown; while in Cleveland, guest of George A. Myers. SOURCE: Cleveland *Gazette*, 23 Sep 1911.

‡At Northern Ohio Conference, AME, "delivered a fine lecture on the Holy Land." SOURCE: Cleveland *Gazette*, 30 Sep 1911.

‡A trustee of Wilberforce, visited from there with Mr. and Mrs. George Myers last week; on way home from conference meetings at Lima and Columbus. SOURCE: Cleveland *Gazette*, 3 Oct 1914.

‡Was here last week as guest of George A. Myers. SOURCE: Cleveland *Gazette*, 10 Apr 1915.

‡Mrs. Anderson joined him here from Washington, DC; considering leaving Wilberforce to locate here or Chicago. SOURCE: Cleveland *Gazette*, 17 Apr 1915.

‡Left 5 May with his wife for Chicago, Denver, San Francisco; will visit Panama-Pacific Exposition, San Francisco, as special representative of *Gazette*. SOURCE: Cleveland *Gazette*, 8 May 1915.

‡Back as guests of Mrs. Della Eubanks and her mother, Mrs. Harmon, 1202 Lakewood Ave.; may locate here. SOURCE: Cleveland *Gazette*, 3 Jul 1915.

‡Resident of Washington, DC; was in Cleveland last week and in Akron to see Sen. Charles Dick. SOURCE: Cleveland *Gazette*, 6 May 1916.

‡Was here last week en route home from Wilberforce to Washington, DC. SOURCE: Cleveland *Gazette*, 24 Jun 1916.

‡Moving to Toledo, as pastor of Warren Chapel, replacing Rev. Charles A. Bundy. SOURCE: Cleveland *Gazette*, 2 Oct 1916.

‡In Toledo. SOURCE: Cleveland *Gazette*, 16 Oct 1919.

‡Speaker in crowded city hall auditorium, Wellsville, OH, on "Man to Man," 300th anniversary celebration of Negroes in America; Rev. Mr. Mason, Wellsville African Methodist Episcopal Church, presided. SOURCE: Cleveland *Gazette*, 11 Jan 1919.

‡Pastor of Warren AME Church will retire at fall conference in Dayton, 13 Sep; Toledo congregation will hold farewell reception 16 Sep, at which time portrait by Frederick D. Allen will be presented to church; previously in Toledo, 1896–97; returned Sep 1916. "Has an enviable Army record," including letter of recommendation for promotion from General Pershing; only colored officer in battle at Santiago; only black member of Military Order of Foreign Wars; wife organized missionary group of Warren Church; they are great travelers, having been to Japan, China, India, Egypt, Palestine, elsewhere; will leave Toledo 1 Oct for Washington, DC, where he has applied for reinstatement in service with Quartermaster Department. SOURCE: Toledo *Blade*, 7 Sep 1918, with picture.

‡Attended Bishop Shaffer funeral, Chicago, with Mrs. Anderson. SOURCE: Cleveland *Gazette*, 19 Apr 1919.

‡Letter, 2215 E. 89th St., Cleveland, appeals for funds for defense of Dr. Leroy N. Bundy, East St. Louis, IL; treasurer of local Bundy fund. SOURCE: Cleveland *Gazette*, 3 May 1919.

‡Cleveland resident; will preach at St. John's African Methodist Episcopal Church, Cadiz, OH, on Sunday. SOURCE: Cleveland *Gazette*, 19 July 1919.

‡Picture of Anderson residence. SOURCE: Joiner, *A Half Century of Freedom*, 122.

‡Mentioned. SOURCE: Work, *The Negro Year Book, 1912*, 76.

‡Died 21 Aug 1934, Cleveland. SOURCE: *Official Army Register*, January 1, 1935.

‡Died this Tuesday at his E. 95th St. residence, age 75; found dead in his room, 9:30 A.M.; widow survives. SOURCE: Cleveland *Gazette*, 25 Aug 1934.

‡Funeral tomorrow, 2 P.M. Secretary to bishop and accountant, Third Episcopal District, African Methodist Episcopal Church, since retirement from Army; William T. Anderson Post, American Legion, bears his name; wife Sada J. survives and is statistician, Women's Parent Mite Missionary Society, African Methodist Episcopal Church, and president, North Ohio Conference Branch, Third Episcopal District. SOURCE: Cleveland *Plain Dealer*, 23 Aug 1934.

‡Ladies Auxiliary, Maj. William T. Anderson Camp, United Spanish War Veterans, No. 70, appeared in uniform at his funeral, St. James African Methodist Episcopal Church. SOURCE: Chicago *Defender*, 15 Sep 1934.

‡Funeral on 24 Aug with eulogy by Bishop R. C. Ransom, African Methodist Episcopal Church; many prominent churchmen attended. SOURCE: Cleveland *Gazette*, 1 Sep 1934.

‡Front-page banner headline, "Major Anderson dies in Sleep," with current picture; body in state at St. James African Methodist Episcopal Church, East 84th and Cedar, 12:30 to 2 P.M., Friday; survived by Mrs. Sada J. Anderson, statistician, Women's Parent Mite Missionary Society, African Methodist Episcopal Church, and president, Northern Ohio Branch, Third Episcopal District; was secretary and accountant to bishop, Third Episcopal District, African Methodist Episcopal Church; 33rd degree Mason. SOURCE: Cleveland *Call & Post*, 25 Aug 1934.

‡Biographical sketch. SOURCE: Logan and Winston, *Dictionary of American Negro Biography*, 15–16.

ANDREWS, Archie; Private; I/25th Inf. Died at Ft McIntosh, TX, on 13 Oct 1908; buried at Fort Sam Houston National Cemetery, Section PE, number 373. SOURCE: Buffalo Soldiers Interred in Fort Sam Houston National Cemetery.

ARCHER, Sylvester; Private; C/10th Cav. Born 1843 in Broome County, NY; married 1 Apr 1862 to Sarah J. Patra, in Binghamton, NY; Civil War veteran; enlisted in F/54th Massachusetts Infantry 8 Apr 1863; Ht 5'6", black hair and brown eyes, brown complexion; occupation farmer; discharged in 1865; enlisted 19 Aug 1867, assigned to C/10th Cavalry; discharged 17 Aug 1872 at Camp Supply, OK; in Strong City, KS, met Abbie Green, born free in Charlotte County, VA, previously married to Jefferson Green with whom she had five children, and whom she left and did not divorce; without divorcing Sarah, Archer married Abbie Green in Topeka 18 Apr [year?]; Barteen born 19 Sep 1885, Gertrude born 7 Dec 1887, Zephyr born 26 Mar 1890, Martha born 30 Jun 1892, Henrietta born 20 May 1894; suffered from palpitation of heart, pleurisy, rheumatism, disease of the eye, and scurvy in later years of life; died 9 Apr 1902, age 59, at Meriden, KS; Sarah J. Archer resided at 26 Wilber St, Binghamton, NY, age 62 when awarded widow's pension from date of Sylvester's death; Sarah Archer died 8 May 1911 at 55 Sherman Place, Binghamton, NY; in Jan 1921 Zephyr Hysten applied for a pension for her mother Abbie Green, alias Ida Jackson Archer, denied because marriage to Archer was not legal. SOURCE: Greene, *Swamp Angels*, 17–18.

ARMFIELD, John; 1st Sgt; G/10th Cav. ‡Corporal, M/10th Cavalry; at Ft Apache, AZ, 1890, subscribed $.50 to testimonial to General Grierson. SOURCE: List of subscriptions, 23 Apr 1890, 10th Cavalry papers, MHI.

‡Private, G/10th Cavalry; qualified as sharpshooter with carbine, 1892, his first qualification. SOURCE: GO 1, AGO, 3 Jan 1893.

‡Private, G/10th Cavalry; served in 10th Cavalry, 1898; remained in U.S. during war with Spain. SOURCE: Cashin, *Under Fire with the Tenth Cavalry*, 345.

First sergeant, G/10th Cavalry; died on 16 Feb 1920; buried at San Antonio National Cemetery, Section D, number 580-a. SOURCE: San Antonio National Cemetery Locator.

ARMS, Benjamin; 1st Sgt; A/24th Inf. ‡Born in McIntosh, GA, 1845; black; enlisted in A/38th Infantry, 14 May 1867; discharged Ft Bliss, TX; reenlisted A/24th Infantry, 17 May 1870–17 May 1875; discharged Ft Ringgold, TX; reenlisted 17 May 1875–16 May 1880; discharged Ft Duncan, TX; reenlisted 17 May 1880–16 May 1885; discharged Ft Reno, Indian Territory; reenlisted Ft Reno, 17 May 1885; noncommissioned staff, Ft Supply, Indian Territory, 18 Jan 1887; promoted to sergeant, A/38th Infantry, 24 Nov 1868; sergeant, A/24th Infantry, until promoted to quartermaster sergeant, 3 Jan 1887, and first sergeant, 8 Apr 1875–16 May 1885; sergeant, A/24th Infantry, 25 Feb 1890. "An excellent soldier and man, sober, intelligent and trustworthy"; each discharge with character excellent; married, no children; deposits $300 ($100 in each year, 1885, 1887, 1888); additional pay $5 per month. SOURCE: Entry dated 25 Feb 1890, Ft Bayard, NM, Descriptive Book, 24 Inf NCS & Band.

‡To report from Ft Reno to Ft Supply, as quartermaster sergeant. SOURCE: *ANJ* 24 (15 Jan 1887): 490.

Sergeant, 24th Infantry, applied for post noncommissioned staff position 1889. SOURCE: Dobak and Phillips, *The Black Regulars*, 302.

‡Senior sergeant, 24th Infantry, with warrant dating from 28 Nov 1868, now stationed at Ft Bayard, sergeant, A/24th Infantry. SOURCE: *ANJ* 27 (3 May 1890): 679.

‡Retires as first sergeant, A/24th Infantry, from Ft Douglas, UT. SOURCE: Cleveland *Gazette*, 26 Jun 1897; *ANJ* 34 (22 May 1897): 705.

ARMSTRONG, Anderson; D/24th Inf. Born in Tennessee; mulatto complexion; cannot read or write, age 27, Jul 1870, at Ft McKavett, TX. SOURCE: Bierschwale, *Fort McKavett*, 96.

ARMSTRONG, Isaac; Private; G/25th Inf. Died 1 Sep 1916; buried in plot W.SID1205-A at San Francisco National Cemetery. SOURCE: San Francisco National Cemetery.

ARMSTRONG, Walter; Private; H/10th Cav. In Troop H/10th Cavalry stationed at Bonita Cañon Camp, AZ, 30 Apr 1886. SOURCE: Tagg, *The Camp at Bonita Cañon*, 231.

‡Honorable mention for services rendered in capture of the Apache Mangas and his band, Rio Bonito, AZ, 18 Oct 1886. SOURCE: Baker, Roster.

ARMSTRONG, William; Private; F/10th Cav. ‡Original member of 10th Cavalry; in troop when organized, Ft Leavenworth, KS, 21 Jun 1867. SOURCE: McMiller, "Buffalo Soldiers," 73.

Died 4 Aug 1867 of cholera at Ft Hays. SOURCE: Regimental Returns, 10th Cavalry, 1867.

ARMSTRONG, Wilson H.; Sergeant; A/9th Cav. ‡Promoted to corporal, A/9th Cavalry, 24 Jul 1893. SOURCE: Roster, 9 Cav, Jul 1893.

Appointed corporal 24 Jul 1893; in A/9th Cavalry at Ft Robinson, NE, Jan 1897. SOURCE: Ninth Cavalry, Roster of NCOs, 1897.

‡Corporal, Ft Robinson, 1894. SOURCE: Investigation of Charges against Chaplain Plummer.

‡Promoted to sergeant. SOURCE: *ANJ* 34 (17 Jul 1897): 854.

‡Sergeant, on special duty instructing recruits, as of 9 May 1902. SOURCE: SD Lists, A/9 Cav, 24 May 1902, Nueva Caceres, Philippines.

ARRINGTON, George; Private; C/24th Inf. ‡Mentioned as among men who recently distinguished themselves; awarded certificate of merit for gallant and meritorious service while escorting Maj. Joseph W. Wham, paymaster, when attacked by robbers between Ft Grant, AZ, and Ft Thomas, AZ; now out of service. SOURCE: GO 18, AGO, 1891.

Cited for bravery against robbers near Cedar Springs, AZ, in May 1889 by Maj. Joseph W. Wham, and awarded certificate of merit; shot through shoulder in fight; left Army before end of 1890. SOURCE: Schubert, *Black Valor*, 93, 95, 98.

Report of Paymaster Wham, describing bravery of escort, published. SOURCE: Schubert, *Voices of the Buffalo Soldier*, 159–62.

‡Born in Halifax, NC, resided Charleston, SC, when enlisted; Distinguished Service Cross awarded in lieu of certificate of merit for gallant and meritorious conduct while escorting Paymaster Wham, 11 May 1889. SOURCE: *Decorations, U.S. Army, Supplement I*, 28.

Awarded certificate of merit for gallant and meritorious conduct while member of escort of Maj. Joseph W. Wham, paymaster, who was ambushed by bandits between Ft Grant and Ft Thomas, 11 May 1889. SOURCE: Gleim, *The Certificate of Merit*, 44.

‡Admitted to Soldiers Home, with disability, on 22 Jul 1890, after serving one year and ten months. SOURCE: SecWar, *AR 1890*, 1043.

‡Mentioned. SOURCE: *Winners of the West* 13 (Jan 1936): 3.

‡His certificate of merit mentioned. SOURCE: *Winners of the West* 14 (Feb 1937).

ASH, John M.; QM Sgt; E/24th Inf. ‡Awarded certificate of merit 11 Jan 1907 for conspicuous gallantry against Pulahanes while sergeant E/24th Infantry; fine example of cool bravery in command of ten soldiers and detachment of constabulary; was surrounded and brought engagement to successful conclusion, at Tabon-Tabon, Leyte, Philippines, 24 Jul 1906. SOURCE: GO 143, AGO, 1 Jul 1907.

Awarded certificate of merit for conspicuous gallantry in action, with command surrounded by bandits, Tabon-Tabon, Leyte, 24 Jul 1906. SOURCE: Gleim, *The Certificate of Merit*, 58.

Born in Henderson, KY; resided Chicago, IL; received Distinguished Service Medal in lieu of certificate of merit. SOURCE: *American Decorations*, 835.

‡In the Philippines, 1906, as sergeant, E/24th Infantry. *See* OTT, **HARRIS**, William C., Sergeant, E/24th Infantry

ASHBERRY, William; Private; K/9th Cav. Died at Ft Davis, TX, on 1 Jun 1868; buried at San Antonio National Cemetery, Section I, number 1467. SOURCE: San Antonio National Cemetery Locator.

ASHBRIDGE, George; Private; L/9th Cav. Enlisted in New Mexico on 10 Jan 1876; discharged at Ft Bliss, TX, 19 Jan 1881, character good. SOURCE: Muster Roll, L/9th Cavalry, 31 Dec 1880–28 Jan 1881.

‡Discharged on expiration of service, Ft Bliss, 19 Jan 1881. SOURCE: Regt Returns, 9 Cav, Jan 1881.

ASHPORT, Lemuel; Corporal; 25th Inf. Born 22 Mar 1846, Taunton MA, son of Noah and Esther Wood Ashport, both born in Massachusetts; Civil War veteran, signed name when enlisted in I/54th Massachusetts Infantry 16 Dec 1863 at West Bridgewater, MA; Ht 5'10", 185 pounds, black-gray hair and brown eyes, brown complexion; occupation shoemaker; discharged 20 Aug 1865; enlisted 15 Aug 1867 in I/39th Infantry; transferred to 25th Infantry 20 Apr 1869, appointed corporal; discharged 15 Aug 1870 at Ft Clark, TX; in Nov 1881 married Elizabeth Pierce, daughter of Albert A. and Sarah Pierce; children Lilian E. born 1 Nov 1882, Ethel H. born 16 Sep 1886, and Pearl E. born 14 Jan 1888; died 29 Feb 1905, age 58, at 22 French Court, Brockton, MA, of cerebral hemorrhage and fall down stairs; buried at Brockton, MA. SOURCE: Greene, *Swamp Angels*, 19.

ASKEW, Blunt; Private; 25th Inf. Born in Cusita, AL; Ht 5'5", black hair and eyes, dark complexion; occupation laborer; enlisted at age 24, Charleston, SC, 27 May 1881; left recruit depot, David's Island, NY, 2 Jul 1881, arrived Ft Randall, SD, 7 Jul 1881. SOURCE: Descriptive & Assignment Rolls of Recruits, 25 Inf.

ASKEW, Preston; 1st Sgt; E/24th Inf. Corporal, awarded certificate of merit for conspicuous gallantry in action with command surrounded by bandits, Tabon-Tabon, Leyte,

Philippines, 24 Jul 1906. SOURCE: Gleim, *The Certificate of Merit*, 58.

‡Awarded certificate of merit on 11 Jan 1907 for conspicuous gallantry as corporal against Pulahanes at Tabon-Tabon, Leyte. SOURCE: GO 143, AGO, 1 Jul 1907.

‡Corporal, cited for bravery under fire against Pulahanes, Tabon-Tabon, 24 Jun 1906, along with Sgt. John Ash, Sgt. William C. Harris, Pvt. Albert W. Piner, and Pvt. Andrew M. Blackman. SOURCE: Muller, *The Twenty Fourth Infantry*, 45

‡At Ft Ontario, NY, 24th Infantry band played at presentation of certificate of merit to 1st Sgt. Preston Askew, E/24th Infantry. SOURCE: *ANJ* (23 May 1908), cited in Fletcher, *"The Negro Soldier and the United States Army."*

First sergeant, received Distinguished Service Medal in lieu of certificate of merit. SOURCE: *American Decorations*, 835.

AUSTIN, Charles; Sergeant; C/25th Inf. ‡Sergeant; C/25th Infantry, died Ft Sam Houston, TX, hospital, after critical abdominal operation; Spanish-American War veteran; wife and family in Virginia; "a brave man, a valiant soldier, and a kind husband." SOURCE: *ANJ* 37 (19 May 1900): 904.

Private, G/25th Infantry, died on 10 May 1900; buried at San Antonio National Cemetery, Section F, number 1123. SOURCE: San Antonio National Cemetery Locator.

AUSTIN, Edward S.; Private; K/25th Inf. Born in Camden County, SC; Ht 5'7", yellow complexion; occupation waiter; enlisted in A/39th Infantry for three years on 22 Nov 1867, age 21, at Boston, MA; extra duty as messenger, HQ, Department of Louisiana; transferred to K/25th Infantry at Jackson Bks, LA, 20 Apr 1869. SOURCE: Descriptive Roll of A/39th Inf.

‡In affidavit, from 267 W. Commerce St., San Antonio, TX, 25 Aug 1890, he claims he was at Ft Sill, Indian Territory, and saw William Branch in hospital after 1874 accident. SOURCE: VA File 2581520, William Branch.

AUSTIN, Frank; Private; E/10th Cav. In Troop E/10th Cavalry stationed at Bonita Cañon Camp, AZ, 28 Feb 1886. SOURCE: Tagg, *The Camp at Bonita Cañon*, 231.

B

BABBITT, Robert; Corporal; L/10th Cav. Died 14 Jan 1877 in hospital at Ft Lancaster, TX. SOURCE: Regimental Returns, 10th Cavalry, 1877.

BACKERS, William; Corporal; E/10th Cav. In K/10th Cavalry; killed 28 Oct 1880 at Ojo Caliente, TX. SOURCE: Regimental Returns, 10th Cavalry, 1880.

‡Killed in action, by Comanches, Ojo Caliente, TX, 28 Oct 1880; Backers Road, Ft Huachuca, AZ, named for him. SOURCE: Orville A. Cochran to H. B. Wharfield, 5 Apr 1965, 10th Cavalry papers, MHI.

BACKUT, Asa; C/25th Inf. Born in South Carolina; mulatto complexion; can read and write, age 24, 5 Sep 1870, at Ft McKavett, TX. SOURCE: Bierschwale, *Fort McKavett,* 109.

BACON, Martin; Sergeant; HQ TRP/9th Cav. ‡Private, E/9th Cavalry; wounded (foot) in action, Camalig, Philippines, 24 Nov 1900. SOURCE: *ANJ* 38 (5 Jan 1901): 455; *Illustrated Review: Ninth Cavalry.*

‡Corporal, G/9th Cavalry, at Ft D. A. Russell, WY, in 1910. SOURCE: *Illustrated Review: Ninth Cavalry.*

Received Philippine Campaign Badge number 11697 for service as sergeant, Headquarters Troop, 9th Cavalry; in 9th Cavalry at Ft Leavenworth, KS, Mar 1905. SOURCE: Philippine Campaign Badge list, 29 May 1905.

Died 16 Jul 1938; buried at San Antonio National Cemetery, Section C, number 478-C. SOURCE: San Antonio National Cemetery Locator.

BADIE, David; 1st Sgt; B/9th Cav. ‡Sergeant, B/9th Cavalry; praised for bravery against Victorio, Nov 1879, by Maj. Albert P. Morrow. SOURCE: Billington, "Black Cavalrymen," 68; Billington, *New Mexico's Buffalo Soldiers,* 93.

Commanded detachment of B Troop that stayed in field tracking Apaches for most of July and August 1881, covering more than one thousand miles. SOURCE: Schubert, *Black Valor,* 83.

‡As sergeant, B/9th Cavalry, 16 Aug 1881, led detachment of fourteen against Indians in Nogal Canyon, NM.

SOURCE: Hamilton, "History of the Ninth Cavalry," 57; Billington, *New Mexico's Buffalo Soldiers,* 105.

· As first sergeant, at Ft Robinson, NE, badgered and provoked soldiers who reported to him, including Sgt. John Denny, who was convicted of insubordination, fined, and reduced, 1884, with sentence remitted, and Cpl. Benjamin Hockins in 1888; served on honor guard when body of Col. Edward Hatch was transported from Ft Robinson, NE, to Ft Leavenworth, KS, in 1889. SOURCE: Kenner, *Buffalo Soldiers and Officers of the Ninth Cavalry,* 48–49, 231.

‡First sergeant, B/9th Cavalry, Ft DuChesne, UT, authorized four-month furlough. SOURCE: *ANJ* 25 (15 Oct 1887): 222.

‡Ranked number 53 among sharpshooters over 90 percent with 91.00 percent, 1887. SOURCE: GO 79, AGO, 31 Dec 1887.

‡First sergeant, I/9th Cavalry as of 25 Jun 1891; sergeant since 1 Oct 1873. SOURCE: Roster, 9 Cav, Jul 1893.

‡Died of disease contracted in line of duty in post hospital, Ft Robinson, 24 Jan 1894. SOURCE: List of Interments, Ft Robinson; Buecker, Fort Robinson Burials.

‡Funeral service at post hall, Ft Robinson, 26 Jan 1894. SOURCE: Order 7, 25 Jan 1894, Post Orders, Ft Robinson.

BAILEY, Albert; Private; E/9th Cav. Strung from tree limb by wrists by Lt. Edward Heyl at San Pedro Springs, TX, Apr 1867, for failure to remove nosebag from his horse promptly. SOURCE: Schubert, *Black Valor,* 16.

‡1st Lt. Edward Heyl charged with superintending tying up Bailey by hands, 9 Apr 1867, at camp near San Antonio, TX.

BAILEY, Battier; Private; B/25th Inf. Mustered in 11 Jul 1898, mustered out B/6th Virginia Infantry 26 Jan 1899; enlisted 25 Sep 1899, discharged private C/48th Infantry 30 Jun 1901, character excellent; reenlisted 24 Jul 1901, discharged private F/25th Infantry 25 Nov 1902, character very good; enlisted 29 Jun 1905, discharged without honor as private 22 Nov 1906, Brownsville, TX. SOURCE: Powell, "Military Record of the Enlisted Men Who Were Discharged Without Honor."

‡Dishonorable discharge, Brownsville. SOURCE: SO 266, AGO, 9 Nov 1906.

BAILEY, Charles; Private; I/10th Cav. Died 19 Dec 1914; buried in plot W 39 at Ft Bayard, NM. SOURCE: "Fort Bayard National Cemetery, Records of Burials."

Buried 19 Dec 1914, section B, row H, plot 39, at Ft Bayard. SOURCE: Erickson, Burials at Fort Bayard National Cemetery, NM.

BAILEY, Ephriam; Private; E/9th Cav. One of ten soldiers charged with mutiny and desertion for role in mutiny at San Pedro Springs, near San Antonio, TX, April 1867; pled guilty to desertion but not mutiny; mutiny charge dropped; convicted of desertion and sentenced to six months confinement at military prison, Ship's Island, MS; sentence remitted before transported to prison. SOURCE: Dobak and Phillips, *The Black Regulars*, 208–10.

BAILEY, Guss; Sergeant; I/9th Cav. ‡Gus Bailey, corporal, B/9th Cavalry, at Ft Robinson, NE, 1884. See OTT, **HERBERT**, Thomas H., Private, K/9th Cavalry

‡In B/9th Cavalry at Ft Robinson, 1889, Pvt. George Waters convicted by garrison court martial for disobeying Cpl. John Downey and for resisting arrest by Corporal Bailey. SOURCE: Order 183, 6 Jun 1889, Post Orders, Ft Robinson.

Appointed sergeant 1 Mar 1894; in I/9th Cavalry at Ft Washakie, WY, Jan 1897. SOURCE: Ninth Cavalry, Roster of NCOs, 1897.

BAILEY, James; Private; B/25th Inf. Enlisted 11 Aug 1905, discharged without honor 22 Nov 1906, Brownsville, TX. SOURCE: Powell, "Military Record of the Enlisted Men Who Were Discharged Without Honor."

‡Dishonorable discharge, Brownsville. SOURCE: SO 266, AGO, 9 Nov 1906.

BAILEY, John H.; Sergeant; 25th Inf. Civil War veteran, enlisted in 4th U.S. Colored Infantry 1863; retired 1891 after twenty-three years as sergeant, 25th Infantry. SOURCE: Dobak and Phillips, *The Black Regulars*, 58.

BAILEY, Willis; Corporal, F/24th Inf. ‡Letter, Adjutant, 10th Cavalry, to Lt. M. Amick, 10th Cavalry, Recruiting Officer, 10 Apr 1867, forwards his enlistment papers and correspondence reporting his occupation, which was listed variously as laborer and boatman. SOURCE: LS, 10 Cav, 1866–67.

‡Private, C/10th Cavalry, on extra duty at Ft Leavenworth, KS, but commander of his company asks that he be immediately relieved because the company is ready to march west without delay. SOURCE: CO, 10 Cav, to Lt. S. W. Bonsall, Adj, Ft Leavenworth, 15 May 1867, LS, 10 Cav, 1866–67.

Private, C/10th Cavalry, served with Pvt. George Washington, C/10th Cavalry, early 1870s. SOURCE: Schubert, *Voices of the Buffalo Soldier*, 234.

‡Private, F/24th Infantry; recruited to teach in Chaplain Allensworth's post school, Ft Bayard, NM, 1888; retained as teacher after promoted to corporal. SOURCE: Billington, *New Mexico's Buffalo Soldiers*, 162.

BAILY, Richard; Private; H/9th Cav. Died 12 Dec 1876; originally buried at Ft Stanton, NM; buried Jun 1896 at Santa Fe National Cemetery, NM, plot B OR 555. SOURCE: Santa Fe National Cemetery, Records of Burials.

BAIMER, John; Trumpeter; B/10th Cav. At Ft Stockton, TX, Apr 1879; charged with beating his wife; Lt. John Bigelow wants to have him reduced to private because Bigelow thinks he will never make a good trumpeter and that he has a hare lip. SOURCE: Kinevan, *Frontier Cavalryman*, 166.

BAKER, Benjamin O.; Private; H/10th Cav. Born in Montrose, PA, Aug 1859; enlisted Pittsburgh, PA, 26 Dec 1882; Ht. 5'4", black complexion, eyes, and hair; assigned to H/10th Cavalry, from Jefferson Barracks, MO, 23 Jan 1883; discharged on surgeon's certificate of disability with lung trouble, Ft Davis, TX, 14 Nov 1884; resided at Binghamton, NY, in 1899; resided at Montrose in 1901. SOURCE: Sayre, *Warriors of Color*, 23–28.

BAKER, Bird; Corporal; H/24th Inf. ‡Sergeant, K/24th Infantry, acquitted, Ft Grant, AZ, of permitting an Indian prisoner to escape; General Grierson, reviewing authority, disapproves and considers Baker an unfit noncommissioned officer. SOURCE: *ANJ* 26 (16 Mar 1889): 377–78.

Died 21 Aug 1892, buried at Ft Bayard, NM, in plot D 38. SOURCE: "Fort Bayard National Cemetery, Records of Burials."

BAKER, Edward L., Jr.; QM Sgt; U.S. Army. ‡Born on Platte River, Laramie Co., WY, 28 Dec 1865; enlisted at Cincinnati, OH, in D/9th Cavalry, 27 Jul 1882; trumpeter, 2 Jul 1883; discharged, 26 Jul 1887; enlisted B/10th Cavalry, 25 Aug 1887; regimental clerk, 4 May 1888; chief trumpeter, 10th Cavalry, 9 Feb 1890; quartermaster sergeant, 10th Cavalry, 28 Jan 1891; enlisted 25 Aug 1892; promoted to sergeant major, 10th Cavalry, 25 Aug 1892; attended cavalry school, Saumar, France, Nov 1896–May 1897; enlisted 25 Aug 1897; appointed first lieutenant, 10th U.S. Volunteer Infantry, 2 August 1898; mustered out and reverted to sergeant major, 10th Cavalry, 8 Mar 1899; appointed captain, 49th Infantry, 9 Sep 1899; mustered out, 30 Jun 1901; discharged from 10th Cavalry, 5 Sep 1901; appointed second lieutenant, Philippine Scouts, 7 Feb 1902; promoted to first lieutenant, 10 Sep 1906; promoted to captain, 12 Sep 1908; resigned, 31 Oct 1909; enlisted, Ft McDowell, CA, post quartermaster sergeant, 7 Nov 1909; retired 12 Jan 1910, in accordance with Special Order 41,

War Department, 6 Jan 1910. SOURCE: VA File XC 2715800, Edward L. Baker.

Life story and bravery in Cuba that led to the award of the Medal of Honor narrated. SOURCE: Schubert, *Black Valor*, 145–61.

Private, 9th Cavalry, when forced into homosexual relationship with 1st Sgt. Richard J. Dickerson; as sergeant, 10th Cavalry, 1891, applied unsuccessfully for post noncommissioned staff position. SOURCE: Dobak and Phillips, *The Black Regulars*, 66, 83, 302.

Private, D/9th Cavalry, almost age 17, reported for duty at Ft Riley, KS, October 1882; he claimed that he was sexually molested by 1st Sgt. James Dickerson, D/9th Cavalry, Ft Riley, Jan 1883; compiled *Roster of Non-commissioned Officers of the 10th U.S. Cavalry, with some Regimental Reminiscences, Appendixes, etc.*, published in 1897. SOURCE: Kenner, *Buffalo Soldiers and Officers of the Ninth Cavalry*, 272–77, 355.

‡"He served in Arizona, New Mexico, Texas, Colorado, Kansas, Indian Territory, Nebraska, Wyoming, Montana. He took part in numerous scouts, arduous marches, and expeditions against isolated bands of Indians and other marauders from 1882 to 1898 on our western frontier." SOURCE: Widow's declaration for pension, 1916, VA File XC 2715800, Edward L. Baker.

‡As chief trumpeter, 10th Cavalry, at Ft Apache, AZ, 1890, subscribed $.50 to testimonial to General Grierson. SOURCE: List of subscriptions, 23 Apr 1890, 10th Cavalry papers, MHI.

‡Married Mary Elizabeth Hawley, born Mary E. Prince and widow of Heber Hawley, Santa Fe, NM, 31 Jul 1887; no previous marriages. SOURCE: VA File XC 2715800, Edward L. Baker.

‡Medical history: typhoid, 1875; kicked by horse, 5 Oct 1882; "constipation in line of duty, cured," 8–9 Mar 1884; dysentery, 1890; gunshot wound, 1898; dysentery, 30 Aug–15 Sep 1898; bronchitis, 1909; "alcoholism acute, not in line of duty," 18–19 Jun 1909. SOURCE: VA File XC 2715800, Edward L. Baker.

‡Stationed at Ft Assiniboine, MT, 1897, with wife and five children: Edward Lee Baker, Eugenia Sheridan Baker, Myrtle Mary Baker, Gwenderlyn James Baker, Dexter Murat Baker; father French; mother American, colored. SOURCE: AGO, Carded Records, Voluntary Organizations, Spanish-American War.

‡Served in 10th Cavalry in Cuba, 1898. SOURCE: Cashin, *Under Fire with the Tenth Cavalry*, 352.

‡Participated in battles at Las Guasimas and San Juan Hill, Cuba; wounded slightly by shrapnel, left side and arm, at San Juan. SOURCE: Regt Returns, 10 Cav, Jun–Jul 1898.

‡Awarded Medal of Honor for heroism, San Juan Hill, 1898. SOURCE: Logan and Winston, *Dictionary of American Negro Biography*, 21.

‡Diary of Cuban campaign of 1898. SOURCE: Steward, *The Colored Regulars*, 255–79.

‡First lieutenant, M/10th U.S. Volunteer Infantry, 1898; captain, L/49th Infantry, 1899; second lieutenant to captain, Philippine Scouts, 1902–09.

His article, "The Environments of the Enlisted Man of the United States Army of Today," *Georgia Baptist* 19 (13 Apr 1899), reprinted. SOURCE: Schubert, *Voices of the Buffalo Soldier*, 208–13.

‡Organized, equipped, commanded L/49th Infantry "and conducted same to the Philippines, and returned to U.S. with every man in excellent health, and every man in the company having deposits with the paymaster." SOURCE: Widow's declaration for pension, 1916, VA File XC 2715800, Edward L. Baker.

‡Died 1914.

‡Biographical sketch. SOURCE: Logan and Winston, *Dictionary of American Negro Biography*, 21.

BAKER, Franklin M.; Sergeant; 9th Cav. Received Philippine Campaign Badge number 11763 for service as sergeant in D/25th Infantry; in 9th Cavalry at Ft Leavenworth, KS, Mar 1905. SOURCE: Philippine Campaign Badge list, 29 May 1905.

BAKER, George; Private; A/10th Cav. ‡Arrived at Ft Leavenworth, KS, from Jefferson Barracks, MO. SOURCE: Adj, Ft Leavenworth, to HQ, Jefferson Bks, 9 Oct 1866.

Died 10 Jul 1867 of cholera at Ft Larned, KS. SOURCE: Regimental Returns, 10th Cavalry, 1867.

BAKER, Peter; F/9th Cav. Born in Kentucky; black complexion; cannot read or write, age 25, Jul 1870, at Ft McKavett, TX. SOURCE: Bierschwale, *Fort McKavett*, 98.

BAKER, Richard; Private; G/10th Cav. Died 17 Dec 1871, cause not stated, at Ft Sill, OK. SOURCE: Regimental Returns, 10th Cavalry, 1871.

Buried at Camp Douglas, UT. SOURCE: Record Book of Interments, Post Cemetery, 252.

BAKER, Thomas; Musician; 24th Inf. Died at Camp Eagle Pass, TX, on 24 Feb 1870; buried at San Antonio National Cemetery, Section F, number 1152. SOURCE: San Antonio National Cemetery Locator.

BAKER, William; Private; 10th Cav. Discharged on completion of enlistment, Ft Sill, OK, 1872; found employment as laborer for post quartermaster at Ft Sill. SOURCE: Dobak and Phillips, *The Black Regulars*, 270.

BAKER, William; Sergeant; H/9th Cav. ‡At Ft Cummings, NM, 1876. SOURCE: Billington, *New Mexico's Buffalo Soldiers*, 113.

‡On detached service from Ft Bliss, TX, 9 Jan–10 Feb 1881. SOURCE: Regt Returns, 9 Cav, Feb 1881.

Citation for gallantry in action from Capt. Henry Carroll; in Aug 1881 action against Nana, ambushed in Gavilan Canyon, NM, broke and ran. SOURCE: Kenner, *Buffalo Soldiers and Officers of the Ninth Cavalry*, 226.

BALDWIN, Buster B.; Private; L/25th Inf. Died 8 Feb 1908, buried at Ft Bayard, NM, in plot P 18. SOURCE: "Fort Bayard National Cemetery, Records of Burials."

Buried 8 Feb 1908, section B, row A, plot 18, at Ft Bayard. SOURCE: Erickson, Burials at Fort Bayard National Cemetery, NM.

BALDWIN, Stephen; Trumpeter; 25th Inf. Born in Washington, GA; Ht 5'6", black hair and eyes, black complexion; served in C/10th Cavalry until 25 Nov 1886; 2nd reenlistment, 25th Infantry at age 32 as trumpeter, Washington, DC, 23 Dec 1886; arrived Ft Snelling, MN, 19 Jan 1887. SOURCE: Descriptive & Assignment Rolls of Recruits, 25 Inf.

BALL, George; Private; D/9th Cav. With Captain Dodge at battle at Milk River, CO, 2–10 Oct 1879. SOURCE: Miller, *Hollow Victory*, 167, 206–7.

‡G. Ball, Corporal, D/9th Cav, with detachment under 1st Lt. John Guilfoyle scouting in Utah Territory, Sep–Oct 1883.

BALL, John F.; Sergeant; 25th Inf. In third enlistment, Ft Snelling, MN, 1885. SOURCE: Dobak and Phillips, *The Black Regulars*, 60.

BALL, W. S.; Private; F/24th Inf. Died at Ft Concho, TX, on 15 Jun 1870; buried at San Antonio National Cemetery, Section D, number 694. SOURCE: San Antonio National Cemetery Locator.

BALLANGER, George; Private; 9th Cav. Received Philippine Campaign Badge number 11710 for service as private, E/9th Cavalry; in 9th Cavalry at Ft Leavenworth, KS, Mar 1905. SOURCE: Philippine Campaign Badge list, 29 May 1905.

BALLENTINE, Cyrus; Private; D/25th Inf. Buried at Ft Bayard, NM. SOURCE: "Buffalo Soldiers Buried at Ft Bayard, NM."

Died 5 Feb 1919; buried at Ft Bayard in plot B K 9. SOURCE: "Fort Bayard National Cemetery, Records of Burials."

Buried 15 Feb 1919, section B, row K, plot 9, at Ft Bayard. SOURCE: Erickson, Burials at Fort Bayard National Cemetery, NM.

BAMBRICK, Joseph; Private; A/39th Inf. Civil War veteran, served in F/81st U.S. Colored Infantry; sentenced to five years for involvement in New Iberia, LA, mutiny, Jul

1867. SOURCE: Dobak and Phillips, *The Black Regulars*, 222.

BANCROFT, George; Private; A/9th Cav. Died at Ft Stockton, TX, on 24 Apr 1871; buried at San Antonio National Cemetery, Section C, number 376. SOURCE: San Antonio National Cemetery Locator.

BANHAM, Jerry; C/25th Inf. Born in Kentucky; mulatto complexion; cannot read or write, age 21, 5 Sep 1870, at Ft McKavett, TX. SOURCE: Bierschwale, *Fort McKavett*, 109.

BANKS, Benjamin; Private; H/10th Cav. Born in Baltimore, MD, Aug 1860; enlisted Pittsburgh, PA, 24 Oct 1882; Ht 5'9"; black complexion, eyes, and hair; never married; died of acute dysentery, Ft Davis, TX, 25 Nov 1884; mother Mary Jane Holcomb, stepfather John Holcomb married 8 Sep 1874, both age 45, when resided at 2218 11th St., NW, Washington, DC, in Mar 1888; mother died 25 Feb 1908. SOURCE: Sayre, *Warriors of Color*, 29–32.

Died of acute dysentery, 25 Nov 1884. SOURCE: Bigelow, *Garrison Tangles*, 67.

Died at Ft Davis on 25 Nov 1884; buried at San Antonio National Cemetery, Section H, number 107. SOURCE: San Antonio National Cemetery Locator.

BANKS, Charles; Private; 24th Inf. Born in Buffalo, WV, in 1880; Delaware Indian mother and white father; raised by a black woman; lived life in black community; joined army at age 18; veteran of Spanish American War; after discharge moved to Colorado Springs, CO; charter member of VFW Post 101; civil rights activist for twenty years; lobbied for passage of Civil Rights Bill of 1935; president of Colorado Springs Chapter of National Association for the Advancement of Colored People for five years; organized strikes and suits against discriminatory practices; died in 1976, last survivor of his regiment. SOURCE: "Pikes Peak Region Black History (part 2): Charles Banks (1880-1976)."

‡Served in Houston, 1917. SOURCE: Haynes, *A Night of Violence*, 122.

BANKS, Jordon; Private; 25th Inf. Born in Charlottesville, VA; Ht 5'5", black hair and eyes, black complexion; discharged from E/9th Cavalry 17 Jan 1886; single, 2nd enlistment at age 26, Denver, CO, 25 Jan 1886; assigned to C/25th Infantry. SOURCE: Descriptive & Assignment Rolls of Recruits, 25 Inf.

BANKS, Plum; Sergeant; B/9th Cav. Sergeant issued Indian Wars Campaign Badge number 1529 on 27 Oct 1909. SOURCE: Carroll, *Indian Wars Campaign Badge*, 44.

‡Veteran of Indian wars, Spanish-American War, and Philippine Insurrection; at Ft D. A. Russell, WY, in 1910;

marksman. SOURCE: *Illustrated Review: Ninth Cavalry*, with picture.

BANKS, Robert; Sergeant; H/10th Cav. In Troop H/10th Cavalry stationed at Bonita Cañon Camp, AZ, 30 Apr 1886. SOURCE: Tagg, *The Camp at Bonita Cañon*, 231.

Died 15 Dec 1888, formerly interred at Ft Apache, AZ; buried 14 Mar 1932 at Santa Fe National Cemetery, NM, plot P 85. SOURCE: Santa Fe National Cemetery, Records of Burials.

BANKS, Robert B.; H/10th Cav. Born in Halifax, PA; enlisted Harrisburg, PA, 20 Jun 1867; Ht. 5'10", brown complexion, black eyes and hair; occupation waiter; twenty years continuous service in H/10th Cavalry; at Ft Wallace, KS, Oct 1868, Apr 1869; at Camp Supply, OK, Jan–Oct 1870; at Ft Sill, OK, Mar 1872; discharged 20 June 1872 and reenlisted 24 July 1872 at Ft Leavenworth, KS; at Ft Sill Aug 1872, March 1874; at Ft Davis, TX, Dec 1875, Apr 1877; discharged and reenlisted 24 July 1877 at Ft Davis; at Ft Davis Oct 1877, Sep 1879; at Eagle Springs, TX, field hospital, Jun 1880; discharged and reenlisted 23–24 July 1882 at Ft Davis; at Ft Davis in 1882, 1883; discharged 23 July 1887 and reenlisted 26 July 1887 at Ft Apache, AZ. SOURCE: Sayre, *Warriors of Color*, 33–34.

BAPTISTE, Andrew J.; Private; C/9th Cav. Died 11 Apr 1920; buried at San Antonio National Cemetery, Section D, number 559-A. SOURCE: San Antonio National Cemetery Locator.

BAQUI, Rodolphe; Sgt Maj; 38th Inf. Before service, free man and bricklayer; Civil War veteran, served as sergeant major, 99th U.S. Colored Infantry and imprisoned at Ft Jefferson, Dry Tortugas, FL, for inciting mutiny. SOURCE: Dobak and Phillips, *The Black Regulars*, 60, 290.

BAQUIE, Leone; Private; 9th Cav. With Pvt. Buck Taylor, sentenced to twenty years for assault on Lt. Robert Webb and desertion, Ft Quitman, TX, 1869. SOURCE: Leiker, *Racial Borders*, 78.

BARDISON George; Private; D/10th Cav. ‡Served in 10th Cavalry, 1898; remained in U.S. during war with Spain. SOURCE: Cashin, *Under Fire with the Tenth Cavalry*, 343.

Died 15 May 1902; buried at Ft Bayard, NM, in plot M 34. SOURCE: "Fort Bayard National Cemetery, Records of Burials."

Buried 15 May 1902; section A, row U, plot 34, at Ft Bayard. SOURCE: Erickson, Burials at Fort Bayard National Cemetery, NM.

BARKER, Alexander; Private; A/9th Cav. Died at Ft Stockton, TX, on 20 Jul 1868; buried at San Antonio Na-

tional Cemetery, Section C, number 415. SOURCE: San Antonio National Cemetery Locator.

BARNER, Moses; Private; H/9th Cav. Born in Lincoln County, TN; Ht 5'7", dark brown hair and brown eyes, dark complexion; occupation laborer; enlisted at age 21, Nashville, TN, 30 Mar 1886; in 25th Infantry, arrived Ft Snelling, MN, 31 Jul 1886. SOURCE: Descriptive & Assignment Rolls of Recruits, 25 Inf.

‡Private, E/25th Infantry; ranked number 76 among expert riflemen, 1905, with 72.33 percent. SOURCE: GO 79, AGO, 1 Jun 1905.

‡At Ft D. A. Russell, WY, in 1910; resident of Fayetteville, TN. SOURCE: *Illustrated Review: Ninth Cavalry*, with picture.

BARNES, Samuel; D/24th Inf. Born in Kentucky; mulatto complexion; cannot read or write, age 23, Jul 1870, at Ft McKavett, TX. SOURCE: Bierschwale, *Fort McKavett*, 96.

BARNES, Samuel; Sergeant; 25th Inf. Reenlisted 1890 with twenty-three-years' service. SOURCE: Dobak and Phillips, *The Black Regulars*, 60–61.

BARNES, William; Private; F/10th Cav. ‡Born in Carter Co., KY, 1856; enlisted 24th Infantry, 1872; participated in Victorio campaign; transferred to 10th Cavalry, 1883; participated in Geronimo campaign, 1885; promoted to sergeant, 1892; served in Cuba, 1899–1900; promoted to first sergeant, 26 Jun 1899; assigned to Samar, Philippines, Apr 1901. SOURCE: *Colored American Magazine* 6 (Feb 1903): 295–97.

‡Born in Kentucky; private, C/24th Infantry, 5 Mar 1878–4 Mar 1883; private, A/10th Cavalry, 4 Apr 1883–3 Apr 1888; transferred to B/10th Cavalry, 19 Apr 1888; corporal, 1 Aug 1888; transferred to F/10th Cavalry, 18 Apr 1892; promoted to sergeant, 21 May 1892. SOURCE: Baker, Roster.

‡At Ft Apache, AZ, 1890, corporal, B/10th Cavalry, subscribed $.50 to testimonial to General Grierson. SOURCE: List of subscriptions, 23 Apr 1890, 10th Cavalry papers, MHI.

‡Served in 10th Cavalry in Cuba, 1898. SOURCE: Cashin, *Under Fire with the Tenth Cavalry*, 343.

In F/10th Cavalry under Lt. Charles A. Romeyn, who described him as ideal first sergeant who was an absolute teetotaler, on the job all the time, knew his paperwork thoroughly, knew all paperwork and responsibilities of supply sergeant, stable sergeant, and mess sergeant, physically active, fine rifle and pistol shot and horseman, able to manhandle a drunk when necessary, tactful with recruits, he reformed or drove out drunkards from troop, anticipated his officers' wishes, studied his men to recommend the best for promotions, studied horses, and absolutely fair with enlisted men and officers. SOURCE: Romeyn, "The First Sergeant," *The Cavalry Journal*

‡Sergeant, F/10th Cavalry, reduced to ranks. SOURCE: SO 91, 10 Cav, 9 Dec 1909, Ft Ethan Allen, VT.

BARNETT, George E.; Corporal; G/9th Cav. Received Philippine Campaign Badge number 11810 for service in G/9th Cavalry as private, 3 Mar 1902–16 Sep 1902; corporal in 9th Cavalry, Ft Leavenworth, KS, Mar 1905. SOURCE: Philippine Campaign Badge Recipients; Philippine Campaign Badge list, 29 May 1905.

BARNETT, John; Private; 25th Inf. Born in Old Town, SC; Ht 5'7", black hair and eyes, dark complexion; occupation laborer; enlisted at age 25, Charleston, SC, 16 Jul 1881; left recruit depot, David's Island, NY, 17 Aug 1881, and after trip on steamer *Thomas Kirby* to Central Depot, New York City, and train via Chicago to Running Water, Dakota Territory, 22 Aug 1881, marched forty-seven miles to Ft Randall, SD, arrived 24 Aug 1881. SOURCE: Descriptive & Assignment Rolls of Recruits, 25 Inf.

Last served in E/25th Infantry; reenlisted at age 30, New York City, 13 Aug 1886; assigned to K/25th Infantry; from Columbus Barracks, OH, arrived Ft Snelling, MN, 17 Sep 1886. SOURCE: Descriptive & Assignment Rolls of Recruits, 25 Inf.

BARRA, Juan; Private; U.S. Army. Seminole Negro Scout, served 1880–82. SOURCE: Schubert, Consolidated List of Seminole Negro Scouts.

Born in Mexico; first enlisted for one year 26 May 1880, at Ft Clark, TX; age 27, Ht 5'6", black hair and eyes, copper complexion; enlisted one additional year at Ft Clark; last discharged at Ft Clark 6 June 1882; 1880 Census lists wife Austacio, white, age 20, and daughter Leonides, white, age 4. SOURCE: Swanson, 2.

BARRERA, Espetacion; Private; U.S. Army. Seminole Negro Scout, served 1878–81. SOURCE: Schubert, Consolidated List of Seminole Negro Scouts.

Born in Mexico; first enlisted for one year 8 Feb 1878, Ft Clark, TX; age 21, Ht 5'7", hair black, eyes hazel, copper complexion; enlisted two additional times, one year each, at Ft Clark; last discharged at Ft. Clark 6 Jun 1881; 1880 Census lists wife Elsa, born in Mexico, black, age 19. SOURCE: Swanson, 2.

BARROW, Blaize; Private; A/24th Inf. Died 15 Mar 1879; buried at San Antonio National Cemetery, Section D, number 770. SOURCE: San Antonio National Cemetery Locator.

BARROW, Stephen B.; Sergeant; 10th Cav. ‡Stationed at Ft Robinson, NE, 1904–05.

‡Author of "Christmas in the United States Army," 1905, *Colored American Magazine*. SOURCE: *Colored American Magazine* 8 (Feb 1905): 95–97.

His article, "Christmas in the Tenth Cavalry," *Colored American Magazine* 8 (Feb 1905), reprinted. SOURCE: Schubert, *Voices of the Buffalo Soldier*, 222–24.

‡"Some knowledge of table arrangement [acquired] in civil life." SOURCE: Barrow, "Christmas in the United States Army," 96.

‡Sergeant, B/10th Cavalry, commissioned second lieutenant, Camp Des Moines, IA, 15 Oct 1917. SOURCE: Glass, *History of the Tenth Cavalry*, appendix M; Sweeney, *History of the American Negro*, 120.

‡Serving as warrant officer at Camp Mara, TX. SOURCE: Work, *The Negro Yearbook, 1925–1926*, 254.

‡Retired as warrant officer, resides at 1668 Harvard Ave., Columbus, OH. SOURCE: Work, *The Negro Yearbook, 1931–1932*, 334.

BARTLETT, Squires; Private; M/9th Cav. Died 27 Sep 1877; buried at Ft Bayard, NM, in plot B 14. SOURCE: "Fort Bayard National Cemetery, Records of Burials."

Squire Bartlett of H/9th Cavalry. SOURCE: "Buffalo Soldiers Buried at Ft Bayard, NM."

Squire Bartlett, M/9th Cavalry, buried 27 Sep 1877, in section A, row B, plot 32 at Ft Bayard. SOURCE: Erickson, Burials at Fort Bayard National Cemetery, NM.

BARTON, George; Private; 25th Inf. Born in Cheatham County, TN; Ht 5'8", black hair and eyes, black complexion; occupation laborer, enlisted at age 24, Nashville, TN, 19 Mar 1886; arrived Ft Snelling, MN, 31 Jul 1886. SOURCE: Descriptive & Assignment Rolls of Recruits, 25 Inf.

BASEY, Henry; M/9th Cav. Born in Louisiana; black complexion; cannot read or write, age 22, Jul 1870, at Ft McKavett, TX. SOURCE: Bierschwale, *Fort McKavett*, 99.

BATES, David; M/9th Cav. Born in Kentucky; mulatto complexion; can read, cannot write, age 27, Jul 1870, at Ft McKavett, TX. SOURCE: Bierschwale, *Fort McKavett*, 99.

BATES, James; Private; H/9th Cav. Awarded certificate of merit for distinguished service in battle, Santiago, Cuba, 1 Jul 1898. SOURCE: Gleim, *The Certificate of Merit*, 45.

‡Cited for gallantry against enemy, 1 Jul 1898. SOURCE: SecWar, *AR 1898*, 708.

‡Commended for gallantry, 1 Jul 1898, and awarded certificate of merit. SOURCE: GO 15, AGO, 13 Feb 1900.

‡Certificate of merit noted. SOURCE: Steward, *The Colored Regulars*, 280.

BATTIES, Edward; Private; 10th Cav. At Ft Hays, KS, 1867, avoided four-month sentence for desertion when trial record failed to note that court members were duly sworn. SOURCE: Dobak and Phillips, *The Black Regulars*, 188.

BATTLE, William P.; Corporal; H/10th Cav. Born in Knoxville, MD, Feb 1858; attended high school in Pittsburgh, PA; on 5 Dec 1883 married Ellen Anderson, born Marietta, PA, Nov 1857; enlisted Pittsburgh, 7 Dec 1883; Ht 5'4", black complexion, brown eyes and black hair; occupation laborer; parents Mary Ellen and Joseph Battle; served in H/10th Cavalry; served 1 Jan–1 Apr 1885 at Ft Davis, TX; Apr–2 May 1885 en route to and at Bowie Station, AZ; May 1885 at Ft Grant, AZ; Jun–26 July 1885 at Ft Apache, AZ; participated in campaigns against Geronimo and Mangus; camped at Bonita Cañon, AZ, 1886; May–31 Dec 1886 at Ft Apache, AZ; discharged 6 Dec 1888 as corporal at San Carlos, AZ; enlisted 27 Jan 1891; discharged 26 Apr 1894 as trumpeter; enlisted 27 Apr 1898, served in Battery B/PA Light Artillery, discharged 27 Nov 1898; reenlisted Nov 1898; served in Battery B/PA Light Artillery; transferred to H/10th Cavalry and served on occupation duty in Cuba, returned to Battery B, mustered out Sep 1902; member in Pennsylvania of Golden Eagle Lodge No. 22, Knights of Pythias, Lincoln Co. No. 17, Uniformed Rank Knights of Pythias, and William H. Carney Post No. 46, American Veterans of Foreign Wars; employed by U.S. Bureau of Mines; Assistant Adjutant General of Pennsylvania; died 17 Jan 1917, address 622 Watts St., Pittsburgh, PA, of pneumonia, survived by wife, who died Apr 1931. SOURCE: Sayre, *Warriors of Color*, 35–44.

A private in Troop H/10th Cavalry stationed at Bonita Cañon Camp, AZ, 30 Apr 1886. SOURCE: Tagg, *The Camp at Bonita Cañon*, 231.

‡Private, H/10th Cavalry, honorable mention for services rendered in capture of Mangas and his band, Rio Bonito, AZ, 18 Oct 1886. SOURCE: Baker, Roster.

BAXTER, William C.; Private; A/25th Inf. Born in Charles County, MD; Ht 5'6", black hair and eyes, black complexion; occupation laborer; resided in Washington, DC, when enlisted 3 Nov 1885, age 20, at Washington, DC; assigned to A/25th Infantry; arrived Ft Snelling, MN, 26 Apr 1886. SOURCE: Descriptive & Assignment Rolls of Recruits, 25 Inf.

BAYNES, Joseph; Private; E/9th Cav. Buried at San Antonio National Cemetery, Section D, number 793. SOURCE: San Antonio National Cemetery Locator.

BEALE, Willington; Private; 25th Inf. Born in Alexandria, VA; Ht 5'6", black hair and eyes, brown complexion; occupation laborer; resided in Alexandria when enlisted at age 22, Washington, DC, 4 Oct 1886; arrived Ft Snelling, MN, 20 Jan 1887. SOURCE: Descriptive & Assignment Rolls of Recruits, 25 Inf.

BEARD, George; Private; 9th Cav. Received Philippine Campaign Badge number 11875 for service as private in C/49th Infantry and H/9th Cavalry; in 9th Cavalry at Ft Leavenworth, KS, Mar 1905. SOURCE: Philippine Campaign Badge list, 29 May 1905.

BEARD, Oatis; Private; G/9th Cav. Received Philippine Campaign Badge number 11821 for service as artificer in B/24th Infantry, 22 May 1900–1 Jul 1902; private in G/9th Cavalry, Ft Leavenworth, KS, Mar 1905. SOURCE: Philippine Campaign Badge Recipients; Philippine Campaign Badge list, 29 May 1905.

BEASLEY, Cole; Private; C/9th Cav. Died 15 Dec 1890, originally buried at Ft Grant, AZ; buried at Santa Fe National Cemetery, NM, plot A-1 752. SOURCE: Santa Fe National Cemetery, Records of Burials.

BEAUMAN, William N.; Private; 10th Cav. Hospitalized at Jefferson Barracks, MO, Sep 1866. SOURCE: Kinevan, *Frontier Cavalryman*, 27.

‡William H. Beauman, Private, 10th Cavalry, recruit for regiment, hospitalized, Jefferson Barracks, 29 Sep 1866; deserted from hospital. SOURCE: McMiller, "Buffalo Soldiers," 45–46.

BECHERES, Isaac; Private; M/10th Cav. Died 10 Feb 1869 of gunshot wound at Medicine Bluff Creek, OK. SOURCE: Regimental Returns, 10th Cavalry, 1869.

Pvt. Jesse Bicherens, M/10th Cavalry, died 11 Feb 1869; buried at Camp Douglas, UT. SOURCE: Record Book of Interments, Post Cemetery, 252.

BECKS, David; 9th Cav. Born in Virginia; mulatto complexion; can read and write, age 27, Sep 1870, at Ft McKavett, TX. SOURCE: Bierschwale, *Fort McKavett*, 106.

BEECHEM, Ardrich R.; Private; L/25th Inf. Died 17 Aug 1915; buried in plot WEST 496-A at San Francisco National Cemetery. SOURCE: San Francisco National Cemetery.

BELL, Arthur; Private; H/10th Cav. ‡Served in 10th Cavalry, 1898; remained in U.S. during war with Spain. SOURCE: Cashin, *Under Fire with the Tenth Cavalry*, 347.

Brother of Medal of Honor recipient Dennis Bell. SOURCE: Schubert, *Black Valor*, 137.

BELL, Dennis; Private; H/10th Cav. Born in Washington, DC; at end of first enlistment in regiment, served in Montana, discharged with character "good"; on second enlistment when awarded Medal of Honor for bravery at Tayabacoa, Cuba, Jun 1898. SOURCE: Schubert, *Black Valor*, 137, 141–42.

‡Served in 10th Cavalry in Cuba, 1898. SOURCE: Cashin, *Under Fire with the Tenth Cavalry*, 347.

‡Awarded Medal of Honor for heroism in Cuba, 1898. See OTT, **THOMPKINS**, William H.; Sergeant; H/25th Infantry

‡Medal of Honor mentioned. SOURCE: Steward, *The Colored Regulars*, 205.

‡Born in Washington, DC; received medal while in hospital, Ft Bliss, TX. SOURCE: Lee, *Negro Medal of Honor Men*, 92, 98.

‡Now out of service; holder of Medal of Honor. SOURCE: *ANJ* 37 (24 Feb 1900): 611.

BELL, James; Private; 9th Cav. Received Philippine Campaign Badge number 11904 for service as private in G/10th Cavalry; in 9th Cavalry at Ft Leavenworth, KS, Mar 1905. SOURCE: Philippine Campaign Badge list, 29 May 1905.

BELL, John; Private; G/9th Cav. Received Philippine Campaign Badge number 11822 for service as private in G/9th Cavalry, 2 Apr 1902–16 Sep 1902; private in 9th Cavalry, Ft Leavenworth, KS, Mar 1905. SOURCE: Philippine Campaign Badge Recipients; Philippine Campaign Badge list, 29 May 1905.

BELL, John; Private; E/25th Inf. ‡Died in the Philippines, 10 Sep 1900. SOURCE: *ANJ* 38 (8 Dec 1900): 355.

John Bel died 10 Sep 1900; buried in plot NADDN926 at San Francisco National Cemetery. SOURCE: San Francisco National Cemetery.

BELL, John B.; Private; 25th Inf. Born in Orange County, VA; Ht 5'4", black hair and brown eyes, brown complexion; occupation laborer; resided in Orange County when enlisted at age 24, Washington, DC, 29 Sep 1886; arrived Ft Snelling, MN, 20 Jan 1887. SOURCE: Descriptive & Assignment Rolls of Recruits, 25 Inf.

BELL, Thomas; Private; A/24th Inf. ‡Died of acute dysentery in the Philippines, 19 Nov 1899. SOURCE: *ANJ* 37 (2 Dec 1899): 327.

Died 19 Nov 1898 in the Philippines; buried in plot EAST 1289 at San Francisco National Cemetery. SOURCE: San Francisco National Cemetery.

BELL, William; QM Sgt; B/10th Cav. ‡Bell's deposition attests to heroism of Pvt. Arthur G. Wheeler, B/10th Cavalry, Las Guasimas, Cuba, 24 Jun 1898; sergeant, recommended for Medal of Honor for heroism in assault on San Juan Hill, 1 Jul 1898. SOURCE: Cashin, *Under Fire with the Tenth Cavalry*, 180, 186, 337.

‡Shot twice by wife with pistol at Ft Robinson, NE, dance in honor of Sergeant Perry, L/10th Cavalry; died 26 Jul 1904. SOURCE: Crawford *Tribune*, 29 Jul 1904.

‡Quartermaster sergeant, died Ft Robinson, 26 Jul 1904; twenty-three-year veteran. SOURCE: Monthly Report, Chaplain William T. Anderson, Ft Robinson, 1 Aug 1904, AGO File 53910.

‡Shot and killed by wife at Ft Robinson dance, 24 July 1904; had resided in southwest part of Crawford, NE. SOURCE: Crawford *Bulletin*, 29 Jul 1904.

Murder by his wife, Ft Robinson, NE, Jul 1904, described in report by Chaplain William Anderson, 10th Cavalry. SOURCE: Schubert, *Voices of the Buffalo Soldier*, 224–25.

‡Buried, Ft Robinson, 27 Jul 1904. SOURCE: List of Interments, Ft Robinson.

BELL, William; Private; A/9th Cav. Died 3 Jan 1899; originally buried at Ft Grant, AZ; buried at Santa Fe National Cemetery, NM, plot A-1 760. SOURCE: Santa Fe National Cemetery, Records of Burials.

BENEFIELD, Edward; Private; G/25th Inf. Buried at San Antonio National Cemetery, Section F, number 1055. SOURCE: San Antonio National Cemetery Locator.

BENJAMIN, Robert A.; Ord Sgt; U.S. Army. ‡Born in Kingston, Jamaica; enlisted at age 21; occupation waiter; Ht 5'6", brown complexion; enlisted, M/9th Cavalry, 2 Jun 1873; continuous service until retirement, 2 Feb 1905; saddler sergeant, 9th Cavalry, 1 Apr 1883; ordnance sergeant, U.S. Army, 9 Oct 1894; at marriage a resident of Orangeburg, SC, married in Columbia, SC; father Isaac Alfred Augustus Benjamin of England; mother Sarah Anne Miller of Jamaica; wife's father James L. Thompson and mother Malinda Simons, both of Richland Co., SC; died 30 Jan 1916, Columbia; first wife, Mary G. Young Benjamin, died 6 Feb 1907, and buried in Highland Cemetery, Geary Co., KS; second wife, Syrene E. Benjamin, widow, address 2506 Taylor St., Columbia, in 1918; had $20 per month in 1922 and lived at 1913 Bambridge St., Philadelphia; pension granted 1917 as Comanche War widow; pension stopped at 2506 Taylor St., Columbia, when she died 14 Nov 1929. SOURCE: VA File WC 927337, Robert A. Benjamin.

‡Born in Kingston, Jamaica; arrived New York, 1869, stayed to 1873; enlisted Philadelphia, 1873; six months at St. Louis, MO, arsenal, then Ft McKavett and Ft Stockton, TX; married eleven years in 1894, with one daughter, Clara. SOURCE: Court Martial Records, Plummer.

Sgt. Benjamin Davis, Post QM Sgt, knew Benjamin from Jun 1874 until his death; soldiered together in Texas, corresponded and kept track of each other; best man at Benjamin's wedding to Mary Young, Junction City, KS.

SOURCE: Affidavit, Davis, 9 Dec 1918, VA File WC 927337, Robert A. Benjamin.

‡At Ft Robinson, NE, authorized four-month furlough. SOURCE: *ANJ* 25 (31 Mar 1888): 714.

‡Sergeant, Ft Robinson; wife expected back at post soon. SOURCE: Cleveland *Gazette*, 12 Jan 1889.

‡With Pvt. John W. Nicholls, I/8th Infantry, ordered to conduct insane Pvt. Lewellen Young, F/9th Cavalry, to asylum, Washington, DC, from Ft Robinson, 14 Jan 1889. SOURCE: Order 10, 12 Jan 1889, Post Orders, Ft Robinson.

‡Recommended by Commander, Ft Robinson, for ordnance sergeant: "sober and reliable and an excellent clerk." SOURCE: Letter to AG, through CO, 9 Cav, Ft Robinson, 18 Mar 1891, LS, Ft Robinson.

‡Promoted to regimental quartermaster sergeant, in accordance with 9th Cavalry Order 27, Ft Robinson, 23 Apr 1891. SOURCE: *Cleveland Gazette*, 16 May 1891.

‡Discharge revoked; returned to regimental saddler sergeant. SOURCE: TWX, AGO, 7 Jan 1892.

‡Assists with regimental clerical work. SOURCE: CO, Ft Robinson, to AAG, DP, 5 May 1892, LS, Ft Robinson.

‡Saddler sergeant since 28 Jun 1888. SOURCE: Roster, 9 Cav, 1893.

‡Examined for ordnance sergeant, Ft Robinson. SOURCE: *ANJ* 30 (1 Jul 1893): 745.

‡Resides at Ft Robinson with wife and child. SOURCE: Medical History, Ft Robinson, Aug 1893.

‡His daughter is student at post Sunday School, 1894; has organ in quarters. SOURCE: Investigation of Charges against Chaplain Plummer.

‡Involved in argument at Ft Robinson, 11 Sep 1894, for which general court martial dishonorably discharged Sgt. David R. Dillon, 24 Sep 1894; at the time lived with wife and mother-in-law, Mrs. Young. SOURCE: Court Martial Records, Dillon.

‡Promoted to ordnance sergeant. SOURCE: *ANJ* 32 (27 Oct 1894): 141.

‡Appointed ordnance sergeant 9 Oct 1894, from saddler sergeant, 9th Cavalry. SOURCE: Dobak, "Staff Noncommissioned Officers."

‡On promotion to ordnance sergeant, Commander, 9th Cavalry, "desires to give expression to the worth of Sgt. Benjamin's long and faithful service in the regiment and in the position he now relinquishes." SOURCE: *ANJ* 32 (3 Nov 1894): 154.

Sgt. Wesley Jefferds, A/9th Cavalry, knew him personally from 1872 until Benjamin's death. SOURCE: Affidavit, Jefferds, 2 Dec 1918, VA File WC 927337, Robert A. Benjamin.

‡Inquired from retirement in 1910 whether War Department objected to his becoming commandant, Claflin College, Orangeburg, SC. SOURCE: AGO File 1607790.

Retired ordnance sergeant when issued Indian Wars Campaign Badge number 1084 on 18 Dec 1908. SOURCE: Carroll, *Indian Wars Campaign Badge*, 31.

BENNET, John; Private; H/10th Cav. In Troop H/10th Cavalry stationed at Bonita Cañon Camp, AZ, 30 Apr 1886. SOURCE: Tagg, *The Camp at Bonita Cañon*, 231.

BENNETT, Aleck; QM Sgt; 9th Cav. ‡Alexander Benett appointed sergeant, E/9th Cavalry, 3 Apr 1893. SOURCE: Roster, 9 Cav, 1893.

Appointed 3 Apr 1893; sergeant at Ft DuChesne, UT, in F/9th Cavalry, Jan 1897. SOURCE: Ninth Cavalry, Roster of NCOs, 1897.

Received Philippine Campaign Badge number 11759 for service as quartermaster sergeant in F/9th Cavalry; in 9th Cavalry at Ft Leavenworth, KS, Mar 1905. SOURCE: Philippine Campaign Badge list, 29 May 1905.

BENNETT, John; Private; M/10th Cav. Shot by civilian, died 17 Jun 1875 at Ft Stockton, TX. SOURCE: Regimental Returns, 10th Cavalry, 1875.

BENNETT, John; Private; H/10th Cav. Born in Bolivar County, MS; enlisted Jefferson Barracks, MO, 11 Apr 1883; Ht 5'4"; black complexion, eyes, and hair; occupation laborer; diagnosed with syphilis, Ft Davis, TX, Jun 1883. SOURCE: Sayre, *Warriors of Color*, 45.

BENNETT, Thomas; Private; D/25th Inf. Died at Ft Clark, TX; buried at Fort Sam Houston National Cemetery, Section PE, number 255. SOURCE: Buffalo Soldiers Interred in Fort Sam Houston National Cemetery.

BENNIN, Thomas; Private; A/10th Cav. ‡Original member of 10th Cavalry; in troop when organized, Ft Leavenworth, KS, 18 Feb 1867. SOURCE: McMiller, "Buffalo Soldiers," 68.

Died of typhoid 21 May 1867 at Ft Larned, KS. SOURCE: Regimental Returns, 10th Cavalry, 1867.

BENSON, Caleb; Sergeant; K/10th Cav. ‡Born in Jacksonville, FL, 25 Jun 1859; enlisted 2 Feb 1875; private, 9th Cavalry, 1875–80; private, B and K/10th Cavalry, 1885–1904; in K/10th Cavalry 1907–08; retired as sergeant from K/10th Cavalry, 29 Sep 1908; married Percilla Smith of Dawes Co., NE, age 27, 26 Mar 1909; died 19 Nov 1937, Crawford, NE, of coronary thrombosis, with B. F. Richards as attending physician; civilian occupation waiter; buried Ft Robinson, NE. SOURCE: VA File XC 2499129, Caleb Benson.

‡Attacked by Indians in Colorado, mouth of Navcos River, Sep 1878. SOURCE: Hamilton, "History of the Ninth Cavalry," 8.

With Captain Dodge at battle at Milk River, CO, 2–10 Oct 1879; received Indian Wars Campaign Badge number 1485. SOURCE: Miller, *Hollow Victory*, 167, 191, 206–7.

‡At Ft Apache, AZ, 1890, private, B/10th Cavalry, subscribed $.50 to testimonial to General Grierson. SOURCE: List of subscriptions, 23 Apr 1890, 10th Cavalry papers, MHI.

‡Private, served in 10th Cavalry, 1898; remained in U.S. during war with Spain. SOURCE: Cashin, *Under Fire with the Tenth Cavalry*, 349.

‡First sergeant, George W. Gaines, A/10th Cavalry was in charge of detachment of regiment camped on timber reserve, Ft Robinson, when sudden storm caused stove explosion that partially blinded Benson. SOURCE: Deposition, Gaines, 25 Aug 1905, VA File XC 2499129, Caleb Benson.

‡First Sergeant Gaines, supports Benson's claim for pension. SOURCE: Deposition, Gaines, 11 Jul 1906, VA File XC 2499129, Caleb Benson.

‡W. F. Clark, Saddler, 10th Cavalry, age 55, and Beverly F. Thornton, Cook, K/10th Cavalry, deposed 11 Jul 1906, and Philip E. Letcher, Sergeant, K/10th Cavalry, Ft Robinson, 1904, age 48 in 1906 wrote deposition in support of pension claim of Caleb Benson. SOURCE: VA File XC 2499129, Caleb Benson.

‡Retired to Crawford after tour in the Philippines, 1909; married Percilla at Crawford in 1909; homesteaded to 1914 when moved to Ft Robinson, where employed first by Captain and Mrs. Whitehead, then Colonel Calvert; then traveled before returning permanently to Crawford. SOURCE: *Souvenir Book: Crawford*, 59.

‡Unable to earn living and "dependent largely upon the good will of my former troop, K 10th Cavalry, for my support"; rejected to finish his thirty years due to disability "after having put in the best years of my life [27] as a soldier in the U.S. Army, and I therefore beg you to hasten the assistance which of right I should have from my Government." SOURCE: Benson, Letter to Commissioner of Pensions, Washington, DC, 22 Aug 1905, VA File XC 2499129, Caleb Benson.

Retired first sergeant when issued Indian Wars Campaign Badge number 1485 on 10 Oct 1910. SOURCE: Carroll, *Indian Wars Campaign Badge*, 43.

Reminiscence of military life published in (Crawford) *Northwest Nebraska News*, August 9, 1934.

‡Buried Ft Robinson, 16 Nov 1937. SOURCE: List of Interments, Ft Robinson.

‡Career summary. SOURCE: Omaha *World-Herald*, 6 Dec 1992.

BENT, John; Sergeant; M/9th Cav. Died at Ft McKavett, TX, on 17 Dec 1872; buried at San Antonio National Cemetery, Section E, number 874. SOURCE: San Antonio National Cemetery Locator.

BENTFORD, David; QM Sgt; 41st Inf. Civil War veteran of 111th U.S. Colored Infantry, spent seven months in Confederate prisoner-of-war camp; regimental quartermaster sergeant. SOURCE: Dobak and Phillips, *The Black Regulars*, 60.

BENTLEY, George; Private; K/9th Cav. ‡Born in Danville, KY; Ht 5'8", mulatto; occupation laborer; character on discharge good; received $147.15 on honorable discharge, completion of enlistment, Ft Davis, TX, 1871, at age 26. SOURCE: Carroll, *The Black Military Experience*, 438–40.

Settled near Ft Davis, married Mexican woman, fathered several children, including George Bentley Jr., who remained in area and married Hispanic woman; "according to other black ex-cavalrymen, Bentley had bayoneted an Indian baby during a campaign years earlier and thus marked his offspring with a curse." SOURCE: Leiker, *Racial Borders*, 88.

BENTON, Mark; Private; M/9th Cav. Born in Spencer County, KY; died and buried at Ft McKavett, TX, before 17 May 1879; body removed to National Cemetery, San Antonio, TX, 23 Nov 1883. SOURCE: Bierschwale, *Fort McKavett,* 122.

BERKLEY, Scott; C/25th Inf. Born in Kentucky; black complexion; can read and write, age 22, 5 Sep 1870, at Ft McKavett, TX. SOURCE: Bierschwale, *Fort McKavett,* 109.

BERRY, Benjamin; Private; I/10th Cav. In Troop I/10th Cavalry stationed at Bonita Cañon Camp, AZ, 30 Jun 1886. SOURCE: Tagg, *The Camp at Bonita Cañon*, 231.

BERRY, Butler; Private; H/10th Cav. Served in unit sometime between 1883 and 1891. SOURCE: Sayre, *Warriors of Color*, 360.

‡Resided at 1808 11th St., NW, Washington, DC, in 1912; could not recall disability of Webb Chatmoun, who was "my bunkie friend," and now lives at 1712 G St., NW, Washington, DC. SOURCE: Affidavit, Butler, 1922, VA File C 2360629, Webb Chatmoun.

BERRY, Edward; Sergeant; H/24th Inf. ‡Born in Virginia, 1830; volunteered 1863, served with F/26th New York Colored Infantry as first sergeant until 7 Oct 1865; enlisted in regular Army at Cleveland, OH, 10 Jan 1868; served in H/41st Infantry and H/24th Infantry; participated in Victorio campaign; quartermaster sergeant of his company for nineteen years; also post commissary sergeant and quartermaster sergeant; died Ft Grant, AZ, of Bright's disease, age 60, 23 Apr 1890. Funeral conducted by Chaplain Weaver; Musician Rounds blew taps; pallbearers commanded by Sgt. William Henson, H/24th Infantry, and included Sgts. John

Johnson, H/24th Infantry, G. D. Powell, C/24th Infantry, W. Pearcall, E/24th Infantry, J. W. Wright and O. Brown, G/10th Cavalry, Pvts. B. Baker, Benjamin Webb, W. Williams, L. Varnes, A. Bailey, and W. H. Booker, H/24th Infantry. SOURCE: Cleveland *Gazette*, 26 Apr 1890.

Died 14 Apr 1890, originally buried at Ft Grant; buried at Santa Fe National Cemetery, NM, plot A-1 737. SOURCE: Santa Fe National Cemetery, Records of Burials.

BERRY, George; Sergeant; G/10th Cav. Served at Ft Sill, OK, 1875; wounded in skirmish with Indians, 6 Apr 1875; carried flags of 10th Cavalry and 3rd Cavalry up San Juan Hill, Cuba, 1 Jul 1898. SOURCE: Schubert, *Voices of the Buffalo Soldier*, 67, 263.

‡Sergeant, D/10th Cavalry; at Ft Apache, AZ, 1890, subscribed $.50 to testimonial to General Grierson. SOURCE: List of subscriptions, 23 Apr 1890, 10th Cavalry papers, MHI.

‡Sergeant, G/10th Cavalry; served in 10th Cavalry in Cuba, 1898. SOURCE: Cashin, *Under Fire with the Tenth Cavalry*, 344.

BERRY, Henry; Private; B/9th Cav. ‡Died of cholera in the Philippines. SOURCE: *ANJ* 39 (9 Aug 1902): 1248.

Died 6 Jun 1902; buried in plot NADDN614 at San Francisco National Cemetery. SOURCE: San Francisco National Cemetery.

BERRY, James F.; Corporal; B/9th Cav. ‡James Berry appointed corporal, 9 Jul 1892. SOURCE: Roster, 9 Cav, 1893.

‡Teaching school at Ft DuChesne, UT, 20 Dec 1892–30 Apr 1893. SOURCE: Report of Schools, Ft DuChesne.

Appointed corporal 22 Dec 1896; in B/9th Cavalry at Ft DuChesne, Jan 1897. SOURCE: Ninth Cavalry, Roster of NCOs, 1897.

BERRYMAN, James; Private; D/9th Cav. Died 15 Dec 1871; buried at San Antonio National Cemetery, Section C, number 475. SOURCE: San Antonio National Cemetery Locator.

BETHEL, Charles; Recruit; 9th Cav. Died 4 Mar 1873; buried at San Antonio National Cemetery, Section D, number 776. SOURCE: San Antonio National Cemetery Locator.

BETHEL, Elijah; Private; I/24th Inf. ‡Enlisted Baltimore, MD, 6 Feb 1899; joined company 23 Feb 1899. SOURCE: Muster Roll, I/24 Inf, Jan–Feb 1899.

‡On detached service at Benicia Barracks, CA, since 8 Apr 1899. SOURCE: Muster Roll, I/24 Inf, Mar–Apr 1899.

‡On detached service at Tarlac, Philippines, since 2 Dec 1899. SOURCE: Muster Roll, I/24 Inf, Nov–Dec 1899.

‡Killed in action in the Philippines, 31 Jul 1900. *See* OTT, SMITH, C. H., Sergeant, I/24th Infantry

Died 1 Aug 1900; buried in plot ESIDE1242 at San Francisco National Cemetery. SOURCE: San Francisco National Cemetery.

BETTERS, James; Corporal; C/9th Cav. ‡Cpl. James Betters, C/9th Cavalry, mortally wounded in Mogollon Mountains, NM, 1876, when his carbine discharged accidentally; buried without ceremony, Ft Bayard, NM. SOURCE: Billington, *New Mexico's Buffalo Soldiers*, 53–54.

Eleven-year veteran, accidentally shot and killed on patrol in Black Mountains, NM, Oct 1877; body unceremoniously and improperly buried, causing scandal. SOURCE: Kenner, *Buffalo Soldiers and Officers of the Ninth Cavalry*, 21.

BETTIS, James; Corporal; C/9th Cav. Died 3 Oct 1877, buried at Ft Bayard, NM, in plot E 35. SOURCE: "Fort Bayard National Cemetery, Records of Burials."

Buried 3 Oct 1877 in section A, row F, plot 38, Ft Bayard. SOURCE: Erickson, Burials at Fort Bayard National Cemetery, NM.

BIAS, Samuel; 25th Inf. Civil War veteran. SOURCE: Dobak and Phillips, *The Black Regulars*, 172.

BICHERENS, Jesse; Private; M/10th Cav. *See* BECHERES, Isaac, Private, M/10th Cavalry

BIDDLE, George; Private; M/10th Cav. ‡Original member of 10th Cavalry; in troop when organized, Ft Riley, KS, 15 Oct 1867. SOURCE: McMiller, "Buffalo Soldiers," 79.

Died 10 Aug 1869 in hospital at Ft Sill, OK. SOURCE: Regimental Returns, 10th Cavalry, 1869.

BIDLEY, Robert; Musician; B/24th Inf. Died at Camp Eagle Pass, TX, on 21 Sep 1878; buried at San Antonio National Cemetery, Section F, number 1142. SOURCE: San Antonio National Cemetery Locator.

BIGGER, William; Sergeant; 9th Cav. Received Philippine Campaign Badge number 11857 for service as sergeant, H/9th Cavalry; in 9th Cavalry at Ft Leavenworth, KS, Mar 1905. SOURCE: Philippine Campaign Badge list, 29 May 1905.

BIRCH, Philip; Private; 25th Inf. Born in Honchester, KY; Ht 5'10", black hair and eyes, yellow complexion; occupation cook; enlisted at age 24, St. Louis, MO, 20 Nov

1886; arrived Ft Snelling, MN, 1 Apr 1887. SOURCE: Descriptive & Assignment Rolls of Recruits, 25 Inf.

BIRD, Zedrick L.; Private; 25th Inf. Stationed at Ft Elliott, TX, 1886, married by magistrate in Mobeetie, TX. SOURCE: Dobak and Phillips, *The Black Regulars*, 140–41.

BIRT, Cape; Private; G/9th Cav. Received Philippine Campaign Badge number 11764 for service as private in G/9th Cavalry; in 9th Cavalry at Ft Leavenworth, KS, Mar 1905. SOURCE: Philippine Campaign Badge list, 29 May 1905.

BISHOP, James; Sergeant; A/39th Inf. Civil War veteran, served in K/80th U.S. Colored Infantry; sentence of twenty years for involvement in New Iberia, LA, mutiny, Jul 1867, reduced to six months. SOURCE: Dobak and Phillips, *The Black Regulars*, 222.

BISMUKES, Samuel; Private; E/10th Cav. In Troop I/10th Cavalry stationed at Bonita Cañon Camp, AZ, 30 Jun 1886. SOURCE: Tagg, *The Camp at Bonita Cañon*, 231.

‡Samuel Bismuckes, Cook, E/9th Cavalry; veteran of Indian wars, Spanish-American War, and Philippine Insurrection; at Ft D. A. Russell, WY, in 1910. SOURCE: *Illustrated Review: Ninth Cavalry*, with picture.

Received Indian Wars Campaign Badge number 759 on 18 Nov 1908 as cook. SOURCE: Carroll, *Indian Wars Campaign Badge*, 22.

BIVANS, George E.; Private; I/24th Infantry. *See* BIVENS, George E., Private, I/24th Infantry

BIVENS, George; Private; I/25th Inf. Died 4 Oct 1902; originally buried at Ft Niobrara, NE; reburied at Ft Leavenworth National Cemetery, plot 3521. SOURCE: Ft Leavenworth National Cemetery.

BIVENS, George E.; Private; I/24th Inf. ‡Name also spelled BIVENS and BIVINS

‡Enlisted in I/24th Infantry, Baltimore, MD, 18 Feb 1899. SOURCE: Muster Roll, I/24 Inf, Jan–Feb 1899.

‡On detached service, Three Rivers, CA, 3 May–21 June 1899; on detached service, Presidio of San Francisco, since 22 Jun 1899. SOURCE: Muster Roll, I/24 Inf, May–Jun 1899.

‡Rejoined company 26 Jul 1899. SOURCE: Muster Roll, I/24 Inf, Jul–Aug 1899.

‡Allotted $5 per month for three months to Emma Buey. SOURCE: Muster Roll, I/24 Inf, Sep–Oct 1899.

‡Wounded in action, 31 Jul 1900. *See* OTT, **SMITH**, C. H.; Sergeant; I/24th Infantry

Received Philippine Campaign Badge number 11876 for service in I/24th Infantry and H/9th Cavalry; in 9th

Cavalry at Ft Leavenworth, KS, Mar 1905. SOURCE: Philippine Campaign Badge list, 29 May 1905.

‡Forced to accompany mutineers, I/24th Infantry, Houston, 1917; died of wounds inflicted by whites. SOURCE: Haynes, *A Night of Violence*, 126, 170.

BIVINS, Horace W.; Ord Sgt; U.S. Army. ‡Born in Pungoteague, Accomack Co., VA, son of Severn S. and Elizabeth Bivins, farmers; at age 15 put in charge of eight-horse farm, one mile from Keller Station, VA; first military training at Hampton Institute, 1885; enlisted Washington, DC, 7 Nov 1887; assigned to E/10th Cavalry and joined troop at Ft Grant, AZ, 19 Oct 1888; transferred to Ft Apache, AZ, Oct 1889; appointed corporal, 15 Jun 1890; an author of *Under Fire with the Tenth Cavalry*; stationed at Ft Sam Houston, TX, 1899. SOURCE: Cashin, *Under Fire with the Tenth Cavalry*, 56–58 (with picture), 344.

Born 1866 of free Negro ancestry; father provided funding for church and school at Pungoteague, VA, 1862, which was burned down the day it was finished; trained briefly at Jefferson Barracks, MO, then joined troop in Arizona Territory; won four gold medals for expert marksmanship with carbine and pistol in 1894; in campaigns against Geronimo; served in Arizona and Montana before 1898; co-authored *Under Fire with the Tenth Cavalry* while stationed in the Philippines; stuffed and mounted specimens of birds, animals, insects which he donated to Billings, MT, library, Hampton Institute, and four government museums; retired 1913; commissioned captain in infantry in 1918; assigned to command reserve labor battalion at Camp Dix, NJ; retired to Billings at close of war; earned thirty-two medals and ribbons; married woman from Billings in 1904; after wife died in 1944 moved to Baltimore to live with niece, Mrs. Isaac Ingraham. SOURCE: "Captain Bivins, 94, Held Many Citations," Baltimore *Evening Sun*, 30 Dec 1955, 15.

‡"A distinguished member of the Tenth U.S. Cavalry—a character worthy of the emulation of every young man of the Negro race"; entered Hampton as work student at age 17; one year later entered Wayland Seminary, Washington, DC; six months later enlisted in Army; joined 10th Cavalry, 19 Jun 1888, and immediately assigned to adjutant as clerk; many marksmanship prizes; offered $75 per week to travel with Buffalo Bill's Wild West show; returned to Hampton on furlough to attend, 3 Dec 1897, and remained until war; "a sober, sensible, industrious Negro, who, in his daily life evinces that kind of race pride that is beautifully commendable and who would have all men thoroughly convinced that the Negro can learn, if given the opportunity, all the arts and cunning performed by any race of men." SOURCE: *Indianapolis Freeman*, 25 Feb 1899.

‡In E/10th Cavalry, 7 Nov 1887–6 Nov 1892; in G/10th Cavalry, 7 Nov 1892–6 Nov 1897; in G/10th Cavalry and on regimental noncommissioned staff, 7 Nov 1897–10 Jul

1901; in Ordnance Department, 11 Jul 1901–15 Jul 1913; foreign service in Cuba, 22 Jun–13 Aug 1898, 7 May 1899–5 Jan 1900; in the Philippines, 14 May 1901–6 Oct 1902, 8 Jun 1906–2 Oct 1907, 3 Feb–15 Nov 1908. SOURCE: Bivins to AG, USA, 1 Jul 1913, AGO File 137634.

‡At Ft Apache, 1890, private, E/10th Cavalry, subscribed $.50 to testimonial to General Grierson. SOURCE: List of subscriptions, 23 Apr 1890, 10th Cavalry papers, MHI.

‡Sharpshooter, as private, E/10th Cavalry, Ft Apache. SOURCE: *ANJ* 28 (4 Jul 1891): 765.

‡Ranked number 6 with revolver, bronze medal, Departments of Dakota and Columbia, Ft Keogh, MT, 15–23 Aug 1892. SOURCE: Baker, Roster; GO 75, AGO, 3 Nov 1892.

‡Second with revolver, silver medal, Departments of Dakota and Columbia, Ft Keogh, 14–22 Aug 1893. SOURCE: Baker, Roster; GO 82, AGO, 24 Oct 1893.

‡First with carbine and revolver, gold medal, Departments of Dakota and Columbia, and Army, distinguished marksman, 1894. SOURCE: Baker, Roster.

‡Won Army gold medal in carbine competition, Ft Sheridan, IL, 16 Oct 1894, with 589 points. SOURCE: Cleveland *Gazette*, 3 Nov 1894; GO 62, AGO, 15 Nov 1894.

Highest carbine score in Army, 1894. SOURCE: *ANJ* 32 (20 Oct 1894): 119.

‡Ranked number 24 among carbine sharpshooters. SOURCE: GO 1, AGO, 2 Jan 1895.

‡Appointed corporal, G/10th Cavalry, 5 Mar 1893; sergeant, 5 Dec 1895; at Ft Assiniboine, MT, 1897. SOURCE: Baker, Roster.

‡Only man ever to win three marksmanship gold medals in one year. SOURCE: Indianapolis *Freeman*, 10 Jul 1897.

‡Ht 5'9", black complexion; distinguished marksman, 1894; served with Hotchkiss gun battery, San Juan, Cuba, 1–3 Jul 1898; promoted from quartermaster sergeant to sergeant major, 2nd Squadron, 10th Cavalry, and on detached service at Bayamo, Cuba, with squadron, 28 Sep–14 Dec 1899; in U.S. with squadron, 2 Jan 1900; married, character excellent; $3 per month additional pay for ten years' continuous service; reenlisted 16 Nov 1900, beginning fourteenth year; ordnance sergeant, U.S. Army, 1 Jul 1901. SOURCE: Descriptive Book, 10 Cav Officers & NCOs.

‡Cited for conspicuous gallantry with Hotchkiss Guns, Cuba, 1 Jul 1898. SOURCE: SecWar, AR 1898, 335; *ANJ* 37 (24 Feb 1900): 611; GO 15, AGO, 13 Feb 1900.

‡Recommended for commission by William H. Heard, late minister resident and consul general to Liberia, as "a brave man and worthy in every way of promotion." SOURCE: Heard to President McKinley, 11 Sep 1899, AGO File 137634.

‡Appointed in colored U.S. Volunteers. SOURCE: AGO File 277172, 16 Sep 1899.

‡Regarding commission in regular Army. SOURCE: AGO File 280745, 26 Sep 1899.

‡Appointed in U.S. Volunteers. SOURCE: AGO File 295452, 24 Oct 1899.

‡On detached service at Ft Clark, TX, 31 Jan 1899–30 Jul 1900, at Ft Brown, TX, 30 Jul–Dec 1900. SOURCE: Muster Roll, Det, Regt NCS, 10 Cav, 31 Dec 1899–31 Dec 1900.

‡On detached service at Pena Colorado, TX, superintending disinterment of bodies of deceased soldiers, 3–7 May 1900. SOURCE: Muster Roll, Det, Regt NCS, 10 Cav, 30 Apr–30 Jun 1900.

‡Discharged end of term, character excellent, with $22.62 clothing allowance; reenlisted, married, 7 Nov 1900. SOURCE: Muster Roll, Det, Regt NCS, 10 Cav, 31 Oct–31 Dec 1900.

‡In charge of detachment, La Granga, Samar, Philippines, 2 Jul–2 Aug 1901, scouting and reconnoitering in northwest corner of island and cleaning out vicinity of insurgents and supplies; marched 655 miles on foot. SOURCE: Bivins to AG, USA, 5 Jul 1916, AGO File 137634.

‡Appointed ordnance sergeant. SOURCE: AGO File 387233, 6 Jul 1901.

‡Ordered to report from residence, 721 5th St., Oakland, CA, to Commander, Presidio of San Francisco, at end of furlough, for transportation to Ft Missoula, MT, for duty. SOURCE: SO 304, AGO, 29 Dec 1902.

‡Reassigned from Ft Missoula to the Philippines. SOURCE: AGO File 1112753, Mar 1906.

‡Expert marksman, 1908, 1909, 1910. SOURCE: AGO File 137634.

‡Stationed at Camp Overton, Philippines. SOURCE: AGO File 1317273, 21 Apr 1908.

‡On arrival at San Francisco, to be sent to Depot of Recruits and Casuals, Ft McDowell, AZ. SOURCE: AGO File 1437874, 21 Apr 1908.

‡Recommended to try out for Cavalry National Rifle Team by Capt. W. H. Hay, 10th Cavalry. SOURCE: AGO File 1511426, 12 Apr 1909.

‡Requests transfer from station at Ft McDowell to Ft Missoula or Ft Mackenzie, WY, preferably latter; mother is aged and unable to travel from Billings, MT, home; Bivins suffering from chronic constipation and would like to serve in cold climate. SOURCE: Bivins to AG, USA, 21 Feb 1909, AGO File 137634.

‡Transferred to Ft Mackenzie. SOURCE: SO 66, AGO, 23 Mar 1909.

‡Ordered from Ft Mackenzie to Ft Ontario, NY. SOURCE: SO 199, AGO, 25 Aug 1910.

‡Ordered to Ft Ethan Allen, VT. SOURCE: AGO File 1728451, 24 Dec 1910.

‡Requests transfer to Ft Mackenzie due to ill health; wife and three children in Billings since 23 Apr 1911 due to poor health in this climate, on advice of doctor.

SOURCE: Bivins to AG, USA, 19 Mar 1913, AGO File 137634.

‡On temporary duty at Ft Mackenzie until eligible to retire. SOURCE: SO 85, AGO, 12 Apr 1913.

‡Retired as of 19 Jul 1913. SOURCE: TWX, CO, Ft Mackenzie to AG, USA, 23 Jul 1913, AGO File 137634.

‡Offers his services as captain in event of call for colored volunteers or guard; outlines his service and states that he was never tried by court martial and that his physical condition is good. SOURCE: Bivins to AG, USA, 5 Jul 1916, AGO File 137634.

‡Repeats 1916 offer: "Refering to letter your office last July I tender you my services to help organize a regiment in my home Virginia." SOURCE: TWX, Bivins to AG, USA, 4 Feb 1917, AGO File 137634.

‡Retired 1930, with thirty-two years' service; was lieutenant of volunteers, 1899; captain, Camp Dix, 1918; resides at Billings. SOURCE: *Crisis* 40 (May 1930): 168.

‡Mrs. Claudia Bivins raised most money for scholarship loan fund of Colored Women's Clubs of Montana, 1930; fund was named for her. SOURCE: Davis, *Lifting as They Climb*, 357.

‡Captain, retired, in accordance with Act of 7 May 1932; captain, Infantry, U.S. Army, 18 Sep 1918; active duty, 12 May–18 Sep 1918. SOURCE: *Official Army Register, 1937*, 1254.

Died 4 Dec 1960 of brief illness; lived with niece, Mrs. Isaac Ingraham, 3432 Piedmont Ave., Baltimore, MD; survivors include son, Charles W. Bivins, Warm Springs, MT; buried in Baltimore National Cemetery. SOURCE: Baltimore *Evening Sun*, 8 Dec 1960.

‡Drawing. SOURCE: Lynk, *The Black Troopers*, 31.

‡Biographical sketch. SOURCE: Logan and Winston, *Dictionary of American Negro Biography*, 45-46.

BLACK, Allen; Private; D/10th Cav. ‡Original member of 10th Cavalry; in troop when organized, Ft Leavenworth, KS, 1 Jun 1867. SOURCE: McMiller, "Buffalo Soldiers," 71.

Died 27 Nov 1868 of consumption at Ft Arbuckle, OK. SOURCE: Regimental Returns, 10th Cavalry, 1868.

Saddler, D/10th Cavalry, died 27 Nov 1868 of consumption, Ft Arbuckle. SOURCE: Regimental Returns, 10th Cavalry, 1868.

BLACK, Top; Private; E/10th Cav. In Troop E/10th Cavalry stationed at Bonita Cañon Camp, AZ, 28 Feb 1886. SOURCE: Tagg, *The Camp at Bonita Cañon*, 231.

BLACKSTONE, Charley; Private; G/9th Cav. ‡With Troutman patrol, Jan 1875; killed Pvt. John Fredericks, Ft Stockton, TX, in dispute over borrowed attorney's fees, Apr 1876. SOURCE: Leckie, *The Buffalo Soldiers*, 108–9.

With Sgt. Edward Troutman and Pvt. John Fredericks, survived attack by Mexicans near Rio Grande, 26 Jan 1875,

in which two cavalrymen were killed; later indicted and jailed, Rio Grande City, TX, for killing one of attackers; at Ft Stockton, Apr 1876, Blackstone killed Fredericks in dispute over responsibility for legal costs. SOURCE: Leiker, *Racial Borders*, 54–55.

BLACKWELL, Isaac; Private; F/24th Inf. Died 4 May 1876; buried at San Antonio National Cemetery, Section F, number 1112. SOURCE: San Antonio National Cemetery Locator.

BLAIR, Henry; Private; E/24th Inf. Died at Ft Griffin, TX, on 19 Sep 1869; buried at San Antonio National Cemetery, Section D, number 742. SOURCE: San Antonio National Cemetery Locator.

BLAKE, Beverly; M/9th Cav. Born in Virginia; mulatto complexion; cannot read or write, age 22, Jul 1870, at Ft McKavett, TX. SOURCE: Bierschwale, *Fort McKavett*, 99.

BLANCH, John; Private; 9th Cav. Received Philippine Campaign Badge number 11716 for service as private in E/9th Cavalry; in 9th Cavalry at Ft Leavenworth, KS, Mar 1905. SOURCE: Philippine Campaign Badge list, 29 May 1905.

BLAND, Harrison; F/9th Cav. Born in Virginia; black complexion; can read and write, age 22, Jul 1870, at Ft McKavett, TX. SOURCE: Bierschwale, *Fort McKavett*, 98.

BLAND, Walter H.; Sergeant; F/9th Cav. Died 3 Mar 1917; buried in plot ES 666-A at San Francisco National Cemetery. SOURCE: San Francisco National Cemetery.

BLANHEIN, John; Private; F/25th Inf. Died 26 Sep 1908; buried in Sec N Addn W Side, plot N 1334, at San Francisco National Cemetery. SOURCE: San Francisco National Cemetery.

BLANTON, Joseph; F/9th Cav. Born in Arizona; black complexion; can read, cannot write, age 21, Jul 1870, at Ft McKavett, TX. SOURCE: Bierschwale, *Fort McKavett*, 96

BLEADSOE, Robert; 1st Sgt; 9th Cav. ‡Sergeant, C/9th Cavalry, veteran of Spanish-American War and Philippine Insurrection; expert rifleman at Ft D. A. Russell, WY, in 1910. SOURCE: *Illustrated Review: Ninth Cavalry*, with picture.

First sergeant, Machine Gun Company, 9th Cavalry, retired; died 2 Aug 1932; buried in plot C 183 at San Francisco National Cemetery. SOURCE: San Francisco National Cemetery.

BLEW, Joseph; Sergeant; G/9th Cav. ‡Born in Pulaski Co., KY, 31 Jan 1858; lived with parents Dave and Celia, brother George, sisters Malinda and Viola, on farm ten miles south of Summerset, Pulaski Co., until 1870; tattoo of girl on right arm; enlisted Louisville, KY, Ht 5'11", Aug 1873; in G/9th Cavalry, Aug 1873–Oct 1889; in A/9th Cavalry, Nov 1889–92; sergeant, 1 Oct 1876; corporal, 26 Mar 1880; sergeant, 17 Sep 1881; private, 16 Sep 1888; corporal, 10 Feb 1889; sergeant, 1 Nov 1891; stationed at Ft Sill, Indian Territory, Oct 1884–Aug 1885, at Ft Niobrara, NE, Aug 1885–Nov 1890, on Sioux campaign, Nov 1890–Mar 1891, and at Ft Robinson, NE, Mar 1891 until discharge, Camp Bettens, WY, Jun 1892; police officer, Omaha, NE, from discharge to death. Married Dora Green (nee Hammett) of Macon Co., MO, 12 Jan 1896, with service performed by Rev. J. W. Braxton, African Methodist Episcopal Church, Omaha. SOURCE: VA File XC 970422, Joseph Blew.

‡Sergeant, G/9th Cavalry; one of six enlisted men of G/9th Cavalry to testify against Lt. John Conline at his 1877 court martial for misconduct, including drunkenness, sexual misconduct, misappropriation of funds belonging to men of his troop, Ft Garland, CO. SOURCE: Billington, *New Mexico's Buffalo Soldiers*, 121–23.

‡Saw Pvt. James F. Jackson, "always a sober quiet peaceable soldier," at Ft Niobrara shortly before Jackson was shot by Moseby of G/9th Cavalry, "a very dangerous man," 12 May 1886. SOURCE: Affidavit, Blew, Omaha, 1899, VA File C 2555351, James F. Jackson.

‡Resided at 6514 21st St., Omaha, with pension of $10 per month in 1896, $17 per month in 1898, $20 per month in 1917. SOURCE: VA File XC 970422, Joseph Blew.

‡Mentioned as surviving veteran of Indian wars. SOURCE: *Winners of the West* 3 (Jun 1926): 7.

‡Wife was loyal follower of Father Divine, resided with daughter Mrs. Alberta Broyles Jackson, who owned "a large old home in the colored section" of Oakland, CA, at 1022 Filbert, until 1948; resided at 2328 23rd St., Oakland, until her death, 31 Jan 1958; daughter worked in cafeteria, Montgomery Ward store, Oakland; pension $12 per month in 1923, $30 per month in 1938, $40 per month in 1944, $48 per month in 1948. SOURCE: VA File XC 970422, Joseph Blew.

‡*See* OTT, **JOHNSON**, Robert T., G/9th Cavalry; OTT, **SHEAFF**, Joseph E., Corporal, G/9th Cavalry; OTT, **TUCKER**, George C., G/9th Cavalry

BLUE, John; Sergeant; F/9th Cav. ‡Died of dysentery at First Reserve Hospital, Manila, Philippines, 12 Aug 1901. SOURCE: *ANJ* 39 (12 Oct 1901): 140.

Died 12 Aug 1901; buried in plot NEW A715 at San Francisco National Cemetery. SOURCE: San Francisco National Cemetery.

BLUFORD, John; Corporal; H/9th Cav. ‡J. Bluford, H/9th Cavalry, sharpshooter with carbine, 75.57 percent, second award, 1892. SOURCE: GO 1, AGO, 3 Jan 1893.

Bluford, John, Corporal, H/9th Cavalry, died 17 Apr 1937; buried in plot D-SOU1191 at San Francisco National Cemetery. SOURCE: San Francisco National Cemetery.

BLUNT, Randall; Private; H/10th Cav. Born in Greenville, NC, 1 Mar 1862; father's name unknown, property of Dr. Blunt; mother Martha Ann Tyson, property of Allen Tyson, stepfather Louis Tyson, property of Allen Tyson; enlisted Baltimore, MD, 2 Jun 1882; Ht. 5'6", black complexion, black eyes and dark brown hair; occupation farmer and laborer; served at Ft Davis, TX, Bowie Station, AZ; Ft Grant, AZ, in field in pursuit of Apache Indians at Pinery Creek, AZ, Camp Bonita Cañon, AZ; discharged Ft Apache, AZ, 1 Jun 1887; married 3 Oct 1895, wife's name unknown, died 1 May 1909, San Francisco, CA; children Randall K. and Thema K. born 10 Nov 1899; resided with daughter Thema Simpson, 231 Duncan Street, San Francisco, CA, 1913; died 5 Apr 1922. SOURCE: Sayre, *Warriors of Color*, 46–50.

Private in H/10th Cavalry stationed at Bonita Cañon Camp, AZ, 30 Apr 1886. SOURCE: Tagg, *The Camp at Bonita Cañon*, 231.

Died 5 Apr 1922; buried in plot A 301 at San Francisco National Cemetery. SOURCE: San Francisco National Cemetery.

BLY, Caesar; Private; 25th Inf. Born in Georgetown, SC; Ht 5'7", black hair and eyes, dark complexion; occupation miner; enlisted at age 21, Charleston, SC, 6 Jun 1881; left recruit depot, David's Island, NY, 2 Jul 1881, arrived Ft Randall, SD, 7 Jul 1881. SOURCE: Descriptive & Assignment Rolls of Recruits, 25 Inf.

BOGGS, Ben; PFC C/351st Machine Gun Bn. Served in F/9th Cavalry; died 3 Sep 1920; buried in plot NAWS 1597-A at San Francisco National Cemetery. SOURCE: San Francisco National Cemetery.

BOGGS, Samuel; Private; G/9th Cav. Died 19 Apr 1901; buried in plot NEW/A440 at San Francisco National Cemetery. SOURCE: San Francisco National Cemetery.

BOHN, Robert; Private; D/9th Cav. With Captain Dodge at battle at Milk River, CO, 2–10 Oct 1879. SOURCE: Miller, *Hollow Victory*, 167, 206–7.

BOLAND, John; Private; I/10th Cav. In Troop I/10th Cavalry stationed at Bonita Cañon Camp, AZ, 30 Jun 1886. SOURCE: Tagg, *The Camp at Bonita Cañon*, 231.

‡Cited for "coolness in action," Cuba, 24 Jun 1898. SOURCE: SecWar, AR 1898, 349.

‡Distinguished service at Las Guasimas, Cuba, mentioned. SOURCE: Steward, *The Colored Regulars*, 137.

‡Citation for distinguished service noted. SOURCE: *ANJ* 37 (24 Feb 1900): 611.

‡Heroism mentioned. SOURCE: Cashin, *Under Fire with the Tenth Cavalry*, 185, 347.

‡Commended for conspicuous courage while wagoner, I/10th Cavalry, in exposing himself to heavy fire and killing Spaniard standing on stone entrenchments and directing fire, thus materially assisting in causing end of Spanish fire at Las Guasimas, 24 Jun 1898. SOURCE: GO 15, AGO, 13 Feb 1900.

BOLLEN, William H.; Wagoner; K/10th Cav. ‡Original member of 10th Cavalry; in troop when organized, Ft Riley, KS, 1 Sep 1867. SOURCE: McMiller, "Buffalo Soldiers," 77.

Died 26 Feb 1868 of an accident at Ft Riley. SOURCE: Regimental Returns, 10th Cavalry, 1868.

BOLLER, Solomon; Private; H/10th Cav. Born in Nottoway County, VA, 15 Jul 1861; owned by family named Campbell; father Henry Boller; mother Fannie Thompson; enlisted Cleveland, OH, 26 Jul 1882; Ht. 5'6", black complexion, eyes and hair; occupation laborer and blacksmith; at Ft Davis, TX, Jan–Apr 1883, 1 Jan 1884–1 Apr 1885; on march to Arizona 1 Apr 1885–2 May 1885; at Ft Grant, AZ, 1 May 1885–26 Jul 1885; in field at Bonita Cañon, AZ, Jul 1885–1 May 1886; discharged Ft Apache, AZ, 25 Jun 1887; married Fannie Thompkins, Gallup, NM, 7 Sep 1888; wife died 12 Nov 1951; died in Los Angeles, CA, 23 Dec 1951, buried Lincoln Cemetery, Los Angeles, CA. SOURCE: Sayre, *Warriors of Color*, 51–61.

"The most of all this time [1885–87] my company was in the field after Chief Geronimo and Mangus, the other Chiefs and their Warriors, and that is where I contracted a severe cold. . . . I was treated while in the field through snow and rain I had to go. Sometimes snow would be up to our knees and I had to shoe horses in snow and rain and there is where I lost my health in the line of my duty trying to protect my country." SOURCE: Sayre, *Warriors of Color*, 55.

Solomen [*sic*] Boller, blacksmith in H/10th Cavalry, stationed at Bonita Cañon Camp, AZ, 30 Apr 1886. SOURCE: Tagg, *The Camp at Bonita Cañon*, 231.

‡Honorable mention for service while blacksmith in H/10th Cavalry in capture of Mangas and his band, Rio Bonito, AZ, 18 Oct 1886. SOURCE: Baker, Roster.

BOLLING, Willie; Corporal; G/9th Cav. ‡William Bolling served in 10th Cavalry in Cuba, 1898. SOURCE: Cashin, *Under Fire with the Tenth Cavalry*, 343.

Received Cuban Campaign Badge for service as private in F/10th Cavalry, 22 Jun 1898–13 Aug 1898. SOURCE: Cuban Campaign Badge Recipients.

Received Philippine Campaign Badge number 11811 for service as corporal, 15 Sep 1900–16 Sep 1902; private in G/9th Cavalry, Ft Leavenworth, KS, Mar 1905. SOURCE: Philippine Campaign Badge Recipients; Philippine Campaign Badge list, 29 May 1905.

BOOKER, Andreson; Private; H/9th Cav. Died 25 Nov 1926; buried at San Antonio National Cemetery, Section B, number 31-A. SOURCE: San Antonio National Cemetery Locator.

BOOKER, William; Private; K/10th Cav. Died 3 May 1873 of rheumatism at Camp Supply, OK. SOURCE: Regimental Returns, 10th Cavalry, 1873.

BOOM, William; Private; L/9th Cav. Enlisted at Louisville, KY, 29 Jul 1875; discharged from L/9th Cavalry 20 Jul 1880 at Ft Bliss, TX, character good; reenlisted 25 Aug 1880. SOURCE: Muster Rolls, L/9th Cavalry, 30 June–31 Aug 1880.

BOONE, Hillard; Private; L/25th Inf. ‡Private Boone, L/25th Infantry, killed in ambush, Philippines, 29 Jan 1900; "a jolly fellow" and "faithful to duty." SOURCE: Richmond *Planet*, 17 Mar 1900.

Pvt. Hillard Boone, L/25th Infantry, died 29 Jan 1900; buried in plot 1101 EAS at San Francisco National Cemetery. SOURCE: San Francisco National Cemetery.

BOOTH, Abraham H.; Private; E/9th Cav. Served against Apaches in New Mexico, 1879. SOURCE: Dobak and Phillips, *The Black Regulars*, 191.

BOOTH, Adam; Private; E/9th Cav. Native of South Carolina; served with troop in New Mexico, 1879; from same town as Sgt. Silas Chapman, E/9th Cavalry; wrote letter to Col. Edward Hatch on behalf of seventeen men of E Troop, complaining about leadership of Capt. Ambrose Hooker; discharged 1880 with character "none" as evaluation by Hooker. SOURCE: Kenner, *Buffalo Soldiers and Officers of the Ninth Cavalry*, 109–11.

BORELAND, Peter; Private; K/25th Inf. Born in New Jersey; Ht 5'2", yellow complexion; occupation soldier; enlisted in A/39th Infantry for three years on 6 Nov 1867, age 27, at Richmond, VA; special duty as messenger, Ships Island, MS–Jackson Bks, LA; transferred to K/25th Infantry at Jackson Bks, 20 Apr 1869. SOURCE: Descriptive Roll of A/39th Inf.

BOROLER, William; Private; F/10th Cav. ‡Original member of 10th Cavalry; in troop when organized, Ft Leavenworth, KS, 21 Jun 1867. SOURCE: McMiller, "Buffalo Soldiers," 73.

Died 7 Jul 1867 of unknown causes at Ft Harker, KS. SOURCE: Regimental Returns, 10th Cavalry, 1867.

BORZOTIE, James; Private; 9th Cav. ‡Pvt. James Borzotra, H/24th Infantry, fined $10 by summary court for violating Article 62, carelessly discharging weapon on guard duty, San Isidro, Philippines, 29 Mar 1902. SOURCE: Register of Summary Court, San Isidro.

Received Philippine Campaign Badge number 11877 for service in H/49th Infantry, United States Volunteers, and H/24th Infantry; in 9th Cavalry at Ft Leavenworth, KS, Mar 1905. SOURCE: Philippine Campaign Badge list, 29 May 1905.

BORZOTRA, James; Private; H/24th Inf. *See* **BORZOTIE**, James, Private, 9th Cavalry

BOSTON, Walter W.; Private; 25th Inf. Struck Pvt. George Williams, 25th Inf, over head with a clawhammer at brothel near Ft Meade, SD. SOURCE: Dobak and Phillips, *The Black Regulars*, 176.

BOTHWELL, William H.; Private; K/48th Inf. ‡Died of variola in the Philippines, 2 Aug 1900. SOURCE: *ANJ* 37 (11 Aug 1901): 1191.

Died 1 Aug 1900; buried in plot NEW A835 at San Francisco National Cemetery. SOURCE: San Francisco National Cemetery.

BOUGHTON, John; Private; D/25th Inf. Company commander sought his discharge in 1889 for excessive drinking. SOURCE: Dobak and Phillips, *The Black Regulars*, 166.

BOUSH, Joseph; Post QM Sgt; U.S. Army. Appointed post quartermaster sergeant 13 Feb 1885, from sergeant, G/24th Infantry. SOURCE: Dobak, "Staff Noncommissioned Officers."

BOWAN, Willie; K/49th Inf. Died 4 May 1900; buried in plot NEW A919 at San Francisco National Cemetery. SOURCE: San Francisco National Cemetery.

BOWEN, Major; Sergeant; G/9th Cav. ‡Major Bowens, sergeant, E/9th Cavalry; with detachment of nineteen that skirmished with insurgents at Tagitay, Philippines, 2 Feb 1901. SOURCE: Hamilton, "History of the Ninth Cavalry," 106; *Illustrated Review: Ninth Cavalry*.

Received Philippine Campaign Badge number 11695 as first sergeant, E/9th Cavalry; in 9th Cavalry at Ft Leavenworth, KS, Mar 1905. SOURCE: Philippine Campaign Badge list, 29 May 1905.

Sergeant issued Indian Wars Campaign Badge number 1522 on 18 Oct 1909. SOURCE: Carroll, *Indian Wars Campaign Badge*, 44.

‡Veteran of Indian wars, Spanish-American War, and Philippine Insurrection; sergeant, G/9th Cavalry, at Ft D. A. Russell, WY, in 1910; marksman; resident of Fort Leaven-

worth. SOURCE: *Illustrated Review: Ninth Cavalry*, with picture.

Sergeant, G/9th Cavalry, buried at Ft Huachuca, AZ, cemetery. SOURCE: U.S. Army Intelligence Center and Fort Huachuca, "Mourning Hearts," 4.

BOWEN, Thomas; Private; 40th Inf. *See* **BOYNE**, Thomas, Private, H/25th Infantry

BOWENS, Major; Sergeant; G/9th Cav. *See* **BOWEN**, Major, Sergeant, G/9th Cavalry

BOWERS, Charles; Private; F/10th Cav. ‡Original member of 10th Cavalry; in troop when organized, Ft Leavenworth, KS, 21 Jun 1867. SOURCE: McMiller, "Buffalo Soldiers," 68.

Died 1 Aug 1867 of cholera at Ft Hays, KS. SOURCE: Regimental Returns, 10th Cavalry, 1867.

BOWERS, Edward; Private; K/9th Cav. One of three troopers killed in pre-dawn Indian attack on Fort Lancaster, TX, 26 Dec 1867. SOURCE: Schubert, *Black Valor*, 17.

‡Killed in action against force of 900 Kickapoos, Navahos, Mexicans, and white renegades, Ft Lancaster, along with Pvts. William Sharpe and Anderson Trimble, K/9th Cavalry, 26 Dec 1867. SOURCE: Hamilton, "History of the Ninth Cavalry," 7; *Illustrated Review: Ninth Cavalry*. *See* **TRIMBLE**, Anderson, Private, K/9th Cavalry

BOWIE, Isaiah; Private; 25th Inf. Convicted by general court martial, Ft Davis, TX, 1872, of neglect of duty, allowing three prisoners in his custody to swim in Rio Grande. SOURCE: Leiker, *Racial Borders*, 78.

BOWIE, James; M/9th Cav. Born in Kentucky; black complexion; cannot read or write, age 22, Jul 1870, at Ft McKavett, TX. SOURCE: Bierschwale, *Fort McKavett*, 99.

BOWLEGS, Cyrus; Private; U.S. Army. Civil War veteran, Seminole Negro Scout, pension file in National Archives. SOURCE: Schubert, Consolidated List of Seminole Negro Scouts.

Civil War veteran, served in I/79th USCT; widow Hagar filed VA file C805615. SOURCE: Schubert, "Seminole-Negro Scouts."

BOWLEGS, David; Sergeant; U.S. Army. Seminole Negro Scout, served 1873–82; pension file in National Archives. SOURCE: Schubert, Consolidated List of Seminole Negro Scouts.

Born in Florida; first enlisted 1 May 1873 at Ft Duncan, TX, for six months; age 42; Ht 5'8", black hair and eyes, black complexion; discharged as corporal, reenlisted 1 Nov 1873 at Ft Duncan; discharged as corporal, reenlisted at

Camp Palafox, TX, 1 May 1874; discharged as corporal 28 Dec 1874 at Ft Duncan where he reenlisted 1 Jan 1875; discharged as sergeant, reenlisted July 1875 at Ft Concho, TX; discharged at Ft Duncan 1 Jan 1876; reenlisted at Ft Clark, TX, 23 Feb 1876; discharged, reenlisted at Camp Pecos, TX, 23 Aug 1876; discharged, reenlisted at Camp Crow Creek, TX, 23 Feb 1877; discharged as sergeant, re-enlisted four additional times for one year each at Ft Clark; last discharged as sergeant at Ft. Clark, 12 May 1882, age 47; wife Nancy, children Priscilla, Leah, Pompey, Sandy, Davis, Camilia, and Noble; on May 1882, with thirty-seven members, returned and stayed with Seminole Nation, Indian Territory, May 1882, only Seminole Negro Indians to return. SOURCE: Swanson, 2.

Age 40, resided at Ft Duncan with Nanny age 30, Priscilla age 10, Leah age 8, Pompey age 5, Sandy age 3, David age 1; detachment first sergeant in 1880; widow Annie filed claim, VA File XC 946437. SOURCE: Schubert, "Seminole-Negro Scouts"; NARA Record Group 393, Special File, M 929, Roll 2; Mulroy, *Freedom on the Border*, 116.

BOWLEGS, Friday; Private; U.S. Army. Seminole Negro Scout, served 1872–85; pension file in National Archives. SOURCE: Schubert, Consolidated List of Seminole Negro Scouts.

Born in Florida; former slave or descended from slave of Seminole Chief Bowlegs (Bowlik); first enlisted for six months 1 Dec 1872 at Ft Duncan, TX; age 45, Ht 6', black hair and eyes, black complexion; discharged and reenlisted two additional times, six months each, at Ft Duncan; discharged 4 Aug 1875 at Ft Concho, TX; reenlisted for six months 1 Sep 1875 at Ft Duncan; discharged 1 Mar 1876 at Ft Duncan; reenlisted for one year and discharged twice at Ft Clark, TX; reenlisted 10 Sep 1880 for one year at San Antonio, TX; discharged and reenlisted for one year 23 Apr 1881 at Ft Clark; discharged and reenlisted four additional times for one year each; last discharge at Ft. Clark 26 Dec 1885, age 50. SOURCE: Swanson, 3.

Resided in 1875 at Ft Duncan with Mary age 38, Annia age 6, Pancho age 12; widow Hannah filed claim, VA File SC 2674005. SOURCE: Schubert, "Seminole-Negro Scouts."

BOWLEGS, George; Private; U.S. Army. Civil War veteran; Seminole Negro Scout; pension file in National Archives. SOURCE: Schubert, Consolidated List of Seminole Negro Scouts.

Served in I/79th U.S. Colored Troops, son William J. Bowlegs applied for claim, VA minor application 375191. SOURCE: Schubert, "Seminole-Negro Scouts."

BOWLEGS, Harkless; Private; U.S. Army. Seminole Negro Scout, served 1881–83. SOURCE: Schubert, Consolidated List of Seminole Negro Scouts.

Born in Mexico; enlisted at Ft Clark, TX, 14 May 1881, age 18; Ht 5'8", hair and eyes black, black complexion; discharged at Ft Clark, 12 May 1882; reenlisted 23 May 1882 at Camp Pecos, TX; discharged 22 May 1883 at Ft Clark where he reenlisted the next day; discharged at Camp Myers, TX, 22 May 1884; reenlisted at Ft Clark 24 Jul 1884; discharged 31 Aug 1884. SOURCE: Swanson, 3.

BOWLEGS, John; Private; U.S. Army. Seminole Negro Scout; died 17 Mar 1895, buried at Seminole Indian Scout Cemetery, Kinney County, TX. SOURCE: Indian Scout Cemetery, Kinney County, Texas.

BOWLEGS, John H.; Private; U.S. Army. Born in Mexico; enlisted for six months at Ft Clark, TX, 6 Aug 1892, age 29; Ht 5'8", black hair and eyes, black complexion; discharged and reenlisted twice for six months each at Ft Ringgold, TX; discharged at San Pedro 25 Feb 1894, reenlisted next day for six months; discharged 25 Aug 1894 and reenlisted next day at Ft Ringgold; discharged at Ft Ringgold 25 Feb 1895 and reenlisted next day for three years; discharged at Ft. Ringgold 24 Feb 1898 and reenlisted next day for three years; discharged at Ft Clark 25 Feb 1901 and reenlisted next day for three years; discharged and reenlisted for three years at Camp Eagle Pass, TX, 24 Feb 1904; last discharge at Ft Clark 25 Feb 1907; died 3 Jul 1937, buried at Seminole Cemetery. SOURCE: Swanson, 3.

Seminole Negro Scout, served 1892–1907; pension file VA file C 2373309 in National Archives. SOURCE: Schubert, Consolidated List of Seminole Negro Scouts; Schubert, "Seminole-Negro Scouts."

Private, Indian scout; died 7 Jul 1934; buried at Seminole Indian Scout Cemetery, Kinney County, TX. SOURCE: Indian Scout Cemetery, Kinney County, Texas.

BOWLEGS, Zack; Private; U.S. Army. Seminole Negro Scout, served 1872–73. SOURCE: Schubert, Consolidated List of Seminole Negro Scouts.

Born in Florida; former slave or descended from slave of Seminole Chief Bowlegs (Bowlik); enlisted for six months 1 Dec 1872 at Ft Duncan, TX, age 45; Ht 6', black hair and eyes, black complexion; discharged at Ft Duncan 1 Jun 1873. SOURCE: Swanson, 4.

BOWMAN; Corporal; 10th Cav. At Ft Stockton, TX, 1878; on field service Oct 1878, had New Testament and volume on Greek mythology in his tent. SOURCE: Kinevan, *Frontier Cavalryman*, 144.

BOWMAN; Sergeant; H/10th Cav. At Fort Davis, TX, Oct 1884. SOURCE: Sayre, *Warriors of Color*, 93.

BOWMAN, Bartley; M/9th Cav. Born in Kentucky; black complexion; can read and write, age 21, Jul 1870, at Ft McKavett, TX. SOURCE: Bierschwale, *Fort McKavett*, 99.

BOWMAN, Jeremiah; Private; D/9th Cav. With Captain Dodge at battle at Milk River, CO, 2–10 Oct 1879. SOURCE: Miller, *Hollow Victory*, 167, 206–7.

BOYD, Daniel; Private; K/9th Cav. Died at Ft Davis, TX, on 16 Mar 1870; buried at San Antonio National Cemetery, Section I, number 1542. SOURCE: San Antonio National Cemetery Locator.

BOYD, Daniel; Sergeant; L/10th Cav. ‡Original member of 10th Cavalry; in troop when organized, Ft Riley, KS, 21 Sep 1867. SOURCE: McMiller, "Buffalo Soldiers," 78.

Drowned 12 Jul 1870 at Ft Sill, OK. SOURCE: Regimental Returns, 10th Cavalry, 1870.

‡Commander, 10th Cavalry, forwards inventory of Sergeant Boyd's personal effects and final statement to Adjutant General. SOURCE: Letter, CO, 10 Cav, to AG, 24 Jul 1870, ES, 10 Cav, 1866–71.

Sergeant, L/10th Cavalry, died 30 Jun 1870, buried at Camp Douglas, UT. SOURCE: Record Book of Interments, Post Cemetery, 252.

BOYD, Edward; Private; A/10th Cav. Died Nov 1874 of pneumonia at Concho River, TX. SOURCE: Regimental Returns, 10th Cavalry, 1874.

BOYD, Hampton; Private; A/24th Inf. Died 2 Jun 1906, buried at Ft Bayard, NM, in plot I 2. SOURCE: "Fort Bayard National Cemetery, Records of Burials."

BOYD, Thomas; Private; 40th Inf. Ht 5'4", could read and write, enlisted 1867. SOURCE: Dobak and Phillips, *The Black Regulars*, 10.

BOYD, Thomas W.; Private; F/24th Inf. Died 31 Mar 1895, buried at Ft Bayard, NM, in plot I 23. SOURCE: "Fort Bayard National Cemetery, Records of Burials."

Buried 31 Mar 1895, section A, row M, plot 26, at Ft Bayard. SOURCE: Erickson, Burials at Fort Bayard National Cemetery, NM.

BOYER; Blacksmith; H/10th Cav. Participated in campaign against Geronimo, 1886. SOURCE: Sayre, *Warriors of Color*, 111.

Participated in Oct 1886 pursuit and capture of Apache Mangus. SOURCE: Schubert, *Voices of the Buffalo Soldier*, 146.

BOYER George W.; Private; D/24th Inf. Died 22 Jun 1894, buried at Ft Bayard, NM, in plot I 25. SOURCE: "Fort Bayard National Cemetery, Records of Burials."

Buried 22 Jun 1897, section A, row M, plot 28 at Ft Bayard, NM. SOURCE: Erickson, Burials at Fort Bayard National Cemetery, NM.

BOYKIN, Charles; Private; 25th Inf. Born in Camden, SC; Ht 5'8", black hair and eyes, dark complexion; occupation laborer; enlisted at age 23, Charleston, SC, 1 Jun 1881; left recruit depot, David's Island, NY, 2 Jul 1881, arrived Ft Randall, SD, 7 Jul 1881. SOURCE: Descriptive & Assignment Rolls of Recruits, 25 Inf.

BOYNE, Thomas; Private; H/25th Inf. ‡Native of Prince Georges Co., MD; won Medal of Honor for two actions against Victorio, Mimbres Mountains, NM, 29 May 1879, and Cuchillo Negro, NM, 27 Sep 1879, while sergeant, C/9th Cavalry. SOURCE: Carroll, *The Black Military Experience*, 411; Koger, *The Maryland Negro in Our Wars*, 23; Lee, *Negro Medal of Honor Men*, 63, 66; Billington, *New Mexico's Buffalo Soldiers*, 88–89.

Civil War veteran, served in B Battery, 2nd Colored Light Artillery, participated in battles during campaign for Richmond, May–Jun 1864, discharged Mar 1866, Brownsville, TX; reenlisted in 40th Infantry, Jan 1867, as Thomas Bowen, of Norfolk, VA; served in 25th Infantry until 1875, when joined 9th Cavalry; received Medal of Honor for valor against Apaches in New Mexico, 1879; frostbitten during winter of 1884–85 while keeping illegal settlers out of Indian Territory, spent Jan 1885 in hospital, Ft Caldwell, KS; reenlisted for 25th Infantry, Ft Meade, SD, Jul 1885; developed hernia while supervising wood-gathering detail, Ft Missoula, MT, Oct 1888; discharged Jan 1889 with disability pension of $8 per month, increased to $10 in Dec 1893; resided in U.S. Soldiers Home until death from consumption, 21 Apr 1896. SOURCE: Schubert, *Black Valor*, 49–50, 53, 57–59, 171.

Medal of Honor for bravery against Apaches in 1879 mentioned. SOURCE: Dobak and Phillips, *The Black Regulars*, 261.

‡Corporal, L/9th Cavalry, on detached service in the field, New Mexico, 21 Jan–24 Feb 1881. SOURCE: Regt Returns, 9 Cav, Feb 1881.

Born in Prince Georges County, MD; Ht 5'6", black hair and eyes, brown complexion; discharged from L/9th Cavalry 17 June 1885; resided in Washington, DC, fifth enlistment 16 Jul 1885, age 37, at Washington, DC; assigned to H/25th Infantry; arrived Ft Snelling, MN, 26 Apr 1886. SOURCE: Descriptive & Assignment Rolls of Recruits, 25 Inf.

‡Admitted to Soldiers Home, from H/25th Infantry, age 43, with twenty-three years and seven months service. SOURCE: SecWar, AR 1889, 1013.

‡Died of consumption at Soldiers Home, age 50, 21 Apr 1896. SOURCE: SecWar, AR 1896, 640.

BRABHAM, Jeremiah; Private; E/24th Inf. ‡Born in Barnwell, SC; occupation drayman; Ht 5'8", dark complexion; enlisted Charleston, SC, age 17, 14 May 1881; assigned to A/24th Infantry; attached to band learning to play, 12 Sep 1883–4 Sep 1884; joined band, Ft Sill, Indian Territory, 4 Nov 1884; garrison court martial fines of $5 and $10 in 1884; discharged, character excellent, with $72 retained pay and $48.14 clothing, 13 May 1886; enlisted Ft Leavenworth, KS, 22 May 1886; joined band, Ft Supply, Indian Territory, 8 Jul 1886; transferred to E/24th Infantry, Ft Sill, character "fair, but disinclined to pay his just debts," single, additional pay $2 per month, clothing $ 37.27, 17 Jan 1888; transferred to Band/24th Infantry, Ft Bayard, NM, character very good, 18 Nov 1890; first class marksman, 1889, and marksman, 1890; discharged, Ft Bayard, character generally good, single, additional pay $5 per month, retained $60.57, clothing $54.24, 7 Jun 1891; enlisted, Ft Leavenworth, 23 Jun 1891; joined, Ft Bayard, 13 Sep 1891; transferred to D/24th Infantry, character good, single, additional pay $3 per month, retained pay $33.33, clothing $52.44, owes $1.08 for subsistence, 2 Apr 1894. SOURCE: Descriptive Book, 24 Inf NCS & Band.

Served in company 1889–91; resided in Albuquerque, NM, 1894–99; resided in California, 1914. SOURCE: Sayre, *Warriors of Color*, 263–64, 282.

Acquainted with Violet Cragg, wife of Sgt. Allen Cragg, 9th Cavalry, at Dodge City and Junction City, KS, and later in Los Angeles, CA. SOURCE: Schubert, *Voices of the Buffalo Soldier*, 250.

BRACKETT, Joseph; Corporal; D/9th Cav. Native of Virginia; completed ten years of service in 9th Cavalry, Dec 1882; corporal, D/9th Cavalry, at Ft Riley, KS, 1882; discharged with character of "good," did not reenlist. SOURCE: Kenner, *Buffalo Soldiers and Officers of the Ninth Cavalry*, 275, 355.

BRADDEN, Alfred; Sergeant; Band/9th Cav. ‡Born in Alabama; Ht 5'9", brown complexion; Civil War veteran, served in 17th U.S. Colored Troops until 25 Apr 1866; served in C/38th Infantry, discharged as sergeant, 17 Nov 1869; in H/24th Infantry, discharged as sergeant, 16 Aug 1875; in B/24th Infantry, discharged as sergeant, 18 Feb 1881; enlisted in Band/24th Infantry, Ft Supply, IT, 19 Feb 1881; principal musician, 1 Oct 1881; resigned 24 Jun 1884; discharged, expiration of service, character excellent, "a good E flat cornet player," married, five children, additional pay $2 per month, retained $60, clothing $59.53, 18 Feb 1886. SOURCE: Descriptive Book, 24 Inf NCS & Band.

Corporal, C/38th Infantry, commanded detachment of ten engaged in skirmish with twenty-five Indians, 21 Jul 1867, near Monument Station, KS. SOURCE: Schubert, *Voices of the Buffalo Soldier*, 146.

‡Sergeant, Band/9th Cavalry, since 11 Aug 1892. SOURCE: Roster, 9 Cav, 1893.

‡Resides with wife at Ft Robinson, NE. SOURCE: Medical History, Ft Robinson.

‡Retires from Ft Robinson, Nov 1893. SOURCE: *ANJ* 31 (4 Nov 1893): 172.

‡Retired post exchange bartender, Ft Robinson, 1894. SOURCE: Investigation of Charges against Chaplain Plummer.

Worked as attendant, post exchange billiard room, for $10.85 per month. SOURCE: Report of Inspection, Ft Robinson, 3 Sep 1894, Reports of Inspection, Dept Platte, II.

‡Lives retired at Ft Robinson, one of six retirees there, four of whom are black. SOURCE: Soldiers on the Retired List Paid in the Department of the Platte by Mail, Misc Records, Dept Platte, 1894–98.

‡Wife Laura died at Ft Robinson, 9 Jun 1910. SOURCE: List of Interments, Ft Robinson.

‡Lives in Crawford, NE, with personal property assessed at $30 and tax of $2 in 1912. SOURCE: Dawes County tax records.

‡No Veterans Administration pension file.

BRADDOCK, Granderson; D/24th Inf. Born in Louisiana; black complexion; cannot read or write, age 24, Jul 1870, at Ft McKavett, TX. SOURCE: Bierschwale, *Fort McKavett*, 96.

BRADDOCK, Thomas; Private; I/10th Cav. In Troop I/10th Cavalry stationed at Bonita Cañon Camp, AZ, 30 Jun 1886. SOURCE: Tagg, *The Camp at Bonita Cañon*, 231.

BRADFORD, George; Private; K/24th Inf. Died at Camp Eagle Pass, TX, on 27 Sep 1870; buried at San Antonio National Cemetery, Section F, number 1151. SOURCE: San Antonio National Cemetery Locator.

BRADFORD, Harrison; Sergeant; E/9th Cav. Tall, light-skinned Civil War veteran, from Scott County, KY, enlisted at age twenty-four, became sergeant in less than six months; led protest against behavior of Lt. Edward Heyl, San Pedro Springs, TX, Apr 1867; killed in confrontation with Heyl and Lt. Fred Smith. SOURCE: Schubert, *Black Valor*, 10, 12, 14.

Role in San Pedro Springs mutiny of 1867 described. SOURCE: Dobak and Phillips, *The Black Regulars*, 205–9, 211.

Born in Kentucky, served during Civil War in 104th U.S. Colored Infantry, age 24 in 1867; sergeant in troop in April 1867, at time of San Pedro Springs, TX, mutiny, protested Heyl's brutality, and was killed during violence; erroneously identified as first sergeant. SOURCE: Kenner, *Buffalo Soldiers and Officers of the Ninth Cavalry*, 76.

‡Led mutiny near San Antonio, TX, spring 1867; shot and killed while resisting arrest, 9 Apr 1867. SOURCE: Hamilton, "History of the Ninth Cavalry," 5; Ninth Cavalry, *Historical and Pictorial Review*, 44.

Shot by Lieutenant Smith, while leading mutiny, 9 Apr 1867. SOURCE: *Illustrated Review: Ninth Cavalry*.

BRADLEY, Levi; Sergeant; E/10th Cav. ‡Born in South Carolina; private, D/10th Cavalry, 20 Apr 1867–20 Apr 1872; in E/10th Cavalry, 10 Sep 1892; corporal, 1 Sep 1877; sergeant, 1 Jan 1878; first sergeant, 1 Jan 1891–31 Mar 1894; sergeant, 1 Apr 1894. SOURCE: Baker, *Roster.*

‡Stationed at San Felipe, TX; marched one hundred miles in command of detachment of eight scouting vicinity of Rio Grande, for murderers of Colson family, 6–13 Jun 1879. SOURCE: SecWar, AR 1879, 112.

In E/10th Cavalry stationed at Bonita Cañon Camp, AZ, 28 Feb 1886. SOURCE: Tagg, *The Camp at Bonita Cañon,* 231.

‡At Ft Apache, AZ, 1890, subscribed $.50 to testimonial to General Grierson. SOURCE: List of subscriptions, 23 Apr 1890, 10th Cavalry papers, MHI.

‡Retires from Ft Custer, MT. SOURCE: *ANJ* 35 (16 Oct 1897): 1117.

BRADLEY, Taylor; Farrier; C/9th Cav. Pvt. Taylor Bradly, C/9th Cavalry, at Fort Sill, OK, 1883. SOURCE: Kenner, *Buffalo Soldiers and Officers of the Ninth Cavalry,* 257.

‡Farrier, C/9th Cavalry, discharged, expiration of service, Ft Robinson, NE, 31 Aug 1885. SOURCE: Regt Returns, 9 Cav, Aug 1885.

BRADLEY, William; F/9th Cav. Born in Virginia; black complexion; cannot read or write, age 22, Jul 1870, at Ft McKavett, TX. SOURCE: Bierschwale, *Fort McKavett,* 97.

BRADLY, Taylor; Private; C/9th Cav. *See* **BRADLEY**, Taylor, Farrier, C/9th Cavalry

BRADY, Isaac; Private; G/9th Cav. Died at Ft Davis, TX, on 30 Mar 1868; buried at San Antonio National Cemetery, Section I, number 1517. SOURCE: San Antonio National Cemetery Locator.

BRADY, Jewel; Private; U.S. Army. Seminole Negro Scout, also known as Brady Jewel, served 1877–78, 1880–81. SOURCE: Schubert, Consolidated List of Seminole Negro Scouts.

Born in Louisiana; enlisted at Ft Clark, TX, 5 Mar 1877, age 32; Ht 5'8", black hair and eyes, dark complexion; discharged at Ft Clark 5 Mar 1878; enlisted at Ft Clark 4 Aug 1880; discharged 8 Aug 1881 at Ft Clark where he reenlisted, age 44, next day; discharged at Camp Myers Spring, TX, 8 Aug 1882. "Formerly enlisted in 10th U.S. Cavalry . . . but said to have been 'neither Seminole, nor Negro, but an Indian, with long hair.'" SOURCE: Swanson, 4, 21.

Private Jewell, once first sergeant, served in 10th Cavalry, 1874–94; at Ft Davis, TX, age 47, left duty as room orderly without being relieved, put in guardhouse 15 Feb 1885; found guilty in general court martial, acquitted with-

out punishment in general court martial 20 Feb 1885. SOURCE: Bigelow, *Garrison Tangles,* 54–55, 82.

BRANCH, Haywood; Corporal; A/10th Cav. Died 20 Apr 1887; buried 15 Mar 1932 at Santa Fe National Cemetery, NM, plot P 87. SOURCE: Santa Fe National Cemetery, Records of Burials.

BRANCH, James; Private; G/25th Inf. Died at Ft Concho, TX, in 1877; buried at San Antonio National Cemetery, Section D, number 696. SOURCE: San Antonio National Cemetery Locator.

BRANCH, William; Private; I/25th Inf. ‡Born in Lunenburg Co., VA; occupation laborer; Ht 5'6"; enlisted Baltimore, MD, 4 Jun 1870; discharged 6 Jun 1875; enlisted 28 Jul 1875; discharged 27 Jul 1880; participated in war against Cheyennes, Kiowas, Comanches, 1874–75. SOURCE: VA File C 2581520, William Branch.

Stationed at Ft Elliott, TX, became involved in construction of housing there. SOURCE: Dobak and Phillips, *The Black Regulars,* 105.

‡Rheumatism caused by accident ten miles from Ft Sill, Indian Territory; coming down steep hill, as rear teamster was locking wagon wheels, mules ran down hill and wheels passed over toes of his right foot; when he got to camp, his right leg numb and his boot half full of blood; sent to hospital in wagon; spent twenty-eight days there and has been lame ever since. SOURCE: Branch to Commissioner of Pensions, 11 Apr 1892, VA File C 2581520, William Branch.

‡Married Rebecca Bryand, 1882, who died in 1886; then Ella Scott, who died 11 Jan 1899; then Ada Livingston, later divorced; then Julia Nelson, married to William Scott, private, D/9th Cavalry, 1894, and divorced 21 May 1908. SOURCE: VA File C 2581520, William Branch.

‡Pension increased from $8 to $20 per month, 4 Mar 1917; addresses in San Antonio, TX: 312 North San Saba, 1903; 905 Castro, 1904; 725 North Laredo, 1905; 409 South Trio, 1906; 101 National, 1909; 129 DeVilbiss, 1915; 740 Barrera, 1918. Died 27 Feb 1941, Station Hospital, Ft Sam Houston, TX; at death mentally incompetent, lived with guardian, Mrs. Willie Young Richardson, 1014 Iowa St., as of 9 May 1940, with pension of $72 per month. SOURCE: VA File C 2581520, William Branch.

‡Served 1870–80; now 80 years old, gets $50 per month pension, belongs to Abraham Lincoln Chapter, No. 30, National Indian War Veterans, San Antonio. SOURCE: *Winners of the West* 7 (Jul 1930): 4.

Works Progress Administration interview with Branch, who was born a slave in Virginia in 1850, and resided at 322 Utah St., San Antonio, TX, in 1930s, reprinted. SOURCE: Schubert, *Voices of the Buffalo Soldier,* 50–53.

‡Subscriber, now age 82. SOURCE: *Winners of the West* 10 (Jan 1933): 1.

Renews subscription; was born in Lunenburg Co., 13 May 1850; discharged Ft Sill. SOURCE: *Winners of the West* 11 (Aug 1934): 3.

‡Died 17 Feb 1941; buried at Fort Sam Houston National Cemetery, Section A, number 67. SOURCE: Buffalo Soldiers Interred in Fort Sam Houston National Cemetery.

See **AUSTIN**, Edward S., Private, K/25th Infantry; OTT, **McKAY**, George, Private, K/24th Infantry; **REDDICK**, Charles, First Sergeant, I/25th Infantry; OTT, **ROE**, John W., I/25th Infantry; OTT, **WILLIAMS**, William H., Private, I/25th Infantry

BRANSON, James; Private; 25th Inf. Born in Martinsburg, VA; Ht 5'5", black hair and brown eyes, brown complexion; occupation laborer; resided Chambersburg, PA, when enlisted at age 28, Harrisburg, PA, 11 Aug 1885; assigned to I/25th Infantry; arrived Ft Snelling, MN, 5 Feb 1886. SOURCE: Descriptive & Assignment Rolls of Recruits, 25 Inf.

BRATCHET, Joseph; Private; D/9th Cav. With Captain Dodge at battle at Milk River, CO, 2–10 Oct 1879. SOURCE: Miller, *Hollow Victory*, 167, 206–7.

BRAUN, Hanson T.; Private; H/10th Cav. Died 24 Jul 1890; buried 15 Mar 1932 at Santa Fe National Cemetery, NM, plot P 77. SOURCE: Santa Fe National Cemetery, Records of Burials.

BRAXTON, Isaiah; Private; K/49th Inf. Died 15 Dec 1900; received for burial 17 Apr 1901; buried in plot NADDN351 at San Francisco National Cemetery. SOURCE: San Francisco National Cemetery.

BRENT, John; M/9th Cav. Born in Virginia; mulatto complexion; can read and write, age 23, Jul 1870, at Ft McKavett, TX. SOURCE: Bierschwale, *Fort McKavett,* 99.

BRENT, William; Private; H/10th Cav. Served at Ft Davis, TX, 1885; resided at corner of 5th and Maple Streets, Leavenworth, KS, in 1897. SOURCE: Sayre, *Warriors of Color*, 10, 12.

BRETT, James; Private; I/25th Inf. Born in Pike County, MS; Ht 5'3", black complexion; occupation soldier; enlisted in A/39th Infantry for three years on 11 Sep 1866, age 21, at Ship Island, MS; promoted to corporal 6 May 1867; reduced for incompetence to private 18 Dec 1867; transferred to K/25th Infantry at Jackson Bks, LA, 20 Apr 1869. SOURCE: Descriptive Roll of A/39th Inf.

BREWSTER, William; M/10th Cav. ‡Original member of 10th Cavalry; in troop when organized, Ft Riley, KS, 15 Oct 1867. SOURCE: McMiller, "Buffalo Soldiers," 79.

Died 10 Oct 1868 in post hospital at Ft Arbuckle, OK. SOURCE: Regimental Returns, 10th Cavalry, 1868.

BRICIÑO, Henry; Sgt Maj; 10th Cav. Discharged Apr 1892. SOURCE: Schubert, *Black Valor*, 148.

BRIDGES, Travis; Private; F/25th Inf. One of twenty men who cycled 1,900 miles from Ft Missoula, MT, to St. Louis, MO, 14 Jun–24 Jul 1897, in 25th Infantry Bicycle Corps to test durability and practicality of bicycles as a means of transportation for troops. SOURCE: File 60178, GC, AGO Records.

BRIGGS, Allen; 9th Cav. Born in North Carolina; black complexion; cannot read or write, age 24, 5 Sep 1870, at Ft McKavett, TX. SOURCE: Bierschwale, *Fort McKavett,* 107.

BRIGGS, Allen; Sergeant; H/9th Cav. Appointed sergeant, 19 May 1881; color sergeant in H/9th Cavalry, Ft Robinson, NE, Jan 1897. SOURCE: Ninth Cavalry, Roster of NCOs, 1897.

‡Sergeant, H/9th Cavalry, since 19 Mar 1881. SOURCE: Roster, 9 Cav, 1893.

‡At Ft Robinson, 1895; sergeant since 1881. SOURCE: *ANJ* 32 (20 Jul 1895): 774.

‡Detailed as regimental standard-bearer, Mar 1896. SOURCE: *ANJ* 33 (28 Mar 1896): 540.

‡Retires from Ft Robinson in accordance with Special Order 170, Adjutant General's Office, 27 Jul 1897. SOURCE: *ANJ* 34 (7 Aug 1897): 909.

‡Retired with $8.30 retained, $60.07 clothing, $100 deposits due him. SOURCE: CO, H/9, to Chief QM, DP, 3 Aug 1897, Descriptive Book, H/9 Cav.

‡Died of consumption, Crawford, NE, 11 Oct 1901; buried, Ft Robinson, 12 Oct 1901. SOURCE: Crawford *Tribune*, 18 Oct 1901.

‡No Veterans Administration pension file.

BRIGHT, William; Corporal; H/10th Cav. Died 7 Oct 1872 of disease at Ft Gibson, OK. SOURCE: Regimental Returns, 10th Cavalry, 1872.

BRINK, Henry; F/9th Cav. Born in Virginia of foreign-born mother and father; black complexion; cannot read or write, age 40, Jul 1870, at Ft McKavett, TX. SOURCE: Bierschwale, *Fort McKavett,* 97.

BRISCOE, Edward; Sergeant; B/10th Cav. ‡Born in St. Mary's, MD; brown complexion; first enlisted 15 May 1875; corporal, 1 Jul 1876; sergeant, 1 Jul 1878; reenlisted Chinati Mountain, TX, 15 May 1880, age 28; private, 27 Aug 1881; corporal, 10 Mar 1882; farrier, 1 Sep 1882; private, 16 Feb

1883; farrier, 28 Jul 1884; corporal, 1 Nov 1884; marksman, 1884; discharged, Whipple Barracks, AZ, character excellent, unmarried, with $60 retained pay, $51 clothing, $160 deposits, 22 May 1885; reenlisted Baltimore, MD, 18 Jun 1885; joined, Whipple Barracks, 19 Aug 1885; corporal, 15 Mar 1887; sergeant, 2 Mar 1888; campaigns against Geronimo and Kid; discharged, Ft Apache, AZ, character excellent, retained pay $60, clothing $37, 17 Jun 1889. SOURCE: Descriptive Book, B/10 Cav, 1880–96.

Enlisted in B/10th Cavalry at age 23, Ht just over 5'6", scar on left thumb and near left eye; promoted to sergeant, demoted to private, promoted to farrier when arrested for drunkenness and disorderly conduct; second sentence remitted to permit his promotion to corporal; served at Ft Concho, TX; described as "excellent soldier" when reenlisted. SOURCE: Wooster, *Soldiers, Suttlers, and Settlers*, 63.

Jul–Aug 1879 led patrol of nine men, B/10th Cavalry, in pursuit of Indians who had stolen horses on Pecos River; involved in effort of noncommissioned officers to start their own mess, Sep 1879. SOURCE: Kinevan, *Frontier Cavalryman*, 204, 208.

‡At Ft Apache, 1890, subscribed $.50 to testimonial to General Grierson. SOURCE: List of subscriptions, 23 Apr 1890, 10th Cavalry papers, MHI.

BRITTEN, Reuben; Private; D/24th Inf. Died at Camp Eagle Pass, TX, on 13 May 1874; buried at San Antonio National Cemetery, Section F, number 1133. SOURCE: San Antonio National Cemetery Locator.

BROADEN, William; Sergeant; H/9th Cav. ‡Corporal, B/10th Cavalry; served in 10th Cavalry in Cuba, 1898. SOURCE: Cashin, *Under Fire with the Tenth Cavalry*, 337.

‡Ranked number 529 among rifle experts, with 68 percent in 1905. SOURCE: GO 101, AGO, 31 May 1906.

Sergeant in H/9th Cavalry when issued Indian Wars Campaign Badge number 1406 on 15 Jul 1909. SOURCE: Carroll, *Indian Wars Campaign Badge*, 40.

BROADUS, Joseph; 1st Sgt; G/9th Cav. ‡Sergeant, one of six enlisted men of G/9th Cavalry to testify against Lt. John Conline at his 1877 court martial for misconduct, including drunkenness, sexual misconduct, misappropriation of funds belonging to men of his troop, Ft Garland, CO. SOURCE: Billington, *New Mexico's Buffalo Soldiers*, 121–23.

In G/9th Cavalry at Ft Garland, 1878, when he twice loaned Lt. John Conline $100. SOURCE: Kenner, *Buffalo Soldiers and Officers of the Ninth Cavalry*, 216.

‡On detached service, Ft Craig, NM, 26 Jan–6 Feb 1881. SOURCE: Regt Returns, 9 Cav, Feb 1881.

BROADUS, Lewis; 1st Sgt; M/25th Inf. ‡Born in Richmond, VA; resided there at enlistment; awarded Distin-

guished Service Cross in lieu of certificate of merit for coolness, presence of mind, bravery in saving lives, Ft Niobrara, NE, 3 Jul 1906. SOURCE: *Decorations. U.S. Army. Supplement I*, 28.

‡Mentioned as extremely efficient noncommissioned officer. SOURCE: Steward, *Fifty Years in the Gospel Ministry*, 352.

‡Ranked number 177 among rifle experts, with 68.67 percent in 1904. SOURCE: GO 79, AGO, 1 Jun 1905.

‡Ranked number 390 among rifle experts, with 69.33 percent in 1905. SOURCE: GO 101, AGO, 31 May 1906.

Awarded certificate of merit for coolness, presence of mind, and bravery, preventing a soldier from firing at his comrades with intent to murder, Ft Niobrara, 3 Jul 1906. SOURCE: Gleim, *The Certificate of Merit*, 58.

Received Distinguished Service Medal in lieu of certificate of merit. SOURCE: *American Decorations*, 836.

‡Twenty-six-year veteran; served in Cuba and the Philippines; prepared ordnance returns, Hartford, CT, armory, at request of state adjutant general, 1917. SOURCE: *Crisis* 14 (June 1917): 84.

‡Commissioned captain, Camp Des Moines, IA, Oct 1917. SOURCE: Sweeney, *History of the American Negro*, 120.

BROCK, Frank W. H.; Private; F/25th Inf. SOURCE: Descriptive & Assignment Rolls of Recruits, 25 Inf.
See **POSEY**, Frank, Private, H/24th Infantry

BROCKO, Frank W. H.; Corporal; F/24th Inf. SOURCE: Sayre, *Warriors of Color*, 397.
See **POSEY**, Frank, Private, H/24th Infantry

BROCKTON, John; M/9th Cav. Born in Pennsylvania; mulatto complexion; can read, cannot write, age 23, Jul 1870, at Ft McKavett, TX. SOURCE: Bierschwale, *Fort McKavett*, 99.

BROMBACK, William; D/24th Inf. Born in Kentucky; black complexion; cannot read or write, age 25, Jul 1870, at Ft McKavett, TX. SOURCE: Bierschwale, *Fort McKavett*, 96.

BRONSON, Joseph; Sergeant; I/48th Inf. Died 14 Nov 1930; buried in plot B 971 at San Francisco National Cemetery. SOURCE: San Francisco National Cemetery.

BRONSTON, Tevis; Private; K/25th Inf. Died 29 Jan 1900 in the Philippines; buried in plot ESIDE1099 at San Francisco National Cemetery. SOURCE: San Francisco National Cemetery.

BROOKINS, Richard; M/9th Cav. Born in Kentucky; mulatto complexion; cannot read or write, age 23, Jul 1870, at Ft McKavett, TX. SOURCE: Bierschwale, *Fort McKavett,* 99.

BROOKS, Clifford; Wagoner; G/9th Cav. Received Philippine Campaign Badge number 11817 for service as private in G/9th Cavalry, 16 Sep 1900–16 Feb 1901; wagoner in 9th Cavalry, Ft Leavenworth, KS, Mar 1905. SOURCE: Philippine Campaign Badge Recipients; Philippine Campaign Badge list, 29 May 1905.

BROOKS, Henry; G/10th Cav. Civil War veteran; served in Independent Battery, U.S. Colored Light Artillery; served in G/10th Cavalry, Jul 1867–Jul 1872; died Hutchinson, KS, 23 Sep 1916. SOURCE: *Organization Index to Pension Files,* rolls 707, 579.

‡Original member of 10th Cavalry; in troop when organized, Ft Leavenworth, KS, 5 Jul 1867. SOURCE: McMiller, "Buffalo Soldiers," 74.

BROOKS, Preston; Corporal; D/9th Cav. Civil War veteran with Robert Hudson according to 5 Dec 1931 letter from Mr. V. C. McKenzie, grandson of Polly Ann Hudson, concerning pension claims for Hudson and Brooks. SOURCE: Letter to Hon. K. D. McKellar, U.S. Senator. Photocopy in authors' files.

‡Stationed at Ft Riley, KS, 1 Jan–19 Jul 1884; at camp on Chicaskia River, Indian Territory, 21 Jul–19 Oct 1884; at Ft Riley, Oct 1884–27 Feb 1885; at camp on Chilicco Creek, Indian Territory, Mar–May 1885; at Ft Riley to 14 Jun 1885; at Ft McKinney, WY, 19 Aug 1885–21 Aug 1887; served as artificer, Quartermaster Department, Ft McKinney, 30 Apr–31 Dec 1886. SOURCE: VA Invalid Claim 1061386, Preston Brooks.

‡Original pension application based on injury to right hip, ankle, back; injured when he fell twenty-eight feet off scaffold while weatherboarding building, Ft McKinney, 16 Dec 1885; then sprained right ankle mounting horse, in line of duty, 10 May 1887; discharged Ft McKinney, 21 Aug 1887; resided Junction City, Geary Co., KS, age 36, yellow complexion, 1891; previously carpenter but now cannot work. SOURCE: VA Invalid Claim 1061386, Preston Brooks.

‡Married to Anna Griffin, Ft Riley; children: Preston Jr., born 4 Jun 1884; Harriet, born Dec 1886; Mary Anna, born Sep 1890. SOURCE: Affidavit, Brooks, 2 May 1902, VA Invalid Claim 1061386, Preston Brooks.

‡Post engineer, Ft Robinson, NE, admonished to guard against fire by wetting down ashes in barrels as required by post orders. SOURCE: Commander, Ft Robinson, to Mr. Preston Brooks, 12 Apr 1893, LS, Ft Robinson.

‡Died 10 Aug 1905; buried at Ft Robinson with Masonic rites and 10th Cavalry band; managed Ft Robinson waterworks and sawmill about fifteen years. SOURCE: Crawford *Tribune,* 15 Aug 1905.

‡Buried, Ft Robinson, 11 Aug 1905. SOURCE: List of Interments, Ft Robinson.

‡Widow Anna resides in Crawford, NE, 1912, with personal property assessed at $49 and taxed at $4. SOURCE: Dawes County tax records.

‡Widow inquired about obtaining pension in 1931. SOURCE: VA Invalid Claim 1061386, Preston Brooks.

Annie Brooks, widow of Preston S. Brooks, born 12 Sep 1855 in Kentucky, daughter of Henry Ford, occupation housework, died of apoplexy, 7 Jun 1930, age 74, at Crawford. SOURCE: Certificate of Death, Dawes County, NE, photocopy in authors' file.

Reburied 22 Jul 1947 at Ft McPherson National Cemetery, Maxwell, Lincoln County, NE, Plot F 0 1043. SOURCE: U.S. Department of Veterans' Affairs, Fort McPherson National Cemetery.

BROOKS, Robert H.; Private; 9th Cav. ‡Enlisted Baltimore, MD, 17 Feb 1899; joined I/24th Infantry 20 Feb 1899. SOURCE: Muster Roll, I/24 Inf, Jan–Feb 1899.

‡On detached service at Three Rivers, CA, 3 May–21 Jun 1899; on detached service at Presidio of San Francisco, 22 Jun 1899. SOURCE: Muster Roll, I/24 Inf, May–Jun 1899.

‡Rejoined company, 26 Jun 1899. SOURCE: Muster Roll, I/24 Inf, Jul–Aug 1899.

‡Fined $1 by summary court, 13 Oct 1899. SOURCE: Muster Roll, I/24 Inf, Sep–Oct 1899.

‡Captured in the Philippines, 31 Jul 1900. *See* OTT, **SMITH**, C. H., Sergeant, I/24th Infantry

Received Philippine Campaign Badge number 11878 for service in I/24th Infantry and H/9th Cavalry; in 9th Cavalry at Ft Leavenworth, KS, Mar 1905. SOURCE: Philippine Campaign Badge list, 29 May 1905.

BROOKS, Thomas; Private; 9th Cav. Received Philippine Campaign Badge number 11765 for service as private in D/9th Cavalry; in 9th Cavalry at Ft Leavenworth, KS, Mar 1905. SOURCE: Philippine Campaign Badge list, 29 May 1905.

BROOKS, William P.; Corporal; G/9th Cav. Enlisted 8 May 1898 at Tuskegee, AL, for three years; honorable discharge, character excellent, 23 May 1901. SOURCE: Certificate in Lieu of Lost or Destroyed Discharge Certificate, 27 Apr 1934, copy in authors' files.

Served in Cuba 20 June 1898–14 Aug 1898; in action at Santiago de Cuba, Cuba, 11 Jul 1898, at El Caney, Cuba, 18 Jul 1898; served in the Philippines 16 Sep 1900–23 May 1901, in engagements with insurgents 9–26 Oct 1900 at or near Lagity, PI; in action at Camalig, PI, 2 Nov 1900; in engagement in hills between Camalig and Dirago, PI, 7 Nov 1900; in engagement at Lagity, PI, 14 Nov 1900; in action at Sulung, PI, 24 Nov 1900; in action at Jovallar, PI, 24 Nov

1900 and near Camalig and Jovallar, 26 Nov 1900. SOURCE: Letter from War Department, Adjutant General's Office, 27 Apr 1934, copy in authors' file.

BROOM, Dargan; Private; 25th Inf. Born in Columbia, SC; Ht 5'8", black hair and eyes, dark complexion; occupation miner; enlisted at age 24, Charleston, SC, 24 May 1881; left recruit depot, David's Island, NY, 2 Jul 1881, arrived Ft Randall, SD, 7 Jul 1881. SOURCE: Descriptive & Assignment Rolls of Recruits, 25 Inf.

BROWN, Albert; Private; E/10th Cav. Died 29 Oct 1868 of dysentery at Ft Arbuckle, OK. SOURCE: Regimental Returns, 10th Cavalry, 1868.

BROWN, Alfred; Private; D/10th Cav. Died 1 Nov 1871 of malaria at Ft Sill, OK. SOURCE: Regimental Returns, 10th Cavalry, 1871.

Died 25 Nov 1871; buried at Camp Douglas, UT. SOURCE: Record Book of Interments, Post Cemetery, 252.

BROWN, Benjamin; Sergeant; C/24th Inf. ‡Born Platte City, MO; occupation packer; Ht 5'8", dark complexion; enlisted, age 25, Ft Leavenworth, KS, 14 Oct 1881, G/24th Infantry, transferred to band; discharged, expiration of service, character excellent, Ft Supply, IT, with $72 retained, $21 clothing, 13 Jul 1886; reenlisted Ft Supply, 16 Jul 1886; discharged, married, character good, Ft Bayard, NM, with additional pay of $2 per month, $65 retained, $11 clothing, 15 Jul 1891; reenlisted Ft Leavenworth, 5 Aug 1891; discharged, married, no children, character very good, Ft Bayard, with additional pay of $3 per month, $53 retained, $7 clothing, 4 Aug 1896. SOURCE: Descriptive Book, 24 Inf NCS & Band.

‡Sergeant, C/24th Infantry, and sharpshooter, stationed at Ft Sill, Indian Territory. SOURCE: *ANJ* 24 (22 Jan 1887): 510.

Born in Platte City, MO; married, no children, excellent shot, and eight-year veteran, senior member of escort for Paymaster Joseph Wham when ambushed by robbers near Cedar Springs, AZ, May 1889; received Medal of Honor for bravery in fight; wounded twice, in abdomen and arm; buried at U.S. Soldiers' and Airmen's Home, Washington, DC. SOURCE: Schubert, *Black Valor*, 93–96, 98, 100, 171.

Medal of Honor for bravery in protecting Paymaster Wham and payroll, Arizona, 1889, mentioned. SOURCE: Dobak and Phillips, *The Black Regulars*, 100, 261.

Report of Paymaster Wham, describing bravery of escort, published. SOURCE: Schubert, *Voices of the Buffalo Soldier*, 159–62.

‡Mentioned among men who distinguished themselves in 1889; Medal of Honor awarded for gallant and meritorious conduct while escorting Maj. Joseph W. Wham, pay-

master, when attacked by band of robbers between Fts Grant and Thomas, AZ. SOURCE: GO 18, AGO, 1891.

‡Awarded Medal of Honor for role in Paymaster Wham fight, Arizona, 1889. SOURCE: Carroll, *The Black Military Experience*, 279; Thompson, "The Negro Regiments."

‡Distinguished marksman, 1889 and 1890. SOURCE: GO 112, AGO, 2 Oct 1890.

‡Sergeant, C/24th Infantry, and one of best marksmen in Army, as he proved at Department of Arizona competition last August. SOURCE: Cleveland *Gazette*, 18 Feb 1893.

‡His six-month furlough rescinded as of 10 Apr 1893 because he loafed around post most of time since 1 Nov 1892, stopped at house of ill fame on north border of military reserve on 8 Apr 1893, and was present when enlisted man of the command was killed there. SOURCE: LTC Henry E. Noyes, 2 Cav, Commander, Ft Huachuca, AZ, to AAG, Department of Arizona, 18 Apr 1893, Letters & Orders Received, 24 Inf, 1893.

‡Distinguished marksman who deserves to compete for place on department rifle team. SOURCE: Commander, C/24, to Adj, Ft Huachuca, 13 Jul 1893, Name File, 24 Inf.

‡Distinguished marksman, eligible for Army team; designated to participate in Department of Arizona rifle meet. SOURCE: Order 119, Ft Huachuca, 10 Aug 1893, Letters & Orders Received, 24 Inf, 1893.

‡Authorized to obey summons to appear before civil court, Tombstone, AZ, with Cpl. Thornton Jackson, C/24th Infantry, and Pvt. Alonzo Warnzer, C/24th Infantry. SOURCE: Order 172, Ft Huachuca, Nov 1893, Letters & Orders Received, 24 Inf, 1893.

‡Succeeds Abbott, appointed ordnance sergeant, as sergeant major, 24th Infantry; Medal of Honor as Wham escort; wounded against Indians; seventeen-year veteran. SOURCE: *ANJ* 34 (7 Aug 1897): 907.

‡Enlisted Ft Douglas, UT, 24 Mar 1898; sick en route to U.S. since 25 Jul 1898; reduced from regimental sergeant major to private, H/24th Infantry. SOURCE: Muster Roll, H/24 Inf, Jul–Aug 1898.

‡Furlough authorized by surgeon's certificate, 12 Sep–11 Oct 1898; on special duty, clerk, Quartermaster Department, 5 Oct 1898; promoted to corporal, 8 Oct 1898. SOURCE: Muster Roll, H/24 Inf, Sep–Oct 1898.

‡Clerk, Quartermaster Department, 5 Oct–24 Dec 1898; sick in hospital since 24 Dec 1898, disease contracted in line of duty. SOURCE: Muster Roll, H/24 Inf, Nov–Dec 1898.

‡Sick in hospital until 7 Jan 1899; clerk, Quartermaster Department since 5 Oct 1898. SOURCE: Muster Roll, H/24 Inf, Jan–Feb 1899.

‡Drum major, 24th Infantry, and ranked number 54 among expert riflemen with 68 percent in 1903. SOURCE: GO 52, AGO, 19 Mar 1904.

Suffered severe stroke at Ft Assiniboine, MT, in 1904; entered U.S. Soldiers Home, Washington, DC, where he died in 1910; buried in Washington, DC. SOURCE: Ball, *Ambush at Bloody Run*, 207–8.

BROWN, Champ; Private; D/10th Cav. Died at Ft Concho, TX, on 15 Feb 1878; buried at San Antonio National Cemetery, Section D, number 540. SOURCE: San Antonio National Cemetery Locator.

BROWN, Charles H.; D/24th Inf. Born in Tennessee; black complexion; can read, cannot write, age 24, Jul 1870, at Ft McKavett, TX. SOURCE: Bierschwale, *Fort McKavett*, 95.

BROWN, Charles R.; Corporal; 9th Cav. ‡Promoted from private, Apr 1902. SOURCE: *ANJ* 39 (10 May 1902): 904.

Received Philippine Campaign Badge number 11760 for service as corporal in F/9th Cavalry; in 9th Cavalry at Ft Leavenworth, KS, Mar 1905. SOURCE: Philippine Campaign Badge list, 29 May 1905.

BROWN, Creed; Private; E/24th Inf. Died 20 Mar 1893; buried at Ft Bayard, NM, in plot I 29. SOURCE: "Fort Bayard National Cemetery, Records of Burials."

Buried 30 Mar 1893, section A, row M, plot 32, at Ft Bayard. SOURCE: Erickson, Burials at Fort Bayard National Cemetery, NM.

BROWN, Daniel; Sergeant; I/10th Cav. ‡Born in Maryland; private, I/10th Cavalry, 26 Jul 1867; corporal, 1 Jan 1871; sergeant, 14 Aug 1872. SOURCE: Baker, Roster.

‡Original member of 10th Cavalry; in troop when organized, Ft Riley, KS, 15 Aug 1867. SOURCE: McMiller, "Buffalo Soldiers," 76.

In Troop I/10th Cavalry stationed at Bonita Cañon Camp, AZ, but absent or on detached service 30 Jun 1886. SOURCE: Tagg, *The Camp at Bonita Cañon*, 231.

‡Retires from Ft Assiniboine, MT. SOURCE: *ANJ* 35 (11 Sep 1897): 23.

BROWN, David; Private; F/9th Cav. Born in Virginia; black complexion; cannot read or write, age 22, Jul 1870, at Ft McKavett, TX. SOURCE: Bierschwale, *Fort McKavett*, 97.

At Fort McKavett, 1870; survived attempt on his life Feb 1870 while guarding civilian prisoner. SOURCE: Kenner, *Buffalo Soldiers and Officers of the Ninth Cavalry*, 94–96.

BROWN, Edmond; Private; A/10th Cav. ‡Died 11 Mar 1870. SOURCE: ES, 10 Cav, 1866–71.

Died 11 Mar 1870 of pneumonia at Camp Supply, OK. SOURCE: Regimental Returns, 10th Cavalry, 1870.

BROWN, Elmer; Private; B/25th Inf. Enlisted 18 May 1892, discharged as private I/10th Cavalry, 17 Aug 1895, character excellent; reenlisted 2 Nov 1895, discharged as private B/25th Infantry, 1 Nov 1898, character very good; reenlisted 2 Nov 1898, discharged as corporal I/25th Infantry 1 Nov 1901, character excellent; reenlisted 7 Nov 1901, discharged as corporal B/25th Infantry 26 Nov 1902, character excellent; reenlisted 25 Feb 1903, discharged as private B/25th Infantry 24 Feb 1906, character excellent; reenlisted 25 Feb 1906, discharged without honor 22 Nov 1906, Brownsville, TX. SOURCE: Powell, "Military Record of the Enlisted Men Who Were Discharged Without Honor."

‡Dishonorable discharge, Brownsville. SOURCE: SO 266, AGO, 9 Nov 1906.

‡Pallbearer for Col. Andrew S. Burt, who had requested that men of 25th Infantry carry his coffin. SOURCE: Curtis, *The Black Soldier*, 49.

BROWN, Frank B.; Private; H/10th Cav. In Troop H/10th Cavalry stationed at Bonita Cañon Camp, AZ, but absent or on detached service 30 Apr 1886. SOURCE: Tagg, *The Camp at Bonita Cañon*, 231.

BROWN, George; Musician; Band/25th Inf. Died at Ft Davis, TX, on 18 Sep 1872; buried at San Antonio National Cemetery, Section I, number 1512. SOURCE: San Antonio National Cemetery Locator.

BROWN, George; Private; B/9th Cav. Served in Indian Territory, 1884–85, keeping illegal settlers off tribal lands; after service, resided in U.S. Soldiers Home. SOURCE: Schubert, *Black Valor*, 59.

‡Admitted to Soldiers Home, with twenty years and seven months' service, age 42. SOURCE: SecWar, AR 1890, 1041.

BROWN,, George; Private; A/48th Inf. Died 2 Jul 1901; buried in plot NADDN417 at San Francisco National Cemetery. SOURCE: San Francisco National Cemetery.

BROWN, Henry; Private; A/25th Inf. Born in Jacksonville, FL; Ht 5'8", black hair and dark eyes, black complexion; occupation waiter; enlisted at age 21, New York City, 9 Aug 1882; arrived Ft Snelling, MN, 21 Nov 1882. SOURCE: Descriptive & Assignment Rolls of Recruits, 25 Inf.

BROWN, J. James; Private; F/10th Cav. *See* **BROWN**, James G., Private, F/10th Cavalry

BROWN, Jacob; Private; 25th Inf. Born in Charleston, SC; Ht 5'5", black hair and eyes, dark complexion; occupation miner; enlisted at age 21, Charleston, 21 May 1881; left recruit depot, David's Island, NY, 2 Jul 1881, arrived Ft Randall, SD, 7 Jul 1881. SOURCE: Descriptive & Assignment Rolls of Recruits, 25 Inf.

BROWN, James; Private; F/10th Cav. ‡Original member of 10th Cavalry; in troop when organized, Ft Leavenworth, KS, 21 Jun 1867. SOURCE: McMiller, "Buffalo Soldiers," 73.

Wounded in action, gunshot wound in right thigh, near Beaver Creek, KS, 21 Aug 1867. SOURCE: LR, DeptMo, 1867.

Wounded in action against Indians at Beaver Creek, 21 Aug 1867. SOURCE: Schubert, *Voices of the Buffalo Soldier*, 20.

BROWN, James; Private; K/10th Cav. ‡Original member of 10th Cavalry; in troop when organized, Ft Riley, KS, 1 Sep 1867. SOURCE: McMiller, "Buffalo Soldiers," 77.

Died 3 Dec 1867, no cause listed, at Ft Riley. SOURCE: Regimental Returns, 10th Cavalry, 1867.

BROWN, James; Private; B/9th Cav. Native of Virginia, age 23, occupation barber; in first year of service when killed in action at Gavilan Canyon, NM, 19 Aug 1881. SOURCE: Kenner, *Buffalo Soldiers and Officers of the Ninth Cavalry*, 229; Schubert, *Black Valor*, 84.

BROWN, James; Private; H/10th Cav. Served in first half of 1880s; resided at 9th and Tays Sts., El Paso, TX, in 1929. SOURCE: Sayre, *Warriors of Color*, 219.

BROWN, James; 1st Sgt; I/10th Cav. ‡"Displayed rare courage and judgment," severely wounded by arrow in running fight with Cheyennes, Kansas, Jun 1867; honorable mention for conspicuous bravery against Cheyennes, Beaver Creek, KS, where he was severely wounded by arrow which pinned his legs together, 18 Oct 1868. SOURCE: Baker, Roster.

‡Original member of 10th Cavalry; in troop when organized, Ft Riley, KS, 15 Aug 1867. SOURCE: McMiller, "Buffalo Soldiers," 76.

‡Reenlisted as first sergeant, I/10th Cavalry, Jul 1877. SOURCE: ES, 10 Cav, 1873–81.

In Troop I/10th Cavalry stationed at Bonita Cañon Camp, AZ, 30 Jun 1886. SOURCE: Tagg, *The Camp at Bonita Cañon*, 231.

‡At Ft Apache, AZ, 1890, subscribed $.50 to testimonial to General Grierson. SOURCE: List of subscriptions, 23 Apr 1890, 10th Cavalry papers, MHI.

‡Cpl. Scott Lovelace, I/10th Cavalry, served in I/10th Cavalry, 1881–86; knew Brown. SOURCE: *Winners of the West* 10 (Jan 1933): 1.

‡In 10th Cavalry since Jul 1867 and I Troop since Aug 1867; promoted to first sergeant, 1 Aug 1872; probably senior first sergeant in Army; recommended for Medal of Honor for heroism, 18 Oct 1868; froze to death in storm en route from Havre, MT, to Ft Assiniboine, MT, 5 Feb 1895. Capt. S. L. Woodward, I/10th Cavalry, called him "in every

sense a gallant and efficient soldier. He knew no fear and there were no difficulties too great for him to attempt to surmount. His untimely death has deprived the regiment and the Army of a model soldier." SOURCE: *ANJ* 32 (23 Feb 1895): 422.

‡His widow of one year taken care of by 10th Cavalry; according to a sergeant, "that woman ain't going to want for bread while the 10th Cav. has a ration left." SOURCE: *ANJ* 33 (7 Dec 1895): 29.

BROWN, James E.; Private; Band/24th Inf. ‡Born in York, PA; brown eyes, brown hair, mulatto; served in F/9th Cavalry, character good, 27 Jun 1878–26 Jun 1883; enlisted, E/24th Infantry, Ft Leavenworth, KS, 11 Aug 1884; joined Band/24th Infantry, Ft Sill, Indian Territory, 6 Feb 1888; returned to E/24th Infantry, 1 Oct 1888. SOURCE: Entry, Ft Bayard, NM, 6 Oct 1888, Descriptive Book, 24 Inf NCS & Band.

Served in E/24th Infantry 1889–91 before transfer to regimental band. SOURCE: Sayre, *Warriors of Color*, 263.

BROWN, James G.; Private; F/10th Cav. Died 6 Mar 1876 in hospital at Ft Concho, TX. SOURCE: Regimental Returns, 10th Cavalry, 1876.

BROWN, James S.; Private; F/10th Cav. Died at Ft Concho, TX, on 6 Mar 1876; buried at San Antonio National Cemetery, Section D, number 667. SOURCE: San Antonio National Cemetery Locator.

J. James Brown died 27 May 1878 of fever at Ft Stockton, TX. SOURCE: Regimental Returns, 10th Cavalry, 1878.

Originally buried at Camp Eagle Pass, TX; buried at San Antonio National Cemetery, Section F, number 1138. SOURCE: San Antonio National Cemetery Locator.

BROWN, John; Private; K/9th Cav. Died 19 Apr 1881, buried at Santa Fe National Cemetery, NM, plot A-3 1031. SOURCE: Santa Fe National Cemetery, Records of Burials.

BROWN, John; Private; 25th Inf. Born in Charleston, SC; Ht 5'5", black hair and eyes, dark complexion; occupation laborer; enlisted at age 21, Charleston, 27 May 1881; left recruit depot, David's Island, NY, 2 Jul 1881, arrived Ft Randall, SD, 7 Jul 1881. SOURCE: Descriptive & Assignment Rolls of Recruits, 25 Inf.

BROWN, John; Private; B/25th Inf. Enlisted 13 Oct 1899, discharged as private 12 Oct 1902, character very good; reenlisted 29 Oct 1902, discharged as cook 28 Oct 1905, character very good; reenlisted 13 Nov 1905, discharged without honor 22 Nov 1906, Brownsville, TX. SOURCE: Powell, "Military Record of the Enlisted Men Who Were Discharged Without Honor."

BROWN, John; Sergeant; C/9th Cav. Served as first sergeant, C/9th Cavalry, prior to Alexander Jones; at Ft Sill, OK, 1884. SOURCE: Kenner, *Buffalo Soldiers and Officers of the Ninth Cavalry*, 262.

BROWN, John; Trumpeter; 25th Inf. Born in Columbus, OH; Ht 5'6", black hair and eyes, black complexion; occupation cook; enlisted as trumpeter at age 26, St Louis, MO, 10 Aug 1886; assigned to D/25th Infantry; arrived Ft Snelling, MN, 25 Apr 1887. SOURCE: Descriptive & Assignment Rolls of Recruits, 25 Inf.

BROWN, John; 9th Cav. Veteran, residing in Denver City, TX, in 1899, wrote letter to Mrs. Julia Henry praising her husband and recalling his service at Ft Sill, OK, under Maj. Guy Henry. SOURCE: Kenner, *Buffalo Soldiers and Officers of the Ninth Cavalry*, 137.

BROWN, John H.; Private; 9th Cav. Received Philippine Campaign Badge number 11717 for service as private, Hospital Corps, 9th Cavalry; in 9th Cavalry at Ft Leavenworth, KS, Mar 1905. SOURCE: Philippine Campaign Badge list, 29 May 1905.

BROWN, John L.; Private; G/10th Cav. Died 28 Nov 1876 of suicide at Ft Griffin, TX. SOURCE: Regimental Returns, 10th Cavalry, 1876.

‡"A letter just received at these Hdqrs signed the Enlisted men of Company G 10th Cavalry states that 'Pvt. John L. Brown on the night of 28th was taken out and tied up, and remained there until he died, and then he was cut down and put in a box, thrown in the ground just as if he was a dog, and that is not all, they put great logs on men and make them carry it until they can't walk and we call on you for protection' "; commander unwilling to credit this statement and wants full report. SOURCE: Adj, 10 Cav, to CO, G/10, 7 Dec 1876, LS, 10 Cav, 1873–83.

‡Followup letter calls attention to 7 Dec 1876 letter, again asks for full report. SOURCE: Adj, 10 Cav, to CO, G/10, 11 Feb 1877, LS, 10 Cav, 1873–83.

‡Adjutant forwards statement of enlisted men of G/10th Cavalry and two earlier requests for full report of commander, G/10th Cavalry; asks for investigation and report without delay. SOURCE: Adj, 10 Cav, to AAG, Department of Texas, 19 Mar 1877, LS, 10 Cav, 1873–83.

‡Commander of 10th Cavalry forwards additional complaints from G/10th Cavalry, Ft Griffin; contends interests of service require further action; writes that commander, G/10th Cavalry, reports Brown a suicide; wants full investigation. SOURCE: CO, 10 Cav, to AAG, Department of Texas, 27 Apr 1877, LS, 10 Cav, 1873–83.

Pvt. John L. Brown, 10th Cavalry, killed by members of his unit, Ft Griffin, 1876, because they suspected he was barracks thief. SOURCE: Dobak and Phillips, *The Black Regulars*, 200.

‡Letter from enlisted men, 10th Cavalry, Ft Concho, TX, who "respectfully request that investigations be made in the case of the murder of John L. Brown, late private of Company G 10th Cavalry," forwarded to Department of the Missouri. SOURCE: CO, 10 Cav, to HQ, Department of the Missouri, 27 Apr 1877, LS, 10 Cav, 1873–83.

Buried at San Antonio National Cemetery, Section D, number 703. SOURCE: San Antonio National Cemetery Locator.

BROWN, John M.; Private; C/9th Cav. Received Philippine Campaign Badge number 11718 for service as private in C/9th Cavalry; in 9th Cavalry at Ft Leavenworth, KS, Mar 1905. SOURCE: Philippine Campaign Badge list, 29 May 1905.

BROWN, John W.; Comsy Sgt; A/9th Cav. ‡Born in Falmouth, Stafford Co., VA, 5 May 1856; enlisted 24 Apr 1876; assigned to D/24th Infantry; discharged as sergeant, 23 Apr 1881; reenlisted, C/9th Cavalry, May 1881; corporal, sergeant, first sergeant, saddler sergeant; commissioned second lieutenant, 9th U.S. Volunteer Infantry, 24 Oct 1898, and joined regiment at San Luis, Cuba, 6 Dec 1898. SOURCE: Coston, *The Spanish-American War Volunteer*, 27.

Appointed sergeant 8 Aug 1886; in A/9th Cavalry at Ft Robinson, NE, Jan 1897. SOURCE: Ninth Cavalry, Roster of NCOs, 1897.

‡Sergeant, A/9th Cavalry, since 8 Aug 1886. SOURCE: Roster, 9 Cav, 1893.

‡Sergeant, A/9th Cavalry, promoted to saddler sergeant, 9th Cavalry, 7 Jul 1897. SOURCE: *ANJ* 34 (17 Jul 1897): 854.

‡Saddler sergeant, 9th Cavalry, commissioned second lieutenant, 9th Volunteer Infantry, 1898. SOURCE: Cashin, *Under Fire with the Tenth Cavalry*, 360; San Francisco *Chronicle*, 15 Nov 1899.

‡Appointed regimental commissary sergeant, Apr 1902. SOURCE: *ANJ* 39 (10 May 1902): 904.

‡Son of John B. and Julia Miner, Falmouth, VA; excellent marksman and former regimental clerk; commissioned in 9th U.S. Volunteer Infantry and served in Cuba; first lieutenant, G/48th Infantry, Philippines; returned to 9th Cavalry after Philippine Insurrection; retired with twenty-seven years as commissary sergeant. SOURCE: Beasley, *Negro Trailblazers*, 298.

BROWN, Joseph; D/24th Inf. Born in Mississippi; black complexion; cannot read or write, age 21, Jul 1870, at Ft McKavett, TX. SOURCE: Bierschwale, *Fort McKavett*, 96.

BROWN, Joseph; Private; G/25th Inf. Born in Marlborough, NY; Ht 5'9", black hair and brown eyes, black complexion; occupation teamster; enlisted 3 Jun 1886, age 21, at Buffalo, NY; assigned to G/25th Infantry; arrived Ft

Snelling, MN, 14 Dec 1886. SOURCE: Descriptive & Assignment Rolls of Recruits, 25 Inf.

BROWN, Lewis; Private; E/9th Cav. *See* **BROWN**, Louis, Private, E/91th Cavalry

BROWN, Louis; Private; E/9th Cav. Witness at court martial of soldiers charged with mutiny and desertion for role in mutiny at San Pedro Springs, near San Antonio, TX, April 1867; pled guilty to desertion but not mutiny; mutiny charge dropped. SOURCE: Dobak and Phillips, *The Black Regulars*, 208–10; Schubert, *Black Valor*, 13–14.

Lewis Brown, private in E/9th Cavalry in Apr 1867, at time of San Pedro Springs mutiny. SOURCE: Kenner, *Buffalo Soldiers and Officers of the Ninth Cavalry*, 76.

BROWN, Primus; C/25th Inf. Born in Pennsylvania; black complexion; can read and write, age 25, 5 Sep 1870, at Ft McKavett, TX. SOURCE: Bierschwale, *Fort McKavett*, 109.

BROWN, Randall; Corporal; A/9th Cav. Native of South Carolina, age 28, light complexion, in second enlistment, at Ft Stanton, NM, and serving as stable guard, Apr 1881, when propositioned by Pvt. Richard Kennedy, A/9th Cavalry. SOURCE: Kenner, *Buffalo Soldiers and Officers of the Ninth Cavalry*, 268–69.

BROWN, Richard; H/25th Inf. Born in Delaware; black complexion; cannot read or write, age 24, 5 Sep 1870, at Ft McKavett, TX. SOURCE: Bierschwale, *Fort McKavett*, 108.

BROWN, Samuel B.; Private; G/25th Inf. Died on 7 Feb 1900; buried at San Antonio National Cemetery, Section I, number 1701. SOURCE: San Antonio National Cemetery Locator.

BROWN, Thomas; Private; C/9th Cav. Died at Ft McIntosh, TX, on 3 Mar 1874; buried at Fort Sam Houston National Cemetery, Section PE, number 417. SOURCE: Buffalo Soldiers Interred in Fort Sam Houston National Cemetery.

BROWN, Thomas H.; Private; C/10th Cav. Died 9 Jul 1875 of shock from gunshot wound at Ft Concho, TX. SOURCE: Regimental Returns, 10th Cavalry, 1875.

BROWN, Walter; Private; 9th Cav. Received Philippine Campaign Badge number 11719 for service as private in E/9th Cavalry; in 9th Cavalry at Ft Leavenworth, KS, Mar 1905. SOURCE: Philippine Campaign Badge list, 29 May 1905.

BROWN, William; Private; B/25th Inf. Enlisted 10 Apr 1899, discharged 30 May 1902, character very good; enlisted 31 Dec 1902, discharged 30 Dec 1905, character very good; reenlisted 23 Feb 1906, discharged without honor 22 Nov 1906, Brownsville, TX. SOURCE: Powell, "Military Record of the Enlisted Men Who Were Discharged Without Honor."

‡Dishonorable discharge, Brownsville. SOURCE: SO 266, AGO, 9 Nov 1906.

BROWN, William W.; 25th Inf. Musician, B/25th Infantry, rode in 25th Infantry Bicycle Corps, Ft Missoula, MT, Summer 1896. SOURCE: Sorenson, List of Buffalo Soldiers Who Rode in the 25 Infantry Bicycle Corps, in authors' files.

‡Alice A. Brown, age 49, 1126 E. 53rd Street, Los Angeles, widow of William W. Brown, veteran of Spanish-American War, who served in A Company and Band/24th Infantry and 25th Infantry, is pensioned, File C 1243461; married to first husband, William H. Oliver, Band/9th Cavalry, by Chaplain George Prioleau, Ft Walla Walla, WA, 1904; Oliver died in Honolulu, HI, before she married Brown. SOURCE: VA File C 1392575, George W. Prioleau.

BROWN, Wilson; Private; A/9th Cav. Private, A/9th Cavalry, Ft Stanton, NM, 1885; claimed to have been sexually molested by Pvt. Israel Monday, A/9th Cavalry. SOURCE: Kenner, *Buffalo Soldiers and Officers of the Ninth Cavalry*, 270.

BROWNING, Andrew; Sergeant; C/9th Cav. Appointed sergeant 2 Jan 1882; in C/9th Cavalry at Ft Robinson, NE, Jan 1897. SOURCE: Ninth Cavalry, Roster of NCOs, 1897.

‡Sergeant, C/9th Cavalry since 2 Jun 1882. SOURCE: Roster, 9 Cav, 1893.

‡At Ft McKinney, WY, granted hunting pass to Big Horn Mountains, 12–18 Sep 1894.

‡Authorized to reenlist as married, Dec 1896.

‡Retired Jul 1901. SOURCE: *ANJ* 38 (27 Jul 1901): 1163.

BRUCE, George; Private; 9th Cav. Veteran of Civil War, served in 32nd U.S. Colored Infantry; served in 40th Infantry and 9th Cavalry. SOURCE: Dobak and Phillips, *The Black Regulars*, 273.

BRUFF, Thomas; Private; H/10th Cav. In Troop H/10th Cavalry stationed at Bonita Cañon Camp, AZ, but absent or on detached service 30 Apr 1886. SOURCE: Tagg, *The Camp at Bonita Cañon*, 231.

‡Honorable mention as private, H/10th Cavalry, in capture of Mangas and his band, Rio Bonito, AZ, 18 Oct 1886. SOURCE: Baker, Roster.

‡Corporal, K/9th Cavalry, since 25 Mar 1892. SOURCE: Roster, 9 Cav, 1893.

‡Private, Band/10th Cavalry, served in 10th Cavalry in Cuba, 1898; died of Cuban fever. SOURCE: Cashin, *Under Fire with the Tenth Cavalry*, 352, 359.

BRUMMSICK, George; 25th Inf. Served three enlistments before working as janitor, Sioux City, IA, post office; funeral in Iowa City conducted by fellow members of colored Masonic Lodge. SOURCE: Dobak and Phillips, *The Black Regulars*, 272, 278.

BRUNER, Cipio; Private; U.S. Army. Seminole Negro Scout, served 1872–74. SOURCE: Schubert, Consolidated List of Seminole Negro Scouts.

Born in Mexico; enlisted at Ft Clark, TX, for six months 12 Aug 1872, age 16; Ht 5'6", black hair and eyes, copper complexion; discharged 6 Mar 1873 and reenlisted for six months three more times at Ft Clark; final discharge, 17 Dec 1874, age 21, at Ft Clark. SOURCE: Swanson, 4.

BRUNER, James; Private; U.S. Army. Seminole Negro Scout, also known as Jim, served 1871–75, 1879–81. SOURCE: Schubert, Consolidated List of Seminole Negro Scouts.

Born in Mexico; enlisted for six months 9 Nov 1871 at Ft Duncan, TX, age 25; Ht 5'10", black hair and eyes, black complexion; discharged and reenlisted for six months five more times at Ft Clark, TX; served as private 9 Nov 1871–11 May 1873; served as sergeant 30 Jun 1873–17 Nov 1873; reenlisted as private 12 Jul 1879 for one year; private, discharged 11 Jul 1880 and reenlisted as corporal next day at Ft Clark; final discharge as corporal at Ft Clark 11 Jul 1881, age 32; 1880 Census lists wife Lucy, and Matilda, age 7, Didia, age 6, and William and James, age 4. SOURCE: Swanson, 4.

BRUNER, Joseph; Private; U.S. Army. Seminole Negro Scout, served 1872–73. SOURCE: Schubert, Consolidated List of Seminole Negro Scouts.

Born in Alabama; enlisted 12 Aug 1872 at Ft Clark, TX, age 52; Ht 5'10", black hair and eyes, black complexion; discharged 6 Mar 1873 at Ft Clark.

BRUNER, Monday; Private; U.S. Army. Seminole Negro Scout, served 1872–75. SOURCE: Schubert, Consolidated List of Seminole Negro Scouts.

Born in Arkansas; enlisted for six months at Ft Duncan, TX, 2 Aug 1872, age 23; Ht 6'2", black hair and eyes, black complexion; discharged at Ft Clark, TX, 2 Feb 1873; enlisted at Ft Clark 7 Mar 1873; discharged 10 Sep 1873 at Ft Clark where he reenlisted 13 Sep 1873; discharged 7 Mar 1874 at Ft Clark where he reenlisted 24 Dec 1874; deserted 17 May 1875. SOURCE: Swanson, 5.

BRUNER, Peter; Private; U.S. Army. Born in Arkansas; enlisted for six months at Ft Duncan, TX, 2 Aug 1872, age 23; Ht 6', black hair and eyes, black complexion; discharged at Ft Duncan, 2 Feb 1873; reenlisted for six months at Ft Clark, TX, 1 May 1873; discharged at Camp Comanche, TX, 1 Nov 1873; enlisted at Ft Duncan 1 Jan 1874; dis-

charged at Camp Palafox, TX, 1 Jul 1874; enlisted at Ft Duncan 5 Apr 1875; discharged at Ft Duncan where he reenlisted 10 Feb 1876; discharged at Camp Pecos, TX, 25 Aug 1876; reenlisted four more times for one year each and discharged at Ft Clark; final discharge at Ft Clark 19 Aug 1881, age 32; 1880 Census lists wife Alvina, age 37, and Adelia, age 3. SOURCE: Swanson, 5.

Seminole Negro Scout, served 1872–81. SOURCE: Schubert, Consolidated List of Seminole Negro Scouts.

BRUNER, Zack; Private; U.S. Army. Seminole Negro Scout, served 1871–75, 1878–80. SOURCE: Schubert, Consolidated List of Seminole Negro Scouts.

Born in Mexico; enlisted at Ft Duncan, TX, 9 Nov 1871, age 17; Ht 5'7", black hair and eyes, black complexion; discharged at Ft Duncan 9 May 1872 where he reenlisted the next day; discharged 10 Nov 1872 at Ft Duncan; enlisted 11 Nov 1872 at Ft Clark, TX; discharged and reenlisted at Ft Clark 11 May 1873; discharged 17 Nov 1873 where he reenlisted 2 Jan 1874; discharged at Ft Concho, TX, 23 Aug 1874; enlisted at Ft Clark 23 Dec 1874; discharged 2 Jun 1875 at Ft Clark where he reenlisted 13 Feb 1878 for one year; discharged at Ft Clark 25 Apr 1879 where he reenlisted 12 Jul 1879; final discharge 22 Jul 1880 at Ft Clark; wife Jennie, children Juno and Susie. SOURCE: Swanson, 6.

BRYANT, John C.; C/25th Inf. Born in Tennessee; mulatto complexion; cannot read or write, age 25, 5 Sep 1870, at Ft McKavett, TX. SOURCE: Bierschwale, *Fort McKavett,* 109.

BRYSON, Walter; Sergeant; 9th Cav. Received Philippine Campaign Badge number 11761 for service as sergeant in F/9th Cavalry; in 9th Cavalry at Ft Leavenworth, KS, Mar 1905. SOURCE: Philippine Campaign Badge list, 29 May 1905.

BUCHANAN, Andrew J.; Corporal; I/9th Cav. Died at Ft Davis, TX, on 4 Oct 1867; buried at San Antonio National Cemetery, Section I, number 1553. SOURCE: San Antonio National Cemetery Locator.

BUCHANAN, Charles; Trumpeter; I/10th Cav. In Troop I/10th Cavalry stationed at Bonita Cañon Camp, AZ, 30 Jun 1886. SOURCE: Tagg, *The Camp at Bonita Cañon,* 231.

BUCHANAN, William; Private; K/9th Cav. Stationed at Ft Clark, TX, in 1872; testified at 1873 court martial of Capt. J. Lee Humfreville. SOURCE: Kenner, *Buffalo Soldiers and Officers of the Ninth Cavalry,* 143.

BUCK, John; QM Sgt; USA. ‡Born in Chapel Hill, TX, 1861; enlisted in 10th Cavalry, 1880; "a man of strong character, an experienced horseman and packer." SOURCE: Steward, *The Colored Regulars*, 149.

‡Private, corporal, sergeant, F/10th Cavalry, from 6 Nov 1880; private, B/10th Cavalry, 22 Oct 1889; corporal, 19 Aug 1890; sergeant, 2 Apr 1893; stationed at Ft Custer, MT, 1897. SOURCE: Baker, Roster.

‡Private, B/10th Cavalry, at Ft Apache, AZ, 1890, subscribed $.50 to testimonial to General Grierson. SOURCE: List of subscriptions, 23 Apr 1890, 10th Cavalry papers, MHI.

‡Authorized four-month furlough from station at Ft Apache. SOURCE: *ANJ* 28 (15 Nov 1890): 188.

‡Ranked fifth with carbine, bronze medal, Departments of Dakota and Columbia, 1892. SOURCE: Baker, Roster.

‡Ranked fifth with revolver, Departments of Dakota and Columbia, at competition, Ft Keogh, MT, 15–23 Aug 1892. SOURCE: GO 75, AGO, 3 Nov 1892.

‡Ranked third with carbine, silver medal, Departments of Dakota and Columbia, 1894. SOURCE: Baker, Roster.

‡Ranked third with revolver, Departments of Dakota and Columbia, at competition, Ft Keogh, 18–27 Sep 1894. SOURCE: GO 62, AGO, 15 Nov 1894.

‡Cited for highly meritorious service leading pack train in severe weather from station at Ft Missoula, MT, across Bitterroot Mountains, ID, Nov 1893, in search of lost party of gentlemen. SOURCE: Steward, *The Colored Regulars*, 237; Baker, Roster.

‡First sergeant, B/10th Cavalry, cited for heroism at Las Guasimas, Cuba, 24 Jun 1898; recommended for Medal of Honor by Capt. J. W. Watson; commissioned second lieutenant, 7th Volunteer Infantry, 1898. SOURCE: Cashin, *Under Fire with the Tenth Cavalry*, 179, 186, 337, 354, 359.

‡Pictures. SOURCE: Cashin, *Under Fire with the Tenth Cavalry*, 353; Indianapolis *Freeman*, 4 Nov 1899.

‡Directed to report to Ft Thomas, KY, as captain, 48th Infantry. SOURCE: *ANJ* 37 (7 Oct 1899): 123.

‡Captain, 48th Infantry, one of nineteen 48th Infantry officers recommended for commissions as second lieutenants in the regular Army. SOURCE: CG, Div PI, Manila, to AG, 8 Feb 1901, AGO File 355163.

‡Drum major, 10th Cavalry, and "an old soldier of long service, has done good work as an officer and enlisted man, in Indian wars, at Santiago, and in the Philippines, and in my opinion is qualified for the position he seeks." SOURCE: Endorsement, CO, 10 Cav, Ft Robinson, NE, 11 Feb 1903, LS, Ft Robinson.

‡Drum major, 10th Cavalry band, and manager, regimental baseball team, Ft Robinson, NE, 1904. SOURCE: Lowe, "Camp Life," 205.

‡Mentioned as retired quartermaster sergeant in acknowledgments. SOURCE: Curtis, *The Black Soldier*, with picture opposite 15.

Retired quartermaster sergeant when issued Indian Wars Campaign Badge number 962 on 31 Oct 1908. SOURCE: Carroll, *Indian Wars Campaign Badge*, 28.

BUCKNEY, Wilson; 1st Sgt; 25th Inf. At Ft Randall, Dakota Territory, 1880, testified in court martial of Captain Geddes for drunkenness. SOURCE: Barnett, *Ungentlemanly Acts*, 197.

BUFORD; Sergeant; 24th Inf. Stationed at Ft Bayard, NM, Jan 1894, attended masquerade ball given by F/24th Infantry, dressed as English dude. SOURCE: Schubert, *Voices of the Buffalo Soldier*, 198.

BULGER, William; Private; D/10th Cav. ‡Honorable mention for bravery against Comanches, Double Mountain Fork, Brazos River, TX, 5 Feb 1874. SOURCE: Baker, Roster.

At Ft Concho, TX, 10 May 1875, complained to company commander that his wife was residing with Sergeant Brown, asked that she be removed from post. SOURCE: Haley, *Fort Concho*, 271.

BULLARD, William H.; Private; 9th Cav. Received Philippine Campaign Badge number 11762 for service as private in F/9th Cavalry; in 9th Cavalry at Ft Leavenworth, KS, Mar 1905. SOURCE: Philippine Campaign Badge list, 29 May 1905.

BUNCH, Thomas; Trumpeter; H/10th Cav. Served in 10th Cavalry, 1898; remained in U.S. during war with Spain. SOURCE: Cashin, *Under Fire with the Tenth Cavalry*, 346.

Buried 20 Oct 1914, section B, row G, plot 46, at Ft Bayard, NM. SOURCE: Erickson, Burials at Fort Bayard National Cemetery, NM.

BUNDY, George W.; M/9th Cav. Born in Kentucky; mulatto complexion; can read and write, age 26, Jul 1870, at Ft McKavett, TX. SOURCE: Bierschwale, *Fort McKavett*, 98.

BUNDY, Paul; Private; D/24th Inf. Buried 25 Jan 1890, section A, row I, plot 16, at Ft Bayard, NM. SOURCE: Erickson, Burials at Fort Bayard National Cemetery, NM.

BUNTON, Mark; Private; N/9th Cav. Born in Kentucky; mulatto complexion; cannot read or write, age 23, Jul 1870, in M/9th Cavalry at Ft McKavett, TX. SOURCE: Bierschwale, *Fort McKavett*, 99.

In N/9th Cavalry, died at Ft McKavett on 15 Jul 1871; buried at San Antonio National Cemetery, Section E, number 836. SOURCE: San Antonio National Cemetery Locator.

BURBE, Lester; Private; H/24th Inf. ‡Enlisted Ft McPherson, GA, 1 Jan 1899; assigned to and joined company Feb 1899; died of disease contracted in line of duty, in hospital, Ft Douglas, UT, Feb 1899; due U.S. for clothing $65.88. SOURCE: Muster Roll, H/24 Inf, Jan–Feb 1899.

‡Lester Burke, 24th Infantry, died 13 Feb 1899; buried Ft Douglas, UT. SOURCE: Clark, "A History of the Twenty-fourth," appendix A.

BURDETTE, Ray; Corporal; B/25th Inf. Ray Burdett enlisted 13 Mar 1901, discharged as private K/9th Cavalry 12 Mar 1904, character good; reenlisted 13 Apr 1904, discharged without honor as corporal 22 Nov 1906, Brownsville, TX. SOURCE: Powell, "Military Record of the Enlisted Men Who Were Discharged Without Honor."

‡Dishonorable discharge, Brownsville. SOURCE: SO 266, AGO, 9 Nov 1906.

BURGE, Benjamin; Private; E/24th Inf. Awarded certificate of merit for gallant and meritorious conduct while member of escort of Maj. Joseph W. Wham, paymaster, in ambush by bandits between Ft Grant, AZ, and Ft Thomas, AZ, 11 May 1889. SOURCE: Gleim, *The Certificate of Merit*, 44.

‡Mentioned among men who distinguished themselves in 1889; awarded certificate of merit for gallant and meritorious conduct while escorting Maj. Joseph W. Wham, paymaster, when attacked by robbers between Ft Grant and Ft Thomas. SOURCE: GO 18, AGO, 1891.

Fourteen-year veteran, cited for bravery against robbers near Cedar Springs, AZ, in May 1889 by Maj. Joseph W. Wham, and awarded certificate of merit; wounded in hand during fight; still in Army at end of 1890. SOURCE: Schubert, *Black Valor*, 93, 95.

Text of Paymaster Wham's report, describing bravery of escort, published. SOURCE: Schubert, *Voices of the Buffalo Soldier*, 159–62.

‡Private, K/24th Infantry, Ft Grant, 1890. SOURCE: SecWar, AR 1890, 289.

BURGESS, Lewis; Corporal; 9th Cav. Received Philippine Campaign Badge number 11767 for service as corporal in F/9th Cavalry; in 9th Cavalry at Ft Leavenworth, KS, Mar 1905. SOURCE: Philippine Campaign Badge list, 29 May 1905.

BURKE, Lester; 24th Inf. *See* **BURBE**, Lester, Private, H/24th Infantry

BURLEY, Robert; Sergeant; D/9th Cav. ‡Private, G/9th Cavalry, on detached service, Ft Stanton, NM, 29 Jan–5 Feb 1881. SOURCE: Regt Returns, 9 Cav, Feb 1881.

‡Sergeant since 10 Nov 1888. SOURCE: Roster, 9 Cav, 1893.

Served on honor guard when body of Col. Edward Hatch was transported from Ft Robinson, NE, to Ft Leavenworth, KS, in 1889. SOURCE: Kenner, *Buffalo Soldiers and Officers of the Ninth Cavalry*, 48–49.

‡Sergeant, I/9th Cavalry, Ft Robinson, NE. SOURCE: *ANJ* 31 (9 Dec 1893): 254.

‡Sergeant, I/9th Cavalry, retires from Ft Robinson, Sep 1895. SOURCE: *ANJ* 33 (14 Sep 1895): 231.

‡No Veterans Administration pension file.

BURNET, John; Sergeant; M/9th Cav. Born in Kentucky; buried at Ft McKavett, TX, before 17 May 1879; body removed to National Cemetery, San Antonio, TX, 23 Nov 1883. SOURCE: Bierschwale, *Fort McKavett*, 123.

BURNETT, John; Private; M/10th Cav. ‡Killed by civilian Pablo Fernandez while member of guard, Ft Stockton, TX, quelling disturbance in neighboring settlement. SOURCE: CO, 10 Cav, to AG, USA, 6 Jul 1875, ES, 10 Cav, 1873–81.

Died at Ft Stockton on 17 Jun 1875; buried at San Antonio National Cemetery, Section C, number 352. SOURCE: San Antonio National Cemetery Locator.

BURNS, George; M/9th Cav. Born in Kentucky; mulatto complexion; can read and write, age 24, Jul 1870, at Ft McKavett, TX. SOURCE: Bierschwale, *Fort McKavett*, 99.

BURTON, Francis; Private; B/25th Inf. Private, issued Indian Wars Campaign Badge number 1528 on 27 Oct 1909. SOURCE: Carroll, *Indian Wars Campaign Badge*, 44.

BURTON, James; Private; I/9th Cav. ‡Deserted from Ft Wingate, NM, 11 Jan 1881. SOURCE: Regt Returns, 9 Cav, Jan 1881.

Private, E/9th Cavalry, deserted from Ft Wingate, Jan 1881; apprehended and released to duty after Nana began series of attacks; rescued under fire by Lieutenant Burnett, Cuchillo Negro, NM, Aug 1881; charges dropped due to gallant conduct in field. SOURCE: Kenner, *Buffalo Soldiers and Officers of the Ninth Cavalry*, 246–47.

With troop in fight against Nana on Cuchillo Negro Creek, August 1881, wounded and saved by Augustus Walley under fire. SOURCE: Schubert, *Black Valor*, 81–82.

BURTON, John; Sergeant; E/24th Inf. ‡Private, I/24th Infantry, at San Carlos, AZ, 1890. See OTT, **HARDEE**, James A., Private, K/24th Infantry

‡Retires as sergeant, E/24th Infantry, from Ft Douglas, UT. SOURCE: *ANJ* 35 (23 Oct 1897): 137.

Died 22 May 1902; buried in plot NADDN903 at San Francisco National Cemetery. SOURCE: San Francisco National Cemetery.

BURTON, John; Saddler; A/9th Cav. Saddler when issued Indian Wars Campaign Badge number 669 on 21 Oct 1908. SOURCE: Carroll, *Indian Wars Campaign Badge*, 19.

‡Veteran of Indian wars and Philippine Insurrection; at Ft D. A. Russell, WY, in 1910; sharpshooter. SOURCE: *Illustrated Review: Ninth Cavalry*, with picture.

BURTON, William E.; Corporal; I/10th Cav. ‡Ranked number 457 among rifle experts with 68.67 percent, 1905. SOURCE: GO 101, AGO, 31 May 1906.

‡Born in Northampton, VA; died, Fort Robinson, NE, age 33, 23 Nov 1906; buried 24 Nov 1906. SOURCE: Monthly Report, Chaplain Anderson, Nov 1906, Ft Robinson; List of Interments, Ft Robinson.

Died of accident in the line of duty. SOURCE: Buecker, *Fort Robinson Burials.*

BUSH, Adam; Sergeant; D/10th Cav. Died 9 Feb 1882 of suicide, shot self, at Ft Concho, TX. SOURCE: Regimental Returns, 10th Cavalry, 1882.

Died at Ft Concho on 9 Feb 1882; buried at San Antonio National Cemetery, Section E, number 826. SOURCE: San Antonio National Cemetery Locator.

BUSH, James W.; Private; H/9th Cav. Born 28 Aug 1842 or 1843 in Lexington, KY; married in slavery at age 20; enlisted as first sergeant, K/54th Massachusetts Infantry for three years on 12 May 1863 at Readville, MA, at age 21; Ht 5'5", black hair and brown eyes, dark complexion; occupation student at Xenia, OH; injured leg at Wateree Junction, SC, while tearing up tracks of Charleston and Savannah railroads; discharged 1865 and returned to Lexington; enlisted Dec 1866 at Lexington and assigned to H/9th Cavalry; transferred to I/9th Cavalry in 1870 and to Troop M in 1872; served in 9th Cavalry 1866–82 at Ft Stockton, TX, Guadaloupe, NM, Ft Quitman, TX, Ft Davis, TX, Ft Concho, TX, Ft Stanton, NM, where he received another leg injury 28 Aug 1878 during pursuit of desperados or bandits at Eagle Creek, NM, and Ft Union, NM; performed field duty at Roswell, NM; under command of 15th Infantry, pursued Victorio and Nana in Mexico; married Alice Curtis 6 July 1883 at Concordia, KS; daughter Mabel Green resided in Lincoln, NE; died 12 Apr 1918 at Lincoln. SOURCE: Greene, *Swamp Angels,* 49–50.

‡J. W. Bush on detached service, Ft Bayard, NM, 29 Jan–10 Feb 1881. SOURCE: Regt Returns, 9 Cav, Feb 1881.

BUSH, Paton; Private; C/10th Cav. Drowned 31 Mar 1871 at Ft Sill, OK. SOURCE: Regimental Returns, 10th Cavalry, 1871.

BUSH, Robert; Wagoner; 9th Cav. Received Philippine Campaign Badge number 11766 for service as wagoner in D/9th Cavalry; in 9th Cavalry at Ft Leavenworth, KS, Mar 1905. SOURCE: Philippine Campaign Badge list, 29 May 1905.

BUSHWAR, John; Private; E/9th Cav. One of ten soldiers charged with mutiny and desertion for role in mutiny at San Pedro Springs, near San Antonio, TX, April 1867; pled guilty to desertion but not mutiny; mutiny charge dropped; convicted of desertion and sentenced to six months confinement at military prison, Ship's Island, MS; sentence remitted before he was transported to prison. SOURCE: Dobak and Phillips, *The Black Regulars,* 208–11.

BUSTER, Jacob; Private; E/24th Inf. Died at Ft McIntosh, TX, on 5 Sep 1880; buried at Fort Sam Houston National Cemetery, Section PE, number 339. SOURCE: Buffalo Soldiers Interred in Fort Sam Houston National Cemetery.

BUTCHER, Henry; Private; C/25th Inf. Born in Ohio; mulatto complexion; can read and write, age 40, 5 Sep 1870, at Ft McKavett, TX. SOURCE: Bierschwale, *Fort McKavett,* 109.

Died at Ft Davis, TX, on 15 Jul 1872; buried at San Antonio National Cemetery, Section I, number 1529. SOURCE: San Antonio National Cemetery Locator.

BUTLER; Corporal; F/10th Cav. Distinguished himself in action against Indians at Beaver Creek, KS, 21 Aug 1867. SOURCE: Schubert, *Voices of the Buffalo Soldier,* 18.

BUTLER; Private; F/10th Cav. In July 1871, absent two days, returned on evening of second day, opened door of barracks, fired six shots at Sergeant Haskins, who was sitting on bunk, then walked to rear of squad room where he either surrendered his weapon or was disarmed. SOURCE: ES, 10 Cav, 1873–81.

BUTLER, Edward; Corporal; C/9th Cav. Died at Ft Davis, TX, on 19 Feb 1869; buried at San Antonio National Cemetery, Section I, number 1514. SOURCE: San Antonio National Cemetery Locator.

BUTLER, Henry; Saddler; E/10th Cav. In Troop E/10th Cavalry stationed at Bonita Cañon Camp, AZ, 28 Feb 1886. SOURCE: Tagg, *The Camp at Bonita Cañon,* 231.

BUTLER, Hiram; Corporal; C/24th Inf. Buried 27 Dec 1904, section A, row O, plot 44 at Ft Bayard, NM. SOURCE: Erickson, Burials at Fort Bayard National Cemetery, NM.

BUTLER, James H.; Musician; 25th Inf. Born in Warrenton, VA; Ht 5'5", black hair and eyes, black complexion; discharged K/24th Infantry 12 Jul 1886; reenlisted, age 27, Washington, DC, 19 Jul 1886; assigned as trumpeter in D/25th Infantry; arrived Ft Snelling, MN, 3 May 1887. SOURCE: Descriptive & Assignment Rolls of Recruits, 25 Inf.

‡Organized brass band at Ft Meade, SD, with Pvt. John H. Cansby, D/25th Infantry, for Christmas, 1887. SOURCE: Cleveland *Gazette,* 7 Jan 1888.

BUTLER, John; D/24th Inf. Born in Tennessee; mulatto complexion; can read and write, age 24, Jul 1870, at Ft McKavett, TX. SOURCE: Bierschwale, *Fort McKavett,* 96.

BUTLER, William; C/25th Inf. Born in Pennsylvania; mulatto complexion; can read and write, age 21, 6 Sep 1870, at Ft McKavett, TX. SOURCE: Bierschwale, *Fort McKavett,* 110.

BUTLER, William; Private; E/10th Cav. In Troop E/10th Cavalry stationed at Bonita Cañon Camp, AZ, 28 Feb 1886. SOURCE: Tagg, *The Camp at Bonita Cañon,* 231.

BUTTON, Francis; Private; G/25th Inf. ‡Authorized to reenlist. SOURCE: TWX, DeptPlatte, 21 May 1895, Post Returns, Ft Robinson.

One of twenty men who cycled 1,900 miles from Ft Missoula, MT, to St. Louis, MO, 14 Jun–24 Jul 1897, in 25th Infantry Bicycle Corps to test durability and practicality of bicycles as a means of transportation for troops. SOURCE: File 60178, GC, AGO Records.

BYRD, Clarence; Private; K/24th Inf. ‡Died of variola in the Philippines, 29 Jul 1900. SOURCE: *ANJ* 37 (11 Aug 1900): 1191.

Clarence Byrd, Private, E/24th Infantry, died 29 Jul 1900; buried in plot N ADD250 at San Francisco National Cemetery. SOURCE: San Francisco National Cemetery.

BYRD, Clarence; Private; B/9th Cav. Died 15 May 1916; buried in plot W SID1015-A at San Francisco National Cemetery. SOURCE: San Francisco National Cemetery.

BYRD, James; Private; F/48th Inf. Died 18 May 1901; buried in plot E SID1313 at San Francisco National Cemetery. SOURCE: San Francisco National Cemetery.

BYTHEWOOD, James; Private; 25th Inf. Born in Barnwell, SC; Ht 5'7", black hair and eyes, fair complexion; occupation striker; enlisted at age 21, Charleston, SC, 8 Jun 1881; left recruit depot, David's Island, NY, 2 Jul 1881, arrived Ft Randall, SD, 7 Jui 1881. SOURCE: Descriptive & Assignment Rolls of Recruits, 25 Inf.

C

CAGER, John T.; QM Sgt; G/9th Cav. Received Cuban Campaign Badge for service as private in B/24th Infantry, 22 Jun 1898–13 Aug 1898; corporal in G/9th Cavalry at Ft Leavenworth, KS, Mar 1905. SOURCE: Cuban Campaign Badge Recipients.

‡Veteran of Spanish-American War and Philippine Insurrection; at Ft D. A. Russell, WY, in 1910. SOURCE: *Illustrated Review: Ninth Cavalry*, with picture.

CAGLE, Walter W.; Sergeant; F/9th Cav. Received Philippine Campaign Badge number 11769 for service as private in E/9th Cavalry; in 9th Cavalry at Ft Leavenworth, KS, Mar 1905. SOURCE: Philippine Campaign Badge list, 29 May 1905.

‡Veteran of Philippine Insurrection; at Ft D. A. Russell, WY, in 1910; sharpshooter; resident of Harrisburg, NC. SOURCE: *Illustrated Review: Ninth Cavalry*, with picture.

CAIN, Adam; Private; 9th Cav. Received Philippine Campaign Badge number 11768 for service as private in F/9th Cavalry; in 9th Cavalry at Ft Leavenworth, KS, Mar 1905. SOURCE: Philippine Campaign Badge list, 29 May 1905.

CAIN, Scott; Private; H/10th Cav. Born in Brookhaven, MS, 1862; enlisted Louisville, KY, 19 Dec 1883; occupation laborer; Ht 5'5", black complexion, hair, and eyes; sentenced, Ft Davis, TX, 24 Jan 1885, to dishonorable discharge and one year hard labor at Leavenworth Military Prison, KS, for theft of greatcoat belonging to Pvt. Peter Dehoney, H/10th Cavalry. SOURCE: Sayre, *Warriors of Color*, 62–76.

CAINE, George; Private; 25th Inf. Born in Caroline County, MD; Ht 5'7", black hair and brown eyes, brown complexion; discharged from F/9th Cavalry, 9 Feb 1887; second enlistment, 25th Infantry at age 34, Baltimore, MD, 12 Mar 1887; assigned to B/25th Infantry, arrived Ft Snelling, MN, 28 May 1887. SOURCE: Descriptive & Assignment Rolls of Recruits, 25 Inf.

‡Discharged, end of term, Ft Robinson, NE, 26 Feb 1887.

CALDWELL; Private; 10th Cav. Discharged soldier, servant of Maj. Anson Mills, 10th Cavalry, at Ft Thomas, AZ, hitched ride on Paymaster Wham's wagons which were robbed on way to Ft Thomas, 11 May 1889. SOURCE: Ball, *Ambush at Bloody Run*, 3.

CALDWELL, Charles; H/25th Inf. Born in Delaware; black complexion; cannot read or write, age 24, 5 Sep 1870, at Ft McKavett, TX. SOURCE: Bierschwale, *Fort McKavett*, 108.

CALDWELL, Henry; Private; 25th Inf. Born in Annapolis, MD; Ht 5'6", black hair and eyes, black complexion; occupation laborer; enlisted at age 26, Chicago, IL, 16 Dec 1886; arrived Ft Snelling, MN, 1 Apr 1887. SOURCE: Descriptive & Assignment Rolls of Recruits, 25 Inf.

CALDWELL, William; Sergeant; 9th Cav. Received Philippine Campaign Badge number 11879 for service as sergeant in B/9th Cavalry; in 9th Cavalry at Ft Leavenworth, KS, Mar 1905. SOURCE: Philippine Campaign Badge list, 29 May 1905.

CALHOUN, James N.; Private; 9th Cav. Received Philippine Campaign Badge number 11880 for service as private in A/9th Cavalry; in 9th Cavalry at Ft Leavenworth, KS, Mar 1905. SOURCE: Philippine Campaign Badge list, 29 May 1905.

CALLOWAY, Charles; Private; F/24th Inf. Born in Nashville, LA; buried at Ft McKavett, TX, before 17 May 1879; body removed to National Cemetery, San Antonio, TX, 23 Nov 1883. SOURCE: Bierschwale, *Fort McKavett*, 123.

Died at Ft McKavett; buried at San Antonio National Cemetery, Section E, number 847. SOURCE: San Antonio National Cemetery Locator.

CAMMEL, Joseph; Private; H/10th Cav. Born in Madison County, KY, 1855; enlisted Cincinnati, OH, 19 Apr 1879; occupation laborer; Ht 5'7", black complexion, hair, and eyes; joined H/10th Cavalry at Jefferson Barracks, MO; at Ft Davis, TX, 5 Jul 1879 where he was discharged and reenlisted 18–19 Apr 1884; at Ft Davis to 7 Feb 1886; Mar–Apr 1885 at Ft Davis and Bowie Station, AZ; May–July 1885 at Ft Grant, AZ; at Pinery Creek, AZ, Aug 1885; in the field in Arizona territory Sept–Oct 1885; in the field Mar–Apr 1886 at Bonita Cañon and on detached duty as courier on White Ranch; in the field and at Ft Apache, AZ, May 1886–Feb 1889; discharged 18 Apr 1889, Ft Apache; unmarried, resided in Albuquerque, NM, 1897–1899; died 15 Dec 1899, buried in Albuquerque. SOURCE: Sayre, *Warriors of Color*, 54, 77–80, 262.

Private in H/10th Cavalry stationed at Bonita Cañon Camp, AZ, 30 Apr 1886. SOURCE: Tagg, *The Camp at Bonita Cañon*, 231.

‡Honorable mention for services rendered in capture of Mangas and his Apache band, Rio Bonito, AZ, 18 Oct 1886. SOURCE: Baker, Roster.

CAMPBELL, Henry; Corporal; L/10th Cav. ‡Original member of 10th Cavalry; in troop when organized, Ft Riley, KS, 21 Sep 1867. SOURCE: McMiller, "Buffalo Soldiers," 78.

Died at Ft Richardson, TX, on 13 Apr 1874; buried at San Antonio National Cemetery, Section D, number 650. SOURCE: San Antonio National Cemetery Locator.

CAMPBELL, Henry; Private; A/10th Cav. Died 14 Jul 1877 in hospital at Ft Concho, TX. SOURCE: Regimental Returns, 10th Cavalry, 1877.

Died at Ft Concho on 20 Jul 1877; buried at San Antonio National Cemetery, Section D, number 598. SOURCE: San Antonio National Cemetery Locator.

CAMPBELL, Isaac; Private; K/24th Inf. Died on 30 Nov 1905; buried at San Antonio National Cemetery, Section F, number 1029. SOURCE: San Antonio National Cemetery Locator.

CAMPBELL, James; Sergeant; 25th Inf. Served in 1876; unable to prepare legible written report or draw a map. SOURCE: Dobak and Phillips, *The Black Regulars*, 127.

CAMPBELL, John; F/9th Cav. Born in Maryland; black complexion; cannot read or write, age 40, Jul 1870, at Ft McKavett, TX. SOURCE: Bierschwale, *Fort McKavett*, 97.

CAMPBELL, John B.; Master Sgt; 10th Cav. ‡Enlisted 9th Cavalry, 1911; transferred to 10th Cavalry and served many years at Ft Huachuca, AZ; retired as master sergeant; resided at 4452 South 21st, Phoenix, AZ, 1972. SOURCE: *9th and 10th Cavalry Association Bulletin* (Jan–Mar 1972).

First time at Ft Huachuca in 1912, F/9th Cavalry; served with all four African American regiments; while at Huachuca was bugler and baseball player, worked as cook and maintenance man; served overseas with 92nd Infantry Division in Meuse-Argonne campaign during World War I;

served overseas during World War II; finally transferred to Army Air Corps; retired 1945 in Portland, OR; attended dedication ceremonies of Buffalo Soldier statue at Ft Huachuca; died 7 Sept 1984, buried in plot 2-114A, Ft Huachuca cemetery. SOURCE: U.S. Army Intelligence Center and Fort Huachuca, "Mourning Hearts," 4

CAMPBELL, Murphy; Private; M/9th Cav. Born in Lexington, KY; died and buried at Ft McKavett, TX, before 17 May 1879. SOURCE: Bierschwale, *Fort McKavett*, 122.

Died at Ft McKavett on 24 Jan 1874; buried at San Antonio National Cemetery, Section E, number 813. SOURCE: San Antonio National Cemetery Locator.

CAMPBELL, Robert; Trumpeter; 10th Cav. In 1889 in guardhouse at Ft Grant, AZ, for killing soldier; he and wife Frankie were gamblers; wife worked as cook at Sierra Bonita ranch before marriage; wife witness to Wham payroll robbery 11 May 1889 between Ft Grant and Ft Thomas, AZ; assisted wounded soldiers. SOURCE: Ball, *Ambush at Bloody Run*, 3, 16.

CANNON, Thomas; D/38th Inf. Buried 4 Aug 1868, section A, row G, plot 37, Ft Bayard, NM. SOURCE: Erickson, Burials at Fort Bayard National Cemetery, NM.

CANNTE, Fred; Private; D/9th Cav. Died 16 Jul 1902; buried in plot NA WS289 at San Francisco National Cemetery. SOURCE: San Francisco National Cemetery.

CANSBY, John H.; Private; Band/25th Inf. Black hair and eyes, black complexion; occupation laborer; enlisted 12 Mar 1886, age 30, at St Louis, MO; assigned to D/25th Infantry; arrived Ft Snelling, MN, 26 Apr 1886. SOURCE: Descriptive & Assignment Rolls of Recruits, 25 Inf.

‡For Christmas 1887, in D/25th Infantry, Ft Meade, SD, 1887, organized brass band with James H. Butler, musician, 25th Infantry. SOURCE: Cleveland *Gazette*, 7 Jan 1888.

‡Born in Calloway County, MO; fourth enlistment, Ft Missoula, MT, 12 Mar 1896; age 39, Ht 5'10", dark brown complexion, single. SOURCE: Descriptive Cards, 25 Inf.

CARLTON, William J.; Private; B/25th Inf. Enlisted 20 Jul 1905, discharged without honor 22 Nov 1906, Brownsville, TX. SOURCE: Powell, "Military Record of the Enlisted Men Who Were Discharged Without Honor."

‡Dishonorable discharge, Brownsville. SOURCE: SO 266, AGO, 9 Nov 1906.

CARMICHAEL, Henry; Private; B/25th Inf. Enlisted 30 Jul 1904, discharged without honor 22 Nov 1906, Brownsville, TX. SOURCE: Powell, "Military Record of the Enlisted Men Who Were Discharged Without Honor."

‡Dishonorable discharge, Brownsville. SOURCE: SO 266, AGO, 9 Nov 1906.

CARMICHAEL, John; Private; K/25th Inf. Born in Davidson County, TN; Ht 5'8", black hair and brown eyes, black complexion; occupation laborer; enlisted at age 26, Nashville, TN, 10 May 1886; arrived Ft Snelling, MN, from Columbus Bks, OH, 17 Sep 1886. SOURCE: Descriptive & Assignment Rolls of Recruits, 25 Inf.

CARPENTER, Allen; Private; M/9th Cav. Born in Kentucky; black complexion; cannot read or write, age 22, Jul 1870, at Ft McKavett, TX. SOURCE: Bierschwale, *Fort McKavett*, 99.

‡Killed by Indians while hunting on North Llano River, TX, 21 Dec 1870. SOURCE: Hamilton, "History of the Ninth Cavalry," 12; *Historical and Pictorial Review*, 45; *Illustrated Review: Ninth Cavalry.*

CARPENTER, Hess; Private; I/10th Cav. Died on 15 Nov 1889; buried at San Antonio National Cemetery, Section D, number 771. SOURCE: San Antonio National Cemetery Locator.

CARPENTER, Robert; H/25th Inf. Born in Delaware; black complexion; cannot read or write, age 24, 5 Sep 1870, at Ft McKavett, TX. SOURCE: Bierschwale, *Fort McKavett*, 108.

CARRICK, James; Private; M/9th Cav. Born in Perryville, KY; died and buried at Ft McKavett, TX, before 17 May 1879. SOURCE: Bierschwale, *Fort McKavett*, 122.

CARROLL, Charles H.; Private; G/9th Cav. Received Cuban Campaign Badge for service as private in C/25th Infantry, 22 Jun 1898–13 Aug 1898. SOURCE: Cuban Campaign Badge Recipients.

Received Philippine Campaign Badge number 11823 for service as private in G/9th Cavalry, 3 Mar 1902–16 Sep 1902; private in G/9th Cavalry, Ft Leavenworth, KS, Mar 1905. SOURCE: Philippine Campaign Badge Recipients; Philippine Campaign Badge list, 29 May 1905.

CARROLL, George; Private; D/9th Cav. Died at Ft Stockton, TX, on 6 Aug 1870; buried at San Antonio National Cemetery, Section C, number 390. SOURCE: San Antonio National Cemetery Locator.

CARROLL Robert T.; Private; A/9th Cav. R. T. Carroll buried at Ft Bayard, NM. SOURCE: "Buffalo Soldiers Buried at Ft Bayard, NM."

R. T. (Robert) Carroll buried 9 Sep 1897 in section A, row F, plot 44 at Ft Bayard. SOURCE: Erickson, Burials at Fort Bayard National Cemetery, NM.

CARROLL, Rufus; Private; 25th Inf. Born at Georges Station, SC; Ht 5'7", black hair and eyes, dark complexion; occupation hostler; enlisted at age 21, Charleston, SC, 1 Jun 1881; left recruit depot, David's Island, NY, 2 Jul 1881, arrived Ft Randall, SD, 7 Jul 1881. SOURCE: Descriptive & Assignment Rolls of Recruits, 25 Inf.

CARSON, Earley; Private; 9th Cav. Received Philippine Campaign Badge number 11770 for service as private in F/9th Cavalry; in 9th Cavalry at Ft Leavenworth, KS, Mar 1905. SOURCE: Philippine Campaign Badge list, 29 May 1905.

CARSON, Willie; Private; M/10th Cav. ‡Died at Ft Robinson, NE, 27 Jun 1902. SOURCE: Medical History, Ft Robinson.

Died of disease. SOURCE: Buecker, Ft Robinson Burials.

‡Buried Ft Robinson, 27 Jun 1902. SOURCE: List of Interments, Ft Robinson.

CARTER, Charles McD.; Sergeant; A/9th Cav. ‡Commander, 10th Cavalry, forwards Carter's application for remission of sentence to commander, E/10th Cavalry, for comment, then forwards application to Adjutant General, approved, late Dec 1876. SOURCE: ES, 10 Cav, 1873–81.

‡Prisoner, late private, E/10th Cavalry, released from Ft Leavenworth, KS. SOURCE: GCMO 22, AGO, 23 Feb 1877.

‡Appointed sergeant 2 May 1893. SOURCE: Roster, 9 Cav, Jul 1893.

Appointed sergeant 2 May 1893; in A/9th Cavalry at Ft Robinson, NE, Jan 1897. SOURCE: Ninth Cavalry, Roster of NCOs, 1897.

‡Wife Helen buried at Ft Robinson, 10 Jan 1898. SOURCE: List of Interments, Ft Robinson.

CARTER, Frank; Private; F/25th Inf. Died 15 May 1913, buried at Ft Bayard, NM, in plot U 41. SOURCE: "Fort Bayard National Cemetery, Records of Burials."

Buried 16 May 1913, section B, row F, plot 41, at Ft Bayard. SOURCE: Erickson, Burials at Fort Bayard National Cemetery, NM.

CARTER, George; Private; F/24th Inf. Died 21 Aug 1899; buried in plot ESIDE495 at San Francisco National Cemetery. SOURCE: San Francisco National Cemetery.

CARTER, Henry; Private; F/24th Inf. Married Lucinda Marshall and later abandoned her at Mobeetie, TX. SOURCE: Schubert, *Voices of the Buffalo Soldier*, 237.

CARTER, Henry; Corporal; F/24th Inf. ‡Retires from Ft Bayard, NM, Apr 1893. SOURCE: *ANJ* 30 (22 Apr 1893): 575.

Corporal, F/24th Infantry, died 12 Jun 1908; buried at Ft Leavenworth National Cemetery, plot G 3642. SOURCE: Ft Leavenworth National Cemetery.

CARTER, John; F/9th Cav. Born in Washington, DC; black complexion; can read, cannot write, age 24, Jul 1870, at Ft McKavett, TX. SOURCE: Bierschwale, *Fort McKavett,* 97.

CARTER, John R.; C/25th Inf. Born in Virginia; mulatto complexion; can read and write, age 26, 5 Sep 1870, at Ft McKavett, TX. SOURCE: Bierschwale, *Fort McKavett,* 109.

CARTER, John T.; Corporal; H/9th Cav. While guarding herd C/9th Cavalry, Cpl. J. T. Carter lost four horses; admonished and threatened with trial and payment of rewards for return, which amounts to $100; a good man. SOURCE: 1LT B. S. Humphrey, CO, C/9, to Adj, Ft Robinson, 14 Sep 1886, LS, Ft Robinson.

Dropped as deserter; recommend his return to duty without trial and payment of reward for horses. SOURCE: CO, Ft Robinson, to AAG, DP, 15 Sep 1886, LS, Ft Robinson.

Recommend approval of Carter's application for restoration to duty; he states why he was frightened away. SOURCE: CO, Ft Robinson, to AAG, DP, 24 Sep 1886, LS, Ft Robinson.

‡Private, H/9th Cavalry, at Ft Robinson, NE, awaiting transportation to Hot Springs, AR, since 17 Nov 1887.

‡Died of pulmonary consumption, Ft Robinson hospital, 23 Mar 1888; funeral 24 Mar 1888. SOURCE: Order 56, 23 Mar 1888, Post Orders, Ft Robinson.

John F. Carter buried Ft Robinson, 23 Aug 1888. SOURCE: List of Interments, Ft Robinson.

Died at age 26. SOURCE: Buecker, Fort Robinson Burials.

CARTER, Lewis; Private; 25th Inf. Born in Westmoreland County, VA; Ht 5'10", black hair and eyes, brown complexion; discharged from I/10th Cavalry 3 Jan 1887; assigned to G/25th Infantry with third enlistment at age 32, Washington, DC, 2 Feb 1887; arrived Ft Snelling, MN, 1 Apr 1887. SOURCE: Descriptive & Assignment Rolls of Recruits, 25 Inf.

In Troop I/10th Cavalry stationed at Bonita Cañon Camp, AZ, 30 Jun 1886. SOURCE: Tagg, *The Camp at Bonita Cañon,* 231.

CARTER, Louis A.; Chaplain; 25th Inf. ‡Successful pastor of large Knoxville, TN, congregation before joining Army. SOURCE: Stover, *Up from Handymen,* 149.

Served as chaplain with each of four black regiments; served in the Philippines; served as chaplain, post schoolmaster, and librarian to 10th Cavalry and 25th Infantry at Ft Huachuca, AZ; achieved rank of colonel; died 19 Jun 1941, buried in plot 4-25 at Ft Huachuca cemetery. SOURCE: U.S. Army Intelligence Center and Fort Huachuca, "Mourning Hearts," 4.

‡Managed 10th Cavalry Wild West show, Ft Ethan Allen, VT, riding hall, Thanksgiving 1911. SOURCE: Fletcher, *The Black Soldier,* 80.

‡First lieutenant, 10th Cavalry. SOURCE: Work, *The Negro Year Book, 1912,* 77.

‡When 10th Cavalry soldier killed a cowboy in response to racial slurs and was accused of murder, Ft Douglas, AZ, 1913, Chaplain Carter led effort to get him a lawyer; soldier was acquitted on basis of self-defense; served with 9th Cavalry in the Philippines, 1915; helped married men provide their own housing, Camp Stotsenburg, PI, to keep them from town. SOURCE: Stover, *Up from Handymen,* 162, 164.

‡Major, 9th Cavalry. SOURCE: Work, *The Negro Yearbook, 1918–1919,* 228.

‡Captain, 25th Infantry, stationed at Camp Henry J. Jones, AZ. SOURCE: Work, *The Negro Yearbook, 1925–1926,* 253.

‡Biographical sketch. SOURCE: Logan and Winston, *Dictionary of American Negro Biography,* 91–92.

CARTER, Neander N.; Private; 10th Cav. Private, unassigned, died 24 June 1905 of disease contracted prior to enlistment at Ft Robinson, NE; buried at Ft Robinson. SOURCE: Buecker, Fort Robinson Burials.

CARTER, Norman F.; Private; 9th Cav. Veteran of 24th Infantry as well as 9th Cavalry, with medical discharges from each when Col. Edward Hatch requested his discharge for fraudulent enlistment in 1884. SOURCE: Dobak and Phillips, *The Black Regulars,* 48.

CARTER, Richard; Private; C/9th Cav. At Ft Robinson, NE, while driving mule team from post to log camp, thrown from loaded wagon, killed instantly 14 Dec 1896. SOURCE: Buecker, Fort Robinson Burials.

‡Buried Ft Robinson, NE, Dec 1896. SOURCE: SO 138, 15 Dec 1896, Post Orders, Ft Robinson; List of Interments, Ft Robinson.

CARTER, Robert L.; H/25th Inf. Born in Virginia; black complexion; cannot read or write, age 25, 5 Sep 1870, at Ft McKavett, TX. SOURCE: Bierschwale, *Fort McKavett,* 108.

CARTER, Samuel; Private; A/9th Cav. Private, A/9th Cavalry, Ft Stanton, NM, 1885; claimed to have been sexually molested by Pvt. Israel Monday, A/9th Cavalry. SOURCE: Kenner, *Buffalo Soldiers and Officers of the Ninth Cavalry,* 270.

CARTER, Thomas; M/9th Cav. Born in Washington, DC; black complexion; can read and write, age 22, Jul 1870, at Ft McKavett, TX. SOURCE: Bierschwale, *Fort McKavett,* 99.

CARTER, William E.; Corporal; 10th Cav. Placed under arrest, Ft Duncan, TX, Dec 1877, for absence without leave, at trader's store during bed check. SOURCE: Kinevan, *Frontier Cavalryman,* 65.

CARTER, William H.; Trumpeter; A/9th Cav. ‡Shot and killed by carbine in hands of friends near A Troop barracks, Ft Niobrara, NE, 16 Jun 1889. Committee that drafted resolution of sympathy for ten-year veteran Carter included 1st Sgt. Solomon Holloman, Sgt. Charles H. Dowd, Trumpeter Robert C. Bland, Blacksmith Nathan Ward, Cpl. Henry Coker, Pvt. James T. Cotton, Pvt. Powhattan E. Booker, Pvt. John Henderson, Jr. SOURCE: *ANJ* 26 (29 Jun 1889): 900.

Died 16 June 1889, buried at Ft Niobrara Post Cemetery. SOURCE: Ft Niobrara Post Cemetery, Complete Listing.

William M. Carter, Musician, A/9th Cavalry; died 16 Jun 1889; originally buried at Ft Niobrara, NE; reburied at Ft Leavenworth National Cemetery, plot G 3565. SOURCE: Ft Leavenworth National Cemetery.

CARVIN, John; Corporal; C/10th Cav. ‡Original member of 10th Cavalry; in troop when organized, Ft Leavenworth, KS, 14 May 1867. SOURCE: McMiller, "Buffalo Soldiers," 70.

Died 5 Aug 1867 of cholera at Camp Grierson, KS. SOURCE: Regimental Returns, 10th Cavalry, 1867.

CASE, Charles L.; Sergeant; B/24th Inf. Died on 6 Apr 1920; buried at San Antonio National Cemetery, Section D, number 497-B. SOURCE: San Antonio National Cemetery Locator.

CASEY, John F.; 1st Sgt; H/10th Cav. Born in Caldwell County, MO, 1851; father white, name unknown; mother Ellen slave owned by David Inyard; enlisted Kansas City, MO, 28 Sep 1872; occupation laborer; Ht 5'10", light complexion, black hair and eyes; lied about his age when he first enlisted, said he was 22 and was only 19; assigned to H/10th Cavalry at Ft Gibson, OK; served continuously in H/10th Cavalry; served in campaigns in pursuit of horse thieves and renegades at Parker, KS; troop transferred to Ft Sill, OK, 1873; served in Indian campaigns at Red River and Washitaw Agency; discharged 30 May 1887, Ft Davis, TX; enlisted 6 Mar 1878; discharged 5 Mar 1883; enlisted 6 Mar 1883; appointed farrier, vice William Allen, who was reduced to private, Ft Davis, 1 Feb 1885; discharged 5 Mar 1888; married Pabla Narra, Ft Davis, 1877, had two children, Mary and Frank; separated, married second wife, Eliza

Turner, 20 Jun 1888, died 28 Apr 1905; married 5 Jul 1906 to third wife, Emma Louise Thomas, born Pettis County, MO, 19 Apr 1861, died 2 Nov 1933; resided at 316 S. 4th St., St. Joseph, MO, 1896–1901, occupation barber, had his own shop; convicted Jan 1885 by general court martial, Ft Davis, of conduct to prejudice of good order and discipline: with Lance Sgt. Robert Anderson, Band/10th Cavalry, on hunting trip, consorted with public women (Pearl Wilson and Rachel Hall) while having lawful wife and family, Oct 1884, reduced from first sergeant to private, fined $10 per month for six months; granted pension of $4 per month, 1893; increased to $6 per month in 1905; increased to $20 per month in 1920, retroactive to 1917; resided in National Military Home, Leavenworth, KS, 1919; died at home, 510 Cedar St., Leavenworth, 11 Aug 1924. SOURCE: Sayre, *Warriors of Color,* 10, 12, 14–16, 26, 81–132.

Promoted to corporal from farrier, H/10th Cavalry, 1 Nov 1885; in H/10th Cavalry stationed at Bonita Cañon Camp, AZ, 30 Apr 1886. SOURCE: Tagg, *The Camp at Bonita Cañon,* 66, 231.

‡Honorable mention for services rendered as corporal in capture of Mangas and his Apache band, Rio Bonito, AZ, 18 Oct 1886. SOURCE: Baker, Roster.

‡Corporal, Ft Apache, AZ, sharpshooter. SOURCE: *ANJ* 24 (27 Nov 1886): 350.

‡First sergeant, Ft Apache, sharpshooter. SOURCE: *ANJ* 25 (13 Aug 1887): 42.

Enlisted Kansas City, 28 Sep 1872, served fifteen years; post-service occupation barber; later resided in Military Soldiers Home, Leavenworth; autobiographical narrative from pension application published. SOURCE: Schubert, *Voices of the Buffalo Soldier,* 141–47.

CASS, Austin; Private; C/9th Cav. Died at Ft Davis, TX, on 4 Jul 1868; buried at San Antonio National Cemetery, Section I, number 1464. SOURCE: San Antonio National Cemetery Locator.

CASSAS, Luce; Private; U.S. Army. Seminole Negro Scout, also known as Louis Cassas; served 1880–84; 1888–89. SOURCE: Schubert, Consolidated List of Seminole Negro Scouts.

Born in Mexico; enlisted at Ft Clark, TX, 9 May 1880, age 29; Ht 5'5", black hair and eyes, black complexion; discharged 12 May 1881 at Ft Clark where he reenlisted and was discharged 12 May 1882; enlisted 21 Jul 1882 at Camp Myers, TX; discharged 20 Jul 1883 at Ft Clark where he reenlisted and was discharged three more times; last reenlistment at Ft Clark 6 Jun 1888; discharged, age 39, at Camp Neville, TX, 28 Feb 1889; 1880 Census lists as white, age 35. SOURCE: Swanson, 6.

CATHAY, William; Private; A/38th Inf. *See* **WILLIAMS,** Cathay, Private, A/38th Infantry

CATHEY, Joseph; Sergeant; G/9th Cav. Received Philippine Campaign Badge number 11824 for service in B/49th United States Volunteers as private, 2 Jan 1900–2 Jun 1901, and in B/24th Infantry as private, 15 Nov 1901–1 Jul 1902; private in G/9th Cavalry, Ft Leavenworth, KS, Mar 1905. SOURCE: Philippine Campaign Badge Recipients; Philippine Campaign Badge list, 29 May 1905.

‡Sergeant, G/9th Cavalry, veteran of Philippine Insurrection; at Ft D. A. Russell, WY, in 1910; sharpshooter. SOURCE: *Illustrated Review: Ninth Cavalry*, with picture.

CATHEY, William; Private; A/38th Inv. *See* **WILLIAMS,** Cathay, Private, A/38th Infantry

CAULDER, Charles; Artificer; 9th Cav. Received Philippine Campaign Badge number 11721 for service as artificer, D/25th Infantry; in 9th Cavalry at Ft Leavenworth, KS, Mar 1905. SOURCE: Philippine Campaign Badge list, 29 May 1905.

CAY, McKinley; E/25th Inf. Buried in section B, row J, plot 18, at Ft Bayard, NM. SOURCE: Erickson, Burials at Fort Bayard National Cemetery, NM.

CEPHAS, Joseph E.; Private; H/10th Cav. Born in Warrenton, VA, 1860; enlisted Philadelphia, PA, 15 Mar 1882; occupation farmer and porter; Ht 5'2"; black complexion, hair and eyes; in campaign against Geronimo, 1886; stationed at Ft Davis, TX, Apr 1882–May 1885; Ft Grant, AZ, May 1885–July 1885; Bonita Cañon, AZ, July 1885–May 1886; Ft Apache, AZ, May 1886–May 1887; discharged, Ft Apache, 14 Mar 1887; married Sarah L. Jackson in Philadelphia, 28 Feb 1889; resided 1935 Alder St., Philadelphia; died 1 Sep 1897; buried in Menon Cemetery, Philadelphia. SOURCE: *Warriors of Color*, 133–35.

Private in H/10th Cavalry stationed at Bonita Cañon Camp, AZ, 30 Apr 1886. SOURCE: Tagg, *The Camp at Bonita Cañon*, 231.

CHAFFIN, John H.; Private; I/24th Inf. Died 23 Feb 1889; buried 15 Mar 1932 at Santa Fe National Cemetery, NM, plot P 94. SOURCE: Santa Fe National Cemetery, Records of Burials.

CHAMBERS, Henry; Corporal; B/25th Inf. Corporal when issued Indian Wars Campaign Badge number 1527 on 27 Oct 1909. SOURCE: Carroll, *Indian Wars Campaign Badge*, 44.

CHAMBERS, William; Sergeant; M/25th Inf. ‡Cited among men who distinguished themselves in 1893: as sergeant, D/25th Infantry, arrested Indian deserter, resisted and defeated nighttime attempt to rescue prisoner; displayed great coolness and bravery, Tongue River Agency, MT, 18 Jun 1893. SOURCE: GO 59, AGO, 10 Nov 1894.

‡As sergeant, H/25th Infantry, accompanied Chaplain Steward on visit to three saloonkeepers near Ft Missoula, MT, to ask them to close on Sunday during services, Jan 1894; all promised to do so. SOURCE: Chaplain T. G. Steward, Monthly Report, 31 Jan 1894, AGO File 4634ACP91.

‡At Bamban, Philippines, 1899. SOURCE: Nankivell, *History of the Twenty-fifth Infantry*, 93, with picture.

Enlisted 1875, served in Texas, Dakota, Montana, Cuba, and the Philippines; listed for bravery in capturing deserter and fending off ambush intended to liberate prisoner; left army in 1900 and applied for pension two years later. SOURCE: Dobak and Phillips, *The Black Regulars*, 262, 279.

CHAMP, Abraham; Private; K/10th Cav. ‡Private, G/9th Cavalry, threatened in saloon, Suggs, WY, 16 Jun 1892, triggering so-called Suggs Affray. SOURCE: Schubert, "The Suggs Affray," 63.

Pled guilty of involvement in affray at Suggs, WY, 1892, and fined $.50, but spent three months in jail awaiting trial. SOURCE: Dobak and Phillips, *The Black Regulars*, 243, 329.

‡Served in 10th Cavalry in Cuba, 1898. SOURCE: Cashin, *Under Fire with the Tenth Cavalry*, 350.

CHANDLER, Richard; Private; 9th Cav. ‡Private, I/9th Cavalry, ordered to report to unit at Ft Wingate, NM. SOURCE: RO 2, 9 Cav, 22 Jan 1879, Name File, 9 Cav.

Died 26 Feb 1880, originally buried at Ft Wingate; buried at Santa Fe National Cemetery, NM, plot A-3 1030. SOURCE: Santa Fe National Cemetery, Records of Burials.

CHAPMAN, Silas; Sergeant; E/9th Cav. Born in South Carolina; enlisted 1875; accumulated $300 in savings; recently promoted to sergeant and in charge of herd guard, near Ojo Caliente, NM, when attacked by Victorio; killed 1 Sept 1879 along with Pvts. Abram Percival, Silas Graddon, William Humphrey, and Lafayette Hooke. SOURCE: Kenner, *Buffalo Soldiers and Officers of the Ninth Cavalry*, 108–9.

‡Sgt. S. Chapman killed in action against Victorio at Camp Ojo Caliente, NM, Sep 1879. SOURCE: Billington, "Black Cavalrymen," 67; Billington, *New Mexico's Buffalo Soldiers*, 89.

‡Was in charge of herd guard, Ojo Caliente, 4 Sep 1879, when Indians jumped herd; he and Pvts. Graddon, Hoke, Murphy, and Percival were killed. SOURCE: Hamilton, "History of the Ninth Cavalry," 44; *Illustrated Review: Ninth Cavalry*.

One of five men of E Troop killed by Victorio's Apaches while guarding troop's horse herd, Ojo Caliente, 4 Sep 1879. SOURCE: Schubert, *Black Valor*, 53.

CHARLES, Irving; Private; E/9th Cav. Private in troop in April 1867 at time of San Pedro Springs, TX, mutiny; among soldiers who attacked Lieutenant Heyl when Sergeant Bradford was killed; death sentence for role in mutiny nullified by reviewing authority and Charles was restored to duty. SOURCE: Kenner, *Buffalo Soldiers and Officers of the Ninth Cavalry*, 77–79.

One of ten soldiers charged with mutiny and desertion for role in mutiny at San Pedro Springs, near San Antonio, TX, April 1867; pled guilty to desertion but not mutiny; mutiny charge dropped; convicted of desertion, sentenced to death, sentence remitted, charges dropped, and soldier restored to duty. SOURCE: Dobak and Phillips, *The Black Regulars*, 208–11; Schubert, *Black Valor*, 14–15.

CHASE, Henry; Private; K/9th Cav. ‡Arrived at Ft Robinson, NE, 28 Jul 1885; unable to march with troop.

While stationed at Ft Robinson, NE, involved in saloon brawl, Crawford, NE, Feb 1887, along with Pvts. George Pumphrey and Lee Irving; convicted by court martial, sentenced to dishonorable discharge, confined for one year, and restored to duty, allowed to reenlist. SOURCE: Kenner, *Buffalo Soldiers and Officers of the Ninth Cavalry*, 150–51.

‡Sentenced to dishonorable discharge and prison, Ft Robinson, NE. SOURCE: GCMO 21, DP, 29 Mar 1887.

‡Commander, Ft Robinson, recommends remission of dishonorable discharge; Chase should be allowed to reenlist; "always a clean soldier," adequately punished for riding horse into Crawford, NE, saloon; original sentence dishonorable discharge and one year. SOURCE: CO, Ft Robinson, to AG, USA, 20 Apr 1888, LS, Ft Robinson.

At Fort Robinson, 1888, rode horse into saloon in Crawford. SOURCE: Dobak and Phillips, *The Black Regulars*, 169.

‡Request for discharge disapproved. SOURCE: Letter, AGO, 3 Oct 1892.

CHASE, Levi; Corporal; L/9th Cav. ‡As recruit, Colored Detachment, Mounted Service, tried by general court martial, Jefferson Barracks, MO, for engaging in disturbance and altercation with Recruit Francis J. Stokes, and trying to take carbine from rack to shoot Stokes, 5 Jul 1889; also tried for profane and abusive language toward Cpl. John M. Edwards, Company B of Instruction, who was conducting him to the guardhouse; convicted of second charge only; fined $10 and jailed for one month. SOURCE: GCMO 48, AGO, 6 Aug 1889.

‡While private, C/9th Cavalry, convicted by garrison court martial, Ft Robinson, NE, for insubordination to first sergeant; sentenced to one month's imprisonment and fined one month's pay. SOURCE: SO 73, 10 Jul 1897, Post Orders, Ft Robinson.

‡Findings of board of officers in his case approved. SOURCE: Letter, DP, 19 Aug 1897, Post Returns, Ft Robinson.

Corporal, L/9th Cavalry, died 16 May 1905; buried at Ft Bayard, NM, in plot H 18. SOURCE: "Fort Bayard National Cemetery, Records of Burials."

Buried 16 May 1905, section A, row K, plot 44 at Ft Bayard. SOURCE: Erickson, Burials at Fort Bayard National Cemetery, NM.

CHASE, William H.; Private; L/25th Inf. Died in the Philippines, 10 Jul 1902; body transferred and buried in 1905 in plot NAWS 892 at San Francisco National Cemetery. SOURCE: San Francisco National Cemetery.

CHATMAN, John; Private; E/9th Cav. ‡Died of variola in the Philippines, 30 Sep 1901. SOURCE: *ANJ* 39 (7 Dec 1901): 339.

Died 29 Sep 1901; buried in plot NADD at San Francisco National Cemetery. SOURCE: San Francisco National Cemetery.

CHATMOUN, Webb; Private; H/10th Cav. ‡Born in Spartanburg Co., SC, 1863; parents unknown; enlisted Cincinnati, OH; Ht 5'8", black, laborer; served 16 Oct 1884–15 Oct 1889, including Apache wars, 1885–86; coal miner after service; incapacitated by rheumatism. SOURCE: VA File C 2360629, Webb Chatmoun.

Served in unit sometime between 1883 and 1891. SOURCE: Sayre, *Warriors of Color*, 360.

Private in H/10th Cavalry stationed at Bonita Cañon Camp, AZ, 30 Apr 1886. SOURCE: Tagg, *The Camp at Bonita Cañon*, 231.

‡Sick in lungs at Ft Davis, TX, hospital, Dec 1884–Jan 1885; sick at Ft Apache, AZ, with weak lungs and rheumatism, 1887 or 1888; sick at San Carlos, AZ, with piles, 1888. SOURCE: Affidavit, Chatmoun, Bevier, MO, 2 Mar 1912, VA File C 2360629, Webb Chatmoun.

‡Died of bronchial pneumonia, age 77. SOURCE: VA File C 2360629, Webb Chatmoun; *Winners of the West* 15 (Nov 1938): 4.

‡Widow Minerva Chatmoun of Bevier, MO, formerly married to Thomas West, who died 1896; pensioned after his death at St. Joseph, MO, 6 Oct 1938; her original widow's claim rejected because she was not married as of 4 Mar 1917; first wife Priscilla Davis Chatmoun died 31 Dec 1925. Probate Judge John V. Goodson, Macon Co., MO, to Veterans Administration, Washington, DC, writes that he does not know law but asks help for Minerva at request of her neighbors; she is "in distress, improperly nourished and dependent on the neighbors for fuel at her residence." SOURCE: VA File C 2360629, Webb Chatmoun.

See OTT, **CLEMENS**, James, Private, H/10th Cavalry; **BERRY**, Butler, Private, H/10th Cavalry

CHEATHAM, Alexander; QM Sgt; I/10th Cav. ‡Original member of 10th Cavalry; in L Troop when organized, Ft Riley, KS, 21 Sep 1867. SOURCE: McMiller, "Buffalo Soldiers," 78.

In Troop I/10th Cavalry stationed at Bonita Cañon Camp, AZ, 30 Jun 1886. SOURCE: Tagg, *The Camp at Bonita Cañon*, 231.

‡In support of Lieutenants Clark and Watson who were chasing marauders, Cheatham rode ninety miles with six mules loaded with supplies from San Carlos, AZ, to Salt River, AZ, from 11 P.M., 6 Mar, to sunset, 7 Mar 1890. SOURCE: Baker, Roster.

‡Cheatham and detachment from San Carlos brought breakfast out on trail of murderers after night march of forty-five miles; "the old fellow looked very tired and worn as he rode up, but his indomitable nerve and pluck carried him on forty-five miles more this day." SOURCE: Watson, "Scouting in Arizona," 131.

‡Sergeant, I/10th Cavalry, at Ft Apache, AZ, 1890, subscribed $.50 to testimonial to General Grierson. SOURCE: List of subscriptions, 23 Apr 1890, 10th Cavalry papers, MHI.

‡Retires as sergeant, C/10th Cavalry, from Ft Assiniboine, MT, 18 Mar 1895. SOURCE: *ANJ* 32 (16 Mar 1895): 52.

CHELF, John; 1st Sgt; P/10th Cav. ‡Private, H/9th Cavalry, at Ft D. A. Russell, WY, in 1910; marksman; resident of Chicago. SOURCE: *Illustrated Review: Ninth Cavalry*, with picture.

Retired 1st Sgt. John Chelf, P/10th Cavalry, died 15 Jan 1938; buried at Ft Leavenworth National Cemetery, plot H 3335-F. SOURCE: Ft Leavenworth National Cemetery.

CHENAULT, Walter; Private; C/10th Cav. ‡Born in Lexington, KY, son of parents he never knew, 6 May 1863; attended Russell Grade School, Lexington; served in 10th Cavalry, 1898–1902, including Cuba; attended Butler University, Indianapolis, IN, 1905–07; earned bachelor of science degree, Normal College, 1911; clerk, Indianapolis post office, 1914–17; licensed to preach in Indiana, Jun 1919; deacon, 1919; elder, 1922; published articles in Indianapolis dailies: *Indianapolis Recorder, Christian Recorder, Southern Christian Recorder*; assistant secretary, Indiana Annual Conference, 1937–43, and chief secretary, 1943; married to Estella Harris of Marion, IN, 1911; children: William, Wade, Charles, Melvin, Harriet, Juanita, Evelyn; member National Association for the Advancement of Colored People; pastor, Shaffer Chapel, Muncie, IN, from Oct 1943. SOURCE: *Encyclopedia of African Methodism*, 64–65.

‡Served in 10th Cavalry, 1898; remained in U.S. during war with Spain. SOURCE: Cashin, *Under Fire with the Tenth Cavalry*, 340.

Biographical sketch in *Encyclopedia of African Methodism* republished. SOURCE: Schubert, *Voices of the Buffalo Soldier*, 256–57.

CHESTER, Rubus; Private; C/10th Cav. Died 3 Aug 1874 of disease at Ft Sill, OK. SOURCE: Regimental Returns, 10th Cavalry, 1874.

CHESTER, Stanley; Private; C/10th Cav. Died 19 Mar 1891; buried at Ft Bayard, NM, in plot G 10. SOURCE: "Fort Bayard National Cemetery, Records of Burials."

Buried 19 Mar 1891, section A, row I, plot 12 at Ft Bayard. SOURCE: Erickson, Burials at Fort Bayard National Cemetery, NM.

CHESTNUT, Grundy; Private; F/9th Cav. Grendy Chestnut born in Tennessee; black complexion; can read, cannot write, age 28, Jul 1870, at Ft McKavett, TX. Died and buried at Ft McKavett before 17 May 1879; body removed to National Cemetery, San Antonio, TX, 23 Nov 1883. SOURCE: Bierschwale, *Fort McKavett*, 97, 123.

Died at Ft McKavett on 18 Jul 1871; buried at San Antonio National Cemetery, Section E, number 869. SOURCE: San Antonio National Cemetery Locator.

Died 18 Jul 1871; buried at Ft Leavenworth National Cemetery, plot E 869. SOURCE: Ft Leavenworth National Cemetery.

CHESTNUT, Henry; Private; H/10th Cav. *See* **CHESTNUTT,**, Henry, Private, H/10th Cavalry

CHESTNUTT, Henry; Private; H/10th Cav. Born in Philadelphia, TN, 1861; enlisted Cincinnati, OH, 7 Jul 1882; occupation farmer; Ht 5'7", mulatto complexion, black hair and eyes; hospitalized four times with gonorrhea, Ft Davis, TX, Mar–Jul 1883. SOURCE: Sayre, *Warriors of Color*, 136.

CHINN, Charles; Ord Sgt; U.S. Army. Native of Kentucky; dark-skinned; served in L/9th Cavalry until he became first sergeant of C/9th Cavalry in 1877; Civil War veteran; author of tribute to late Senator Charles Sumner that appeared in *ANJ*, 25 Apr 1874, while member of L/9th Cavalry, at Ft Ringgold, TX; promoted to ordnance sergeant 1887; aged 56 in 1897 when ordered to Ft McPherson, GA, and sued State of Georgia when ordered into Jim Crow railroad car. SOURCE: Kenner, *Buffalo Soldiers and Officers of the Ninth Cavalry*, 15, 175–76.

Saddler sergeant, 9th Cavalry, stationed at Ringgold Barracks, TX, Mar 1874, signed resolution of mourning at death of Senator Charles Sumner, as chairman of committee. SOURCE: Schubert, *Voices of the Buffalo Soldier*, 63–64.

Appointed ordnance sergeant 10 Jul 1888, from sergeant, E/24th Infantry. SOURCE: Dobak, "Staff Noncommissioned Officers."

CHISHOLM, Lee; Private; 24th Inf. *See* **CHRISHOLM,** Lee, Private, 24th Infantry

CHOLIKELY, Alonzo; Private; H/9th Cav. Received Philippine Campaign Badge number 11886; in 9th Cavalry at Ft Leavenworth, KS, Mar 1905. SOURCE: Philippine Campaign Badge list, 29 May 1905.

CHRISHOLM, Lee; Private; 24th Inf. Severely injured in face with pocketknife by Pvt. Dick Richardson, Ft Bayard, NM, 1889; responded by pulling razor; confined for one month. SOURCE: Dobak and Phillips, *The Black Regulars*, 200.

‡Pvt. Lee Chisholm, 24th Infantry, involved in fight with Pvt. Dick Richardson, 24th Infantry, Ft Bayard, Christmas 1889. SOURCE: Billington, *New Mexico's Buffalo Soldiers*, 164.

CHRISTOPHER, Albert; Private; H/10th Cav. Died 8 Apr 1881, cause not stated, at Ft Davis, TX. SOURCE: Regimental Returns, 10th Cavalry, 1881.

CHRISTOPHER, Albert; Private; H/9th Cav. Died at Ft McKavett, TX, on 18 Jul 1881; buried at San Antonio National Cemetery, Section I, number 1504. SOURCE: San Antonio National Cemetery Locator.

CHRISTOPHER, Andrew; M/9th Cav. Born in Kentucky; black complexion; cannot read or write, age 25, Jul 1870, at Ft McKavett, TX. SOURCE: Bierschwale, *Fort McKavett*, 99.

CHRISTY, William; Sergeant; F/10th Cav. ‡Was 10th Cavalry's first fatality, near Ft Hays, KS, summer 1867; Christy a farmer from Pennsylvania with two months in regiment. SOURCE: Leckie, *The Buffalo Soldiers*, 22.

‡Shot through head and killed during attack by seventy-five Indians, 2 Aug 1867. SOURCE: Armes, *Ups and Downs*, 237.

‡Killed in action by Indians, Saline Reservation, n.d.; Christy Avenue, Ft Huachuca, AZ, named for him. SOURCE: Orville A. Cochran to H. B. Wharfield, 5 Apr 1965, 10th Cavalry papers, MHI.

Killed in action 2 Aug 1867 at Saline River, KS. SOURCE: Regimental Returns, 10th Cavalry, 1867.

Killed in action against Cheyennes about 40 miles northeast of Ft Hays, KS, 2 Aug 1867. SOURCE: Kinevan, *Frontier Cavalryman*, 28.

CLAGGETT, Joseph; Saddler; H/10th Cav. Born in Prince Georges County, MD, 1846; enlisted Washington, DC, 9 Jul 1867; occupation laborer; Ht 5'4"; dark brown skin, black hair and eyes; served thirty continuous years, all in H/10th Cavalry; discharged and reenlisted 8–9 Jul 1872, Ft Sill, OK; at Ft Sill, 1873; at Ft Davis, TX, 1875–77; discharged and reenlisted, 8–9 Jul 1877, Ft Davis; discharged and reenlisted 8–9 Jul 1882, Ft Davis; discharged 8 Jul 1887, Ft Apache, AZ; enlisted 21 Jul 1887, Ft Apache; discharged and reenlisted 20–21 Jul 1892, Ft Buford, ND; discharged and reenlisted 20-21 July 1897, Ft Assiniboine, MT; discharged 20 Sep 1897, Box Elder, MT; resided at Helena City, MT. SOURCE: Sayre, *Warriors of Color*, 65, 137–38.

‡Original member of 10th Cavalry; in troop when organized, Ft Leavenworth, KS, 21 Jul 1867. SOURCE: McMiller, "Buffalo Soldiers," 75.

‡As sergeant he led patrol after Comanches from Ft Davis into Guadalupe Mountains, early summer 1877. SOURCE: Leckie, *The Buffalo Soldiers*, 157.

Private in H/10th Cavalry stationed at Bonita Cañon Camp, AZ, 30 Apr 1886. SOURCE: Tagg, *The Camp at Bonita Cañon*, 231.

‡At Ft Apache, 1890, subscribed $.50 to testimonial to General Grierson. SOURCE: List of subscriptions, 23 Apr 1890, 10th Cavalry papers, MHI.

‡Was private and original member of troop; will retire soon and return "to his old Maryland home to enjoy a well earned rest." SOURCE: Baker, Roster.

‡Retires as saddler from Ft Assiniboine. SOURCE: *ANJ* 35 (18 Sep 1897): 40.

CLARIDY, Henry; Private; B/23rd Kansas Inf. Died 11 Feb 1941; buried at Ft Leavenworth National Cemetery, plot E 869. SOURCE: Ft Leavenworth National Cemetery.

CLARK, Alexander; Private; M/9th Cav. Born in Louisville, KY; mulatto complexion; cannot read or write, age 28, Jul 1870, at Ft McKavett, TX; died and buried at Ft McKavett before 27 May 1879. SOURCE: Bierschwale, *Fort McKavett*, 99, 122.

Died at Ft McKavett; buried at San Antonio National Cemetery, Section I, number 1504. SOURCE: San Antonio National Cemetery Locator.

CLARK, Allen; Private; Band/10th Cav. Died 23 Nov 1881 of typho-malaria at Ft Concho, TX. SOURCE: Regimental Returns, 10th Cavalry, 1881.

Died at Ft Concho on 23 Nov 1881; buried at San Antonio National Cemetery, Section E, number 802. SOURCE: San Antonio National Cemetery Locator.

CLARK, Charles; Sergeant; D/10th Cav. ‡Original member of 10th Cavalry; in troop when organized, Ft

Leavenworth, KS, 1 Jun 1867. SOURCE: McMiller, "Buffalo Soldiers," 71.

Died 4 Oct 1870 of Bright's disease at Ft Sill, OK. SOURCE: Regimental Returns, 10th Cavalry, 1870.

‡Commander, 10th Cavalry, forwards final statement of late Private Clark to Adjutant General, U.S. Army, 13 Oct 1870. SOURCE: ES, 10 Cav, 1866–71.

Sergeant, D/10th Cavalry, died 3 Oct 1870, buried at Camp Douglas, UT. SOURCE: Record Book of Interments, Post Cemetery, 252.

CLARK, Cornelius; Corporal; E/9th Cav. Private, received Philippine Campaign Badge number 11720 for service as private in E/9th Cavalry; in 9th Cavalry at Ft Leavenworth, KS, Mar 1905. SOURCE: Philippine Campaign Badge list, 29 May 1905.

Corporal, died 6 May 1907, buried at Ft Bayard, NM, in plot P 10. SOURCE: "Fort Bayard National Cemetery, Records of Burials."

Buried 6 May 1907, section B, row A, plot 10 at Ft Bayard. SOURCE: Erickson, Burials at Fort Bayard National Cemetery, NM.

CLARK, Edward; Private; G/48th Inf. Died in the Philippines 14 Dec 1900; transferred for reburial in Apr 1902; buried in plot NADD 815 at San Francisco National Cemetery. SOURCE: San Francisco National Cemetery.

CLARK, Henry; Private; 25th Inf. Born in Charleston, SC; Ht 5'9", black hair and grey eyes, yellow complexion; occupation laborer; resided Boston, MA, when he enlisted at age 31, Philadelphia, PA, 22 Dec 1885; assigned to B/25th Infantry; arrived Ft Snelling, MN, 5 Feb 1886. SOURCE: Descriptive & Assignment Rolls of Recruits, 25 Inf.

CLARK, J. N.; Private; A/10th Cav. See **CLARKE**, John H., Private, A/10th Cavalry

CLARK, James; 9th Cav. Born in Tennessee; black complexion; can read and write, age 23, 5 Sep 1870, at Ft McKavett, TX. SOURCE: Bierschwale, Fort McKavett, 107.

CLARK, James A.; D/24th Inf. Born in Ohio; mulatto complexion; can read and write, age 24, Jul 1870, at Ft McKavett, TX. SOURCE: Bierschwale, Fort McKavett, 96.

CLARK, James T.; D/24th Inf. Born in Kentucky; mulatto complexion; can read and write, age 24, Jul 1870, at Ft McKavett, TX. SOURCE: Bierschwale, Fort McKavett, 95.

CLARK, John W.; Private; E/10th Cav. Died 29 Mar 1869 in hospital at Ft Arbuckle, OK. SOURCE: Regimental Returns, 10th Cavalry, 1869.

CLARK, Lig J.; Corporal; H/24th Inf. ‡Enlisted Dallas, TX, 10 Jun 1898. SOURCE: Muster Roll, H/24 Inf, Sep–Oct 1898.

‡Present for duty. SOURCE: Muster Roll, H/24 Inf, Nov–Dec 1898.

‡Discharged 29 Jan 1899, character excellent, single, deposits $50, clothing $2.71; reenlisted Ft Douglas, UT, 30 Jan 1899. SOURCE: Muster Roll, H/24 Inf, Jan–Feb 1899.

‡Recommended for certificate of merit for gallantry at Naguilian, Luzon, Philippines, 7 Dec 1899. SOURCE: ANJ 39 (15 Feb 1902): 594–95.

Pvt. Lig J. Clark, H/24th Infantry, awarded certificate of merit for most distinguished gallantry in action at Naguilian, Luzon, 7 Dec 1899. SOURCE: Gleim, The Certificate of Merit, 50.

‡Awarded certificate of merit for distinguished gallantry, Naguilian, Luzon, 7 Dec 1899; discharged 18 Jan 1902; awarded 10 Mar 1902. SOURCE: GO 86, AGO, 24 Jul 1902.

See OTT, **WILLIAMS**, Walter B., Sergeant Major, 24th Infantry

‡Born in Brownwood, TX, 1878; resided Temple, TX; stationed at Tampa, FL, during Cuban campaign; mustered out, Ft Douglass [sic], 29 Jan 1899; reenlisted 30 Jan 1899; sailed to the Philippines, 13 Jul 1899; in "fierce battle at Arayat," 12 Oct 1899, and many others; promoted to corporal, 14 Jul 1900; bought house for his mother on return; died of typhoid, 21 Apr 1902. "All Temple was proud of Lig J. Clark, and now mourn his death with a sorrow second only to that of his loving mother and two sisters who survive him. His discharge spoke of him as 'an excellent noncommissioned officer'; we say 'an excellent son and citizen.'" SOURCE: Letter, R. E. L. Holland, M.D., Temple, TX, to Editor, Indianapolis Freeman, 20 Sep 1902.

CLARK, Louis; M/9th Cav. Born in Kentucky; mulatto complexion; can read and write, age 23, Jul 1870, at Ft McKavett, TX. SOURCE: Bierschwale, Fort McKavett, 99.

CLARK, Oscar; Private; D/9th Cav. Private when issued Indian Wars Campaign Badge number 658 on 20 Oct 1908. SOURCE: Carroll, Indian Wars Campaign Badge, 19.

CLARK, William; Private; E/10th Cav. Died 1 Aug 1870; buried at Camp Douglas, UT. SOURCE: Record Book of Interments, Post Cemetery, 252.

CLARK, William; 10th Cav. Resided in Anacostia, DC, 1903. SOURCE: Sayre, Warriors of Color, 141.

CLARKE, John H.; Private; A/10th Cav. J. N. Clark or John H. Clarke died 25 Oct 1868; buried at Ft Leavenworth National Cemetery, plot C 2023. SOURCE: Ft Leavenworth National Cemetery.

CLARKE, Ollie; 1st Sgt; 9th Cav. Received Philippine Campaign Badge number 11853 for service as first sergeant, H/9th Cavalry; in 9th Cavalry at Ft Leavenworth, KS, Mar 1905. SOURCE: Philippine Campaign Badge list, 29 May 1905.

CLARKE, Thomas H. R.; 2nd Lt; 8th Inf, USV. Served at Fort Thomas, KY, and Chickamauga, GA, 1898; article on Benjamin O. Davis in *Colored American Magazine* (Washington, DC), 18 May 1901, reprinted. SOURCE: Schubert, *Voices of the Buffalo Soldier*, 218–20.

CLAUGHS, Frank; Recruit; 10th Cav. Died 13 Sep 1867 of dysentery at Ft Riley, KS. SOURCE: Regimental Returns, 10th Cavalry, 1867.

CLAVON, Merritt; Private; G/25th Inf. Born in Petersburg, VA; Ht 5'8", black hair and brown eyes, brown complexion; occupation sailor; resided in Baltimore, MD, when he enlisted 25 Aug 1886, age 21, at Baltimore; assigned to G/25th Infantry; arrived Ft Snelling, MN, 14 Dec 1886. SOURCE: Descriptive & Assignment Rolls of Recruits, 25 Inf.

CLAY, Henry; Private; M/10th Cav. ‡Mentioned as newly enlisted, Apr 1873. SOURCE: ES, 10 Cav, 1873–81.

Died 18 May 1874 of disease at Camp Benson. SOURCE: Regimental Returns, 10th Cavalry, 1874.

‡Died 18 May 1874; regiment commander forwards final statement and inventory of effects. SOURCE: CO, 10 Cav, to AG, USA, 27 May 1874, ES, 10 Cav, 1873–81.

CLAY, Matthew G.; Private; M/9th Cav. ‡Sentenced by general court martial. SOURCE: SO 171, DeptMo, 7 Sep 1903.

‡At Ft D. A. Russell, WY, in 1910; resident of Evansville, IN. SOURCE: *Illustrated Review: Ninth Cavalry,* with picture.

Buried 16 Dec 1916, section B, row I, plot 16 at Ft Bayard, NM. SOURCE: Erickson, Burials at Fort Bayard National Cemetery, NM.

CLAY, Samuel; Private; D/10th Cav. Died 14 Jun 1873 of typhoid at Ft Griffin, TX. SOURCE: Regimental Returns, 10th Cavalry, 1873.

Died at Ft Griffin on 14 Jun 1873; buried at San Antonio National Cemetery, Section D, number 654. SOURCE: San Antonio National Cemetery Locator.

CLAY, William; Private; E/9th Cav. 15-year veteran, at Ft McKinney, WY, 1886. SOURCE: Kenner, *Buffalo Soldiers and Officers of the Ninth Cavalry*, 232.

CLAY, William; Private; C/9th Cav. ‡Died in the Philippines, 8 Sep 1900. SOURCE: *ANJ* 38 (10 Nov 1900): 259.

‡Drowned while bathing, Nagasaki, 8 Sep 1900; buried there. SOURCE: Hamilton, "History of the Ninth Cavalry," 92; *Illustrated Review: Ninth Cavalry*.

Willie Clay, Private, G/9th Cavalry, died 8 Sep 1900 in Japan; received for burial 30 Mar 1902; buried in plot NADD 901 at San Francisco National Cemetery. SOURCE: San Francisco National Cemetery.

CLAYBORNE, Peter; Sergeant; E/10th Cav. ‡Born in South Carolina; private, B/10th Cavalry, 7 Mar 1867–7 Mar 1872; private, corporal, sergeant, 4 Apr 1872–4 Apr 1877; private, E/10th Cavalry, 14 Apr 1877–13 Apr 1887; in D/10th Cavalry, 13 May 1887–12 May 1892; corporal, 8 Dec 1894; sergeant, 5 Mar 1897. SOURCE: Baker, Roster.

‡An original 10th Cavalryman, he came into regiment at its origin, Ft Leavenworth, KS; first action against Indians on Republican River, KS, May 1867, and Salt Creek, KS, 1867; in repulse of Black Kettle, Ft Dodge, KS, 1868; Foster Springs, TX, fight; engagement at Saragossa, Mexico, against Lipans and Kickapoos, 1876. SOURCE: Baker, Roster.

Private in Troop E/10th Cavalry stationed at Bonita Cañon Camp, AZ, 28 Feb 1886. SOURCE: Tagg, *The Camp at Bonita Cañon*, 231.

‡At Ft Apache, AZ, 1890, subscribed $.50 to testimonial to General Grierson. SOURCE: List of subscriptions, 23 Apr 1890, 10th Cavalry papers, MHI.

‡Retires from Ft Assiniboine, MT. SOURCE: *ANJ* 34 (26 Jun 1897): 801.

CLAYTON, Sie; Private; U.S. Army. Seminole Negro Scout, served in 1894. SOURCE: Schubert, Consolidated List of Seminole Negro Scouts.

Married. SOURCE: NARA, M 929, Roll 2.

CLEAVER, Solomon; Private; E/10th Cav. Died 13 Dec 1880 of consumption at Ft Concho, TX. SOURCE: Regimental Returns, 10th Cavalry, 1880.

CLEMENS, Benjamin; M/9th Cav. Born in Kentucky; black complexion; cannot read or write, age 23, Jul 1870, at Ft McKavett, TX. SOURCE: Bierschwale, *Fort McKavett*, 99.

CLEMENT, Thomas; Sergeant; K/10th Cav. ‡Born in Texas; parents Virginians; educated at Hampton Institute, minister and teacher; worked as coal miner, hotel and railroad man, soldier, musician; in ninth year as minister, largest black congregation in Texas, at Wesley Chapel, Houston, 1947. SOURCE: *Encyclopedia of African Methodism*, 67.

‡Private, Ft Robinson, NE, 1904–05; captain and right halfback, K/10th Cavalry football team; author of "Athletics in the American Army," *Colored American Magazine*. SOURCE: *Colored American Magazine* 8 (Jan 1905): 21–29.

‡No Veterans Administration pension file.

Biographical sketch in *Encyclopedia of African Methodism* republished. SOURCE: Schubert, *Voices of the Buffalo Soldier*, 257.

CLEMENTS, Charles F.; Private; H/24th Inf. Died 11 Jul 1915; buried at Ft Bayard, NM, in plot W 17; source questions last name. SOURCE: "Fort Bayard National Cemetery, Records of Burials."

Buried 11 Jul 1915, section B, row H, plot 17, at Ft Bayard, NM. SOURCE: Erickson, Burials at Fort Bayard National Cemetery, NM.

CLIFFORD, Charles; Corporal; K/25th Inf. Corporal when issued Indian Wars Campaign Badge number 1398 on 13 Jul 1909. SOURCE: Carroll, *Indian Wars Campaign Badge*, 40.

CLIFFORD, Rubin; Private; A/10th Cav. Died 26 Jun 1881, cause not stated, at Pecos Crossing, TX. SOURCE: Regimental Returns, 10th Cavalry, 1881.

CLYDE, W. F.; 1st Sgt; D/9th Cav. Sergeant, D/9th Cavalry, at Ft Riley, KS, Jan 1883; replaced James Dickerson as first sergeant; deserted in early 1885. SOURCE: Kenner, *Buffalo Soldiers and Officers of the Ninth Cavalry*, 272, 278.

CO, Jefferson; F/9th Cav. Born in Virginia; black complexion; can read and write, age 24, Jul 1870, at Ft McKavett, TX. SOURCE: Bierschwale, *Fort McKavett*, 98.

COBB, Edward F.; Corporal; A/10th Cav. ‡Served in 10th Cavalry in Cuba, 1898; drowned 22 Jun 1898. SOURCE: Cashin, *Under Fire with the Tenth Cavalry*, 337, 338.

Drowned when landing craft overturned, Daiquiri, Cuba, 22 Jun 1898. SOURCE: Schubert, *Black Valor*, 145.

COFFEE, Nathan; Private; A/24th Inf. ‡Died of malaria in the Philippines, 28 Jan 1900. SOURCE: *ANJ* 37 (10 Feb 1900): 562.

Died 28 Jan 1900; buried in plot 773 at San Francisco National Cemetery. SOURCE: San Francisco National Cemetery.

COLBERT, Elias; 9th Cav. Born in Virginia; black complexion; can read, cannot write, age 24, 5 Sep 1870, at Ft McKavett, TX. SOURCE: Bierschwale, *Fort McKavett*, 107.

COLBERT, John A.; Private; A/38th Inf. Died 3 Nov 1869; buried at Ft Leavenworth National Cemetery, plot C 2049. SOURCE: Ft Leavenworth National Cemetery.

COLE, Gonza; Corporal; A/9th Cav. Born in Charles County, MD; Ht 5'9", black hair and eyes, black complex-

ion; occupation laborer; resided in Montgomery County, MD, when enlisted 25 Aug 1886, age 23, at Washington, DC; assigned to G/25th Infantry; arrived Ft Snelling, MN, 14 Dec 1886. SOURCE: Descriptive & Assignment Rolls of Recruits, 25 Inf.

‡Private, A/9th Cavalry, detailed to special duty as post librarian, Ft Robinson, NE. SOURCE: Order 184, 29 Oct 1892, Post Orders, Ft Robinson.

‡Relieved from special duty as librarian. SOURCE: Order 9, 2 Feb 1894, Post Orders, Ft Robinson.

Appointed corporal 13 Sep 1896; in A/9th Cavalry at Ft Robinson, Jan 1897. SOURCE: Ninth Cavalry, Roster of NCOs, 1897.

COLE, Pollard; Sergeant; H/10th Cav. Born in Georgetown, KY, 1842; served in Civil War, K/12th U.S. Colored Heavy Artillery, 7 Oct 1864–24 Apr 1866; enlisted Louisville, KY, 14 June 1867; occupation soldier; Ht 5'6", black complexion, hair, and eyes; served continuously in H/10th Cavalry; at Ft Leavenworth, KS, July 1867; at Ft Sill, OK, Nov 1870; discharged 13 Jun 1872, Ft Sill; enlisted 20 Jun 1872, Ft Sill; discharged and reenlisted 19–20 Jun 1877, Ft Davis, TX; in field at Eagle Springs, TX, Jun 1880; at camp near Presidio, TX, Jun–Aug 1881; discharged and reenlisted 19–20 Jun 1882, Ft Davis; acting first sergeant, Ft Davis, Jan 1885; participated in campaign against Geronimo, 1886; discharged and reenlisted 19–20 Jun 1887, Ft Apache, AZ; discharged and reenlisted 19–20 Jun 1892; discharged Ft Buford, ND, 13 Aug 1894; married Estephana Gonzales, Ft Davis, 27 Sep 1882; son Joseph Cole born 26 Dec 1894; died 20 May 1900; buried Georgetown, KY; widow and son resided on H. J. Green ranch, Rancho Verde, CA, in 1911–12. SOURCE: Sayre, *Warriors of Color*, 67–68, 111, 139–43.

‡Original member of 10th Cavalry; in troop when organized, Ft Leavenworth, KS, 21 Jul 1867. SOURCE: McMiller, "Buffalo Soldiers," 75.

‡Farrier, 1874; cited for gallantry against Kiowas and Comanches, Wichita Agency, Indian Territory, 22–23 Aug 1874. SOURCE: Baker, Roster.

Reduced from first sergeant to sergeant, 15 Dec 1885; in H/10th Cavalry stationed at Bonita Cañon Camp, AZ, 30 Apr 1886. SOURCE: Tagg, *The Camp at Bonita Cañon*, 66, 231.

Sergeant Cole, H/10th Cavalry, participated in Oct 1886 pursuit and capture of Apache Mangus. SOURCE: Schubert, *Voices of the Buffalo Soldier*, 146–47.

‡Honorable mention for services rendered in capture of Mangas and his Apache band, Rio Bonito, AZ, 18 Oct 1886. SOURCE: Baker, Roster.

‡Sergeant, authorized four-month furlough from Ft Apache. SOURCE: *ANJ* 24 (25 Jun 1887): 954.

‡At Ft Apache, 1890, subscribed $.50 to testimonial to General Grierson. SOURCE: List of subscriptions, 23 Apr 1890, 10th Cavalry papers, MHI.

‡Retires as sergeant from Ft Buford, 13 Aug 1894. SOURCE: Baker, Roster; *ANJ* 31 (14 Jul 1894): 803.

COLEMAN, Archie; Private; E/10th Cav. In Troop E/10th Cavalry stationed at Bonita Cañon Camp, AZ, 28 Feb 1886. SOURCE: Tagg, *The Camp at Bonita Cañon*, 231.

COLEMAN, Henry; Private; K/9th Cav. Served in second half of 1890s; resided at 627 W. 4th St., Cincinnati, OH, in 1907. SOURCE: Sayre, *Warriors of Color*, 498.

COLEMAN, Jordan; Private; C/38th Inf. Died 6 Aug 1867; originally buried at Ft Hays, KS; reburied at Ft Leavenworth National Cemetery, plot 3292. SOURCE: Ft Leavenworth National Cemetery.

COLEMAN, Mitchell; Private; A/25th Inf. Died 1 Feb 1872; buried at San Antonio National Cemetery, Section D, number 777. SOURCE: San Antonio National Cemetery Locator.

COLEMAN, Reuben; Sergeant; F/9th Cav. Died at Ft Davis, TX, on 14 Jul 1867; buried at San Antonio National Cemetery, Section I, number 1509. SOURCE: San Antonio National Cemetery Locator.

COLEMAN, Robert; M/9th Cav. Born in Kentucky; black complexion; cannot read or write, age 23, Jul 1870, at Ft McKavett, TX. SOURCE: Bierschwale, *Fort McKavett*, 99.

COLLIER, Gilbert; F/9th Cav. Born in Georgia; black complexion; cannot read or write, age 24, Jul 1870, at Ft McKavett, TX. SOURCE: Bierschwale, *Fort McKavett*, 97.

COLLINS, Dudley; Private; E/10th Cav. Died 10 Jan 1872 of consumption at Ft Sill, OK. SOURCE: Regimental Returns, 10th Cavalry, 1872.

Died 9 Jan 1872, buried at Camp Douglas, UT. SOURCE: Record Book of Interments, Post Cemetery, 252.

COLLINS, Francis; Private; H/9th Cav. ‡On detached service at Jefferson Barracks, MO, 4 Aug 1880–10 Feb 1881. SOURCE: Regt Returns, 9 Cav, Feb 1881.

Private, H/9th Cavalry, at Ft Riley, KS, 1882. SOURCE: Kenner, *Buffalo Soldiers and Officers of the Ninth Cavalry*, 275.

COLLINS, Frederick; Private; A/39th Inf. Civil War veteran, served in C/10th Heavy Artillery; sentence of nine years for involvement in New Iberia, LA, mutiny, Jul 1867, reduced to one year. SOURCE: Dobak and Phillips, *The Black Regulars*, 222.

COLLINS, Melvin R.; H/25th Inf. Born in Maryland; black complexion; can read and write, age 24, 5 Sep 1870, at Ft McKavett, TX. SOURCE: Bierschwale, *Fort McKavett*, 107.

COLLINS, Robert; M/9th Cav. Born in Kentucky; mulatto complexion; cannot read or write, age 26, Jul 1870, at Ft McKavett, TX. SOURCE: Bierschwale, *Fort McKavett*, 99.

COLLINS, Thomas; Private; M/9th Cav. Killed Sgt. Frank Washington, B/9th Cavalry, at Ft DuChesne, UT, Oct 1887. SOURCE: Kenner, *Buffalo Soldiers and Officers of the Ninth Cavalry*, 339.

COLLINS, William Thomas; Private; B/10th Cav. Served in 1881; resided at 21 N. Sharpe St., Baltimore, MD, at age 37, in May 1891; resided at 216 Sharp St. Alley in 1894. SOURCE: Sayre, *Warriors of Color*, 407.

COLTRANE, James A.; Corporal; B/25th Inf. Jones A. Coltrane enlisted 30 Nov 1900, discharged as private 29 Nov 1903, character excellent; reenlisted 30 Nov 1903, discharged without honor as corporal 22 Nov 1906, Brownsville, TX. SOURCE: Powell, "Military Record of the Enlisted Men Who Were Discharged Without Honor."

‡Dishonorable discharge, Brownsville. SOURCE: SO 266, AGO, 9 Nov 1906.

‡One of fourteen cleared of involvement in Brownsville raid and allowed to reenlist. SOURCE: Weaver, *The Brownsville Raid*, 248.

COLUMBUS, Robert H.; Private; K/25th Inf. Born in Gloucester, VA; Ht 5'3", black complexion; occupation farmer; enlisted in A/39th Infantry for three years on 9 Aug 1867, age 27, at Philadelphia, PA; transferred to K/25th Infantry at Jackson Bks, LA, 20 Apr 1869. SOURCE: Descriptive Roll of A/39th Inf.

COMAGER, Charles W.; Sergeant; I/9th Cav. ‡Charles W. Comagor promoted from corporal, Ft Robinson, NE, May 1895. SOURCE: *ANJ* 32 (18 May 1895): 626.

Appointed sergeant 1 May 1895; in I/9th Cavalry at Ft Washakie, WY, Jan 1897. SOURCE: Ninth Cavalry, Roster of NCOs, 1897.

COMAGER, Charles W.; Sergeant; I/9th Cav. *See* COMANGER, Charles W., Sergeant, I/9th Cavalry

Combs, H.; H/38th Inf. Died 29 Jun 1867; buried at Ft Leavenworth National Cemetery, plot 1304. SOURCE: Ft Leavenworth National Cemetery.

COMBS, Henry; Corporal; 9th Cav. Died at Ft Clark, TX; buried at Fort Sam Houston National Cemetery, Section PE, number 47. SOURCE: Buffalo Soldiers Interred in Fort Sam Houston National Cemetery.

COMBS, Richard; Cook; B/10th Cav. ‡Private, at Ft Apache, AZ, 1890, subscribed $.50 to testimonial to General Grierson. SOURCE: List of subscriptions, 23 Apr 1890, 10th Cavalry papers, MHI.

‡Private, served in 10th Cavalry in Cuba, 1898. SOURCE: Cashin, *Under Fire with the Tenth Cavalry*, 338.

‡Retires. SOURCE: SO 117, AGO, 18 May 1904.

Retired cook issued Indian Wars Campaign Badge number 1155 on 24 Mar 1909. SOURCE: Carroll, *Indian Wars Campaign Badge*, 32.

Buried at old Ft Crook cemetery, now on Offutt Air Force Base, Omaha, NE. SOURCE: Photograph of Richard Combs gravestone in authors' files.

COMER, Levi; Private; K/9th Cav. ‡Served 1872–73. *See* **SLAUGHTER**, Rufus, Private, K/9th Cavalry

Brutally treated by Capt. J. Lee Humfreville at camp near Ft Richardson, TX, and on return march to Ft Clark, TX, summer 1872, resulting in hospitalization at Ft McKavett, TX; deserted during last half of 1875. SOURCE: Kenner, *Buffalo Soldiers and Officers of the Ninth Cavalry*, 141–45, 336.

Court martial order convicting Capt. J. Lee Humfreville of brutality published. SOURCE: Schubert, *Voices of the Buffalo Soldier*, 55–62.

COMFREY, Charles; F/9th Cav. Born in Kentucky; black complexion; cannot read or write, age 21, Jul 1870, at Ft McKavett, TX. SOURCE: Bierschwale, *Fort McKavett*, 97.

CONE, Willis; Private; D/10th Cav. Died 4 Sep 1868 of disease at Ft Arbuckle, OK. SOURCE: Regimental Returns, 10th Cavalry, 1868.

CONLEY, Paschall; QM Sgt; 10th Cav. ‡Born in Huntsville, AL; enlisted H/24th Infantry, age 20, occupation clerk, Ht 5'5", mulatto, Memphis, TN, 26 Mar 1879; discharged, character excellent, 25 Mar 1884; reenlisted, D/24th Infantry, 1 Jul 1884; corporal, 16 Jul 1884; sergeant, 1 Jul 1886; marksman, 1883, 1884, 1887, 1888, and member, Department of the Missouri rifle team, 1886; fined $10 by garrison court martial, Ft Supply, Indian Territory, 1887; reduced to private and fined $10 per month for six months by garrison court martial, Ft Supply, 1888; sergeant major, 5 Oct 1888; reduced at own request and transferred to D/24th Infantry, 1 Feb 1889; character good, married, one child. SOURCE: Descriptive Book, 24 Inf NCS & Band.

Private, regimental clerk, 24th Infantry, Ft Supply, OK, 1882, reported that post library subscribed to black Huntsville, AL, *Gazette*, at his suggestion. SOURCE: Dobak and Phillips, *The Black Regulars*, 154.

‡Sharpshooter as corporal, D/24th Infantry, Ft Supply. SOURCE: *ANJ* 24 (21 Aug 1886): 70.

‡Private, L/10th Cavalry, 1 Jul 1889; corporal, 1 Mar 1890; transferred to H/10th Cavalry, 25 Aug 1890; quarter-master sergeant, 10th Cavalry, 14 May 1893; at Ft Assiniboine, MT, 1897. SOURCE: Baker, Roster.

‡An excellent noncommissioned officer who should be commissioned, according to John E. Lewis, H/10th Cavalry, in letter from Lakeland, FL, 5 Jun 1898. SOURCE: Gatewood, "Smoked Yankees," 37.

‡Sergeant, M/10th Cavalry, 1898; remained in U.S. during war with Spain; narrates Spanish-American War experience. SOURCE: Cashin, *Under Fire with the Tenth Cavalry*, 351, 262–63.

‡Appointed squadron sergeant major, 10th Cavalry, 13 Jun 1899; served at Holguin, Cuba, 17 May 1899–12 May 1902; allotted $25 per month to Mrs. Mary J. Conley, 1 Jan–20 Jun 1900, 1 Oct 1900–31 Mar 1901, and $20 per month, 1 Jul–31 Dec 1901; discharged, character excellent, married, four minor children, 30 Jun 1902; reenlisted as squadron sergeant major, Ft Robinson, NE, 1 Jul 1902, wife and children residing in Havre, MT; reenlisted as regimental quartermaster sergeant, Ft Robinson, 1 Jul 1905; retired, character excellent, with $350 deposits and $250 due him for clothing, 19 Nov 1906. SOURCE: Descriptive Book, 10 Cav Officers & NCOs.

‡Guest with his wife at K/10th Cavalry Thanksgiving dinner, Ft Robinson, 1904. SOURCE: Simmons, "Thanksgiving Day," 664.

‡Sister Sallie married Beverly Thornton, Cook, K/10th Cavalry, at Ft Robinson.

‡Celebrated twentieth wedding anniversary, with large number of invited guests from Ft Robinson and Crawford, NE, 25 Apr 1905; to retire in about one year. SOURCE: Crawford *Tribune*, 5 May 1905.

‡Retired after thirty years with pension of $30 per month. SOURCE: Cleveland *Gazette*, 29 Dec 1906.

CONN, George; Private; B/25th Inf. Enlisted 3 Oct 1904, discharged without honor, 22 Nov 1906, Brownsville, TX. SOURCE: Powell, "Military Record of the Enlisted Men Who Were Discharged Without Honor."

‡Dishonorable discharge, Brownsville. SOURCE: SO 266, AGO, 9 Nov 1906.

CONNELL, Jim; Private; 25th Inf. Born in Goodlettsville, TN; Ht 5'7", black hair and eyes, yellow complexion; occupation laborer; enlisted at age 24, Nashville, TN, 19 Mar 1886; arrived Ft Snelling, MN, 31 Jul 1886. SOURCE: Descriptive & Assignment Rolls of Recruits, 25 Inf.

CONNER, Charles; Sergeant; 24th Inf. Wife Louisa was hospital matron, Ft Duncan, TX, 1870s. SOURCE: Dobak and Phillips, *The Black Regulars*, 174.

CONNOR; M/9th Cav. Born in Kentucky; mulatto complexion; cannot read or write, age 22, Jul 1870, at Ft McKavett, TX. SOURCE: Bierschwale, *Fort McKavett*, 98.

CONRAD, George, Jr.; Private; 9th Inf. Enlisted 1883; learned to read and write in the Army. SOURCE: Dobak and Phillips, *The Black Regulars*, 47.

CONTEE, James S.; 1st Sgt; H/9th Cav. ‡Sergeant, H/9th Cavalry, with detachment engaged against enemy, Lumagua, Philippines, 9 May 1901. SOURCE: Hamilton, "History of the Ninth Cavalry," 107; *Illustrated Review, Ninth Cavalry.*

Received Philippine Campaign Badge number 11855 for service as sergeant, H/9th Cavalry; in 9th Cavalry at Ft Leavenworth, KS, Mar 1905. SOURCE: Philippine Campaign Badge list, 29 May 1905.

‡First sergeant, H/9th Cavalry, veteran of Spanish-American War and Philippine Insurrection; at Ft D. A. Russell, WY, in 1910; sharpshooter, resident of Washington, DC. SOURCE: *Illustrated Review, Ninth Cavalry.*

CONTEE, William; Private; M/25th Inf. Died 29 Apr 1902; buried in plot 1114 at San Francisco National Cemetery. SOURCE: San Francisco National Cemetery.

CONWAY, Johnson; Private; 25th Inf. Born in Fredericksburg, VA; Ht 5'6", black hair and eyes, brown complexion; discharged from L/10th Cavalry 13 Feb 1887; 2nd reenlistment, 25th Infantry at age 29, Washington, DC, 12 Mar 1887; assigned to F/25th Infantry, arrived Ft Snelling, MN, 28 May 1887. SOURCE: Descriptive & Assignment Rolls of Recruits, 25 Inf.

CONYERS, Boyd; Private; B/25th Inf. Enlisted 11 Aug 1905, discharged without honor 19 Nov 1906. SOURCE: Powell, "Military Record of the Enlisted Men Who Were Discharged Without Honor."

‡Dishonorable discharge, Brownsville. SOURCE: SO 266, AGO, 9 Nov 1906.

‡Mrs. Boyd Conyers, age 85, of Monroe, GA, regarding Brownsville: "He never talked about it. The only thing he would say was he didn't do it." SOURCE: *Newsweek*, 16 Oct 1972.

CONYERS, Jerry; Private; E/10th Cav. Died 25 Aug 1880 of diarrhea in the field. SOURCE: Regimental Returns, 10th Cavalry, 1880.

COOK, Alexander; Private; D/9th Cav. With Captain Dodge at battle at Milk River, CO, 2–10 Oct 1879. SOURCE: Miller, *Hollow Victory*, 167, 206–7.

COOK, Alexander; Private; 24th Inf. Resident of Nashville, TN; attended Fort Reno, OK, wedding of Cpl. Henry Giles, 1887. SOURCE: Dobak and Phillips, *The Black Regulars*, 141.

‡A. Cook, K/24th Infantry, at Ft Reno, Indian Territory, 1887. See **GILES**, Henry, Sergeant, C/24th Infantry

COOK, Charles; Private; A/24th Inf. Served at Ft Supply, IT, 1882–83; three letters to Anna Payne, Dodge City, KS, published. SOURCE: Schubert, *Voices of the Buffalo Soldier*, 123–26.

COOK, Cyrus; Private; I/10th Cav. ‡Cycire Cook, original member of 10th Cavalry; in troop when organized, Ft Riley, KS, 15 Aug 1867. SOURCE: McMiller, "Buffalo Soldiers," 76.

Died 17 Jul 1868, shot by accident, at Republican River, KS. SOURCE: Regimental Returns, 10th Cavalry, 1868.

COOK, Edward; H/25th Inf. Born in North Carolina; mulatto complexion; can read, cannot write, age 22, 5 Sep 1870, in H/25th Infantry at Ft McKavett, TX. SOURCE: Bierschwale, *Fort McKavett,* 107.

COOK, Ermine; Private; E/24th Inf. ‡Died of typhoid in the Philippines. SOURCE: *ANJ* 38 (9 Oct 1900): 187.

Died 9 Oct 1900; buried in plot ESIDE1230 at San Francisco National Cemetery. SOURCE: San Francisco National Cemetery.

COOK, French; Private; C/24th Inf. Born in Bowling Green, KY; buried at Ft McKavett, TX, before 17 May 1879; body removed to National Cemetery, San Antonio, TX, 23 Nov 1883. SOURCE: Bierschwale, *Fort McKavett,* 123.

Died at Ft McKavett on 11 Jun 1872; buried at San Antonio National Cemetery, Section E, number 843. SOURCE: San Antonio National Cemetery Locator.

COOK, George; F/9th Cav. Born in Kentucky; black complexion; cannot read or write, age 22, Jul 1870, at Ft McKavett, TX. SOURCE: Bierschwale, *Fort McKavett,* 97.

COOK, James R.; Private; 40th Inf. Company clerk, one of three enlisted men, with Sgt. John Stanley and Pvt. John H. Hedgeman, sent with officer to establish recruiting office, New York City, Nov 1867. SOURCE: Dobak and Phillips, *The Black Regulars*, 6.

COOK, Joe; Private; U.S. Army. Seminole Negro Scout, served 1872–82, 1886. SOURCE: Schubert, Consolidated List of Seminole Negro Scouts.

Born in Arkansas; enlisted Ft Duncan, TX, 2 Aug 1872, age 38; Ht 5'4", black hair and eyes, black complexion; discharged Ft Duncan 2 Feb 1873; enlisted Ft Clark, TX, 23 Apr 1873; blacksmith in 1873; discharged at Ft Clark, 23 Oct 1873; enlisted 21 Dec 1874 at Ft Clark where he was discharged 26 Jun 1875; saddler in 1876; enlisted Ft Clark 17 Oct 1876; discharged at Camp Painted Comanche, TX, 17 Apr 1877; enlisted 17 Apr 1877 at Ft Clark where he was discharged 7 May 1878; enlisted 20 May 1879 at Ft Clark where he was discharged 27 May 1880; enlisted 28 May 1880 at Ft Clark where he was discharged 23 May

1881; enlisted Ft Clark 17 Dec 1881; discharged 16 Dec 1882 at Camp Myers, TX; enlisted Ft Clark 24 Jun 1886; killed by railroad cars at Maxon Spring, TX, 26 Dec 1886; buried at Camp Pena, CO. SOURCE: Swanson, 6.

COOK, John; Private; B/25th Inf. One of twenty men who cycled 1,900 miles from Ft Missoula, MT, to St. Louis, MO, 14 Jun–24 Jul 1897, in 25th Infantry Bicycle Corps to test durability and practicality of bicycles as a means of transportation for troops. SOURCE: File 60178, GC, AGO Records.

‡Dishonorable discharge, Brownsville, TX. SOURCE: SO 266, AGO, 9 Nov 1906.

COOMBS, Isaac; Private; K/9th Cav. Died 20 Apr 1902; buried in plot NADD 1383 at San Francisco National Cemetery. SOURCE: San Francisco National Cemetery.

COON, Joe; Private; U.S. Army. Seminole Negro Scout, served 1872–79; father of Scout John Jefferson. SOURCE: Schubert, Consolidated List of Seminole Negro Scouts; Porter, *The Negro on the American frontier*, 474.

Born in Arkansas; son of John Cavallo, also known as Gopher John Horse or Chief John Horse; mother was probably Horse's first wife; enlisted at Ft Duncan, TX, 2 Aug 1872, age 38; Ht 5'8", black hair and eyes, dark complexion; discharged 2 Feb 1873, reenlisted 1 May 1873 at Ft Duncan; discharged at Camp Comanche, TX, 1 Nov 1873; enlisted 24 Dec 1874, discharged 24 Jun 1875 at Ft Clark, TX; enlisted 4 Feb 1876 at Ft Duncan; discharged at Camp Pecos, TX, 7 Aug 1876; enlisted 23 Apr 1877 at Ft Clark; discharged, reenlisted at Camp Painted Comanche, TX, 23 Apr 1878; discharged at Ft Clark 23 Apr 1879. SOURCE: Swanson, 6.

COOPER, Archie; Corporal; G/9th Cav. ‡Corporal, G/9th Cavalry; veteran of Philippine Insurrection; at Ft D. A. Russell, WY, in 1910; sharpshooter; resident of Cuero, TX. SOURCE: *Illustrated Review: Ninth Cavalry*, with picture.

Archie Cooper, first sergeant, E/9th Cavalry, died 23 Nov 1934; buried in San Francisco National Cemetery. SOURCE: San Francisco National Cemetery.

COOPER, Barney; Private; 24th Inf. With his wife Amanda of St. Louis, MO, attended Fort Reno, OK, wedding of Cpl. Henry Giles, 1887. SOURCE: Dobak and Phillips, *The Black Regulars*, 141.

COOPER, Charles E.; Private; B/25th Inf. Enlisted 15 Sep 1899, discharged as private Company B, 48th Infantry 30 Jun 1901, character excellent; reenlisted 1 Aug 1901, discharged as private B/25th Infantry 31 Jul 1904, character excellent; reenlisted 9 Aug 1904, discharged without honor 19 Nov 1906. SOURCE: Powell, "Military Record of the Enlisted Men Who Were Discharged Without Honor."

‡Dishonorable discharge, Brownsville, TX. SOURCE: SO 266, AGO, 9 Nov 1906.

COOPER, Horace; Color Sgt; 9th Cav. ‡Private, restored to duty without trial. SOURCE: SO 278, AGO, 23 Nov 1891.

‡Corporal, C/9th Cavalry, since 6 Sep 1892. SOURCE: Roster, 9 Cav.

‡Promoted to sergeant, C/9th Cavalry, Ft Robinson, NE, Apr 1895. SOURCE: *ANJ* 32 (11 May 1895): 608.

‡Sergeant, authorized to reenlist as married. SOURCE: Letter, AGO, 2 Jun 1896, Post Returns, Ft Robinson.

Appointed sergeant 28 Apr 1895; in C/9th Cavalry at Ft Robinson, Jan 1897. SOURCE: Ninth Cavalry, Roster of NCOs, 1897.

‡Sergeant, on recruiting duty, early 1898. SOURCE: Cashin, *Under Fire with the Tenth Cavalry*, 112.

‡Appointed regimental color sergeant, May 1901. SOURCE: *ANJ* 38 (1 Jun 1901): 966.

COOPER, James D.; Sergeant; 25th Inf. At Ft Snelling, MN, 1880s, served as post librarian and school overseer, delivered patient to government asylum, Washington, DC. SOURCE: Dobak and Phillips, *The Black Regulars*, 259.

COOPER, John; Corporal; F/9th Cav. Appointed corporal 28 Jan 1896; in F/9th Cavalry at Ft DuChesne, UT, Jan 1897. SOURCE: Ninth Cavalry, Roster of NCOs, 1897.

COOPER, John; 1st Sgt; D/9th Cav. ‡Sergeant, on special duty in charge of recruits, Nueva Caceres, Philippines, 23–24 May 1902. SOURCE: SD List, D/9 Cav.

Sergeant when issued Indian Wars Campaign Badge number 659 on 20 Oct 1908. SOURCE: Carroll, *Indian Wars Campaign Badge*, 19.

‡Veteran of Indian wars and Philippine Insurrection, first sergeant, at Ft D. A. Russell, WY, in 1910. SOURCE: *Illustrated Review, Ninth Cavalry*, with picture.

COOPER, Robert A.; 1st Sgt; 24th Inf. Attended Fort Reno, OK, wedding of Cpl. Henry Giles, with his wife, 1887. SOURCE: Dobak and Phillips, *The Black Regulars*, 141.

COOPER, William H.; C/25th Inf. Born in Kentucky; black complexion; cannot read or write, age 21, 5 Sep 1870, at Ft McKavett, TX. SOURCE: Bierschwale, *Fort McKavett*, 109.

COPELAND, Benjamine; Private; A/25th Inf. Died 5 Feb 1882, buried Plot 2 20, Ft Meade National Cemetery, SD. SOURCE: Ft Meade National Cemetery, VA database.

COPELAND, Samuel; Private; A/24th Inf. Born in Lynchburg, VA; resided in Washington, DC; at Naguilian,

Luzon, Philippines, 7 Dec 1899, volunteered to swim Rio Grande de Cagayan in face of a well-entrenched enemy, swam the river, returned with raft for small arms and ammunition, crossed again, took part in attack that drove off superior enemy force; awarded Distinguished Service Cross in 1925. SOURCE: *American Decorations*, 228.

CORBITT, George; Corporal; F/9th Cav. Private, received Philippine Campaign Badge number 11881 for service as private in H/9th Cavalry; in 9th Cavalry at Ft Leavenworth, KS, Mar 1905. SOURCE: Philippine Campaign Badge list, 29 May 1905.

‡Corporal, F/9th Cavalry, veteran of Philippine Insurrection; at Ft D. A. Russell, WY, in 1910. SOURCE: *Illustrated Review, Ninth Cavalry*, with picture.

CORNELIUS, George W.; Private; K/25th Inf. Born in Providence, RI; Ht 5'7", black hair and brown eyes, black complexion; occupation soldier; enlisted at age 25, Boston, MA, 26 Mar 1886; arrived Ft Snelling, MN, 5 Aug 1886. SOURCE: Descriptive & Assignment Rolls of Recruits, 25 Inf.

‡Admitted to Soldiers Home with disability, with three years and nine months service, age 32, 20 Dec 1890. SOURCE: SecWar, *AR 1891*, 751.

CORNFOWL, Henry; Corporal; L/10th Cav. Died 3 Apr 1874 in hospital at Ft Richardson, TX. SOURCE: Regimental Returns, 10th Cavalry, 1874.

CORSEAU, Clarkson W.; D/24th Inf. Born in Ohio; mulatto complexion; can read and write, age 24, Jul 1870, at Ft McKavett, TX. SOURCE: Bierschwale, *Fort McKavett*, 96.

COSBY, Edward; Private; D/10th Cav. Died 26 Jun 1882, fell off horse, at Ft Concho, TX. SOURCE: Regimental Returns, 10th Cavalry, 1882.

COSBY, Nick; Private; F/10th Cav. ‡Private Cosby, F/10th Cavalry, wounded in battle against Indians, Kansas, 21 Aug 1867. SOURCE: Armes, *Ups and Downs*, 247.

Wounded in action, gunshot wound in left thigh, near Beaver Creek, KS, 21 Aug 1867. SOURCE: LR, DeptMo, 1867.

COSY, Levi; Sergeant; G/25th Inf. Died at Ft Concho, TX, on 23 Apr 1870; buried at San Antonio National Cemetery, Section D, number 539. SOURCE: San Antonio National Cemetery Locator.

COTMAN, James O.; Private; 25th Inf. At Ft Meade, SD, 1880s, served as hospital nurse. SOURCE: Dobak and Phillips, *The Black Regulars*, 147.

COTTMAN, Thomas; Corporal; I/10th Cav. In Troop I/10th Cavalry stationed at Bonita Cañon Camp, AZ, 30 Jun 1886. Tagg questions spelling of Cottman. SOURCE: Tagg, *The Camp at Bonita Cañon*, 231.

COTTRELL, Robert H.; Private; K/25th Inf. Born in Northumberland, VA; Ht 5'5", bright complexion; occupation laborer; enlisted in A/39th Infantry for three years on 5 Nov 1867, age 27, at Richmond, VA; transferred to K/25th Infantry at Jackson Bks, LA, 20 Apr 1869. SOURCE: Descriptive Roll of A/39th Inf.

COUNTEE, Thomas W.; Sergeant; F/24th Inf. ‡Drowned while crossing San Mateo River, Philippines, 21 Aug 1899. SOURCE: Richmond *Planet*, 2 Sep 1899.

Sergeant, F/24th Infantry, died 21 Aug 1899; buried in plot ESIDE621 at San Francisco National Cemetery. SOURCE: San Francisco National Cemetery.

COVINGTON, James C.; Private; E/24th Inf. Born in Louisville, KY; Ht 5'5", black hair and eyes, brown complexion; occupation waiter; enlisted in 25th Infantry at age 23, Chicago, IL, 16 Dec 1886; arrived Ft Snelling, MN, 1 Apr 1887. SOURCE: Descriptive & Assignment Rolls of Recruits, 25 Inf.

‡In K/24th Infantry at San Carlos, AZ, 1890; contributed $1 to Henry Thompson and wife Ruth, daughter of John Brown. SOURCE: Cleveland *Gazette*, 7 Jun 1890.

‡Resident of Chicago; to be discharged from E/24th Infantry at end of term, Ft Bayard, NM, 15 Dec 1891. SOURCE: Cleveland *Gazette*, 12 Dec 1891.

COVINGTON, Samuel; Corporal; C/10th Cav. ‡Promoted to corporal, G/9th Cavalry, since 28 Jul 1893. SOURCE: Roster, 9 Cav.

‡Alternate for 9th Cavalry regimental color guard, Ft Robinson, NE, Mar 1896. SOURCE: *ANJ* 33 (28 Mar 1896): 540.

Appointed sergeant 1 Nov 1896; in G/9th Cavalry at Ft Robinson, Jan 1897. SOURCE: Ninth Cavalry, Roster of NCOs, 1897.

‡Corporal, C/10th Cavalry, served in 10th Cavalry in Cuba, 1898. SOURCE: Cashin, *Under Fire with the Tenth Cavalry*, 339.

COWAN, James D.; Private; 25th Inf. Born in Philadelphia, PA; Ht 5'7", black hair and dark brown eyes, black complexion; occupation laborer; resided in Philadelphia when he enlisted at age 21, Philadelphia, 6 Sep 1886; arrived Ft Snelling, MN, 20 Jan 1887. SOURCE: Descriptive & Assignment Rolls of Recruits, 25 Inf.

COX, James; Private; G/10th Cav. Died 22 Sep 1888; originally buried at Ft Grant, AZ; buried at Santa Fe National Cemetery, NM, plot A-1 757. SOURCE: Santa Fe National Cemetery, Records of Burials.

CRAGG, Allen; Sergeant; E/9th Cav. Allen Crage born in Kentucky; mulatto complexion; can read and write, age 22, Jul 1870, in F/9th Cavalry at Ft McKavett, TX. SOURCE: Bierschwale, *Fort McKavett*, 98.

Born in Kentucky; served in G/117th U.S. Colored Troops during Civil War; married Violet Cragg, Junction City, KS, 1 Jun 1885; Violet Cragg was born into slavery, worked as nurse during Civil War, and later worked variety of menial jobs in western towns and garrisons, resided in Los Angeles, CA, after husband died; daughter Ella, born ca. 1866, St. Louis, MO, was fathered by white Howard Whitney, later married Chief Trumpeter Stephen Taylor, 9th Cavalry, lived in Santa Fe, NM, 1906. SOURCE: Schubert, *Voices of the Buffalo Soldier*, 248–51.

‡Sergeant, E/9th Cavalry, since 17 Jul 1885. SOURCE: Roster, 9 Cav.

‡Wife is one of three laundresses authorized E/9th Cavalry, Ft Robinson, NE, and authorized quartermaster stove and utensils, Jun 1891. SOURCE: Post Adj to Post QM, Ft Robinson, 22 Jul 1891, LS, Ft Robinson.

‡Resides on Laundress Row with wife, Aug 1893. SOURCE: Medical History, Ft Robinson.

‡At Ft Robinson since 1885. SOURCE: *ANJ* 32 (4 May 1895): 591.

‡Retires from Ft Robinson, May 1885. SOURCE: *ANJ* 32 (11 May 1895): 609.

‡Retires to Sacramento, CA. SOURCE: Order 29, 11 May 1895, Post Orders, Ft Robinson.

‡Veterans Administration pension application 881404, by widow Violet Cragg, 16 Dec 1907, not found in search at National Archives.

CRAIG, George; Private; L/10th Cav. Died 29 Aug 1869 in hospital at Ft Sill, OK. SOURCE: Regimental Returns, 10th Cavalry, 1869.

Died 29 Aug 1869; buried at Camp Douglas, UT. SOURCE: Record Book of Interments, Post Cemetery, 252.

CRAIG, John; M/9th Cav. Born in Kentucky; cannot read or write, age 22, Jul 1870, at Ft McKavett, TX. SOURCE: Bierschwale, *Fort McKavett*, 99.

CRAIG, Thomas B.; Sergeant; E/9th Cav. Corporal, received Philippine Campaign Badge number 11700 for service as corporal in E/9th Cavalry; in 9th Cavalry at Ft Leavenworth, KS, Mar 1905. SOURCE: Philippine Campaign Badge list, 29 May 1905.

‡Veteran of Spanish-American War and Philippine Insurrection; sergeant, D/9th Cavalry, wounded in action, San Juan, Cuba, 1 Jul 1898; sharpshooter; sergeant, E/9th Cavalry, at Ft D. A. Russell, WY, in 1910; resident of Washing-

ton, DC. SOURCE: *Historical Review, Ninth Cavalry*, with picture.

CRAIGE, Richard; Corporal; F/25th Inf. At Ft Randall, Dakota Territory, 1880, testified in court martial of Capt. Andrew Geddes for drunkenness. SOURCE: Barnett, *Ungentlemanly Acts*, 197–98.

CRANSHAW, Tennie; Sergeant; K/24th Inf. ‡With seventy-five men of K Company, engaged 150 insurgents at Santa Ana, Philippines, 6 Oct 1899; repulsed enemy. SOURCE: Muller, *The Twenty Fourth Infantry*, 30.

Awarded certificate of merit for coolness and good judgment in action at Santa Ana, 6 Oct 1899. SOURCE: Gleim, *The Certificate of Merit*, 49.

‡Awarded certificate of merit for coolness and judgment in attack by insurgents, Santa Ana, 6 Oct 1899; discharged 9 Sep 1901. SOURCE: GO 32, AGO, 6 Feb 1904.

CRAVEN, Luther; Private; E/9th Cav. Served against Apaches in New Mexico, 1879. SOURCE: Dobak and Phillips, *The Black Regulars*, 192.

CRAWFORD, Hartley; Private; F/9th Cav. Native of South Carolina; on first enlistment in 1878, could read and write. SOURCE: Kenner, *Buffalo Soldiers and Officers of the Ninth Cavalry*, 106–7.

CRAWFORD, Henry; Corporal; C/9th Cav. Appointed corporal 15 Dec 1894; in C/9th Cavalry at Ft Robinson, NE, Jan 1897. SOURCE: Ninth Cavalry, Roster of NCOs, 1897.

‡Promoted from lance corporal to corporal, C/9th Cavalry. SOURCE: *ANJ* 32 (22 Dec 1894): 278.

‡Authorized to reenlist in A/9th Cavalry as married. SOURCE: Letter, AGO, 22 Jan 1897.

CRAWFORD, John; Private; D/9th Cav. With Captain Dodge at battle at Milk River, CO, 2–10 Oct 1879. SOURCE: Miller, *Hollow Victory*, 167, 206–7.

CRAWFORD, Preston; Private; D/10th Cav. ‡Mentioned, Feb 1873. SOURCE: LS, 10 Cav, 1873–77.

Died 30 Oct 1872 of disease at Ft Dodge, KS. SOURCE: Regimental Returns, 10th Cavalry, 1872.

‡Recruit, died in hospital, Ft Dodge. SOURCE: Letter, CO, 10 Cav, Ft Gibson, Indian Territory, to AG, USA, 20 Feb 1873, ES, 10 Cav, 1873–81.

CROCHERON, Luther; Private; D/25th Inf. Born in Mattewan [*sic*], NJ; Ht 5'8", black hair and brown eyes, yellow complexion; occupation laborer; resided in Mamaroneck, NY, when he enlisted 18 Nov 1885, age 20, at Davis Island, NY; assigned to D/25th Infantry; arrived

Ft Snelling, MN, 26 Apr 1886. SOURCE: Descriptive & Assignment Rolls of Recruits, 25 Inf.

Deserted during tenure of 1st Sgt. John Franklin, Jan 1869–May 1871. SOURCE: Dobak and Phillips, *The Black Regulars*, 300.

CROCKET, George H.; Private; 25th Inf. Born in Philadelphia, PA; Ht 5'8", brown hair and eyes, brown complexion; occupation teamster; enlisted at age 21, Philadelphia, 9 Apr 1886; arrived Ft Snelling, MN, 19 Aug 1886. SOURCE: Descriptive & Assignment Rolls of Recruits, 25 Inf.

CROOM, Mills B.; Private; D/24th Inf. Died 24 Dec 1894; buried at Ft Bayard, NM, in plot I 24. SOURCE: "Fort Bayard National Cemetery, Records of Burials."

Mills B. Groom of D/24th Infantry buried at Ft Bayard. SOURCE: "Buffalo Soldiers Buried at Ft Bayard, NM."

Buried 24 Dec 1894, section A, row M, plot 27, at Ft Bayard. SOURCE: Erickson, Burials at Fort Bayard National Cemetery, NM.

CROPPER, John S.; Private; Band/10th Cav. Died 4 Jun 1872 of disease at Ft Sill, OK. SOURCE: Regimental Returns, 10th Cavalry, 1872.

Buried at Camp Douglas, UT. SOURCE: Record Book of Interments, Post Cemetery, 252.

CROPPER, Samuel; Private; G/24th Inf. Served in K/10th Cavalry 1882–87, when he reenlisted for G/24th Infantry; age 67 in 1924, resided at 1335 T Street, NW, Washington, DC. SOURCE: Sayre, *Warriors of Color*, 184.

‡Assisted Lt. John Bigelow in planning Christmas program at Mowry Mine, AZ, along with Private Hazzard, K/10th Cavalry, 1885. SOURCE: Bigelow, *On the Bloody Trail of Geronimo*, 103.

Private in D/24th Infantry when issued Indian Wars Campaign Badge number 680 on 22 Oct 1908. SOURCE: Carroll, *Indian Wars Campaign Badge*, 19.

See OTT, **BRANSFORD**, Wesley, Private, K/10th Cavalry

CROSBY, Scott; Corporal; A/24th Inf. ‡While sergeant, D/24th Infantry, Ft Bayard, NM, reduced to ranks, confined for four months, and fined $10 per month for four months for being drunk on guard and allowing others on guard to get drunk. SOURCE: *ANJ* 28 (11 Oct 1890): 105.

Awarded certificate of merit for distinguished service in battle, Santiago, Cuba, 1 Jul 1898. SOURCE: Gleim, *The Certificate of Merit*, 46.

‡Awarded certificate of merit for distinguished service while private, A/24th Infantry, battle of Santiago, 1 Jul 1898. SOURCE: GO 15, AGO, 13 Feb 1900.

Born in Marion County, TN; received Distinguished Service Medal in lieu of certificate of merit. SOURCE: *American Decorations*, 836.

‡Certificate of merit mentioned. SOURCE: Steward, *Colored Regulars*, 280; *ANJ* 37 (24 Feb 1900): 611; Scipio, *Last of the Black Regulars*, 130.

CROSBY, T.; Private; F/10th Cav. Wounded in action against Indians at Beaver Creek, KS, 21 Aug 1867. SOURCE: Schubert, *Voices of the Buffalo Soldier*, 20.

CROSS, J. C.; Private; 24th Inf. Died on detached duty; buried in section A, row W, plot 11 at Ft Bayard, NM. SOURCE: Erickson, Burials at Fort Bayard National Cemetery, NM.

CROSS, Joseph; Private; 25th Inf. Born in Marietta, OH; Ht 5'8", light brown hair and grey eyes, yellow complexion; occupation laborer; enlisted at age 19, Cincinnati, OH, 19 Apr 1886; arrived Ft Snelling, MN, 31 Jul 1886. SOURCE: Descriptive & Assignment Rolls of Recruits, 25 Inf.

CROUCH, Edward; Private; 10th Cav. Served in Montana, 1894. SOURCE: Dobak and Phillips, *The Black Regulars*, 156.

CROW, James; F/9th Cav. Born in Kentucky; mulatto complexion; cannot read or write, age 23, Jul 1870, at Ft McKavett, TX. SOURCE: Bierschwale, *Fort McKavett*, 98.

CROWDER, Daniel; Farrier; F/9th Cav. Died 1 Jun 1900; buried at San Antonio National Cemetery, Section F, number 1126. SOURCE: San Antonio National Cemetery Locator.

CROWDER, Julius; Corporal; G/9th Cav. Received Philippine Campaign Badge number 11812 for service as private in G/9th Cavalry, 16 Sep 1900–16 Feb 1901; corporal in 9th Cavalry, Ft Leavenworth, KS, Mar 1905. SOURCE: Philippine Campaign Badge Recipients; Philippine Campaign Badge list, 29 May 1905.

CROWDER, Rufus; Corporal; 9th Cav. Received Philippine Campaign Badge number 11865 for service as corporal in B/9th Cavalry; in 9th Cavalry at Ft Leavenworth, KS, Mar 1905. SOURCE: Philippine Campaign Badge list, 29 May 1905.

CROWDER, William A.; Private; 9th Cav. Received Philippine Campaign Badge number 11882 for service as private, H/9th Cavalry; in 9th Cavalry at Ft Leavenworth, KS,

Mar 1905. SOURCE: Philippine Campaign Badge list, 29 May 1905.

CROWDIS, David; F/9th Cav. Born in Kentucky; black complexion; cannot read or write, age 24, Jul 1870, at Ft McKavett, TX. SOURCE: Bierschwale, *Fort McKavett,* 97.

CRUMMEL, C.A.; Sergeant; F/10th Cav. Distinguished himself in action against Indians at Beaver Creek, KS, 21 Aug 1867. SOURCE: Schubert, *Voices of the Buffalo Soldier*, 18.

CRUMP, Edward W.; Private; C/9th Cav. Born in Bayou Sara, LA; Ht 5'8", black hair and eyes, black complexion; occupation laborer; enlisted in 25th Infantry at age 20, Washington, DC, 19 Apr 1886; arrived Ft Snelling, MN, 17 Sep 1886. SOURCE: Descriptive & Assignment Rolls of Recruits, 25 Inf.

‡Born in St. Francisville, LA, to Lewis and Maria Crump, 1867; enlisted Washington, DC; Ht 5'9", occupation porter, 16 Apr 1885; discharged, Ft Meade, SD, as sergeant, H/25th Infantry; enlisted Baltimore, MD, 10 Jun 1889; discharged Ft Leavenworth, KS, 9 Sep 1892; retired from Washington public schools as steam engineer, with $100 per month pension, 1932; military pension $45 per month, 1932; wife earned $3,100 from Washington public schools, 1932; died 21 Nov 1947; buried Arlington National Cemetery. SOURCE: VA File C 2359804, Edward W. Crump.

‡Served with Sgt. Barney McKay, C/9th Cavalry, Ft DuChesne, UT, 1889–90; was with detachment commanded by McKay which went to crossing of Uintah River, around thirteen miles from post, as escort for Chaplain Scott, Mar 1889; with river over banks, waded through cold water from around 9 A.M. to sundown; many contracted colds and rheumatism, including McKay, who was hospitalized. SOURCE: Affidavit, Crump, 1917, VA File XC 2659455, Barney McKay.

‡Lived with wife Sadie in Washington at 406 Franklin Street, NW, in 1894; at 1903 9 1/2 Street, NW, in 1895; at 117 U Street, NW, from 1933; pension of $55 per month as of 12 Aug 1942, increased to $60 as of 5 Jun 1944. SOURCE: VA Vile C 2359804, Edward W. Crump.

Renews subscription; is in good health, never drank, smoked, or gambled. SOURCE: *Winners of the West* 15 (Jul 1938): 8.

CULLINS, John; Private; G/10th Cav. Died 19 Jul 1867 of cholera at Ft Harker, KS. SOURCE: Regimental Returns, 10th Cavalry, 1867.

CUMBY, George; Trumpeter; H/9th Cav. ‡Died of variola in the Philippines, 31 Dec 1901. SOURCE: *ANJ* 39 (1 Mar 1902): 645.

CUMMINGS, Cicero; 24th Inf. *See* **STARKS**, Cicero, 24th Infantry

CUMMINGS, Robert; Private; G/9th Cav. Died at Ft Stockton, TX, on 5 Nov 1873; buried at San Antonio National Cemetery, Section C, number 442. SOURCE: San Antonio National Cemetery Locator.

CUMMINS, George; F/9th Cav. Born in Panama, Central America; black complexion; can read and write, age 23, Jul 1870, at Ft McKavett, TX. SOURCE: Bierschwale, *Fort McKavett,* 98.

CUNNINGHAM, Charles; Private; K/9th Cav. Born 1844 in Franklin County, PA, son of Mary Ann Brady; sister Jennie V. Cunningham; Civil War veteran; enlisted in F/54th Massachusetts Regiment on 8 Apr 1863; Ht 5'8", black hair and eyes, black complexion; discharged 20 Aug 1865; married Frances Smith in Middletown, Dauphin County, PA, 1868; daughters Sarah Williams born 1870 and Charlotte Finkbone born around 1872; married to Mary Ray, who died; enlisted 16 Dec 1872, assigned to K/9th Cavalry; served at Ft Lewis, CO; Ft Henry, NM; Ft Stanton, NM; Ft Bayard, NM; Rock Creek, CO, and Ft Wingate, NM; attacked by Mexican with an axe while asleep at Pedro's Ranch 1 Jan 1880, on duty as mounted courier between Rio Peidea and Animas City, CO; suffered wound to face; discharged because of disability 6 June 1888; mother lived at 308 Mulberry St., Dauphin, PA, in 1898; he died 8 Aug 1906 of Bright's disease. SOURCE: Greene, *Swamp Angels*, 74.

CUNNINGHAM, George; Private; H/10th Cav. ‡Sick in Ft Robinson, NE, hospital, 19 Sep–20 Oct 1904.

Died 29 Jan 1905; buried at Ft Bayard, NM, in plot H 12. SOURCE: "Fort Bayard National Cemetery, Records of Burials."

Buried 29 Jan 1905, section A, row K, plot 14 at Ft Bayard. SOURCE: Erickson, Burials at Fort Bayard National Cemetery, NM.

CUNNINGHAM, Henry; Private; F/24th Inf. Died 18 Dec 1899; buried in plot NADD 476 at San Francisco National Cemetery. SOURCE: San Francisco National Cemetery.

CURTIS, John H.; Private; M/9th Cav. Died 21 Jul 1879; originally buried at Ft Stanton, NM; buried Jun 1896 at Santa Fe National Cemetery, NM, plot B 559. SOURCE: Santa Fe National Cemetery, Records of Burials.

CURTIS, William H.; F/9th Cav. Born in Massachusetts; mulatto complexion; can read and write, age 24, Jul 1870, at Ft McKavett, TX. SOURCE: Bierschwale, *Fort McKavett,* 98.

CUSTARD, Elijah; Corporal; M/25th Inf. ‡Promoted from private, Aug 1905; died Sep 1905.

Died 17 Sep 1905; buried at Ft Niobrara Post Cemetery. SOURCE: Ft Niobrara Post Cemetery, Complete Listing.

Died 17 Sep 1905; originally buried at Ft Niobrara, NE; reburied at Ft Leavenworth National Cemetery, plot 3536. SOURCE: Ft Leavenworth National Cemetery.

CUTHBERT, John F.; Sergeant; G/9th Cav. Received Cuban Campaign Badge for service as private in C/25th Infantry, 22 Jun 1898–13 Aug 1898. SOURCE: Cuban Campaign Badge Recipients.

Received Philippine Campaign Badge number 11807 for service as private in G/9th Cavalry, 3 Mar 1902–16 Sep 1902; sergeant in G/9th Cavalry, Ft Leavenworth, KS, Mar 1905. SOURCE: Philippine Campaign Badge Recipients; Philippine Campaign Badge list, 29 May 1905.

D

DADE, Allen; Private; B/9th Cav. Recruited from St. Louis, MO; threatened at gunpoint by Sgt. Brent Woods, Apr 1880. SOURCE: Kenner, *Buffalo Soldiers and Officers of the Ninth Cavalry*, 228.

‡Pvt. Allan Dade, B/9th Cavalry, on detached service, Ft Bayard, NM, 16 Jan–9 Feb 1881. SOURCE: Regt Returns, 9 Cav, Feb 1881.

DALE, Thomas; Corporal; H/9th Cav. ‡Served in Lincoln County, NM, war, 1878. SOURCE: Leckie, *The Buffalo Soldiers*, 198.

‡Assigned with three privates to aid sheriff in maintaining order, Lincoln, NM, Apr 1878. SOURCE: Billington, *New Mexico's Buffalo Soldiers*, 75.

DALLAS, George M.; Private; G/25th Inf. Died at Ft Davis, TX, 5 May 1872; buried at San Antonio National Cemetery, Section I, number 1508. SOURCE: San Antonio National Cemetery Locator.

DAMMOND, John W.; Private; E/10th Cav. In Troop E/10th Cavalry stationed at Bonita Cañon Camp, AZ, 28 Feb 1886. Tagg questions spelling of Dammond. SOURCE: Tagg, *The Camp at Bonita Cañon*, 231.

DANCE, William; Private; K/24th Inf. ‡Died of malaria in the Philippines, 25 Nov 1899. SOURCE: *ANJ* 37 (13 Jan 1900): 463.

‡Native of Richmond, died of fever in the Philippines "through bad treatment." SOURCE: Richmond *Planet,* 14 Apr 1900.

Died 25 Nov 1899; buried in plot 1245 at San Francisco National Cemetery. SOURCE: San Francisco National Cemetery.

DANDRIDGE, Luther; Private; G/10th Cav. Pvt. Luther Dandridge, C/10th Cavalry, acquitted by military court of mutiny, 1871. SOURCE: Dobak and Phillips, *The Black Regulars*, 324–25.

‡Commander, 10th Cavalry, refers the charges of petty larceny against him to field officers' court for trial, 19 Jun 1873. SOURCE: ES, 10 Cav, 1873–83.

DANDRIDGE, Richard; Private; F/10th Cav. ‡Original member of 10th Cavalry; in troop when organized, Ft Leavenworth, KS, 21 Jun 1867. SOURCE: McMiller, "Buffalo Soldiers," 73.

Died 1 Aug 1867 of cholera at Ft Hays, KS. SOURCE: Regimental Returns, 10th Cavalry, 1867.

DANIEL, Lawrence; Private; B/25th Inf. Enlisted 2 Jun 1905, discharged without honor 19 Nov 1906. SOURCE: Powell, "Military Record of the Enlisted Men Who Were Discharged Without Honor."

Dishonorable discharge, Brownsville, TX. SOURCE: SO 266, AGO, 9 Nov 1906.

DANIELS, Caesar; Private; U.S. Army. Born in Texas; enlisted at Ft Clark, TX, 8 Mar 1901, age 29, occupation horse breaker; Ht 5'8", black hair, brown eyes, dark complexion; discharged 7 Mar 1904 at Ft Ringgold, TX, where he reenlisted next day; discharged 7 Mar 1907 at Ft Clark where he reenlisted next day; discharged and reenlisted 7 Mar 1910 at Ft Clark; discharged 7 Mar 1913 at Ft Clark where he reenlisted next day; honorably discharged at Ft Clark 31 Aug 1914 with thirteen years five months service; died 19 Jun 1919; buried at Seminole Cemetery. SOURCE: Swanson, 7.

Seminole Negro Scout, served 1901–14. SOURCE: Schubert, Consolidated List of Seminole Negro Scouts.

Buried at Seminole Indian Scout Cemetery, Kinney County, TX. SOURCE: Indian Scout Cemetery, Kinney County, Texas.

DANIELS, Charles; Sergeant; U.S. Army. Born in Mexico; enlisted at Ft Duncan, TX, 7 Oct 1871, age 17; Ht 5'8", black hair and eyes, black complexion; discharged 7 Apr 1872 at Ft Duncan, enlisted next day; discharged and reenlisted at Ft Clark, TX, 14 Oct 1872; discharged 14 Oct 1872 at Ft Clark, reenlisted next day; discharged, reenlisted for six months three more times at Ft Clark; discharged at Camp Pecos, TX, 7 Aug 1876; enlisted 29 Jan 1877, discharged 19 Jan 1878 at Ft Clark; three times enlisted for one year, discharged as private at Ft Clark, 1 Feb 1878–12 May 1881; corporal 1 Feb 1879; twice enlisted, discharged as sergeant at Ft Clark 13 May 1881–22 May 1883;

discharged as sergeant at Camp Myers, TX, 22 May 1884; enlisted at Ft Clark 26 May 1884; discharged as private 3 Jun 1885, reenlisted as private next day at Camp Neville, TX; discharged 3 June 1886 at Ft Clark; enlisted at Ft Clark 16 Aug 1892; discharged 15 Feb 1893, enlisted next day at Camp Agua Nueva, TX; discharged 15 July 1893, reenlisted next day at Ft Ringgold, TX; discharged as corporal 15 Feb 1894, reenlisted next day at Camp San Pedro, TX; discharged as sergeant 15 Aug 1894, reenlisted for six months next day at Ft Ringgold; discharged as sergeant 14 Feb 1895, reenlisted for three years four times as sergeant 17 Feb 1898–17 Feb 1907 at Ft Ringgold; retired at Ft Clark as sergeant 4 Oct 1909; died 10 Jan 1931; buried Brackettville, TX, cemetery. SOURCE: Swanson, 8.

Seminole Negro Scout, served 1871–86, 1892–1909; retired. SOURCE: Schubert, Consolidated List of Seminole Negro Scouts.

Charlie Daniels, Seminole Negro Scout. SOURCE: Schubert, *Black Valor*, 36.

Promoted from private to first sergeant Jun 1884. SOURCE: NARA, M929, Roll 2.

DANIELS, Edward L.; Corporal; B/25th Inf. Enlisted 18 Jan 1894, discharged as private K/25th Infantry 17 Jan 1899, character excellent; reenlisted 18 Jan 1899, discharged sergeant 17 Jan 1902, character excellent; reenlisted 18 Jan 1902, discharged as sergeant L/25th Infantry 26 Nov 1902, character excellent; enlisted 18 July 1904, discharged without honor as corporal 22 Nov 1906, Brownsville, TX. SOURCE: Powell, "Military Record of the Enlisted Men Who Were Discharged Without Honor."

‡Dishonorable discharge, Brownsville. SOURCE: SO 266, AGO, 9 Nov 1906.

‡Veteran of Cuban campaign, skilled at topographical sketches; one of fourteen cleared of involvement in Brownsville raid by court in 1910 and authorized to reenlist. SOURCE: Weaver, *The Brownsville Raid*, 32, 298.

DANIELS, Elijah; Private; U.S. Army. Seminole Negro Scout, served 1871–76; father of Bill Daniels and Scout John Daniels; pension file in National Archives. SOURCE: Schubert, Consolidated List of Seminole Negro Scouts.

Born in Arkansas; enlisted at Ft Duncan, TX, 7 Oct 1871, age 40; Ht 5'10", black hair and eyes, black complexion; discharged 24 Apr 1872 at Ft Duncan where he reenlisted; discharged 14 Oct 1872 at Ft Clark, TX; enlisted 9 Oct 1872, discharged 9 Apr 1873 as private at Ft Clark; enlisted 10 Apr 1873, discharged as sergeant 10 Oct 1873 at Ft Clark; reenlisted 10 Oct 1873, discharged as private 10 Apr 1874 at Ft Clark; reenlisted 10 Apr 1874, discharged as sergeant 11 Dec 1874 at Ft Clark; enlisted 26 Dec 1874, discharged as sergeant 22 Jun 1875 at Ft Clark; enlisted 27 Nov 1875 at Ft Clark; discharged as private at Camp Pecos, TX, 2 May 1876; enlisted 20 May 1876, discharged as private 21 Nov 1876 at Ft Clark; may have been

"chief" of the Seminole Negroes at Ft Clark after 7 Sep 1878 death of Scout John Kibbitts; died 12 Jan 1908; buried at Seminole Cemetery. SOURCE: Swanson, 9, 27.

Leader of Creek Negroes on Nueces River, Uvalde County, TX, 1870; first sergeant in 1876; invalid claim, VA invalid claim 1411757 filed 1906. SOURCE: NARA Record Group 393, Special File; Porter, *Negro on the American Frontier,* 474; Schubert, "Seminole-Negro Scouts."

Buried at Seminole Indian Scout Cemetery, Kinney County, TX. SOURCE: Indian Scout Cemetery, Kinney County, Texas.

DANIELS, Hayes; Private; G/9th Cav. ‡Served in 10th Cavalry, 1898; remained in U.S. during war with Spain. SOURCE: Cashin, *Under Fire with the Tenth Cavalry*, 350.

Received Philippine Campaign Badge number 11825 for service starting in 3 Nov 1901 as private in M/25th Infantry; private in G/9th Cavalry, Ft Leavenworth, KS, Mar 1905. SOURCE: Philippine Campaign Badge Recipients; Philippine Campaign Badge list, 29 May 1905.

DANIELS, Jerremiah; Private; F/9th Cav. Died at Ft Davis, TX, 31 Jan 1868; buried at San Antonio National Cemetery, Section I, number 1551. SOURCE: San Antonio National Cemetery Locator.

DANIELS, Jerry; Sergeant; U.S. Army. Born in Mexico; enlisted at Ft Duncan, TX, 31 Aug 1871, age 22; Ht 5'10", black hair and eyes, black complexion; discharged, reenlisted 29 Feb 1872 at Ft Duncan; discharged 30 Aug 1872 at Ft Clark, TX, where he reenlisted for six months three consecutive times starting 9 Sept 1872; discharged at Ft Clark 27 Mar 1874; enlisted 18 Jun 1874; discharged 25 Dec 1874 at Ft Clark where he reenlisted 8 Feb 1876; discharged as corporal 7 Aug 1876 at Ft Clark; enlisted 9 Feb 1878, discharged as corporal 24 Feb 1879 at Ft Clark; enlisted 25 Apr 1879 at Ft Clark; appointed sergeant 31 May 1879 by SO 113; discharged at Ft Clark 1 May 1880; 1880 Census lists occupation as farmer, wife Jam age 24, daughter Judia age 7; died 29 Jan 1925; buried at Seminole Cemetery. SOURCE: Swanson, 9.

Invalid VA claim filed in 1913. SOURCE: NARA Record Group 393, Special File.

Seminole Negro Scout, served 1871–76, 1878–80; pension file in National Archives. SOURCE: Schubert, Consolidated List of Seminole Negro Scouts.

Buried at Seminole Indian Scout Cemetery, Kinney County, TX. SOURCE: Indian Scout Cemetery, Kinney County, Texas.

DANIELS, John; Private; U.S. Army. Born in Texas; enlisted at Ft Clark, TX, 29 June 1907, age 37; Ht 5'7", black hair and eyes, black complexion; discharged 28 Jun 1910, reenlisted next day at Ft Clark; discharged 28 Jun 1913, reenlisted next day at Ft Clark; honorably discharged 31

June 1914, age 43, when actively enlisted Seminole Scouts were terminated; died 5 July 1923; buried at Seminole Cemetery. SOURCE: Swanson, 10.

Seminole Negro Scout, served 1907–14; brother of Bill Daniels and son of Scout Elijah Daniels. SOURCE: Schubert, Consolidated List of Seminole Negro Scouts; Porter, "Negro on the American Frontier," 474.

Buried at Seminole Indian Scout Cemetery, Kinney County, TX. SOURCE: Indian Scout Cemetery, Kinney County, Texas.

DANIELS, Thomas; Private; U.S. Army. Seminole Negro Scout, served 1894–1909. SOURCE: Schubert, Consolidated List of Seminole Negro Scouts.

Born in Texas; enlisted at Ft Clark, TX, 23 Jan 1894, age 22; Ht 5'6", black hair and eyes, black complexion; discharged 22 July 1894 at Ft Ringgold, TX, where he reenlisted next day; discharged 30 Nov 1894 at Ft Ringgold; enlisted 4 Oct 1897 at Ft Clark; discharged 2 Oct 1900 at Ft Ringgold where he reenlisted next day; discharged 3 Oct 1903 at Ft Ringgold where he reenlisted next day; discharged at Ft Clark 4 Oct 1906; reenlisted 6 Oct 1906 at age 31; discharged 5 Oct 1909 at Ft Clark; died 5 Jul 1923; buried at Seminole Cemetery. SOURCE: Swanson, 10.

DANNELL, Milton; Private; B/10th Cav. Died 7 Oct 1878, cause not stated, at Ft Clark, TX. SOURCE: Regimental Returns, 10th Cavalry, 1878.

DANNELS, Milton; Private; 10th Cav. Died, post hospital, Ft Stockton, TX, Apr 1879; mother, Mrs. Arnold, resides in Macon, GA. SOURCE: Kinevan, *Frontier Cavalryman*, 162.

DAVIS, Benjamin F.; Private; G/10th Cav. Died 25 Jul 1867 of cholera at Wilson Creek, KS. SOURCE: Regimental Returns, 10th Cavalry, 1867.

DAVIS, Benjamin F.; Post QM Sgt; U.S. Army. ‡Original member of M/10th Cavalry; in troop when organized, Ft Riley, KS, 15 Oct 1867. SOURCE: McMiller, "Buffalo Soldiers," 79.

‡Joined regiment in 1867; retired as post quartermaster sergeant. SOURCE: Baker, Roster.

‡Appointed post quartermaster sergeant, from regimental sergeant major, 9th Cavalry, 20 Jan 1885. SOURCE: Roster, 9 Cav.

Appointed post quartermaster sergeant 8 Jan 1885, from regimental sergeant major, 9th Cavalry. SOURCE: Dobak, "Staff Noncommissioned Officers."

Born in Pennsylvania; veteran of 32nd U.S. Colored Infantry; served two enlistments in 10th Cavalry before serving for five years as sergeant major, 9th Cavalry; became post quartermaster sergeant, 1885; married 1886 at home of Sgt. and Mrs. John H. Ferguson, 9th Cavalry. SOURCE: Dobak and Phillips, *The Black Regulars*, 82, 141.

‡Retired Ft Robinson, NE, after reception and banquet, 23 Apr 1895, with nineteen years as regimental sergeant major and post quartermaster sergeant. SOURCE: Cleveland *Gazette*, 4 May 1895.

‡Knew Robert Benjamin from Jun 1874 until his death; soldiered together in Texas, corresponded and kept track of each other; best man at Benjamin's wedding to Mary Young, Junction City, KS; now age 69 and residing at 1615 17th St., NW, Washington, DC. SOURCE: Affidavit, Davis, 9 Dec 1918, VA File WC 927337, Robert A. Benjamin.

Retired sergeant, issued Indian Wars Campaign Badge number 1102 on 4 Jan 1909; badge reported lost 24 Feb 1911, replaced by number 1494. SOURCE: Carroll, *Indian Wars Campaign Badge*, 32.

‡Born in Chester Co., PA, 1849; Civil War veteran; served over thirty-one years; appointed quartermaster sergeant, 1885; died 9 Nov 1921; buried with military honors, Soldiers Home Cemetery, Washington, DC; survived by widow, three daughters, three grandchildren; was member of National Association for the Advancement of Colored People. SOURCE: *Crisis* 24 (May 1922): 27.

DAVIS, Benjamin O.; Brig Gen; U.S. Army. Life and career summarized; sergeant at Ft DuChesne, UT, mentored and tutored for qualifying examination for commission by Lt. Charles Young in 1901. SOURCE: Kenner, *Buffalo Soldiers and Officers of the Ninth Cavalry*, 308–9.

Served as first lieutenant, G/8th Inf, USV, at Fort Thomas, KY, and Chickamauga, GA, 1898; article on him by Thomas H. R. Clarke, in *Colored American Magazine* (Washington, DC), 18 May 1901, reprinted. SOURCE: Schubert, *Voices of the Buffalo Soldier*, 218–20.

‡First colored man to pass examination for regular Army commission, Ft Leavenworth, KS, and scored third of eighteen who took test; son of Messenger Davis of office of Secretary of the Interior; was major, Washington Colored High School cadet corps; former lieutenant, 8th U.S. Volunteer Infantry; then enlisted in 9th Cavalry and served one year as squadron sergeant major. SOURCE: Richmond *Planet*, 30 Mar 1901.

One of two blacks among 1,464 men who received regular Army commissions between 30 Dec 1898 and 30 Jun 1901. SOURCE: Schubert, *Black Valor*, 158.

‡Appointment as second lieutenant, 10th Cavalry, dates from 2 Feb 1901. SOURCE: *ANJ* 38 (1 Jun 1901): 966.

‡First black officer commissioned from ranks into regular Army. SOURCE: Indianapolis *Freeman*, 15 Jun 1901.

‡Graduate of Washington Colored High School. SOURCE: *The Voice of the Negro* 1 (Jun 1904): 222.

‡Arrived Ft Washakie, WY, from Rawlins, WY. SOURCE: Fremont *Clipper*, 22 Aug 1902.

‡Was in Lander, WY, shopping with his wife last Saturday. SOURCE: Fremont *Clipper*, 19 Dec 1902.

‡One of 300 enlisted men commissioned from the ranks into regular Army, 1898–1902, but one of only two, with John E. Green, who were black. SOURCE: Fletcher, *The Black Soldier*, 165.

‡Returned to Ft Washakie from thirty-day leave in Washington, DC, where his wife will spend winter. SOURCE: Fremont *Clipper*, 30 Dec 1904.

‡Promoted to first lieutenant, Apr 1905; arrived Ft Robinson, NE, 21 Apr 1905; commander, M/10th Cavalry, 24–29 May and 23–28 Jun 1905; absent with leave, 4–15 Jun 1905; on detached service at Wilberforce University, OH, 27 Aug 1905, in accordance with Special Order 166, Adjutant General's Office, 1905. SOURCE: Post Returns, Ft Robinson.

‡Detailed to Wilberforce as military instructor. SOURCE: Indianapolis *Freeman*, 21 Oct 1905.

‡Dropped from post returns, Ft Robinson, May 1907; still at Wilberforce. Named military attaché to Liberia, a new position established to develop closer relations. SOURCE: Cleveland *Gazette*, 4 Dec 1909.

‡Will return from Liberia to duty with 9th Cavalry, Ft D. A. Russell, WY. SOURCE: Cleveland *Gazette*, 13 Jan 1912.

‡Joined regiment from duty as military attaché in Africa. SOURCE: Cheyenne *State Leader*, 19 Jan 1912.

‡Mentioned. SOURCE: Work, *The Negro Yearbook, 1912*, 77.

‡Assigned as military instructor at Wilberforce. SOURCE: Cleveland *Gazette*, 5 Sep 1914.

‡As military instructor and commander at Wilberforce. SOURCE: Joiner, *A Half Century of Freedom*, 108.

‡Recently promoted to lieutenant colonel from major. SOURCE: Cleveland *Gazette*, 14 Sep 1918.

‡Mentioned. SOURCE: Work, *The Negro Yearbook, 1918–1919*, 228.

DAVIS, Charles; D/24th Inf. Born in Kentucky; black complexion; can read and write, age 24, Jul 1870, at Ft McKavett, TX. SOURCE: Bierschwale, *Fort McKavett,* 95.

DAVIS, Charles D.; Private; 9th Cav. Received Philippine Campaign Badge number 11722 for service as private in D/49th Infantry, United States Volunteers; in 9th Cavalry at Ft Leavenworth, KS, Mar 1905. SOURCE: Philippine Campaign Badge list, 29 May 1905.

DAVIS, Charles H.; M/9th Cav. Born in Pennsylvania; mulatto complexion; can read and write, age 24, Jul 1870, at Ft McKavett, TX. SOURCE: Bierschwale, *Fort McKavett*, 99.

DAVIS, Edward; 9th Cav. Born in England; mulatto complexion; can read and write, age 22, Jul 1870, at Ft McKavett, TX. SOURCE: Bierschwale, *Fort McKavett*, 106.

DAVIS, Edward; Private; K/9th Cav. ‡Private, D/9th Cavalry, in hands of civil authorities, Buffalo, WY, 1–18 May 1890, and Crawford, NE, 28–30 Mar 1893. SOURCE: Regt Returns, 9 Cav.

‡Discharge disapproved. SOURCE: Letter, AGO, 15 Apr 1895.

‡Charges withdrawn. SOURCE: Letter, DP, 11 Sep 1895.

‡Discharged, end of term, private, H/9th Cavalry, with $8 clothing and $47 retained pay, 22 Apr 1897. SOURCE: CO, H/9, to Chief PM, DP, 17 Apr 1897, LS, H/9 Cav.

‡Wounded in action at San Juan, Cuba, 2 Jul 1898; suffering from scalp wound, blood streaming down his face, he waited only long enough for bandage, then joined troops in advance. SOURCE: SecWar, AR 1898, 707, 709.

‡Awarded certificate of merit for distinguished service in Cuba, Jul 1898. SOURCE: Steward, *The Colored Regulars*, 280; *ANJ* 37 (24 Feb 1900): 611.

Private, H/9th Cavalry, awarded certificate of merit for distinguished service in battle, Santiago, Cuba, 1 Jul 1898. SOURCE: Gleim, *The Certificate of Merit*, 45.

Born in Nashville, TN; resided San Antonio, TX; received Distinguished Service Medal in lieu of certificate of merit. SOURCE: *American Decorations*, 835.

‡Commended for gallantry, 1 Jul 1898. SOURCE: GO 15, AGO, 13 Feb 1900.

Received Philippine Campaign Badge number 11826 for service as private in G/9th Cavalry, 3 Mar 1902–16 Sep 1902; private in G/9th Cavalry, Ft Leavenworth, KS, Mar 1905. SOURCE: Philippine Campaign Badge Recipients; Philippine Campaign Badge list, 29 May 1905.

‡Veteran of Indian wars, Spanish-American War, and Philippine Insurrection; private, K/9th Cavalry, at Ft D. A. Russell, WY, in 1910; resident of Galveston, TX. SOURCE: *Illustrated Review: Ninth Cavalry*, with picture.

Retired sergeant, K/9th Cavalry; died 10 Apr 1934; buried in plot C 830 at San Francisco National Cemetery. SOURCE: San Francisco National Cemetery.

DAVIS, Edward; Corporal; 9th Cav. Received Philippine Campaign Badge number 11871 for service as corporal in L/9th Cavalry; in 9th Cavalry at Ft Leavenworth, KS, Mar 1905. SOURCE: Philippine Campaign Badge list, 29 May 1905.

DAVIS, Edward; Private; K/9th Cav. Issued Indian Wars Campaign Badge number 1544 on 3 Dec 1909. SOURCE: Carroll, *Indian Wars Campaign Badge*, 45.

DAVIS, George; F/9th Cav. Born in Louisiana; mulatto complexion; cannot read or write, age 23, Jul 1870, at Ft McKavett, TX. SOURCE: Bierschwale, *Fort McKavett*, 97.

DAVIS, George; F/9th Cav. Born in Kentucky; black complexion; can read, cannot write, age 21, Jul 1870, at Ft McKavett, TX. SOURCE: Bierschwale, *Fort McKavett*, 96

DAVIS Henry; Private; D/25th Inf. Died 10 Mar 1902; buried in plot WSIDE363 NA at San Francisco National Cemetery. SOURCE: San Francisco National Cemetery.

DAVIS, Isom; Private; D/9th Cav. Died at Ft Stockton, TX, on 21 Jul 1868; buried at San Antonio National Cemetery, Section C, number 414. SOURCE: San Antonio National Cemetery Locator.

DAVIS, Jacob P.; Private; B/10th Cav. Died 22 Jun 1881 in hospital at Ft Concho, TX. SOURCE: Regimental Returns, 10th Cavalry, 1881.

Died at Ft Concho on 22 Jun 1881; buried at San Antonio National Cemetery, Section E, number 829. SOURCE: San Antonio National Cemetery Locator.

DAVIS, James; Corporal; M/10th Cav. ‡Original member of 10th Cavalry; in troop when organized, Ft Riley, KS, 15 Sep 1867. SOURCE: McMiller, "Buffalo Soldiers," 79.

Injured by horse, died 14 Aug 1868 at Ft Arbuckle, OK. SOURCE: Regimental Returns, 10th Cavalry, 1868.

DAVIS, James A.; Saddler; E/9th Cav. Died 20 Sep 1901; buried in plot NADD 1387 at San Francisco National Cemetery. SOURCE: San Francisco National Cemetery.

DAVIS, Jerry; Sergeant; U.S. Army. Seminole Negro Scout, served 1878–79. SOURCE: Schubert, Consolidated List of Seminole Negro Scouts.

Promoted from private to corporal Mar 1878; appointed sergeant May 1878. SOURCE: NARA, M 929, Roll 2.

DAVIS, Jerry A.; Private; G/9th Cav. ‡Admonished by commander, Ft Robinson, NE, that he is obligated to send his school-age children to class; under no circumstances will they be allowed to loiter around barracks during school hours. SOURCE: CO, Ft Robinson, to Private Davis, 22 Mar 1893, LS, Ft Robinson.

‡His wife's sister is visiting Ft Robinson, early Apr 1893. SOURCE: Ft Robinson Weekly Bulletin, 5 Apr 1893, filed with Court Martial Records, McKay.

Died 6 Apr 1893 of disease in post hospital, Ft Robinson. SOURCE: Buecker, Fort Robinson Burials.

‡His funeral at Ft Robinson, 7 Apr 1893. SOURCE: Order 26, 6 Apr 1893, Post Orders, Ft Robinson; List of Interments, Ft Robinson.

DAVIS, John; Corporal; F/24th Inf. Died at Ft Davis, TX, on 13 Jan 1872; buried at San Antonio National Cemetery, Section I, number 1549. SOURCE: San Antonio National Cemetery Locator.

DAVIS, John; Private; E/10th Cav. In Troop E/10th Cavalry stationed at Bonita Cañon Camp, AZ, 28 Feb 1886. SOURCE: Tagg, *The Camp at Bonita Cañon*, 231.

DAVIS, John; Private; E/9th Cav. Died 9 Aug 1888; originally buried at Ft Grant, AZ, buried at Santa Fe National Cemetery, NM, plot A-1 783. SOURCE: Santa Fe National Cemetery, Records of Burials.

DAVIS, John W.; Private; 25th Inf. Born in Sandy Spring, MD; Ht 5'6", black hair and eyes, black complexion; occupation laborer; enlisted at age 21, Washington, DC, 21 May 1886; arrived Ft Snelling, MN, 17 Sep 1886. SOURCE: Descriptive & Assignment Rolls of Recruits, 25 Inf.

DAVIS, Joseph; C/25th Inf. Born in Ohio; black complexion; can read and write, age 22, 6 Sep 1870, at Ft McKavett, TX. SOURCE: Bierschwale, *Fort McKavett*, 110.

DAVIS, Martin; Private; C/10th Cav. ‡Stationed at Ft Davis, TX, at time of death. SOURCE: SecWar, AR 1880, 149.

‡Killed in action against Victorio, Eagle Springs, TX, 30 Jul 1880; street in Wharry housing area, Ft Huachuca, AZ, formerly named for him. SOURCE: Orville A. Cochran to H. B. Wharfield, 5 Apr 1965, 10th Cavalry papers, MHI; Leckie, *The Buffalo Soldiers*, 225.

Killed in action, 30 Jul 1880. SOURCE: Regimental Returns, 10th Cavalry, 1880.

DAVIS, Nelson E.; Private; H/10th Cav. In Troop H/10th Cavalry stationed at Bonita Cañon Camp, AZ, but absent or on detached service 30 Apr 1886. SOURCE: Tagg, *The Camp at Bonita Cañon*, 231.

DAVIS, Richard; Corporal; F/24th Inf. Died 1 Jul 1888; buried at Ft Bayard, NM, in plot G 21. SOURCE: "Fort Bayard National Cemetery, Records of Burials."

Buried 1 Jul 1888, section A, row I, plot 23 at Ft Bayard. SOURCE: Erickson, Burials at Fort Bayard National Cemetery, NM.

DAVIS, Robert; Corporal; A/38th Inf. ‡At Ft Cummings, NM, autumn 1867; tried at Ft Selden, NM, Jan 1868, for role in soldier revolt; convicted of participation sentenced to dishonorable discharge and ten years at penitentiary, Jefferson City, MO. SOURCE: Billington, *New Mexico's Buffalo Soldiers*, 39–41.

Only one of seven 38th Infantrymen charged and convicted by military court of mutiny, New Mexico, 1868; others were acquitted. SOURCE: Dobak and Phillips, *The Black Regulars*, 324.

At Ft Selden, Jan 1868 trial of Cpl. Robert Davis, C/38th Infantry, defense counsel Thomas B. Catron challenged witness Yeatman's intelligence and competency to stand as witness, "being a Colored Man"; deemed competent by the Court, and Judge Advocate (prosecutor) would examine the witness Yeatman as he thought proper. SOURCE: Dobak, "Trial of Corporal Robert Davis."

DAVIS, S.; Sergeant; 38th Inf. Commanded detachment in skirmish with Indians, thirty miles west of Fort Hays, KS, 28–29 Jul 1867. SOURCE: Schubert, *Voices of the Buffalo Soldier*, 9.

DAVIS, Thomas J.; Private; D/9th Cav. ‡Died of dysentery at Pasacao, Philippines, 11 Oct 1900. SOURCE: Hamilton, "History of the Ninth Cavalry," 103; *Illustrated Review: Ninth Cavalry*.

Died 11 Oct 1900; buried in plot NADDN459 at San Francisco National Cemetery. SOURCE: San Francisco National Cemetery.

DAVIS, Will; Private; E/25th Inf. Died 18 Nov 1915; buried in plot WSIDE818-A at San Francisco National Cemetery. SOURCE: San Francisco National Cemetery.

DAVIS, William; Private; F/9th Cav. At Ft Reno, OK, Aug 1883, involved in argument with 1st Sgt. Emanuel Stance. SOURCE: Schubert, *Voices of the Buffalo Soldier*, 132.

Barracks dispute with Sgt. Emanuel Stance, Fort Reno, 1883, led to attempt by Pvt. Moses Green to kill Stance. SOURCE: Kenner, *Buffalo Soldiers and Officers of the Ninth Cavalry*, 166–67.

DAVIS, William H.; Ord Sgt; U.S. Army. Appointed ordnance sergeant 25 May 1886, from first sergeant, D/25th Infantry. SOURCE: Dobak, "Staff Noncommissioned Officers."

‡In D/25th Infantry served as first sergeant of company when soldier stuck fork in Pvt. George D. Crockett's eye; now age 50 and residing at Beaufort, Carteret Co., NC. SOURCE: Affidavit, Davis, 16 Feb 1891, VA File XC 2624113, George D. Crockett.

DAVIS, William J.; Private; I/25th Inf. ‡Died at Ft Niobrara, NE, 28 Mar 1906. SOURCE: Monthly Report, Chaplain Steward, 31 Mar 1906.

Died 28 Mar 1906, buried at Ft Niobrara Post Cemetery. SOURCE: Ft Niobrara Post Cemetery, Complete Listing.

DAWSON, John W.; Private; I/24th Inf. ‡Enlisted Raleigh, NC, 23 Mar 1899. SOURCE: Muster Roll, I/24 Inf, Mar–Apr 1899.

‡Absent sick in Manila, Philippines, since 9 Sep 1899. SOURCE: Muster Roll, I/24 Inf, Nov–Dec 1899.

Died 19 Jan 1911, buried at Ft Bayard, NM, in plot S 35. SOURCE: "Fort Bayard National Cemetery, Records of Burials."

Buried 19 Jan 1911, section B, row D, plot 35 at Ft Bayard. SOURCE: Erickson, Burials at Fort Bayard National Cemetery, NM.

DAWSON, Joseph; Sergeant; F/25th Inf. Died at Ft Stockton, TX, on 1 Feb 1879; buried at San Antonio National Cemetery, Section C, number 350. SOURCE: San Antonio National Cemetery Locator.

DAWSON, William; Private; I/10th Cav. In Troop I/10th Cavalry stationed at Bonita Cañon Camp, AZ, 30 Jun 1886. SOURCE: Tagg, *The Camp at Bonita Cañon*, 231.

DAY, Abram; 9th Cav. Born in Tennessee; mulatto complexion; can read, cannot write, age 22, 5 Sep 1870, at Ft McKavett, TX. SOURCE: Bierschwale, *Fort McKavett*, 107.

DAY, Charles W.; Private; 24th Inf. Mentioned. SOURCE: Dobak and Phillips, *The Black Regulars*, 164.

DAY, John; Private; I/9th Cav. Received as private Indian Wars Campaign Badge number 1885 on 23 Dec 1920. SOURCE: Carroll, *Indian Wars Campaign Badge*, 55.

DAY, Louis; Corporal; E/10th Cav. In Troop E/10th Cavalry stationed at Bonita Cañon Camp, AZ, but absent or on detached service 28 Feb 1886. SOURCE: Tagg, *The Camp at Bonita Cañon*, 231.

‡Sergeant, E/10th Cavalry, at Ft Apache, AZ, 1890, subscribed $.50 to testimonial to General Grierson. SOURCE: List of subscriptions, 23 Apr 1890, 10th Cavalry papers, MHI.

DAYES, Joseph; Private; F/9th Cav. Native of Mobile, AL; veteran of infantry service in New Mexico; discharged for disability; remained in New Mexico and worked as cook and servant for officers; enlisted in 9th Cavalry, age 29, Apr 1877; beaten and terrorized by Capt. Henry Carroll after failing to respond properly to commands; deserted, apprehended, received dishonorable discharge and two years, Jan 1880. SOURCE: Kenner, *Buffalo Soldiers and Officers of the Ninth Cavalry*, 159–60.

DeALEXANDER, Alexis; Private; K/25th Inf. Born in Chicago, IL; Ht 6'0", dark hair and brown eyes, yellow complexion; occupation miner; enlisted 18 Dec 1885, age 23, at St Louis, MO; assigned to K/25th Infantry; arrived Ft Snelling, MN, 26 Apr 1886. SOURCE: Descriptive & Assignment Rolls of Recruits, 25 Inf.

DEAN, John; Private; F/24th Inf. ‡Drowned crossing San Mateo River, Philippines, 21 Aug 1899. SOURCE: Richmond *Planet*, 2 Sep 1899.

Private, F/24th Infantry, died 21 Aug 1899; buried in plot 556 ESDE at San Francisco National Cemetery. SOURCE: San Francisco National Cemetery.

DEARING, Ruben; Private; C/10th Cav. ‡Saddler, L/10th Cavalry, served in regiment 1898; remained in U.S. during war with Spain. SOURCE: Cashin, *Under Fire with the Tenth Cavalry*, 350.

Received as private Indian Wars Campaign Badge number 1407 on 15 Jul 1909. SOURCE: Carroll, *Indian Wars Campaign Badge*, 40.

DeGRAFFEURILL, John; 9th Cav. Born in Kentucky; black complexion; can read and write, age 24, 5 Sep 1870, at Ft McKavett, TX. SOURCE: Bierschwale, *Fort McKavett*, 107.

DeGROAT, Curtis; Private; H/10th Cav. In Troop E/10th Cavalry stationed at Bonita Cañon Camp, AZ, 28 Feb 1886. SOURCE: Tagg, *The Camp at Bonita Cañon*, 231.

‡Private Degroat, H/10th Cavalry, at Ft Apache, AZ, 1890, subscribed $.50 to testimonial to General Grierson. SOURCE: List of subscriptions, 23 Apr 1890, 10th Cavalry papers, MHI.

DEHONEY, Peter; Private; C/10th Cav. Born in Columbia, KY, 6 Jul 1865; father Clark Dehoney enslaved, farmer, resided near Milltown, Adair County, KY; mother Livonia died of brain fever 1871; sister Lucilla C. Johnson, 777 West 25th St., Indianapolis, IN; brothers George A., John, James L., Abraham L., and Reason; enlisted Cleveland, OH, 8 Nov 1882; Ht 5'6"; dark complexion, dark brown eyes, black hair; occupation laborer and waiter; served in H/10th Cavalry; served at Ft Davis, TX, 1883–Apr 1885; at Ft Davis, Jan 1885, cavalry greatcoat stolen by Pvt. Scott Cain; at Ft Grant, AZ, May 1885; in the field July–Aug 1885 at Bonita Cañon, AZ; Apr–June 1885 on detached service at Whites Ranch and Turkey Creek, AZ; discharged Ft Apache, AZ, 7 Nov 1887; enlisted Ft Grant, 28 Jun 1889; discharged Ft Assiniboine, MT, 27 Sep 1892; married Elisa White, Moorhead, MN, 16 Feb 1916, no children; resided in Bismarck, ND, Minneapolis, MN, Fargo, ND; died 19 Oct 1951 at home, 567 8th Ave. N., Minneapolis; buried at Ft Snelling, MN, National Cemetery. SOURCE: Sayre, *Warriors of Color*, 23–28, 62–63, 144–56, 219.

In Troop H/10th Cavalry stationed at Bonita Cañon Camp, AZ, 30 Apr 1886. SOURCE: Tagg, *The Camp at Bonita Cañon*, 231.

DEMBY, Sheridan; Private; 25th Inf. Born in Philadelphia, PA; Ht 5'7", black hair and brown eyes, brown complexion; occupation sailor; enlisted at age 21, Baltimore, MD, 7 May 1886; arrived Ft Snelling, MN, 19 Aug 1886. SOURCE: Descriptive & Assignment Rolls of Recruits, 25 Inf.

Deserted during tenure of John Franklin as first sergeant, Jan 1869–May 1871. SOURCE: Dobak and Phillips, *The Black Regulars*, 300.

DEMPSEY, Patrick; Private; D/9th Cav. Died on 1 Sep 1907; buried at San Antonio National Cemetery, Section E, number 905. SOURCE: San Antonio National Cemetery Locator.

DENIS, John H.; Corporal; H/25th Inf. Private, 25th Infantry, born in Dorchester County, MD; Ht 5'9", black hair and eyes, brown complexion; occupation soldier; enlisted at age 30, Baltimore, MD, 2 Aug 1886; arrived Ft Snelling, MN, 17 Sep 1886. SOURCE: Descriptive & Assignment Rolls of Recruits, 25 Inf.

Corporal, H/25th Infantry, died 30 Nov 1900 on U.S. Army Transport *Hancock* en route to Manila, Philippines; buried in plot 1059 EAS at San Francisco National Cemetery. SOURCE: San Francisco National Cemetery.

DENMARK, Hamilton; Private; C/10th Cav. Died 13 Feb 1868 of disease at Ft Riley, KS. SOURCE: Regimental Returns, 10th Cavalry, 1868.

DENNIS, Albert; Private; I/9th Cav. Convicted of stealing gold watch from citizen, sentenced to dishonorable discharge and two years, but sentence overturned on technicality by reviewing authority, 1881. SOURCE: Kenner, *Buffalo Soldiers and Officers of the Ninth Cavalry*, 25.

DENNY, John; Sergeant; H/9th Cav. ‡Born in Big Flats, NY; Medal of Honor for service against Victorio in 1880 awarded to him later at Ft Robinson, NE. SOURCE: Carroll, *The Black Military Experience*, 413–14.

Led eight men on five-week scout of Magdalena Mountains, NM, winter 1877; chased deserters from Ft Bayard, NM, to town of Hillsborough, NM, 150 miles, with seven men, 1879. SOURCE: Dobak and Phillips, *The Black Regulars*, 258.

Life and career, including bravery against Apaches in 1879 for which he received the Medal of Honor, narrated. SOURCE: Schubert, *Black Valor*, 54–57, 83–86, 117, 171.

Struck by rheumatism, reduced to private in B/9th Cavalry, assigned as barracks orderly, Aug 1880; private in Apr 1881, carried dispatches by horseback between Deming, NM, and Ft Cummings, NM. SOURCE: Kenner, *Buffalo Soldiers and Officers of the Ninth Cavalry*, 228–29.

‡Awarded Medal of Honor for rescue of Private Freeland during battle of Las Animas, NM, Sep 1879. SOURCE: Billington, *New Mexico's Buffalo Soldiers*, 91.

‡Medal of Honor transmitted to him in letter, Adjutant General, U.S. Army, 10 Jan 1895.

‡Awarded Medal of Honor for distinguished service as private, C/9th Cavalry, against Apaches, removed wounded comrade to safety under fire, 18 Sep 1879; regimental commander, Col. James Biddle, says that "such acts of gallantry not only reflect credit upon the individual, but also on the organization to which he belongs, and the 9th Cavalry may well feel proud of having in its ranks a man so signally honored." SOURCE: *ANJ* 32 (26 Jan 1895): 358.

‡Promoted from lance corporal to corporal, C/9th Cavalry, Ft Robinson, NE, 23 Mar 1895. SOURCE: *ANJ* 32 (6 Apr 1895): 523; Ninth Cavalry, Roster of NCOs, 1897.

‡To retire, Ft Robinson, 11 Sep 1897. SOURCE: SO 205, AGO, 7 Sep 1897.

‡Employed at post exchange, Ft Robinson, Jan–Jun 1899; paid $10 per month. SOURCE: QM Consolidated File, Ft Robinson.

‡No Veterans Administration pension file.

DENT, Allen; F/9th Cav. Born in Maryland; black complexion; can read and write, age 22, Jul 1870, at Ft McKavett, TX. SOURCE: Bierschwale, *Fort McKavett*, 98.

DENT, Charles; F/9th Cav. Born in Washington, DC; black complexion; cannot read or write, age 21, Jul 1870, at Ft McKavett, TX. SOURCE: Bierschwale, *Fort McKavett*, 97.

DENT, Henry; Private; D/9th Cav. ‡Born in St. Mary's Co., MD, 29 Oct 1856; parents Henry L. Dent and Julia Dorsey of Maryland; Ht 5'6", enlisted, black complexion, occupation butler, 4 Jan 1878; served at Ft Riley, KS, Fts Selden and Craig, NM, Fts Garland and Lewis, CO, "which I helped to build"; discharged 3 Jan 1883; married Rosa B. Ross, age 25, Baltimore, MD, 27 Apr 1897; resided at 1434 Presstman, Baltimore; pensions: $30 per month, 5 Mar 1927, $40, 29 Oct 1928, $50, 1 Apr 1935, $55, 1 Sep 1937, $72, 26 Nov 1937; died 12 Sep 1938. Widow's pension $30 per month, 16 Sep 1938, $40, 21 Mar 1944; moved to 822 Carrollton Avenue, Baltimore, in 1947; died 11 Jan 1949. SOURCE: VA File C 2363092, Henry Dent.

With Captain Dodge at battle at Milk River, CO, 2–10 Oct 1879. SOURCE: Miller, *Hollow Victory*, 167, 206–7.

‡Former comrades in D/9th Cavalry, with locations, 6 Jul 1895: Edward Scott, private, Forest Glen, Montgomery Co., MD; Moses Coleman, private, Junction City, Geary Co., KS; Samuel Cornish, private, 122 Sharp Street, Baltimore; James Haskins, private, Pueblo, CO. SOURCE: VA File C 2363092, Henry Dent.

‡Served 1878–83; member, Camp 11, National Indian War Veterans, St. Joseph, MO; died recently, Baltimore. SOURCE: *Winners of the West* 16 (Dec 1938): 2.

DENT, Robert I.; Private; C/9th Cav. Died 13 Jan 1917; buried in plot ESIDE653-A at San Francisco National Cemetery. SOURCE: San Francisco National Cemetery.

DERCHILD, Joseph; Private; C/9th Cav. Died 13 Jun 1879; buried at Ft Bayard, NM, in plot B 12. SOURCE: "Fort Bayard National Cemetery, Records of Burials."

Joseph Derchilo, C/9th Cavalry, buried at Ft Bayard. SOURCE: "Fort Bayard National Cemetery, Records of Burials."

Buried 13 Jun 1879, section A, row B, plot 31 at Ft Bayard. SOURCE: Erickson, Burials at Fort Bayard National Cemetery, NM.

DERRICK, Samuel; Sergeant; G/24th Inf. Died 15 Jan 1892; buried at Ft Bayard, NM, in plot I 34. SOURCE: "Fort Bayard National Cemetery, Records of Burials."

Samuel Derrick, Sergeant, C/24th Infantry, buried at Ft Bayard. SOURCE: "Buffalo Soldiers Buried at Ft Bayard, NM."

Buried 15 Jan 1892, section A, row M, plot 37 at Ft Bayard. SOURCE: Erickson, Burials at Fort Bayard National Cemetery, NM.

DERWIN, Isaac; Private; A/10th Cav. ‡Died on Staked Plains expedition, Aug 1877. SOURCE: Leckie, *The Buffalo Soldiers*, 161.

Died 31 Jul 1877 of exhaustion at Staked Plains, TX. SOURCE: Regimental Returns, 10th Cavalry, 1877.

‡Final statement of deceased Derwin transmitted by commander, 10th Cavalry, to Adjutant General's Office, 3 Sep 1877. SOURCE: ES, 10 Cav, 1873–81.

DESAUSSURE, Carolina; Private; B/25th Inf. Enlisted 12 Apr 1899, discharged as private C/25th Infantry 30 May 1902, character very good; reenlisted 8 Aug 1902, discharged as private B/25th Infantry 7 Aug 1905, character very good; reenlisted 18 Aug 1905, discharged without honor 19 Nov 1906. SOURCE: Powell, "Military Record of the Enlisted Men Who Were Discharged Without Honor."

‡Dishonorable discharge, Brownsville, TX. SOURCE: SO 266, AGO, 9 Nov 1906.

DICKERSON, David; Private; 25th Inf. Lost left thumb in shooting accident; lived in Austin, TX, after discharge and could only do light work. SOURCE: Dobak and Phillips, *The Black Regulars*, 272.

DICKERSON, Richard T.; 1st Sgt; D/9th Cav. Native of Virginia; former schoolteacher, age 24, very dark complexion, almost six feet tall when he enlisted in Cincinnati, OH, mid-1879; assigned to duty as clerk in office of regimental adjutant; returned to D Troop early 1881; shortly after return replaced Israel Murphy as first sergeant; accused of sexually molesting soldiers, including Pvt. Edward L. Baker, Ft Riley, KS, Jan 1883; claimed charges were part of plot by Sgt. Richard Miller to remove him and become first sergeant; sentenced to dishonorable discharge, spring 1883.

SOURCE: Kenner, *Buffalo Soldiers and Officers of the Ninth Cavalry*, 270–76.

DICKERSON, William; G/9th Cav. Received Philippine Campaign Badge number 11827 for service as private in L/9th Cavalry, 3 Mar 1902–16 Sep 1902; private in G/9th Cavalry, Ft Leavenworth, KS, Mar 1905. SOURCE: Philippine Campaign Badge Recipients; Philippine Campaign Badge list, 29 May 1905.

DICKSON, Solomon; Private; C/10th Cav. ‡Solomon Diekson, C/10th Cavalry; original member of 10th Cavalry; in troop when organized, Ft Leavenworth, KS, 14 May 1867. SOURCE: McMiller, "Buffalo Soldiers," 70.

Deserted during tenure of George Garnett as first sergeant, Jan 1869–May 1871. SOURCE: Dobak and Phillips, *The Black Regulars*, 300.

DIEKSON, Solomon; C/10th Cav. *See* **DICKSON,** Solomon, Private, C/10th Cavalry

DILLARD, James H.; Private; H/10th Cav. Born in Todd County, KY, 1861; enlisted Cincinnati, OH, 26 Jun 1882; Ht 5'7"; black complexion, eyes, and hair; occupation farmer; discharged Ft Apache, AZ, 25 Jun 1887; enlisted Ft Apache, 26 Jun 1887. SOURCE: Sayre, *Warriors of Color*, 157.

In Troop H/10th Cavalry stationed at Bonita Cañon Camp, AZ, 30 Apr 1886. SOURCE: Tagg, *The Camp at Bonita Cañon*, 231.

‡Honorable mention for services rendered in capture of Mangas and his Apache band, Rio Bonito, AZ, 18 Oct 1886. SOURCE: Baker, Roster.

DILLWOOD, Thomas; Private; B/10th Cav. *See* **DILWOOD,** Thomas J., B/10th Cavalry

DILWOOD, Thomas J.; B/10th Cav. At Ft Duncan, TX, Dec 1877–Jan 1878, served as Lt. John Bigelow's orderly; discharged Feb 1878. SOURCE: Kinevan, *Frontier Cavalryman*, 54, 93, 282.

After service Pvt. Thomas J. Dillwood, 10th Cavalry, worked as post office janitor, San Antonio, TX. SOURCE: Dobak and Phillips, *The Black Regulars*, 272.

‡Lives in San Antonio; would like to hear from old comrades. SOURCE: *Winners of the West* 5 (May 1928): 5.

‡Commander of new all-black Abraham Lincoln Camp No. 30, National Indian War Veterans, San Antonio, organized 14 Oct 1929. SOURCE: *Winners of the West* 6 (Oct 1929): 7.

‡Picture, with three comrades of Camp 30, National Indian War Veterans. SOURCE: *Winners of the West* 9 (Mar 1932): 7.

‡Age 83; served ten years. SOURCE: *Winners of the West* 10 (Aug 1933): 3.

‡Congratulates editor on efforts for veterans; can hardly talk, is paralyzed, weak, and feeble; aged wife and son help him get around. SOURCE: *Winners of the West* 11 (Sep 1933): 3.

DIMERY, Henry; Private; U.S. Army. *See* **DINNY,** Henry, Private, U.S. Army

DINGMAN, Hiram L. B.; Private; F/25th Inf. One of twenty men who cycled 1,900 miles from Ft Missoula, MT, to St. Louis, MO, 14 Jun–24 Jul 1897, in 25th Infantry Bicycle Corps to test durability and practicality of bicycles as a means of transportation for troops. SOURCE: File 60178, GC, AGO Records.

DINNIWIDDLE, Daniel; Sergeant; K/25th Inf. Died 9 Feb 1881, buried in plot 1 9, Ft Meade National Cemetery, SD. SOURCE: Ft Meade National Cemetery, VA database.

DINNY, Henry; Private; U.S. Army. Seminole Negro Scout, also known as Henry Dimery, served 1893–98. SOURCE: Schubert, Consolidated List of Seminole Negro Scouts.

Henry Dimery born in Mexico; enlisted at Ft Ringgold, TX, 17 Jul 1893, age 23; Ht 5'8", black hair and eyes, black complexion; discharged 16 Jan 1894, reenlisted next day at Camp San Pedro, TX; discharged 16 Jul 1894 at Ft Ringgold; enlisted 17 Jul 1895, discharged 16 Jan 1898 at Ft Ringgold. SOURCE: Swanson, 10.

Married. SOURCE: NARA, M 929, Roll 2.

DIRKS, Harrison; Private; H/48th Inf. ‡Committed suicide in the Philippines. SOURCE: *ANJ* 37 (26 May 1900): 927.

Pvt. Harrison Dirks, K/48th Infantry, died 15 May 1900; buried in plot NADDN967 at San Francisco National Cemetery. SOURCE: San Francisco National Cemetery.

DIXIE, Joe; Private; U.S. Army. Born in Mexico; an initial enlistee in Seminole Scouts at Ft Duncan, TX, 15 Aug 1870, age 18; name given by Major Bliss at enlistment; Ht 5'7", black hair and eyes, copper complexion; discharged 15 Feb 1871 at Ft Duncan where he enlisted for four more six-month terms; dishonorably discharged by general court martial 072, Dept of TX, 5 Dec 1872; died 1 Aug 1941; buried Seminole Cemetery. SOURCE: Swanson, 10.

Seminole Negro Scout, served 1870–72; sister Rose married Scout Adam Fay. SOURCE: Schubert, Consolidated List of Seminole Negro Scouts.

Name also spelled Dixey and Dixon; in original detachment of Scouts at Ft Duncan; sister Rose born ca. 1860, married Adam Fay. SOURCE: NARA Record Group

393, Special File; Porter, "Negro on the American Frontier," 474.

Buried at Seminole Indian Scout Cemetery, Kinney County, TX. SOURCE: Indian Scout Cemetery, Kinney County, Texas.

DIXON, Carrol; Private; 9th Cav. Received Philippine Campaign Badge number 11723 for service as private in D/25th Infantry; in 9th Cavalry at Ft Leavenworth, KS, Mar 1905. SOURCE: Philippine Campaign Badge list, 29 May 1905.

DIXON, Charles; Private; 10th Cav. At Ft Stockton, TX, Apr 1879; tried for theft and avoided imprisonment by what Lt. John Bigelow called "a mere technical quibble." SOURCE: Kinevan, *Frontier Cavalryman*, 167.

DIXON, Joe; Private; U.S. Army. Seminole Negro Scout, served 1883–84. SOURCE: Schubert, Consolidated List of Seminole Negro Scouts.

Born in Mexico; enlisted at Ft Clark, TX, 30 Aug 1883, age 26; Ht 5'9", black hair and eyes, black complexion; discharged 31 Aug 1884 at Ft Clark. SOURCE: Swanson, 11.

DIXON, Joseph; Private; U.S. Army. Born in Mexico; Seminole Negro Scout, enlisted at Ft Clark, TX, 6 Jan 1885, age 29; Ht 5'6", black hair and eyes, black complexion; discharged 5 Jan 1886 at Ft Clark where he reenlisted for one year three more times; discharged 9 Jan 1889 at Ft Clark; enlisted for six months 5 Jan 1893, age 32, at San Antonio, TX; discharged at Ft Ringgold, TX, 4 Jul 1893. SOURCE: Swanson, 11.

DIXON, Joseph; Corporal; I/10th Cav. In Troop I/10th Cavalry stationed at Bonita Cañon Camp, AZ, 30 Jun 1886. SOURCE: Tagg, *The Camp at Bonita Cañon*, 231.

‡Acquitted at Whipple Barracks, AZ, of calling troop commander "a damned old scoundrel" and "an old drunken sot." SOURCE: *ANJ* 25 (19 Nov 1887): 323.

DOBLER, Fred; 1st Lt; 49th Inf. Died 7 Aug 1927; buried in plot OS 5 PLOT 2 at San Francisco National Cemetery. SOURCE: San Francisco National Cemetery.

DOBSON, Theophilus; Private; E/9th Cav. Died 11 Jul 1890 of pneumonia in post hospital, Ft Robinson, NE. SOURCE: Buecker, Fort Robinson Burials.

‡Buried at Ft Robinson, 11 Jun 1890. SOURCE: List of Interments, Ft Robinson.

DOLBY, Ulysses; Private; 10th Cav. Dark-complected white man, enlisted in 10th Cavalry 1887, served 2.5 years; became frustrated at lack of promotion, revealed his secret, and received discharge. SOURCE: Dobak and Phillips, *The Black Regulars*, 84.

DOMGIE, Joseph C.; M/9th Cav. Born in Virginia; mulatto complexion; can read and write, age 29, Jul 1870, at Ft McKavett, TX. SOURCE: Bierschwale, *Fort McKavett*, 99.

DOMSON, James; Private; I/10th Cav. In Troop I/10th Cavalry stationed at Bonita Cañon Camp, AZ, but absent or on detached service 30 Jun 1886. Tagg questions spelling of Domson. SOURCE: Tagg, *The Camp at Bonita Cañon*, 231.

DONOHOE, John; Private; M/9th Cav. Born in Newark, NJ; died and buried at Ft McKavett, TX, before 17 May 1879. SOURCE: Bierschwale, *Fort McKavett*, 122.

Died at Ft McKavett on 29 Dec 1869; buried at San Antonio National Cemetery, Section E, number 832. SOURCE: San Antonio National Cemetery Locator.

DOOMS, Thomas; Corporal; M/10th Cav. ‡Born in Kentucky; private, corporal, sergeant, C/10th Cavalry, 4 Jan 1887–3 Jan 1892; private, 29 Sep 1892; corporal, 1 Feb 1897; stationed at Ft Assiniboine, MT, 1897. SOURCE: Baker, Roster.

‡Corporal, C/10th Cavalry, served in 10th Cavalry in Cuba, 1898. SOURCE: Cashin, *Under Fire with the Tenth Cavalry*, 339.

‡Born in Bourbon Co., KY; corporal, M/10th Cavalry, age 42, fourteen years' service, died of disease contracted in line of duty, Ft Robinson, NE, 17 Mar 1904. SOURCE: ‡Monthly Report, Chaplain Anderson, AGO File 53901.

Died of disease contracted in line of duty. SOURCE: Buecker, Fort Robinson Burials.

‡Buried at Ft Robinson, 17 Mar 1904. SOURCE: List of Interments, Ft Robinson.

DORSETT, Edward; Private; G/10th Cav. ‡Edward Dorset an original member of 10th Cavalry; in troop when organized, Ft Leavenworth, KS, 5 Jul 1867. SOURCE: McMiller, "Buffalo Soldiers," 74.

Died 27 Aug 1867 of cholera at Ft Harker, KS. SOURCE: Regimental Returns, 10th Cavalry, 1867.

DORSEY, A. J.; Sergeant; H/24th Inf. Died at Ft McIntosh, TX, on 7 Jan 1879; buried at Fort Sam Houston National Cemetery, Section PE, number 345. SOURCE: Buffalo Soldiers Interred in Fort Sam Houston National Cemetery.

DORSEY, Caleb; Farrier; G/10th Cav. Died 24 Jul 1882 of apoplexy at Ft Stockton, TX. SOURCE: Regimental Returns, 10th Cavalry, 1882.

Died at Ft Stockton on 24 Jul 1882; buried at San Antonio National Cemetery, Section C, number 356. SOURCE: San Antonio National Cemetery Locator.

DORSEY, Ephraim; Private; I/25th Inf. Born in Philadelphia, PA; Ht 5'7", black hair and dark brown eyes, black complexion; occupation laborer; enlisted at age 22, New York City, 6 Sep 1882; arrived Ft Snelling, MN, 21 Nov 1882. SOURCE: Descriptive & Assignment Rolls of Recruits, 25 Inf.

DORSEY, Frank; Private; M/9th Cav. Killed in action against Victorio, Black Mountains, NM, May 1879. SOURCE: Kenner, *Buffalo Soldiers and Officers of the Ninth Cavalry*, 255.

‡Private, C/9th Cavalry, killed in action against Victorio, Mimbres Mountains, NM, 28 May 1879; Pvt. George W. Moore wounded in same fight. SOURCE: Hamilton, "History of the Ninth Cavalry," 43; *Illustrated Review: Ninth Cavalry*.

‡Buried where he fell, in well-marked grave. SOURCE: Billington, "Black Cavalrymen," 64.

DORSEY, George; Trumpeter; 9th Cav. Received Philippine Campaign Badge number 11771 for service as trumpeter in F/9th Cavalry; in 9th Cavalry at Ft Leavenworth, KS, Mar 1905. SOURCE: Philippine Campaign Badge list, 29 May 1905.

DORSEY, Horace A.; H/25th Inf. Born in Maryland; black complexion; can read and write, age 21, 5 Sep 1870, in H/25th Infantry at Ft McKavett, TX. SOURCE: Bierschwale, *Fort McKavett*, 107.

DORSEY, James; Private; M/10th Cav. ‡Original member of 10th Cavalry; in troop when organized, Ft Riley, KS, 15 Oct 1867. SOURCE: McMiller, "Buffalo Soldiers," 79.

Died 15 Feb 1870 in hospital at Ft Arbuckle, OK. SOURCE: Regimental Returns, 10th Cavalry, 1870.

DORSEY, William H.; Corporal; A/24th Inf. ‡Private on extra duty as blacksmith, Quartermaster Department. SOURCE: Order 52, Ft Huachuca, AZ, 7 Apr 1893, Name File, 24 Inf.

‡Died in the Philippines, 5 Apr 1901. SOURCE: *ANJ* 38 (13 Apr 1901): 803.

Corporal, died 5 Apr 1901; buried in plot NADDN390 at San Francisco National Cemetery. SOURCE: San Francisco National Cemetery.

DOTY, Timothy; Private; 25th Inf. Born in Lancaster, KY; Ht 5'9", black hair and eyes, brown complexion; occupation farmer; enlisted at age 27, Cincinnati, OH, 1 Dec 1886; arrived Ft Snelling, MN, 1 Apr 1887. SOURCE: Descriptive & Assignment Rolls of Recruits, 25 Inf.

DOUGLAS, Joseph; 1st Sgt; E/9th Cav. Civil War veteran, present at San Pedro, TX, mutiny, Apr 1867. SOURCE: Schubert, *Black Valor*, 14

‡Witness in court martial of 1st Lt. E. M. Heyl, 9th Cavalry, for brutality, camp near San Antonio, TX, Apr 1867; other witnesses: Sgt. Johnson Smith, Corporal Lock, Cpl. Henry Cants, all of E/9th Cavalry.

DOUGLAS, Lewis; Private; D/9th Cav. Died 13 Dec 1877; buried at Santa Fe National Cemetery, NM, plot K 387. SOURCE: Santa Fe National Cemetery, Records of Burials.

DOUGLAS, Will; Private; C/9th Cav. Born 25 Dec 1890; died 10 Apr 1956; buried at Santa Fe National Cemetery, NM, plot V 526. SOURCE: Santa Fe National Cemetery, Records of Burials.

DOUGLAS, William; Private; 25th Inf. Born in Washington, DC; Ht 5'9", black hair and brown eyes, brown complexion; occupation waiter; resided Washington, DC, when he enlisted at age 24, Boston, MA, 28 Sep 1885; assigned to C/25th Infantry; arrived Ft Snelling, MN, 5 Feb 1886. SOURCE: Descriptive & Assignment Rolls of Recruits, 25 Inf.

DOUGLASS, John H.; Private; K/10th Cav. ‡Detailed as teamster, Camp Supply, Indian Territory. SOURCE: SO 54, HQ, Det 10 Cav, 31 Jul 1869, Orders, Det 10 Cav.

Died 11 Mar 1870 of pneumonia at Camp Supply, OK. SOURCE: Regimental Returns, 10th Cavalry, 1870.

‡Inventory of his effects and final statement transmitted. SOURCE: CO, K/10, to CO, 10 Cav, Apr 1870, ES, 10 Cav, 1866–71.

DOUGLASS, Primas; Private; E/10th Cav. In Troop E/10th Cavalry stationed at Bonita Cañon Camp, AZ, 28 Feb 1886. SOURCE: Tagg, *The Camp at Bonita Cañon*, 231.

In regiment summer 1889. SOURCE: Dobak and Phillips, *The Black Regulars*, 202.

DOWNS, Allen; Private; 24th Inf. Civil War veteran; after discharge from 24th Infantry, worked as cook in Denver and Pueblo, CO, and Las Vegas, NE. SOURCE: Dobak and Phillips, *The Black Regulars*, 141.

DOWTHA, Washington; Private; D/24th Inf. Born in Kentucky; black complexion; cannot read or write, age 24, Jul 1870, at Ft McKavett, TX; buried at Ft McKavett before 17 May 1879; body removed to National Cemetery, San Antonio, TX, 23 Nov 1883. SOURCE: Bierschwale, *Fort McKavett*, 96.

Died at Ft McKavett on 29 Jun 1870; buried at San Antonio National Cemetery, Section E, number 845. SOURCE: San Antonio National Cemetery Locator.

DRAIN, Peter; Private; 25th Inf. Born in Knoxville, TN; Ht 5'9", black hair and eyes, brown complexion; occupation laborer; enlisted at age 21, St. Louis, MO, 29 Nov 1886; arrived Ft Snelling, MN, 1 Apr 1887. SOURCE: Descriptive & Assignment Rolls of Recruits, 25 Inf.

DRAKE, Luther; Private; B/9th Cav. Buried 9 Dec 1905, section A, row K, plot 32 at Ft Bayard, NM. SOURCE: Erickson, Burials at Fort Bayard National Cemetery, NM.

DRATON, Charles; Private; C/9th Cav. Died 14 Jul 1889; originally buried at Ft DuChesne, UT; buried at Santa Fe National Cemetery, NM, plot A-4 1095. SOURCE: Santa Fe National Cemetery, Records of Burials.

DREW, Albert; Sergeant; H/9th Cav. ‡Private, fined $5 and costs for fast riding in town, Buffalo, WY, Sep 1886. SOURCE: *Big Horn Sentinel*, 2 Oct 1886.

‡Ranked number 47 among carbine sharpshooters with 72 percent, 1890. SOURCE: GO 1, AGO, 2 Jan 1891.

‡Sergeant, H/9th Cavalry, since 5 Nov 1885. SOURCE: Roster, 9 Cav.

Appointed sergeant 5 Nov 1885; in H/9th Cavalry at Ft Robinson, NE, Jan 1897. SOURCE: Ninth Cavalry, Roster of NCOs, 1897.

‡Sergeant, H/9th Cavalry, Ft Robinson, deposited $30 with paymaster, 1897.

DUBOISE, Stephen H.; Private; I/10th Cav. In Troop I/10th Cavalry stationed at Bonita Cañon Camp, AZ, 30 Jun 1886. SOURCE: Tagg, *The Camp at Bonita Cañon*, 231.

‡Served in 10th Cavalry in Cuba, 1898. SOURCE: Cashin, *Under Fire with the Tenth Cavalry*, 348.

DUDLEY, John H.; Corporal; H/24th Inf. Born in Delaware; black complexion; can read and write, age 24, 5 Sep 1870, in H/25th Infantry at Ft McKavett, TX. SOURCE: Bierschwale, *Fort McKavett*, 108.

‡Born in Wilmington, DE; occupation musician; first enlistment, H/25th Infantry, Aug 1870; second discharge, Band/10th Cavalry, 17 Mar 1878; third discharge, Band/10th Cavalry, 17 Mar 1883; fourth discharge, married, character excellent, Ft Reno, Indian Territory, 12 Apr 1888; deposits, $500, 1885–87, clothing $127.05, retained $60; additional pay $3 per month; fifth enlistment, Ft Supply, Indian Territory, 13 Apr 1888; discharged, married, no children, character excellent, Ft Bayard, NM, 12 Apr 1893; deposits, $225, 1888–92, clothing $155.69, retained $60; additional pay $4 per month; enlisted Ft Bayard, 13 Apr 1893; transferred from band to E/24th Infantry, character very good, married, no children, 15 Jul 1893; deposits $250, retained $3.07; additional pay $5 per month. SOURCE: Descriptive Book, 24 Inf NCS & Band.

‡Mentioned as not absent without leave, Jan 1874. SOURCE: LS, 10 Cav, 1873–77.

‡Deposited $60 with paymaster. SOURCE: CO, 10 Cav, to Paymaster General, 26 Dec 1876, 12 Mar, 7 May 1877, LS, 10 Cav, 1873–77.

‡Enlisted 13 Apr 1898, Ft Douglas, UT; promoted from private to corporal, Tampa, FL, 10 May 1898; twenty-nine years' continuous service. SOURCE: Muster Roll, H/24 Inf, May–Jun 1898.

‡Wounded in action, San Juan, Cuba, 2 Jul 1898; returned to U.S. for treatment. SOURCE: Muster Roll, H/24 Inf, Jul–Aug 1898.

‡On furlough, authorized by surgeon's certificate, 15 Aug–13 Oct 1899; on special duty as clerk, Subsistence Department, since 15 Oct 1898. SOURCE: Muster Roll, H/24 Inf, Nov–Dec 1898 and Jan–Feb 1899.

‡Corporal, H/24th Infantry, wounded in action, Cuba, 1898. SOURCE: Muller, *The Twenty Fourth Infantry*, 96.

‡Picture. SOURCE: Indianapolis *Freeman*, 18 Mar 1899.

‡Corporal, H/24th Infantry, retired May 1901. SOURCE: *ANJ* 37 (19 May 1900): 895.

Retired corporal received Indian Wars Campaign Badge number 1076 on 9 Dec 1908; badge reported lost on 12 Jun 1914, not replaced. SOURCE: Carroll, *Indian Wars Campaign Badge*, 31.

DUDLEY, Joseph P.; Private; E/24th Inf. Died at Ft McIntosh, TX, on 12 May 1879; buried at Fort Sam Houston National Cemetery, Section PE, number 427. SOURCE: Buffalo Soldiers Interred in Fort Sam Houston National Cemetery.

DUMAS, Clark; Sergeant; M/10th Cav. ‡Mentioned as deceased, Sep 1877. SOURCE: ES, 10 Cav, 1873–81.

Died 29 Jul 1877 of disease at Pecos River, TX. SOURCE: Regimental Returns, 10th Cavalry, 1877.

DUNCAN, Austin; Corporal; I/10th Cav. ‡Original member of 10th Cavalry; in troop when organized, Ft Leavenworth, KS, 14 May 1867. SOURCE: McMiller, "Buffalo Soldiers," 70.

‡In C/10th Cavalry, papers in case of State of Kentucky v. Austin Duncan forwarded to Adjutant General, U.S. Army, 8 Jun 1867; Duncan removed by civil authorities from rendezvous where enlisted and held without cause. SOURCE: ES, 10 Cav, 1866–71.

In I/10th Cavalry, died 11 May 1868 of disease at Ft Hays, KS. SOURCE: Regimental Returns, 10th Cavalry, 1868.

DUNIHY, Smith; M/9th Cav. Born in Kentucky; mulatto complexion; cannot read or write, age 26, Jul 1870, at Ft McKavett, TX. SOURCE: Bierschwale, *Fort McKavett*, 99.

DUNLAP, George; D/24th Inf. Born in Louisiana; black complexion; cannot read or write, age 28, Jul 1870, at Ft McKavett, TX. SOURCE: Bierschwale, *Fort McKavett,* 96.

DUNN, Nathan; Private; 25th Inf. Born in Raleigh, NC; Ht 5'7", black hair and brown eyes, black complexion; occupation laborer; enlisted at age 21, Harrisburg, PA, 24 May 1886; arrived Ft Snelling, MN, 17 Sep 1886. SOURCE: Descriptive & Assignment Rolls of Recruits, 25 Inf.

DUOTTE, Edward; Private; H/9th Cav. Died on 21 Apr 1898; buried at San Antonio National Cemetery, Section I, number 1662. SOURCE: San Antonio National Cemetery Locator.

DUPRE, Louis; Private; F/10th Cav. Died Dec 1876 of pistol shot in personal affray at Ft Duncan, TX. SOURCE: Regimental Returns, 10th Cavalry, 1876.

‡Louis Dupee died 30 Dec 1876. SOURCE: ES, 10 Cav, 1873–81.

DUPREE, John; Private; H/10th Cav. Born in Lincoln County, NC, 1856; Ht 5'7", brown complexion, brown eyes, black hair; occupation laborer; enlisted 14 Jan 1877; discharged Ft Davis, TX, 13 Jan 1882; enlisted Ft Davis, 14 Jan 1882; dishonorable discharge and six months for assault with knife of Pvt. Samuel Porter, H/10th Cavalry, 24 Aug 1884. SOURCE: Sayre, *Warriors of Color,* 158–62.

DUPREE, Luzienne; Private; 25th Inf. Civil War veteran; after service, bought a farm in Louisiana. SOURCE: Dobak and Phillips, *The Black Regulars,* 17.

DUVAL, George; Private; K/9th Cav. Testified at court martial of Capt. Jacob Lee Humfreville, 1874. SOURCE: Kenner, *Buffalo Soldiers and Officers of the Ninth Cavalry,* 335.

DYER, Joshua; H/25th Inf. Born in Pennsylvania; mulatto complexion; can read and write, age 27, 5 Sep 1870, at Ft McKavett, TX. SOURCE: Bierschwale, *Fort McKavett,* 108.

DYSON, John; Private; F/10th Cav. Died 4 Aug 1878 of typhoid at Ft Concho, TX. SOURCE: Regimental Returns, 10th Cavalry, 1878.

Died at Ft Concho on 13 Aug 1878; buried at San Antonio National Cemetery, Section D, number 669. SOURCE: San Antonio National Cemetery Locator.

DYSON, Thomas C.; Private; 25th Inf. Served at Ft Stockton, TX, 1880; fought with Pvt. Joseph Hale, 25th Infantry, over a prostitute. SOURCE: Dobak and Phillips, *The Black Regulars,* 177.

E

EADS, Norman; Sergeant; M/10th Cav. Died 11 Aug 1889; buried at Ft Bayard, NM, in plot G 17. SOURCE: "Fort Bayard National Cemetery, Records of Burials."

Norman Eades buried 11 Aug 1889, section A, row I, plot 19, at Ft Bayard. SOURCE: Erickson, Burials at Fort Bayard National Cemetery, NM.

EARL, Elijah; 10th Cav. After leaving service, settled in Shackelford County, TX, and became leader of black community. SOURCE: Smith, *U.S. Army and the Texas Frontier Economy*, 180.

EARL, Robert; Private; D/25th Inf. At Ft McIntosh, TX, 1900; arrested in Laredo, TX, Oct 1900, with Pvts. Joshua Nichols and Benjamin Hover, for beating local police officer. SOURCE: Leiker, *Racial Borders*, 123.

EARLES, Armstead; 1st Sgt; G/10th Cav. ‡Sergeant, C/10th Cavalry, at San Carlos, AZ, authorized two-month furlough. SOURCE: *ANJ* 25 (28 Apr 1888): 794.

‡First sergeant, G/10th Cavalry, retired 1 Aug 1892. SOURCE: Baker, Roster.

‡Retired, convicted by general court martial, Ft Grant, AZ, of embezzlement and sentenced to dishonorable discharge and forfeiture of pay and allowances; Brig. Gen. Elwell S. Otis approved but mitigated sentence on recommendation of court to reimbursement of $89.40, which was cost of his subsistence and transportation for trial from Ft Clark, TX; clemency was due to his long and honorable service and restitution of funds. SOURCE: *ANJ* 34 (3 Jul 1897): 821.

Retired; died at Ft Grant, 3 Nov 1897; buried at Santa Fe National Cemetery, NM, plot 730. SOURCE: Santa Fe National Cemetery, Records of Burials.

EARLY, Anthony; Corporal; D/9th Cav. ‡Enlistment in I/9th Cavalry authorized. SOURCE: Letter, AGO, 27 Sep 1893, Post Returns, Ft Robinson.

‡Promoted from lance corporal, D/9th Cavalry, to corporal, Jul 1895. SOURCE: *ANJ* 32 (13 Jul 1895): 758.

Appointed corporal 1 Jul 1895; in D/9th Cavalry at Ft Washakie, WY, Jan 1897. SOURCE: Ninth Cavalry, Roster of NCOs, 1897.

‡Mentioned as surviving Indian war veteran. SOURCE: *Winners of the West* 3 (Jul 1926): 7.

EBSTEIN, Oscar; Private; A/10th Cav. Died at Ft Concho, TX, on 27 Nov 1874; buried at San Antonio National Cemetery, Section D, number 676. SOURCE: San Antonio National Cemetery Locator.

ECKLER, William; Private; 41st Inf. "Was corresponding with" a white woman near Ft Concho, TX, 1869. SOURCE: Dobak and Phillips, *The Black Regulars*, 175.

EDMORE, James; 1st Sgt; 24th Inf. Died at Ft Stockton, TX, on 16 Apr 1872; buried at San Antonio National Cemetery, Section C, number 435. SOURCE: San Antonio National Cemetery Locator.

EDMUNDSON, George; Private; A/9th Cav. Died at Ft Stockton, TX, on 31 Oct 1871; buried at San Antonio National Cemetery, Section C, number 412. SOURCE: San Antonio National Cemetery Locator.

EDWARDS, Charles; Private; G/9th Cav. Died 5 Apr 1913; buried at Ft Bayard, NM, in plot F 1255. SOURCE: "Fort Bayard National Cemetery, Records of Burials."

Buried 5 Apr 1913, section B, row F, plot 33 at Ft Bayard. SOURCE: Erickson, Burials at Fort Bayard National Cemetery, NM.

EDWARDS James; Private; H/9th Cav. Originally buried Jun 1896 at Ft Stanton, NM; buried at Santa Fe National Cemetery, NM, plot B 554. SOURCE: Santa Fe National Cemetery, Records of Burials.

EDWARDS, John; Private; H/24th Inf. Died 23 Jan 1902; buried at Ft Bayard, NM, in plot M 20. SOURCE: "Fort Bayard National Cemetery, Records of Burials."

Buried 23 Jan 1902, section A, row U, plot 20, at Ft Bayard. SOURCE: Erickson, Burials at Fort Bayard National Cemetery, NM.

EDWARDS, Lewis; Private; 25th Inf. Born in Charleston, SC; enlisted, age 23, Ht 5'9", dark complexion, black hair and eyes, occupation driver, Charleston, 15 Jul 1881; left recruit depot, David's Island, NY, 17 Aug 1881, and after trip on steamer *Thomas Kirby* to Central Depot, New York City, and train via Chicago to Running Water, Dakota Territory, 22 Aug 1881, marched forty-seven miles to Ft Randall, SD, arrived 24 Aug 1881. SOURCE: Descriptive & Assignment Cards, 25 Inf.

EDWARDS, Robert; Private; 9th Cav. ‡Served as private, H/10th Cavalry, 1898; remained in U.S. during war with Spain. SOURCE: Cashin, *Under Fire with the Tenth Cavalry*, 346.

Received Philippine Campaign Badge number 11883 for service as private, H/9th Cavalry; in 9th Cavalry at Ft Leavenworth, KS, Mar 1905. SOURCE: Philippine Campaign Badge list, 29 May 1905.

‡Veteran of Spanish-American War and Philippine Insurrection; at Ft D. A. Russell, WY, in 1910; resident of St. Louis, MO. SOURCE: *Illustrated Review: Ninth Cavalry*, with picture.

EDWARDS, Samuel; M/9th Cav. Born in Kentucky; mulatto complexion; cannot read or write, age 24, Jul 1870, at Ft McKavett, TX. SOURCE: Bierschwale, *Fort McKavett*, 99.

EGLI, Edward; Private; G/25th Inf. Died 20 Dec 1867; buried at San Antonio National Cemetery, Section B, number 119. SOURCE: San Antonio National Cemetery Locator.

ELDERBERRY, Hiram; C/25th Inf. Born in Kentucky; mulatto complexion; can read and write, age 24, 5 Sep 1870, at Ft McKavett, TX. SOURCE: Bierschwale, *Fort McKavett*, 109.

ELLIOTT, _all; Private; G/10th Cav. Died 26 Nov 1878 of malaria at Ft Sill, OK. SOURCE: Regimental Returns, 10th Cavalry, 1878.

ELLIOTT, James; Sergeant; D/10th Cav. ‡Born in Georgia; private, farrier, corporal, in M, C, D/10th Cavalry, 16 May 1887–15 May 1892; private, 15 Jun 1892; sergeant, 18 Jun 1893; stationed at Ft Assiniboine, MT, 1897. SOURCE: Baker, Roster.

‡Former deserter, "now a very active and consistent Christian," assisting Chaplain Steward with series of Gospel meetings, Ft Missoula, MT, Feb 1893. SOURCE: Monthly report, Chaplain Steward, 1 Mar 1893.

‡Served in 10th Cavalry in Cuba, 1898. SOURCE: Cashin, *Under Fire with the Tenth Cavalry*, 340–41.

‡Commended for distinguished service, battle of Santiago, Cuba, 1 Jul 1898. SOURCE: GO 15, AGO, 13 Feb 1900; SecWar, *AR 1898*, 709–10.

Awarded certificate of merit for distinguished service in battle of Santiago, 1 Jul 1898. SOURCE: Gleim, *The Certificate of Merit*, 45.

‡Activities in Cuba mentioned. SOURCE: Bigelow, *Reminiscences of Santiago*, 105, 114–15, 120–21, 130, 163.

‡Heroism mentioned in unsigned letter, Montauk, NY, 8 Oct 1898. SOURCE: Gatewood, *"Smoked Yankees,"* 80.

‡Awarded certificate of merit for distinguished service in Cuba, 1 Jul 1898. SOURCE: *ANJ* 37 (24 Feb 1900): 611; Steward, *The Colored Regulars*, 280.

ELLIS, George W.; Private; H/24th Inf. Received as private Indian Wars Campaign Badge number 1187 on 23 Jan 1909. SOURCE: Carroll, *Indian Wars Campaign Badge*, 34.

ELLIS, Robert; Private; E/24th Inf. Died 23 Mar 1893; buried at Ft Bayard, NM, in plot I 30. SOURCE: "Fort Bayard National Cemetery, Records of Burials."

Buried 23 Mar 1893, section A, row M, plot 33 at Ft Bayard. SOURCE: Erickson, Burials at Fort Bayard National Cemetery, NM.

ELY, Absolom; Sergeant; D/9th Cav. Enlisted early 1870s, age 21, mulatto, farmer from Virginia, served at Ft Stockton, TX; promoted to sergeant months after induction. SOURCE: Kenner, *Buffalo Soldiers and Officers of the Ninth Cavalry*, 84.

EMANUEL, George H.; Private; D/9th Cav. With Captain Dodge at battle at Milk River, CO, 2–10 Oct 1879. SOURCE: Miller, *Hollow Victory*, 167, 206–7.

EMERY, Andrew J.; Private; H/10th Cav. Born in Richmond, KY, 25 Feb 1862; enlisted Cincinnati, OH, 9 Jan 1882, Ht 5'9", brown complexion, black eyes and hair; served as post librarian, Ft Davis, TX, for more than one year; injured by falling horse, Ft Davis, May 1886; discharged Ft Apache, AZ, 8 Jan 1887; granted invalid pension of $4 per month, 1888, increased to $6 in 1895, unchanged until he died; resided at Minnetonka Beach, MN, in 1896; married Dora M. Packard, 26 Nov 1900; children: Arthur J., born 9 Apr 1900, Hazel May, born 28 May 1901, Charles Clifford, born 15 Oct 1904, Dolly, born 5 Sep 1905, Grant D., born 18 Nov 1906; died 21 Jul 1919. SOURCE: Sayre, *Warriors of Color*, 10, 12, 163–71.

Private in H/10th Cavalry stationed at Bonita Cañon Camp, AZ, but absent or on detached service 30 Apr 1886. SOURCE: Tagg, *The Camp at Bonita Cañon*, 231.

EMORY, Robert; Private; L/9th Cav. Died 20 Feb 1868; buried at San Antonio National Cemetery, Section F, number 1159. SOURCE: San Antonio National Cemetery Locator.

ENGLISH, Ernest; Private; B/25th Inf. Enlisted 16 Oct 1899, discharged as private Company K, 49th USV Infantry 30 May 1901, character very good; reenlisted 31 May 1901, discharged as private B/25th Infantry 30 May 1904, character very good; reenlisted 13 Jun 1904, discharged without honor 19 Nov 1906. SOURCE: Powell, "Military Record of the Enlisted Men Who Were Discharged Without Honor."

Dishonorable discharge, Brownsville, TX. SOURCE: SO 266, AGO, 9 Nov 1906.

ENGLISH, George; Private; B/10th Cav. ‡Served in 10th Cavalry in Cuba, 1898; drowned there, 22 Jun 1898. SOURCE: Cashin, *Under Fire with the Tenth Cavalry*, 338.

Drowned when landing craft overturned, Daiquiri, Cuba, 22 Jun 1898. SOURCE: Schubert, *Black Valor*, 145.

‡Died in Cuba, 22 Jun 1898. SOURCE: *ANJ* 36 (11 Feb 1899): 567.

ENNIS, Joseph; F/9th Cav. Born in Maryland; black complexion; can read and write, age 27, Jul 1870, at Ft McKavett, TX. SOURCE: Bierschwale, *Fort McKavett*, 96.

EPPS, Richard; Private; C/9th Cav. Cited for bravery against Apaches in the Florida Mountains, New Mexico, in January 1877 by Lt. Henry Wright. SOURCE: Schubert, *Black Valor*, 45–46.

‡Commended for bravery, Florida Mountains, 1877. SOURCE: Billington, "Black Cavalrymen," 62; Billington, *New Mexico's Buffalo Soldiers*, 91.

EUSTILL, Clayborne; Private; B/10th Cav. Died 22 Jun 1872 of disease at Ft Sill, OK. SOURCE: Regimental Returns, 10th Cavalry, 1872.

EVANS, Edward; Private; 9th Cav. Received Philippine Campaign Badge number 11884 for service as private in M/9th Cavalry and H/9th Cavalry; in 9th Cavalry at Ft Leavenworth, KS, Mar 1905. SOURCE: Philippine Campaign Badge list, 29 May 1905.

EVANS Elijah; Private; F/10th Cav. Died 20 Jun 1903; buried at Ft Bayard, NM, in plot L 31. SOURCE: "Fort Bayard National Cemetery, Records of Burials."

Buried 20 Jun 1903, section A, row S, plot 35 at Ft Bayard. SOURCE: Erickson, *Burials at Fort Bayard National Cemetery, NM.*

EVANS, Fred; Private; D/9th Cav. Fined $20 for attacking 1st Sgt. Israel Murphy with intent to do bodily harm, Jan 1881; ceased attack when a sergeant "broke a carbine over his head." SOURCE: Kenner, *Buffalo Soldiers and Officers of the Ninth Cavalry*, 19–20, 271.

EVANS, James; Private; K/25th Inf. Born in Harrison County, MS; Ht 5'6", brown complexion; occupation laborer; enlisted in A/39th Infantry for three years on 29 Oct 1866, age 24, at New Orleans, LA; detached service as HQ messenger, Department of Louisiana; transferred to K/25th Infantry at Jackson Bks, LA, 20 Apr 1869. SOURCE: Descriptive Roll of A/39th Inf.

EVANS, John; Private; C/49th Inf. ‡Drowned in Cagayan River, Alcala, Philippines, 22 Jul 1900. SOURCE: *ANJ* 38 (20 Oct 1900): 186; *ANJ* 37 (11 Aug 1900): 1191.

‡Drowned because he got cramp while bathing and could not swim against swift current. SOURCE: Fletcher, *The Black Soldier*, 297.

Private, G/49th Infantry, died 21 Jul 1900; buried in plot 965 NEW at San Francisco National Cemetery. SOURCE: San Francisco National Cemetery.

EVANS, Robert; Sergeant; C/10th Cav. ‡Killed in action, Gayleysville Canyon, AZ, 3 Jul 1886; Evans Road, Ft Huachuca, AZ, named for him. SOURCE: Orville A. Cochran to H. B. Wharfield, 5 Apr 1965, 10th Cavalry papers, MHI; Baker, Roster.

Buried in plot 900 at San Francisco National Cemetery. SOURCE: San Francisco National Cemetery.

EVERETT, Frank; Private; K/10th Cav. Died at Ft Davis, TX, on 1 Jul 1881; buried at San Antonio National Cemetery, Section I, number 1526. SOURCE: San Antonio National Cemetery Locator.

EWELL, Levi; Private; K/10th Cav. Died 16 May 1887; originally buried at Ft Grant, AZ; buried at Santa Fe National Cemetery, NM, plot A-1 784. SOURCE: Santa Fe National Cemetery, Records of Burials.

EWEN, Peter; Private; D/9th Cav. With Captain Dodge at battle at Milk River, CO, 2–10 Oct 1879. SOURCE: Miller, *Hollow Victory*, 167, 206–7.

EWING, John; Private; 24th Inf. Served at Ringgold Barracks, TX, 1877; fought with Pvt. David Lyons after argument over prostitutes, cut Lyons and drew blood; sentenced to dishonorable discharge and three years. SOURCE: Dobak and Phillips, *The Black Regulars*, 177.

F

FACCETT, William; Private; I/10th Cav. In Troop I/10th Cavalry stationed at Bonita Cañon Camp, AZ, but absent or on detached service 30 Jun 1886. Tagg questions spelling of Faccett. SOURCE: Tagg, *The Camp at Bonita Cañon,* 231.

FACTOR, Allen; Private; U.S. Army. Seminole Negro Scout, age 44, served 1873–84. SOURCE: Schubert, Consolidated List of Seminole Negro Scouts.

Born in Florida; enlisted at Ft Duncan, TX, 5 Dec 1873, age 40; Ht 5'6", black hair and eyes, black complexion; discharged 5 June 1874 at Camp Palafox, TX; enlisted 11 June 1874 at Camp Eagle Pass, TX; discharged 11 Dec 1874, reenlisted 1 Jan 1875 at Ft Duncan; discharged, reenlisted 2 Jul 1875, age 46, at Ft Concho, TX; died of apoplexy at Ft Duncan 28 Dec 1875; buried at Eagle Pass. SOURCE: Swanson, 11.

Resided in 1875 at Ft Duncan with Silvia age 37, Suzie age 7. SOURCE: NARA Record Group 393, Special File.

FACTOR, Dembo; Private; U.S. Army. Seminole Negro Scout, served 1878–83. SOURCE: Schubert, Consolidated List of Seminole Negro Scouts.

Born in Florida; former slave of Nelly Factor in Florida; enlisted at Ft Clark, TX, 8 Feb 1878, age 62; Ht 5'7", black hair and eyes, black complexion; discharged 24 Apr 1879 at Ft Clark where he reenlisted for one-year terms four more times; last discharge at Camp Myers Spring, TX, 22 Jan 1883; died 15 July 1891; buried at Seminole Cemetery. SOURCE: Swanson, 11.

Demdo Factor buried at Seminole Indian Scout Cemetery, Kinney County, TX. SOURCE: Indian Scout Cemetery, Kinney County Texas.

FACTOR, Dindie; Private; U.S. Army. Seminole Negro Scout, served 1870–76, 1879–80; pension file in National Archives. SOURCE: Schubert, Consolidated List of Seminole Negro Scouts.

Born in Arkansas; descendant of former slave of Nelly Factor of Florida; enlisted at Ft Duncan, TX, 16 Aug 1870, age 28; Ht 5'11", black hair and eyes, black complexion; discharged 15 Feb 1871, reenlisted next day at Ft Duncan; discharged, enlisted at Ft Duncan 31 Aug 1871; discharged at Ft Duncan 29 Feb 1872, reenlisted next day; discharged 31 Aug 1872, reenlisted 7 Sep 1872 at Ft Duncan; discharged 10 Mar 1873 at Camp Comanche, TX, 1 Nov 1873; enlisted 1 Jan 1874 at Ft Duncan; discharged 11 Jul 1874 at Camp Palafox, TX; enlisted 2 Dec 1874 at Ft Clark, TX; discharged 25 Jun 1875, reenlisted at Ft Clark; discharged 1 Jan 1876 at Ft Duncan; enlisted 26 May 1879 at Ft Clark where he was discharged 25 May 1880; enlisted 26 May 1880 at Ft Clark where he was discharged 12 June 1881; father of Scout Pompey Factor. SOURCE: Swanson, 12.

In original detachment of Scouts enlisted at Ft Duncan Aug 1870, age 29; widow Josephine filed claim, VA widow claim 15619035. SOURCE: NARA Record Group 393, Special File; Schubert, "Seminole-Negro Scouts."

FACTOR, Hardy; Private; U.S. Army. Seminole Negro Scout, served 1870–72, 1876–77, 1879–80; father of Scout Pompey Factor. SOURCE: Schubert, Consolidated List of Seminole Negro Scouts.

Hardie Factor born in Florida; former slave of Nelly Factor of Florida; one of two Scouts from Florida given warrior status with a Seminole name, Yah Ha Las lo Nocky; one of twenty chosen fit for Scout service by Major Bliss; enlisted at Ft Duncan, TX, 16 Aug 1870, age 64; Ht 5'9", black hair and eyes, black complexion; discharged 15 Feb 1871 at Ft Duncan where he reenlisted next day; twice discharged, reenlisted 31 Aug 1871 and 29 Feb 1872 at Ft Duncan; discharged at Ft Duncan 29 Aug 1872; enlisted Ft Clark, TX, 11 Oct 1876; discharged Camp Painted Comanche, TX, 11 Apr 1877; enlisted 25 May 1879 at Ft Clark where he was discharged 27 May 1880; 1880 Census lists wife Esther age 60, son Hardy age 12. SOURCE: Swanson, 12.

FACTOR, Hardy; Private; U.S. Army. Born in Florida; enlisted at Ft Duncan, TX, 10 Jan 1874, age 40; Ht 5'8", black hair and eyes, black complexion; discharged 1 Jul 1874 at Camp Palafox, TX; enlisted at Ft Duncan 1 Jan 1875; discharged and reenlisted 1 Jul 1875 at Ft Concho, TX; discharged at Ft Duncan 1 July 1876. SOURCE: Swanson, 12.

Resided in 1875 at Ft Duncan with Hester age 45, Frederic age 3. SOURCE: NARA Record Group 393, Special File; Porter, *The Negro on the American Frontier*, 474.

FACTOR, Pompey; Private; 24th Inf. Seminole Negro Scout; age 21 when first enlisted in 1870; received Medal of Honor for valor with Lt. John Bullis on Pecos River, TX, Apr 1875; unable to write his name; deserted after shooting of Adam Payne, Jan 1877, returned from Mexico May 1879 and was restored to duty; discharged 1880; farmed along border near Brackettville, TX, until he died 28 Mar 1928; awarded pension shortly before death; buried nearby in Seminole Negro community cemetery on Los Moras Creek. SOURCE: Schubert, *Black Valor*, 34, 36, 38–39.

Born in Arkansas; enlisted at Ft Duncan, TX, 16 Aug 1870, age 21; Ht 5'8", black hair and eyes, black complexion; discharged 2 Feb 1871, reenlisted 15 Feb 1871 at Ft Duncan; discharged 31 Aug 1871, reenlisted 7 Oct 1871 at Ft Duncan; twice discharged, reenlisted next day at Ft Duncan, 17 Apr 1872–9 Oct 1872; discharged 9 Apr 1873, reenlisted 1 May 1873 at Ft Duncan; discharged at Camp Comanche, TX, 1 Nov 1873; enlisted 1 Nov 1873 at Ft Duncan; discharged 1 Jul 1874 at Camp Palafox, TX; enlisted 2 Dec 1874, discharged 3 June 1875 at Ft Clark, TX; enlisted 1 Sept 1875, discharged 5 Mar 1876 at Ft Duncan; enlisted at Ft Clark 26 Oct 1874; discharged 13 Apr 1877, reenlisted next day at Camp Painted Comanche, TX; deserted 13 Apr 1877 when Scout Adam Payne was gunned down by a sheriff at a dance, went to Mexico with others; restored to duty without trial by SO 113, 31 May 1878, Dept of TX, if he made good time lost to government, forfeited all pay and allowances for time of absence; enlisted 16 Sep 1879, age 30; discharged at Black Water Hole, TX, 14 Nov 1880. SOURCE: Swanson, 13.

Seminole Negro Scout, served 1870–77, 1879–80, pension file in National Archives. SOURCE: Schubert, Consolidated List of Seminole Negro Scouts.

‡Seminole Negro Scout; won Medal of Honor for heroism, with Lieutenant Bullis, Pecos River, TX, 26 Apr 1875. SOURCE: Carroll, *The Black Military Experience*, 390.

In original detachment of Scouts enlisted at Ft Duncan, age 16, Aug 1870; signed name with "X" in 1876; restored to duty from desertion May 1878; son Dindie Factor born ca. 1874. SOURCE: NARA Record Group 383, Special File; Porter, *The Negro on the American Frontier*, 474.

FACTOR, Tobe; Private; U.S. Army. Seminole Negro Scout, served 1893–98. SOURCE: Schubert, Consolidated List of Seminole Negro Scouts.

Born in Mexico; enlisted at Ft Clark, TX, 13 Jan 1893, age 29; Ht 5'7", black hair and eyes, black complexion; discharged 12 Jul 1893, reenlisted next day at Ft Ringgold, TX; discharged 12 Jan 1894, reenlisted next day at Camp San Pedro, TX; discharged, reenlisted next day at Ft Ringgold 12 Jul 1894 for six months and 12 Jan 1895 for

three years; discharged 12 Jan 1898 at Ft Ringgold. SOURCE: Swanson, 13.

Married. SOURCE: NARA, M 929, Roll 2.

FAIN, Frank; Sergeant; E/9th Cav. Appointed sergeant 16 Jan 1892; in E/9th Cavalry at Ft Robinson, NE, Jan 1897. SOURCE: Ninth Cavalry, Roster of NCOs, 1897; Roster, 9 Cav.

‡First sergeant as of 16 Jul 1892. SOURCE: Roster, 9 Cav.

FAIR, Robert; I/9th Cav. Civil War service in K/122nd Infantry, United States Colored Troops; married Pabla Nalla, former wife of 1st Sgt. John F. Casey, H/10th Cavalry, at Ft Davis, TX, 8 Mar 1889; died 12 Dec 1905. SOURCE: Sayre, *Warriors of Color*, 128.

FANTROY, Basil; M/9th Cav. Born in Kentucky; black complexion; can read, cannot write, age 19, Jul 1870, at Ft McKavett, TX. SOURCE: Bierschwale, *Fort McKavett*, 99.

FARLEY, Beauford; Private; G/9th Cav. Received Philippine Campaign Badge number 11829 for service as private in G/9th Cavalry, 18 Apr 1902–16 Sep 1902; private in G/9th Cavalry, Ft Leavenworth, KS, Mar 1905. SOURCE: Philippine Campaign Badge Recipients; Philippine Campaign Badge list, 29 May 1905.

FARRELL, Louis; Private; 9th Cav. Received Philippine Campaign Badge number 11867 for service as private in H/9th Cavalry; in 9th Cavalry at Ft Leavenworth, KS, Mar 1905. SOURCE: Philippine Campaign Badge list, 29 May 1905.

FARRINGTON, George W.; Private; I/9th Cav. *See* OTT, FEARINGTON, George W., Private, I/9th Cavalry

FASIT, Benjamin; Sergeant; E/10th Cav. ‡Served in 10th Cavalry in Cuba, 1898. SOURCE: Cashin, *Under Fire with the Tenth Cavalry*, 342.

‡Commended for distinguished service, battle of Santiago, Cuba, 1 Jul 1898. SOURCE: GO 15, AGO, 13 Feb 1900.

Awarded certificate of merit for distinguished service in battle of Santiago, 1 Jul 1898. SOURCE: Gleim, *The Certificate of Merit*, 45.

‡Awarded certificate of merit. SOURCE: Steward, *The Colored Regulars*, 280; *ANJ* 37 (24 Feb 1900): 611.

FAULKNER, Charles S. C.; Private; F/10th Cav. Born in Garrett County, KY, 1850; enlisted Cincinnati, OH, 29 Jul 1879, Ht 5'7", black complexion, brown eyes, black hair; served continuously in 10th Cavalry; at Ft Davis, TX, 1883; discharged and reenlisted 28–29 Jul 1884 at Ft Davis; discharged and reenlisted 28–29 Jul 1889, Ft Apache, AZ; discharged and reenlisted 28–29 July 1894, Ft Buford, ND; served on occupation duty at Manzanillo, Cuba, 1899; discharged and reenlisted 28–29 July 1899, Manzanillo; discharged and reenlisted 28–29 July 1902 at sea on U.S. Army Transport *Thomas*; discharged and reenlisted 28–29 Jul 1907 at Ft Mackenzie, WY; discharged 7 Feb 1907 at Ft D. A. Russell; enlisted 18 Feb 1907 at Ft D. A. Russell, WY; sister Ruth Watts resided 4237 Sacramento Ave., St. Louis, MO; first wife Julia, second wife Mollie Brown. SOURCE: Sayre, *Warriors of Color*, 172–73.

‡Born in Kentucky; private, H/10th Cavalry, 29 Jul 1879; corporal, 20 Mar 1881; sergeant, 11 Sep 1881; stationed at Ft Assiniboine, MT, 1897. SOURCE: Baker, Roster.

Quartermaster sergeant in H/10th Cavalry stationed at Bonita Cañon Camp, AZ, 30 Apr 1886. SOURCE: Tagg, *The Camp at Bonita Cañon*, 231.

‡Sergeant, H/10th Cavalry, at Ft Apache, 1890, subscribed $.50 to testimonial to General Grierson. SOURCE: List of subscriptions, 23 Apr 1890, 10th Cavalry papers, MHI.

‡Sergeant, F/10th Cavalry, national standard bearer. SOURCE: *ANJ* 35 (19 Feb 1898): 458.

‡Served in 10th Cavalry in Cuba, 1898. SOURCE: Cashin, *Under Fire with the Tenth Cavalry*, 346.

FAY, Adam; Private; U.S. Army. Seminole Negro Scout, served 1870–88; married Scout Joe Dixie's sister Rose; pension file in National Archives. SOURCE: Schubert, Consolidated List of Seminole Negro Scouts.

Born in Mexico; enlisted at Ft Duncan, TX, 16 Aug 1870, age 17; discharged and reenlisted for six months five times at Ft Duncan, 5 Feb 1871–1 May 1873; discharged 1 Nov 1873 at Camp Comanche, TX; enlisted Ft Duncan 8 Jan 1874; discharged 4 Jul 1874 at Camp Palafox, TX; enlisted 1 Oct 1874 at Ft Clark, TX, where he was discharged 1 Apr 1875; enlisted 1 Oct 1875 at Camp Supply, IT; discharged 17 Apr 1876 as corporal where he reenlisted day before at Ft Clark; discharged 13 Oct 1876 as private and reenlisted same day at Ft Clark; discharged 13 Apr 1877 and reenlisted same day at Camp Painted Comanche, TX; discharged at Ft Clark 13 Apr 1878, reenlisted same day at Howards Camp; discharged 24 Apr 1879 at Ft Clark where he reenlisted 3 May 1879, blacksmith 1 May 1879; discharged and reenlisted for one year same day at Ft Clark on 2 May 1880, 12 May 1881, 12 May 1882, 12 May 1883 when he was discharged as corporal; discharged at Camp Myers Spring, TX, 12 May 1884, reenlisted same day at Ft Clark; discharged 31 Aug 1884. SOURCE: Swanson, 14.

In original detachment of Scouts enlisted at Ft Duncan, age 18, Aug 1870; died 8 Jul 1908; widow Rose born ca. 1860, sister of Scout Joe Dixie, filed pension claim, VA file XC 2659982, in 1917; widow resided Brackettville, TX, in 1942. SOURCE: Schubert, "Seminole-Negro Scouts"; Porter, *The Negro on the American Frontier*, 474.

FAY, John; Private; U.S. Army. Seminole Negro Scout, served continuously 1870–88; pension file in National Archives. SOURCE: Schubert, Consolidated List of Seminole Negro Scouts; Schubert, *Black Valor*, 30.

FAY, Sandy; Sergeant; U.S. Army. Seminole Negro Scout, served 1872–1905; retired. SOURCE: Schubert, Consolidated List of Seminole Negro Scouts.

Born in Mexico; enlisted at Ft Duncan, TX, 10 Sep 1872, age 18; Ht 5'4", black hair and eyes, black complexion; discharged and reenlisted for six-month terms twice at Ft Duncan 10 Mar 1873–16 Dec 1873; discharged 16 Jun 1874 at Ft Clark, TX, and reenlisted next day; discharged 17 Dec 1874 at Ft Clark where he reenlisted 24 Jan 1875; discharged at Camp Supply, IT, 9 Sep 1875; enlisted 9 Feb 1876 at Ft Clark; discharged and reenlisted 9 Aug 1876 at Camp Pecos, TX; discharged 9 Feb 1877 and reenlisted seven times for one-year terms at Ft Clark; discharged at Camp Myers Spring, TX, 22 May 1884; enlisted for six months 23 May 1884 at Ft Clark where he was discharged 30 Nov 1884; enlisted three times for one year starting 27 Dec 1884 at Ft Clark, ending with discharge at Camp Neville Springs, TX; enlisted Camp Neville Springs 1 Jul 1890; discharged 31 Dec 1890 at Ft Clark where he reenlisted next day; discharged 30 Jun 1891 and 31 Dec 1891 at Camp Palvo, TX, where twice he reenlisted next day for six months; discharged 30 Jun 1892 at Camp Presidio, TX, where he reenlisted next day; discharged 31 Dec 1892 at Camp Artenlas; reenlisted 1 Jan 1893 at Ft Ringgold, TX; discharged 30 Jun 1893 and reenlisted next day at Camp Carrizo, NM; discharged 31 Dec 1893 at Camp San Pedro, TX, where he reenlisted next day; discharged at Camp Roma, TX, 30 Jun 1894; enlisted 1 Jul 1894 at Ft Ringgold where he was discharged 31 Dec 1894; reenlisted at Ft Ringgold four times for three years starting 1 Jan 1895; sergeant in last term of service, retired 27 Apr 1905. SOURCE: Swanson, 15.

FEARINGTON, George W.; Sergeant; F/25th Inf. Private, I/9th Cavalry, awarded certificate of merit for excellent conduct and heroic service putting out barracks fire, Ft DuChesne, UT, 13 Dec 1899. SOURCE: Gleim, *The Certificate of Merit*, 50.

Born in Durham County, NC; resided Durham, NC; received Distinguished Service Medal in lieu of certificate of merit. SOURCE: *American Decorations*, 837.

‡Awarded certificate of merit, 24 Nov 1903, for excellent conduct and heroic service when troop barrack was destroyed by fire, Ft DuChesne, 13 Dec 1899; took position on peak of building and stayed there applying water, although in serious danger, until fire was brought under control. SOURCE: GO 32, AGO, 6 Feb 1904.

‡At post hospital, Presidio of San Francisco, CA, with hole in chest; shot by Cpl. Walter Lockett, I/9th Cavalry, while in tent, early morning, 7 Nov 1902; Lockett was

apparently drunk; both are ten-year men and veterans of Cuba and the Philippines; commander is Capt. Charles Young, whose troop "has always enjoyed a splendid reputation for discipline and good behavior." SOURCE: San Francisco *Chronicle*, 8 Nov 1902.

‡Veteran of Philippine Insurrection; at Ft D. A. Russell, WY, in 1910; sharpshooter; resident of Durham, NC. SOURCE: *Illustrated Review: Ninth Cavalry*, with picture.

Sergeant, F/25th Infantry, died 20 Nov 1933; buried in plot C 655 at San Francisco National Cemetery. SOURCE: San Francisco National Cemetery.

FERGUSON, James; Private; G/10th Cav. ‡Original member of 10th Cavalry; in troop when organized, Ft Leavenworth, KS, 5 Jul 1867. SOURCE: McMiller, "Buffalo Soldiers," 74.

Died 24 Jul 1867 of cholera at Wilson Creek, KS. SOURCE: Regimental Returns, 10th Cavalry, 1867.

FERGUSON, John H.; Sergeant; A/9th Cav. ‡Discharged. SOURCE: SO 257, AGO, 4 Nov 1891.

Post QM Sgt. Benjamin F. Davis married at home of Sgt. and Mrs. John H. Ferguson, 9th Cavalry, at Ft Niobrara, NE, in 1886. SOURCE: Dobak and Phillips, *The Black Regulars*, 141.

FIELDING, Frank; Private; 10th Cav. National chaplain of National Indian War Veterans, 1929. SOURCE: Dobak and Phillips, *The Black Regulars*, 277.

FIELDS, Harvey; 1st Sgt; H/25th Inf. Born in Kentucky; mulatto complexion; can read and write, age 24, 5 Sep 1870, in H/25th Infantry at Ft McKavett, TX. SOURCE: Bierschwale, *Fort McKavett*, 107.

‡Sergeant, H/25th Infantry, led detachment of thirteen men of I/20th Infantry and C and H/10th Cavalry, 665 miles from camp at Seven Springs, TX, in pursuit of Indian raiders; discovered no recent signs or information on depredations, 30 Jul–1 Dec 1879. SOURCE: SecWar, *AR 1880*, 137.

‡Retires as first sergeant from Ft Missoula, MT, Sep 1894. SOURCE: *ANJ* 32 (6 Oct 1894): 86.

FIELDS, Henry; Private; D/10th Cav. Died 9 Sep 1870 of disease at Ft Sill, OK. SOURCE: Regimental Returns, 10th Cavalry, 1870.

‡Commander, 10th Cavalry, forwards final statement of late Private Fields to Adjutant General, 10 Sep 1870. SOURCE: ES, 10 Cav, 1866–71.

Private, D/10th Cavalry, died 10 Sep 1870, buried at Camp Douglas, UT. SOURCE: Record Book of Interments, Post Cemetery, 252.

FIELDS, Henry; Sergeant; G/9th ‡Sergeant, G/9th Cavalry, since 11 Jun 1889. SOURCE: Roster, 9 Cav.

Appointed sergeant 11 Jun 1889; in G/9th Cavalry at Ft Robinson, NE, Jan 1897. SOURCE: Ninth Cavalry, Roster of NCOs, 1897.

‡At Ft Robinson, 1892.

‡With detachment fired on by insurgents at Donsoll, Philippines, 4 Jun 1901; also in small engagement at Bonga River, 27 Jun 1901. SOURCE: Hamilton, "History of the Ninth Cavalry," 107; *Illustrated Review: Ninth Cavalry*.

FIELDS, John; Sergeant; 9th Cav. At Fort Hays, KS, 1882, quick action averted armed clash between soldiers and civilians, after civilian shot and killed Cpl. Thornton Jackson. SOURCE: Dobak and Phillips, *The Black Regulars*, 199.

FIELDS, Picket; Private; I/10th Cav. In Troop I/10th Cavalry stationed at Bonita Cañon Camp, AZ, 30 Jun 1886. SOURCE: Tagg, *The Camp at Bonita Cañon*, 231.

FIELDS, Wallace; Private; D/10th Cav. Died 27 Jan 1913; buried at San Antonio National Cemetery, Section B, number 131. SOURCE: San Antonio National Cemetery Locator.

FINDLEY, John; Private; F/25th Inf. Private, F/25th Infantry, rode in 25th Infantry Bicycle Corps, Ft. Missoula, MT, summer 1896. SOURCE: Sorenson, List of Buffalo Soldiers Who Rode in the 25th Infantry Bicycle Corps, in authors' files.

One of twenty men who cycled 1,900 miles from Ft Missoula to St. Louis, MO, 14 Jun–24 Jul 1897, in the 25th Infantry Bicycle Corps to test durability and practicality of bicycles as a means of transportation for troops; served as cyclist mechanic on trip. SOURCE: File 60178, GC, AGO Records.

Member of 25th Infantry bicycle corps, 1896, Ft Missoula, expert cyclist and chief mechanic. SOURCE: Dobak and Phillips, *The Black Regulars*, 324.

FINLEY, Augustus; Private; G/9th Cav. ‡Enlisted in D/9th Cavalry, Ft McKinney, WY, 10 Feb 1888.

‡Commander, Captain Finley, G/9th Cavalry, calls him "a gambling, ill-natured, sulky man . . . captious, fault-finding soldier." SOURCE: Report of inspection, Ft Robinson, NE, 21 Aug 1893, Reports of Inspections, DP.

‡Turned over to civil authorities, 30 Aug 1893. SOURCE: CO, Ft Robinson, to CO, G/9, 1 Sep 1893, LS, Ft Robinson.

‡Alleged to have stolen some money; case not reported to post commander until U.S. Marshal Ledyard appeared with warrant. SOURCE: CO, Ft Robinson, to AAG, DP, 25 Nov 1893, LS, Ft Robinson.

‡In hands of civil authorities, Omaha, NE, 30 Aug–14 Dec 1893. SOURCE: Regt Returns, 9 Cav.

Died 5 Dec 1897 of disease contracted in line of duty. SOURCE: Buecker, Fort Robinson Burials.

‡Funeral, Ft Robinson, NE, 6 Dec 1897. SOURCE: SO 161, 5 Dec 1897, Post Orders, Ft Robinson.

‡Money due deceased Private Finley from sale of his personal effects $15.60, money he left $16.50, pay $21, sent to Department of the Platte. SOURCE: CO, G/9, to Chief Paymaster, DP, 21 Jan 1898, Miscellaneous Records, DP.

FINLEY, Lewis G.; Private; D/25th Inf. *See* **FINLEY**, Louis G., Private, D/25th Infantry

FINLEY, Louis G.; Private; D/25th Inf. ‡Died of acute diarrhea aboard U.S. Army Transport *Thomas*, bound for San Francisco, CA, 5 Jul 1901. SOURCE: *ANJ* 39 (9 Aug 1902): 1249.

Pvt. Lewis G. Finley, D/25th Infantry, died 6 July 1902 on U.S. Army Transport *Thomas* en route from Manila, Philippines, to San Francisco; buried in plot NADD 1147 at San Francisco National Cemetery. SOURCE: San Francisco National Cemetery.

FINLEY, Rae; Private; H/25th Inf. Born in Kentucky; black complexion; cannot read or write, age 28, 5 Sep 1870, in H/25th Infantry at Ft McKavett, TX. SOURCE: Bierschwale, *Fort McKavett,* 107.

‡Retired from F/24th Infantry, Ft Douglas, UT. SOURCE: *ANJ* 34 (7 Aug 1897): 909.

FINNEGAN, Michael; Private; G/24th Cav. Born in Madison County, FL, 16 Mar 1862; enlisted Detroit, MI, 9 Jun 1884, Ht 5'7", mulatto complexion, black eyes and hair; occupation laborer, hostler, painter, ship steward; assigned to H/10th Cavalry; discharged Ft Apache, AZ, 9 Jun 1889; reenlisted Fort Apache, 9 Jun 1889; discharged 8 Sep 1892; enlisted Chicago, IL, 9 Nov 1892; assigned to G/24th Infantry; discharged, Ft Bayard, NM, 6 May 1895; claimed invalid pension on basis of fractured skull incurred when waylaid while delivering post mail from Maxey, AZ, to Ft Thomas, AZ, Apr 1891; resided Baltimore, MD, and Philadelphia, PA; received invalid pension of $6 per month, 1896, increased to $8 in 1898, increased to $12 in 1916; sailed on transatlantic steamers 1914–17, survived German torpedo attack that sank steamer *East Wales* off coast of Britain, 14 Oct 1917; never married; died 8 Jun 1918; buried National Soldiers Home Cemetery, Elizabeth City County, VA. SOURCE: Sayre, *Warriors of Color*, 174–81.

Appointed from private to wagoner 1 Nov 1885; wagoner in H/10th Cavalry stationed at Bonita Cañon Camp, AZ, 30 Apr 1886. SOURCE: Tagg, *The Camp at Bonita Cañon*, 66, 231.

‡Corporal, H/10th Cavalry, sharpshooter, at Ft Apache. SOURCE: *ANJ* 25 (21 Jul 1888): 1034.

‡Acquitted of assault on civilian employee of Quartermaster Department, Ft Apache. SOURCE: *ANJ* 27 (28 Dec 1889): 352.

‡First sergeant, H/10th Cavalry, at Ft Apache, 1890, subscribed $.50 to testimonial to General Grierson. SOURCE: List of subscriptions, 23 Apr 1890, 10th Cavalry papers, MHI.

‡As corporal, A/10th Cavalry, ranked number 9 with carbine, Departments of Arizona and Texas, bronze medal, Ft Wingate, NM, 17–22 Aug 1891. SOURCE: Baker, Roster; GO 81, AGO, 6 Oct 1891.

‡Ranked number 49 among carbine sharpshooters with over 72 percent, 1891. SOURCE: GO 1, AGO, 2 Jan 1892.

‡As sergeant, A/10th Cavalry, ranked number 5 with carbine, Departments of Columbia and Dakota, bronze medal, Ft Keogh, MT, 15–21 Aug 1892. SOURCE: Baker, Roster; GO 75, AGO, 3 Nov 1892.

FINNEY, Lewis; Sergeant; 25th Inf. Warned Pvt. George W. Newman, 25th Infantry, that carrying a razor could result in a prison term, Ft Davis, TX, 1873. SOURCE: Dobak and Phillips, *The Black Regulars*, 200.

FINNEY, Will; Private; M/10th Cav. Died 24 Dec 1907; buried at Ft Bayard, NM, in plot P 20. SOURCE: "Fort Bayard National Cemetery, Records of Burials."

Will Finny, M/10th Cavalry, buried at Ft Bayard. SOURCE: "Buffalo Soldiers Buried at Ft Bayard, NM."

Buried 24 Dec 1907, section B, row A, plot 20, at Ft Bayard. SOURCE: Erickson, Burials at Fort Bayard National Cemetery, NM.

FISH, Henry R.; F/9th Cav. Born in Washington, DC; mulatto complexion; cannot read or write, age 24, Jul 1870, at Ft McKavett, TX. SOURCE: Bierschwale, *Fort McKavett,* 98.

‡Served 1869–74; resides in Washington, DC. SOURCE: *Winners of the West* 4 (May 1927): 2.

FISHER, Henry; Private; I/25th Inf. Born in Norristown, PA; Ht 5'9", dark hair and eyes, yellow complexion; occupation laborer; enlisted at age 21, Philadelphia, PA, 18 Aug 1881; arrived Ft Snelling, MN, 21 Nov 1882. SOURCE: Descriptive & Assignment Rolls of Recruits, 25 Inf.

FISHER, Samuel; Private; C/10th Cav. ‡Original member of 10th Cavalry; in troop when organized, Ft Leavenworth, KS, 14 May 1867. SOURCE: McMiller, "Buffalo Soldiers," 70.

Died 11 Aug 1867 of cholera at Camp Grierson, KS. SOURCE: Regimental Returns, 10th Cavalry, 1867.

FISHER, William J.; Private; D/25th Inf. Born in Jamaica, West Indies; Ht 5'6", black hair and brown eyes, brown complexion; occupation laborer; resided in Mount Vernon, NY, when enlisted 9 Nov 1885, age 21, at Davis Island, NY; assigned to D/25th Infantry; arrived Ft Snelling, MN, 26 Apr 1886. SOURCE: Descriptive & Assignment Rolls of Recruits, 25 Inf.

FITZGERALD, James; Private; 25th Inf. Born in Nottoway County, VA; Ht 5'4", black hair and eyes, black complexion; served in K/10th Cavalry to 2 Jan 1887; second reenlistment at age 34, St. Louis, MO, 24 Jan 1887; arrived Ft Snelling, MN, 22 Mar 1887. SOURCE: Descriptive & Assignment Rolls of Recruits, 25 Inf.

FITZGERALD, John; Ord Sgt; U.S. Army. ‡Born in Philadelphia, PA; served first enlistment with I/24th Infantry, discharged as sergeant, 27 Mar 1870; appointed regimental quartermaster sergeant, 1 Mar 1877; fifth enlistment, Ft Supply, Indian Territory, single, character excellent, 26 Mar 1885; additional pay $4 per month; deposits $300 in 1881, $150 in 1882, retained $60, clothing $159; appointed ordnance sergeant, U.S. Army, 28 May 1885. SOURCE: Descriptive Book, 24 Inf NCS & Band.

Appointed ordnance sergeant, 28 May 1885, from quartermaster sergeant, 24th Infantry. SOURCE: Dobak, "Staff Noncommissioned Officers."

FLADGER, John J.; Private; 25th Inf. Born in Marion, SC; enlisted Charleston, SC, age 27, occupation brakeman, Ht 5'9", dark complexion, black eyes and hair, 20 Jun 1881; left recruit depot, David's Island, NY, 17 Aug 1881, and after trip on steamer *Thomas Kirby* to Central Depot, New York City, and train via Chicago to Running Water, Dakota Territory, 22 Aug 1881, marched forty-seven miles to Ft Randall, SD, arrived 24 Aug 1881. SOURCE: Descriptive & Assignment Rolls, 25 Inf.

FLANBEAU, Adam; 1st Sgt; F/24th Inf. Died at Ft McIntosh, TX, on 7 May 1874; buried at Fort Sam Houston National Cemetery, Section PE, number 415. SOURCE: Buffalo Soldiers Interred in Fort Sam Houston National Cemetery.

FLEETWOOD, Miles E.; Corporal; M/10th Cav. Served 2 Feb 1882–1 Feb 1887; regimental clerk, Ft Davis, TX, 1882–83; resided at 312 E. 6th St., Cincinnati, OH, in 1896; resided at 528 Plum St., Cincinnati, in 1897, occupation barber, age 42; testifies correct name is Marcuius E. Fleetwood. SOURCE: Sayre, *Warriors of Color*, 8–9, 12–13.

FLEMMING, Will; Private; 10th Cav. At San Carlos, AZ, Jul 1889, complained of harassment by 1st Sgt. James Logan; considered to be "worthless soldier" by Capt. Lewis Johnson; murdered by fellow soldiers, possibly at instigation of Sergeant Logan; all accused were acquitted after

two years of legal proceedings. SOURCE: Dobak and Phillips, *The Black Regulars*, 201–2.

FLETCHER, David; F/9th Cav. Born in Washington, DC; mulatto complexion; cannot read or write, age 24, Jul 1870, at Ft McKavett, TX. SOURCE: Bierschwale, *Fort McKavett*, 98.

FLETCHER, Edward; 1st Sgt; F/9th Cav. ‡Sergeant as of 1 Jan 1887. SOURCE: Roster, 9 Cav.

‡At Ft Robinson, NE, 1887–91. *See* OTT, **ROSS**, Edward, Private, G/9th Cavalry; OTT, **SMITH**, Walter, Private, F/9th Cavalry; OTT, **WILLIAMS**, Charles, Private, F/9th Cavalry

‡Fined $10 by garrison court martial for allowing and engaging in gambling in barracks after taps; leniency due to his good record. SOURCE: Order 132, Jul 1888, Post Orders, Ft Robinson.

‡First sergeant, F/9th Cavalry, 1891. *See* OTT, **BRADFORD**, Rudolph, Private, F/9th Cavalry

Appointed sergeant 1 Jan 1887; in F/9th Cavalry at Ft DuChesne, UT, Jan 1897. SOURCE: Ninth Cavalry, Roster of NCOs, 1897.

Received Philippine Campaign Badge number 11772 for service as first sergeant in F/9th Cavalry; in 9th Cavalry at Ft Leavenworth, KS, Mar 1905. SOURCE: Philippine Campaign Badge list, 29 May 1905.

FLETCHER, George; Private; H/10th Cav. Served at Fort Davis, TX, with William Allen. SOURCE: Sayre, *Warriors of Color*, 12.

FLETCHER, Humphrey; Private; L/9th Cav. At Ft Duncan, TX, 1870, owned pig stolen by Pvts. Humphrey Williams and Frank Thomas. SOURCE: Kenner, *Buffalo Soldiers and Officers of the Ninth Cavalry*, 177.

FLETCHER, James Robert; Trumpeter; K/10th Cav. Born in Winchester, VA, 15 Nov 1861; father George born in West Virginia; mother Lucy B. Ford born in West Virginia; brother Charles; sisters Luvinia and Edmonia; enlisted Philadelphia, PA, 1 Sep 1882; Ht 5'3", black complexion, eyes, and hair; occupation barber, janitor; discharged from H/10th Cavalry, 31 Aug 1887; reenlisted 26 Sep 1887; discharged from K/10th Cavalry, Ft Thomas, AZ, 20 Apr 1892; resided in Washington, DC, from 1892; married Lucy Beatrice Williams, Washington, DC, 9 May 1901; children Lee James, born 9 Dec 1901, Lavinia B. Sullivan, born 10 Apr 1908, Norman E., born 30 Jan 1909, Evelyn A. Bowen, born 4 Apr 1911, Roland S., born 19 May 1913, Earnestine C., born 4 Oct 1920; received pension of $20 per month in 1924, increased to $25 in 1928, increased to $30 in 1929, increased to $55, then $72 in 1937; janitor, Precinct 8, Washington, DC, Police Force; died Washington, DC, 24 Mar 1942; buried at Arlington National Cemetery; wife died age 92, Washington, DC, 17 Jun 1975. SOURCE: Sayre, *Warriors of Color*, 182–91, 220, 234.

Trumpeter in H/10th Cavalry stationed at Bonita Cañon Camp, AZ, 30 Apr 1886. SOURCE: Tagg, *The Camp at Bonita Cañon*, 231.

‡Trumpeter J. R. Fletcher at Ft Apache, AZ, 1890, subscribed $.25 to testimonial to General Grierson. SOURCE: List of subscriptions, 23 Apr 1890, 10th Cavalry papers, MHI.

FLETCHER, Nathan; 1st Sgt; E/9th Cav. ‡Fifteen years' continuous service in Army; now in F/9th Cavalry. SOURCE: Cleveland *Gazette*, 26 Jul 1886.

‡Sergeant, F/9th Cavalry, as of 3 Feb 1880. SOURCE: Roster, 9 Cav.

‡Authorized four-month furlough from Ft Robinson, NE. SOURCE: *ANJ* 24 (25 Jun 1887): 954.

‡Replaced recently killed first sergeant (*see* **STANCE**, Emanuel, First Sergeant, F/9th Cavalry) just before arrival of Simpson Mann in troop. SOURCE: Rickey, Mann interview.

Replaced 1st Sgt. Emanuel Stance in 1887; departed Ft Robinson on four-month furlough, 26 May 1887; "the longest tenured and most dependable non-commissioned officer in the company"; served on honor guard when body of Col. Edward Hatch was transported from Ft Robinson to Ft Leavenworth, KS, in 1889. SOURCE: Kenner, *Buffalo Soldiers and Officers of the Ninth Cavalry*, 48–49, 170.

‡Mrs. Fannie Fletcher, wife of 1st Sgt. Nathan Fletcher, to be directed to leave post with understanding that she is never to return. SOURCE: Post QM, Ft Robinson, to CO, Ft Robinson, 29 Mar 1888, Register of Correspondence, Ft Robinson.

‡Sergeant, F/9th Cavalry, on special duty as post provost sergeant, Ft Robinson, vice Sgt. Arthur Ransom, G/9th Cavalry. SOURCE: Order 5, 16 Jan 1893, Post Orders, Ft Robinson.

Appointed 1 Jan 1895; in E/9th Cavalry at Ft Robinson, Jan 1897. SOURCE: Ninth Cavalry, Roster of NCOs, 1897.

‡Reenlistment as first sergeant, E/9th Cavalry, married, authorized. SOURCE: Letter, AGO, 14 Jun 1897.

FLIPPER, Henry O.; 2nd Lt; 10th Cav. ‡Biographical sketch. SOURCE: Logan and Winston, *Dictionary of American Negro Biography*, 227–28.

‡Mentioned as 1877 graduate of U.S. Military Academy. SOURCE: Billington, *New Mexico's Buffalo Soldiers*, 190.

Aware of lengths to which his men would go to continue gambling. SOURCE: Dobak and Phillips, *The Black Regulars*, 161–62.

Report of scouting expedition, Feb–Mar 1880, from Ft Sill, OK, with G/10th Cavalry, published. SOURCE: Schubert, *Voices of the Buffalo Soldier*, 87–89.

‡Offered services to government in war with Spain, 1898. SOURCE: Clark, "A History of the Twenty-fourth," 87.

FLOYD, Caleb H.; F/9th Cav. Born in Virginia; black complexion; cannot read or write, age 21, Jul 1870, at Ft McKavett, TX. SOURCE: Bierschwale, *Fort McKavett*, 98.

FLOYD, John; QM Sgt; M/9th Cav. ‡Lance corporal, I/9th Cavalry, promoted to corporal vice Bailey, promoted. SOURCE: *ANJ* 31 (19 May 1894): 663.

‡Promoted to sergeant, Ft Washakie, WY, Nov 1895. SOURCE: *ANJ* 33 (16 Nov 1895): 179.

Appointed sergeant 5 Nov 1895; in I/9th Cavalry at Ft Washakie, Jan 1897. SOURCE: Ninth Cavalry, Roster of NCOs, 1897.

‡Quartermaster sergeant, M/9th Cavalry, ranked number 5, Army pistol competition, and number 9, Northern Division pistol competition, both at Ft Sheridan, IL, 1906. SOURCE: GO 198, AGO, 6 Dec 1906.

‡Veteran of Spanish-American War and Philippine Insurrection; sergeant, at Ft D. A. Russell, WY, in 1910; marksman. SOURCE: *Illustrated Review: Ninth Cavalry*, with picture.

FORD; Private; 10th Cav. At Ft Davis, TX, 15 Jan 1885. SOURCE: Bigelow, *Garrison Tangles*, 46.

FORD, Albert; Private; D/10th Cav. Died 2 Jun 1879 of knife fight at San Angela, TX. SOURCE: Regimental Returns, 10th Cavalry, 1879.

Died at Ft Concho, TX, on 2 Jun 1879; buried at San Antonio National Cemetery, Section E, number 807. SOURCE: San Antonio National Cemetery Locator.

FORD, George W.; QM Sgt; 10th Cav. ‡Lived on Duke Street, Alexandria, VA, between St. Asaph and Columbia; moved with parents to farm at Gum Spring, adjoining Mount Vernon estate, 1857; went to live with aunt Mary V. Bell, 543 Broome St., New York, NY, Mar 1860; returned late winter, 1861. SOURCE: Affidavit, Ford, 28 Nov 1921, VA File C 2580332, George W. Ford.

‡Father a free man, owned farm inherited from West Ford; baptized at age 5, St. Paul's Episcopal Church, where Washingtonians worshiped; family were respected and active communicants of Episcopal Church; as lad he sold pictures at entrance to Mount Vernon; grandfather was wheelwright, carpenter, overseer of house servants at Mount Vernon, slaves at Mount Vernon frequently did chores on Ford farm; in New York City with parents during draft riots; delegate from Kansas to 1900 Republican convention in Philadelphia, voted for Theodore Roosevelt as vice president; wife a native of Charleston, SC, speaks with clear English accent acquired as girl living with English family in Brooklyn, NY, is daughter of well-known Baptist

minister. SOURCE: Rev. Gay C. White, "From Mt. Vernon to Springfield," (Springfield) *Illinois State Register*, 17 Jan 1937.

‡Born in Fairfax Co., VA; enlisted Washington, DC, age 21, farmer, Ht 5'7", yellow complexion, 10 Sep 1867; assigned to L/10th Cavalry; discharged, expiration of service, as first sergeant, Ft Sill, OK, 10 Sep 1872; enlisted Ft Sill, 11 Sep 1872; assigned to the field and staff, 10th Cavalry; discharged Ft Concho, TX, expiration of service, quartermaster sergeant, "character most excellent," 11 Sep 1877. SOURCE: Register of Enlistments.

‡Original member of 10th Cavalry; in L Troop when organized, Ft Riley, KS, 21 Sep 1867. SOURCE: McMiller, "Buffalo Soldiers," 78.

‡Enlisted at age 19, 1867; served two enlistments; appointed superintendent of Negro section, Chattanooga National Cemetery, 1878; supervised several national cemeteries; granted leave of absence to serve as major, 23rd Kansas Infantry, 1898; retired 1930. SOURCE: Rickey, *Forty Miles a Day on Beans and Hay*, 344.

‡"Dear Sir: I feel that my first duty should be an apology for intruding on your valuable time on a subject for which you possibly have little or no interest. I have been wondering if I am the last man or are there any survivors of the 10th Cavalry who were in at its organization. I enlisted Sept. 10, 1867. Discharged Sept. 11, 1877. I entered the regiment at the age of 19 as trumpeter, served seven years as first sergeant of L Troop, and was discharged as Q.M. Sergt. in 1877 through the recommendation of Col. B. H. Grierson, our commander. I received an appointment as Supt. National Cemeteries and served in that position for fifty-three years, retiring in August, 1930. At the outbreak of the Spanish-American War, I was stationed at the National Cemetery at Fort Scott, Kansas. Through the recommendation of Colonel Grierson I was commissioned Major of the 23rd Kansas Volunteers, and served with my regiment in Cuba having obtained leave of absence from my cemeterial duties. I just imagined you might have knowledge of another survivor. I must in closing ask you to kindly overlook any defects in this letter. You know a man 89 years old is not expected to be a good penman. Sincerely yours, Geo. W. Ford." Letter, Ford to Sergeant Major, 10th Cavalry, West Point, NY, 17 Nov 1936. SOURCE: *Cavalry Journal* 46 (Jul–Aug 1937): 394.

‡Among Ford's most prized possessions is letter from Lt. Col. N. B. Briscoe, Commander, 10th Cavalry, Ft Leavenworth, KS, 27 Nov 1936: "I am most pleased to hear from one of the charter members of the tenth cavalry, and am taking the liberty of publishing your letter in the regiment, and of making inquiry through the service papers for other original members. The long and honorable record attained during the years since 1867 is a great pride to those of us now in the regiment and I am sure you will be gratified to learn that we hold annually an organization day celebration on July 28. Among the men in the regiment

there are about fifteen whose fathers also served in the 10th Cavalry. . . . It is a great pleasure to hear from you and I assure you that anything you want from the 10th Cavalry is yours." SOURCE: Rev. Gay C. White, "From Mt. Vernon to Springfield," (Springfield) *Illinois State Register*, 17 Jan 1937.

‡Born in Virginia; 10th Cavalry, 1867–77, discharged as quartermaster sergeant; superintendent, Military Cemetery, Springfield, 1916. SOURCE: *Crisis* 11 (Apr 1916): 290.

‡Honorable mention for gallantry against Kiowas and Comanches, Wichita Agency, Indian Territory, 22–23 Aug 1874. SOURCE: Baker, Roster.

‡Served as mail courier in L/10th Cavalry and D/10th Cavalry, between Ft Arbuckle, KS, and Ft Gibson, Indian Territory, winter 1868: "This was no pleasure ride when one considers that besides fording the icy waters of the Canadian, the Washita, and Wild Horse, there was also the danger of capture by Indians"; Filmore Roberts, "a boy of 19," drowned in Canadian River with his pouch; reported as absent without leave when he did not arrive at Ft Arbuckle; body found months later. From Ford letter, dated Rural Route 1, Springfield, IL. SOURCE: *Winners of the West* 1 (Apr 1924): 1.

‡Pvt. John Randall, G/10th Cavalry, was wounded eleven times with lances and shot in hip about forty-five miles west of Ft Hays, KS, while hiding in hole under railroad cut, Oct 1867; Sgt. Charles H. Davis performed gallantly in main battle. SOURCE: *Winners of the West* 2 (Nov 1925): 2.

‡First sergeant, L/10th Cavalry, accidentally shot in leg by loaded revolver he unpacked from arms chest, while issuing arms to guard, Ft Sill, Sep 1871. SOURCE: Affidavit, Thomas J. Spencer, former first lieutenant, 10th Cavalry, Washington, DC, 23 May 1890, VA File C 2580332, George W. Ford.

‡Former comrade Joseph A. Blackburn saw Ford accidentally wounded with Colt revolver in line of duty. SOURCE: Affidavit, Blackburn, former first sergeant, L/10th Cavalry, Henrietta, Clay Co., TX, 16 May 1890, VA File C 2580332, George W. Ford.

‡Ford writes from Ft Scott, KS, that he was commended in General Order 53, 1874, for gallantry in action; desires to know if conditions permit issue to him of Medal of Honor. SOURCE: J. D. Bowersock, Member of Congress, to Secretary of War, 23 Apr 1902, AGO File 431605.

‡War Department reports to Bowersock no indication of recommendation for Medal of Honor or certificate of merit for Ford. SOURCE: AAG to Bowersock, 3 May 1902, AGO File 431605.

‡First Sergeant Ford present Jul–Aug 1874; L/10th Cavalry in accordance with Special Order 155, Headquarters, Ft Richardson, TX, 12 Aug, left 14 Aug, arrived Ft Sill 18 Aug; left post 21 Aug, arrived Wichita Agency 22 Aug, engaged Nocomi and Kiowa Indians with one noncommissioned officer wounded in action; marched 160

miles. SOURCE: Report of Rolls Division, AGO, 26 Apr 1902, AGO File 431605.

‡Born 23 Nov 1847; lived with parents, Fairfax Co., VA, until he went to school in New York City; returned and lived one year with sister; enlisted Washington, DC, 10 Sep 1867; served ten years to discharge as quartermaster sergeant, noncommissioned staff, 10th Cavalry, Ft Concho, 11 Sep 1877; worked at Arlington National Cemetery, Mar–May 1878; transferred to Chattanooga Cemetery until Nov 1878; then Beaufort, SC, National Cemetery to Aug 1894; Ft Scott until 1904; Port Hudson, LA, until Nov 1906; enlisted Topeka, KS, 15 Jul 1898; discharged Ft Leavenworth, 10 Apr 1899. SOURCE: Affidavit, Ford, 29 Dec 1931, VA File C 2580332, George W. Ford.

‡Children: George, Jr., born 1880, resided at 10750 Glenroy, Chicago, IL; Noel B., born 1881, deceased; Harriet C., born 1884, married Goin, resided at 920 Shipman, Peoria, IL; James I., born 1886, resided at 1605 East Capitol, Springfield; Donald G., born 1888, deceased; Cecil B., born 1891, resided at 303 Gale, Peoria; Elise, married Jenkins, 1414 Pine, Columbia, SC; Vera, married E. C. Powell, 916 First Avenue, Charleston, WV. SOURCE: VA File C 2580332, George W. Ford.

‡Major, 23rd Kansas, and commander, 2nd Battalion. SOURCE: Beasley, *Negro Trailblazers*, 284.

‡President has referred to War Department Ford letter of 21 Jun 1899, asking authority to recruit Negro regiment for service in the Philippines; Secretary of War says present plans do not include additional volunteer regiments for Philippine service; Ford letter to remain on file for future consideration. SOURCE: AAG to Ford, 27 Jun 1899, AGO File 246901.

‡Ford asks return of papers he filed when commissioned in Volunteers. SOURCE: Ford to SecWar, 2 Nov 1899, AGO File 246901.

‡War Department complies with Ford request for return of papers. SOURCE: AAG to Ford, 17 Nov 1899, AGO File 246901.

‡Letter, Theodore Roosevelt to "My Dear Major Ford," dated Oyster Bay, NY, 9 Jul 1900, responds to Ford query regarding Roosevelt's attacks on black troops; Roosevelt explains his respect for black soldiers and his pointing out of shortcomings of others. SOURCE: Morison and Blum, *Letters of Theodore Roosevelt*, II.

‡Ford request for position in colored regiment has been placed on file and will receive due consideration at proper time. SOURCE: AG to J. D. Bowersock, 21 Jan 1901, AGO File 246901.

‡In response to inquiry, informed that vacancies in Philippine Scouts are filled at lieutenant level; Ford letter to president will be referred to General Chaffee. SOURCE: AG to Ford, 2 Dec 1901, AGO File 246901.

‡"Should the present crisis demand that men be enlisted and drilled for the defense of the country, I beg to offer my services and ask that when needed, I be authorized to enlist and prepare a regiment of Colored Men, more if necessary, to be used in any emergency that may arise. The Colored Men of Illinois are loyal and ready to defend their country whenever called upon. My military experience has been gained by ten years' service as a non. com. officer in the regular Army, and one year as Major, 23 Kans Vol., War with Spain." SOURCE: Ford to SecWar, 6 Feb 1917, AGO File 246901.

‡Born in Alexandria, 23 Nov 1850; educated in grade schools of New York City; "have been a student of drill regulations for the past 40 years, have drilled and instructed several cos. of the National Guard"; speaks and reads Spanish fairly well; physical condition "nearly perfect." SOURCE: Ford, questionnaire, AGO, 9 Feb 1917, AGO File 246901.

‡Son Cecil B. Ford served as dental assistant, 8th Illinois Infantry Hospital Corps, 370th Infantry (National Guard), 24 Jul 1917–24 Jan 1918. SOURCE: Affidavit, Ford, 1 Oct 1921, VA File, C 2580332, George W. Ford.

Writings in *Winners of the West* quoted. SOURCE: Dobak and Phillips, *The Black Regulars*, 278.

Article "Winning the West," in *Winners of the West* (Apr 1924), reproduced. SOURCE: Schubert, *Voices of the Buffalo Soldier*, 68.

‡Pension: $20 per month, 4 Mar 1917; $24 per month, 16 Jun 1920; $30 per month, 23 Nov 1922; $72 per month, 4 May 1931; $60 per month, 29 Dec 1931; $72 per month, 13 Aug 1935; $100 per month, 9 Jun 1938. SOURCE: VA File C 2580332, George W. Ford.

‡Complains about veto of pension bill by President Coolidge. SOURCE: *Winners of the West* 1 (Jul 1924): 1.

‡Complains about unfair pension treatment. SOURCE: *Winners of the West* 1 (Oct 1924): 4.

‡Renews subscription; expresses gratitude for pension fight carried on by magazine. SOURCE: *Winners of the West* 4 (Aug 1927): 4.

‡Said goodbye to boyhood friend Joseph A. Blackburn, Ft Worth, TX, 12 Sep 1877; "recently saw his name in your magazine and you have helped me locate him and have reunion." SOURCE: *Winners of the West* 5 (Sep 1928): 3.

‡Ford: "I sometimes wonder if some white persons hope to inherit a different and separate heaven and let us have such a one as is depicted in *Green Pastures*. I am fully aware of the shortcomings of many of my people, but the great majority are peaceful and law abiding. There are very many noble and high-minded white people, who do not subscribe to the treatment to which we are subjected, but they lack the courage and the interest to come out in the open and protest against it. Many persons think of us as the carefree, shiftless characters shown in the farcical skit of 'Amos 'n' Andy' "; calls attention to *Harper's* 1859 article ["Mount Vernon as it is," *Harper's Monthly* 18 (March 1859)] and his grandfather West Ford, whom he recalled as a "picturesque old fellow" and privileged character at Mount Vernon and Alexandria. SOURCE: Rev. Gay C. White,

"From Mt. Vernon to Springfield," (Springfield) *Illinois State Register*, 17 Jan 1937.

‡Ford and wife are sick but improving; he was 90 on 23 Nov 1937; "am the only living survivor of the original regiment, the 10th U.S. Cavalry, who marched away toward the Rio Grande, 1,225 strong in 1867"; renews subscription. SOURCE: *Winners of the West* 15 (Feb 1938): 3.

‡Picture, "Oldest Known Survivor"; with letter, Sgt. Maj. L. M. Carter, 10th Cavalry, Ft Leavenworth, KS, requesting photograph of Ford for regimental archives. SOURCE: *Winners of the West* 15 (Jun 1938): 7.

‡Superintendent, National Cemetery, Chattanooga, 1878; then cemeteries at Beaufort, Ft Scott, Port Hudson; superintendent at Camp Butler, IL, 1906–30; died at home, Springfield, 30 Jun 1939; survived by wife, to whom he was married 28 Aug 1879, three daughters, one sister, eight grandchildren; buried at Camp Butler. SOURCE: *Winners of the West* 16 (Aug 1939): 1.

‡Ford died of bronchial pneumonia; father William Ford of Alexandria; mother Henrietta Bruce Ford of Virginia; buried at Camp Butler National Cemetery, IL; widow Harriett E. (Bythewood) Ford born 16 Sep 1861; married at Beaufort, 28 Aug 1879; resided at 1525 South 11th, Springfield; resided at 916 First Avenue, Charleston, 30 Aug 1939; pension $50 per month, 1 Apr 1944. SOURCE: VA File C 2580332, George W. Ford.

See OTT, **ANDERSON**, Henry, Private, L/10th Cavalry

FORD, John; Private; 9th Cav. Died 26 Nov 1871; buried at San Antonio National Cemetery, Section D, number 783. SOURCE: San Antonio National Cemetery Locator.

FORD, Samuel; Private; B/10th Cav. At Ft Stockton, TX, 1879; witness in court martial of Lt. William H. Beck, 10th Cavalry, San Antonio, TX, Feb 1879. SOURCE: Kinevan, *Frontier Cavalryman*, 287.

FORD, Steven; Corporal; B/10th Cav. At Ft Duncan, TX, Dec 1877–Sep 1879; 1878, replaced Cpl. Robert Reinhart as Lt. John Bigelow's orderly. SOURCE: Kinevan, *Frontier Cavalryman*, 83, 162, 282.

FORD, Thomas; Private; C/10th Cav. Served with Pvt. George Washington, C/10th Cavalry, early 1870s. SOURCE: Schubert, *Voices of the Buffalo Soldier*, 234.

FORD, Wiley; Private; 25th Inf. Born in Franklin, VA; Ht 6'0", black hair and eyes, saddle complexion; occupation laborer, enlisted at age 23, Cincinnati, OH, 3 Dec 1886; arrived Ft Snelling, MN, 1 Apr 1887. SOURCE: Descriptive & Assignment Rolls of Recruits, 25 Inf.

FORMAN, Andrew; Corporal; D/24th Inf. Died 7 Jan 1893; buried at Ft Bayard, NM, in plot I 31. SOURCE: "Fort Bayard National Cemetery, Records of Burials."

Buried 7 Jan 1893, section A, row M, plot 30, at Ft Bayard. SOURCE: Erickson, Burials at Fort Bayard National Cemetery, NM.

FORMAN, Elwood A.; Corporal; H/25th Inf. Private, H/25th Infantry, rode in 25th Infantry Bicycle Corps, Ft. Missoula, MT, summer 1896. SOURCE: Sorenson, List of Buffalo Soldiers Who Rode in the 25th Infantry Bicycle Corps, in authors' files.

One of twenty men who cycled 1,900 miles from Ft Missoula to St. Louis, MO, 14 Jun–24 Jul 1897, in 25th Infantry Bicycle Corps to test durability and practicality of bicycles as a means of transportation for troops. SOURCE: File 60178, GC, AGO Records.

‡Corporal, H/25th Infantry, died in the Philippines, 22 Apr 1901. SOURCE: *ANJ* 38 (4 May 1901): 876.

FORNISS, George; 24th Inf. In 1871 married Cesaria Perazo, El Paso, TX, stayed together until her death in 1886; worked as tailor; in 1892 resided with Severiana Tijeria, moved to Brownsville, TX, married her in 1903, when daughter Josephine was 10 years old. SOURCE: Leiker, *Racial Borders*, 87–88.

FORSTER, George W.; Private; H/10th Cav. Died 22 Feb 1891; buried 10 Mar 1932 at Santa Fe National Cemetery, NM, plot P.102. SOURCE: Santa Fe National Cemetery, Records of Burials.

FORT, Lewis; Private; H/9th Cav. ‡Born in Alexandria, VA; in D/9th Cavalry, Sep 1878–Jan 1896; transferred to H/9th Cavalry, age 37, Ht 5'8", seventeen years' continuous service, $4 per month additional pay, 25 Jan 1896; seven summary court martial convictions, Ft Robinson, NE, 1896–97. SOURCE: Descriptive Book, H/9 Cav.

With Captain Dodge at battle at Milk River, CO, 2–10 Oct 1879. SOURCE: Miller, *Hollow Victory*, 167, 206–7.

Participated in battle with Utes on Milk River, Sep–Oct 1878; private, D/9th Cavalry, wrote affidavit attesting to Henry Johnson's bravery at Milk River while serving at Ft McKinney, WY, 1890. SOURCE: Schubert, *Black Valor*, 68.

‡Reenlistment in D/9th Cavalry, married, authorized. SOURCE: Letter, AGO, 28 Jul 1893.

‡Wife Bertie G. Fort writes Secretary of War from Crawford, NE, asking for quarters at Ft Robinson, 28 Jul 1894; she left post in Apr 1894 of her own accord "to keep from having trouble with a man, I would not do as he wanted me to do"; commander said when she returned that he could not give her permission to reside on post; husband has fifteen years' service, married nine years; she worked for Capt.

John Loud, 1886–93: "I always did my duty as a servant"; commander, Ft Robinson, defends his position as based on fact that there are too many enlisted men's wives on post, 8 Aug 1894; Adjutant General supports commander, 14 Aug 1894. SOURCE: QM Consolidated File, Ft Robinson.

‡Killed in action, San Juan, Cuba, 2 Jul 1898. SOURCE: SecWar, *AR 1898*, 707; *ANJ* 36 (11 Feb 1899): 567.

‡Killed in action, Cuba, 1898. SOURCE: Scipio, *Last of the Black Regulars*, 29.

FOSTER; Corporal; H/10th Cav. Participated in campaign against Geronimo, 1886. SOURCE: Sayre, *Warriors of Color*, 111.

FOSTER, Allen; Corporal; E/9th Cav. Cursed and abused by Capt. Ambrose Hooker, New Mexico, 1879. SOURCE: Kenner, *Buffalo Soldiers and Officers of the Ninth Cavalry*, 107.

FOSTER, George; Private; M/10th Cav. Died at Ft Davis, TX, on 3 May 1883; buried at San Antonio National Cemetery, Section I, number 1497. SOURCE: San Antonio National Cemetery Locator.

FOSTER, George; Sergeant; H/10th Cav. ‡Private, wounded in battle with Indians near Sulphur Springs, TX, while part of Capt. M. L. Courtney's command of H/10th Cavalry and H/25th Infantry, Jul 1879; two Indians also killed. SOURCE: SecWar, *AR 1879*, 107.

‡Honorable mention as private, H/10th Cavalry, for services rendered in capture of Mangas and his Apache band, Rio Bonito, AZ, 18 Oct 1886. SOURCE: Baker, Roster.

Corporal Foster, H/10th Cavalry, participated in Oct 1886 pursuit and capture of Apache Mangus. SOURCE: Schubert, *Voices of the Buffalo Soldier*, 146.

‡Sergeant, H/10th Cavalry, shot by interpreter John Glass, Ft Apache, AZ, 20 Feb 1891, and died two days later; Glass in guardhouse to await action of civil authorities; "Sergt. Foster was a good soldier of twenty-one years service in the 10th Cavalry, and bore on his body the marks of a wound received in an Indian fight. His death is much regretted by all who knew him." SOURCE: *ANJ* 28 (14 Mar 1891): 493.

FOSTER, George W.; Private; H/10th Cav. In Troop H/10th Cavalry stationed at Bonita Cañon Camp, AZ, 30 Apr 1886. SOURCE: Tagg, *The Camp at Bonita Cañon*, 231.

FOSTER, Henry; Private; C/24th Inf. Died 3 Jun 1907; buried at San Antonio National Cemetery, Section F, number 974. SOURCE: San Antonio National Cemetery Locator.

FOSTER, Larkin; Wagoner; B/10th Cav. ‡Lankin Foster original member of 10th Cavalry; in troop when organized, Ft Leavenworth, KS, 1 Apr 1867. SOURCE: McMiller, "Buffalo Soldiers," 69.

Died 19 Sep 1871; killed in action at Foster Springs, Indian Territory. SOURCE: Regimental Returns, 10th Cavalry, 1871.

FOSTER, Leon D.; Private; A/9th Cav. Died 24 Jan 1910; buried at Ft Bayard, NM, in plot S 16. SOURCE: "Fort Bayard National Cemetery, Records of Burials."

Buried 24 Jan 1910, section B, row D, plot 16, at Ft Bayard. SOURCE: Erickson, Burials at Fort Bayard National Cemetery, NM.

FOSTER, Perrent; Corporal; L/25th Inf. Died in the Philippines 29 Aug 1900; body received for reburial 15 Apr 1902 at San Francisco National Cemetery, buried in plot NADDN947. SOURCE: San Francisco National Cemetery.

FOSTER, Saint; 1st Sgt; 10th Cav. ‡Born in Texas; private, D/25th Infantry, 12 Nov 1875–11 Nov 1880; private, corporal, sergeant, first sergeant, M and C/10th Cavalry; private, corporal, sergeant, D/10th Cavalry, 12 Feb 1881–27 Apr 1893; private, G/10th Cavalry, 2 Mar 1896; sergeant, 9 Mar 1896; first sergeant, 5 Sep 1896; stationed at Ft Assiniboine, MT, as first sergeant, G/10th Cavalry, 1897. SOURCE: Baker, Roster.

‡Sharpshooter, stationed at Ft McDowell, AZ. SOURCE: *ANJ* 24 (18 Jun 1887): 934.

‡Honorable mention for skill in trailing raiding parties in Arizona, 1888. SOURCE: Baker, Roster; Steward, *The Colored Regulars*, 244.

‡First sergeant, M/10th Cavalry, at Ft Apache, AZ, 1890, subscribed $.50 to testimonial to General Grierson. SOURCE: List of subscriptions, 23 Apr 1890, 10th Cavalry papers, MHI.

‡First sergeant, G/10th Cavalry, served in 10th Cavalry in Cuba, 1898. SOURCE: Cashin, *Under Fire with the Tenth Cavalry*, 344.

‡Commanded G/10th Cavalry at Las Guasimas, Cuba, 1898, and won commission due to success with troops in battle. SOURCE: Steward, *The Colored Regulars*, 139.

‡Second lieutenant, 10th Infantry, U.S. Volunteers. SOURCE: Cashin, *Under Fire with the Tenth Cavalry*, 320, with picture.

Served in 10th Cavalry as first sergeant under Lt. Charles A. Romeyn who called him close to the ideal first sergeant and among the finest soldiers he had known. SOURCE: Romeyn, "The First Sergeant," *Cavalry Journal*.

FOSTER, Samuel; Private; 9th Cav. Received Philippine Campaign Badge number 11885 for service as private in I/49th Infantry, United States Volunteers, and H/9th Cavalry;

in 9th Cavalry at Ft Leavenworth, KS, Mar 1905. SOURCE: Philippine Campaign Badge list, 29 May 1905.

FOSTER, William; F/9th Cav. Born in Tennessee; black complexion; cannot read or write, age 26, Jul 1870, at Ft McKavett, TX. SOURCE: Bierschwale, *Fort McKavett*, 98.

FOSTER, William; Sergeant; 24th Inf. Married to Theodora Sanches, Matamoras, Mexico, 1872; threatened life of Pvt. George Steele, 24th Infantry, for ruining his relationship with a woman; Steele thereupon deserted; was apprehended, convicted by military court in San Antonio, TX, and fined $80. SOURCE: Dobak and Phillips, *The Black Regulars*, 198, 317.

FOWLER, Albert; 1st Sgt; D/9th Cav. With Captain Dodge at battle at Milk River, CO, 2–10 Oct 1879. SOURCE: Miller, *Hollow Victory*, 167, 206–7.

Sergeant Fowler, "lightest in color and most intelligent" among soldiers of D/9th Cavalry, greeted by 5th Cavalry band and several hundred people upon arrival by train at Cheyenne, WY; Lieutenant Hughes said the colored soldiers compared well with white solders, having been tried several times and never found wanting, and displayed great coolness and determination; the company proceeded via Denver on train to Ft Union, NM. SOURCE: "Colored Troops," *Cheyenne Daily Leader*, 22 Oct 1879.

FOWLER, Arthur; Recruit; 25th Inf. Died 14 Sept 1917; buried at Ft Bayard, NM, in plot Z. SOURCE: "Fort Bayard National Cemetery, Records of Burials."

Buried 14 Sep 1917, section B, row K, plot 42 at Ft Bayard. SOURCE: Erickson, Burials at Fort Bayard National Cemetery, NM.

FOX, Lafayette; 24th Inf. Died 3 Nov 1896; buried at Ft Bayard, NM, in plot I 21. SOURCE: "Fort Bayard National Cemetery, Records of Burials."

FOX, Oscar; Sergeant; D/25th Inf. ‡In D/25th Infantry, ranked fourth among infantry marksmen, Department of Dakota, and on department team. SOURCE: *ANJ* 35 (25 Sep 1897): 55.

‡Resident of Flushing, NY; thirteen years' service, including heroism at El Caney, Cuba, 1898; discharged, character excellent; expected to reenlist after home leave; presented medal for valor by fellow townsmen, 1899. SOURCE: *ANJ* 38 (3 Aug 1901): 1187.

Pvt. Oscar Fox, 24th Infantry; New Yorker and three-year veteran when served with escort for Paymaster Joseph Wham when ambushed by robbers near Cedar Springs, AZ, in May 1889; did not contribute significantly to defense. SOURCE: Schubert, *Black Valor*, 93–96.

‡Third best marksman, Department of the Missouri, 1903. SOURCE: SecWar, *AR 1903*, 1:427.

‡Ranked number 24 among expert riflemen with 72.6 percent, 1904. SOURCE: GO 52, AGO, 19 Mar 1904.

‡Ranked number 17 in Northern Division rifle team competition, Ft Sheridan, IL, awarded bronze medal, 1904. SOURCE: GO 167, AGO, 28 Oct 1904.

‡Ranked number 14 among expert riflemen with 79.67 percent, 1905. SOURCE: GO 79, AGO, 1 Jun 1905.

‡Distinguished marksman, 1905. SOURCE: GO 173, AGO, 20 Oct 1905.

‡Ranked number 160 among expert riflemen with 72.67 percent, 1906. SOURCE: GO 101, AGO, 31 May 1906.

‡Ranked number 10 on U.S. infantry team that won first place, National Rifle Match, Sea Girt, NJ, 1906; each member of team won $300 and medal. SOURCE: GO 190, AGO, 15 Nov 1906.

‡Member of U.S. Army infantry team of seventeen riflemen, 1907. SOURCE: GO 162, AGO, 1 Aug 1907.

‡Ranked number 6 on ninth-place U.S. Army team, National Rifle Match, Camp Perry, OH, 28–31 Aug 1907. SOURCE: GO 4, AGO, 6 Jan 1908.

FRAGER, Robert; Private; 25th Inf. Born on Johns Island, SC; Ht 5'5", black hair and eyes, dark complexion; occupation laborer; enlisted at age 22, Charleston, SC, 6 Jun 1881; left recruit depot, David's Island, NY, 2 Jul 1881, arrived Ft Randall, SD, 7 Jul 1881. SOURCE: Descriptive & Assignment Rolls of Recruits, 25 Inf.

At Ft Snelling, MN, 1883, confined for twenty days for absence without leave. SOURCE: Dobak and Phillips, *The Black Regulars*, 185.

FRANCIS, James; Corporal; 38th Inf. One of seven 38th Infantrymen acquitted by military court of mutiny, New Mexico, 1868. SOURCE: Dobak and Phillips, *The Black Regulars*, 324.

FRANGE, Taseo; D/24th Inf. Born in Georgia; mulatto complexion; cannot read or write, age 25, Jul 1870, at Ft McKavett, TX. SOURCE: Bierschwale, *Fort McKavett*, 96.

FRANK, Jacob; Private; G/10th Cav. Died 11 Jun 1873; buried at San Antonio National Cemetery, Section C, number 280. SOURCE: San Antonio National Cemetery Locator.

FRANKLIN, Anthony; Corporal; B/25th Inf. Enlisted 29 Sep 1894, discharged as private 28 Sep 1897, character good; reenlisted 29 Sep 1897, discharged as private 28 Sep 1900, character very good; reenlisted 12 Feb 1901, discharged as private L/25th Infantry 11 Feb 1904, character excellent; reenlisted 18 Aug 1905, discharged without honor November 22, 1906. SOURCE: Powell, "Military Record of the Enlisted Men Who Were Discharged Without Honor."

‡Dishonorable discharge, Brownsville, TX. SOURCE: SO 266, AGO, 9 Nov 1906.

FRANKLIN, Isaac; Private; I/10th Cav. In Troop I/10th Cavalry stationed at Bonita Cañon Camp, AZ, 30 Jun 1886. SOURCE: Tagg, *The Camp at Bonita Cañon*, 231.

FRANKLIN, John; 1st Sgt; D/25th Inf. Offered cash to soldiers who did not approve of his leadership and deserted. SOURCE: Dobak and Phillips, *The Black Regulars*, 300.

‡At Ft Custer, MT. SOURCE: *ANJ* 26 (16 Feb 1889): 491.

FRANKLIN, William; Sergeant; 10th Cav. At Ft Apache, AZ, 1888, conducted religious services for men of his regiment and 24th Infantry. SOURCE: Dobak and Phillips, *The Black Regulars*, 119.

FRANKLIN, William M.; Private; E/25th Inf. Died 2 Jan 1901 on U.S. Army Transport *Warren* from Philippines; buried in plot E SID1344 at San Francisco National Cemetery. SOURCE: San Francisco National Cemetery.

FRANKS, Benjamin; Private; E/25th Inf. ‡Died of dysentery in the Philippines, 26 Aug 1900. SOURCE: *ANJ* 38 (8 Sep 1900): 43.

‡Died in the Philippines, 25 Aug 1900. SOURCE: Richmond *Planet*, 8 Sep 1900.

Died 26 Aug 1900; buried in plot NEW A944 at San Francisco National Cemetery. SOURCE: San Francisco National Cemetery.

FRASER, Carlos; Corporal; F/10th Cav. Born in Waterboro, SC; enlisted in 25th Infantry, Charleston, SC, age 22, laborer, Ht 5'6", black complexion, eyes, hair, 18 Jun 1881; left recruit depot, David's Island, NY, 17 Aug 1881, and after trip on steamer *Thomas Kirby* to Central Depot, New York City, and train via Chicago to Running Water, Dakota Territory, 22 Aug 1881, marched forty-seven miles to Ft Randall, SD, arrived 24 Aug 1881. SOURCE: Descriptive & Assignment Cards, 25 Inf.

‡Corporal, F/10th Cavalry; ranked number 10 in revolver competition, Departments of Arizona and California, bronze medal, Ft Wingate, NM, 1889. SOURCE: GO 78, AGO, 12 Oct 1889; Baker, Roster.

FRAUSTO, Gregario; Private; U.S. Army. Son of Scout Vector Frausto, Seminole Negro Scout, served 1878–84. SOURCE: Schubert, Consolidated List of Seminole Negro Scouts.

Born in Mexico; enlisted at Ft Clark, TX, 7 Mar 1878, age 25; Ht 5'7", black hair and eyes, black complexion; discharged 24 Apr 1879 at Ft Clark where he reenlisted five times for one-year terms; last discharge at Ft Clark 31 Aug 1884; 1880 Census lists wife Jausua age 20, daughter

Leventha age 8 and son Beto age 1; reportedly living 19 Aug 1941 in Del Rio, TX; buried at Cemeterio Viejo Loma de la Cruz, Round Mountain, Del Rio. SOURCE: Swanson, 16.

FRAUSTO, Quirino; Private; U.S. Army. Son of Scout Vector Frausto, Seminole Negro Scout, served 1878–84. SOURCE: Schubert, Consolidated List of Seminole Negro Scouts.

Born in Mexico; enlisted at Ft Clark, TX, 1 Mar 1878, age 26; Ht 5'7", black hair and eyes, copper complexion; discharged 29 Apr 1879 at Ft Clark where he reenlisted next day; discharged 1 May 1880 at Ft Clark; enlisted 12 Aug 1882 at Camp Myers Spring, TX; discharged 13 Aug 1883 at Ft. Clark where he reenlisted day before; discharged 11 Aug 1884 at Ft Clark where he reenlisted 13 Aug 1884; discharged 31 Aug 1884 at Ft Clark; died 1905; buried at Cemeterio Viejo Loma de la Cruz, Round Mountain, Del Rio, TX. SOURCE: Swanson, 16.

FRAUSTO, Thomas; Private; U.S. Army. Son of Scout Vector Frausto, Seminole Negro Scout, served 1878–79. SOURCE: Schubert, Consolidated List of Seminole Negro Scouts.

Born in Mexico; enlisted at Ft Clark, TX, 29 May 1878, age 33; Ht 5'5", black hair, brown eyes, copper complexion; discharged 28 May 1879 at Ft Clark; died 1897?; buried at Cemeterio Viejo Loma de la Cruz, Round Mountain, Del Rio, TX. SOURCE: Swanson, 16.

FRAUSTO, Vector; Private; U.S. Army. Seminole Negro Scout, served 1878–79; father of Scouts Gregario, Quirino, and Thomas Frausto. SOURCE: Schubert, Consolidated List of Seminole Negro Scouts.

Born in Mexico; enlisted at Ft Clark, TX, 7 May 1878, age 49; Ht 5'7", black hair, brown eyes, copper complexion; discharged 5 May 1879 at Ft Clark; probably father of Scouts Gregario and Quirino Frausto; buried at Cemeterio Viejo Loma de la Cruz, Round Mountain, Del Rio, TX. SOURCE: Swanson, 16.

FRAZER, Carlos; Corporal; F/10th Cav. *See* **FRASER,** Carlos, Corporal, F/10th Cavalry

FRAZIER, Lewis; Sergeant; D/10th Cav. Died 3 May 1914; buried at Ft Bayard, NM, in plot V 37. SOURCE: "Fort Bayard National Cemetery, Records of Burials."

Buried 3 May 1914, section B, row G, plot 37 at Ft Bayard. SOURCE: Erickson, Burials at Fort Bayard National Cemetery, NM.

FRAZIER, Petrum R.; Private; A/9th Cav. ‡On special duty as cook, Nueva Caceres, Philippines, as of 19 Apr 1902. SOURCE: Special Duty List, A/9 Cav.

Was retired when he died 9 May 1908; buried at Post Cemetery, Presidio of Monterey: Section I, number 24. SOURCE: Post Cemetery Record Book.

FREDERICKS, John; Private; G/9th Cav. With Sgt. Edward Troutman and Pvt. Charley Blackstone, survived attack by Mexicans near Rio Grande, 26 Jan 1875, in which two cavalrymen were killed; later indicted and jailed, Rio Grande City, TX, for killing one of attackers; at Ft Stockton, TX, Apr 1876, killed by Blackstone in dispute over responsibility for legal costs. SOURCE: Leiker, *Racial Borders*, 54–55.

‡Served 1875–76. *See* **BLACKSTONE**, Charley, Private, G/9th Cavalry; **TROUTMAN**, Edward, Sergeant, G/9th Cavalry

Died at Ft Stockton on 17 Aug 1875 [*sic*]; buried at San Antonio National Cemetery, Section C, number 351. SOURCE: San Antonio National Cemetery Locator.

FREELAIN, William; Private; 9th Cav. Received Philippine Campaign Badge number 11702 for service as private in E/9th Cavalry; in 9th Cavalry at Ft Leavenworth, KS, Mar 1905. SOURCE: Philippine Campaign Badge list, 29 May 1905.

FREELAND, A.; Private; B/9th Cav. Wounded in action, Las Animas Creek, NM, 16 Sep 1879, and rescued under fire by Sgt. John Denny; recovered and returned to duty by October 1879. SOURCE: Schubert, *Black Valor*, 54–56.

‡With Private Caump, B/9th Cavalry, wounded in action on Animas River against Indians, 18 Sep 1879; Caump later died of wounds. SOURCE: Hamilton, "History of the Ninth Cavalry," 42; *Illustrated Review: Ninth Cavalry*. *See* **DENNY**, John, Sergeant, H/9th Cavalry

FREEMAN, Andrew P.; Private; E/24th Inf. *See* **FREMAN**, Andrew P., Private, E/24th Infantry

FREEMAN, Fred; Private; A/9th Cav. At Ft Elliott, TX, Nov 1883, sentenced to three months' confinement and discharged for giving two saddle blankets to woman so she could keep her children warm. SOURCE: Kenner, *Buffalo Soldiers and Officers of the Ninth Cavalry*, 24.

FREEMAN, George L.; Private; 25th Inf. Served during 1880s. SOURCE: Dobak and Phillips, *The Black Regulars*, 186.

FREEMAN, James; M/9th Cav. Born in Kentucky; mulatto complexion; cannot read or write, age 24, Jul 1870, at Ft McKavett, TX. SOURCE: Bierschwale, *Fort McKavett,* 99.

FREEMAN, Jerry R.; Private; A/10th Cav. ‡Mentioned 1873. SOURCE: ES, 10 Cav, 1873–81.

Died at Ft Davis, TX, on 2 Nov 1884; buried at San Antonio National Cemetery, Section I, number 1567. SOURCE: San Antonio National Cemetery Locator.

FREEMAN, Johnson; Private; Band/25th Inf. *See* **JOHNSON**, Freeman, Private, Band/25th Infantry

FREMAN, Andrew P.; Private; E/24th Inf. Died 5 Jul 1889; headstone reads Freeman but all records indicate Freman; buried at Santa Fe National Cemetery, NM, plot A1 796. SOURCE: Santa Fe National Cemetery, Records of Burials.

FRIERSON, Eugene; Sgt Maj; 10th Cav. ‡Born in Tennessee; private, K/10th Cavalry, 19 Oct 1892; corporal, 13 Jun 1895; stationed at Ft Custer, MT, 1897. SOURCE: Baker, Roster.

‡Born in Columbia, TN, around 1873; Ht 5'6", brown complexion; marksman, 1893, 1894, 1900; sharpshooter, 1896, 1897, 1901, 1902; lance corporal, corporal, sergeant, 17 Oct 1894–1 Dec 1902; squadron sergeant major, 1 Dec 1902; served in Cuba, 22 May 1899–30 Oct 1900, 13 Dec 1900–5 May 1902; reenlisted, character excellent, $3 per month additional pay for ten years' continuous service, 19 Oct 1902; married to Julia E. Frierson, one child; deposits $250, 13 Nov 1900, $15, 11 Mar 1903, $30, 9 Apr 1903; proficient at noncommissioned officers' school, Ft Robinson, NE, in Army regulations, minor tactics, hippology, drill regulations, and as expert rifleman, 13 Jul 1905. SOURCE: Descriptive Book, 10 Cav Officers & NCOs.

‡At Ft Robinson as corporal, K/10th Cavalry, for cavalry competition, Sep 1897.

‡Served in 10th Cavalry, 1898; remained in U.S. during war with Spain. SOURCE: Cashin, *Under Fire with the Tenth Cavalry*, 349.

‡Guest of former troop, K/10th Cavalry, at Christmas dinner, 1904, with wife. SOURCE: Barrow, "Christmas in the United States Army," 96–97.

‡Ranked number 16 among marksmen, Northern Division cavalry, 1905. SOURCE: Glass, *History of the Tenth Cavalry*, 45.

‡Author of "An Adventure in the Big Horn Mountains, or, the Trials and Tribulations of a Recruit," in *Colored American Magazine*. SOURCE: *Colored American Magazine* 8 (Apr 1905): 196–99; (May 1905): 277–79; (Jun 1905): 338–40.

Pvt. Eugene P. Frierson, K/10th Cavalry, wrote three-part article on experiences on practice march, Big Horn Mountains, Montana, 1893, in *Colored American Magazine*, 1905, reprinted. SOURCE: Schubert, *Voices of the Buffalo Soldier*, 188–97.

‡Ranked number 16, Northern Division cavalry competition, bronze medal, Ft Riley, KS, 1905. SOURCE: GO 173, AGO, 20 Oct 1905.

‡Ranked number 133 among expert riflemen with 73.33 percent, 1905. SOURCE: GO 101, AGO, 31 May 1906.

‡Regimental sergeant major, 1914, first lieutenant, 8th Illinois Infantry, 1916; first lieutenant, 9th Cavalry, 1916; passed examination for commission, Ft Huachuca, AZ, May 1914; commissioned at El Paso, TX, 1916; retired with thirty years, 1919. SOURCE: *Crisis* 9 (Nov 1914): 13; 12 (Sep 1916): 247; 17 (Sep 1919): 259.

‡Author of preface to *The Black Soldier*. SOURCE: Curtis, *The Black Soldier*.

‡As sergeant major, 10th Cavalry, Ft Huachuca, 28 Aug 1914, he wrote: "If there is any doubt on the part of any citizen as to our valor, courage, and obedience in the Army, I simply refer him to the records of the War Department, in Washington, DC. . . . Men are not superior by reason of the accident of race or color. They are superior who have the best heart and the best brain. Superiority is born of honesty, of virtue, of charity, and above all of the love of liberty." SOURCE: Curtis, *The Black Soldier*, 56, with pictures.

‡Regimental sergeant major, 10th Cavalry, commissioned second lieutenant from training camp at Leon Springs, TX. SOURCE: Glass, *History of the Tenth Cavalry*, appendix M.

FRIERSON, Watts; Farrier; E/9th Cav. ‡Corporal, K/10th Cavalry, served in 10th Cavalry, 1898; remained in U.S. during war with Spain. SOURCE: Cashin, *Under Fire with the Tenth Cavalry*, 349.

‡Private, G/24th Infantry, ranked number 207 among rifle experts with 68 percent, 1904. SOURCE: GO 79, AGO, 1 Jul 1905.

‡Farrier, E/9th Cavalry, at Ft D. A. Russell, WY, in 1910; sharpshooter. SOURCE: *Illustrated Review: Ninth Cavalry*, with picture.

Born in Tennessee; died 29 Apr 1918, age 51; body sent to Ft Huachuca Cemetery for burial. SOURCE: Sage, Ft. Huachuca Cemetery.

FRINK, George; Sergeant; I/10th Cav. In Troop I/10th Cavalry stationed at Bonita Cañon Camp, AZ, 30 Jun 1886. SOURCE: Tagg, *The Camp at Bonita Cañon*, 231.

FRISBY, John T.; Private; G/24th Inf. Died 12 Mar 1906; buried at Ft Bayard, NM, in plot H 38. SOURCE: "Fort Bayard National Cemetery, Records of Burials."

Buried 12 Mar 1906, section A, row K, plot 45, at Ft Bayard. SOURCE: Erickson, Burials at Fort Bayard National Cemetery, NM.

FRY, Frank; Farrier; E/10th Cav. ‡At Ft Apache, AZ, 1890, subscribed $.50 to testimonial to General Grierson. SOURCE: List of subscriptions, 23 Apr 1890, 10th Cavalry papers, MHI.

‡Served in 10th Cavalry, 1898; remained in U.S. during war with Spain. SOURCE: Cashin, *Under Fire with the Tenth Cavalry*, 343.

‡Farrier, drowned in Rio Grandera, Samar, Philippines, 28 Jun 1901; body recovered. SOURCE: *ANJ* 39 (28 Sep 1901): 81.

Died 28 Jun 1901; buried in plot N ADD at San Francisco National Cemetery. SOURCE: San Francisco National Cemetery.

FRY, Henry; Private; I/10th Cav. Died 18 Mar 1909; buried at San Francisco National Cemetery. SOURCE: San Francisco National Cemetery.

FRY, James; Corporal; C/25th Inf. Died at Ft Stockton, TX, on 20 Jul 1879; buried at San Antonio National Cemetery, Section C, number 348. SOURCE: San Antonio National Cemetery Locator.

FRY, John; Private; A/10th Cav. ‡As surviving Indian war veteran. SOURCE: *Winners of the West* 3 (Jun 1926): 7.

Died 31 Aug 1931; buried at San Antonio National Cemetery, Section J, number 311. SOURCE: San Antonio National Cemetery Locator.

FULLER, Cornelius; QM Sgt; 24th Inf. ‡Born in Cartersville, GA; first enlisted in G/24th Infantry; discharged as corporal, 16 Nov 1884; reenlisted, Ft Leavenworth, KS, age 26, Ht 5'5", black complexion, 21 Nov 1884; transferred to Band/24th Infantry, Ft Supply, Indian Territory, 10 Apr 1885; fined $5 by garrison court martial, Ft Bayard, NM, 1889; discharged, end of term, Ft Bayard, character very good, single, with $2 per month additional pay, deposits $15, retained $60, clothing $41.59, 20 Nov 1889; reenlisted, Ft Bayard, 21 Nov 1889; discharged, end of term, Ft Bayard, character excellent, married, no children, with $3 per month additional pay, retained $60, clothing $48.83, owes government $7.06 for subsistence stores, 20 Nov 1894. SOURCE: Descriptive Book, 24 Inf NCS & Band.

‡Retires as quartermaster sergeant, 24th Infantry, with thirty years' service and $30 per month pension. SOURCE: Cleveland *Gazette*, 29 Dec 1906.

Cpl. Comelius Fuller, Band/24th Infantry, died 23 Apr 1930; buried in plot B 777 at San Francisco National Cemetery. SOURCE: San Francisco National Cemetery.

FULSOME, Albert; Private; B/10th Cav. At Ft Stockton, TX, 1879; witness in court martial of Lt. William H. Beck, 10th Cavalry, San Antonio, TX, Feb 1879. SOURCE: Kinevan, *Frontier Cavalryman*, 287.

FUQUA, Eulous; Private; G/9th Cav. Received Philippine Campaign Badge number 11828 for service as private in F/9th Cavalry, 16 Sep 1900–22 Jul 1901; private in G/9th Cavalry, Ft Leavenworth, KS, Mar 1905. SOURCE: Philippine Campaign Badge Recipients; Philippine Campaign Badge list, 29 May 1905.

FURMAN, John; Private; C/48th Inf. Died 9 May 1900; buried in plot NEW A888 at San Francisco National Cemetery. SOURCE: San Francisco National Cemetery.

G

GABBARD, Monroe; Private; B/10th Cav. At Ft Riley, KS, 1867, sentenced to three months for absence without leave after brutal treatment by Capt. John B. Vande Wiele. SOURCE: Dobak and Phillips, *The Black Regulars*, 186–87.

GADDESS, John; Trumpeter; A/10th Cav. Died 25 Nov 1882 of pneumonia at Ft Davis, TX. SOURCE: Regimental Returns, 10th Cavalry, 1882.

Died at Ft Davis, TX, on 25 Nov 1885; buried at San Antonio National Cemetery, Section I, number 1538. SOURCE: San Antonio National Cemetery Locator.

See **GADDIS**, John, Private, Band/10th Cavalry

GADDIS, John; Private; Band/10th Cav. ‡Deposited $100 with paymaster. SOURCE: CO, 10 Cav, to PMG, 13 Jan 1874, LS, 10 Cav, 1873–77.

‡Deposited $100 with paymaster. SOURCE: CO, 10 Cav, to PMG, 4 May 1874, LS, 10 Cav, 1873–77.

‡Former private, Band/10th Cavalry, plays very important instrument; regimental commander recommends approval of his enlistment. SOURCE: CO, 10 Cav, to AG, USA, 31 Dec 1874, LS, 10 Cav, 1873–77.

John Gaddess, Trumpeter, A/10th Cavalry, died 25 Nov 1882 of pneumonia at Ft Davis, TX. SOURCE: Regimental Returns, 10th Cavalry, 1882.

John Gaddess, died at Ft Davis, on 25 Nov 1885; buried at San Antonio National Cemetery, Section I, number 1538. SOURCE: San Antonio National Cemetery Locator.

GADSDEN, Peter; Sergeant; A/9th Cav. ‡Retires Apr 1901. SOURCE: *ANJ* 38 (27 Apr 1901): 843.

Retired sergeant, received Indian Wars Campaign Badge number 1451 on 22 Oct 1909. SOURCE: Carroll, *Indian Wars Campaign Badge*, 42.

GAINES, George W.; 1st Sgt; A/10th Cav. In Troop E/10th Cavalry stationed at Bonita Cañon Camp, AZ, 28 Feb 1886. SOURCE: Tagg, *The Camp at Bonita Cañon*, 231.

‡At Wounded Knee Creek, SD, at time of massacre as private, E/9th Cavalry; sergeant, A/10th Cavalry, Ft Robinson, NE, 1906. SOURCE: Ricker Tablet no. 35, NSHS.

‡Promoted to corporal, E/9th Cavalry, in accordance with regimental order 27, Ft Robinson, 23 Apr 1891. SOURCE: Cleveland *Gazette*, 16 May 1891.

‡Sergeant, E/9th Cavalry, since 15 Mar 1893. SOURCE: Roster, 9 Cav.

Appointed sergeant 15 Mar 1893; in E/9th Cavalry at Ft Robinson, Jan 1897. SOURCE: Ninth Cavalry, Roster of NCOs, 1897.

‡As sergeant, E/9th Cavalry, led detachment of one private from each troop, which proceeded to Ft Robinson's wood reservation to cut for new corral fence, 25 Mar 1895; carried three days' rations; accompanied by four mules and one civilian packer. SOURCE: Post Order 18, 23 Mar 1895, Post Orders, Ft Robinson.

‡Reenlistment for A/10th Cavalry authorized. SOURCE: TWX, AGO, USA, 6 Nov 1897.

‡Served in A/10th Cavalry, 1898; remained in U.S. during war with Spain. SOURCE: Cashin, *Under Fire with the Tenth Cavalry*, 337

‡Promoted to corporal, Sep 1899. SOURCE: *ANJ* 37 (23 Sep 1899): 80.

‡First sergeant, A/10th Cavalry; was in charge of detachment of regiment camped on timber reserve, Ft Robinson, when sudden storm caused stove explosion that partially blinded Caleb Benson. SOURCE: Deposition, Gaines, 25 Aug 1905, VA File XC 2499129, Caleb Benson.

‡First sergeant, A/10th Cavalry, age 51; supports Benson's claim for pension. SOURCE: Deposition, Gaines, 11 Jul 1906, VA File XC 2499129, Caleb Benson.

GAINES, Henry; Private; E/38th Inf. Died 12 Feb 1869; originally buried at Ft Hays, KS; reburied at Ft Leavenworth National Cemetery, plot 3365. SOURCE: Ft Leavenworth National Cemetery.

GAINES, Levin S.; Corporal; E/38th Inf. Died 21 Dec 1867; originally buried at Ft Hays, KS; reburied at Ft Leavenworth National Cemetery, plot 3327. SOURCE: Ft Leavenworth National Cemetery.

GAINES, Nathan; Private; I/9th Cav. Private, I/9th Cavalry, wounded in chest, Cuchillo Negro, NM, Aug 1881.

SOURCE: Kenner, *Buffalo Soldiers and Officers of the Ninth Cavalry*, 245.

GAINES, Norman E.; Private; 9th Cav. Born in Virginia; enlisted in Baltimore, MD, age 24; occupation waiter; wounded in action against Apaches in 1881. SOURCE: Dobak and Phillips, *The Black Regulars*, 251, 330.

GAIRY, William; Private. At Ft Duncan, TX, 1871, dishonorably discharged for cohabiting with Seminole Negro woman after arranging a mock wedding. SOURCE: Leiker, *Racial Borders*, 83.

GAITHER, Ozrow; Sergeant; E/10th Cav. ‡Served in 10th Cavalry in Cuba, 1898. SOURCE: Cashin, *Under Fire with the Tenth Cavalry*, 342.

‡Commended for distinguished service, battle of Santiago, Cuba, 1 Jul 1898; now out of service. SOURCE: GO 15, AGO, 13 Feb 1900.

Ozrow Gather, Sergeant, E/10th Cavalry, awarded certificate of merit for distinguished service in battle, Santiago, 1 Jul 1898. SOURCE: Gleim, *The Certificate of Merit*, 45.

‡Born and enlisted in Nashville, TN; awarded certificate of merit for distinguished service in Cuba. SOURCE: *ANJ* 36 (10 Jun 1899): 967.

‡Certificate of merit mentioned. SOURCE: Steward, *The Colored Regulars*, 280; *ANJ* 37 (24 Feb 1900): 611.

GALLAGHAN, W. E.; Private; B/10th Cav. Died at Ft McKavett, TX, on 11 Dec 1877; buried at San Antonio National Cemetery, Section E, number 866. SOURCE: San Antonio National Cemetery Locator.

GALLAGHER, Samuel; Private; L/10th Cav. Died 30 May 1868 of disease at Ft Arbuckle, OK. SOURCE: Regimental Returns, 10th Cavalry, 1868.

GALLOWAY, Lawrence; Blacksmith; H/9th Inf. ‡Born in Augusta, GA; age 46 in Apr 1895; Ht 5'6", complexion yellow; $5 per month additional pay for twenty years' continuous service, all in H Troop. SOURCE: Descriptive Book, H/9 Cav.

Became involved in barracks fight with Pvt. John Denny, Ft DuChesne, UT, prior to Jan 1895. SOURCE: Schubert, *Black Valor*, 56–57.

GAMBLE, John; Sergeant; K/25th Inf. Born in Eufala, AL; Ht 5'11", black hair and eyes, black complexion; occupation waiter; enlisted at age 22, Cincinnati, OH, 17 May 1886; from Columbus Bks, OH, arrived Ft Snelling, MN, 17 Sep 1886. SOURCE: Descriptive & Assignment Rolls of Recruits, 25 Inf.

‡Sergeant, K/25th Infantry, at Ft Niobrara, NE, 1904. SOURCE: Wilson, "History of Fort Niobrara."

GAMBLE, John E.; Private; K/25th Inf. Born 1848? in West Indies; parents' names unknown, mother born in Liverpool, England; widower, usual occupation farmer; died 23 Mar 1945, age 97, of arteriosclerotic nephritis with uremia at Veterans' Hospital, Knoxville, IA. SOURCE: Iowa State Department of Health Certificate of Death, John E. Gamble, photocopy in authors' files.

Norfolk [NE] *Daily News* reported in 2 Dec 1908 that he didn't remember where he was born, was servant to an officer on Civil War blockade-running British ship that was captured by Union forces, taken to New Orleans, LA; took name of Gamble after Gamble of Proctor & Gamble family who employed him; served in Ohio state troops for two years before he enlisted in Cincinnati in 1886; in 25th Infantry for nineteen years; rose to noncommissioned officer rank; served in Sitting Bull campaign in South Dakota in winter of 1890–91; in battle of Wounded Knee and performed scouting duty in Pine Ridge reservation country; in charge of hill of El Caney, Cuba; in constabulary in the Philippines in 1900; married a native Filipina; lived first in Niobrara, NE; moved to Norfolk, NE, about 1904 where resident until 1943; described in 1908 as lanky janitor who worked for numerous families in Norfolk; resided for many years at 214 South 14th St. in Norfolk; wife returned to the Philippines in 1920s; collapsed on Omaha, NE, street in winter of 1943, hospitalized at Veterans' Hospital in Knoxville, IA, for eighteen months until death in Mar 1945; survived by daughters Mrs. Henry Jones of Norfolk and Mrs. Robert Wright of Omaha, sons Heistand a sergeant in the Army and King in the Navy; buried at Ft Leavenworth, KS, National Cemetery, 26 Mar 1945. SOURCE: *Norfolk Daily News*, April 1945, photocopy in authors' files.

Born in Eufala, AL; Ht 5'11", black hair and eyes, black complexion; occupation waiter; enlisted at age 22, Cincinnati, 17 May 1886; from Columbus Bks, OH, arrived Ft Snelling, MN, 17 Sep 1886. SOURCE: Descriptive & Assignment Rolls of Recruits, 25 Inf.

Died 23 Mar 1945; buried 26 Mar 1945 at Ft Leavenworth National Cemetery, plot C 2182. SOURCE: Ft Leavenworth National Cemetery.

GANAWAY, Joseph; Musician; K/25th Inf. Born in Franklin, LA; Ht 5'6", black complexion; occupation soldier; enlisted in A/39th Infantry for three years on 25 Mar 1867, age 21, at Greenville, LA; appointed musician 25 Mar 1867; transferred to K/25th Infantry at Jackson Bks, LA, 20 Apr 1869. SOURCE: Descriptive Roll of A/39th Inf.

GANT, John; Private; H/24th Inf. ‡Enlisted Ft Douglas, UT, twenty-ninth year of continuous service, 14 Feb 1899. SOURCE: Muster Roll, H/24 Inf, Jan–Feb 1899.

Was retired when died 9 May 1904; buried at Ft Bayard, NM, in plot J 11. SOURCE: "Fort Bayard National Cemetery, Records of Burials."

Buried 9 May 1904, section A, row O, plot 12, at Ft Bayard. SOURCE: Erickson, Burials at Fort Bayard National Cemetery, NM.

GANT, Joseph; F/9th Cav. Born in Maryland; black complexion; cannot read or write, age 19, Jul 1870, at Ft McKavett, TX. SOURCE: Bierschwale, *Fort McKavett,* 98.

GARCIA, Ignacio; Private; A/10th Cav. Died 26 Nov 1908; buried at Santa Fe National Cemetery, NM, plot H 717. SOURCE: Santa Fe National Cemetery, Records of Burials.

GARDNER, William; Corporal; 9th Cav. Received Philippine Campaign Badge number 11705 as corporal in L/9th Cavalry; in 9th Cavalry at Ft Leavenworth, KS, Mar 1905. SOURCE: Philippine Campaign Badge list, 29 May 1905.

Died 28 Mar 1877; buried at Ft Leavenworth National Cemetery, plot 1475. SOURCE: Ft Leavenworth National Cemetery.

GAREY, Charles; Sergeant; B/10th Cav. ‡Original member of 10th Cavalry; in troop when organized, Ft Leavenworth, KS, 1 Apr 1867. SOURCE: McMiller, "Buffalo Soldiers," 69.

Died 23 Mar 1877 on furlough at Leavenworth City, KS. SOURCE: Regimental Returns, 10th Cavalry, 1877.

‡Mentioned Apr 1877 as formerly in B/10th Cavalry. SOURCE: ES, 10 Cav, 1873–81.

GARFIELD, James; Farrier; 9th Cav. Received Philippine Campaign Badge number 11774 for service as farrier in E/9th Cavalry; in 9th Cavalry at Ft Leavenworth, KS, Mar 1905. SOURCE: Philippine Campaign Badge list, 29 May 1905.

GARNER, James; Private; K/10th Cav. Died at Ft Davis, TX, on 18 Nov 1884; buried at San Antonio National Cemetery, Section I, number 1566. SOURCE: San Antonio National Cemetery Locator.

GARNETT, George; Private; C/10th Cav. While first sergeant of C Troop for twenty-nine months (Jan 1869–May 1871), browbeat, insulted, brutalized his men, and thirty-two of 10th Cavalry's 108 desertions came from his troop; acquitted by military court of mutiny, 1871. SOURCE: Dobak and Phillips, *The Black Regulars,* 64, 324–25.

GARNETT, William; 9th Cav. Born in Kentucky; mulatto complexion; can read and write, age 21, 5 Sep 1870, at Ft McKavett, TX. SOURCE: Bierschwale, *Fort McKavett,* 107.

GARRETT, George; Private; C/10th Cav. Served with Pvt. George Washington, C/10th Cavalry, early 1870s. SOURCE: Schubert, *Voices of the Buffalo Soldier,* 234.

GARRETT, William; Private; 10th Cav. Did odd jobs in Silver City, NM, after discharge. SOURCE: Dobak and Phillips, *The Black Regulars,* 272.

GARROD, James; Private; G/10th Cav. Died 19 Jan 1868 in hospital at Ft Riley, KS. SOURCE: Regimental Returns, 10th Cavalry, 1868.

GARTRILL, Charles; Private; F/10th Cav. Wounded in action against Indians at Beaver Creek, KS, 21 Aug 1867. SOURCE: Schubert, *Voices of the Buffalo Soldier,* 20.

Wounded in action, gunshot wound in scalp, near Beaver Creek, 21 Aug 1867. SOURCE: LR, DeptMo, 1867.

GASKINS, John; Private; L/49th Inf. ‡Drowned in the Philippines, 5 May 1900. SOURCE: *ANJ* 37 (30 Jun 1900): 1046.

Died 5 May 1900; buried in plot NEW A959 at San Francisco National Cemetery. SOURCE: San Francisco National Cemetery.

GASKINS, William E.; Private; D/9th Cav. ‡Lance corporal, D/9th Cavalry, on special duty, troop clerk, Nueva Caceres, Philippines, since 10 Mar 1902. SOURCE: Special Duty List, D/9 Cav, 24 May 1902.

Died 18 Jul 1906; buried at Ft Bayard, NM, in plot O 17. SOURCE: "Fort Bayard National Cemetery, Records of Burials."

Buried 28 Jul 1906, section A, row W, plot 17 at Ft Bayard. SOURCE: Erickson, Burials at Fort Bayard National Cemetery, NM.

GASTON, Edward; Sergeant; D/9th Cav. Enlisted early 1870s, age 21, mulatto, laborer from West Virginia; served at Ft Stockton, TX, promoted to sergeant only months after induction. SOURCE: Kenner, *Buffalo Soldiers and Officers of the Ninth Cavalry,* 84.

GATE, John; Private; C/10th Cav. Died 7 Aug 1867 of cholera at Camp Grierson, KS. SOURCE: Regimental Returns, 10th Cavalry, 1867.

GATHER, Ozrow; Sergeant; E/10th Cav. See **GAITHER,** Ozrow, Sergeant, E/10th Cavalry

GAY, McKinley; Private; E/25th Inf. Died 2 Sep 1917; buried at Ft Bayard, NM, in plot Y 18. SOURCE: "Fort Bayard National Cemetery, Records of Burials."

GEAVY, Charles M.; Sergeant; B/10th Cav. *See* **GAREY**, Charles, Sergeant, B/10th Cavalry

GEE, Marion; Private; F/10th Cav. Died on 1 May 1901; buried at San Antonio National Cemetery, Section F, number 1071. SOURCE: San Antonio National Cemetery Locator.

GEORGE, William; Private; K/9th Cav. Died at Ft Griffin, TX, on 30 Sep 1870; buried at San Antonio National Cemetery, Section D, number 726. SOURCE: San Antonio National Cemetery Locator.

GERRY, William; Private; U.S. Army. Born in Fayette County, KY; enlisted at Ft Duncan, TX, 1 May 1873, age 28; discharged 1 Nov 1873 at Camp Comanche, TX; enlisted 23 Feb 1874 at Ft Clark, TX; discharged 23 Aug 1874 at Ft Concho, TX; enlisted 4 Dec 1874 at Ft Clark where he was discharged 4 June 1875; probably a discharged soldier married to a Seminole; buried Jun 1907 at Seminole Cemetery. SOURCE: Swanson, 17.

Seminole Negro Scout, served 1873–75. SOURCE: Schubert, Consolidated List of Seminole Negro Scouts.

Born in Kentucky about 1845; married to Seminole woman; died 1907; buried at Seminole Indian Scout Cemetery, Kinney County, TX. SOURCE: Indian Scout Cemetery, Kinney County, Texas.

GIBBS, Algernon; H/25th Inf. Born in Pennsylvania; mulatto complexion; can read and write, age 24, 5 Sep 1870, at Ft McKavett, TX. SOURCE: Bierschwale, *Fort McKavett*, 107.

GIBBS, Thomas; Private; 25th Inf. Born in Columbia, SC; Ht 5'6", black hair and eyes, dark complexion; occupation lumberman; enlisted at age 21, Charleston, SC, 19 May 1881; left recruit depot, David's Island, NY, 2 Jul 1881, arrived Ft Randall, SD, 7 Jul 1881. SOURCE: Descriptive & Assignment Rolls of Recruits, 25 Inf.

GIBBS, Thomas; Private; 25th Inf. Born in Charleston, SC; Ht 5'5", black hair and eyes, dark complexion; occupation drayman; enlisted at age 22, Charleston, 24 May 1881; left recruit depot, David's Island, NY, 2 Jul 1881, arrived Ft Randall, SD, 7 Jul 1881. SOURCE: Descriptive & Assignment Rolls of Recruits, 25 Inf.

GIBBS, William; Private; A/9th Cav. ‡Died of pneumonia, Ft Robinson, NE, Apr 1888. SOURCE: Medical History, Ft Robinson.

Died 17 Apr 1888 of pneumonia contracted in line of duty in post hospital, Ft Robinson. SOURCE: Buecker, Fort Robinson Burials.

‡Funeral, Ft Robinson, 18 Apr 1888. SOURCE: Post Order 74, Ft Robinson, 17 Apr 1888; List of Interments, Ft Robinson.

GIBSON, Edward; Sergeant; G/24th Inf. ‡E. D. Gibson born in Wythe Co., VA, 4 Dec 1852; enlisted in 10th Cavalry, Nov 1869; saw "many hard fights with the Indians"; transferred to 24th Infantry, 1880; wrote narrative of 24th Infantry in Cuba. SOURCE: Johnson, *History of Negro Soldiers*, 145–47.

First enlisted in 24th Infantry in 1869; second enlistment was as sergeant, 10th Cavalry; learned to sign name during service. SOURCE: Dobak and Phillips, *The Black Regulars*, 81, 124.

‡Pvt. E. D. Gibson, K/24th Infantry, at San Carlos, AZ, 1890 contributed $.50 for destitute daughter and son-in-law of John Brown. SOURCE: Cleveland *Gazette*, 7 Jun 1890. *See* OTT, **HARDEE**, James A., Private, K/24th Infantry

GIBSON, George; Private; C/9th Cav. Private, C/9th Cavalry, at Ft Sill, OK, 1884, claimed that Bertha Livingston, fiancée of 1st Sgt. Jason Jackson, was a prostitute. SOURCE: Kenner, *Buffalo Soldiers and Officers of the Ninth Cavalry*, 264.

GIBSON, Henry; Private; H/10th Cav. In Troop H/10th Cavalry stationed at Bonita Cañon Camp, AZ, 30 Apr 1886. SOURCE: Tagg, *The Camp at Bonita Cañon*, 231.

GIBSON, James; Private; H/25th Inf. Died 21 Sep 1880; buried at plot 1 7, Ft Meade National Cemetery, SD. SOURCE: Ft Meade National Cemetery, VA database.

GIBSON, James; Private; H/10th Cav. In Troop H/10th Cavalry stationed at Bonita Cañon Camp, AZ, 30 Apr 1886. SOURCE: Tagg, *The Camp at Bonita Cañon*, 231.

‡Honorable mention for services rendered in capture of Mangas and his Apache band, Rio Bonito, AZ, 18 Oct 1886. SOURCE: Baker, Roster.

GIBSON, James W.; Private; H/10th Cav. Born in St. Charles, MO, 1846; enlisted Indianapolis, IN, 17 Jul 1867, Ht 5'5", brown complexion, black eyes and hair; occupation laborer; served at Ft Davis, TX, 1877. SOURCE: Sayre, *Warriors of Color*, 192.

‡James W. Gibson, I/10th Cavalry, original member of 10th Cavalry; in troop when organized, Ft Riley, KS, 15 Aug 1867. SOURCE: McMiller, "Buffalo Soldiers," 76.

GIBSON, Murry; Private; E/10th Cav. Pvt. Murray Gibson in E/10th Cavalry stationed at Bonita Cañon Camp, AZ, 28 Feb 1886. SOURCE: Tagg, *The Camp at Bonita Cañon*, 231.

‡At Ft Apache, AZ, 1890, subscribed $.50 to testimonial to General Grierson. SOURCE: List of subscriptions, 23 Apr 1890, 10th Cavalry papers, MHI.

‡Served in 10th Cavalry in Cuba, 1898. SOURCE: Cashin, *Under Fire with the Tenth Cavalry*, 342.

GIBSON, Thomas; Private; K/9th Cav. Served in second half of 1890s; mailing address Station K, College Hill, Cincinnati, OH, in 1907. SOURCE: Sayre, *Warriors of Color*, 498.

GIBSON, Thomas; Private; D/24th Inf. Died on 22 Apr 1909; buried at San Antonio National Cemetery, Section B, number 44. SOURCE: San Antonio National Cemetery Locator.

GIBSON, William; Sergeant; C/10th Cav. ‡Original member of 10th Cavalry; in troop when organized, Ft Leavenworth, KS, 14 May 1867. SOURCE: McMiller, "Buffalo Soldiers," 70.

In troop during Sgt. George Garnett's tenure as first sergeant, testified against Garnett at 1871 court martial. SOURCE: Dobak and Phillips, *The Black Regulars*, 64.

GILBERT, Charles; Corporal; G/9th Cav. Received Philippine Campaign Badge number 11887 for service as corporal, F/9th Cavalry; in 9th Cavalry at Ft Leavenworth, KS, Mar 1905. SOURCE: Philippine Campaign Badge list, 29 May 1905.

Private, G/9th Cavalry; died 21 Mar 1909; buried at Ft Leavenworth National Cemetery, plot G 3648. SOURCE: Ft Leavenworth National Cemetery.

GILBERT, Saint; Sergeant; F/9th Cav. ‡Promoted from corporal, Apr 1902. SOURCE: *ANJ* 39 (10 May 1902): 904.

Received Philippine Campaign Badge number 11775 for service as sergeant in F/9th Cavalry. SOURCE: Philippine Campaign Badge list, 29 May 1905.

‡Veteran of Philippine Insurrection; at Ft D. A. Russell, WY, in 1910; sharpshooter; resident of Manchester, KY. SOURCE: *Illustrated Review: Ninth Cavalry*, with picture.

GILES, Henry; Sergeant; C/24th Inf. ‡Corporal, K/24th Infantry, married Miss Maria Smith of Washington, DC, at Ft Reno, Indian Territory, Apr 1887; best men: A. Cook of Nashville, TN, and William A. Foreman of Louisville, KY, both in K/24th Infantry. SOURCE: Cleveland *Gazette*, 23 Apr 1887.

Cpl. Henry Giles, 24th Infantry, married at Fort Reno, OK, 1887; wedding described in Cleveland *Gazette* article written by Pvt. Prince A. Moulton. SOURCE: Dobak and Phillips, *The Black Regulars*, 141, 151.

‡Corporal, K/24th Infantry, San Carlos, AZ, 1890. *See* OTT, **HARDEE**, James A., Private, K/24th Infantry

‡Resided at 1130 East Third South, Salt Lake City, UT, in 1898. SOURCE: Clark, "A History of the Twenty-fourth," appendix E.

‡Sergeant, C/24th Infantry; drowned in the Philippines, 23 Aug 1900. SOURCE: *ANJ* 38 (1 Sep 1900): 19.

GILL, Spencer; M/9th Cav. Born in Kentucky; mulatto complexion; cannot read or write, age 24, Jul 1870, at Ft McKavett, TX. SOURCE: Bierschwale, *Fort McKavett*, 99.

GILLESPIE, Archibald Honduras; Sergeant; A/9th Cav. Enlisted 17 Oct 1898, age 16; served with 9th and 10th Cavalry and 24th and 25th Infantry, 1898–1926; served in the Philippines, 1901–09; in 1916–17 Mexican expedition under Gen. John Pershing to capture Pancho Villa; commissioned captain 15 Oct 1917; reverted to sergeant 14 Apr 1918; cavalry instructor at U.S. Military Academy, West Point, NY, where he retired and is buried; nephew of QM Sgt. James R. Gillespie. SOURCE: "The Buffalo Sailor," American Forces Information Service News Articles, April 4, 2000.

‡Private, A/9th Cavalry, at Ft D. A. Russell, WY, in 1910; sharpshooter. SOURCE: *Illustrated Review: Ninth Cavalry*, with picture.

GILLESPIE, James R.; Post QM Sgt; U.S. Army. *See* **GILLISPIE**, James R., Quartermaster Sergeant, U.S. Army

GILLET, John W.; Private; I/10th Cav. In Troop I/10th Cavalry stationed at Bonita Cañon Camp, AZ, 30 Jun 1886. SOURCE: Tagg, *The Camp at Bonita Cañon*, 231.

GILLIAM, Chauncey; Private; 25th Inf. Born in Charleston, SC; enlisted Charleston, occupation miner, age 22, Ht 5'6", dark complexion, black eyes and hair, 16 Jun 1881; left recruit depot, David's Island, NY, 17 Aug 1881, and after trip on steamer *Thomas Kirby* to Central Depot, New York City, and train via Chicago to Running Water, Dakota Territory, 22 Aug 1881, marched forty-seven miles to Ft Randall, SD, arrived 24 Aug 1881. SOURCE: Descriptive & Assignment Rolls, 25 Inf.

GILLISPIE, James R.; QM Sgt; U.S. Army. ‡Corporal, A/10th Cavalry, at Ft Apache, AZ, 1890, subscribed $.50 to testimonial to General Grierson. SOURCE: List of subscriptions, 23 Apr 1890, 10th Cavalry papers, MHI.

‡Sergeant, A/10th Cavalry, stationed at Ft Grant, AZ; to report to Lt. Col. Edward P. Pearson, 24th Infantry, president, board of officers, Ft Grant, for examination for position of post quartermaster sergeant. SOURCE: *ANJ* 28 (21 Mar 1891): 510.

‡Appointed post quartermaster sergeant from sergeant, A/10th Cavalry, 5 May 1891. SOURCE: Baker, Roster; Dobak, "Staff Noncommissioned Officers."

‡Ordered from Ft Grant to Ft Missoula, MT; comrades "regret his and his amiable wife's departure." SOURCE: Cleveland *Gazette*, 19 Mar 1892.

‡His child baptized by Chaplain Steward, Ft Missoula, 25 Dec 1892. SOURCE: Monthly Report, Chaplain Steward, Dec 1892.

‡Sends $1.50 from Ft DuChesne, UT, for one-year subscription to Richmond *Planet*; writes that every colored man who can afford a paper should have *Planet*; praises paper's "bold and manly stand," prays for journalistic unity, wishes *Planet* "a greater success and a long and useful life." SOURCE: Richmond *Planet*, 2 Feb 1895.

‡An excellent noncommissioned officer who should be commissioned, according to John E. Lewis, H/10th Cavalry, in letter from Lakeland, FL, 5 Jun 1898. SOURCE: Gatewood, *"Smoked Yankees,"* 36.

‡First lieutenant of volunteers, 1898. SOURCE: Steward, *The Colored Regulars*, 291.

James R. Gillespie, enlisted 1 Aug 1881; rose to rank of master sergeant; commissioned as first lieutenant in 8th Volunteer Infantry in Havana, Cuba, 17 Jun 1898; served in 9th and 10th Cavalry and 25th Infantry; retired 13 May 1907; called back to active duty 11 Oct 1915; commissioned captain in Liberian Frontier Force; served in Monrovia, Liberia, as American military attaché; uncle of Sgt. Archibald Honduras Gillespie, A/9th Cavalry. SOURCE: "The Buffalo Sailor," American Forces Information Service News Articles, April 4, 2000. Printout in authors' files.

‡Retired Army officer and veteran of Spanish-American War and Philippines; now captain of Liberian Frontier Police with $1,600 per year pay and $250 per year quarters allowance. SOURCE: Cleveland *Gazette*, 18 Dec 1915.

‡No Veterans Administration pension file.

GIVENS, Adam; D/24th Inf. Born in Kentucky; mulatto complexion; cannot read or write, age 22, Jul 1870, at Ft McKavett, TX. SOURCE: Bierschwale, *Fort McKavett*, 96.

GIVENS, John C.; Private; L/9th Cav. Died 28 Apr 1915; buried at Ft Bayard, NM, in plot W 18. SOURCE: "Fort Bayard National Cemetery, Records of Burials."

Buried 26 Apr 1915, section B, row H, plot 16, at Ft Bayard. SOURCE: Erickson, Burials at Fort Bayard National Cemetery, NM.

GIVENS, William H.; QM Sgt; B/10th Cav. ‡Born in Kentucky; private, sergeant, quartermaster sergeant, B/10th Cavalry, 20 Aug 1869–20 Aug 1874; private, corporal, sergeant, first sergeant, B/10th Cavalry, 1 Aug 1876–4 Aug 1881; private, first sergeant, quartermaster sergeant, sergeant, first sergeant, K/10th Cavalry, 8 Nov 1881–21 Nov

1891; private, F/9th Cavalry, 14 Nov 1893–10 Apr 1894; private, H/10th Cavalry, 10 Apr 1894; corporal, 9 May 1894; sergeant, 12 Mar 1895; stationed at Ft Assiniboine, MT, 1897. SOURCE: Baker, Roster.

‡Enlisted 1869; served on Mexican border, 1876–78, and in Victorio campaign; commended by Lt. Col. Theodore J. Wint for service in Cuba, 1898. SOURCE: Steward, *The Colored Regulars*, 245.

Born in Kentucky; at Ft Duncan, TX, Dec 1877, struck Pvt. James Harris, B/10th Cavalry, who refused order to stop talking, confined to quarters; at Ft Stockton, TX, 1879; witness in court martial of Lt. William H. Beck, 10th Cavalry, San Antonio, TX, Feb 1879; "an excellent man in many respects; he is clear headed, conscientious and energetic," according to Lt. John Bigelow, Ft Stockton, Apr 1879. In 1898 with Lieutenant Bigelow wounded, led D/10th Cavalry up San Juan Hill and "conducted himself like the thorough soldier which I have long known him to be," according to Lieutenant Bigelow; one of six 10th Cavalry sergeants to receive volunteer commissions for their performance in Cuba. SOURCE: Kinevan, *Frontier Cavalryman*, 63–64, 165, 238, 287.

‡At Ft Grant, AZ; to be examined for ordnance sergeant. SOURCE: *ANJ* 24 (14 May 1887): 834.

‡At Ft Grant; to be examined for post quartermaster sergeant. SOURCE: *ANJ* 25 (7 Jan 1888): 462.

‡First sergeant, K/10th Cavalry; at Ft Apache, AZ, 1890, subscribed $.50 to testimonial to General Grierson. SOURCE: List of subscriptions, 23 Apr 1890, 10th Cavalry papers, MHI.

‡At Ft Thomas, AZ; to enter Army and Navy Hospital, Hot Springs, AR. SOURCE: *ANJ* 27 (21 Jun 1890): 808.

‡At San Carlos, AZ; to be examined for commissary sergeant. SOURCE: *ANJ* 28 (25 Apr 1891): 595.

‡Authorized six-month furlough from Ft Grant. SOURCE: *ANJ* 29 (14 Nov 1891): 198.

First sergeant, K/10th Cavalry, discharged 17 Nov 1892, replaced by William McBryar. SOURCE: Register of Enlistments, NA. Notes in authors' files.

Transferred to H/10th Cavalry. SOURCE: SO 83, AGO, 9 Apr 1894.

‡At Ft Assiniboine, 1895; examined for ordnance sergeant. SOURCE: *ANJ* 33 (16 Nov 1895): 179.

‡Served in 10th Cavalry in Cuba, 1898. SOURCE: Cashin, *Under Fire with the Tenth Cavalry*, 340.

First sergeant, 10th Cavalry, Capt. John Bigelow's company, 1898; had served as sergeant in Bigelow's company when Bigelow joined regiment in 1877. SOURCE: Dobak and Phillips, *The Black Regulars*, 331.

‡Commanded company at Las Guasimas, Cuba, and won commission due to success with troops in battle. SOURCE: Steward, *The Colored Regulars*, 139.

‡At San Juan, Cuba, exercised "a steadying and encouraging influence upon the men" and conducted himself

like "the thorough soldier which I have long known him to be," according to Capt. John Bigelow. SOURCE: SecWar, *AR 1898*, 711.

‡Cited for distinguished service in Cuba. SOURCE: *ANJ* 37 (24 Feb 1900): 611.

‡As first sergeant, D/10th Cavalry, commended "for exercising a steady and encouraging influence upon the men of his troop and conducting himself in a thoroughly efficient manner," at battle of Santiago, Cuba, 1 Jul 1898. SOURCE: GO 15, AGO, 13 Feb 1900.

‡Should be commissioned, according to John E. Lewis, H/10th Cavalry, in letter from Lakeland, FL, ca. 1 Aug 1898. SOURCE: Gatewood, *"Smoked Yankees,"* 580.

‡Commissioned second lieutenant, 10th U.S. Volunteer Infantry. SOURCE: Cashin, *Under Fire with the Tenth Cavalry*, 361.

‡Capt. John Bigelow's recollections of his service with Givens on the frontier and in Cuba. SOURCE: Bigelow, *Reminiscences of Santiago*, 9, 96–97, 133, 135, 163, 166–67.

‡Retired Jun 1901. SOURCE: *ANJ* 38 (29 Jun 1901): 1067.

GLASBY; Private; I/9th Cav. Almost cut off by Indians in action at Cuchillo Negro Creek, NM, Aug 1879. SOURCE: Schubert, *Black Valor*, 81–82.

GLASBY, Edward; F/9th Cav. Born in North Carolina; black complexion; cannot read or write, age 23, Jul 1870, at Ft McKavett, TX. SOURCE: Bierschwale, *Fort McKavett*, 97.

GLASS, James; Private; M/9th Cav. Private, M/9th Cavalry, at Ft Washakie, WY, 1887; resided in quarters of Sgt. Edward Hanson, 9th Cavalry, and his laundress wife when they went on furlough, and moonlighted as laundress; convicted of making indecent proposal to white laundress, sentenced to dishonorable discharge and five years, obtained release with assistance of Milwaukee attorney Alfred H. Bright, Mar 1888. SOURCE: Kenner, *Buffalo Soldiers and Officers of the Ninth Cavalry*, 251–53.

GLASS, John T.; Private; A/10th Cav. Died 27 Mar 1908; buried at Santa Fe National Cemetery, NM, plot H 710. SOURCE: Santa Fe National Cemetery, Records of Burials.

GLENN, Frank; Private; E/24th Inf. Died at Ft Davis, TX, on 15 May 1871; buried at San Antonio National Cemetery, Section H, number 111. SOURCE: San Antonio National Cemetery Locator.

GLOVER, William; Private; D/9th Cav. Died 15 Oct 1913; buried at San Antonio National Cemetery, Section

B, number 134. SOURCE: San Antonio National Cemetery Locator.

GLYNN, George; Private; L/9th Cav. Died 30 Sep 1892; buried at Santa Fe National Cemetery, NM, plot I 450. SOURCE: Santa Fe National Cemetery, Records of Burials.

GOFF, George W.; Sergeant; K/9th Cav. ‡Recording secretary, Diamond Club, K/9th Cavalry, Ft Robinson, NE. SOURCE: *ANJ* 28 (2 May 1891): 620.

‡Promoted from lance corporal to corporal, Ft Robinson, 2 Sep 1895. SOURCE: *ANJ* 33 (14 Sep 1895): 23.

‡Corporal, K/9th Cavalry, alternate for regimental color guard, Ft Robinson. SOURCE: *ANJ* 33 (28 Mar 1896): 540.

Appointed corporal 2 Sep 1895; in K/9th Cavalry at Ft Robinson, Jan 1897. SOURCE: Ninth Cavalry, Roster of NCOs, 1897.

‡Sir Knight Captain, Crispus Attucks Lodge No. 3, Knights of Pythias, State of Nebraska. SOURCE: Richmond *Planet*, 18 Dec 1897.

‡Enlisted Memphis, TN; sergeant, won certificate of merit for service in Cuba, 1898; now out of service. SOURCE: *ANJ* 36 (10 Jun 1899): 967.

‡Commended for gallantry in Cuba, 1 Jul 1898; awarded certificate of merit; now out of service. SOURCE: GO 15, AGO, 13 Feb 1900.

‡Sergeant, awarded certificate of merit for service in Cuba, 1 Jul 1898; now out of service. SOURCE: Steward, *The Colored Regulars*, 280; *ANJ* 37 (24 Feb 1900): 611; Gleim, *The Certificate of Merit*, 45.

GOHEINS, Samuel; H/38th Inf. Buried at Ft Leavenworth National Cemetery, plot 1612. SOURCE: Ft Leavenworth National Cemetery.

GOINGS, Alfred; Sergeant; K/25th Inf. Born in Bayou Sara, LA; Ht 5'8", griffe [black/mulatto or black/Indian] complexion; occupation laborer; enlisted in A/39th Infantry for three years on 29 Aug 1866, age 21, at New Orleans, LA; appointed sergeant 23 Mar 1867; transferred to K/25th Infantry at Jackson Bks, LA, 20 Apr 1869. SOURCE: Descriptive Roll of A/39th Inf.

First sergeant, A/39th Infantry, Civil War veteran, served in E/10th Heavy Artillery; sentence of five years for involvement in New Iberia, LA, mutiny, Jul 1867, overturned. SOURCE: Dobak and Phillips, *The Black Regulars*, 222.

GOINS, Joshua Van Buren; D/24th Inf. Joshua Goins born in Florida; mulatto complexion; can read and write, age 24, Jul 1870, at Ft McKavett, TX. SOURCE: Bierschwale, *Fort McKavett*, 96.

‡Born in Xenia, OH, 2 Feb 1848; enlisted Jul 1863; during enlistment led many soldier comrades to Jesus; discharged, end of term, Ft McKavett, Jul 1870; licensed to preach, San Antonio, TX, 1870; made career as itinerant preacher, Texas, Louisiana, Indian Territory; established Delhi Institute, Delhi, LA, and was president for four years; twenty years as trustee, Paul Quinn College; three-time delegate to general conference, African Methodist Episcopal Church; oldest active itinerant minister in Texas. SOURCE: Talbert, *The Sons of Allen*, 218–19.

GOINS, Thomas E.; Private; B/10th Cav. Died 13 Feb 1877 of consumption at Ft Clark, TX. SOURCE: Regimental Returns, 10th Cavalry, 1877.

GOLDEN, John; Sergeant; H/9th Cav. ‡Ranked number 4, Pacific Division pistol team competition, Ord Barracks, CA, 1904. SOURCE: GO 167, AGO, 28 Oct 1904.

Corporal, 9th Cavalry, received Philippine Campaign Badge number 11859 for service as corporal in H/9th Cavalry; in 9th Cavalry at Ft Leavenworth, KS, Mar 1905. SOURCE: Philippine Campaign Badge list, 29 May 1905.

GOLDEN, Thomas; Saddler; B/9th Cav. Pvt. Thomas Golding, B/9th Cavalry, native of Georgia; enlisted Dec 1871, self-described musician; deserted six months later but surrendered in three weeks and allowed to serve; received "good" evaluation at end of enlistment; age 35 and completing second enlistment when killed in action, Aug 1881; had served as saddler for five years. SOURCE: Kenner, *Buffalo Soldiers and Officers of the Ninth Cavalry*, 229.

‡Thomas Golden , Saddler, B/9th Cavalry, on detached service at Ft Craig, NM, 20 Dec 1880–20 Feb 1881. SOURCE: Regt Returns, 9 Cav, Feb 1881.

Pvt. Thomas Golding, I/9th Cavalry, killed in action, Gavilan Canyon, NM, 19 Aug 1879. SOURCE: Schubert, *Black Valor*, 84.

‡Thomas Golden killed in action at Gavillon Pass in Mimbres Mountains, NM, 19 Aug 1881; Pvts. James Brown and Monroe Overstreet of B/9th Cavalry also killed; Pvt. William A. Hollins wounded. SOURCE: Hamilton, "History of the Ninth Cavalry," 57; Billington, *New Mexico's Buffalo Soldiers*, 105; *Illustrated Review: Ninth Cavalry*.

GOLDING, Thomas; Saddler; B/9th Cav. *See* **GOLDEN**, Thomas, Saddler, B/9th Cavalry

GOLDSBOROUGH, George; 10th Cav. Served two years in white 7th Cavalry before joining and serving ten years in 10th Cavalry, according to Pvt. Thomas Dillwood, B/10th Cavalry, Ft Duncan, TX, Jan 1878. SOURCE: Kinevan, *Frontier Cavalryman*, 95.

GOLDSBOROUGH, William H.; 1st Sgt; 24th Inf. Received medical discharge from Ft Supply, OK, 1883, then did odd jobs at Caldwell, KS, took up claim in Oklahoma, 1889. SOURCE: Dobak and Phillips, *The Black Regulars*, 271.

GOLDSBY, George; 1st Sgt; G/10th Cav. Civil War veteran, served in (white) 21st Pennsylvania Cavalry; enlisted 10th Cavalry in 1867. SOURCE: Dobak and Phillips, *The Black Regulars*, 300–301.

‡Born in Selma, AL; enlisted 1867; became sergeant major; reenlisted, 1872, as first sergeant, D/10th Cavalry; led soldiers on raid to avenge insults, from Ft Concho, TX, into San Angelo, TX, 1877, then deserted. SOURCE: Leckie, *The Buffalo Soldiers*, 164.

Married Cherokee woman Ellen Beck, son Crawford born 1876; deserted 1878 after dispute with white Texans; Crawford later known as Cherokee Bill, hanged for murder at Ft Smith, AR, 1896. SOURCE: Leiker, *Racial Borders*, 88.

‡First sergeant, G/10th Cavalry, Ft Lyon, CO, Mar 1869. SOURCE: LR, Det 10 Cav, 1868–69.

According to Ellen Beck in 1922, Goldsby, who sometimes used pseudonym of William Scott, E/21st Pennsylvania Cavalry, left her in 1880. SOURCE: Sayre, *Warriors of Color*, 335, 339–40. *See* **LYNCH**, William, Private, K/9th Cavalry

‡Ex-sergeant, first sergeant, sergeant major, 10th Cavalry; according to W. A. Haynes and Fred Scott of San Francisco, he is really Pancho Villa. SOURCE: Cleveland *Gazette*, 7 Mar 1914.

GOOD, Talton; M/9th Cav. Born in Kentucky; mulatto complexion; cannot read or write, age 25, Jul 1870, at Ft McKavett, TX. SOURCE: Bierschwale, *Fort McKavett*, 99.

GOODE, Benjamin H.; Private; H/24th Inf. ‡Enlisted Ft McPherson, GA, 20 Jan 1899. SOURCE: Muster Roll, H/24 Inf, Jan–Feb 1899.

‡Awarded certificate of merit for distinguished gallantry, Naguilian, Luzon, Philippines, 7 Dec 1899; award made 10 Mar 1902; discharged 18 Jan 1902. SOURCE: *ANJ* 39 (15 Feb 1902): 594–95; GO 86, AGO, 24 Jul 1902.

Awarded certificate of merit for most distinguished gallantry in action at Naguilian, Luzon, 7 Dec 1899. SOURCE: Gleim, *The Certificate of Merit*, 50.

Born and resided in Abbeville County, SC; received Distinguished Service Medal in lieu of certificate of merit. SOURCE: *American Decorations*, 838.

GOODE, Pleasant; Private; 25th Inf. Born in Petersburg, VA; Ht 5'9", black hair and eyes, brown complexion; served in C/10th Cavalry to 30 Dec 1886; second reenlistment at age 27, St. Louis, MO, 11 Jan 1887; arrived Ft Snelling, MN, 22 Mar 1887. SOURCE: Descriptive & Assignment Rolls of Recruits, 25 Inf.

GOODEN, William H.; Private; D/25th Inf. Discharged in 1896 with $506.50 in savings. SOURCE: Dobak and Phillips, *The Black Regulars*, 167.

GOODLOE, Thomas; Sgt Maj; 9th Cav. ‡In I/9th Cavalry, married, desires to reenlist with six-month furlough, Mar 1890.

Sergeant, G/9th Cavalry, since 11 Dec 1891; first sergeant as of 15 Dec 1891. SOURCE: Roster, 9 Cav.

‡At Ft Robinson, NE, 1893; heard by Sgt. A. E. Ransom to say regarding Barney McKay affair: "The niggers won't hang together; they are always ready to hang one another." SOURCE: Court Martial Records, McKay.

See **JEFFERSON**, Charles W., Sergeant, B/9th Cavalry

‡Resided with wife and mother-in-law at quarters of Captain Day, 9th Cavalry, Ft Robinson, Aug 1893. SOURCE: Medical History, Ft Robinson.

‡Reenlistment, married, authorized. SOURCE: TWX, AGO, 17 Feb 1896.

‡Convicted of conduct to prejudice of good order and discipline by garrison court martial, Ft Robinson; sentenced to $10 fine and public reprimand, in consideration of his previous good character. SOURCE: *ANJ* 33 (11 Jul 1896): 816.

‡Born in Nashville, TN; knew Archy Wall, born in Franklin, Maury Co., TN, since boyhood; enlisted around same time in 1876; served together in 24th Infantry for number of years; saw each other and kept in touch for nearly fifty years, including when in different regiments; resides at 1319 66th Street, Berkeley, CA, age 72. SOURCE: Affidavit, Goodloe, 18 May 1931, VA File C 2643745, Archy Wall.

Thomas Goodlow appointed sergeant 15 Dec 1891; in G/9th Cavalry at Ft Robinson, Jan 1897. SOURCE: Ninth Cavalry, Roster of NCOs, 1897.

Regimental Sgt. Maj. Thomas Goodlow, 9th Cavalry, died 6 Nov 1936; buried in plot D-SOU1425 at San Francisco National Cemetery. SOURCE: San Francisco National Cemetery.

GOODLOW, Thomas; Sergeant; G/9th Cav. *See* **GOODLOE**, Thomas, Sergeant Major, 9th Cavalry

GOODMAN, Alphonse; Private; E/9th Cav. Strung from tree limb by wrists by Lt. Edward Heyl at San Pedro Springs, TX, Apr 1867, for failure to remove nosebag from his horse promptly. SOURCE: Schubert, *Black Valor*, 16.

‡1st Lt. Edward Heyl charged with ordering Goodman tied up by the hands for one hour as punishment for disobedience, Apr 1867.

GOODMAN, George W.; Private; D/9th Cav. With Captain Dodge at battle at Milk River, CO, 2–10 Oct 1879. SOURCE: Miller, *Hollow Victory*, 167, 206–7.

GOODPASTURE, Logan; Corporal; 24th Inf. Fined $5 for beating Appolenos Romero, servant of Col. Edward Hatch, 1873, after Romero had rejected invitation to attend a dance, saying he "did not dance with niggers." SOURCE: Dobak and Phillips, *The Black Regulars*, 152.

GOODRUM, Jack; Private; 9th Cav. Received Philippine Campaign Badge number 11711 for service as private, E/9th Cavalry; in 9th Cavalry at Ft Leavenworth, KS, Mar 1905. SOURCE: Philippine Campaign Badge list, 29 May 1905.

GOODSON, Robert; F/9th Cav. Born in Virginia; black complexion; cannot read or write, age 19, Jul 1870, at Ft McKavett, TX. SOURCE: Bierschwale, *Fort McKavett*, 97.

GOODWINE, Nathan; Private; 9th Cav. Received Philippine Campaign Badge number 11712 for service as private in E/9th Cavalry; in 9th Cavalry at Ft Leavenworth, KS, Mar 1905. SOURCE: Philippine Campaign Badge list, 29 May 1905.

GOOLSBY, Isaac; Private; B/25th Inf. Enlisted 14 Nov 1900, discharged as artificer of B/25th Infantry, 3 Nov 1903, character good; reenlisted 1 Dec 1903, discharged without honor 19 Nov 1906. SOURCE: Powell, "Military Record of the Enlisted Men Who Were Discharged Without Honor."

Dishonorable discharge, Brownsville, TX. SOURCE: SO 266, AGO, 9 Nov 1906.

GORAM, Richard; F/9th Cav. Born in North Carolina; black complexion; cannot read or write, age 25, Jul 1870, at Ft McKavett, TX. SOURCE: Bierschwale, *Fort McKavett*, 98.

GORDON, Charles; M/9th Cav. Born in East India; mulatto complexion; cannot read or write, age 26, Jul 1870, at Ft McKavett, TX. SOURCE: Bierschwale, *Fort McKavett*, 99.

GORDON, Edward; Private; 10th Cav. Died on detached service 25 Jul 1909; buried in plot NADD 1359 at San Francisco National Cemetery. SOURCE: San Francisco National Cemetery.

GORDON, Henry; Private; U.S. Army. Born in Jones County, GA; enlisted at Ft Clark, TX, 12 Aug 1872, age 41; Ht 5'8", black hair and eyes, black complexion; discharged 6 Mar 1873, reenlisted next day at Ft Clark; discharged 10 Sep 1873, reenlisted 19 Dec 1873 at Ft Clark; discharged Jun 1874. SOURCE: Swanson, 17.

Seminole Negro Scout, served 1872–74. SOURCE: Schubert, Consolidated List of Seminole Negro Scouts.

GORDON, Isaac; Private; G/10th Cav. Died 28 Jan 1870 in hospital at Ft Dodge, KS. SOURCE: Regimental Returns, 10th Cavalry, 1870.

GORDON, Isaac; Private; U.S. Army. Seminole Negro Scout, served 1873–84, 1886–87. SOURCE: Schubert, Consolidated List of Seminole Negro Scouts.

Born in Florida; enlisted at Ft Duncan, TX, 5 Dec 1873, age 35; Ht 5'7", black hair and eyes, black complexion; discharged at Camp Palafox, TX, 5 Jun 1874; enlisted 11 Jun 1874 at Camp Eagle Pass, TX; discharged 10 Dec 1874, reenlisted next day at Ft Duncan; discharged 1 Jul 1875, reenlisted same day at Ft Concho, TX; discharged 1 Jan 1876 at Ft. Duncan; enlisted 12 Aug 1876, discharged 12 Mar 1877 at Ft Clark, TX; enlisted 12 Mar 1877, discharged as corporal 12 Mar 1878 at Ft Clark; twice enlisted as private, discharged at Ft Clark for one year, 2 May 1879–12 May 1881; enlisted 13 May 1881, discharged as corporal 16 May 1882 at Ft Clark; enlisted 17 May 1882, discharged as sergeant 16 May 1883 at Ft Clark; enlisted 17 May 1883 at Ft Clark; discharged as private at Camp Myers Spring, TX, 16 May 1884; enlisted 18 Jan 1886, age 47, discharged as private 17 Jan 1887 at Ft Clark; 1880 Census lists wife Sukey age 30, George age 9, Charity age 8, Cilla age 5, and Tina age 1. SOURCE: Swanson, 18.

Age 35, resided at Ft Duncan in 1875 with Sukey age 36, George age 9, Charity age 8, Cilla age 5, Tina age 1. SOURCE: NARA Record Group 393, Special File.

GORDON, Isaac; H/25th Inf. Born in Indiana; black complexion; married in Dec 1869; cannot read or write, age 24, 5 Sep 1870, at Ft McKavett, TX. SOURCE: Bierschwale, *Fort McKavett,* 108.

GORDON, Jacob V.; F/9th Cav. Born in Washington, DC; black complexion; cannot read or write, age 21, Jul 1870, at Ft McKavett, TX. SOURCE: Bierschwale, *Fort McKavett,* 98.

GORDON, John T.; Private; A/10th Cav. ‡Died on Staked Plains expedition, Aug 1877. SOURCE: Leckie, *The Buffalo Soldiers,* 161–62.

Died 30 Jul 1877 of exhaustion at Staked Plains, TX. SOURCE: Regimental Returns, 10th Cavalry, 1877.

‡Commander, 10th Cavalry, transmits final statement of deceased Gordon to Adjutant General, 3 Sep 1877. SOURCE: ES, 10 Cav, 1873–81.

GORDON, Sam; Private; U.S. Army. Born in Mexico; enlisted at Ft Clark, TX, 13 Jan 1893, age 26; Ht 5'9", black hair and eyes, mulatto complexion; discharged 12 Jul 1893 at Ft Ringgold, TX, where he reenlisted next day; discharged 12 Jan 1894 at Camp San Pedro, TX, where he reenlisted next day; discharged 12 Apr 1894 at Ft Ringgold; died 22 Mar 1905; buried at Seminole Cemetery. SOURCE: Swanson, 18.

Seminole Negro Scout, served 1893–94. SOURCE: Schubert, Consolidated List of Seminole Negro Scouts.

Buried at Seminole Indian Scout Cemetery, Kinney County, TX. SOURCE: Indian Scout Cemetery, Kinney County, Texas.

GORDON, Thomas; Private; 25th Inf. Born in Charleston, SC; Ht 5'6", black hair and eyes, dark complexion; occupation miner; enlisted at age 22, Charleston, 23 May 1881; left recruit depot, David's Island, NY, 2 Jul 1881, arrived Ft Randall, SD, 7 Jul 1881. SOURCE: Descriptive & Assignment Rolls of Recruits, 25 Inf.

GOSLINE, John A.; Comsy Sgt; U.S. Army. Appointed commissary sergeant 17 May 1897 from first sergeant, D/25th Infantry. SOURCE: Dobak, "Staff Noncommissioned Officers."

GOSS, Isaac; Private; K/25th Inf. Born in Arkansas; Ht 5'5", black complexion; occupation soldier; enlisted in A/39th Infantry for three years on 29 Aug 1866, age 21, at Ft St Philip, LA; promoted to corporal 18 Dec 1867; reduced for incompetence 1 Dec 1868; transferred to K/25th Infantry at Jackson Bks, LA, 20 Apr 1869. SOURCE: Descriptive Roll of A/39th Inf.

GOULD, Peter; Private; K/25th Inf. Born in Rahway, NJ; Ht 5'8", black complexion; occupation soldier; enlisted in A/39th Infantry for three years on 21 Aug 1867, age 23, at Philadelphia, PA; daily duty as post QM since 1 Apr 1869; transferred to K/25th Infantry at Jackson Bks, LA, 20 Apr 1869. SOURCE: Descriptive Roll of A/39th Inf.

GOVER, John W.; F/9th Cav. Born in Kentucky; black complexion; cannot read or write, age 21, Jul 1870, at Ft McKavett, TX. SOURCE: Bierschwale, *Fort McKavett,* 96.

GRADDON, Silas; Private; E/9th Cav. One of five men of E Troop killed by Victorio's Apaches while guarding troop's horse herd, Ojo Caliente, NM, 4 Sep 1879. SOURCE: Schubert, *Black Valor,* 53.

In fourth year of service when on duty in Sgt. Silas Chapman's herd guard, near Ojo Caliente, Sep 1879, and attacked by Victorio; killed along with Chapman, Pvts. Abram Percival, William Humphrey, and Lafayette Hooke. SOURCE: Kenner, *Buffalo Soldiers and Officers of the Ninth Cavalry,* 108.

‡Private Graddon, E/9th Cavalry, killed in action 4 Sep 1879. *See* **CHAPMAN**, Silas, Sergeant, E/9th Cavalry

GRAFTON, William; Private; H/10th Cav. Born in Kansas City, MO, 1855; enlisted Cincinnati, OH, 1 Mar 1882,

Ht 5'6", black complexion, eyes, and hair; occupation laborer. SOURCE: Sayre, *Warriors of Color*, 193.

Private in H/10th Cavalry stationed at Bonita Cañon Camp, AZ, but absent or on detached service 30 Apr 1886. SOURCE: Tagg, *The Camp at Bonita Cañon*, 231.

GRAHAM, Charles; Private; K/25th Inf. Born in Richmond, VA; Ht 5'2", black complexion; occupation cooper; enlisted in A/39th Infantry for three years on 10 Oct 1867, age 21, at Richmond, VA; daily duty to post bakery since 1 Apr 1869; transferred to K/25th Infantry at Jackson Bks, LA, 20 Apr 1869. SOURCE: Descriptive Roll of A/39th Inf.

GRAHAM, John; Sergeant; D/25th Inf. ‡Born in Virginia; private, D/10th Cavalry, 14 Feb 1877–13 Feb 1882; transferred to K/10th Cavalry, 13 Mar 1882–12 Mar 1887; transferred to E/10th Cavalry, 21 Mar 1887; corporal, 21 Mar 1887; sergeant, 1 Feb 1892; stationed at Ft Custer, MT, 1897. SOURCE: Baker, Roster.

‡Corporal, E/10th Cavalry, subscribed $.50 to testimonial to General Grierson. SOURCE: List of subscriptions, 23 Apr 1890, 10th Cavalry papers, MHI.

‡Sergeant, E/10th Cavalry, served in 10th Cavalry in Cuba, 1898. SOURCE: Cashin, *Under Fire with the Tenth Cavalry*, 342.

Awarded certificate of merit for distinguished service in battle, Santiago, Cuba, 1 Jul 1898. SOURCE: Gleim, *The Certificate of Merit*, 45.

‡Awarded certificate of merit for distinguished service, Cuba, 1 Jul 1898. SOURCE: Steward, *The Colored Regulars*, 280; *ANJ* 37 (24 Feb 1900): 611.

‡Sergeant, D/25th Infantry, 1900. SOURCE: GO 15, AGO, 13 Feb 1900.

‡Retired, Aug 1902. SOURCE: *ANJ* 39 (30 Aug 1902): 1315.

‡No Veterans Administration pension file.

GRAHAM, John W.; Private; A/25th Inf. Born in Baltimore, MD; Ht 5'6", black hair and brown eyes, mulatto complexion; occupation soldier; discharged from B/10th Cavalry 7 Dec 1885; second reenlistment, 26 Dec 1885, age 30, at Baltimore; assigned to A/25th Infantry; arrived Ft Snelling, MN, 12 Apr 1886. SOURCE: Descriptive & Assignment Rolls of Recruits, 25 Inf.

GRAHAM, Joseph; Private; 25th Inf. Born in Waterboro, SC; enlisted, age 33, occupation rock miner, dark complexion, black hair and eyes, Charleston, SC, 21 Jun 1881; left recruit depot, David's Island, NY, 17 Aug 1881, and after trip on steamer *Thomas Kirby* to Central Depot, New York City, and train via Chicago to Running Water, Dakota Territory, 22 Aug 1881, marched forty-seven miles to Ft Randall, SD, arrived 24 Aug 1881. SOURCE: Descriptive & Assignment Rolls, 25 Inf.

GRAHAM, William; Private; 9th Cav. Received Philippine Campaign Badge number 11773 for service as private in I/24th Infantry; in 9th Cavalry at Ft Leavenworth, KS, Mar 1905. SOURCE: Philippine Campaign Badge list, 29 May 1905.

GRAN, George; Private; I/10th Cav. Buried 27 Feb 1901, section A, row V, plot 21 at Ft Bayard, NM. SOURCE: Erickson, Burials at Fort Bayard National Cemetery, NM.

GRANT, Henry C.; Private; D/9th Cav. With Captain Dodge at battle at Milk River, CO, 2–10 Oct 1879. SOURCE: Miller, *Hollow Victory*, 167, 206–7.

GRANT, Henry C.; Sergeant; M/10th Cav. Died 13 Dec 1888; buried at Ft Bayard, NM, in plot G 19. SOURCE: "Fort Bayard National Cemetery, Records of Burials."

Buried 13 Dec 1888, section A, row I, plot 21, at Ft Bayard. SOURCE: Erickson, Burials at Fort Bayard National Cemetery, NM.

GRANT, John; C/25th Inf. Born in Ohio; mulatto complexion; cannot read or write, age 21, 6 Sep 1870, at Ft McKavett, TX. SOURCE: Bierschwale, *Fort McKavett*, 110.

GRANT, Matthew; Private; 24th Inf. Married Catarina Vega at Silver City, NM, 1889. SOURCE: Dobak and Phillips, *The Black Regulars*, 317.

GRANT, William; Private; B/10th Cav. Died 18 Jul 1886; originally buried at Ft Grant, AZ; buried at Santa Fe National Cemetery, NM, plot A-1 754. SOURCE: Santa Fe National Cemetery, Records of Burials.

GRANT, William; Private; 10th Cav. ‡Killed by fellow prisoner during fight in guardhouse, Ft Davis, TX, Jun 1878. SOURCE: Carroll, *The Black Military Experience*, 276.

Beaten and stabbed to death while confined in guardhouse, Ft Davis, 1878. SOURCE: Dobak and Phillips, *The Black Regulars*, 200.

GRANT, William D.; 9th Cav. Received Philippine Campaign Badge number 11860 for service as saddler, K/9th Cavalry; in 9th Cavalry at Ft Leavenworth, KS, Mar 1905. SOURCE: Philippine Campaign Badge list, 29 May 1905.

GRASHEN, Rudolph; Private; H/9th Cav. Died 1 Aug 1902; buried in plot NEW A805 at San Francisco National Cemetery. SOURCE: San Francisco National Cemetery.

GRAVES, John; Saddler; F/9th Cav. Born in Lexington, KY; black complexion; cannot read or write, age 28, Jul 1870, at Ft McKavett, TX; died and buried at Ft McKavett, before 17 May 1879; body removed to National Cemetery,

San Antonio, TX, 23 Nov 1883. SOURCE: Bierschwale, *Fort McKavett*, 96, 123.

Fined $5 for argument and fight with Sgt. Emanuel Stance, F/9th Cavalry, Ft Davis, TX, 1879. SOURCE: Schubert, *Black Valor*, 18.

Died at Ft McKavett on 7 Nov 1871; buried at San Antonio National Cemetery, Section E, number 873. SOURCE: San Antonio National Cemetery Locator.

GRAVES, John J.; Private; D/9th Cav. Died at Ft Stockton, TX, on 23 Apr 1872; buried at San Antonio National Cemetery, Section C, number 436. SOURCE: San Antonio National Cemetery Locator.

GRAVES, William; Private; F/25th Inf. Born in Madison Court House, VA; Ht 5'6", black hair and brown eyes, brown complexion; occupation waiter; resided Madison Court House when enlisted at age 25, Harrisburg, PA, 21 Jul 1885; assigned to F/25th Infantry; arrived Ft Snelling, MN, 5 Feb 1886. SOURCE: Descriptive & Assignment Rolls of Recruits, 25 Inf.

GRAY, Charles; Private; D/24th Inf. Born in Towson, MD, 2 Apr 1861; enlisted Baltimore, MD, 12 Jul 1882, Ht 5'9", brown complexion, brown eyes, black hair; occupation laborer; served in H/10th Cavalry; at Ft Davis, TX, 13 Aug 1882–6 Jul 1883; in the field scouting from Presidio west to Viejo Pass, TX, 6 Jul–31 Aug 1883; 31 Aug 1883–1 Apr 1885 at Ft Davis; 1 Apr 1885–19 May 1885 at Ft Grant, AZ; in the field in pursuit of Apache Indians, 19 Jun 1885–26 Jul 1885; at Bonita Cañon, AZ, 7 Aug–1 May 1886; at Ft Apache, AZ, 1 May 1886 until discharged 11 Jul 1887; enlisted 18 Jul 1887; served in H/10th Cavalry; discharged 10 Apr 1892; enlisted 8 Sep 1892, served in D/24th Infantry; discharged 8 Dec 1895; resided Phoenix, AZ, 1927; received pension of $20, increased to $30, per month 1928; died 10 Jan 1929; buried at Ajo Cemetery, Ajo, AZ. SOURCE: Sayre, *Warriors of Color*, 194–97.

GRAY, Charles; Sergeant; A/9th Cav. ‡Private in H/10th Cavalry stationed at Bonita Cañon Camp, AZ, 30 Apr 1886. SOURCE: Tagg, *The Camp at Bonita Cañon*, 231.

‡Trumpeter, H/10th Cavalry, at Ft Apache, AZ, 1890, subscribed $.50 to testimonial to General Grierson. SOURCE: List of subscriptions, 23 Apr 1890, 10th Cavalry papers, MHI.

‡Promoted to corporal, B/9th Cavalry, from private, Ft DuChesne, UT, Apr 1895. SOURCE: *ANJ* 32 (4 May 1895): 590.

‡Promoted to sergeant, G/10th Cavalry, from corporal, Jun 1902. SOURCE: *ANJ* 39 (7 Jun 1902): 1004.

Received as sergeant Indian Wars Campaign Badge number 668 on 21 Oct 1908. SOURCE: Carroll, *Indian Wars Campaign Badge*, 19.

‡Veteran of Indian wars and Philippine Insurrection; sergeant, A/9th Cavalry, at Ft D. A. Russell, WY, in 1910. SOURCE: *Illustrated Review: Ninth Cavalry*, with picture.

GRAY, Gilbert; Private; 9th Cav. Died 28 Feb 1909; buried at Ft Bayard, NM, in plot R 13. SOURCE: "Fort Bayard National Cemetery, Records of Burials."

Died on detached service; buried 28 Feb 1909, section B, row C, plot 13 at Ft Bayard. SOURCE: Erickson, Burials at Fort Bayard National Cemetery, NM.

GRAY, James; Private; K/25th Inf. Born in Washington County, NC; Ht 5'8", black complexion; occupation blacksmith; enlisted in A/39th Infantry for three years on 12 Oct 1867, age 21, at Norfolk, VA; daily duty to post garden since 10 Apr 1869; transferred to K/25th Infantry at Jackson Bks, LA, 20 Apr 1869. SOURCE: Descriptive Roll of A/39th Inf.

GRAY, Robert; Corporal; Band/25th Inf. ‡Private, Band/25th Infantry, fined $1 by summary court for absence from drill, Ft Missoula, MT, 3 Aug 1896. SOURCE: Descriptive & Assignment Cards, 25 Inf.

‡Fined $1 by summary court for absence from retreat, Iba, Zambales, Philippines, 25 Oct 1900. SOURCE: Misc Records, 25 Inf.

Died 6 Jul 1905; buried at Ft Bayard, NM, in plot H 9. SOURCE: "Fort Bayard National Cemetery, Records of Burials."

Buried 6 Jul 1905, section A, row K, plot 11, at Ft Bayard. SOURCE: Erickson, Burials at Fort Bayard National Cemetery, NM.

GRAYER, Frank; Private; G/9th Cav. Received Philippine Campaign Badge number 11830 for service as private in L/9th Cavalry, 16 May 1900–16 Sep 1902; private in G/9th Cavalry, Ft Leavenworth, KS, Mar 1905. SOURCE: Philippine Campaign Badge Recipients; Philippine Campaign Badge list, 29 May 1905.

GRAYSON; Corporal; E/9th Cav. ‡Wife is one of three laundresses authorized for E/9th Cavalry; authorized use of cooking stove and utensils, Ft Robinson, NE. SOURCE: Post Adj to Post QM, 22 Jun 1891, LS, Ft Robinson.

Wife, Mattie, died 18 Aug 1891, buried at Ft Robinson. SOURCE: Buecker, Fort Robinson Burials.

GRAYSON, Abraham; Private; E/9th Cav. Company clerk at Ft DuChesne, UT, 1887. SOURCE: Kenner, *Buffalo Soldiers and Officers of the Ninth Cavalry*, 233.

GRAYSON, Renty; Private; U.S. Army. Born in Mexico; claimed to be Negro without Indian blood; enlisted at Ft Duncan, TX, 7 Oct 1871, age 19; Ht 5'7", black hair and eyes, black complexion; discharged 7 Apr 1872, reenlisted next day at Ft Duncan; discharged 8 Oct 1872 at Ft Clark, TX, where he reenlisted five more times for six-month terms, 9 Oct 1872–1 Feb 1875; captured Lipan Chief Costillito during Col. Ranald Slidell Mackenzie's raid at Remolino, Mexico, May 1873; involved in Kickapoo Spring, TX, skirmish with Lieutenant Hudson, Dec 1873; on detached service as guide for A/4th Cavalry and guide in Palo Duro Canyon, TX, skirmish; killed an Indian in hand-to-hand battle at Palo Duro Canyon Aug 1875; discharged, reenlisted 18 Sep 1875 at Camp Supply, Indian Territory; discharged 13 Apr 1876 at Ft Clark where he reenlisted three times for one-year terms; last discharge at Ft Clark 13 July 1893; 1880 Census lists daughter Louise, age 9, son Anel, age 6; 10 Jul 1914 letter from 14th Cavalry HQ authorized Grayson to remain and reside at Ft Clark; impoverished 1920–23; R. Stratton, Brackettville ex-trooper, helped him get pension as Indian War veteran back-dated to 11 Mar 1917 to Nov 1923 in the amount of $1,600 with $20 per month pension; died 31 May 1929; buried Seminole Cemetery. SOURCE: Swanson, 19.

Lassoed Chief Costillito in expedition against Lipan and Kickapoo at Remolino, Mexico, 18 May 1873, which resulted in destruction of three villages, killing of nineteen warriors, and capture of forty prisoners, including the chief and his daughter Teresita, who later married Scout James Perryman. SOURCE: Porter, *The Negro on the American Frontier*, 479.

Seminole Negro Scout, served 1871–79, 1893; pension file in National Archives. SOURCE: Schubert, Consolidated List of Seminole Negro Scouts.

Buried at Seminole Indian Scout Cemetery, Kinney County, TX. SOURCE: Indian Scout Cemetery, Kinney County, Texas.

GREAR, Charles O.; Private; H/24th Inf. Buried 6 Mar 1914, section B, row G, plot 33, at Ft Bayard, NM. SOURCE: Erickson, Burials at Fort Bayard National Cemetery, NM.

GREAVES, Clinton; Corporal; C/9th Cav. Born in Madison County, VA, in 1855; resided in Prince Georges County, MD, and employed as laborer when he enlisted in 1872; received Medal of Honor for bravery against Apaches in the Florida Mountains, New Mexico, in January 1877; re-enlisted in H/9th Cavalry, Nov 1877; after fifteen years in 9th Cavalry, transferred to Colored Detachment, Columbus Barracks, OH, served five years; married Bertha Williams of Appomattox Court House, VA; left Army in 1893; worked as civilian for Quartermaster Department at Columbus Barracks until death in 1906; widow supported herself by doing housework until she died in 1936; Greaves's bravery commemorated by statue at Ft Bayard, NM. SOURCE: Schubert, *Black Valor*, 45–48, 169.

‡Born in Madison Co., VA; resided in Prince Georges Co., MD; Ht 5'7"; won Medal of Honor for heroism against

Apaches, Florida Mountains, 24 Jan 1877; stationed at Ft Cummings, NM, at time. SOURCE: Leckie, *The Buffalo Soldiers*, 178–79; Carroll, *The Black Military Experience*, 407; Lee, *Negro Medal of Honor Men*, 61–63; Koger, *The Maryland Negro in Our Wars*, 23; Billington, "Black Cavalrymen," 62; Billington, *New Mexico's Buffalo Soldiers*, 51.

‡Joined Army, age 22, in 1872; served over twenty years; retired to Columbus, OH, where he died, 1906. SOURCE: Amos, *Above and Beyond in the West*, 8.

GREEN, Alfred; Private; 25th Inf. Born in Santee, SC; enlisted Charleston, SC, age 23, occupation brakeman; Ht 5'7", dark complexion, black eyes and hair; left recruit depot, David's Island, NY, 17 Aug 1881, and after trip on steamer *Thomas Kirby* to Central Depot, New York City, and train via Chicago to Running Water, Dakota Territory, 22 Aug 1881, marched forty-seven miles to Ft Randall, SD, arrived 24 Aug 1881. SOURCE: Descriptive & Assignment Rolls, 25 Inf.

GREEN, Bailey; 1st Sgt; C/9th Cav. Sergeant, L/9th Cavalry, at Ft Duncan, TX, Apr 1871. SOURCE: Kenner, *Buffalo Soldiers and Officers of the Ninth Cavalry*, 177.

‡First sergeant, C/9th Cavalry, authorized four-month furlough from Ft Leavenworth, KS. SOURCE: *ANJ* 25 (19 Nov 1887): 322.

‡At Ft Leavenworth; warrant as noncommissioned officer dates from 1 Dec 1873. SOURCE: *ANJ* 25 (18 Feb 1888): 586.

‡Transferred from Ft Leavenworth to Army and Navy Hospital, Hot Springs, AR. SOURCE: *ANJ* 27 (14 Sep 1889): 42.

‡Recovered; returned from hospital to his company at Ft Leavenworth. SOURCE: *ANJ* 27 (4 Jan 1890): 368.

‡Retired as first sergeant, C/9th Cavalry, 2 Sep 1892. SOURCE: Roster, 9 Cav.

GREEN, Charles A.; Private; H/10th Cav. Born in Ann Arundel County, MD, 1862; enlisted Baltimore, MD, 27 Mar 1883; Ht. 5'4", black complexion, eyes, and hair; occupation hostler; at Ft Davis, TX, May–Dec 1883; discharged 20 Mar 1888; enlisted Newark, NJ, 9 Jan 1889. SOURCE: Sayre, *Warriors of Color*, 198.

Private in H/10th Cavalry stationed at Bonita Cañon Camp, AZ, but absent or on detached service 30 Apr 1886. SOURCE: Tagg, *The Camp at Bonita Cañon*, 232.

Honorable mention for services rendered in capture of Mangas and his Apache band, Rio Bonito, AZ, 18 Oct 1886. SOURCE: Baker, Roster.

GREEN, Dalbert P.; Master Sgt; 25th Inf. ‡Born 25 Mar 1873; enlisted Washington, DC; served in B and E/25th Infantry, 27 Aug 1891–26 Aug 1896; B/25th Infantry and Noncommissioned Staff/25th Infantry, 27 Aug 1896–26

Aug 1899; on Noncommissioned Staff/25th Infantry, 27 Aug 1899–retirement, Schofield Barracks, HI, 30 Aug 1916; corporal, 12 Jun 1893; sergeant, 19 Jan 1895; commissary sergeant, 23 Mar 1895; regimental supply sergeant, 7 Aug 1916; served in Cuba, 22 Jun–13 Aug 1898, and in the Philippines, 31 Jun 1899–17 Jul 1902 and 13 Sep 1907–11 Sep 1909; character on all discharges excellent; retired in accordance with Special Order 189, War Department, 14 Aug 1916; resided at 31 Pierce Street, NW, Washington, DC.

Sergeant, B/25th Infantry, rode in 25th Infantry Bicycle Corps, Ft. Missoula, MT, Summer 1896. SOURCE: Sorenson, List of Buffalo Soldiers Who Rode in the 25th Infantry Bicycle Corps, in authors' files.

Commissary sergeant, 25th Infantry, cycled with Lieutenant Moss to Yellowstone, 1896; captain, manager, and historian, 25th Infantry. SOURCE: Dobak and Phillips, *The Black Regulars*, 279.

‡At Bamban, Philippines, 1899. SOURCE: Nankivell, *History of the Twenty-fifth Infantry*, 93, with picture.

‡In charge of commissary while commissary officer, Lt. R. J. Burt, was absent with 1st Battalion. SOURCE: Richmond *Planet*, 27 Jan 1900.

‡Heroism in the Philippines, 2 Dec 1899, discussed. SOURCE: *Leslie's Weekly* 90 (10 Feb 1900): 107.

‡*Leslie's* story reprinted. SOURCE: Richmond *Planet*, 17 Feb 1900; Cleveland *Gazette*, 10 Mar 1900.

‡Mentioned. SOURCE: Richmond *Planet*, 28 Jul 1900.

‡"Indignant Sergeant D. P. Green, 25th Inf., sent a protest recently to the Manila *Times* for referring to the ballplayers of that command as 'darkies.'. . . The *Times* made a manly apology." SOURCE: *ANJ* 35 (22 Jul 1901): 1049.

‡Along with regimental noncommissioned staff, initiated move to buy Brig. Gen. Andrew Burt a retirement gift. SOURCE: Richmond *Planet*, 7 Dec 1901.

‡Letter to editor. SOURCE: Manila *Times*, 8 May 1901.

‡"Mickey" Green "a man of great gallantry," who saved life of Sgt. George Thompson, Band/25th Infantry, according to Colonel Burt in Chicago speech, 11 Sep 1902. SOURCE: Cleveland *Gazette*, 11 Oct 1902.

‡Retired 1916 with over twenty-five years' service. SOURCE: *Crisis* 13 (Dec 1916): 93.

‡When retired, Honolulu *Star-Gazette* wrote that Green "has been the best known and most liked man in the 25th for years. He has well earned his retirement and can proceed to his home feeling that he has given the active years of his life to his country and has a splendid record behind him of duty well performed." SOURCE: Cleveland *Gazette*, 25 Nov 1917.

‡Former captain, manager, coach of regimental baseball team, 1894–1908, "the happiest days of my life"; now master sergeant, retired; thanked for assistance in preparation of chapter on regimental baseball team. SOURCE: Nankivell, *History of the Twenty-fifth Infantry*, introduction, 163.

GREEN, David; Blacksmith; C/10th Cav. Died 23 Apr 1879 of consumption at Ft Clark, TX. SOURCE: Regimental Returns, 10th Cavalry, 1879.

GREEN, Ezekiel; 1st Sgt; L/10th Cav. ‡Served in 10th Cavalry, 1898; remained in U.S. during war with Spain. SOURCE: Cashin, *Under Fire with the Tenth Cavalry*, 349.

‡Ranked number 360 among rifle experts with 69.67 percent, 1905. SOURCE: GO 101, AGO, 31 May 1906.

Received as sergeant Indian Wars Campaign Badge number 1555 on 18 Jan 1910. SOURCE: Carroll, *Indian Wars Campaign Badge*, 45.

GREEN, Freeman; Sergeant; F/9th Cav. Died at Ft Davis, TX, on 13 Oct 1867; buried at San Antonio National Cemetery, Section I, number 1516. SOURCE: San Antonio National Cemetery Locator.

GREEN, George; Private; E/10th Cav. ‡Original member of 10th Cavalry; in troop when organized, Ft Leavenworth, KS, 15 Jun 1867. SOURCE: McMiller, "Buffalo Soldiers," 72.

Died 28 Jul 1867 of disease at Ft Gibson, OK. SOURCE: Regimental Returns, 10th Cavalry, 1867.

GREEN, George; Private; F/10th Cav. ‡Original member of 10th Cavalry; in troop when organized, Ft Leavenworth, KS, 21 Jun 1867. SOURCE: McMiller, "Buffalo Soldiers," 73.

Died 1 Aug 1867 of cholera at Ft Hays, KS. SOURCE: Regimental Returns, 10th Cavalry, 1867.

GREEN, George; Private; H/25th Inf. Died 18 Nov 1902, buried at Ft Bayard, NM, in plot PB 19E. SOURCE: "Fort Bayard National Cemetery, Records of Burials."

Buried 18 Nov 1902, section A, row S, plot 4, at Ft Bayard. SOURCE: Erickson, Burials at Fort Bayard National Cemetery, NM.

GREEN, Henry; 1st Sgt; M/9th Cav. Native of Washington, DC; completed three-year term in infantry 1869, enlisted in 9th Cavalry; became first sergeant after mass desertion Oct 1870; brawled with Sgt. Emanuel Stance Dec 1872; reduced to ranks Dec 1873; discharged at end of term Oct 1874. SOURCE: Kenner, *Buffalo Soldiers and Officers of the Ninth Cavalry*, 163–64.

Born in Virginia; black complexion; can read and write, age 23, Jul 1870, at Ft McKavett, TX. SOURCE: Bierschwale, *Fort McKavett*, 99.

‡First sergeant in M/9th Cavalry at Ft McKavett, TX, 1872–73. *See* **STANCE**, Emanuel, First Sergeant, F/9th Cavalry

GREEN, Isom; Private; E/9th Cav. Served with troop in New Mexico, 1879; at Ojo Caliente, NM, Sept 1879.

SOURCE: Kenner, *Buffalo Soldiers and Officers of the Ninth Cavalry*, 109.

GREEN, John; Private; I/10th Cav. ‡Original member of 10th Cavalry; in troop when organized, Ft Riley, KS, 15 Aug 1867. SOURCE: McMiller, "Buffalo Soldiers," 76.

Died 5 Dec 1868 of accidental pistol shot at Ft Wallace, KS. SOURCE: Regimental Returns, 10th Cavalry, 1868.

GREEN, John E.; Lt Col; U.S. Army. ‡Enlisted by Chaplain Allensworth, 24th Infantry, Louisville, KY, 1898, while student at Walden University, Nashville, TN; served as Allensworth's clerk while in H/24th Infantry, 1899; later commissioned in 25th Infantry. SOURCE: Alexander, *Battles and Victories*, 364, 392.

‡Green and Benjamin O. Davis were the only two blacks among 300 enlisted men commissioned from the ranks, 1898–1902. SOURCE: Fletcher, *The Black Soldier*, 165.

One of two blacks among 1,464 men who received regular Army commissions between 30 Dec 1898 and 30 Jun 1901. SOURCE: Schubert, *Black Valor*, 158.

‡Corporal, H/24th Infantry, when appointed second lieutenant, 25th Infantry. SOURCE: Cleveland *Gazette*, 13 Jul 1901.

‡Appointed second lieutenant, 25th Infantry. SOURCE: Indianapolis *Freeman*, 20 Jul 1901.

‡Second lieutenant, 1901; first lieutenant, 1916, Mexican border; military attaché to Liberia; lieutenant colonel and chief, Military Department, Wilberforce University, 1920; retired, Camp Henry J. Jones, AZ, 1929. SOURCE: *Crisis* 12 (Jun 1916): 62; *Crisis* 20 (May 1920): 270; *Crisis* 38 (Jul 1929): 218.

‡Second lieutenant, 25th Infantry, led detachment against bandits, Indang, Batangas, Philippines, 29 Nov 1901. SOURCE: *ANJ* 39 (18 Jan 1902): 487.

‡In the Philippines, 1906. *See* **WOODS**, Robert Gordon, Captain, I/49th Infantry

‡Mentioned as first lieutenant. SOURCE: Work, *The Negro Year Book, 1912*, 77.

‡First lieutenant, stationed at Wilberforce; appointed chairman of board of judges to pass on annual competitive drill of separate battalion, high-school cadets, Washington, DC. SOURCE: Cleveland *Gazette*, 17 May 1913.

‡Promoted to captain, stationed in Liberia. SOURCE: Cleveland *Gazette*, 18 Nov 1916.

‡Lieutenant colonel, military attaché in Liberia. SOURCE: Work, *The Negro Yearbook, 1918–1919*, 228.

‡Lieutenant colonel at Camp Henry J. Jones. SOURCE: Work, *The Negro Yearbook, 1925–1926*, 253.

GREEN, John S.; F/9th Cav. Born in Pennsylvania; mulatto complexion; cannot read or write, age 24, Jul 1870, at Ft McKavett, TX. SOURCE: Bierschwale, *Fort McKavett*, 98.

GREEN, Lewis T.; Sergeant; H/9th Cav. ‡Sergeant since 12 Feb 1885. SOURCE: Roster, 9 Cav.

‡At Ft Robinson, NE, 1895; sergeant since 12 Feb 1885. SOURCE: *ANJ* 32 (13 Jun 1895): 758.

Appointed sergeant 12 Feb 1885; in H/9th Cavalry at Ft Robinson, Jan 1897. SOURCE: Ninth Cavalry, Roster of NCOs, 1897.

‡Deposits with paymaster, 1897–98: $35.

Retired sergeant, received Indian Wars Campaign Badge number 1114 on 30 Jan 1909. SOURCE: Carroll, *Indian Wars Campaign Badge*, 32.

GREEN, M. J.; Private; G/9th Cav. Died at Ft Concho, TX, on 26 Oct 1871; buried at San Antonio National Cemetery, Section D, number 721. SOURCE: San Antonio National Cemetery Locator.

GREEN, Moses; Private; 25th Inf. Born on St. Johns Island, SC; Ht 5'11", black hair and eyes, dark complexion; occupation butcher, enlisted at age 24, Charleston, SC, 20 May 1881; left recruit depot, David's Island, NY, 2 Jul 1881, arrived Ft Randall, SD, 7 Jul 1881. SOURCE: Descriptive & Assignment Rolls of Recruits, 25 Inf.

GREEN, Moses; Private; F/9th Cav. Native of Virginia; age 23 when court martialed and convicted of premeditated deadly assault on Sgt. Emanuel Stance, Ft Reno, OK, 1883; sentenced to nine months' hard labor on post and forfeited $10 per month for same period; married 1886 and completed enlistment with character "very good." SOURCE: Kenner, *Buffalo Soldiers and Officers of the Ninth Cavalry*, 166–67.

Record of his court martial for striking 1st Sgt. Emanuel Stance, F/9th Cavalry, on the head, Ft Reno, OK, 1883, published. SOURCE: Schubert, *Voices of the Buffalo Soldier*, 129–36.

‡Intends to marry, Ft Robinson, NE, Christmas 1886. SOURCE: Cleveland *Gazette*, 27 Nov 1886.

GREEN, Walter; 2nd Lt; H/48th Inf. ‡Born in North Carolina; private, K/25th Infantry, 2 Aug 1879–1 Aug 1884; private, corporal, sergeant, first sergeant, I/9th Cavalry, 9 Aug 1884–8 Aug 1889; private, K/10th Cavalry, 13 Aug 1889; corporal, 15 Jan 1890; sergeant, 10 May 1890; first sergeant, 16 Feb 1894; stationed at Ft Custer, MT, 1897. SOURCE: Baker, Roster.

First sergeant, I/9th Cavalry, Ft Robinson, NE, 1889. *See* OTT, **WHITEN**, Walter J., Private, 24th Infantry

Third enlistment, Chicago, IL, 13 Aug 1889; replaced 1st Sgt. William McBryar in K/10th Cavalry 15 Feb 1894; remained first sergeant through Spanish-American War.

SOURCE: Register of Enlistments, NA. Notes in authors' files.

‡Served in 10th Cavalry, 1898; remained in U.S. during war with Spain. SOURCE: Cashin, *Under Fire with the Tenth Cavalry*, 349.

‡First sergeant, K/10th Cavalry, discharged to take commission in 48th Infantry. SOURCE: *ANJ* 37 (25 Nov 1899): 294.

‡Mentioned as second lieutenant, H/48th Infantry. SOURCE: Beasley, *Negro Trailblazers*, 284.

‡Commissioned captain, Camp Des Moines, IA, Oct 1917. SOURCE: Glass, *History of the Tenth Cavalry*, appendix M.

GREEN, William; Private; L/9th Cav. Enlisted at Ft Union, NM, 5 Jun 1876; discharged at Ft Bliss, TX, Jun 1881, character good. SOURCE: Muster Roll, L/9th Cavalry, 30 Apr–30 Jun 1881.

GREEN, William; Private; F/9th Cav. At Ft Reno, OK, Aug 1883, witnessed dispute between Pvt. Moses Green and 1st Sgt. Emanuel Stance. SOURCE: Schubert, *Voices of the Buffalo Soldier*, 132.

GREEN, William H.; Private; 38th Inf. Civil War veteran, served with 38th Infantry in Kansas; returned to Marietta, GA, worked in National Cemetery there. SOURCE: Dobak and Phillips, *The Black Regulars*, 272.

GREEN, William L.; D/24th Inf. Born in North Carolina; mulatto complexion; can read and write, age 21, Jul 1870, at Ft McKavett, TX. SOURCE: Bierschwale, *Fort McKavett*, 96.

GREENE, William H.; Signal Corps. Graduate of City College of New York; second in class of eight in Signal Corps class, 1884; first black Signal Corps member, assigned to Pensacola, FL, weather station, then Rochester, NY, discharged June 1887 for undisclosed offenses. SOURCE: Dobak and Phillips, *The Black Regulars*, 79–80, 83. See OTT, **GREENE**, Hallett, Signal Corps

GREER, Pierce; Private; 25th Inf. Born in Atlanta, GA; Ht 5'7", brown hair and black eyes, fair complexion; occupation laborer; enlisted at age 23, Charleston, SC, 27 May 1881; left recruit depot, David's Island, NY, 2 Jul 1881, arrived Ft Randall, SD, 7 Jul 1881. SOURCE: Descriptive & Assignment Rolls of Recruits, 25 Inf.

GREGOIRE, Gabriel; Private; K/25th Inf. Born in New Orleans, LA; Ht 5'6", brown complexion; occupation laborer; enlisted in A/39th Infantry for three years on 1 Oct 1867, age 22, at New Orleans; extra duty as post hospital attendant since 30 Mar 1869; transferred to K/25th Infan-

try at Jackson Bks, LA, 20 Apr 1869. SOURCE: Descriptive Roll of A/39th Inf.

GREGORY, Andrew; Private; K/25th Inf. Born in Edenton, NC; Ht 5'9", light complexion; occupation teamster; enlisted in A/39th Infantry for three years on 4 Oct 1866, age 20, at New Orleans, LA; confined fifteen days; transferred to K/25th Infantry at Jackson Bks, LA, 20 Apr 1869. SOURCE: Descriptive Roll of A/39th Inf.

GREGORY, Robert; Private; A/9th Cav. With Pvt. George Washington, K/25th Infantry, convicted, Ft Stockton, TX, Dec 1871, of breaking into and looting home of local black citizen, sentenced to dishonorable discharge and four years, Ft Quitman, TX, 1869. SOURCE: Leiker, *Racial Borders*, 79, 207.

GRESS, J. G.; Private; 24th Inf. *See* **GROSS**, James J., Private, 24th Infantry

GREY, Charles H.; Private; K/9th Cav. ‡Died 16 Mar 1890 at Ft Robinson, NE. SOURCE: List of Interments, Ft Robinson.

Died of pneumonia. SOURCE: Buecker, Fort Robinson Burials.

‡Funeral at Ft Robinson, 17 Mar 1890. SOURCE: Order 54, 16 Mar 1890, Post Orders, Ft Robinson.

GREY, James; M/9th Cav. Born in Kentucky; black complexion; cannot read or write, age 22, Jul 1870, at Ft McKavett, TX. SOURCE: Bierschwale, *Fort McKavett*, 99.

GRICE, Perry; Private; 10th Cav. Died on detached service; buried 16 Jan 1910, section B, row C, plot 35, at Ft Bayard, NM. SOURCE: Erickson, Burials at Fort Bayard National Cemetery, NM.

GRIFFIN, Charles; Private; I/10th Cav. In Troop I/10th Cavalry stationed at Bonita Cañon Camp, AZ, 30 Jun 1886. SOURCE: Tagg, *The Camp at Bonita Cañon*, 231.

GRIFFIN, George; C/25th Inf. Born in Louisiana; mulatto complexion; cannot read or write, age 24, 5 Sep 1870, at Ft McKavett, TX. SOURCE: Bierschwale, *Fort McKavett*, 109.

GRIFFIN, George; Musician; 25th Inf. With regiment at Fort Snelling, MN, 1880s; served continuously from first enlistment in 39th Infantry, Oct 1866. SOURCE: Dobak and Phillips, *The Black Regulars*, 93.

‡Musician George Griffin, G/25th Infantry, retires. SOURCE: *ANJ* 28 (17 Jan 1891): 349.

GRIFFIN, George; Private; H/25th Inf. Buried 28 Aug 1900, section A, row V, plot 13, at Ft Bayard, NM. SOURCE: Erickson, *Burials at Fort Bayard National Cemetery, NM.*

GRIFFIN, Isaac; Private; D/24th Inf. Born in Georgia; black complexion; cannot read or write, age 24, Jul 1870, at Ft McKavett, TX. SOURCE: Bierschwale, *Fort McKavett,* 96.

‡His sentence in accordance with General Court Martial Order 3, Department of Texas, 4 Feb 1876, to be carried out at Kansas Penitentiary, Leavenworth. SOURCE: GCMO 42, AGO, 4 Apr 1876.

Died on 21 Jan 1932; buried at Fort Sam Houston National Cemetery, Section A, number 21. SOURCE: Buffalo Soldiers Interred in Fort Sam Houston National Cemetery.

GRIFFIN, Jeremiah; Private; K/10th Cav. ‡Killed in action, Ojo Caliente, TX, 28 Oct 1880. SOURCE: Leckie, *The Buffalo Soldiers,* 230.

‡Killed in action, Ojo Caliente, 29 Oct 1880. SOURCE: Baker, Roster.

Died 28 Oct 1880, killed in action, Ojo Caliente. SOURCE: Regimental Returns, 10th Cavalry, 1880.

GRIM, James; Private; B/9th Cav. Died 10 Dec 1899; originally buried at Ft Wingate, NM; buried at Santa Fe National Cemetery, NM, plot A-2 965. SOURCE: Santa Fe National Cemetery, Records of Burials.

GRIMDER, Henry; M/9th Cav. Born in Kentucky; black complexion; can read, cannot write, age 24, Jul 1870, at Ft McKavett, TX. SOURCE: Bierschwale, *Fort McKavett,* 99.

GRIMDY, Edward; M/9th Cav. Born in Kentucky; black complexion; cannot read or write, age 22, Jul 1870, at Ft McKavett, TX. SOURCE: Bierschwale, *Fort McKavett,* 99.

GRIMKE, Washington; Private; 9th Cav. *See* **GRUNKE,** Washington, Private, 9th Cavalry

GRINIER, Dallas; Private; U.S. Army. Seminole Negro Scout, served 1872–76, 1886–88. SOURCE: Schubert, Consolidated List of Seminole Negro Scouts.

Dallas Griner, born in Cherokee Nation, IT; enlisted at Ft Clark, TX, 9 Sep 1872, age 20; Ht 5'5", hair and eyes black, black complexion; discharged 9 Mar 1873 at Ft Clark where he enlisted four times for six-month terms; at Ft McKavett, TX, 17 Dec 1875 left field command without permission on completion of enlistment, desertion excused and returned to duty at Ft Clark 7 Mar 1876; with Isaac Payne indicted by Kinney County, TX, grand jury 6 Sep 1876 for theft of prized gelding owned by Deputy Sheriff Windus; reenlisted for one year 9 Jan 1886 at Ft Clark where

he was discharged and reenlisted twice for one-year terms; died of cholera morbus at Ft Clark 29 May 1888; buried at Seminole Cemetery. SOURCE: Swanson, 19. *See* **KIBBETTS,** Robert, Corporal, U.S. Army

Signed name with "X" in 1876. SOURCE: NARA, M 929, Roll 2.

Dallas Griner buried at Seminole Indian Scout Cemetery, Kinney County, TX. SOURCE: Indian Scout Cemetery, Kinney County, Texas.

GROOM, Mills B.; Private; D/24th Inf. *See* **CROOM,** Mills B., Private, D/24th Infantry

GROSS, Daniel; Sergeant; 9th Cav. Gunner on mountain howitzer when killed in action at Rio Perches, NM, Jan 1880. SOURCE: Kenner, *Buffalo Soldiers and Officers of the Ninth Cavalry,* 228.

‡Sgt. D. J. Gross, F/9th Cavalry, killed in action on headwaters of Rio Perches, 12 Jan 1880, along with Pvt. I. H. James, F/9th Cavalry. SOURCE: Hamilton, "History of the Ninth Cavalry," 52; *Illustrated Review: Ninth Cavalry.*

GROSS, James J.; Private; 24th Inf. Died while on casual detachment, 2 Oct 1906; buried at Ft Bayard, NM, in plot 0 12. SOURCE: "Fort Bayard National Cemetery, Records of Burials."

J. G. Gress, 24th Infantry, died while on casual detachment; buried at Ft Bayard. SOURCE: "Buffalo Soldiers Buried at Ft Bayard, NM."

GROSS, Thomas; Private; C/9th Cav. ‡Recruit, Colored Detachment, Mounted Service, Jefferson Barracks, MO, 1888. *See* OTT, **GUNTER,** William H., Recruit, Colored Detachment/Mounted Service

‡Enlisted Ft McKinney, WY, 12 Mar 1894.

‡Charges against him contained in letter, Department of the Platte, 7 Sep 1895, are withdrawn by letter, Department of the Platte, 16 Sep 1895.

‡Reenlistment, married, authorized by letter, Adjutant General's Office, 14 Oct 1896.

Died on detached service 7 May 1915; buried at Ft Leavenworth National Cemetery, plot H 3390 A. SOURCE: Ft Leavenworth National Cemetery.

GRUNKE, Washington; Private; 9th Cav. Washington Grimke killed along with Sgt. Bushrod Johnson, Jul 1882, by horse thief they were escorting to Ft Sill, OK. SOURCE: Kenner, *Buffalo Soldiers and Officers of the Ninth Cavalry,* 22.

‡He and Sgt. Bush Johnson killed by "a desperate horse thief," while taking him from Henrietta, TX, to Ft Sill, Indian Territory, Aug 1882. SOURCE: Hamilton, "History of the Ninth Cavalry," 64; *Illustrated Review: Ninth Cavalry.*

GUDDY, Lusk; Trumpeter; D/9th Cav. With Captain Dodge at battle at Milk River, CO, 2–10 Oct 1879. SOURCE: Miller, *Hollow Victory*, 167, 206–7.

GUDDY, Zeke; Private; 9th Cav. *See* **GULLEY**, Zeikel, Private, 9th Cavalry

GUIDINE, Olive; Sergeant; K/25 Inf. Died 28 Oct 1886; buried in plot 4 68, Ft Meade National Cemetery, SD. SOURCE: Ft Meade National Cemetery, VA database.

GUINN, Floyd; Private; B/9th Cav. Military prisoner, died 17 Nov 1882; buried at Ft Leavenworth National Cemetery, plot 1790. SOURCE: Ft Leavenworth National Cemetery.

GUIRDIN, Eugene; Private; 25th Inf. Born in Charleston, SC; Ht 5'7", brown hair and hazel eyes, fair complexion; occupation hostler; enlisted at age 22, Charleston, 17 May 1881; left recruit depot, David's Island, NY, 2 Jul 1881, arrived Ft Randall, SD, 7 Jul 1881. SOURCE: Descriptive & Assignment Rolls of Recruits, 25 Inf.

GULLEY, Zeikel; Private; 9th Cav. Name sometimes written "Zeke Guddy" by Pension Office employees. SOURCE: Dobak and Phillips, *The Black Regulars*, 331.

GUY, John; Private; 25th Inf. Born in York, PA; Ht 5'5", black hair and eyes, black complexion; occupation laborer; enlisted at age 30, Harrisburg, PA, 22 Jul 1886; arrived Ft Snelling, MN, 19 Aug 1886. SOURCE: Descriptive & Assignment Rolls of Recruits, 25 Inf.

GUYSON, Edward; Private; E/10th Cav. In Troop E/10th Cavalry stationed at Bonita Cañon Camp, AZ, but absent or on detached service 28 Feb 1886. SOURCE: Tagg, *The Camp at Bonita Cañon*, 231.

GWYNN, Edward; Private; E/10th Cav. Received as private Indian Wars Campaign Badge number 1404 on 15 Jul 1909. SOURCE: Carroll, *Indian Wars Campaign Badge*, 40.

H

HAGEN, Abram; Sergeant; G/24th Inf. ‡Wounded in action in Cuba, 1898. SOURCE: Muller, *The Twenty Fourth Infantry*, 98.

‡Commended for distinguished service, battle of Santiago, Cuba, 1 Jul 1898, as corporal, G/24th Infantry; awarded certificate of merit. SOURCE: GO 15, AGO, 13 Feb 1900.

‡Certificate of merit mentioned. SOURCE: Steward, *The Colored Regulars*, 280; *ANJ* 37 (24 Feb 1900): 611; Scipio, *Last of the Black Regulars*, 130.

Awarded certificate of merit for distinguished service in battle, Santiago, 1 Jul 1898. SOURCE: Gleim, *The Certificate of Merit*, 46.

HAGGER, William; Private; G/9th Cav. Died at Ft Clark, TX; buried at Fort Sam Houston National Cemetery, Section PE, number 102. SOURCE: Buffalo Soldiers Interred in Fort Sam Houston National Cemetery.

HAGINS, William H.; H/25th Inf. Born in North Carolina; mulatto complexion; can read and write, age 24, 5 Sep 1870, at Ft McKavett, TX. SOURCE: Bierschwale, *Fort McKavett*, 107.

HAGUE, Lucius J.; Corporal; E/9th Cav. ‡Lucious J. Hague promoted from lance corporal, E/9th Cavalry, Ft Robinson, NE, 10 May 1895. SOURCE: *ANJ* 32 (25 May 1895): 642.

Appointed corporal 10 May 1895; in E/9th Cavalry at Ft Robinson, Jan 1897. SOURCE: Ninth Cavalry, Roster of NCOs, 1897.

‡Corporal, K/9th Cavalry, ranked number 75 among rifle experts with 75 percent, 1905. SOURCE: GO 101, AGO, 31 May 1906.

‡Veteran of Spanish-American War and Philippine Insurrection; corporal, E/9th Cavalry, at Ft D. A. Russell, WY, in 1910; sharpshooter. SOURCE: *Illustrated Review: Ninth Cavalry*, with picture.

HAINER, Levi; Private; M/10th Cav. *See* **HAINES**, Levi, Private, M/10th Cavalry

HAINES, Andrew J.; Private; 10th Cav. Died 10 Feb 1922; buried at San Antonio National Cemetery, Section D, number 733-B. SOURCE: San Antonio National Cemetery Locator.

HAINES, John; C/25th Inf. Born in Louisiana; mulatto complexion; cannot read or write, age 26, 5 Sep 1870, at Ft McKavett, TX. SOURCE: Bierschwale, *Fort McKavett*, 109.

HAINES, Levi; Private; M/10th Cav. ‡Levi Hainer original member of M/10th Cavalry; in troop when organized, Ft Riley, KS, 15 Oct 1867. SOURCE: McMiller, "Buffalo Soldiers," 79.

1st Sgt. Levi Hainer, M/10th Cavalry, served at Ft Sill, OK, 1874. SOURCE: Schubert, *Voices of the Buffalo Soldier*, 67.

Pvt. Levi Haines, M/10th Cavalry, drowned 6 May 1881 at Morgan Creek, TX. SOURCE: Regimental Returns, 10th Cavalry, 1881.

HAIRSTON, Charley; Private; B/25th Inf. Enlisted 26 May 1905, discharged without honor 19 Nov 1906. SOURCE: Powell, "Military Record of the Enlisted Men Who Were Discharged Without Honor."

Dishonorable discharge, Brownsville, TX. SOURCE: SO 266, AGO, 9 Nov 1906.

HALE, Joseph; Private; 25th Inf. Served at Ft Stockton, TX, 1880; fought with Pvt. Thomas C. Dyson, 25th Infantry, over a prostitute. SOURCE: Dobak and Phillips, *The Black Regulars*, 177.

HALL, Allen; Private; I/10th Cav. In Troop I/10th Cavalry stationed at Bonita Cañon Camp, AZ, 30 Jun 1886. SOURCE: Tagg, *The Camp at Bonita Cañon*, 231.

HALL, Charles; Corporal; M/9th Cav. Died at Ft Stockton, TX, on 4 Jul 1874; buried at San Antonio National Cemetery, Section C, number 355. SOURCE: San Antonio National Cemetery Locator.

HALL, Edward M.; Private; G/25th Inf. Born in Reading, PA; Ht 5'5", black hair and brown eyes, brown complexion; occupation waiter; resided in York, PA, when he enlisted 18 Aug 1886, age 23, at Harrisburg, PA; assigned to G/25th Infantry; arrived Ft Snelling, MN, 14 Dec 1886. SOURCE: Descriptive & Assignment Rolls of Recruits, 25 Inf.

HALL, Fayette; Private; E/9th Cav. Strung from tree limb by wrists by Lt. Edward Heyl at San Pedro Springs, TX, Apr 1867, for failure to remove nosebag from his horse promptly. SOURCE: Schubert, *Black Valor*, 16.

‡1st Lt. Edward Heyl charged with tying Hall up by the thumbs and striking him with sabre, camp near San Antonio, TX, 9 Apr 1867.

HALL, Frank W.; Private; H/25th Inf. Born in Warrenton, NC, 25 Feb 1862; enlisted Baltimore, MD, 12 Apr 1883; Ht 5'6", mulatto complexion, brown eyes, black hair; occupations laborer, waiter, coachman, janitor, miner; served in H/10th Cavalry; discharged Ft Apache, AZ, 11 Apr 1888; enlisted Washington, DC, 10 May 1888, served in H/25th Infantry; discharged Ft Missoula, MT, 9 May 1893; enlisted St. Paul, MN, 26 May 1893; transferred 18 Feb 1894 from H/25th Infantry to Hospital Corps; discharged Hot Springs, AR, 25 May 1898; married Rachel Ann Norman, Hot Springs, 26 Jul 1897, divorced 10 Feb 1904; children Catherine Beatrice, born 16 Jun 1898, married name Brooks resided at 620 Harrison St., Tacoma, WA, in 1920, and Frank Eisele Wade, born 9 Nov 1899, served as steward, U.S. Navy, World War I, and resided at same Tacoma, WA, address in 1920; received pension of $6 per month, 1901, increased to $12 per month in 1903, increased to $20 in 1924, increased to $40 in 1927, increased to $50 in 1928; resided in National Home for Disabled Veteran Soldiers, Ohio, 1907; resided in National Military Home, Leavenworth, KS, 1908; resided at 1011 New York Ave., Washington, DC, in 1914, before admission to United States Soldiers Home, Washington, DC, 30 Jun 1914; discharged from home Sep 1915 and readmitted Dec 1915; discharged from home Sept 1917 and readmitted Apr 1920; discharged from Soldiers Home Jan 1925; admitted to Southern Branch, National Home for Disabled Volunteer Soldiers, Elizabeth City County, VA, Oct 1925; died in Warrenton, 12 Jan 1934; buried in Plummer Cemetery, Warrenton. SOURCE: Sayre, *Warriors of Color*, 199–208.

Private in H/10th Cavalry, sick in hospital at Fort Bowie, AZ, 10 Dec 1885; returned to Bonita Cañon Camp, AZ, by 28 Feb 1886; private in H/10th Cavalry stationed at Bonita Cañon Camp, 30 Apr 1886. SOURCE: Tagg, *The Camp at Bonita Cañon*, 67, 232.

HALL, Grooms; Private; K/25th Inf. Died at Ft Stockton, TX, on 28 Jul 1871; buried at San Antonio National Cemetery, Section C, number 382. SOURCE: San Antonio National Cemetery Locator.

HALL, Joseph; Private; M/10th Cav. Died at Camp Pena, CO, on 18 Jul 1884; buried at San Antonio National Cemetery, Section F, number 1119. SOURCE: San Antonio National Cemetery Locator.

HALL, Morell; Private; U.S. Army. Born in Mississippi; enlisted at Ft Duncan, TX, 1 Sep 1875, age 22; Ht 5'7", black hair and eyes, black complexion; discharged at Ft Duncan 1 Mar 1876; enlisted 13 May 1883 at Ft Clark, TX; discharged 14 May 1884 at Camp Myers Spring, TX; enlisted 27 May 1884, age 36, at Ft Clark where discharged 31 Aug 1884; ex-soldier from colored regiment, intermarried; pastor of Seminole Baptist Church for fifty years; buried 15 May 1929 at Seminole Cemetery. SOURCE: Swanson, 20.

Seminole Negro Scout, served 1875–76, 1883–84. SOURCE: Schubert, Consolidated List of Seminole Negro Scouts.

Morrell Halls, died 14 May 1929; buried at Seminole Indian Scout Cemetery, Kinney County, TX. SOURCE: Indian Scout Cemetery, Kinney County, Texas.

HALL, Thomas; C/25th Inf. Born in Georgia; mulatto complexion; cannot read or write, age 21, 5 Sep 1870, at Ft McKavett, TX. SOURCE: Bierschwale, *Fort McKavett*, 109.

HALL, Thomas; Private; Band/24th Inf. Died 12 Oct 1884; buried at Ft Leavenworth National Cemetery, plot G 3060. SOURCE: Ft Leavenworth National Cemetery.

HALL, Thornton; Private; C/10th Cav. Died 18 Jul 1867 of cholera at Camp Grierson, KS. SOURCE: Regimental Returns, 10th Cavalry, 1867.

HALLON, Ross; Corporal; A/25th Inf. Killed Sturgis, SD, druggist H. P. Lynch in Aug 1885, after Lynch treated Minnie Lewis, whom Hallon had beaten; Hallon was subsequently jailed and lynched in Sturgis. SOURCE: Dobak and Phillips, *The Black Regulars*, 240.

Died 24 Aug 1885; buried in plot 1 59, Ft Meade National Cemetery, SD. SOURCE: Ft Meade National Cemetery, VA database.

HAMILTON, Charles; Private; 25th Inf. Born in Leesville, VA; Ht 5'8", black hair and eyes, black complexion; occupation laborer; resided in Alexandria County, VA, when enlisted at age 28, Washington, DC, 6 Sep 1886; arrived Ft Snelling, MN, 20 Jan 1887. SOURCE: Descriptive & Assignment Rolls of Recruits, 25 Inf.

HAMILTON, Edward; Private; C/9th Cav. Tried by court martial, Ft Sill, OK, Aug 1884, on charges stemming from his reaction to ill treatment by sergeant; his statement to court published. SOURCE: Schubert, *Voices of the Buffalo Soldier*, 137–38.

‡Deserted from Ft Robinson, NE, 17 Jul 1886.

HAMILTON, Ernest; Private; K/9th Cav. Received Philippine Campaign Badge number 11725 for service as private in K/9th Cavalry; in 9th Cavalry at Ft Leavenworth, KS, Mar 1905. SOURCE: Philippine Campaign Badge list, 29 May 1905.

HAMILTON, Nelson; Private; 9th Cav. Received Philippine Campaign Badge number 11724 for service as private in E/9th Cavalry; in 9th Cavalry at Ft Leavenworth, KS, Mar 1905. SOURCE: Philippine Campaign Badge list, 29 May 1905.

HAMILTON, Thomas; Private; 25th Inf. Born in Christ Church, SC; Ht 5'8", black hair and eyes, dark complexion; occupation laborer; enlisted at age 24, Charleston, SC, 14 Jun 1881; left recruit depot, David's Island, NY, 2 Jul 1881, arrived Ft Randall, SD, 7 Jul 1881. SOURCE: Descriptive & Assignment Rolls of Recruits, 25 Inf.

HAMMANS, Isaac; Trumpeter; 10th Cav. *See* **HAMMONS**, Isaiah, Private, 10th Cavalry

HAMMONS, Isaiah; Private; 10th Cav. ‡Enlisted by recruiting officer, Santa Fe, NM, 17 Dec 1866. SOURCE: CO, 10 Cav, to Lt George McDermott, 10 May 1867, ES, 10 Cav, 1866–71.

‡Regimental headquarters has final statement but no inventory of effects for late Private Hammons. SOURCE: CO, 10 Cav, to Lt T. A. Jennings, K/25, 22 Apr 1867, LS, 10 Cav, 1866–67.

Isaac Hammans, Trumpeter, 10th Cavalry, died 27 Mar 1867; buried at Ft Leavenworth National Cemetery, plot C 2063. SOURCE: Ft Leavenworth National Cemetery.

HAMPTON, George W.; Sergeant; Band/10th Cav. ‡Sergeant at San Marcelino, Philippines, witness to Pvt. William R. Fulbright's disrespectful language toward and challenge to fight Sgt. John H. Jackson, Band/25th Infantry, 31 Oct 1900. SOURCE: Misc Records, 25 Inf.

‡Private acquitted of absence from concert by summary court, Iba, Zambales, Philippines, 25 Oct 1900. SOURCE: Misc Records, 25 Inf.

‡At Ft Niobrara, NE, Mar 1903; his "disease appears fatal and [he] has reached a remarkably clear faith and awaits his earthly end with perfect composure. His bible has become to him his trusted guide." SOURCE: Monthly Report, Chaplain Steward, Mar 1903.

Died 6 May 1903; buried at Ft Bayard, NM, in plot L 26. SOURCE: "Fort Bayard National Cemetery, Records of Burials"; "Buffalo Soldiers Buried at Ft Bayard, NM."

In Band, 25th Infantry, buried 6 May 1903, section A, row S, plot 29, at Ft Bayard. SOURCE: Erickson, Burials at Fort Bayard National Cemetery, NM.

HAMPTON, Thornton; Private; 10th Cav. Served in 1880s. SOURCE: Dobak and Phillips, *The Black Regulars*, 186–87.

HAMPTON, Wade; Private; D/10th Cav. Choctaw father and African American mother; enlisted Ft Gibson, OK, Apr 1867, served as company farrier and blacksmith; after discharge employed at Ft Sill, OK, as blacksmith; died at Okmulgee, OK, 1932. SOURCE: Dobak and Phillips, *The Black Regulars*, 270, 334.

‡Served five years; recent subscriber. SOURCE: *Winners of the West* 4 (Mar 1927): 8.

‡Subscriber and member, Camp 11, National Indian War Veterans, St. Joseph, MO; served 1867–72; died at Okmulgee, OK, 14 Dec 1932. SOURCE: *Winners of the West* 10 (Jan 1933): 3.

HAMS, Thornton; Private; C/10th Cav. ‡Mentioned among men who distinguished themselves in 1889; awarded certificate of merit for gallant and meritorious service while escort for Maj. Joseph W. Wham, paymaster, when attacked by robbers between Fts Grant and Thomas, AZ. SOURCE: GO 18, AGO, 1891.

Report of Paymaster Wham, describing bravery of escort, published. SOURCE: Schubert, *Voices of the Buffalo Soldier*, 159–62.

Cited for bravery against robbers near Cedar Springs, AZ, in May 1889 by Maj. Joseph W. Wham, and awarded certificate of merit; wounded during fight; still in Army at end of 1890. SOURCE: Schubert, *Black Valor*, 93, 95.

‡At Ft Grant, 1890; certificate of merit mentioned. SOURCE: SecWar, *AR 1890*, 289; Baker, Roster.

Awarded certificate of merit for gallant and meritorious conduct while member of escort of Maj. Joseph W. Wham, paymaster, who was ambushed by bandits between Fts Grant and Thomas, 11 May 1889. SOURCE: Gleim, *The Certificate of Merit*, 44.

‡Letter, Adjutant General's Office, 1 May 1896, concerns his enlistment for A/9th Cavalry.

HANAON, James S.; Private; F/10th Cav. Died 26 Mar 1870; buried at Ft Leavenworth National Cemetery, plot D 1338. SOURCE: Ft Leavenworth National Cemetery.

HANCE, George W.; Private; B/25th Inf. Born in Zanesville, OH; Ht 6'2", black hair and eyes, black complexion; discharged from D/24th Infantry 26 Apr 1886; fourth enlistment at age 37, Columbus Barracks, OH, 19 May 1886; assigned to B/25th Infantry; arrived Ft Snelling, MN, 29 Jun 1886. SOURCE: Descriptive & Assignment Rolls of Recruits, 25 Inf.

Pvt. George W. Hance, E/9th Cavalry, served against Apaches in New Mexico, 1879. SOURCE: Dobak and Phillips, *The Black Regulars*, 191.

‡Died of valvular heart disease on arrival at U.S. Soldiers Home, age 57, 15 Mar 1904. SOURCE: SecWar, *AR 1904*, 4:289.

HANDY, Frank; Private; E/9th Cav. Cursed and menaced by Lt. Edward Heyl, morning of 9 Apr 1867; one of ten soldiers charged with mutiny and desertion for role in mutiny at San Pedro Springs, near San Antonio, TX, April 1867; pled guilty to desertion but not mutiny; mutiny charge dropped; convicted of desertion and sentenced to six months' confinement at military prison, Ship's Island, MS; sentence remitted before he was transported to prison. SOURCE: Dobak and Phillips, *The Black Regulars*, 208–11; Schubert, *Black Valor*, 13.

HANLEY, Edward; Private; F/10th Cav. Died 28 Jun 1873 of disease at Ft Concho, TX. SOURCE: Regimental Returns, 10th Cavalry, 1873.

‡Deceased; final statement sent to Adjutant General, 27 Jul 1873. SOURCE: LS, 10 Cav, 1873–83.

HANSON, Edward; Sergeant; B/9th Cav. Born in Virginia; black complexion; can read and write, age 26, Jul 1870, in F/9th Cavalry at Ft McKavett, TX; wife Mary, born in Kentucky, mulatto complexion, occupation washerwoman, can read and write, age 25, living with daughter Sarah J., age 1, at Ft McKavett July 1870. SOURCE: Bierschwale, *Fort McKavett,* 97, 101.

‡Appointed sergeant, 8 Apr 1877. SOURCE: Roster, 9 Cav.

Sergeant, at Fort Washakie, WY, 1887, went on furlough with his laundress wife. SOURCE: Kenner, *Buffalo Soldiers and Officers of the Ninth Cavalry*, 251.

‡Stationed at Ft DuChesne, UT; to report for examination for appointment as ordnance sergeant. SOURCE: *ANJ* 28 (1 Aug 1891): 539.

‡Retires from Ft DuChesne, Apr 1895. SOURCE: *ANJ* 32 (13 Apr 1895): 539.

Died 27 May 1908; buried at San Antonio National Cemetery, Section C, number 474. SOURCE: San Antonio National Cemetery Locator.

HANSON, John; Private; L/9th Cav. Native of Maryland; fined $5 and made to carry a log in Apr 1874; at Ft Union, NM, Mar 1876, in fourth year of service, age 27, when killed by white gunfighter David Crockett in shootout at bar in Cimarron, NM, with Pvts. George Small and Anthony Harvey, L/9th Cavalry. SOURCE: Kenner, *Buffalo Soldiers and Officers of the Ninth Cavalry*, 180.

‡Killed by cattle herders at Cimarron, NM, 24 Jan 1876, along with Pvts. Anthony Harvey and George Smallow, L/9th Cavalry. SOURCE: Hamilton, "History of the Ninth Cavalry," 28; *Illustrated Review: Ninth Cavalry*.

‡Killed in saloon shootout with Pvts. Anthony Harvey and George Small, L/9th Cavalry, Cimarron, Apr 1876; buried at Ft Union, NM. SOURCE: Billington, *New Mexico's Buffalo Soldiers*, 67.

HAPER; Sergeant; H/25th Inf. Children buried at Ft McKavett, TX, before 17 May 1879; bodies removed to National Cemetery, San Antonio, TX, 23 Nov 1883. SOURCE: Bierschwale, *Fort McKavett,* 123.

HARASHAW, James; Private; 25th Inf. Civil War veteran; at Ft Bliss, TX, convicted Oct 1871 of desertion, dishonorably discharged and sentenced to one year at hard labor, after passing out after drinking spree in Mexico and being apprehended by Mexican police. SOURCE: Leiker, *Racial Borders*, 84, 208.

HARDEN, William; Private; B/25th Inf. Enlisted 13 Aug 1898, discharged as private Company I, 25th Infantry, 27 Feb 1899, character excellent; enlisted 21 Jul 1905, discharged without honor 19 Nov 1906. SOURCE: Powell, "Military Record of the Enlisted Men Who Were Discharged Without Honor."

‡Dishonorable discharge, Brownsville, TX. SOURCE: SO 266, AGO, 9 Nov 1906.

HARDEN, William J.; Private; 9th Cav. Received Philippine Campaign Badge number 11726; in 9th Cavalry at Ft Leavenworth, KS, Mar 1905. SOURCE: Philippine Campaign Badge list, 29 May 1905.

HARDY, James; Corporal; 24th Inf. Circulated letter asking for money to support surviving members of abolitionist John Brown's family, in 1890. SOURCE: Dobak and Phillips, *The Black Regulars*, 144.

HARE, Solomon; Private; F/25th Inf. Soloman Hare born in Virginia; black complexion; cannot read or write, age 26, 5 Sep 1870, in C/25th Infantry at Ft McKavett, TX. SOURCE: Bierschwale, *Fort McKavett,* 108.

Sgt. Solomon Hare, 25th Infantry, Civil War veteran; served at Ft Snelling, MN, 1880s; reduced to private at Ft Missoula, MT, during his sixth enlistment, for gambling. SOURCE: Dobak and Phillips, *The Black Regulars*, 299, 313.

‡Sergeant, I/25th Infantry, authorized two-month furlough from Ft Missoula. SOURCE: *ANJ* 27 (22 Feb 1890): 491.

‡Reduced from sergeant, F/25th Infantry, to private, Ft Missoula; while sergeant of guard, gambled with prisoner under sentence; portion of sentence calling for three months' confinement remitted by Brig. Gen. Thomas H. Ruger. SOURCE: *ANJ* 28 (18 Oct 1890): 121.

‡Private, F/25th Infantry, retires from Ft Missoula, Dec 1892. SOURCE: *ANJ* 30 (17 Dec 1892): 271.

HARMON, Charles; Private; G/10th Cav. ‡Original member of 10th Cavalry; in troop when organized, Ft Leavenworth, KS, 5 Jul 1867. SOURCE: McMiller, "Buffalo Soldiers," 74.

Died 25 Jul 1867 of cholera at Wilson Creek, KS. SOURCE: Regimental Returns, 10th Cavalry, 1867.

HAROLD, Aleck; Private; A/10th Cav. Died 24 Jul 1867 of disease at Ft Larned, KS. SOURCE: Regimental Returns, 10th Cavalry, 1867.

HARPER, Clay; QM Sgt; E/9th Cav. Received Philippine Campaign Badge number 11727 for service as corporal, D/48th Infantry, United States Volunteers; in 9th Cavalry at Ft Leavenworth, KS, Mar 1905. SOURCE: Philippine Campaign Badge list, 29 May 1905.

‡Veteran of Philippine Insurrection; at Ft D. A. Russell, WY, in 1910. SOURCE: *Illustrated Review: Ninth Cavalry*, with picture.

HARPER, Henry; Private; H/10th Cav. ‡Original member of 10th Cavalry; in troop when organized, Ft Leavenworth, KS, 21 Jul 1867. SOURCE: McMiller, "Buffalo Soldiers," 75.

Died 2 Oct 1867 of disease at Big Creek, KS. SOURCE: Regimental Returns, 10th Cavalry, 1867.

HARPER Henry; Private; D/24th Inf. Died 7 Mar 1889; buried at Ft Bayard, NM, in plot G 18. SOURCE: "Fort Bayard National Cemetery, Records of Burials."

Buried 7 Mar 1889, section A, row I, plot 20, at Ft Bayard. SOURCE: Erickson, Burials at Fort Bayard National Cemetery, NM.

HARPER, Henry; Private; H/10th Cav. At Ft Apache, AZ, 1890, subscribed $.50 to testimonial to General Grierson. SOURCE: List of subscriptions, 23 Apr 1890, 10th Cavalry papers, MHI.

HARPER, John W.; 1st Sgt; H/25th Inf. Born in Virginia; mulatto complexion; can read and write; married Oct or Dec 1869; age 28, 5 Sep 1870, in H/25th Infantry at Ft McKavett, TX; wife Fannie, born in Louisiana, mulatto complexion, cannot read or write, occupation washerwoman, living in tent at Ft McKavett 6 Sep 1870. SOURCE: Bierschwale, *Fort McKavett*, 107, 110.

‡At Ft Davis, TX, 1878; best marksman in company, tied for fourth in regiment. SOURCE: Scrapbook, 25 Inf, I.

‡Son born to wife Fanny, Ft Davis, 30 Aug 1879. SOURCE: Thompson, "The Negro Regiments."

Sergeant Haper, H/25th Infantry, children buried at Ft McKavett, TX, before 17 May 1879; bodies removed to National Cemetery, San Antonio, TX, 23 Nov 1883. SOURCE: Bierschwale, *Fort McKavett*, 123.

Appointed ordnance sergeant 25 Oct 1887, from first sergeant, H/25th Infantry. SOURCE: Dobak, "Staff Non-commissioned Officers."

HARPER, Robert H.; Private; 24th Inf. After service recalled that Brackettville near Ft Clark, TX, offered ample opportunities to gamble. SOURCE: Dobak and Phillips, *The Black Regulars*, 169.

HARPER, William H.; Corporal; E/9th Cav. Appointed corporal 7 Oct 1893; in E/9th Cavalry at Ft Robinson, NE, Jan 1897. SOURCE: Ninth Cavalry, Roster of NCOs, 1897.

‡At Ft Robinson, 1894. *See* **TURNER**, Peter H., Blacksmith, E/9th Cavalry

‡On permanent color guard, Ft Robinson, 1895. SOURCE: *ANJ* 32 (3 Aug 1895): 807. *See* **LYMAN**, George, Color Sergeant, 9th Cavalry

‡Appointed to regimental color guard, Ft Robinson, Mar 1896. SOURCE: *ANJ* 33 (28 Mar 1896): 540.

HARRIS, Abram; Private; 25th Inf. Born in Abbeville, SC; Ht 6'2", black hair and eyes, fair complexion; occupation waiter, enlisted at age 21, Charleston, SC, 1 Jun 1881; left recruit depot, David's Island, NY, 2 Jul 1881, arrived Ft Randall, SD, 7 Jul 1881. SOURCE: Descriptive & Assignment Rolls of Recruits, 25 Inf.

HARRIS, Albert; Private; M/25th Inf. Died in Philippine Islands on 8 Nov 1900; buried at San Antonio National Cemetery, Section F, number 1068. SOURCE: San Antonio National Cemetery Locator.

HARRIS, Alexander; Private; K/25th Inf. Born in Wilmington, DE; Ht 5'3", black complexion; occupation blacksmith; enlisted in A/39th Infantry for three years on 12 Jul 1867, age 21, at Philadelphia, PA; appointed sergeant 23 Mar 1867; transferred to K/25th Infantry at Jackson Bks, LA, 20 Apr 1869. SOURCE: Descriptive Roll of A/39th Inf.

HARRIS, Anderson; Sergeant; B/25th Inf. Died 6 Feb 1894; buried at San Antonio National Cemetery, Section I, number 1597. SOURCE: San Antonio National Cemetery Locator.

HARRIS, Charles L.; D/24th Inf. Born in Indiana; black complexion; can read and write, age 24, Jul 1870, at Ft McKavett, TX. SOURCE: Bierschwale, *Fort McKavett*, 95.

HARRIS, David; Private; L/25th Inf. Died 25 May 1905; originally buried at Ft Niobrara, NE; reburied at Ft Leavenworth National Cemetery, plot G 3535. SOURCE: Ft Leavenworth National Cemetery.

HARRIS, Edward H.; Private; Band/10th Cav. ‡Deposited $20 with paymaster. SOURCE: CO, 10 Cav, to PMG, 4 May 1874, LS, 10 Cav, 1873–83.

At Ft Concho, TX, 1877, the only man on post with any knowledge of printing, but required supervision by an officer. SOURCE: Dobak and Phillips, *The Black Regulars*, 52.

HARRIS, Foster; Private; G/23rd Kan Inf. Died 15 Apr 1899; buried at Ft Leavenworth National Cemetery, plot 3177. SOURCE: Ft Leavenworth National Cemetery.

HARRIS, George; F/9th Cav. Born in Maryland; black complexion; cannot read or write, age 24, Jul 1870, at Ft McKavett, TX. SOURCE: Bierschwale, *Fort McKavett*, 97.

HARRIS, George; Private; I/10th Cav. In Troop I/10th Cavalry stationed at Bonita Cañon Camp, AZ, 30 Jun 1886. SOURCE: Tagg, *The Camp at Bonita Cañon*, 231.

HARRIS, George; Farrier; E/10th Cav. Received as farrier Indian Wars Campaign Badge number 1405 on 15 Jul 1909; badge reported lost 24 Oct 1912, replaced with number 1684. SOURCE: Carroll, *Indian Wars Campaign Badge*, 40, 49.

HARRIS, George G.; Private; H/10th Cav. In Troop H/10th Cavalry stationed at Bonita Cañon Camp, AZ, 30 Apr 1886. SOURCE: Tagg, *The Camp at Bonita Cañon*, 232.

HARRIS, George W.; M/10th Cav. Sergeant, 4th U.S. Colored Infantry; resides at 932 L. Pine St, Baltimore, MD. SOURCE: United States Colored Troops Resident in Baltimore at the Time of the 1890 Census.

‡Original member of 10th Cavalry; in troop when organized, Ft Riley, KS, 15 Oct 1867. SOURCE: McMiller, "Buffalo Soldiers," 79.

HARRIS, George W.; Sergeant; I/9th Cav. Died at Ft Davis, TX, on 20 Aug 1872; buried at San Antonio National Cemetery, Section I, number 1543. SOURCE: San Antonio National Cemetery Locator.

HARRIS, Henry; Private; 25th Inf. Born in Nashville, TN; Ht 5'10", black hair and eyes, black complexion; occupation laborer; enlisted at age 21, Nashville, 25 Feb 1886; arrived Ft Snelling, MN, 31 Jul 1886. SOURCE: Descriptive & Assignment Rolls of Recruits, 25 Inf.

HARRIS, Hyder; Private; H/10th Cav. Born in Caroline County, VA, 1851; enlisted Baltimore, MD, 25 Feb 1881; Ht 5'3", black complexion, eyes, and hair; occupation laborer and farmer; discharged Bonita Canyon, AZ, 24 Feb 1886; married Jane Holland, Elkridge, MD, 6 Oct 1887,

died 4 Sep 1930; no children; died 22 Jan 1903. SOURCE: Sayre, *Warriors of Color*, 209–25.

Corporal, H/10th Cavalry, honorably discharged 24 Feb 1886. SOURCE: Tagg, *The Camp at Bonita Cañon*, 66.

HARRIS, James; Private; 25th Inf. At Ft Duncan, TX, Dec 1877; struck by Sgt. William Givens, 10th Cavalry, for failure to obey order; confined to quarters for disobedience; at Ft Stockton, TX, 1878. SOURCE: Kinevan, *Frontier Cavalryman*, 63–64, 283.

HARRIS, Jeremiah; Private; A/10th Cav. ‡Dishonorably discharged, then enlisted Ft Sill, Indian Territory, 12 Feb 1870, under assumption he was discharged by mistake for another man in company of same name. SOURCE: CO, 10 Cav, to CO, A/10, 28 Feb 1870, ES, 10 Cav, 1866–71.

‡Dishonorably discharged in accordance with Special Order 106, War Department, 16 May 1869; dropped from rolls, 20 Apr 1870. SOURCE: CO, A/10 Cav, to CO, 10 Cav, 20 Apr 1870, ES, 10 Cav, 1866–71.

Former 10th Cavalryman who found employment with blacksmith at Fort Sill, OK. SOURCE: Dobak and Phillips, *The Black Regulars*, 268.

HARRIS, John; Private; M/10th Cav. Died 11 Nov 1889; buried at Ft Bayard, NM, in plot G 15. SOURCE: "Fort Bayard National Cemetery, Records of Burials."

Buried 11 Nov 1889, section A, row I, plot 17 at Ft Bayard. SOURCE: Erickson, Burials at Fort Bayard National Cemetery, NM.

HARRIS, John W.; Private; K/10th Cav. ‡Born in Winchester, VA; died, age 49, with twenty-seven years' service, Ft Robinson, NE, 27 Jun 1904. SOURCE: Monthly Report, Chaplain Anderson, 1 Jul 1904.

‡Buried, Ft Robinson, 27 Jun 1904. SOURCE: List of Interments, Ft Robinson.

Died of disease in line of duty. SOURCE: Buecker, Fort Robinson Burials.

HARRIS, Joseph; Sergeant; A/10th Cav. ‡Died of pistol shot wound, 6 Apr 1870. SOURCE: CO, A/10, to CO, 10 Cav, 12 Apr 1870, ES, 10 Cav, 1866–71.

Died 8 Apr 1870 of pistol shot at Camp Supply, OK. SOURCE: Regimental Returns, 10th Cavalry, 1870.

HARRIS, Lafayette; Corporal; A/24th Inf. Died at Camp Eagle Pass, TX, on 20 Sep 1879; buried at San Antonio National Cemetery, Section F, number 1144. SOURCE: San Antonio National Cemetery Locator.

HARRIS, Lewis; Farrier; H/10th Cav. Promoted from private 1 Nov 1885; in Troop H/10th Cavalry stationed at Bonita Cañon Camp, AZ, 30 Apr 1886. SOURCE: Tagg, *The Camp at Bonita Cañon*, 66, 231.

HARRIS, Sam H.; Private; 10th Cav. Wounded and escaped from battle at Carrizal, Mexico, 1916; recovered from wound at Ft Bliss, TX, hospital; described in newspapers as "the little yellow fellow." SOURCE: Leiker, *Racial Borders*, 166.

HARRIS, Sherman; Farrier; I/10th Cav. Private in Troop I/10th Cavalry stationed at Bonita Cañon Camp, AZ, but absent or on detached service 30 Jun 1886. SOURCE: Tagg, *The Camp at Bonita Cañon*, 231.

‡Served in 10th Cavalry in Cuba, 1898. SOURCE: Cashin, *Under Fire with the Tenth Cavalry*, 347.

‡Testified as witness for Pvt. George Wilson, I/10th Cavalry, who served with Hotchkiss gun detachment which landed in Cuba, 22 Jun 1898; took part in battle at San Juan; cared for fever patients and got fever. SOURCE: Affidavit, 1933, VA File C2323163, George Wilson.

‡Cited for conspicuous coolness and gallantry under fire, Las Guasimas, Cuba, 24 Jun 1898. SOURCE: SecWar, *AR 1898*, 349; GO 15, AGO, 13 Feb 1900; *ANJ* 37 (24 Feb 1900): 611; Cashin, *Under Fire with the Tenth Cavalry*, 185; Steward, *The Colored Regulars*, 137.

‡Resides in Cuba, 1933. *See* OTT, **WILSON**, George, Private, I/10th Cavalry

HARRIS, Silas; Private; G/9th Cav. Received Philippine Campaign Badge number 11849 for service as private in G/9th Cavalry, 12 Apr 1902–16 Sep 1902; private in G/9th Cavalry, Ft Leavenworth, KS, Mar 1905. SOURCE: Philippine Campaign Badge Recipients; Philippine Campaign Badge list, 29 May 1905.

‡Veteran of Philippine Insurrection; at Ft D. A. Russell, WY, in 1910; resident of Macon, GA. SOURCE: *Illustrated Review: Ninth Cavalry*, with picture.

HARRIS, Simon P.; Regt QM Sgt; 9th Cav. ‡Sergeant, D/9th Cavalry, promoted to saddler sergeant, 9th Cavalry, Ft Robinson, NE, 23 Apr 1891. SOURCE: Cleveland *Gazette*, 16 May 1891.

‡Appointed regimental quartermaster sergeant, 12 Oct 1892. SOURCE: Roster, 9 Cav.

‡Shares duplex on post with Sergeant Major Jones, Ft Robinson, 1894. SOURCE: Investigation of Charges against Chaplain Plummer.

Appointed regimental quartermaster 12 Oct 1891; in 9th Cavalry at Ft Robinson, Jan 1897. SOURCE: Ninth Cavalry, Roster of NCOs, 1897.

HARRIS, Theodore; 9th Cav. ‡Married Miss Frances Jones in Crawford, NE [should read NE], 18 Nov 1896, at home of Mrs. L. Jackson. SOURCE: Crawford *Tribune*, 20 Nov 1896.

‡No Veterans Administration pension file.

HARRIS, Wesley; Private; H/9th Cav. Native of Ohio; in third year of service when wounded in chest, Gavilan Canyon, NM, Aug 1881. SOURCE: Kenner, *Buffalo Soldiers and Officers of the Ninth Cavalry*, 230.

‡Seriously wounded in action against Nana, 19 Aug 1881. SOURCE: *Illustrated Review: Ninth Cavalry*.

See **WILLIAMS**, John, Private, H/9th Cavalry

HARRIS, William; Private; 9th Cav. Received Philippine Campaign Badge number 11728, for service as private, F/48th Infantry, United States Volunteers; in 9th Cavalry at Ft Leavenworth, KS, Mar 1905. SOURCE: Philippine Campaign Badge list, 29 May 1905.

HARRISON, Henry; Cav. Former cavalryman who found work as Pullman porter. SOURCE: Dobak and Phillips, *The Black Regulars*, 272.

HARRISON, Isaac; Private; A/9th Cav. With Pvt. William Nelson, rescued Capt. Michael Cooney when thrown by his horse during Indian ambush en route to Ft Clark, TX, from Ft Stockton, TX, Apr 1872. SOURCE: Kenner, *Buffalo Soldiers and Officers of the Ninth Cavalry*, 56–57.

‡Served 1872. *See* **NELSON**, William, Trumpeter, A/9th Cavalry

HARRISON, John; Private; C/9th Cav. Praised for gallantry in action against Lipan Apaches, near Ft Davis, TX, Sep 1868. SOURCE: Kenner, *Buffalo Soldiers and Officers of the Ninth Cavalry*, 53.

HARRISON,, Julius; Private; K/24th Inf. ‡Mentioned among men who distinguished themselves in B/24th Infantry, 1889; awarded certificate of merit for gallant and meritorious service while escort for Maj. Joseph W. Wham, paymaster, when attacked by robbers between Fts Grant and Thomas, AZ. SOURCE: GO 18, AGO, 1891.

Private, B/24th Infantry, fourteen-year veteran, cited for bravery against robbers near Cedar Springs, AZ, in May 1889 by Maj. Joseph W. Wham, and awarded certificate of merit; wounded during fight; still in Army at end of 1890. SOURCE: Schubert, *Black Valor*, 93, 95.

Report of Paymaster Wham, describing bravery of escort, published. SOURCE: Schubert, *Voices of the Buffalo Soldier*, 159–62.

‡At Ft Grant, 1890; certificate of merit mentioned. SOURCE: SecWar, *AR 1890*, 289.

Private, B/24th Infantry, awarded certificate of merit for gallant and meritorious conduct while member of escort of Maj. Joseph W. Wham, paymaster, who was ambushed by bandits between Fts Grant and Thomas, 11 May 1889. SOURCE: Gleim, *The Certificate of Merit*, 44.

K/24th Infantry; died 23 Jun 1891; buried 11 Mar 1894 at Ft Bayard, NM, in plot I 26. SOURCE: "Fort Bayard National Cemetery, Records of Burials."

Julius Harrison, H/24th Infantry, buried at Ft Bayard. SOURCE: "Buffalo Soldiers Buried at Ft Bayard, NM."

H/24th Infantry, died 23 Jun 1891, buried 11 Mar 1894, section A, row M, plot 29, at Ft Bayard. SOURCE: Erickson, *Burials at Fort Bayard National Cemetery.*

HARRISON, Milford; Private; K/24th Inf. Died at Camp Eagle Pass, TX, on 5 Mar 1870; buried at San Antonio National Cemetery, Section F, number 1153. SOURCE: San Antonio National Cemetery Locator.

HARRISON, Richard; Sergeant; C/9th Cav. In C/9th Cavalry, at Ft Sill, OK, 1882–84, promoted to sergeant 1884. SOURCE: Kenner, *Buffalo Soldiers and Officers of the Ninth Cavalry*, 266.

Buried 26 Oct 1906, section A, row W, plot 14, at Ft Bayard, NM. SOURCE: Erickson, *Burials at Fort Bayard National Cemetery, NM.*

HARRISON, William H.; Private; H/10th Cav. Served at Ft Davis, TX, 1885. SOURCE: Sayre, *Warriors of Color*, 70.

In Troop H/10th Cavalry stationed at Bonita Cañon Camp, AZ, but absent or on detached service 30 Apr 1886. SOURCE: Tagg, *The Camp at Bonita Cañon*, 232.

HARTWELL, Benjamin; Private; M/10th Cav. Born in slavery, recalled being sold with others while with his grandmother; died 8 Mar 1934 at age 88; came to Ft Robinson, NE, area thirty-five to forty years earlier and lived at the McClain place five miles south of Crawford, NE; funeral conducted by Rev. Herbert Bletson, pastor of AME Church; military funeral ceremonies performed at Ft Robinson. SOURCE: Buecker, Fort Robinson Burials.

HARVEY, Anthony; Private; L/9th Cav. Native of Prince Edward Island, Canada; occupation fisherman; enlisted Dec 1872; fined $3 in Jun 1875; at Ft Union, NM, Mar 1876, when killed by white gunfighter David Crockett in shootout at bar in Cimarron, NM, with Pvts. George Small and John Hanson, L/9th Cavalry. SOURCE: Kenner, *Buffalo Soldiers and Officers of the Ninth Cavalry*, 180.

‡Killed by cattle herders at Cimarron, 24 Jan 1876, along with Pvts. John Hanson and George Smallow, L/9th Cavalry. SOURCE: Hamilton, "History of the Ninth Cavalry," 28; *Illustrated Review: Ninth Cavalry.*

HARVEY, Howard; 9th Cav. Born in Georgia; black complexion; can read and write, age 26, 5 Sep 1870, at Ft McKavett, TX. SOURCE: Bierschwale, *Fort McKavett*, 107.

HASKINS, David; 1st Sgt; F/10th Cav. ‡Born in Virginia; private, sergeant, quartermaster sergeant, first sergeant, L/10th Cavalry, and sergeant major, F/10th Cavalry, 6 Sep 1867–5 Sep 1882; private, F/10th Cavalry, 17 Feb 1883; sergeant, 22 Feb 1883; first sergeant, 1 Mar 1883. SOURCE: Baker, Roster.

‡Original member of 10th Cavalry; in L Troop when organized, Ft Riley, KS, 21 Sep 1867. SOURCE: McMiller, "Buffalo Soldiers," 78.

In July 1871, Private Butler of F/10th Cavalry was absent two days, returned on evening of second day, opened door of barracks, fired six shots at Sergeant Haskins, who was sitting on bunk, then walked to rear of squad room where he either surrendered his weapon or was disarmed. SOURCE: ES, 10 Cav, 1873–81.

‡His request for reduction to the ranks approved by commander, L/10th Cavalry, but not by regimental commander, Feb 1873; proper application for resignation of warrant will be considered; order reducing him to ranks would imply misconduct on his part. SOURCE: ES, 10 Cav, 1873–81.

‡Resignation as first sergeant accepted. SOURCE: CO, 10 Cav, to CO, L/10 Cav, 20 Mar 1873, ES, 10 Cav, 1873–81.

Former slave; as first sergeant, 10th Cavalry, applied for position as ordnance sergeant, 1879. SOURCE: Dobak and Phillips, *The Black Regulars*, 83.

‡First sergeant, F/10th Cavalry, at Ft Grant, AZ, to be examined for post quartermaster sergeant. SOURCE: *ANJ* 24 (26 Feb 1887): 610.

‡First sergeant, F/10th Cavalry, at Ft Apache, AZ, 1890, subscribed $.50 to testimonial to General Grierson. SOURCE: List of subscriptions, 23 Apr 1890, 10th Cavalry papers, MHI.

‡Retires from Ft Assiniboine, MT, as first sergeant, F/10th Cavalry. SOURCE: *ANJ* 35 (12 Mar 1898): 519.

Retired first sergeant, received Indian Wars Campaign Badge number 1150 on 16 Mar 1909. SOURCE: Carroll, *Indian Wars Campaign Badge*, 33.

HASKINS, James; Private; D/9th Cav. With Captain Dodge at battle at Milk River, CO, 2–10 Oct 1879. SOURCE: Miller, *Hollow Victory*, 167, 206–7.

‡Resided in Pueblo, CO, 1895. *See* DENT, Henry, Private, D/9th Cavalry

HATCHET, John R.; Corporal; D/9th Cav. With Captain Dodge at battle at Milk River, CO, 2–10 Oct 1879. SOURCE: Miller, *Hollow Victory*, 167, 206–7.

Private, D/9th Cavalry, died 11 Mar 1881; buried at Ft Leavenworth National Cemetery, plot 1974. SOURCE: Ft Leavenworth National Cemetery.

HATCHETT, John; Private; D/9th Cav. Native of Virginia; age 30 with nine years of service when he died of gunshot wound received in fight with Pvt. William Nance, Feb 1879; Nance sentenced to six months and fined $10 per month for six months, with leniency due to good record.

SOURCE: Kenner, *Buffalo Soldiers and Officers of the Ninth Cavalry*, 271.

HAWKINS, Henry; Private; 10th Cav. Served with Pvt. George Washington, C/10th Cavalry, early 1870s; resided northeast of Geary, OK, after service. SOURCE: Schubert, *Voices of the Buffalo Soldier*, 230.

HAWKINS, James H.; Private; G/24th Inf. Served Aug 1879–Aug 1884, including at Eagle Springs, TX; resided at 426 Burgundy Alley, Baltimore, MD, at age 50 in 1911. SOURCE: Sayre, *Warriors of Color*, 418.

HAWKINS, Jordon; Private; C/9th Cav. Died at Camp Eagle Pass, TX, on 22 Dec 1872; buried at San Antonio National Cemetery, Section F, number 1161. SOURCE: San Antonio National Cemetery Locator.

HAWKINS, William; Sergeant; H/10th Cav. Born near Upper Marlboro, Prince Georges Co., MD, 18 Sep 1867; father Charles Hawkins; mother Sarah Brown; brothers Charles B. and Fielder Hawkins; half brother, Anthony, married to Vertie Brown; enlisted Baltimore, MD, 11 Feb 1882; Ht 5'8", complexion yellow, black eyes and hair; occupation laborer; served Jan 1884–28 Feb 1885 at Ft Davis, TX; Mar–7 Apr 1885, Bowie Station, AZ; May–Jun 1885, Ft Grant, AZ; Jul–Aug 1885, Pnievy [*sic*] Creek, AZ; Sep, Oct 1885–30 Apr 1886, Bonita Cañon, AZ; Jun 1886–10 Feb 1887 when discharged at Ft Apache, AZ; resided in Washington, DC, area from autumn 1891; married Ivy Lee Johnson, Washington, DC, 8 Apr 1901; wife employed as charwoman, Treasury Department; daughter Mary M. J. born 30 May 1902, daughter Mildred Elizabeth born 31 Aug 1904, daughter Ethel Teresa born 8 Apr 1907, son William Anthony born 14 Dec 1909, daughter Ivy Elizabeth born 20 Jul 1912, son Joseph Edward born 20 Jul 1912, daughter Sarah Catherine born 18 Aug 1915, son Charles L. born 19 Jan 1919, son James H. born 30 Aug 1923; employed continuously as laborer, Government Printing Office, from 1906 to 1929; received $50 per month pension 1928; admitted to U.S. Soldiers Home, Washington DC, Sep 1930; died 9 May 1931; buried at Mt. Olivet Cemetery, Bladensburg Rd., Washington, DC; widow received $48 per month pension 1931, reduced to $30 per month in 1937, increased to $48 per month in Jan 1951; widow died 5 Jun 1952. SOURCE: Sayre, *Warriors of Color*, 221, 226–54.

Corporal in H/10th Cavalry stationed at Bonita Cañon Camp, AZ, but absent or on detached service 30 Apr 1886. SOURCE: Tagg, *The Camp at Bonita Cañon*, 231.

‡Honorable mention for services rendered in capture of Mangas and his Apache band, Rio Bonito, AZ, 18 Oct 1886. SOURCE: Baker, Roster.

Pvt. William Hawkins, 10th Cavalry, part of delegation of veterans attending President Herbert Hoover's inau-

guration parade, 1929. SOURCE: Dobak and Phillips, *The Black Regulars*, 277.

HAWKINS, William H.; Private; L/24th Inf. Died 19 May 1905; buried at Ft Bayard, NM, in plot H 37. SOURCE: "Fort Bayard National Cemetery, Records of Burials."

Buried 18 May 1905, section A, row K, plot 44, at Ft Bayard. SOURCE: Erickson, Burials at Fort Bayard National Cemetery, NM.

HAYDEN; Private; G/9th Cav. With Sgt. Charles Johnson, G/9th Cavalry, rescued white miner and his family from drowning, Uncompahgre River, CO, 1877. SOURCE: Kenner, *Buffalo Soldiers and Officers of the Ninth Cavalry*, 217.

HAYES, Fred; Private; B/10th Cav. Private in B/10th Cavalry at Ft Duncan, TX, Jan 1878. SOURCE: Kinevan, *Frontier Cavalryman*, 81.

HAYMAN, Perry A.; B/25th Inf. ‡Born in Sharon Hill, PA; enlisted, age 20, Philadelphia, PA; served ten years; Charles Holder, M/10th Cavalry, shot peddler to steal whisky, was turned over to civil authorities, Ft Smith, AR, Apr 1874; Cpl. George Berry was wounded in fight at Cheyenne Agency, OK, Apr 1875; participated in battle at Cheyenne Agency and served at Ft Reno, Indian Territory; then served in 25th Infantry; now age 71. SOURCE: *Winners of the West* 2 (Mar 1925): 2–3.

‡Corporal, M/10th Cavalry, wounded in Cheyenne Agency fight, 6 Apr 1875. SOURCE: Leckie, *The Buffalo Soldiers*, 139.

Recollections of service as private with Tenth Cavalry, 1874–75, republished. SOURCE: Schubert, *Voices of the Buffalo Soldier*, 65–69.

HAYNES, William; Lance Cpl; F/25th Inf. Private, F/25th Infantry, rode in 25th Infantry Bicycle Corps, Ft. Missoula, MT, summer 1896. SOURCE: Sorenson, List of Buffalo Soldiers Who Rode in the 25th Infantry Bicycle Corps, in authors' files.

One of twenty men who cycled 1,900 miles from Ft Missoula to St. Louis, MO, 14 Jun–24 Jul 1897, in 25th Infantry Bicycle Corps to test durability and practicality of bicycles as a means of transportation for troops. SOURCE: File 60178, GC, AGO Records.

HAYWOOD, Charles; Private; D/9th Cav. ‡Killed in action, Pine Ridge, SD, 30 Dec 1890, while part of wagon guard. SOURCE: Hamilton, "History of the Ninth Cavalry," 74; *Illustrated Review: Ninth Cavalry.*

‡Killed along with horse when troop, commanded by Capt. John Loud, repulsed Sioux attack on regiment's wagon train. SOURCE: Kelley, *Pine Ridge, 1890*, 192.

‡Killed by Indian in cavalry uniform in "exchange of a few shots." SOURCE: Perry, "The Ninth U.S. Cavalry in the Sioux Campaign of 1890," 39.

Killed by hostile Indians about 6:45 A.M. while on duty as advance guard D/9th Cavalry escort for wagon train, near Pine Ridge Agency, SD; originally buried at Pine Ridge Cemetery with 7th Cavalry casualties. SOURCE: Buecker, Fort Robinson Burials.

‡Buried at Ft Robinson, NE. SOURCE: List of Interments, Ft Robinson.

HAYWOOD, James; Private; 25th Inf. Born in Alamance County, NC; Ht 5'10", black hair and eyes, brown complexion; in E/24th Infantry to 1 Mar 1887; third enlistment at age 39, St. Louis, MO, 17 Mar 1887; arrived Ft Snelling, MN, 1 Apr 1887. SOURCE: Descriptive & Assignment Rolls of Recruits, 25 Inf.

HAYWOOD, Joseph; Private; 25th Inf. Born in East Florida, FL; Ht 5'10", black hair and eyes, fair complexion; occupation drayman; enlisted at age 23, Charleston, SC, 23 May 1881; left recruit depot, David's Island, NY, 2 Jul 1881, arrived Ft Randall, SD, 7 Jul 1881. SOURCE: Descriptive & Assignment Rolls of Recruits, 25 Inf.

HAZZARD, Charles; Trumpeter; M/10th Cav. Served at Ft Sill, OK, 1874. SOURCE: Schubert, *Voices of the Buffalo Soldier*, 67.

HECTOR, Herman, Jr.; Private; E/9th Cav. Private, E/9th Cavalry, confined for one month for insubordination to Sgt. Brent Woods, at Ft DuChesne, UT, 1887. SOURCE: Kenner, *Buffalo Soldiers and Officers of the Ninth Cavalry*, 235.

‡Enlisted Ft Washakie, WY, 25 Dec 1889. SOURCE: Regt Returns, 9 Cav, Dec 1889.

‡Relieved of special duty as clerk, Adjutant's Office, Ft Robinson, NE. SOURCE: Order 71, 30 Apr 1892, Post Orders, Ft Robinson.

‡Wife is pyromaniac although "a very good quiet woman of excellent character." SOURCE: CO, Ft Robinson, to AAG, DP, 8 and 9 Aug 1893, LS, Ft Robinson.

‡Teacher, Ft Robinson schools, 4 Nov 1893–30 Apr 1894. SOURCE: Reports of Schools, Ft Robinson.

‡Relieved of extra duty as schoolteacher, Ft Robinson. SOURCE: Order 27, 29 Apr 1894, Post Orders, Ft Robinson.

‡Child buried at Ft Robinson, 1894. SOURCE: List of Interments, Ft Robinson.

‡Enlisted 22 Oct 1886; sentenced to dishonorable discharge and one year, Ft Washakie, 2 Dec 1888, in accordance with General Court Martial Order 103, Department of the Platte, Nov 1888; reenlisted, 23 Dec 1889, in accordance with message, Adjutant General's Office, 23 Dec 1889; convicted of theft of gold watch and chain worth $59 from Blacksmith Peter H. Turner, E/9th Cavalry, in accor-

dance with Special Order 100, Department of the Platte, 27 Sep 1894; sentenced to dishonorable discharge and eighteen months; was his own counsel at court martial. SOURCE: Court Martial Records, Hector.

‡Military Convict Hector conducted to Ft Omaha, NE, with Military Convict George Washington, 9th Cavalry, by 1st Sgt. George Tracy and Pvt. Harry Rice, D/9th Cavalry. SOURCE: Order 77, 3 Oct 1894, Post Orders, Ft Robinson.

HEDGEMAN, John H.; Private; 40th Inf. One of three enlisted men, with Sgt. John Stanley and Pvt. James R. Cook, sent with officer to establish recruiting office, New York City, Nov 1867. SOURCE: Dobak and Phillips, *The Black Regulars*, 6.

HEISER, Richard; Private; L/9th Cav. Enlisted 24 Aug 1875 at Louisville, KY; at Ft Bliss, TX, Nov–Dec 1879; with L/9th Cavalry, left camp on Rio Mimbres, NM, on 8 Jul 1880 and marched twenty miles to Ft Cummings, NM; left Ft Cummings 8 Aug on march to Leas Ferry on Rio Grande and returned to camp after march of 104 miles; discharged in the field at Ft Cummings, 20 Aug 1880, character good. SOURCE: Muster Rolls, L/9th Cavalry, 31 Oct 1879–29 Feb 1880, 30 June–31 Aug 1880.

HELM, Benjamin; 1st Sgt; C/10th Cav. Former sergeant major, 6th U.S. Colored Infantry; enlisted Louisville, KY, Feb 1867. SOURCE: Dobak and Phillips, *The Black Regulars*, 204.

HELM, Benjamin; Corporal; K/10th Cav. Died at Ft Davis, TX, on 6 Jan 1882; buried at San Antonio National Cemetery, Section I, number 1561. SOURCE: San Antonio National Cemetery Locator.

HELM, Joshua; Corporal; C/25th Inf. Born in Kentucky; mulatto complexion; cannot read or write, age 26, 5 Sep 1870, in C/25th Infantry at Ft McKavett, TX. SOURCE: Bierschwale, *Fort McKavett*, 109.

‡Private, F/114th U.S. Colored Troops; corporal, C/25th Infantry; reenlisted in C/25th Infantry, served at Newport Bks, KY; adjutant, 10th Cavalry, forwards check for $90 to Adjutant General to pay Helm's claim. SOURCE: Adj, 10 Cav, to AG, USA, 27 Feb 1875, LS, 10 Cav, 1873–83.

HENDERSON, George; Private; G/9th Cav. Received Philippine Campaign Badge number 11831 for service as private in G/9th Cavalry, 16 Sep 1900–16 Sep 1902; private in G/9th Cavalry, Ft Leavenworth, KS, Mar 1905. SOURCE: Philippine Campaign Badge Recipients; Philippine Campaign Badge list, 29 May 1905.

HENDERSON, James W.; 1st Sgt; K/9th Cav. Received as first sergeant Indian Wars Campaign Badge number 1835 on 22 May 1918. SOURCE: Carroll, *Indian Wars Campaign Badge*, 53.

HENDERSON, Joseph; Corporal; L/9th Cav. Enlisted at Louisville, KY, 17 Aug 1880; discharged at Ft Bliss, TX, 18 Aug 1880. SOURCE: Muster Rolls, L/9th Cavalry, 30 June–31 Aug 1880.

HENDERSON, Nevel T.; Sergeant; 25th Inf. At Ft Concho, TX, 1878, arrested and restricted to quarters for causing disturbance in town of San Angelo. SOURCE: Dobak and Phillips, *The Black Regulars*, 169.

HENDERSON, Thomas; F/9th Cav. Born in Tennessee; black complexion; cannot read or write, age 27, Jul 1870, at Ft McKavett, TX. SOURCE: Bierschwale, *Fort McKavett*, 97.

HENDERSON, William; Private; 25th Inf. Born in Georges Station, SC; Ht 5'9", black hair and eyes, dark complexion; occupation miner; enlisted at age 21, Charleston, SC, 1 Jun 1881; left recruit depot, David's Island, NY, 2 Jul 1881, arrived Ft Randall, SD, 7 Jul 1881.

Ht 5'10", black complexion; occupation soldier; reenlisted at age 26, St Louis, MO, 21 Aug 1886; from Columbus Bks, OH, arrived Ft Snelling, MN, 17 Sep 1886. SOURCE: Descriptive & Assignment Rolls of Recruits, 25 Inf.

HENDRICKS, Louie; Private; D/10th Cav. Died 10 Jul 1890; buried at Ft Bayard, NM, in plot E 11. SOURCE: "Fort Bayard National Cemetery, Records of Burials."

L. W. (Louis) Hendricks buried 10 Jul 1890, section A, row I, plot 13, at Ft Bayard. SOURCE: Erickson, Burials at Fort Bayard National Cemetery, NM.

HENRY, Boston; Private; F/9th Cav. Pvt. Boston Henry, 41st Infantry, shot and killed by white civilians near Ft Concho, TX, 1869. SOURCE: Dobak and Phillips, *The Black Regulars*, 175.

‡Private, 9th Cavalry, killed by white civilian, San Angelo, TX, Jun 1869. SOURCE: Carroll, *The Black Military Experience*, 454.

Private, 9th Cavalry, murdered by civilian near Menard, TX, Jun 1869. SOURCE: Kenner, *Buffalo Soldiers and Officers of the Ninth Cavalry*, 92.

HENRY, Charles; Corporal; I/24th Inf. Died 10 Oct 1900; buried in plot EAST 1306 at San Francisco National Cemetery. SOURCE: San Francisco National Cemetery.

HENRY, Frank; Trumpeter; H/10th Cav. On expedition to Tayabacoa, Cuba, with Lieutenant Carter, Jun 1898. SOURCE: Schubert, *Black Valor*, 139.

‡Pvt. Frank Henry at Camp Forse, AL, Nov 1898. SOURCE: Richmond *Planet*, 3 Dec 1898.

‡Served in 10th Cavalry in Cuba, 1898. SOURCE: Cashin, *Under Fire with the Tenth Cavalry*, 345.

HENRY, Jesse; Musician; K/25th Inf. Born in Fayette County, KY; Ht 5'7", black complexion; occupation farmer; enlisted in A/39th Infantry for three years on 8 Oct 1866, age 21, at Greenville, LA; detached service to regimental band since 23 Jan 1869; transferred to K/25th Infantry at Jackson Bks, LA, 20 Apr 1869. SOURCE: Descriptive Roll of A/39th Inf.

HENRY, Lewis; Private; K/25th Inf. Born in Attakapas, LA; Ht 5'10", black complexion; occupation soldier; enlisted in A/39th Infantry for three years on 5 Oct 1866, age 21, at New Orleans, LA; detached service to regimental band since 19 Jan 1869; transferred to K/25th Infantry at Jackson Bks, LA, 20 Apr 1869. SOURCE: Descriptive Roll of A/39th Inf.

HENRY, Oscar D.; Private; L/24th Inf. Died 4 May 1901; buried at Ft Bayard, NM, in plot N 30-194. SOURCE: "Fort Bayard National Cemetery, Records of Burials."

O. D. (Oskar) Henry buried 4 May 1901, section A, row V, plot 30, at Ft Bayard. SOURCE: Erickson, Burials at Fort Bayard National Cemetery, NM.

HENRY, Robert; F/9th Cav. Born in Tennessee; black complexion; cannot read or write, age 23, Jul 1870, at Ft McKavett, TX. SOURCE: Bierschwale, *Fort McKavett*, 98.

HENRY, William; Private; H/38th Inf. Died 6 Jul 1867; buried at Ft Leavenworth National Cemetery, plot C 1571. SOURCE: Ft Leavenworth National Cemetery.

HENRY, William; Private; 9th Cav. Died 14 Jun 1866; buried at San Antonio National Cemetery, Section D, number 799. SOURCE: San Antonio National Cemetery Locator.

HENSON, Mahlon S.; Private; E/10th Cav. Died 9 Jul 1873 of consumption at Ft Richardson, TX. SOURCE: Regimental Returns, 10th Cavalry, 1873.

Died at Ft Richardson on 9 Jul 1873; buried at San Antonio National Cemetery, Section D, number 608. SOURCE: San Antonio National Cemetery Locator.

HENSON, William; Sergeant; H/24th Inf. ‡Authorized six-month furlough from San Carlos, AZ. SOURCE: *ANJ* 26 (22 Jun 1889): 882.

‡At Ft Grant, AZ, Apr 1890, served as pallbearer at funeral for Sgt. Edward Berry, H/24th Infantry. SOURCE: Cleveland *Gazette*, 26 Apr 1890.

HERBERT, Thomas H.; Corporal; E/10th Cav. ‡Private, B/9th Cavalry; sentenced to thirty days by garrison court martial, Ft Robinson, NE, for vile and obscene language toward Pvts. Charles Daniels and William Davis; threw rock at Davis and hit Pvt. James H. Cook; resisted arrest by Cpl. Gus Bailey, 26 Dec 1888. SOURCE: Order 255, 30 Dec 1888, Post Orders, Ft Robinson.

‡Served in 10th Cavalry in Cuba, 1898. SOURCE: Cashin, *Under Fire with the Tenth Cavalry*, 342.

‡Commended for distinguished service, battle of Santiago, Cuba, 1 Jul 1898, as corporal, E/10th Cavalry. SOURCE: GO 15, AGO, 13 Feb 1900.

‡Awarded certificate of merit for distinguished service in Cuba, 1 Jul 1898. SOURCE: *ANJ* 37 (24 Feb 1900): 611; Steward, *The Colored Regulars*, 280.

‡Born in Montgomery Co., MD; received Distinguished Service Medal for distinguished service, battle of Santiago, 1 Jul 1898. SOURCE: Koger, *The Maryland Negro in Our Wars*, 23.

‡Veteran of Spanish-American War and Philippine Insurrection; private, K/9th Cavalry, at Ft D. A. Russell, WY, in 1910; resident of Montgomery, AL. SOURCE: *Illustrated Review: Ninth Cavalry*, with picture.

Awarded certificate of merit for distinguished service in battle, Santiago, 1 Jul 1898. SOURCE: Gleim, *The Certificate of Merit*, 45.

Born in Montgomery County, MD; resided Washington, DC; received Distinguished Service Medal in lieu of certificate of merit. SOURCE: *American Decorations*, 838.

HERD, Ira; F/9th Cav. Born in Georgia; mulatto complexion; cannot read or write, age 24, Jul 1870, at Ft McKavett, TX. SOURCE: Bierschwale, *Fort McKavett*, 98.

HIBBITT, John; Private; H/10th Cav. Born in Sumner County, TN, 1861; enlisted Indianapolis, IN, 28 Jan 1882; occupation laborer; Ht 5'6", yellow complexion, black hair and eyes; joined H/10th Cavalry from Jefferson Bks, MO, 13 Aug 1882; at Ft Davis, TX, 1 Jan 1884–1 Apr 1885; at Ft Grant, AZ, 2 May 1885–26 Jul 1885; camped 7 Aug 1885–1 May 1886 at Bonita Cañon, AZ; at Ft Apache, AZ, 17 May 1886–28 Jul 1887; served in Geronimo campaign; discharged Ft Apache, 27 Jul 1887; married to Jennie Johnson, Gallatin, TN, 2 Oct 1887; daughter Savada born 10 Jun 1890, son John Jr. born 18 Apr 1892, son Willie born 27 Dec 1895, son Harry born 15 Nov 1898, daughter Mary born 29 Jan 1900; resided in Arlington, Lincoln County, OK; died 6 Oct 1901; buried in Oklahoma. SOURCE: Sayre, *Warriors of Color*, 255–57.

Private in H/10th Cavalry stationed at Bonita Cañon Camp, 30 Apr 1886. SOURCE: Tagg, *The Camp at Bonita Cañon*, 232.

HICKMAN, French; Private; 24th Inf. Served in 1873; Lt. John L. Bullis persuaded commanding officer to drop disorderly conduct charges because of Hickman's extreme youth. SOURCE: Dobak and Phillips, *The Black Regulars*, 195.

HICKMAN, John H.; C/25th Inf. Born in Louisiana; black complexion; can read and write, age 24, 5 Sep 1870, at Ft McKavett, TX. SOURCE: Bierschwale, *Fort McKavett,* 109.

HICKS, William B.; Private; G/9th Cav. Died of apoplexy and chronic Bright's disease in hospital, Ft Robinson, NE; Ellen Biddle in *Reminiscences of a Soldier's Wife* remembers funeral was attended by all who were at a luncheon, including General Coppinger, Captain Emmet, and Colonel Biddle. SOURCE: Buecker, Fort Robinson Burials.

‡Funeral, Ft Robinson, 8 Oct 1896, handled by regular Army and Navy Union of Ft Robinson. SOURCE: SO 114, 7 Oct 1896, Post Orders, Ft Robinson.

‡Buried at Ft Robinson. SOURCE: List of Interments, Ft Robinson.

‡His effects sold for $27, which sum was forwarded to department headquarters. SOURCE: 2nd Lt M. Batson, CO, G/9 Cav, to Chief PM, DP, 2 Feb 1897, Miscellaneous Records, DeptPlatte.

HIESKEL, Pleasant; D/24th Inf. Born in Virginia; mulatto complexion; cannot read or write, age 23, Jul 1870, at Ft McKavett, TX. SOURCE: Bierschwale, *Fort McKavett,* 95.

HIGH, John H.; Private; L/10th Cav. ‡Original member of 10th Cavalry; in troop when organized, Ft Riley, KS, 21 Sep 1867. SOURCE: McMiller, "Buffalo Soldiers," 78.

Died 12 Sep 1868 of dysentery at Ft Arbuckle, OK. SOURCE: Regimental Returns, 10th Cavalry, 1868.

‡William C. Drew, Chief, Claims Division, asked commander, 10th Cavalry, whether High had ever served with K/9th U.S. Colored Troops, Feb 1870.

HILL, Bolton H.; Corporal; 9th Cav. Received Philippine Campaign Badge number 11701 for service as corporal in E/9th Cavalry; in 9th Cavalry at Ft Leavenworth, KS, Mar 1905. SOURCE: Philippine Campaign Badge list, 29 May 1905.

HILL, Charles; Musician; Band/25th Inf. ‡Charles Hill, Principal Musician, 9th Cavalry, killed by civilian, Ft Davis, TX, Jul 1876. SOURCE: Carroll, *The Black Military Experience*, 279.

Died at Ft Davis, 5 Jul 1876; buried at San Antonio National Cemetery, Section I, number 1568. SOURCE: San Antonio National Cemetery Locator.

HILL, Colony; Private; M/9th Cav. Private in F/9th Cavalry born in Lebanon, KY; died and buried at Ft McKavett,

TX, before 17 May 1879; body removed to National Cemetery, San Antonio, TX, 23 Nov 1883. SOURCE: Bierschwale, *Fort McKavett,* 123.

Private in M/9th Cavalry died on 25 Jul 1871; buried at San Antonio National Cemetery, Section E, number 872. SOURCE: San Antonio National Cemetery Locator.

HILL, Conway; M/9th Cav. Born in Kentucky; mulatto complexion; cannot read or write, age 23, Jul 1870, at Ft McKavett, TX. SOURCE: Bierschwale, *Fort McKavett,* 99.

HILL, Ezekiel H.; Private; 25th Inf. E. H. Hill, 24th Infantry, married "Spanish lady, name unknown," Ft Elliott, TX, Dec 1885. SOURCE: Cleveland *Gazette,* 9 Jan 1886.

Pvt. Ezekiel H. Hill stationed at Ft Elliott, 1886, married by magistrate in Mobeetie, TX. SOURCE: Dobak and Phillips, *The Black Regulars,* 140–41.

‡Cpl. Ezekiel Hill, B/24th Infantry, on detached service as scorer, department rifle meet, Ft Bayard, NM. SOURCE: Order 118, Ft Huachuca, 9 Aug 1893, Name File, 24 Inf.

HILL, Issam; Private; C/10th Cav. Accidentally shot, died 27 Jul 1872 at Sand Creek, Indian Territory. SOURCE: Regimental Returns, 10th Cavalry, 1872.

HILL, Jacob; Corporal; D/9th Cav. ‡Veteran of Spanish-American War and Philippine Insurrection; at Ft D. A. Russell, WY, in 1910; resident of Baltimore, MD. SOURCE: *Illustrated Review: Ninth Cavalry,* with picture.

Received as corporal Indian Wars Campaign Badge number 1362 on 28 May 1909. SOURCE: Carroll, *Indian Wars Campaign Badge,* 39.

HILL, John; Private; E/9th Cav. Private in troop in April 1867 at time of San Pedro Springs, TX, mutiny; trussed and suspended by wrists from tree for failing to remove nosebag from horse promptly by Lt. Edward Heyl. SOURCE: Kenner, *Buffalo Soldiers and Officers of the Ninth Cavalry,* 76.

HILL, Moses; F/9th Cav. Born in Virginia; black complexion; cannot read or write, age 26, Jul 1870, at Ft McKavett, TX. SOURCE: Bierschwale, *Fort McKavett,* 98.

HILL, Thomas; Private; H/48th Inf. Died 27 Apr 1900; buried in plot NEW A950 at San Francisco National Cemetery. SOURCE: San Francisco National Cemetery.

HILL, William H.; Comsy Sgt; 10th Cav. ‡Born in St. Francis Co., MO; served in A/9th Cavalry, 20 May 1890–1 Aug 1893; in K/10th Cavalry, 4 Oct 1893–24 Oct 1899; drum major, Band/10th Cavalry, 25 Oct–8 Dec 1899; commissary sergeant, 10 Dec 1901; stationed in Cuba, 21 May 1899–20 May 1902; character excellent; married to Mrs.

Missouri Hill, no children; deposits $105, 1900, $70, 1901; clothing $49; enlisted Ft Robinson, NE, 9 Dec 1902, character excellent; discharge, 8 Dec 1905, character excellent, clothing $97. SOURCE: Descriptive Book, 10 Cav Officers & NCOs.

‡Private, A/9th Cavalry, teacher, Ft Robinson school, 1 Nov 1892–30 Apr 1893. SOURCE: Report of Schools, Ft Robinson, 1892–96; Order 33, 29 Apr 1893, Post Orders, Ft Robinson.

‡Sergeant, served in K/10th Cavalry, 1898; remained in U.S. during war with Spain. SOURCE: Cashin, *Under Fire with the Tenth Cavalry,* 349.

‡Commissary sergeant, guest with wife at K/10th Cavalry Thanksgiving dinner. SOURCE: Simmons, "Thanksgiving Day," 663.

Retired post commissary sergeant, received Indian Wars Campaign Badge number 1501 on 9 Sep 1909. SOURCE: Carroll, *Indian Wars Campaign Badge,* 43.

HINES, Clinton; Private; D/25th Inf. Died 21 Oct 1884; buried in plot 1 48, Ft Meade National Cemetery, SD. SOURCE: Ft Meade National Cemetery, VA database.

HIPSHER, Wiley; Corporal; E/9th Cav. ‡Private, E/9th Cavalry, relieved from extra duty as teamster with Quartermaster Department, Ft Robinson, NE. SOURCE: SO 86, 8 Aug 1896, Post Orders, Ft Robinson.

‡Served as private, A/10th Cavalry, in Cuba, 1898; wounded in action, 1 Jul 1898. SOURCE: Cashin, *Under Fire with the Tenth Cavalry,* 336–37.

‡Wounded at Santiago, Cuba, 1 Jul 1898. SOURCE: SecWar, *AR 1898,* 324.

‡Veteran of Spanish-American War and Philippine Insurrection; sergeant, E/9th Cavalry, at Ft D. A. Russell, WY, in 1910; sharpshooter. SOURCE: *Illustrated Review: Ninth Cavalry,* with picture.

Received Philippine Campaign Badge number 11699 for service as corporal in E/9th Cavalry; in 9th Cavalry at Ft Leavenworth, KS, Mar 1905. SOURCE: Philippine Campaign Badge list, 29 May 1905.

HITE, Leonard P.; Sergeant; G/9th Cav. Died on 8 Jul 1882; buried at San Antonio National Cemetery, Section C, number 325. SOURCE: San Antonio National Cemetery Locator.

Died 8 Jul 1882; struck by lightning at Ft Stockton, TX. SOURCE: Regimental Returns, 10th Cavalry, 1882.

HOBBS, John H.; Private; H/9th Cav. Died 10 Jul 1902; buried in plot NEW A796 at San Francisco National Cemetery. SOURCE: San Francisco National Cemetery.

HOBSON, John; Private; D/24th Inf. Died 17 Sep 1890; buried at Ft Leavenworth National Cemetery, plot 2787. SOURCE: Ft Leavenworth National Cemetery.

HOCKADAY, William; Private; 9th Cav. Received Philippine Campaign Badge number 11888 for service as private in B/48th Infantry, United States Volunteers, and G/24th Infantry; in 9th Cavalry at Ft Leavenworth, KS, Mar 1905. SOURCE: Philippine Campaign Badge list, 29 May 1905.

HOCKINS, Benjamin; Corporal; E/9th Cav. Native of Kentucky; listed on Census rolls 1870 as illiterate; gradually became "quite proficient in grammatical skills"; at Ft Davis, TX, 1876; private with fourteen years' service by Jul 1880, when arrested for absence without leave; called a "god damned black son of a bitch" by Lt. F. Beers Taylor, and objected, "I don't think it is right for an officer to call an enlisted man a God damned black son of a bitch. My mother was black . . . but she was a lady and no bitch"; convicted of resisting and threatening Taylor, sentenced to dishonorable discharge and one year, but pardoned after serving six months and allowed to reenlist; at Ft McKinney, WY, 1886; corporal, E/9th Cavalry, convicted at Ft Robinson, NE, of insubordination to 1st Sgt. David Badie, B/9th Cavalry, 1888. SOURCE: Kenner, *Buffalo Soldiers and Officers of the Ninth Cavalry*, 14–15, 112–14, 231, 233, 316, 349.

‡1st Lt. F. Bears Taylor said to Hockins, "Don't look at me, God damn you," "I could kill you," and "Go on, you God damn black son of a bitch," also struck him several blows on head, face, shoulders with carbine after Hockins was on the ground, helpless, handcuffed, shackled, while in E/9th Cavalry at Ft Cummings, NM, 21 Oct 1880. SOURCE: GCMO 61, AGO, 4 Nov 1881.

At Ft Robinson, 1st Sgt. David Badie badgered and provoked soldiers who reported to him, including Cpl. Benjamin Hockins in 1888. SOURCE: Kenner, *Buffalo Soldiers and Officers of the Ninth Cavalry*, 48–49, 231.

‡Transferred to B/9th Cavalry, Ft DuChesne, UT. SOURCE: Order 22, 9 Cav, 1 May 1888.

‡Corporal, B/9th Cavalry, fined $5 by garrison court martial, Ft Robinson, for insubordination to 1st Sgt. David Badie, B/9th Cavalry. SOURCE: Order 162, 22 Aug 1888, Post Orders, Ft Robinson.

‡Appointed corporal, G/9th Cavalry, 17 Jul 1892. SOURCE: Roster, 9 Cav.

HODSDEN, Euclid T.; Private; 9th Cav. Served in Philippine Campaign as private in E/9th Cavalry; in 9th Cavalry at Ft Leavenworth, KS, Mar 1905. SOURCE: Philippine Campaign Badge list, 29 May 1905

HOGAN, James; Corporal; K/25th Inf. Born in Montgomery County, PA; Ht 6'0", black complexion; occupation teamster; enlisted in A/39th Infantry for three years on 29 Aug 1867, age 22, at Philadelphia, PA; transferred to K/25th Infantry at Jackson Bks, LA, 20 Apr 1869. SOURCE: Descriptive Roll of A/39th Inf.

HOGINS, Jerry; Private; H/10th Cav. ‡Original member of 10th Cavalry; in troop when organized, Ft Leavenworth, KS, 21 Jul 1867. SOURCE: McMiller, "Buffalo Soldiers," 75.

Died 3 Sep 1867 of cholera in Kansas. SOURCE: Regimental Returns, 10th Cavalry, 1867.

HOKE, Lafayette E.; Private; E/9th Cav. One of five men of E Troop killed by Victorio's Apaches while guarding troop's horse herd, Ojo Caliente, NM, 4 Sep 1879. SOURCE: Schubert, *Black Valor*, 53.

‡Private Hoke, E/9th Cavalry, killed in action against Victorio, Camp Ojo Caliente, 4 Sep 1879. SOURCE: Billington, "Black Cavalrymen," 67; Billington, *New Mexico's Buffalo Soldiers*, 89.

Pvt. Lafayette Hooke [*sic*], E/9th Cavalry., native of North Carolina; enlisted summer 1879, age 21, occupation waiter; on duty in Sgt. Silas Chapman's herd guard near Ojo Caliente, Sep 1879, when attacked by Victorio; killed along with Chapman, Pvts. Abram Percival, William Humphrey, and Silas Graddon. SOURCE: Kenner, *Buffalo Soldiers and Officers of the Ninth Cavalry*, 108.

See **CHAPMAN**, Silas, Sergeant, E/9th Cavalry

HOLDEN, Charles; Private; C/10th Cav. Served at Ft Sill, OK, 1874, shot and wounded peddler, killed peddler's son in robbery attempt, was turned over to civil authorities. SOURCE: Schubert, *Voices of the Buffalo Soldier*, 66.

HOLDEN, James; Sergeant; K/9th Cav. ‡Appointed corporal, 10 Jul 1892. SOURCE: 9 Cav, Roster.

‡Promoted to sergeant, Ft Robinson, NE, 26 Aug 1895. SOURCE: *ANJ* 33 (7 Sep 1895): 7.

Appointed sergeant 26 Aug 1895; in K/9th Cavalry at Ft Robinson, Jan 1897. SOURCE: Ninth Cavalry, Roster of NCOs, 1897.

HOLDEN, Joseph D.; Corporal; D/9th Cav. Appointed corporal 20 Jan 1896; in D/9th Cavalry at Ft Washakie, WY, Jan 1897. SOURCE: Ninth Cavalry, Roster of NCOs, 1897.

HOLLAND, Elijah; Private; H/48th Inf. ‡Died of variola in the Philippines, 25 Jun 1900. SOURCE: *ANJ* 37 (7 Jul 1900): 1071.

Died in the Philippines 28 Jun 1900; body received 15 Apr 1902 at San Francisco National Cemetery; buried in plot NEW A838. SOURCE: San Francisco National Cemetery.

HOLLAND, Ernest; Private; I/9th Cav. Died 22 Sep 1899; originally buried at Ft DuChesne, UT; buried at Santa Fe National Cemetery, NM, plot A-4 1097. SOURCE: Santa Fe National Cemetery, Records of Burials.

HOLLAND, Moses; 1st Sgt; K/9th Cav. "Yellow" complexion; reported for duty with K Troop summer 1870; reduced to the ranks in 1874. SOURCE: Kenner, *Buffalo Soldiers and Officers of the Ninth Cavalry*, 141, 145.

HOLLAND, Robert C.; Private; H/9th Cav. ‡Died of cholera in the Philippines, 15 Jun 1902. SOURCE: *ANJ* 39 (9 Aug 1902): 1248.

Died 15 Jun 1902; buried in plot NAWS 803 at San Francisco National Cemetery. SOURCE: San Francisco National Cemetery.

HOLLIDAY, William F.; Private; D/9th Cav. With Captain Dodge at battle at Milk River, CO, 2–10 Oct 1879. SOURCE: Miller, *Hollow Victory*, 167, 206–7.

HOLLINS, Robert; Private; 9th Cav. Received Philippine Campaign Badge number 11889 for service as private in E/25th Infantry; in 9th Cavalry at Ft Leavenworth, KS, Mar 1905. SOURCE: Philippine Campaign Badge list, 29 May 1905.

HOLLINS, William A.; Private; B/9th Cav. ‡Severely wounded in action against Apaches, Gabaldon [*sic*] Canyon, NM, 19 Aug 1881. SOURCE: Billington, *New Mexico's Buffalo Soldiers*, 105.

Shot through lungs, Gavilan Canyon, NM, Aug 1881; discharged five months later at end of enlistment, character excellent. SOURCE: Kenner, *Buffalo Soldiers and Officers of the Ninth Cavalry*, 230.

See **GOLDEN**, Thomas, Saddler, B/9th Cavalry

HOLLOMAN, Solomon; 1st Sgt; A/9th Cav. Born in Jacksonville, SC; signed with an X when enlisted in 40th Infantry at Jacksonville, Ht 5'7", black hair and brown eyes, olive complexion, occupation laborer, age 22, Oct 1866; signed his name when reenlisted in K/25th Infantry, occupation soldier, age 25, at Jackson Bks, LA; reenlisted in K/25th Infantry at stated age of 28, not married, 20 Oct 1879 at Ft Concho, TX; enlisted in Chicago, IL, age 37, occupation hostler, 16 Feb 1884, entitled to reenlisted pay; no enlistment paper for 1889; enlisted in A/9th Cavalry, first sergeant at Ft Robinson, NE, age 46, married, 16 Feb 1894. SOURCE: Register of Enlistments. Notes in authors' files.

In 25th Infantry at Ft Stockton, TX, July 1873, organized protest over treatment of Pvt. John Taylor, with Sgt. Ellis Russell, 25th Infantry; later admitted his role and became witness for prosecution at court martial along with others convicted of attending an unauthorized meeting. SOURCE: Kenner, *Buffalo Soldiers and Officers of the Ninth Cavalry*, 87, 89–90.

‡At Ft Niobrara, NE, 1889. *See* **CARTER**, William H., Trumpeter, A/9th Cavalry

‡Sergeant as of 1 Mar 1889; first sergeant as of 10 Mar 1889. SOURCE: Roster, 9 Cav.

‡Author of resolution of tribute to deceased Sgt. Israel Valentine, Ft Robinson, 1892. SOURCE: *ANJ* 28 (2 Jun 1892): 782.

‡Resides with wife, mother-in-law, and brother-in-law on Laundress Row, Ft Robinson, 1893. SOURCE: Medical History, Ft Robinson.

‡Reenlistment, married, authorized, by letter, Adjutant General's Office, 11 Jan 1894.

‡Daughter Ida Rebecca, age sixteen months, died of capillary bronchitis, complication of pneumonia, Ft Robinson, 20 Feb 1897. SOURCE: Post Surgeon to Surgeon General, USA, 6 Apr 1897, LS, Post Surgeon, Ft Robinson.

Appointed first sergeant 10 Mar 1889; in A/9th Cavalry at Ft Robinson, Jan 1897. SOURCE: Ninth Cavalry, Roster of NCOs, 1897.

‡Transferred from Reserve Divisional Hospital, Siboney, Cuba, with yellow fever, on U.S. Army Transport *Concho* to Fortress Monroe, VA, 24 Jun 1898. SOURCE: Hospital Papers, Spanish-American War.

Retired sergeant, received Indian Wars Campaign Badge number 1220 on 12 Jul 1909. SOURCE: Carroll, *Indian Wars Campaign Badge*, 35.

HOLLOMON, Solomon; 1st Sgt; A/9th Cav. *See* **HOLLOMAN**, Solomon, First Sergeant, A/9th Cavalry

HOLMES, Walter S.; Trumpeter; G/9th Cav. Received Philippine Campaign Badge number 11817 for service as private in A/25th Infantry, 16 Oct 1900–28 June 1902; trumpeter in G/9th Cavalry, Ft Leavenworth, KS, Mar 1905. SOURCE: Philippine Campaign Badge Recipients; Philippine Campaign Badge list, 29 May 1905.

HOLOMON, John; Private; B/25th Inf. Enlisted 17 Jun 1898, discharged as private B/9th Cavalry, 28 Jan 1899, character good; enlisted 16 Jun 1899, discharged as corporal B/25th Infantry 15 Jun 1902, character excellent; reenlisted 21 Aug 1902, discharged as private 20 Aug 1905, character very good; reenlisted 21 Aug 1905, discharged without honor 16 Nov 1906. SOURCE: Powell, "Military Record of the Enlisted Men Who Were Discharged Without Honor."

Dishonorable discharge, Brownsville, TX. SOURCE: SO 266, AGO, 9 Nov 1906.

HOLT, James; Private; 24th Inf. At Ringgold Bks, TX, 1874, fought with Pvt. George McKay, K/24th Infantry, over Mexican woman. SOURCE: Leiker, *Racial Borders*, 86.

HOLT, John; Private; A/38th Inf. ‡At Ft Cummings, NM, autumn 1867; acquitted of involvement in soldiers' revolt.

SOURCE: Billington, *New Mexico's Buffalo Soldiers*, 41–42.

One of seven 38th Infantrymen acquitted by military court of mutiny, New Mexico, 1868. SOURCE: Dobak and Phillips, *The Black Regulars*, 324.

HOLT, Richard; Private; E/10th Cav. In Troop E/10th Cavalry stationed at Bonita Cañon Camp, AZ, 28 Feb 1886. SOURCE: Tagg, *The Camp at Bonita Cañon*, 231.

HOMES, Marcus; Private; K/25th Inf. Born in Monroe County, GA; Ht 5'9", yellow complexion; occupation wheelwright; enlisted in A/39th Infantry for three years on 3 Sep 1867, age 34, at Greenville, LA; transferred to K/25th Infantry at Jackson Bks, LA, 20 Apr 1869. SOURCE: Descriptive Roll of A/39th Inf.

HONESTY, Gustavus; Corporal; A/25th Inf. Died 26 Jan 1873; buried at San Antonio National Cemetery, Section D, number 778. SOURCE: San Antonio National Cemetery Locator.

HOOD, John; Sergeant; 9th Cav. Received Philippine Campaign Badge number 11706 for service as sergeant in H/9th Cavalry; in 9th Cavalry at Ft Leavenworth, KS, Mar 1905. SOURCE: Philippine Campaign Badge list, 29 May 1905.

Sergeant, 9th Cavalry, died 14 Feb 1907; buried at Ft Bayard, NM, in plot 37. SOURCE: "Fort Bayard National Cemetery, Records of Burials."

Buried 14 Feb 1907, section A, row W, plot 37 at Ft Bayard. SOURCE: Erickson, Burials at Fort Bayard National Cemetery, NM.

HOOPER, George; H/25th Inf. Born in Maryland; black complexion; cannot read or write, age 23, 5 Sep 1870, at Ft McKavett, TX. SOURCE: Bierschwale, *Fort McKavett*, 108.

HOPE, Jasper Pickens; 1st Sgt; D/9th Cav. With troop in fight against Utes on Milk River, Oct 1879. SOURCE: Schubert, *Black Valor*, 63.

Sergeant Hope, F/9th Cavalry, at Ft Reno, OK, Aug 1883, broke up dispute between 1st Sgt. Emanuel Stance and Pvt. William Davis. SOURCE: Schubert, *Voices of the Buffalo Soldier*, 132.

‡Served in F/9th Cavalry, 1875–85; now age 81. SOURCE: *Winners of the West* 12 (Nov 1935): 3.

HOPKINS, Julius; Private; G/25th Inf. Born in Charleston, SC; Ht 5'9", black hair and eyes, dark complexion; occupation laborer; enlisted at age 21, Charleston, 18 May 1881; left recruit depot, David's Island, NY, 2 Jul 1881, arrived Ft Randall, SD, 7 Jul 1881. SOURCE: Descriptive & Assignment Rolls of Recruits, 25 Inf.

Died 15 Dec 1899; buried at San Antonio National Cemetery, Section I, number 1694. SOURCE: San Antonio National Cemetery Locator.

HOPKINS, Pleasant; F/9th Cav. Born in Tennessee; black complexion; cannot read or write, age 21, Jul 1870, at Ft McKavett, TX. SOURCE: Bierschwale, *Fort McKavett*, 97.

HOPKINS, Robert L.; Private; C/10th Cav. Deserted during tenure of George Garnett as first sergeant, Jan 1869–May 1871. SOURCE: Dobak and Phillips, *The Black Regulars*, 300.

HOPKINS, Val; Corporal; E/10th Cav. ‡Voll Hopkins, Corporal, 24th Infantry, at Ft Elliott, TX, 1885. SOURCE: Cleveland *Gazette*, 9 Jan 1886.

‡Corporal, E/10th Cavalry, at Ft Apache, AZ, 1890, subscribed $.50 to testimonial to General Grierson. SOURCE: List of subscriptions, 23 Apr 1890, 10th Cavalry papers, MHI.

‡Sharpshooter, Ft Apache, 1891. SOURCE: *ANJ* 31 (4 Jul 1891): 765.

Died 23 Nov 1891; headstone shows first name as Vol, but A 11 records show Val as the first name; buried at Santa Fe National Cemetery, NM, plot A-1 743. SOURCE: Santa Fe National Cemetery, Records of Burials.

HORN, Leroy; Cook; B/25th Inf. Mustered in 11 Jul 1898, discharged as private D/7th U.S. Volunteers 28 Feb 1899; enlisted 9 Oct 1899, discharged as private F/48th U.S. Volunteers 30 Jun 1901; reenlisted 18 Jul 1901, discharged as private H/25th Infantry 26 Jul 1904, character very good; reenlisted 28 Jul 1904, discharged without honor as cook, 22 Nov 1906, Brownsville, TX. SOURCE: Powell, "Military Record of the Enlisted Men Who Were Discharged Without Honor."

‡Dishonorable discharge, Brownsville. SOURCE: SO 266, AGO, 9 Nov 1906.

HORSLER, Waddy; D/38th Infantry. Buried 12 Jul 1868, section G, row I, plot 39, Ft Bayard. SOURCE: National Cemetery, NM.

HORTON, George; Sergeant; C/25th Inf. ‡Authorized three-month furlough from Ft Shaw, MT. SOURCE: *ANJ* 28 (7 Mar 1891): 474.

Taught in post school, Ft Shaw. SOURCE: Dobak and Phillips, *The Black Regulars*, 132.

HORTON, George; Saddler; H/10th Cav. Enlisted after four years of marriage, continued to send money to wife in Washington, DC; came home and tried civilian life for almost one year; reenlisted for two more terms, and continued to send money home. SOURCE: Dobak and Phillips, *The Black Regulars*, 142.

Served at Ft Davis, TX, 1885; resided at 40 DeFries St., Washington, DC, in 1896. SOURCE: Sayre, *Warriors of Color*, 10.

Appointed from private to saddler 1 Nov 1885; in Troop H/10th Cavalry camped at Bonita Cañon Camp, AZ, 30 Apr 1886. SOURCE: Tagg, *The Camp at Bonita Cañon*, 67, 231.

‡Sentenced to six months and $60 fine for false allegations of assault and abuse against Capt. C. D. Viele, 10th Cavalry, Ft Apache, AZ. SOURCE: *ANJ* 25 (28 Jan 1887): 527.

HORTON, Lewis; Private; I/49th Inf. Died 25 Oct 1900; body received 8 Jul 1902 at San Francisco National Cemetery, buried in plot NEW A1056. SOURCE: San Francisco National Cemetery.

HORTON, Louis; Private; M/9th Cav. Served in M Troop, Ft Stanton, NM, Dec 1876, and helped prevent Trumpeter George Washington from killing Sgt. Emanuel Stance. SOURCE: Kenner, *Buffalo Soldiers and Officers of the Ninth Cavalry*, 165.

HORTON, Louis; Private; D/9th Cav. Private, D/9th Cavalry, Ft Riley, KS, 1882; testified that Pvt. Edward Baker was coerced by Sgt. Richard Miller into testifying that 1st Sgt. James Dickerson molested him. SOURCE: Kenner, *Buffalo Soldiers and Officers of the Ninth Cavalry*, 274

HORTON, Walter; A/38th Inf. Buried 23 Sep 1868 in section A, row G, plot 39, Ft Bayard, NM. SOURCE: Erickson, *Burials at Fort Bayard National Cemetery, NM*.

HOSKINS, Isaac M.; Private; H/48th Inf. Died 13 May 1900; buried in plot NEW A968 at San Francisco National Cemetery. SOURCE: San Francisco National Cemetery.

HOSKINS, Thomas; Private; U.S. Army. Seminole Negro Scout, served 1883–84. SOURCE: Schubert, *Consolidated List of Seminole Negro Scouts*.

Born in Texas; enlisted at Ft Clark, TX, 27 Dec 1883, age 25; Ht 5'10", black hair and eyes, black complexion; discharged at Camp Myers Spring, TX, where he reenlisted for one year 27 Dec 1883; discharged 31 Aug 1884, early release at Ft Clark for benefit of service. SOURCE: Swanson, 20.

HOUSTON, Adam; Sergeant; QM Corps. ‡Born in Pulaski Co., VA, 1858; Ht 5'10", brown complexion; served in Cuba 23 Jun–3 Jul 1898, 8 May 1899–24 Apr 1902; twenty-two years' continuous service as of 21 Jan 1901; $2 per month additional pay for certificate of merit; $5 per

month additional pay for twenty years' continuous service; married, no children; sergeant, B/10th Cavalry, promoted to color sergeant, 10th Cavalry, 10 Mar 1901; reenlisted 21 Jan 1904; promoted to regimental quartermaster sergeant, 27 Dec 1906; widowed by 20 Jan 1907. SOURCE: Descriptive Book, 10 Cav Officers & NCOs.

‡Private, corporal, sergeant, K/24th Infantry, 1 Dec 1879–30 Nov 1884; private, corporal, sergeant, B/10th Cavalry, 29 Dec 1884–28 Dec 1889; private, C/10th Cavalry, 20 Jan 1890; corporal, 1 Jul 1890; sergeant, 15 Mar 1891; first sergeant, 20 Jul 1891; stationed at Ft Assiniboine, MT, 1897. SOURCE: Baker, *Roster*.

‡Served with Thomas Allsup in K/24th Infantry, Ft Concho, TX, Jul 1880; after divorce, Allsup's first wife married Sgt. Lewis M. Smith, E/10th Cavalry, Ft Apache, AZ; now age 66, resides at Soldiers Home, California. SOURCE: Affidavit, Houston, 14 Apr 1926, VA File XC 2659797, Thomas H. Allsup.

‡Served in C/10th Cavalry in Cuba, 1898. SOURCE: Cashin, *Under Fire with the Tenth Cavalry*, 190, 360.

Wounded in action, Santiago, Cuba, 1 Jul 1898. SOURCE: SecWar, *AR 1898*, 324.

‡His heroism in Cuba slighted according to unsigned letter [Cpl. John E. Lewis], Montauk, NY, n.d. SOURCE: Gatewood, *"Smoked Yankees,"* 78.

As first sergeant, C/10th Cavalry, awarded certificate of merit for distinguished service in battle, Santiago, 1 Jul 1898. SOURCE: Gleim, *The Certificate of Merit*, 45.

‡Awarded certificate of merit for distinguished service in Cuba, 1 Jul 1898. SOURCE: *ANJ* 37 (24 Feb 1900): 611; Steward, *The Colored Regulars*, 280.

‡Commended for distinguished service, battle of Santiago, 1 Jul 1898. SOURCE: GO 15, AGO, 13 Feb 1900.

Born and resided in Pulaski County, VA; received Distinguished Service Medal in lieu of certificate of merit. SOURCE: *American Decorations*, 838.

Retired sergeant, QM Corps; received Indian Wars Campaign Badge number 1887 on 24 Jan 1921. SOURCE: Carroll, *Indian Wars Campaign Badge*, 55.

HOUSTON, Andrew; Private; 9th Cav. Received Philippine Campaign Badge number 11730 for service as private in E/9th Cavalry; in 9th Cavalry at Ft Leavenworth, KS, Mar 1905. SOURCE: Philippine Campaign Badge list, 29 May 1905.

HOUSTON, Monroe; Sergeant; F/9th Cav. Sergeant, F/9th Cavalry, 1872–73. SOURCE: Kenner, *Buffalo Soldiers and Officers of the Ninth Cavalry*, 338.

HOVER, Benjamin; Private; D/25th Inf. At Ft McIntosh, TX, 1900; arrested in Laredo, TX, Oct 1900, with Pvts. Joshua Nichols and Robert Earl for beating local police officer. SOURCE: Leiker, *Racial Borders*, 123.

HOWARD, James; Private; F/9th Cav. Died 19 May 1866; buried at San Antonio National Cemetery, Section D, number 796. SOURCE: San Antonio National Cemetery Locator.

HOWARD, John; Private; E/9th Cav. Served with troop in New Mexico in 1879 near Ojo Caliente, Sep 1879, when attacked by Victorio. SOURCE: Kenner, *Buffalo Soldiers and Officers of the Ninth Cavalry*, 109.

HOWARD, John A.; K/10th Cav. ‡Original member of 10th Cavalry; in troop when organized, Ft Riley, KS, 1 Sep 1867. SOURCE: McMiller, "Buffalo Soldiers," 77.

After service Pvt. John A. Howard, 10th Cavalry, employed as janitor in post office, San Antonio, TX. SOURCE: Dobak and Phillips, *The Black Regulars*, 272.

HOWARD, Joseph; M/9th Cav. Born in Kentucky; mulatto complexion; cannot read or write, age 21, Jul 1870, at Ft McKavett, TX. SOURCE: Bierschwale, *Fort McKavett*, 99.

HOWARD, Julius; Private; I/25th Inf. Born in San Antonio, TX; Ht 5'4", black hair and brown eyes, mulatto complexion; occupation waiter; enlisted at age 24, Boston, MA, 28 Sep 1885; assigned to I/25th Infantry; arrived Ft Snelling, MN, 5 Feb 1886. SOURCE: Descriptive & Assignment Rolls of Recruits, 25 Inf.

HOWARD, Lewis; C/25th Inf. Born in Maryland; mulatto complexion; cannot read or write, age 21, 5 Sep 1870, at Ft McKavett, TX. SOURCE: Bierschwale, *Fort McKavett*, 109.

HOWARD, Nathaniel; Sergeant; L/9th Cav. Enlisted at Pittsburgh, PA, 13 Aug 1875 for five years; discharged from L/9th Cavalry 12 Aug 1880 at Ft Bliss, TX, character good; reenlisted 2 Oct 1880. SOURCE: Muster Rolls, L/9th Cavalry, 30 June–31 Aug 1880.

HOWARD, Silas; Private; 9th Cav. Civil War veteran, served in 4th U.S. Colored Infantry. SOURCE: Dobak and Phillips, *The Black Regulars*, 22.

HOWARD, William; Sergeant; E/9th Cav. An original member of E/9th Cavalry; listed on Census rolls 1870 as illiterate; gradually became "quite proficient in grammatical skills"; one of three original members still in troop in 1879, with James Williams and Zekiel Sykes; retired as 30-year man in the late 1890s. SOURCE: Kenner, *Buffalo Soldiers and Officers of the Ninth Cavalry*, 14–15, 316, 326.

‡Wife is one of three authorized laundresses, E/9th Cavalry, and so entitled to Quartermaster stove and utensils if available, Ft Robinson, NE, Jun 1891. SOURCE: Post Adj to Post QM, 22 Jun 1891, LS, Ft Robinson.

‡Retires from Ft Robinson as sergeant, E/9th Cavalry, 14 Feb 1893. SOURCE: *ANJ* 30 (11 Mar 1893): 479; Roster, 9 Cav.

‡Retired; lives with wife in old barrack, Ft Robinson. SOURCE: Medical History, Ft Robinson.

‡Retired; employed as laborer, Ft Robinson post exchange, at $5 per month. SOURCE: Report of Inspection, Ft Robinson, 3 Sep 1894, Reports of Inspections, DeptPlatte, 2.

‡Emma Howard, washerwoman, resided at Ft Robinson, 1894. SOURCE: Court Martial Records, Plummer.

‡One of six retirees, four of whom are black, at Ft Robinson. SOURCE: Misc Records, DeptPlatte, 1894–98.

‡Wife Emma buried at Ft Robinson, 20 Aug 1908. SOURCE: List of Interments, Ft Robinson.

Resided in Crawford, NE, 1912, with personal property assessed at $21 and paid $2 tax; personal property assessed at $10 and paid $1 tax, 1916.

‡Resided in Crawford, 1921, age 75, with no income except retired pay; knew Louisa McClain from time of her marriage to Henry McClain; identified as "respected by everyone and . . . credited with being truthful and honest in each and every respect" by Veterans Administration Special Examiner C. R. Franks. SOURCE: VA File XC 2705872, Henry McClain.

Retired sergeant, received Indian Wars Campaign Badge no. 1147 on 10 Mar 1909. SOURCE: Carroll, *Indian Wars Campaign Badge*, 33.

HOWELL, James; Private; C/9th Cav. Died 10 Oct 1902; buried in plot 1203 NEW at San Francisco National Cemetery. SOURCE: San Francisco National Cemetery.

HOWERTON, John C.; Private; A/10th Cav. ‡Born 16 Apr 1854; enlisted Indianapolis, IN, Ht 5'5", mulatto, served 26 Sep 1882–25 Sep 1887, including Geronimo campaign; married Mary Eliza Pollard, Braidwood, IL, 1888; laborer for city of Chicago, IL; pensioned at $4 per month, 21 Feb 1890, with injury to right shoulder and rheumatism; resided at 2971 Dearborn, Chicago; sons Robert and Dewey, daughter Ursula; wife died 1931; he died 11 May 1934. SOURCE: VA File XC 896871, John C. Howerton.

‡Horse fell on Howerton, Ft Stockton, TX, Apr 1884. SOURCE: Affidavit, Green Trice (age 28, Hiram, OH, former private, L/10 Cav), 19 Feb 1894, VA File XC 896871, John C. Howerton.

‡Howerton was thrown from horse while herd guide. SOURCE: Affidavit, Robert Anderson (sergeant, B/10th Cavalry, Ft Custer, MT), 14 Sep 1893, VA File XC 896871, John C. Howerton.

‡Died in Chicago; late member, Camp 11, National Indian War Veterans. SOURCE: *Winners of the West* 11 (May 1934): 3.

‡Born 16 Apr 1854, slave of William B. Bruce, on farm five miles north of Brunswick, MO; mother also belonged to Bruce; father Henry Howerton, slave of Joseph Howerton, was sold South in 1860 or 1861; year later learned of father's death; in 1860–63 was at home "with my old master William B. Bruce"; mother loaded all four children in wagon she had hired to escape to LaClede, MO, 1864; there hidden by white man, fed for two to three days in his cellar, he was put on Hannibal & St. Joseph Railroad to St. Joseph, MO, where he was told to cross to Kansas when he could; crossed Missouri River on ferry of Captain Blackston, taken to Mr. Bryant's farm, Doniphan Co.; stayed until he returned to St. Joseph, summer 1869; then got work on farm of John Britton, nineteen miles west of Omaha and three miles south of Elkhorn Station, on Union Pacific Railroad; stayed there until 1871. SOURCE: Affidavit, Howerton, 10 Sep 1927, VA File XC 896871, John C. Howerton.

Text of Pvt. John C. Howerton, L/10th Cavalry, account of his escape from slavery with his mother and siblings autumn 1864, published. SOURCE: Schubert, *Voices of the Buffalo Soldier*, 127–28.

HUBBARD, George; Private; M/10th Cav. Died 6 Oct 1873 of disease at Ft Sill, OK. SOURCE: Regimental Returns, 10th Cavalry, 1873.

HUCKSTEP, Henderson; Sergeant; G/9th Cav. ‡Private, L/10th Cavalry, assaulted female servant of post trader, Ft Bayard, NM, Aug 1890. SOURCE: Billington, *New Mexico's Buffalo Soldiers*, 166.

‡Promoted from private to corporal, Ft Robinson, NE, Oct 1895. SOURCE: *ANJ* 33 (12 Oct 1895): 87.

Received Philippine Campaign Badge number 11805 for service as sergeant in 9th Cavalry, 16 Sep 1900–16 Sep 1902; sergeant in G/9th Cavalry, Ft Leavenworth, KS, Mar 1905. SOURCE: Philippine Campaign Badge Recipients; Philippine Campaign Badge list, 29 May 1905.

HUDDLESTON, William; Private; B/24th Inf. Died 10 Nov 1901; buried at Ft Bayard, NM, in plot N 43. SOURCE: "Fort Bayard National Cemetery, Records of Burials."

Buried 10 Nov 1901, section A, row V, plot 43, at Ft Bayard. SOURCE: Erickson, Burials at Fort Bayard National Cemetery, NM.

HUFF, John; C/25th Inf. Born in Kentucky; mulatto complexion; can read and write, age 26, 5 Sep 1870, at Ft McKavett, TX. SOURCE: Bierschwale, *Fort McKavett,* 109.

HUFFMAN, Wyatt; 1st Lt; C/49th Inf. ‡Served in G/25th Infantry, 10 Jan 1872–10 Jan 1897; corporal, 25 May 1875; sergeant, 1 Aug 1876; first sergeant, 1 Jan–1 Sep 1891; sergeant, 1 Sep 1891–29 Jul 1898; second lieutenant, 8th Infantry, U.S. Volunteers, 29 Jul 1898–6 Mar 1899; in M/25th Infantry, 14 Mar–9 Sep 1899; second lieutenant, 49th In-

fantry, 9 Sep 1899; first lieutenant, 2 Jan 1901; served at El Caney and Santiago, Cuba, 1898; marksman and sharpshooter. SOURCE: Descriptive Book, C/49 Inf.

‡With G/25th Infantry in Cuba, 1898; "one of the finest soldiers in the regiment and carried so many service stripes on his arm that little of his sleeve showed," according to Col. Reynolds J. Burt. SOURCE: Nankivell, *History of the Twenty-fifth Infantry*, 67.

Sergeant, 25th Infantry, recommended for commission in immune regiment by Lt. Col. Aaron S. Daggett, 25th Infantry, even before regiment left Cuba, Aug 1898. SOURCE: Schubert, *Black Valor*, 110.

‡Commissioned second lieutenant, 8th Volunteer Infantry. SOURCE: Cashin, *Under Fire with the Tenth Cavalry*, 360.

‡Resident of Tennessee; commissioned for bravery at El Caney. SOURCE: Johnson, *History of Negro Soldiers*, 32.

‡Commissioned for gallantry and meritorious service around Santiago. SOURCE: New York *Journal*, quoted in Thweatt, *What the Newspapers Say*, 10; Richmond *Planet*, 13 Aug 1898.

‡Philippine service mentioned. SOURCE: Villard, "The Negro in the Regular Army," 724.

‡Second lieutenant, K/49th Infantry, on detached service with 25th Infantry, 22 Sep 1899–30 May 1900; commander, K/49th Infantry, 23 Jul–1 Aug and 14 Sep–5 Oct 1900.

‡Promoted to first lieutenant, 49th Infantry, 2 Jan 1901. SOURCE: *ANJ* 38 (19 Jan 1901): 503.

HUGGINS, Cumsey; Private; 25th Inf. Born in Christ Church, SC; enlisted Charleston, SC, age 22, Ht 5'6", dark complexion, black hair and eyes, occupation farmer, 28 Jun 1881; left recruit depot, David's Island, NY, 17 Aug 1881, and after trip on steamer *Thomas Kirby* to Central Depot, New York City, and train via Chicago to Running Water, Dakota Territory, 22 Aug 1881, marched forty-seven miles to Ft Randall, SD, arrived 24 Aug 1881. SOURCE: Descriptive & Assignment Rolls, 25 Inf.

HUGHES, Carter; C/25th Inf. Born in Tennessee; black complexion; can read and write, age 23, 5 Sep 1870, at Ft McKavett, TX. SOURCE: Bierschwale, *Fort McKavett,* 109.

HUGHES, Charles; Private; G/9th Cav. Private, U.S. Army, Seminole Negro Scout, served 1893–94. SOURCE: Schubert, Consolidated List of Seminole Negro Scouts.

Born in Kentucky; enlisted as Seminole Negro Scout at Ft Clark, TX, 16 Jan 1893, age 45; Ht 5'8", grey hair, black eyes, dark complexion; discharged 16 Jul 1893 at Ft Ringgold, TX, where he reenlisted 13 Aug 1893; discharged 12 Feb 1894 at Camp San Pedro, TX, where he reenlisted next day; discharged as corporal at Ft Ringgold; transferred to G/9th Cavalry 13 Feb 1895; 1880 Census lists Hughes as black male, age 32. SOURCE: Swanson, 20.

HUGHES, David; Farrier; E/10th Cav. In Troop E/10th Cavalry stationed at Bonita Cañon Camp, AZ, 28 Feb 1886. SOURCE: Tagg, *The Camp at Bonita Cañon*, 231.

HUGHES, Isaac; Private; C/10th Cav. ‡Isack Hughes, C/10th Cavalry, original member of 10th Cavalry; in troop when organized, Ft Leavenworth, KS, 14 May 1867. SOURCE: McMiller, "Buffalo Soldiers," 70.

Served with Pvt. George Washington, C/10th Cavalry, early 1870s; also known as Ike; resided northeast of Geary, OK, after service. SOURCE: Schubert, *Voices of the Buffalo Soldier*, 230, 234.

HUGHES, John; Private; H/10th Cav. Died at Ft Concho, TX, on 2 Aug 1883; buried at San Antonio National Cemetery, Section O, number 1537. SOURCE: San Antonio National Cemetery Locator.

Buried at San Antonio National Cemetery, Section D, number 712. SOURCE: San Antonio National Cemetery Locator.

HULL, Moses; Private; G/10th Cav. Shot while trying to escape from guard; died 21 Aug 1873 at Ft Sill, OK. SOURCE: Regimental Returns, 10th Cavalry, 1873.

HUMPHREY, John; Private; F/10th Cav. Died 2 Aug 1867 of cholera at Ft Hays, KS. SOURCE: Regimental Returns, 10th Cavalry, 1867.

HUMPHREY, John A.; Private; I/10th Cav. ‡Private, H/24th Infantry, relieved from extra duty as laborer, and detailed on extra duty as plasterer, Quartermaster Department, Ft Huachuca, AZ. SOURCE: Order 16, Ft Huachuca, 1 Feb 1893, Name File, 24 Inf.

‡Served as private, I/10th Cavalry in Cuba, 1898. SOURCE: Cashin, *Under Fire with the Tenth Cavalry*, 348.

‡Certificate of merit awarded for gallant conduct in voluntarily clearing path up side of hill through heavy and impassible weeds and brush while under heavy fire, Las Guasimas, Cuba, 24 Jun 1898, when private, I/10th Cavalry; discharged as artificer, 24th Infantry, 7 Jun 1903.

As artificer, awarded certificate of merit for gallant conduct, voluntarily cutting and clearing path up hill through heavy brush while under fire, Las Guasimas, 24 Jun 1898. SOURCE: Gleim, *The Certificate of Merit*, 45.

‡Heroism mentioned. SOURCE: Cashin, *Under Fire with the Tenth Cavalry*, 185.

‡Private, H/24th Infantry, fined $3 by summary court, San Isidro, Philippines, for being drunk in quarters, 31 Mar 1902, first conviction. SOURCE: Register of Summary Court, San Isidro.

HUMPHREY, William; Private; E/9th Cav. In fourth year of service when on duty in Sgt. Silas Chapman's herd guard, near Ojo Caliente, NM, Sep 1879, and attacked by Victorio; killed along with Chapman, Pvts. Abram Percival, Silas Graddon, and Lafayette Hooke. SOURCE: Kenner, *Buffalo Soldiers and Officers of the Ninth Cavalry*, 108.

HUMPHRIES, Samuel; Private; E/10th Cav. In Troop E/10th Cavalry stationed at Bonita Cañon Camp, AZ, 28 Feb 1886. SOURCE: Tagg, *The Camp at Bonita Cañon*, 231.

HUNLEY, Edward; Private; F/10th Cav. Died at Ft Concho, TX, on 27 Jun 1873; buried at San Antonio National Cemetery, Section D, number 672. SOURCE: San Antonio National Cemetery Locator.

HUNT, Eugene; Private; 9th Cav. Received Philippine Campaign Badge number 11776 for service as private in F/9th Cavalry; in 9th Cavalry at Ft Leavenworth, KS, Mar 1905. SOURCE: Philippine Campaign Badge list, 29 May 1905.

HUNTER, George; Private; H/10th Cav. Accidentally shot, died 7 Aug 1873 at Ft Sill, OK. SOURCE: Regimental Returns, 10th Cavalry, 1873.

HUNTER, Isaac; Sergeant; I/9th Cav. ‡Served as private, L/10th Cavalry, 1898; remained in U.S. during war with Spain. SOURCE: Cashin, *Under Fire with the Tenth Cavalry*, 351.

‡Expert rifleman and horseshoer, I/9th Cavalry, at Ft D. A. Russell, WY, in 1910; resident of Enfield, NC. SOURCE: *Illustrated Review: Ninth Cavalry*, with picture.

Sergeant, I/9th Cavalry; died 25 Feb 1937; buried in plot D-SOU1263 at San Francisco National Cemetery. SOURCE: San Francisco National Cemetery.

HUNTER, John; C/25th Inf. Born in Virginia; mulatto complexion; can read and write, age 23, 5 Sep 1870, at Ft McKavett, TX. SOURCE: Bierschwale, *Fort McKavett*, 108.

HUNTER, John G.; H/25th Inf. Born in Indiana; mulatto complexion; can read, cannot write, age 21, 5 Sep 1870, at Ft McKavett, TX. SOURCE: Bierschwale, *Fort McKavett*, 108.

HUNTER, Jordan; Saddler; D/9th Cav. Born in Virginia; black complexion; cannot read or write, age 29, Jul 1870, at Ft McKavett, TX. SOURCE: Bierschwale, *Fort McKavett*, 98.

‡Retires from Ft Washakie, WY. SOURCE: *ANJ* 34 (8 May 1897): 663.

HUNTER, Lewis; F/9th Cav. Born in Kentucky; black complexion; cannot read or write, age 24, Jul 1870, at Ft McKavett, TX. SOURCE: Bierschwale, *Fort McKavett,* 97.

HUNTER, Robert; Private; D/10th Cav. Died 22 Jul 1887; buried at Santa Fe National Cemetery, NM, plot A-1 751. SOURCE: Santa Fe National Cemetery, Records of Burials.

HUNTINGDON, Sylvester; Private; C/10th Cav. Died 25 Jan 1873; buried at Ft Leavenworth National Cemetery, plot C 2055. SOURCE: Ft Leavenworth National Cemetery.

HURBERT, David; Private; 25th Inf. Born in Hampton, VA; Ht 5'7", black hair and brown eyes, brown complexion; occupation cook; resided Boston, MA, when enlisted at age 25, Boston, 28 Sep 1885; assigned to B/25th Infantry; arrived Ft Snelling, MN, 5 Feb 1886. SOURCE: Descriptive & Assignment Rolls of Recruits, 25 Inf.

Hurley, Bartholomew A.; Corporal; L/49th Inf. Died 10 Mar 1937; buried in plot D SOU1215 at San Francisco National Cemetery. SOURCE: San Francisco National Cemetery.

HUSTON, Charles; Private; A/9th Cav. Died at Ft Stockton, TX, on 19 Jul 1871; buried at San Antonio National Cemetery, Section C, number 338. SOURCE: San Antonio National Cemetery Locator.

HUTCHENS, George H.; Private; I/10th Cav. In Troop I/10th Cavalry stationed at Bonita Cañon Camp, AZ, 30 Jun 1886. SOURCE: Tagg, *The Camp at Bonita Cañon,* 231.

HUTCHINSON, George; Blacksmith; A/10th Cav. Served in H/10th Cavalry in 1880; in A/10th Cavalry during 1882; age 56, resides in Albuquerque, NM, 1897; still in Albuquerque with $23 per month pension in 1914. SOURCE: Sayre, *Warriors of Color,* 262, 278.

HUTCHISON, Robert; Private; B/38th Inf. Died 29 Aug 1967; buried at Ft Leavenworth National Cemetery, plot C 1649. SOURCE: Ft Leavenworth National Cemetery.

HUTCHISON, George; F/9th Cav. Born in Kentucky; black complexion; can read, cannot write, age 21, Jul 1870, at Ft McKavett, TX. SOURCE: Bierschwale, *Fort McKavett,* 96.

HUTTON, William A.; Private; H/9th Cav. Received Philippine Campaign Badge number 11890 for service as private in C/9th Cavalry; in 9th Cavalry at Ft Leavenworth, KS, Mar 1905. SOURCE: Philippine Campaign Badge list, 29 May 1905.

‡Veteran of Philippine Insurrection; at Ft D. A. Russell, WY, in 1910; resident of Washington, DC. SOURCE: *Illustrated Review: Ninth Cavalry,* with picture.

HYMES, Pompy; Private; G/49th Inf. ‡Died of variola in the Philippines, 9 Mar 1900. SOURCE: *ANJ* 37 (14 Apr 1900): 779.

Died 9 Mar 1900; buried in plot NEW A317 at San Francisco National Cemetery. SOURCE: San Francisco National Cemetery.

I

IMES, James; Private; K/9th Cav. ‡Served 1872–73. *See* **SLAUGHTER**, Rufus, Private, K/9th Cavalry; **WILLIAMS**, Jerry, Private, K/9th Cavalry

Brutal treatment at Ft Clark, TX, by Capt. J. Lee Humfreville, summer 1872, described; discharged on certificate of disability early 1875. SOURCE: Kenner, *Buffalo Soldiers and Officers of the Ninth Cavalry*, 141–45, 336.

Text of court martial order convicting Capt. J. Lee Humfreville of brutality published. SOURCE: Schubert, *Voices of the Buffalo Soldier*, 55–62.

INGOMAN, Madison; QM Sgt; D/9th Cav. ‡Served in G/10th Cavalry, 1873. SOURCE: ES, 10 Cav, 1872–81.

With Captain Dodge at battle at Milk River, CO, 2–10 Oct 1879. SOURCE: Miller, *Hollow Victory*, 167, 206–7.

‡Sergeant, D/9th Cavalry, from 1 May 1880. SOURCE: Roster, 9 Cav.

‡Ambushed while commanding wagon train escort of six privates between Ft Craig, NM, and Camp Ojo Caliente, NM, Jan 1881; Pvt. William Jones severely wounded and died next day. SOURCE: Billington, *New Mexico's Buffalo Soldiers*, 101.

Ingoman Madison, sergeant in D/9th Cavalry, awarded certificate of merit for gallantry in action, charging and routing Indians who twice attacked wagon train under his escort en route to Ojo Caliente, 23 Jan 1881, in canyon of Canada Alamosa, NM, 25 Jan 1881. SOURCE: Gleim, *The Certificate of Merit*, 43.

‡Sergeant, D/9th Cavalry, at Ft Robinson, NE, as witness in Brown and Wormsley court martial, 26 Oct–27 Dec 1889; then returned to station at Ft McKinney, WY.

With troop in fight against Utes, Milk River, Oct 1879; wrote affidavit attesting to Henry Johnson's bravery at Milk River while serving at Ft McKinney, 1890. SOURCE: Schubert, *Black Valor*, 64, 68.

‡Admonished by commander, Ft Robinson, that while his family resides on post, his children of proper school age must attend post school or some other school; under no circumstances will they loiter around barracks during school hours. SOURCE: CO to Sgt. Ingoman, 22 Mar 1893, LS, Ft Robinson.

‡Resides at Ft Robinson on Laundress Row with wife, three children, and sister-in-law with one child. SOURCE: Medical History, Ft Robinson, Entry for Aug 1893.

Appointed sergeant 1 May 1880; in D/9th Cavalry at Ft Washakie, WY, Jan 1897. SOURCE: Ninth Cavalry, Roster of NCOs, 1897.

‡Quartermaster sergeant, D/9th Cavalry, died in Cuba, 8 Aug 1898. SOURCE: *ANJ* 36 (11 Feb 1899): 567.

Native of Kentucky, five-year veteran of 10th Cavalry, age 33, when transferred to 9th Cavalry in 1878; cited for bravery against Apaches, Ojo Caliente, Jan 1881, and awarded certificate of merit; replaced W. F. Clyde as first sergeant, D/9th Cavalry, Ft Riley, KS, early 1885; served as first sergeant for three years, became quartermaster sergeant in 1889 and remained in that rank until he died of yellow fever in Cuba, 8 Aug 1898. SOURCE: Kenner, *Buffalo Soldiers and Officers of the Ninth Cavalry*, 278–79.

‡Died of fever in Cuba and buried with honors, Ft Leavenworth, KS, 3 Mar 1900; two citations for actions against Apaches en route to Ojo Caliente, 21 Jan 1881, and at Canada Alamosa, NM, 25 Jan 1881. SOURCE: *ANJ* 37 (10 Mar 1900): 651.

Sgt. Matteson Ingoman, A/9th Cavalry, died 8 Aug 1899; originally buried at Santiago, Cuba; reburied at Ft Leavenworth National Cemetery, plot A 3187. SOURCE: Ft Leavenworth National Cemetery.

INGOMAN, Matteson; Sergeant; A/9th Cav. *See* **INGOMAN**, Madison, Quartermaster Sergeant, D/9th Cavalry

INGRAHAM, Roden; Private; C/38th Inf. Roden Ingraham or Hoden Ingrahem died 7 Aug 1887; buried at Ft Leavenworth National Cemetery, plot 3293. SOURCE: Ft Leavenworth National Cemetery.

INGRAHEM, Hoden; Private; C/38th Inf. *See* **INGRAHAM**, Roden, Private, C/38th Infantry

INGRAM, Roy; Private; 9th Cav. Received Philippine Campaign Badge number 11777 for service as private in E/9th Cavalry; in 9th Cavalry at Ft Leavenworth, KS, Mar

1905. SOURCE: Philippine Campaign Badge list, 29 May 1905.

INGRAM, W. H.; B/9th Cav. Served three years in B/9th Cavalry; participated in battle at Pine Ridge Agency, SD, in 1890; discharged at Ft DuChesne, UT, in 1892; in Kansas City, MO, in 1898 revived a Negro company of so-called governor's guards and serves as captain of best drilled Negroes in Kansas. SOURCE: "Ex-Consul Waller Will Fight, Kansas City Negroes Preparing for the War," *Leavenworth Times*, 25 Jun 1898.

IRVIN, Allen; Private; K/25th Inf. Born in Fayette County, KY; Ht 5'5", brown complexion; occupation farmer; enlisted in A/39th Infantry for three years on 12 Oct 1866, age 22, at Greenville, LA; transferred to K/25th Infantry at Jackson Bks, LA, 20 Apr 1869. SOURCE: Descriptive Roll of A/39th Inf.

IRVING, Lee; Private; B/10th Cav. Born in Ohio; mulatto complexion; can read, cannot write, age 21, 5 Sep 1870, in 9th Cavalry at Ft McKavett, TX. SOURCE: Bierschwale, *Fort McKavett,* 107.

While stationed in K/9th at Ft Robinson, NE, involved in saloon brawl, Crawford, NE, Feb 1887, along with Pvts. George Pumphrey and Henry Chase; convicted by court martial and confined for three months. SOURCE: Kenner, *Buffalo Soldiers and Officers of the Ninth Cavalry,* 150–51.

‡Private, K/9th Cavalry, directed to leave Ft Robinson with Pvt. Walter R. Fisher, K/9th Cavalry, and three days' rations to repair telegraph line to Running Water, 18 Jul 1888. SOURCE: Order 135, 17 Jul 1888, Post Orders, Ft Robinson.

‡Private, K/9th Cavalry, wounded in action at Pine Ridge, SD, 1890; returned to Ft Robinson, 4 Jan 1891. SOURCE: Kelley, *Pine Ridge, 1890,* 219.

‡Retires from Ft Custer, MT, as private, B/10th Cavalry, 28 Apr 1896. SOURCE: *ANJ* 33 (25 Apr 1896): 616; Baker, Roster.

IRWIN, Samuel; Private; F/9th Cav. Died 28 Jan 1902; buried in plot 751 at San Francisco National Cemetery. SOURCE: San Francisco National Cemetery.

ISAM, Frank J.; Saddler; I/10th Cav. In Troop I/10th Cavalry stationed at Bonita Cañon Camp, AZ, 30 Jun 1886. SOURCE: Tagg, *The Camp at Bonita Cañon,* 231.

‡At Ft Apache, AZ, 1890, subscribed $.50 to testimonial to General Grierson. SOURCE: List of subscriptions, 23 Apr 1890, 10th Cavalry papers, MHI.

IVANS, Lewis; Farrier; 9th Cav. Received Philippine Campaign Badge number 11891 for service as farrier in F/9th Cavalry; in 9th Cavalry at Ft Leavenworth, KS, Mar 1905. SOURCE: Philippine Campaign Badge list, 29 May 1905.

J

JACKSON, Abram; Corporal; A/25th Inf. Died at Ft Davis, TX, on 11 Nov 1876; buried at San Antonio National Cemetery, Section I, number 1499. SOURCE: San Antonio National Cemetery Locator.

JACKSON, Andrew; C/25th Inf. Born in New Jersey; mulatto complexion; can read and write, age 21, 5 Sep 1870, at Ft McKavett, TX. SOURCE: Bierschwale, *Fort McKavett,* 109.

JACKSON, Anthony; Sergeant; E/25th Inf. Died at Ft Davis, TX, on 5 Jul 1874; buried at San Antonio National Cemetery, Section I, number 1461. SOURCE: San Antonio National Cemetery Locator.

JACKSON, Arthur; Private; D/25th Inf. Discharged 1871, with notation on his papers saying he was "deficient in intellect and generally worthless." SOURCE: Dobak and Phillips, *The Black Regulars,* 257.

JACKSON, Benjamin; Corporal; H/10th Cav. Enlisted 26 Apr 1879; on scout at Eagle Springs, TX; served at Ft Davis, TX, 1882–83; discharged on surgeon's certificate of disability, 24 Mar 1883; resided in Georgetown, KY; at 817 Hopkins St., Cincinnati, OH, in 1896 and 1897, age 38, occupation laborer; pension $6 per month in 1897. SOURCE: Sayre, *Warriors of Color,* 8, 13.

JACKSON, Charles; Private; H/41st Inf. At Ft Quitman, TX, 1869, assaulted Francisca Ortiz, hospital matron, for insulting him; convicted of conduct prejudicial to good order and military discipline, fined $20 per month for three months. SOURCE: Leiker, *Racial Borders,* 86, 208.

JACKSON, Charles; Private; F/25th Inf. Died 21 Nov 1900; buried in plot East 1080 at San Francisco National Cemetery. SOURCE: San Francisco National Cemetery.

JACKSON, Charles; Private; 9th Cav. Received Philippine Campaign Badge number 11779 for service as private in F/9th Cavalry; in 9th Cavalry at Ft Leavenworth, KS, Mar 1905. SOURCE: Philippine Campaign Badge list, 29 May 1905.

JACKSON, Daniel; M/9th Cav. Born in Virginia; black complexion; can read and write, age 23, Jul 1870, at Ft McKavett, TX. SOURCE: Bierschwale, *Fort McKavett,* 100.

JACKSON, Elisha; Sergeant; H/9th Cav. ‡Appointed corporal, H/9th Cavalry, 19 Apr 1893. SOURCE: Roster, 9 Cav.

‡Promoted to sergeant from corporal, Ft Robinson, NE, Dec 1894. SOURCE: *ANJ* 32 (22 Dec 1894): 278.

Appointed sergeant 8 Dec 1894; in H/9th Cavalry at Ft Robinson, Jan 1897. SOURCE: Ninth Cavalry, Roster of NCOs, 1897.

‡To be discharged from H/9th Cavalry, 24 May 1897, with $175 deposits, $92 clothing, $48 retained. SOURCE: CO, H/9, to Chief QM, DeptPlatte, May 1897, LS, H/9 Cav.

‡Born in Richmond Co., VA; enlisted, age 31, Ft Robinson, 20 May 1897, with ten years' continuous service in M and H/9th Cavalry; married without children; commissioned second lieutenant, 10th Infantry, U.S. Volunteers. SOURCE: Descriptive Book, H/9 Cav.

‡Married widow of Saddler Sgt. Charles H. Dowd, 9th Cavalry, Ft Robinson, 15 Jun 1897. SOURCE: CO, 9 Cav, to AG, USA, 17 Jun 1897, LS, Ft Robinson.

‡On point, Cuba, 1 Jul 1898, and "ever in front and by his example encouraged all about him." SOURCE: SecWar, *AR 1898,* 708.

Sergeant, H/9th Cavalry, commissioned second lieutenant, 10th Volunteer Infantry, after Spanish-American War. SOURCE: Cashin, *Under Fire with the Tenth Cavalry,* 360.

‡Awarded certificate of merit for meritorious service, Cuba, 1898; out of service by 1900. SOURCE: *ANJ* 37 (24 Feb 1900): 611; Steward, *The Colored Regulars,* 280.

‡Commended for gallantry, 1 Jul 1898; now out of service. SOURCE: GO 15, AGO, 13 Feb 1900.

As sergeant, H/9th Cavalry, awarded certificate of merit for distinguished service in battle, Santiago, Cuba, 1 Jul 1898. SOURCE: Gleim, *The Certificate of Merit,* 45.

JACKSON, Frank; Private; G/25th Inf. Died 20 Feb 1916; buried in plot WSIDE850A at San Francisco National Cemetery. SOURCE: San Francisco National Cemetery.

JACKSON, George; Sergeant; B/25th Inf. ‡Enlisted 1898. SOURCE: Weaver, *The Brownsville Raid*, 71.

Mustered in 16 Jul 1898, mustered out as corporal, Company G, 23rd Kansas Volunteer Infantry, 10 Apr 1899; enlisted 3 Dec 1900, discharged as sergeant Company B, 25th Infantry 3 Dec 1903, character excellent; reenlisted 3 Dec 1903, discharged without honor as sergeant November 16, 1906. SOURCE: Powell, "Military Record of the Enlisted Men Who Were Discharged Without Honor."

‡Ranked number 16, Northern Division Infantry Team competition, Ft Sheridan, IL, 1904. SOURCE: GO 167, AGO, 28 Oct 1904.

‡Dishonorable discharge, Brownsville, TX. SOURCE: SO 266, AGO, 9 Nov 1906.

JACKSON, Hamilton; Private; 39th Inf. Contracted venereal disease while in service. SOURCE: Dobak and Phillips, *The Black Regulars*, 172.

JACKSON, Harvey; Private; D/24th Inf. Died at Ft McIntosh, TX, on 19 Oct 1872; buried at Fort Sam Houston National Cemetery, Section PE, number 424. SOURCE: Buffalo Soldiers Interred in Fort Sam Houston National Cemetery.

JACKSON, Henry C.; M/9th Cav. Born in Kentucky; black complexion; cannot read or write, age 25, Jul 1870, at Ft McKavett, TX. SOURCE: Bierschwale, *Fort McKavett*, 100.

JACKSON, Hilary; Private; L/9th Cav. Enlisted at Baltimore, MD, 23 Jan 1879. SOURCE: Muster Roll, L/9th Cavalry, 31 Oct 1879–31 Dec 1879.

‡Pvt. H. Jackson, L/9th Cavalry, on detached service in the field, New Mexico, 21 Jan–24 Feb 1881. SOURCE: Regt Returns, 9 Cav, Feb 1881.

JACKSON, Isaac; Sergeant; H/10th Cav. Born in Louisville, KY, 1847; served during Civil War, K/109th Infantry, U.S. Colored Troops, 16 Jul 1863–16 Oct 1865; in field hospital for two months in 1864 at Catlettsburg, KY, for camp diarrhea; enlisted at Indianapolis, IN, 5 Dec 1873, Ht 5'5", complexion dark brown, black eyes and hair; occupation laborer; served as blacksmith in A/10th Cavalry and in H/10th Cavalry; discharged 5 Dec 1878 at Ft Davis; enlisted 6 Dec 1878 at Ft Davis; served in H/10th Cavalry; discharged 5 Dec 1883, Ft Davis; enlisted 6 Dec 1883, Ft Davis; served in H/10th Cavalry; company clerk; in campaign against Geronimo; discharged San Carlos, AZ, 5 Dec 1888; enlisted for E/24th Infantry, San Carlos, 23 Oct 1889; discharged San Carlos, 17 May 1891, not physically strong enough for continued service; wife Julia Berry of Bellville, TX, born 30 Jul 1868, married Jackson in Albuquerque, NM, 20 May 1901, after divorcing Andrew Smith of Big Spring, TX, at Albuquerque in 1900; resided at Albuquer-

que in 1896–1899, occupation porter, saloonkeeper, city jailor; $6 per month pension 1901 increased to $12 same year and to $14 before he died; collapsed on the street, cardiac arrest, and died in Albuquerque 24 Oct 1902; buried in Fairview Cemetery, Albuquerque; widow Julia owned and operated Seattle Rooming House and Julian Café, Medford, OR, in 1914; continues to apply unsuccessfully for widow's pension up to Nov 1940 when she is 72. SOURCE: Sayre, *Warriors of Color*, 10, 12, 16, 52, 54, 79, 258–326.

Sergeant in H/10th Cavalry stationed at Bonita Cañon Camp, AZ, but absent or on detached service 30 Apr 1886. SOURCE: Tagg, *The Camp at Bonita Cañon*, 231.

‡Honorable mention for services rendered in capture of Mangas and his Apache band, Rio Bonito, AZ, 18 Oct 1886. SOURCE: Baker, Roster.

JACKSON, James; Private; G/10th Cav. ‡Original member of 10th Cavalry; in troop when organized, Ft Leavenworth, KS, 5 Jul 1867. SOURCE: McMiller, "Buffalo Soldiers," 74.

Died 31 Jul 1867 of cholera at Wilson Creek, KS. SOURCE: Regimental Returns, 10th Cavalry, 1867.

JACKSON, James; Private; B/9th Cav. With troop in fight against Victorio, Las Animas Creek, NM, 18 Sep 1879. SOURCE: Schubert, *Black Valor*, 55–56.

JACKSON, James; Private; E/9th Cav. Died 2 Mar 1906; buried at Ft Leavenworth National Cemetery, plot 3450. SOURCE: Ft Leavenworth National Cemetery.

JACKSON, Jason K.; 1st Sgt; C/9th Cav. Sergeant, C/9th Cavalry, at Ft Sill, OK, 1884, replaced Alexander Jones as first sergeant; engaged to Bertha Livingston, a prostitute according to Pvt. George Gibson; had fight with predecessor Sep 1884. SOURCE: Kenner, *Buffalo Soldiers and Officers of the Ninth Cavalry*, 262, 264–67.

Jason J. Jackson, first sergeant, 9th Cavalry, accused by Sgt. Alexander Jones at Ft Sill of bringing "his whore" into the barracks. SOURCE: Dobak and Phillips, *The Black Regulars*, 274.

JACKSON, John; Sergeant; C/9th Cav. ‡Private, C/9th Cavalry; child buried at Ft Robinson, NE, 28 Aug 1886. SOURCE: List of Interments, Ft Robinson.

At Ft Robinson, eighth child of Loseto Ormalus, Ella Jackson, born 27 June 1886, died 28 Aug 1886 of chronic entine colitis; father Pvt. John Jackson, age 47, K/9th Cavalry, Negro; mother, age 34, Mexican. SOURCE: Buecker, Fort Robinson Burials.

‡Appointed sergeant, 22 Aug 1887. SOURCE: Roster, 9 Cav.

‡Killed Artificer Cornelius Donovan, C/8th Infantry, in line of duty as sergeant of guard, Ft Robinson, "greatly

outraged by the most insulting language"; Donovan threatened him and he had to take threat literally; nine years of service in D/9th Cavalry and his officers consider him "thoroughly good and reliable." SOURCE: CO, Ft Robinson, to AAG, DP, 16 and 19 Oct 1891, LS, Ft Robinson.

‡In hands of civil authorities, Omaha, NE, 25 Oct–21 Dec 1891. SOURCE: Regt Returns, 9 Cav.

‡Resided in quarters adjacent to Saddler Sergeant Benjamin, Ft Robinson, 1894. SOURCE: Court Martial Records, Dillon.

‡Ordered from Ft Robinson to Douglas, WY, to receive deserter Myles Smith, D/9th Cavalry, from city marshal. SOURCE: Order 89, 30 Nov 1894, Post Orders, Ft Robinson.

‡At Ft Washakie, WY, 1896.

Appointed sergeant 22 Aug 1887; in D/9th Cavalry at Ft Washakie, Jan 1897. SOURCE: Ninth Cavalry, Roster of NCOs, 1897.

JACKSON, John; Private; 9th Cav. Received Philippine Campaign Badge number 11778 for service as private in F/9th Cavalry; in 9th Cavalry at Ft Leavenworth, KS, Mar 1905. SOURCE: Philippine Campaign Badge list, 29 May 1905.

JACKSON, John H.; Private; 24th Inf. Left Army in 1870, spent rest of his life near Ft Davis, TX, farming and occasionally driving wagons for post quartermaster. SOURCE: Dobak and Phillips, *The Black Regulars*, 268.

JACKSON, John J.; 1st Sgt; C/9th Cav. ‡Captain of Ft Robinson, NE, baseball team. SOURCE: Cleveland *Gazette*, 24 Jul 1886.

‡Sergeant, to open dancing school for enlisted men, Ft Robinson, 1 Dec 1886. SOURCE: Cleveland *Gazette*, 27 Nov 1886.

‡Appointed sergeant, 6 Sep 1892. SOURCE: Roster, 9 Cav.

‡Promoted to first sergeant, Ft Robinson, vice Mason, retired. SOURCE: *ANJ* 32 (11 May 1895): 608.

Appointed first sergeant 26 Apr 1895; in C/9th Cavalry at Ft Robinson, Jan 1897. SOURCE: Ninth Cavalry, Roster of NCOs, 1897.

Awarded certificate of merit for distinguished service in battle, Santiago, Cuba, 1 Jul 1898. SOURCE: Gleim, *The Certificate of Merit*, 45.

‡Awarded certificate of merit for gallantry, Cuba, 1 Jul 1898. SOURCE: GO 15, AGO, 13 Feb 1900; Steward, *The Colored Regulars*, 245; *ANJ* 37 (24 Feb 1900): 611.

‡Shot and killed, Ft Douglas, UT, 8 Aug 1899, by Pvt. W. H. Carter, C/9th Cavalry, who was then chased into Salt Lake City and shot fatally by pursuers. SOURCE: *ANJ* 36 (19 Aug 1899): 1214.

‡Buried at Ft Douglas. SOURCE: Clark, "A History of the Twenty-fourth," appendix A.

JACKSON, Julius; Private; E/25th Inf. Awarded certificate of merit for saving comrade from drowning at risk of own life, Malabang, Mindanao, Philippines, 16 Dec 1907. SOURCE: Gleim, *The Certificate of Merit*, 59.

‡Awarded certificate of merit, 12 Sep 1908, for saving comrade from drowning at risk of own life, Malabang, Mindanao, 16 Dec 1907. SOURCE: GO 134, AGO, 1 Jul 1909.

JACKSON, Lawrence M.; Private; C/8th Ill Inf. Served as private in M/25th Infantry; died 25 Mar 1914; buried in plot WSIDE1354 at San Francisco National Cemetery. SOURCE: San Francisco National Cemetery.

JACKSON, Peter; Private; 10th Cav. Shot and killed by white civilians while taking message from commander from Ft Concho, TX, to San Angelo, TX. SOURCE: Schubert, *Voices of the Buffalo Soldier*, 116.

JACKSON, Peter; Sergeant; G/24th Inf. ‡Awarded certificate of merit for service in Cuban campaign, 1898. SOURCE: Scipio, *Last of the Black Regulars*, 130.

Awarded certificate of merit for distinguished service in battle, Santiago, Cuba, 1 Jul 1898. SOURCE: Gleim, *The Certificate of Merit*, 46.

‡Commended for distinguished service, battle of Santiago, 1 Jul 1898, as corporal; now sergeant; awarded certificate of merit. SOURCE: GO 15, AGO, 13 Feb 1900; Steward, *The Colored Regulars*, 280; *ANJ* 37 (24 Feb 1900): 611.

Born and resided in New York City; received Distinguished Service Medal in lieu of certificate of merit. SOURCE: *American Decorations*, 839

‡Ranked number 67 among expert riflemen with 73 percent, 1904. SOURCE: GO 79, AGO, 1 Jun 1905.

JACKSON, Pettis; Private; B/9th Cav. At Ft DuChesne, UT, 1897, member of troop baseball team. SOURCE: Kenner, *Buffalo Soldiers and Officers of the Ninth Cavalry*, 19.

JACKSON, Richard; M/9th Cav. Born in Virginia; black complexion; cannot read or write, age 25, Jul 1870, at Ft McKavett, TX. SOURCE: Bierschwale, *Fort McKavett*, 99.

JACKSON, Romeo; Private; K/24th Inf. ‡Died of variola in the Philippines. SOURCE: *ANJ* 37 (24 Mar 1900): 707.

Died 9 Mar 1900; buried in plot 261 at San Francisco National Cemetery. SOURCE: San Francisco National Cemetery.

JACKSON, Samuel; Private; Band/10th Cav. Died 30 Apr 1871 of consumption at Ft Sill, OK. SOURCE: Regimental Returns, 10th Cavalry, 1871.

Buried at Camp Douglas, UT. SOURCE: Record Book of Interments, Post Cemetery, 252.

JACKSON, Smith; Sergeant; I/9th Cav. Died at Ft Davis, TX, on 26 Oct 1871; buried at San Antonio National Cemetery, Section I, number 1460. SOURCE: San Antonio National Cemetery Locator.

JACKSON, Squire; Sergeant; B/9th Cav. Died 28 Feb 1901; buried at Santa Fe National Cemetery, NM, plot I 435. SOURCE: Santa Fe National Cemetery, Records of Burials.

JACKSON, Thomas; M/9th Cav. Born in Kentucky; mulatto complexion; cannot read or write, age 24, Jul 1870, at Ft McKavett, TX. SOURCE: Bierschwale, *Fort McKavett,* 99.

JACKSON, Thomas; M/9th Cav. Born in Kentucky; black complexion; cannot read or write, age 25, Jul 1870, at Ft McKavett, TX. SOURCE: Bierschwale, *Fort McKavett,* 99.

JACKSON, Thornton; Corporal; C/24th Inf. Private, E/9th Cavalry, from New England; at Ft Wingate, NM, 1875, brutalized by Capt. Ambrose Hooker for improperly packing Hooker's tent on scout. SOURCE: Kenner, *Buffalo Soldiers and Officers of the Ninth Cavalry,* 105.

Cpl. Thornton Jackson, E/9th Cavalry, forced by Capt. Ambrose Hooker to march dismounted for five days, handcuffed to company wagon, New Mexico, 1879, because Hooker claimed that Jackson had threatened him with a revolver; shot and killed by civilian at Fort Hays, KS, 1882. SOURCE: Dobak and Phillips, *The Black Regulars,* 193, 199.

Corporal, C/24th Infantry, when he died 18 Jan 1882; originally buried at Ft Hays, KS; reburied at Ft Leavenworth National Cemetery, plot H 3378. SOURCE: Ft Leavenworth National Cemetery.

JACKSON, William; Private; Band/10th Cav. Shot with pistol by Corporal Snead, F/10th Cavalry, in personal affray; died 28 Nov 1876 at Ft Griffin, TX. SOURCE: Regimental Returns, 10th Cavalry, 1876.

‡Commander, 10th Cavalry, forwards effects of late Private Jackson to Adjutant General, 30 Jan 1877. SOURCE: ES, 10 Cav, 1872–81.

JACKSON, William; Private; F/48th Inf. Died 9 Nov 1900; buried in plot 864 at San Francisco National Cemetery. SOURCE: San Francisco National Cemetery.

JACKSON, William C.; Private; I/25th Inf. Died 4 Dec 1900; buried in plot 946 at San Francisco National Cemetery. SOURCE: San Francisco National Cemetery.

JACKSON, William J.; D/24th Inf. Born in Ohio; mulatto complexion; can read and write, age 24, Jul 1870, at Ft McKavett, TX. SOURCE: Bierschwale, *Fort McKavett,* 96.

JACKSON, William L.; Private; K/25th Inf. Born in Chester County, PA; Ht 6'0", black complexion; occupation farmer; enlisted in A/39th Infantry for three years on 27 Aug 1867, age 34, at Philadelphia, PA; detached service, Subsistence Department, New Orleans, since 27 Feb 1869; transferred to K/25th Infantry at Jackson Bks, LA, 20 Apr 1869. SOURCE: Descriptive Roll of A/39th Inf.

JACOBS, George; Private; M/9th Cav. Born in Maryland; mulatto complexion; cannot read or write, age 22, at Ft McKavett, TX, Jul 1870; born in Washington, DC; died and buried at Ft McKavett before 17 May 1879; body removed to National Cemetery, San Antonio, TX, 23 Nov 1883. SOURCE: Bierschwale, *Fort McKavett,* 100, 123.

Native of Washington, DC; age 21, in first year of enlistment, when shot and killed trying to escape from guardhouse Dec 1870. SOURCE: Kenner, *Buffalo Soldiers and Officers of the Ninth Cavalry,* 163.

Died at Ft McKavett on 7 Dec 1870; buried at San Antonio National Cemetery, Section E, number 894. SOURCE: San Antonio National Cemetery Locator.

JACOBS, Innocent; Saddler; D/9th Cav. With Captain Dodge at battle at Milk River, CO, 2–10 Oct 1879. SOURCE: Miller, *Hollow Victory,* 167, 206–7.

JAMES, Augustus; Private; I/10th Cav. ‡Original member of 10th Cavalry; in troop when organized, Ft Riley, KS, 15 Aug 1867. SOURCE: McMiller, "Buffalo Soldiers," 76.

Died 18 Feb 1870 of typhoid at Camp Supply, OK. SOURCE: Regimental Returns, 10th Cavalry, 1870.

‡Deceased; commander, I/10th Cavalry, forwards copies of final statement and inventory of his personal effects, Mar 1870. SOURCE: ES, 10 Cav, 1866–71.

JAMES, Charles; Private; 25th Inf. Born in Kent County, MD; Ht 5'5", black hair and brown eyes, brown complexion; occupation laborer; enlisted at age 26, Baltimore, MD, 13 Dec 1886; assigned to G/25th Infantry; arrived Ft Snelling, MN, 1 Apr 1887. SOURCE: Descriptive & Assignment Rolls of Recruits, 25 Inf.

JAMES, Edward; Private; 25th Inf. Born in Richmond, VA; Ht 5'8", brown hair and eyes, yellow complexion; occupation cook; resided Richmond when enlisted at age 21, New York City, 13 Sep 1886; arrived Ft Snelling, MN, 20 Jan 1887. SOURCE: Descriptive & Assignment Rolls of Recruits, 25 Inf.

JAMES, Henry; Recruit; 10th Cav. Unassigned, died 14 Apr 1876 of disease at Ft Concho, TX. SOURCE: Regimental Returns, 10th Cavalry, 1876.

JAMES, Isaac H.; Private; F/9th Cav. ‡Private I. H. James, F/9th Cavalry, killed in action, 12 Jan 1880, on headwaters of Rio Perches. SOURCE: Hamilton, "History of the Ninth Cavalry," 52.

Isaac James, Farrier, F/9th Cavalry, died 15 Apr 1880; originally buried at Ft Stanton, NM; buried at Santa Fe National Cemetery, NM, plot B 560. SOURCE: Santa Fe National Cemetery, Records of Burials.

JAMES, John; Blacksmith; G/9th Cav. Received Cuban Campaign Badge for service as blacksmith in D/9th Cavalry, 22 Jun 1898–13 Aug 1898. SOURCE: Cuban Campaign Badge Recipients.

Received Philippine Campaign Badge number 11815 for service as private G/9th Cavalry, 16 Sep 1900–16 Sep 1902; blacksmith in G/9th Cavalry, Ft Leavenworth, KS, Mar 1905. SOURCE: Philippine Campaign Badge Recipients; Philippine Campaign Badge list, 29 May 1905.

JAMES, Richard; Private; E/10th Cav. In Troop E/10th Cavalry stationed at Bonita Cañon Camp, AZ, but absent or on detached service 28 Feb 1886. SOURCE: Tagg, *The Camp at Bonita Cañon*, 231.

JAMES, Robert; Private; C/49th Inf. ‡Died of dysentery in the Philippines, 3 Jan 1901. SOURCE: *ANJ* 38 (19 Jan 1901): 503.

Died 31 Dec 1900; body received for burial at San Francisco National Cemetery 15 Apr 1902. SOURCE: San Francisco National Cemetery.

JAMES, William; Blacksmith; D/9th Cav. With Captain Dodge at battle at Milk River, CO, 2–10 Oct 1879. SOURCE: Miller, *Hollow Victory*, 167, 206–7.

JAMES, William H.; Private; I/24th Inf. ‡Enlisted Ft D. A. Russell, WY, 13 Feb 1899. SOURCE: Muster Roll, I/24 Inf, Jan–Feb 1899.

‡Fined $.50 by summary court, San Francisco, CA, 22 Apr 1899. SOURCE: Muster Roll, I/24 Inf, Mar–Apr 1899.

‡Fined $2 by summary court, 10 May 1899; fined $3 by summary court, 23 May 1899. SOURCE: Muster Roll, I/24 Inf, May–Jun 1899.

‡Fined one month's pay by summary court, 8 Aug 1899. SOURCE: Muster Roll, I/24 Inf, Jul–Aug 1899.

‡Absent sick in Manila, Philippines, since 11 Oct 1899. SOURCE: Muster Roll, I/24 Inf, Sep–Oct 1899.

‡Captured by insurgents, 10 Oct 1900; killed same day while attempting to escape. *See* OTT, **BURNS**, William J., Corporal, I/24th Infantry

Died 10 Oct 1900; buried in plot 1255 at San Francisco National Cemetery. SOURCE: San Francisco National Cemetery.

JARIMO, Juan; Private; I/10th Cav. Died 12 Jul 1892; originally buried at Ft Wingate, NM; buried at Santa Fe National Cemetery, NM, plot A-2 985. SOURCE: Santa Fe National Cemetery, Records of Burials.

JARRETT, Jacob; D/24th Inf. Born in Tennessee; black complexion; can read, cannot write, age 25, Jul 1870, at Ft McKavett, TX. SOURCE: Bierschwale, *Fort McKavett*, 96.

JASON, William; Private; G/10th Cav. Died 26 Dec 1870 of disease at Ft Dodge, KS. SOURCE: Regimental Returns, 10th Cavalry, 1870.

JEFFERDS, Wesley; Sergeant; A/9th Cav. Three-year Civil War veteran when first enlisted in 9th Cavalry, 1867. SOURCE: Schubert, *Black Valor*, 10.

‡In L/9th Cavalry, on detached service in the field, New Mexico, 21 Jan–24 Feb 1881. SOURCE: Regt Returns, 9 Cav, Feb 1881.

‡In A/9th Cavalry at Ft Niobrara, NE; to be examined for appointment as ordnance sergeant. SOURCE: *ANJ* 26 (3 Aug 1889): 1002.

‡At Ft Niobrara; to be examined for appointment as ordnance sergeant. SOURCE: *ANJ* 27 (23 Aug 1890): 902.

Retires from Ft Robinson, NE, Apr 1892. SOURCE: *ANJ* 29 (30 Apr 1892): 625.

‡Retired as sergeant, A/9th Cavalry, 29 Apr 1892. SOURCE: Roster, 9 Cav.

‡Resided at 306 Third Street, SE, Washington, DC, in 1906; served over ten years with Sgt. Maj. Jeremiah Jones, 9th Cavalry. SOURCE: Affidavit, Jefferds, 19 May 1906, VA File WC 611769, Jeremiah Jones.

Retired Sgt. Wesley Jefferds received Indian Wars Campaign Badge number 1109 on 15 Jan 1909. SOURCE: Carroll, *Indian Wars Campaign Badge*, 32.

‡Age 69; resided at 306 Third Street, SE, Washington, DC, in 1918; knew Sgt. Robert Benjamin personally from 1872 until Benjamin's death. SOURCE: Affidavit, Jefferds, 2 Dec 1918, VA File WC 927337, Robert A. Benjamin.

JEFFERS, David B.; Comsy Sgt; U.S. Army. Born in Indiana; enlisted Cincinnati, OH; sergeant 24th Infantry and regimental quartermaster sergeant 9th Cavalry before appointment as post commissary sergeant. SOURCE: Dobak and Phillips, *The Black Regulars*, 82.

Appointed commissary sergeant 5 Jun 1879, from quartermaster sergeant, 9th Cavalry. SOURCE: Dobak, "Staff Noncommissioned Officers."

‡Appointed commissary sergeant, U.S. Army, 5 Jun 1879. SOURCE: Roster, 9 Cav.

‡One of only two blacks in noncommissioned general staff positions, along with Commissary Sergeant Sullivant, 1879.

‡At Ft McKinney, WY, friend to Chaplain Plummer and Sergeant Benjamin, as quartermaster sergeant, 9th Cavalry; from Angel Island, CA, 1894, wrote threatening letter to Mrs. Robert Benjamin, warning against testimony about Plummer; former quartermaster sergeant, 9th Cavalry, Ft McKinney. SOURCE: Court Martial Records, Plummer.

‡Retires from Ft Custer, MT. SOURCE: ANJ 34 (22 May 1897): 705.

‡To report as second lieutenant, 48th Infantry, to Ft Thomas, KY. SOURCE: ANJ 37 (30 Sep 1899): 101.

‡First lieutenant, E/48th Infantry, and veteran of thirty years. SOURCE: San Francisco Chronicle, 15 Nov 1899.

Retired post commissary sergeant, received Indian Wars Campaign Badge number 1498 on 6 Dec 1911. SOURCE: Carroll, Indian Wars Campaign Badge, 43.

JEFFERSON, Charles W.; Sergeant; B/9th Cav. ‡Enlisted in 9th Cavalry, 23 May 1890; corporal, G/9th Cavalry, 1 Jan 1895; discharged 23 May 1895; reenlisted in B/9th Cavalry, 28 May 1895, promoted to corporal, sergeant, first sergeant; discharged 27 May 1898; reenlisted 28 May 1898; discharged 3 Feb 1899; reenlisted 4 Feb 1899; appointed captain, 49th Infantry, 9 Sep 1899; resigned in accordance with Special Order 226, Adjutant General's Office, Oct 1900. SOURCE: Descriptive Book, A/49 Inf.

‡At Ft Robinson, NE, 1893, refused to serve meal to prisoner Diggs in guardhouse; told by First Sergeant Goodloe, "Any of you men that don't want to carry this man's meals don't have to, but hereafter you had better walk the chalk." Testimony of Sgt. Arthur E. Ransom. SOURCE: Court Martial Records, McKay.

‡Lance corporal, B/9th Cavalry, conducted deserter Hiram Tolmatier, H/8th Infantry, from Ft Robinson to Ft D. A. Russell, WY. SOURCE: Order 9, 10 Feb 1895, Post Orders, Ft Robinson.

‡Lance corporal, promoted to corporal, Ft Robinson, 11 Feb 1895. SOURCE: ANJ 32 (9 Mar 1895): 434.

‡Corporal, G/9th Cavalry, discharged May 1895. SOURCE: ANJ 32 (8 Jun 1895): 674.

‡Promoted from private to corporal, B/9th Cavalry, Ft DuChesne, UT, Nov 1895. SOURCE: ANJ 33 (7 Dec 1895): 236.

Appointed corporal 27 Nov 1895; in B/9th Cavalry at Ft DuChesne, Jan 1897. SOURCE: Ninth Cavalry, Roster of NCOs, 1897.

‡Wounded in action, El Caney, Cuba, 1898; recommended for certificate of merit by troop and squadron commanders. SOURCE: Cashin, Under Fire with the Tenth Cavalry, 116–17; Illustrated Review: Ninth Cavalry.

‡Commended and awarded certificate of merit for distinguished service, battle of Santiago, Cuba, as first ser-

geant, B/9th Cavalry. SOURCE: GO 15, AGO, 13 Feb 1900; Steward, The Colored Regulars, 280; ANJ 37 (9 Dec 1899): 345.

‡Promoted to captain, 49th Infantry. SOURCE: ANJ 37 (9 Dec 1899): 345.

‡Mentioned as captain, A/49th Infantry. SOURCE: Beasley, Negro Trailblazers, 284.

As first sergeant, B/9th Cavalry, awarded certificate of merit for distinguished service in battle, Santiago, 1 Jul 1898. SOURCE: Gleim, The Certificate of Merit, 47.

In B/9th Cavalry, received Indian Wars Campaign Badge number 580 on 28 Sep 1908. SOURCE: Carroll, Indian Wars Campaign Badge, 16.

‡Veteran of Indian wars, Spanish-American War, and Philippine Insurrection; expert rifleman; sergeant, B/9th Cavalry, at Ft D. A. Russell in 1910. SOURCE: Illustrated Review: Ninth Cavalry, with picture.

JEFFERSON, Curley; Private; U.S. Army. Born at Ft Clark, TX; enlisted at Ft Clark 13 Aug 1908, age 26; Ht 5'7", black hair, brown eyes, black complexion; discharged 14 Aug 1911, reenlisted 14 Aug 1911 at Ft Clark; honorably discharged 31 Jul 1914. SOURCE: Swanson, 21.

Born in 1881. SOURCE: Porter, The Negro on the American Frontier, 474.

Seminole Negro Scout, served 1908–1914. SOURCE: Schubert, Consolidated List of Seminole Negro Scouts.

Born 18 Jan 1881 at Ft Clark; died 25 Jul 1959; buried at Seminole Indian Scout Cemetery, Kinney County, TX. SOURCE: Indian Scout Cemetery, Kinney County, Texas.

JEFFERSON, John; 1st Sgt; C/10th Cav. Born at Ft Clark, TX; enlisted at Ft Clark 16 May 1905, age 28; Ht 5'10", black hair and eyes, black complexion; discharged 15 May 1908, reenlisted next day at Ft Clark; discharged 15 May 1911, reenlisted same day at Ft Clark for three years; discharged 15 May 1914; enlistments frozen pending termination of Seminole Scouts 31 June 1914; 1908 photograph, A. No. 603, of John Jefferson in Old Guardhouse Museum, Brackettville, TX. SOURCE: Swanson, 21.

Private, U.S. Army, Seminole Negro Scout, served 1905–14; son of Scout Joe Coon and grandson of Chief John Horse. SOURCE: Schubert, Consolidated List of Seminole Negro Scouts.

Born 1879; after service as Scout joined 10th Cavalry; resided in Del Rio, TX, 1941. SOURCE: Porter, The Negro on the American Frontier, 474.

Born 30 Sep 1878; first sergeant, C/10th Cavalry; died 5 Sep 1954; buried at Seminole Indian Scout Cemetery, Kinney County, TX. SOURCE: Indian Scout Cemetery, Kinney County, Texas.

JEFFERSON, John D.; Corporal; E/25th Inf. Died 5 Jul 1902; buried in plot SEC N765 at San Francisco National Cemetery. SOURCE: San Francisco National Cemetery.

JEFFERSON, Sam; Private; U.S. Army. Born in Mexico; enlisted at Ft Clark, TX, 30 Apr 1894, age 26; Ht 5'5", black hair and eyes, black complexion; discharged at Ft Ringgold, TX, 29 Oct 1894. SOURCE: Swanson, 21.

Seminole Negro Scout, served 1894. SOURCE: Schubert, Consolidated List of Seminole Negro Scouts.

Born about 1868, died 14 Jul 1914; buried at Seminole Indian Scout Cemetery, Kinney County, TX. SOURCE: Indian Scout Cemetery, Kinney County, Texas.

JEFFERSON, William; Sergeant; M/10th Cav. ‡Original member of 10th Cavalry; in troop when organized, Ft Riley, KS, 15 Oct 1867. SOURCE: McMiller, "Buffalo Soldiers," 79.

Drowned 31 Aug 1869 at Canadian River, OK. SOURCE: Regimental Returns, 10th Cavalry, 1869.

‡Commander of M/10th Cavalry reports incomplete company records so cannot furnish final statement regarding Jefferson as casualty. SOURCE: ES, 10 Cav, 1866–71.

JEFFREY, Albert; Private; K/25th Inf. Born in Iberville, LA; Ht 5'8", black complexion; occupation soldier; enlisted in A/39th Infantry for three years on 29 Aug 1866, age 21, at Ft St. Philip, LA; transferred to K/25th Infantry at Jackson Bks, LA, 20 Apr 1869. SOURCE: Descriptive Roll of A/39th Inf.

Pvt. Albert Jeffrey, A/39th Infantry, Civil War veteran, served in D/10th Heavy Artillery; sentence of five years for involvement in New Iberia, LA, mutiny, Jul 1867, overturned. SOURCE: Dobak and Phillips, *The Black Regulars*, 222.

JENIFER, Henry; Private; 9th Cav. Previously discharged from 40th Infantry with chronic syphilis, Apr 1869, but managed to enlist in 9th Cavalry five months later. SOURCE: Dobak and Phillips, *The Black Regulars*, 65.

JENIFER, William; Sergeant; K/9th Cav. Enlisted in Washington, DC, for K/9th Cavalry, Oct 1869, with prior infantry experience. SOURCE: Kenner, *Buffalo Soldiers and Officers of the Ninth Cavalry*, 335.

‡Admitted to Soldiers Home with disability at age 39 with sixteen years and five months' service, 16 Jun 1886. SOURCE: SecWar, *AR 1886*, 738.

JENKINS, Adam; C/25th Inf. Born in Alabama; mulatto complexion; cannot read or write, age 26, 5 Sep 1870, at Ft McKavett, TX. SOURCE: Bierschwale, *Fort McKavett,* 109.

JENKINS, Daniel; Private; A/9th Cav. Died 31 Dec 1889; originally buried at Ft Niobrara, NE; reburied at Ft Leavenworth National Cemetery, plot 3568. SOURCE: Ft Leavenworth National Cemetery.

JENKINS, Filmen; Private; A/10th Cav. Died 6 Feb 1867; buried at Ft Leavenworth National Cemetery, plot C 726. SOURCE: Ft Leavenworth National Cemetery.

JENKINS, Frank; QM Sgt; D/25th Inf. Received as quartermaster sergeant Indian Wars Campaign Badge number 1609 on 27 Oct 1910. SOURCE: Carroll, *Indian Wars Campaign Badge*, 46.

JENKINS, Jerry; Private; 24th Inf. Discharged at end of enlistment in 1870, tried civilian life, decided to enlist again. SOURCE: Dobak and Phillips, *The Black Regulars*, 23.

JENKINS, Jerry A.; C/25th Inf. Born in Tennessee; black complexion; can read and write, age 22, 5 Sep 1870, at Ft McKavett, TX. SOURCE: Bierschwale, *Fort McKavett,* 108.

JENKINS, Tillman; Recruit; 10th Cav. Unassigned, died 4 Feb 1867 of pneumonia at Ft Leavenworth, KS. SOURCE: Regimental Returns, 10th Cavalry, 1867.

Tillmon Jenkins, recruit from Jefferson Bks, MO, died in Ft Leavenworth hospital shortly after arrival on post, early 1867. SOURCE: McMiller, "Buffalo Soldiers," 52.

JENKINS, William; Sergeant; F/9th Cav. ‡Wagoner, Ft Robinson, NE, 1891.

‡Served 1894. *See* OTT, **DILLON**, David R., Sergeant, Band/9th Cavalry

Promoted from lance corporal to corporal. SOURCE: *ANJ* 34 (21 Nov 1896): 196.

Appointed corporal 14 Nov 1896; corporal in F/9th Cavalry at Ft DuChesne, UT, Jan 1897. SOURCE: Ninth Cavalry, Roster of NCOs, 1897.

Received Philippine Campaign Badge number 11780 for service as quartermaster sergeant in F/9th Cavalry; in 9th Cavalry at Ft Leavenworth, KS, Mar 1905. SOURCE: Philippine Campaign Badge list, 29 May 1905.

Sergeant, F/9th Cavalry, received Indian Wars Campaign Badge number 1370 on 1 Jun 1909. SOURCE: Carroll, *Indian Wars Campaign Badge*, 39.

JENNINGS, Oliver; Private; K/10th Cav. ‡Original member of 10th Cavalry; in troop when organized, Ft Riley, KS, 1 Sep 1867. SOURCE: McMiller, "Buffalo Soldiers," 77.

‡Died 24 Jan 1869 on San Francisco Creek, Indian Territory, of wounds inflicted 23 Jan 1869. SOURCE: Baker, Roster.

Died 24 Jan 1869; killed in action, San Francisco Creek, Indian Territory. SOURCE: Regimental Returns, 10th Cavalry, 1869.

JENNISON, Perry; Private; L/10th Cav. ‡Original member of 10th Cavalry; in troop when organized, Ft Riley, KS, 21 Sep 1867. SOURCE: McMiller, "Buffalo Soldiers," 78.

Died 19 Sep 1868 of hemorrhage at Ft Arbuckle, OK. SOURCE: Regimental Returns, 10th Cavalry, 1868.

JENNY, John; Sergeant; B/9th Cavalry. 1st Sgt. David Badie badgered and provoked soldiers who reported to him, including Sgt. John Jenny, who was convicted of insubordination, fined, and reduced, 1884, with sentence remitted. SOURCE: Kenner, *Buffalo Soldiers and Officers of the Ninth Cavalry*, 48–49, 231.

JEWEL, Brady; Private; U.S. Army. *See* **BRADY,** Jewel, Private, U.S. Army

JINKINS, Joseph; Private; H/9th Cav. ‡Died of cholera in the Philippines, 8 Jun 1902. SOURCE: *ANJ* 39 (9 Aug 1902): 1248.

Died 8 Jun 1902 in the Philippines; buried in plot N ADD795 at San Francisco National Cemetery. SOURCE: San Francisco National Cemetery.

JOHNS, Alfred; Private; G/10th Cav. *See* OTT, JOHNSON, Alfred, Private, G/10th Cavalry

JOHNS, Joseph; Private; D/9th Cav. With Captain Dodge at battle at Milk River, CO, 2–10 Oct 1879. SOURCE: Miller, *Hollow Victory*, 167, 206–7.

JOHNSON, Alfred; Private; G/10th Cav. ‡Died of disease, Ft Griffin, TX, 2 Dec 1874. SOURCE: CO, 10 Cav, to AG, USA, 19 Dec 1874, LS, 10 Cav, 1873–83.

Pvt. Alfred Johns, G/10th Cavalry, died at Ft Concho, TX, on 2 Dec 1874; buried at San Antonio National Cemetery, Section D, number 699. SOURCE: San Antonio National Cemetery Locator.

JOHNSON, Alfred; Private; I/10th Cav. In Troop I/10th Cavalry stationed at Bonita Cañon Camp, AZ, but absent or on detached service 30 Jun 1886. SOURCE: Tagg, *The Camp at Bonita Cañon*, 231.

JOHNSON, Benjamin; Private; 25th Inf. Born in Smyrna, DE; Ht 5'7", black hair and brown eyes, brown complexion; occupation teamster; enlisted at age 25, Philadelphia, PA, 9 Apr 1886; arrived Ft Snelling, MN, 19 Aug 1886. SOURCE: Descriptive & Assignment Rolls of Recruits, 25 Inf.

JOHNSON, Beverly; M/9th Cav. Born in Kentucky; mulatto complexion; can read and write, age 30, Jul 1870, at Ft McKavett, TX. SOURCE: Bierschwale, *Fort McKavett,* 98.

JOHNSON, Bushrod; Sergeant; G/9th Cav. ‡Sgt. Bush Johnson left in charge of unit garden and property by Lt. Patrick Cusack when unit departed for field duty, Sep 1881.

SOURCE: Billington, *New Mexico's Buffalo Soldiers*, 114–15.

‡Killed by horse thief, Aug 1882. *See* **GRUNKE,** Washington, Private, 9th Cavalry

Killed along with Private Washington Grimke, Jul 1882, by horse thief they were escorting to Ft Sill, OK. SOURCE: Kenner, *Buffalo Soldiers and Officers of the Ninth Cavalry*, 22.

JOHNSON, Carter; Private; G/9th Cav. Died at Ft Davis, TX, on 12 Feb 1879; buried at San Antonio National Cemetery, Section D, number 767. SOURCE: San Antonio National Cemetery Locator.

JOHNSON, Charles; D/24th Inf. Born in Pennsylvania; black complexion; can read and write, age 30, Jul 1870, at Ft McKavett, TX. SOURCE: Bierschwale, *Fort McKavett,* 95.

JOHNSON, Charles; M/9th Cav. Born in Virginia; black complexion; cannot read or write, age 28, Jul 1870, at Ft McKavett, TX. SOURCE: Bierschwale, *Fort McKavett,* 100.

JOHNSON, Charles; Trumpeter; G/9th Cav. Served with troop at Ft Garland, CO, 1877. SOURCE: Kenner, *Buffalo Soldiers and Officers of the Ninth Cavalry*, 218.

‡One of six enlisted men of G/9th Cavalry to testify against Lt. John Conline at his 1877 court martial for misconduct, including drunkenness, sexual misconduct, and misappropriation of funds belonging to men of his troop, Ft Garland. SOURCE: Billington, *New Mexico's Buffalo Soldiers*, 121–23.

JOHNSON, Charles; Private; C/9th Cav. Resident of Baltimore, MD, before enlistment; died 13 Apr 1886, age 27, of acute double pneumonia in hospital at Ft Robinson, NE; funeral at Ft Robinson 14 Apr 1886. SOURCE: Buecker, Fort Robinson Burials.

‡Buried at Ft Robinson, 13 Apr 1886. SOURCE: List of Interments, Ft Robinson.

JOHNSON, Charles; Private; 25th Inf. Born in Harrodsburg, KY; Ht 5'8", black hair and eyes, black complexion; occupation blacksmith; enlisted at age 31, Columbus Bks, OH, 31 Dec 1881. SOURCE: Descriptive & Assignment Rolls of Recruits, 25 Inf.

JOHNSON, Charles; Private; H/10th Cav. Died 28 Mar 1889; buried 15 Mar 1952 at Santa Fe National Cemetery, NM, plot P 63. SOURCE: Santa Fe National Cemetery, Records of Burials.

JOHNSON, Charles; Private; B/24th Inf. Buried 29 Mar 1912, section B, row E, plot 40, at Ft Bayard, NM.

SOURCE: Erickson, Burials at Fort Bayard National Cemetery, NM.

JOHNSON, Dan; Private; U.S. Army. Seminole Negro Scout, served 1872–75. SOURCE: Schubert, Consolidated List of Seminole Negro Scouts.

Born in Florida; former slave of a Seminole in Florida; enlisted at Ft Duncan, TX, 1 Dec 1872, age 45; Ht 5'9", black hair and eyes, black complexion; discharged at Ft Duncan, 1 Jun 1873; enlisted 11 Oct 1873 at Ft Clark, TX, where discharged 1 Apr 1874. SOURCE: Swanson, 22.

JOHNSON, Daniel; Sergeant; K/40th Inf. Enlisted in New York City, 1867, listed occupation as "orator." SOURCE: Dobak and Phillips, *The Black Regulars*, 24.

JOHNSON, Daniel; Private; U.S. Army. Seminole Negro Scout, served 1872–74, 1876. SOURCE: Schubert, Consolidated List of Seminole Negro Scouts.

Born in Mexico; enlisted at Ft Duncan, TX, 2 Aug 1872, age 21; Ht 5'11", black hair and eyes, black complexion; discharged 8 Feb 1873, reenlisted 1 May 1873 at Ft Duncan; discharged 1 Jan 1874 at Camp Comanche, TX; enlisted 5 Jan 1874, discharged 5 Jul 1874 at Ft Duncan; enlisted 31 Mar 1876, age 20, at Ft Duncan; discharged at Ft Clark, TX, 31 Aug 1876; restrained from shooting Caesar Payne 15 Sep 1876; threatened Lieutenant Bullis with carbine 15 Oct 1876, arrested and jailed next day; jailed with Benjamin Wilson 15 Nov 1876. SOURCE: Swanson, 22.

Wounded in same barroom gun battle in which Cpl. George Washington was killed, Eagle Pass, TX, 1875. SOURCE: Porter, *The Negro on the American Frontier*, 485. *See* **WASHINGTON,** George, Private, U.S. Army

JOHNSON, David; Private; C/9th Cav. Died at Ft Davis, TX, on 14 May 1868; buried at San Antonio National Cemetery, Section I, number 1555. SOURCE: San Antonio National Cemetery Locator.

JOHNSON, Dennis; Private; G/9th Cav. Died 8 Mar 1912; buried in plot W SID364 at San Francisco National Cemetery. SOURCE: San Francisco National Cemetery.

JOHNSON, Dorsey; Private; H/10th Cav. Died at Ft Davis, TX, on 5 Mar 1883; buried at San Antonio National Cemetery, Section I, number 1463. SOURCE: San Antonio National Cemetery Locator.

JOHNSON, E.; Private; C/9th Cav. Died 25 Dec 1878; buried at Ft Bayard, NM, in plot B 5. SOURCE: "Fort Bayard National Cemetery, Records of Burials."

Buried 9 Sep 1897, section A, row F, plot 44 at Ft Bayard. SOURCE: Erickson, Burials at Fort Bayard National Cemetery, NM.

JOHNSON, Edward; Private; F/10th Cav. ‡Original member of 10th Cavalry; in troop when organized, Ft Leavenworth, KS, 21 Jun 1867. SOURCE: McMiller, "Buffalo Soldiers," 73.

Died 1 Aug 1867 of cholera at Ft Hays, KS. SOURCE: Regimental Returns, 10th Cavalry, 1867.

Buried at Ft Leavenworth National Cemetery, plot 3277. SOURCE: Ft Leavenworth National Cemetery.

JOHNSON, Elias; Musician; F/25th Inf. One of twenty men who cycled 1,900 miles from Ft Missoula, MT, to St. Louis, MO, 14 Jun–24 Jul 1897, in 25th Infantry Bicycle Corps to test durability and practicality of bicycles as a means of transportation for troops. SOURCE: File 60178, GC, AGO Records.

JOHNSON, Frank L.; Private; B/25th Inf. Private, B/25th Infantry, rode in 25th Infantry Bicycle Corps, Ft. Missoula, MT, summer 1896. SOURCE: Sorenson, List of Buffalo Soldiers Who Rode in the 25th Infantry Bicycle Corps, in authors' files.

One of twenty men who cycled 1,900 miles from Ft Missoula to St. Louis, MO, 14 Jun–24 Jul 1897, in 25th Infantry Bicycle Corps to test durability and practicality of bicycles as a means of transportation for troops. SOURCE: File 60178, GC, AGO Records.

JOHNSON, Freeman; Private; Band/25th Inf. Died 1 Nov 1906; buried at Ft Bayard, NM, in plot O 27. SOURCE: "Fort Bayard National Cemetery, Records of Burials."

Johnson Freeman, Private, Band/25th Infantry, buried at Ft Bayard. SOURCE: "Buffalo Soldiers Buried at Ft Bayard, NM."

Buried 11 Nov 1906, section A, row w, plot 27, at Ft Bayard. SOURCE: Erickson, Burials at Fort Bayard National Cemetery, NM.

JOHNSON, George; Private; 9th Cav. When he enlisted in 1867 he was unable to sign his name; during fifth enlistment transferred to Hospital Corps. SOURCE: Dobak and Phillips, *The Black Regulars*, 81.

JOHNSON, George; Private; H/10th Cav. Died 18 Jul 1872 of disease at Ft Sill, OK. SOURCE: Regimental Returns, 10th Cavalry, 1872.

JOHNSON, George; Corporal; Band/10th Cav. ‡Private, served in 10th Cavalry, 1898; remained in U.S. during war with Spain. SOURCE: Cashin, *Under Fire with the Tenth Cavalry*, 359.

Died 26 Jun 1902 of chronic nephritis, chronic uremia, general arteriosclerosis disease contracted in line of duty, at Ft Robinson, NE. SOURCE: Buecker, Fort Robinson Burials.

‡Died at Ft Robinson, Jun 1902; buried, Ft Robinson, 26 Jun 1902. SOURCE: Medical History, Ft Robinson; List of Interments, Ft Robinson.

JOHNSON, George H.; 1st Sgt; H/9th Cav. ‡Sergeant since 1 Jul 1880; first sergeant since 17 Jul 1881. SOURCE: Roster, 9 Cav.

‡Authorized five-month furlough. SOURCE: *ANJ* 25 (14 Jul 1888): 1014.

Appointed first sergeant 17 Jan 1881; in H/9th Cavalry at Ft Robinson, NE, Jan 1897. SOURCE: Ninth Cavalry, Roster of NCOs, 1897.

JOHNSON, George S.; Private; B/9th Cav. Died 26 Mar 1904; buried at Post Cemetery, Presidio of Monterey: Section I, number 1; originally buried in Alabama. SOURCE: Post Cemetery Record Book.

JOHNSON, Green; Private; C/10th Cav. ‡Original member of 10th Cavalry; in troop when organized, Ft Leavenworth, KS, 14 May 1867. SOURCE: McMiller, "Buffalo Soldiers," 70.

Served with Pvt. George Washington, C/10th Cavalry, early 1870s; deceased before Dec 1905. SOURCE: Schubert, *Voice of the Buffalo Soldier*, 234.

JOHNSON, Harry; Private; B/9th Cav. Buried at Santa Fe National Cemetery, NM, plot A-1 762. SOURCE: Santa Fe National Cemetery, Records of Burials.

JOHNSON, Harry; Private; L/9th Cav. Died at Ft Stockton, TX, on 2 Mar 1883; buried at San Antonio National Cemetery, Section C, number 339. SOURCE: San Antonio National Cemetery Locator.

JOHNSON, Henry; Private; E/9th Cav. One of ten soldiers charged with mutiny and desertion for role in mutiny at San Pedro Springs, near San Antonio, TX, April 1867; pled guilty to desertion but not mutiny; mutiny charge dropped; convicted of desertion and sentenced to six months' confinement at military prison, Ship's Island, MS; sentence remitted before transported to prison. SOURCE: Dobak and Phillips, *The Black Regulars*, 208–11.

JOHNSON, Henry; F/9th Cav. Born in Tennessee; black complexion; cannot read or write, age 29, Jul 1870, at Ft McKavett, TX. SOURCE: Bierschwale, *Fort McKavett,* 98.

JOHNSON, Henry; Private; 25th Inf. Discharged for drunkenness 1874, stayed with company as cook without pay, asked to be allowed to enlist again, and permitted to do so. SOURCE: Dobak and Phillips, *The Black Regulars*, 166.

JOHNSON, Henry; Private; 10th Cav. After discharge at Ft Sill, OK, found employment with Quartermaster Depart-

ment. SOURCE: Dobak and Phillips, *The Black Regulars*, 334.

JOHNSON, Henry; Private; G/10th Cav. Died 30 Sep 1885; buried at Santa Fe National Cemetery, NM, plot A-1 785. SOURCE: Santa Fe National Cemetery, Records of Burials.

JOHNSON, Henry; Private; K/9th Cav. Born in Boynton, VA; as 21-year-old laborer enlisted in 1867; with Captain Dodge at battle at Milk River, CO, 2–10 Oct 1879; awarded Medal of Honor 22 Sep 1890 for bravery at Milk River; retired 1898 and settled in Washington, DC; died 1905 and buried in Arlington National Cemetery. SOURCE: Miller, *Hollow Victory*, 100, 167, 183, 114 with picture, 183, 206–7.

Life, career, and bravery at battle at Milk River against Utes, Oct 1879, for which he received Medal of Honor, narrated. SOURCE: Schubert, *Black Valor*, 61–71, 117–18.

Enlisted in Baltimore; service at Milk River in 1879 mentioned. SOURCE: Kinevan, *Frontier Cavalryman*, 224, 233.

‡Enlisted Baltimore, MD, Jun 1877; Medal of Honor awarded at Ft Robinson, NE, 1890. SOURCE: Lee, *Negro Medal of Honor Men*, 68–71.

‡Born in Boynton, VA; awarded Medal of Honor for distinguished service, Milk River, Sep 1879. SOURCE: Carroll, *The Black Military Experience*, 386.

Spoke at grand reception given by citizens of Denver, CO, at YMCA hall, Oct 1879, after coming to aid of troops ambushed on Milk River by Utes, Sep 1879; became drunk, threatened to shoot Mexican woman, fined $10 per month for three months, Feb 1881. SOURCE: Kenner, *Buffalo Soldiers and Officers of the Ninth Cavalry*, 69–70, 271.

‡Sergeant, D/9th Cavalry, when awarded Medal of Honor. SOURCE: Leckie, *The Buffalo Soldiers*, 208.

‡Reduced from sergeant, K/9th Cavalry, to private for abusive language to bartender, post canteen, Ft Robinson, when told he could have no more beer. SOURCE: *ANJ* 27 (28 Dec 1889): 352.

‡Private, K/9th Cavalry, authorized to wear knot in lieu of Medal of Honor, by letter, Adjutant General's Office, 7 Sep 1897.

‡Reported to Ft Robinson from furlough, Jul 1898; retired and went home to Washington, DC, 29 Aug 1898, in accordance with telegram, Adjutant General's Office, 29 Jul 1898.

‡Retires to his home, Washington, DC, from Ft Robinson, as private, K/9th Cavalry. SOURCE: *ANJ* 35 (6 Aug 1898): 1007; SO 112, 29 Aug 1898, Post Orders, Ft Robinson.

JOHNSON, Henry; Private; H/10th Cav. Served in first half of 1880s. SOURCE: Sayre, *Warriors of Color*, 219.

JOHNSON, Henry; Private; H/10th Cav. Born and raised in Alexandria, LA; enlisted Little Rock, AR, 9 May 1899; discharged three years later, Ilo, Philippines; tailor, post office address 812 5th St., Alexandria, but lives in unnumbered house on lower Third Street, age 56, in 1929. SOURCE: Sayre, *Warriors of Color*, 222.

JOHNSON, Horace; Sergeant; M/9th Cav. Born in Louisiana; black complexion; cannot read or write, age 29, Jul 1870, in M/9th Cavalry at Ft McKavett, TX. SOURCE: Bierschwale, *Fort McKavett*, 99.

‡Sergeant stationed in M/9th Cavalry at Ft McKavett, 1872–73. *See* **STANCE**, Emanuel, First Sergeant, F/9th Cavalry

Sergeant, F/9th Cavalry, 1872–73. SOURCE: Kenner, *Buffalo Soldiers and Officers of the Ninth Cavalry*, 338.

JOHNSON, Horace; Private; G/10th Cav. Died 10 or 11 Mar 1889; originally buried at Ft Grant, AZ; buried at Santa Fe National Cemetery, NM, plot A-1 778. SOURCE: Santa Fe National Cemetery, Records of Burials.

JOHNSON, Isaiah; Private; I/9th Cav. Pvt. Isaiah Johnson, 24th Infantry, enlisted in 9th Cavalry 1884, unable to write his name; reenlisted in 24th Infantry 1889, from Hospital Corps, could sign his name shakily. SOURCE: Dobak and Phillips, *The Black Regulars*, 81.

‡Private, C/9th Cavalry, Ft Robinson, NE, 1886.

‡Transferred to Hospital Corps, Ft Robinson, Oct 1887.

Private, L/9th Cavalry, Ft Leavenworth, KS, transferred to Hospital Corps and assigned to Ft Missoula, MT. SOURCE: *ANJ* 26 (17 Nov 1888): 226.

Appointed corporal 2 May 1896; in I/9th Cavalry at Ft Washakie, WY, Jan 1897. SOURCE: Ninth Cavalry, Roster of NCOs, 1897.

‡Private, F/9th Cavalry, being tried by general court martial, Ft DuChesne, UT, with Lt. H. A. Barker, 9th Cavalry, as his counsel. SOURCE: *ANJ* 35 (22 Jan 1898): 382.

‡Private, I/9th Cavalry, in hands of civil authorities, Cheyenne, WY, 30 Aug 1897–23 Feb 1898; sentenced to ten years in Wyoming State Penitentiary, Laramie. SOURCE: Regt Returns, 9 Cav.

JOHNSON, James; Artificer; K/25th Inf. Born in Richmond, VA; Ht 5'8", bright complexion; occupation carpenter; enlisted in A/39th Infantry for three years on 1 Nov 1867, age 21, at Richmond; appointed artificer 1 Jan 1868; transferred to K/25th Infantry at Jackson Bks, LA, 20 Apr 1869. SOURCE: Descriptive Roll of A/39th Inf.

JOHNSON, James; Private; I/9th Cav. Died at Ft Davis, TX, on 17 Sep 1883; buried at San Antonio National Cemetery, Section I, number 1552. SOURCE: San Antonio National Cemetery Locator.

JOHNSON, James; Private; B/25th Inf. Born in Jackson, MS; Ht 5'5", brown hair and eyes, black complexion; occupation cook; enlisted at age 22, New York City, 9 Dec 1886; assigned to B/25th Infantry; arrived Ft Snelling, MN, 1 Apr 1887. SOURCE: Descriptive & Assignment Rolls of Recruits, 25 Inf.

JOHNSON, James; Private; B/25th Inf. Enlisted 21 Mar 1901, discharged as private B/25th Infantry 20 Mar 1904, character good; reenlisted 21 Mar 1904, discharged without honor 22 Nov 1906, Brownsville, TX. SOURCE: Powell, "Military Record of the Enlisted Men Who Were Discharged Without Honor."

‡Dishonorable discharge, Brownsville. SOURCE: SO 266, AGO, 9 Nov 1906.

JOHNSON, James E.; Private; E/10th Cav. ‡Original member of 10th Cavalry; in troop when organized, Ft Leavenworth, KS, 15 Jun 1867. SOURCE: McMiller, "Buffalo Soldiers," 72.

Died 29 Oct 1869 in hospital at Ft Sill, OK. SOURCE: Regimental Returns, 10th Cavalry, 1869.

Died 29 Oct 1869; buried at Camp Douglas, UT. SOURCE: Record Book of Interments, Post Cemetery, 252.

JOHNSON, James G.; Private; F/24th Inf. ‡Pvt. J. E. Johnson, 24th Infantry, drowned crossing San Mateo River, Philippines, 21 Aug 1899. SOURCE: Richmond *Planet*, 2 Sep 1899.

Pvt. James G. Johnson, F/24th Infantry, died 21 Aug 1899; buried in plot ES 560 at San Francisco National Cemetery. SOURCE: San Francisco National Cemetery.

JOHNSON, James O.; Private; A/10th Cav. Died on 19 Sep 1895; buried at San Antonio National Cemetery, Section I, number 1615. SOURCE: San Antonio National Cemetery Locator.

JOHNSON, John; Private; L/9th Cav. Born in Virginia; in mid-30s when killed 30 Sep 1879 in action with Pvt. Major Woodard, L/9th Cavalry, Cuchillo Negro Canyon, NM, where he was buried. SOURCE: Kenner, *Buffalo Soldiers and Officers of the Ninth Cavalry*, 188.

‡Private Johnson killed in action, Mimbres Mountains, New Mexico, along with Private Woodward, 30 Sep 1879. SOURCE: Hamilton, "History of the Ninth Cavalry," 47; *Illustrated Review: Ninth Cavalry*.

One of two troopers killed in action against Apaches, Mimbres Mountains, 30 Sep 1879. SOURCE: Schubert, *Black Valor*, 57.

Died 30 Sep 1879; killed by Indians near New Mexico, buried 14 Oct 1891 at Ft Bayard, NM, in plot Y 36. SOURCE: "Fort Bayard National Cemetery, Records of Burials."

Buried 30 Sep 1879, section A, row M, plot 39 at Ft Bayard, NM. SOURCE: Erickson, Burials at Fort Bayard National Cemetery, NM.

JOHNSON, John A.; Sergeant; K/10th Cav. Died 7 Oct 1908; buried in plot N ADD1352 at San Francisco National Cemetery. SOURCE: San Francisco National Cemetery.

JOHNSON, John H.; Corporal; H/24th Inf. ‡At Ft Grant, AZ, 1890, he and comrades Cpl. O. R. Lawrence, Sgt. J. Holden, Pvts. William Richardson, Charles H. Thompson, Albert Steed, John C. Perkins, and others, bought casket for burial of Sgt. Edward Berry, H/24th Infantry, because they were dissatisfied with casket provided by government. SOURCE: Cleveland *Gazette*, 26 Apr 1890.

Sergeant, H/24th Infantry, commanded pallbearers at funeral for Sgt. Edward Berry, H/24th Infantry, at Ft Grant, Apr 1890. SOURCE: Cleveland *Gazette*, 26 Apr 1890.

‡Gave speech at picnic of E/24th Infantry band, Ft Grant, Jun 1890. SOURCE: Cleveland *Gazette*, 28 Jun 1890.

Acquitted of neglect of duty, Ft Bayard, NM. SOURCE: *ANJ* 28 (3 Jan 1891): 313.

‡Enlisted Ft Bayard, 10 Jul 1896, with ten years' continuous service; promoted from private to corporal, Tampa, FL, 10 May 1898. SOURCE: Muster Roll, H/24 Inf, May–Jun 1898.

‡Is presently sick, disease contracted in line of duty, since 1 Oct 1898. SOURCE: Muster Roll, H/24 Inf, Nov–Dec 1898.

‡Sick until 27 Jan 1899; on special duty as painter, Quartermaster Department, since 1 Feb 1899. SOURCE: Muster Roll, H/24 Inf, Jan–Feb 1899.

‡Recommended for certificate of merit for gallantry, Naguilian, Luzon, Philippines, 7 Dec 1899. SOURCE: *ANJ* 39 (15 Feb 1902): 595.

Cpl. John W. Johnson, H/24th Infantry, awarded certificate of merit for most distinguished gallantry in action at Naguilian, Luzon, 7 Dec 1899. SOURCE: Gleim, *The Certificate of Merit*, 50.

‡Certificate of merit for distinguished gallantry, Naguilian, Luzon, 7 Dec 1899, awarded 10 Mar 1902. SOURCE: GO 86, AGO, 24 Jul 1902.

‡Corporal, drowned in the Philippines. SOURCE: Muller, *The Twenty Fourth Infantry*, 34.

JOHNSON, John J.; Private; 24th Inf. Died on detached service 24 Apr 1908; buried in plot N ADD1260 at San Francisco National Cemetery. SOURCE: San Francisco National Cemetery.

JOHNSON, John W.; Private; L/10th Cav. Died 25 Jul 1876 of disease at Ft Concho, TX. SOURCE: Regimental Returns, 10th Cavalry, 1876.

Died on 25 Jul 1876; buried at San Antonio National Cemetery, Section D, number 593. SOURCE: San Antonio National Cemetery Locator.

JOHNSON, John W.; Private; A/10th Cav. ‡At Ft Apache, AZ, 1890, subscribed $.50 to testimonial to General Grierson. SOURCE: List of subscriptions, 23 Apr 1890, 10th Cav papers, MHI.

Buried at Ft Leavenworth National Cemetery, plot 2701. SOURCE: Ft Leavenworth National Cemetery.

JOHNSON, John W.; Private; D/9th Cav. With Captain Dodge at battle at Milk River, CO, 2–10 Oct 1879. SOURCE: Miller, *Hollow Victory*, 167, 206–7.

JOHNSON, John W. L.; Private; Band/9th Cav. ‡Died at Ft Robinson, NE, hospital, 14 Dec 1897. SOURCE: Crawford *Tribune*, 17 Dec 1897.

‡Funeral, Ft Robinson, 15 Dec 1897. SOURCE: SO 168, 15 Dec 1897, Post Orders, Ft Robinson; List of Interments, Ft Robinson.

Died 1 Dec 1897 of disease contracted in line of duty at Ft Robinson. SOURCE: Buecker, Fort Robinson Burials.

JOHNSON, Joseph; Private; B/9th Cav. Died on 8 May 1909; buried at San Antonio National Cemetery, Section I, number 1645. SOURCE: San Antonio National Cemetery Locator.

JOHNSON, Joshua; Private; 10th Cav. Civil War veteran; enlisted in regular Army to get treatment for his hemorrhoids; spent most of a year incapacitated at Ft Sill, OK, but completed enlistment. SOURCE: Dobak and Phillips, *The Black Regulars*, 47.

JOHNSON, King; Private; D/25th Inf. Completed enlistment by 1889; returned to service because he thought opportunity there was better than in civilian life. SOURCE: Dobak and Phillips, *The Black Regulars*, 60.

JOHNSON, Lawrence; Corporal; M/9th Cav. Served in M Troop Dec 1872, witness at Emanuel Stance court martial. SOURCE: Kenner, *Buffalo Soldiers and Officers of the Ninth Cavalry*, 164.

‡At Ft McKavett, TX, 1872–73. See **STANCE**, Emanuel, First Sergeant, F/9th Cavalry

JOHNSON, Lewis; Private; G/9th Cav. Received Philippine Campaign Badge number 11832 for service as private in G/9th Cavalry, 3 Mar 1902–16 Sep 1902; private in G/9th Cavalry, Ft Leavenworth, KS, Mar 1905. SOURCE: Philippine Campaign Badge Recipients; Philippine Campaign Badge list, 29 May 1905.

JOHNSON, Luke J.; 9th Cav. Died 20 Mar 1908; buried in plot N ADD1247 at San Francisco National Cemetery. SOURCE: San Francisco National Cemetery.

JOHNSON, Mack; Private; I/10th Cav. In Troop I/10th Cavalry stationed at Bonita Cañon Camp, AZ, but absent or on detached service 30 Apr 1886. SOURCE: Tagg, *The Camp at Bonita Cañon*, 231.

JOHNSON, Merrit; M/9th Cav. Born in Kentucky; black complexion; cannot read or write, age 21, Jul 1870, at Ft McKavett, TX. SOURCE: Bierschwale, *Fort McKavett*, 100.

JOHNSON, Monroe; Sergeant; M/9th Cav. ‡Sergeant, M/9th Cavalry, at Ft McKavett, TX, 1872–73. *See* **STANCE**, Emanuel, First Sergeant, F/9th Cavalry

Civil War veteran, enlisted in New Orleans, LA, Jan 1867; learned to sign name during second enlistment; age 35 and in third enlistment when wounded in action against Apaches in 1881. SOURCE: Dobak and Phillips, *The Black Regulars*, 251, 330.

Corporal, I/9th Cavalry, wounded in right foot, Cuchillo Negro, NM, Aug 1881. SOURCE: Kenner, *Buffalo Soldiers and Officers of the Ninth Cavalry*, 245.

Sergeant, M/9th Cavalry; died 28 Feb 1900; buried at Ft Leavenworth National Cemetery, plot 3186. SOURCE: Ft Leavenworth National Cemetery.

JOHNSON, Oliver; Private; C/9th Cav. Died at Ft Davis, TX, on 6 Jul 1868; buried at San Antonio National Cemetery, Section I, number 1545. SOURCE: San Antonio National Cemetery Locator.

JOHNSON, Peter; Private; 25th Inf. Born in Waterboro, SC; Ht 5'7", black hair and eyes, dark complexion; occupation drayman; enlisted at age 25, Charleston, SC, 20 May 1881; left recruit depot, David's Island, NY, 2 Jul 1881, arrived Ft Randall, SD, 7 Jul 1881. SOURCE: Descriptive & Assignment Rolls of Recruits, 25 Inf.

JOHNSON, Randall; Private; B/9th Cav. Died at Ft Stockton, TX, on 7 Oct 1868; buried at San Antonio National Cemetery, Section C, number 413. SOURCE: San Antonio National Cemetery Locator.

JOHNSON, Richard; Private; C/10th Cav. ‡Original member of 10th Cavalry; in troop when organized, Ft Leavenworth, KS, 14 May 1867. SOURCE: McMiller, "Buffalo Soldiers," 70.

Died 5 Oct 1868 of disease at Ft Harker, KS. SOURCE: Regimental Returns, 10th Cavalry, 1868.

JOHNSON, Richard; Private; E/10th Cav. In Troop E/10th Cavalry stationed at Bonita Cañon Camp, AZ, 28 Feb 1886. SOURCE: Tagg, *The Camp at Bonita Cañon*, 231.

JOHNSON, Richard; Private; C/24th Inf. Died 18 Jul 1902; buried in plot 1137 at San Francisco National Cemetery. SOURCE: San Francisco National Cemetery.

JOHNSON, Robert D.; Private; L/24th Inf. Died 26 Oct 1915; buried in plot WS 501-A at San Francisco National Cemetery. SOURCE: San Francisco National Cemetery.

JOHNSON, Robert J.; Corporal; K/9th Cav. As private received Indian Wars Campaign Badge number 1363 on 28 May 1909; later received duplicate badge number 1767. SOURCE: Carroll, *Indian Wars Campaign Badge*, 39, 51.

Veteran of Indian wars, Spanish-American War, and Philippine Insurrection; at Ft D. A. Russell, WY, in 1910; sharpshooter; resident of Moffat's Creek, VA. SOURCE: *Illustrated Review: Ninth Cavalry*, with picture.

JOHNSON, Robert T.; Sergeant; G/9th Cav. ‡Was recruit at St. Louis, MO, with Joseph Blew, Oct 1873; then served together in G/9th Cavalry until discharged in 1883; met again in Omaha, NE, 1904, when Johnson was working on the Overland Limited train. SOURCE: Affidavit, Johnson, age 70, 916 Cypress, Oakland, CA, 31 May 1924, VA File XC 970422, Joseph Blew.

With Private Hayden, G/9th Cavalry, rescued white miner and his family, Uncompahgre River, CO, 1877. SOURCE: Kenner, *Buffalo Soldiers and Officers of the Ninth Cavalry*, 217, 347.

JOHNSON, Sam; Private; G/25th Inf. One of twenty men who cycled 1,900 miles from Ft Missoula, MT, to St. Louis, MO, 14 Jun–24 Jul 1897, in 25th Infantry Bicycle Corps to test durability and practicality of bicycles as a means of transportation for troops. SOURCE: File 60178, GC, AGO Records.

JOHNSON, Sidney; Private; H/10th Cav. Died at Ft Davis, TX, on 17 Mar 1883; buried at San Antonio National Cemetery, Section I, number 1530. SOURCE: San Antonio National Cemetery Locator.

JOHNSON, Silas; QM Sgt; D/10th Cav. ‡Farrier, served in 10th Cavalry in Cuba, 1898. SOURCE: Cashin, *Under Fire with the Tenth Cavalry*, 341.

‡President McKinley congratulated him and shook his hand on trip from New York City to Long Island City, NY. SOURCE: Cleveland *Gazette*, 17 Sep 1898.

‡Son born to wife at Ft Robinson, NE, 10 Feb 1906. SOURCE: Monthly Report, Chaplain Anderson, Mar 1906.

Quartermaster sergeant, received Indian Wars Campaign Badge number 1564 on 21 Feb 1910. SOURCE: Carroll, *Indian Wars Campaign Badge*, 45.

JOHNSON, Simon; Private; 9th Cav. Received Philippine Campaign Badge number 11731 for service as private in E/9th Cavalry; in 9th Cavalry at Ft Leavenworth, KS, Mar 1905. SOURCE: Philippine Campaign Badge list, 29 May 1905.

JOHNSON, Solomon; Cook; B/25th Inf. Enlisted 28 Sep 1899, discharged corporal L/48th Infantry 30 Jun 1901, character excellent; reenlisted 31 Jul 1901, was discharged as private K/25th Infantry 26 Nov 1902, character excellent; reenlisted 6 May 1903, discharged as private B/25th Infantry 5 May 1906, character excellent; reenlisted 8 May 1906, discharged without honor as cook 22 Nov 1906, Brownsville, TX. SOURCE: Powell, "Military Record of the Enlisted Men Who Were Discharged Without Honor."

‡Private, E/9th Cavalry, letter. SOURCE: *ANJ* 39 (12 Oct 1901): 141.

‡Dishonorable discharge, Brownsville. SOURCE: SO 266, AGO, 9 Nov 1906.

JOHNSON, Thomas; Private; I/10th Cav. Died 24 Sep 1878, cause not stated, at Ft Sill, OK. SOURCE: Regimental Returns, 10th Cavalry, 1878.

JOHNSON, Thomas; Private; A/10th Cav. Died 10 Mar 1879 of pistol accident at Ft Elliott, TX. SOURCE: Regimental Returns, 10th Cavalry, 1879.

JOHNSON, Thomas; Private; Band/25th Inf. At Ft Missoula, MT, reported to Regimental QM Sgt. John Williams that Pvt. Samuel Lundy had eloped with Williams's 16-year-old daughter Etta. SOURCE: Dobak and Phillips, *The Black Regulars*, 142.

JOHNSON, Thomas; Cook; D/24th Inf. Retired, died 4 Apr 1911; buried at Ft Bayard, NM, in plot T 17. SOURCE: "Fort Bayard National Cemetery, Records of Burials."

Died 10 Apr 1911; buried 4 Apr 1911, section A, row F, plot 44 at Ft Bayard. SOURCE: Erickson, Burials at Fort Bayard National Cemetery, NM.

JOHNSON, Thomas; 1st Sgt; I/24th Inf. Awarded certificate of merit for distinguished service, pursuing and disarming, at risk of his own life, soldier bent on murdering his first sergeant, at Camp McGrath, Batangas, Philippines, 22 Aug 1912. SOURCE: Gleim, *The Certificate of Merit*, 61.

‡Commended in general orders by Maj. Gen. J. Franklin Bell, Commanding General, Department of the Philippines, for distinguished service, Camp McGrath, Batangas. SOURCE: Curtis, *The Black Soldier*, 42.

Born in Woodford County, KY; resided Louisville, KY; received Distinguished Service Medal in lieu of certificate of merit. SOURCE: *American Decorations*, 839.

Awarded certificate of merit for distinguished service at risk of his own life in pursuit and disarming of enlisted man bent on murdering his first sergeant, Camp McGrath, Batangas, Philippines, 22 Aug 1912. SOURCE: AGO, Bulletin 29, 13 Jul 1914.

JOHNSON, William; Private; C/9th Cav. Originally buried at Ft Grant, AZ; buried at Santa Fe National Cemetery, NM, plot A-1 761. SOURCE: Santa Fe National Cemetery, Records of Burials.

JOHNSON, William; Private; F/10th Cav. ‡Original member of 10th Cavalry; in troop when organized, Ft Leavenworth, KS, 21 Jun 1867. SOURCE: McMiller, "Buffalo Soldiers," 73.

Sergeant, F/10th Cavalry, wounded in action, gunshot wound in left thigh, near Beaver Creek, KS, 21 Aug 1867. SOURCE: LR, DeptMo, 1867.

Wounded in action against Indians at Beaver Creek, 21 Aug 1867. SOURCE: Schubert, *Voices of the Buffalo Soldier*, 20.

Sergeant, convicted by garrison court martial, Ft Lyon, CO, of neglect of duty, failure to obey standing troop order to lead, not ride, horses to water on march near Saline River, 20 Aug 1868; reduced to private. SOURCE: GCMO 25, DeptMo, 16 Apr 1869.

Private, mentioned Mar 1873. SOURCE: LS, 10 Cav, 1873–83.

‡"One of the few colored telegraph operators," died Ft Grant, AZ, 15 Jul 1887. SOURCE: Cleveland *Gazette*, 30 Jul 1887.

Died 15 Jul 1887; originally buried at Ft Grant; buried at Santa Fe National Cemetery, NM, plot A-1 779. SOURCE: Santa Fe National Cemetery, Records of Burials.

JOHNSON, William; Sergeant; 10th Cav. Reduced to private at Ft Concho, TX, 1878, for absence without leave but acquitted of assault of woman with whom he had had two-year relationship that had started at Ft Clark, TX, in 1876; could not read or write, and Sgt. William Richardson had read her letters to him in the field and written his replies. SOURCE: Dobak and Phillips, *The Black Regulars*, 143.

JOHNSON, William; C/25th Inf. Born in Virginia; mulatto complexion; cannot read or write, age 24, 5 Sep 1870, at Ft McKavett, TX. SOURCE: Bierschwale, *Fort McKavett*, 109.

JOHNSON, William; M/9th Cav. Born in Kentucky; black complexion; cannot read or write, age 22, Jul 1870, at Ft McKavett, TX. SOURCE: Bierschwale, *Fort McKavett*, 100.

JOHNSON, William; Private; I/10th Cav. In Troop I/10th Cavalry stationed at Bonita Cañon Camp, AZ, but absent or on detached service 30 Jun 1886. SOURCE: Tagg, *The Camp at Bonita Cañon*, 231.

JOHNSON, William; Private; 25th Inf. Born in New Rochelle, NY; Ht 5'5", black hair and eyes, brown complexion; with K/24th Infantry until 4 Sep 1886; reenlisted at age 33, New York City, 8 Dec 1886; arrived Ft Snelling, MN, 20 Jan 1887. SOURCE: Descriptive & Assignment Rolls of Recruits, 25 Inf.

‡Resident of New York City; discharged, end of term, from Ft Bayard, NM, 7 Dec 1891. SOURCE: Cleveland *Gazette*, 12 Dec 1891.

JOHNSON, William; Private; M/9th Cav. Died 19 Mar 1899; buried at Santa Fe National Cemetery, NM, plot 761. SOURCE: Santa Fe National Cemetery, Records of Burials.

JOHNSON, William; Private; G/49th Inf. Died 18 Oct 1900; buried in plot NEW A377 at San Francisco National Cemetery. SOURCE: San Francisco National Cemetery.

JOHNSON, William; Corporal; F/25th Inf. ‡Private, F/25th Infantry, drowned, body recovered, in the Philippines, 27 Feb 1901. SOURCE: *ANJ* 38 (16 Mar 1901): 703.

Corporal, F/25th Infantry, died 27 Feb 1901; buried in plot NEW A949 at San Francisco National Cemetery. SOURCE: San Francisco National Cemetery.

JOHNSON, William D.; Master Sgt; 25th Inf. ‡Private, K/25th Infantry, at Ft Niobrara, NE, 1904. SOURCE: Wilson, "History of Fort Niobrara."

‡Master sergeant at Camp Stephen D. Little, Nogales, AZ, 1925. SOURCE: Nankivell, *History of the Twenty-fifth Infantry*, 159.

Died 23 Jun 1935; buried in plot C 1398 at San Francisco National Cemetery. SOURCE: San Francisco National Cemetery.

JOHNSON, William H.; 1st Sgt; E/10th Cav. Trumpeter, E/10th Cavalry, in Troop E/10th Cavalry stationed at Bonita Cañon Camp, AZ, 28 Feb 1886. SOURCE: Tagg, *The Camp at Bonita Cañon*, 231.

‡Corporal, at Ft Apache, AZ, 1890, subscribed $.50 to testimonial to General Grierson. SOURCE: List of subscriptions, 23 Apr 1890, 10th Cavalry papers, MHI.

‡Trumpeter, served in 10th Cavalry in Cuba, 1898. SOURCE: Cashin, *Under Fire with the Tenth Cavalry*, 342.

‡Wounded in action at Santiago, Cuba, 24 Jun 1898. SOURCE: SecWar, *AR 1898*, 355.

‡Retired "with fine record" as first sergeant. SOURCE: Fremont *Clipper*, 30 Nov 1906.

JOHNSON, William J.; Private; C/9th Cav. Died 25 Oct 1900; buried in plot NEW A1208 at San Francisco National Cemetery. SOURCE: San Francisco National Cemetery.

JOHNSON, William M.; Private; F/9th Cav. ‡Recruit from depot arrived at Ft Robinson, NE, 1 Mar 1887.

‡Deserted from Ft Robinson, 23 Apr 1887.

Died of disease 24 Oct 1890 at Ft Robinson. SOURCE: Buecker, Fort Robinson Burials.

‡Buried at Ft Robinson, 24 Oct 1890. SOURCE: List of Interments, Ft Robinson.

JOHNSON, Willie; Private; G/49th Inf. ‡Died in the Philippines, 18 Oct 1900. SOURCE: *ANJ* 38 (10 Nov 1900): 259.

Died 18 Oct 1900; buried in plot N ADD377 at San Francisco National Cemetery. SOURCE: San Francisco National Cemetery.

JOHNSON, York; Private; C/10th Cav. ‡Original member of 10th Cavalry; in troop when organized, Ft Leavenworth, KS, 14 May 1867. SOURCE: McMiller, "Buffalo Soldiers," 70.

‡Recruit on extra duty, Ft Leavenworth, assigned to C/10th Cavalry. SOURCE: CO, 10 Cav, to Adjutant, Ft Leavenworth, 15 May 1867, LS, 10 Cav, 1866–67.

‡Shot to death along with Pvt. Charles Smith by Lt. Robert Price in fit of rage after quarrel en route to Santa Fe, NM, summer 1871. SOURCE: Leckie, *The Buffalo Soldiers*, 66.

Died 22 Jun 1871, shot by 2nd Lt. Robert Price at Galisteo, NM. SOURCE: Regimental Returns, 10th Cavalry, 1871.

JOHNSTON, Albert; F/9th Cav. Born in Kentucky; black complexion; cannot read or write, age 23, Jul 1870, at Ft McKavett, TX. SOURCE: Bierschwale, *Fort McKavett*, 97.

JOHNSTON, Charles; Sergeant; D/25th Inf. From LaGrange County, GA; at Ft Davis, TX, secretly married Mexican woman, deserted in Jan 1884 with valuables and money entrusted to him by soldiers, apprehended near Presidio del Norte, Mexico, by Mexican police. SOURCE: Leiker, *Racial Borders*, 85.

JOHNSTON, Perry; Private; D/9th Cav. With Captain Dodge at battle at Milk River, CO, 2–10 Oct 1879. SOURCE: Miller, *Hollow Victory*, 167, 206–7.

JOHNSTON, William B.; Private; 9th Cav. Received Philippine Campaign Badge number 11732 for service as private in E/9th Cavalry; in 9th Cavalry at Ft Leavenworth, KS, Mar 1905. SOURCE: Philippine Campaign Badge list, 29 May 1905.

JOINER, Gabriel; Corporal; D/9th Cav. With Captain Dodge at battle at Milk River, CO, 2–10 Oct 1879. SOURCE: Miller, *Hollow Victory*, 167, 206–7.

JOINER, Oliver; H/25th Inf. Born in North Carolina; black complexion; can read and write, age 26, 5 Sep 1870, at Ft McKavett, TX. SOURCE: Bierschwale, *Fort McKavett*, 107.

JONES, Alexander; 1st Sgt; C/9th Cav. ‡Discharged, end of term, as first sergeant, D/24th Infantry, 4 Oct 1873; entitled to reenlistment pay. SOURCE: AG, USA, to CG, DivMo, 4 Apr 1877, ES, 10 Cav, 1872–81.

‡Mentioned Mar 1877 as discharged 4 Oct 1876 and reenlisted as private, D/10th Cavalry, 26 Oct 1876. SOURCE: ES, 10 Cav, 1872–81.

‡First sergeant, C/9th Cavalry; inspector general says he has justifiable complaint regarding excessive guard and fatigue details, Ft Robinson, NE, Nov 1886. SOURCE: Report of Inspection, Ft Robinson, 15 Nov 1886, Reports of Inspections, DeptPlatte.

Native of Georgia, mulatto; joined C/9th Cavalry 1882; first sergeant, C/9th Cavalry, at Ft Sill, OK, 1884, with prior service in 24th Infantry and 10th Cavalry; filed formal complaint against Capt. Charles Beyer for appropriating for use of his family government rations intended to feed soldiers and for using troops as laborers for personal use; fought in barracks with successor 1st Sgt. Jason J. Jackson Sep 1884; restored as first sergeant after Beyer's dismissal; discharged without character 1887, although Beyer had been convicted and dismissed from the service. SOURCE: Kenner, *Buffalo Soldiers and Officers of the Ninth Cavalry*, 261–67.

Sergeant, 9th Cavalry, served at Fort Sill, complained that 1st Sgt. Jason Jackson brought "his whore" into the barracks. SOURCE: Dobak and Phillips, *The Black Regulars*, 274.

JONES, Andrew; 9th Cav. Born in Virginia; black complexion; cannot read or write, age 20, 5 Sep 1870, at Ft McKavett, TX. SOURCE: Bierschwale, *Fort McKavett*, 107.

JONES, Andrew; Sergeant; H/9th Cav. ‡Born in King Co., VA; age 49 in 1895; Ht 5'8"; three years in 38th Infantry; five years in E/24th Infantry; twenty years in H/9th Cavalry; $6 per month additional pay for twenty-five years' continuous service; character excellent, single. SOURCE: Descriptive Book, H/9 Cav.

‡Sergeant since 1 Jan 1881. SOURCE: *ANJ* 32 (8 Jun 1895): 674.

‡Sergeant since 17 Jan 1881. SOURCE: Roster, 9 Cav.

Appointed sergeant 1 Jan 1881; in H/9th Cavalry at Ft Robinson, NE, Jan 1897. SOURCE: Ninth Cavalry, Roster of NCOs, 1897.

‡Retires from Ft Robinson as sergeant, H/9th Cavalry. SOURCE: *ANJ* 34 (22 May 1897): 705.

JONES, Beverly; M/9th Cav. Born in Maryland; mulatto complexion; can read and write, age 23, Jul 1870, at Ft McKavett, TX. SOURCE: Bierschwale, *Fort McKavett*, 100.

‡Admitted to Soldiers Home with disability at age 40 with nineteen years and eight months' service, 23 Jan 1888. SOURCE: SecWar, *AR 1888*, 902.

JONES, Bular; Private; G/25th Inf. Born in Rappahannock County, VA; Ht 5'8", black hair and eyes, black complexion; occupation laborer; enlisted 18 Aug 1886, age 21, at Harrisburg, PA; assigned to G/25th Infantry; arrived Ft Snelling, MN, 14 Dec 1886. SOURCE: Descriptive & Assignment Rolls of Recruits, 25 Inf.

JONES, Charles; Private; L/9th Cavalry. Enlisted at Baltimore, MD, 23 Jan 1879; at Ft Bliss, TX. SOURCE: Muster Roll, L/9th Cavalry, 31 Oct 1879–31 Dec 1879.

Died 9 Dec 1881; buried at Ft Leavenworth National Cemetery, plot 2772. SOURCE: Ft Leavenworth National Cemetery.

JONES, Clayton; Private; I/10th Cav. In Troop I/10th Cavalry stationed at Bonita Cañon Camp, AZ, 30 Jun 1886. SOURCE: Tagg, *The Camp at Bonita Cañon*, 232.

JONES, David; Blacksmith; I/10th Cav. In Troop I/10th Cavalry stationed at Bonita Cañon Camp, AZ, 30 Jun 1886. SOURCE: Tagg, *The Camp at Bonita Cañon*, 231.

JONES, Douglas; Private; F/9th Cav. Died 18 Apr 1879; originally buried at Ft Stanton, NM; buried Jun 1896 at Santa Fe National Cemetery, NM, plot H11 558 or B 558. SOURCE: Santa Fe National Cemetery, Records of Burials.

JONES, Edmund; Private; E/25th Inf. Died 1 Apr 1905; buried at Ft Bayard, NM, in plot H 5. SOURCE: "Fort Bayard National Cemetery, Records of Burials."

Buried 1 Apr 1905, section A, row K, plot 7 at Ft Bayard. SOURCE: Erickson, Burials at Fort Bayard National Cemetery, NM.

JONES, Edward; Private; I/24th Inf. Died at Ft Concho, TX, on 2 Dec 1869; buried at San Antonio National Cemetery, Section D, number 597. SOURCE: San Antonio National Cemetery Locator.

JONES, Edward; Corporal; C/10th Cav. Served in second half of 1880s; resided at 1039 Hopkins St., Cincinnati, OH, in 1907. SOURCE: Sayre, *Warriors of Color*, 498.

JONES, Edward; Private; F/24th Inf. ‡Drowned crossing San Mateo River, Philippines, 21 Aug 1899. SOURCE: Richmond *Planet*, 2 Sep 1899.

Private, F/24th Infantry, died in the Philippines 21 Aug 1899; body received for burial 24 Feb 1900 at San Francisco National Cemetery, buried in plot EAST 506. SOURCE: San Francisco National Cemetery.

JONES, Edward; Private; D/24th Inf. Died 22 Sep 1915; buried in plot WEST 489-A at San Francisco National Cemetery. SOURCE: San Francisco National Cemetery.

JONES, Eldridge T.; Private; D/9th Cav. ‡Killed in action near Ft Lancaster, TX, by Kickapoos, 11 Oct 1867, while escorting Camp Hudson-Ft Stockton, TX, mail along with Cpl. Samuel Wright, D/9th Cavalry. SOURCE: Leckie, *The Buffalo Soldiers*, 84–85; Hamilton, "History of the Ninth Cavalry," 7.

See OTT, **WRIGHT**, Samuel, Corporal, D/9th Cavalry

Killed while delivering mail from Ft Lancaster, Oct 1867. SOURCE: Schubert, *Black Valor*, 17.

JONES, Eugene; Private; H/25th Inf. One of twenty men who began to cycle 1,900 miles from Ft Missoula, MT, to St. Louis, MO, 14 Jun–24 Jul 1897, in 25th Infantry Bicycle Corps to test durability and practicality of bicycles as a means of transportation for troops. Commander considered him a habitual troublemaker and sent him back to Ft Missoula from St. Joseph, MO. SOURCE: File 60178, GC, AGO Records.

‡In H/25th Infantry; member of bicycle corps that rode from Ft Missoula to St. Joseph and was sent back ill; only one of twenty who became sick and was faking, according to 2nd Lt. James A. Moss. SOURCE: *ANJ* 35 (2 Oct 1897): 71.

‡Wounded in action, El Caney, Cuba, 1 Jul 1898. SOURCE: Nankivell, *History of the Twenty-fifth Infantry*, 83.

JONES, Frank; Private; B/25th Inf. Enlisted 7 Oct 1898, discharged as private G/24th Infantry 2 Feb 1899, character good; reenlisted 23 Feb 1899, discharged as private K/24th Infantry 22 Feb 1902, character good; reenlisted 8 May 1902, discharged as private L/24th Infantry 5 May 1905, character excellent; enlisted 6 Jul [no year], discharged without honor 19 Nov 1906. SOURCE: Powell, "Military Record of the Enlisted Men Who Were Discharged Without Honor."

Dishonorable discharge, Brownsville, TX. SOURCE: SO 266, AGO, 9 Nov 1906.

JONES, Henry; Private; B/25th Inf. Enlisted 19 Mar 1904, discharged without honor 19 Nov 1906. SOURCE: Powell, "Military Record of the Enlisted Men Who Were Discharged Without Honor."

Dishonorable discharge, Brownsville, TX. SOURCE: SO 266, AGO, 9 Nov 1906.

JONES, Henry C.; Private; E/10th Cav. ‡Born in Montgomery Co., TX; Ht 5'9", brown eyes and black hair, dark brown complexion; discharged from Band/10th Cavalry, 2 Apr 1895; fourth enlistment in B/25th Infantry, Ft Missoula, MT, 2 Jun 1895. SOURCE: Misc Records, 25 Inf.

In Troop E/10th Cavalry stationed at Bonita Cañon Camp, AZ, 28 Feb 1886. SOURCE: Tagg, *The Camp at Bonita Cañon*, 231.

‡Transferred from E/10th Cavalry to Hospital Corps, Ft Grant, AZ. SOURCE: *ANJ* 25 (10 Dec 1887): 382.

‡In E/10th Cavalry, at Ft Apache, AZ, 1890, subscribed $.50 to testimonial to General Grierson. SOURCE: List of subscriptions, 23 Apr 1890, 10th Cavalry papers, MHI.

‡Served in Band/10th Cavalry in Cuba, 1898. SOURCE: Cashin, *Under Fire with the Tenth Cavalry*, 359.

Private in Band/10th Cavalry, received Indian Wars Campaign Badge number 1426 on 19 Aug 1909. SOURCE: Carroll, *Indian Wars Campaign Badge*, 41.

JONES, Ira; Private; E/24th Inf. ‡Drowned near Mount Arayat, Philippines, 15 Oct 1899, while trying to swim with comrade after a carabao. SOURCE: Manila *Times*, 19 Oct 1899.

Died 15 Oct 1899; buried in plot EAST 563 at San Francisco National Cemetery. SOURCE: San Francisco National Cemetery.

JONES, Jacob; Private; 25th Inf. Born in Charleston, SC; Ht 5'9", black hair and eyes, dark complexion; occupation miner; enlisted at age 21, Charleston, 29 May 1881; left recruit depot, David's Island, NY, 2 Jul 1881, arrived Ft Randall, SD, 7 Jul 1881. SOURCE: Descriptive & Assignment Rolls of Recruits, 25 Inf.

‡Fined $25 at Missoula, MT, Dec 1889, for assault on Lizzie Maroney of "notorious 'four-mile' house." SOURCE: Fowler, *The Black Infantry*, 68.

JONES, Jehu; Sergeant; 25th Inf. Returned to Army for second enlistment after break in service in New York City, 1870. SOURCE: Dobak and Phillips, *The Black Regulars*, 61.

JONES, Jeremiah; Ord Sgt; U.S. Army. ‡Born in Charles Co., MD, 18 Oct 1861; Ht 5'7", black complexion; private, corporal, sergeant, sergeant major, 9th Cavalry, 22 Jan 1881–21 Jan 1896; had syphilis, 1881; served as ordnance sergeant at Ft Huachuca, AZ, Jefferson Bks, MO, Ft Logan, CO; died of pneumonia while on active duty as ordnance sergeant, Ft Logan, 20 Mar 1906; married Annie L. Brown at 431 8th Street, SW, Washington, DC; widow resided at 1812 11th St., NW, until 1906, then moved to 431 8th Street, SW. SOURCE: VA File WC 611769, Jeremiah Jones.

See OTT, **JEFFERDS**, Wesley, Sergeant, A/9th Cavalry

‡Date of rank as regimental sergeant major, 9th Cavalry, 12 Feb 1885. SOURCE: *ANJ* 25 (18 Feb 1888): 586; Roster, 9 Cav.

‡Deposited $450 with paymaster, Ft McKinney, WY, 21 Jan 1886. SOURCE: CO, 9 Cav, to Paymaster General, USA, 15 Feb 1886, LS, 9 Cav.

‡Senior man on Ft Robinson, NE, canteen committee of nine noncommissioned officers, five of whom are in 9th Cavalry, others 8th Infantry, appointed to make recommendations to canteen council. SOURCE: Order 136, 1 Jul 1890, Post Orders, Ft Robinson.

‡With regiment on practice march from Ft Robinson, Aug 1890.

‡Authorized six-month furlough by Special Order 108, Division of the Missouri, 26 Dec 1890. SOURCE: *ANJ* 28 (3 Jan 1891): 312.

‡Furlough revoked by telegram, Adjutant General's Office, 8 Apr 1891.

‡Acts as chief clerk and is so busy attending to proper classification and administrative details that he has little time for clerical work; forced with adjutant to work far into night, far more than regular hours. SOURCE: CO, Ft Robinson, to AAG, DP, 5 May 1892, LS, Ft Robinson.

‡On expedition from Ft Robinson to Butte, MT, and back, under Lt. Col. Reuben Bernard, 18–31 Jul 1894.

‡Managed church benefit concerts for Chaplain Plummer, also sang; shared duplex on old post with QM Sgt. Simon Harris, 9th Cavalry. SOURCE: Investigation of Charges against Chaplain Plummer.

‡Examined for ordnance sergeant, Ft Robinson, Nov 1895. SOURCE: *ANJ* 33 (16 Nov 1895): 179.

‡Reenlisted at Ft Robinson, 22 Jan 1896. SOURCE: *ANJ* 33 (1 Feb 1896): 388.

Regimental sergeant major appointed 12 Feb 1885; at Ft Robinson, Jan 1897. SOURCE: Ninth Cavalry, Roster of NCOs, 1897.

Appointed ordnance sergeant 22 Jun 1897, from regimental sergeant major, 9th Cavalry. SOURCE: Dobak, "Staff Noncommissioned Officers."

‡Appointed ordnance sergeant as of 22 Jun 1897; departed Ft Robinson 24 Jun 1897, for duty at Whipple Barracks, AZ. SOURCE: SO 80, 23 Jul 1897, Post Orders, Ft Robinson.

JONES, Jesse; Corporal, 9th Cav. Received Philippine Campaign Badge number 11754 for service as corporal in M/49th Infantry, United States Volunteers; in 9th Cavalry at Ft Leavenworth, KS, Mar 1905. SOURCE: Philippine Campaign Badge list, 29 May 1905.

JONES, John; Private; K/10th Cav. ‡Died spring 1870. SOURCE: ES, 10 Cav, 1866–71.

Died 28 Mar 1870 of pneumonia at Camp Supply, OK. SOURCE: Regimental Returns, 10th Cavalry, 1870.

JONES, John; Sergeant; E/10th Cav. Killed by Pvt. Edward Townsend, E/10th Cavalry, 15 Sep 1876, at San Felipe, TX. SOURCE: Regimental Returns, 10th Cavalry, 1876.

JONES, John; F/9th Cav. Born in Kentucky; black complexion; cannot read or write, age 21, Jul 1870, at Ft McKavett, TX. SOURCE: Bierschwale, *Fort McKavett,* 97.

JONES, John; Private; 25th Inf. Born in Charleston, SC; Ht 5'7", black hair and eyes, fair complexion; occupation miner; enlisted at age 21, Charleston, 6 Jun 1881; left recruit depot, David's Island, NY, 2 Jul 1881, arrived Ft Randall, SD, 7 Jul 1881. SOURCE: Descriptive & Assignment Rolls of Recruits, 25 Inf.

JONES, John A.; Private; H/9th Cav. Wife Helen, lived in Crawford, NE, fell dead on sidewalk, died of a hemorrhage of the lungs. SOURCE: Buecker, Fort Robinson Burials.

Wife buried at Ft Robinson, NE, 25 Nov 1897. SOURCE: List of Interments, Ft Robinson.

JONES, John R.; Corporal; 25th Inf. Civil War veteran; served one enlistment; offered promotion to quartermaster sergeant but declined to reenlist because of better opportunities in civilian life. SOURCE: Dobak and Phillips, *The Black Regulars,* 143.

JONES, John S.; Private; K/25th Inf. Born in Columbia, TN; Ht 5'8", black hair and eyes, black complexion; occupation stone cutter; enlisted at age 22, Nashville, TN, 28 Apr 1886; from Columbus Bks, OH, arrived Ft Snelling, MN, 17 Sep 1886. SOURCE: Descriptive & Assignment Rolls of Recruits, 25 Inf.

JONES, Joseph; Private; H/10th Cav. Died 10 Sep 1869 in hospital at Ft Sill, OK. SOURCE: Regimental Returns, 10th Cavalry, 1869.

Died 10 Sep 1869; buried at Camp Douglas, UT. SOURCE: Record Book of Interments, Post Cemetery, 252.

JONES, Leroy C.; Private; H/48th Inf. ‡Died of variola in the Philippines, 21 Jun 1900. SOURCE: *ANJ* 37 (7 Jul 1900): 1071.

Died 21 Jun 1900; buried in plot NADDN823 at San Francisco National Cemetery. SOURCE: San Francisco National Cemetery.

JONES, Lewis; Private; B/9th Cav. As private, received Indian Wars Campaign Badge number 1919 on 7 Jan 1925. SOURCE: Carroll, *Indian Wars Campaign Badge,* 56.

JONES, Nathan; Private; F/9th Cav. Killed in action by Indians, Eagle Springs, TX, 100 miles from Ft Davis, TX, while escorting mail, 5 Dec 1867. SOURCE: Hamilton, "History of the Ninth Cavalry," 7; *Illustrated Review: Ninth Cavalry*; Ninth Cavalry, *Historical and Pictorial Review*, 45.

Killed while delivering mail from Ft Davis at Eagle Springs, Dec 1867. SOURCE: Schubert, *Black Valor*, 17.

JONES, Nelson; Saddler; E/10th Cav. ‡Recently died, Oct 1870. SOURCE: ES, 10 Cav, 1866–71.

Died 14 Oct 1870 of typhoid at Ft Sill, OK. SOURCE: Regimental Returns, 10th Cavalry, 1870.

Private, E/10th Cavalry, died 13 Oct 1870, buried at Camp Douglas, UT. SOURCE: Record Book of Interments, Post Cemetery, 252.

JONES, Philip; Corporal; H/10th Cav. ‡Born in Virginia; private, M/10th Cavalry, 27 Sep 1867–27 Sep 1872; private, corporal, sergeant, 5 Oct 1874–4 Oct 1882; private, corporal, sergeant, D/10th Cavalry, 5 Oct 1882–4 Oct 1892; private, 11 Oct 1892; sergeant, 12 Oct 1892; private, H/10th Cavalry, 1 Sep 1896; corporal, 3 Sep 1896; at Ft Assiniboine, MT, 1897. SOURCE: Baker, Roster.

Sgt. Philip Jones, 10th Cavalry, enlisted in Boston, MA, 1867; second enlistment at Ft Sill, OK, 1872; third enlistment Ft Clark, TX, 1877; fourth enlistment Ft Davis, TX, 1882; fifth enlistment San Carlos, AZ, 1887; sixth enlistment Ft Keogh, MT, 1892. SOURCE: Dobak and Phillips, *The Black Regulars*, 40.

‡Original member of 10th Cavalry; in troop when organized, Ft Riley, KS, 15 Oct 1867. SOURCE: McMiller, "Buffalo Soldiers," 79.

‡An original member of M Troop; involved in his first Indian fight around Ft Sill, Indian Territory, under 2nd Lt. William R. Harman, defending beef, wood, and hay contractors with employees; participated in arrest of Satanta and Satank, Ft Sill, Apr 1871; performed much duty as courier between Indian Territory and Texas post in early days. SOURCE: Baker, Roster.

‡Sergeant, D/10th Cavalry, at Ft Apache, AZ, 1890, subscribed $.50 to testimonial to General Grierson. SOURCE: List of subscriptions, 23 Apr 1890, 10th Cavalry papers, MHI.

‡Retired from Ft Assiniboine and moved to Havre, MT, 28 Nov 1897. SOURCE: *ANJ* 36 (13 Nov 1897): 192; Indianapolis *Freeman*, 11 Dec 1897.

JONES, Samuel G.; Corporal; G/9th Cav. Appointed corporal 2 Sep 1896; in G/9th Cavalry at Ft Robinson, NE, Jan 1897. SOURCE: Ninth Cavalry, Roster of NCOs, 1897.

JONES, Sidney; Saddler; B/10th Cav. At Ft Duncan, TX, Jan 1878. SOURCE: Kinevan, *Frontier Cavalryman*, 287.

JONES, Silas; Private; H/10th Cav. Born in Saline County, MO, 1846; enlisted Memphis, TN, 29 Jun 1867; Ht 5'5", black complexion, eyes, and hair; served in H/10th Cavalry; discharged 18 Jun 1872 at Ft Sill, OK; enlisted 29 Jun 1872 at Ft Sill; served in H/10th Cavalry; discharged 28 Jun 1877 at Ft Davis, TX; enlisted 29 Jun 1877 at Ft Davis; served in H/10th Cavalry; discharged 28 June 1882 at Ft Davis; enlisted 4 July 1882 at Ft Davis; served in H/10th Cavalry; discharged 3 Jul 1887 at Ft Apache, AZ; enlisted 4 Jul 1887 at Ft Apache; served in H/10th Cavalry; discharged 3 July 1892 at Ft Buford, ND; enlisted 8 Jul 1892, Ft Buford; served in H/10th Cavalry; letter "H" tattooed on left arm; wife Nellie; died Havre, MT, 12 Jul 1936. SOURCE: Sayre, *Warriors of Color*, 327–29.

‡Original member of 10th Cavalry; in troop when organized, Ft Leavenworth, KS, 21 Jul 1867. SOURCE: McMiller, "Buffalo Soldiers," 75.

Trumpeter in H/10th Cavalry stationed at Bonita Cañon Camp, AZ, 30 Apr 1886. SOURCE: Tagg, *The Camp at Bonita Cañon*, 231.

‡In H/10th Cavalry since it was organized; honorable mention for service rendered in capture of Mangas and his Apache band, Rio Bonito, AZ, 18 Oct 1886. SOURCE: Baker, Roster.

‡Retires from Ft Assiniboine, MT. SOURCE: *ANJ* 34 (7 Aug 1897): 909.

JONES, Thomas; C/25th Inf. Born in Virginia; black complexion; can read and write, age 22, 5 Sep 1870, at Ft McKavett, TX. SOURCE: Bierschwale, *Fort McKavett*, 109.

JONES, Thomas (1); Private; D/9th Cav. With Captain Dodge at battle at Milk River, CO, 2–10 Oct 1879. SOURCE: Miller, *Hollow Victory*, 167, 206–7.

JONES, Thomas (2); Private; D/9th Cav. With Captain Dodge at battle at Milk River, CO, 2–10 Oct 1879. SOURCE: Miller, *Hollow Victory*, 167, 206–7.

JONES, Walker; Private; E/9th Cav. One of ten soldiers charged with mutiny and desertion for role in mutiny at San Pedro Springs, near San Antonio, TX, April 1867; pled guilty to desertion but not mutiny; mutiny charge dropped; convicted of desertion and sentenced to six months' confinement at military prison, Ship's Island, MS; sentence remitted before he was transported to prison. SOURCE: Dobak and Phillips, *The Black Regulars*, 208–11.

JONES, Wiley; Private; B/10th Cav. At Ft Duncan, TX, 1877. SOURCE: Kinevan, *Frontier Cavalryman*, 79.

JONES, William; Private; F/25th Inf. Died at Camp Eagle Pass, TX, on 10 Apr 1872; buried at San Antonio National

Cemetery, Section F, number 1157. SOURCE: San Antonio National Cemetery Locator.

JONES, William; Private; L/9th Cav. Born in Kentucky; blue eyes, mulatto; occupation plasterer; acquitted of murder for killing in barroom, Las Animas, CO, Aug 1876, along with Blacksmith James Payne and Pvt. Nathan Trent, L/9th Cavalry. SOURCE: Kenner, *Buffalo Soldiers and Officers of the Ninth Cavalry*, 183–84.

JONES, William; Private; D/9th Cav. ‡In I/9th Cavalry; cited for gallantry against Victorio, Nov 1879, by Maj. Albert P. Morrow. SOURCE: Billington, "Black Cavalrymen," 68; Billington, *New Mexico's Buffalo Soldiers*, 93.

Private, D/9th Cavalry, when killed in action against Apaches, Ojo Caliente, NM, Jan 1881. SOURCE: Kenner, *Buffalo Soldiers and Officers of the Ninth Cavalry*, 279.

‡Killed in action by Indians, Canada, NM, while on escort duty, 27 Jan 1881. SOURCE: Regt Return, 9 Cav, Jan 1881; Hamilton, "History of the Ninth Cavalry," 58; *Illustrated Review: Ninth Cavalry*.

JONES, William; Private; 25th Inf. Born in Sussex County, VA; Ht 5'8", black hair and eyes, coffee complexion; occupation coachman; enlisted at age 24, New York City, 8 Sep 1886; arrived Ft Snelling, MN, 20 Jan 1887. SOURCE: Descriptive & Assignment Rolls of Recruits, 25 Inf.

JONES, William; Corporal; B/9th Cav. ‡Promoted from private, Ft DuChesne, UT, Jun 1895. SOURCE: *ANJ* 32 (22 Jun 1895): 706.

At Ft DuChesne, Jan 1897; appointed 3 Jun 1895. SOURCE: Ninth Cavalry, Roster of NCOs, 1897.

JONES, William; Private; F/25th Inf. Died 27 Nov 1898; buried at Ft Bayard, NM, in plot F15 149. SOURCE: "Fort Bayard National Cemetery, Records of Burials."

Buried 27 Nov 1898, section A, row M, plot 17, at Ft Bayard. SOURCE: Erickson, Burials at Fort Bayard National Cemetery, NM.

JONES, William B.; Private; 25th Inf. Born in Atlanta, GA; Ht 5'8", black hair and brown eyes, yellow complexion; occupation waiter; enlisted at age 27, Chicago, IL, 29 Nov 1886; arrived Ft Snelling, MN, 1 Apr 1887. SOURCE: Descriptive & Assignment Rolls of Recruits, 25 Inf.

JONES, William T.; Private; G/25th Inf. Born in Gettysburg, PA; Ht 5'9", black hair and eyes, yellow complexion; occupation barber; enlisted 5 Aug 1886, age 27, New York City; assigned to G/25th Infantry; arrived Ft Snelling, MN, 14 Dec 1886. SOURCE: Descriptive & Assignment Rolls of Recruits, 25 Inf.

JONES, Wilmer; D/24th Inf. Born in Virginia; mulatto complexion; cannot read or write, age 24, Jul 1870, at Ft McKavett, TX. SOURCE: Bierschwale, *Fort McKavett*, 96.

JORDAN, Albert E.; Private; F/23rd Kan Inf. Died 31 Mar 1937; buried at Ft Leavenworth National Cemetery, plot H 3315-F. SOURCE: Ft Leavenworth National Cemetery.

JORDAN, George; 1st Sgt; K/9th Cav. ‡Born in Williamson Co., KY; enlisted, age 19, Nashville, TN, 25 Dec 1866; occupation farmer; Ht 5'4", black complexion. SOURCE: Register of Enlistments, 1866.

‡Second enlistment, Ft Davis, TX, 3 Jan 1870, as corporal. SOURCE: Register of Enlistments, 1870.

Native of Tennessee; transferred in 1870 to 9th Cavalry after three years in infantry; listed on Census rolls 1870 as illiterate; gradually became "quite proficient in grammatical skills"; as private, K/9th Cavalry, at Ft Richardson, TX, in 1874, only member of troop to defend Capt. Jacob Lee Humfreville in latter's trial for brutality, denied that Humfreville had bribed him but acknowledged receiving $2.50 from Humfreville for Christmas; promoted to corporal Sep 1874; at Ft Davis, TX, 1876; promoted to sergeant 1879; in 1884 organized the "Diamond Club" at Camp Supply, OK, with Sgt. Thomas Shaw; Diamond Club staged gala balls on Christmas Eve 1884, 27 Jul 1889, Jan 1890, and 20 Apr 1891 at Ft Robinson, NE; valor in Victorio war and Medal of Honor mentioned; informed by adjutant general that the denial of right to vote was the prerogative of local officials. SOURCE: Kenner, *Buffalo Soldiers and Officers of the Ninth Cavalry*, 14–15, 145–47, 152–55, 316.

‡Third enlistment, Ft Griffin, TX, 3 Jan 1875, as corporal. SOURCE: Register of Enlistments, 1875.

‡Fourth enlistment, Farmington, NM, 3 Jan 1880, as sergeant; discharged, Ft Supply, Indian Territory, 2 Jan 1880, character good. SOURCE: Register of Enlistments, 1880.

‡Won Medal of Honor for organizing and directing defense of civilian settlement at old Ft Tularosa, NM, against Victorio. SOURCE: Leckie, *The Buffalo Soldiers*, 221.

Life, career, and bravery against Apaches, for which he received Medal of Honor, narrated. SOURCE: Schubert, *Black Valor*, 69, 74–75, 77–79, 87–88, 115, 117–18.

‡Rifleman with "sure finger and keen eyesight," commanded detachment of twenty-five that repulsed 100 Apaches, 14 May 1880, old Ft Tularosa; with nineteen men forced Apaches back in Carrizo Canyon, NM, 12 Aug 1881; [erroneously states] Jordan retired to U.S. Soldiers Home, Washington, DC. SOURCE: Lee, *Negro Medal of Honor Men*, 70–71; Billington, *New Mexico's Buffalo Soldiers*, 95–96, 105.

‡Heroism on Aug 1881 mentioned. SOURCE: Carroll, *The Black Military Experience*, 378.

Sergeant, K/9th Cavalry, awarded certificate of merit for gallantry in action while commanding right wing of detachment of nineteen keeping a large number of the enemy from surrounding the command, Carrizo Canyon, 12 Aug 1881. SOURCE: Gleim, *The Certificate of Merit*, 43.

Appointed first sergeant 20 Jul 1886; in K/9th Cavalry at Ft Robinson, Jan 1897. SOURCE: Ninth Cavalry, Roster of NCOs, 1897.

‡Commended by post commander, Ft Robinson, for role in capture of escapee, 24 Jan 1887. SOURCE: CO, Ft Robinson, to CO, K/9 Cav, 24 Jan 1887, LS, Ft Robinson.

‡Fifth enlistment, Ft Supply, 3 Jan 1885, as first sergeant; discharged, Ft Robinson, 2 Jan 1890, character very good. SOURCE: Register of Enlistments, 1885.

‡Sixth enlistment, Ft Robinson, 3 Jan 1890; discharged 2 Jan 1895, character excellent. SOURCE: Register of Enlistments, 1890.

‡Award of Medal of Honor published in Order 23, 9th Cavalry, 4 Jan 1890.

‡President, Diamond Club, K/9th Cavalry, Ft Robinson. SOURCE: *ANJ* 28 (2 May 1891): 620.

‡First sergeant, K/9th Cavalry, since 20 Jul 1896. SOURCE: Roster, 9 Cav.

‡Retires from Ft Robinson in accordance with Special Order 73, Adjutant General's Office, 30 Mar 1897.

‡Affidavit, from Crawford, NE, 13 Dec 1898. SOURCE: VA File XC 2648848, Rufus Slaughter.

‡Assessed value of personal property, 1902, was $11.

‡Died in Crawford 24 Oct 1904; thirty-year veteran, at Ft Robinson 1885–98; retired and lived in Crawford; buried with military honors, Ft Robinson. SOURCE: Crawford *Tribune*, 28 Oct 1904.

‡Funeral, Ft Robinson, 26 Oct 1904, attended by entire command; died preceding day; according to Dr. J. H. Hartwell of Crawford, "First Sergt. George Jordan, retired, died for the want of proper attention. He lived alone and had no one to attend to his wants. The Doctor made two applications for his admittance into Fort Robinson Hospital and was refused." SOURCE: Monthly Report, Chaplain Anderson, 1 Nov 1904.

‡Jordan applied for admission to hospital when Col. Jacob Augur was absent; hospital did not have facilities and Jordan was not destitute; he was advised to go to Soldiers Home but said he could not due to business at Crawford. SOURCE: Endorsement, Colonel Augur, to Monthly Report, Chaplain Anderson, 1 Nov 1904.

‡Surgeon General states that retiree has no right to treatment in military hospitals; privilege may be granted on decision of commander with advice of surgeon based on situation; "at the same time, surgeons should be careful to show all practicable consideration towards retired soldiers, especially when their records and services are as excellent as were those of 1st Sergeant George Jordan, Retired." SOURCE: Endorsement, Surgeon General, to Monthly Report, Chaplain Anderson, 1 Nov 1904.

‡Biography erroneously follows Lee regarding Jordan's retirement. SOURCE: Reasons and Patrick, *They Had a Dream*.

‡Biographical sketch. SOURCE: Logan and Winston, eds., *Dictionary of American Negro Biography*, 371–72.

‡No Veterans Administration pension file.

JORDAN, Moses; Sergeant; K/9th Cav. ‡Corporal as of 16 Apr 1892. SOURCE: Roster, 9 Cav.

‡Promoted to sergeant, Ft Robinson, NE, Mar 1895. SOURCE: *ANJ* 32 (30 Mar 1895): 506.

Appointed sergeant 16 Mar 1895; in K/9th Cavalry at Ft Robinson, Jan 1897. SOURCE: Ninth Cavalry, Roster of NCOs, 1897.

‡Stationed at Ft Meyer, VA, 1894. SOURCE: *ANJ* 31 (7 Jul 1894): 786.

JORDON, John; Musician; G/25th Inf. Died on 27 Mar 1899; buried at San Antonio National Cemetery, Section I, number 1688. SOURCE: San Antonio National Cemetery Locator.

JORDON, Robert; Corporal; 9th Cav. Received Philippine Campaign Badge number 11734 for service as corporal, D/25th Infantry; in 9th Cavalry at Ft Leavenworth, KS, Mar 1905. SOURCE: Philippine Campaign Badge list, 29 May 1905.

JOSEPH, Leon; Private; A/39th Inf. Civil War veteran, served in D/10th Heavy Artillery; sentence of death for involvement in New Iberia, LA, mutiny, Jul 1867, reduced to ten years. SOURCE: Dobak and Phillips, *The Black Regulars*, 222.

JULY, Benjamin; 1st Sgt; U.S. Army. Seminole Negro Scout, born in Mexico; enlisted at Ft Clark, TX, 21 Sep 1882, age 19; Ht 5'11", black hair and eyes, black complexion; discharged 20 Sep 1883, reenlisted next day at Ft Clark; discharged 31 Aug 1884, reenlisted 27 Dec 1884 at Ft Clark; discharged 26 Dec 1885 at Camp Neville Springs, TX; enlisted 9 Jan 1886 for one year at Ft Clark where he was discharged, reenlisted for one year three more times; discharged 9 Jan 1890, reenlisted for six months the same day at Ft Clark; discharged at Camp Neville Springs 8 Jul 1890; enlisted 9 Jan 1891 at Ft Clark; discharged, reenlisted 8 Jul 1891; discharged, reenlisted 9 Jan 1892 at Camp Palvo, TX; discharged 19 Jul 1892, reenlisted at Camp Presidio, TX; discharged 18 Jan 1893 and 18 Jul 1893, reenlisted next day at Ft Ringgold, TX; promoted to sergeant Jun 1893; promoted to first sergeant Jun 1894; served as first sergeant at Ft Ringgold from 1894 to 1904; at Ft Clark 1907 for discharge with disability 28 May 1907; retired first sergeant at Washington, DC; died 14 Sep 1912; buried at Seminole Cemetery. SOURCE: Swanson, 23.

Son of Scout Sampson July, Seminole Negro Scout, served 1882–1907. SOURCE: Schubert, Consolidated List of Seminole Negro Scouts.

Married man in 1894; widow Martha filed claim in 1918. SOURCE: NARA, M 929, Roll 2.

JULY, Billy; Private; 10th Cav. Born in Mexico; enlisted as Seminole Negro Scout at Ft Clark, TX, 29 May 1884, age 20; discharged 31 Aug 1884; enlisted and served at Ft Clark 19 Jan 1886–8 Jan 1890; enlisted at Ft Clark 9 Jan 1890; discharged 8 Jul 1890, where he reenlisted next day at Camp Neville Springs, TX; discharged at Ft Clark 8 Jan 1891, reenlisted next day; discharged 8 Jul 1891 at Camp Palvo, TX, where he reenlisted, discharged 8 Jul 1892; enlisted 9 Jul 1892 at Camp Neville Springs; discharged at Camp Palvo 8 Jan 1892; enlisted at Camp Neville Springs 9 Jan 1892; discharged, reenlisted 9 Jul 1892 at Camp Presidio, TX; discharged 8 Jan 1893 at Camp Salinno; reenlisted 9 Jul 1893 at Ft Ringgold, TX; discharged 8 Jan 1893 as sergeant at Camp San Pedro, TX; reenlisted at Camp Salenio, TX, 9 Jan 1893; discharged as sergeant 8 Jul 1893 at Ft Ringgold; reenlisted at Camp San Pedro 9 Jan 1894; discharged as corporal 8 Jul 1894, reenlisted next day at Ft Ringgold; discharged as corporal 8 Jan 1895, reenlisted for three years next day at Ft Ringgold; discharged as private 8 Jan 1898, reenlisted 10 Jan 1898 at Ft Ringgold; discharged as private 9 Jan 1901, reenlisted next day at Ft Ringgold; discharged as corporal 9 Jan 1904, reenlisted next day at Ft Ringgold; discharged as private 9 Jan 1907, reenlisted next day at Ft Clark; discharged as private 9 Jan 1913, reenlisted next day, age 46 at Ft Clark; transferred to 10th Cavalry 16 Jul 1914. SOURCE: Swanson, 24.

Son of Scout Sampson July, Seminole Negro Scout, served 1884, 1886–1913. SOURCE: Schubert, Consolidated List of Seminole Negro Scouts.

Private, U.S. Army, Seminole Negro Scout; married Dolly, born ca. 1870, daughter of Scout Sgt. John Ward. SOURCE: Schubert, *Black Valor*, 30; Porter, *The Negro on the American Frontier*, 474.

Born in Texas, private, 10th Cavalry; died 4 Apr 1914; buried at Seminole Indian Scout Cemetery, Kinney County, TX. SOURCE: Indian Scout Cemetery, Kinney County, Texas.

JULY, Carolina; Private; U.S. Army. Seminole Negro Scout, born in Mexico; enlisted at Ft Duncan, TX, 1 Jan 1874, age 18; Ht 5'4", black hair and eyes, black complexion; discharged 7 Jul 1874 at Camp Palafox, TX; reenlisted 7 Jul 1874 at Ft Duncan where he was discharged 11 Feb 1875; enlisted 1 Feb 1875 at Ft Clark, TX; discharged 18 Sep 1875 at Camp Supply, IT; enlisted 4 Oct 1875 at Ft Clark where he was discharged 4 Feb 1876; enlisted 13 Oct 1876 at Ft Duncan; discharged 13 Apr 1877 at Camp Painted Comanche, TX, where he reenlisted same day; discharged

13 Apr 1878 at Camp Howard C. where he reenlisted same day; discharged 24 Apr 1879 at Ft Clark; reenlisted and discharged at Ft Clark for one-year term, 2 May 1879–1 Apr 1880; son of Sampson July; died 13 Apr 1884; buried at Seminole Cemetery. SOURCE: Swanson, 25.

Son of Scout Sampson July, Seminole Negro Scout, served 1873–82; pension file in National Archives. SOURCE: Schubert, Consolidated List of Seminole Negro Scouts.

Widow Jhonar Laslie filed pension claim, VA file SC 3021675. SOURCE: Schubert, "Seminole-Negro Scouts."

Died 18 Apr 1884; buried at Seminole Indian Scout Cemetery, Kinney County, TX. SOURCE: Indian Scout Cemetery, Kinney County, Texas.

JULY, Charles; Private; U.S. Army. Born in Mexico, also called Cabo July, son of Jim July; enlisted at Ft Clark, TX, 5 Jun 1875, age 18; Ht 5'6", black hair and eyes, black complexion; discharged 21 Dec 1875 at Ft Clark; enlisted 4 Jan 1876 at Ft Duncan, TX; discharged 8 Aug 1876 at Camp Pecos, TX; enlisted 1 Oct 1876 at Camp Eagle Pass, TX; discharged, reenlisted 1 Apr 1877 at Camp Painted Comanche, TX; discharged 20 Apr 1878, reenlisted 7 May 1878 at Ft Clark; discharged 6 May 1879, reenlisted next day at Ft Clark; accidentally shot and killed himself at Camp Pecos 5 Nov 1879; buried in Seminole Cemetery. SOURCE: Swanson, 25.

Seminole Negro Scout, served 1875–79. SOURCE: Schubert, Consolidated List of Seminole Negro Scouts.

Buried at Seminole Indian Scout Cemetery, Kinney County, TX. SOURCE: Indian Scout Cemetery, Kinney County, Texas.

JULY, Charles J.; Private; U.S. Army. Born at Ft Clark, TX; enlisted at Ft Clark 5 Jun 1875, age 18; Ht 5'7", black hair and eyes, black complexion; enlisted 12 Oct 1908, discharged 11 Oct 1911 at Ft Clark; reenlisted 12 Oct 1911, discharged 31 Jul 1914 at Ft Clark. SOURCE: Swanson, 25.

Seminole Negro Scout, served 1908–14. SOURCE: Schubert, Consolidated List of Seminole Negro Scouts.

JULY, Fay; Private; U.S. Army. Born in Mexico; enlisted at Ft Clark, TX, 16 Sep 1893, age 21; Ht 5'5", black hair and eyes, black complexion; discharged 15 Mar 1894, reenlisted next day at Camp San Pedro, TX; discharged 15 May 1894 at Ft Ringgold, TX; enlisted 5 Apr 1894 at Ft Clark; discharged, reenlisted next day 4 Apr 1898 at Ft Ringgold; discharged 4 Apr 1901, reenlisted next day at Ft Ringgold; discharged 4 Apr 1904, reenlisted next day at Ft Ringgold; discharged 4 Apr 1907, reenlisted next day at Ft Clark; discharged as first sergeant 4 Apr 1913, reenlisted 6 Apr 1913 at Ft Clark; discharged as private 31 Jul 1914; photograph, A. No. 601, with William Shields and alone, photograph A. No. 602, at Old Guardhouse Museum, Brackettville, TX; died 6 Aug 1940; buried at Seminole Cemetery. SOURCE: Swanson, 24.

Son of Scout Sampson July, Seminole Negro Scout, served 1893–1913; pension file VA file C 2348766 in National Archives. SOURCE: Schubert, Consolidated List of Seminole Negro Scouts; Schubert, "Seminole-Negro Scouts."

Buried at Seminole Indian Scout Cemetery, Kinney County, TX. SOURCE: Indian Scout Cemetery, Kinney County, Texas.

JULY, John; Private; U.S. Army. Born in Mexico; enlisted at Ft Duncan, TX, 5 Jun 1875, age 17; Ht 5'6", black hair and eyes, black complexion; discharged 1 Jan 1876 at Ft Duncan where he reenlisted 5 Jan 1876; discharged 8 Aug 1876 at Camp Pecos, TX; reenlisted 13 Nov 1876 at Ft Duncan; discharged 13 May 1877 at Ft Clark, TX, where he reenlisted same day; discharged 13 May 1877 at Camp Devils River, TX; enlisted 14 May 1878 at Camp Howards C; discharged 13 May 1879 at Ft Clark where he reenlisted same day; discharged 27 May 1880 at Ft Clark where he reenlisted 14 May 1881; discharged 28 May 1882 at Camp Myers Spring, TX, where he reenlisted next day; discharged 28 May 1883 at Ft Clark where he reenlisted next day; discharged 28 May 1885 at Camp Myers, TX, where he reenlisted next day; discharged 31 Aug 1884 at Ft Clark where he reenlisted 27 Dec 1884; discharged at Camp Neville, TX, 26 Dec 1885; enlisted four times for one-year terms at Ft Clark where he was discharged; enlisted at Ft Clark 9 Jan 1890; discharged 9 Jul 1890 at Camp Neville where he reenlisted same day; discharged 8 Jan 1891 at Ft Clark where he reenlisted next day; discharged 8 Jul 1891 at Camp Palvo, TX, where he reenlisted for two consecutive 6-month terms; discharged 18 Jul 1892 at Camp Presidio, TX, where he reenlisted next day; discharged 18 Jan 1893 at Ft Ringgold, TX, where he reenlisted next day; discharged as corporal 18 Jul 1893 at Ft Ringgold where he reenlisted next day; discharged as corporal 18 Jan 1894 at Camp San Pedro, TX, where he reenlisted next day; discharged as sergeant 18 Jul 1894 at Camp San Pedro; enlisted 19 Jul 1894 at Ft Ringgold where he was discharged 18 Jan 1895 as sergeant; enlisted 19 Jan 1895 at Ft Ringgold where he was discharged

as private 18 Jan 1898; enlisted 25 Jan 1898; sergeant, died of cirrhosis of liver, 3 Mar 1900. SOURCE: Swanson, 26.

Son of Scout Sampson July, Seminole Negro Scout, served 1875–1900; widow Molly, VA file XC 3102675, in National Archives. SOURCE: Schubert, Consolidated List of Seminole Negro Scouts; Schubert, "Seminole-Negro Scouts."

Buried at Alexandria National Cemetery, Pineville, LA. SOURCE: Gordon, Photos.

JULY, Sampson; Sergeant; U.S. Army. Born in Tampa Bay, FL, at Indian village Tholonoto-sasa, Micanopy reserve; former slave of Micanopy, chief of Seminole Nation; Ht 5'10", black hair and eyes, black complexion; enlisted at Ft Duncan, TX, 4 Mar 1875, age 49; discharged, reenlisted 10 Oct 1875 at Camp Supply, TX; discharged, reenlisted 10 Apr 1876 at Ft Duncan; discharged, reenlisted 10 Apr 1877 at Camp Painted Comanche, TX; discharged, reenlisted 11 Apr 1878 at Camp Howard C.; discharged, reenlisted for one year at Ft Clark, TX, five times, 1 May 1880–13 May 1883; last discharged 12 May 1884 at Camp Myers, TX; wife Mary, children Jim, Fate, and Scouts John, Ben, and Bill July; died 16 May 1918; buried at Seminole Cemetery. SOURCE: Swanson, 26.

Seminole Negro Scout, served 1875–84; father of Scouts Benjamin, Billy, Carolina, Fay, and John July; daughter Rebecca, niece of Chief John Horse, married Scout Billy Wilson. SOURCE: Schubert, Consolidated List of Seminole Negro Scouts.

In 1875 age 45, resided at Ft Duncan with Mary age 42, Carolina age 20, Cato age 18, Jim age 7, John age 16, Fate age 3, Ben age 11, Bill age 10. SOURCE: NARA, M 929, Roll 2; Porter, *The Negro on the American Frontier*, 476.

Seminole Negro Scout; daughter married Scout Bill Williams. SOURCE: Schubert, *Black Valor*, 30.

Born about 1826; buried at Seminole Indian Scout Cemetery, Kinney County, TX. SOURCE: Indian Scout Cemetery, Kinney County, Texas.

JUNIOR, Joe; Private; F/10th Cav. Died 21 Mar 1904; buried at Ft Bayard, NM, in plot J 1. SOURCE: "Fort Bayard National Cemetery, Records of Burials."

K

KAHOLOKULA, John; Private; I/10th Cav. Born in Maui, HI, enlisted 1898; served for three enlistments in 10th Cavalry, one enlistment in 24th Infantry, and one enlistment in 9th Cavalry. SOURCE: Enlistment Registers, notes in authors' files.

‡Served in 10th Cavalry, 1898; remained in U.S. during war with Spain. SOURCE: Cashin, *Under Fire with the Tenth Cavalry*, 348.

‡Stationed at Ft Robinson, NE, 1903.

KANE, Simon; D/24th Inf. Born in Alabama; black complexion; can read and write, age 24, Jul 1870, at Ft McKavett, TX. SOURCE: Bierschwale, *Fort McKavett*, 96.

KARRICK, James; Private; M/9th Cav. Died at Ft McKavett, TX, on 16 Dec 1869; buried at San Antonio National Cemetery, Section E, number 833. SOURCE: San Antonio National Cemetery Locator.

KAY, Alexander; C/25th Inf. Born in Mississippi; black complexion; can read and write, age 22, 5 Sep 1870, at Ft McKavett, TX. SOURCE: Bierschwale, *Fort McKavett*, 109.

KEATES, Charles; Private; G/10th Cav. ‡Original member of 10th Cavalry; in troop when organized, Ft Leavenworth, KS, 5 Jul 1867. SOURCE: McMiller, "Buffalo Soldiers," 74.

Died from accidental discharge of carbine at camp on Union Pacific Railroad, 1 Sep 1867. SOURCE: Regimental Returns, 10th Cavalry, 1867.

KEENE, Howard; Private; I/10th Cav. In Troop I/10th Cavalry stationed at Bonita Cañon Camp, AZ, 30 Jun 1886. SOURCE: Tagg, *The Camp at Bonita Cañon*, 232.

KELHAM, Henry; Private; M/10th Cav. ‡Private Kelhany, M/10th Cavalry, mentioned as recently died, Mar 1874. SOURCE: ES, 10 Cav, 1872–81.

Died 1 May 1874 of disease at Camp Benson. SOURCE: Regimental Returns, 10th Cavalry, 1874.

KELLAM, Alfred; Sergeant; H/9th Cav. ‡Promoted to corporal, H/9th Cavalry, from lance corporal, Ft DuChesne, UT, Dec 1894. SOURCE: *ANJ* 32 (22 Dec 1894): 278.

Appointed corporal 8 Dec 1894; in H/9th Cavalry at Ft Robinson, NE, Jan 1897. SOURCE: Ninth Cavalry, Roster of NCOs, 1897.

Alfred Keliam received Philippine Campaign Badge number 11856 for service as sergeant in H/9th Cavalry; in 9th Cavalry at Ft Leavenworth, KS, Mar 1905. SOURCE: Philippine Campaign Badge list, 29 May 1905.

‡Veteran of Philippine Insurrection; sergeant, H/9th Cavalry, at Ft D. A. Russell, WY, in 1910; sharpshooter; resident of Fairmount Heights, MD. SOURCE: *Illustrated Review: Ninth Cavalry*, with picture.

KELLEY, George B.; 1st Sgt; C/9th Cav. ‡Born in Galipolis, OH; served in G/24th Infantry, 27 Aug 1897–18 Jun 1899; age 23 in 1900; served in D/49th Infantry before becoming battalion sergeant major, 7 Oct 1900; served at Tuguegarao, Cagayan, Philippines, Nov 1900; regimental sergeant major, 23 Dec 1900; reduced to private and confined 14 Feb–14 Jul 1900; discharged, character excellent; wife is Mrs. Rena B. Kelley, 267 Everett Street, Portland, OR. SOURCE: Descriptive Book, 49 Inf NCS.

‡Served in Cuba at San Juan and Santiago; spent forty days at Siboney, Cuba, hospital; private and corporal, G/24th Infantry; enlisted in 49th Infantry, San Francisco; second lieutenant, K/49th Infantry, 6 Feb 1901; discharged Aparri, Philippines, 20 May 1901, character excellent. SOURCE: Descriptive Book, K/49 Inf.

‡Stationed at Ord Barracks, Monterey, CA, 1903; president of Literary and Social Club organized with civilians of Pacific Grove, CA; manager of squadron baseball team that lost to 15th Infantry. SOURCE: Indianapolis *Freeman*, 5 Dec 1903.

‡Letter to editor, n.d., on opportunities in the Philippines, observes that there are no windfalls available and opportunities for small capital investment have leveled off; success "depends on the man himself for a successful grasping of them as elsewhere." SOURCE: Indianapolis *Freeman*, 20 Feb 1904.

Received Philippine Campaign Badge number 11892 for service as private in H/9th Cavalry; in 9th Cavalry at Ft

Leavenworth, KS, Mar 1905. SOURCE: Philippine Campaign Badge list, 29 May 1905.

‡Former private, G/24th Infantry; died in Minnesota, 9 Oct 1938. SOURCE: Taylor, "Minnesota Black Spanish-American War Veterans."

KELLEY, James; Trumpeter; L/9th Cav. *See* **KELLY,** James, Trumpeter, L/9th Cavalry

KELLEY, Richard; Private; D/9th Cav. With Captain Dodge at battle at Milk River, CO, 2–10 Oct 1879. SOURCE: Miller, *Hollow Victory*, 167, 206–7.

KELLY, George C.; Private; G/10th Cav. Died 24 Jul 1867 of cholera at Wilson Creek, KS. SOURCE: Regimental Returns, 10th Cavalry, 1867.

KELLY, James; Trumpeter; L/9th Cav. Enlisted at Ft Lyons, CO, on 25 Nov 1876; discharged at Ft Bliss, TX, 2 Jan 1881 with surgeon's certificate of disability, bursa of left hip, contracted in line of duty, character good. SOURCE: Muster Roll, L/9th Cavalry, 31 Dec 1880–28 Feb 1881.

‡Discharged on certificate of disability, Ft Bliss, 2 Jan 1881. SOURCE: Regt Returns, 9 Cav, Jan 1881.

Kelly, Joseph, Jr.; Private; K/24th Inf. Died 14 Apr 1902; buried at Ft Bayard, NM, in plot N 37. SOURCE: "Fort Bayard National Cemetery, Records of Burials."

Buried 14 Apr 1902, section A, row V, plot 37, at Ft Bayard. SOURCE: Erickson, Burials at Fort Bayard National Cemetery, NM.

KELLY, Joseph W.; Private; I/25th Inf. Died at Ft McIntosh, TX, on 1 Apr 1907; buried at Fort Sam Houston National Cemetery, Section PE, number 400. SOURCE: Buffalo Soldiers Interred in Fort Sam Houston National Cemetery.

KELLY, Vernon; Private; H/24th Inf. ‡Fined $10 by summary court, San Isidro, Philippines, for being drunk and disorderly in street, 30 Jan 1902, fourth conviction; sentenced to two days in solitary confinement on bread and water and fined one month's pay for disobeying legal order to remain in quarters, 13 Feb 1902; fined $5 for being drunk in street, 6 Apr 1902. SOURCE: Register of Summary Court, San Isidro.

Died in the Philippines 9 May 1902; body received for burial 12 Jun 1905 at San Francisco National Cemetery, buried in plot NADD/833. SOURCE: San Francisco National Cemetery.

KELLY, Walter; Private; G/25th Inf. Born in Princess Anne County, VA; Ht 5'8", black hair and brown eyes, brown complexion; occupation farmer; resided in Kemperville,

VA, when enlisted 1 Sep 1886, age 24, at Baltimore, MD; assigned to G/25th Infantry; arrived Ft Snelling, MN, 14 Dec 1886. SOURCE: Descriptive & Assignment Rolls of Recruits, 25 Inf.

KELLY, William H.; K/10th Cav. ‡Sergeant-at-arms, Camp 30, National Indian War Veterans, San Antonio, TX. SOURCE: *Winners of the West* 6 (Oct 1929): 7.

‡Commander, Camp 30; World War I veteran. SOURCE: *Winners of the West* 7 (Oct 1930): 7.

‡Fought in Apache campaign, 1885–86, while at Ft Grant, AZ; recalls that Pvt. Frank Scott was killed in action; Bill Gibbons was first sergeant. SOURCE: *Winners of the West* 15 (Jan 1938): 7.

Died on 2 Feb 1940; buried at Fort Sam Houston National Cemetery, Section A, number 84. SOURCE: Buffalo Soldiers Interred in Fort Sam Houston National Cemetery.

KELSEY, Edward; Private; D/9th Cav. With Captain Dodge at battle at Milk River, CO, 2–10 Oct 1879. SOURCE: Miller, *Hollow Victory*, 167, 206–7.

‡In D/9th Cavalry, Ft Craig, NM, 1881; killed Nov 1881 by deserter Pvt. William Richardson, D/9th Cavalry, who was tracked by detachment under Sergeant Dickerson and found by Pvt. Edward Kelsey. SOURCE: Billington, *New Mexico's Buffalo Soldiers*, 131.

Died 17 Nov 1881; buried at Ft Leavenworth National Cemetery, plot C 1975. SOURCE: Ft Leavenworth National Cemetery.

Kemp, Charlie; Private; F/49th Inf. Died 28 Feb 1945; buried at Ft Leavenworth National Cemetery, plot C 2175. SOURCE: Ft Leavenworth National Cemetery.

KENDAL, Hampton; Private; 24th Inf. *See* **KENDALL,** Hampton, Private, F/24th Infantry

KENDALL, Hampton; Private; F/24th Inf. ‡Drowned crossing San Mateo River, Philippines, 21 Aug 1899. SOURCE: Richmond *Planet*, 2 Sep 1899.

Private, F/24th Infantry, died 21 Aug 1899; buried in plot E 8 593 at San Francisco National Cemetery. SOURCE: San Francisco National Cemetery.

KENDALL, Jackson; Private; K/10th Cav. ‡Served in 10th Cavalry, 1898; remained in U.S. during war with Spain. SOURCE: Cashin, *Under Fire with the Tenth Cavalry*, 349.

Received Philippine Campaign Badge number 11714 for service as private in E/9th Cavalry; in 9th Cavalry at Ft Leavenworth, KS, Mar 1905. SOURCE: Philippine Campaign Badge list, 29 May 1905.

KENDRICK, David; Private; F/9th Cav. ‡Recruit from depot, arrived Ft Robinson, NE, 1 Mar 1887.

At Ft Robinson, Jun 1887, assaulted Pvt. William Smith in dining hall after Smith drew a knife; both acquitted by court martial. SOURCE: Kenner, *Buffalo Soldiers and Officers of the Ninth Cavalry*, 170.

‡Released by garrison court martial, Ft Robinson, which determined he did strike Pvt. W. Smith, F/9th Cavalry, on head with bowl in troop dining room, but not to prejudice of good order and discipline. SOURCE: Order 140, 13 Jul 1887, Post Orders, Ft Robinson.

‡Prisoner in guardhouse, Ft Robinson, Dec 1889; complained to inspector general that before he was tried, letter from his mother, asking his discharge as her only support, was returned by his commander to Washington with claim that Kendrick had written it himself; Military Convict Jones, F/9th Cavalry, acknowledges writing letter. SOURCE: Report of Inspection, 2 Dec 1889, Reports of Inspections, DP, I.

KENDRICK, Lindsay; Sergeant; I/10th Cav. ‡Served 1876. *See* OTT, **BRITTON**, William H., Recruit, Mounted Service

‡Deposited $20 with paymaster, Ft Concho, TX, 1877. SOURCE: LS, 10 Cav, 1873–83.

Cpl. Lindsey Kindricks, I/10th Cavalry, stationed at Bonita Cañon Camp, AZ, but absent or on detached service 30 Jun 1886. SOURCE: Tagg, *The Camp at Bonita Cañon*, 231.

‡At Fort Apache, AZ, 1890, subscribed $.50 to testimonial to General Grierson. SOURCE: List of subscriptions, 23 Apr 1890, 10th Cavalry papers, MHI.

KENNEDY, Henry; Private; L/10th Cav. ‡Original member of 10th Cavalry; in troop when organized, Ft Riley, KS, 21 Sep 1867. SOURCE: McMiller, "Buffalo Soldiers," 78.

Died 27 Jul 1870 of chronic diarrhea at Ft Sill, OK. SOURCE: Regimental Returns, 10th Cavalry, 1870.

Private, L/10th Cavalry, died 26 Jul 1870, buried at Camp Douglas, UT. SOURCE: Record Book of Interments, Post Cemetery, 252.

KENNEDY, John; Corporal; D/10th Cav. Died 21 Feb 1875 in hospital at Ft Sill, OK. SOURCE: Regimental Returns, 10th Cavalry, 1875.

KENNEDY, Richard; Private; A/9th Cav. Enlisted age 21, Baltimore, MD, May 1880; dark complexion, Ht 5'8"; joined troop at Ft Stanton, NM, 13 Oct 1880 after preliminary training at Jefferson Bks, MO; assigned to tend post garden near Mescalero Indian Agency, Feb 1881; convicted of homosexual advances toward Cpl. Randall Brown, A/9th Cavalry, sentenced to dishonorable discharge and one year. SOURCE: Kenner, *Buffalo Soldiers and Officers of the Ninth Cavalry*, 268–69.

‡In A/9th Cavalry at Ft Stanton, 1881. SOURCE: Regt Returns, 9 Cav, Jan 1881.

KENNY, Isaac; Private; I/10th Cav. Died 12 Jan 1869 of no listed cause at Ft Wallace, KS. SOURCE: Regimental Returns, 10th Cavalry, 1869.

KERNAN, William; Private; B/25th Inf. Enlisted 13 Jan 1900, discharged as private M/24th Infantry 24 Nov 1902, character very good; enlisted 18 Feb 1905, discharged without honor 19 Nov 1906. SOURCE: Powell, "Military Record of the Enlisted Men Who Were Discharged Without Honor."

Dishonorable discharge, Brownsville, TX. SOURCE: SO 266, AGO, 9 Nov 1906.

KERSHAW, Francis; C/25th Inf. Born in Virginia; mulatto complexion; can read and write, age 24, 5 Sep 1870, at Ft McKavett, TX. SOURCE: Bierschwale, *Fort McKavett*, 109.

KEY, Charles; Ord Sgt; U.S. Army. ‡Original member of E/10th Cavalry; in troop when organized, Ft Leavenworth, KS, 15 Jun 1867. SOURCE: McMiller, "Buffalo Soldiers," 72.

‡Mentioned as private, formerly sergeant, E/10th Cavalry, Mar 1874. SOURCE: ES, 10 Cav, 1872–81.

‡Private, E/10th Cavalry; honorable mention for gallantry against Kiowas and Comanches, Wichita Agency, Indian Territory, 22–23 Aug 1874. SOURCE: Baker, Roster.

‡Appointed ordnance sergeant from sergeant, E/10th Cavalry, 8 Feb 1889. SOURCE: Baker, Roster.

Quartermaster sergeant in Troop E/10th Cavalry stationed at Bonita Cañon Camp, AZ, 28 Feb 1886. SOURCE: Tagg, *The Camp at Bonita Cañon*, 231.

Appointed ordnance sergeant 8 Feb 1889, from sergeant, E/10th Cavalry. SOURCE: Dobak, "Staff Noncommissioned Officers."

‡Ordnance sergeant at Ft Trumbull, CT, with twenty-seven years of service. SOURCE: Cleveland *Gazette*, 12 Mar 1892.

Resided in Philadelphia, 1896, in same house as veteran James Logan, 10th Cavalry; resided in Cape May, NJ, 1902. SOURCE: Sayre, *Warriors of Color*, 360.

KIBBETTS, George; Private; U.S. Army. Born at Ft Duncan, TX; Ht 5'5", black hair and eyes, black complexion; enlisted at Ft Clark, TX, 3 May 1894, age 22; discharged 1 Nov 1894 at Ft Ringgold, TX; enlisted starting 25 Jun 1902 for three years at Ft Clark where he was discharged, 25 Jun 1914, age 37; Seminole Scouts terminated 30 Jun 1914; buried at Seminole Cemetery. SOURCE: Swanson, 27.

Possibly son of Bobby Kibbetts; Seminole Negro Scout, served 1894, 1902–14; claim filed 1932, VA file C 2612717 in National Archives. SOURCE: Schubert, Consolidated List of Seminole Negro Scouts; Schubert, "Seminole-Negro Scouts."

KIBBETTS, John; 1st Sgt; 24th Inf. Born in Florida, a slave or descendent of Kub-bit-che, Seminole chief; Seminole warrior name Sit-tee-tas-to-nach-y, "Tearing Warrior"; second in command of Seminole Negro Indian band under Chief John Horse in Mexico; band split in two after moving to Texas from Naciemiento, Mexico, and Laguna de Parras, Mexico; Kibbetts became chief of Naciemiento group; asked Captain DeGress at Ft Duncan, TX, to return to Indian Territory; Ht 5'11", black hair and eyes, black complexion; enlisted as sergeant at Ft Duncan, 16 Sep 1870, age 62; served as sergeant, enlisted and discharged continuously at Ft Duncan to 1 Jul 1874; enlisted 1 Jan 1875 at Ft Duncan; discharged at Ft Concho, TX, 1 Jul 1875, reenlisted same day; discharged 1 Jan 1876 at Ft Duncan; enlisted 12 Sep 1876, discharged as first sergeant 12 Mar 1877 at Ft Clark, TX; enlisted 12 Mar 1877 as first sergeant, discharged 12 Mar 1878 at Ft Clark; son Scout Robert Kibbetts; elected and remained chief of Seminole at military reservations until his death 7 Sep 1878; succeeded by Scout Elijah Daniels; buried at Seminole Cemetery. SOURCE: Swanson, 27, 28.

Seminole Negro Scout, leader of first group of ten Scouts to enlist Aug 1870 and made sergeant. SOURCE: Schubert, *Black Valor*, 28–29, 34.

Second in command after Chief John Horse of 250 Seminole-Negroes in Mexico in 1870; 100 under Kibbetts at Nacimiento, Coahuila, near Eagle Pass, TX; age 70, resided at Ft Duncan in 1875 with wife Nancy age 60 and Missouri age 15; step-granddaughter Julia (ca. 1862–1946) was wife of Isaac Payne. SOURCE: NARA Record Group 393, Special File; Porter, *The Negro on the American Frontier*, 474, 476.

KIBBETTS, Robert; Corporal; U.S. Army. Born in Arkansas; also known as Bobby; son of Scout John Kibbetts; Ht 5'9", black hair and eyes, black complexion; enlisted at Ft Duncan, TX, 16 Aug 1870, age 26; discharged, reenlisted continuously at Ft Duncan through 1 Feb 1875; discharged at Ft Concho, TX, 1 Aug 1875; enlisted 1 Sep 1875, discharged 1 Mar 1876 at Ft Duncan; enlisted 11 Apr 1876, discharged 11 Oct 1876 at Ft Clark, TX; reenlisted 11 Oct 1876 at Ft Clark; after Deputy Windus shot Scout Adam Payne on 1 Jan 1877, reportedly jumped Deputy Windus and Sheriff Croswell, John Thomas wrestled Kibbetts off Windus while Scouts Isaac Payne and Dallas Griner and others escaped to Naciemientos, Mexico; Kibbetts charged with attempted murder of deputy in performance of duty, grand jury found him not guilty of charge 12 May 1877; discharged, reenlisted 11 Apr 1877 at Camp Painted Comanche, TX; discharged, reenlisted 11 Apr 1878, Camp Howards C.; discharged, reenlisted 24 Apr 1879 at Ft Clark; discharged as corporal 1 May 1880, reenlisted next day at Ft Clark; discharged as sergeant 12 May 1881, reenlisted, discharged as sergeant through 19 May 1882; discharged as first sergeant 18 May 1883, reenlisted next day at Ft Clark; discharged as sergeant 18 May 1884 at Camp Myers, TX; enlisted 30 May 1884 at Ft Clark; discharged 5 Jun 1885, reenlisted 11 Jun 1885 at Camp Neville Springs, TX; discharged as sergeant 3 Jun 1886 at Ft Clark; enlisted at Camp Neville Springs 4 June 1886; discharged 3 Jun 1887, reenlisted 6 Jun 1887 at Ft Clark; discharged 3 Jun 1888, reenlisted next day at Camp Pena Colorado, TX; discharged 3 Jun 1889, reenlisted next day at Ft Clark; discharged, reenlisted for six months as sergeant at Camp Neville Springs 3 Dec 1889–4 Dec 1890; discharged 3 Jun 1891 at Camp Palvo, TX, reenlisted next day as private; discharged as private 3 Jun 1892 at Camp Presidio, TX; enlisted 3 Jun 1892 at Ft Clark; discharged 2 Jan 1893, reenlisted next day at Ft Ringgold; discharged 12 Jul 1894, reenlisted next day at Ft Ringgold; discharged 12 Jul 1894 at Camp Hot Springs, AR; enlisted 15 Nov 1895 at Ft Clark; discharged as corporal 14 Nov 1898, reenlisted next day at Ft Ringgold; discharged 14 Nov 1904 as corporal, reenlisted next day for three years at age 57 at Ft Clark; died of exhaustion from chronic bronchitis and chronic asthma 26 Apr 1905; buried at Seminole Cemetery; 1880 Census lists wife Philes and children Washington and Marin. SOURCE: Swanson, 28.

Seminole Negro Scout, served 1870–1904; pension file in National Archives. SOURCE: Schubert, Consolidated List of Seminole Negro Scouts.

Promoted from private to corporal May 1878; promoted from private to sergeant June 1884; widow Phyllis; VA Pension file XC 2681380. SOURCE: NARA, M929, Roll 2.

In original detachment of Scouts enlisted at Ft Duncan, Aug 1870, age 20; in 1875, age 30, resided with Phyllis age 25, George age 2. SOURCE: NARA Record Group 393, Special File.

Served thirty-one years as Indian Scout; died 26 Apr 1905; buried at Seminole Indian Scout Cemetery, Kinney County, TX. SOURCE: Indian Scout Cemetery, Kinney County, Texas.

KIBBITS, "L" H.; Corporal; U.S. Army. Seminole Negro Scout; died 1873; buried at Seminole Indian Scout Cemetery, Kinney County, TX. SOURCE: Indian Scout Cemetery, Kinney County, Texas.

KIDD, Henry; Private; C/10th Cav. ‡Original member of 10th Cavalry; in troop when organized, Ft Leavenworth, KS, 14 May 1867. SOURCE: McMiller, "Buffalo Soldiers," 70.

Served with Pvt. George Washington, C/10th Cavalry, early 1870s. SOURCE: Schubert, *Voices of the Buffalo Soldier*, 234.

Kiler, Samuel H., Jr.; Corporal; M/25th Inf. Died in the Philippines 4 Aug 1901; buried in plot NEW A299 at San Francisco National Cemetery. SOURCE: San Francisco National Cemetery.

KIMBALL, Richard; Private; B/10th Cav. On march to Ft Stockton, TX, Feb 1878 refused to help fill water kegs; required to march all day on foot, leading his horse. SOURCE: Kinevan, *Frontier Cavalryman*, 104.

KIMBER, John; Private; H/10th Cav. Born in Robinson County, TN, 1860; enlisted Louisville, KY, 18 Dec 1883; Ht 5'8"; black complexion, eyes, and hair; occupation laborer. SOURCE: Sayre, *Warriors of Color*, 330.

John Krinber in Troop H/10th Cavalry stationed at Bonita Cañon Camp, AZ, but absent or on detached service 30 Apr 1886. SOURCE: Tagg, *The Camp at Bonita Cañon*, 232.

KIMBLERN, Calvin; Private; D/25th Inf. ‡Cited among men who distinguished themselves in 1893 for promptness, perseverance, rapidity in pursuit and capture, after severe struggle, of deserter at Sheridan, WY, 12–13 Oct; and endurance in long ride from Ft Custer, MT, to Sheridan. SOURCE: GO 56, AGO, 10 Nov 1894.

Mentioned in order in 1894 for capture of deserter after pursuit from Ft Custer to Sheridan. SOURCE: Dobak and Phillips, *The Black Regulars*, 262.

KINDRED, Jacob; D/24th Inf. Born in North Carolina; black complexion; can read and write, age 21, Jul 1870, at Ft McKavett, TX. SOURCE: Bierschwale, *Fort McKavett*, 96.

KING, Ben; Private; U.S. Army. Seminole Negro Scout, served in 1875. SOURCE: Schubert, Consolidated List of Seminole Negro Scouts.

Born in Florida; Ht 5'6", black hair and eyes, black complexion; enlisted at Ft Clark, TX, 1 May 1875, age 19; discharged at Ft Clark 21 Dec 1875. SOURCE: Swanson, 27.

KING, James H.; H/25th Inf. Born in Washington, DC; mulatto complexion; can read and write, age 25, 5 Sep 1870, at Ft McKavett, TX. SOURCE: Bierschwale, *Fort McKavett*, 107.

King, Jason C.; Private; K/25th Inf. Died 26 Aug 1907; buried in plot NAWS 1206 at San Francisco National Cemetery. SOURCE: San Francisco National Cemetery.

KING, Willie; Private; A/9th Cav. Received Philippine Campaign Badge number 11733 for service as private, E/9th Cavalry; in 9th Cavalry at Ft Leavenworth, KS, Mar 1905. SOURCE: Philippine Campaign Badge list, 29 May 1905.

‡Veteran of Philippine Insurrection; at Ft D. A. Russell, WY, in 1910. SOURCE: *Illustrated Review: Ninth Cavalry*.

Kinney, Isaac; Private; I/10th Cav. Died 22 Jan 1869; buried at Ft Leavenworth National Cemetery, plot C 1938. SOURCE: Ft Leavenworth National Cemetery.

KINNEY, Sanford; Private; G/25th Inf. Died at Ft Davis, TX, on 6 Sep 1872; buried at San Antonio National Cemetery, Section I, number 1532. SOURCE: San Antonio National Cemetery Locator.

KIPPER, John; Sergeant; A/25th Inf. Spanish-American War veteran; at Ft Bliss, TX, 1900; convicted of murder in attempt to free two soldiers from jail, El Paso, TX, Feb 1900. SOURCE: Leiker, *Racial Borders*, 130.

‡Sentenced to life in prison for leading mob of Negro soldiers against El Paso police station, 17 Feb 1900, and for murder of policeman Newton Stewart. SOURCE: *ANJ* 37 (12 May 1900): 869.

KIRK, William; Private; C/25th Inf. Born in Conestoga, PA; Ht 5'7", black hair and brown eyes, brown complexion; occupation waiter; resided Steelton, PA, when enlisted at age 21, Harrisburg, PA, 24 Jul 1885; assigned to C/25th Infantry; arrived Ft Snelling, MN, 5 Feb 1886. SOURCE: Descriptive & Assignment Rolls of Recruits, 25 Inf.

KIRKLEY, Samuel; Corporal; G/9th Cav. ‡One of six enlisted men of G/9th Cavalry to testify against Lt. John Conline at his 1877 court martial for misconduct, including drunkenness, sexual misconduct, and misappropriation of funds belonging to men of his troop, Ft Garland, CO. SOURCE: Billington, *New Mexico's Buffalo Soldiers*, 121–23.

Private, G/9th Cavalry, at Ft Garland, 1878, when he loaned $83 to Lieutenant Conline. SOURCE: Kenner, *Buffalo Soldiers and Officers of the Ninth Cavalry*, 216.

KITCHEN, George; Private; K/24th Inf. ‡Died of cerebral hemorrhage in the Philippines, 24 Dec 1899. SOURCE: *ANJ* 37 (20 Jan 1900): 488.

Died in the Philippines 14 Dec 1899; body received for burial 29 Mar 1901 at San Francisco National Cemetery, buried in plot NEW A335. SOURCE: San Francisco National Cemetery.

Kline, Louis; Private; E/48th Inf. Died in the Philippines on 9 Nov 1900; body received for burial 15 Apr 1902 at San Francisco National Cemetery. SOURCE: San Francisco National Cemetery, buried in plot NEW A820.

Knight, Daniel; Private; K/49th Inf. Died 21 Mar 1900; buried in plot ES 829 at San Francisco National Cemetery. SOURCE: San Francisco National Cemetery.

KNOWLES, Columbus; M/9th Cav. Born in Kentucky; black complexion; cannot read or write, age 22, Jul 1870, at Ft McKavett, TX. SOURCE: Bierschwale, *Fort McKavett,* 100.

Knox, Marion; Private; K/10th Cav. Originally buried at Ft Grant, AZ; buried at Santa Fe National Cemetery, NM, plot A-1 782. SOURCE: Santa Fe National Cemetery, Records of Burials.

Kurtz, Arthur; Private; C/25th Inf. Died 16 Jul 1902; buried in plot 574 at San Francisco National Cemetery. SOURCE: San Francisco National Cemetery.

L

LACY, George; Private; B/24th Inf. ‡At Cabanatuan, Philippines, 1901; witness in trial of Wade Hampton, Private, B/24th Infantry.

Received Philippine Campaign Badge number 11735 for service as private in C/9th Cavalry; in 9th Cavalry at Ft Leavenworth, KS, Mar 1905. SOURCE: Philippine Campaign Badge list, 29 May 1905.

LAFFERTY, Benjamin; Sqdn Sgt Maj; 9th Cav. ‡Promoted from lance corporal to corporal, I/9th Cavalry, Ft DuChesne, UT, Feb 1896. SOURCE: *ANJ* 33 (7 Mar 1896): 480.

Appointed corporal 24 Feb 1896; in I/9th Cavalry, Ft Washakie, WY, Jan 1897. SOURCE: Ninth Cavalry, Roster of NCOs, 1897.

‡Promoted from first sergeant, C/9th Cavalry, to sergeant major, first squadron/9th Cavalry, Apr 1902. SOURCE: *ANJ* 39 (7 Jun 1902): 1004.

LaFORCE, David; M/9th Cav. Born in Indiana; mulatto complexion; can read and write, age 21, Jul 1870, at Ft McKavett, TX. SOURCE: Bierschwale, *Fort McKavett,* 100.

LAMKINS, Amanias; Sergeant; I/10th Cav. *See* LUMKINS, Ananias, Sergeant, I/10th Cavalry

LANCASTER, Henry; Private; C/25th Inf. Died at Ft Griffin, TX, on 22 Aug 1872; buried at San Antonio National Cemetery, Section D, number 724. SOURCE: San Antonio National Cemetery Locator.

LANDERS, Bass; Private; G/10th Cav. Died 28 Jul 1867 of cholera at Wilson Creek, KS. SOURCE: Regimental Returns, 10th Cavalry, 1867.

LANDERS, George; Private; C/10th Cav. Deserted during tenure of George Garnett as first sergeant, Jan 1869–May 1871. SOURCE: Dobak and Phillips, *The Black Regulars,* 300.

LANE, Edward; 1st Sgt; C/10th Cav. ‡Born in Virginia; private, corporal, sergeant, A/9th Cavalry, 13 Sep 1886–12 Sep 1891; private, C/10th Cavalry, 24 Sep 1891; corporal,

1 Sep 1894; sergeant, 21 Mar 1895; at Ft Assiniboine, MT, 1897. SOURCE: Baker, Roster.

‡Served in 10th Cavalry in Cuba, 1898. SOURCE: Cashin, *Under Fire with the Tenth Cavalry,* 339.

‡Wounded in action, Santiago, Cuba, 1 Jul 1898. SOURCE: SecWar, *AR 1898,* 324.

‡First sergeant, C/10th Cavalry, posted $300 bond for prostitute Lizzie Carr, Crawford, NE, arrested for assault, 1 Apr 1904. SOURCE: Police Court Docket, Crawford, NE.

As first sergeant received Indian Wars Campaign Badge number 1408 on 15 Jul 1909. SOURCE: Carroll, *Indian Wars Campaign Badge,* 42.

Retired first sergeant, died 20 Jun 1916; buried at Ft Leavenworth National Cemetery, plot 3315D. SOURCE: Ft Leavenworth National Cemetery.

LANE, Pope; M/9th Cav. Born in Alabama; mulatto complexion; cannot read or write, age 24, Jul 1870, at Ft McKavett, TX. SOURCE: Bierschwale, *Fort McKavett,* 100.

LANGSTER, John; M/9th Cav. Born in Kentucky; mulatto complexion; cannot read or write, age 22, Jul 1870, at Ft McKavett, TX. SOURCE: Bierschwale, *Fort McKavett,* 100.

LANGSTON, John; Private; M/9th Cav. Born in Kentucky; buried at Ft McKavett, TX, before 17 May 1879; body removed to National Cemetery, San Antonio, TX, 23 Nov 1883. SOURCE: Bierschwale, *Fort McKavett,* 123.

Died at Ft McKavett on 1 Nov 1871; buried at San Antonio National Cemetery, Section E, number 875. SOURCE: San Antonio National Cemetery Locator.

LANGWOOD, William; Private; D/9th Cav. With Captain Dodge at battle at Milk River, CO, 2–10 Oct 1879. SOURCE: Miller, *Hollow Victory,* 167, 206–7.

LANIER, Frank; Private; 10th Cav. Born in Nashville, TN, 17 Jul 1856; enlisted Cincinnati, OH, 17 Oct 1879; Ht 5'7"; complexion mulatto, black eyes and hair; occupation laborer; served in H/10th Cavalry on scout to Eagle Pass, TX, from Ft Davis, TX; discharged Ft Davis, 16 Oct 1884;

married Nannie China Collins, Cincinnati, 17 Jul 1896; resided at 237 W. 6th St., Cincinnati, in 1896; resided at 617 Webb Alley, Cincinnati, in 1897, age 48; occupation cook, Cincinnati, Hamilton & Dayton Railroad, 1896–97; resided 4831 Langley Ave., Chicago, IL, 1929; received $40 per month pension Apr 1929, increased to $50 in Jul 1929, increased to $55 and to $72 in Nov 1937 as he is in need of regular aid or attendance of another person; died 30 Mar 1938; buried in lot 37, section 15, row 1, Lincoln Cemetery, 123rd & Medzie Avenue, Chicago. SOURCE: Sayre, *Warriors of Color*, 8, 13, 219, 331–34.

LANKFORD, Henry; Private; E/25th Inf. Died 20 Oct 1904; buried at Ft Bayard, NM, in plot J 34. SOURCE: "Fort Bayard National Cemetery, Records of Burials."

Buried 20 Oct 1904, section A, row O, plot 39, at Ft Bayard. SOURCE: Erickson, Burials at Fort Bayard National Cemetery, NM.

LARK, Aaron; Private; 25th Inf. Born in Roanoke County, VA; Ht 5'5", black hair and eyes, black complexion; occupation laborer; enlisted at age 30, Columbus Bks, OH, 16 Dec 1886; arrived Ft Snelling, MN, 1 Apr 1887. SOURCE: Descriptive & Assignment Rolls of Recruits, 25 Inf.

LATIMER, George A.; C/25th Inf. Born in Massachusetts; mulatto complexion; can read and write, age 26, 5 Sep 1870, at Ft McKavett, TX. SOURCE: Bierschwale, *Fort McKavett*, 109.

LATIMER, Grant; Private; E/48th Inf. ‡Died of variola in the Philippines, 8 Dec 1900. SOURCE: *ANJ* 38 (15 Dec 1900): 373.

Died in the Philippines 8 Dec 1900; buried in plot NEW A824 at San Francisco National Cemetery. SOURCE: San Francisco National Cemetery.

LAWRENCE, Earnest; Private; I/9th Cav. ‡Veteran of Philippine Insurrection; trumpeter, I/9th Cavalry, at Ft D. A. Russell, WY, in 1910; sharpshooter; resident of Chattanooga, TN. SOURCE: *Illustrated Review: Ninth Cavalry*, with picture.

Received Philippine Campaign Badge number 11872 for service as trumpeter in E/9th Cavalry; in 9th Cavalry at Ft Leavenworth, KS, Mar 1905. SOURCE: Philippine Campaign Badge list, 29 May 1905.

‡Private, I/9th Cavalry, killed by Raymond Hall, late of F/9th Cavalry, at Autumn Leaf Club dance last night at Keefe Hall, Cheyenne, WY; Raymond Hall escaped. SOURCE: Cheyenne *State Leader*, 13 Oct 1911.

LAWRENCE, James O.; Private; B/24th Inf. Died 24 Aug 1892; buried at Ft Bayard, NM, in plot I 33. SOURCE: "Fort Bayard National Cemetery, Records of Burials."

J. O. Lawrence, Private, E/24th Infantry, buried at Ft Bayard. SOURCE: "Buffalo Soldiers Buried at Ft Bayard, NM."

Buried 24 Aug 1892, section A, row M, plot 36, at Ft Bayard. SOURCE: Erickson, Burials at Fort Bayard National Cemetery, NM.

LAWRENCE, Thomas A.; Private; C/25th Inf. Died 18 Feb 1913; buried in plot WS 1009 at San Francisco National Cemetery. SOURCE: San Francisco National Cemetery.

LAWS, Alfred; Private; A/9th Cav. Died at Ft Concho, TX, on 1 Jul 1873; buried at San Antonio National Cemetery, Section D, number 671. SOURCE: San Antonio National Cemetery Locator.

LAWS, Clinton; Private; M/10th Cav. ‡Recently deceased, Aug 1874.

Died 12 Jul 1874 of typhoid at Wichita Agency, OK. SOURCE: Regimental Returns, 10th Cavalry, 1874.

LAWS, James; Private; 25th Inf. Born in Berrysville, VA; Ht 5'7", black hair and brown eyes, mulatto complexion; occupation laborer; enlisted at age 22, Pittsburgh, PA, 5 Apr 1886; arrived Ft Snelling, MN, 31 Jul 1886. SOURCE: Descriptive & Assignment Rolls of Recruits, 25 Inf.

LAWSON, Davis; Private; 9th Cav. Received Philippine Campaign Badge number 11709 for service as private in E/9th Cavalry; in 9th Cavalry at Ft Leavenworth, KS, Mar 1905. SOURCE: Philippine Campaign Badge list, 29 May 1905.

LAWSON, Frank; Private; 9th Cav. Received Philippine Campaign Badge number 11893 for service as private in H/9th Cavalry; in 9th Cavalry at Ft Leavenworth, KS, Mar 1905. SOURCE: Philippine Campaign Badge list, 29 May 1905.

LAWSON, George; Private; B/25th Inf. Enlisted 7 Aug 1905, discharged without honor 19 Nov 1906. SOURCE: Powell, "Military Record of the Enlisted Men Who Were Discharged Without Honor."

‡Dishonorable discharge, Brownsville, TX. SOURCE: SO 266, AGO, 9 Nov 1906.

LAWSON, Walter; E/25th Inf. Born in Clark County, VA; Ht 5'9", black hair and eyes, black complexion; occupation laborer; enlisted as Walker Lawson at age 24, Pittsburgh, PA, 5 Apr 1886; arrived Ft Snelling, MN, 31 Jul 1886. SOURCE: Descriptive & Assignment Rolls of Recruits, 25 Inf.

‡Alias Walker Lawson; widow Millie gets private bill passed for $20 per month pension. SOURCE: *Winners of the West* 3 (Apr 1926): 2.

LAYTON, Charles; H/25th Inf. Mulatto complexion; cannot read or write, age 24, 5 Sep 1870, at Ft McKavett, TX. SOURCE: Bierschwale, *Fort McKavett,* 108.

LEAKE, Lawrence M.; Private; 9th Cav. Received Philippine Campaign Badge number 11736 for service as private, E/46th Infantry, United States Volunteers; in 9th Cavalry at Ft Leavenworth, KS, Mar 1905. SOURCE: Philippine Campaign Badge list, 29 May 1905.

LEAUMONT, Henry; 1st Sgt; F/25th Inf. Died at Ft Stockton, TX, on 25 Nov 1874; buried at San Antonio National Cemetery, Section C, number 353. SOURCE: San Antonio National Cemetery Locator.

LEDUC, Pierre A.; Sergeant; 39th Inf. Considered "a reliable soldier and a very intelligent man" by Capt. James F. Randlett. SOURCE: Dobak and Phillips, *The Black Regulars,* 10.

LEE; Corporal; 25th Inf. At Ft Stockton, TX, 1873. *See* **MEW**, Benjamin, Sergeant, 25th Infantry

LEE, Charles; Private; E/10th Cav. In Troop E/10th Cavalry stationed at Bonita Cañon Camp, AZ, but absent or on detached service 28 Feb 1886. SOURCE: Tagg, *The Camp at Bonita Cañon,* 232.

LEE, Fitz; Private; L/9th Cav. Born in Dinwiddie County, VA; served from 1889 to 1899; received Medal of Honor for bravery in rescue at Tayabacoa, Cuba, Jun 1898; died after long illness, age 33, at Leavenworth, KS, 14 Sep 1899. SOURCE: Schubert, *Black Valor,* 137, 140–41.

‡Private, M/10th Cavalry, served in 10th Cavalry, 1898. SOURCE: Cashin, *Under Fire with the Tenth Cavalry,* 351–52.

‡Awarded Medal of Honor for service in Cuba, 1898. *See* **THOMPKINS**, William H., Sergeant, D/25th Infantry

‡Medal of Honor mentioned; Lee out of service in 1900. SOURCE: *ANJ* 37 (24 Feb 1900): 611; Steward, *The Colored Regulars,* 205.

‡Born in Dinwiddie Co., VA; received medal 3 Jun 1899 while in hospital, Ft Bliss, TX. SOURCE: Lee, *Negro Medal of Honor Men,* 92, 98.

LEE, James; Corporal; C/9th Cav. Appointed corporal 11 Jun 1894; in C/9th Cavalry at Ft Robinson, NE, Jan 1897. SOURCE: Ninth Cavalry, Roster of NCOs, 1897.

LEE, James; Private; E/24th Inf. Died 5 Apr 1915; buried in plot WSIDE393E at San Francisco National Cemetery. SOURCE: San Francisco National Cemetery.

LEE, Joseph; Private; K/10th Cav. Died 28 Mar 1878 in hospital at Ft Clark, TX. SOURCE: Regimental Returns, 10th Cavalry, 1878.

LEE, Ples; Private; F/9th Cav. Died 30 Mar 1909; buried in plot NA WS1456 at San Francisco National Cemetery. SOURCE: San Francisco National Cemetery.

LEE, Robert E.; Sergeant; F/24th Inf. ‡Born in Mercer Co., KY; Ht 5'10", black complexion; occupation laborer; enlisted, age 23, Ft Leavenworth, KS, 15 Nov 1883; transferred from H/24th Infantry to Band/24th Infantry, 1 Oct 1888; discharged, end of term, Ft Bayard, NM, single, character excellent, 14 Nov 1888; retained $72, clothing overdrawn $9; reenlisted, Ft Bayard, 15 Nov 1888; transferred to F/24th Infantry, single, character very good, retained $60, clothing overdrawn $23, 12 Nov 1893; reenlisted 21 Nov 1893. SOURCE: Descriptive Book, 24 Inf NCS & Band.

‡Wagoner, F/24th Infantry, married Miss R. Rainey, Ft Bayard, Sep 1891. SOURCE: *ANJ* 29 (17 Oct 1891): 133.

Sergeant, Band/24th Infantry, died 8 Jun 1921; buried in plot E.S. 1225A at San Francisco National Cemetery. SOURCE: San Francisco National Cemetery.

LEE, Ulysses G.; Private; F/9th Cav. Born in Washington, DC; Ht 5'6", black hair and brown eyes, dark brown complexion; occupation laborer; enlisted in 25th Infantry at age 21, Harrisburg, PA, 9 Dec 1886; assigned to I/25th Infantry, arrived Ft Snelling, MN, 5 Aug 1886. SOURCE: Descriptive & Assignment Rolls of Recruits, 25 Inf.

LEE, William; Private; D/25th Inf. Deserted during tenure of John Franklin as first sergeant, Jan 1869–May 1871. SOURCE: Dobak and Phillips, *The Black Regulars,* 300.

LEE, William; Private; F/9th Cav. Served at Ft Reno, OK, 1883. SOURCE: Schubert, *Voices of the Buffalo Soldier,* 133.

LEE, William; Private; 25th Inf. Born in Richmond, VA; Ht 5'8", black hair and brown eyes, brown complexion; occupation sailor; enlisted at age 24, Baltimore, MD, 7 Apr 1886; arrived Ft Snelling, MN, 19 Aug 1886. SOURCE: Descriptive & Assignment Rolls of Recruits, 25 Inf.

LEE, William H.; Private; 25th Inf. Born in Richmond, VA; Ht 5'4", black hair and brown eyes, brown complexion; occupation teamster; enlisted at age 22, Philadelphia, PA, 4 Apr 1886; assigned to C/25th Infantry; arrived Ft Snelling, MN, 1 Apr 1887. SOURCE: Descriptive & Assignment Rolls of Recruits, 25 Inf.

LEEK, Allen; Private; F/25th Inf. Died at Ft Stockton, TX, on 19 Mar 1873; buried at San Antonio National Cemetery, Section C, number 440. SOURCE: San Antonio National Cemetery Locator.

LEELY, Robert; Private; D/10th Cav. ‡Original member of 10th Cavalry; in troop when organized, Ft Leavenworth, KS, 1 Jun 1867. SOURCE: McMiller, "Buffalo Soldiers," 71.

Died 3 Jul 1867 of heart disease at Ft Arbuckle, OK. SOURCE: Regimental Returns, 10th Cavalry, 1867.

LEMONS, Willie; Private; B/25th Inf. Enlisted 13 Apr 1899, discharged as private 30 May 1902, character good; reenlisted 28 Jun 1902, discharged as private M/24th Infantry 27 Jun 1905, character good; reenlisted 4 Jul 1905, discharged without honor 22 Nov 1906, Brownsville, TX. SOURCE: Powell, "Military Record of the Enlisted Men Who Were Discharged Without Honor."

‡Dishonorable discharge, Brownsville. SOURCE: SO 266, AGO, 9 Nov 1906.

LEONARD, John E.; Sergeant; H/9th Cav. Received Philippine Campaign Badge number 11866 for service as private in D/9th Cavalry; in 9th Cavalry at Ft Leavenworth, KS, Mar 1905. SOURCE: Philippine Campaign Badge list, 29 May 1905.

‡Veteran of Philippine Insurrection; sergeant, H/9th Cavalry, at Ft D. A. Russell, WY, in 1910; marksman; resident of Boston. SOURCE: *Illustrated Review: Ninth Cavalry*, with picture.

LEONARD Thomas; Private; F/24th Inf. Died 15 Apr 1893; buried at Ft Bayard, NM, in plot 1 27. SOURCE: "Fort Bayard National Cemetery, Records of Burials."

Buried 15 Apr 1893, section A, row M, plot 30, at Ft Bayard. SOURCE: Erickson, Burials at Fort Bayard National Cemetery, NM.

LeRUCK, Samuel E.; Private; 10th Cav. *See* RUCK, Samuel E., Private, 10th Cavalry

LETCHER, Philip; Sergeant; K/10th Cav. ‡Born in Kentucky; private, corporal, sergeant, F/10th Cavalry, 17 Oct 1879–16 Oct 1884; private, corporal, sergeant, K/10th Cavalry, 28 Oct 1884–27 Oct 1889; private, K/10th Cavalry, 21 Nov 1889; sergeant, 13 Jan 1890; at Ft Custer, MT, 1897. SOURCE: Baker, Roster.

‡Served as quartermaster sergeant, K/10th Cavalry, 1898; remained in U.S. during war with Spain. SOURCE: Cashin, *Under Fire with the Tenth Cavalry*, 349.

‡Quartermaster sergeant, A/10th Cavalry, Ft Robinson, NE, 1902, detailed to color guard. SOURCE: SO 62, 10 Cav, 9 Jul 1902.

‡Sergeant, K/10th Cavalry, Ft Robinson, 1904.

‡Age 48 in 1906 when he wrote deposition in support of pension claim of Caleb Benson. SOURCE: VA File XC 2499129, Caleb Benson.

‡Enlisted Ft Leavenworth, KS, 1879; retired at Ft Robinson, 1906; after retirement worked nearly twenty years in postal service; resides at 3415 N. 28th Street, Omaha, NE; recently visited regiment. SOURCE: *Cavalry Journal* 46 (Nov 1937): 578.

Retired quartermaster sergeant, received Indian Wars Campaign Badge number 1466 on 10 Feb 1910. SOURCE: Carroll, *Indian Wars Campaign Badge*, 32.

LETT, William; Private; C/25th Inf. Died at Ft Stockton, TX, on 7 Oct 1879; buried at San Antonio National Cemetery, Section C, number 3345. SOURCE: San Antonio National Cemetery Locator.

LEVERETT, Hark; Private; H/9th Cav. Died 8 Jun 1902; buried in plot N ADD794 at San Francisco National Cemetery. SOURCE: San Francisco National Cemetery.

LEWIS; Private; M/10th Cav. As provost guard on 21 Apr 1871 shot Pvt. Jeremiah Spencer, L/10th Cavalry, who died 28 Apr 1871 at Ft Sill, OK. SOURCE: Regimental Returns, 10th Cavalry, 1871.

LEWIS, Charles; Private; 25th Inf. Born in Caroline County, VA; Ht 5'4", black hair and eyes, black complexion; occupation laborer; recruited as trumpeter, enlisted at age 18, Pittsburgh, PA, 12 Jun 1882; arrived Ft Snelling, MN, 21 Nov 1882. SOURCE: Descriptive & Assignment Rolls of Recruits, 25 Inf.

LEWIS, Edward; F/9th Cav. Born in Kentucky; black complexion; cannot read or write, age 21, Jul 1870, at Ft McKavett, TX. SOURCE: Bierschwale, *Fort McKavett,* 97.

LEWIS, Hamilton; Private; B/24th Inf. Among men who distinguished themselves in 1889; awarded certificate of merit for gallant and meritorious conduct while escorting paymaster Maj. Joseph W. Wham when attacked by robbers between Fts Grant and Thomas, AZ; now out of service. SOURCE: GO 18, AGO, 1891.

Text of report of Paymaster Wham, describing bravery of escort, published. SOURCE: Schubert, *Voices of the Buffalo Soldier*, 159–62.

Awarded certificate of merit for gallant and meritorious conduct while member of escort of Maj. Joseph W. Wham, paymaster, who was ambushed by bandits between Fts Grant and Thomas, 11 May 1889. SOURCE: Gleim, *The Certificate of Merit*, 44.

‡At Ft Grant, 1890; certificate of merit mentioned. SOURCE: SecWar, *AR 1890*, 289.

Twelve-year veteran, drove paymaster's wagon and cited for bravery against robbers near Cedar Springs, AZ, in May 1889 by Maj. Joseph W. Wham, and awarded certificate of merit; wounded during fight; left Army before end of 1890. SOURCE: Schubert, *Black Valor*, 93, 95, 98.

LEWIS, James J.; Private; F/9th Cav. Died 14 Jun 1902; buried in plot NA WS540 at San Francisco National Cemetery. SOURCE: San Francisco National Cemetery.

LEWIS, John; Private; E/10th Cav. In Troop E/10th Cavalry stationed at Bonita Cañon Camp, AZ; on detached service at Ft Grant, AZ, 31 Aug 1885–30 Apr 1886. SOURCE: Tagg, *The Camp at Bonita Cañon*, 67, 232.

LEWIS, Minor; Private; I/10th Cav. In Troop I/10th Cavalry stationed at Bonita Cañon Camp, AZ, 30 Jun 1886. SOURCE: Tagg, *The Camp at Bonita Cañon*, 232.

LEWIS, Richard D.; Private; H/25th Inf. ‡Died in the Philippines, 2 Apr 1901. SOURCE: *ANJ* 38 (13 Apr 1901): 803.

Died 2 Apr 1901; buried in plot NEW A838 at San Francisco National Cemetery. SOURCE: San Francisco National Cemetery.

LEWIS, Robert; Artificer; K/25th Inf. Born in Suffolk County, VA; Ht 5'3", black complexion; occupation laborer; enlisted in A/39th Infantry for three years on 5 Aug 1867, age 22, at Philadelphia, PA; transferred to K/25th Infantry at Jackson Bks, LA, 20 Apr 1869. SOURCE: Descriptive Roll of A/39th Inf.

LEWIS, William; Sergeant; F/25th Inf. Sergeant, received Indian Wars Campaign Badge number 1257 on 17 Feb 1909. SOURCE: Carroll, *Indian Wars Campaign Badge*, 36.

LEWIS, William F. C.; C/25th Inf. Born in South Carolina; mulatto complexion; can read and write, age 25, 5 Sep 1870, at Ft McKavett, TX. SOURCE: Bierschwale, *Fort McKavett,* 109.

LIGGINS, Edward C.; Sergeant; 10th Cav. Listed as sick in quarters, Ft Davis, TX, 14 Jan 1885; wife, Elta A., holds baby of Mary and Lt. John Bigelow, Jr., during their meals. SOURCE: Bigelow, *Garrison Tangles*, 44, 79.

LIGHTFOOT, James R.; Sergeant; K/25th Inf. ‡Born in Culpeper Co., VA; moved to Washington, DC, as child; enlisted in C/25th Infantry, 1895; served in Montana; discharged mid-1898 and reenlisted for duty in Cuba; never fully recovered from yellow fever contracted in Cuba; transferred to K/25th Infantry as corporal, then promoted to sergeant; killed eight miles north of San Felipe, Philippines, in enemy attack. SOURCE: Richmond *Planet*, 8 Sep 1900.

Awarded certificate of merit for distinguished gallantry in advance on concealed enemy at capture of insurgent stronghold, Camansi, Luzon, Philippines, 5 Jan 1900; killed in action, 14 Jul 1900. SOURCE: GO 32, AGO, 6 Feb 1904; Gleim, *The Certificate of Merit*, 50.

‡Virginian who showed "vim and coolheadedness"; wounded in arm and chest in ambush, 29 Jan 1900. SOURCE: Richmond *Planet*, 17 Mar 1900.

‡Killed in action, Cabangan, Luzon, 15 Jul 1900. SOURCE: *ANJ* 37 (28 Jul 1900): 1142; Cleveland *Gazette*, 15 Sep 1900.

LINCOLN, Daniel; Private; 40th Inf. Civil War veteran, served in 4th U.S. Colored Infantry. SOURCE: Dobak and Phillips, *The Black Regulars*, 22.

LINCOLN, Robert; Private; 25th Cav. Born in Beaufort, SC; occupation laborer; fair complexion, Ht 5'4 1/2"; enlisted, age 22, Charleston, SC, 2 Jul 1881; left recruit depot, David's Island, NY, 17 Aug 1881, and after trip on steamer *Thomas Kirby* to Central Depot, New York City, and train via Chicago to Running Water, Dakota Territory, 22 Aug 1881, marched forty-seven miles to Ft Randall, SD, arrived 24 Aug 1881. SOURCE: Descriptive & Assignment Rolls, 25 Inf.

Convicted with Pvt. Edward Mack, 25th Infantry, of raping Sioux woman, held as prisoner of war at Fort Randall, 1882; served thirty-eight months of ten-year sentence. SOURCE: Dobak and Phillips, *The Black Regulars*, 179.

LINDSAY, Charles; Private; D/25th Inf. Deserted during tenure of John Franklin as first sergeant, Jan 1869–May 1871. SOURCE: Dobak and Phillips, *The Black Regulars*, 300.

LISBY, Frank A.; Private; A/10th Cav. Died 20 Aug 1877 of disease at Ft Concho, TX. SOURCE: Regimental Returns, 10th Cavalry, 1877.

LISBY, John; Private; H/10th Cav. Died 29 Jun 1877 of disease at Ft Davis, TX. SOURCE: Regimental Returns, 10th Cavalry, 1877.

Died at Ft Davis on 27 Nov 1877; buried at San Antonio National Cemetery, Section I, number 1536. SOURCE: San Antonio National Cemetery Locator.

LIVINGSTON, George W.; Private; M/9th Cav. Born in Kentucky; died and buried at Ft McKavett, TX, before 17 May 1879. SOURCE: Bierschwale, *Fort McKavett,* 122.

Died at Ft McKavett on 23 Nov 1869; buried at San Antonio National Cemetery, Section E, number 835. SOURCE: San Antonio National Cemetery Locator.

LLOYD, Jerry; Private; E/10th Cav. In Troop E/10th Cavalry stationed at Bonita Cañon Camp, AZ, 28 Feb 1886. SOURCE: Tagg, *The Camp at Bonita Cañon*, 231.

LOCHLIN, William; Private; 25th Inf. Born in Maysville, KY; Ht 5'5", black hair and eyes, saddle complexion; occupation laborer; enlisted at age 23, Cincinnati, OH, 7 Dec 1886; arrived Ft Snelling, MN, 1 Apr 1887. SOURCE: Descriptive & Assignment Rolls of Recruits, 25 Inf.

LOCK, James; Corporal; E/9th Cav. ‡Corporal Lock, E/9th Cavalry, served in 1867. *See* **DOUGLAS**, Joseph, First Sergeant, E/9th Cavalry

One of ten soldiers charged with mutiny and desertion for role in mutiny at San Pedro Springs near San Antonio, TX, April 1867; pled guilty to desertion but not mutiny; mutiny charge dropped; convicted of desertion and sentenced to six months' confinement at military prison, Ship's Island, MS; sentence remitted before he was transported to prison. SOURCE: Dobak and Phillips, *The Black Regulars*, 208–11.

LOCKADOO, Nathan; Private; K/25th Inf. Born in Jackson County, OH; Ht 6'0", black hair and hazel eyes, dark complexion; occupation farmer; enlisted 15 Oct 1885, age 32, at Columbus Bks, OH; assigned to K/25th Infantry; arrived Ft Snelling, MN, 26 Apr 1886. SOURCE: Descriptive & Assignment Rolls of Recruits, 25 Inf.

LOCKS, George; Private; C/10th Cav. Died 3 Aug 1880, killed in action at Eagle Springs, TX. SOURCE: Regimental Returns, 10th Cavalry, 1880.

LOGAN, James; 1st Sgt; E/10th Cav. Served in E/10th Cavalry 1867–94; two years as volunteer; resided in Philadelphia, PA, in 1896 in same house as 10th Cavalry veteran Charles Key; resided 860 N. Darien St., Philadelphia; occupation laborer, age 63, in 1902. SOURCE: Sayre, *Warriors of Color*, 359.

In Troop E/10th Cavalry stationed at Bonita Cañon Camp, AZ, 28 Feb 1886. SOURCE: Tagg, *The Camp at Bonita Cañon*, 231.

Civil War veteran, in fifth enlistment, at San Carlos, AZ, Jul 1889, when accused of harassing and later involvement in murder of Pvt. Will Flemming; acquitted after two years of legal proceedings. SOURCE: Dobak and Phillips, *The Black Regulars*, 201–2, 323.

LOGAN, John; Private; F/10th Cav. ‡Original member of 10th Cavalry; in troop when organized, Ft Leavenworth, KS, 21 Jun 1867. SOURCE: McMiller, "Buffalo Soldiers," 73.

Died 2 Aug 1867 of cholera at Ft Hays, KS. SOURCE: Regimental Returns, 10th Cavalry, 1867.

LOGAN, John A.; Sgt Maj; 9th Cav. ‡Promoted from lance corporal, C/9th Cavalry, Ft Robinson, NE, Apr 1895. SOURCE: *ANJ* 32 (11 May 1895): 608.

‡Reduced to ranks, C/9th Cavalry, Ft Robinson, Oct 1895. SOURCE: *ANJ* 33 (12 Oct 1895): 87.

‡Enlisted Chattanooga, TN, 23 Aug 1892, and assigned to C/9th Cavalry; served five years in C/9th Cavalry, six years in L/9th Cavalry, and six years on regimental noncommissioned staff; veteran of Spanish-American War and Philippine Insurrection; sergeant major since 29 Aug 1904; marksman, 1907. SOURCE: *Illustrated Review: Ninth Cavalry*, with picture.

‡Sergeant major, on soldiers' boycott committee, Cheyenne, WY. SOURCE: Cheyenne *State Leader*, 15 Jan 1911.

Died 16 Sep 1916; buried in plot WS 1035-A at San Francisco National Cemetery. SOURCE: San Francisco National Cemetery.

LOGAN, Robert D.; Private; D/10th Cav. Drowned 7 Sep 1878 at Ft Concho, TX. SOURCE: Regimental Returns, 10th Cavalry, 1878.

Died at Ft Concho on 7 Sep 1878; buried at San Antonio National Cemetery, Section E, number 820. SOURCE: San Antonio National Cemetery Locator.

LONG, David; 9th Cav. Born in Kentucky; mulatto complexion; can read and write, age 23, 5 Sep 1870, at Ft McKavett, TX. SOURCE: Bierschwale, *Fort McKavett*, 107.

LONG, Gid; Private; L/10th Cav. ‡Served in 10th Cavalry, 1898; remained in U.S. during war with Spain. SOURCE: Cashin, *Under Fire with the Tenth Cavalry*, 351.

Died 15 Sep 1901; buried at Ft Bayard, NM, in plot N 36200. SOURCE: "Fort Bayard National Cemetery, Records of Burials."

Buried 15 Sep 1901, section A, row V, plot 36, at Ft Bayard. SOURCE: Erickson, Burials at Fort Bayard National Cemetery, NM.

LONG, William; Private; U.S. Army. Seminole Negro Scout, served 1873–76. SOURCE: Schubert, Consolidated List of Seminole Negro Scouts.

Born in Washington, DC; possibly not Seminole but intermarried; Ht 5'7", black hair and eyes, black complexion; enlisted at Ft Clark, TX, 22 Apr 1873, age 23; discharged 22 Oct 1873 at Ft Clark where he reenlisted same day; discharged 22 Apr 1874 at Ft Clark where he reenlisted 1 Mar 1875; discharged 14 Sep 1875 at Camp Supply, TX, where he reenlisted same day; discharged 13 Apr 1876. SOURCE: Swanson, 29.

LONGORIO, Julian; Corporal; U.S. Army. Born in Mexico; captured by Indians at early age with Manuel Longorio; served as paid civilian scout at Ft Clark, TX, and acted as a spy on Mexican Indians for Colonel Mackenzie and Lt. Col. William R. Shafter; when jailed as

American Army spy in Piedra Negras, Mexico, Mar 1877, Shafter and troops surrounded Piedra Negras but found jail empty; Ht 5'6", black hair, hazel eyes, copper complexion; enlisted at Ft Clark, 5 May 1879, age 40; discharged 6 May 1880 at Ft Clark where he reenlisted same day; discharged as corporal 12 May 1881 at Ft Clark where he reenlisted next day; discharged as private 12 May 1882 at Ft Clark; enlisted 3 June 1882 at Camp Neville Springs, TX; discharged as corporal 3 June 1883 at Ft Clark where he reenlisted same day; discharged as sergeant 3 Jun 1884 at Camp Neville Springs; reenlisted 4 Jun 1884 at Camp Myers, TX; discharged as corporal 3 Jun 1885 at Camp Neville Springs where he reenlisted next day; discharged 3 Jun 1886 at Ft Clark; reenlisted at Camp Neville Springs 4 Jun 1886; discharged 3 Jun 1887 at Camp San Carlos; reenlisted 4 June 1887 at Ft Clark; discharged 3 Jun 1888 at Camp Pena Colorado, TX, where he reenlisted next day; discharged as corporal 3 Jun 1889 at Camp Neville Springs; 1880 Census lists Julian Longorio as white male age 30, white wife Refugio, white children Arthur age 1 and Matildia age 3. SOURCE: Swanson, 29.

Seminole Negro Scout, served 1879–89. SOURCE: Schubert, Consolidated List of Seminole Negro Scouts.

Promoted from corporal to sergeant Jun 1884. SOURCE: NARA, M 929, Roll 2.

LONGORIO, Manuel; Private; U.S. Army. Seminole Negro Scout, served 1880–86. SOURCE: Schubert, Consolidated List of Seminole Negro Scouts.

Born in Mexico; raised with Julian Longorio by Indians in Mexico; Ht 5'6", black hair and eyes, dark complexion; enlisted at Ft Clark, TX, 6 May 1880, age 26; discharged 12 May 1881 at Ft Clark where he reenlisted same day; discharged as corporal 12 May 1882 at Ft Clark where he reenlisted 18 June 1883; discharged 12 Jun 1884 as private at Camp Myers Spring, TX, where he reenlisted 19 Jun 1884; discharged 31 Aug 1884 at Ft Clark where he reenlisted 6 Jan 1885; discharged as private 5 Jan 1886 at Ft Clark; died 11 Mar 1920; buried at St Mary's, Brackettville, TX. SOURCE: Swanson, 29.

LOOKERS, William; Private; I/10th Cav. Died 14 May 1876 of consumption at Ft Concho, TX. SOURCE: Regimental Returns, 10th Cavalry, 1876.

Died at Ft Concho on 14 May 1876; buried at San Antonio National Cemetery, Section E, number 814. SOURCE: San Antonio National Cemetery Locator.

LOOMIS, Richard; Private; F/9th Cav. Died at Ft Davis, TX, on 19 Mar 1868; buried at San Antonio National Cemetery, Section I, number 1513. SOURCE: San Antonio National Cemetery Locator.

LOVE, Charles H.; Sergeant; E/10th Cav. Private, E/10th Cavalry stationed at Bonita Cañon Camp, AZ, but absent or on detached service 28 Feb 1886. SOURCE: Tagg, *The Camp at Bonita Cañon*, 231.

‡Private, E/10th Cavalry, at Ft Apache, AZ, 1890, subscribed $.50 to testimonial to General Grierson. SOURCE: List of subscriptions, 23 Apr 1890, 10th Cavalry papers, MHI.

Retired sergeant, received Indian Wars Campaign Badge number 1219 on 15 Jul 1909; later received duplicate number 1769. SOURCE: Carroll, *Indian Wars Campaign Badge*, 35.

‡Retired as sergeant, E/10th Cavalry, 13 Jun 1894. SOURCE: Baker, Roster.

LOVE, Frank W.; Sqdn Sgt Maj; 9th Cav. ‡Born in Kansas City, MO, 20 Nov 1877; enlisted Kansas City, 18 Aug 1900; served in D/25th Infantry, 18 Aug 1900–17 Aug 1903; E/9th Cavalry, 18 Aug 1903–17 Aug 1906; E/9th Cavalry and on noncommissioned staff, 9th Cavalry, Aug 1906–17 Aug 1909; appointed sergeant major, first squadron, 9th Cavalry, from sergeant, E/9th Cavalry, 16 Aug 1909; marksman, 1906; sharpshooter, 1908; expert rifleman, 1909; at Ft D. A. Russell, WY, in 1910. SOURCE: *Illustrated Review: Ninth Cavalry*, with picture.

Received Philippine Campaign Badge number 11708 for service as private, D/25th Infantry; in 9th Cavalry at Ft Leavenworth, KS, Mar 1905. SOURCE: Philippine Campaign Badge list, 29 May 1905.

LOVE, Milton; Sergeant; C/10th Cav. Died 17 Aug 1867 of cholera at Camp Grierson, KS. SOURCE: Regimental Returns, 10th Cavalry, 1867.

LOVE, Samuel; 9th Cav. Born in Tennessee; black complexion; cannot read or write, age 21, 5 Sep 1870, at Ft McKavett, TX. SOURCE: Bierschwale, *Fort McKavett,* 107.

LUCKADOE, Joseph; Sergeant; B/25th Inf. Private, 40th Infantry, on board steamer *Flambeau* when it sank off Wilmington, NC, lost Civil War discharge papers from 4th U.S. Colored Infantry; led Pvts. Joshua L. Newby, Benedict Thomas, and Henry Williams, 25th Infantry, in defense of Eagle Springs, TX, mail station against attack, New Year's Eve, 1873. SOURCE: Dobak and Phillips, *The Black Regulars*, 11, 258–59, 332.

LUCKY, Frank; 9th Cav. Born in Alabama; mulatto complexion; cannot read or write, age 21, 5 Sep 1870, at Ft McKavett, TX. SOURCE: Bierschwale, *Fort McKavett,* 107.

LUMKINS, Ananias; Sergeant; I/10th Cav. Private, I/10th Cavalry, stationed at Bonita Cañon Camp, AZ, 30 Jun 1886. SOURCE: Tagg, *The Camp at Bonita Cañon*, 232.

‡Born in Virginia; private, I/10th Cavalry, 5 Jan 1884; corporal, 14 Oct 1892; sergeant, 5 Oct 1894; at Ft Assiniboine, MT, 1897. SOURCE: Baker, Roster.

‡Served in I/10th Cavalry in Cuba, 1898. SOURCE: Cashin, *Under Fire with the Tenth Cavalry*, 347.

Sergeant, D/10th Cavalry, received Indian Wars Campaign Badge number 754 on 11 Nov 1908. SOURCE: Carroll, *Indian Wars Campaign Badge*, 21.

LUNDY, Samuel; Private; 25th Inf. At Ft Missoula, MT, eloped with Etta Williams, 16-year-old daughter of Regimental QM Sgt. John Williams; caught, charged with desertion, charges reduced to absence without leave when Etta testified that their departure was due to death threats from her father; sentenced to three months, which he served at Ft Missoula. SOURCE: Dobak and Phillips, *The Black Regulars*, 142.

LUNNEY, Mack; Private; 25th Inf. Born in Darlington, SC; enlisted age 22, occupation miner, Ht 5'8", dark complexion, black eyes and hair, Charleston, SC, 25 May 1881; left recruit depot, David's Island, NY, 17 Aug 1881, and after trip on steamer *Thomas Kirby* to Central Depot, New York City, and train via Chicago to Running Water, Dakota Territory, 22 Aug 1881, marched forty-seven miles to Ft Randall, SD, arrived 24 Aug 1881. SOURCE: Descriptive & Assignment Rolls, 25 Inf.

LUSK, Green; Private; G/9th Cav. Died at Ft Davis, TX; buried at San Antonio National Cemetery, Section D, number 798. SOURCE: San Antonio National Cemetery Locator.

LUSK, James; Private; K/25th Inf. Died at Ft Davis, TX, on 13 Jun 1877; buried at San Antonio National Cemetery, Section I, number 1498. SOURCE: San Antonio National Cemetery Locator.

LUST, Houston; Sergeant; D/9th Cav. Born in Tennessee; black complexion; can read and write, age 24, Jul 1870, at Ft McKavett, TX. SOURCE: Bierschwale, *Fort McKavett*, 107.

‡Private, H/9th Cavalry, on detached service, Ft Bayard, NM, 29 Jan–16 Feb 1881. SOURCE: Regt Returns, 9 Cav, Feb 1881.

‡Sergeant, I/9th Cavalry, witness at trial of Joe Jemson, Private, I/9th Cavalry, Ft Robinson, NE, 6 May 1891. SOURCE: Summary Court Record, Ft Robinson, I.

‡Sergeant, D/9th Cavalry, appointed 1 Mar 1884. SOURCE: Roster, 9 Cav.

Appointed sergeant 1 Mar 1884; in D/9th Cavalry at Ft Washakie, WY, Jan 1897. SOURCE: Ninth Cavalry, Roster of NCOs, 1897.

‡Resides at Ft Robinson with wife and one child, Aug 1893. SOURCE: Medical History, Ft Robinson.

‡Sergeant of guard, 11 Sep 1894, who arrested Sgts. David Dillon and Robert Benjamin; lived in quarters on post with wife. SOURCE: Court Martial Records, Dillon.

‡Sergeant, D/9th Cavalry, at Ft Robinson, 1895; sergeant since 1884. SOURCE: *ANJ* 32 (23 Mar 1895): 490.

‡Retires as sergeant, D/9th Cavalry, from Ft Washakie. SOURCE: *ANJ* 34 (20 Mar 1897): 525.

Retired sergeant, received Indian Wars Campaign Badge number 1724 on 21 Feb 1914. SOURCE: Carroll, *Indian Wars Campaign Badge*, 50.

LUSTER, Charles; Sergeant; H/25th Inf. Sergeant, received Indian Wars Campaign Badge number 1310 on 20 Mar 1909. SOURCE: Carroll, *Indian Wars Campaign Badge*, 38.

LYMAN, George; Color Sgt; 9th Cav. Native of Kentucky; Ht 5'9", mulatto, age 21 when enlisted Lexington, KY, Nov 1871; on reenlistment promoted to sergeant; cited for gallantry against Apaches, Black Mountains, New Mexico, May 1879; reduced to private for absence without leave Feb 1881; sergeant when convicted by court martial, Ft Sill, OK, Jan 1884, of illicit relationship with white Cecilia Bow, sentenced to dishonorable discharge and two years, reduced by reviewing authority to nine months' confinement and return to duty; transferred to D/9th Cavalry, Ft Riley, KS, 1884; reappointed sergeant 1886; reenlisted 1887, transferred to A/9th Cavalry. SOURCE: Kenner, *Buffalo Soldiers and Officers of the Ninth Cavalry*, 253–59.

‡Singled out by Capt. Charles D. Beyer for bravery and gallantry against Victorio, Jun 1879. SOURCE: Billington, "Black Cavalrymen," 64; Billington, *New Mexico's Buffalo Soldiers*, 88–89.

‡Sergeant, C/9th Cavalry, at Ft Cummings, NM, 1881; on detached service in field in charge of five privates, C/9th Cavalry, scouting, 30 Jan–3 Feb 1881. SOURCE: Regt Returns, 9 Cav, Feb 1881.

‡Served with Henry Briscoe, Nov 1879–Jul 1882; in campaign against Victorio, including fight at Santa Rita Mountains, and remembers that someone was wounded. SOURCE: Affidavit, Leavenworth, KS, 29 Apr 1922, VA File C 2349975, Henry Briscoe.

‡Appointed corporal A/9th Cavalry, 26 Jun 1892. SOURCE: Roster, 9 Cav.

‡Corporal, A/9th Cavalry, Ft Robinson, NE, 1894.

‡Corporal, E/9th Cavalry, detailed as permanent color guard, 9th Cavalry, Ft Robinson, Jul 1895, with Cpl. W. H. Harper, E/9th Cavalry, and Cpl. E. N. Reynolds, H/9th Cavalry. SOURCE: *ANJ* 32 (3 Aug 1895): 807.

‡Corporal, A/9th Cavalry, appointed to regimental color guard, Ft Robinson, Mar 1896. SOURCE: *ANJ* 33 (28 Mar 1896): 540.

‡Sergeant, A/9th Cavalry, authorized to reenlist as married soldier by letter, Adjutant General's Office, 29 Dec 1896.

‡Ranked number 3, carbine competition, Departments of Dakota, Columbia, and the Platte, at Ft Robinson, 27–30 Sep 1897. SOURCE: GO 64, AGO, 18 Nov 1897.

‡Color sergeant, 9th Cavalry, second best marksman in Department of the Platte, 1898. SOURCE: Cleveland *Gazette*, 21 May 1898.

‡Sergeant, 9th Cavalry, color-bearer in Cuba, 1898. SOURCE: Cashin, *Under Fire with the Tenth Cavalry*, 117.

Appointed sergeant 3 Dec 1896; in A/9th Cavalry at Ft Robinson, Jan 1897. SOURCE: Ninth Cavalry, Roster of NCOs, 1897.

Retired sergeant, received Indian Wars Campaign Badge number 969 on 7 Nov 1908. SOURCE: Carroll, *Indian Wars Campaign Badge*, 28.

LYNCH, William; Private; K/9th Cav. Born in Waynesville, OH, 1862; enlisted Cincinnati, OH, 5 Jul 1882; Ht 5'3"; brown complexion, black eyes and hair; occupation laborer; served in H/10th Cavalry; discharged 4 Jul 1887; enlisted Ft Gibson, OK, 9 Aug 1889; served in K/9th Cavalry at Ft Robinson, NE, 1 Jan–27 Apr 1890; en route to and at Pine Ridge Indian Agency, SD; en route to and at Ft Robinson, 1 May–Nov or Dec 1890; in the field at Pine Ridge, SD, end of 1890–24 Mar 1891; en route to and at Ft Meyer, VA, 24 Mar–31 Dec 1891, discharged Ft Meyer, 8 Aug 1894; married Ellen Beck, born 10 Feb 1859, at Muskogee, OK; Beck died 17 Dec 1932, former wife of Sgt. George Goldsby, 10th Cavalry, with whom she had four children, including Georgia Ellen, born Jul 1874, and Crawford J., born 8 Feb 1876; died 17 Jan 1916; buried Citizen Cemetery, Ft Gibson; widow Ellen never divorced Goldsby, also known as William Scott, and after 1922 signed all documents relating to pension applications "Ellen Goldsby." SOURCE: Sayre, *Warriors of Color*, 335–40.

In Troop H/10th Cavalry stationed at Bonita Cañon Camp, AZ, 30 Apr 1886. SOURCE: Tagg, *The Camp at Bonita Cañon*, 232.

LYONS, Daniel; Corporal; H/24th Inf. ‡Enlisted Dallas, TX, 7 Jun 1898; joined company 6 Sep 1898; owes U.S. $1 for ordnance (canteen, canteen straps, tin cup). SOURCE: Muster Roll, H/24 Inf, Sep–Oct 1898.

‡Private, discharged Ft Douglas, UT, character excellent, single, 29 Jan 1899; due soldier $2.77 for clothing; reenlisted Ft Douglas, 30 Jan 1899; formerly served under name Daniel Lyon, Sep 1898–Jan 1899.

‡Died of variola in the Philippines, 14 Mar 1900. SOURCE: *ANJ* 37 (24 Mar 1900): 707.

Corporal, H/24th Infantry, died 11 Mar 1900; buried in plot 262 at San Francisco National Cemetery. SOURCE: San Francisco National Cemetery.

LYONS, David; Private; 24th Inf. Served at Ringgold Barracks, TX, 1877; injured in fight with Pvt. John Ewing after argument over prostitutes. SOURCE: Dobak and Phillips, *The Black Regulars*, 177.

LYONS, David; Musician; D/24th Inf. Died 2 Feb 1890; buried at Ft Bayard, NM, in plot G 13. SOURCE: "Fort Bayard National Cemetery, Records of Burials."

Buried 2 Feb 1890, section A, row I, plot 15, at Ft Bayard. SOURCE: Erickson, Burials at Fort Bayard National Cemetery, NM.

LYONS, John R.; Private; D/10th Cav. ‡Risked life to save drowning comrade at Mallets Bay near Ft Ethan Allen, VT, 6 Jul 1911; certificate of merit awarded 21 Aug 1911. SOURCE: AGO, Bulletin 9, 1912.

Awarded certificate of merit for risking life in rescue of drowning comrade, Ft Ethan Allen, 6 Jul 1911. SOURCE: Gleim, *The Certificate of Merit*, 61.

M

McBAIN, Edward; Private; G/9th Cav. ‡Pvt. E. McBain, G/9th Cavalry, on detached service at Ft Stanton, NM, 29 Jan–5 Feb 1881. SOURCE: Regt Returns, 9 Cav, Feb 1881.

Private, G/9th Cavalry, sentenced to three months' confinement for stealing sack of potatoes, spring 1881; sentence remitted by reviewing authority. SOURCE: Kenner, *Buffalo Soldiers and Officers of the Ninth Cavalry*, 24–25.

McBRYAR, William; Sergeant; 9th Cav. ‡Born in Elizabethtown, NC; Ht 5'5 1/2", brown complexion. SOURCE: Descriptive & Assignment Cards of Recruits, 25 Inf.

‡First enlisted New York City, 3 Jan 1887. SOURCE: Lee, *Negro Medal of Honor Men*, 80–81.

‡Served as private, corporal, sergeant, first sergeant, K/10th Cavalry, and private, corporal, sergeant, and quartermaster sergeant, H/25th Infantry, 3 Jan 1887–8 Sep 1898; second lieutenant, 8th Volunteer Infantry, 29 Jul 1898; first lieutenant, 7 Sep 1898; discharged 6 Mar 1899; private and battalion sergeant major, 25th Infantry, 9 Mar–9 Sep 1899; second lieutenant, 49th Infantry, 30 Sep 1899; on detached service with 25th Infantry, 30 Sep 1899–30 Jul 1900; commander, K/49th Infantry, 5 Jan–27 Mar 1901. SOURCE: Descriptive Book, K/49 Inf.

‡Stationed at Ft Thomas, AZ, when he won Medal of Honor in engagement against Apaches, Salt River, AZ, 7 Mar 1890. SOURCE: SecWar, *AR 1890*, 290; Baker, Roster; Carroll, *The Black Military Experience*, 421.

‡Cited among men who distinguished themselves in 1890 for coolness, bravery, and good marksmanship against Apaches, Salt River. SOURCE: GO 100, AGO, 17 Dec 1891.

Medal of Honor for bravery against Apaches in 1890 mentioned. SOURCE: Dobak and Phillips, *The Black Regulars*, 260–61.

Life, career, and bravery in action against Apache guerrilla Kid in 1890, for which he received Medal of Honor, narrated. SOURCE: Schubert, *Black Valor*, 101–15, 155, 158, 161, 166–67.

‡Sergeant, K/10th Cavalry at Ft Apache, AZ, 1890, subscribed $.50 to testimonial to General Grierson. SOURCE: List of subscriptions, 23 Apr 1890, 10th Cavalry papers, MHI.

Replaced 1st Sgt. William H. Givens, K/10th Cavalry; second enlistment, Ft Grant, AZ, 3 Jan 1892; relieved 5 Oct 1893 at own request; replaced by Washington Brown whom he replaced 19 Nov 1893; relieved as first sergeant 16 Feb 1894 and replaced by Walter Green. SOURCE: Register of Enlistments, NA; notes in authors' files.

‡Commissioned first lieutenant, 8th Volunteer Infantry, after Spanish-American War. SOURCE: Cashin, *Under Fire with the Tenth Cavalry*, 360.

‡Picture. SOURCE: Cashin, *Under Fire with the Tenth Cavalry*, 134.

‡Won commission for gallantry and meritorious service around Santiago, Cuba, 1898. SOURCE: Thweatt, *What the Newspapers Say*, 9–10.

‡Commissioned for bravery at El Caney, Cuba. SOURCE: Johnson, *History of Negro Soldiers*, 32.

‡Sergeant, H/25th Infantry, commissioned for gallantry at Santiago, 1–2 Jul 1898. SOURCE: Richmond *Planet*, 13 Aug 1898.

‡Enlisted in 25th Infantry, Chattanooga, TN, 9 Mar 1899; most recent service in M/8th Volunteer Infantry; thirteen years' continuous service; arrived from furlough at Ft Logan, CO, 30 May 1899. SOURCE: Descriptive & Assignment Cards of Recruits, 25 Inf.

‡Appointed second lieutenant, 49th Infantry, from sergeant major, 25th Infantry. SOURCE: *ANJ* 37 (9 Dec 1899): 345b.

‡Second lieutenant, M/49th Infantry, as of 9 Sep 1899. SOURCE: Descriptive Book, M/49 Inf.

‡First lieutenant, 49th Infantry, as of 6 Oct 1900. SOURCE: *ANJ* 38 (24 Nov 1900): 307.

‡Philippine service mentioned. SOURCE: Villard, "The Negro in the Regular Army," 724.

Received Cuban Campaign Badge for service as quartermaster sergeant in H/25th Infantry, 22 Jun 1898–13 Aug 1898; in 9th Cavalry at Ft Leavenworth, KS, Mar 1905. SOURCE: Cuban Campaign Badge Recipients.

Text of application for active service for border troubles with Mexico, 1914, published. SOURCE: Schubert, *Voices of the Buffalo Soldier*, 252–53.

McCABBIN, Care; Private; H/10th Cav. Born in Bourbon County, KY, 1862; enlisted Cincinnati, OH, 19 May

1884; Ht 5'4"; black complexion, eyes and hair; occupation laborer. SOURCE: Sayre, *Warriors of Color*, 374.

McCABE, William; Sergeant; E/9th Cav. ‡Appointed sergeant Jul 1889. SOURCE: Roster, 9 Cav.

Appointed sergeant 19 Jul 1889; in E/9th Cavalry at Ft Robinson, NE, Jan 1897. SOURCE: Ninth Cavalry, Roster of NCOs, 1897.

McCALLEY, Charles; Private; 24th Inf. At Ft Sill, OK, 1882–84, reported on unit activities to Huntsville, AL, *Gazette*. SOURCE: Dobak and Phillips, *The Black Regulars*, 313–14.

McCALLEY, Wiley; Private; D/25th Inf. Died 23 Nov 1902; buried at Ft Bayard, NM, in plot L 4. SOURCE: "Fort Bayard National Cemetery, Records of Burials."

Wiley McCalley, A/25th Infantry, buried at Ft Bayard. SOURCE: "Buffalo Soldiers Buried at Ft Bayard, NM."

Buried 23 Nov 1902, section A, row W, plot 5, at Ft Bayard. SOURCE: Erickson, Burials at Fort Bayard National Cemetery, NM.

McCALLIP, Pleasants; Private; U.S. Army. Seminole Negro Scout, born in Miriand City, AL; former slave or descendant of slave of James McKellop, Scotsman who married Mary Perryman, daughter of Benjamin Perryman of prominent Creek family, adherents of McKintosh faction; Ht 5'7", black hair and eyes, black complexion; enlisted at Ft Clark, TX, 12 Aug 1872, age 25; discharged 6 Mar 1873 at Ft Clark where he reenlisted next day; discharged 10 Sep 1873 at Ft Clark where he reenlisted 12 Sep 1873; discharged 1 Apr 1874 at Ft Clark where he reenlisted 16 May 1874; appointed blacksmith 3 Oct 1874; discharged 11 Dec 1874 at Ft Clark where he reenlisted 26 Dec 1874; appointed farrier 31 Dec 1874; discharged 26 Jun 1875 at Ft Clark; enlisted 29 Feb 1876 at Ft Clark; discharged 29 Aug 1876 at Camp Pecos, TX, where he reenlisted same day; deserted 5 Jan 1877. SOURCE: Swanson, 30.

McCAMPBELL, George; Sergeant; M/9th Cav. ‡Sergeant, M/9th Cavalry, on pass in Lander, WY, 31 Dec 1887–7 Jan 1888; died of spinal meningitis at Ft Washakie, WY, 3 Feb 1888.

Corporal, M/9th Cavalry, Ft Stanton, NM; in Dec 1876 helped prevent Sgt. Emanuel Stance from killing Trumpeter George Washington. SOURCE: Kenner, *Buffalo Soldiers and Officers of the Ninth Cavalry*, 165.

McCANTS, William; Private; 25th Inf. Born in Mount Pleasant, SC; occupation farmer; Ht 5'4 1/2", fair complexion, black hair and eyes; enlisted Charleston, SC, age 21, 14 Jun 1881; left recruit depot, David's Island, NY, 17 Aug 1881, and after trip on steamer *Thomas Kirby* to Central

Depot, New York City, and train via Chicago to Running Water, Dakota Territory, 22 Aug 1881, marched forty-seven miles to Ft Randall, SD, arrived 24 Aug 1881. SOURCE: Descriptive and Assignment Rolls, 25 Inf.

McCAW, Melvin; Sergeant; F/9th Cav. ‡Promoted from lance corporal to corporal, Ft DuChesne, UT, 1 Jul 1895. SOURCE: *ANJ* 32 (13 Jul 1895): 758.

‡Promoted to sergeant. SOURCE: *ANJ* 34 (21 Nov 1896): 196.

Appointed sergeant 14 Nov 1896; in F/9th Cavalry at Ft DuChesne, Jan 1897. SOURCE: Ninth Cavalry, Roster of NCOs, 1897.

Received Philippine Campaign Badge number 11781 for service as sergeant in F/9th Cavalry; in 9th Cavalry at Ft Leavenworth, KS, Mar 1905. SOURCE: Philippine Campaign Badge list, 29 May 1905.

McCLAIN, Adam; Private; U.S. Army. Seminole Negro Scout, served 1898–1901. SOURCE: Schubert, Consolidated List of Seminole Negro Scouts.

Born in Texas; Ht 5'6", black hair and eyes, black complexion; enlisted at Ft Clark, TX, 26 Feb 1898, age 21; discharged 25 Feb 1901 at Ft Ringgold, TX; died 12 Sep 1950. SOURCE: Swanson, 31.

Buried at Seminole Indian Scout Cemetery, Kinney County, TX. SOURCE: Indian Scout Cemetery, Kinney County, Texas.

McCLARE, Allen; Cook; L/9th Cav. Born 7 Dec 1879; enlisted from Virginia, occupation cook; died 19 Aug 1944; buried at Prospect Hill, Omaha, NE. SOURCE: Fort Robinson, NE, annotated notes on photocopy in authors' files of McClare entry in OTT.

‡At Ft D. A. Russell, WY, in 1910; marksman; resident of Greenwood, SC. SOURCE: *Illustrated Review: Ninth Cavalry*, with picture.

McCLATCHIE, Henry; Private; 25th Inf. Born in Holly Springs, MS; Ht 5'11", black hair and eyes, black complexion; served in I/10th Cavalry to 2 Mar 1887; second reenlistment in 25th Infantry at age 31, St Louis, MO, 16 Mar 1887; arrived Ft Snelling, MN, 1 Apr 1887. SOURCE: Descriptive & Assignment Rolls of Recruits, 25 Inf.

Henry McClatchia in Troop I/10th Cavalry stationed at Bonita Cañon Camp, AZ, 30 Jun 1886. SOURCE: Tagg, *The Camp at Bonita Cañon*, 232.

McCOLUM, Virgil; Private; I/24th Inf. Died at Ft Richardson, TX, on 26 Oct 1869; buried at San Antonio National Cemetery, Section D, number 629. SOURCE: San Antonio National Cemetery Locator.

McCOWN, Peter; Ord Sgt; U.S. Army. ‡Born in Detroit; resided in Cincinnati, on enlistment; awarded Distinguished

Service Medal for gallantry at Santiago, Cuba, 1 Jul 1898, in lieu of certificate of merit. SOURCE: *Decorations, U.S. Army, Supplement I*, 36.

‡Private, D/10th Cavalry, 4 Dec 1885–3 Dec 1890, 12 Dec 1890–31 May 1891; transferred to E/10th Cavalry, 1 Jun 1891; corporal, 1 Feb 1892; sergeant, 16 Jun 1893; at Ft Custer, MT, 1897. SOURCE: Baker, Roster.

Pvt. Peter McCown, 10th Cavalry, at Ft Bayard, NM, was confined for previously allowing prisoner to escape while serving as guard; Jan 1889 planned and carried out escape with Pvt. Albert S. Crouch, 10th Cavalry; both captured at Deming, NM. SOURCE: Billington, *New Mexico's Buffalo Soldiers*, 168–69.

‡Private, D/10th Cavalry, twice found in room of female servant of officer at reveille, Ft Bayard. SOURCE: Billington, *New Mexico's Buffalo Soldiers*, 166.

‡Served as first sergeant, E/10th Cavalry in Cuba, 1898. SOURCE: Cashin, *Under Fire with the Tenth Cavalry*, 342.

As first sergeant in E/10th Cavalry awarded certificate of merit for distinguished service in battle, Santiago, 1 Jul 1898. SOURCE: Gleim, *The Certificate of Merit*, 45.

‡Enlisted Philadelphia, 1885; won certificate of merit for distinguished service in battle of Santiago, 1898. SOURCE: *ANJ* 37 (24 Feb 1900): 610; Steward, *The Colored Regulars*, 280; GO 15, AGO, 13 Feb 1900.

‡Narrates Spanish-American War experience. SOURCE: Cashin, *Under Fire with the Tenth Cavalry*, 217–20.

‡Commissioned second lieutenant, 7th Volunteer Infantry, after Spanish-American War. SOURCE: Cashin, *Under Fire with the Tenth Cavalry*, 359.

‡Mentioned as first lieutenant, 48th Infantry. SOURCE: *ANJ* 37 (7 Oct 1899): 123; Beasley, *Negro Trailblazers*, 285.

‡Mentioned. SOURCE: San Francisco *Chronicle*, 15 Nov 1899.

Picture as first lieutenant, 48th Infantry. SOURCE: Indianapolis *Freeman*, 18 Nov 1899.

‡One of nineteen officers of 48th Infantry recommended as regular Army second lieutenants. SOURCE: CG, DivPI, Manila, 8 Feb 1901, to AGO, AGO File 355163.

See OTT, **CROUCH**, Albert S., Private, 10th Cavalry; **SMITH**, Jacob Clay, Saddler Sergeant, 10th Cavalry

Ordnance sergeant, received Indian Wars Campaign Badge number 648 on 16 Oct 1908; reported it lost on 3 Dec 1910; received badge number 1497. SOURCE: Carroll, *Indian Wars Campaign Badge*, 18.

McCROSKEY, Lee; 9th Cav. Born in Tennessee; mulatto complexion; can read and write, age 24, 5 Sep 1870, at Ft McKavett, TX. SOURCE: Bierschwale, *Fort McKavett*, 107.

McCURDY, Walter; QM Sgt; B/25th Inf. Enlisted 5 Jul 1890; discharged as sergeant 4 Jul 1895, character excellent; reenlisted 5 Jul 1895, discharged as sergeant 4 Jul 1898,

character excellent; reenlisted 5 Jul 1898, discharged as sergeant 3 Mar 1899, character excellent; reenlisted 4 Mar 1899, discharged as quartermaster sergeant 3 Mar 1902, character excellent; reenlisted 4 Mar 1902, discharged as corporal 3 Mar 1905, character excellent; reenlisted 4 Mar 1905, discharged without honor as quartermaster sergeant November 22, 1906. SOURCE: Powell, "Military Record of the Enlisted Men Who Were Discharged Without Honor."

‡In the Philippines, 1899. SOURCE: Richmond *Planet*, 27 Jan 1900.

‡Developed bad leg cramp on march from Magalong to Mt Arayat, Philippines, 20 Dec 1899. SOURCE: Richmond *Planet*, 10 Feb 1900.

‡Before Brownsville, never charged with violation of discipline. SOURCE: Cleveland *Gazette*, 23 Feb 1907.

Dishonorable discharge, Brownsville, TX. SOURCE: SO 266, AGO, 9 Nov 1906.

‡Acting quartermaster sergeant, B/25th Infantry, and 16-year veteran with Cuban and Philippine service when discharged. SOURCE: Weaver, *The Brownsville Raid*, 179.

McDANIEL, Nathanial or Nathan; Private; H/10th Cav. *See* **McDANIELS**, Nathaniel, Private, C/10th Cavalry

McDANIELS, Henry; Private; M/24th Inf. Born 17 Sep 1876; died 20 May 1947; buried 5 Jun 1956 in plot NAWS 16013 at San Francisco National Cemetery. SOURCE: San Francisco National Cemetery.

McDANIELS, Nathaniel; Private; C/10th Cav. Born in Lynchburg, VA, 1853 although other evidence had birth year of 1862; father James McDaniel; mother Parthenia Hunt; enlisted Harrisburg, PA, 30 Mar 1883; Ht 6'; "Indian color" complexion, black eyes and hair; occupation laborer; served in H/10th Cavalry; discharged Ft Apache, AZ, 29 Mar 1888; enlisted Harrisburg, 14 Nov 1890; served in C/10th Cavalry; discharged on surgeon's certificate of disability, Washington, DC, 28 Oct 1891; married Hannah Johnson, parents William and Ciley Johnson, Campbell County, VA, 10 Mar 1877; married Sarah Scott, parents James and Sarah Scott, Lynchburg, 20 Dec 1888; in St. Elizabeth's Hospital, Washington, DC, 8 Sep–1 Dec 1891, with acute dementia; 31 Mar 1897 married Catherine Cooley, parents Henry and Eliza Powell Cooley, Petersburg, VA; one child with Sarah Scott lived only a few weeks; died 30 Oct 1898 at Jersey City, NJ, age 45?; buried in New York Bay Cemetery. SOURCE: Sayre, *Warriors of Color*, 341–73.

In Troop H/10th Cavalry stationed at Bonita Cañon Camp, AZ, 30 Apr 1886. SOURCE: Tagg, *The Camp at Bonita Cañon*, 232.

‡Taken to asylum in Washington, DC, as insane, Sep 1892, by Sgt. B. Perea, Band/24th Infantry. SOURCE: Descriptive Book, 24 Inf NCS & Band.

McDONALD, Robert; Farrier; B/10th Cav. At Ft Duncan, TX, Dec 1877, as sergeant sought to resign warrant and be reduced to ranks; Lt. John Bigelow denied his request as unauthorized; succeeded in getting him reduced to private, Ft Stockton, TX, Apr 1879. SOURCE: Kinevan, *Frontier Cavalryman*, 70, 147, 159–60.

‡Reduced from sergeant to private, fined $30, and jailed for three months for allowing prisoner to escape through carelessness, Ft Thomas, AZ. SOURCE: *ANJ* 25 (24 Mar 1888): 694.

‡At Ft Apache, AZ, 1890, subscribed $.50 to testimonial to General Grierson. SOURCE: List of subscriptions, 23 Apr 1890, 10th Cavalry papers, MHI.

‡Served as farrier in B/10th Cavalry in Cuba, 1898. SOURCE: Cashin, *Under Fire with the Tenth Cavalry*, 338.

‡Stabbed to death in Havana, Cuba, 12 Feb 1899. SOURCE: *ANJ* 36 (18 Feb 1899): 582.

McDOUGAL, Barney; 24th Inf. Also called McKay. *See* **McKAY**, Barney, Sergeant, G/9th Cavalry

McDOUGALE, John H.; Private; L/25th Inf. Died 13 Dec 1901; originally buried at Castellijos Zambelle, Philippines; buried 20 Jun 1902 in plot NA 979 at San Francisco National Cemetery. SOURCE: San Francisco National Cemetery.

MACE, William; Private; D/10th Cav. ‡Convicted of murder and won appeal, 1877. SOURCE: Leckie, *The Buffalo Soldiers*, 164.

At Ft Concho, TX, 1878; convicted of murder for role in barroom shooting, Feb 1878; death sentence successfully appealed. SOURCE: Leiker, *Racial Borders*, 90.

McFERRIN, Jesse L.; Corporal; C/25th Inf. Died 21 Apr 1903; buried at Ft Leavenworth National Cemetery, plot 3532. SOURCE: Ft Leavenworth National Cemetery.

McGAROCK, William; D/24th Inf. Born in Tennessee; mulatto complexion; cannot read or write, age 24, Jul 1870, at Ft McKavett, TX. SOURCE: Bierschwale, *Fort McKavett*, 96.

McGHEE, Oscar; Sergeant; D/9th Cav. ‡Certificates of final statements of Pvts. Luke Steed and Oscar McGhee, D/9th Cavalry, Ft Washakie, WY, transmitted by chief paymaster, Department of the Platte, to Maj. John S. Loud, Ft Washakie, 20 Jul 1897. SOURCE: Misc Records, DP.

‡Veteran of Philippine Insurrection; sergeant, D/9th Cavalry, at Ft D. A. Russell, WY, in 1910. SOURCE: *Illustrated Review: Ninth Cavalry*, with picture.

At Ringgold Barracks, TX, 1899; "had meager familiarity with Spanish." SOURCE: Leiker, *Racial Borders*, 126.

McGHEE, Samuel; Private; B/25th Inf. Mustered in 16 Jan 1899, mustered out as private H/8th U.S. Volunteers 6 Mar 1899; reenlisted 9 Mar 1899, discharged as private A/24th Infantry 22 Mar 1902, character very good; reenlisted 10 May 1902, discharged as private K/24th Infantry 9 May 1905, character excellent; reenlisted 5 Jul 1905, discharged without honor 19 Nov 1906. SOURCE: Powell, "Military Record of the Enlisted Men Who Were Discharged Without Honor."

‡Dishonorable discharge, Brownsville, TX. SOURCE: SO 266, AGO, 9 Nov 1906.

McGINTY, Joseph; Private; E/10th Cav. Died 16 Mar 1892; buried at San Antonio National Cemetery, Section I, number 1572. SOURCE: San Antonio National Cemetery Locator.

McINTOSH, Henry; Private; 25th Inf. Born in Sumter, SC; Ht 5'5 1/2", black hair and eyes, dark complexion; occupation laborer; enlisted, age 28, Charleston, SC, 2 Jul 1881; left recruit depot, David's Island, NY, 17 Aug 1881, and after trip on steamer *Thomas Kirby* to Central Depot, New York City, and train via Chicago to Running Water, Dakota Territory, 22 Aug 1881, marched forty-seven miles to Ft Randall, SD, arrived 24 Aug 1881. SOURCE: Descriptive & Assignment Rolls, 25 Inf.

McINTOSH, Robert; Private; I/24th Inf. ‡Enlisted Baltimore, MD, 28 Mar 1899. SOURCE: Muster Roll, I/24 Inf, Mar–Apr 1899.

‡On detached service, Arayat, Philippines, since 3 Oct 1899. SOURCE: Muster Roll, I/24 Inf, Sep–Oct 1899.

Died 16 May 1901; buried EAST 1314 in plot NAWS 16013 at San Francisco National Cemetery. SOURCE: San Francisco National Cemetery.

MACK, Clayborn; Private; B/10th Cav. On march, Oct 1878, from Ft Stockton, TX, Lt. William H. Beck called him a "god damned black ignorant son of a bitch"; when he objected and told Beck that his mother "although a colored woman, was a lady," he was made to walk three days, then perform hard labor from reveille to retreat for five days. SOURCE: Kinevan, *Frontier Cavalryman*, 145.

‡1st Lt. W. H. Beck, 10th Cavalry, was convicted of forcing Mack without cause to walk three days to camp at Pena Blanco, TX, 16–18 Oct 1878; Mack claimed that Beck called him "You Goddamn black ignorant son of a bitch," and that Mack respectfully informed Beck that his mother was a lady, although a colored woman, but that this was deleted from finding of guilty. SOURCE: GCMO 34, AGO, 30 May 1879.

MACK, Edward; Private; 25th Inf. Convicted with Pvt. Robert Lincoln, 25th Infantry, of raping Sioux woman, held as prisoner of war at Fort Randall, SD, 1882; served thirty-eight months of fifteen-year sentence. SOURCE: Dobak and Phillips, *The Black Regulars*, 179.

MACK, William; F/9th Cav. Born in Kentucky; black complexion; cannot read or write, age 23, Jul 1870, at Ft McKavett, TX. SOURCE: Bierschwale, *Fort McKavett*, 97.

MACK, William; Private; L/24th Inf. Died 5 Nov 1901; buried at Ft Bayard, NM, in plot N 42. SOURCE: "Fort Bayard National Cemetery, Records of Burials."

Buried 5 Nov 1901, section A, row V, plot 42, at Ft Bayard. SOURCE: Erickson, *Burials at Fort Bayard National Cemetery, NM*.

MACKADOO, Richard; Private; C/9th Cav. Pvt. Rick Mackadoo, C/9th Cavalry, cited for bravery against Apaches in Florida Mountains, New Mexico, in January 1877 by Lt. Henry Wright. SOURCE: Schubert, *Black Valor*, 45–46.

‡Commended for bravery in fight against Apaches, Florida Mountains, 24 Jan 1877. SOURCE: Leckie, *The Buffalo Soldiers*, 179; Billington, "Black Cavalrymen," 62; Billington, *New Mexico's Buffalo Soldiers*, 51.

‡Private bill passed for $20 per month pension. SOURCE: *Winners of the West* 3 (Apr 1926): 2.

‡Mentioned as surviving Indian war veteran. SOURCE: *Winners of the West* 3 (Jun 1926): 7.

‡Name also spelled Mackadew.

McKAY, Barney; Sergeant; G/9th Cav. ‡Also known as McDougal.

‡Born in Kentucky, son of Barney McKay and Mary McDougal; one sister Hannah Taylor; occupation laborer; complexion brown; enlisted Indianapolis, IN, 16 Aug 1881, as private, general dismounted service; honorably discharged, 12 Jan 1892. SOURCE: VA File XC 2659455, Barney McKay.

Sgt. Barney McDougal, 24th Infantry, fired pistol shots at Pvt. Jefferson Weedon because Weedon was rumored to have made advances to McDougal's wife. SOURCE: Dobak and Phillips, *The Black Regulars*, 177.

‡Injured left leg on march from Ft Sill to Boulder Creek, Indian Territory, when thrown from baggage wagon which overturned, May 1882; reinjured when thrown by mule, 4 Aug 1884; had surgery on knee for floating cartilage, by Dr. Adair, Ft Robinson, NE, spring 1892. SOURCE: Affidavit, McKay, 1417 17th Street, Washington, DC, 24 Jan 1916, VA File XC 2659455, Barney McKay.

‡Private, C/9th Cavalry, arrived Ft Robinson from depot, 1 Mar 1887.

‡Corporal, C/9th Cavalry, promoted to sergeant. SOURCE: Order 46, 9 Cav, 20 Sep 1888.

‡Sergeant, G/9th Cavalry, sentenced to dishonorable discharge and two years for "circulating an incendiary circular" among Ft Robinson troops inciting them to lawless acts against civilians of Crawford, NE. SOURCE: *ANJ* 30 (22 Jul 1893): 795.

‡George W. Jackson met McKay right after he was released from military prison; friend Drayton Moffett in same regiment and company had written that McKay was in prison; Moffett was trying to enlist support to get him out. SOURCE: Affidavit, George W. Jackson, 1211 Linden Street, NE, Washington, DC, occupation bookkeeper, age 71, 5 Nov 1925, VA File XC 2659455, Barney McKay.

Worked in 1896 and subsequent political campaigns. SOURCE: Affidavit, Thomas H. R. Clarke, 6 Nov 1925, VA File XC 2659455, Barney McKay.

‡Ella Farrell first knew McKay around Jan 1897, when he resided at house of Mrs. Lacey's family on K Street, between 17th and 18th Streets, NW; husband Charles J. Farrell, chauffeur, served with McKay in 9th Cavalry. SOURCE: Affidavit, Ella Farrell, 1416 P Street, NW, Washington, age 48, 30 Oct 1925, VA File XC 2659455, Barney McKay.

‡Coauthor with T. H. R. Clarke of *A Republican Text-Book for Colored Voters*, 1900, 48 pages.

Julia McKay, born and raised in Hillsdale, Bergen Co., NJ, daughter of Samuel and Mary Moore, met McKay in Washington, 1900, while he worked for law firm of Lambert and Baker; married in Washington, 5 Jun 1902; no children; he had come to Washington after military service, was Pullman porter for some time, then ran newspaper in Camden, NJ, for a few months; notice of wedding published in Denver *Statesman* because he had number of friends in the West whom he wanted to inform of marriage. SOURCE: Affidavit, Julia McKay, age 60, occupation dressmaker, 28 Oct 1925, VA File XC 2659455, Barney McKay.

‡Before enlistment worked as railroad porter and iron puddler and incapable of doing either; worked on New York Central Railroad, Oct 1896–May 1897, until knee and back gave way on New York-Chicago run; was carried off train at Buffalo, NY. SOURCE: McKay to Commissioner of Pensions Vespasian Warner, 13 Oct 1905, VA File XC 2659455, Barney McKay.

‡Letter, from 1620 L Street, NW, Washington, protests support by department commander Mitchell, of Spanish-American War Veterans of dismissal of 25th Infantry battalion after Brownsville affray. SOURCE: Washington *Post*, 25 Jan 1907.

‡Mentioned. SOURCE: Acknowledgements to Curtis, *The Black Soldier*.

‡Editor, *Jersey Tribune* and *New England Torch-Light*; author of *Republican Text-Book for Colored Voters* (1896), *Republican Party and the Negro* (1904), and *Hughes' Attitude Towards the Negro* (1916). SOURCE: Business card, "SERGT. B. M. MCKAY," VA File XC 2659455, Barney McKay.

Text of declaration, 1917, and letter to Secretary of the Interior Franklin Lane, 1918, both from pension application, published. SOURCE: Schubert, *Voices of the Buffalo Soldier*, 178–87.

‡Had $6 per month pension for injury to left knee; increased to $20 per month on 26 Oct 1922 based on syrionitis and floating cartilage in left knee; died 30 Apr 1925; widow, 1340 Corcoran Street, NW, Washington, died 2 Apr 1941. SOURCE: VA File XC 2659455, Barney McKay.

‡Born 27 Oct 1862; occupation watchman and government service; died at 1340 Corcoran Street from arteriosclerotic nephritis, myocarditis, and oremic toxemia; buried Harmony Cemetery, E. R. Jones, undertaker, 3 May 1925. SOURCE: Certificate of Death #2915000, District of Columbia, VA File XC 2659455, Barney McKay.

See OTT, **CREGG**, John L., Private, G/9th Cavalry; **CRUMP**, Edward W., Private, C/9th Cavalry; OTT, **EDWARDS**, William D., Corporal, A/10th Cavalry; OTT, **PAYNE**, Hayes B., Sergeant, K/24th Infantry; OTT, **POWELL**, George D., Sergeant Major, 24th Infantry

McKAY, George; Musician; 24th Inf. Lived with Faustina Sanchez. SOURCE: Dobak and Phillips, *The Black Regulars*, 172.

McKEE, Henry; Private; D/25th Inf. ‡At Ft Niobrara, NE, 1902. *See* OTT, **MORRIS**, Edward, Private, D/25th Infantry

Died 17 Sep 1902; originally buried at Ft Niobrara; reburied at Ft Leavenworth National Cemetery, plot 3524. SOURCE: Ft Leavenworth National Cemetery.

McKENNON, John; 1st Sgt; 25th Inf. Left Army and became policeman, New Orleans, LA. SOURCE: Dobak and Phillips, *The Black Regulars*, 17.

McKENZIE, Edward; Sergeant; B/9th Cav. ‡Sergeant, I/9th Cavalry, since 1 Aug 1880. SOURCE: Roster, 9 Cav.

Sergeant, I/9th Cavalry, served on honor guard when body of Col. Edward Hatch was transported from Ft Robinson, NE, to Ft Leavenworth, KS, in 1889. SOURCE: Kenner, *Buffalo Soldiers and Officers of the Ninth Cavalry*, 48–49.

‡On extra duty as wagonmaster, Ft Robinson. SOURCE: Order 92, 4 Mar 1891, Post Orders, Ft Robinson.

‡Denies signing petition for removal of Capt. John Guilfoyle as commander of I Troop. SOURCE: CO, Ft Robinson, to AAG, Department of the Platte, 1 May 1891, LS, Ft Robinson.

‡Resides with wife and five children in old barrack, Ft Robinson, Aug 1893. SOURCE: Medical History, Ft Robinson.

‡In I/9th Cavalry; wife Annie died of paralysis, Ft Robinson, Feb 1895; she was sister of wife of 1st Sgt. George Mason, C/9th Cavalry; buried at post cemetery, 16 Feb 1895. SOURCE: *ANJ* 32 (2 Mar 1895): 439; List of Interments, Ft Robinson.

Retires from B/9th Cavalry, Ft DuChesne, UT. SOURCE: *ANJ* 35 (25 Dec 1897): 311.

MACKEY, Robert; Private; A/39th Inf. Civil War veteran, served in D/10th Heavy Artillery; sentence of ten years for involvement in New Iberia, LA, mutiny, Jul 1867, reduced to three years. SOURCE: Dobak and Phillips, *The Black Regulars*, 222.

MACKI, Edward; Private; 25th Inf. Born in Summerville, SC; Ht 5'5", black hair and eyes, fair complexion; occupation laborer; enlisted at age 22, Charleston, SC, 23 May 1881; left recruit depot, David's Island, NY, 2 Jul 1881, arrived Ft Randall, SD, 7 Jul 1881. SOURCE: Descriptive & Assignment Rolls of Recruits, 25 Inf.

McKIBBIN, Care; Private; H/10th Cav. In Troop H/10th Cavalry stationed at Bonita Cañon Camp, AZ, but absent or on detached service 30 Apr 1886. SOURCE: Tagg, *The Camp at Bonita Cañon*, 232.

‡Honorable mention for services rendered in capture of Mangas and his Apache band, Rio Bonito, AZ, 18 Oct 1886. SOURCE: Baker, Roster.

McKINEY, Claud W.; Private; K/24th Inf. Died 23 Dec 1915; buried in plot 651-A WE at San Francisco National Cemetery. SOURCE: San Francisco National Cemetery.

McKINNEY, Mack; Private; 9th Cav. Could not sign name when he enlisted in 1867; in 1870 published humorous poem titled "Ode to a Pair of Tight Breeches" about Army uniforms in *Army and Navy Journal*, SOURCE: Dobak and Phillips, *The Black Regulars*, 177.

McMAHON, Andrew; Private; E/38th Inf. Died 29 Jul 1867; originally buried at Ft Hays, KS; reburied at Ft Leavenworth National Cemetery, plot 3374. SOURCE: Ft Leavenworth National Cemetery.

McMICKEN, William; Private; E/9th Cav. Served in the Philippines as private in E/9th Cavalry; in 9th Cavalry at Ft Leavenworth, KS, Mar 1905. SOURCE: Philippine Campaign Badge list, 29 May 1905.

‡Veteran of Philippine Insurrection; at Ft D. A. Russell, WY, in 1910. SOURCE: *Illustrated Review: Ninth Cavalry*, with picture.

McMILLAN, Emmett; Private; F/24th Inf. ‡Drowned crossing San Mateo River, Philippines, 21 Aug 1899. SOURCE: Richmond *Planet*, 2 Sep 1899.

Private, F/24th Infantry, buried in plot 507 at San Francisco National Cemetery. SOURCE: San Francisco National Cemetery.

McNARY, Presley; Private; A/24th Inf. Died at Ft McIntosh, TX, on 28 Jan 1877; buried at Fort Sam Houston National Cemetery, Section PE, number 295. SOURCE:

Buffalo Soldiers Interred in Fort Sam Houston National Cemetery.

McREYNOLDS, Cunen; Private; B/10th Cav. At Ft Duncan, TX, Dec 1877, convicted of mistreating horse and fined $5. SOURCE: Kinevan, *Frontier Cavalryman*, 82.

McREYNOLDS, Willis; Private; B/10th Cav. At Ft Stockton, TX, Sep 1879, lectured new recruit about showing proper respect for old soldiers. SOURCE: Kinevan, *Frontier Cavalryman*, 214.

MADDOX, Thomas; Sergeant; C/10th Cav. Died at Ft Stockton, TX, on 24 Jun 1884; buried at San Antonio National Cemetery, Section C, number 400. SOURCE: San Antonio National Cemetery Locator.

MADEN, Ebbert; Color Sgt. ‡Enlisted in F/9th Cavalry, 1880; saddler, K/9th Cavalry, 1888; corporal, F and E/9th Cavalry, 1890; participated in Sioux campaign, 1890–91; served in Cuban campaign, 1898. SOURCE: *ANJ* 37 (18 Nov 1899): 278.

‡First sergeant, F/9th Cavalry; married Miss Annie Ewing, "one of Omaha's belles," at Chadron, NE. SOURCE: Cleveland *Gazette*, 24 Jul 1886.

‡Assigned south-end quarters, Laundress Row, Ft Robinson, NE. SOURCE: CO to QM, Ft Robinson, 30 Oct 1886, LS, Ft Robinson.

‡Son buried at Ft Robinson [1886?]. SOURCE: List of Interments, Ft Robinson.

‡Sergeant, F/9th Cavalry, at Ft Robinson, 1887. *See* OTT, **HARRIS**, Robert, Sergeant, F/9th Cavalry

When sergeant in F/9th Cavalry at Ft Robinson, Nov 1887, became involved in stables fight with another sergeant and reduced to ranks. SOURCE: Kenner, *Buffalo Soldiers and Officers of the Ninth Cavalry*, 171.

‡Reduced to ranks by garrison court martial, Ft Robinson, for quarrel with Sgt. Robert Harris, F/9th Cavalry, 13 Nov 1887; also careless with candle in stable, 12 Nov 1887. SOURCE: Order 226, 18 Nov 1887, Post Orders, Ft Robinson.

‡Private, F/9th Cavalry, transferred to K/9th Cavalry. SOURCE: Order 12, 9 Cav, 13 Mar 1888.

‡Private, F/9th Cavalry, assigned daily duty at post canteen, Ft Robinson. SOURCE: Order 36, 24 Feb 1890, Post Orders, Ft Robinson.

‡Private, F/9th Cavalry, assigned daily duty at post canteen, Ft Robinson, vice Pvt. William B. Griffith, B/9th Cavalry. SOURCE: Order 131, Jun 1890, Post Orders, Ft Robinson.

‡Private, F/9th Cavalry, assigned daily duty at post canteen, Ft Robinson. SOURCE: Order 183, 31 Aug 1890, Post Orders, Ft Robinson.

‡Relieved from duty at canteen. SOURCE: Order 248, 18 Nov 1890, Post Orders, Ft Robinson.

‡On special duty as assistant, post canteen, Ft Robinson. SOURCE: Order 61, 31 Mar 1891, Post Orders, Ft Robinson.

Appointed corporal, F/9th Cavalry, 3 Nov 1891. SOURCE: Roster, 9 Cav.

‡Commander recognizes his prompt notification of guard of escape of prisoner and his energy and good judgment in capture and return of prisoner: "Such devotion to the interest of the service when off as well as on duty is a worthy example to all"; corporal, F/9th Cavalry. SOURCE: Order 77, 7 May 1892, Post Orders, Ft Robinson.

‡Ranked number 8 in carbine competition, Departments of the East, California, and the Platte, Bellevue, NE, 18–25 Sep 1894. SOURCE: GO 62, AGO, 15 Nov 1894.

‡At Ft Robinson, 1895; corporal since 3 Nov 1892. SOURCE: *ANJ* 32 (23 Feb 1895): 422.

‡Promoted to sergeant, Ft Robinson, 10 May 1895. SOURCE: *ANJ* 32 (25 May 1895): 642.

Appointed sergeant 10 May 1895; in E/9th Cavalry at Ft Robinson, NE, Jan 1897. SOURCE: Ninth Cavalry, Roster of NCOs, 1897.

‡Reenlistment as married soldier authorized by letter, Adjutant General's Office, 14 Jan 1898.

‡Family resides at Ft Robinson and claims to be indigent, dependent on charity of garrison for subsistence. SOURCE: CO, Ft Robinson, to CO, 9 Cav, 25 Jul 1898, LS, Ft Robinson.

‡First lieutenant, B/49th Infantry, as of 9 Sep 1899; transferred to M/49th Infantry, 28 Oct 1899; promoted to captain, 14 Nov 1899. SOURCE: Descriptive Book, B/49 Inf.

Retired color sergeant; received Indian Wars Campaign Badge number 1759 on 28 Oct 1914. SOURCE: Carroll, Indian Wars Campaign Badge, 51.

MADISON, Ingoman; QM Sgt; D/9th Cav. *See* **INGOMAN**, Madison, Quartermaster Sergeant, D/9th Cavalry

MADISON, John; Private; H/10th Cav. Born 1850? in Shelbyville, KY; discharged from D/24th Infantry 10 Sep 1883; enlisted H/10th Cavalry, San Antonio, TX, 4 Jan 1884; Ht 5'7", dark brown complexion, black eyes and hair; occupation porter. SOURCE: Sayre, *Warriors of Color*, 12, 341.

Private in H/10th Cavalry stationed at Bonita Cañon Camp, AZ, but absent or on detached service 30 Apr 1886. SOURCE: Tagg, *The Camp at Bonita Cañon*, 232.

MAGEE, Alfred; Artificer; K/25th Inf. Born in Liberty, MS; Ht 5'7", black complexion; occupation soldier; enlisted in A/39th Infantry for three years on 20 Aug 1866, age 23, at Ft St Philip, LA; promoted to sergeant 23 Mar 1867; reduced as incompetent 8 Feb 1869; transferred to K/25th Infantry at Jackson Bks, LA, 20 Apr 1869. SOURCE: Descriptive Roll of A/39th Inf.

MAHO, Thomas; Corporal; D/9th Cav. Died at Ft Stockton, TX, on 28 Oct 1871; buried at San Antonio National Cemetery, Section C, number 411. SOURCE: San Antonio National Cemetery Locator.

MAHUE, Martin; Private; L/10th Cav. Died 11 Aug 1868 of disease at Ft Arbuckle, OK. SOURCE: Regimental Returns, 10th Cavalry, 1868.

MAJOR, Alfred; Private; I/9th Cav. Buried 20 Sep 1903, section A, row Q, plot 13, at Ft Bayard, NM. SOURCE: Erickson, Burials at Fort Bayard National Cemetery, NM.

MAJORS, Harry; Corporal; F/49th Inf. Died 16 May 1936; buried at Ft Leavenworth National Cemetery, plot I 165. SOURCE: Ft Leavenworth National Cemetery.

MANN, Henry; Private; K/9th Cav. Served in second half of 1890s; resided at 1021 Hopkins St., Cincinnati, OH, in 1907. SOURCE: Sayre, *Warriors of Color*, 498.

MANN, Simpson; Private; F/9th Cav. ‡Resided Mickles Mill, Monroe Co., WV; enlisted, age 27, Cincinnati, OH, 1888; served one three-year enlistment at Ft Robinson, NE. SOURCE: Rickey, Mann interview.

‡Convicted by garrison court martial of absence without permission over night of 2–3 Nov 1889; $5 retained from pay until discharge. SOURCE: Order 233, 8 Nov 1899, Post Orders, Ft Robinson.

‡One hundred-three-year-old veteran awarded Indian wars campaign medal at Wadsworth Hospital, 13 May 1965. SOURCE: Rickey, "The Negro Regulars," 1.

Text of notes of Don Rickey's interview with Mann, Wadsworth Veterans Hospital, Leavenworth, KS, Jan 1965, published. SOURCE: Schubert, *Voices of the Buffalo Soldier*, 153–58.

MANOLT, Joseph; Private; K/25th Inf. Born in Bayou La Fouche, LA; Ht 5'11", black complexion; occupation soldier; enlisted in A/39th Infantry for three years on 29 Aug 1866, age 21, at Ft St Philip, LA; promoted to sergeant 24 Mar 1867; reduced as incompetent 15 Mar 1868; transferred to K/25th Infantry at Jackson Bks, LA, 20 Apr 1869. SOURCE: Descriptive Roll of A/39th Inf.

MANSFIELD, Harry; Private; 10th Cav. Native of New York, enlisted in 10th Cavalry at age 18; five-year veteran with reputation as nondrinker when he took his first drink, missed roll call, and disappeared from Ft Davis, TX. SOURCE: Leiker, *Racial Borders*, 83.

MANSON, William D.; Private; D/24th Inf. ‡Letter from Ft Supply, Indian Territory, described Christmas, 1885. SOURCE: Cleveland *Gazette*, 9 Jan 1886.

Sentenced to one year for firing shotgun through door of wife's quarters. SOURCE: Dobak and Phillips, *The Black Regulars*, 197.

MANWELL, George; Private; C/10th Cav. Died 3 Mar 1869; buried at Ft Douglas, UT. SOURCE: Record Book of Interments, Post Cemetery, 252.

MAPP, Solomon; Private; I/25th Inf. Died at Ft Davis, TX, on 26 Oct 1879; buried at San Antonio National Cemetery, Section I, number 1524. SOURCE: San Antonio National Cemetery Locator.

MARASCHAL, Natividad; Private; U.S. Army. Seminole Negro Scout, served 1876–84. SOURCE: Schubert, Consolidated List of Seminole Negro Scouts.

Born in Mexico; Ht 5'6", black hair and eyes, black complexion; enlisted at Ft Clark, TX, 12 Sep 1876, age 26; discharged and reenlisted for one year seven times, 12 Mar 1877–15 May 1883; discharged, age 33 at Camp Myers Spring, TX, 14 May 1884. SOURCE: Swanson, 30.

MARASCHAL, Trinida; Private; U.S. Army. Born in Mexico; Ht 5'6", black hair and eyes, black complexion; enlisted at Ft Duncan, TX, 12 Dec 1873, age 23; discharged 11 Jun 1874, reenlisted next day at Camp Eagle Pass, TX; discharged 12 Dec 1874, reenlisted 1 Feb 1875 at Ft Duncan; discharged 1 Aug 1875 at Ft Clark, TX; enlisted 1 Sep 1875 at Ft Duncan where he was discharged 5 Mar 1876. SOURCE: Swanson, 30.

Seminole Negro Scout, served 1873–76. SOURCE: Schubert, Consolidated List of Seminole Negro Scouts.

In 1875, age 30, resided at Ft Duncan with Molly age 30, Amanda age 3, female child age 1. SOURCE: NARA Record Group 393, Special File.

MARCHBANKS, Vance H.; Sergeant; C/10th Cav. ‡Private, A/9th Cavalry, detailed on special duty as assistant librarian, Ft Robinson, NE. SOURCE: SO 103, 16 Sep 1896, Post Orders, Ft Robinson.

‡Transferred to Hospital Corps in accordance with Special Order 274, Adjutant General's Office, 22 Nov 1897.

‡Squadron sergeant major, 10th Cavalry, at Ft Washakie, WY; letter. SOURCE: *The Voice of the Negro* (Dec 1906).

Squadron sergeant major, stationed at Ft Washakie, 1906; text of letter to editor, *The Voice of the Negro*, concerning shooting involving 25th Infantry, Brownsville, TX, Aug 1906, published. SOURCE: Schubert, *Voices of the Buffalo Soldier*, 123–26.

‡Sergeant, C/10th Cavalry, commissioned captain at Camp Des Moines, IA, 15 Oct 1917. SOURCE: Glass, *History of the Tenth Cavalry*, appendix M; Sweeney, *History of the American Negro in the Great War*, 126.

‡Warrant officer, at Ft Huachuca, AZ. SOURCE: Work, *The Negro Yearbook, 1925–1926*, 254; Work, *The Negro Yearbook, 1931–1932*, 334.

MAREE, James B.; Private; 25th Inf. Born in Charleston, SC; occupation laborer; Ht 5'8", fair complexion, black hair and eyes; enlisted, age 21, Charleston, 21 Jan 1881; left recruit depot, David's Island, NY, 17 Aug 1881, and after trip on steamer *Thomas Kirby* to Central Depot, New York City, and train via Chicago to Running Water, Dakota Territory, 22 Aug 1881, marched forty-seven miles to Ft Randall, SD, arrived 24 Aug 1881. SOURCE: Descriptive & Assignment Rolls, 25 Inf.

MARLOWE, William; Private; C/10th Cav. Served with Pvt. George Washington, C/10th Cavalry, early 1870s. SOURCE: Schubert, *Voices of the Buffalo Soldier*, 234.

MARSHALL, Albert; Corporal; F/9th Cav. Cpl. Alfred Marshall, native of Kentucky, age 23, former farmer, at Ft McKavett, TX, 1870; murdered 2 Feb 1870 while guarding civilian prisoner John Jackson. SOURCE: Kenner, *Buffalo Soldiers and Officers of the Ninth Cavalry*, 94–95.

‡Killed by white civilian John Jackson at Ft McKavett, 1870. SOURCE: Leckie, *The Buffalo Soldiers*, 99.

‡Killed near Manadrill, TX, 2 Feb 1870. SOURCE: *Historical and Pictorial Review, Second Cavalry Division*, 45.

‡Killed in vicinity of San Angelo, TX, 1870. SOURCE: Carroll, *The Black Military Experience*, 456.

‡Killed along with Pvt. Charles Murray, 9th Cavalry, by friends of Jackson while standing guard at Jackson home. SOURCE: Sullivan, "Fort McKavett," 144.

Died at Ft Concho, TX, on 2 Feb 1871; buried at San Antonio National Cemetery, Section E, number 891. SOURCE: San Antonio National Cemetery Locator.

MARSHALL, Hoyle; 1st Sgt; A/10th Cav. ‡Born in South Carolina; private, A/10th Cavalry, 12 Jul 1882; corporal, 1 Sep 1889; sergeant, 1 Feb 1892; at Ft Custer, MT, 1897. SOURCE: Baker, Roster.

Corporal received Indian Wars Campaign Badge number 1403 on 15 Jul 1909. SOURCE: Carroll, *Indian Wars Campaign Badge*, 40.

First sergeant, A/10th Cavalry, died 14 May 1938; buried in plot D-WES960 at San Francisco National Cemetery. SOURCE: San Francisco National Cemetery.

MARSHALL, Isaac; Private; F/10th Cav. ‡Issac Marshall, F/10th Cavalry, original member of 10th Cavalry; in troop when organized, Ft Leavenworth, KS, 21 Jun 1867. SOURCE: McMiller, "Buffalo Soldiers," 73.

Wounded in action, gunshot wound in right leg, near Beaver Creek, KS, 21 Aug 1867. SOURCE: LR, DeptMo, 1867.

Wounded in action against Indians at Beaver Creek, 21 Aug 1867. SOURCE: Schubert, *Voices of the Buffalo Soldier*, 20; Armes, *Ups and Downs*, 247.

MARSHALL, John; Sergeant; A/10th Cav. ‡Original member of 10th Cavalry; in troop when organized, Ft Leavenworth, KS, 18 Feb 1867. SOURCE: McMiller, "Buffalo Soldiers," 68.

‡Led patrol that intercepted eight Indians and killed one, near Catfish Creek, TX, 6 May 1875. SOURCE: Leckie, *The Buffalo Soldiers*, 142.

Served at Ft Concho, TX, 1875; led detachment in pursuit of Indians, May 1875; text of report, written with assistance of Sgt. Maj. Joseph Parker, signed with an "X," published. SOURCE: Schubert, *Voices of the Buffalo Soldier*, 73–74.

MARSHALL, Joseph; Private; F/9th Cav. Born in Louisiana; black complexion; can read, cannot write, age 21, Jul 1870, at Ft McKavett, TX. SOURCE: Bierschwale, *Fort McKavett*, 96.

Private, F/9th Cavalry, died 1 Aug 1870; buried at Camp Douglas, UT. SOURCE: Record Book of Interments, Post Cemetery, 252.

MARSHALL, Louis; Private; C/10th Cav. ‡Served in 10th Cavalry in Cuba, 1898. SOURCE: Cashin, *Under Fire with the Tenth Cavalry*, 340.

‡Wounded in action at Santiago, Cuba, 1 Jul 1898. SOURCE: SecWar, *AR 1898*, 324.

Rescued by Sgt. Maj. Edward Baker after sustaining wound and falling into San Juan River, Cuba, 1 Jul 1898; first name also spelled "Lewis." SOURCE: Schubert, *Black Valor*, 151.

MARSHALL, Moses; Private; H/25th Inf. ‡Sergeant at Ft Davis, TX, 1878. *See* **ROBINSON**, Richard, Corporal, H/25th Infantry

At Ft Davis, shot and killed Cpl. Richard Robinson in his bed for negative comments about his wife. SOURCE: Leiker, *Racial Borders*, 78.

‡Convicted of murder, District Court, Presidio Co., TX, and sentenced to nine years in Texas State Penitentiary, Huntsville, 9 Apr 1879. SOURCE: Report of Trials, Department of Texas, 1878–79.

MARTIN, Abram; Lance Cpl; 25th Inf. Born in Charleston, SC; Ht 5'8", black hair and eyes, fair complexion; occupation hostler; enlisted at age 21, Charleston, 23 May 1881; left recruit depot, David's Island, NY, 2 Jul 1881, arrived Ft Randall, SD, 7 Jul 1881. SOURCE: Descriptive & Assignment Rolls of Recruits, 25 Inf.

One of twenty men in B/25th Infantry who cycled 1,900 miles from Ft Missoula, MT, to St. Louis, MO, 14 Jun–24 Jul 1897, in 25th Infantry Bicycle Corps to test durability and practicality of bicycles as a means of transportation for troops. SOURCE: File 60178, GC, AGO Records.

MARTIN, Adkins; F/9th Cav. Born in Alabama; black complexion; can read and write, age 22, Jul 1870, at Ft McKavett, TX. SOURCE: Bierschwale, *Fort McKavett,* 97.

MARTIN, Charles; Private; F/10th Cav. Died 17 Jul 1867 of unknown causes at Ft Harker, KS. SOURCE: Regimental Returns, 10th Cavalry, 1867.

MARTIN, Daniel; Private; B/24th Inf. Died at Camp Eagle Pass, TX, on 27 Aug 1879; buried at San Antonio National Cemetery, Section F, number 1143. SOURCE: San Antonio National Cemetery Locator.

MARTIN, David G.; Private; I/9th Cav. Rescued under fire by Lt. George R. Burnett, Cuchillo Negro, NM, Aug 1881. SOURCE: Kenner, *Buffalo Soldiers and Officers of the Ninth Cavalry,* 245.

Became disoriented and confused in fight against Nana on Cuchillo Negro Creek, NM, 16 Aug 1881, and was guided to safety by Lt. George Burnett and Pvt. Augustus Walley. SOURCE: Schubert, *Black Valor,* 82.

MARTIN, George; D/24th Inf. Born in Pennsylvania; mulatto complexion; can read, cannot write, age 24, Jul 1870, at Ft McKavett, TX. SOURCE: Bierschwale, *Fort McKavett,* 95.

MARTIN, George; Private; F/25th Inf. Born in New Brunswick, NJ; Ht 5'11", black hair and eyes, dark complexion; occupation waiter; resided New Brunswick when enlisted at age 25, New York City, 7 Sep 1885; assigned to F/25th Infantry; arrived Ft Snelling, MN, 5 Feb 1886. SOURCE: Descriptive & Assignment Rolls of Recruits, 25 Inf.

MARTIN, James; Private; 10th Cav. Born in Canada; frequently confined by courts martial; deserted from Ft Davis, TX, 1883. SOURCE: Leiker, *Racial Borders,* 85.

MARTIN, John; Private; H/9th Cav. Died at Ft Davis, TX, on 15 Apr 1868; buried at San Antonio National Cemetery, Section O, number 1558. SOURCE: San Antonio National Cemetery Locator.

MARTIN, John; Private; G/9th Cav. Received Philippine Campaign Badge number 11833 for service as private in A/25th Infantry, 7 Nov 1900–28 Jun 1902; private in G/9th Cavalry, Ft Leavenworth, KS, Mar 1905. SOURCE: Philippine Campaign Badge Recipients; Philippine Campaign Badge list, 29 May 1905.

Died 17 Apr 1907; buried at Ft Bayard, NM, in plot 8. SOURCE: "Fort Bayard National Cemetery, Records of Burials."

Buried 17 Apr 1907, section B, row A, plot 8 at Ft Bayard. SOURCE: Erickson, Burials at Fort Bayard National Cemetery, NM.

MARTIN, John H.; Ord Sgt; U.S. Army. Appointed ordnance sergeant 20 Jan 1889 from first sergeant, E/25th Infantry. SOURCE: Dobak, "Staff Noncommissioned Officers."

MARTIN, Lloyd D.; Private; 9th Cav. Received Philippine Campaign Badge number 11783 for service as private in F/9th Cavalry; in 9th Cavalry at Ft Leavenworth, KS, Mar 1905. SOURCE: Philippine Campaign Badge list, 29 May 1905.

MARTIN, Richard; Corporal; G/9th Cav. ‡Farrier, G/9th Cavalry, at Ft Robinson, NE; deposited $125 with paymaster. SOURCE: Misc Records, DP, 1894–98.

Appointed corporal 19 Dec 1896; in G/9th Cavalry at Ft Robinson, Jan 1897. SOURCE: Ninth Cavalry, Roster of NCOs, 1897.

MARTIN, Shadrach; Private; F/9th Cav. Died at Ft Davis, TX; buried at San Antonio National Cemetery, Section I, number 1523. SOURCE: San Antonio National Cemetery Locator.

MARTIN, William J.; Private; G/24th Inf. ‡Died of septicemia and shock following operation in the Philippines, 17 Jun 1902. SOURCE: *ANJ* 39 (9 Aug 1902): 1248.

Died 17 Jun 1902; buried in plot NEW A1146 at San Francisco National Cemetery. SOURCE: San Francisco National Cemetery.

MARTS, Harry; Private; F/10th Cav. Died 9 Oct 1914; buried at Ft Bayard, NM, in plot V 43. SOURCE: "Fort Bayard National Cemetery, Records of Burials."

Buried 9 Oct 1914, section B, row G, plot 43 at Ft Bayard. SOURCE: Erickson, Burials at Fort Bayard National Cemetery, NM.

MASON, Alexander; Private; A/9th Cav. Died 27 Aug 1901; buried at San Antonio National Cemetery, Section F, number 1077. SOURCE: San Antonio National Cemetery Locator.

MASON, Charles; Private; F/25th Inf. Died 10 Jun 1912; buried at Ft Bayard, NM, in plot T 33. SOURCE: "Fort Bayard National Cemetery, Records of Burials."

Buried 20 Jun 1912, section B, row E, plot 33, at Ft Bayard. SOURCE: Erickson, Burials at Fort Bayard National Cemetery, NM.

MASON, George; 1st Sgt; C/9th Cav. Native of Kentucky; dark-skinned; enlisted at age 18 in 1867; listed as illiterate in 1870 Census; consistent "excellent" character ratings; served as sergeant for L/9th, 1867–89; troop moved from Ft Union, NM, in June 1876 to Ft Lyon, CO; L/9th Cavalry detached to serve at Ft Leavenworth, KS, Oct 1886. SOURCE: Kenner, *Buffalo Soldiers and Officers of the Ninth Cavalry,* 53, 175–76, 189, 341.

‡First sergeant, L/9th Cavalry, Ft Leavenworth, with warrant dating from 3 Jan 1872. SOURCE: *ANJ* 25 (18 Feb 1888): 586.

‡First sergeant, C/9th Cavalry, since 1 Oct 1892; sergeant since 1 Aug 1889. SOURCE: Roster, 9 Cav.

‡First sergeant, C/9th Cavalry; letter, Adjutant General's Office, 14 Apr 1895, concerns his retirement.

‡Married, stationed at Ft Robinson, NE, 1895; wife is sister of wife of Sgt. Edward McKenzie, I/9th Cavalry. SOURCE: *ANJ* 32 (2 Mar 1895): 439.

‡Retires from Ft Robinson, Apr 1895. SOURCE: *ANJ* 32 (20 Apr 1895): 555.

‡Praised by commander, Capt. Charles W. Taylor, upon retirement. SOURCE: *ANJ* 32 (11 May 1895): 608.

‡Retired and residing in Crawford, NE, one of six retirees there, four of whom are black. SOURCE: Soldiers on the Retired List Paid in the Department of the Platte by Mail, Misc Records, DP, 1894–98.

‡Died at home in Crawford with asthma, 15 Apr 1916; 9th Cavalry retiree and twenty-year resident; "was very agreeable and pleasant in all his dealings with his fellow men." SOURCE: Crawford *Tribune,* 17 Apr 1916.

‡Buried at Ft Robinson, 15 Apr 1916. SOURCE: List of Interments, Ft Robinson.

MASON, Henry; Private; E/25th Inf. On duty 5 July 1881 at Ft Hale, Dakota Territory, in boat's crew in Quartermaster Department and replied to order issued by Cpl. George Williams, C/25th Infantry, to turn out and help make a trip across the Missouri River, by stating "It's no use to wake me, for I won't get up, I won't get up before reveille; it ain't reveille and I won't get up for nobody not on government business," and willfully failed and neglected to obey the order; tried for violation of Article of War 21 in general court martial convened 19 Aug 1881 at Ft Sully, Dakota Territory; found not guilty but guilty of conduct to the prejudice of good order and military discipline; fined $15 of pay; court was lenient because of hard work of boat's crew on 4 July. SOURCE: General Court-Martial Orders No. 99, Ft Snelling, MN, 19 Aug 1881.

MASON, Henry; Private; A/24th Inf. Died 29 Sep 1905; buried at Ft Bayard, NM, in plot H 21. SOURCE: "Fort Bayard National Cemetery, Records of Burials."

Buried 29 Sep 1905, section A, row K, plot 24, at Ft Bayard. SOURCE: Erickson, Burials at Fort Bayard National Cemetery, NM.

MASON, John; Sergeant; H/9th Cav. ‡Born in Wytheville, TN; Ht 5'4 1/2", occupation waiter; enlisted, age 21, Bristol, TN, 6 Dec 1894; discharged, end of term, character excellent, Ft Robinson, NE, 5 Dec 1897; fined $.50 by summary court, 7 Nov 1895, and $2.50, 18 Sep 1896; deposits $5, retained $8.80, clothing $12.71. SOURCE: Descriptive Book, H/9 Cav.

Appointed corporal 17 Jul 1896; in H/9th Cavalry at Ft Robinson, Jan 1897. SOURCE: Ninth Cavalry, Roster of NCOs, 1897.

‡Corporal, H/9th Cavalry, wounded in action, San Juan, Cuba, 2 Jul 1898; despite bad wound he charged up hill near head of troops. SOURCE: SecWar, *AR 1898,* 707–8; *Illustrated Review: Ninth Cavalry.*

‡Corporal, H/9th Cavalry, returned from furlough to duty, Ft Robinson, 7 Oct 1898.

‡Commended for gallantry in charging at head of troops up San Juan Hill in battle of Santiago, Cuba, in which he was seriously wounded; now sergeant, H/9th Cavalry. SOURCE: GO 15, AGO, 13 Feb 1900.

MASON, John H.; Corporal; D/10th Cav. ‡Admitted to Soldiers Home with disability at age 40 with ten years and ten months' service, 18 May 1886; died later in year. SOURCE: SecWar, *AR 1886,* 738.

Died at Ft Davis, TX, on 19 Jan 1886; buried at San Antonio National Cemetery, Section I, number 1564. SOURCE: San Antonio National Cemetery Locator.

Mason, John H.; Private; C/24th Inf. Died 31 Jul 1901; buried in plot ADDN 425 at San Francisco National Cemetery. SOURCE: San Francisco National Cemetery.

MASON, Lewis; M/9th Cav. Born in Kentucky; black complexion; cannot read or write, age 21, Jul 1870, at Ft McKavett, TX. SOURCE: Bierschwale, *Fort McKavett,* 98.

MASON, Samuel; H/25th Inf. Born in Louisiana; black complexion; cannot read or write, age 26, 5 Sep 1870, at Ft McKavett, TX. SOURCE: Bierschwale, *Fort McKavett,* 108.

MASON, Surrie; Private; K/25th Inf. Born in Bayou La Fouche, LA; Ht 5'4", black complexion; occupation laborer; enlisted in A/39th Infantry for three years on 26 Oct 1866, age 22, at Greenville, LA; transferred to K/25th Infantry at Jackson Bks, LA, 20 Apr 1869. SOURCE: Descriptive Roll of A/39th Inf.

MASON, Thomas; Private; A/10th Cav. ‡Arrived at Ft Leavenworth, KS, from Jefferson Bks, MO, Oct 1866.

‡Died at Ft Concho, TX, 5 Jul 1875. SOURCE: ES, 10 Cav, 1872–81.

Died 5 Jul 1875 in hospital at Ft Concho. SOURCE: Regimental Returns, 10th Cavalry, 1875.

MASON, William; Saddler; C/10th Cav. Saddler, C/9th Cavalry, one of best marksmen in regiment, at Ft Sill, OK, 1883. SOURCE: Kenner, *Buffalo Soldiers and Officers of the Ninth Cavalry*, 257.

‡Private, B/9th Cavalry, ranked number 8 with carbine, Department of the Platte competition, Bellevue, NE, 17–22 Aug 1891, bronze medal. SOURCE: Baker, Roster.

‡Private, B/9th Cavalry, qualified for first time as carbine sharpshooter with 74.86 percent. SOURCE: GO 1, AGO, 3 Jan 1893.

‡Saddler, C/10th Cavalry, and distinguished marksman, ranked number 8 with revolver and number 9 with carbine, Departments of Dakota and the Columbia, two bronze medals, 1893. SOURCE: Baker, Roster.

‡Distinguished marksman, carbine, 1891, and carbine and revolver, 1893. SOURCE: GO 82, AGO, 24 Oct 1893.

Ranked number 50 among carbine sharpshooters with 74.14 percent, 1893. SOURCE: GO 1, AGO, 2 Jan 1894.

MASSEY, James; Private; I/10th Cav. In Troop I/10th Cavalry stationed at Bonita Cañon Camp, AZ, 30 Jun 1886. SOURCE: Tagg, *The Camp at Bonita Cañon*, 232.

MASSIE, Adam; Private. Died 4 Jul 1899; buried at San Antonio National Cemetery, Section I, number 1692. SOURCE: San Antonio National Cemetery Locator.

MATHEWS, J.; Private; C/9th Cav. *See corrected entry,* **MATHEWS,** William, Private, C/9th Cavalry

MATHEWS, Jessie; Private; E/10th Cav. In Troop E/10th Cavalry stationed at Bonita Cañon Camp, AZ, but absent or on detached service 28 Feb 1886. SOURCE: Tagg, *The Camp at Bonita Cañon*, 232.

MATHEWS, Levi; Private; L/9th Cav. Enlisted 10 Jun 1879 at Baltimore, MD; at Ft Bliss, TX. SOURCE: Muster Roll, L/9th Cavalry, 31 Oct 1879–31 Dec 1879.

MATHEWS, Stephen; Private; I/10th Cav. Died 27 Mar 1871 of meningitis at Camp Supply, OK. SOURCE: Regimental Returns, 10th Cavalry, 1871.

MATHEWS, William; Private; C/9th Cav. ‡Died of pulmonary disease at Ft Robinson, NE, 16 Feb 1888. SOURCE: Medical History, Ft Robinson.

Pvt. William H. Mathews, C/9th Cavalry, died 16 Feb 1888 of bronchitis contracted in line of duty at post hospital; died of pulmonary edema at post hospital; buried at Ft Robinson. SOURCE: Buecker, Fort Robinson Burials

‡Funeral at Ft Robinson, 18 Feb 1888. SOURCE: Order 35, 17 Feb 1888, Post Orders, and List of Interments, Ft Robinson.

MATHIGLEY, Henry; Sergeant; C/9th Cav. Died 13 Jun 1879; buried at Ft Bayard, NM, in plot B 36. SOURCE: "Fort Bayard National Cemetery, Records of Burials."

Sgt. Heny Mathigly, buried 13 Jun 1879, section A, row F, plot 39 at Ft Bayard. SOURCE: Erickson, Burials at Fort Bayard National Cemetery, NM.

MATTHEWS, Daniel; Private; 9th Cav. Received Philippine Campaign Badge number 11784 for service as private in F/9th Cavalry; in 9th Cavalry at Ft Leavenworth, KS, Mar 1905. SOURCE: Philippine Campaign Badge list, 29 May 1905.

MATTHEWS, George; M/9th Cav. Born in Missouri; mulatto complexion; cannot read or write, age 22, Jul 1870, at Ft McKavett, TX. SOURCE: Bierschwale, *Fort McKavett*, 100.

MATTHEWS, William H.; Private; M/10th Cav. Died 11 Jun 1882 of dysentery at Ft Concho, TX. SOURCE: Regimental Returns, 10th Cavalry, 1882.

MAULSBY, William; Private; F/24th Inf. Convicted by court martial, Ft Duncan, TX, Dec 1877, of beating hospital matron, confined for eight months; at Ft Elliott, TX, 1881, convicted of feigning illness and malingering. SOURCE: Kinevan, *Frontier Cavalryman*, 82–83.

MAXWELL, Albert E.; Private; l/25th Inf. Died 24 Mar 1905; originally buried at Ft Niobrara, NE; reburied at Ft Leavenworth National Cemetery, plot 3539. SOURCE: Ft Leavenworth National Cemetery.

MAXWELL, William; Private; G/9th Cav. Received Philippine Campaign Badge number 11834 for service as private in C/25th Infantry, 28 Jun 1902–20 Jul 1902; private in G/9th Cavalry, Ft Leavenworth, KS, Mar 1905. SOURCE: Philippine Campaign Badge Recipients; Philippine Campaign Badge list, 29 May 1905

MAYFIELD, Walter; Private; C/25th Inf. Died 10 Apr 1918; buried at Ft Bayard, NM, in plot Z 24. SOURCE: "Fort Bayard National Cemetery, Records of Burials."

Buried 10 Apr 1918, section B, row K, plot 24, at Ft Bayard. SOURCE: Erickson, Burials at Fort Bayard National Cemetery, NM.

MAYS, Isaiah; Corporal; B/24th Inf. ‡Born in Carter's Ridge, VA. SOURCE: Carroll, *The Black Military Experience*, 278, 417.

Born in Carter's Ridge; 8-year veteran when he served with escort of Paymaster Joseph Wham near Cedar Springs, AZ, against robbers, and received Medal of Honor for bravery, running through heavy fire to get help; reenlisted, character "excellent," Sep 1891; sought discharge Feb 1892 to return to Virginia and take care of his parents, but War Department rejected application; reassigned to D/24th Infantry, Ft Bayard, NM, June 1892, after losing stripes and being fined $10 per month for six months for disrespect of commanding officer; discharged summer 1893, and resided in various Arizona towns, working as laborer, at least until 1922. SOURCE: Schubert, *Black Valor*, 93, 95–96, 98–99.

Medal of Honor for bravery in protecting Paymaster Wham and payroll, Arizona, 1889, mentioned. SOURCE: Dobak and Phillips, *The Black Regulars*, 100, 261.

‡Among men who distinguished themselves in 1889; awarded Medal of Honor for gallant and meritorious service while escort for Maj. Joseph W. Wham, paymaster, when attacked by robbers between Fts Grant and Thomas, AZ, 11 May 1889. SOURCE: GO 18, AGO, 1891.

Text of report of Paymaster Wham, describing bravery of escort, published. SOURCE: Schubert, *Voices of the Buffalo Soldier*, 159–62.

Forced out of Army due to disciplinary problems in 1893; worked as miner; lost his Medal of Honor in flood near Clifton, AZ, in late 1890s; pension application refused in 1920; died 1925 at Arizona State Hospital, Phoenix; buried in hospital cemetery; veterans placed bronze headstone on grave. SOURCE: Ball, *Ambush at Bloody Run*, photo 112, 208.

MAZIQUE, Sanco; Private. *See* **MOZIQUE**, Edward, Private, E/10th Cavalry

MEADE, William; Private; 25th Inf. Born in Tappahannock, VA; Ht 6'0", black hair and dark brown eyes, brown complexion; occupation waiter; enlisted at age 26, Philadelphia, PA, 29 Nov 1886; assigned to F/25th Infantry; arrived Ft Snelling, MN, 1 Apr 1887. SOURCE: Descriptive & Assignment Rolls of Recruits, 25 Inf.

MEBANE, Samuel; Private; 25th Inf. Born in Rockingham County, NC; Ht 5'9", black hair and eyes, black complexion; occupation laborer; resided in Wentworth, NC, when enlisted at age 22, Washington, DC, 4 Dec 1886; arrived Ft Snelling, MN, 20 Jan 1887. SOURCE: Descriptive & Assignment Rolls of Recruits, 25 Inf.

MEEHAN, George H.; Private; M/25th Inf. Buried 20 Mar 1907, section B, row A, plot 17, at Ft Bayard, NM. SOURCE: Erickson, Burials at Fort Bayard National Cemetery, NM.

MEEKS, Joseph; Private; D/25th Inf. Born in Prince Georges Co., MD; Ht 5'7", black hair and brown eyes, black complexion; discharged from H/9th Cavalry, 21 Jan 1886; second enlistment 5 Feb 1886, age 21, at Washington, DC; assigned to D/25th Infantry; arrived Ft Snelling, MN, 26

Apr 1886. SOURCE: Descriptive & Assignment Rolls of Recruits, 25 Inf.

MEHAMITT, Jeremiah; Private; D/10th Cav. Died 1 Mar 1900; buried at San Antonio National Cemetery, Section I, number 1702. SOURCE: San Antonio National Cemetery Locator.

MEILLBROWN, Robert; Sergeant; I/10th Cav. In Troop I/10th Cavalry stationed at Bonita Cañon Camp, AZ, 30 Jun 1886. SOURCE: Tagg, *The Camp at Bonita Cañon*, 231.

MERMIER, Joseph; D/24th Inf. Born in New York; mulatto complexion; cannot read or write, age 24, Jul 1870, at Ft McKavett, TX. SOURCE: Bierschwale, *Fort McKavett*, 96.

MERRILL, Robert; 9th Cav. Born in Tennessee; black complexion; can read and write, age 21, 5 Sep 1870, at Ft McKavett, TX. SOURCE: Bierschwale, *Fort McKavett*, 107.

MERRIWEATHER, Henry; Private; 25th Inf. Born in Richmond, VA; Ht 5'7", black hair and brown eyes, brown complexion; occupation hostler; enlisted at age 22, Baltimore, MD, 27 Apr 1886; arrived Ft Snelling, MN, 19 Aug 1886. SOURCE: Descriptive & Assignment Rolls of Recruits, 25 Inf.

MERRIWETHER, James H.; Private; 9th Cav. Murdered near Ft Davis, TX, 1870. SOURCE: Dobak and Phillips, *The Black Regulars*, 328.

MERRYWEATHER, A.; Musician; Band/9th Cav. Died at Ft Davis, TX, on 15 Oct 1870; buried at San Antonio National Cemetery, Section I, number 1550. SOURCE: San Antonio National Cemetery Locator.

MEW, Benjamin; Sergeant; 25th Inf. At Ft Stockton, TX, 1873, conviction for attempting to poison wife Martha and her lover Corporal Lee set aside by Department of Texas commander, Gen. Christopher C. Augur. SOURCE: Barnett, *Ungentlemanly Acts*, 171.

MEYERS, William; Private; H/10th Cav. Died at Ft Davis, TX, on 6 Oct 1879; buried at San Antonio National Cemetery, Section I, number 1502. SOURCE: San Antonio National Cemetery Locator.

MICHAEL, Doc; Private; H/10th Cav. *See* **MOCFIELD**, Doc, Private, H/10th Cavalry

MIDDLETON, Charles; Private; 25th Inf. Born in Charleston, SC; Ht 5'4", black hair and eyes, fair complexion; occupation laborer; enlisted, age 22, Charleston, 9 Jun

1881; left recruit depot, David's Island, NY, 2 Jul 1881, arrived Ft Randall, SD, 7 Jul 1881. SOURCE: Descriptive & Assignment Rolls of Recruits, 25 Inf.

MIDDLETON, Richard; Private; 25th Inf. Born in Georgetown, SC; Ht 5'8", occupation soldier, black hair and eyes, brown complexion; enlisted, age 27, St Louis, MO, 14 Sep 1886; arrived Ft Snelling, MN, 9 Oct 1886. SOURCE: Descriptive & Assignment Rolls, 25 Inf.

MIDDLETON, Robert; Private; 25th Inf. Born in Barnwell Court House, SC; Ht 5'4 1/2", black hair and eyes, dark complexion; occupation farmer; enlisted, age 22, Charleston, SC, 13 Jun 1881; left recruit depot, David's Island, NY, 17 Aug 1881, and after trip on steamer *Thomas Kirby* to Central Depot, New York City, and train via Chicago to Running Water, Dakota Territory, 22 Aug 1881, marched forty-seven miles to Ft Randall, SD, arrived 24 Aug 1881. SOURCE: Descriptive & Assignment Rolls, 25 Inf.

MILES, James; Private; F/25th Inf. Died 17 Nov 1896; buried at Ft Bayard, NM, in plot I 16. SOURCE: "Fort Bayard National Cemetery, Records of Burials."

Buried 17 Nov 1898, section A, row M, plot 19, at Ft Bayard. SOURCE: Erickson, Burials at Fort Bayard National Cemetery, NM.

MILES, Julius; Blacksmith; M/10th Cav. ‡Original member of L/10th Cavalry; in troop when organized, Ft Riley, KS, 21 Sep 1867. SOURCE: McMiller, "Buffalo Soldiers," 78.

In M/10th Cavalry, died 18 Oct 1869 in hospital at Ft Sill, OK. SOURCE: Regimental Returns, 10th Cavalry, 1869.

Died 18 Oct 1869; buried at Camp Douglas, UT. SOURCE: Record Book of Interments, Post Cemetery, 252.

MILESTON, Fillmore; Private; F/10th Cav. Died 3 Aug 1867; originally buried at Ft Hays, KS; reburied at Ft Leavenworth National Cemetery, plot 3287. SOURCE: Ft Leavenworth National Cemetery.

MILLER, Alexander; Private; 25th Inf. Born in Bibb County, AL; Ht 5'7", black hair and hazel eyes, copper complexion; occupation machinist; enlisted at age 25, Cincinnati, OH, 22 Mar 1886; arrived Ft Snelling, MN, 31 Jul 1886. SOURCE: Descriptive & Assignment Rolls of Recruits, 25 Inf.

MILLER, Charles; F/9th Cav. Born in Kentucky; black complexion; cannot read or write, age 21, Jul 1870, at Ft McKavett, TX. SOURCE: Bierschwale, *Fort McKavett*, 97.

MILLER, Colonel E.; Sergeant; H/10th Cav. Born in Elkton, MD, 2 Mar 1862; enlisted 7 May 1879; Ht 5'11", light brown complexion, brown eyes, black hair; occupation sailor, porter, teamster; served thirteen years in H/10th Cavalry; discharged 6 May 1884, enlisted May 1884, Ft Davis, TX; discharged 5 May 1889, Ft Apache, AZ; enlisted 23 Aug 1889; discharged 22 Nov 1892, Ft Buford, ND; participated in campaign against Geronimo, 1886; never married; sought pension based on accident at target practice, Ft Apache, 1886, which severely damaged right eye, in correspondence dated 1905–07; resided in Baltimore, MD, and Kansas City, MO. SOURCE: Sayre, *Warriors of Color*, 375–78.

Private in H/10th Cavalry stationed at Bonita Cañon Camp, AZ, 30 Apr 1886. SOURCE: Tagg, *The Camp at Bonita Cañon*, 232.

Pvt. C. E. Miller, H/10th Cavalry, participated in Oct 1886 pursuit and capture of Apache Mangus. SOURCE: Schubert, *Voices of the Buffalo Soldier*, 146.

‡Honorable mention for services rendered as private in capture of Mangas and his Apache band, Rio Bonito, AZ, 18 Oct 1886. SOURCE: Baker, Roster.

‡Sergeant, authorized four-month furlough from Ft Apache. SOURCE: *ANJ* 29 (14 Nov 1891): 198.

‡Served with Webb Chatmoun in 1880s; resided at 300 Walnut Street, Kansas City, MO, in 1913. SOURCE: VA File C 2360629, Webb Chatmoun.

MILLER, Daniel; Recruit; 10th Cav. Died 5 Nov 1867 at Ft Riley, KS. SOURCE: Regimental Returns, 10th Cavalry, 1867.

MILLER, David A.; Private; B/25th Inf. Born in Chambersburg, PA; Ht 5'9", black hair and eyes, brown complexion; occupation soldier; enlisted at age 38, Washington, DC, 14 Nov 1881; arrived Ft Snelling, MN, 21 Nov 1882. SOURCE: Descriptive & Assignment Rolls of Recruits, 25 Inf.

MILLER, Frank; Private; 25th Inf. Born in Baltimore, MD; Ht 5'6", black hair and brown eyes, brown complexion; occupation laborer; enlisted at age 24, Baltimore, 29 Nov 1886; assigned to B/25th Infantry; arrived Ft Snelling, MN, 1 Apr 1887. SOURCE: Descriptive & Assignment Rolls of Recruits, 25 Inf.

MILLER, George; Private; G/9th Cav. Died 13 Jun 1909; buried at Santa Fe National Cemetery, NM, plot B 902. SOURCE: Santa Fe National Cemetery, Records of Burials.

MILLER, Girard; 1st Sgt; H/10th Cav. Born in Washington, DC, 1 Nov 1865; mother Elizabeth Johnson; enlisted Washington, 23 Nov 1881; Ht 5'9"; light brown complexion, brown eyes, black hair; occupation laborer; discharged as first sergeant, Ft Apache, AZ, 22 Nov 1886, character excellent; resided in Washington in 1901; married Martha A. Parrish, Philadelphia, PA, 15 Aug 1909, who died 14 May 1963; children William L. born 1910, Gerrard Jr. born 1911, Carrall born 1914, Elizabeth born 1917 married name Rainey; received $30 per month pension Nov 1931, increased to $40 Jul 1937, increased to $45 in Nov 1937; employed as sanitary inspector, City of Buffalo Health Department, 1937; died at residence, 210 Clinton St., Buffalo, NY, 11 June 1938; buried in grave 2532, section 40, at Forest Lawn Cemetery, Buffalo; widow received pension of $30 per month Jul 1938. SOURCE: *Warriors of Color*, 26, 360, 379–90.

Enlisted in Washington, DC, 23 Nov 1881; corporal in H/10th Cavalry stationed at Bonita Cañon Camp, AZ, 30 Apr 1886. SOURCE: Tagg, *The Camp at Bonita Cañon*, 67, 231.

MILLER, Henry C.; Saddler Sgt; NCS/10th Cav. ‡Sergeant, 10th Cavalry, mentioned 1873 as deceased. SOURCE: ES, 10 Cav, 1872–81.

Died 17 Jan 1873, cause not stated, at Ft Gibson, OK. SOURCE: Regimental Returns, 10th Cavalry, 1873.

MILLER, James; Private; L/9th Cav. Born in Philadelphia, PA; mulatto; Ht 5'11"; enlisted at age 19; at Ft McIntosh, TX, 1872; at Ft McIntosh, convicted of assault on Mexican, Laredo, TX, Jul 1872, and imprisoned until Oct 1872; at Ft Ringgold, TX, 1873; fined $8 for minor offense Oct 1874; trekked from Ft Brown, TX, to Ft Union, NM, Sep 1875–Jan 1876; June 1876 to Ft Lyon, CO; convicted of murder for killing in barroom, Las Animas, CO, Aug 1876; hanged at Las Animas, Sep 1877. SOURCE: Kenner, *Buffalo Soldiers and Officers of the Ninth Cavalry*, 178, 180–88.

MILLER, John; Private; K/25th Inf. Born in Washington County, VA; Ht 5'4", black hair and eyes; occupation laborer; enlisted at age 23, Cincinnati, OH, 20 Apr 1886; from Columbus Bks, OH, arrived Ft Snelling, MN, 17 Sep 1886. SOURCE: Descriptive & Assignment Rolls of Recruits, 25 Inf.

MILLER, John D.; Sergeant; D/9th Cav. ‡Private, D/9th Cavalry, at Ft Robinson, NE, 1894, resided with wife Elizabell in room at Chaplain Plummer's quarters. SOURCE: Investigation of Charges against Chaplain Plummer.

‡Private, D/9th Cavalry, on recruiting duty early 1898. SOURCE: Cashin, *Under Fire with the Tenth Cavalry*, 112.

Sergeant, received Indian Wars Campaign Badge number 660 on 20 Oct 1908. SOURCE: Carroll, *Indian Wars Campaign Badge*, 19.

‡Sergeant, D/9th Cavalry, at Ft D. A. Russell, WY, in 1910. SOURCE: *Illustrated Review: Ninth Cavalry*, with picture.

MILLER, John E.; 1st Sgt; K/9th Cav. ‡Private, teacher at Ft Robinson, NE, school, 15 Nov 1894–31 Jan 1895, 1 Feb–30 Apr 1895. SOURCE: Reports of Schools, Ft Robinson, 1892–96.

‡Lance corporal, relieved from extra duty as schoolteacher, Ft Robinson. SOURCE: Order 26, 29 Apr 1895, Post Orders, Ft Robinson.

‡Promoted to corporal, Ft Robinson, 9 May 1895. SOURCE: *ANJ* 32 (18 May 1895): 626.

‡Promoted to sergeant, Ft Robinson, 1 Oct 1895. SOURCE: *ANJ* 33 (12 Oct 1895): 87.

Appointed first sergeant 19 Dec 1896; in G/9th Cavalry at Ft Robinson, Jan 1897. SOURCE: Ninth Cavalry, Roster of NCOs, 1897.

‡Sergeant, G/9th Cavalry, authorized to reenlist as married, K/9th Cavalry, by letter, Adjutant General's Office, 28 Dec 1897.

MILLER, John W.; Private; I/10th Cav. In Troop I/10th Cavalry stationed at Bonita Cañon Camp, AZ, 30 Jun 1886. SOURCE: Tagg, *The Camp at Bonita Cañon*, 232.

MILLER, Lounie; Private; F/9th Cav. Died 29 Mar 1913; buried at Ft Leavenworth National Cemetery, plot E 2488-A. SOURCE: Ft Leavenworth National Cemetery.

MILLER, Richard; Color Sgt; 9th Cav. Native of Kentucky, enlisted 1879, assigned to D/9th Cavalry; sergeant, age 26, D/9th Cavalry, 1881, disappointed by selection of James Dickerson to be first sergeant; four-month furlough, summer 1882; discharged 1884, remained civilian for eighteen months, then enlisted in 10th Cavalry; cited for bravery against Apache outlaw on San Carlos Reservation, AZ, Aug 1886; trumpeter, 1890–95; rejoined 9th Cavalry, stationed at Ft DuChesne, UT, reappointed sergeant 1897, helped organize band and served as drum major; served in Cuba and the Philippines, received certificate of merit, became regimental color sergeant. SOURCE: Kenner, *Buffalo Soldiers and Officers of the Ninth Cavalry*, 271–78, 354–55.

Involved in scandal over homosexuality of 1st Sgt. Richard Dickerson. SOURCE: Dobak and Phillips, *The Black Regulars*, 65–66.

‡Corporal, B/10th Cavalry, honorable mention for daring effort to capture Indian outlaw, San Carlos, AZ, 28 Aug 1886. SOURCE: Baker, Roster.

‡Trumpeter, B/10th Cavalry; at Ft Apache, AZ, 1890, subscribed $.50 to testimonial to General Grierson. SOURCE: List of subscriptions, 23 Apr 1890, 10th Cavalry papers, MHI.

Appointed sergeant 16 Jul 1895; in F/9th Cavalry at Ft DuChesne, Jan 1897. SOURCE: Ninth Cavalry, Roster of NCOs, 1897.

‡Sergeant, F/9th Cavalry, and drum major, troop band, Ft DuChesne. SOURCE: *ANJ* 34 (29 May 1897): 733.

‡Seriously wounded in thigh, Guinobatan, Albay, Philippines, 17 Dec 1900. SOURCE: *ANJ* 38 (2 Feb 1901): 555; Hamilton, "History of the Ninth Cavalry," 103; *Illustrated Review: Ninth Cavalry*.

As sergeant in F/9th Cavalry, awarded certificate of merit for distinguished conduct in engagement with enemy where he was attacked and wounded by several bolomen, Tagbac, Albay, 17 Dec 1900. SOURCE: Gleim, *The Certificate of Merit*, 54.

‡Appointed regimental color sergeant, May 1901. SOURCE: *ANJ* 38 (1 Jun 1901): 966.

‡Awarded certificate of merit, 17 Dec 1903, for distinguished conduct in engagement with insurgents, Tagbac, Albay, 17 Dec 1900, where he was attacked and wounded by several bolomen while sergeant, F/9th Cavalry. SOURCE: GO 32, AGO, 6 Feb 1904.

Born in Madison County, KY; resided Louisville, KY; received Distinguished Service Medal in lieu of certificate of merit. SOURCE: *American Decorations*, 841.

MILLER, Samuel; Blacksmith; H/9th Cav. Received Philippine Campaign Badge number 11868 for service as blacksmith in K/9th Cavalry; in 9th Cavalry at Ft Leavenworth, KS, Mar 1905. SOURCE: Philippine Campaign Badge list, 29 May 1905.

‡Veteran of Philippine Insurrection; at Ft D. A. Russell, WY, in 1910; sharpshooter; resident of Atlanta, GA. SOURCE: *Illustrated Review: Ninth Cavalry*, with picture.

MILLER, Stephen; D/24th Inf. Born in Kentucky; mulatto complexion; cannot read or write, age 41, Jul 1870, at Ft McKavett, TX. SOURCE: Bierschwale, *Fort McKavett*, 96.

MILLER, Sylvester; Private; I/25th Inf. Died 7 Sep 1900; buried at Ft Bayard, NM, in plot A 164. SOURCE: "Fort Bayard National Cemetery, Records of Burials."

Buried 7 Sep 1900, section A, row V, plot 10 at Ft Bayard. SOURCE: Erickson, Burials at Fort Bayard National Cemetery, NM.

MILLER, Thomas; Private; K/10th Cav. ‡Original member of 10th Cavalry; in troop when organized, Ft Riley, KS, 1 Sep 1867. SOURCE: McMiller, "Buffalo Soldiers," 77.

Died 30 Mar 1869 of accidental gunshot wound at Cimarron Crossing, KS. SOURCE: Regimental Returns, 10th Cavalry, 1869.

MILLER, Toler; 1st Sgt; D/9th Cav. As first sergeant, received Indian Wars Campaign Badge number 662 on 20

Oct 1908. SOURCE: Carroll, *Indian Wars Campaign Badge*, 19.

MILLER, William; Sergeant; U.S. Army. Seminole Negro Scout, served 1874–78. SOURCE: Schubert, Consolidated List of Seminole Negro Scouts.

Born in Mexico; not Seminole, probably German and Mexican with Indian background; Ht 5'5", black hair and eyes, yellow complexion; enlisted at Ft Clark, TX, 14 May 1874, age 19; discharged 24 Dec 1874 at Ft Clark where he reenlisted 22 Mar 1875; discharged 22 Sep 1875 at Camp Supply, TX, where he reenlisted as sergeant same day; on 15 Oct 1875 with Lieutenant Bullis and two other Scouts stole thirty horses from Indian camp in Mexico; in Jan 1876 went into Comanche and Apache camp in Mexico as spy for five days; discharged 13 Apr 1876 and reenlisted as sergeant for six months twice at Ft Clark; discharged 13 Apr 1877 at Camp Painted Comanche, TX, where he reenlisted for one year on same day; discharged as sergeant, age 22, 7 May 1878 at Ft Clark. SOURCE: Swanson, 31.

MILLER, William; Private; G/10th Cav. Died 23 Apr 1890; originally buried at Ft Grant, AZ; buried at Santa Fe National Cemetery, NM, plot I-780. SOURCE: Santa Fe National Cemetery, Records of Burials.

MILLIMAN, Jerry; Farrier; L/10th Cav. Born in Glen Falls, NY, in 1840; age 23 when he enlisted in G/54th Massachusetts Regiment for three years 9 Apr 1863 at Readville, MA; Ht 5'5", black hair and eyes, dark complexion; occupation boatman and farmer; present for duty at skirmish on James Island, SC, 16 Jul 1863 and Ft Wagner, SC, 18 Jul 1863; promoted to corporal 22 Jun 1863; at Battle of Honey Hill, SC, 30 Nov 1864; discharged 20 Aug 1865; enlisted 4 Jan 1869; appointed as farrier and served in L/10th Cavalry; served at Ft Sill, OK, Ft Concho, TX, and Ft Stanton, NM; married to Rosa Ann Jackson who died Mar 1878; married Elizabeth Van on 30 Nov 1879 in San Antonio; she and her first husband Henry Randall belonged to Seth Randall who moved from Talladega, AL, to Texas; she used her father's name Van after Emancipation; Milliman died 27 Dec 1896; widow applied for pension. SOURCE: Greene, *Swamp Angels*, 184.

MILLS, Andrew; M/9th Cav. Born in Kentucky; black complexion; cannot read or write, age 23, Jul 1870, at Ft McKavett, TX. SOURCE: Bierschwale, *Fort McKavett*, 100.

MILLS, George; Private; B/10th Cav. ‡Killed in action at Ojo Caliente, TX, 29 Oct 1880. SOURCE: Baker, Roster; Leckie, *The Buffalo Soldiers*, 230; Regimental Returns, 10th Cavalry, 1880.

MILLS, William; Private; 25th Inf. Born in Caroline County, VA; Ht 5'10", black hair and brown eyes, brown complexion; occupation laborer; enlisted at age 22, Baltimore, MD, 7 Apr 1886; arrived Ft Snelling, MN, 19 Aug 1886. SOURCE: Descriptive & Assignment Rolls of Recruits, 25 Inf.

MILLSTONE, Tillmon; Private; F/10th Cav. Died 2 Aug 1867 of cholera at Ft Hays, KS. SOURCE: Regimental Returns, 10th Cavalry, 1867.

MIMS John; Private; B/25th Inf. Died 10 Nov 1902; buried in plot N ADD1180 at San Francisco National Cemetery. SOURCE: San Francisco National Cemetery.

MIMS, Lewis; Private; 9th Cav. Received Philippine Campaign Badge number 11785 for service as private in F/9th Cavalry; in 9th Cavalry at Ft Leavenworth, KS, Mar 1905. SOURCE: Philippine Campaign Badge list, 29 May 1905.

‡Private, E/9th Cavalry, at Ft D. A. Russell, WY, in 1910; resident of 254 Chestnut St., Macon, GA. SOURCE: *Illustrated Review, Ninth Cavalry*, with picture.

MINAR, James L.; Sergeant; M/10th Cav. ‡Born in Virginia; private, F/10th Cavalry, 1 Dec 1876–30 Nov 1881; private, 7 Dec 1881; corporal, 31 Oct 1883; sergeant, 11 Sep 1884; at Ft Assiniboine, MT, 1897. SOURCE: Baker, Roster.

‡Sergeant, F/10th Cavalry, at Ft Apache, AZ, 1890, subscribed $.50 to testimonial to General Grierson. SOURCE: List of subscriptions, 23 Apr 1890, 10th Cavalry papers, MHI.

‡Sergeant, F/10th Cavalry, reduced to ranks. SOURCE: *ANJ* 35 (12 Mar 1898): 518.

‡Served as sergeant, M/10th Cavalry, in Cuba, 1898. SOURCE: Cashin, *Under Fire with the Tenth Cavalry*, 352.

One of four sergeants accompanying Lt. Carter Johnson on expedition to southern Cuba to deliver arms to insurgents, June 1898. SOURCE: Schubert, *Black Valor*, 135.

‡Retires as sergeant, M/10th Cavalry, in accordance with Special Order 300, Adjutant General's Office, 11 Dec 1903.

MINFIELD, Caleb; Private; A/10th Cav. Drowned 5 Nov 1874 at Ft Concho, TX. SOURCE: Regimental Returns, 10th Cavalry, 1874.

MINGO, Arthur; Sergeant; 10th Cav. ‡Private, C/9th Cavalry; veteran of Philippine Insurrection; at Ft D. A. Russell, WY, in 1910; resident of 21 Douglas St., Chattanooga, TN. SOURCE: *Illustrated Review: Ninth Cavalry*, with picture.

Sergeant, 10th Cavalry; died 31 Jul 1936; buried in plot D-WES641 at San Francisco National Cemetery. SOURCE: San Francisco National Cemetery.

MINUS, Washington; Private; L/9th Cavalry. Enlisted 9 July 1879 at Baltimore, MD; at Ft Bliss, TX. SOURCE: Muster Roll, L/9th Cavalry, 31 Oct 1879–31 Dec 1879.

MITCHELL, Andrew; Private; 25th Inf. Born in Upperville, VA; Ht 6'0", black hair and eyes, colored complexion; occupation farmer; enlisted at age 25, Philadelphia, PA, 8 Jun 1881; left recruit depot, David's Island, NY, 2 Jul 1881, arrived Ft Randall, SD, 7 Jul 1881. SOURCE: Descriptive & Assignment Rolls of Recruits, 25 Inf.

MITCHELL, Frederick; Private; 10th Cav. At Ft Concho, TX, Feb 1881 one of post printers who produced broadside warning civilians to respect rights of soldiers. SOURCE: Dobak and Phillips, *The Black Regulars*, 238–39.

MITCHELL, George; Private; B/10th Cav. Transferred from L/10th Cavalry, Ft Stockton, TX, Apr 1879; a competent clerk; kicked by horse Sep 1879 and disabled. SOURCE: Kinevan, *Frontier Cavalryman*, 160, 207.

MITCHELL, George W.; Private; B/25th Inf. Enlisted 5 Jul 1904, discharged without honor 22 Nov 1906, Brownsville, TX. SOURCE: Powell, "Military Record of the Enlisted Men Who Were Discharged Without Honor."

‡Dishonorable discharge, Brownsville. SOURCE: SO 266, AGO, 9 Nov 1906.

MITCHELL, J. S.; Private; C/10th Cav. Died at Ft Davis, TX, on 9 Jul 1881; buried at San Antonio National Cemetery, Section I, number 1527. SOURCE: San Antonio National Cemetery Locator.

MITCHELL, James; Private; B/25th Inf. ‡Died of dysentery at Palauig, Luzon, Philippines, 2 Jul 1901. SOURCE: *ANJ* 38 (24 Aug 1901): 1256.

Died 2 Jul 1901; buried in plot 985 at San Francisco National Cemetery. SOURCE: San Francisco National Cemetery.

MITCHELL, John H.; 1st Sgt; M/9th Cav. Born in Kentucky; mulatto complexion; can read and write, age 22, Jul 1870, at Ft McKavett, TX. SOURCE: Bierschwale, *Fort McKavett*, 98.

First sergeant, deserted along with six other men, Oct 1870. SOURCE: Kenner, *Buffalo Soldiers and Officers of the Ninth Cavalry*, 163.

MITCHELL, Paul; Private; A/39th Inf. Civil War veteran, served in D/81st U.S. Colored Infantry; sentence of twenty years for involvement in New Iberia, LA, mutiny, Jul 1867, reduced to two years. SOURCE: Dobak and Phillips, *The Black Regulars*, 222.

MITCHELL, Price L.; Sergeant; 39th Inf. Thirty years after discharge, remembered drilling twice per day as a recruit. SOURCE: Dobak and Phillips, *The Black Regulars*, 12.

MITCHELL Thomas C.; Private; I/25th Inf. Died 26 Apr 1902; buried in plot 869 at San Francisco National Cemetery. SOURCE: San Francisco National Cemetery.

MITCHELL, William; Private; K/10th Cav. ‡Original member of 10th Cavalry; in troop when organized, Ft Riley, KS, 1 Sep 1867. SOURCE: McMiller, "Buffalo Soldiers," 77.

Died 31 May 1868 in the field in Kansas after shooting self accidentally. SOURCE: Regimental Returns, 10th Cavalry, 1868.

MOBLEY, David; Private; I/9th Cav. Died at Ft Concho, TX, on 27 Nov 1870; buried at San Antonio National Cemetery, Section D, number 678. SOURCE: San Antonio National Cemetery Locator.

MOCFIELD, Doc; Private; H/10th Cav. In Troop H/10th Cavalry stationed at Bonita Cañon Camp, AZ, 30 Apr 1886; name could also be Doc Michael. SOURCE: Tagg, *The Camp at Bonita Cañon*, 232.

MODE, Henry; Recruit; 9th Cav. Died 20 Mar 1873; buried at San Antonio National Cemetery, Section D, number 775. SOURCE: San Antonio National Cemetery Locator.

MOISE, Augustine; Private; K/25th Inf. Born in Iberville, LA; Ht 5'5", black complexion; occupation soldier; enlisted in A/39th Infantry for three years on 29 Aug 1866, age 24, at Ft St Philip, LA; transferred to K/25th Infantry at Jackson Bks, LA, 20 Apr 1869. SOURCE: Descriptive Roll of A/39th Inf.

MONDAY, Israel; Private; A/9th Cav. Assigned to A/9th Cavalry 1882; accused of molesting Pvt. Thomas Polk, A/9th Cavalry, Ft Stanton, NM, Nov 1885; Pvts. Samuel Carter and Wilson Brown also claimed to have been victims of Monday; convicted of molesting Polk and sentenced to dishonorable discharge and two years. SOURCE: Kenner, *Buffalo Soldiers and Officers of the Ninth Cavalry*, 269–70.

MONROE, Edward M.; Private; A/24th Inf. Born and resided in Philadelphia, PA; at Naguilian, Luzon, Philippines, 7 Dec 1899, volunteered to swim the Rio Grande de Cagayan in face of a well-entrenched enemy, swam the river, returned with raft for small arms and ammunition, crossed again, took part in attack that drove off superior enemy force; awarded Distinguished Service Cross in 1925. SOURCE: *American Decorations*, 456.

‡Awarded Distinguished Service Cross for heroism in the Philippines, 7 Dec 1899. SOURCE: *Crisis* 30 (June 1925): 78.

MONROE, George; Sergeant; A/9th Cav. ‡Appointed sergeant, 30 Apr 1892. SOURCE: Roster, 9 Cav.

Appointed sergeant 30 Apr 1892; in A/9th Cavalry at Ft Robinson, NE, Jan 1897. SOURCE: Ninth Cavalry, Roster of NCOs, 1897.

‡Wife Sallie buried at Ft Robinson, 1894. SOURCE: List of Interments, Ft Robinson.

‡At Ft Robinson, 1895. SOURCE: *ANJ* 32 (23 Feb 1895): 422.

MONROE, James; Private; 9th Cav. Received Philippine Campaign Badge number 11738 for service as private in E/9th Cavalry; in 9th Cavalry at Ft Leavenworth, KS, Mar 1905. SOURCE: Philippine Campaign Badge list, 29 May 1905.

MONROE, John; D/24th Inf. Born in Kentucky; black complexion; cannot read or write, age 24, Jul 1870, at Ft McKavett, TX. SOURCE: Bierschwale, *Fort McKavett*, 96.

MONROE, William; Private; 10th Cav. Received dishonorable discharge in 1867 for fellating a fellow soldier. SOURCE: Dobak and Phillips, *The Black Regulars*, 300.

MONTGOMERY, Everett; 9th Cav. Born in Georgia; mulatto complexion; can read, cannot write, age 22, 5 Sep 1870, at Ft McKavett, TX. SOURCE: Bierschwale, *Fort McKavett*, 107.

MONTGOMERY, Seaborn; A/10th Cav. Civil War veteran; served in Independent Battery, U.S. Colored Light Artillery. SOURCE: *Organization Index to Pension Files*.

‡Original member of 10th Cavalry; in troop when organized, Ft Leavenworth, KS, 18 Feb 1867. SOURCE: McMiller, "Buffalo Soldiers," 68.

MOODY, Alex; Private; F/9th Cav. At Ft Robinson, NE, 1887; brawled with and wounded fellow soldier, Crawford, NE; deserted, apprehended; dishonorably discharged and sentenced to two years' confinement. SOURCE: Kenner, *Buffalo Soldiers and Officers of the Ninth Cavalry*, 169.

MOON, John; Private; 10th Cav. Served with Pvt. George Washington, C/10th Cavalry, early 1870s. SOURCE: Schubert, *Voices of the Buffalo Soldier*, 230.

MOORE, Adam; Sergeant; C/9th Cav. ‡Appointed corporal, C/9th Cavalry, 23 Mar 1889. SOURCE: Roster, 9 Cav.

‡Promoted to sergeant, vice Rock, retired, Ft Robinson, NE, Dec 1894. SOURCE: *ANJ* 32 (22 Dec 1894): 278.

Appointed sergeant 15 Dec 1894; in C/9th Cavalry at Ft Robinson, Jan 1897. SOURCE: Ninth Cavalry, Roster of NCOs, 1897.

‡Commended for gallantry in charge up San Juan Hill, battle of Santiago, Cuba, 1 Jul 1898; now out of service. SOURCE: GO 15, AGO, 13 Feb 1900; *ANJ* 37 (24 Feb 1900): 611.

‡Wounded in action at San Juan, Cuba, 1 Jul 1898. SOURCE: *Illustrated Review: Ninth Cavalry*, with picture.

MOORE, Arthur L.; Private; M/10th Cav. Died 9 May 1907; buried at Ft Bayard, NM, in plot P 15. SOURCE: "Fort Bayard National Cemetery, Records of Burials."

Buried 9 May 1907, section B, row A, plot 15, at Ft Bayard. SOURCE: Erickson, Burials at Fort Bayard National Cemetery, NM.

MOORE, David Miles; Musician; F/25th Inf. *See* MOORE, Miles, Musician, F/25th Infantry

MOORE, Fredrick Thomas; Private; D/9th Cav. Born 10 Jun 1859 in Cecil County, MD; father Benjamin Moore; enlisted 21 Aug 1880 in Baltimore, MD; discharged 29 Aug 1885, Ft McKinney, WY; applied for benefits, claim XC 258253; died 7 Jun 1944, Hill City, KS; daughter Frida Dotson resided Hill City. SOURCE: Application for Burial Allowance, Veteran Frederick Moore, Claim No. XC 2 568 253, photocopy in authors' files.

MOORE, John; Private; F/10th Cav. ‡Original member of 10th Cavalry; in troop when organized, Ft Leavenworth, KS, 21 Jun 1867. SOURCE: McMiller, "Buffalo Soldiers," 73.

Died 16 Sep 1869 in hospital at Ft Sill, OK. SOURCE: Regimental Returns, 10th Cavalry, 1869.

Died 11 Sep 1869; buried at Camp Douglas, UT. SOURCE: Record Book of Interments, Post Cemetery, 252.

MOORE, Joseph; QM Sgt; 9th Cav. ‡Private, arrived at Ft Robinson, NE, from Jefferson Bks, MO, 14 Aug 1885. SOURCE: Monthly Return, Ft Robinson, Aug 1885.

‡Along with E. Marshall, 9th Cavalry, responsible for establishment of Sunday School at Ft Robinson. SOURCE: Cleveland *Gazette*, 11 Aug 1886.

At Ft Robinson, Aug 1886, appointed acting sergeant major. SOURCE: Kenner, *Buffalo Soldiers and Officers of the Ninth Cavalry*, 172.

‡Private, F/9th Cavalry, relieved from extra duty as schoolteacher, Ft Robinson. SOURCE: Order 111, 4 Jun 1887, Post Orders, Ft Robinson.

‡Corporal, F/9th Cavalry, relieved from extra duty as schoolteacher, Ft Robinson. SOURCE: Order 217, 7 Nov 1887, Post Orders, Ft Robinson.

‡Sergeant, F/9th Cavalry, on extra duty as schoolteacher, Ft Robinson. SOURCE: Order 226, 31 Oct 1889, Post Orders, Ft Robinson.

‡Relieved from extra duty as schoolteacher, Ft Robinson. SOURCE: Order 61, 25 Mar 1890, Post Orders, Ft Robinson.

‡Proposes to raise sufficient money among four colored regiments to buy site of John Brown fort, Harper's Ferry, WV, for monument. SOURCE: Cleveland *Gazette*, 9 Aug 1890.

‡Private, A/9th Cavalry, relieves Sgt. Harry S. Ogilvie, C/8th Infantry, as schoolteacher, Ft Robinson. SOURCE: Order 88, 29 Apr 1891, Post Orders, Ft Robinson.

‡Commander, Ft Robinson, asks for report from superintendent of post schools on qualifications of Private Moore as schoolteacher. SOURCE: CO, Ft Robinson, to Chaplain Plummer, 28 Apr 1891, LS, Ft Robinson.

‡On extra duty as schoolteacher, Ft Robinson. SOURCE: Order 183, 19 Sep 1891, Post Orders, Ft Robinson.

‡Corporal, retained on extra duty as schoolteacher in accordance with telegram, Adjutant General's Office, 4 Dec 1891.

‡Teacher, Ft Robinson, 1 Nov 1891–30 Apr 1892. SOURCE: Reports of Schools, Ft Robinson, 1892–96.

‡Commander, Ft Robinson, asks authority to keep Corporal Moore on as schoolteacher because of his experience; Moore has organized post schools for enlisted men and children under direction of chaplain; his relief would seriously hinder progress. SOURCE: CO, Ft Robinson, to AG, USA, 15 Nov 1891, LS, Ft Robinson.

‡Appointed sergeant, A/9th Cavalry, 26 Jun 1892. SOURCE: Roster, 9 Cav.

Appointed sergeant 26 Jun 1892; in A/9th Cavalry at Ft Robinson, Jan 1897. SOURCE: Ninth Cavalry, Roster of NCOs, 1897.

‡Letter, Ft Robinson, to editor. SOURCE: Cleveland *Gazette*, 4 Mar 1895.

‡Sergeant, on special regimental recruiting duty with 1st Lt. Montgomery D. Parker, 9th Cavalry, at Cincinnati. SOURCE: *ANJ* 32 (24 Aug 1895): 855.

‡Examined for ordnance sergeant at Ft Robinson, Nov 1895, while sergeant, A/9th Cavalry. SOURCE: *ANJ* 33 (16 Nov 1895): 179.

‡Reenlistment authorized by letter, Adjutant General's Office, 19 Jan 1898.

‡Sergeant, A/9th Cavalry; commissioned first lieutenant, 8th Volunteer Infantry, after Spanish-American War. SOURCE: Cashin, *Under Fire with the Tenth Cavalry*, 355, 359, with picture in uniform of 8th Volunteer Infantry.

‡Mentioned. SOURCE: San Francisco *Chronicle*, 15 Nov 1899.

‡Mentioned as second lieutenant, F/48th Infantry. SOURCE: Beasley, *Negro Trailblazers*, 284.

‡Formerly with 8th and 48th Volunteer Infantry regiments; now quartermaster sergeant, 9th Cavalry, Ord Bks, CA, with first squadron. SOURCE: Indianapolis *Freeman*, 5 Dec 1903.

MOORE, Loney; Corporal; L/24th Inf. ‡Wounded in Cuba, 1898. SOURCE: Muller, *The Twenty Fourth Infantry*, 16.

‡Commended for distinguished service as private, A/24th Infantry, battle of Santiago, Cuba, 1 Jul 1898; awarded certificate of merit. SOURCE: GO 15, AGO, 13 Feb 1900.

‡Certificate of merit mentioned. SOURCE: Steward, *The Colored Regulars*, 280; *ANJ* 37 (24 Feb 1900): 611.

Awarded certificate of merit for distinguished service as private, A/24th Infantry, in battle of Santiago, 1 Jul 1898. SOURCE: Gleim, *The Certificate of Merit*, 46.

‡Corporal, L/24th Infantry, awarded certificate of merit for service in Cuban campaign, 1898. SOURCE: Scipio, *Last of the Black Regulars*, 130.

MOORE, Miles; Musician; F/25th Inf. Born David Miles Moore on 8 Apr 1848 in Ithaca, NY; mother Elizabeth, father David Moore born in Elmira, NY; Civil War veteran; enlisted in H/54th Massachusetts Regiment 29 Apr 1863 at Readville, MA; Ht 5'10", black hair mixed with gray, brown eyes, mulatto complexion; discharged 20 Aug 1865; enlisted in E/39th Infantry 13 May 1868; served at Ft Columbus, NY, as musician; transferred to F/25th Infantry 30 Apr 1870; discharged 30 Aug 1870 at Ft Clark, TX; married Ardelle Rosemary on 16 Dec 1875 at New Orleans, LA; Richard born 1874, August born 22 Oct 1877, Arthur born 12 Jan 1883, Elizabeth born 12 Oct 1888, George born 9 Mar 1890; lived at 63 Walwork St., Saratoga Springs, NY; died in hospital at Saratoga Springs 30 May 1904. SOURCE: Greene, *Swamp Angels*, 191.

MOORE, Robert; M/9th Cav. Born in Kentucky; black complexion; cannot read or write, age 26, Jul 1870, at Ft McKavett, TX. SOURCE: Bierschwale, *Fort McKavett*, 100.

MOORE, Ross; Private; 9th Cav. At Ft Duncan, TX, 1870; stole carbine from soldier, disposed of it in Eagle Pass, convicted of desertion, sentenced to dishonorable discharge and five years. SOURCE: Leiker, *Racial Borders*, 83, 208.

MOORE, Russell; Private; G/9th Cav. Received Philippine Campaign Badge number 11836 for service as private in E/24th Infantry, 16 Aug 1899–16 Feb 1901; private in G/9th Cavalry, Ft Leavenworth, KS, Mar 1905. SOURCE: Philippine Campaign Badge Recipients; Philippine Campaign Badge list, 29 May 1905.

MOORE, Sam B.; Private; G/9th Cav. Received Philippine Campaign Badge number 11837 for service as private in G/9th Cavalry, 12 Apr 1902–16 Sep 1902; private in G/9th Cavalry, Ft Leavenworth, KS, Mar 1905. SOURCE: Philippine Campaign Badge Recipients; Philippine Campaign Badge list, 29 May 1905.

MOORE, William T.; Private; F/9th Cav. ‡Died of variola in the Philippines, 19 Jul 1901. SOURCE: *ANJ* 39 (21 Sep 1901): 59.

Died 19 Jul 1901; buried in plot N ADD1384 at San Francisco National Cemetery. SOURCE: San Francisco National Cemetery.

MORAN, Charles; Private; 25th Inf. Born in Charleston, SC; Ht 5'7", black hair and eyes, fair complexion; occupation hostler; enlisted at age 23, Charleston, 14 Jun 1881; left recruit depot, David's Island, NY, 2 Jul 1881, arrived Ft Randall, SD, 7 Jul 1881. SOURCE: Descriptive & Assignment Rolls of Recruits, 25 Inf.

MORANEY, Elihu; Private; 25th Inf. Born in Greenville, SC; Ht 6'0", black hair and eyes, fair complexion; occupation farmer; enlisted at age 21, Charleston, SC, 23 May 1881; left recruit depot, David's Island, NY, 2 Jul 1881, arrived Ft Randall, SD, 7 Jul 1881. SOURCE: Descriptive & Assignment Rolls of Recruits, 25 Inf.

MORE, Samuel; Private; 25th Inf. Born in Baltimore, MD; Ht 5'7", black hair and eyes, brown complexion; discharged from F/9th Cavalry 28 Feb 1887; second reenlistment, 25th Infantry, at age 27, Baltimore, 14 Mar 1887; assigned to B/25th Infantry, arrived Ft Snelling, MN, 28 May 1887. SOURCE: Descriptive & Assignment Rolls of Recruits, 25 Inf.

MORELL, Benjamin; F/9th Cav. *See* **MORRELL**, Benjamin, Ordinance Sergeant, U.S. Army

MORGAN, David; Private; 24th Inf. Discharged in 1871; died destitute at Brownsville, TX, 1917; officers at Ft Brown, TX, and local Grand Army of the Republic post paid for his funeral. SOURCE: Dobak and Phillips, *The Black Regulars*, 278.

MORGAN, John M.; Private; H/10th Cav. Died 2 Nov 1877 of gunshot wounds at Ft Davis, TX. SOURCE: Regimental Returns, 10th Cavalry, 1877.

Died at Ft Davis on 27 Nov 1877; buried at San Antonio National Cemetery, Section I. SOURCE: San Antonio National Cemetery Locator.

MORGAN, Paul; Private; I/9th Cav. Died at Ft Stockton, TX, on Jun 1869; buried at San Antonio National Cemetery, Section C, number 406. SOURCE: San Antonio National Cemetery Locator.

MORRELL, Benjamin; Ord Sgt; U.S. Army. Born in Kentucky; black complexion; can read, cannot write, age 21, Jul 1870, at Ft McKavett, TX. SOURCE: Bierschwale, *Fort McKavett*, 97.

Born in Madison County, KY; Ht 5'11", black hair and dark eyes, yellow complexion; occupation soldier; served in A/25th Infantry during third enlistment, earned additional $4 per month for fifteen years' continuous service, discharged 3 Nov 1882; fourth reenlistment in A/25th Infantry at age 41, Washington, DC, 22 Dec 1882; arrived Ft Snelling, MN, 1 Jul 1883. SOURCE: Descriptive & Assignment Rolls of Recruits, 25 Inf.

‡First sergeant, A/25th Infantry, at Ft Concho, TX, 1878; best marksman in company and eighth in regiment. SOURCE: 25 Inf, Scrapbook, I:145.

Appointed ordnance sergeant 28 May 1885, from regimental sergeant major, 25th Cavalry. SOURCE: Dobak, "Staff Noncommissioned Officers."

‡Wrote two letters to Richmond *Planet* from Dutch Island, Jamestown, RI, contributing money to defense of three black women accused of murder in Lunenburg Co., VA; letter of 26 Aug 1895 contained $2.50; letter of 17 Jul 1896 contained $2.25, including $1 from his wife and $.25 from his young son Freddie. SOURCE: Richmond *Planet*, 21 Sep 1895 and 25 Jul 1896.

MORRIS, Emanuel; Private; D/9th Cav. With Captain Dodge at battle at Milk River, CO, 2–10 Oct 1879. SOURCE: Miller, *Hollow Victory*, 167, 206–7.

MORRIS, Henry; F/9th Cav. Born in Georgia; black complexion; cannot read or write, age 25, Jul 1870, at Ft McKavett, TX. SOURCE: Bierschwale, *Fort McKavett*, 98.

MORRIS, Peter; Private; B/10th Cav. Deserted while on march to Ft Stockton, TX, Feb 1878. SOURCE: Kinevan, *Frontier Cavalryman*, 100.

MORRIS, Reuben B.; Private; D/9th Cav. ‡Letter, Department of the Platte, 20 Jun 1894, concerns his application for transfer.

‡In hands of civil authorities, Crawford, NE, 11–23 Jan 1895. SOURCE: Regt Returns, 9 Cav, Jan 1895.

Private, G/9th Cavalry; died 10 Sep 1902; buried in plot NEW A1181 at San Francisco National Cemetery. SOURCE: San Francisco National Cemetery.

MORRIS, William; Corporal; 9th Cav. Stationed at Ft DuChesne, UT, won both 100-yard and 220-yard dashes at 1896 track competition of all units in Department of the Colorado. SOURCE: Dobak and Phillips, *The Black Regulars*, 149.

Private, B/9th Cavalry, at Ft DuChesne, 1896; won 100-yard and 220-yard dashes at Denver, CO, track meet held for Department of the Colorado troops, Oct 1896. SOURCE: Kenner, *Buffalo Soldiers and Officers of the Ninth Cavalry*, 19–20.

MORRIS, William S.; Sergeant; E/9th Cav. ‡Private, E/9th Cavalry, on special duty as assistant librarian, Ft Robinson, NE. SOURCE: Order 48, 18 Jul 1894, Post Orders, Ft Robinson.

Sergeant, received Indian Wars Campaign Badge number 1361 on 28 May 1909. SOURCE: Carroll, *Indian Wars Campaign Badge*, 39.

‡Veteran of Indian wars, Spanish-American War, and Philippine Insurrection; sergeant, E/9th Cavalry, at Ft D. A. Russell, WY, in 1910. SOURCE: *Illustrated Review: Ninth Cavalry*, with picture.

MORRISON, Charles; C/25th Inf. Born in Virginia; black complexion; cannot read or write, age 22, 5 Sep 1870, at Ft McKavett, TX. SOURCE: Bierschwale, *Fort McKavett*, 109.

MORSE, James; Private; E/9th Cav. Received Philippine Campaign Badge number 11704 for service as private in E/9th Cavalry; in 9th Cavalry at Ft Leavenworth, KS, Mar 1905. SOURCE: Philippine Campaign Badge list, 29 May 1905.

MORSE, William; Private; K/25th Inf. Born in Richmond, VA; Ht 5'3", black complexion; occupation painter; enlisted in A/39th Infantry for three years on 21 Oct 1867, age 23, at Richmond; detached service to regimental band since 19 Jan 1868; transferred to K/25th Infantry at Jackson Bks, LA, 20 Apr 1869. SOURCE: Descriptive Roll of A/39th Inf.

MORTON, Alexander; 10th Cav. Died 27 Feb 1870; buried at Ft Leavenworth National Cemetery, D 1340. SOURCE: Ft Leavenworth National Cemetery.

MORTON, George; Sergeant; A/9th Cav. ‡Private, attendant at Ft Robinson, NE, post exchange store at $15 per month. SOURCE: Reports of Inspections, Department of the Platte, II.

‡Promoted to corporal at Ft Robinson, 21 Jan 1895. SOURCE: *ANJ* 32 (2 Feb 1895): 374.

Appointed corporal 21 Jan 1895; in A/9th Cavalry at Ft Robinson, Jan 1897. SOURCE: Ninth Cavalry, Roster of NCOs, 1897.

‡Sergeant, on special duty as provost sergeant since 27 Jan 1901. SOURCE: SD List, A/9, Nueva Caceres, Philippines, 24 May 1902.

Sergeant, A/9th Cavalry, received Indian Wars Campaign Badge number 667 on 21 Oct 1908. SOURCE: Carroll, *Indian Wars Campaign Badge*, 19.

‡Veteran of Indian wars, Spanish-American War, and Philippine Insurrection; at Ft D. A. Russell, WY, in 1910. SOURCE: *Illustrated Review: Ninth Cavalry*, with picture.

MORTON, Henry; Private; G/25th Inf. Died at Ft Concho, TX, on 1 Jun 1878; buried at San Antonio National

Cemetery, Section D, number 639. SOURCE: San Antonio National Cemetery Locator.

MORTON, Willis; Private; U.S. Army. Seminole Negro Scout, served 1876–78. SOURCE: Schubert, Consolidated List of Seminole Negro Scouts.

Born in Mexico; may have been slave or adopted name of Army doctor Samuel Morton, who accompanied Cherokees on Trail of Tears to Arkansas reservation; Ht 5'4", black hair and eyes, black complexion; enlisted at Ft Clark, TX, 14 Nov 1876, age 30; discharged 17 May 1877 at Camp Painted Comanche, TX, where he reenlisted same day; discharged 29 May 1878 at Ft Clark. SOURCE: Swanson, 31.

MOSBY, James A.; Corporal; I/9th Cav. Born 22 Dec 1876; died 4 Feb 1937; buried in plot D-SOU1298 at San Francisco National Cemetery. SOURCE: San Francisco National Cemetery.

MOSBY, Thomas; Private; 25th Inf. ‡Born in Whiteville, NC; occupation laborer; Ht 5'4 1/2", brown complexion, black eyes and hair; enlisted, age 21, Charleston, SC, 18 Jul 1881; left recruit depot, David's Island, NY, 17 Aug 1881, and after trip on steamer *Thomas Kirby* to Central Depot, New York City, and train via Chicago to Running Water, Dakota Territory, 22 Aug 1881, marched forty-seven miles to Ft Randall, SD, arrived 24 Aug 1881. SOURCE: Descriptive & Assignment Rolls, 25 Inf.

MOSBY Thomas; Private; G/9th Cav. ‡Private Moseby, G/9th Cavalry, at Ft Niobrara, NE, 1886. *See* **BLEW**, Joseph, Sergeant, G/9th Cavalry

Died 12 May 1886; buried at Ft Leavenworth National Cemetery, plot G 3551. SOURCE: Ft Leavenworth National Cemetery.

MOSEBY; Private; G/9th Cav. *See* **Mosby**, Thomas, Private, G/9th Cavalry

MOSEBY, Houry; D/24th Inf. Born in Kentucky; mulatto complexion; can read and write, age 23, Jul 1870, at Ft McKavett, TX. SOURCE: *Fort McKavett*, 95.

MOSES, Paul S.; D/24th Inf. Died 28 May 1919; buried at Ft Bayard, NM, in plot U 11. SOURCE: "Fort Bayard National Cemetery, Records of Burials."

MOSLEY, Robert; Private; 25th Inf. Born in Kent County, VA; Ht 5'4", black hair and dark brown eyes, brown complexion; occupation waiter; resided in Philadelphia, PA, where he enlisted at age 22, 15 Sep 1886; arrived Ft Snelling, MN, 20 Jan 1887. SOURCE: Descriptive & Assignment Rolls of Recruits, 25 Inf.

MOSLEY, Zechoriah; Trumpeter; M/10th Cav. ‡Original member of 10th Cavalry; in troop when organized, Ft Riley, KS, 15 Oct 1867. SOURCE: McMiller, "Buffalo Soldiers," 79.

‡Sharpshooter at Ft McDowell, AZ. SOURCE: *ANJ* 24 (18 Jun 1887): 934.

Pvt. Zack Morris, 10th Cavalry, after discharge employed by Quartermaster Department at Ft Sill, OK. SOURCE: Dobak and Phillips, *The Black Regulars*, 334.

MOTIN, Harry; Private; B/9th Cav. Born in Tennessee; black complexion; cannot read or write, age 24, 5 Sep 1870, in 9th Cavalry at Ft McKavett, TX. SOURCE: Bierschwale, *Fort McKavett*, 107.

Died 6 Dec 1895; originally buried at Ft DuChesne, UT, reburied at Santa Fe National Cemetery, NM, plot A-4 1107. SOURCE: Santa Fe National Cemetery, Records of Burials.

MOTLEY, George; Private; H/24th Inf. ‡Died of general debility in the Philippines, 11 Dec 1899. SOURCE: *ANJ* 37 (30 Dec 1899): 412.

Died in Ilagan, Philippines, 11 Dec 1899; buried in plot NADD 402 at San Francisco National Cemetery. SOURCE: San Francisco National Cemetery.

MOTT, William; Private; 9th Cav. Received Philippine Campaign Badge number 11739 for service as private, E/9th Cavalry; in 9th Cavalry at Ft Leavenworth, KS, Mar 1905. SOURCE: Philippine Campaign Badge list, 29 May 1905.

MOULTON, Prince A.; Musician; K/24th Inf. ‡Musician P. A. Moulton, Musician, 24th Infantry, wrote letter from Ft Reno, Indian Territory, 14 Apr 1887; plays bass drum in Ft Reno band. SOURCE: Cleveland *Gazette*, 23 Apr 1887.

Pvt. Prince A. Moulton, 24th Infantry, attended Fort Reno wedding of Cpl. Henry Giles, with his wife, 1887; he reported affair to Cleveland *Gazette*. SOURCE: Dobak and Phillips, *The Black Regulars*, 141.

‡Musician P. A. Moulton, K/24th Infantry, at San Carlos, AZ, 1890. *See* OTT, **HARDEE**, James A., Private, K/24th Infantry

MOZIQUE, Edward; Private; E/10th Cav. Also known as Sancho; born 10 Jun 1849 in Columbia, SC, father French Creole from New Orleans, LA; slave owned by Widow Green who gave Mozique, his mother, and six siblings to her nephew Dr. Edward Fleming in Spartanburg, SC; returned to Columbia after Civil War; enlisted 23 Feb 1875, age 26, occupation carpenter; assigned to E/10th Cavalry, sent to Jefferson Bks, MO, for training; after 230-mile march from Austin, TX, arrived at Ft Concho, TX, Jul 1875; assigned to carpenter's shop, received $10.60 more per month above private's pay; active member of band; discharged 24 Feb 1880 at Ft Concho; lived and worked in San Angelo, TX, as carpenter and cook; worked as cook for M. L. Mertz at Kickapoo Springs, TX, corral in 1885; in San Angelo married Alice Johnson, born 4 Jul 1875, daughter of Belva Johnson, born in Kentucky, and Angeline Taylor, born in Louisiana; retired from cooking at J. D. Sugg ranch in 1931 to care for wife who died Oct 1988 of influenza and toxemia; wife buried at Fairmont Cemetery in San Angelo; 100th birthday interview published in *San Angelo Standard Times*, 10 Jun 1949; lived with son Edward, 1951; died 20 Apr 1951 in hospital, funeral in San Angelo. SOURCE: Pollard and Hagen, "Edward 'Sancho' Mozique," with photo of Mozique, figure 4.

Pvt. Sanco Mazique, born in slavery, 1849, in South Carolina; enlisted 1875; served briefly at Jefferson Barracks, when transferred to Ft Concho; after discharge settled in San Angelo area as cook. SOURCE: Wooster, *Soldiers, Suttlers, and Settlers*, 205.

MUNDY, LaFayette; Recruit; 10th Cav. Pvt. Lafayette Munday, 40th Infantry, Civil War veteran, ruptured his testicles while in 4th U.S. Colored Cavalry in 1865; enlisted in 40th Infantry 1866. SOURCE: Dobak and Phillips, *The Black Regulars*, 8.

‡Sergeant, L/10th Cavalry, Feb 1873; commander disapproves troop order reducing him to ranks and says trial by court martial would be appropriate. SOURCE: ES, 10 Cav, 1872–81.

‡Resignation of his warrant as sergeant approved. SOURCE: CO, 10 Cav, to CO, L/10, 17 Mar 1873, ES, 10 Cav, 1872–81.

‡Mentioned May 1875 as recruit at St. Louis, MO, depot awaiting assignment to regiment. SOURCE: LS, 10 Cav, 1873–83.

MUNROE, Daniel; Private; D/24th Inf. Died 6 Nov 1888; buried at Ft Bayard, NM, in plot G 20. SOURCE: "Fort Bayard National Cemetery, Records of Burials."

Buried 16 Nov 1888, section A, row I, plot 22, at Ft Bayard. SOURCE: Erickson, Burials at Fort Bayard National Cemetery, NM.

MURDOCK, Richard; H/25th Inf. Born in Pennsylvania; black complexion; can read and write, age 30, 5 Sep 1870, at Ft McKavett, TX. SOURCE: Bierschwale, *Fort McKavett*, 108.

MURE, John; Private; 10th Cav. Served in 9th and 10th Cavalry; widow Nannie L. Mure, age 79, had $12 per month pension in 1924. SOURCE: Dobak and Phillips, *The Black Regulars*, 277.

MURMAN, Charley; Private; K/10th Cav. See **NORMAN**, Charley, Private, K/10th Cavalry

MURPHY, Israel B.; 1st Sgt; B/9th Cav. Born in Virginia; black complexion; cannot read or write, age 25, Jul 1870, in F/9th Cavalry at Ft McKavett, TX. SOURCE: Bierschwale, *Fort McKavett*, 96.

Israel Murphy, 9th Cavalry, Civil War veteran; served in same troop with Allen Cragg; knew Violet Cragg at Junction City, KS, and later in Los Angeles, CA. SOURCE: Schubert, *Voices of the Buffalo Soldier*, 250.

‡Sergeant since 8 Apr 1877; first sergeant since 1 Jan 1886. SOURCE: Roster, 9 Cav.

In D/9th Cavalry, assaulted by Pvt. Fred Evans, D/9th Cavalry, Jan 1881; replaced by Richard Dickerson as first sergeant early in 1881. SOURCE: Kenner, *Buffalo Soldiers and Officers of the Ninth Cavalry*, 271.

‡Ranked number 6 in revolver competition, Departments of Dakota and the Platte, at Bellevue, NE, 4–9 Aug 1890. SOURCE: GO 112, AGO, 2 Oct 1890.

‡First sergeant, B/9th Cavalry, to be examined for ordnance sergeant, Ft DuChesne, UT. SOURCE: *ANJ* 29 (31 Oct 1891): 159.

‡Retires from Ft DuChesne, May 1895. SOURCE: *ANJ* 32 (18 May 1895): 627.

Retired first sergeant, received Indian Wars Campaign Badge number 1217 on 12 Jul 1909. SOURCE: Carroll, *Indian Wars Campaign Badge*, 35.

‡Retired soldier, resident of 1666 West 35th, Los Angeles, for thirty years; served as sergeant, F/9th Cavalry, at Ft Concho, TX, 1873. SOURCE: Affidavit, Murphy, age 81, 13 Apr 1926, VA File XC 2659797, Thomas H. Allsup.

MURPHY, William; Private; E/9th Cav. One of five men of E Troop killed by Victorio's Apaches while guarding troop's horse herd, Ojo Caliente, NM, 4 Sep 1879. SOURCE: Schubert, *Black Valor*, 53.

‡Private Murphy, E/9th Cavalry, killed in action at Camp Ojo Caliente, 4 Sep 1879. SOURCE: Billington, "Black Cavalrymen," 67; Billington, *New Mexico's Buffalo Soldiers*, 89. See **CHAPMAN**, Silas, Sergeant, E/9th Cavalry

MURRALL, George; Corporal; M/10th Cav. Died 2 Mar 1869 of accidental gunshot wound at Cache Creek, OK. SOURCE: Regimental Returns, 10th Cavalry, 1869.

MURRAY, Andrew; Corporal; F/9th Cav. ‡A. Murray promoted from lance corporal, Ft DuChesne, UT. SOURCE: *ANJ* 33 (26 Oct 1895): 119.

Appointed corporal 15 Oct 1895; in F/9th Cavalry at Ft DuChesne, Jan 1897. SOURCE: Ninth Cavalry, Roster of NCOs, 1897.

MURRAY, Charles; Private; F/10th Cav. ‡Pvt. Charles Murry, original member of F/10th Cavalry; in troop when organized, Ft Leavenworth, KS, 21 Jun 1867. SOURCE: McMiller, "Buffalo Soldiers," 73.

Wounded in action against Indians at Beaver Creek, KS, 21 Aug 1867. SOURCE: Schubert, *Voices of the Buffalo Soldier*, 20.

‡Private C. Murray, F/10th Cavalry, wounded in action in Kansas, 21 Aug 1867. SOURCE: Armes, *Ups and Downs*, 247.

Wounded in action, arrow wound in left leg, near Beaver Creek, 21 Aug 1867. SOURCE: LR, DeptMo, 1867.

MURRAY, Charles; Private; F/9th Cav. Native of Virginia, age 24, at Fort McKavett, TX, 1870; murdered Feb 1870 while guarding civilian prisoner. SOURCE: Kenner, *Buffalo Soldiers and Officers of the Ninth Cavalry*, 94.

‡Killed along with Pvt. Albert Marshall, 9th Cavalry, by friends of John Jackson while standing guard at Jackson home. SOURCE: Sullivan, "Fort McKavett," 144. *See* **MARSHALL**, Albert, Corporal, F/9th Cavalry

Buried at Ft McKavett; body removed to National Cemetery, San Antonio, TX, 23 Nov 1883. SOURCE: Bierschwale, *Fort McKavett*, 123.

Private, D/9th Cavalry, died at Ft Concho, TX, on 2 Feb 1870; buried at San Antonio National Cemetery, Section E, number 890. SOURCE: San Antonio National Cemetery Locator.

MURRAY, Clinton; Private; G/9th Cav. Received Philippine Campaign Badge number 11838 for service as private in B/24th Infantry, 15 Nov 1901–1 Jul 1902; private in G/9th Cavalry, Ft Leavenworth, KS, Mar 1905. SOURCE: Philippine Campaign Badge Recipients; Philippine Campaign Badge list, 29 May 1905.

MURRAY, Enos; Private; F/25th Inf. Died at Camp Eagle Pass, TX, on 7 Jul 1872; buried at San Antonio National Cemetery, Section F, number 1158. SOURCE: San Antonio National Cemetery Locator.

MURRAY, Henry; Corporal; F/9th Cav. Died 7 Oct 1902; buried in plot NADD 1228 at San Francisco National Cemetery. SOURCE: San Francisco National Cemetery.

MURRAY, James H.; Sergeant; 9th Cav. Received Philippine Campaign Badge number 11858 for service as sergeant, H/9th Cavalry; in 9th Cavalry at Ft Leavenworth, KS, Mar 1905. SOURCE: Philippine Campaign Badge list, 29 May 1905.

MURRAY, John A.; Corporal; I/10th Cav. ‡Private John Murray, I/10th Cavalry, died 24 Apr 1870. SOURCE: ES, 10 Cav, 1866–71.

Died 24 Apr 1870 of smallpox at Ft Leavenworth, KS. SOURCE: Regimental Returns, 10th Cavalry, 1870.

Cpl. John A. Murray died 24 Apr 1870; buried at Ft Leavenworth National Cemetery, plot D 1337. SOURCE: Ft Leavenworth National Cemetery.

MURRY, Charles; Private; F/10th Cav. *See* **MURRAY**, Charles, Private, F/10th Cavalry

MYERS, Alfred; Corporal; B/10th Cav. Confined to quarters, Ft Duncan, TX, Jan 1878 for being absent from bed check. SOURCE: Kinevan, *Frontier Cavalryman*, 145.

MYERS, Anson; Private; 24th Inf. When he applied for transfer to Hospital Corps in 1887 his company commander called him a good cook and nurse but noted that he could not read or write; reenlisted in 24th Infantry. SOURCE: Dobak and Phillips, *The Black Regulars*, 81.

MYERS, John E.; Private; Band/9th Cav. Died 9 Jul 1879; buried at Santa Fe National Cemetery, NM, plot K 306. SOURCE: Santa Fe National Cemetery, Records of Burials.

MYERS, William; Private; C/10th Cav. Died 26 Oct 1879 of smallpox at Ft Davis, TX. SOURCE: Regimental Returns, 10th Cavalry, 1879.

MYERS, William H.; Sergeant; K/24th Inf. Born in Georgetown, SC; occupation waiter; Ht 5'8", dark complexion, black hair and eyes; enlisted in 25th Infantry, age 20, Charleston, SC, 15 Jul 1881; left recruit depot, David's Island, NY, 17 Aug 1881, and after trip on steamer *Thomas Kirby* to Central Depot, New York City, and train via Chicago to Running Water, Dakota Territory, 22 Aug 1881, marched forty-seven miles to Ft Randall, SD, arrived 24 Aug 1881. SOURCE: Descriptive & Assignment Rolls, 25 Inf.

‡Private, K/24th Infantry, at San Carlos, AZ, 1890.

‡James A. Hardee, Private, K/24th Infantry, at San Carlos, reports in letter, 30 May 1890, collection of $23 for destitute daughter and son-in-law of John Brown; W. H. Myers contributed $.50. SOURCE: Cleveland *Gazette*, 7 Jun 1890.

‡Private, I/24th Infantry; enlisted Ft Grant, AZ, 3 Sep 1896; eighteen years' continuous service in 1899; absent on furlough since 20 Feb 1899. SOURCE: Muster Roll, I/24 Inf, May–Jun 1899.

‡Transferred to K/24th Infantry. SOURCE: Muster Roll, I/24 Inf, Mar–Apr 1899.

‡Retires as sergeant, K/24th Infantry, Feb 1901. SOURCE: *ANJ* 38 (23 Feb 1901): 623.

Retired sergeant, K/24th Infantry, died 12 Oct 1921; buried in plot A 178 at San Francisco National Cemetery. SOURCE: San Francisco National Cemetery.

N

NANCE, David; Private; E/9th Cav. Died at Ft Concho, TX, on 3 Jul 1873; buried at San Antonio National Cemetery, Section D, number 670. SOURCE: San Antonio National Cemetery Locator.

NANCE, George; Private; F/9th Cav. Native of Ohio with ten years' service in 1878. SOURCE: Kenner, *Buffalo Soldiers and Officers of the Ninth Cavalry*, 106–7.

NANCE, William; Private; D/9th Cav. Fatally wounded Pvt. John Hatchett in fight, Feb 1879; sentenced to six months and fined $10 per month for six months, with leniency due to good record. SOURCE: Kenner, *Buffalo Soldiers and Officers of the Ninth Cavalry*, 271.

NANCE, William H.; Private; L/9th Cav. Died 22 Nov 1886; buried at Ft Leavenworth National Cemetery, plot 2129. SOURCE: Ft Leavenworth National Cemetery.

NEAL, Burr; Private; E/10th Cav. ‡Private, contributed $1 of $3.25 sent by men of A/10th Cavalry to Richmond *Planet* for defense fund of three black women accused of murder, Lunenburg Co., VA, Sep 1895. SOURCE: Richmond *Planet*, 21 Sep 1895.

‡Served in 10th Cavalry in Cuba, 1898. SOURCE: Cashin, *Under Fire with the Tenth Cavalry*, 342.

‡Showed "great gallantry" before Santiago, Cuba, 24 Jun 1898; helped Captain Ayres and Pvts. W. R. Nelson, A. Wally, and A. C. White drag Major Bell, 1st Cavalry, who had been wounded in action, to safety. SOURCE: SecWar, *AR 1898*, 355.

‡Murdered at Ft Washakie, WY, 31 May 1905.

Died 31 May 1905; buried at Ft Leavenworth National Cemetery, plot G 3510. SOURCE: Ft Leavenworth National Cemetery.

NECO, Isidro; Private; U.S. Army. Seminole Negro Scout, served in 1880. SOURCE: Schubert, Consolidated List of Seminole Negro Scouts.

Born in Louisiana; black hair and eyes, complexion copper; enlisted at Ft Clark, TX, 27 May 1880, age 43; deserted from Ft Clark 31 Aug 1880. SOURCE: Swanson, 31.

Born in Texas; Ht 5'5", black hair, brown eyes, dark complexion; enlisted at Ft Clark, 7 Jan 1886, age 15; discharged 8 Jan 1887 and reenlisted for one year three more times; final discharge 25 Feb 1890 at Camp Neville Springs, TX. SOURCE: Swanson, 32.

NEELY, George; Private; L/9th Cav. Enlisted 1 Mar 1877 at Ft Lyon, CO; on duty as company cook at Ft Bliss, TX. SOURCE: Muster Roll, L/9th Cavalry, 31 Oct 1879–31 Dec 1879.

NEFF, William; Private; D/9th Cav. Died at Ft Stockton, TX, on 18 Dec 1868; buried at San Antonio National Cemetery, Section C, number 409. SOURCE: San Antonio National Cemetery Locator.

NEIL, Jeff J.; Private; E/9th Cav. Died 21 Apr 1882; buried at Ft Leavenworth National Cemetery, plot 3380. SOURCE: Ft Leavenworth National Cemetery.

NELSON, John; Private; M/10th Cav. Died 30 Mar 1881 of inflammation of bowels at Ft Concho, TX. SOURCE: Regimental Returns, 10th Cavalry, 1881.

Died at Ft Concho on 20 May 1881; buried at San Antonio National Cemetery, Section E, number 828. SOURCE: San Antonio National Cemetery Locator.

NELSON, Samuel A.; Corporal; F/25th Inf. ‡Convicted of murder by general court martial, Iba, Philippines; death sentence commuted to life in prison at Leavenworth, KS, by President McKinley. SOURCE: *ANJ* 38 (22 Dec 1900): 399.

‡Died of dysentery in the Philippines, 25 Dec 1900. SOURCE: *ANJ* 38 (12 Jan 1901): 479.

Died 25 Dec 1900; body received for burial 15 Apr 1902 at San Francisco National Cemetery, buried in plot NEW A994. SOURCE: San Francisco National Cemetery.

NELSON, William; Trumpeter; A/9th Cav. ‡With Pvt. Isaac Harrison, rescued his commander, Capt. Michael Cooney, near Howard's Well on the El Paso-San Antonio, TX, road, Apr 1872. SOURCE: Leckie, *The Buffalo Soldiers*, 101.

With Pvt. Isaac Harrison, rescued Capt. Michael Cooney, who was thrown by his horse during Indian ambush between Ft Stockton, TX, and Fort Clark, TX, Apr 1872. SOURCE: Kenner, *Buffalo Soldiers and Officers of the Ninth Cavalry*, 57.

NEW, Benjamin; Private; K/25th Inf. Died at Ft Stockton, TX, on 3 Sep 1874; buried at San Antonio National Cemetery, Section C, number 354. SOURCE: San Antonio National Cemetery Locator.

NEWBY, Joshua; Private; B/25th Inf. Member of three-man detachment led by Sgt. Joseph Luckadoe, along with Pvts. Benedict Thomas and Henry Williams, 25th Infantry, who defended Eagle Springs, TX, mail station against attack, New Year's Eve, 1873. SOURCE: Dobak and Phillips, *The Black Regulars*, 258–59, 332.

NEWHOUSE, Robert; Private; K/24th Inf. ‡Born in Chicago; resided in Chicago on enlistment; awarded Distinguished Service Medal in lieu of certificate of merit for rescue of comrade from drowning near Camp McGrath, Philippines, 12 Nov 1914. SOURCE: *Decorations, U.S. Army, Supplement I*, 36

Awarded certificate of merit for rescuing fellow soldier from drowning at risk of his own life, near Camp McGrath, Batangas, PI, 12 Nov 1914. SOURCE: Gleim, *The Certificate of Merit*, 63.

NEWLANDS, Goodson M.; Private; C/24th Inf. ‡Born in Asheville, NC; resided in Summerville, SC; occupation foreman; Ht 5'11", brown complexion; enlisted, age 22, Charleston, SC, 20 Feb 1888; assigned to F/24th Infantry, 27 Jul 1888; regimental clerk, 17 Jun 1889; fined three times by courts martial; sentenced to seven days' confinement when not on duty in adjutant's office, Ft Bayard, NM, 6 Jul 1891; discharged, end of term, single, character excellent, 19 Feb 1893, with $5 deposits, $72 retained, $8 clothing. SOURCE: Descriptive Book, 24 Inf NCS & Band.

‡At Ft Bayard, 1890. *See* OTT, **HENDRICKS**, Lewis, 24th Infantry

‡Enlisted San Francisco, 24 Feb 1893; joined Band/24th Infantry, 27 Feb 1893; on special duty as regimental clerk, 1 Mar 1893; also clerk in Subsistence Department, 3 Mar 1893; single; at Ft Douglas, UT, $45 clothing and $37 retained, 1 Nov 1896. SOURCE: Descriptive Book, 24 Inf NCS & Band.

In C/24th Infantry at Ft Bayard when wife Nora E. Newland, born in Montgomery, AL, 25 Dec 1875, daughter of Phyllis Spurling, died 6 Jul at age 19, buried 6 Jul 1895 at Ft Bayard. SOURCE: Patricia Erickson, 12 Mar 2003 e-mail message, printout in authors' files.

NEWMAN, George H.; Private; H/10th Cav. Born in Middleburg, VA, 1855; enlisted Baltimore, MD, 15 Jan 1877; Ht 5'6", brown complexion, black eyes and hair; occupation waiter; served in D/10th Cavalry; discharged 14 Jan 1882; enlisted Washington, DC, 1 Feb 1882; jerked by horse, causing sprain in small of back, Ft Davis, TX, 31 Jul 1882; bitten by horse, Ft Davis, 9 Feb 1883; served as corporal at Ft Davis, Jan 1885; tattoos of crossed sabers on right arm and "Wichita" on left arm. SOURCE: Sayre, *Warriors of Color*, 66, 391.

Reduced from corporal 1 Nov 1885; private in H/10th Cavalry stationed at Bonita Cañon Camp, AZ, 30 Apr 1886. SOURCE: Tagg, *The Camp at Bonita Cañon*, 68, 232.

Received as corporal H/10th Cavalry, Indian Wars Campaign Badge number 1916 on 26 Apr 1924. SOURCE: Carroll, *Indian Wars Campaign Badge*, 56.

NEWMAN, George W.; Private; 25th Inf. Warned by Sgt. Lewis Finney, 25th Infantry, that carrying a razor could result in a prison term, Ft Davis, TX, 1873. SOURCE: Dobak and Phillips, *The Black Regulars*, 200.

NEWMAN, George W.; Private; 25th Inf. Born in Washington, DC; Ht 5'6", black hair and eyes, black complexion; occupation laborer; enlisted at age 24, Washington, DC, 27 Nov 1886; assigned to C/25th Infantry; arrived Ft Snelling, MN, 1 Apr 1887. SOURCE: Descriptive & Assignment Rolls of Recruits, 25 Inf.

NEWMAN, Henry; Private; E/10th Cav. In Troop E/10th Cavalry stationed at Bonita Cañon Camp, AZ, but absent or on detached service 28 Feb 1886. SOURCE: Tagg, *The Camp at Bonita Cañon*, 232.

NEWMAN, Henry; Private; F/25th Inf. Born in Fauquier County, VA; Ht 5'6", black hair and eyes, brown complexion; occupation laborer; enlisted at age 23, Washington, DC, 13 Dec 1886; assigned to F/25th Infantry; arrived Ft Snelling, MN, 1 Apr 1887. SOURCE: Descriptive & Assignment Rolls of Recruits, 25 Inf.

NEWMAN, William T.; Private; F/10th Cav. Died 7 Mar 1890; originally buried at Ft Grant, AZ; reburied at Santa Fe National Cemetery, NM, plot A-1 756. SOURCE: Santa Fe National Cemetery, Records of Burials.

NEWSOM, James H.; Private; E/10th Cav. In Troop E/10th Cavalry stationed at Bonita Cañon Camp, AZ, 28 Feb 1886. SOURCE: Tagg, *The Camp at Bonita Cañon*, 232.

NEWSOME, Felix; Private; 25th Inf. Born in Williamson County, TN; Ht 5'8", black hair and eyes, black complexion; occupation laborer; enlisted at age 23, Nashville, TN, 8 Apr 1886; arrived Ft Snelling, MN, 31 Jul 1886. SOURCE: Descriptive & Assignment Rolls of Recruits, 25 Inf.

NEWSON, Sylvester; Corporal; A/39th Inf. Civil War veteran, served in F/10th Heavy Artillery; sentence of five years for involvement in New Iberia, LA, mutiny, Jul 1867, reduced to one year. SOURCE: Dobak and Phillips, *The Black Regulars*, 222.

NICHERSON, Floyd; Private; F/25th Inf. *See* **NICKERSON**, Floyd, Private, F/25th Infantry

NICHOLAS, William; Private; B/23rd Kan Inf. Born 30 Mar 1879; died 3 Nov 1947; buried at Ft Leavenworth National Cemetery, plot I 229-B. SOURCE: Ft Leavenworth National Cemetery.

NICHOLS, Joshua; Private; D/25th Inf. At Ft McIntosh, TX, 1899; arrested in Laredo, TX, Oct 1899, with Pvts. Robert Earl and Benjamin Hover, for beating local police officer. SOURCE: Leiker, *Racial Borders*, 123.

NICHOLS, Leroy; Private; M/25th Inf. Died 12 Mar 1915; buried in plot WS 406A at San Francisco National Cemetery. SOURCE: San Francisco National Cemetery.

NICHOLS, Richard; Private; G/10th Cav. ‡Pvt. Richard Nicols, Company G, original member of 10th Cavalry; in troop when organized, Ft Leavenworth, KS, 5 Jul 1867. SOURCE: McMiller, "Buffalo Soldiers," 74.

Died when gored by buffalo at Ft Hays, KS, 28 Sep 1867. SOURCE: Regimental Returns, 10th Cavalry, 1867.

Pvt. Richard Nichols, G/10th Cavalry, died 28 Sep 1867; buried at Ft Leavenworth National Cemetery, plot 3304. SOURCE: Ft Leavenworth National Cemetery.

NICHOLSON, Edward; Private; L/9th Cav. ‡Served as private, C/10th Cavalry in Cuba, 1898. SOURCE: Cashin, *Under Fire with the Tenth Cavalry*, 340.

‡Died of cerebral hemorrhage aboard U.S. Army Transport *Logan*, bound from San Francisco to Manila, Philippines, 24 May 1907. SOURCE: Hamilton, "History of the Ninth Cavalry," 116.

Died 24 May 1907; buried in plot NADD1182 at San Francisco National Cemetery. SOURCE: San Francisco National Cemetery.

NICHOLSON, Thomas; Private; D/9th Cav. Five-year veteran, at Ringgold Barracks, TX, 1899; shot in back by local residents, Rio Grande City, TX, while trying to get back to post after street disturbance, Oct 1899. SOURCE: Leiker, *Racial Borders*, 124.

NICKERSON, Floyd; Private; F/25th Inf. Died 9 Mar 1899; buried at Ft Bayard, NM, in plot I 14. SOURCE: "Fort Bayard National Cemetery, Records of Burials."

Floyd Nicherson, F/25th Infantry, buried at Ft Bayard. SOURCE: "Buffalo Soldiers Buried at Ft Bayard, NM."

Buried 9 Mar 1899, section A, row M, plot 16, at Ft Bayard. SOURCE: Erickson, Burials at Fort Bayard National Cemetery, NM.

NICOLS, Richard; G/10th Cav. *See* **NICHOLS**, Richard, Private, G/10th Cavalry

NOAL, Robert J.; Sergeant; M/10th Cav. ‡Born in Maryland; private and corporal, G/10th Cavalry, 2 Mar 1883–1 Mar 1888; private, 28 Mar 1888; corporal, 25 Jan 1889; sergeant, 14 Mar 1897. SOURCE: Baker, Roster.

‡Corporal, G/10th Cavalry, at Ft Apache, AZ, 1890, subscribed $.50 to testimonial to General Grierson. SOURCE: List of subscriptions, 23 Apr 1890, 10th Cavalry papers, MHI.

‡Served as sergeant, M/10th Cavalry, in Cuba, 1898. SOURCE: Cashin, *Under Fire with the Tenth Cavalry*, 352.

In 10th Cavalry; one of four sergeants accompanying Lt. Carter Johnson on expedition to southern Cuba to deliver arms to insurgents, June 1898. SOURCE: Schubert, *Black Valor*, 135.

Robert Noal received as sergeant Indian Wars Campaign Badge number 1526 on 27 Oct 1909. SOURCE: Carroll, *Indian Wars Campaign Badge*, 44.

NOBLE, John; Private; 25th Inf. Born in Peedee, SC; Ht 5'5", black hair and eyes, fair complexion; occupation laborer; enlisted at age 22, Charleston, SC, 24 May 1881; left recruit depot, David's Island, NY, 2 Jul 1881, arrived Ft Randall, SD, 7 Jul 1881. SOURCE: Descriptive & Assignment Rolls of Recruits, 25 Inf.

NOBLE, John; Trumpeter; I/10th Cav. Stationed at Bonita Cañon Camp, AZ, 30 Jun 1886. SOURCE: Tagg, *The Camp at Bonita Cañon*, 231.

‡Trumpeter John Nuble, I/10th Cavalry, served in 10th Cavalry in Cuba, 1898. SOURCE: Cashin, *Under Fire with the Tenth Cavalry*, 347.

NOLAND, Howard; Sergeant; G/9th Cav. Died 16 Jun 1888; buried at Ft Leavenworth National Cemetery, plot 3563. SOURCE: Ft Leavenworth National Cemetery.

NORMAN, Benjamin; Private; 24th Inf. In Sep 1871 received letter offering exact facsimiles of U.S. currency, passed letter to Sgt. Harrison Wilson, who sent it up the chain of command to the Secretary of War; Norman was complimented for his honesty. SOURCE: Dobak and Phillips, *The Black Regulars*, 144, 313.

NORMAN, Charley; Private; K/10th Cav. Died 19 Apr 1906; buried at Ft Bayard, NM, in plot 1 6. SOURCE: "Fort Bayard National Cemetery, Records of Burials."

Charley Murman, K/10th Cavalry, buried at Ft Bayard. SOURCE: "Buffalo Soldiers Buried at Ft Bayard, NM."

Buried 19 Apr 1906, section A, row M, plot 7, at Ft Bayard. SOURCE: Erickson, Burials at Fort Bayard National Cemetery, NM.

NORRIS, Jefferson; Private; M/24th Inf. Died 18 Jun 1909; buried at Ft Bayard, NM, in plot R 46. SOURCE: "Fort Bayard National Cemetery, Records of Burials."

Buried 18 Jun 1909, section B, row C, plot 46, at Ft Bayard. SOURCE: Erickson, Burials at Fort Bayard National Cemetery, NM.

NORTON, West; Private; 9th Cav. Received Philippine Campaign Badge number 11862 for service as private in K/9th Cavalry and H/9th United States Cavalry; in 9th Cavalry at Ft Leavenworth, KS, Mar 1905. SOURCE: Philippine Campaign Badge list, 29 May 1905.

NOYED, James; Private; E/24th Inf. Died 12 Aug 1899; body received for burial 24 Feb 1900 at San Francisco National Cemetery, buried in plot ES 653. SOURCE: San Francisco National Cemetery.

NUBLE, John; Trumpeter; I/10th Cav. *See* **NOBLE,** John, Trumpeter, I/10th Cavalry

NUGENT, William; Private; H/10th Cav. Born in Louisiana, 1854; Ht 5'4", brown complexion, black eyes and hair; occupation blacksmith; discharged from H/25th Infantry, 3 Jun 1880; enlisted San Antonio, TX, 2 May 1884. SOURCE: Sayre, *Warriors of Color*, 392.

NUNN, Bess; H/25th Inf. Born in Kentucky; black complexion; can read, cannot write, age 22, 5 Sep 1870, at Ft McKavett, TX. SOURCE: Bierschwale, *Fort McKavett*, 107.

NUNN, Moses J.; Private; F/8th Ill Inf. Born 12 Dec 1874; died 14 Jul 1954; buried at Ft Leavenworth National Cemetery, plot E 1466. SOURCE: Ft Leavenworth National Cemetery.

O

ODEN, Oscar N.; Trumpeter; I/10th Cav. ‡Served in 10th Cavalry in Cuba, 1898. SOURCE: Cashin, *Under Fire with the Tenth Cavalry*, 185, 347.

‡Commended for distinguished service as trumpeter, I/10th Cavalry, Battle of Santiago, Cuba, 1 Jul 1898. SOURCE: GO 15, AGO, 13 Feb 1900.

‡Awarded certificate of merit for distinguished service as trumpeter, I/10th Cavalry, in Cuba, 1898. SOURCE: *ANJ* 37 (24 Feb 1900): 611; Steward, *The Colored Regulars*, 280.

Awarded certificate of merit for distinguished service in battle, Santiago, 1 Jul 1898. SOURCE: Gleim, *The Certificate of Merit*, 45.

Born in Eaton County, MI; resided San Francisco, CA; received Distinguished Service Medal in lieu of certificate of merit. SOURCE: *American Decorations*, 841.

‡Convicted by general court martial, Holguin, Cuba, of carelessly wounding soldier with revolver; sentenced to five months' confinement and loss of pay. SOURCE: *ANJ* 38 (8 Jun 1901): 993.

ODOM, Henry; Musician; B/25th Inf. Henry Odum, Musician, B/25th Infantry, enlisted 16 Jun 1899, discharged 15 Jun 1902, character very good; reenlisted 21 Aug 1902, discharged 20 Aug 1905, character very good; reenlisted 23 Aug 1905, discharged without honor 22 Nov 1906, Brownsville, TX. SOURCE: Powell, "Military Record of the Enlisted Men Who Were Discharged Without Honor."

‡Dishonorable discharge, Brownsville. SOURCE: SO 266, AGO, 9 Nov 1906.

OGDEN, Harvey; Private; Band/10th Cav. ‡Died at Santa Fe, NM. SOURCE: *ANJ* 25 (7 Jun 1888): 994.

Not assigned to troop; died 24 Jun 1888; buried at Santa Fe National Cemetery, NM, plot I 415. SOURCE: Santa Fe National Cemetery, Records of Burials.

OGLESBY, Walter; Private; K/25th Inf. Born in Chattanooga, TN; Ht 5'11", black hair and eyes, dark complexion; occupation broom maker; enlisted at age 22, Cincinnati, OH, 27 Apr 1886; from Columbus Bks, OH, arrived Ft Snelling, MN, 17 Sep 1886. SOURCE: Descriptive & Assignment Rolls of Recruits, 25 Inf.

OILDS, James; Private; K/25th Inf. Born in Lucala County, TN; Ht 5'7", black hair and eyes, yellow complexion; occupation laborer; enlisted at age 26, Nashville, TN, 19 Apr 1886; from Columbus Bks, OH, arrived Ft Snelling, MN, 17 Sep 1886. SOURCE: Descriptive & Assignment Rolls of Recruits, 25 Inf.

OLEVIA, Felix; 1st Sgt; A/9th Cav. In 1864 joined 81st U.S. Colored Infantry; Civil War veteran; at Ft Quitman, TX, frequently crossed border without permission to visit Mexican woman, for which he was reduced to ranks and fined $10 per month for one year. SOURCE: Leiker, *Racial Borders*, 82, 208.

OLFORD, Isaac; M/9th Cav. Born in Kentucky; mulatto complexion; cannot read or write, age 22, Jul 1870, at Ft McKavett, TX. SOURCE: Bierschwale, *Fort McKavett*, 99.

OLIVER Floyd; Private; F/9th Cav. Died 7 Oct 1905; buried at Ft Leavenworth National Cemetery, plot 3263. SOURCE: Ft Leavenworth National Cemetery.

OLIVER, Joe; Private; 10th Cav. Captured after battle at Carrizal, Mexico; returned to Ft Bliss, TX, 29 Jun 1916. SOURCE: Leiker, *Racial Borders*, 167–68.

OLIVER, William H.; Principal Musician; 25th Inf. ‡At Ft Walla Walla, WA, 1904. *See* OTT, **BROWN**, William W., 24th and 25th Infantry

‡Chief trumpeter, Band/9th Cavalry; veteran of Philippine Insurrection; at Ft D. A. Russell, WY, in 1910; resident of Richmond, TX. SOURCE: *Illustrated Review: Ninth Cavalry*, with picture.

Principal musician, 25th Infantry; died 23 Sep 1915; buried in plot WSIDE635A at San Francisco National Cemetery. SOURCE: San Francisco National Cemetery.

ONLEY, John; Sergeant; D/9th Cav. With Captain Dodge at battle at Milk River, CO, 2–10 Oct 1879. SOURCE: Miller, *Hollow Victory*, 167, 206–7.

Sgt. John Olney told story of coming to aid of troops ambushed on Milk River, CO, by Utes, Sep 1879, at reception given by citizens of Denver, CO, Oct 1879. SOURCE: Kenner, *Buffalo Soldiers and Officers of the Ninth Cavalry*, 70–71.

ONLEY, Joseph; Private; L/9th Cav. Enlisted 16 Aug 1875 at Ft Ringgold, TX; at Ft Bliss, TX. SOURCE: Muster Roll, L/9th Cavalry, 31 Oct 1879–31 Dec 1879.

OPPERMAN, Henry; Private; E/9th Cav. Died 14 Aug 1878; buried at Santa Fe National Cemetery, NM, plot D 386. SOURCE: Santa Fe National Cemetery, Records of Burials.

ORTIZ, Enrique; Private; U.S. Army. Seminole Negro Scout, served 1886–90. SOURCE: Schubert, Consolidated List of Seminole Negro Scouts.

Born in Texas; Ht 5'5", black hair, brown eyes, dark complexion; enlisted at Ft Clark, 7 Jan 1886, age 25; discharged and reenlisted for one year at Ft Clark three times; final discharge at Camp Neville Springs, TX, 25 Feb 1890. SOURCE: Swanson, 32.

OSBORNE, James; Private; I/24th Inf. Died at Ft Richardson, TX, on 18 Sep 1869; buried at San Antonio National Cemetery, Section D, number 631. SOURCE: San Antonio National Cemetery Locator.

OTEY, James; Private; 25th Inf. Reenlisted 1890, Ft Missoula, MT; only experienced carpenter and wheelwright on post. SOURCE: Dobak and Phillips, *The Black Regulars*, 61.

OUTLEND, Jerry R.; Corporal; E/10th Cav. In Troop E/10th Cavalry stationed at Bonita Cañon Camp, AZ, 28 Feb 1886. SOURCE: Tagg, *The Camp at Bonita Cañon*, 231.

OVERR, Oscar; 2nd Lt; 23rd Kans Inf. ‡Resident of Allensworth, CA; first black justice of the peace in California; owns twenty-four acres and has claim on 640 acres of nearby government land; has contract for irrigation water, four wells, and pumping station; irrigates 1,300 acres; raises chickens, turkeys, ducks, cattle; failed in "untiring efforts" to locate polytechnic school in Allensworth. SOURCE: Beasley, *Negro Trailblazers*, 157, 285.

‡First black justice of the peace in California, 1914, when Allensworth became judicial district. SOURCE: *New York Times*, 22 Oct 1972.

See **ALLENSWORTH**, Allen, Chaplain, 24th Infantry

OVERSTREET, Monroe; Private; B/9th Cav. Native of Kentucky, age 36, two years into second enlistment, serving as B Troop teamster when killed in action at Gavilan Pass, NM, Aug 1881. SOURCE: Kenner, *Buffalo Soldiers and Officers of the Ninth Cavalry*, 229.

Private, I/9th Cavalry, killed in action, Gavilan Canyon, NM, 19 Aug 1879. SOURCE: Schubert, *Black Valor*, 84.

‡Killed in action against Apaches, Gabaldon Canyon, NM, 19 Aug 1881. SOURCE: Billington, *New Mexico's Buffalo Soldiers*, 105. *See* **GOLDEN**, Thomas, Saddler, B/9th Cavalry

OWENS, Charles H.; Post QM Sgt; U.S. Army. ‡Born in Philadelphia; dark complexion, Ht 5'4"; enlisted, Philadelphia, age 22, 13 Nov 1886; formerly served in E/10th Cavalry; in D/24th Infantry, 11 Jan 1887; corporal, 1 Oct 1888; sergeant, 1 Jan 1890; regimental quartermaster sergeant, 25 Feb 1890; discharged, end of term, character excellent, single, Ft Bayard, NM, 12 Nov 1891, with $60 retained and $10.65 clothing, owing government $4.70 for subsistence stores; enlisted Ft Bayard, 13 Nov 1891; became post quartermaster sergeant, U.S. Army, 1 Feb 1895, and transferred to Ft Custer, MT, with $50.67 retained, owing government $7.36 for subsistence stores. SOURCE: Descriptive Book, 24 Inf NCS & Band.

Private in Troop E/10th Cavalry stationed at Bonita Cañon Camp, AZ, 28 Feb 1886. SOURCE: Tagg, *The Camp at Bonita Cañon*, 232.

Appointed post quartermaster sergeant 1 Feb 1895, from quartermaster sergeant, 24th Infantry. SOURCE: Dobak, "Staff Noncommissioned Officers."

OWENS, James; Private; F/9th Cav. Died 6 Jan 1907; buried at Ft Leavenworth National Cemetery, plot 3467. SOURCE: Ft Leavenworth National Cemetery.

OWENS, Richard; Private; C/25th Inf. ‡Died of peritonitis in the Philippines, 21 Oct 1901. SOURCE: *ANJ* 39 (18 Jan 1902): 502.

Died 21 Oct 1901; buried in plot NEW A883 at San Francisco National Cemetery. SOURCE: San Francisco National Cemetery.

OWENS, Wesley; Private; 10th Cav. After five years' service in 10th Cavalry worked as bodyguard for Charles Howard, Texas district judge involved in El Paso salt war of 1877. SOURCE: Leiker, *Racial Borders*, 65.

OWENS, William; Sergeant; H/9th Cav. ‡Committed suicide at Guinobatan, Luzon, Philippines, 9 Aug 1901. SOURCE: *ANJ* 39 (12 Oct 1901): 140.

Died 9 Aug 1901; buried in plot NAWS 273 at San Francisco National Cemetery. SOURCE: San Francisco National Cemetery.

OWINGS, Alfred; Private; H/10th Cav. Died 18 Feb 1871 of accidental carbine shot at Ft Sill, OK. SOURCE: Regimental Returns, 10th Cavalry, 1871.

Died 18 Feb 1871; buried at Camp Douglas, UT. SOURCE: Record Book of Interments, Post Cemetery, 252.

P

PAGE, Bassett; Private; E/24th Inf. Born in North Carolina; mulatto complexion; can read and write, age 26, 5 Sep 1870, in C/25th Infantry at Ft McKavett, TX. SOURCE: Bierschwale, *Fort McKavett,* 109.

Civil War veteran; among first soldiers to retire from regular Army in early 1890s after law authorizing retirement with Civil War time counted as double. SOURCE: Dobak and Phillips, *The Black Regulars,* 334.

‡Retires from Ft Bayard, NM, Feb 1892. SOURCE: *ANJ* 29 (6 Feb 1892): 411.

PAGE Edwin; Private; K/38th Inf. Died 20 Aug 1867; buried at Ft Leavenworth National Cemetery, plot E 2536. SOURCE: Ft Leavenworth National Cemetery.

PAINE, Adam; Private; 24th Inf. *See* **PAYNE,** Adam, Private, 24th Infantry

PARKER, Charles; Blacksmith; G/10th Cav. At base of San Juan Hill, Cuba, along San Juan River, 1 Jul 1898, tried to dissuade Sergeant Major Baker from attempting rescue of wounded Private Marshall. SOURCE: Schubert, *Black Valor,* 151–52.

PARKER, Charles E.; 1st Sgt; 10th Cav. ‡Private, L/10th Cavalry, at Camp Santa Rosa, TX, May 1879; excused from duty by Surgeon M. F. Price because of fever and debility but kept at work by Capt. George A. Armes, causing suffering and impeding recovery. SOURCE: GCMO 36, AGO, 27 May 1880.

‡Farrier, at Ft Apache, AZ, 1890, subscribed $.50 to testimonial to General Grierson. SOURCE: List of subscriptions, 23 Apr 1890, 10th Cavalry papers, MHI.

‡Served as corporal in G/10th Cavalry in Cuba, 1898. SOURCE: Cashin, *Under Fire with the Tenth Cavalry,* 345.

First sergeant, died on 14 Feb 1909; buried at San Antonio National Cemetery, Section F, number 965. SOURCE: San Antonio National Cemetery Locator.

PARKER, George; Private; I/10th Cav. In Troop I/10th Cavalry stationed at Bonita Cañon Camp, AZ, 30 Jun 1886. SOURCE: Tagg, *The Camp at Bonita Cañon,* 232.

PARKER, Henry; Sergeant; D/10th Cav. Escaped his slave master in Apton Valley, KY; Civil War veteran; joined USCT, age 18; served three years as private; at White's Ranch, TX; in Jan 1865 at Scottsboro, AL, and Larkinsville, AL; in Mar 1865 at Boyd's Station, AL, and Stevenson's Gap, AL; enlisted for five years by 18 May 1867 at Memphis, TN, age 21, Ht 5'9", black hair and eyes, mulatto complexion, occupation groom; assigned to D/10th Cavalry; discharged 18 May 1872 at Ft. Sill, OK, as private; reenlisted for five years at Ft Sill 6 June 1872, Ht 5'11", assigned to D/10th Cavalry; promoted to sergeant, served in color guard; discharged Ft Concho, TX, 6 Jun 1877, character excellent. SOURCE: "Buffalo Soldiers & Indian Wars," Part 1.

PARKER Henry; Private; C/38th Inf. Died 3 Aug 1867; originally buried at Ft Hays, KS; reburied at Ft Leavenworth National Cemetery, plot 3286. SOURCE: Ft Leavenworth National Cemetery.

PARKER, James; Private; E/10th Cav. Died 29 Dec 1870; buried at Camp Douglas, UT. SOURCE: Record Book of Interments, Post Cemetery, 252.

PARKER, James E.; 1st Sgt; 10th Cav. ‡Private, M/10th Cavalry, original member of M/10th Cavalry; in troop when organized, Ft Riley, KS, 15 Oct 1867. SOURCE: McMiller, "Buffalo Soldiers," 79.

‡Mentioned as sergeant, D/10th Cavalry, Dec 1875. SOURCE: ES, 10 Cav, 1873–83.

‡Mentioned as private, M/10th Cavalry, transferred from A/10th Cavalry, May 1877. SOURCE: ES, 10 Cav, 1873–83.

First sergeant, beaten with club in 1879 by Lt. Charles Nordstrom, causing Nordstrom to be suspended from rank for six months and fined $75 per month for six months. SOURCE: Dobak and Phillips, *The Black Regulars,* 189.

PARKER, Jesse E.; Artificer; D/24th Inf. Awarded certificate of merit for brave and faithful conduct, assisting wounded officer to safety while under heavy fire, Santiago, Cuba, 1 Jul 1898. SOURCE: Gleim, *The Certificate of Merit,* 46.

Born and resided in Charleston, WV; received Distinguished Service Medal in lieu of certificate of merit. SOURCE: *American Decorations*, 842.

‡Pvt. 1st Class Jesse C. Parker, Hospital Corps, 1906, commended for assisting wounded officer to safety, Santiago, 1 Jul 1898, while artificer, D/24th Infantry. SOURCE: Cleveland *Gazette*, 24 Nov 1906.

PARKER, John; Private; E/10th Cav. ‡Original member of 10th Cavalry; in troop when organized, Ft Leavenworth, KS, 15 Jun 1867. SOURCE: McMiller, "Buffalo Soldiers," 72.

Died 10 Dec 1870 of accidental wound at Ft Sill, OK. SOURCE: Regimental Returns, 10th Cavalry, 1870.

PARKER, Joseph; Sgt Maj; 10th Cav. ‡Private, K/10th Cavalry, detailed for duty at detachment headquarters, Ft Lyon, CO. SOURCE: SO 1, Det 10 Cav, 22 Feb 1869, Orders, Det 10 Cav, 1868–69.

‡Reported absent without leave, Jan 1873, but on recruiting duty. SOURCE: ES, 10 Cav, 1873–83.

‡Sergeant, K/10th Cavalry; commander, 10th Cavalry, asks orders transferring Parker to Ft Gibson, Indian Territory, as saddler sergeant, 10th Cavalry. SOURCE: CO, 10 Cav, to AAG, Department of Texas, 21 Feb 1873, LS, 10 Cav, 1873–83.

Sergeant major, 10th Cavalry, at Ft Concho, TX, 1875; helped Sgt. John Marshall write his report of pursuit of Indians, May 1875. SOURCE: Schubert, *Voices of the Buffalo Soldier*, 73.

‡Sergeant major, 10th Cavalry, deposited $25 with paymaster, Ft Concho, Sep 1881. SOURCE: TS, 10 Cav.

Died 20 Jan 1882 of heart disease at Ft Concho. SOURCE: Regimental Returns, 10th Cavalry, 1882.

Died at Ft Concho on 21 Jan 1882; buried at San Antonio National Cemetery, Section E, number 809. SOURCE: San Antonio National Cemetery Locator.

PARKER, William; C/25th Inf. Born in Virginia; mulatto complexion; married Feb 1870; can read, cannot write, age 21, 5 Sep 1870, at Ft McKavett, TX. SOURCE: Bierschwale, *Fort McKavett,* 108.

PARKER, William; Private; F/9th Cav. Died at Ft Clark, TX, on 19 Sep 1905; buried at Fort Sam Houston National Cemetery, Section PE, number 41. SOURCE: Buffalo Soldiers Interred in Fort Sam Houston National Cemetery.

PARNELL, Edward; Trumpeter; E/25th Inf. ‡Trumpeter, 10th Cavalry; at Ft Bayard, NM, 1890; competed in Department of Arizona marksmanship contest. SOURCE: Billington, *New Mexico's Buffalo Soldiers*, 154.

‡Trumpeter, D/10th Cavalry, at Ft Apache, AZ, 1890, subscribed $.50 to testimonial to General Grierson.

SOURCE: List of subscriptions, 23 Apr 1890, 10th Cavalry papers, MHI.

‡Trumpeter, E/25th Infantry, died of enteritis in the Philippines. SOURCE: *ANJ* 37 (21 Oct 1899): 178.

‡Died of heart failure in attack on La Loma Church, Philippines; veteran of twenty-nine years. SOURCE: Cleveland *Gazette*, 18 Nov 1899.

Died 9 Oct 1899; buried 24 Apr 1900 in plot E 671 at San Francisco National Cemetery. SOURCE: San Francisco National Cemetery.

PATON, Jerome; Sergeant; E/9th Cav. ‡In hands of civil authorities, Omaha, NE, 29 Jan–23 May 1893. SOURCE: Regt Returns, 9 Cav.

‡Appointed sergeant, 7 Jul 1893. SOURCE: Roster, 9 Cav.

‡At Ft Robinson, NE; date of rank 7 Jul 1893. SOURCE: *ANJ* 32 (9 Feb 1895): 390.

‡Convicted by garrison court martial, Ft Robinson, of failure to repair at correct time for stable duty; fined $5. SOURCE: Order 50, 21 Jul 1894, Post Orders, Ft Robinson.

Appointed sergeant 7 Jul 1893; in E/9th Cavalry at Ft Robinson, Jan 1897. SOURCE: Ninth Cavalry, Roster of NCOs, 1897.

PATRICK, George; Private; I/9th Cav. Died at Ft Davis, TX, on 5 Jul 1874; buried at San Antonio National Cemetery, Section I, number 1539. SOURCE: San Antonio National Cemetery Locator.

PATTERSON, Andrew J.; Sergeant; C/10th Cav. Retired sergeant, received Indian Wars Campaign Badge number 1099 on 30 Dec 1908. SOURCE: Carroll, *Indian Wars Campaign Badge*, 31.

‡Former sergeant, C/10th Cavalry and surviving Indian war veteran. SOURCE: *Winners of the West* 3 (Jan 1926): 7.

PATTERSON, William; Private; C/10th Cav. ‡Original member of 10th Cavalry; in troop when organized, Ft Leavenworth, KS, 14 May 1867. SOURCE: McMiller, "Buffalo Soldiers," 70.

Died 28 Jul 1876 of cholera at Ft Leavenworth. SOURCE: Regimental Returns, 10th Cavalry, 1867.

PATTERSON, William; QM Sgt; G/9th Cav. Received Cuban Campaign Badge for service as sergeant in G/9th Cavalry, 22 Jun 1898–13 Aug 1898. SOURCE: Cuban Campaign Badge Recipients.

Received Philippine Campaign Badge number 11804 for service as sergeant in G/9th Cavalry, 16 Sep 1900–16 Sep 1902; quartermaster sergeant in G/9th Cavalry, Ft Leavenworth, KS, Mar 1905. SOURCE: Philippine Campaign Badge Recipients; Philippine Campaign Badge list, 29 May 1905.

PAULEY, Charles J.; Private; D/9th Cav. ‡Shot dead in barracks by Cpl. Isher Johnson, I/9th Cavalry, in dispute over monte game, Ft Washakie, WY, 14 Aug 1897; buried on post with full military honors. SOURCE: Fremont *Clipper*, 20 Aug 1897.

‡Deposit of $48.90 made to account of deceased Private Pauley. SOURCE: CO, D/9, to Chief Paymaster, DP, 16 Sep 1897, Misc Records, DP.

Died 15 Aug 1897; originally buried at Ft Washakie; reburied at Ft Leavenworth National Cemetery, plot 3514. SOURCE: Ft Leavenworth National Cemetery.

PAYNE, Aaron; Private; U.S. Army. Born in Mexico; probably descendant of slaves belonging to Seminole Head Chief King Payne; Ht 5'5", black hair and eyes, black complexion; enlisted at Ft Duncan, TX, 7 Oct 1871, age 17; discharged 7 Apr 1872 at Ft Duncan where he reenlisted for six months three times; discharged at Ft Duncan 10 Oct 1873; enlisted at Ft Clark, TX, 10 Oct 1873; discharged 10 Apr 1874 at Ft Clark; enlisted 17 Jun 1874 at Ft Duncan; discharged 17 Dec 1874 at Ft Clark; enlisted 2 Feb 1876 at Ft Clark; discharged 7 Aug 1876 at Camp Pecos, TX; enlisted 29 Jan 1877 at Ft Clark where he was discharged 29 Jan 1878; enlisted for one year 8 Feb 1878 at Ft Clark; died of accidental pistol shot near Ft Clark 27 Jan 1879; buried at Seminole Cemetery. SOURCE: Swanson, 32.

Seminole Negro Scout, served 1871–79. SOURCE: Schubert, Consolidated List of Seminole Negro Scouts.

Buried at Seminole Indian Scout Cemetery, Kinney County, TX. SOURCE: Indian Scout Cemetery, Kinney County, Texas.

PAYNE, Adam; Private; 24th Inf. Seminole Negro Scout; born in Florida, participated in forced migration known as Trail of Tears as child; 5'7" and over 30 years old when he enlisted 12 Nov 1873, Ft Duncan, TX; served two six-month enlistments and discharged Feb 1875; received Medal of Honor for valor during Red River expedition Sep 1874; wanted for stabbing black soldier at dance near Ft Clark, TX, when shot and killed 1 Jan 1877 by Deputy Sheriff Clarion Windus, himself a Medal of Honor hero. SOURCE: Schubert, *Black Valor*, 32–34, 38, 165.

Seminole Negro Scout, also known as Adam Paine, served 1873–75. SOURCE: Schubert, Consolidated List of Seminole Negro Scouts.

Born in Florida; Ht 5'7", black hair and eyes, black complexion; enlisted at Ft Duncan, 2 Nov 1873, age 30; discharged 12 May 1874 at Camp Palafox, TX; fought in Red River ward, known by scout Henry Strong as "Bad Man" who wore headdress of buffalo horns; enlisted 1 Jun 1874 at Ft Clark; cited by Colonel Mackenzie as "most daring of any scout I have ever known" for action 20 Sept 1874 when attacked by superior force of Indians, for which he received Medal of Honor as Adam Paine; discharged 19 Feb 1875 at Ft Clark; Deputy Sheriff Clarion Windus had

warrant issued for his arrest due to stabbing of soldier in Brownsville, TX; shot point blank by Windus at New Year's Eve fandango and died 1 Jan 1877; buried at Seminole Cemetery. SOURCE: Swanson, 32. *See* **KIBBETTS**, Robert, Corporal, U.S. Army

Buried at Seminole Indian Scout Cemetery, Kinney County, TX. SOURCE: Indian Scout Cemetery, Kinney County, Texas.

PAYNE, Adam; Private; U.S. Army. Seminole Negro Scout, served 1893–94. SOURCE: Schubert, Consolidated List of Seminole Negro Scouts.

Born in Mexico; Ht 5'2", black hair and eyes, black complexion; enlisted at Ft Clark, TX, 17 Jan 1893, age 25; discharged 16 Jul 1893 at Ft Ringgold, TX; enlisted at Ft Clark 27 Feb 1894; discharged 26 Aug 1894 at Ft Ringgold. SOURCE: Swanson, 33.

PAYNE, Billy; Private; U.S. Army. Bully Payne born in Mexico; Ht 5'8", black hair and eyes, mulatto complexion; enlisted at Ft Clark, TX, 14 Jan 1893, age 25; discharged 13 Jul 1893, reenlisted next day at Ft Ringgold, TX; discharged and reenlisted for six months three times at Ft Ringgold, 14 Jul 1893–14 Jul 1894; final discharge 13 Jan 1895 at Camp San Pedro, TX. SOURCE: Swanson, 33.

Seminole Negro Scout, served 1893–95. SOURCE: Schubert, Consolidated List of Seminole Negro Scouts.

Married. SOURCE: NARA, M 929, Roll 2.

PAYNE, Caesar; Private; U.S. Army. Seminole Negro Scout, served 1871–74, 1877–79. SOURCE: Schubert, Consolidated List of Seminole Negro Scouts.

Born in Florida; probably descendant of slaves of Seminole Head Chief King Payne; Ht 5'10", black hair and eyes, black complexion; enlisted at Ft Duncan, TX, 4 Oct 1871, age 46; discharged 7 Apr 1872, reenlisted next day at Ft Duncan; discharged 8 Oct 1872, reenlisted next day at Ft Duncan; discharged 9 Apr 1873 at Ft Duncan; enlisted 10 Apr 1873 at Ft Clark, TX; discharged, reenlisted 10 Oct 1873 at Ft Clark; discharged, reenlisted 10 Apr 1874 at Ft Clark; discharged 1 Oct 1874 at Ft Clark; Daniel Johnson restrained from shooting Caesar Payne 15 Sep 1876; arrested by Sheriff Crowell 15 Oct 1876 as accessory in theft with Scott Warrior of five horses from McKee's pasture; enlisted 23 Apr 1877 at Ft Clark; discharged 13 Apr 1878, reenlisted 23 Apr 1878 at Camp Painted Comanche, TX; discharged 23 Apr 1879 at Ft Clark.

PAYNE, Charles; Private; U.S. Army. Seminole Negro Scout, served 1894–1901. SOURCE: Schubert, Consolidated List of Seminole Negro Scouts.

Born in Texas; Ht 5'3", black hair and eyes, black complexion; enlisted 30 Apr 1894 at Ft Clark, TX, age 21; discharged 29 Oct 1894 at Ft Ringgold, TX; enlisted 26 Feb

1898 at Ft Clark; discharged 25 Feb 1901 at Ft Ringgold. SOURCE: Swanson, 33.

PAYNE, Daniel; Private; U.S. Army. Born in Mexico; Ht 5'9", black hair and eyes, dark complexion; enlisted at Ft Duncan, TX, 26 Nov 1873, age 18; discharged 26 May 1874 at Camp Palafox, TX; enlisted 22 June 1874 at Camp Eagle Pass, TX; discharged 22 Dec 1874 at Ft Duncan where he reenlisted 1 Feb 1875; discharged 1 Aug 1875 at Ft Concho, TX; reenlisted 1 Aug 1875 at Camp Supply, TX; discharged 1 Apr 1875 at Ft Duncan. SOURCE: Swanson, 34.

Seminole Negro Scout, served 1873–76. SOURCE: Schubert, Consolidated List of Seminole Negro Scouts.

Age 35, resided at Ft Duncan in 1875 with mother Leah age 50 and Scout Robert Payne age 23. SOURCE: NARA Record Group 393, Special File.

PAYNE, David; Private; U.S. Army. Seminole Negro Scout; born in Mexico; Ht 5'7", black hair and eyes, black complexion; enlisted at Ft Duncan, TX, 1 Feb 1876, age 22; discharged 8 Aug 1876 at Camp Pecos, TX; enlisted for one year 31 Jan 1877, discharged 31 Jul 1878 at Ft Clark, TX; reenlisted 11 Feb 1878 at Ft Clark where discharged 24 Apr 1879; buried at Seminole Cemetery, 1879. SOURCE: Swanson, 34.

Died in 1879; buried at Seminole Indian Scout Cemetery, Kinney County, TX. SOURCE: Indian Scout Cemetery, Kinney County, Texas.

PAYNE, Harry; Private; E/10th Cav. Died 24 Jul 1908; buried in plot NW 1340 at San Francisco National Cemetery. SOURCE: San Francisco National Cemetery.

PAYNE, Isaac; Private; 24th Inf. Born in Mexico; Ht 5'8", black hair and eyes, black complexion; enlisted Ft Duncan, TX, 7 Oct 1871, age 17; discharged 7 Apr 1872, reenlisted next day at Ft Duncan; discharged 8 Oct 1872, reenlisted 25 Oct 1872 at Ft Duncan; discharged 25 Apr 1873 at Ft Duncan; reenlisted 25 Apr 1873 at Ft Clark, TX; discharged, reenlisted 22 Oct 1873 at Ft Clark; discharged 22 Apr 1874 at Ft Clark where he reenlisted 1 Jun 1874; discharged 11 Dec 1874 at Ft Clark where he reenlisted for six months 24 Jan 1875; deserted 28 Jul 1875 at Ft McKavett, TX, when he left field command three days after expiration of enlistment; returned, reported to duty at Ft Clark where he was formally discharged 28 Feb 1876; enlisted for one year and discharged at Ft Clark five times, 29 Jan 1877–22 Jun 1883; enlisted 23 Jun 1883 at Ft Clark; discharged as corporal 22 Jun 1884, reenlisted 24 Jun 1884 at Camp Myers, TX; discharged as private 26 Jun 1885, reenlisted 24 Jun 1885 at Camp Neville Springs, TX; discharged 26 Jun 1886 at Ft Clark; enlisted 27 Jun 1886 at Camp Neville Springs; discharged 23 Jun 1887 at Ft Clark; enlisted 1 Jul 1888 at Ft Clark; discharged, reenlisted for six months at Ft Ringgold, TX, three times, 16 Jul 1893–17 Jul 1894; discharged 15

Jan 1895 at Camp San Carlos, TX; enlisted for three years 17 Jan 1895 at Ft Ringgold; discharged 16 Jan 1898, reenlisted for three years 22 Jan 1898 at Ft Ringgold; discharged 21 Jan 1901 at Ft Ringgold, age 47; died 12 Jan 1904; buried at Nacimiento, Coahuila, Mexico. SOURCE: Swanson, 34.

Seminole Negro Scout; born in Mexico, age 21 when enlisted; served numerous six-month enlistments between 1871 and 1901; received Medal of Honor for valor with Lt. John Bullis on Pecos River, TX, Apr 1875; applied for pension 1903; died in Mexico 1904. SOURCE: Schubert, *Black Valor*, 30, 34, 39.

Served 1871–1901; wife Julia, born ca. 1862, died 1946, was step-granddaughter of Scout John Kibbetts. SOURCE: Schubert, Consolidated List of Seminole Negro Scouts; Schubert, "Seminole-Negro Scouts." *See* **KIBBETTS,** Robert, Corporal, U.S. Army

‡Trumpeter, 10th Cavalry; Seminole Negro Scout; awarded Medal of Honor for heroism with Lieutenant Bullis, Pecos River, TX, 26 Apr 1875. SOURCE: Carroll, *The Black Military Experience*, 390.

Born 1854; died 12 Jan 1904; buried at Indian Scout Cemetery. SOURCE: Indian Scout Cemetery, Kinney County, Texas.

PAYNE, James; Blacksmith; L/9th Cav. Born in Kentucky; acquitted of murder for killing in barroom, Las Animas, CO, Aug 1876, along with Pvts. Nathan Trent and William Jones, L/9th Cavalry. SOURCE: Kenner, *Buffalo Soldiers and Officers of the Ninth Cavalry*, 183.

PAYNE, James L.; Private; F/25th Inf. Died 17 Sep 1914; buried in plot WEST 1418 at San Francisco National Cemetery. SOURCE: San Francisco National Cemetery.

PAYNE, Jesse; Private; C/10th Cav. Died 17 Dec 1870 of disease at Ft Sill, OK.

SOURCE: Regimental Returns, 10th Cavalry, 1870. Died 15 Dec 1870; buried at Camp Douglas, UT. SOURCE: Record Book of Interments, Post Cemetery, 252.

PAYNE, John; M/9th Cav. Born in North Carolina; black complexion; cannot read or write, age 26, Jul 1870, at Ft McKavett, TX. SOURCE: Bierschwale, *Fort McKavett,* 100.

PAYNE, Plantz; Private; U.S. Army. Seminole Negro Scout, served 1889–90. SOURCE: Schubert, Consolidated List of Seminole Negro Scouts.

Born in Mexico; Ht 5'7", black hair and eyes, black complexion; enlisted at Ft Clark, TX, 11 Nov 1889, age 23; discharged 28 Feb 1890 at Camp Neville Springs, TX. SOURCE: Swanson, 35.

PAYNE, Robert; Private; U.S. Army. Born in Mexico; Ht 5'8", black hair and eyes, black complexion; enlisted at Ft Duncan, TX, 26 Nov 1873, age 16; discharged 26 May 1874

at Camp Palafox, TX; enlisted 2 Oct 1874, discharged 2 Apr 1875 at Ft Clark, TX; enlisted 1 Apr 1875 at Ft Duncan; discharged, reenlisted 7 Oct 1875 at Camp Supply, TX; discharged 13 Apr 1876 at Ft Clark; enlisted 26 Apr 1876 at Camp Brazos, TX; discharged, reenlisted 26 Oct 1876 at Ft Clark; discharged, reenlisted 26 Apr 1877 at Camp Painted Comanche, TX; discharged, reenlisted 26 Apr 1878 at Camp Painted Comanche; dishonorably discharged, general court martial 31 May 1879; enlisted 15 May 1882 at Ft Clark; discharged 14 May 1883, reenlisted next day at Ft Clark; discharged 14 May 1884, reenlisted 18 May 1884 at Ft Myers, TX; discharged 31 Aug 1884 at Ft Clark; enlisted 3 Sep 1890 at Ft Clark; discharged 2 Mar 1891, reenlisted next day at Camp Neville Springs, TX; discharged 2 Sep 1891 at Camp Neville Springs; enlisted 4 Nov 1891 at Ft Clark; discharged at Camp Presidio, TX, 14 May 1892; enlisted 13 Jan 1893 at Ft Clark; discharged 12 Jul 1893, reenlisted next day at Ft Ringgold, TX; discharged 12 Jan 1894 at Ft Ringgold; enlisted for six months 7 Feb 1894 at Ft Clark; died 31 Mar 1894 at Ft Ringgold. SOURCE: Swanson, 35.

Seminole Negro Scout, served 1873–79, 1882–84, 1890–94, and perhaps more. SOURCE: Schubert, *Black Valor*, 30; Schubert, Consolidated List of Seminole Negro Scouts.

Resided at Ft Duncan, age 23, in 1875, with mother Leah age 50 and Scout Daniel Payne age 35. SOURCE: NARA Record Group 393, Special File; NARA M 929, Roll 2.

Robt Paine, Seminole Scout, buried at Alexandria National Cemetery, Pineville, LA. SOURCE: Gordon, Photos.

PAYNE, Titus; Private; U.S. Army. Seminole Negro Scout, served 1871–72. SOURCE: Schubert, Consolidated List of Seminole Negro Scouts.

Born in Florida; slave or descendant of slaves belonging to Seminole Head Chief King Payne; Ht 5'8", black hair and eyes, black complexion; enlisted at Ft Duncan, TX, 7 Oct 1871, age 40; discharged 7 Apr 1872 and reenlisted next day at Ft Duncan; discharged 14 Oct 1872 at Ft Clark, TX; assassinated 19 May 1876 at Ft Clark in company of John Horse, who was wounded in four places. SOURCE: Swanson, 35.

Seminole Negro Scout, shot and killed by unknown assailants, Ft Clark, May 1876. SOURCE: Schubert, *Black Valor*, 37.

PAYNE, William; QM Sgt; E/10th Cav. ‡Enlisted, age 16, 4 Feb 1892; at Ft Keogh, MT, when Spanish-American War broke out; narrates war experience. SOURCE: Cashin, *Under Fire with the Tenth Cavalry*, 220–24.

‡Served in 10th Cavalry in Cuba, 1898; wounded in action. SOURCE: Cashin, *Under Fire with the Tenth Cavalry*, 342; SecWar, *AR 1898*, 324.

‡Awarded certificate of merit for distinguished service in Cuba, 1 Jul 1898. SOURCE: *ANJ* 37 (24 Feb 1900): 611; Steward, *The Colored Regulars*, 280.

‡Commended for distinguished service as sergeant, E/10th Cavalry, battle of Santiago, Cuba, 1 Jul 1898. SOURCE: GO 15, AGO, 13 Feb 1898.

Awarded certificate of merit for distinguished service in battle, Santiago, 1 Jul 1898. SOURCE: Gleim, *The Certificate of Merit*, 45.

Born in Nashville, TN; resided Chattanooga, TN; received Distinguished Service Medal in lieu of certificate of merit. SOURCE: *American Decorations*, 842.

‡At Ft Huachuca, AZ, 1914; passed examination for commission as captain of volunteers, May 1914. SOURCE: *Crisis* 9 (Nov 1914): 14.

PEAKER, Stephen P.; Private; 39th Inf. Civil War veteran, served in 24th U.S. Colored Infantry. SOURCE: Dobak and Phillips, *The Black Regulars*, 335.

PEARSON, Frank; Private; K/24th Inf. ‡Died of disease of liver in the Philippines, 18 Jan 1902. SOURCE: *ANJ* 39 (15 Mar 1902): 706.

Died 18 Jan 1902; buried in plot NEW801 at San Francisco National Cemetery. SOURCE: San Francisco National Cemetery.

PEARSON, Oliver; Private; E/9th Cav. Died 17 Jul 1894; buried at Santa Fe National Cemetery, NM, plot I 447. SOURCE: Santa Fe National Cemetery, Records of Burials.

PEDEE, Martin; Private; 25th Inf. ‡Musician, convicted of attempted rape of white wife of corporal in same company, 25th Infantry, Ft Davis, TX, Nov 1872. SOURCE: Carroll, *The Black Military Experience*, 274–75.

Pvt. Martin Peede, musician, 25th Infantry, convicted by court martial, Ft Davis, 1872, of attempted rape of comrade's wife; sentence of dishonorable discharge and seven years reduced to one year's confinement at Ft Davis. SOURCE: Dobak and Phillips, *The Black Regulars*, 197.

At Ft Davis, Nov 1872, in second enlistment, convicted of raping comrade's wife, sentence of dishonorable discharge and seven years reduced to twelve months by Judge Advocate General. SOURCE: Kenner, *Buffalo Soldiers and Officers of the Ninth Cavalry*, 58.

PENDERGRASS, John C.; Sgt Maj; 10th Cav. ‡Born in Jamestown, IL; Ht 5'9", mulatto; served in A/10th Cavalry, 5 Dec 1881–4 Dec 1886, 1 Jun 1887–31 May 1892, 1 Jun 1892–31 May 1897, 1 Jun 1897–18 Aug 1898, character excellent on all discharges; served in Cuba 14 Jun–14 Aug 1898 and 12 Dec 1900–25 Apr 1902; sergeant, A/10th Cavalry, 10 Mar 1900; first sergeant, A/10th Cavalry, 11 Mar 1900; sharpshooter 1885, 1888, 1889, 1891, 1893, 1894,

1896, 1901; wounded in right arm and bone broken, 1 1/2" above elbow, with carbine during sham battle, Manzanillo, Cuba, 8 May 1901; in hospital in Cuba, 8–26 May 1901; promoted to regimental color sergeant, 5 Jun 1901; married to Mrs. Amanda Pendergrass, 118 11th Street, Springfield, IL, no children; deposits Jul–Sep 1902 $123, clothing $83; reenlisted Ft Robinson, NE, 13 Nov 1903; expert rifleman 1904 and 1905; wife at Ft Robinson; deposits, $700 in 1903, $100 in 1904, $100 in 1905, $300 in 1906; clothing $106; sharpshooter 1906. SOURCE: Descriptive Book, 10 Cav Officers and NCOs.

‡Born in Illinois; private, corporal, sergeant, A/10th Cavalry, 5 Dec 1881–4 Dec 1886; private, 1 Jun 1887; sergeant, 10 Oct 1887; first sergeant, 1 Feb 1888. SOURCE: Baker, Roster.

‡Distinguished marksman, 1884 and 1885. SOURCE: GO 78, AGO, 20 Oct 1886.

‡Distinguished marksman, 1886; fifth in Division of the Pacific with rifle, silver medal. SOURCE: Baker, Roster.

‡First sergeant, A/10th Cavalry, sharpshooter, at Ft Apache, AZ, 1888. SOURCE: *ANJ* 25 (21 Jul 1888): 1034.

‡Ranked number 10 in competition of Army carbine team of distinguished marksmen as first sergeant, A/10th Cavalry, 1889. SOURCE: GO 78, AGO, 12 Oct 1889.

‡First sergeant, A/10th Cavalry, at Ft Apache, 1890, subscribed $.50 to testimonial to General Grierson. SOURCE: List of subscriptions, 23 Apr 1890, 10th Cavalry papers, MHI.

‡Served as first sergeant, A/10th Cavalry, in Cuba, 1898. SOURCE: Cashin, *Under Fire with the Tenth Cavalry*, 336.

‡Picture. SOURCE: Cashin, *Under Fire with the Tenth Cavalry*, 250.

‡Letter from Santiago, Cuba, no date. SOURCE: Gatewood, *"Smoked Yankees,"* 50–52.

‡Commissioned second lieutenant, 10th Volunteer Infantry, after Spanish-American War. SOURCE: Cashin, *Under Fire with the Tenth Cavalry*, 360–61; Johnson, *History of Negro Soldiers*, 50.

‡Color sergeant, 10th Cavalry; commander asks authority to detail him as schoolteacher in emergency; no other competent man available. SOURCE: CO, Ft Robinson, to AGO, 24 Oct 1902, LS, Ft Robinson.

‡Ranked number 123 among expert riflemen with 70.33 percent in 1904. SOURCE: GO 79, AGO, 1 Jun 1905.

‡Ranked number 589 among expert riflemen with 67 percent in 1905. SOURCE: GO 101, AGO, 31 May 1906.

Sergeant major, 10th Cavalry, received Indian Wars Campaign Badge number 537 on 16 Apr 1909. SOURCE: Carroll, *Indian Wars Campaign Badge*, 15.

PENDLETON, Joseph; Sergeant; I/25th Inf. Born in Louisa County, VA; Ht 5'7", black hair and eyes, brown complexion; occupation soldier; enlisted at age 28, Wash-

ington, DC, 5 Jan 1882. SOURCE: Descriptive & Assignment Rolls of Recruits, 25 Inf.

Sergeant, 25th Infantry, delivered insane soldier of 11th Infantry to asylum in Washington, DC, 1884. SOURCE: Dobak and Phillips, *The Black Regulars*, 259.

‡Authorized two-month furlough from Ft Snelling, MN. SOURCE: *ANJ* 24 (25 Dec 1886): 430.

‡Transferred from Ft Missoula, MT, to take charge of Ft Snelling mess. SOURCE: *ANJ* 25 (14 Jul 1888): 1015.

PENN, Delemar; Sergeant; I/9th Cav. Commanded right flank of Capt. Charles Beyer's attack against Victorio, Mimbres Mountains, New Mexico, 29 May 1879; cited for bravery by Beyer; name also spelled "Delaware." SOURCE: Schubert, *Black Valor*, 51–53.

‡Sgt. Delaware Penn, I/9th Cavalry, cited for gallantry against Victorio, Jun 1879, by Capt. Charles D. Beyer. SOURCE: Billington, "Black Cavalrymen," 64; Billington, *New Mexico's Buffalo Soldiers*, 88–89.

PENN, Will; Private; L/10th Cav. Died 26 May 1914; buried 14 Mar 1932 at Santa Fe National Cemetery, NM, plot P 137. SOURCE: Santa Fe National Cemetery, Records of Burials.

PENN, William H.; 1st Sgt; K/9th Cav. ‡Born in Baltimore, MD, 1863; enlisted 1880 and served against Indians, and in Cuba, the Philippines, and Samoa; many years as ranking sergeant in 3rd Squadron, 9th Cavalry; retired 4 Feb 1908. SOURCE: *Crisis* 27 (Jan 1924): 126.

‡On furlough from Ft Robinson, NE, at Crawford, NE, Mar 1887.

‡Appointed sergeant, 30 Dec 1889. SOURCE: Roster, 9 Cav.

William N. Penn appointed sergeant 30 Dec 1889; in K/9th Cavalry at Ft Robinson, Jan 1897. SOURCE: Ninth Cavalry, Roster of NCOs, 1897.

‡Detached as provost sergeant, Ft Meyer, VA. SOURCE: *ANJ* 31 (14 Apr 1894): 570.

‡Relieved from extra duty with Quartermaster Department, Ft Meyer. SOURCE: *ANJ* 32 (5 Jan 1895): 310.

‡Sergeant, K/9th Cavalry, sent to Hot Springs, SD, to pick up deserter, Pvt. William Smith, E/9th Cavalry. SOURCE: SO 129, 21 Nov 1896, Post Orders, Ft Robinson.

‡Reenlistment as married soldier at Ft Robinson authorized by letter, Adjutant General's Office, 3 Dec 1897.

‡When first sergeant, K/9th Cavalry, 1901, met William Washington and his first wife; Washington remained unmarried 1903–10; Penn retired and resided at 1012 6 1/2 Street, SE, Washington, DC, in 1920. SOURCE: VA File WC 894780, William Washington.

PENNINGTON, Wash; Private; K/9th Cav. Native of Kentucky, wounded in action against Nana, Carrizo Canyon, NM, Aug 1881; spent more than a year in hospital, recovered, discharged on surgeon's certificate of disability. SOURCE: Kenner, *Buffalo Soldiers and Officers of the Ninth Cavalry*, 149.

PERCIVAL, Abram; Private; E/9th Cav. Native of West Indies; on at least second enlistment when on duty in Sgt. Silas Chapman's herd guard near Ojo Caliente, NM, Sep 1879, and attacked by Victorio; killed along with Chapman, Pvts. Silas Graddon, William Humphrey, and Lafayette Hooke. SOURCE: Kenner, *Buffalo Soldiers and Officers of the Ninth Cavalry*, 108.

‡Private Percival killed in action at Camp Ojo Caliente, NM, 4 Sep 1879. SOURCE: Billington, "Black Cavalrymen," 67; Billington, *New Mexico's Buffalo Soldiers*, 89; *Illustrated Review: Ninth Cavalry. See* **CHAPMAN**, Silas, Sergeant, E/9th Cavalry

One of five men of E Troop killed by Victorio's Apaches while guarding troop's horse herd, Ojo Caliente, 4 Sep 1879. SOURCE: Schubert, *Black Valor*, 53.

PERKINS, Frank; E/10th Cav. Civil War veteran; also used name Franklin Spencer; served in Independent Battery, U.S. Colored Light Artillery; served in E and B/10th Cavalry, 1867–77. SOURCE: Cunningham e-mail message, 28 Jan 2000, in authors' files.

‡Original member of 10th Cavalry; in troop when organized, Ft Leavenworth, KS, 15 Jun 1867. SOURCE: McMiller, "Buffalo Soldiers," 72.

PERKINS, Levi; H/25th Inf. Born in England; mulatto complexion; can read and write, age 21, 5 Sep 1870, at Ft McKavett, TX. SOURCE: Bierschwale, *Fort McKavett*, 108.

PERKINS, William; Private; 25th Inf. At Ft Meade, SD, company cook who doubled his income by baking and selling pies and cakes to his comrades. SOURCE: Dobak and Phillips, *The Black Regulars*, 137.

PERRY, Alfred; H/25th Inf. Born in North Carolina; mulatto complexion; cannot read or write, age 25, 5 Sep 1870, at Ft McKavett, TX. SOURCE: Bierschwale, *Fort McKavett*, 108.

PERRY, Charles; Private; K/9th Cav. Born in South America; accumulated $335 in savings, in second enlistment, when killed in action against Nana, Carrizo Canyon, NM, Aug 1881. SOURCE: Kenner, *Buffalo Soldiers and Officers of the Ninth Cavalry*, 149.

‡Killed in action against Nana, Carrizo Canyon, 12 Aug 1881. SOURCE: Leckie, *The Buffalo Soldiers*, 232; Billington, *New Mexico's Buffalo Soldiers*, 105.

PERRY, Charles; QM Sgt; L/10th Cav. ‡Born in Missouri; private, corporal, sergeant, first sergeant, B/10th Cavalry, 26 Feb 1877–25 Feb 1892; private, E/10th Cav-

alry, 26 Feb 1892; corporal, 16 Apr 1892. SOURCE: Baker, Roster.

‡Sergeant, 10th Cavalry, led patrol at Ojo Caliente, NM, 28 Oct 1880, in which five enlisted men were killed. SOURCE: Leckie, *The Buffalo Soldiers*, 230.

‡First sergeant, B/10th Cavalry, at Ft Apache, AZ, 1890, subscribed $.50 to testimonial to General Grierson. SOURCE: List of subscriptions, 23 Apr 1890, 10th Cavalry papers, MHI.

‡Served as first sergeant, L/10th Cavalry, 1898; remained in U.S. during war with Spain. SOURCE: Cashin, *Under Fire with the Tenth Cavalry*, 350.

‡Appointed from sergeant, E/10th Cavalry, to first lieutenant, 49th Infantry; to report at New York City. SOURCE: *ANJ* 37 (7 Oct 1899): 122.

‡First lieutenant as of 9 Sep 1899; to report for duty at Jefferson Barracks, MO. SOURCE: *ANJ* 37 (14 Oct 1899): 147.

‡As first lieutenant, E/49th Infantry, led detachment of twenty that wounded an insurgent and captured him and another at Laguna de Bay, Philippines, Feb 1900; first capture by 49th Infantry. SOURCE: Cleveland *Gazette*, 24 Mar 1900.

‡Twenty-four years' continuous service; police officer on board U.S. Army Transport *Warren*, 10 Dec 1899–11 Jan 1900, and on board U.S. Army Transport *Thomas*, 27 May 1901; commander of detachment that captured insurgent outpost near Laguna de Bay, and detachment that repulsed and captured insurgents who assaulted Alaminos, Philippines, 2 Jan 1901. SOURCE: Descriptive Book, E/49 Inf.

‡Rejoined his troop of 10th Cavalry as quartermaster sergeant after discharge from 49th Infantry. SOURCE: Fletcher, "The Negro Soldier in the United States Army," 297.

‡Dance given in his honor, Ft Robinson, NE, 25 Jul 1904. SOURCE: Crawford *Tribune*, 29 Jul 1904.

Retired first sergeant, received Indian Wars Campaign Badge number 1070 on 31 Dec 1908. SOURCE: Carroll, *Indian Wars Campaign Badge*, 30.

PERRY, Denbar; Private; L/9th Cav. At Ft Duncan, TX, 1870; sentenced to fifteen years' imprisonment for mutinous conduct toward Lt. Frederic A. Kendall, 25th Infantry, Dec 1870. SOURCE: Kenner, *Buffalo Soldiers and Officers of the Ninth Cavalry*, 177.

PERRYMAN, Ignacio; Private; U.S. Army. Seminole Negro Scout, served 1893–94, 1907–14. SOURCE: Schubert, Consolidated List of Seminole Negro Scouts.

Born in Mexico; Ht 5'6", black hair and eyes, black complexion; enlisted at Ft Clark, TX, 3 Jan 1893, age 21; discharged 12 Jul 1893, reenlisted next day at Ft Ringgold, TX; discharged 12 Jan 1894 at Camp San Pedro, TX; enlisted 12 Mar 1907 at Ft Clark where he was discharged 11

Mar 1910; enlisted 12 Mar 1910 at Ft Clark where he was discharged 11 Mar 1913; enlisted 12 Mar 1913 for seven years, age 38; honorably discharged 31 Jul 1914; died 20 May 1933; buried at Seminole Indian Scout Cemetery, Kinney County, TX. SOURCE: Swanson, 36.

PERRYMAN, Isaac; Sergeant; U.S. Army. Seminole Negro Scout, served 1873–85, 1889–1907; retired; pension file in National Archives. SOURCE: Schubert, Consolidated List of Seminole Negro Scouts.

Born in Arkansas; Ht 5'5', black hair and eyes, black complexion; enlisted at Ft Duncan, TX, 1 May 1873, age 29; discharged 1 Nov 1873 at Camp Comanche, TX; enlisted 1 Jan 1874 at Ft Duncan; discharged 1 Jul 1874 at Camp Palafox, TX; enlisted 1 Jan 1875 at Ft Duncan; discharged, reenlisted 1 Jul 1875 at Ft Concho, TX; discharged 1 Jan 1876 at Ft Duncan; enlisted 14 Apr 1876 at Ft Clark, TX; discharged, reenlisted 14 Oct 1876 at Ft Clark; discharged 14 Apr 1877 at Camp Painted Comanche, TX; enlisted 18 May 1877 at Ft Clark; discharged, reenlisted 18 May 1878 at Camp Devil R; discharged, reenlisted 17 May 1879 at Ft Clark; discharged 27 May 1880, reenlisted next day at Ft Clark; discharged 5 Jun 1881, reenlisted next day at Ft Clark; discharged 2 Jun 1882, reenlisted 23 Jun 1882 at Camp Myers Spring, TX; discharged 22 Jun 1884, reenlisted 24 Jun 1884 at Camp Myers Spring; discharged 31 Aug 1884 at Ft Clark; enlisted 27 Dec 1884 at Ft Clark; discharged 26 Dec 1885 at Camp Neville Springs, TX; enlisted 10 Jan 1889 at Ft Clark; discharged 9 Jan 1890, reenlisted next day at Ft Clark; discharged 9 Jul 1890, reenlisted next day at Camp Neville Springs; discharged 9 Jan 1891, reenlisted next day at Ft Clark; discharged 9 Jul 1891 at Camp Palvo, TX; enlisted 9 Jul 1891 at Ft Clark; discharged, reenlisted 19 Jan 1892 at Camp Palvo; discharged 18 Jul 1892 at Camp Presidio, TX; enlisted 16 Aug 1892 at Ft Clark; discharged 15 Feb 1893 at Tepeguaje, TX; enlisted 16 Feb 1893 at Agua Nueva, TX; discharged 15 Aug 1893 at Ft Ringgold, TX; reenlisted at Ft Ringgold where he was discharged 3 Dec 1894; enlisted 2 Apr 1895 at Ft Ringgold; discharged, reenlisted 22 Apr 1901 at Ft Clark; discharged 21 Apr 1904 at Ft Sill, OK; enlisted 22 Apr 1904 at Ft Clark; discharged 21 Apr 1907, reenlisted next day at Ft Clark; retired as sergeant 10 Jul 1908 at Ft Clark; died 12 Sep 1918; buried at Seminole Indian Scout Cemetery, Kinney County, TX. SOURCE: Swanson, 37.

Age 30, resided at Ft Duncan in 1875 with Scout Jim Perryman age 25 and mother Nelia age 50; signed name with an "X" in 1876; widow Lea pension certificate 9302. SOURCE: NARA Record Group 393, Special File; NARA, M 929, Roll 2.

PERRYMAN, James; Private; U.S. Army. Seminole Negro Scout, also known as Jim, served 1873–80, 1882–84; pension in National Archives. SOURCE: Schubert, Consolidated List of Seminole Negro Scouts.

Born in Mexico; also known as Jim; Ht 5'5", black hair and eyes, black complexion; enlisted at Ft Duncan, TX, 1 May 1873; discharged 1 Nov 1873 at Camp Comanche, TX; enlisted 1 Jan 1874 at Ft Duncan; discharged 1 Jul 1874 at Camp Palafox, TX; enlisted 1 Jan 1875 at Ft Duncan; discharged, reenlisted 1 Jul 1875 at Ft Concho, TX; discharged 1 Jan 1876 at Ft Duncan; enlisted 29 Jan 1877, discharged 29 Jan 1878 at Ft Clark, TX; enlisted 7 Aug 1878, discharged 12 Sep 1879 at Ft Clark; enlisted 13 Sep 1879 for one year at Ft Clark; discharged 19 Nov 1880 at Camp Blackwater; enlisted for one year 13 May 1882 at Ft Clark; discharged 12 May 1883, reenlisted for one year next day at Ft Clark; discharged 12 May 1884 at Camp Myers, TX; discharged 27 May 1884, reenlisted next day for one year at Ft Clark where he was discharged 31 Aug 1884; enlisted for one year 27 Dec 1884; discharged at Camp Neville Springs, TX; married daughter of Lipan Chief Costillito, both of whom were captured in Mackenzie's Raid on Remolino, May 1873; died 26 Sep 1930; buried at Seminole Indian Scout Cemetery, Kinney County, TX. SOURCE: Swanson, 36. *See* **GRAYSON**, Renty, Private, U.S. Army

Seminole Negro Scout; married Teresita, daughter of Lipan chief captured in Col. Ranald Mackenzie's raid into Mexico, 1879; ceremony performed by Lt. John L. Bullis. SOURCE: Schubert, *Black Valor*, 32.

At age 25 resided in 1875 at Ft Duncan with Scout Isaac Perryman age 30 and mother Nelia age 50; wife Teresita bore son Deacon Warren Juan Perryman who died 1881, buried in Scouts' cemetery near Ft Clark; widow pension certificate 9302, widow Lea. SOURCE: NARA Record Group 393, Special File; Porter, *The Negro on the American Frontier*, 479; Mulroy, *Freedom on the Border*, 119.

PERRYMAN, Pompey; Private; U.S. Army. Seminole Negro Scout, served 1878–80, 1884. SOURCE: Schubert, Consolidated List of Seminole Negro Scouts.

Born in Arkansas; Ht 5'7", black hair and eyes, black complexion; enlisted at Ft Clark, TX, 8 Feb 1878, age 30; discharged 24 Apr 1879, reenlisted next day at Ft Clark; discharged 1 May 1880, reenlisted next day at Ft Clark; discharged 12 May 1881, reenlisted next day at Ft Clark; discharged as corporal 22 May 1883 at Ft Clark; enlisted 23 May 1883 at Ft Clark; discharged as sergeant 22 May 1884 at Camp Myers, TX; enlisted 26 May 1884 at Ft Clark where he was discharged as sergeant 31 May 1885; enlisted 16 May 1886, discharged as private 11 Aug 1886 at Ft Clark; enlisted 17 Sep 1886 at Ft Clark, discharged 15 Sep 1887 at Camp Neville Springs, TX; enlisted 17 Sep 1888 at Ft Clark, discharged 16 Sep 1889, reenlisted next day at Ft Clark; discharged 16 Mar 1890, reenlisted next day at Camp Neville Springs; discharged 16 Sep 1890 at Camp Neville Springs, enlisted 17 Sep 1890 at Devil's R; discharged 16 Mar 1891, reenlisted next day at Camp Neville Springs; discharged 16 Sep 1891, reenlisted next day at Camp Palvo, TX; discharged 16 Mar 1892 at Camp Palvo, enlisted 17

Mar 1892 at Camp Presidio, TX; discharged 16 Sep 1892, reenlisted next day at Camp Eagle Pass, TX; discharged 16 Mar 1893, reenlisted next day at Ramirez R.; discharged 16 Sep 1893, reenlisted next day at Ft Ringgold, TX; discharged 16 Mar 1894 at Camp San Pedro, TX; died 5 Jan 1923; buried at Seminole Indian Scout Cemetery, Kinney County, TX. SOURCE: Swanson, 38.

Promoted from private to sergeant Jun 1884. SOURCE: NARA, M929, Roll 2.

PETERS, David; Corporal; E/9th Cav. Cursed and abused by Capt. Ambrose Hooker in New Mexico, 1879. SOURCE: Kenner, *Buffalo Soldiers and Officers of the Ninth Cavalry*, 107.

PETERS, Richard W.; Sergeant; E/9th Cav. ‡Authorized to enlist in K/9th Cavalry by letter, Adjutant General's Office, 23 May 1895.

Received Philippine Campaign Badge number 11703 for service as corporal in K/9th Cavalry; in 9th Cavalry at Ft Leavenworth, KS, Mar 1905. SOURCE: Philippine Campaign Badge list, 29 May 1905.

‡Sergeant, E/9th Cavalry, veteran of Spanish-American War and Philippine Insurrection, at Ft D. A. Russell, WY, in 1910; sharpshooter. SOURCE: *Illustrated Review, Ninth Cavalry*.

PETERSON, John; Private; 25th Inf. Born in Rome, NY; Ht 5'3", black hair and eyes, black complexion; occupation soldier; enlisted at age 29, Buffalo, NY, 21 Dec 1881. SOURCE: Descriptive & Assignment Rolls of Recruits, 25 Inf.

PETRY, Andrew; Private; B/10th Cav. Confined to guardhouse, Ft Duncan, TX, Feb 1878 for intoxication. SOURCE: Kinevan, *Frontier Cavalryman*, 99.

PETTIE, Samuel; QM Sgt; B/9th Cav. ‡Appointed corporal, B/9th Cavalry, 16 Dec 1891. SOURCE: Roster, 9 Cav.

‡Promoted to sergeant, B/9th Cavalry, Ft DuChesne, UT, Dec 1894. SOURCE: *ANJ* 32 (15 Dec 1894): 262.

Appointed sergeant 1 Dec 1894; in B/9th Cavalry at Ft DuChesne, Jan 1897. SOURCE: Ninth Cavalry, Roster of NCOs, 1897.

‡First sergeant, B/9th Cavalry, second in competition of Pacific Division cavalry team, Ord Bks, CA, 1904. SOURCE: GO 167, AGO, 28 Oct 1904.

‡Ranked sixth in Northern Division cavalry competition, Ft Riley, KS, 1905; silver medal. SOURCE: GO 173, AGO, 20 Oct 1905.

‡Ranked number 474 among rifle experts with 68.67 percent, 1905. SOURCE: GO 101, AGO, 31 May 1906.

‡Distinguished marksman, ranked second, Division of the Pacific, 1904; ranked sixth, Northern Division, 1905;

ranked number 13, Division of the Philippines, 1908. SOURCE: GO 207, AGO, 19 Dec 1908.

‡Expert rifleman and veteran of Spanish-American War and Philippine Insurrection; quartermaster sergeant, B/9th Cavalry, at Ft D. A. Russell, WY, in 1910. SOURCE: *Illustrated Review: Ninth Cavalry*, with picture.

PETTIGREW, William M.; Private; G/9th Cav. Received Philippine Campaign Badge number 11840 for service as corporal in C/48th United States Volunteers, 26 Jan 1900–30 May 1901, and as private in G/25th Infantry, 16 Sep 1901–28 Jun 1902; private in G/9th Cavalry, Ft Leavenworth, KS, Mar 1905. SOURCE: Philippine Campaign Badge Recipients; Philippine Campaign Badge list, 29 May 1905.

PETTIS, Charles M.; Private; 9th Cav. Received Philippine Campaign Badge number 11740 for service as private in H/9th Cavalry; in 9th Cavalry at Ft Leavenworth, KS, Mar 1905. SOURCE: Philippine Campaign Badge list, 29 May 1905.

PETTIT, John; Private; 25th Inf. Mentioned. SOURCE: Dobak and Phillips, *The Black Regulars*, 274.

PHELPS, William; Private; F/25th Inf. Served as Capt. Andrew Geddes's orderly at Ft Stockton, TX, 1879. SOURCE: Barnett, *Ungentlemanly Acts*, 133.

PHILIPS, Joe; Private; U.S. Army. Seminole Negro Scout, served 1872–77. SOURCE: Schubert, Consolidated List of Seminole Negro Scouts.

Joe Phillips, born in Mexico; Ht 5'4", black hair and eyes, black complexion; enlisted at Ft Duncan, TX, 2 Aug 1872, age 17; discharged 2 Feb 1873, Ft Duncan; enlisted 22 Apr 1873 at Ft Clark, TX, discharged 22 Apr 1874 at Ft Clark; enlisted 14 Jun 1874 at Ft Clark, discharged 17 Dec 1874; enlisted 1 Jan 1875 at Ft Clark, discharged 5 Jul 1875 at Ft Clark; enlisted 4 Oct 1875 at Ft Clark, discharged 4 Feb 1876; enlisted 8 Aug 1876 at Camp Pecos, TX; deserted from Ft Clark 5 Jan 1877 when Scout Adam Payne was shot 1 Jan 1877 by deputy sheriff.

PHILIPS, John; Private; U.S. Army. Seminole Negro Scout, served 1871–80. SOURCE: Schubert, Consolidated List of Seminole Negro Scouts.

John Phillips born in Florida; probably slave or descendant of slave, Joe Phillips, who was informer on King Philip, father of Coacoochee; Ht 5'10", black hair and eyes, black complexion; enlisted at Ft Duncan, TX, 7 Oct 1871, age 30; discharged 7 Apr 1872, reenlisted next day at Ft Duncan; discharged, reenlisted 8 Oct 1872 at Ft Duncan; discharged 9 Apr 1873 at Ft Duncan, enlisted 1 May 1873 at Ft Duncan; discharged 1 Nov 1873 at Camp Comanche, TX, enlisted 13 Dec 1873 at Ft Duncan; discharged 13 Jun

1874 at Camp Palafox, TX; enlisted 28 Feb 1876 at Camp Pecos, TX; discharged 25 Aug 1876, reenlisted 28 Aug 1876 at Camp Pecos; discharged at Camp Crow Creek, TX, re-enlisted at Camp Crow Creek 28 Feb 1877; discharged 28 Feb 1878, reenlisted next day at Ft Clark, TX; discharged 24 Apr 1879 at Ft Clark; discharged for one year 12 Jul 1879 at Ft Clark; died of heart disease 14 Jun 1880 at Ft Clark; buried at Seminole Indian Scout Cemetery, Kinney County, TX. SOURCE: Swanson, 38.

PHILIPS, Joseph; Private; U.S. Army. Seminole Negro Scout, served 1893–94, 1900–1909. SOURCE: Schubert, Consolidated List of Seminole Negro Scouts; Schubert, *Black Valor*, 31.

Joseph Phillips born in Mexico; Ht 5'7", black hair and eyes, black complexion; enlisted at Ft Clark, TX, 22 Oct 1893, age 34; discharged 10 Apr 1894 at Ft Ringgold, TX; enlisted 3 May 1894 at Ft Clark, discharged 2 Nov 1894 at Ft Ringgold; enlisted 11 May 1900 at Ft Ringgold, discharged 10 May 1903, reenlisted next day at Ft Ringgold; discharged 10 May 1906, reenlisted next day at Ft Clark; discharged 10 May 1909 at Ft Clark; died 13 Aug 1935; buried at Seminole Indian Scout Cemetery, Kinney County, TX. SOURCE: Swanson, 39.

PHILIPS, Ned; Private; U.S. Army. Seminole Negro Scout, served 1870–72. SOURCE: Schubert, Consolidated List of Seminole Negro Scouts.

Born in Florida, former slave or descendant of slave of King Philip, father of Coacoochee (Wild Cat); Ht 5'8", black hair and eyes, black complexion; enlisted at Ft Duncan, TX, 1 Oct 1870, age 42; discharged 15 Feb 1871, reen-listed next day at Ft Duncan; discharged, reenlisted 31 Aug 1871 at Ft Duncan; discharged 29 Feb 1872 at Ft Duncan. SOURCE: Swanson, 39.

PHILLIPS, Andrew; Corporal; G/10th Cav. ‡Original member of 10th Cavalry; in troop when organized, Ft Leavenworth, KS, 5 Jul 1867. SOURCE: McMiller, "Buffalo Soldiers," 74.

Died 21 Jul 1867 of unknown causes at Ft Harker, KS. SOURCE: Regimental Returns, 10th Cavalry, 1867.

PHILLIPS, James D.; Private; I/9th Cav. ‡Deserted from Ft Wingate, NM, 30 Jan 1881. SOURCE: Regt Returns, 9 Cav, Jan 1881.

Pvt. James Phillips, E/9th Cavalry, deserted from Ft Wingate, Jan 1881; apprehended and released to duty after Nana began series of attacks; charges later dropped because of gallant conduct in Aug 1881 at Cuchillo Negro, NM. SOURCE: Kenner, *Buffalo Soldiers and Officers of the Ninth Cavalry*, 246–47.

PHILLIPS, Shardon; Private; H/9th Cav. Died 25 Dec 1899; originally buried at Ft Wingate, NM; reburied at Santa Fe National Cemetery, NM, plot A-2 962. SOURCE: Santa Fe National Cemetery, Records of Burials.

PHILLIPS, Stephen F.; Private; 10th Cav. ‡Unassigned private, deceased, Nov 1875. SOURCE: ES, 10 Cav, 1873–83.

Died 28 Sep 1875 in hospital at Ft Concho, TX. SOURCE: Regimental Returns, 10th Cavalry, 1875.

PHILLIPS, Thomas; Sergeant; E/9th Cav. ‡Enlisted, Private, C/9th Cavalry, Ft Robinson, NE, 16 Aug 1895.

Received Philippine Campaign Badge number 11698 for service as sergeant, E/9th Cavalry; in 9th Cavalry at Ft Leavenworth, KS, Mar 1905. SOURCE: Philippine Campaign Badge list, 29 May 1905.

Corporal, E/9th Cavalry, received Indian Wars Campaign Badge number 1360 on 28 May 1909. SOURCE: Carroll, *Indian Wars Campaign Badge*, 39.

PICKENS, Edward; Corporal; I/10th Cav. In Troop I/10th Cavalry stationed at Bonita Cañon Camp, AZ, 30 Jun 1886. SOURCE: Tagg, *The Camp at Bonita Cañon*, 231.

PICKENS, Peter; Private; F/10th Cav. ‡Original member of 10th Cavalry; in troop when organized, Ft Leavenworth, KS, 21 Jun 1867. SOURCE: McMiller, "Buffalo Soldiers," 73.

Died 3 Aug 1867 of cholera at Ft Hays, KS. SOURCE: Regimental Returns, 10th Cavalry, 1867.

Pvt. Peter Pickins, F/10th Cavalry, died 3 Aug 1867; originally buried at Ft Hays; reburied at Ft Leavenworth National Cemetery, plot 3288. SOURCE: Ft Leavenworth National Cemetery.

PICKET, Soney; Private; D/9th Cav. *See* **PICKETT**, Sonny, Private, D/9th Cavalry

PICKETT, Anthony; H/25th Inf. Born in North Carolina; mulatto complexion; can read and write, age 19, 5 Sep 1870, at Ft McKavett, TX. SOURCE: Bierschwale, *Fort McKavett*, 107.

PICKETT, Sonny; Private; D/9th Cav. Soney Picket, Private, D/9th Cavalry, with Captain Dodge at battle at Milk River, CO, 2–10 Oct 1879. SOURCE: Miller, *Hollow Victory*, 167, 206–7.

‡Sonny Pickett, D/9th Cavalry, served 1875–80; subscribes to *Winners of the West*; age 84. SOURCE: *Winners of the West* 10 (Jan 1933): 3.

PICKINGPACK, Thomas J.; Private; G/9th Cav. Received Philippine Campaign Badge number 11839 for service as private in E/25th Infantry, 1 Jun 1901–28 Jun 1902; private in G/9th Cavalry, Ft Leavenworth, KS, Mar 1905.

SOURCE: Philippine Campaign Badge Recipients; Philippine Campaign Badge list, 29 May 1905.

PICKINS, Peter; Private; F/10th Cav. *See* **PICKENS**, Peter, Private, F/10th Cavalry

PILLOW, Alexander; Ord Sgt; U.S. Army. ‡Sergeant, G/25th Infantry, examined for ordnance sergeant, Ft Missoula, MT, 1893. SOURCE: *ANJ* 30 (1 Jul 1893): 745.

‡Promoted to ordnance sergeant. SOURCE: *ANJ* 32 (27 Oct 1894): 141.

Appointed ordnance sergeant 9 Oct 1894, from sergeant, G/25th Infantry. SOURCE: Dobak, "Staff Noncommissioned Officers."

PINKARD, James; Private; F/24th Inf. Born in Arkansas; buried at Ft McKavett, TX, before 17 May 1879; body removed to National Cemetery, San Antonio, TX, 23 Nov 1883. SOURCE: Bierschwale, *Fort McKavett,* 123.

Died at Ft McKavett on 30 Sep 1870; buried at San Antonio National Cemetery, Section E, number 848. SOURCE: San Antonio National Cemetery Locator.

PINKNEY, John C.; Private; L/9th Cavalry. Enlisted 24 Aug 1875 at Louisville, KY; at Ft Bliss, TX. SOURCE: Muster Roll, L/9th Cavalry, 31 Oct 1879–31 Dec 1879.

PINN, Nathan; Recruit; 10th Cav. Died 12 Oct 1867 of meningitis at Ft Riley, KS. SOURCE: Regimental Returns, 10th Cavalry, 1867.

PINN, Newton; Recruit; 10th Cav. Died 1 Dec 1867, no cause listed, at Ft Riley, KS. SOURCE: Regimental Returns, 10th Cavalry, 1867.

PIPES, Nelson; Private; E/10th Cav. ‡Unassigned recruit, 10th Cavalry, on temporary duty for training at Ft Bascom, NM. SOURCE: SO 3, District of NM, 23 Jan 1867.

‡Original member of E/10th Cavalry; in troop when organized, Ft Leavenworth, KS, 15 Jun 1867. SOURCE: McMiller, "Buffalo Soldiers," 72.

Nelson Piper, E/10th Cavalry, died 5[?] Aug 1869 in hospital at Ft Sill, OK. SOURCE: Regimental Returns, 10th Cavalry, 1869.

Died 7 Aug 1869; buried at Camp Douglas, UT. SOURCE: Record Book of Interments, Post Cemetery, 252.

PIPKINS, Charles H.; Corporal; E/10th Cav. In Troop E/10th Cavalry stationed at Bonita Cañon Camp, AZ, 28 Feb 1886. SOURCE: Tagg, *The Camp at Bonita Cañon,* 231.

PITMAN, Samuel; M/9th Cav. Born in Kentucky; black complexion; cannot read or write, age 26, Jul 1870, at Ft McKavett, TX. SOURCE: Bierschwale, *Fort McKavett,* 100.

PITTS, Anthony; Private; A/24th Inf. Died at Camp Eagle Pass, TX, on 28 May 1878; buried at San Antonio National Cemetery, Section F, number 1139. SOURCE: San Antonio National Cemetery Locator.

PITTS, Hoppie; Private; 9th Cav. Received Philippine Campaign Badge number 11894 for service as private in E/9th Cavalry; in 9th Cavalry at Ft Leavenworth, KS, Mar 1905. SOURCE: Philippine Campaign Badge list, 29 May 1905.

PLANT, James W.; Private; C/24th Inf. Born in New York; buried at Ft McKavett, TX, before 17 May 1879; body removed to National Cemetery, San Antonio, TX, 23 Nov 1883. SOURCE: Bierschwale, *Fort McKavett,* 123.

Died at Ft McKavett on 12 Sep 1872; buried at San Antonio National Cemetery, Section E, number 849. SOURCE: San Antonio National Cemetery Locator.

PLEASANT, Hardaway; Private; I/10th Cav. In Troop I/10th Cavalry stationed at Bonita Cañon Camp, AZ, 30 Apr 1886. SOURCE: Tagg, *The Camp at Bonita Cañon,* 232.

PLEASANT, John; Private; F/25th Inf. ‡Died of malaria in the Philippines, 11 Jan 1900. SOURCE: *ANJ* 37 (10 Feb 1900): 562.

Died in Manila, Philippines, 11 Jan 1900; body received for burial 15 Apr 1902 at San Francisco National Cemetery, buried in plot NEW A990. SOURCE: San Francisco National Cemetery.

PLEASANTS, Thomas; Private; Band/9th Cav. Born in Goochland County, VA, 1862; enlisted Pittsburgh, PA, 5 Dec 1883; Ht 5'5", black complexion, eyes and hair; occupation laborer; discharged from H/10th Cavalry, 4 Dec 1888; enlisted Washington, DC, 14 Dec 1888; served in K/10th Cavalry; discharged 13 Dec 1893; enlisted Ft Robinson, NE, 19 Dec 1893, served in Band/9th Cavalry; tattoos of head and breast of woman on right forearm and woman on left forearm. SOURCE: Sayre, *Warriors of Color,* 393.

Private in H/10th Cavalry stationed at Bonita Cañon Camp, AZ, 30 Jun 1886. SOURCE: Tagg, *The Camp at Bonita Cañon,* 232.

PLUMMER, Henry Vinton; Chaplain; 9th Cav. ‡Family biography. SOURCE: Nellie Arnold Plummer, *Out of the Depths.*

‡During Civil War, served in U.S. Navy aboard gunboat USS *Coeur de Leon* of Potomac Flotilla and at

Washington Navy Yard; married to Julia Lomax by Sandy Alexander, minister of Second Baptist Church, Washington, DC, at Hyattsville, MD, 22 Jun 1867. SOURCE: VA File WC 17458, Henry V. Plummer.

‡Not accompanying regimental headquarters from Ft McKinney, WY, to Ft Robinson, NE, because of scarcity of quarters. SOURCE: *ANJ* 24 (30 Apr 1887): 794.

‡Mentioned as first African-American chaplain. SOURCE: Cleveland *Gazette*, 29 Aug 1891.

‡Resides at Ft Robinson with wife, sister, four of his six children, two servants, Aug 1893; married twenty-eight years. SOURCE: Medical History, Ft Robinson; Court Martial Records, Plummer.

‡Editor of Fort Robinson *Weekly Bulletin*, four pages, one folded sheet, $.05 per issue.

‡Author of "Resident Manager," "Fort Robinson Department," Omaha *Progress*, 1893.

‡Convicted by general court martial, Ft Robinson, of conduct unbecoming an officer and a gentleman, Sep 1894; sentenced to dishonorable discharge. SOURCE: Stover, "Chaplain Henry V. Plummer, His Ministry and His Court Martial."

Pre-service life, military career, interest in soldier education, and court martial conviction discussed. SOURCE: Dobak and Phillips, *The Black Regulars*, 116–17, 122, 129, 131–32, 152–53.

‡Charles R. Lee and James A. Lee of Kansas City, KS, testify to Plummer's heart trouble, indigestion, lumbago, all of which incapacitate him for manual labor; also testify to Plummer's lack of any other means of support except daily labor, 11 Feb 1895; applied for invalid pension through Attorney Allan Rutherford, Washington, DC, 23 Feb 1895; granted $8 per month from 21 Jun 1899, approved 24 Mar 1900, based on "partial inability to earn a support by manual labor." SOURCE: VA File WC 17458, Henry V. Plummer.

Pastor, Second Baptist Church, 533 North Wichita, Wichita, KS, 1901–02; resided at 911 Washington Avenue, Kansas City.

‡Picture in uniform. SOURCE: Wichita *Searchlight*, 2 Nov 1901.

‡Living children, 1903: Adam F. Plummer, born 30 Sep 1868; Charles Sumner Plummer, born 8 Feb 1872; Henry V. Plummer, Jr., born 7 Dec 1879; Ulysses S. G. Plummer, born 16 Mar 1881; Ferdinand G. H. Plummer, born 3 Apr 1887; Hannibal L. Plummer, born 18 Mar 1889. SOURCE: VA File WC 17458, Henry V. Plummer.

Text of letter to *U.S. Army Visitor*, monthly newspaper of U.S. Army Mutual Aid Association, Apr 1893, published. SOURCE: Schubert, *Voices of the Buffalo Soldier*, 175–76.

‡Seriously ill. SOURCE: Kansas City (KS) *American Citizen*, 3 Feb 1905.

‡Died in Kansas City, 10 Feb 1905. SOURCE: Kansas City *American Citizen*, 17 Feb 1905.

‡Undertaker W. B. Raymond, 431 Minnesota Avenue, Kansas City, shipped Plummer's remains to Washington,

DC, 12 Feb 1905. SOURCE: VA File WC 17458, Henry V. Plummer.

‡Brother Elias Plummer, Hutchinson, Reno Co., KS, resided in Washington, DC, 1867; resided with brother until latter died; African Methodist Episcopal minister for twenty years; address Box 328B, East Hutchinson, KS. SOURCE: VA File WC 17458, Henry V. Plummer.

‡Widow Julia (Lomax) Plummer filed application for widow's pension from 911 Washington Avenue, Kansas City, 27 Feb 1905; pension of $8 per month began 27 Feb 1905; increased to $12 per month 19 Apr 1908; widow resided at 1313 T Street, NW, Washington, DC, when she died of bronchial pneumonia 4 Oct 1915, with $540 equity in real estate; Henry V. Plummer, Jr., age 38, resided in Washington, DC, 1915. SOURCE: VA File WC 17458, Henry V. Plummer.

‡Biographical sketch. SOURCE: Logan and Winston, eds., *Dictionary of American Negro Biography*, 15–16.

See AGO File 6474 ACP 81.

Service, court martial, and dismissal, Ft Robinson, narrated. SOURCE: Kenner, *Buffalo Soldiers and Officers of the Ninth Cavalry*, 283–92.

PLUMMER, Solomon; Sergeant; D/9th Cav. Appointed sergeant 3 Feb 1887; in D/9th Cavalry at Ft Washakie, WY, Jan 1897. SOURCE: Ninth Cavalry, Roster of NCOs, 1897.

‡Appointed sergeant 3 Feb 1888. SOURCE: Roster, 9 Cav.

‡On special duty as exchange steward, Ft Robinson, NE, vice Sgt. James Donohue, C/8th Infantry. SOURCE: Order 12, 4 Feb 1893, Post Orders, Ft Robinson.

‡In M/9th Cavalry; reenlistment for third term celebrated with dinner and hop, Ft DuChesne, UT. SOURCE: *ANJ* 36 (16 Mar 1899): 572.

‡Granted four-month furlough. SOURCE: *ANJ* 36 (30 Mar 1899): 619.

‡With detachment of nineteen men of D/9th Cavalry that engaged insurgents, captured a Remington rifle; stationed at San Fernando, Philippines. SOURCE: Hamilton, "History of the Ninth Cavalry," 106; Manila *Times*, 11 Feb 1901; *Illustrated Review: Ninth Cavalry*.

POKE, Samuel; Private; 25th Inf. Born in Nashville, TN; Ht 5'5", black hair and eyes, black complexion; served in K/10th Cavalry to 6 Jan 1887; fourth reenlistment at age 38, St. Louis, MO, 17 Jan 1887; arrived Ft Snelling, MN, 22 Mar 1887. SOURCE: Descriptive & Assignment Rolls of Recruits, 25 Inf.

POLK, James K.; Private; 9th Cav. Died 24 Mar 1876; buried at Santa Fe National Cemetery, NM, plot B 553. SOURCE: Santa Fe National Cemetery, Records of Burials.

POLK, Thomas; Private; A/9th Cav. Private in fourth year of service in A/9th Cavalry, Ft Stanton, NM, Nov 1885, when sexually molested by Pvt. Israel Monday, A/9th Cavalry. SOURCE: Kenner, *Buffalo Soldiers and Officers of the Ninth Cavalry*, 269–70, 354.

Saddler, A/9th Cavalry, reenlistment as married authorized by letter, Adjutant General's Office, 4 Aug 1893.

Private, received Indian Wars Campaign Badge number 671 on 21 Oct 1908. SOURCE: Carroll, *Indian Wars Campaign Badge*, 19.

POLK, Thomas; Cook; B/9th Cav. Retired cook, died 13 Sep 1911; buried at Post Cemetery, Presidio of Monterey, CA, Section I, number 1; wife Elsie Polk, died 11 Jan 1912, buried at Post Cemetery, Presidio of Monterey, Section B, number 42. SOURCE: Post Cemetery Record Book.

POLK, Thomas Elzey; Sergeant; C/9th Cav. Born 11 Jun 1860, third child of Morris and Rebecca Polk; enlisted 2 Mar 1882, age 21; Ht 5'6", black hair and eyes; assigned to C/9th Calvary; promoted to sergeant, character excellent; discharged at Ft Robinson, NE, 1 Mar 1887; enlisted 6 Sep 1887 in Baltimore, MD, age 26; served in L/9th Cavalry; discharged 5 Sept 1892, Ft Leavenworth, KS, character good; with first wife Alice King of Allen, MD, had children Viola, Lelia, Ulysses, Winifred, and Winifred's twin Bicille who died in 1904; died 24 June 1940. SOURCE: "Thomas Elzey Polk," one page undated manuscript, copy in authors' files.

Born in Allen, MD; father was granted freedom in 1829; first enlisted at Baltimore, described as illiterate; learned to read and write during first tour of duty, wrote letters from Ft Sill, IT, and Ft Robinson, NE; married twice; fathered eight children including Celestine, Thomas Jr., and Everett; last surviving child Everett, a World War II veteran, passed Civil Service examination, worked as page for U.S. government in Washington, DC; resides in Florida; Condra Wilfred Williams and Velmar Polk Nutter published *History of the Polk Family of Allen, Maryland: A Genealogical History of the Family of Morris and Rebecca Black Polk* in 1976. SOURCE: "Polk/Dorman Family Traces Roots Back to 1829," *Baltimore Afro-American* (27 Aug 1994), B1.

Performed cooking, supply duties; stationed at Ft Sill; at Ft Leavenworth, KS; at Ft Robinson, 1885–87; last served in C/9th Cavalry. SOURCE: Letter from Wanda Polk Peyton to Thomas Buecker, 25 Jan 1995, photocopy in authors' files.

‡Thomas Polk, sergeant, C/9th Cavalry, at Ft Robinson, 1886; deposited $231 with paymaster.

‡Discharged, end of term, character excellent, Mar 1887.

At Ft Robinson; sergeant, C/9th Cavalry, for two years. SOURCE: Letter from Thomas E. Polk, 2 Oct 1885, photocopy in authors' files.

‡Subscriber; served 1882–92. SOURCE: *Winners of the West* 9 (Nov 1932): 1.

‡Reader since 1932; member, Camp 11, National Indian War Veterans; died Eden, MD, 24 Jun 1940. SOURCE: *Winners of the West* 17 (Jul 1940): 2.

POPE, Malachi; Private; K/9th Cav. Brutal treatment by Capt. J. Lee Humfreville, summer 1872, described. SOURCE: Kenner, *Buffalo Soldiers and Officers of the Ninth Cavalry*, 142–45.

‡Thrown into cold stream by Capt. J. Lee Humfreville, Ft Richardson, TX, 15 Dec 1872, and forced into hospital by subsequent illness. SOURCE: GCMO 23, AGO, 3 Apr 1874.

Text of court martial order convicting Capt. J. Lee Humfreville of brutality published. SOURCE: Schubert, *Voices of the Buffalo Soldier*, 55–62.

POPE, Zachariah; 1st Sgt; C/25th Inf. Enlisted in 10th Cavalry 1867; discharged 1877, went home to East Carondelet, IL, knifed a man, enlisted in 25th Infantry; retired with thirty years in 1897. SOURCE: Dobak and Phillips, *The Black Regulars*, 47.

‡Original member of B/10th Cavalry; in troop when organized, Ft Leavenworth, KS, 1 Apr 1867. SOURCE: McMiller, "Buffalo Soldiers," 69.

‡Mentioned as having served in 1867. SOURCE: Baker, Roster.

‡Retires as first sergeant, C/25th Infantry, from Tampa, FL. SOURCE: *ANJ* 35 (11 Jun 1898): 816.

Retired sergeant, received Indian Wars Campaign Badge number 1059 on 25 Nov 1908. SOURCE: Carroll, *Indian Wars Campaign Badge*, 30.

PORTEE, Wade H.; Corporal; G/9th Cav. Received Philippine Campaign Badge number 11813 for service in B/48th United States Volunteers as private, 25 Jan 1900–31 May 1901, and in G/9th Cavalry as private, 12 Apr 1902–16 Sep 1902; corporal in G/9th Cavalry, Ft Leavenworth, KS, Mar 1905. SOURCE: Philippine Campaign Badge Recipients; Philippine Campaign Badge list, 29 May 1905.

PORTER, Augustus; Private; G/49th Inf. Died 4 Feb 1900 in Manila, Philippines; buried in plot 738 at San Francisco National Cemetery. SOURCE: San Francisco National Cemetery.

PORTER, C. C.; Private; F/10th Cav. *See* **PORTER,** Clark C., Private, F/10th Cavalry

PORTER, Charles; Private; G/10th Cav. Died 11 Jun 1876 of disease at Ft Concho, TX. SOURCE: Regimental Returns, 10th Cavalry, 1876.

PORTER, Charles W.; Private; L/9th Cav. Charles W. Porter born 9 Aug 1881, died 12 Feb 1959; buried at Ft

Leavenworth National Cemetery, plot M 3760. SOURCE: Ft Leavenworth National Cemetery.

PORTER, Clark C.; Private; F/10th Cav. ‡C. C. Porter, private, F/10th Cavalry, died of tuberculosis complicated by pneumonia, Ft Washakie, WY, 26 Dec 1905.

Died 25 Dec 1905; originally buried at Ft Washakie; reburied at Ft Leavenworth National Cemetery, plot G 3511. SOURCE: Ft Leavenworth National Cemetery.

PORTER, James; Private; F/10th Cav. Died 27 Jul 1888; originally buried at Ft Grant, AZ; reburied at Santa Fe National Cemetery, NM, plot A-1 777. SOURCE: Santa Fe National Cemetery, Records of Burials.

PORTER, John H.; C/25th Inf. Born in Maryland; black complexion; can read. cannot write, age 21, 5 Sep 1870, at Ft McKavett, TX. SOURCE: Bierschwale, *Fort McKavett,* 109.

‡Letter from Mr. and Mrs. Alonzo Miller, El Paso, TX, reports that Porter died at age 71, fourteen months ago at Miller home after living with them for eighteen years. SOURCE: *Winners of the West* 5 (Apr 1928): 2.

PORTER, John L.; Musician; H/24th Inf. ‡Enlisted Ft Douglas, UT, 14 May 1898; assigned to H/24th Infantry, 16 Sep 1898; musician, 17 Sep 1898. SOURCE: Muster Roll, H/24 Inf, Sep–Oct 1898.

‡Fined $1 by summary court, 18 Nov 1898. SOURCE: Muster Roll, H/24 Inf, Nov–Dec 1898.

‡Discharged, character good, single, 29 Jan 1899; due $2.48 for clothing; reenlisted at Ft Douglas, 30 Jan 1899; appointment as musician continued; fined $.50 by summary court, 15 Feb 1899. SOURCE: Muster Roll, H/24 Inf, Jan–Feb 1899.

‡Wounded in action in the Philippines, 7 Dec 1899. SOURCE: Muller, *The Twenty Fourth Infantry,* 35.

‡Died of diphtheria in the Philippines, 2 Jan 1900. SOURCE: *ANJ* 37 (20 Jan 1900): 488.

Died in Manila, PI, 2 Jan 1900; buried in plot NEW A387 at San Francisco National Cemetery. SOURCE: San Francisco National Cemetery.

PORTER, Joseph H.; H/25th Inf. Born in Maryland; black complexion; cannot read or write, age 24, 5 Sep 1870, at Ft McKavett, TX. SOURCE: Bierschwale, *Fort McKavett,* 108.

PORTER, Samuel H.; Private; H/24th Inf. Born in Nashville, TN, 1855; enlisted Memphis, TN, 25 Jan 1877; Ht 5'6", black complexion, eyes and hair; occupation laborer; served in F/10th Cavalry; treated at Ft Concho, TX, in June and October 1878 for neuralgia and fever; treated at Ft Elliott, TX, and Ft Sill, IT, for 15 Nov 1879 gunshot wound; discharged 24 Jan 1882; enlisted St. Louis, MO, 9 Mar 1882; served in H/10th Cavalry; kicked by horse in Sept 1882 at

Ft Davis, TX; hospitalized three times with gonorrhea, Ft Davis, 1883; discharged 8 Mar 1887; enlisted Ft Lyon, CO, 13 Aug 1887; served in H/24th Infantry. SOURCE: Sayre, *Warriors of Color,* 394–95.

Private in H/10th Cavalry stationed at Bonita Cañon Camp, AZ, but absent or on detached service 30 Apr 1886. SOURCE: Tagg, *The Camp at Bonita Cañon,* 232.

PORTER, Sanford; Private; C/9th Cav. Died at Ft Davis, TX, on 6 Aug 1868; buried at San Antonio National Cemetery, Section I, number 1466. SOURCE: San Antonio National Cemetery Locator.

PORTER, Wesley; Private; L/9th Cav. Enlisted 24 Sep 1875 at Louisville, KY; sick with rheumatism contracted in line of duty, in post hospital at Ft Bliss, TX. SOURCE: Muster Roll, L/9th Cavalry, 31 Oct 1879–31 Dec 1879.

‡Private, reenlistment authorized by letter, Adjutant General's Office, 17 Jan 1896.

‡Sergeant, Band/9th Cavalry, retires Dec 1900. SOURCE: *ANJ* 38 (29 Dec 1900): 431.

PORTER, William; Private; 10th Cav. On expedition to Tayabacoa, Cuba, with Lieutenant Carter, Jun 1898. SOURCE: Schubert, *Black Valor,* 139.

POSEY, Frank; Private; H/24th Inf. Born in Montgomery County, MD, 1860; enlisted as Frank Posey in Baltimore, MD, 21 Nov 1881; Ht 5'6", mulatto complexion, brown eyes, black hair; occupation laborer; served in H/10th Cavalry; treated for various ailments at Ft Davis, TX, 1882–83; deserted at Ft Davis, 27 Feb 1885, under threat of arrest by civil authorities; enlisted Cleveland, OH, 1 Jul 1885, as Frank Brocko; joined F/25th Infantry, Ft Snelling, MN, 13 Apr 1886; appointed corporal 1 Feb 1887; apprehended at Ft Snelling, 15 May 1888; convicted at Ft Shaw, MT, 2 Jul 1888, sentenced to dishonorable discharge and two years at hard labor; confinement reduced to one year and reduced further to time served, 14 Nov 1888; wife resided at 473 Jackson St., St. Paul, MN, 1888; order for his release from unexecuted portion of sentence 14 Nov 1888. SOURCE: Sayre, *Warriors of Color,* 396–99.

Born in Carroll County, MD; Ht 5'10", black hair and brown eyes, yellow complexion; occupation blacksmith; enlisted as Frank Brock 1 Jul 1885, age 22, Cleveland, OH; assigned to F/25th Infantry; arrived Ft Snelling, MN, 12 Apr 1886. SOURCE: Descriptive & Assignment Rolls of Recruits, 25 Inf.

POSEY, John; Private; F/24th Inf. ‡Died of abscess of liver, Dagupan, Luzon, Philippines, 2 Jul 1901. SOURCE: *ANJ* 38 (24 Aug 1901): 1256.

Died in the Philippines 2 Jul 1901; buried in plot NA 1197 at San Francisco National Cemetery. SOURCE: San Francisco National Cemetery.

POSY; Private; F/10th Cav. Had horse shot out from under him in fight against Indians, Saline River, KS, 2 Aug 1867. SOURCE: Schubert, *Voices of the Buffalo Soldier*, 13.

POTTS, Benjamin F.; QM Sgt; 10th Cav. Sgt. Ben Potts, I/10th Cavalry, stationed at Bonita Cañon Camp, AZ, 30 Jun 1886. SOURCE: Tagg, *The Camp at Bonita Cañon*, 231.

‡Private, I/10th Cavalry, at Ft Apache, AZ, 1890, subscribed $.25 to testimonial to General Grierson. SOURCE: List of subscriptions, 23 Apr 1890, 10th Cavalry papers, MHI.

‡Served as sergeant, I/10th Cavalry, in Cuba, 1898. SOURCE: Cashin, *Under Fire with the Tenth Cavalry*, 347.

‡Retired as quartermaster sergeant, 10th Cavalry, Jan 1901. SOURCE: *ANJ* 38 (2 Feb 1901): 547.

POWELL; Private; D/10th Cav. Drunk and disorderly on parade ground at Ft Davis, TX, Dec 1884. SOURCE: Bigelow, *Garrison Tangles*, 33.

POWELL, G. D.; Sergeant; C/24th Inf. Died 14 Apr 1890; originally buried at Ft Grant, AZ; reburied at Santa Fe National Cemetery, NM, plot A-1 737. SOURCE: Santa Fe National Cemetery, Records of Burials.

POWELL, Robert; Private; K/9th Cav. Died 31 Aug 1908; buried in plot NAWS 1310 at San Francisco National Cemetery. SOURCE: San Francisco National Cemetery.

POWELL, Toby; Private; E/25th Inf. Died at Ft Davis, TX, on 10 May 1877; buried at San Antonio National Cemetery, Section I, number 1491. SOURCE: San Antonio National Cemetery Locator.

POWERS, Alfred; Private; D/10th Cav. ‡Original member of 10th Cavalry; in troop when organized, Ft Leavenworth, KS, 1 Jun 1867. SOURCE: McMiller, "Buffalo Soldiers," 71.

Died 1 Sep 1867 of cholera at Ft Gibson, OK. SOURCE: Regimental Returns, 10th Cavalry, 1867.

POWERS, William A.; Chief Trumpeter; 10th Cav. Died 9 Feb 1890; reburied 14 Mar 1932 at Santa Fe National Cemetery, NM, plot P 129. SOURCE: Santa Fe National Cemetery, Records of Burials.

PRATER, Lonie; Private; 9th Cav. Received Philippine Campaign Badge number 11741 for service as private, E/9th Cavalry; in 9th Cavalry at Ft Leavenworth, KS, Mar 1905. SOURCE: Philippine Campaign Badge list, 29 May 1905.

PRATHER, W. H.; Private; I/9th Cav. ‡Poem regarding Pine Ridge campaign, 1891. SOURCE: Foner, *The United States Soldier*, 135.

Text of two of his poems published. SOURCE: Schubert, *Voices of the Buffalo Soldier*, 170–72.

PRATT, Richard; Private; G/25th Inf. Born in Church Hill, MD; Ht 5'4", black hair and brown eyes, brown complexion; occupation soldier; discharged from C/10th Cavalry, 2 Dec 1885; fourth reenlistment, 11 Jan 1886, age 39, at Baltimore, MD; assigned to G/25th Infantry; arrived Ft Snelling, MN, 12 Apr 1886. SOURCE: Descriptive & Assignment Rolls of Recruits, 25 Inf.

PRESTER, Daniel; Private; C/25th Inf. Died at Ft Stockton, TX, on 5 May 1880; buried at San Antonio National Cemetery, Section C, number 344. SOURCE: San Antonio National Cemetery Locator.

PRESTON, Lloyd; Private; E/10th Cav. In Troop E/10th Cavalry stationed at Bonita Cañon Camp, AZ, but absent or on detached service 28 Feb 1886. SOURCE: Tagg, *The Camp at Bonita Cañon*, 232.

PRESTON, Perry; Private; E/10th Cav. Died 23 Mar 1881 of pneumonia at Ft Concho, TX. SOURCE: Regimental Returns, 10th Cavalry, 1881.

PRESTON, William; Private; 25th Inf. Born in Havre de Grace, MD; Ht 5'6", black hair and brown eyes, brown complexion; occupation laborer; enlisted at age 22, Baltimore, MD, 3 Apr 1886; arrived Ft Snelling, MN, 19 Aug 1886. SOURCE: Descriptive & Assignment Rolls of Recruits, 25 Inf.

PREWIT, David; Private; D/9th Cav. With Captain Dodge at battle at Milk River, CO, 2–10 Oct 1879. SOURCE: Miller, *Hollow Victory*, 167, 206–7.

PRICE, Brady D.; Private; G/9th Cav. Received Philippine Campaign Badge number 11841 for service as private in G/25th Infantry, 28 Mar 1901–15 Sep 1902; private in G/9th Cavalry, Ft Leavenworth, KS, Mar 1905. SOURCE: Philippine Campaign Badge Recipients; Philippine Campaign Badge list, 29 May 1905.

PRICE, George; Private; G/48th Inf. Died 1 Jul 1901; buried in plot E SID1238 at San Francisco National Cemetery. SOURCE: San Francisco National Cemetery.

PRICE, Joseph; Private; A/9th Cav. ‡On daily duty at post garden, Ft Robinson, NE. SOURCE: Order 48, 10 Mar 1890, Post Orders, Ft Robinson.

‡At Ft Robinson, 1892.

Private, received Indian Wars Campaign Badge number 672 on 21 Oct 1908. SOURCE: Carroll, *Indian Wars Campaign Badge*, 19.

PRICE, Moses; Private; C/10th Cav. Drowned 15 Oct 1873 at Clear Fork, TX. SOURCE: Regimental Returns, 10th Cavalry, 1873.

Died at Ft Griffin, TX, on 15 Oct 1873; buried at San Antonio National Cemetery, Section D, number 655. SOURCE: San Antonio National Cemetery Locator.

PRIDE, Alfred; Private; K/9th Cav. ‡Born and reared at Amelia Court House, VA, near Richmond; occupation laborer; ran away from home at age 16; enlisted Washington, DC, 1865; appointed sergeant, Ft Robinson, NE, K/9th Cavalry, 1 Jul 1888; married Matilda Hawkins of Washington, age 32, in Washington, 5 May 1898; first marriage for both; resided in Washington thirty years. SOURCE: VA File WC 10020, Alfred Pride.

‡Private, B/10th Cavalry, transferred to Ft Sill, IT. SOURCE: Special Order 57, HQ, Det 10 Cav, Camp Supply, Indian Territory, 10 Aug 1869.

At Ft Duncan, TX, 1877, with assistance of Lt. John Bigelow wrote letter of complaint to paymaster about not receiving pay for six months. SOURCE: Kinevan, *Frontier Cavalryman*, 60–61.

‡Sergeant, K/9th Cavalry, and sergeant of guard, Ft Robinson, when he allowed prisoner to escape and was reduced to private and fined $20: "But for his long service and good character the sentence would have been more severe." SOURCE: *ANJ* 28 (8 Nov 1890): 120.

‡Retires as private, K/9th Cavalry. SOURCE: SO 70, AGO, 25 Mar 1898.

‡Widow Matilda Pride received $12 per month pension as of 4 Mar 1917; resided at 2600 I Street, NW, Washington, when she died 20 Mar 1928 with a pension of $30 per month; late husband served in B/10th Cavalry, F/24th Infantry, 1878–83, and K/9th Cavalry, 1883–98; he died of apoplexy in Washington, 2 Aug 1910; buried at Arlington Cemetery, 5 Aug 1910. SOURCE: VA File WC 10020, Alfred Pride.

‡Survived by brother George Allen Pride, messenger, Department of the Treasury, 1237 22nd Street, NW, Washington; also brother John Henry Pride, blacksmith, Amelia Court House; brother Moses, laborer, 1411 Massachusetts Avenue, NW, Washington; sister Marcella, wife of laborer Charles Helm, U.S. Navy Yard, Washington; sister Mary Ann, wife of farmer Eugene Morton, Rumney, NH. SOURCE: VA File WC 10020, Alfred Pride.

PRIEST, I. A.; Chief Musician; 25th Inf. Died at Ft Clark, TX, on 8 Aug 1870; buried at Fort Sam Houston National Cemetery, Section PE, number 12. SOURCE: Buffalo Soldiers Interred in Fort Sam Houston National Cemetery.

PRIESTLY, Joseph A.; Private; L/10th Cav. ‡Served in 10th Cavalry, 1898; remained in U.S. during war with Spain. SOURCE: Cashin, *Under Fire with the Tenth Cavalry*, 350.

Died on 19 Mar 1899; buried at San Antonio National Cemetery, Section I, number 1684. SOURCE: San Antonio National Cemetery Locator.

PRINGLE, Edward; Corporal; I/9th Cav. Served during operations against "boomers" in Indian Territory, 1884. SOURCE: Kenner, *Buffalo Soldiers and Officers of the Ninth Cavalry*, 200.

PRIOLEAU, George W.; Chaplain; U.S. Army. ‡Born in Charleston, SC; educated at Claflin College; taught in public schools; graduated from Wilberforce University in 1884; entered Army as captain, 9th Cavalry, 1895; transferred to 10th Cavalry, 1915; transferred to 25th Infantry, 1916; promoted to major, 9 Aug 1917. SOURCE: *Crisis* 16 (May 1918): 15.

‡Born a slave in Charleston, 15 May 1856; now on second tour of duty in the Philippines, Camp McGrath, Batangas. SOURCE: *Colored American Magazine* 16 (Apr 1909): 224.

‡Parents L. S. and Susan Prolix, slaves; educated in public schools of Charleston and Avery Institute; attended Claflin College, Orangeburg, SC, 1875; taught primary public school, Lyons Township, Orangeburg Co., SC; joined African Methodist Episcopal Church, of which father was pastor, St. Mathews, SC; joined Columbia, SC, conference, Dec 1879; sent to Wilberforce, Dec 1880; retired as oldest ranking chaplain in Army. SOURCE: Beasley, *Negro Trailblazers*, 292–93.

‡Taught in public schools, Selma, OH, Sep 1884–Sep 1885; pastor, Hamilton, OH, 1885, and Troy, OH, 1887; organized William H. Carney Lodge, No. 89, Grand Union of Odd Fellows; doctor of divinity, Payne Theological Seminary, 1895, which he disclaimed before preaching baccalaureate sermon at Wilberforce, 1910, due to his high conception of meaning of degree and prevailing abuse of it. SOURCE: Wright, *Centennial Encyclopedia of the AME Church*, 181.

‡Under administration of President B. F. Lee, Wilberforce University graduated a "brilliant galaxy of cultured young men and women," including Prolix, now chaplain of 9th Cavalry. SOURCE: Richings, *Evidences of Progress among Colored People*, 107.

‡"Among the many [Wilberforce graduates] who have reached eminence." SOURCE: Hartshorne, *An Era of Progress and Promise*, 281.

‡Troy minister, just returned from "very pleasant" visit to Indianapolis. SOURCE: Cleveland *Gazette*, 2 Jun 1888.

‡Wife Anna L. Scovell, B.S., Wilberforce, 1885; earned diploma from Wilberforce Normal Department, 1890. SOURCE: Cleveland *Gazette*, 28 Jun 1890.

‡Professor of Theology and Homiletics, Wilberforce; taught historical and pastoral theology at Payne Theological Seminary, formerly Theology Department, Wilberforce, 1890–94; resigned to take chaplaincy. SOURCE: McGinnis, *A History and an Interpretation of Wilberforce University*, 143–44.

‡In Wilberforce, OH, after extended tour of the South. SOURCE: Cleveland *Gazette*, 16 Dec 1892.

‡Preached sermon from Judges, Chapter 14, Verse 14, at Congregational Church, Crawford, NE, Sunday, 24 Jan 1897, "most ably and eloquently." SOURCE: Crawford *Tribune*, 29 Jan 1897.

‡Letter from Ft Robinson, NE, 8 Feb 1897, states pay and benefits. SOURCE: Cleveland *Gazette*, 20 Feb 1897.

‡Authorized one and one-half month's leave from Ft Robinson as of 15 Jul 1897. SOURCE: *ANJ* 34 (10 Jul 1897): 838.

‡Author of "Is the Chaplain's Work in the Army a Necessity?" in Steward, *Active Service*. SOURCE: Indianapolis *Freeman*, 11 Sep 1897.

‡Letter from Ft Robinson describes military routine and opportunities for black men. SOURCE: Cleveland *Gazette*, 5 Mar 1898.

‡Letters from Tampa, FL, 13 May 1898, regarding racism there; from Montauk, NY, Sep 1898; from Ft Grant, AZ, Oct 1898, on spread of Negrophobia. SOURCE: Gatewood, *"Smoked Yankees,"* 27–29, 74–75, 82–84.

‡Bedridden with malaria and remained in Tampa when 9th Cavalry went to Cuba (SOURCE: SO 55, 9 Cav, 13 May 1898); on regimental recruiting duty, Orangeburg (SOURCE: SO 14, 9 Cav, 14 May 1898). SOURCE: Cashin, *Under Fire with the Tenth Cavalry*, 110.

‡Relieved of regimental recruiting duty, Charleston, and directed to join portion of regiment in Florida. SOURCE: *ANJ* 35 (6 Aug 1898): 1009.

‡Letter from Ft Grant, AZ, Nov 1898, praises *Gazette*'s consistent stand against "lynching and mobocracy." SOURCE: Cleveland *Gazette*, 26 Nov 1898.

Text of Aug 1899 letter to Cleveland *Gazette* discussing Jim Crow railroad accommodations. SOURCE: Schubert, *Voices of the Buffalo Soldier*, 214–16.

‡On leave in New Orleans: "We glory in the prestige won by our regiments." SOURCE: *ANJ* 36 (29 Jul 1899): 1138

‡Letter from New Orleans, no date: went there on leave from Ft Grant; at El Paso, TX, forced onto Jim Crow car with "greasy Mexicans"; Southern Pacific Railroad yielded to his demand to travel without such company and hitched a separate car on the train for him. SOURCE: Cleveland *Gazette*, 19 Aug 1899.

‡Letter from New Orleans, no date, regarding subjugation of black Americans: "Strange that the American people fail to learn the lesson of their own independence." SOURCE: Cleveland *Gazette*, 26 Aug 1899.

‡Letter, dated "Jim Crow Car, Texas," 25 Aug 1899: wife not well enough to leave New Orleans; has railroad car all to himself on return to Ft Grant; breakfasted with whites in Alpine, TX, this morning. SOURCE: Cleveland *Gazette*, 9 Sep 1899.

‡Letter, Ft Grant, 21 May 1900, informs of new law authorizing thirty dentists for regular Army, at least four of whom should be black; War Department should know "we are up again for recognition in the Army." SOURCE: Cleveland *Gazette*, 2 Jun 1900.

‡As of 31 Dec 1900 on duty with regiment, Nueva Caceres, Philippines. SOURCE: Hamilton, "History of the Ninth Cavalry," 100.

‡En route home to New Orleans from the Philippines, writes that "there is greater pacification among the Filipinos where our troops are stationed and that the natives will fight most fiercely white troops but will welcome our troops without resistance." SOURCE: Cleveland *Gazette*, 12 Apr 1902.

‡First wife, Annie L. Prioleau, race mixed, born in New Orleans to Noah Scovell and Lucy A. Flowers, 18 Dec 1862, occupation teacher, died of uremia, 26 Feb 1903. SOURCE: VA File C 1392575, George W. Prioleau.

‡Wife died at Ft Walla Walla, WA, 26 Feb 1903; to be buried at New Orleans. SOURCE: Cleveland *Gazette*, 21 Mar 1903.

‡Aaron R. Prioleau defrauded out of congressional seat, 1st District, South Carolina, by George S. Legare; "though a Negro, is the rightful claimant." SOURCE: Indianapolis *Freeman*, 20 Feb 1904.

‡Aaron R. Prioleau is related to Chaplain Prioleau and "a successful farmer, merchant, & miller." SOURCE: Indianapolis *Freeman*, 12 Aug 1905.

‡Married Miss Ethel Stafford of Kansas City, KS, 20 Feb 1905; three children; first wife died 27 Feb 1902 [*sic*]; thirty-third degree Mason and member of Odd Fellows and Knights of Pythias; owns "an elegant modern home" at Raymond and West 35th Place, Los Angeles, where he will reside, and other valuable properties. SOURCE: Beasley, *Negro Trailblazers*, 293.

‡To conduct service, Cheyenne, WY, African Methodist Episcopal Church, Sunday, 15 Aug 1909. SOURCE: Cheyenne *Daily Leader*, 15 Aug 1909.

‡Veteran of Philippine Insurrection; at Ft D. A. Russell, WY, in 1910; sharpshooter. SOURCE: *Illustrated Review: Ninth Cavalry*, with picture.

‡Mentioned. SOURCE: Work, *Negro Year Book, 1912*, 77, and *Negro Yearbook, 1918–1919*, 228.

‡To be transferred from 10th Cavalry to 25th Infantry and stationed in Hawaii. SOURCE: Cleveland *Gazette*, 10 Jun 1916.

‡Promoted to major as of 9 Aug 1917; reports that 25th Infantry has collected $3,200 for National Association for the Advancement of Colored People, $325 of that amount

for refugees from East St. Louis, IL. SOURCE: Cleveland *Gazette*, 6 Oct 1917.

‡Retired chaplain, resides in Los Angeles. SOURCE: Work, *The Negro Yearbook, 1925–1926*, 253.

‡Organized Bethel African Methodist Episcopal Church, Los Angeles. SOURCE: *Encyclopedia of African Methodism*, 175.

‡Daughter Ethel Suzanna born 21 Jun 1914; son George Wesley born 18 Mar 1917, Kapiolani Maternity Home, Honolulu, HI; daughter Lois Emma born 18 Jun 1924, Los Angeles; retired as major on 15 May 1920 with continuous service since 29 Apr 1895; resided at 1311 West 35th Street, Los Angeles, when he died in Jul 1927; on death, widow received $8,018 in U.S. Government Life Insurance; widow's pension $22.50 per month in 1934, with $4.50 additional for one minor child. SOURCE: VA File C 1392575, George W. Prioleau.

‡Biographical sketch. SOURCE: Logan and Winston, eds., *Dictionary of American Negro Biography*, 13–14; Stover, *Up from Handymen*, 53–57.

Career mentioned. SOURCE: Dobak and Phillips, *The Black Regulars*, 117, 119.

PROCTOR, Charles R.; Private; 9th Cav. Received Philippine Campaign Badge number 11895 for service as private, H/9th Cavalry; in 9th Cavalry at Ft Leavenworth, KS, Mar 1905. SOURCE: Philippine Campaign Badge list, 29 May 1905.

PROCTOR, Ernest; Private; B/24th Inf. Died 6 Oct 1896; originally buried at Ft Grant, AZ; reburied at Santa Fe National Cemetery, NM, plot A-1 795; also recorded as Ernest Procter and Earnest Proctor. SOURCE: Santa Fe National Cemetery, Records of Burials.

PROCTOR, John C.; Color Sgt; 9th Cav. ‡Born in Prince Georges Co., MD; occupation laborer; yellow complexion; enlisted in L/10th Cavalry, age 21, 6 Dec 1881; reenlisted 13 Dec 1886; transferred to A/10th Cavalry, 15 Feb 1891; reenlisted as sergeant, I/9th Cavalry, 17 Dec 1891; reenlisted 17 Dec 1896; discharged as first sergeant, I/9th Cavalry, 19 Jul 1898; first lieutenant, 8th Volunteer Infantry, 4 Aug 1898–6 Mar 1899; enlisted as corporal, I/9th Cavalry, 14 Jun 1899; enlisted as first sergeant, E/24th Infantry, 16 Jun 1902; reenlisted as sergeant, C/9th Cavalry, 17 Jun 1905; reenlisted 18 Feb 1907; appointed color sergeant, 9th Cavalry, 14 Jun 1908; retired 17 Sep 1908; resided at 113 Howard Avenue, Anacostia, Washington, DC; died 24 Jun 1917. SOURCE: VA File XC 2659372, John C. Proctor.

‡Appointed sergeant, I/9th Cavalry, 13 Oct 1892. SOURCE: Roster, 9 Cav.

‡Resides with wife, one white adopted child, and Ella Johnson, on Laundress Row, Ft Robinson, NE, Aug 1893. SOURCE: Medical History, Ft Robinson.

‡Ranked number 4 in revolver competition, Departments of the East, the Platte, and California, Bellevue, NE, as sergeant, I/9th Cavalry. SOURCE: GO 82, AGO, 24 Oct 1893.

‡Mrs. Proctor "has been a trouble to the commanding officer" on several occasions; this time she hid a woman of bad character in her quarters. SOURCE: CO, Ft Robinson, to CO, I/9, Ft Robinson, 23 Dec 1894, LS, Ft Robinson.

Appointed sergeant 13 Oct 1892; in I/9th Cavalry at Ft Washakie, WY, Jan 1897. SOURCE: Ninth Cavalry, Roster of NCOs, 1897.

‡First sergeant, I/9th Cavalry, at Ft Robinson, for cavalry competition, Sep 1897.

‡First sergeant, A/9th Cavalry, commissioned first lieutenant, 8th Volunteer Infantry, after Spanish-American War. SOURCE: Cashin, *Under Fire with the Tenth Cavalry*, 360, with picture, 356.

‡Commissioned for gallantry and meritorious service around Santiago, Cuba, 1–2 Jul 1898. SOURCE: Thweatt, *What the Newspapers Say*, 9; Richmond *Planet*, 13 Aug 1898; Johnson, *History of Negro Soldiers*, 50.

‡Lieutenant, 8th Volunteer Infantry; had a white "hill billy" put in guardhouse for failure to salute, Chickamauga, TN. SOURCE: Indianapolis *Freeman*, 24 Dec 1898.

‡To report for duty as captain, F/49th Infantry, at Jefferson Bks, MO. SOURCE: *ANJ* 37 (30 Sep 1899): 101.

‡Private, saddler, farrier, corporal, sergeant, L and A/10th Cavalry, 6 Dec 1881–12 Dec 1891; private, farrier, corporal, sergeant, and first sergeant, I/9th Cavalry; first lieutenant, 8th Volunteer Infantry, 29 Jul 1898–6 Mar 1899; private, sergeant, first sergeant, I/9th Cavalry, 14 Jun 1899–present, on furlough; captain, 49th Infantry, 9 Sep 1899. SOURCE: Descriptive Book, F/49 Inf.

One of twenty-three officers of 49th Infantry recommended as regular Army second lieutenants. SOURCE: CG, DivPI, Manila, 8 Feb 1901, to AGO, AGO File 355163.

‡Quartermaster sergeant, E/24th Infantry, ranked number 1, Northern Division rifle team, Ft Sheridan, IL, 1904; awarded gold medal. SOURCE: GO 167, AGO, 28 Oct 1904.

‡Resided at 1019 North 21st Street, Omaha, NE, in 1904.

‡Louisa Proctor, age 59, resided at 2124 North 27th Avenue, Omaha, in 1920, was twice married to John Proctor: "I am not going to tell why I married him twice"; first married him, Crawford, NE, around 1900; last saw Proctor in Omaha, Dec 1909; divorced at Washington, DC, 1912; had no children; raised boy named Claude who died 15 Oct 1919; previously married at age 16 to Henry Chambers, F/24th Infantry, Ft Elliott, TX; resided together seven to eight years; he got divorce. SOURCE: Affidavit, Louisa Proctor, 28 May 1920, VA File XC 2659372, John C. Proctor.

‡Widow Martha E. Proctor born in Oxon Hill, MD, 22 Aug 1878; parents Alexander Butler and Georgianna

Locker; no previous marriages; resided at 1055 Sumner Road, Anacostia, Washington, DC, and worked as laborer in 1920; resided at 2603 12th Place, SE, Washington, in 1957; pension increased from $40 to $48 per month, 19 Feb 1951; died 18 Jun 1957; survived by sister, Sarah Waters. SOURCE: VA File SC 2659372, John C. Proctor.

See **SMITH**, Jacob Clay, Saddler Sergeant, 10th Cavalry; **WATKINS**, James M., Quartermaster Sergeant, C/10th Cavalry

PROCTOR, William; Private; I/10th Cav. In Troop I/10th Cavalry stationed at Bonita Cañon Camp, AZ, 30 Jun 1886. SOURCE: Tagg, *The Camp at Bonita Cañon*, 232.

PROCTOR, William; Private; B/25th Inf. Private, B/25th Infantry, rode in 25th Infantry Bicycle Corps, Ft. Missoula, MT, summer 1896. SOURCE: Sorenson, List of Buffalo Soldiers Who Rode in the 25th Infantry Bicycle Corps, in authors' files.

One of twenty men who cycled 1,900 miles from Ft Missoula to St. Louis, MO, 14 Jun–24 Jul 1897, in 25th Infantry Bicycle Corps to test durability and practicality of bicycles as a means of transportation for troops. SOURCE: File 60178, GC, AGO Records.

PROFFETT, Shannon; Private; I/25th Inf. ‡Murdered by comrade in the Philippines, 22 Jul 1900. SOURCE: *ANJ* 37 (4 Aug 1900): 1166.

‡Killed with .45-caliber pistol by Pvt. John H. Smith, H/25th Infantry, San Felipe, Zambales, Philippines, 23 Jul 1900. SOURCE: Manila *Times*, 31 Jul 1900.

‡Native of Xenia, OH; shot and killed by Private Smith, H/25th Infantry; both "noted for reckless bravery and daring," got into gambling dispute. SOURCE: Richmond *Planet*, 20 Oct 1900.

Pvt. Shannon Proffitt, I/25th Infantry, died in the Philippines, 25 Jul 1900; body received for burial 15 Apr 1902 at San Francisco National Cemetery, buried 20 Jun 1902 in plot N ADD996. SOURCE: San Francisco National Cemetery.

PROFFITT, Shannon; Private; I/25th Inf. *See* **PROFFETT**, Shannon, Private, I/25th Infantry

PRUETT, Hugh; Private; G/38th Inf. Died 21 Jul 1867; buried at Ft Leavenworth National Cemetery, plot 3385. SOURCE: Ft Leavenworth National Cemetery.

PRYOR, James; Private; K/24th Inf. ‡Drowned in the Philippines, 28 Feb 1900. SOURCE: *ANJ* 37 (10 Mar 1900): 659.

Private, K/24th Infantry; died 28 Feb 1900; buried in plot E.S 1271 at San Francisco National Cemetery. SOURCE: San Francisco National Cemetery.

PUGH, Alvin; Pvt 1st Cl; F/25th Inf. ‡Private first class, 24th Infantry; served in Houston, TX, 1917; tried unsuccessfully at court martial to establish alibi for being off post during riot; sentenced to two years. SOURCE: Haynes, *A Night of Violence*, 268, 271.

Private first class, F/25th Infantry; died 6 May 1938; buried in plot E-EAS1702 at San Francisco National Cemetery. SOURCE: San Francisco National Cemetery.

PUMPHREY, George W.; Sergeant; H/9th Cav. ‡Recognized as deserter from B/9th Cavalry while serving with K/9th Cavalry, Ft Robinson, NE, as George Hunter and confined, Jan 1886. SOURCE: Post Returns, Ft Robinson.

‡Restored to duty in accordance with General Court Martial Order 7, Department of the Platte, 22 Jan 1886.

‡Transferred to K/9th Cavalry by Special Order 102, Adjutant General's Office, 1 May 1886.

‡Complains that his captain curses and abuses the men and that they are poorly fed, seldom having more than coffee and bread for supper. SOURCE: Report of Inspection, Ft Robinson, 2 Aug 1888, Reports of Inspections, DP, I.

‡Private, H/9th Cavalry; authorized to reenlist as married soldier by letter, Adjutant General's Office, 16 Feb 1897.

Deposited with paymaster, Ft Robinson, $167 in 1897 and $40 in 1898.

‡Cited for gallantry in action, Cuba, 1 Jul 1898. SOURCE: SecWar, *AR 1898*, 708.

As corporal in H/9th Cavalry, awarded certificate of merit for distinguished service in battle, Santiago, Cuba, 1 Jul 1898. SOURCE: Gleim, *The Certificate of Merit*, 45.

‡Awarded certificate of merit for gallantry as corporal, H/9th Cavalry, 1 Jul 1898. SOURCE: GO 16, AGO, 13 Feb 1900; *ANJ* 37 (24 Feb 1900): 611; Steward, *The Colored Regulars*, 280.

‡Born in Anne Arundel Co., MD; awarded Distinguished Service Medal for gallantry, Santiago, Cuba, 1 Jul 1898. SOURCE: Koger, *The Maryland Negro in Our Wars*, 23.

Born in Anne Arundel County, MD; resided Baltimore, MD; received Distinguished Service Medal in lieu of certificate of merit. SOURCE: *American Decorations*, 842.

Received Philippine Campaign Badge number 11861 for service as sergeant, H/9th Cavalry; in 9th Cavalry at Ft Leavenworth, KS, Mar 1905. SOURCE: Philippine Campaign Badge list, 29 May 1905.

PUMPHREY, James H.; Sergeant; K/9th Cav. J. H. Pumphrey, native of Maryland, veteran of two years, stationed at Ft Robinson, NE, when he was involved in saloon brawl, Crawford, NE, Feb 1887, along with Pvts. Lee Irving and Henry Chase; convicted by court martial and confined for six months; objected to presence on court of 2nd Lt. William McAnaney because of McAnaney's derogatory remarks about black soldiers. SOURCE: Kenner, *Buffalo Soldiers and Officers of the Ninth Cavalry*, 150–51, 168.

‡J. H. Pumphrey, saddler, B/10th Cavalry, at Ft Apache, AZ, 1890, subscribed $.50 to testimonial to General Grierson. SOURCE: List of subscriptions, 23 Apr 1890, 10th Cavalry papers, MHI.

‡J. H. Pumphrey promoted to lance corporal from private, Ft Robinson, Feb 1895. SOURCE: *ANJ* 32 (9 Mar 1895): 454.

Appointed corporal 24 Feb 1895; in K/9th Cavalry at Ft Robinson, Jan 1897. SOURCE: Ninth Cavalry, Roster of NCOs, 1897.

Sergeant, H/10th Cavalry, received Indian Wars Campaign Badge number 540 on 16 Apr 1909. SOURCE: Carroll, *Indian Wars Campaign Badge*, 15.

PURNELL, George; Pvt 1st Cl; Supply Troop/9th Cav. ‡Private, M/9th Cavalry, at Ft D. A. Russell, WY, in 1910. SOURCE: *Illustrated Review: Ninth Cavalry*, with picture.

Private first class, Supply Troop/9th Cavalry; died 11 Jun 1921; buried in plot A 147 at San Francisco National Cemetery. SOURCE: San Francisco National Cemetery.

PURNELL, William Whipple; Captain; 48th Inf. ‡Born in Philadelphia, PA, 25 Jan 1869; son of James W. and Julia A. Purnell; attended Howard University Normal and Preparatory Departments, 1880–85; graduated from pharmacy school, Howard University, 1890, and medical school, Howard University, 1893; assistant instructor, eyes, ears, nose, and throat, Howard University, 1893–98; first lieutenant and assistant surgeon, 8th Volunteer Infantry, and captain, surgeon, 48th Infantry; a leading Negro physician of San Francisco area with "a rapidly growing practice among Italians, Spanish and members of his own race"; married Miss Theodora Lee of Chicago, granddaughter of late John Jones, 1895; son Lee Julian educated at Berkeley, CA, high school and University of California, will graduate as electrical engineer, 1914; member of Oakland Chamber of Commerce; an organizer of Elks Lodge, director of Knights of Pythias, member of Foresters and Masons; wife an organizer of Florence Nightingale Auxiliary, Oakland Red Cross, "devoted member" of St Augustin Mission of Episcopal Church and on Old Folks Home executive board. SOURCE: Beasley, *Negro Trailblazers*, 300.

‡Resident of Omaha, NE. SOURCE: Indianapolis *Freeman*, 30 Sep 1899.

‡Mentioned. SOURCE: San Francisco *Chronicle*, 15 Nov 1899.

Died 2 Jan 1935; buried in plot OSA 3 PLOT 1 at San Francisco National Cemetery. SOURCE: San Francisco National Cemetery.

Q

QUARLES, John; Private; L/9th Cav. Died 27 Apr 1916; buried in plot WEST 839-A at San Francisco National Cemetery. SOURCE: San Francisco National Cemetery.

QUEEN, Edgar; Private; Hospital Corps. ‡Born in Prince William Co., VA; Ht 5'7"; enlisted Washington, DC, age 26, 28 Jul 1892; five years' previous service in K/9th Cavalry; joined H/9th Cavalry, Ft DuChesne, UT, 10 Oct 1892; deserted from Ft Robinson, NE, 30 Dec 1894; surrendered at Omaha, NE, 5 Mar 1895; sentenced by general court martial to six months' confinement and loss of pay; fined twice by summary courts, Ft Robinson, 1896; discharged without character, end of term, single, Ft Robinson, 2 Oct 1897. SOURCE: Descriptive Book, H/9 Cav.

‡Letter, Department of the Platte, 25 Mar 1895, concerns charges against Queen.

‡Returned to duty at Ft Robinson from furlough, 24 Sep 1898.

Private, Hospital Corps, received Indian Wars Campaign Badge number 873 on 11 Jan 1909. SOURCE: Carroll, *Indian Wars Campaign Badge*, 25.

R

RAILY, Andrew; Private; 9th Cav. At Ft McKavett, TX, 1870, confined for six months for drunkenness on duty. SOURCE: Dobak and Phillips, *The Black Regulars*, 165.

RAINS, Henry R.; Private; 10th Cav. Died 17 Jul 1908 while on detached duty; buried at Ft Bayard, NM, in plot Q 18. SOURCE: "Fort Bayard National Cemetery, Records of Burials."

H. R. (Henry) Raines died while on detached duty; buried 17 Jul 1908, section B, row B, plot 18, at Ft Bayard. SOURCE: Erickson, Burials at Fort Bayard National Cemetery, NM.

RALPY, Andrew; M/9th Cav. Born in Kentucky; black complexion; cannot read or write, age 22, Jul 1870, at Ft McKavett, TX. SOURCE: Bierschwale, *Fort McKavett*, 100.

RAMLER, Edmond; Private; U.S. Army. Seminole Negro Scout, served in 1894. SOURCE: NARA, M 929, Roll 2.

RAMSEY, Henry; Private; 9th Cav. Received Philippine Campaign Badge for service as private in B/9th Cavalry; in 9th Cavalry at Ft Leavenworth, KS, Mar 1905. SOURCE: Philippine Campaign Badge list, 29 May 1905.

RAMSEY, Horace W.; Private; 24th Inf. Served in 1880s. SOURCE: Dobak and Phillips, *The Black Regulars*, 186.

RANDALL, Wesley; Private; A/48th Inf. Died in the Philippines 4 Feb 1900; buried in plot 751 at San Francisco National Cemetery. SOURCE: San Francisco National Cemetery.

RANDOLPH, Adolphus; E/10th Cav. Civil War veteran; also used name Lewis Todd; served in Independent Battery, U.S. Colored Light Artillery; served in E/10th Cavalry, 1869–71. SOURCE: *Organization Index to Pension Files*.

RANDOLPH, F. B.; Sergeant; G/10th Cav. Murdered 12 Jan 1868 at Junction City, KS. SOURCE: Regimental Returns, 10th Cavalry, 1868.

RANDOLPH, James; Sergeant; L/9th Cav. ‡Attacked twenty-four cattle thieves near Havana Ranch, TX, capturing one and scattering rest, Nov 1874. SOURCE: Hamilton, "History of the Ninth Cavalry," 21.

At Ft Ringgold, TX, 1874; led patrol of three privates, surprised party of rustlers, captured one, scattered others, Nov 1874; dishonorably discharged Mar 1879 for stealing five sacks of corn. SOURCE: Kenner, *Buffalo Soldiers and Officers of the Ninth Cavalry*, 178–79.

RANDOLPH, William; General Prisoner; L/25th Inf. Died 30 Nov 1916; buried in New Addition West Wide, plot 186 at San Francisco National Cemetery. SOURCE: San Francisco National Cemetery.

RANKINS, Marcus; Private; I/10th Cav. Died 22 Jun 1873 of disease at Ft Richardson, TX. SOURCE: Regimental Returns, 10th Cavalry, 1873.

Died at Ft Richardson on 22 Jun 1873; buried at San Antonio National Cemetery, Section D, number 609. SOURCE: San Antonio National Cemetery Locator.

RATCLIFF, Toney; QM Sgt; 10th Cav. ‡Toney Ratcliff, original member of E/10th Cavalry; in troop when organized, Ft Leavenworth, KS, 15 Jun 1867. SOURCE: McMiller, "Buffalo Soldiers."

Quartermaster sergeant, recommended for reenlistment as "a good soldier, and . . . an intelligent man" by Capt. Louis Carpenter, 1875. SOURCE: Dobak and Phillips, *The Black Regulars*, 60.

RAY; Private; E/10th Cav. Private Abner Wooded, E/10th Cavalry, died 23 Dec 1880 from wounds inflicted by Private Ray at Grierson Springs, TX. SOURCE: Regimental Returns, 10th Cavalry, 1880.

RAY, Albert; Sergeant; 25th Inf. At Ft Snelling, MN, 1885. SOURCE: Dobak and Phillips, *The Black Regulars*, 147.

‡First sergeant, F/25th Infantry, at Ft Shaw, MT; to be discharged in accordance with Special Order, Adjutant General's Office, 2 Jun 1890. SOURCE: *ANJ* 27 (7 Jun 1890): 775.

RAY, Alfred M.; QM Sgt. ‡Born in Tennessee; private, saddler sergeant, first sergeant, F/10th Cavalry, 17 May 1872–16 May 1882; private, 13 Feb 1885; corporal, 1 Jul 1885; sergeant, 15 Dec 1885; at Ft Assiniboine, MT, 1897. SOURCE: Baker, Roster.

‡Born in Washington Co., TN, 16 May 1856; in 10th Cavalry, 1872–82, 1885–98; first lieutenant, 10th Volunteer Infantry, 2 Aug 1898–8 Mar 1899; color sergeant, 10th Cavalry, in Cuba, 1898; second lieutenant, L/49th Infantry, 9 Sep 1899; first lieutenant, 10 Oct 1900; transferred to H/49th Infantry, 20 Dec 1900; wife resides in Jonesboro, TN. SOURCE: Descriptive Book, L/49th Inf.

‡Color sergeant, 10th Cavalry, 1897; quartermaster sergeant, F/10th Cavalry, 1898; commissioned first lieutenant, 10th Volunteer Infantry, after Spanish-American War; served in regiment, Aug 1898–Mar 1899. SOURCE: *ANJ* 37 (4 Nov 1899): 219; Cashin, *Under Fire with the Tenth Cavalry*, 360.

‡Color sergeant, 10th Cavalry. SOURCE: *ANJ* 35 (19 Feb 1898): 458.

‡Capt. John Bigelow arrived at Chattanooga, TN, from Washington, en route to join his troop at Chickamauga: "At the station I saw a tall, fine-looking cavalryman, whom I recognized as Sergeant Ray, Color Sergeant of the Tenth Cavalry, and learned from him that there was no train to Lytle that would get me there much before midnight." SOURCE: Bigelow, *Reminiscences of Santiago*, 7.

‡Served in F/10th Cavalry in Cuba, 1898. SOURCE: Cashin, *Under Fire with the Tenth Cavalry*, 343.

‡Had twenty-six [*sic*] years in 10th Cavalry and 10th Volunteer Infantry when commissioned in 49th Infantry. SOURCE: Fletcher, *The Black Soldier*, 64.

‡To report to Jefferson Bks, MO, as second lieutenant, 49th Infantry. SOURCE: *ANJ* 37 (7 Oct 1899): 123.

Sixteen-year veteran of 10th Cavalry; served as first lieutenant in L/49th Infantry under Capt. Edward L. Baker, Jr., and alongside Lt. Macon Russell, seventeen-year veteran; commanded detachment at Pamplona, Luzon, Philippines. SOURCE: Schubert, *Black Valor*, 155, 157.

‡Picture. SOURCE: Indianapolis *Freeman*, 21 Oct 1899.

‡Went to the Philippines with L/49th Infantry on U.S. Army Transport *Sherman*, Dec 1899.

Retired quartermaster sergeant, received Indian Wars Campaign Badge number 1499 on 6 Dec 1911. SOURCE: Carroll, *Indian Wars Campaign Badge*, 43.

RAY, Joseph; M/9th Cav. Born in Kentucky; black complexion; cannot read or write, age 23, Jul 1870, at Ft McKavett, TX. SOURCE: Bierschwale, *Fort McKavett*, 100.

RAYNOR, Isaiah; Private; B/25th Inf. Enlisted 16 Sep 1899, discharged as private B/48th Infantry 30 Jun 1901, character excellent; reenlisted 7 Aug 1901, discharged as private B/25th Infantry 6 Aug 1904, character very good;

reenlisted 12 Aug 1904, discharged without honor 19 Nov 1906. SOURCE: Powell, "Military Record of the Enlisted Men Who Were Discharged Without Honor."

‡Dishonorable discharge, Brownsville, TX. SOURCE: SO 266, AGO, 9 Nov 1906.

READ, Scott; Private; E/10th Cav. Died 5 Jun 1874, cause not stated, at Ft Sill, OK. SOURCE: Regimental Returns, 10th Cavalry, 1874.

REDDICK, Charles; 1st Sgt; I/25th Inf. ‡Served with William Branch at Ft Sill, Indian Territory, as sergeant, I/25th Infantry. SOURCE: Affidavit, Reddick, Bedford City, VA, VA File C2581520, William Branch.

First sergeant of company for at least ten years, at Ft Snelling, MN, 1885. SOURCE: Dobak and Phillips, *The Black Regulars*, 93.

‡Authorized four-month furlough from Ft Missoula, MT. SOURCE: *ANJ* 27 (17 May 1890): 719.

‡Retires. SOURCE: *ANJ* 28 (17 Jan 1891): 349.

REDDICK, David F.; Corporal; D/9th Cav. With Captain Dodge at battle at Milk River, CO, 2–10 Oct 1879. SOURCE: Miller, *Hollow Victory*, 167, 206–7.

REDDON, Shelton; F/9th Cav. Born in Kentucky; mulatto complexion; cannot read or write, age 25, Jul 1870, at Ft McKavett, TX. SOURCE: Bierschwale, *Fort McKavett*, 98.

REDMAN, Jesse I.; Saddler; H/9th Cav. Received Philippine Campaign Badge number 11870 for service as saddler in H/9th Cavalry; in 9th Cavalry at Ft Leavenworth, KS, Mar 1905. SOURCE: Philippine Campaign Badge list, 29 May 1905.

‡Veteran of Philippine Insurrection; at Ft D. A. Russell, WY, in 1910; sharpshooter; resident of Pleasantville, NJ. SOURCE: *Illustrated Review: Ninth Cavalry,* with picture.

REDMAN, William; Private; E/10th Cav. In Troop E/10th Cavalry stationed at Bonita Cañon Camp, AZ, 28 Feb 1886. SOURCE: Tagg, *The Camp at Bonita Cañon*, 232.

REDMOND, Francis; Private; K/9th Cav. From Montreal, Canada. SOURCE: Letter from William Dobak, 25 Aug 1998, in authors' files.

‡Assigned duty as clerk, regimental headquarters, Santa Fe, NM. SOURCE: Regimental Order 48, 9 Cav, 29 Sep 1879.

Described Oklahoma and Arkansas boomer relations with soldiers in letter dated 31 Jul 1884 from Camp Russell, OK, and 20 Aug 1884 from camp on Cimarron River, Oklahoma. SOURCE: *ANR* (23 Aug 1884): 4, and (30 Aug 1884): 12.

‡Convicted by garrison court martial, Ft Robinson, NE, of conduct to prejudice of good order and discipline; jailed for ten days and fined $5. SOURCE: Order 4, 9 Jan 1886, Post Orders, Ft Robinson.

In K/9th Cavalry, Ft Robinson; refused to make muster rolls and payrolls for troop, claiming neuralgia prevented him from clerical work, 19 Feb 1886; ordered by Capt. Charles Parker to commence work on muster and payrolls for troop, replied he preferred to go to guardhouse, 20 Feb 1886; found guilty in general court martial of disobedience of orders and conduct to prejudice of good order and military discipline, sentenced to hard labor and forfeit of $10 of pay for six months; reviewing officer not satisfied of evil intent by the accused and disapproved findings and sentence; Private Redmond released from confinement and returned to duty. SOURCE: HQ DeptPlatte, General Court-Martial Orders No 29, Omaha, NE, 25 Mar 1886; photocopy in authors' files.

‡Applied for copy of proceedings of general court martial in his case, as reported in General Court Martial Order 29, Department of the Platte, 25 Mar 1886, but received no response; inspector general says he has legitimate complaint. SOURCE: Report of Inspection, Ft Robinson, 15 Nov 1886, Reports of Inspection, DP, I.

‡On daily duty as clerk for post adjutant, Ft Robinson. SOURCE: Order 214, 31 Oct 1887, Post Orders, Ft Robinson.

REED, Charles; Private; H/10th Cav. Born in Louisville, KY, 1850; enlisted San Antonio, TX, 14 Dec 1883; Ht 5'6", black complexion, eyes, and hair; occupation laborer. SOURCE: Sayre, *Warriors of Color*, 400.

In Troop H/10th Cavalry stationed at Bonita Cañon Camp, AZ, 30 Apr 1886. SOURCE: Tagg, *The Camp at Bonita Cañon*, 232.

REED, Charles; Sergeant; G/24th Inf. ‡Age 70; served 1884–94. SOURCE: *Winners of the West* 12 (Nov 1935): 3.

Sergeant, G/24th Infantry; died 13 Sep 1936; buried in plot DSOUT580 at San Francisco National Cemetery. SOURCE: San Francisco National Cemetery.

REED, Charles; Private; D/24th Inf. Died 22 Jan 1903; buried at Ft Bayard, NM, in plot L 15. SOURCE: "Fort Bayard National Cemetery, Records of Burials."

Chas (Charlie) Reed, B/24th Infantry, buried 23 Jan 1903, section A, row S, plot 18, at Ft Bayard. SOURCE: Erickson, Burials at Fort Bayard National Cemetery, NM.

REED, Charles; Sergeant; L/24th Inf. Died 29 Nov 1915; buried at Ft Bayard, NM, in plot X 34. SOURCE: "Fort Bayard National Cemetery, Records of Burials."

Buried 29 Nov 1915, section B, row I, plot 34, at Ft Bayard. SOURCE: Erickson, Burials at Fort Bayard National Cemetery, NM.

REED, George; Private; I/10th Cav. In Troop I/10th Cavalry stationed at Bonita Cañon Camp, AZ, 30 Jun 1886. SOURCE: Tagg, *The Camp at Bonita Cañon*, 232.

REED, John W.; Private; F/10th Cav. Died 22 Sep 1872 of disease at Ft Sill, OK. SOURCE: Regimental Returns, 10th Cavalry, 1872.

REED, Samuel C.; Private; C/9th Cav. Died 13 Jun 1897; buried at Ft Leavenworth National Cemetery, plot 3159. SOURCE: Ft Leavenworth National Cemetery.

REED, William; Private; D/9th Cav. With Captain Dodge at battle at Milk River, CO, 2–10 Oct 1879. SOURCE: Miller, *Hollow Victory*, 167, 206–7.

REED, William C.; Corporal; F/10th Cav. Died 10 Nov 1887; originally buried at Ft Grant, AZ; buried at Santa Fe National Cemetery, NM, plot A-1 744. SOURCE: Santa Fe National Cemetery, Records of Burials.

REEDE, Aleck; Private; D/25th Inf. Died on 28 Apr 1902; buried at San Antonio National Cemetery, Section F. SOURCE: San Antonio National Cemetery Locator.

REEDER, James A.; Private; 9th Cav. Recommended for discharge by Capt. Patrick Cusack because he lacked sufficient confidence in himself to be of use. SOURCE: Dobak and Phillips, *The Black Regulars*, 257.

REESE, Cicero; Private; 9th Cav. Received Philippine Campaign Badge number 11743 for service as private in E/9th Cavalry; in 9th Cavalry at Ft Leavenworth, KS, Mar 1905. SOURCE: Philippine Campaign Badge list, 29 May 1905.

REEVES, Isaac; Private; B/48th Inf. ‡Died in the Philippines, 26 Nov 1900. SOURCE: *ANJ* 38 (8 Dec 1900): 355.

Died 26 Nov 1900; buried 20 Jun 1902 in plot NEW A993 at San Francisco National Cemetery. SOURCE: San Francisco National Cemetery.

REEVES, Thornton; Sergeant; 38th Inf. ‡Implicated in soldiers' revolt at Ft Cummings, NM, autumn 1867; acquitted by court martial of involvement. SOURCE: Billington, *New Mexico's Buffalo Soldiers*, 39, 42.

One of six 38th Infantrymen acquitted by military court of mutiny, New Mexico, 1868. SOURCE: Dobak and Phillips, *The Black Regulars*, 324.

REID, Edward C.; Sergeant; E/9th Cav. Received Philippine Campaign Badge number 11707 for service as private in E/9th Cavalry; in 9th Cavalry at Ft Leavenworth, KS, Mar 1905. SOURCE: Philippine Campaign Badge list, 29 May 1905.

‡Sergeant, E/9th Cavalry, veteran of Philippine Insurrection; at Ft D. A. Russell, WY, in 1910. SOURCE: *Illustrated Review: Ninth Cavalry,* with picture.

REID, James R.; Sergeant; B/25th Inf. Enlisted 17 May 1898, honorably discharged as private 1 Mar 1899, character very good; reenlisted 7 Mar 1899, discharged as sergeant 6 March 1902, character excellent; reenlisted 7 Mar 1902, discharged as sergeant 6 Mar 1905, character excellent; reenlisted 7 Mar 1905, discharged without honor as sergeant 16 Nov 1906. SOURCE: Powell, "Military Record of the Enlisted Men Who Were Discharged Without Honor."

‡Dishonorable discharge, Brownsville, TX. SOURCE: SO 266, AGO, 9 Nov 1906.

REID, John; Sergeant; C/38th Inf. Commanded ten-man escort for ration wagons when they repelled attack by approximately 400 Indians at White Rock Station, KS, 3 Aug 1867. SOURCE: Schubert, *Voices of the Buffalo Soldier,* 10–11.

REID, John; Sergeant; B/10th Cav. ‡Fined $10 and $5.80 costs for carrying concealed weapon, Crawford, NE, 30 Jan 1904; paid $14.30 and spent one day in jail. SOURCE: Police Court Records, Crawford.

‡Sergeant; request dated 10 Dec 1905 for four-month furlough to visit relatives in Omaha, NE, approved; only one furlough in seven years' previous service. SOURCE: AG File 1206256.

‡In hands of civil authorities 13 May 1906; reduced to private 5 Jun 1906. SOURCE: AG File 1206256.

Crawford *Tribune* reported 18 May 1906 that Pvt. Jordan Taylor, B/10th Cavalry, escaped from Ewing building, Crawford, and was shot by assembled crowd; before he died of wounds, Taylor stated that Reid shot Moss and could be found in the Ewing house. SOURCE: Buecker, Fort Robinson Burials.

‡Sentenced to seven years' confinement by Dawes County, NE, court for manslaughter; killed Deputy Marshal Art Moss of Crawford, May 1906; Department of the Missouri commander approved request of commander, Ft Robinson, for authority to discharge Reid without honor, 1 Feb 1907. SOURCE: AG File 1206256.

REID, Samuel; Private; G/25th Inf. One of twenty men who cycled 1,900 miles from Ft Missoula, MT, to St. Louis, MO, 14 Jun–24 Jul 1897, in 25th Infantry Bicycle Corps to test durability and practicality of bicycles as a means of transportation for troops. SOURCE: File 60178, GC, AGO Records.

REINHART, Robert; Corporal; B/10th Cav. At Ft Duncan, TX, Feb 1878, replaced Pvt. Thomas Dillwood as Lt. John Bigelow's orderly. SOURCE: Kinevan, *Frontier Cavalryman,* 103, 282.

REMO, John F.; Sergeant; U.S. Army. Seminole Negro Scout, served 1875–94, 1905–11; retired. SOURCE: Schubert, Consolidated List of Seminole Negro Scouts.

Born in Cherokee Nation, IT; also known as Joe; Ht 5'11", black hair and eyes, black complexion; enlisted at Ft Clark, TX, 23 Oct 1875; discharged 23 Apr 1876 at Ft Clark; enlisted 23 Apr 1876 at Beaver Lake, TX; discharged 23 Oct 1876, reenlisted at Ft Clark; discharged 25 Apr 1877, reenlisted next day at Camp Painted Comanche, TX; discharged 7 May 1878; enlisted 3 May 1879 at Ft Clark; discharged 2 May 1880; enlisted 24 May 1881 at Ft Clark; discharged 23 May 1882, reenlisted 29 May 1882 at Camp Myers Spring, TX; discharged 28 May 1883, reenlisted next day at Ft Clark; discharged as corporal 28 May 1884, reenlisted 30 May 1884 at Camp Myers Spring; discharged as private 31 Aug 1884 at Ft Clark; enlisted 27 Dec 1884 at Ft Clark; discharged as corporal 26 Dec 1885 at Camp Neville Springs, TX; enlisted 22 Jan 1886 at Ft Clark; discharged as corporal 6 Feb 1887, reenlisted next day at Camp Neville Springs; discharged as corporal 6 Feb 1888 at Fort Clark; enlisted 7 Feb 1888 at Camp Neville Springs, discharged as corporal and reenlisted five times, 6 Feb 1889–7 Feb 1891; discharged as corporal 6 Aug 1891 at Camp Palvo, TX; enlisted 9 Aug 1891 at Ft Clark; discharged as corporal 8 Mar 1892, enlisted next day at Camp Presidio, TX; discharged as corporal 8 Aug 1892, enlisted next day at Ft Clark; discharged as corporal 3 Mar 1893 at Ft Ringgold, TX; discharged as private 8 Mar 1894 at Camp San Pedro, TX; enlisted 9 Mar 1893 at Camp Rameriz R; discharged as private 8 Aug 1893 at Ft Ringgold; enlisted 16 Apr 1894 at Ft Clark; discharged as private 15 Oct 1894 at Ft Ringgold; enlisted 28 Jul 1905 at Ft Clark; discharged as private 27 Jul 1908, reenlisted for three years next day at Ft Clark; retired as sergeant 1 Jul 1911 at Ft Clark; died 10 Mar 1930; buried at Seminole Indian Scout Cemetery, Kinney County, TX. SOURCE: Swanson, 39.

Promoted from private to corporal Jun 1884. SOURCE: NARA, M 929, Roll 2.

REY, Joseph; Sgt Maj; 9th Cav. Stationed at Ringgold Barracks, TX, Mar 1874, signed resolution of mourning at death of Senator Charles Sumner, as secretary of committee. SOURCE: Schubert, *Voices of the Buffalo Soldier,* 63–64.

REYNOLDS, Eleazer N.; Corporal; H/9th Cav. ‡Appointed corporal 21 Jun 1893. SOURCE: Roster, 9 Cav.

‡At Ft Robinson, NE, 1895; member of permanent color guard. SOURCE: *ANJ* 32 (3 Aug 1895): 807. *See* **LYMAN**, George, Color Sergeant, 9th Cavalry

‡Alternate, regimental color guard, Ft Robinson, Mar 1896. SOURCE: *ANJ* 33 (28 Mar 1896): 540.

Appointed corporal 21 Jun 1893; in H/9th Cavalry at Ft Robinson, Jan 1897. SOURCE: Ninth Cavalry, Roster of NCOs, 1897.

RHODES, Charles; F/9th Cav. Born in Kentucky; mulatto complexion; cannot read or write, age 23, Jul 1870, at Ft McKavett, TX. SOURCE: Bierschwale, *Fort McKavett,* 98.

RHODES, Roy; Private; B/24th Inf. Died 4 Jun 1904; buried at Ft Bayard, NM, in plot J 16. SOURCE: "Fort Bayard National Cemetery, Records of Burials."

Ray Rhodes, B/24th Infantry, buried at Ft Bayard. SOURCE: "Buffalo Soldiers Buried at Ft Bayard, NM."

Buried 4 Jun 1904, section A, row O, plot 18, at Ft Bayard. SOURCE: Erickson, Burials at Fort Bayard National Cemetery, NM.

RICE; Blacksmith; F/10th Cav. Killed Pvt. Walter Smith, F/10th Cavalry, 28 Aug 1882, at Concho River, Texas. SOURCE: Regimental Returns, 10th Cavalry, 1882.

RICE, Ernest; Private; A/48th Inf. ‡Died of typhoid in the Philippines, 21 Aug 1901. SOURCE: *ANJ* 38 (1 Sep 1900): 19.

Died 21 Aug 1900; buried in plot E S 982 at San Francisco National Cemetery. SOURCE: San Francisco National Cemetery.

RICE, Henry; Saddler; D/9th Cav. Saddler, received Indian Wars Campaign Badge number 661 on 20 Oct 1908. SOURCE: Carroll, *Indian Wars Campaign Badge,* 19.

RICE, John; Private; K/25th Inf. Born in Jackson, LA; Ht 5'8", black complexion; occupation soldier; enlisted in A/39th Infantry for three years on 23 Mar 1867, age 21, at Greenville, LA; detached service to regimental band since 19 Jan 1868; transferred to K/25th Infantry at Jackson Bks, LA, 20 Apr 1869. SOURCE: Descriptive Roll of A/39th Inf.

RICHARD, Raymond; Sergeant; HQ/9th Cav. ‡Enlisted in 9th Cavalry band from Georgia, age 13, 1887; lived to be 91 in Oakland, CA, area. SOURCE: Clark, "A History of the Twenty-fourth," 95.

‡Resided at 315 South 13th East, Salt Lake City, UT, with John Queen. SOURCE: Clark, "A History of the Twenty-fourth," appendix E.

Sgt. Raymond Richard, Sr., HQ/24th Infantry; born 18 Feb 1874; died 27 Mar 1965; buried in plot PPNA 84 at San Francisco National Cemetery. SOURCE: San Francisco National Cemetery.

RICHARDS, Hayden; Sergeant; D/25th Inf. Discharged in 1896 with $216.50 in savings. SOURCE: Dobak and Phillips, *The Black Regulars,* 167.

‡Wounded in action at El Caney, Cuba, 1 Jul 1898. SOURCE: Nankivell, *History of the Twenty-fifth Infantry,* 83.

‡Transferred from Reserve Divisional Hospital, Siboney, Cuba, to U.S. on U.S. Army Transport *Santiago* with yellow fever, 25 Jul 1898. SOURCE: Hospital Papers, Spanish-American War.

RICHARDS, James A.; Signal Sgt; U.S. Army. ‡Born in England; resident of Jamaica from age 12; veteran of twelve years in U.S. Navy; enlisted at age 15 and discharged as signal quartermaster petty officer; served in D/10th Cavalry as telegraph operator, 1885–89; then 24th Infantry until 13 May 1897, when he was transferred to Signal Corps; in war with Spain, went to Tampa, FL, with balloon corps; promoted to sergeant 16 May 1899; now stationed in Cuba. SOURCE: Cleveland *Gazette,* 28 Oct 1899.

Private, 24th Infantry, requested transfer from Arizona to Presidio of San Francisco, CA, for telegraphy school but was reassigned to regimental headquarters, Ft Bayard, NM, 1890. SOURCE: Dobak and Phillips, *The Black Regulars,* 52.

RICHARDS, Solomen; Private; I/10th Cav. In Troop I/10th Cavalry stationed at Bonita Cañon Camp, AZ, 30 Jun 1886. SOURCE: Tagg, *The Camp at Bonita Cañon,* 232.

RICHARDSON, Alexander V.; Comsy Sgt; 24th Inf. ‡Born in Gallatin, TN, 13 Dec 1858; six months' formal schooling; left home at age 16; enlisted in B/24th Infantry, 10 Mar 1876; corporal, 1 May 1877; sergeant, 28 Jul 1880; first sergeant, 31 Mar 1889; sergeant until appointed first lieutenant, 9th Volunteer Infantry, 26 Oct 1898. SOURCE: Coston, *The Spanish-American War Volunteer,* 82.

‡On four-month furlough from Ft Elliott, TX. SOURCE: *ANJ* 24 (9 Oct 1886): 210.

‡First sergeant, A/24th Infantry; commissioned first lieutenant, 9th Volunteer Infantry, after Spanish-American War. SOURCE: Cashin, *Under Fire with the Tenth Cavalry,* 360.

‡Mentioned as captain, 48th Infantry. SOURCE: *ANJ* 37 (9 Dec 1899): 345b.

‡Mentioned as captain, B/48th Infantry. SOURCE: Beasley, *Negro Trailblazers,* 285.

‡Captain, B/48th Infantry; twenty-six-year veteran [*sic*]; sergeant at San Juan Hill, Cuba, 1898. SOURCE: San Francisco *Chronicle,* 15 Nov 1899.

‡Ranked number 342 among rifle experts with 69.67 percent in 1905. SOURCE: GO 101, AGO, 31 May 1906.

‡Retires as commissary sergeant, 24th Infantry. SOURCE: *ANR* 38 (7 Oct 1905): 21.

Retired commissary sergeant, received Indian Wars Campaign Badge number 1203 on 24 May 1909. SOURCE: Carroll, *Indian Wars Campaign Badge,* 34.

RICHARDSON, Arthur; Private; M/9th Cav. Died 13 May 1907; buried at Ft Leavenworth National Cemetery, plot 3472. SOURCE: Ft Leavenworth National Cemetery.

RICHARDSON, Dick; Private; 24th Inf. Severely injured Pvt. Lee Chrisholm in face with pocketknife, Ft Bayard, NM, 1889; confined for two months. SOURCE: Dobak and Phillips, *The Black Regulars*, 200.

‡Involved in fight with Pvt. Lee Chisholm, 24th Infantry, Ft Bayard, Christmas 1889. SOURCE: Billington, *New Mexico's Buffalo Soldiers*, 164.

RICHARDSON, Jacob; Sgt Maj; 24th Inf. Died at Ft Stockton, TX, on 24 Jun 1889; buried at San Antonio National Cemetery, Section D, number 756. SOURCE: San Antonio National Cemetery Locator.

RICHARDSON, Thomas; Private; F/9th Cav. Reported to duty at Ft Robinson, NE, Jun 1887; in Aug 1887, involved in barracks fight with Sgt. Emanuel Stance, sentenced to ten months' confinement; after release, again defied authority and sentenced to dishonorable discharge and four years in 1888. SOURCE: Kenner, *Buffalo Soldiers and Officers of the Ninth Cavalry*, 170–71, 340.

RICHARDSON, William; Sergeant; 10th Cav. At Ft Concho, TX, 1878; assisted Sgt. William Johnson, who could not read or write, by reading to him letters from Johnson's girlfriend, preparing replies. SOURCE: Dobak and Phillips, *The Black Regulars*, 143.

RICHARDSON, William; Private; D/9th Cav. ‡Deserted from Ft Craig, NM, Nov 1881, after breaking into his sergeant's locker and stealing $550 belonging to three men of company; tracked by detachment under Sergeant Dickerson and found by Pvt. Edward Kelsey; killed Kelsey and swam across Rio Grande; found and disarmed by Sergeant Stewart and Private West, who recovered $180 and killed him when he tried to escape. SOURCE: Billington, *New Mexico's Buffalo Soldiers*, 131.

Died 15 or 17 Nov 1881; buried at Ft Leavenworth National Cemetery, plot C 1976. SOURCE: Ft Leavenworth National Cemetery.

RICKERT, Eugene; Wagoner; 9th Cav. Received Philippine Campaign Badge number 11786 for service as wagoner in F/9th Cavalry; in 9th Cavalry at Ft Leavenworth, KS, Mar 1905. SOURCE: Philippine Campaign Badge list, 29 May 1905.

RIDDLE, Alfred; Private; H/24th Inf. ‡Private, E/24th Infantry, wounded in action in Cuba, 1898. SOURCE: Muller, *The Twenty Fourth Infantry*, 18.

‡Twenty-eight-year veteran shot in abdomen at San Juan Hill, Cuba; is in St. Peter's Hospital, Brooklyn, NY. SOURCE: *ANJ* 35 (30 Jul 1898): 985.

‡Enlisted New York City, 9 Nov 1898; twenty-nine years' continuous service. SOURCE: Muster Roll, H/24 Inf, Nov–Dec 1898.

‡Sick in hospital since 18 Feb 1899, "wound in line of duty." SOURCE: Muster Roll, H/24 Inf, Jan–Feb 1899.

Private, E/24th Infantry; died 16 Sep 1919; buried at San Francisco National Cemetery. SOURCE: San Francisco National Cemetery.

RIDDLE, George; Private; M/10th Cav. Died 11 Aug 1869; buried at Camp Douglas, UT. SOURCE: Record Book of Interments, Post Cemetery, 252.

RIDEOUT, Albert; Private; L/25th Inf. ‡Died of dysentery in the Philippines, 10 Nov 1901. SOURCE: *ANJ* 39 (18 Jan 1902): 503.

Died 10 Nov 1901; buried in plot N ADD1008 at San Francisco National Cemetery. SOURCE: San Francisco National Cemetery.

RIDEOUT, William. *See* WILLIAMS, William H., Private, A/9th Cavalry

RILE, Augustus M.; Private; H/48th Inf. Died 20 Aug 1900; buried in plot NA 859 at San Francisco National Cemetery. SOURCE: San Francisco National Cemetery.

RILEY, James; Private; B/10th Cav. At Ft Stockton, TX, 1879; jailed in nearby town for firing pistol in town. SOURCE: Kinevan, *Frontier Cavalryman*, 207.

RILEY, William; Private; I/25th Inf. Died at Ft Davis, TX, on 5 Jul 1874; buried at San Antonio National Cemetery, Section I, number 1534. SOURCE: San Antonio National Cemetery Locator.

RINGO, Walter; Corporal; F/24th Inf. Corporal, received Indian Wars Campaign Badge number 787 on 31 Mar 1909. SOURCE: Carroll, *Indian Wars Campaign Badge*, 22.

RINGGOLD, George; Private; K/25th Inf. Born in Philadelphia, PA; Ht 5'9", mulatto complexion; occupation soldier; enlisted in A/39th Infantry for three years on 17 Sep 1867, age 21, at Philadelphia; extra duty at post hospital since 30 Mar 1869; transferred to K/25th Infantry at Jackson Bks, LA, 20 Apr 1869. SOURCE: Descriptive Roll of A/39th Inf.

RINGGOLD, Henry; Private; 25th Inf. Born in Queenstown, MD; Ht 5'6", black hair and brown eyes, black complexion; occupation brick maker; enlisted at age 25, Harrisburg, PA, 26 Mar 1886; arrived Ft Snelling, MN, 17 Sep 1886. SOURCE: Descriptive & Assignment Rolls of Recruits, 25 Inf.

RIVERS, Richard; Private; 25th Inf. Served with Frank Hall; married Hall's former wife Rachel Ann Norman; resided in Washington, DC; died 1913 at St. Elizabeth's Hospital, Washington, DC. SOURCE: Sayre, *Warriors of Color*, 199, 204.

RIVERS, Samuel; Private; G/9th Cav. Born in Giles County, TN; Ht 5'8", black hair and eyes, black complexion; occupation waiter; enlisted in 25th Infantry at age 21, Nashville, TN, 6 Apr 1886; arrived Ft Snelling, MN, 31 Jul 1886. SOURCE: Descriptive & Assignment Rolls of Recruits, 25 Inf.

‡In G/9th Cavalry, defense witness at Barney McKay court martial at Ft Robinson, NE, 1893. SOURCE: Court Martial Records, McKay.

ROACH, Frank; Private; C/9th Cav. Died at Ft Davis, TX, on 28 Apr 1868; buried at San Antonio National Cemetery, Section I, number 1540. SOURCE: San Antonio National Cemetery Locator.

ROACH, George W.; Corporal; C/10th Cav. Died 19 Apr 1869; buried at Camp Douglas, UT. SOURCE: Record Book of Interments, Post Cemetery, 252.

ROADS, Charles A. E.; Private; G/25th Inf. Born in Richmond, VA; Ht 5'9", black hair and eyes, black complexion; occupation laborer; resided in York, PA, when enlisted 17 Aug 1886, age 21, at Harrisburg, PA; assigned to G/25th Infantry; arrived Ft Snelling, MN, 14 Dec 1886. SOURCE: Descriptive & Assignment Rolls of Recruits, 25 Inf.

ROBBS, William; Private; 25th Inf. Born in Wilson Co., TN; Ht 5'5", black hair and brown eyes, brown complexion; occupation confectioner; enlisted at age 22, Philadelphia, PA, 13 Dec 1886; assigned to C/25th Infantry; arrived Ft Snelling, MN, 1 Apr 1887. SOURCE: Descriptive & Assignment Rolls of Recruits, 25 Inf.

ROBERSON, Robert; Corporal; M/25th Inf. *See* **ROBERTSON**, Robert, Corporal, M/25th Infantry

ROBERTS, Dennis; Sergeant; B/24th Inf. Sergeant, received Indian Wars Campaign Badge number 622 on 13 Oct 1908. SOURCE: Carroll, *Indian Wars Campaign Badge*, 17.

ROBERTS, Filmore; Private; L/10th Cav. ‡Original member of 10th Cavalry; in troop when organized, Ft Riley, KS, 21 Sep 1867. SOURCE: McMiller, "Buffalo Soldiers," 78.

‡Assigned to Ft Arbuckle-Ft Gibson, Indian Territory, mail route, winter of 1867–68; drowned en route. SOURCE: Leckie, *The Buffalo Soldiers*, 29.

Drowned with mail 20 May 1868 at Little River, OK. SOURCE: Regimental Returns, 10th Cavalry, 1868.

See **FORD**, George W., Quartermaster Sergeant, 10th Cavalry

ROBERTS, George W.; 1st Sgt; D/9th Cav. Native of Louisiana; sergeant in D/9th Cavalry when he reenlisted at Ft Stockton, TX, in 1871 at age 28; transferred briefly to 25th Infantry; returned to D/9th Cavalry and appointed first sergeant; involved in protest over treatment of Pvt. John Taylor, Ft Stockton, summer 1873; convicted by court martial of attending unauthorized meeting; received dishonorable discharge. SOURCE: Kenner, *Buffalo Soldiers and Officers of the Ninth Cavalry*, 84, 89.

ROBERTS, Henry; C/25th Inf. Born in Maryland; mulatto complexion; can read and write, age 21, 5 Sep 1870, at Ft McKavett, TX. SOURCE: Bierschwale, *Fort McKavett*, 109.

ROBERTS, John; Private; K/25th Inf. Died 11 Feb 1885; buried in plot 1 51, Ft Meade National Cemetery, SD. SOURCE: Ft Meade National Cemetery, VA database.

ROBERTS, John T.; Private; K/25th Inf. Born in Southampton, VA; Ht 5'8", black complexion; occupation tailor; enlisted in A/39th Infantry for three years on 8 Sep 1867, age 28, at Norfolk, VA; transferred to K/25th Infantry at Jackson Bks, LA, 20 Apr 1869. SOURCE: Descriptive Roll of A/39th Inf.

ROBERTS, Louis; D/24th Inf. Born in Pennsylvania; black complexion; can read and write, age 24, Jul 1870, at Ft McKavett, TX. SOURCE: Bierschwale, *Fort McKavett*, 95.

ROBERTS, Philip; Sergeant; I/10th Cav. ‡Born in Maryland; private, I/10th Cavalry, 21 Mar 1882–20 Mar 1887; private, general mounted service and I/10th Cavalry, 18 Apr 1887; corporal, 7 Aug 1889; sergeant, 14 Oct 1893; ranked number 10 with revolver, Department of the Missouri, with bronze medal, 1893; at Ft Assiniboine, MT, 1897. SOURCE: Baker, Roster.

In Troop I/10th Cavalry stationed at Bonita Cañon Camp, AZ, 30 Jun 1886. SOURCE: Tagg, *The Camp at Bonita Cañon*, 232.

‡Served in 10th Cavalry, 1898; remained in U.S. during war with Spain. SOURCE: Cashin, *Under Fire with the Tenth Cavalry*, 348.

ROBERTS, Stansberry; Private; B/25th Inf. Enlisted 4 Nov 1900, discharged as private 3 Nov 1903, character very good; reenlisted 3 Dec 1903, discharged without honor 13 Nov 1906. SOURCE: Powell, "Military Record of the Enlisted Men Who Were Discharged Without Honor."

‡Dishonorable discharge, Brownsville, TX. SOURCE: SO 266, AGO, 9 Nov 1906.

ROBERTSON, Daniel; Private; K/25th Inf. Died on 3 Oct 1872; buried at San Antonio National Cemetery,

Section C, number 439. SOURCE: San Antonio National Cemetery Locator.

ROBERTSON, Robert; Corporal; M/25th Inf. Died 1 Mar 1901; buried in plot EAST 1139 at San Francisco National Cemetery; Cpls. Robert Roberson and Robert Robison also listed as buried in same plot; Robison death date 28 Feb 1901. SOURCE: San Francisco National Cemetery.

ROBERTSON, Victor; C/25th Inf. Born in Louisiana; mulatto complexion; cannot read or write, age 25, 5 Sep 1870, at Ft McKavett, TX. SOURCE: Bierschwale, *Fort McKavett,* 109.

ROBESIN, Peter; Private; 9th Cav. Received Philippine Campaign Badge number 11896 for service as private in A/9th Cavalry; in 9th Cavalry at Ft Leavenworth, KS, Mar 1905. SOURCE: Philippine Campaign Badge list, 29 May 1905.

‡At Ft D. A. Russell, WY, in 1910; resident of Baltimore, MD. SOURCE: *Illustrated Review: Ninth Cavalry,* with picture.

ROBESON, William; Private; 25th Inf. At Ft Meade, SD, 1880s, served as hospital nurse. SOURCE: Dobak and Phillips, *The Black Regulars,* 147.

ROBINSON, Andrew; Private; M/49th Inf. Died 13 Apr 1933; buried in plot C 445 at San Francisco National Cemetery. SOURCE: San Francisco National Cemetery.

ROBINSON, Berry; Blacksmith; G/9th Cav. Private, E/9th Cavalry, at Ft DuChesne, UT, 1887. SOURCE: Kenner, *Buffalo Soldiers and Officers of the Ninth Cavalry,* 234.

‡Private, H/9th Cavalry; served in Lincoln, NM, Jul 1878. SOURCE: Billington, *New Mexico's Buffalo Soldiers,* 78–79.

‡Reenlistment authorized by telegram, Adjutant General's Office, 18 Feb 1897.

‡Retired, Dec 1901. SOURCE: *ANJ* 39 (21 Dec 1901): 394.

ROBINSON, Charles; Private; A/10th Cav. Died at Ft Davis, TX, on 30 Sep 1883; buried at San Antonio National Cemetery, Section I, number 1562. SOURCE: San Antonio National Cemetery Locator.

ROBINSON, Charles; Private; H/25th Inf. Born in Washington, DC; Ht 5'6", black hair and brown eyes, brown complexion; occupation soldier; enlisted at age 35, Washington, DC, 19 Aug 1886; arrived Ft Snelling, MN, 17 Sep 1886. SOURCE: Descriptive & Assignment Rolls of Recruits, 25 Inf.

‡Admitted to Soldiers Home with disability, age 37, after twelve years and eleven months' service, 24 Aug 1889. SOURCE: SecWar, *AR 1889,* 1014.

ROBINSON, Charles; Private; K/25th Inf. Born in Atlanta, GA; Ht 5'5", black hair and eyes, black complexion; occupation laborer; enlisted at age 24, Nashville, TN, 9 May 1886; from Columbus Bks, OH, arrived Ft Snelling, MN, 17 Sep 1886. SOURCE: Descriptive & Assignment Rolls of Recruits, 25 Inf.

ROBINSON, Charley; Private; L/9th Cav. Enlisted 30 Dec 1876 at Santa Fe, NM; in confinement in post guardhouse at Ft Bliss, TX, awaiting trial by general court martial. SOURCE: Muster Roll, L/9th Cavalry, 31 Oct 1879–31 Dec 1879.

ROBINSON, Daniel; H/25th Inf. Born in Pennsylvania; black complexion; cannot read or write, age 24, 5 Sep 1870, at Ft McKavett, TX. SOURCE: Bierschwale, *Fort McKavett,* 108.

ROBINSON, Daniel C.; Corporal; E/9th Cav. Appointed corporal 4 Oct 1893; in E/9th Cavalry at Ft Robinson, NE, Jan 1897. SOURCE: Ninth Cavalry, Roster of NCOs, 1897.

ROBINSON, G. H.; Private; H/10th Cav. Former cavalryman and comrade of Dennis Bell, with whom he visited former 1st Sgt. Lewis Smith, who had retired with wife to Alexandria, VA, by 1906. SOURCE: Schubert, *Black Valor,* 141.

ROBINSON, George; Private; K/25th Inf. Born in Bayou Sara, LA; Ht 5'4", black complexion; occupation soldier; enlisted in A/39th Infantry for three years on 29 Aug 1867, age 21, at Ft St. Philip, LA; promoted to corporal 23 Mar 1867; reduced as incompetent 21 Jun 1867; transferred to K/25th Infantry at Jackson Bks, LA, 20 Apr 1869. SOURCE: Descriptive Roll of A/39th Inf.

ROBINSON, Harry; Corporal; E/49th Inf. ‡Died of dysentery at Calamba, Luzon, Philippines, 25 May 1901. SOURCE: *ANJ* 38 (27 Jul 1901): 1169.

Died 25 May 1901; buried in plot NEW A938 at San Francisco National Cemetery. SOURCE: San Francisco National Cemetery.

ROBINSON, Henry; QM Sgt; C/10th Cav. ‡Born in Kentucky; private, corporal, sergeant, first sergeant, C/10th Cavalry, 5 Mar 1867–4 Mar 1882; private, 15 Mar 1886; sergeant, 1 May 1886. SOURCE: Baker, Roster.

‡Original member of C/10th Cavalry; in troop when organized, Ft Leavenworth, KS, 14 May 1867. SOURCE: McMiller, "Buffalo Soldiers," 70.

‡Honorable mention for gallantry against Kiowas and Comanches, Wichita Agency, Indian Territory, 22–23 Aug 1874. SOURCE: Baker, *Roster.*

‡Authorized two-month furlough from Ft Apache, AZ. SOURCE: *ANJ* 24 (12 Mar 1887): 650.

‡At Ft Apache, 1890, subscribed $.25 to testimonial to General Grierson. SOURCE: List of subscriptions, 23 Apr 1890, 10th Cavalry papers, MHI.

‡Retired from the Presidio of San Francisco, CA, as quartermaster sergeant, C/10th Cavalry. SOURCE: *ANJ* 37 (28 Jul 1900): 1143.

Retired quartermaster sergeant, received Indian Wars Campaign Badge number 1197 on 5 May 1909. SOURCE: Carroll, *Indian Wars Campaign Badge,* 34.

ROBINSON, Henry; Private; K/9th Cav. ‡Served in 1872–73. *See* **SLAUGHTER**, Rufus, Private, K/9th Cavalry

Text of court martial order convicting Capt. J. Lee Humfreville of brutality published. SOURCE: Schubert, *Voices of the Buffalo Soldier,* 55–62.

ROBINSON, Henry; Private; 25th Inf. Born in Charleston, SC; occupation fisherman; age 26, Ht 5'5"; enlisted 1 Jun 1881; left recruit depot, David's Island, NY, 17 Aug 1881, and after trip on steamer *Thomas Kirby* to Central Depot, New York City, and train via Chicago to Running Water, Dakota Territory, 22 Aug 1881, marched forty-seven miles to Ft Randall, SD, arrived 24 Aug 1881. SOURCE: Descriptive & Assignment Rolls, 25 Inf.

ROBINSON, Henry C.; Private; 25th Inf. Born in Albemarle County, VA; Ht 5'4", black hair and brown eyes, brown complexion; occupation waiter; enlisted at age 22, Washington, DC, 27 Sep 1886; arrived Ft Snelling, MN, 20 Jan 1887. SOURCE: Descriptive & Assignment Rolls of Recruits, 25 Inf.

ROBINSON, Houston; Private; K/10th Cav. While prisoner in custody of Pvt. King Adams, H/10th Cavalry, Ft Grant, AZ, 10 Dec 1885, he was allowed to wander out of guard's sight. SOURCE: Sayre, *Warriors of Color,* 2.

ROBINSON, James; Private; D/9th Cav. Died at Ft Concho, TX, on 16 Nov 1868; buried at San Antonio National Cemetery, Section C, number 410. SOURCE: San Antonio National Cemetery Locator.

ROBINSON, James; Blacksmith; I/10th Cav. Shot accidentally, died 9 Dec 1875 at Ft Concho, TX. SOURCE: Regimental Returns, 10th Cavalry, 1875.

ROBINSON, James; Corporal; L/49th Inf. ‡Died of tuberculosis in the Philippines, 2 Oct 1900. SOURCE: *ANJ* 38 (20 Oct 1900): 187.

‡Stationed at Claveria, Philippines; died in hospital of "acute tuberculosis of both lungs," Aparri, Philippines, 30 Nov 1900. SOURCE: Regt Returns, 49th Infantry.

Died 2 Oct 1900; body received 26 Jun 1901 at San Francisco National Cemetery, buried in plot NEW A468. SOURCE: San Francisco National Cemetery.

ROBINSON, James; Private; 9th Cav. Died 30 Jan 1908 while on detached duty; buried at Ft Bayard, NM, in plot P 24. SOURCE: "Fort Bayard National Cemetery, Records of Burials."

Died while on detached service; buried 30 Jan 1908, section B, row A, plot 24, at Ft Bayard. SOURCE: Erickson, *Burials at Fort Bayard National Cemetery, NM.*

ROBINSON, John; Blacksmith; E/10th Cav. In Troop E/10th Cavalry stationed at Bonita Cañon Camp, AZ, 28 Feb 1886. SOURCE: Tagg, *The Camp at Bonita Cañon,* 231.

ROBINSON, John; Corporal; F/10th Cav. Born in Virginia; private, corporal, sergeant, F/10th Cavalry, 7 Mar 1882–6 Mar 1887; private, corporal, sergeant, first sergeant, 14 Mar 1887–13 Mar 1892; private and sergeant, general recruiting service, 2 Apr 1892–21 Apr 1894; private, F/10th Cavalry, 14 Sep 1894; corporal, 25 Feb 1895. SOURCE: Baker, *Roster.*

Born in Stafford County, VA; Ht 5'8", black hair and eyes, black complexion; served in F/10th Cavalry to 5 Mar 1887; second reenlistment in 25th Infantry at age 29, Columbus Bks, OH, 14 Mar 1887; arrived Ft Snelling, MN, 1 Apr 1887. SOURCE: Descriptive & Assignment Rolls of Recruits, 25 Inf.

ROBINSON, John; Private; 9th Cav. Received Philippine Campaign Badge number 11897 for service as private in C/48th Infantry, United States Volunteers, and E/24th Infantry; in 9th Cavalry at Ft Leavenworth, KS, Mar 1905. SOURCE: Philippine Campaign Badge list, 29 May 1905.

ROBINSON, John H.; Private; H/9th Cav. Died on 29 Mar 1895; buried at San Antonio National Cemetery, Section D, number 496. SOURCE: San Antonio National Cemetery Locator.

ROBINSON, John W.; Corporal; F/10th Cav. ‡Original member of F/10th Cavalry; in troop when organized, Ft Leavenworth, KS, 21 Jun 1867. SOURCE: McMiller, "Buffalo Soldiers," 73.

Wounded in action, gunshot wound in left leg, near Beaver Creek, KS, 21 Aug 1867. SOURCE: LR, DeptMo, 1867.

Pvt. John W. Robinson, F/10th Cavalry, wounded in action against Indians at Beaver Creek, 21 Aug 1867. SOURCE: Schubert, *Voices of the Buffalo Soldier,* 20.

‡Wounded in action against Indians, Kansas, 21 Sep 1867. SOURCE: Armes, *Ups and Downs*, 248.

ROBINSON, John W.; Corporal; F/10th Cav. ‡Born in Virginia; private, corporal, sergeant, F/10th Cavalry, 7 Mar 1882–6 Mar 1887; private, corporal, sergeant, first sergeant in E/25th Infantry, 14 Mar 1887–13 Mar 1892; private and sergeant, general recruiting service, 2 Apr 1892–21 Apr 1894; private, F/10th Cavalry, 14 Sep 1894; corporal, 25 Feb 1895. SOURCE: Baker, Roster. *Corrected entry.*

ROBINSON, Lewis; Private; 25th Inf. Born in Hamilton County, TN; Ht 5'9", black hair and eyes, black complexion; occupation laborer; enlisted at age 22, Nashville, TN, 7 Apr 1886; arrived Ft Snelling, MN, 31 Jul 1886. SOURCE: Descriptive & Assignment Rolls of Recruits, 25 Inf.

ROBINSON, Richard; Corporal; H/25th Inf. ‡Shot dead through head with Springfield rifle while asleep on bunk, Ft Davis, TX, Sep 1878, by Sgt. Moses Marshall. SOURCE: Carroll, *The Black Military Experience*, 276.

At Ft Davis, shot and killed in his bed by Sgt. Moses Marshall for negative comments about Marshall's wife. SOURCE: Leiker, *Racial Borders*, 78.

ROBINSON, Scott; Private; 25th Inf. Born in Darlington, SC; Ht 5'11", black hair and eyes, fair complexion; occupation cotton hand; enlisted at age 22, Charleston, SC, 20 May 1881; left recruit depot, David's Island, NY, 2 Jul 1881; arrived Ft Randall, SD, 7 Jul 1881. SOURCE: Descriptive & Assignment Rolls of Recruits, 25 Inf.

ROBINSON, Solomon; Corporal; F/9th Cav. Died 11 Aug 1880; buried at Ft Bayard, NM, in plot E 37. SOURCE: "Fort Bayard National Cemetery, Records of Burials."

Buried 11 Aug 1880, section A, row F, plot 40 at Ft Bayard. SOURCE: Erickson, Burials at Fort Bayard National Cemetery, NM.

ROBINSON, Stephen V.; Private; L/9th Cav. Enlisted 21 Jan 1879 at Baltimore, MD; on daily duty as stable police at Ft Bliss, TX. SOURCE: Muster Roll, L/9th Cavalry, 31 Oct 1879–31 Dec 1879.

‡Served 1879–84; died at Baltimore, age 80. SOURCE: *Winners of the West* 11 (Jun 1934): 3.

ROBINSON, William; Private; A/39th Inf. Civil War veteran; sentence of death for involvement in New Iberia, LA, mutiny, Jul 1867, reduced to ten years. SOURCE: Dobak and Phillips, *The Black Regulars*, 222.

ROBISON, George; Private; L/9th Cav. Enlisted 12 Feb 1878 at Santa Fe, NM; on daily duty at regimental head-

quarters, Santa Fe, per RO 10, 10 Jul 1878. SOURCE: Muster Roll, L/9th Cavalry, 31 Oct 1879–31 Dec 1879.

ROBISON, Robert; Corporal; M/25th Inf. *See* **ROBERTSON**, Robert, Corporal, M/25th Infantry

ROCHE, Michael F.; Private; M/25th Inf. Died 22 Apr 1902; buried in plot NA 1100 at San Francisco National Cemetery. SOURCE: San Francisco National Cemetery.

ROCHESTER, Nicholas; M/9th Cav. Born in Kentucky; mulatto complexion; can read, cannot write, age 20, Jul 1870, at Ft McKavett, TX. SOURCE: Bierschwale, *Fort McKavett,* 100.

ROCK, Pierre; Sergeant; L/9th Cav. Sergeant in C/9th Cavalry, led eleven men on 200-mile scout along Rio Grande, TX, summer 1872. SOURCE: Dobak and Phillips, *The Black Regulars*, 258.

‡In C/9th Cavalry, appointed sergeant 3 Sep 1892. SOURCE: Roster, 9 Cav.

At Ft Robinson, NE, 1894; married. SOURCE: Kenner, *Buffalo Soldiers and Officers of the Ninth Cavalry*, 189.

‡Retires from Ft Robinson, Dec 1894. SOURCE: *ANJ* 32 (22 Dec 1894): 278.

RODGERS, Henry R.; Private; B/9th Cav. ‡Transferred to Reserve Divisional Hospital, Siboney, Cuba, with remittent yellow fever, 22 Jul 1898. SOURCE: Hospital Papers, Spanish-American War.

Sergeant, B/9th Cavalry, died 3 Dec 1930; buried in plot B 983 at San Francisco National Cemetery. SOURCE: San Francisco National Cemetery.

ROGERS, John; Trumpeter; I/9th Cav. ‡Corporal, clothing destroyed when fighting fire, Ft Wingate, NM, 15 Dec 1876. SOURCE: Billington, *New Mexico's Buffalo Soldiers*, 110.

Corporal, I/9th Cavalry, at Ft Wingate, Nov 1877, complained to Secretary of War that Lt. Col. Wesley Merritt repeatedly tried to break into his quarters when he was absent and his wife was in bed; corporal, risked life to carry message from Lieutenant Burnett to Lieutenant Valois under fire, Cuchillo Negro, NM, Aug 1881; sergeant, I/9th Cavalry, served during operations against "boomers" in Indian Territory, Apr 1884. SOURCE: Kenner, *Buffalo Soldiers and Officers of the Ninth Cavalry*, 201, 238, 244.

‡Trumpeter, I/9th Cavalry, volunteered to carry message seeking reinforcements when detachment was ambushed by Apaches, Cuchillo Negro Mountains, 16 Aug 1881. SOURCE: Billington, *New Mexico's Buffalo Soldiers*, 106.

‡Trumpeter, I/9th Cavalry, in action against Apache Nana, Aug 1881. SOURCE: Leckie, *The Buffalo Soldiers*, 232.

After brave conduct in action against Apaches in Aug 1881, applied for certificate of merit. SOURCE: Dobak and Phillips, *The Black Regulars*, 261.

‡Cited for heroic action, Cuchillo Negro Mountains, in carrying message under heavy fire to commander, Lt. Gustavus Valois, Aug 1881. SOURCE: Carroll, *The Black Military Experience*, 367.

Trumpeter in I/9th Cavalry, awarded certificate of merit for distinguished gallantry in action, voluntarily carrying dispatch for help, under severe fire, through lines of enemy encircling command, Cuchillo Negro Mountains, 16 Aug 1881. SOURCE: Gleim, *The Certificate of Merit*, 43.

‡Corporal, I/9th Cavalry; family put out of quarters and off Ft Robinson, NE, reservation, for engaging in row, May 1891. SOURCE: LS, Ft Robinson.

‡Asked other enlisted men of I/9th Cavalry to sign petition for transfer of Capt. John Guilfoyle from command of troop. SOURCE: CO, Ft Robinson, to AAG, DP, 26 Jun 1891, LS, Ft Robinson.

‡Trumpeter, G/9th Cavalry, ordered by post commander, Ft Robinson, to see that his children attended school and did not loiter around barracks during school hours. SOURCE: CO, Ft Robinson, to Rogers, 22 Mar 1893, LS, Ft Robinson.

‡Resides with wife, two children, and brother-in-law in old barrack, Ft Robinson, Aug 1893. SOURCE: Medical History, Ft Robinson.

‡Trumpeter, G/9th Cavalry, with quarters on post with wife, Ft Robinson, 1894. SOURCE: Court Martial Records, Dillon.

‡Trumpeter, I/9th Cavalry; Ft Robinson commander disapproves his request; does not consider it in best interest of service to allow Mrs. Rogers to return to post. SOURCE: CO, Ft Robinson, to Rogers, 9 Oct 1895, LS, Ft Robinson.

ROGERS, Nathan; Private; E/38th Inf. Died 12 Sep 1868; originally buried at Ft Hays, KS; reburied at Ft Leavenworth National Cemetery, plot 3368. SOURCE: Ft Leavenworth National Cemetery.

ROLAND, Samuel; Private; C/10th Cav. ‡Original member of 10th Cavalry; in troop when organized, Ft Leavenworth, KS, 14 May 1867. SOURCE: McMiller, "Buffalo Soldiers," 70.

Died 3 Jul 1869 in hospital at Ft Wichita, KS. SOURCE: Regimental Returns, 10th Cavalry, 1869.

ROLLINS, John; Private; 10th Cav. Died 28 Feb 1870; buried at Ft Leavenworth National Cemetery, plot D 1339. SOURCE: Ft Leavenworth National Cemetery.

ROLLINS, John; Private; F/24th Inf. ‡2nd Lt. Theodore Decker, 24th Infantry, visited Rollins's mistress, a Mexican prostitute named Refugia Estrada, in town of Eagle Pass,

TX, 12 Apr 1880, and engaged in disgraceful shooting fray with Rollins in which Estrada was killed and Decker was shot in face and shoulder; Decker dismissed from service. SOURCE: GCMO 50, AGO, 23 Aug 1880.

Court martial order convicting Lt. Theodore Decker, 24th Infantry, for conduct unbecoming an officer, arising out of competition between Decker and Rollins for same woman, published. SOURCE: Schubert, *Voices of the Buffalo Soldier*, 111–13.

ROONEY, James; 9th Cav. Born in Tennessee; mulatto complexion; can read and write, age 22, Sep 1870, at Ft McKavett, TX. SOURCE: Bierschwale, *Fort McKavett*, 107.

ROPER, Charles H.; 1st Sgt; D/9th Cav. ‡Private, C/9th Cavalry; application for transfer disapproved by letter, Adjutant General's Office, 24 Apr 1894.

‡Lance corporal, I/9th Cavalry, promoted to corporal, Ft DuChesne, UT, Jan 1896. SOURCE: *ANJ* 33 (18 Jan 1896): 348.

Appointed sergeant 2 May 1896; in I/9th Cavalry at Ft Washakie, WY, Jan 1897. SOURCE: Ninth Cavalry, Roster of NCOs, 1897.

‡First sergeant, D/9th Cavalry, killed by accident in the Philippines, 2 Mar 1901. SOURCE: *ANJ* 38 (30 Mar 1901): 755.

Died 2 Mar 1901; buried in New Add, plot 416 at San Francisco National Cemetery. SOURCE: San Francisco National Cemetery.

ROSE, David; Sergeant; B/9th Cav. ‡Private, on detached service, Ft Bayard, NM, 16–31 Jan 1881. SOURCE: Regt Returns, 9 Cav, Jan 1881.

Sergeant, died 13 Apr 1881; buried at Santa Fe National Cemetery, NM, plot K 350. SOURCE: Santa Fe National Cemetery, Records of Burials.

ROSE, William B.; Ord Sgt; U.S. Army. ‡At Ft Elliott, TX, 1885. SOURCE: Cleveland *Gazette*, 9 Jan 1886.

‡At Ft Elliott, 1886. *See* **SMITH**, Jacob Clay, Saddler Sergeant, 10th Cavalry

First sergeant, F/24th Infantry, reduced to ranks and fined $60, Ft Elliott, 1886, for role in soldiers' meeting called to censure comrades who did not resist train robbers while on official escort duty. SOURCE: Dobak and Phillips, *The Black Regulars*, 252.

‡Reduced from first sergeant to private, fined $60, confined for six months by general court martial, Ft Elliott, for allowing and participating in 15 Dec 1886 protest meeting. SOURCE: *ANJ* 24 (26 Mar 1887): 695.

Text of resolution of censure and related articles from *Army and Navy Journal* published; sergeant, stationed at Ft Bayard, NM, Jan 1894, one of three managers of masquerade ball given by company. SOURCE: Schubert, *Voices of the Buffalo Soldier*, 149–52, 198.

‡Sergeant, F/24th Infantry, authorized four-month furlough from Ft Bayard. SOURCE: *ANJ* 26 (6 Jul 1889): 923.

‡First sergeant, F/24th Infantry, sharpshooter, Ft Bayard. SOURCE: *ANJ* 28 (27 Sep 1890): 70.

‡Sergeant, F/24th Infantry, examined for ordnance sergeant, Ft Bayard. SOURCE: *ANJ* 30 (8 Jul 1893): 767.

‡First sergeant, F/24th Infantry, promoted to ordnance sergeant. SOURCE: *ANJ* 32 (27 Oct 1894): 141.

Appointed ordnance sergeant 9 Oct 1894, from first sergeant, F/24th Infantry. SOURCE: Dobak, "Staff Noncommissioned Officers."

ROSS, Alfred; Private; C/9th Cav. Private, C/9th Cavalry, and personal servant of Capt. Charles Beyer at Ft Sill, OK, 1883. SOURCE: Kenner, *Buffalo Soldiers and Officers of the Ninth Cavalry*, 255.

‡At Ft Sill, 1883–88. *See* **COLE**, Private, C/9th Cavalry

Served in Indian Territory, 1884–85, keeping illegal settlers off tribal lands; after service, resided in U.S. Soldiers Home. SOURCE: Schubert, *Black Valor*, 59.

‡Discharged on surgeon's certificate, 1 Feb 1887.

‡Admitted to Soldiers Home with disability, age 36, after five years' service, 21 May 1888. SOURCE: SecWar, *AR 1888*, 903.

ROSS, Asa; Private; U.S. Army. Seminole Negro Scout, served 1873–80; retired. SOURCE: Schubert, Consolidated List of Seminole Negro Scouts.

Born in Goliad, TX; Ht 5'7", black hair and eyes, black complexion; enlisted 14 May 1873 at Ft Clark, TX, discharged 14 Nov 1873; enlisted 14 Nov 1873 at Ft Clark, age 23, discharged 14 May 1874 at Ft Clark; enlisted 24 Feb 1875 at Ft Clark, discharged 7 Sep 1875 at Camp Supply, TX; enlisted 6 Jan 1877 at Ft Clark, discharged 6 Jan 1878; enlisted 1 Feb 1878 at Ft Clark, discharged 1 Feb 1879; enlisted 1 Feb 1879 at Ft Clark, discharged 21 Mar 1880 at Camp Chinati, TX. SOURCE: Swanson, 40.

ROSS, Hercules; Private; G/10th Cav. ‡Original member of 10th Cavalry; in troop when organized, Ft Leavenworth, KS, 5 Jul 1867. SOURCE: McMiller, "Buffalo Soldiers," 74.

Drowned 19 Jun 1869 at Pawnee Creek, KS. SOURCE: Regimental Returns, 10th Cavalry, 1869.

ROSS, Joseph; Corporal; 9th Cav. At Ft Quitman, TX, 1870, court martialed for mutinous language. SOURCE: Leiker, *Racial Borders*, 82.

ROSS, Leon; Private; M/9th Cav. Buried 1 Mar 1907, section A, row W, plot 44 at Ft Bayard, NM. SOURCE: Erickson, Burials at Fort Bayard National Cemetery, NM.

Private, B/9th Cavalry, died 1 Mar 1907; buried at Ft Bayard in plot 0 44. SOURCE: "Fort Bayard National Cemetery, Records of Burials."

Leon Ross, M/9th Cavalry, buried at Ft Bayard. SOURCE: "Buffalo Soldiers Buried at Ft Bayard, NM."

ROSS, Lewis; D/24th Inf. Born in Kentucky; black complexion; cannot read or write, age 21, Jul 1870, at Ft McKavett, TX. SOURCE: Bierschwale, *Fort McKavett,* 96.

ROSS, Patrick; Blacksmith; B/9th Cav. Former member of 25th Infantry, received permission to reenlist in 1890, provided he paid his own way to nearest 9th Cavalry post; stationed at Ft DuChesne, UT, won three events at 1896 track competition of all units in Department of the Colorado and General's Medal for highest individual score. SOURCE: Dobak and Phillips, *The Black Regulars*, 62, 149.

At Ft DuChesne, Oct 1896; won three of eight contests designed for cavalrymen at Denver competition for troops of Department of the Colorado, Oct 1896; received "general's medal" from Gen. Frank Wheaton's daughter Octavia as the outstanding contestant. SOURCE: Kenner, *Buffalo Soldiers and Officers of the Ninth Cavalry*, 20–21.

ROSS, Revo; Private; B/25th Inf. Died 29 May 1906; buried at Ft Leavenworth National Cemetery, plot 3538. SOURCE: Ft Leavenworth National Cemetery.

ROSS, William H.; Private; H/10th Cav. Died 12 Feb 1914; buried at Ft Bayard, NM, in plot V 20. SOURCE: "Fort Bayard National Cemetery, Records of Burials."

Buried 12 Feb 1914, section B, row G, plot 20, at Ft Bayard. SOURCE: Erickson, Burials at Fort Bayard National Cemetery, NM.

ROUNDS; Musician; H/24th Inf. ‡At Ft Grant, AZ, blew taps at funeral of Sgt. Edward Berry, H/24th Infantry, Apr 1890. SOURCE: Cleveland *Gazette*, 26 Apr 1890.

ROUSE, Curtis; Private; G/9th Cav. Served as private, F/9th Cavalry, at Ft Reno, OK, 1883; witness in court martial of Pvt. Moses Green for striking Sgt. Emanuel Stance. SOURCE: Schubert, *Voices of the Buffalo Soldier*, 134–35.

‡Sergeant, I/9th Cavalry, authorized thirty-day absence from Ft Robinson, NE, hunting with one corporal and four privates of I/9th Cavalry. SOURCE: Order 216, 9 Oct 1890, Post Orders, Ft Robinson.

‡Sergeant, I/9th Cavalry, asked other men of troop to sign petition to transfer commander, Capt. John Guilfoyle. SOURCE: CO, Ft Robinson, to AAG, DP, 26 Jun 1891, LS, Ft Robinson.

‡Private, G/9th Cavalry, witness for defense in Barney McKay court martial, Ft Robinson, 1893. SOURCE: Court Martial Records, McKay.

ROUSEY, Joseph; Private; I/10th Cav. Born in Staunton, VA, 1855; enlisted Baltimore, MD, 20 Nov 1876; Ht 5'6", chestnut brown complexion, brown eyes, black hair; occupation laborer; served in I/10th Cavalry; discharged Camp near Presidio, TX, 19 Nov 1881; enlisted Baltimore, 1 Feb 1882; served in H/10th Cavalry; discharged Ft Apache, AZ, 31 Jan 1887; enlisted Jefferson Bks, MO, 5 May 1887; served in I/10th Cavalry; discharged Ft Apache, 20 Apr 1892; married Catherine in Baltimore, 10 May 1898, who died Dec 1924; died in University Hospital, Baltimore, 27 Feb 1902; buried at Sharp Street Cemetery, Baltimore. SOURCE: Sayre, *Warriors of Color*, 401–5.

Promoted to first sergeant 13 Dec 1885; first sergeant in Troop H/10th Cavalry stationed at Bonita Cañon Camp, AZ, 30 Apr 1886; reduced to private 9 Jun 1886. SOURCE: Tagg, *The Camp at Bonita Cañon*, 68, 231.

‡Honorable mention for services rendered in capture of Mangas and his Apache band, Rio Bonito, AZ, 18 Oct 1886. SOURCE: Baker, Roster.

ROUT, Richard; Private; H/25th Inf. Born in Stafford, KY; Ht 5'5", black hair and eyes, black complexion; occupation laborer; enlisted in 25th Infantry at age 23, Cincinnati, OH, 29 Nov 1886; arrived Ft Snelling, MN, 1 Apr 1887. SOURCE: Descriptive & Assignment Rolls of Recruits, 25 Inf.

One of twenty men in H/25th Infantry who cycled 1,900 miles from Ft Missoula, MT, to St. Louis, MO, 14 Jun–24 Jul 1897, in 25th Infantry Bicycle Corps to test durability and practicality of bicycles as a means of transportation for troops. SOURCE: File 60178, GC, AGO Records.

ROWERSON, Prince; Private; A/25th Inf. Died 11 May 1872; buried at San Antonio National Cemetery, Section D, number 779. SOURCE: San Antonio National Cemetery Locator.

ROWLAND, Samuel; Private; C/10th Cav. Died 3 Jul 1869; buried at Camp Douglas, UT. SOURCE: Record Book of Interments, Post Cemetery, 252.

ROWLETT, John C.; 9th Cav. Received Philippine Campaign Badge number 11744 for service as corporal, D/49th Infantry, United States Volunteers; in 9th Cavalry at Ft Leavenworth, KS, Mar 1905. SOURCE: Philippine Campaign Badge list, 29 May 1905.

ROY, Johnson; Sergeant; I/25th Inf. Died on 7 Nov 1909; buried at San Antonio National Cemetery, Section C, number 370. SOURCE: San Antonio National Cemetery Locator.

ROYSTER, Charles; Private; F/9th Cav. At Ft Robinson, NE, Jun 1887, confined for ten days for negligence in watering horses and insolent response to Sgt. Emanuel Stance.

SOURCE: Kenner, *Buffalo Soldiers and Officers of the Ninth Cavalry*, 170.

RUCK, Samuel E.; Private; 10th Cav. Died 1 Feb 1909 while on detached duty; buried at Ft Bayard, NM, in plot R 6. SOURCE: "Fort Bayard National Cemetery, Records of Burials."

Sam LeRuck, on detached duty, 10th Cavalry; buried at Ft Bayard. SOURCE: "Buffalo Soldiers Buried at Ft Bayard, NM."

Died on detached duty, buried 1 Feb 1909, section B, row C, plot 6, at Ft Bayard. SOURCE: Erickson, Burials at Fort Bayard National Cemetery, NM.

RUDDLE, John; Private; M/10th Cav. Died 16 Aug 1917; buried at Ft Bayard, NM, in plot Y 17. SOURCE: "Fort Bayard National Cemetery, Records of Burials."

Buried 16 Aug 1917, section B, row J, plot 17, at Ft Bayard. SOURCE: Erickson, Burials at Fort Bayard National Cemetery, NM.

RUSSEL, Solomon; Private; B/25th Inf. Died 11 Apr 1901; buried at Ft Bayard, NM, in plot N 29. SOURCE: "Fort Bayard National Cemetery, Records of Burials."

Buried 11 Apr 1901, section A, row V, plot 29 at Ft Bayard. SOURCE: Erickson, Burials at Fort Bayard National Cemetery, NM.

RUSSELL, Charles A.; Private; L/49th Inf. Died 26 Dec 1939; buried 29 Dec 1930 [*sic*] in plot E EAS1004 at San Francisco National Cemetery. SOURCE: San Francisco National Cemetery.

RUSSELL, Clarence; Private; 9th Cav. Received Philippine Campaign Badge number 11787 for service as private in D/9th Cavalry; in 9th Cavalry at Ft Leavenworth, KS, Mar 1905. SOURCE: Philippine Campaign Badge list, 29 May 1905.

RUSSELL, Ellis; Sergeant; 25th Inf. At Ft Stockton, TX, July 1873, organized protest over treatment of Pvt. John Taylor, with Sgt. Solomon Holloman, 25th Infantry. SOURCE: Kenner, *Buffalo Soldiers and Officers of the Ninth Cavalry*, 86.

RUSSELL, Jeremiah; Private; C/10th Cav. Died 20 Jul 1867 of cholera at Camp Grierson, KS. SOURCE: Regimental Returns, 10th Cavalry, 1867.

RUSSELL, Macon; 1st Lt; L/49th Inf. ‡Born in Mecklenburg Co., VA, 17 Jul 1858; in F/24th Infantry, 4 Jul 1881–3 Jul 1886; in H/25th Infantry, 20 Sep 1887–8 Sep 1898; second lieutenant, 8th Volunteer Infantry, 15 Sep 1898–6 Mar 1899; in H/25th Infantry, 21 Mar–21 Sep 1899; first lieutenant, 9 Sep 1899; lieutenant, H/25th Infantry, 21 Sep

1899–9 Feb 1900; mother Mrs. Claris Russell, Sugar Creek, NC. SOURCE: Descriptive Book, L/49 Inf.

‡First sergeant, H/25th Infantry; transferred from Reserve Divisional Hospital, Siboney, Cuba, to U.S. on U.S. Army Transport *Santiago* with yellow fever, 25 Jul 1898. SOURCE: Hospital Papers, Spanish-American War.

Sergeant, 25th Infantry, recommended for commission in immune regiment by Lt. Col. Andrew S. Daggett, 25th Infantry, even before regiment left Cuba, Aug 1898; seventeen-year veteran, served in L/49th Infantry under Capt. Edward L. Baker, Jr., and alongside Lt. Alfred Ray, sixteen-year veteran; commanded detachment at Sanchez Mira, Luzon, Philippines. SOURCE: Schubert, *Black Valor*, 110, 155, 157.

‡To proceed to Ft Thomas, KY, to receive commission in 8th U.S. Volunteer Infantry. SOURCE: *ANJ* 36 (17 Sep 1898): 69.

‡Commissioned second lieutenant, 8th Volunteer Infantry, after Spanish-American War. SOURCE: Cashin, *Under Fire with the Tenth Cavalry*, 360.

‡Won commission for gallantry and meritorious service around Santiago, Cuba. SOURCE: Thweatt, *What the Newspapers Say*, 4.

‡Commissioned for gallantry at Santiago, 1–2 Jul 1898. SOURCE: Richmond *Planet*, 13 Aug 1898.

‡Commissioned for bravery at El Caney, Cuba. SOURCE: Johnson, *History of Negro Soldiers*, 32.

‡Joined L/49th Infantry after it arrived in the Philippines; was already in Manila when 49th Infantry departed San Francisco, Dec 1899. SOURCE: Regt Returns, 49 Inf.

‡Mentioned. SOURCE: *ANJ* 38 (6 Oct 1900): 131.

‡Service in the Philippines mentioned. SOURCE: Villard, "The Negro in the Regular Army," 726.

RUSSELL, Thomas; Private; 24th Inf. ‡Drowned crossing San Mateo River, Philippines, 21 Aug 1899. SOURCE: Richmond *Planet*, 2 Sep 1899.

Private, F/24th Infantry; died 21 Aug 1899; buried in plot ES OF512 at San Francisco National Cemetery. SOURCE: San Francisco National Cemetery.

S

ST. CLAIR, Jean; Private; D/25th Inf. Jean Stclair born 15 Aug 1887; died 4 Oct 1945; buried at Ft Leavenworth National Cemetery, plot E 2983. SOURCE: Ft Leavenworth National Cemetery.

SALLEY, Coleman; Private; B/10th Cav. ‡Original member of 10th Cavalry; in troop when organized, Ft Leavenworth, KS, 1 Apr 1867. SOURCE: McMiller, "Buffalo Soldiers," 69.

Drowned 19 May 1867 at Buffalo Creek, KS. SOURCE: Regimental Returns, 10th Cavalry, 1867.

SALLY, John M.; Corporal; M/25th Inf. Died 5 Jul 1902; buried in plot NEW A1152 at San Francisco National Cemetery. SOURCE: San Francisco National Cemetery.

SAMMONS, William H.; Private; F/24th Inf. ‡Enlisted Ft Douglas, UT, 20 Oct 1897, with five years' continuous service; formerly corporal, F/24th Infantry; transferred to H/24th Infantry as private, 6 Oct 1898; on special duty as clerk, Subsistence Department, 12 Oct 1898. SOURCE: Muster Roll, H/24 Inf, Sep–Oct 1898.

‡Private, F/24th Infantry; transferred from Reserve Divisional Hospital, Siboney, Cuba, to U.S. on U.S. Army Transport *Santiago* with remittent yellow fever, 25 Jun 1898. SOURCE: Hospital Papers, Spanish-American War.

‡Promoted to corporal, 7 Nov 1898. SOURCE: Muster Roll, H/24 Inf, Nov–Dec 1898.

‡On special duty as clerk, Subsistence Department, through February 1899. SOURCE: Muster Roll, H/24 Inf, Jan–Feb 1899.

Private, F/24th Infantry; died 26 Jan 1915; buried in plot W S 228-A at San Francisco National Cemetery. SOURCE: San Francisco National Cemetery.

SAMPSON, Marshall; D/24th Inf. Born in Georgia; black complexion; cannot read or write, age 21, Jul 1870, at Ft McKavett, TX. SOURCE: Bierschwale, *Fort McKavett*, 96.

SAMUEL, George; Private; M/9th Cav. *See* SAMUELS, George, Private, M/9th Cavalry

SAMUELS, George; Private; M/9th Cav. Served in M/9th Cavalry, Dec 1872, witness at Emanuel Stance court martial. SOURCE: Kenner, *Buffalo Soldiers and Officers of the Ninth Cavalry*, 164.

‡Pvt. George Samuel, M/9th Cavalry, at Ft McKavett, TX, 1872–73. *See* STANCE, Emanuel, First Sergeant, F/9th Cavalry

SANCHEZ, Antonio; Private; U.S. Army. Antonio Sanches, born in Mexico; Ht 5'5", grey hair, black eyes, dark complexion; enlisted 13 Jan 1887 at Ft Clark, TX, age 45; discharged 6 Feb 1888 at Ft Clark; enlisted 16 Jan 1893 at Ft Clark; discharged 15 Jul 1893, reenlisted next day at Ft Ringgold, TX; discharged 15 Jan 1894, reenlisted next day at Camp San Pedro, TX; discharged 15 Jul 1894, reenlisted next day at Ft Ringgold; discharged 15 Jan 1895 at Camp San Carlo; enlisted 16 Jan 1895 at Ft Ringgold where he was discharged 16 Jan 1898; enlisted 1 Apr 1898 at Ft Ringgold; discharged 31 Mar 1901, reenlisted next day at Ft Clark; discharged, reenlisted for three years four more times at Ft Clark, 31 Mar 1904–1 Apr 1913; honorably discharged 30 Sep 1914. SOURCE: Swanson, 40.

Seminole Negro Scout, served 1887–89, 1893–1914. SOURCE: Schubert, Consolidated List of Seminole Negro Scouts.

Married. SOURCE: NARA, M 929, Roll 2.

SANDERS, Arthur; Private; B/10th Cav. Confined to guardhouse, Ft Duncan, TX, Jan 1878 for being absent from bed check. SOURCE: Kinevan, *Frontier Cavalryman*, 93.

SANDERS, George S.; Private; G/24th Inf. Died 20 Feb 1912; buried in plot W S 861 at San Francisco National Cemetery. SOURCE: San Francisco National Cemetery.

SANDERS, James C.; Cook; F/10th Cav. ‡Served in 10th Cavalry in Cuba, 1898. SOURCE: Cashin, *Under Fire with the Tenth Cavalry*, 343.

Died 23 Apr 1916; buried at Ft Leavenworth National Cemetery, plot H 3356-B. SOURCE: Ft Leavenworth National Cemetery.

SANDERS, Joseph; Private; K/25th Inf. Born in North Carolina; Ht 5'8", black complexion; occupation soldier; enlisted in A/39th Infantry for three years on 1 Dec 1866, age 22, at Greenville, LA; transferred to K/25th Infantry at Jackson Bks, LA, 20 Apr 1869. SOURCE: Descriptive Roll of A/39th Inf.

SANDERS, Mingo; 1st Sgt; B/25th Inf. ‡Born in Marion, SC; attended school there until he learned to read and write; enlisted Charleston, SC, 16 May 1881, after seeing advertisement for soldiers in Marion newspaper; in Dakota for considerable period; one-fourth blind after being hit in eye by exploding soda bottle; at El Caney, Cuba, with party that cut wire under heavy fire, 1 Jul 1898; at Santiago, Cuba, 2–3 and 10–11 Jul 1898; he and his company gladly shared their hardtack with Theodore Roosevelt's regiment in Cuba at Roosevelt's request; served in the Philippines at La Loma, 9 Oct 1899, at O'Donnell, 18 Oct 1899, at Commizi, 5 Jan 1900, at Subig, 29 Jan, 9–10 Feb, 21 and 23 Sep 1900; led two men through insurrectionist lines from Bam Bam to O'Donnell, 28 Nov 1899, with message from Gen. Andrew Burt to commander, 9th Infantry; captured several insurgents and weapons while in the Philippines as first sergeant, B/25th Infantry; General Burt wrote Mary Church Terrell that "Mingo Sanders is the best non-commissioned officer I have ever known." SOURCE: Terrell, "A Sketch of Mingo Sanders," 128–31.

‡Recruit, age 24, occupation cotton hand, Ht 5'8", black hair and eyes, fair complexion; enlisted Charleston, 16 May 1881; en route from depot, David's Island, NY, to Ft Randall, Dakota Territory, 2–7 Jul 1881. SOURCE: Descriptive & Assignment Rolls, 25 Inf.

‡Enlisted 16 May 1881; served in Cuba and the Philippines. SOURCE: *Colored American Magazine* 12 (Feb 1907): 147.

‡Authorized to reenlist as married soldier, with defective vision, 23 Apr 1896. SOURCE: AGO File 36224.

One of twenty men in B/25th Infantry who cycled 1,900 miles from Ft Missoula, MT, to St. Louis, MO, 14 Jun–24 Jul 1897, in 25th Infantry Bicycle Corps to test durability and practicality of bicycles as a means of transportation for troops. SOURCE: File 60178, GC, AGO Records.

‡Returned to unit from furlough in the U.S.; arrived at La Loma in time to take part in battle, 9 Oct 1900. SOURCE: Richmond *Planet*, 20 Jan 1900.

‡Located enemy outpost near Cabangan, Philippines, and captured enemy first sergeant and his rifle there. SOURCE: Richmond *Planet*, 23 Mar 1901.

‡Dishonorable discharge, Brownsville, TX. SOURCE: SO 266, AGO, 9 Nov 1906.

Discharged as corporal May 15, 1886, character very good; reenlisted 16 May 1886; discharged as sergeant 15 May 1891, character very good; reenlisted 16 May 1891; discharged as sergeant 15 May 1896, "a faithful and reliable soldier"; reenlisted 15 May 1896; discharged as ser-

geant 15 May 1899, character excellent; reenlisted 16 May 1899; discharged as first sergeant 15 May 1902, character excellent; reenlisted 16 May 1902; discharged as first sergeant 15 May 1905, character excellent; reenlisted 16 May 1905; discharged as first sergeant without honor 22 November 1906. SOURCE: Powell, "Military Record of the Enlisted Men Who Were Discharged Without Honor."

‡Sanders "has the respect and esteem of every officer in his regiment, and now, in his old age, blind of an eye, and within a few months of . . . a pension, he is cast out 'without honor' from the service he loves and the flag he fought for, to make a struggle in civil life for his bread and butter. The old soldier divided the bread of his company with the hungry Rough Riders at El Caney, upon the request of him whose order now drives him out to beg." SOURCE: Cleveland *Gazette*, 1 Dec 1906.

‡At discharge had one year, five months, and twenty-three days to serve before retirement. SOURCE: Cleveland *Gazette*, 23 Feb 1907.

‡2nd Lt. George C. Lawrason, 25th Infantry, Ft Reno, OK, believes Sanders was totally innocent of participation in or knowledge of Brownsville affray, 17 Dec 1906. SOURCE: AGO File 1192148.

‡Maj. G. W. Penrose, 25th Infantry, Ft Reno, makes statement regarding Brownsville that tends to exonerate Sanders, 20 Dec 1906. SOURCE: AGO File 1193156.

‡Poem "Sergeant Mingo Sanders," by R. L., published in New York *Sun* and reprinted in Indianapolis *Freeman*, 12 Jan 1907.

‡Applied for reenlistment; went to Judge Advocate General to make statement but his attorney kept him from taking oath; they fear Army plans to reenlist him to send him to the Philippines or Alaska to keep him from testifying before Senate. SOURCE: Washington *Post*, 25 Jan 1907.

Text of Mary Church Terrell's "A Sketch of Mingo Saunders," from *Voice of the Negro*, Mar 1907. SOURCE: Schubert, *Voices of the Buffalo Soldier*, 55–62.

‡Honorable Henry Cabot Lodge makes telephone request for information regarding his service, 8 Jun 1907. SOURCE: AGO File 1250511.

‡Honorable Joseph B. Foraker requests record of one conviction against him, 8 Jul 1907. SOURCE: AGO File 1250511.

‡Address in October 1908: 146 M Street, SE, Washington, DC. SOURCE: VA File XC 2625648 Mingo Sanders (kept by Veterans Administration and not turned over to National Archives).

‡Letter to President Roosevelt asks reinstatement; his savings have vanished and his wife's health is failing; first two discharges with character very good; next four discharges with character excellent. SOURCE: Cleveland *Gazette*, 31 Oct 1908.

‡President of U.S. instructs that he never be allowed to return to Army, 7 Feb 1909. SOURCE: AGO File 1763692.

‡Entered Freedmen's Hospital, Howard University, Washington, DC, with diabetic gangrenous infection of foot, 12 Aug 1929; died 15 Aug 1929. SOURCE: Pittsburgh *Courier*, 31 Aug 1929.

‡Died after leg was amputated; employed with Interior Department until death; resided at 463 New York Avenue, NW, Washington, DC. SOURCE: New York *Age*, 31 Aug 1929.

‡Leaves wife Luella and "a host of other relatives and friends"; remains are at John T. Rhines funeral chapel, Third and I Streets, SW, Washington, DC. SOURCE: Washington *Star*, 23 Aug 1929.

‡Former member and past patron, Ada Chapter, No. 2, Order of the Eastern Star. SOURCE: Washington *Star*, 24 Aug 1929.

‡Former Masonic grand master; members of Grand Lodge met at Masonic Temple, 1111 19th Street, NW, Washington, DC, 24 Aug 1929, to arrange funeral, which is scheduled for 26 Aug 1929. SOURCE: Washington *Star*, 24 Aug 1929.

‡Funeral scheduled for 1 P.M., 26 Aug 1929, with interment at Arlington National Cemetery. SOURCE: Washington *Star*, 25 Aug 1929.

‡Buried at Arlington Cemetery; survived by widow, Luella M. Sanders. SOURCE: Chicago *Defender*, 31 Aug 1929.

‡Biographical information. SOURCE: Weaver, *The Brownsville Raid*, 37, 95, 108, 121, 141, 242–45.

SANFORD, Sol; Wagoner; H/9th Cav. Received Philippine Campaign Badge number 11898 for service as private in L/9th Cavalry; in 9th Cavalry at Ft Leavenworth, KS, Mar 1905. SOURCE: Philippine Campaign Badge list, 29 May 1905.

‡Veteran of Philippine Insurrection; at Ft D. A. Russell, WY, in 1910; sharpshooter; resident of Milledgeville, GA. SOURCE: *Illustrated Review: Ninth Cavalry*, with picture.

SATCHELL, James; QM Sgt; K/24th Inf. ‡Commended for distinguished service as sergeant, A/24th Infantry, at battle of Santiago, Cuba, 1 Jul 1898, and awarded certificate of merit. SOURCE: GO 15, AGO, 13 Feb 1900.

‡Awarded certificate of merit for service in Cuban campaign, 1898. SOURCE: Scipio, *Last of the Black Regulars*, 130; Steward, *The Colored Regulars*, 280; *ANJ* 37 (24 Feb 1900): 611.

Awarded certificate of merit for distinguished service in battle, Santiago, Cuba, 1 Jul 1898. SOURCE: Gleim, *The Certificate of Merit*, 46.

Born and resided in Eastville, VA; received Distinguished Service Medal in lieu of certificate of merit. SOURCE: *American Decorations*, 842.

‡Quartermaster sergeant, A/24th Infantry; ranked number 185 among rifle experts with 68.67 percent in 1904. SOURCE: GO 79, AGO, 1 Jun 1905.

‡Quartermaster sergeant, K/24th Infantry, and distinguished marksman. SOURCE: GO 173, AGO, 20 Oct 1905.

SATTERTHWAITE, Romeo; Private; H/10th Cav. Born in Pitt County, NC, 17 Aug 1852, enslaved; enlisted Baltimore, MD, 11 Aug 1879; Ht 5'10", dark brown complexion, black eyes and hair; occupation laborer; at Eagle Springs, TX, and fought at Salt Lake, TX, summer of 1880; hospitalized Aug–Nov 1880 at Ft Davis, TX; present 31 Aug 1881 for duty at post near Presidio, TX; on duty 31 Dec 1881 at Pena Colorado, TX; discharged at Ft Davis, 11 Aug 1884; married in North Carolina, 18 Oct 1876, wife died 29 Jul 1910 in Baltimore; children Joseph J. born 10 Sep 1889 and Viola Bessie born 6 Jul 1894; resided at 729 Spring St., Baltimore, in 1894. SOURCE: Sayre, *Warriors of Color*, 406–25.

SAUNDERS, Alexander; H/25th Inf. Born in Virginia; mulatto complexion; can read and write, age 22, 5 Sep 1870, in H/25th Infantry at Ft McKavett, TX. SOURCE: Bierschwale, *Fort McKavett*, 107.

‡Pvt. Alexander Sanders, formerly of H/25th Infantry, resides in Phoebus, VA: "What has become of the boys of Company H, 25th U.S. Infantry, 1870 to 1875?"; encloses subscription order. SOURCE: *Winners of the West* 5 (May 1928): 5.

‡Wants to hear from old comrades. SOURCE: *Winners of the West* 6 (May 1929): 2.

SAUNDERS, James H.; Private; K/9th Cav. Died 1 Jan 1900; originally buried at Ft DuChesne, UT; reburied at Santa Fe National Cemetery, NM, plot A-4 1104. SOURCE: Santa Fe National Cemetery, Records of Burials.

SAUNDERS, Stephen; M/9th Cav. Born in Kentucky; black complexion; cannot read or write, age 21, Jul 1870, at Ft McKavett, TX. SOURCE: Bierschwale, *Fort McKavett*, 98.

SAUNDERS, William H.; Private; F/9th Cav. Died 28 Jul 1880; originally buried at Ft Stanton, NM; reburied at Santa Fe National Cemetery, NM, plot B 562. SOURCE: Santa Fe National Cemetery, Records of Burials.

SAUTER, Marcus; Private; I/25th Inf. Buried at San Antonio National Cemetery, Section B, number 130. SOURCE: San Antonio National Cemetery Locator.

SAVAGE, Jesse; Private; F/25th Inf. Born in Northampton, VA; Ht 5'9", black hair and eyes, black complexion; discharged from A/9th Cavalry 1 Jun 1886; reenlisted in 25th Infantry at age 35, occupation cook, Baltimore, MD, 12 Oct 1887; arrived Ft Snelling, MN, 7 Nov 1887. SOURCE: Descriptive & Assignment Rolls of Recruits, 25 Inf.

‡Served 1881–97; recent subscriber. SOURCE: *Winners of the West* 4 (Mar 1927): 8.

SCANDRICH, Jerry; 9th Cav. Born in Georgia; black complexion; can read and write, age 24, 5 Sep 1870, at Ft McKavett, TX. SOURCE: Bierschwale, *Fort McKavett,* 107.

SCHLOSS, Columbus; Recruit; C/10th Cav. ‡Recruit Columbus Schlass, C/10th Cavalry, original member of 10th Cavalry; in troop when organized, Ft Leavenworth, KS, 14 May 1867. SOURCE: McMiller, "Buffalo Soldiers," 70.

Recruit Columbus Schloss died 28 Jul 1867 of cholera at Camp Grierson, KS. SOURCE: Regimental Returns, 10th Cavalry, 1867.

SCHOENOCKER, John; H/25th Inf. Born in Maryland; black complexion; can read and write, age 24, 5 Sep 1870, at Ft McKavett, TX. SOURCE: Bierschwale, *Fort McKavett,* 108.

SCOTT, Alonzo; Sergeant; 24th Inf. Corporal, E/9th Cavalry, at Ft DuChesne, UT, Dec 1887. SOURCE: Kenner, *Buffalo Soldiers and Officers of the Ninth Cavalry*, 235.

‡Private, E/24th Infantry, at Ft Douglas, UT, not permitted to run in competition because he was so much faster than rest of men. SOURCE: Clark, "A History of the Twenty-fourth," 70.

Sergeant, 24th Infantry, at Ft DuChesne, placed second in both 100-yard and 220-yard dashes at 1896 track competition of all units in Department of the Colorado. SOURCE: Dobak and Phillips, *The Black Regulars*, 149.

SCOTT, Beverly; Private; D/10th Cav. Died 16 Mar 1873 of disease at Camp Supply, OK. SOURCE: Regimental Returns, 10th Cavalry, 1873.

‡Commander, 10th Cavalry, forwarded final statement and inventory of personal effects regarding Scott, formerly stationed at Camp Supply, to Adjutant General, 2 Apr 1873. SOURCE: ES, 10 Cav, 1873–83.

Died 16 Mar 1873; buried at Ft Leavenworth National Cemetery, plot G 3042. SOURCE: Ft Leavenworth National Cemetery.

SCOTT, Burley; Private; K/25th Inf. *See* SCOTT, Praley, Private, K/25th Infantry

SCOTT, Edward; Corporal; K/10th Cav. Private, D/9th Cavalry, with Captain Dodge at battle at Milk River, CO, 2–10 Oct 1879. SOURCE: Miller, *Hollow Victory*, 167, 206–7.

Former member of D/9th Cavalry and veteran of 1879 fight at Milk River, leg shattered in firefight against Apaches and rescued by Lt. Powhattan Clarke, 1886. SOURCE: Dobak and Phillips, *The Black Regulars*, 40–41.

Text of Lieutenant Clark's account of his rescue of Corporal Scott, from letter to his father, May 1886, published. SOURCE: Schubert, *Voices of the Buffalo Soldier*, 139–40.

‡Corporal, K/10th Cavalry, wounded in action against Geronimo, Pineto Mountains, Mexico, 3 May 1886. SOURCE: Baker, Roster.

‡Admitted to Soldiers Home with disability, age 30, after eight years and four months' service, 27 May 1886. SOURCE: SecWar, *AR 1884*, 748.

‡Resided at Forest Glen, Montgomery Co., MD, in 1895. SOURCE: VA File C 2363092, Henry Dent.

SCOTT, Frank; Private; K/10th Cav. Died 8 Jan 1897; buried at San Antonio National Cemetery, Section I, number 1642. SOURCE: San Antonio National Cemetery Locator.

SCOTT, George; Private; G/10th Cav. Died 22 Dec 1867, no cause listed, at Ft Hays, KS. SOURCE: Regimental Returns, 10th Cavalry, 1868.

SCOTT, George; Private; F/25th Inf. One of twenty men who cycled 1,900 miles from Ft Missoula, MT, to St. Louis, MO, 14 Jun–24 Jul 1897, in 25th Infantry Bicycle Corps to test durability and practicality of bicycles as a means of transportation for troops. SOURCE: File 60178, GC, AGO Records.

SCOTT, Henry; M/9th Cav. Born in Kentucky; mulatto complexion; cannot read or write, age 27, Jul 1870, at Ft McKavett, TX. SOURCE: Bierschwale, *Fort McKavett,* 100.

SCOTT, James; M/9th Cav. Born in Kentucky; black complexion; cannot read or write, age 24, Jul 1870, at Ft McKavett, TX. SOURCE: Bierschwale, *Fort McKavett,* 100.

SCOTT, John; Sergeant; E/24th Inf. Born in Woodstock, CT; Ht 5'9", black hair and brown eyes, brown complexion; occupation farmer; enlisted in 25th Infantry at age 21, Boston, MA, 9 Dec 1886; assigned to I/25th Infantry, arrived Ft Snelling, MN, 28 May 1887. SOURCE: Descriptive & Assignment Rolls of Recruits, 25 Inf.

‡Resident of Boston; sergeant to be discharged at end of term, Ft Bayard, NM, 8 Dec 1891. SOURCE: Cleveland *Gazette*, 12 Dec 1891.

SCOTT, John H.; I/10th Cav. Second sergeant, 30th Maryland Volunteers; resides at Baltimore, MD. SOURCE: United States Colored Troops Resident in Baltimore at the Time of the 1890 Census.

‡Original member of 10th Cavalry; in troop when organized, Ft Riley, KS, 15 Aug 1867. SOURCE: McMiller, "Buffalo Soldiers," 76.

SCOTT, Joseph; Private; 9th Cav. Received Philippine Campaign Badge number 11789 for service as private in D/9th Cavalry; in 9th Cavalry at Ft Leavenworth, KS, Mar 1905. SOURCE: Philippine Campaign Badge list, 29 May 1905.

‡Veteran of Philippine Insurrection; at Ft D. A. Russell, WY, in 1910; resident of Washington, DC. SOURCE: *Illustrated Review: Ninth Cavalry*, with picture.

SCOTT, Nelson; Lance Cpl; G/9th Cav. ‡Private, B/9th Cavalry, at Ft Duchesne, UT; teacher in post school, 1 Nov 1891–31 Jan 1892, 14 Dec 1892–30 Apr 1893. SOURCE: Reports of Schools, Fort Duchesne.

‡Assigned to extra duty as teacher, Ft Robinson, NE. SOURCE: Order 67, 24 Sep 1895, Post Orders, Ft Robinson.

‡At Ft Robinson; teacher in post school, Sep 1895–Feb 1896. SOURCE: Reports of Schools, Fort Duchesne.

‡Lance corporal, G/9th Cavalry; relieved from extra duty as schoolteacher, Ft Robinson. SOURCE: SO 14, 2 Feb 1897, Post Orders, Ft Robinson.

Sergeant, G/9th Cavalry, born in Mississippi; died 24 Aug 1936; buried in plot D-SOU1445 at San Francisco National Cemetery. SOURCE: San Francisco National Cemetery.

SCOTT, Praley; Private; K/25th Inf. Born in Georgia; Ht 5'6", black complexion; occupation laborer; enlisted in A/39th Infantry for three years on 10 Oct 1866, age 21, at New Orleans, LA; daily duty to post garden since 10 Apr 1869; transferred to K/25th Infantry at Jackson Bks, LA, 20 Apr 1869. SOURCE: Descriptive Roll of A/39th Inf.

Private, A/39th Infantry, Civil War veteran, served in D/82nd U.S. Colored Infantry; acquitted of involvement in New Iberia, LA, mutiny, Jul 1867. SOURCE: Dobak and Phillips, *The Black Regulars*, 222.

‡Pvt. Burley Scott, K/25th Infantry, born in Maringo, AL; Ht 5'6", dark complexion, black hair and eyes; occupation laborer; enlisted New Orleans, LA, age 24, 1 Oct 1866; initially assigned to A/39th Infantry; discharged, end of term, Jackson Bks, LA, Oct 1869. SOURCE: Register of Enlistments.

Died 10 Jan 1873 of disease at Ft Sill, OK. SOURCE: Regimental Returns, 10th Cavalry, 1873.

SCOTT, Sterling; Private; E/38th Inf. Died 5 Nov 1867; originally buried at Ft Hays, KS; reburied at Ft Leavenworth National Cemetery, plot 3352. SOURCE: Ft Leavenworth National Cemetery.

SCOTT, Thomas J.; Private; M/9th Cav. ‡Died of "saritonitis" at Ft Washakie, WY, 24 Mar 1887. SOURCE: Regt Returns, 9 Cav, Mar 1887.

Died 24 Mar 1887; originally buried at Ft Washakie; reburied at Ft Leavenworth National Cemetery, plot 3503. SOURCE: Ft Leavenworth National Cemetery.

SCOTT, Walter; D/24th Inf. Born in Ohio; mulatto complexion; can read, cannot write, age 24, Jul 1870, at Ft McKavett, TX. SOURCE: Bierschwale, *Fort McKavett*, 95.

SCOTT, Wesley; Private; L/9th Cav. Died 2 Feb 1877; buried at Ft Leavenworth National Cemetery, plot 2253. SOURCE: Ft Leavenworth National Cemetery.

SCOTT, William; Private; 10th Cav. At Ft Concho, TX, 1876, stole sack of corn from stables and sold it to nearby civilian. SOURCE: Dobak and Phillips, *The Black Regulars*, 195–96.

SCOTT, William; Private; U.S. Army. Seminole Negro Scout, served 1888–89. SOURCE: Schubert, Consolidated List of Seminole Negro Scouts.

Born in Texas; Ht 6', black hair and eyes, black complexion; enlisted at Ft Clark, TX, 26 Dec 1888; discharged at Camp Neville Springs, TX, 28 Feb 1889. SOURCE: Swanson, 40.

SCOTT, William; Private; 9th Cav. Received Philippine Campaign Badge number 11788 for service as private in F/9th Cavalry; in 9th Cavalry at Ft Leavenworth, KS, Mar 1905. SOURCE: Philippine Campaign Badge list 29 May 1905.

SCRUGGINS, Marshal; Private; L/9th Cav. Died at Ft McIntosh, TX, on 24 Jul 1872; buried at Fort Sam Houston National Cemetery, Section PE, number 422. SOURCE: Buffalo Soldiers Interred in Fort Sam Houston National Cemetery.

SEAWRIGHT, Albert; Corporal; 9th Cav. ‡Pvt. Albert Searight, G/10th Cavalry, served in 10th Cavalry, 1898; remained in U.S. during war with Spain. SOURCE: Cashin, *Under Fire with the Tenth Cavalry*, 333.

Received Philippine Campaign Badge number 11745 for service as corporal in H/48th Infantry, United States Volunteers; in 9th Cavalry at Ft Leavenworth, KS, Mar 1905. SOURCE: Philippine Campaign Badge list, 29 May 1905.

SEBASTON; Lewis; Private; 9th Cav. Received Philippine Campaign Badge number 11790 for service as private in H/25th Infantry; in 9th Cavalry at Ft Leavenworth, KS, Mar 1905. SOURCE: Philippine Campaign Badge list, 29 May 1905.

SEIGLER, Fred; Pvt 1st Class; A/9th Cav. *See* SEIGLER, Fred, Private 1st Class, A/9th Cavalry

SELLERS, Isaac; F/9th Cav. Born in Virginia; black complexion; cannot read or write, age 22, Jul 1870, at Ft McKavett, TX. SOURCE: Bierschwale, *Fort McKavett*, 97.

SETTLERS, James; Private; E/9th Cav. ‡Mentioned in orders among men who distinguished themselves in 1889 for meritorious conduct while private, E/9th Cavalry; saved his commander from drowning while crossing Wind River, Wyoming, at risk of his own life, 19 Jul 1889. SOURCE: GO 18, AGO, 1891; Dobak and Phillips, *The Black Regulars*, 262.

‡Private, F/9th Cavalry; relieved of extra duty with Quartermaster Department, Ft Robinson, NE. SOURCE: Order 181, 25 Oct 1892, Post Orders, Ft Robinson.

‡Transferred from 9th Cavalry to 25th Infantry. SOURCE: SO 244, AGO, 23 Oct 1893.

‡Certificate of merit for 1889 rescue awarded 16 Jan 1900; discharged 29 Sep 1900. SOURCE: *ANJ* 39 (2 Aug 1902): 1219; GO 86, AGO, 24 Jul 1902.

Private in E/9th Cavalry, awarded certificate of merit for saving his commanding officer from death by drowning, Wind River, 19 Jul 1889. SOURCE: Gleim, *The Certificate of Merit*, 44.

SEWALL, B.; Private; L/9th Cav. *See* SOWELL, Berry, Corporal, L/9th Cavalry

SEWARD, William; G/9th Cav. ‡Born in Harden Co., KY; occupation farmer; Ht 5'7 1/2", black complexion, hair, and eyes; enlisted Louisville, age 25, 24 Nov 1871; discharged, end of term, Ft Ringgold, TX, 23 Sep 1874. SOURCE: Register of Enlistments.

Slept on sentry duty, but had been made preceding night to carry saddle from retreat to reveille, Department of Texas, 1873. SOURCE: Dobak and Phillips, *The Black Regulars*, 182.

SEWELL, Isaiah; Private; E/25th Inf. Died 24 May 1898; buried at San Antonio National Cemetery, Section I, number 1665. SOURCE: San Antonio National Cemetery Locator.

SEWELL, James; Private; G/9th Cav. Died at Ft Griffin, TX, on 27 Mar 1872; buried at San Antonio National Cemetery, Section D, number 690. SOURCE: San Antonio National Cemetery Locator.

SHANDS, Charles; F/9th Cav. Born in Virginia; black complexion; can read and write, age 23, Jul 1870, at Ft McKavett, TX. SOURCE: Bierschwale, *Fort McKavett*, 98.

SHARP, G. W.; Private; M/9th Cav. Born in Louisville, KY; black complexion; cannot read or write, age 26, Jul 1870, at Ft McKavett, TX; buried at Ft McKavett before 17 May 1879; body removed to National Cemetery, San Antonio, TX, 23 Nov 1883. SOURCE: Bierschwale, *Fort McKavett*, 100, 123.

Died at Ft McKavett, 3 Jan 1872; buried at San Antonio National Cemetery, Section E, number 876. SOURCE: San Antonio National Cemetery Locator.

SHARPE, William; Private; K/9th Cav. ‡Killed in action, 26 Dec 1867. SOURCE: Leckie, *The Buffalo Soldiers*, 85; *Illustrated Review: Ninth Cavalry*. *See* BOWERS, Edward, Private, K/9th Cavalry; TRIMBLE, Anderson, Private, K/9th Cavalry

One of three troopers killed in pre-dawn Indian attack on Fort Lancaster, TX, 26 Dec 1867. SOURCE: Schubert, *Black Valor*, 17.

SHAW, Perry; Private; D/10th Cav. ‡Private in M/10th Cavalry at Ft McDowell, AZ, 1887. SOURCE: Misc Records, 10 Cav.

‡At Ft Apache, AZ, 1890, subscribed $.50 to testimonial to General Grierson. SOURCE: List of subscriptions, 23 Apr 1890, 10th Cavalry papers, MHI.

Private, D/10th Cavalry, died 21 Nov 1891; buried at Ft Bayard, NM, in plot I 35. SOURCE: "Fort Bayard National Cemetery, Records of Burials."

Buried 21 Nov 1891, section A, row M, plot 38, at Ft Bayard. SOURCE: Erickson, Burials at Fort Bayard National Cemetery, NM.

SHAW, Thomas; Sergeant; K/9th Cav. ‡Born in Covington, KY; awarded Medal of Honor for heroism against Apache Nana while sergeant, K/9th Cavalry, Carrizo Canyon, NM, 19 Jul 1881. SOURCE: Carroll, *The Black Military Experience*, 397–98; Leckie, *The Buffalo Soldiers*, 232.

Life, career, and valor against Apaches, for which he received Medal of Honor, narrated. SOURCE: Schubert, *Black Valor*, 69, 77–79, 87–88, 117.

‡Medal of Honor for heroism in action against Nana, Carrizo Canyon, 12 Aug 1881. SOURCE: Billington, *New Mexico's Buffalo Soldiers*, 105.

‡First sergeant, B/9th Cavalry, at Ft Bayard, NM, 1877. *See* OTT, RICHTER, William J., B/9th Cavalry

‡On furlough from Ft Cummings, NM, 20 Dec 1880–18 Feb 1881. SOURCE: Regt Returns, 9 Cav, Dec 1880–Feb 1881.

‡Enlisted as private, Ft Robinson, NE, 7 Dec 1886. SOURCE: Post Returns, Ft Robinson, Dec 1886.

‡Date of rank as sergeant 10 Dec 1886. SOURCE: Roster, 9 Cav.

‡At Ft Robinson, 1888; wife visiting in Kansas City, MO. SOURCE: Cleveland *Gazette*, 12 Jan 1889.

‡Treasurer of Diamond Club, K/9th Cavalry, as sergeant, Ft Robinson. SOURCE: *ANJ* 28 (2 May 1891): 620.

Ran away from master to enlist in Union Army at age 18 in 1864; as first sergeant in K/9th Cavalry, valor in Victorio war in 1881 and Medal of Honor discussed; served on honor guard when body of Col. Edward Hatch was transported from Ft Robinson to Ft Leavenworth, KS, in 1889; at Ft Meyer, VA, retired in 1894; settled in Rosslyn, VA; died 1895. SOURCE: Kenner, *Buffalo Soldiers and Officers of the Ninth Cavalry*, 48–49, 147–49, 154.

SHELTON, Houston; Private; D/9th Cav. At Ft Stockton, TX, July 1873, participated in protest over treatment of Pvt. John Taylor; convicted by court martial of attending unauthorized meeting and dishonorably discharged. SOURCE: Kenner, *Buffalo Soldiers and Officers of the Ninth Cavalry*, 89.

SHELTON, Leonard; Private; F/9th Cav. Born in Clark County, KY; black complexion; cannot read or write, age 19, Jul 1870, at Ft McKavett, TX; buried at Ft McKavett before 17 May 1879; body removed to National Cemetery, San Antonio, TX, 23 Nov 1883. SOURCE: Bierschwale, *Fort McKavett*, 97, 123.

Died at Ft McKavett on 3 Sep 1873; buried at San Antonio National Cemetery, Section E, number 850. SOURCE: San Antonio National Cemetery Locator.

SHELTON, Thomas D.; 1st Sgt; K/9th Cav. ‡Private, sick in Ft Robinson, NE, hospital, 22 May–Jun 1891. SOURCE: Regt Returns, 9 Cav, May–Jun 1891.

‡Corporal as of 4 Oct 1893; at Ft Robinson, 1895. SOURCE: *ANJ* 32 (1 Jun 1895): 658.

‡Reenlistment as married soldier authorized by letter, Adjutant General's Office, 1 May 1895.

Appointed corporal 4 Oct 1893; in K/9th Cavalry at Ft Robinson, Jan 1897. SOURCE: Ninth Cavalry, Roster of NCOs, 1897.

Sergeant, K/9th Cavalry, received Indian Wars Campaign Badge number 1364 on 28 May 1909. SOURCE: Carroll, *Indian Wars Campaign Badge*, 39.

‡Veteran of Indian wars, Spanish-American War, and Philippine Insurrection; first sergeant, at Ft D. A. Russell, WY, in 1910; marksman; resident of Albemarle Co., VA. SOURCE: *Illustrated Review: Ninth Cavalry*, with picture.

Died 22 Feb 1935; buried in plot C 1243 at San Francisco National Cemetery. SOURCE: San Francisco National Cemetery.

SHEPARD, Thomas; Corporal; F/10th Cav. ‡Original member of 10th Cavalry; in troop when organized, Ft Leavenworth, KS, 21 Jun 1867. SOURCE: McMiller, "Buffalo Soldiers," 73.

‡Wounded in action against Indians in Kansas, 21 Aug 1867. SOURCE: Armes, *Ups and Downs*, 247.

Cpl. Thomas Shepherd, F/10th Cavalry, wounded in action against Indians at Beaver Creek, KS, 21 Aug 1867. SOURCE: Schubert, *Voices of the Buffalo Soldier*, 20.

Cpl. Thomas Sheppard, F/10th Cavalry, wounded in action, arrow wound in right side of neck, near Beaver Creek, 21 Aug 1867. SOURCE: LR, DeptMo, 1867.

SHEPARDSON, George; Private; A/49th Inf. ‡Deserted from Cordin, Philippines, 24 Dec 1900, after trying to kill 1st Sgt. Peter G. Gibson and killing a native. SOURCE: Descriptive Book, A/49 Inf.

Died 27 Dec 1900; buried in plot 1136 at San Francisco National Cemetery. SOURCE: San Francisco National Cemetery.

SHEPHERD, Thomas; Corporal; F/10th Cav. *See* SHEPARD, Thomas, Corporal, F/10th Cavalry

SHEPPARD, Horace; Musician; Band/25th Inf. Died at Ft Clark, TX; buried at Fort Sam Houston National Cemetery, Section PE, number 165. SOURCE: Buffalo Soldiers Interred in Fort Sam Houston National Cemetery.

SHEPPARD, Thomas; Corporal; F/10th Cav. *See* SHEPARD, Thomas, Corporal, F/10th Cavalry

SHIDELL, John S.; Corporal; B/9th Cav. ‡Private, K/9th Cavalry, wounded in action against Nana, Carrizo Canyon, NM, Aug 1881; returned to duty after convalescence, promoted to sergeant before he reenlisted in 1885. SOURCE: Kenner, *Buffalo Soldiers and Officers of the Ninth Cavalry*, 149.

‡In C/9th Cavalry; child Willie Slidell died and was buried at Ft Robinson, NE, 3 Apr 1886. SOURCE: List of Interments, Ft Robinson.

Child Willie, age 3 months, 3 days, died of entracolitis 3 Apr 1886; child Walter Shidell died of premature birth in eighth month, 21 Sep 1886, buried at Ft Robinson, father mulatto, mother Mexican. SOURCE: Buecker, Fort Robinson Burials.

Pvt. John S. Shidell appointed corporal 6 Jul 1896; in B/9th Cavalry at Ft DuChesne, UT, Jan 1897. SOURCE: Ninth Cavalry, Roster of NCOs, 1897.

‡Pvt. John J. Shidell, B/9th Cavalry, in hands of civil authorities, Price, UT, and Salt Lake City, UT, 2 Oct 1897– 18 Apr 1898. SOURCE: Regt Returns, 9 Cav, Oct 1897– Apr 1898.

SHIELDS, Archibald; Private; U.S. Army. Seminole Negro Scout, served 1881–88. SOURCE: Schubert, Consolidated List of Seminole Negro Scouts.

Born in South Carolina; Ht 5'6", black hair and eyes, yellow complexion; enlisted at Ft Clark, TX, 14 May 1881, age 49; discharged 13 May 1882, reenlisted next day at Ft Clark; discharged 13 May 1883, reenlisted next day at Ft Clark; discharged 13 May 1884 at Camp Neville Springs, TX; enlisted for one year 13 May 1884 at Ft Clark; enlistment terminated for convenience of government 31 Aug 1884 at Ft Clark; enlisted 6 Jan 1885 at Ft Clark where he was discharged 5 Jan 1886; enlisted 9 Jan 1886 at Ft Clark where he was discharged 3 Jan 1887; enlisted 3 Jan 1887 at Ft Clark where he was discharged 3 Jan 1888; enlisted for one year 9 Jan 1888 at Ft Clark; discharged for disability 4 Nov 1888. SOURCE: Swanson, 41.

Archibald R. Shields, born in South Carolina, private, Indian Scouts, died 7 Jun 1907; buried at Seminole Indian

Scout Cemetery, Kinney County, TX. SOURCE: Indian Scout Cemetery, Kinney County, Texas.

SHIELDS, Frank H.; 9th Cav. Received Philippine Campaign Badge number 11899 for service as farrier in H/9th Cavalry; in 9th Cavalry at Ft Leavenworth, KS, Mar 1905. SOURCE: Philippine Campaign Badge list, 29 May 1905.

SHIELDS, James; M/10th Cav. Private, 39th USCT; resides at 806 Pierce Ave., Baltimore, MD. SOURCE: United States Colored Troops Resident in Baltimore, 1890 Census.

‡Original member of 10th Cavalry; in troop when organized, Ft Riley, KS, 15 Oct 1867. SOURCE: McMiller, "Buffalo Soldiers," 79.

SHIELDS, John; Sergeant; U.S. Army. Seminole Negro Scout, served 1894, 1898–1914. SOURCE: Schubert, Consolidated List of Seminole Negro Scouts.

Born in Texas; Ht 5'7", black hair and eyes, black complexion; enlisted at Ft Clark, TX, 8 Sep 1894, age 22; discharged 30 Nov 1894 at Ft Clark; enlisted 16 Feb 1898 at Ft Clark where he was discharged 21 Feb 1901; enlisted at Camp Eagle Pass, TX, 26 Feb 1904; discharged 25 Feb 1907, reenlisted next day at Ft Clark; discharged as sergeant 25 Feb 1910, reenlisted next day at Ft Clark; honorably discharged 30 Sep 1914; died 19 Apr 1928; buried at Seminole Indian Scout Cemetery, Kinney County, TX. SOURCE: Swanson, 41.

SHIELDS, William; Corporal; U.S. Army. Seminole Negro Scout, served 1887–1908. SOURCE: Schubert, Consolidated List of Seminole Negro Scouts.

Born in Mexico; Ht 5'6", black hair and eyes, black complexion; enlisted at Ft Clark, TX, 3 Jan 1887, age 21; discharged 2 Jan 1888, reenlisted 5 Jan 1888 at Ft Clark; discharged 4 Jan 1889 at Camp Neville Springs, TX; enlisted 7 Jan 1889 at Ft Clark; discharged 6 Jan 1890, reenlisted next day at Ft Clark; discharged 6 Jul 1890, reenlisted next day at Camp Neville Springs; discharged 6 Jan 1891, reenlisted next day at Ft Clark; discharged 6 Jul 1891, reenlisted next day at Camp Palvo, TX; discharged 6 Jan 1892, reenlisted next day at Camp Palvo; discharged 6 Jul 1892 at Camp Presidio, TX; enlisted 17 Aug 1893 at Ft Ringgold, TX; discharged 16 Feb 1894 at Camp Salienas, TX; enlisted 17 Feb 1894 at Camp San Pedro, TX; discharged 15 Aug 1894, reenlisted next day at Ft Ringgold; discharged and reenlisted for three years twice at Ft Ringgold, 16 Feb 1895–17 Feb 1898; discharged 16 Feb 1901 at Ft Ringgold; enlisted 17 Feb 1901 at Ft Clark; discharged 16 Feb 1904, reenlisted next day at Camp Eagle Pass, TX; discharged 17 Feb 1907, reenlisted next day at Ft Clark; discharged as corporal for disability 28 Sep 1908 at Ft Clark; photograph, A.C. #601, of Shields and Fay July in Old Guardhouse Museum, Brackettville, TX. SOURCE: Swanson, 42.

SHIPLEY, John; Private; D/9th Cav. With Captain Dodge at battle at Milk River, CO, 2–10 Oct 1879; received Indian Wars Campaign Medal. SOURCE: Miller, *Hollow Victory*, 167, 191, 206–7.

SHIPLEY, John; Sergeant; A/9th Cav. ‡Private, H/9th Cavalry, at Ft McKinney, WY, 1888. SOURCE: Regt Returns, 9 Cav.

‡Reenlisted as private, H/9th Cavalry, Ft Robinson, NE, and requests retirement, 14 Aug 1898; discharge at end of previous term was with character, good. SOURCE: Regt Returns, 9 Cav, Aug 1898.

‡Retired as sergeant, A/9th Cavalry, Ft Grant, AZ, Dec 1899. SOURCE: *ANJ* 37 (23 Dec 1899): 395.

Retired sergeant; received Indian Wars Campaign Badge number 1075 on 9 Dec 1908. SOURCE: Carroll, *Indian Wars Campaign Badge*, 31.

‡No Veterans Administration pension file.

SHOOP, Thomas; Private; A/10th Cav. Died 16 Dec 1903; buried at San Antonio National Cemetery, Section F, number 1059. SOURCE: San Antonio National Cemetery Locator.

SHORT, George; Private; 24th Inf. Part of escort for Paymaster Joseph Wham when he was ambushed by robbers near Cedar Springs, AZ, in May 1889; did not contribute significantly to defense. SOURCE: Schubert, *Black Valor*, 93, 95, 96.

SHROPSHIRE, Shelvin; 1st Sgt; H/10th Cav. ‡Born in Alabama; private and corporal, F/15th U.S. Colored Troops, 18 Jan 1864–13 May 1866; private, corporal, sergeant, first sergeant, C/10th Cavalry, and regimental quartermaster sergeant, 10th Cavalry, 1 Mar 1867–1 Mar 1882; private, B/10th Cavalry, 8 Aug 1883; corporal, 1 Nov 1883; transferred to L/10th Cavalry, 5 Nov 1884; sergeant, 1 Mar 1888; first sergeant, 23 Jun 1888; transferred to H/10th Cavalry, 23 Oct 1890; at Ft Assiniboine, MT, 1897. SOURCE: Baker, Roster.

‡Constituent member of C/10th Cavalry when organized at Ft Leavenworth, 16 May 1867, and "a conspicuous figure in regimental history since"; first Indian action against Cheyennes, at Great Bend of Arkansas River; at Galestee [*sic*], NM, disarmed a second lieutenant of regiment who had already shot and killed two men and thus prevented mutiny; mentioned for bravery in action against Kiowas and Comanches at Wichita Agency, Indian Territory, 22–23 Aug 1874; "rendered excellent service through the Geronimo campaign of 1885–86." SOURCE: Baker, Roster.

‡At Ft Bayard, NM, 1891. *See* OTT, STARGALL, Charlie, Private, 10th Cavalry

Served in C/10th Cavalry with Pvt. George Washington, early 1870s; account of early frontier campaigns and relations between sergeants and privates published in article by Frederic Remington in *Cosmopolitan*, February 1897.

SOURCE: Schubert, *Voices of the Buffalo Soldier*, 21–22, 234.

‡Conversation with Frederic Remington reported. SOURCE: Remington, "Vagabonding with the Tenth," *Cosmopolitan Magazine* 22 (Feb 1897).

‡Served in 10th Cavalry, 1898; remained in U.S. during war with Spain. SOURCE: Cashin, *Under Fire with the Tenth Cavalry*, 346.

‡At Camp Forse, AL, Nov 1898; feet were so sore he could not attend Thanksgiving dinner and was served in his tent.

‡By 1898 soldiers were relatively well educated and frequently resented discipline by noncommissioned officers who could barely read and write, such as Shropshire. SOURCE: Fletcher, "The Negro Soldier," 31.

‡Retirement with thirty-three years' service celebrated by regimental parade; elaborate dinner dance held in his honor by his troop on following day. SOURCE: Fletcher, "The Negro Soldier," 95.

‡No Veterans Administration pension file.

SIEGLER, Fred; Private; A/9th Cav. Private 1st Class Fred Siegler died 20 June 1919; buried at Ft Bayard, NM, in plot U 16. SOURCE: "Fort Bayard National Cemetery, Record of Burials."

Private Fred Siegler, buried 20 Jun 1919, section D, row F, plot 16, at Ft Bayard. SOURCE: Erickson, Burials at Fort Bayard National Cemetery, NM.

SIMMONS, Charles; Private; B/25th Inf. Born in Mecklenburg, KY; Ht 5'7", black hair and brown eyes, brown complexion; occupation soldier; discharged from D/24th Infantry, 1 May 1886; second reenlistment, 18 May 1886, age 27, at St Louis, MO; assigned to B/25th Infantry; arrived Ft Snelling, MN, 4 Jul 1886. SOURCE: Descriptive & Assignment Rolls of Recruits, 25 Inf.

SIMMONS, George; Private; U.S. Army. Seminole Negro Scout, served 1872–75, 1879–80, 1882–84. SOURCE: Schubert, Consolidated List of Seminole Negro Scouts.

Born in Mississippi; Ht 5'5", black hair and eyes, black complexion; enlisted at Ft Clark, TX, 12 Aug 1872, age 27; discharged 12 Feb 1873 at Ft Clark; enlisted 25 Aug 1873 at Ft Clark where he was discharged 25 Feb 1874; enlisted 29 Jan 1875 at Ft Clark; discharged 19 Sep 1875 at Camp Supply, TX; enlisted 13 Feb 1878, age 40, at Ft Clark where he was discharged 29 Apr 1879; enlisted 2 May 1879 at Ft Clark where he was discharged 1 May 1880; enlisted 13 May 1882 at Ft Clark where he was discharged 14 May 1883; enlisted 13 May 1883 at Ft Clark; discharged 12 May 1884 at Camp Myers, TX; enlisted 12 May 1884 at Ft Clark where enlistment was terminated for convenience of government 31 Aug 1884; 1880 Census lists George Simmons, age 45, wife Lucy age 25, children Nelly, Henry, Sally, Catherine, Hepey. SOURCE: Swanson, 42.

SIMMONS, Joseph; Private; E/10th Cav. Died 16 Feb 1875 of wounds received in quarrel, Ft Richardson, TX. SOURCE: Regimental Returns, 10th Cavalry, 1875.

Died at Ft Richardson on 16 Feb 1875; buried at San Antonio National Cemetery, Section D, number 606. SOURCE: San Antonio National Cemetery Locator.

SIMMONS, Marcus; Private; 25th Inf. Born in Charleston, SC; occupation laborer; Ht 5'8 1/2", dark complexion, black hair and eyes; enlisted, age 20, Charleston, 5 Jul 1881; left recruit depot, David's Island, NY, 17 Aug 1881, and after trip on steamer *Thomas Kirby* to Central Depot, New York City, and train via Chicago to Running Water, Dakota Territory, 22 Aug 1881, marched forty-seven miles to Ft Randall, SD, arrived 24 Aug 1881. SOURCE: Descriptive & Assignment Rolls, 25 Inf.

SIMMONS, Peter; Private; 25th Inf. Born in Charleston, SC; occupation laborer; Ht 5'4 1/4", fair complexion, black hair and eyes; enlisted, age 24, Charleston, 27 May 1881; left recruit depot, David's Island, NY, 17 Aug 1881, and after trip on steamer *Thomas Kirby* to Central Depot, New York City, and train via Chicago to Running Water, Dakota Territory, 22 Aug 1881, marched forty-seven miles to Ft Randall, SD, arrived 24 Aug 1881. SOURCE: Descriptive & Assignment Rolls, 25 Inf.

SIMMONS, William; B/9th Cav. Buried at Santa Fe National Cemetery, NM, plot A-1 759. SOURCE: Santa Fe National Cemetery, Records of Burials.

SIMMONS, William; Trumpeter; L/10th Cav. ‡Excused from duty, Camp Santa Rosa, TX, by Assistant Surgeon M. F. Price because of dysentery, May 1879, but kept at menial tasks by Capt. George A. Armes, 10th Cavalry; locked in barracks by Pvt. John W. Woods on orders of Armes, 11 Jun 1879, Ft Stockton, TX, in defiance of post commander's orders that Simmons be hospitalized; due to Armes's actions, disease worsened and Simmons died, Ft Stockton, 7 Sep 1879. SOURCE: GCMO 36, AGO, 27 May 1880.

See OTT, COLLINS, George, Private, L/10th Cavalry

At Ft Stockton, Aug 1879, sick in hospital with dysentery. SOURCE: Armes, *Ups and Downs*, 473.

Died 7 Sep 1879 of consumption at Ft Stockton. SOURCE: Regimental Returns, 10th Cavalry, 1879.

Died at Ft Stockton on 7 Sep 1879; buried at San Antonio National Cemetery, Section C, number 346. SOURCE: San Antonio National Cemetery Locator.

SIMONS, Henry; Private; D/25th Inf. Born in Prince Georges County, MD; Ht 6'0", black hair and brown eyes, black complexion; occupation laborer; resided in Washington, DC, when he enlisted 28 Dec 1885, age 27, at Washington, DC; assigned to D/25th Infantry; arrived Ft Snelling,

MN, 26 Apr 1886. SOURCE: Descriptive & Assignment Rolls of Recruits, 25 Inf.

SIMPSON, Wig; Private; F/48th Inf. Died 5 Jul 1901; buried in plot NEW A386 at San Francisco National Cemetery; also listed as Simpson Wig. SOURCE: San Francisco National Cemetery.

SIMPSON, William; Private; G/38th Inf. Died 21 Jul 1867; originally buried at Ft Hays, KS; reburied at Ft Leavenworth National Cemetery, plot 3323. SOURCE: Ft Leavenworth National Cemetery.

SIMS, John; Private; 25th Inf. Initially enlisted at Washington, DC, for 40th Infantry; served total of eight years and returned to Washington; died in 1928 and buried at Arlington National Cemetery. SOURCE: Dobak and Phillips, *The Black Regulars*, 278.

SIMS, Lewis; Private; K/25th Inf. ‡At Ft Niobrara, NE, 1904. SOURCE: Wilson, "History of Fort Niobrara."

Private, received Indian Wars Campaign Badge number 1399 on 13 Jul 1909. SOURCE: Carroll, *Indian Wars Campaign Badge*, 40.

SINCLAIR, Thomas; Private; 25th Inf. Born in Charleston, SC; Ht 5'5", black hair and eyes, fair complexion; occupation laborer; enlisted at age 22, Charleston, 21 May 1881; left recruit depot, David's Island, NY, 2 Jul 1881, arrived Ft Randall, SD, 7 Jul 1881. SOURCE: Descriptive & Assignment Rolls of Recruits, 25 Inf.

SINGLETON, Charles; Private; D/38th Inf. Died 31 Aug 1867; buried at Ft Leavenworth National Cemetery, plot E 2537. SOURCE: Ft Leavenworth National Cemetery.

SKIDRICK, Frank; Sergeant; I/10th Cav. ‡Died of accidental gunshot wound late 1870. SOURCE: Leckie, *The Buffalo Soldiers*, 56.

Died 23 Jul 1870 of gunshot wound at Camp Supply, OK. SOURCE: Regimental Returns, 10th Cavalry, 1870.

‡Final statement sent to Adjutant General. SOURCE: CO, 10 Cav, to AG, 21 Aug 1870, ES, 10 Cav, 1866–71.

SLAMP, Demer; Private; F/24th Inf. Died 23 Apr 1897; buried at Santa Fe National Cemetery, NM, plot I 435. SOURCE: Santa Fe National Cemetery, Records of Burials.

SLAUGHTER, Rufus; Private; K/9th Cav. ‡Served in E/13th Artillery, Mar 1864–Nov 1865; served continuously from 1866 to 1886; got rheumatism in right shoulder, hip, knees, from explosion, Ft Supply, Indian Territory, Jul 1884; filed claim for invalid pension from Crawford, NE, at age

54, 8 Apr 1891; at time of death on 12 Oct 1907, former wife Ella Slaughter resided at 119 Sweetwater Street, Hot Springs, SD. SOURCE: VA File XC 2648848, Rufus Slaughter.

Brutal treatment by Capt. J. Lee Humfreville, summer 1872, described. SOURCE: Kenner, *Buffalo Soldiers and Officers of the Ninth Cavalry*, 141–45.

‡Capt. Lee Humfreville, 9th Cavalry, convicted by general court martial of handcuffing in pairs Slaughter and Pvts. James Imes, Jerry Williams, Levi Comer, Henry Robinson, and Jim Wade and Farrier E. Tucker, pulling them 450 miles by a rope hitched to an Army wagon from Ft Richardson, TX, to Ft McKavett, TX, in a nineteen-day period, allowing them only bread and meat and no fire in their camp, 15 Dec 1872–20 Jan 1873. SOURCE: GCMO 23, AGO, 3 Apr 1874.

Text of court martial order convicting Capt. J. Lee Humfreville of brutality published. SOURCE: Schubert, *Voices of the Buffalo Soldier*, 55–62.

‡Wife Ella is visiting sister-in-law in Louisville. SOURCE: Cleveland *Gazette*, 14 Aug 1886.

‡Discharged as trumpeter, K/9th Cavalry, end of term, Ft Robinson, NE, 25 Dec 1886.

‡Completed twenty years in regular Army on 29 Dec 1886; has joined his family on farm three miles from Ft Robinson, NE, where he will try civilian life. SOURCE: Cleveland *Gazette*, 1 Jan 1887.

‡Unmarried, divorced from Ella Slaughter of Hot Springs, SD, 1892; two children: Gertrude, born 1876, and Sam, born 1878. SOURCE: Bureau of Pensions Questionnaire, 27 Jun 1898, VA File XC 2648848, Rufus Slaughter.

‡"Resented the carving up of his coat Saturday night by Brooks," and knocked down and chastised Brooks. SOURCE: Crawford *Tribune*, 27 Dec 1901.

‡Lived alone in 1904, but was nursed through difficult attack of rheumatism by former comrade Henry Wilson, Crawford, 1904. SOURCE: Schubert, *Buffalo Soldiers, Braves, and the Brass*, 155.

‡Resident of Crawford, 1905, with personal property assessed at $51, on which he paid $2 tax. SOURCE: Dawes County tax records.

‡Died at Alliance, NE, Oct 1907, an "old colored pioneer" of Crawford. SOURCE: Crawford *Tribune*, 18 Oct 1907.

‡Pension at time of death was $6 per month. SOURCE: VA File XC 2648848, Rufus Slaughter.

‡Son Sam resided in Crawford, 1907, with no assessed personal property of value. SOURCE: Dawes County tax records.

See JORDAN, George, First Sergeant, K/9th Cavalry; OTT, WASHINGTON, William, 9th Cavalry; OTT, WRIGHT, Daniel, Sergeant, K/9th Cavalry

SLAUTER, William; Corporal; G/9th Cav. ‡Appointed corporal 23 Oct 1891. SOURCE: Roster, 9 Cav.

‡Post gardener, Ft Robinson, NE. SOURCE: Order 54, 16 Aug 1895, Post Orders, Ft Robinson.

‡Discharged at Ft Robinson, Oct 1895. SOURCE: *ANJ* 33 (12 Oct 1895): 87.

Appointed corporal 12 Dec 1896; in G/9th Cavalry at Ft Robinson, Jan 1897. SOURCE: Ninth Cavalry, Roster of NCOs, 1897.

SLIDELL; Private; C/9th Cav. *See* SHIDELL, John S., Corporal, B/9th Cavalry

SLOAN, Miles; Private; A/10th Cav. Died 4 Feb 1867; buried at Ft Leavenworth National Cemetery, plot C 725. SOURCE: Ft Leavenworth National Cemetery.

SMALL, Benjamin; Private; C/10th Cav. Died 23 Mar 1880 of consumption at Ft Davis, TX. SOURCE: Regimental Returns, 10th Cavalry, 1880.

SMALL, George; Private; L/9th Cav. Native of Kentucky; fined $10 by court martial, Jun 1874, and $3 in Jun 1875; age 25 at Ft Union, NM, Mar 1876, when killed by white gunfighter David Crockett in shootout at bar in Cimarron, NM, with Pvts. Anthony Harvey and John Hanson, L/9th Cavalry; had accumulated savings of $167. SOURCE: Kenner, *Buffalo Soldiers and Officers of the Ninth Cavalry*, 180.

‡Killed in saloon shootout along with Pvts. John Hanson and Anthony Harvey, L/9th Cavalry, Cimarron, Apr 1876; buried at Ft Union, NM. SOURCE: Billington, *New Mexico's Buffalo Soldiers*, 67.

SMALL, Thomas; Private; I/10th Cav. ‡Original member of 10th Cavalry; in troop when organized, Ft Riley, KS, 15 Aug 1867. SOURCE: McMiller, "Buffalo Soldiers," 76.

Died 26 Feb 1870 of typhoid at Camp Supply, OK. SOURCE: Regimental Returns, 10th Cavalry, 1870.

‡Final statement and inventories of effects of Pvts. Small and Augustus James, I/10th Cavalry, forwarded to Adjutant General by commander, 10th Cavalry, Mar 1870. SOURCE: ES, 10 Cav, 1866–71.

SMALLEY, Benjamin; Private; G/10th Cav. Died at Ft Davis, TX, on 25 Mar 1880; buried at San Antonio National Cemetery, Section I, number 1505. SOURCE: San Antonio National Cemetery Locator.

SMALLS, Henry; Private; 25th Inf. Born in Charleston, SC; occupation shoemaker; Ht 5'4 1/4", dark complexion, black hair and eyes; enlisted, age 26, Charleston, 12 Jul 1881; left recruit depot, David's Island, NY, 17 Aug 1881, and after trip on steamer *Thomas Kirby* to Central Depot, New York City, and train via Chicago to Running Water, Dakota Territory, 22 Aug 1881, marched forty-seven miles to Ft Randall, SD, arrived 24 Aug 1881. SOURCE: Descriptive & Assignment Rolls, 25 Inf.

SMALLWOOD, Eli; Musician; Band/25th Inf. Died at Ft Davis, TX, on 2 Nov 1872; buried at San Antonio National Cemetery, Section I, number 1547. SOURCE: San Antonio National Cemetery Locator.

SMALLWOOD, Lee; Private; E/10th Cav. Born in Bertie County, NC; Ht 5'11", black hair and eyes, brown complexion; served in E/10th Cavalry to 17 Jan 1887; second reenlistment in 25th Infantry at age 26, Cincinnati, OH, 2 Feb 1887; arrived Ft Snelling, MN, 1 Apr 1887. SOURCE: Descriptive & Assignment Rolls of Recruits, 25 Inf.

In Troop E/10th Cavalry stationed at Bonita Cañon Camp, AZ, but absent or on detached service 28 Feb 1886. SOURCE: Tagg, *The Camp at Bonita Cañon*, 232.

SMART, Ransom; Private; 25th Inf. Born in Beaufort, SC; Ht 5'9", black hair and eyes, fair complexion; occupation waiter; enlisted at age 24, Charleston, SC, 16 May 1881; left recruit depot, David's Island, NY, 2 Jul 1881, arrived Ft Randall, SD, 7 Jul 1881. SOURCE: Descriptive & Assignment Rolls of Recruits, 25 Inf.

Black complexion; last in F/25th Infantry; reenlisted at age 30, Washington, DC, 14 Jun 1886; assigned to A/25th Infantry; arrived Ft Snelling, MN, 5 Aug 1886. SOURCE: Descriptive & Assignment Rolls of Recruits, 25 Inf.

SMART, Robert; Private; G/9th Cav. Received Philippine Campaign Badge number 11746 for service as private in E/9th Cavalry, 3 Mar 1902–16 Sep 1902; private in G/9th Cavalry, Ft Leavenworth, KS, Mar 1905. SOURCE: Philippine Campaign Badge Recipients; Philippine Campaign Badge list, 29 May 1905.

SMITH, Aaron; Private; H/25th Inf. Died at Ft Davis, TX, on 25 Mar 1880; buried at San Antonio National Cemetery, Section I, number 1535. SOURCE: San Antonio National Cemetery Locator.

SMITH, Adam T.; Private; A/10th Cav. Died at Ft Concho, TX, on 25 Sep 1873; buried at San Antonio National Cemetery, Section D, number 681. SOURCE: San Antonio National Cemetery Locator.

‡Commander, 10th Cavalry, forwards final statement of late Private Smith to Adjutant General, 8 Dec 1873. SOURCE: ES, 10 Cav, 1873–83.

SMITH, Admerson; Private; D/24th Inf. Died 5 Mar 1895; buried at San Antonio National Cemetery, Section I, number 1608. SOURCE: San Antonio National Cemetery Locator.

SMITH, Alfred; H/25th Inf. Born in Louisiana; mulatto complexion; cannot read or write, age 23, 5 Sep 1870, at Ft McKavett, TX. SOURCE: Bierschwale, *Fort McKavett,* 108.

SMITH, Alon T.; Private; E/10th Cav. Died Nov 1873 in hospital at Ft Concho, TX. SOURCE: Regimental Returns, 10th Cavalry, 1873.

SMITH, Andrew J.; Drum Maj; Band/25th Inf. ‡Private, C/10th Cavalry, 1869. SOURCE: Baker, Roster.

‡Sergeant, C/10th Cavalry, cited for gallantry against Kiowas and Comanches, Wichita Agency, Indian Territory, 22–23 Aug 1874. SOURCE: Baker, Roster.

‡First sergeant, B/25th Infantry, authorized fifty-day furlough from Ft Snelling, MN. SOURCE: *ANJ* 24 (20 Nov 1886): 230.

‡First sergeant, B/25th Infantry, at Ft Buford, ND; examined for ordnance sergeant. SOURCE: *ANJ* 30 (1 Jul 1893): 745.

‡North Carolinian, commissioned for bravery at El Caney, Cuba, 1898. SOURCE: Johnson, *History of Negro Soldiers,* 32.

‡Commissioned in volunteers for gallantry at Santiago, Cuba, 1–2 Jul 1898. SOURCE: Richmond *Planet,* 13 Aug 1898; Thweatt, *What the Newspapers Say,* 10.

Sergeant, recommended for commission in immune regiment by Lt. Col. Andrew S. Daggett, 25th Infantry, even before regiment left Cuba, Aug 1898. SOURCE: Schubert, *Black Valor,* 110.

‡Sergeant, B/25th Infantry, commissioned second lieutenant, 8th Volunteer Infantry, after Spanish-American War. SOURCE: Cashin, *Under Fire with the Tenth Cavalry,* 360, with picture, 133.

‡In the Philippines, 1900. SOURCE: Richmond *Planet,* 28 Jul 1898.

‡Drum major, Band/25th Infantry, transferred from Manila, Philippines, to San Francisco. SOURCE: *ANJ* 38 (8 Dec 1900): 355.

SMITH, Archie; 10th Cav. After leaving service, settled at Ft Davis, TX, and built prosperous ranch. SOURCE: Smith, *U.S. Army and the Texas Frontier Economy,* 180.

In Dec 1884, Lt. John Bigelow, Jr., attended service at Catholic chapel located in Archie Smith's home, about a mile from Ft Davis; former soldier Smith married local Mexican woman. SOURCE: Bigelow, *Garrison Tangles,* 39, 74.

SMITH, Augustus; C/25th Inf. Born in New York; mulatto complexion; can read and write, age 26, 5 Sep 1870, at Ft McKavett, TX. SOURCE: Bierschwale, *Fort McKavett,* 108.

SMITH, Benjamin; Private; L/9th Cav. Born in Kentucky; age 26, when convicted with Pvt. James Miller,

L/9th Cavalry, of murder for killing in barroom, Las Animas, CO, Aug 1876; death sentence commuted to life in prison. SOURCE: Kenner, *Buffalo Soldiers and Officers of the Ninth Cavalry,* 183–84.

SMITH, C. O.; 1st Sgt; B/10th Cav. After discharge went into business in Texas, hunting deserters, asked Lt. John Bigelow for list of deserters at large, 1879. SOURCE: Kinevan, *Frontier Cavalryman,* 158–59.

SMITH, Charles; Private; C/10th Cav. ‡Killed in 1871. *See* JOHNSON, York, Private, C/10th Cavalry

Died 22 Jun 1871, shot by 2nd Lt. Robert Price at Galisteo, NM. SOURCE: Regimental Returns, 10th Cavalry, 1871.

SMITH, Edward; Corporal; D/10th Cav. Died at Ft Davis, TX, on 17 Jul 1885; buried at San Antonio National Cemetery, Section D, number 763. SOURCE: San Antonio National Cemetery Locator.

SMITH, Edward; Private; D/9th Cav. Private, received Indian Wars Campaign Badge number 1818 on 2 Nov 1917. SOURCE: Carroll, *Indian Wars Campaign Badge,* 53.

SMITH, Emile; Private; E/9th Cav. ‡On special duty as clerk, Adjutant's Office, Ft Robinson, NE. SOURCE: Order 71, 30 Apr 1892, Post Orders, Ft Robinson.

‡Involved in affray at Suggs, WY, Jun 1892. SOURCE: Schubert, "The Suggs Affray," 63.

Involved in affray at Suggs, 1892, and fined $.50, but spent three months in jail awaiting trial. SOURCE: Dobak and Phillips, *The Black Regulars,* 243, 329.

‡On special duty as post librarian, Ft Robinson. SOURCE: Order 161, 23 Sep 1892, Post Orders, Ft Robinson.

‡Teacher, Ft Robinson school, 9 Dec 1892–1 Feb 1893. SOURCE: Reports of Schools, DP.

‡Acquitted by garrison court martial, Ft Robinson, of disobeying order issued by commander through 1st Sgt. William Clay. SOURCE: Order 16, 23 Feb 1893, Post Orders, Ft Robinson.

SMITH, Ewing; Sergeant; C/10th Cav. ‡Original member of 10th Cavalry; in troop when organized, Ft Leavenworth, KS, 14 May 1867. SOURCE: McMiller, "Buffalo Soldiers," 70.

Died 9 Jul 1868, shot by accident, at Ft Wallace, KS. SOURCE: Regimental Returns, 10th Cavalry, 1868.

Died 9 Jul 1868; buried at Ft Leavenworth National Cemetery, plot C 1926. SOURCE: Ft Leavenworth National Cemetery.

SMITH, Frank; Private; 40th Inf. Orderly at regimental headquarters until spring 1868, when he was sent to New

York City for duty with regimental recruiter. SOURCE: Dobak and Phillips, *The Black Regulars*, 6.

SMITH, George; 9th Cav. Born in Tennessee; black complexion; cannot read or write, age 26, Sep 1870, at Ft McKavett, TX. SOURCE: Bierschwale, *Fort McKavett*, 107.

SMITH, George; H/25th Inf. Born in Virginia; mulatto complexion; can read and write, age 24, 5 Sep 1870, at Ft McKavett, TX. SOURCE: Bierschwale, *Fort McKavett*, 108.

SMITH, George; Private; F/10th Cav. Served at Ft Concho, TX, 1875; part of detachment led by Sgt. John Marshall, A/10th Cavalry, in pursuit of Indians, May 1875; bravery mentioned in Marshall's report. SOURCE: Schubert, *Voices of the Buffalo Soldier*, 74.

SMITH, George; Private; K/25th Inf. Died 8 Mar 1881; buried plot 1 8, Ft Meade National Cemetery. SOURCE: Ft Meade National Cemetery, VA database.

SMITH, George H.; Private; 25th Inf. Born in Fairfax County, VA; Ht 5'4", black hair and eyes, black complexion; occupation laborer; resided in Fairfax County when he enlisted at age 21, Washington, DC, 20 Sep 1886; arrived Ft Snelling, MN, 20 Jan 1887. SOURCE: Descriptive & Assignment Rolls of Recruits, 25 Inf.

SMITH, Henry; Private; M/10th Cav. ‡Original member of 10th Cavalry; in troop when organized, Ft Riley, KS, 15 Oct 1867. SOURCE: McMiller, "Buffalo Soldiers," 79.
Died 4 Sep 1868 of gunshot wound at Ft Riley. SOURCE: Regimental Returns, 10th Cavalry, 1868.

SMITH, Henry; M/9th Cav. Born in Kentucky; black complexion; can read and write, age 29, Jul 1870, at Ft McKavett, TX. SOURCE: Bierschwale, *Fort McKavett*, 98.

SMITH, Henry N.; Private; M/10th Cav. Died 11 Aug 1877 of disease at Ft Clark, TX. SOURCE: Regimental Returns, 10th Cavalry, 1877.
‡Recently deceased; final statement transmitted. SOURCE: CO, 10 Cav, to AG, USA, 2 Sep 1877, ES, 10 Cav, 1873–83.

SMITH, Jacob; Private; B/10th Cav. Died 3 Mar 1876 of pistol shot at Ft Griffin, TX. SOURCE: Regimental Returns, 10th Cavalry, 1876.

SMITH, Jacob Clay; Saddler Sgt; 10th Cav. ‡Born in Taylorsville, KY, 25 Jun 1857; enlisted 20 Jan 1880; joined I/24th Infantry, Ringgold Bks, TX, 16 Mar 1880; transferred to F/24th Infantry, 31 Mar 1881; corporal, 4 Aug 1882; sergeant, 23 Feb 1883; transferred to 10th Cavalry, Oct 1887; private, M/10th Cavalry and E/10th Cavalry, 5 Nov

1887–20 Jan 1890; transferred to C/10th Cavalry, 6 Feb 1890; sergeant, 1 Apr 1890; saddler sergeant, 5 Oct 1894; commissioned second lieutenant, K/9th Volunteer Infantry, 27 Oct 1898; served with 9th Infantry, Cruisto, Cuba, Jan 1899. SOURCE: Baker, Roster; Coston, *The Spanish-American War Volunteer*, 77.
Claimed to have had some theatrical experience before enlisting; organized "a dramatic and minstrel troupe" among men of his regiment and 3rd Cavalry, Ft Elliott, TX, 1885. SOURCE: Dobak and Phillips, *The Black Regulars*, 153.
‡Letters, Ft Elliott, 26 Oct and 29 Dec 1885. SOURCE: Cleveland *Gazette*, 2 Nov 1885 and 9 Jan 1886, respectively.
‡Called meeting at Ft Elliott, 15 Dec 1886, which condemned ineptitude of Sgt. Charles Connor and two privates who allowed prisoner to escape en route to Ft Leavenworth, KS; Smith served as secretary of meeting; chaired first by temporary chairman Sgt. M. Wilcox, then chairman Sgt. William Wilkes; committee that drafted resolution: 1st Sgt. William Rose, Pvt. Asa L. Lewis, and Sergeant Spurling, all of F/24th Infantry. SOURCE: *ANJ* 24 (25 Dec 1886): 43.
Corporal, F/24th Infantry, called meeting that resulted in resolution of censure, Ft Elliott, 1886; resolution and related articles from *Army and Navy Journal* published. SOURCE: Schubert, *Voices of the Buffalo Soldier*, 149–52.
‡Made speech at picnic of E/24th Infantry band, Ft Grant, AZ, Jun 1890. SOURCE: Cleveland *Gazette*, 28 Jun 1890.
‡To report to regiment commander, Ft Custer, MT, as saddler sergeant. SOURCE: *ANJ* 32 (13 Oct 1894): 102.
‡Examined at Ft Assiniboine, MT, for post quartermaster sergeant, Jan 1896. SOURCE: *ANJ* 33 (18 Jan 1896): 349.
‡Met a little black boy who needed clothes at Chattanooga, 1898; took him to clothing store, bought him complete outfit, hat to shoes, for $10. SOURCE: Fletcher, "The Negro Soldier," 189.
‡Served as saddler sergeant, 10th Cavalry, in Cuba, 1898. SOURCE: Cashin, *Under Fire with the Tenth Cavalry*, 352.
Initiated request for Medal of Honor for Edward L. Baker, 1898, because he was eyewitness and no commissioned officers were present. SOURCE: Schubert, *Black Valor*, 155.
‡Commissioned second lieutenant, 9th Volunteer Infantry, after Spanish-American War. SOURCE: Cashin, *Under Fire with the Tenth Cavalry*, 360.
‡Lieutenant, 48th Infantry, and Cuba veteran. SOURCE: San Francisco *Chronicle*, 15 Nov 1899.
‡First lieutenant, K/48th Infantry. SOURCE: Beasley, *Negro Trailblazers*, 284.
‡Real estate agent, age 62, resided at 1117 N Street, SE, Washington, DC, in 1920; knew Martha C. Proctor,

wife of John C. Proctor, at least ten years and her late husband from 1882; Louisa Proctor's first husband, Henry Chambers, was in F/24th Infantry; was best man in Chambers-Proctor wedding, Mobeetie, TX, ca. 1884–85; Chambers later remarried; Peter McCown married sister of Henry Chambers's second wife. SOURCE: Affidavit, Smith, 1920, VA File XC 2659372, John C. Proctor.

Born in Anniston, AL; resided in Rushville, IN; at San Juan, Cuba, 1 Jul 1898, cut fences or obstructions of four to five strands of barbed wire under heavy fire, enabled A Troop to advance and take position to which it had been ordered; awarded Distinguished Service Cross in 1925. SOURCE: *American Decorations*, 456.

‡Resided at 1117 N Street in Washington in 1926; knew Thomas H. Allsup well, from 1880 until 1905; retired in 1908. SOURCE: Affidavit, Smith, 24 Jan 1926, VA File XC 2659797, Thomas H. Allsup.

‡Picture. SOURCE: Mary Curtis, *The Black Soldier*, opposite 52.

SMITH, James; Sergeant; D/24th Inf. Died 22 Apr 1913; buried in plot WEST 1122 at San Francisco National Cemetery. SOURCE: San Francisco National Cemetery.

SMITH, John; Private; A/10th Cav. ‡Served against Cheyennes and Kiowas, 1866 [*sic*]; died 1900; widow Mary Smith, Indianapolis, has $12 per month pension after fifteen years of effort, which is her total income. SOURCE: *Winners of the West* 1 (Nov 1924): 2, 5.

Text of widow Mary Smith's letter in *Winners of the West*, Nov 1924, describing her dire financial straits, published. SOURCE: Schubert, *Voices of the Buffalo Soldier*, 255.

SMITH, John; Recruit; 10th Cav. Died 12 Oct 1867 of meningitis at Ft Riley, KS. SOURCE: Regimental Returns, 10th Cavalry, 1867.

SMITH, John; D/24th Inf. Born in Virginia; black complexion; can read and write, age 21, Jul 1870, at Ft McKavett, TX. SOURCE: Bierschwale, *Fort McKavett*, 96.

SMITH, John; Private; A/10th Cav. Drowned 26 Sep 1874 at Ft Concho, OK. SOURCE: Regimental Returns, 10th Cavalry, 1874.

Died at Ft Concho on 28 Sep 1874; buried at San Antonio National Cemetery, Section E, number 888. SOURCE: San Antonio National Cemetery Locator.

SMITH, John; Private; Band/9th Cav. Died 30 Apr 1880; buried at Santa Fe National Cemetery, NM, plot K 304. SOURCE: Santa Fe National Cemetery, Records of Burials.

SMITH, John; Private; E/10th Cav. In Troop E/10th Cavalry stationed at Bonita Cañon Camp, AZ, 28 Feb 1886. SOURCE: Tagg, *The Camp at Bonita Cañon*, 232.

SMITH, John; Corporal; E/24th Inf. ‡Certificate of merit awarded 8 Dec 1903 for conspicuous bravery in rescue of comrade from drowning in Rio Grande near Cabanatuan, Philippines, 22 Nov 1899, when private, E/24th Infantry; discharged 16 Jan 1902. SOURCE: GO 32, AGO, 6 Feb 1904.

Awarded certificate of merit for conspicuous bravery in rescuing comrade from drowning in Rio Grande, 22 Nov 1899. SOURCE: Gleim, *The Certificate of Merit*, 49.

SMITH, John; Private; E/10th Cav. Died 9 Jul 1904; originally buried at Ft Washakie, WY; reburied at Ft Leavenworth National Cemetery, plot 3508. SOURCE: Ft Leavenworth National Cemetery.

SMITH, John; Private; E/25th Inf. Died at Ft Clark, TX; buried at Fort Sam Houston National Cemetery, Section PE, number 114. SOURCE: Buffalo Soldiers Interred in Fort Sam Houston National Cemetery.

SMITH, John H.; Private; D/25th Inf. Died at Ft Stockton, TX, on 21 Aug 1879; buried at San Antonio National Cemetery, Section C, number 347. SOURCE: San Antonio National Cemetery Locator.

SMITH, Joseph; Private; G/38th Inf. Died 4 Mar 1868; buried at Ft Leavenworth National Cemetery, plot 3313. SOURCE: Ft Leavenworth National Cemetery.

SMITH, Joseph C.; Corporal; G/25th Inf. ‡Musician, E/25th Infantry, Ft Buford, ND, 1893; catcher, regimental baseball team, "one of the gamiest [*sic*] and scrappiest players that ever donned a baseball suit," according to Sgt. D. P. Green. SOURCE: Nankivell, *History of the Twenty-fifth Infantry*, 164.

‡Corporal, G/25th Infantry, second best infantry marksman, Department of the Missouri, 1903. SOURCE: SecWar, *AR 1903*, 1:427.

‡Ranked first with gold medal, Southern Division infantry team competition, Ft Reno, OK, 1904. SOURCE: GO 167, AGO, 28 Oct 1904.

‡Distinguished marksman, with Department of Missouri silver medal, 1903, and Southwestern Division gold medals, 1904 and 1905. SOURCE: GO 173, AGO, 20 Oct 1905.

‡Ranked number 180 among rifle experts, 1904, with 68.67 percent. SOURCE: GO 79, AGO, 1 Jun 1905.

‡First place at Army's Ft Sheridan, IL, rifle competition, 3 Aug 1905; broke all records with 181 out of 200 slow fire and 97 out of 100 rapid fire. SOURCE: New York *Age*, 10 Aug 1905.

‡Ranked number 358 among rifle experts, 1905, with 69.67 percent. SOURCE: GO 101, AGO, 31 May 1906.

Corporal, received Indian Wars Campaign Badge number 755 on 17 Nov 1908. SOURCE: Carroll, *Indian Wars Campaign Badge*, 21.

SMITH, Lawson; Sergeant; L/9th Cav. At Ft Duncan, TX, 1871. SOURCE: Kenner, *Buffalo Soldiers and Officers of the Ninth Cavalry*, 177.

SMITH, Lewis M.; 1st Sgt; M/10th Cav. ‡Born in Virginia; private, I/10th Cavalry, 28 Apr 1875–27 Apr 1880; private, C/24th Infantry, 13 May 1880–13 Jul 1881; private, E/10th Cavalry, 13 Jul 1881; corporal, 1 Jul 1882; sergeant, 1 Feb 1884; first sergeant, 1 Apr 1894; at Ft Custer, MT, 1897. SOURCE: Baker, Roster.

Sergeant in Troop E/10th Cavalry stationed at Bonita Cañon Camp, AZ, 28 Feb 1886. SOURCE: Tagg, *The Camp at Bonita Cañon*, 231.

‡Born in Warrenton, VA, 15 Jul 1854; enlisted at age 21 for I/10th Cavalry; Indian campaigns in Arizona, Idaho, Texas, and Indian Territory; commanded company in battle in Cuba. SOURCE: Lynk, *The Black Troopers*, 52.

‡Authorized six-month furlough from Ft Apache, AZ. SOURCE: *ANJ* 27 (15 Mar 1890): 542.

‡Sergeant, E/10th Cavalry; at Ft Apache, 1890, subscribed $.50 to testimonial to General Grierson. SOURCE: List of subscriptions, 23 Apr 1890, 10th Cavalry papers, MHI.

‡At Ft Apache, 1891; sharpshooter. SOURCE: *ANJ* 31 (4 Jul 1891): 765.

‡Ranked number 2 with revolver, Departments of Arizona and Texas, 1891, silver medal; ranked number 6 with revolver, Departments of Dakota and Columbia, 1894, silver medal. SOURCE: Baker, Roster.

‡Ranked number 2 in revolver competition, Departments of Texas and Arizona, Ft Wingate, NM, 17–22 Aug 1891. SOURCE: GO 81, AGO, 6 Oct 1891.

‡Ranked number 17 among carbine sharpshooters with over 72 percent, 1891. SOURCE: GO 1, AGO, 2 Jan 1892.

‡Ranked number 6 in revolver competition, Departments of Dakota and Columbia, Ft Keogh, MT, 18–27 Sep 1894. SOURCE: GO 62, AGO, 15 Nov 1894.

‡First sergeant, E/10th Cavalry, at Ft Robinson, NE, for cavalry competition, Sep 1897. SOURCE: Monthly Returns, Ft Robinson, Sep 1897.

As acting first sergeant, M/10th Cavalry, 23-year veteran was one of four sergeants accompanying Lt. Carter Johnson on expedition to southern Cuba to deliver arms to insurgents, June 1898; lived in retirement with wife, Alexandria, VA, 1906. SOURCE: Schubert, *Black Valor*, 135, 141.

‡Served as first sergeant, M/10th Cavalry in Cuba, 1898. SOURCE: Cashin, *Under Fire with the Tenth Cavalry*, 352.

‡First lieutenant, 48th Infantry, as of 9 Sep 1899, ordered to Ft Thomas, KY. SOURCE: *ANJ* 37 (14 Oct 1899): 147.

‡Mentioned as first lieutenant, I/48th Infantry. SOURCE: Beasley, *Negro Trailblazers*, 284.

‡Stationed at San Fernando de la Union, Philippines; led detachment of I/48th Infantry that captured thirty of enemy, Jun 1900; Cpl. Daniel Lee, I/48th Infantry, cited for gallantry in this action. SOURCE: Richmond *Planet*, 28 Jul 1900.

‡Retires as first sergeant, M/10th Cavalry, in accordance with Special Order 272, Adjutant General's Office, 19 Nov 1902.

‡Widow Jennie remarried in Alexandria, VA, 1907, resided at 132 S. Newberry, York, PA. SOURCE: Chief, Bureau of Pensions, to Commissioner of Pensions, 7 Apr 1926, VA File XC 2659797, Thomas H. Allsup.

See OTT, HOUSTON, Adam, Sergeant, Quartermaster Corps

SMITH, Luscious; Private; D/10th Cav. ‡Luchious Smith served as corporal, D/10th Cavalry, in Cuba, 1898. SOURCE: Cashin, *Under Fire with the Tenth Cavalry*, 341.

‡Distinguished himself at San Juan Hill and promoted to corporal. SOURCE: SecWar, *AR 1898*, 710.

‡In going up San Juan Hill, three men of D/10th Cavalry distinguished themselves: Smith, Cpl. John Walker, and Sergeant Elliot; Smith and Elliot "were during the ascent of the hill constantly among the bolder few who voluntarily made themselves ground-scouts, drawing the attention of the enemy from the main line upon themselves." SOURCE: Bigelow, *Reminiscences of Santiago*, 130–31.

‡Commended for distinguished service in battle of Santiago, Cuba, 1 Jul 1898; now out of service. SOURCE: GO 15, AGO, 13 Feb 1900.

‡Certificate of merit mentioned. SOURCE: Steward, *The Colored Regulars*, 280; *ANJ* 37 (24 Feb 1900): 611.

‡Corporal; heroism in Cuba mentioned. SOURCE: Gatewood, *"Smoked Yankees,"* 80.

Awarded certificate of merit for distinguished service in battle, Santiago, 1 Jul 1898. SOURCE: Gleim, *The Certificate of Merit*, 45.

Born in Etowah County, AL; resided in Pittsburgh, PA; received Distinguished Service Medal in lieu of certificate of merit. SOURCE: *American Decorations*, 843.

‡Private, D/10th Cavalry, at Ft Robinson, NE; in hands of civil authorities, Crawford, NE, 15–17 May 1903. SOURCE: Regt Returns, 10 Cav, May 1903.

SMITH, Nathan; Private; C/10th Cav. Deserted during tenure of George Garnett as first sergeant, Jan 1869–May 1871. SOURCE: Dobak and Phillips, *The Black Regulars*, 300.

Served with Pvt. George Washington, C/10th Cavalry, in Texas, early 1870s. SOURCE: Schubert, *Voices of the Buffalo Soldier*, 234.

SMITH, Richard; Private; D/9th Cav. Died 17 Apr 1876; buried at Santa Fe National Cemetery, NM, plot K 390. SOURCE: Santa Fe National Cemetery, Records of Burials.

SMITH, Richard; Private; E/24th Inf. Born in Pulaski County, VA; Ht 5'5", black hair and eyes, black complexion; occupation farmer; enlisted in 25th Infantry at age 28, Cincinnati, OH, 7 Dec 1886; arrived Ft Snelling, MN, 1 Apr 1887. SOURCE: Descriptive & Assignment Rolls of Recruits, 25 Inf.

‡Resident of Cincinnati; to be discharged from E/24th Infantry at end of term from Ft Bayard, NM, 6 Dec 1891. SOURCE: Cleveland *Gazette*, 12 Dec 1891.

SMITH, Robert; Corporal; K/25th Inf. Born in Baltimore, MD; Ht 5'4", black complexion; occupation painter; enlisted in A/39th Infantry for three years on 24 Jan 1867, age 30, at Greenville, LA; promoted to corporal 18 Dec 1867; transferred to K/25th Infantry at Jackson Bks, LA, 20 Apr 1869. SOURCE: Descriptive Roll of A/39th Inf.

SMITH, Robert; Private; G/9th Cav. ‡1st Lt. Francis S. Davidson acquitted by general court martial, Ft Brown, TX, 22 Jul 1875, of failure to equip Smith with serviceable cartridge box. SOURCE: GCMO 93, AGO, 15 Nov 1875.

‡With detachment attacked by Indians at Agua Chiquita, NM; Pvt. Robert Smith and Pvt. Daniel Stanton killed in action; stationed at Ft Stanton, NM. SOURCE: Hamilton, "History of the Ninth Cavalry," 53; *Illustrated Review: Ninth Cavalry*.

‡Attacked by Apaches, Agua Chiquita Canyon, Sep 1880. SOURCE: Billington, *New Mexico's Buffalo Soldiers*, 97–98.

Died 4 Sep 1880; originally buried at Ft Stanton; reburied at Santa Fe National Cemetery, NM, plot B 626. SOURCE: Santa Fe National Cemetery, Records of Burials.

SMITH, Robert; Private; D/10th Cav. Died at Ft Concho, TX, on 13 Mar 1907; buried at San Antonio National Cemetery, Section E, number 817. SOURCE: San Antonio National Cemetery Locator.

SMITH, Solomon; Private; H/24th Inf. ‡Enlisted Camp G. H. Thomas, GA, 29 Apr 1898. SOURCE: Muster Roll, H/24 Inf, May–Jun 1898.

‡Sick, disease contracted in line of duty, and returned to U.S. for treatment. SOURCE: Muster Roll, H/24 Inf, Sep–Oct 1898.

‡Transferred from Reserve Divisional Hospital, Siboney, Cuba, to U.S. on U.S. Army Transport *Santiago* with remittent malarial fever, 25 Jul 1898. SOURCE: Hospital Papers, Spanish-American War.

‡Authorized furlough on surgeon's certificate, 19 Sep–18 Oct 1898. SOURCE: Muster Roll, H/24 Inf, Sep–Oct 1898.

‡Discharged, end of term, character good, single, Ft Douglas, UT, 27 Jan 1899; deposits $45; due U.S. for clothing $38.69. SOURCE: Muster Roll, H/24 Inf, Jan–Feb 1899.

‡Youngest soldier in regular Army. SOURCE: Indianapolis *Freeman*, 4 Feb 1899, with picture.

Served in Cuban campaign as private, 22 Jun 1898–13 Aug 1898; reenlisted 27 Feb 1905. SOURCE: Cuban Campaign Badge Recipients.

SMITH, Stanley; Private; 9th Cav. Received Philippine Campaign Badge number 11791 for service as private in F/9th Cavalry; in 9th Cavalry at Ft Leavenworth, KS, Mar 1905. SOURCE: Philippine Campaign Badge list, 29 May 1905.

SMITH, Thomas; Private; F/10th Cav. ‡Original member of 10th Cavalry; in troop when organized, Ft Leavenworth, KS, 21 Jun 1867. SOURCE: McMiller, "Buffalo Soldiers," 73.

Killed in action 2 Aug 1867 at Middle Fork, KS. SOURCE: Regimental Returns, 10th Cavalry, 1867.

Killed in action and scalped, near Beaver Creek, KS, 21 Aug 1867. SOURCE: LR, DeptMo, 1867.

SMITH, Thompson W.; Private; E/10th Cav. ‡Lieutenant Wallace, 6th Cavalry, Recruiting Officer, Baltimore, notifies commander, Ft Concho, TX, of apprehension of Smith from desertion in Washington, DC, 4 Jan 1876. SOURCE: ES, 10 Cav, 1873–83.

‡Convicted of desertion by general court martial, St. Louis Bks, MO; sentenced to dishonorable discharge and three years. SOURCE: GCMO 30, AGO, 16 Mar 1876.

‡Prisoner number 331, U.S. Military Prison, Ft Leavenworth, KS; married, age 24, resident of Washington, DC, before enlistment; died 15 Sep 1876 of gunshot wound received while trying to escape from guard. SOURCE: Certificates of Disability, DivMo, 1875–87.

Military prisoner died 15 Sep 1876; buried at Ft Leavenworth National Cemetery, plot 1466. SOURCE: Ft Leavenworth National Cemetery.

SMITH, Walter; Private; F/10th Cav. Killed by Blacksmith Rice, F/10th Cavalry, 28 Aug 1882, Concho River, TX. SOURCE: Regimental Returns, 10th Cavalry, 1882.

SMITH, Wesley P.; H/25th Inf. Born in Pennsylvania; mulatto complexion; can read and write, age 21, 5 Sep 1870, at Ft McKavett, TX. SOURCE: Bierschwale, *Fort McKavett*, 108.

SMITH, William; M/9th Cav. Born in Kentucky; mulatto complexion; cannot read or write, age 22, Jul 1870, at Ft McKavett, TX. SOURCE: Bierschwale, *Fort McKavett*, 100.

SMITH, William; Private; F/9th Cav. Private, F/9th Cavalry, 1872–73. SOURCE: Kenner, *Buffalo Soldiers and Officers of the Ninth Cavalry*, 338.

SMITH, William; Private; 10th Cav. After discharge at Ft Sill, OK, found employment with Quartermaster Department. SOURCE: Dobak and Phillips, *The Black Regulars*, 334.

SMITH, William; Private; F/9th Cav. At Ft Robinson, NE, Jun 1887, assaulted by Pvt. David Kendrick in dining hall after Smith drew a knife; both acquitted by court martial. SOURCE: Kenner, *Buffalo Soldiers and Officers of the Ninth Cavalry*, 170.
See KENDRICK, David, Private, F/9th Cavalry

SMITH, William; Private; B/25th Inf. Enlisted 29 Oct 1898, discharged as private 28 Oct 1901, character good; enlisted 17 Jun 1905, discharged without honor 19 Nov 1906. SOURCE: Powell, "Military Record of the Enlisted Men Who Were Discharged Without Honor."
‡Dishonorable discharge, Brownsville, TX. SOURCE: SO 266, AGO, 9 Nov 1906

SMITH, William; Private; I/48th Inf. ‡Died of pneumonia in the Philippines, 22 Aug 1900. SOURCE: *ANJ* 38 (8 Sep 1900): 43.
‡Died in the Philippines, 31 Aug 1900. SOURCE: Richmond *Planet*, 8 Sep 1900.
Died 31 Aug 1900; body received 15 Apr 1902 at San Francisco National Cemetery, buried in plot NEW A1021. SOURCE: San Francisco National Cemetery.

SMITH, William E.; Private; B/10th Cav. Native of Harrison County; joined B/10th Cavalry in 1881, age 25; received $5 fine and sentence of one year at hard labor; also sent to Alcatraz for forgery and overdrawing clothing and ordnance allowances; given dishonorable discharge. SOURCE: Wooster, *Soldiers, Sutlers, and Settlers*, 62.

SMITH, William H.; Private; I/25th Inf. Born in Leesburg, VA; Ht 5'6", brown hair and eyes, dark complexion; occupation laborer; enlisted at age 32, Providence, RI, 13 Jul 1881; arrived Ft Snelling, MN, 21 Nov 1882. SOURCE: Descriptive & Assignment Rolls of Recruits, 25 Inf.

SMITH, William J.; Private; L/9th Cav. Enlisted 5 Jun 1879 at Baltimore, MD; at Ft Bliss, TX. SOURCE: Muster Roll, L/9th Cavalry, 31 Oct 1879–31 Dec 1879.

SNEAD; Corporal; F/10th Cav. Shot and killed with pistol Pvt. William Jackson, Band/10th Cavalry, at San Angelo, TX, 28 Nov 1876. SOURCE: Regimental Returns, 10th Cavalry, 1876.

SNEED, John; Private; E/25th Inf. Enlisted 4 Dec 1886; assigned to E/25th Infantry; arrived Ft Snelling, MN, 1 Apr 1887. SOURCE: Descriptive & Assignment Rolls of Recruits, 25 Inf.
‡Born in Accomack Co., VA; occupation hostler; Ht 5'7 1/2", brown eyes, black hair, brown complexion; enlisted Baltimore, MD, age 22, 14 Dec 1886; discharged, end of term, character excellent, Ft Buford, ND, 31 Dec 1891. SOURCE: Register of Enlistments.
Resident of Baltimore; to be discharged at end of term from Ft Bayard, NM, 3 Dec 1891. SOURCE: Cleveland *Gazette*, 12 Dec 1891.

SNOTEN, Peter; Sergeant; G/9th Cav. ‡Born in Somers Co., TN; parents unknown; occupation laborer; Ht 5'11", black complexion; enlisted in A/24th Infantry, 8 Apr 1876; transferred to G/9th Cavalry, 5 May 1885; transferred to L/9th Cavalry, 26 Jul 1900; transferred to G/9th Cavalry, 20 Aug 1902; retired as sergeant, G/9th Cavalry, 14 Jun 1905; wife Fannie, 516 E. 1st Street, Los Angeles, died 14 Apr 1923; then married Sarah B. Snoten, divorced from Sam Skinner, Beaumont, TX, 15 Aug 1910; died at age 72, at Soldiers Home, Sawtelle, CA; Sarah Snoten's attorney without fee C. W. Cordin of National Military Home, CA, 1927; after Snoten's death, she married Coleman Moore, late private, D/3rd North Carolina Infantry; she sold eggs on street and chickens door-to-door for eight years, could find no stable work, pleaded for help from Mrs. Franklin Roosevelt, 30 Nov 1936: lived "with not even enough shoes and stockings to meet the winter." SOURCE: VA File XC 978555, Peter Snoten.
‡Veteran of Spanish-American War; wife Fannie resided in Crawford, NE, 1899. SOURCE: Crawford *Tribune*, 27 Jan 1899.
Received Philippine Campaign Badge number 11808 for service as corporal in L/9th Cavalry, 16 May 1900–15 May 1901; corporal in G/9th Cavalry, Ft Leavenworth, KS, Mar 1905. SOURCE: Philippine Campaign Badge Recipients; Philippine Campaign Badge list, 29 May 1905.
Retired sergeant, received Indian Wars Campaign Badge number 1204 on 24 May 1909. SOURCE: Carroll, *Indian Wars Campaign Badge*, 34.
‡Resided at 1326 E. 28th Street, Los Angeles, from 1905 until 1926; was in G/9th Cavalry in 1891 on detached service at Ft Custer, MT, when he met Sgt. and Mrs. Thomas H. Allsup. SOURCE: Affidavit, Snoten, 15 Apr 1926, VA File XC 2659797, Thomas H. Allsup.

SOLOMAN, Henry; Private; H/9th Cav. Died at Ft Davis, TX, on 3 Dec 1867; buried at San Antonio National Cemetery, Section I, number 1544. SOURCE: San Antonio National Cemetery Locator.

SOLOMON[?], Miles; Recruit; 10th Cav. Died 4 Feb 1867 of pneumonia at Ft Leavenworth, KS. SOURCE: Regimental Returns, 10th Cavalry, 1867.

SOLOMON, Robert; Private; C/24th Cav. Died 25 Mar 1889; buried at Santa Fe National Cemetery, NM, plot A-1 797. SOURCE: Santa Fe National Cemetery, Records of Burials.

SOMERS, Charles; Private; L/9th Cav. Enlisted 23 Jul 1878 at New York, NY; at Ft Bliss, TX. SOURCE: Muster Roll, L/9th Cavalry, 31 Oct 1879–31 Dec 1879.

SOMMERVILLE, Edward; F/25th Inf. Edward Somerville, 25th Infantry, completed six enlistments by 1894 and was two years short of retirement when surgeon declared him unfit for service because of shortness of breath and weak heart and refused to authorize his reenlistment; entered U.S. Soldiers Home and applied for disability pension. SOURCE: Dobak and Phillips, *The Black Regulars*, 274.

Pvt. Edward Somerville, C/25th Infantry, born in North Carolina; mulatto complexion; can read and write, age 25, 5 Sep 1870, at Ft McKavett, TX. SOURCE: Bierschwale, *Fort McKavett*, 108.

‡Edward Sommerville, F/25th Infantry, died at U.S. Soldiers Home of heart disease, age 51, 25 Mar 1896. SOURCE: SecWar, *AR 1896*, 640.

SORRELL, Frank; Private; E/10th Cav. In Troop E/10th Cavalry stationed at Bonita Cañon Camp, AZ, but absent or on detached service 28 Feb 1886. SOURCE: Tagg, *The Camp at Bonita Cañon*, 232.

SOWELL, Berry; Corporal; L/9th Cav. Enlisted 9 Aug 1875 at Ft Brown, TX; private at Ft Bliss, TX, Nov 1879–Feb 1880; corporal, discharged at Ft Bliss 8 Aug 1880, character good; reenlisted 26 Aug 1880. SOURCE: Muster Rolls, L/9th Cavalry, 30 June–31 Aug 1880.

‡Pvt. B. Sewall, L/9th Cavalry, on detached service in the field, New Mexico, 21 Jan–24 Feb 1881. SOURCE: Regt Returns, 9 Cav, Feb 1881.

SPARKS, Augustus; Private; H/10th Cav. In Troop H/10th Cavalry stationed at Bonita Cañon Camp, AZ, but absent or on detached service 30 Apr 1886. SOURCE: Tagg, *The Camp at Bonita Cañon*, 232.

Private, H/10th Cavalry, participated in campaign against Geronimo, 1886. SOURCE: Sayre, *Warriors of Color*, 111.

Participated in Oct 1886 pursuit and capture of Apache Mangus. SOURCE: Schubert, *Voices of the Buffalo Soldier*, 146.

‡Ranked number 8 in revolver competition, Departments of California and Arizona, Ft Wingate, NM, 1889, bronze medal. SOURCE: GO 78, AGO, 12 Oct 1889; Baker, Roster.

‡At Ft Apache, AZ, 1890, subscribed $.50 to testimonial to General Grierson. SOURCE: List of subscriptions, 23 Apr 1890, 10th Cavalry papers, MHI.

SPEAKES, James; Sergeant; E/10th Cav. Civil War veteran of 25th U.S. Colored Infantry; as lance sergeant, led party of fourteen recruits from Philadelphia, PA, to Ft Leavenworth, KS, 1867. SOURCE: Dobak and Phillips, *The Black Regulars*, 12.

‡James Speaks, original member of 10th Cavalry; in E troop when organized, Ft Leavenworth, KS, 15 Jun 1867. SOURCE: McMiller, "Buffalo Soldiers," 72.

SPEAKES, William; Private; C/25th Inf. Born in Frederick, MD; Ht 5'5", black hair and grey eyes, brown complexion; occupation blacksmith; resided Philadelphia, PA, when enlisted at age 21, Harrisburg, PA, 13 Aug 1885; assigned to C/25th Infantry; arrived Ft Snelling, MN, 5 Feb 1886. SOURCE: Descriptive & Assignment Rolls of Recruits, 25 Inf.

SPEAKS, James; E/10th Cav. *See* SPEAKES, James, Sergeant, E/10th Cavalry

SPEAR, James; Sergeant; E/10th Cav. In Troop E/10th Cavalry stationed at Bonita Cañon Camp, AZ, 28 Feb 1886. SOURCE: Tagg, *The Camp at Bonita Cañon*, 231.

‡Authorized two-month furlough from Ft Thomas, AZ. SOURCE: *ANJ* 26 (12 Jan 1888): 386.

‡At Ft Apache, AZ, 1890, subscribed $.50 to testimonial to General Grierson. SOURCE: List of subscriptions, 23 Apr 1890, 10th Cavalry papers, MHI.

SPENCE, William; Band/24th Inf. ‡Remained in Tayug, Philippines, after service. SOURCE: Funston papers, KSHS.

William S. Spence died 13 Dec 1930; buried 18 Dec 1930 in plot B 1064 at San Francisco National Cemetery. SOURCE: San Francisco National Cemetery.

SPENCER, Franklin; Private; 9th Cav. *See* PERKINS, Frank, E/10th Cavalry

SPENCER, George; 9th Cav. Born in Georgia; black complexion; can read and write, age 24, Sep 1870, at Ft McKavett, TX. SOURCE: Bierschwale, *Fort McKavett*, 107.

SPENCER, Jeremiah; Private; L/10th Cav. Died 28 Apr 1871, shot 21 Apr 1871 by Private Lewis, provost guard, M/10th Cavalry, at Ft Sill, OK. SOURCE: Regimental Returns, 10th Cavalry, 1871.

Died 23 Apr 1871; buried at Camp Douglas, UT. SOURCE: Record Book of Interments, Post Cemetery, 252.

SPERLIN, George; Private; 25th Inf. Born in Adair County, KY; Ht 5'7", black hair and eyes, black complexion; served in F/10th Cavalry to 3 Feb 1887; second reenlistment in 25th Infantry at age 29, Cincinnati, OH, 2 Mar 1887; arrived Ft Snelling, MN, 1 Apr 1887. SOURCE: Descriptive & Assignment Rolls of Recruits, 25 Inf.

SPILLER, Noah; Private; 40th Inf. Survived wreck of steamer *Flambeau* off Wilmington, NC. SOURCE: Dobak and Phillips, *The Black Regulars*, 10.

SPILLMAN, John; Private; 9th Cav. At Ft Quitman, TX, 1869, acquitted of crossing border, assaulting Mexican, stealing his blanket and overcoat. SOURCE: Leiker, *Racial Borders*, 83–84.

SPINNER, John; Private; I/10th Cav. Died at Ft Davis, TX, on 18 Nov 1884; buried at San Antonio National Cemetery, Section H, number 110. SOURCE: San Antonio National Cemetery Locator.

SPRIGGS, Eliord; Corporal; F/10th Cav. ‡Original member of 10th Cavalry; in F Troop when organized, Ft Leavenworth, KS, 21 Jun 1867. SOURCE: McMiller, "Buffalo Soldiers," 73.

Had horse shot out from under him in fight against Indians, Saline River, KS, 2 Aug 1867. SOURCE: Schubert, *Voices of the Buffalo Soldier*, 13.

SPRIGGS, John; Private; 25th Inf. Born in Washington, DC; Ht 5'7", black hair and brown eyes, brown complexion; occupation laborer; enlisted at age 21, Baltimore, MD, 23 Apr 1886; arrived Ft Snelling, MN, 19 Aug 1886. SOURCE: Descriptive & Assignment Rolls of Recruits, 25 Inf.

SPRIGGS, Stephen; Private; L/9th Cav. Enlisted at Baltimore, MD, 2 Feb 1880; sick in hospital with bruised foot, troop in the field in New Mexico Jul–Aug 1880; in confinement at Ft Cummings, NM, Sept–Oct 1880; dishonorably discharged at Ft Bliss, TX, 17 Jan 1881. SOURCE: Muster Rolls, L/9th Cavalry, 30 Jun–31 Oct 1880; 31 Dec 1880–28 Feb 1881.

‡Discharged at Ft Bliss in accordance with General Court Martial Order 1, Department of the Missouri. SOURCE: Regt Returns, 9 Cav, Jan 1881.

STAFF, Edward; Corporal; C/9th Cav. Born in Warrenton, VA; enlisted 20 Feb 1887, occupation soldier; character very good when discharged at Ft Leavenworth, KS, 19 Feb 1892, age 31, Ht 5'8", black hair, brown eyes, complexion mulatto. SOURCE: Discharge, Edward Staff, 19 Feb 1892; photocopy in author's files.

‡Appointed corporal 3 Sep 1898. SOURCE: Roster, 9 Cav.

‡Died of abscess on brain, Ft McKinney, WY, 26 Oct 1893. SOURCE: Regt Returns, 9 Cav, Oct 1893.

‡Killed recently at Buffalo, WY, and buried with honors at National Cemetery, Ft Leavenworth. SOURCE: *ANJ* 31 (11 Nov 1893): 191.

Died 28 Oct 1893; buried at Ft Leavenworth National Cemetery, plot 3005. SOURCE: Ft Leavenworth National Cemetery.

STAFF, William R.; Captain; B/49th Inf. ‡Born in Washington, DC, 1 Jan 1873; educated and enlisted at Leavenworth, KS; mentioned for gallantry at San Juan, Cuba, 1 Jul 1898. SOURCE: *ANJ* 37 (20 Jan 1900): 478.

‡Private, corporal, sergeant, C/24th Infantry, 30 Jun 1892–25 Mar 1899; battalion sergeant major, 24th Infantry, 25 Mar 1899; participated in battles of San Juan and Santiago, Cuba, 1–15 Jul 1898; at yellow fever camp, Siboney, Cuba, 16 Jul–25 Aug 1898; arrived in the Philippines 2 Jan 1900; participated in engagements at Las Pinas, Philippines, 24 and 26 Sep 1900. SOURCE: Descriptive Book, B/49 Inf.

‡Private, C/24th Infantry, on extra duty as painter, Quartermaster Department, Ft Huachuca, AZ. SOURCE: Order 81, Ft Huachuca, 6 Jun 1893, Name File, 24 Inf.

‡Relieved of extra duty as painter, Quartermaster Department, Ft Huachuca. SOURCE: Order 96, Ft Huachuca, 30 Jun 1893, Name File, 24 Inf.

‡Relieved of extra duty as painter, Quartermaster Department, Ft Huachuca. SOURCE: Order 165, Ft Huachuca, 10 Nov 1893, Name File, 24 Inf.

Corporal, C/24th Infantry, stationed at Ft Huachuca, 1895; texts of letter to Adjutant General requesting change in his records to show his complexion as "mulatto" rather than "Negro," and response, published. SOURCE: Schubert, *Voices of the Buffalo Soldier*, 204–5.

‡Stationed at Vancouver Barracks, WA, 1899. SOURCE: San Francisco *Chronicle*, 15 Sep 1899.

‡Engaged insurgents at Zapote Bridge, Las Pinas, Philippines, 24 Sep 1900. SOURCE: *ANJ* 38 (1 Dec 1900): 333.

‡Won victory over insurgents, San Pueblo, Philippines, Jan 1901. SOURCE: *ANJ* 38 (30 Mar 1901): 753.

‡Mentioned as captain, B/49th Infantry. SOURCE: Beasley, *Negro Trailblazers*, 217.

STAFFORD, James N.; Private; H/24th Inf. ‡Enlisted Chicago, 23 Nov 1896, with five years' service. SOURCE: Muster Roll, H/24 Inf, May–Jun 1898.

‡Wounded in action on San Juan Hill, Santiago, Cuba, 1 Jul 1898; returned to U.S. for treatment. SOURCE: Muster Roll, H/24 Inf, Sep–Oct 1898.

‡Wounded in Cuba, 1898. SOURCE: Muller, *The Twenty Fourth Infantry*, 19.

‡On furlough authorized by surgeon's certificate, 24 Sep–23 Oct 1898. SOURCE: Muster Roll, H/24 Inf, Sep–Oct 1898.

‡On special duty as laborer with Quartermaster Department, 18 Nov 1898–28 Feb 1899. SOURCE: Muster Roll, H/24 Inf, Nov–Dec 1898 and Jan–Feb 1899.

Pvt. James M. Stafford, H/24th Infantry, died 15 Aug 1932; buried in plot C 163 at San Francisco National Cemetery. SOURCE: San Francisco National Cemetery.

STANCE, Emanuel; 1st Sgt; F/9th Cav. Emanuel Stanz born in Louisiana; mulatto complexion; can read and write, age 22, Jul 1870, in F/9th Cavalry at Ft McKavett, TX. SOURCE: Bierschwale, *Fort McKavett,* 97.

‡Born in Carroll Parish, LA; occupation farmer; Ht 5'1 1/2", black complexion; enlisted, age 19, 2 Oct 1866; reenlisted, Ht 5'5 1/2", 1876. SOURCE: Register of Enlistments.

‡Enlisted 1867 [*sic*]; scarcely five feet tall; native of Charleston, SC; stationed at Ft McKavett, TX, 1870; had five successful encounters with Indians in two years; received Medal of Honor. SOURCE: Leckie, *The Buffalo Soldiers*, 10.

Life, career, and bravery in action against Indians, 1870, for which he received Medal of Honor, narrated. SOURCE: Schubert, *Black Valor*, 9–26, 46, 50, 78–79, 117, 166.

‡With five enlisted men of F/9th Cavalry, surprised and attacked small village at Kickapoo Springs, TX, about fourteen miles from Ft McKavett, wounded four Indians, recaptured two white boys and fifteen horses, 19–20 May 1870. SOURCE: Hutcheson, "The Ninth Regiment of Cavalry"; Hamilton, "History of the Ninth Cavalry," 12; *Illustrated Review: Ninth Cavalry*.

‡Mentioned. SOURCE: Carroll, *The Black Military Experience in the American West*, 72, 403.

‡Expressed appreciation for Medal of Honor in letter to Adjutant General, U.S. Army, 24 Jul 1870: "I will cherish the gift as a thing of priceless value and endeavor by my future conduct to merit the high honor conferred upon me." SOURCE: Lee, *Negro Medal of Honor Men*, 59, 61.

‡While sergeant, M/9th Cavalry, convicted by general court martial, Ft McKavett, 3 Jan 1873, of being drunk to prejudice of good order and discipline at stables, Ft McKavett, 26 Dec 1872; of telling 1st Sgt. Henry Green, "If you reported that I was drunk you reported a God-damned lie and God-damn you you can't whip me"; and of "mayhem, to the prejudice of good order and discipline," assaulting Sergeant Green and biting off a portion of his lower lip, all on same day; prosecution witnesses: First Sergeant Green, Sgt. Horace Johnson, Sgt. Monroe Johnson,

and Pvt. William Smith, all of M/9th Cavalry; defense witnesses: Pvt. George Samuel and Cpl. Lawrence Johnson, M/9th Cavalry; sentenced to reduction to private and six months' confinement and loss of pay. SOURCE: GCMO 1, Department of Texas, 11 Jan 1873, appended to Court Martial Records, Stance.

‡Fined $10 by garrison court martial, Ft Robinson, NE. SOURCE: Order 6, 12 Jan 1886, Post Orders, Ft Robinson.

‡Authorized four-month furlough by Special Order 136, Division of the Missouri, 6 Sep 1886.

Completed twenty years of service on 25 Dec 1886; unit will give dinner and dance in his honor. SOURCE: Cleveland *Gazette*, 1 Jan 1887.

‡Reenlisted Ft Robinson, 26 Dec 1886. SOURCE: Post Returns, Ft Robinson, Dec 1886.

‡With detachment from Ft Robinson "scouting for robbers," 11–12 Jan 1887. SOURCE: Monthly Returns, 9 Cav, Jan 1887.

‡Regarding Stance at Ft Robinson in 1887, *see* OTT, GLENN, Louis, Private, F/9th Cavalry; OTT, ROYSTER, Henry, Private, F/9th Cavalry; WATERFORD, George, Blacksmith, F/9th Cavalry

‡Found dead on public highway between Ft Robinson and Crawford, NE, with four gunshot wounds, between 7:30 and 8:30 in the morning, 25 Dec 1887. SOURCE: Medical History, Ft Robinson.

‡Pvt. Simpson Mann heard that just before his 1888 arrival at Ft Robinson two or three soldiers had killed a sergeant who had beaten soldiers and told their captain lies about them; sergeant had been "dirty mean." SOURCE: Rickey, Mann interview.

‡Died at post hospital, Ft Robinson; funeral scheduled for 2 P.M., 27 Dec 1887. SOURCE: Post Surgeon to CO, Ft Robinson, 26 Dec 1887, Register of Correspondence, Post Surgeon, Ft Robinson.

‡Funeral scheduled for 10 A.M., 28 Dec 1887. SOURCE: Order 253, 27 Dec 1887, Post Orders, Ft Robinson.

‡Buried at Ft Robinson, 25 Dec 1887. SOURCE: List of Interments, Ft Robinson.

‡*See* Schubert, "The Violent World of Emanuel Stance."

Death at Ft Robinson in 1887, discussed. SOURCE: Dobak and Phillips, *The Black Regulars*, 200–201.

‡"As he was a very strict disciplinarian, it is believed he was killed by one of his own men. He stood high in the esteem of his superiors and wore a medal awarded by Congress for bravery in rescuing children from Indians." SOURCE: *ANJ* 25 (31 Dec 1887): 442.

‡"He was a Congressional medal man and left it and a manuscript of his life, with drawings, which should go to the Army Museum. Great effort has been made to discover the perpetrators of this villainous murder by members of this garrison. Stance was very strict. But his troop needed a strong hand, and it took a pretty nervy man to be 1st sergeant." SOURCE: *ANJ* 25 (14 Jan 1888): 482.

‡Biographical sketch. SOURCE: Logan and Winston, eds., *Dictionary of American Negro Biography*, 568–69.

Service in Texas described; mentioned as recipient of Medal of Honor; subsequent career and death narrated. SOURCE: Kenner, *Buffalo Soldiers and Officers of the Ninth Cavalry*, 159–74.

STANILY, William; Sergeant; B/10th Cav. *See* STAN-LEY, William, Sergeant, B/10th Cavalry

STANLEY, James; Private; K/10th Cav. ‡Killed in action, Ojo Caliente, TX, 29 Oct 1880. SOURCE: Baker, Roster; Leckie, *The Buffalo Soldiers*, 230.

Died 28 Oct 1880 at Ojo Caliente. SOURCE: Regimental Returns, 10th Cavalry, 1880.

STANLEY, John; Sergeant; 40th Inf. One of three enlisted men, with Pvts. James R. Cook and John H. Hedgeman, sent with officer to establish recruiting office, New York City, Nov 1867; completed enlistment as first sergeant, B/40th Infantry, and reenlisted. SOURCE: Dobak and Phillips, *The Black Regulars*, 6, 288.

STANLEY, William; Sergeant; B/10th Cav. ‡Born in Newbern, NC; black complexion; enlisted San Antonio, TX, 13 Jan 1880, with five years' continuous service; trumpeter as of 1880 enlistment; does not write his name; retained $60, clothing $24.15, deposits, 1880–83, $50; reenlisted Ft Davis, TX, 13 Jan 1885, unmarried, trumpeter, retained $60 and clothing $59; enlisted Ft Apache, AZ, 13 Jan 1890, single; marksman, 1883–85, 1888, 1890–91; sharpshooter, 1884–85; discharged, character excellent, Ft Custer, MT, 12 Jan 1895; retained $60, clothing $85, deposits $40; enlisted 13 Jan 1895. SOURCE: Descriptive Book, B/10 Cav.

‡Trumpeter, B/10th Cavalry, at Ft Apache, 1890, subscribed $.50 to testimonial to General Grierson. SOURCE: List of subscriptions, 23 Apr 1890, 10th Cavalry papers, MHI.

‡Served as trumpeter, B/10th Cavalry in Cuba, 1898. SOURCE: Cashin, *Under Fire with the Tenth Cavalry*, 338.

‡Retired Mar 1902 as sergeant, B/10th Cavalry. SOURCE: *ANJ* 39 (8 Mar 1902): 671.

Retired Sgt. William Stanily, B/10th Cavalry, died 9 Jun 1912; buried at Ft Leavenworth National Cemetery, plot E 137-A. SOURCE: Ft Leavenworth National Cemetery.

STANSON, John J.; Private; 24th Inf. Died on detached service 25 Sep 1906; buried in plot NADD 1194 at San Francisco National Cemetery. SOURCE: San Francisco National Cemetery.

STANTON, Daniel; Private; G/9th Cav. Killed in action in New Mexico, 1 Sep 1880, with detachment attacked by Indians at Agua Chiquita, NM; two privates, Robert Smith and Daniel Stanton, killed in action; stationed at Ft Stanton, NM. SOURCE: Hamilton, "History of the Ninth Cavalry," 53; *Illustrated Review: Ninth Cavalry*.

Attacked by Apaches, Agua Chiquita Canyon, while in command of detachment, Sep 1880. SOURCE: Billington, *New Mexico's Buffalo Soldiers*, 97–98.

Died 3 Sep 1880; buried at Santa Fe National Cemetery, NM, plot B 563. SOURCE: Santa Fe National Cemetery, Records of Burials.

STANTON, R. W.; Corporal; H/25th Inf. Died 11 Mar 1884; buried plot 1 43, Ft Meade National Cemetery. SOURCE: Ft Meade National Cemetery, VA database.

STAPLETON, Charles; Private; E/9th Cav. One of ten soldiers charged with mutiny and desertion for role in mutiny at San Pedro Springs, near San Antonio, TX, April 1867; pled guilty to desertion but not mutiny; mutiny charge dropped; convicted of desertion and sentenced to six months' confinement at military prison, Ship's Island, MS; sentence remitted before he was transported to prison. SOURCE: Dobak and Phillips, *The Black Regulars*, 208–11.

STARKS, Cicero; 24th Inf. Born into slavery, enlisted and served under name of Cicero Cummings, then found his father Moses Starks and changed his name to Cicero Starks. SOURCE: Dobak and Phillips, *The Black Regulars*, 300.

STARKS, Daniel; Private; L/10th Cav. Died at Ft Stockton, TX, on 4 Jan 1882; buried at San Antonio National Cemetery, Section C, number 340. SOURCE: San Antonio National Cemetery Locator.

STARKS, Solomon; Private; F/9th Cav. Died at Ft Davis, TX, on 7 Aug 1868; buried at San Antonio National Cemetery, Section I, number 1554. SOURCE: San Antonio National Cemetery Locator.

STCLAIR, Jean; Private; D/25th Inf. *See* ST. CLAIR, Jean, Private, D/25th Infantry

STEAD, Eugene; Private; F/9th Cav. ‡Died of cholera in the Philippines, 15 Jun 1902. SOURCE: *ANJ* 39 (9 Aug 1902): 1248.

Died in 15 Jun 1902; buried in plot N ADD529 at San Francisco National Cemetery. SOURCE: San Francisco National Cemetery.

STEARNS, George W.; A/38th Inf. Buried 24 Dec 1868 in section A, row G, plot 44, Ft Bayard, NM. SOURCE: Erickson, Burials at Fort Bayard National Cemetery, NM.

STEEL, Albert; Private; 10th Cav. Deserted from Ft Davis, TX, 1884. SOURCE: Leiker, *Racial Borders*, 82.

STEELE, George; Private; 24th Inf. Deserted after Sgt. William Foster threatened his life; was apprehended, convicted by military court in San Antonio, TX, and fined $80. SOURCE: Dobak and Phillips, *The Black Regulars*, 198.

STEELE, James T.; Sergeant; I/24th Inf. Died 24 Feb 1901; buried at Santa Fe National Cemetery, NM, plot K 385. SOURCE: Santa Fe National Cemetery, Records of Burials.

STEPHENS, Avery; Private; C/10th Cav. Died 17 Jun 1867 of consumption at Camp Grierson, KS. SOURCE: Regimental Returns, 10th Cavalry, 1867.

STEPHENS, Isaac; H/25th Inf. Born in New York; black complexion; can read and write, age 35, 5 Sep 1870, at Ft McKavett, TX. SOURCE: Bierschwale, *Fort McKavett*, 108.

STEVENS, Albert; Private; A/10th Cav. Died 22 Dec 1875 of disease at Ft Concho, TX. SOURCE: Regimental Returns, 10th Cavalry, 1875.

‡Commander, 10th Cavalry, forwards final statement and inventory of effects of deceased Private Stevens to Adjutant General, 3 Jan 1876. SOURCE: ES, 10 Cav, 1873–83.

STEVENS, Jacob W.; 1st Sgt; K/24th Inf. ‡Born in Baltimore, MD; awarded Distinguished Service Medal for role in engagement near Santa Ana, Philippines, 6 Oct 1899. SOURCE: Koger, *The Maryland Negro in Our Wars*, 23.

At Cabanatuan, Philippines, 1900–1901; witnessed Pvt. Frank Myers's failure and neglect to turn out guard at approach to his post of officer of the day, 3 Apr 1901; testified that Pvt. Thomas Morris took weapon from quarters, although ordered by noncommissioned officer not to, fired it, and caused alarm in camp, 12 Apr 1901; testified that Pvt. John H. Faggins failed to repair for reveille, 22 Apr 1901; Pvt. John C. Hargraves, drunk and disorderly in camp, told 1st Sgt. Jacob W. Stevens that he would be damned if he would go on detached service and would go back to saloon and drink more, 24 Apr 1901; testified that Pvt. Lee Shaver was too drunk to fall in for pay, 17 May 1901; witnessed Pvt. Isaiah Cook too drunk to perform duties, 19 May 1901; witnessed Pvt. Clarence Sales's absence without leave from pay table, 17 May 1901, his abusive and threatening language, 28 May 1901, and his taking rifle from barracks to use against Pvt. Samuel Stevens, D/24th Infantry; testified that Sgt. James Ingman and Pvt. Joseph McHenry failed to repair for retreat, 31 May 1901; witnessed Pvt. Thomas M. Harris's failure to repair for reveille, 2 Jun 1902; Pvt. William Lee, disorderly in camp, loud and disrespectful, handled weapon in threatening manner and refused order to give it to first sergeant. SOURCE: Name File, 24 Inf.

Awarded certificate of merit for coolness and good judgment in action at Santa Ana, Philippines, 6 Oct 1899. SOURCE: Gleim, *The Certificate of Merit*, 49.

‡Certificate of merit awarded 8 Dec 1903 for coolness and good judgment under fire as first sergeant, K/24th Infantry, in engagement at Santa Ana, 6 Oct 1899. SOURCE: GO 32, AGO, 6 Feb 1904.

Born in Franktown, VA; resided in Baltimore; received Distinguished Service Medal in lieu of certificate of merit. SOURCE: *American Decorations*, 843.

STEVENSON, James; Sergeant; B/10th Cav. Private, 19th Maryland; lives at 2120 Lemmon St., Baltimore, MD. SOURCE: United States Colored Troops Resident in Baltimore, 1890 Census.

‡At Ft Lyon, CO, Mar 1869. SOURCE: LR, Det 10 Cav, 1868–69.

STEVENSON, Samuel; Private; A/10th Cav. Died 23 Oct 1880 of consumption at Ft Stockton, TX. SOURCE: Regimental Returns, 10th Cavalry, 1880.

Died at Ft Stockton on 23 Oct 1880; buried at San Antonio National Cemetery, Section C, number 341. SOURCE: San Antonio National Cemetery Locator.

STEVENSON, Peter; F/9th Cav. Born in Louisiana; black complexion; can read, cannot write, age 23, Jul 1870, at Ft McKavett, TX. SOURCE: Bierschwale, *Fort McKavett*, 97.

STEWARD, David; Private; 25th Inf. Born in Fredericksburg, VA; Ht 5'1", black hair and eyes, black complexion; occupation laborer; recruited as trumpeter, enlisted at age 16, Pittsburgh, PA, 19 Jun 1882; arrived Ft Snelling, MN, 21 Nov 1882. SOURCE: Descriptive & Assignment Rolls of Recruits, 25 Inf.

STEWARD, Edward; Private; I/10th Cav. In Troop I/10th Cavalry stationed at Bonita Cañon Camp, AZ, 30 Jun 1886. SOURCE: Tagg, *The Camp at Bonita Cañon*, 232.

STEWARD, James; Sergeant; L/9th Cav. Died in 26 Jan 1904; buried in plot NA WS325 at San Francisco National Cemetery. SOURCE: San Francisco National Cemetery.

STEWARD, John; Private; H/10th Cav. Served in early 1880s. SOURCE: Sayre, *Warriors of Color*, 403.

STEWARD, John; Saddler; E/9th Cav. Saddler, E/9th Cavalry, assaulted soldier with poker, dining room, Ft DuChesne, UT, Dec 1887, and fined $10. SOURCE: Kenner, *Buffalo Soldiers and Officers of the Ninth Cavalry*, 235.

STEWARD, Theophilus G.; Chaplain; 25th Inf. Born 17 Apr 1843 in Gouldtown community in Bridgeton, NJ; father James, mother Rebecca, brother William; earned divinity degree in 1880 from Protestant Episcopal Divinity School; married Elizabeth Gadsden in 1866; description of reasons for enlisting as chaplain and service at Ft Missoula, MT, 24 Aug 1891–10 Apr 1898; remained in U.S. recruiting and writing during Spanish-American War; served at Ft Niobrara, NE, near Valentine, 27 Aug 1902–spring 1906; served at Ft McIntosh, TX; retired 17 Apr 1907; son James died in Washington, DC, at age 24, Jun 1893; wife died 2 Nov 1893, buried in New Jersey; two sons, age 8 and 14 in 1893; in Brooklyn, NY, 1896, married Dr. Susan McKinney, widow of William McKinney, an itinerant preacher; served as professor and administrator at Wilberforce University, Ohio, until his death in 1924; buried in New Jersey. SOURCE: Seraile, "Saving Souls on the Frontier."

‡Belongs to old colored family which goes back to pre-Revolutionary War New Jersey freemen; chaplain since 1891; wife a medical doctor at Wilberforce University; six sons: two Harvard graduates, one in medical school at University of Minnesota, three at Wilberforce. SOURCE: San Francisco *Chronicle*, 22 Oct 1899.

‡Career abstract: taught school, 1863–64; entered ministry; taught school, Marion, SC, and Stewart Co., GA, while in South; cashier, Freedmen's Bank, Macon, GA; in Delaware, 1871–73; in Haiti, Dec 1874; pastor of Bridge Street African Methodist Episcopal Church, Brooklyn, 1875–77; in West Philadelphia, PA, Divinity School of Protestant Episcopal Church, 1877–80, graduating at head of class; one year in Frankford, PA; two years in Delaware; two years in Union Church, Philadelphia; then Metropolitan African Methodist Episcopal Church, Washington, DC. SOURCE: AGO File 4634 ACP 91, T. G. Steward.

‡Spent 1865–67 in South Carolina and Georgia "doing missionary work"; large brick church in Macon built during his management and named Steward's Church over his protest; registrar and elections judge, Stewart Co., GA; wrote Republican platform in Delaware, 1872–73; member of state central committee, Brooklyn, 1875–78, when he knew Dr. Susan McKinney; now one of few delegates of African Methodist Episcopal Church in Ecumenical Conference planned for Washington, DC, this November. SOURCE: Steward, 1410 Pierce Place, Washington, DC, to John R. Lynch, 2 Jun 1891, AGO File 4634 ACP 91, T. G. Steward.

‡Accompanied Bishop D. A. Payne and sailed from New York to Charleston, SC, on U.S. government vessel *Arago*, 9 May 1865; then "itinerant licentiate," became deacon of South Carolina Conference, organized 16 May 1865 at colored Presbyterian Church, Calhoun Street (then Boundary Street) at northern limit of Charleston near King Street. SOURCE: Payne, *History of the African Methodist Episcopal Church*, 469.

‡At opening session of African Methodist Episcopal Conference, Charleston, Zion Presbyterian Church, May 1865, Steward was assigned to Beaufort, SC. SOURCE: Taylor, *The Negro in South Carolina*, 113–14.

‡President B. F. Lee of Wilberforce University resigned 1884; teachers' committee endorsed Steward as successor; in election John G. Mitchell got seventeen of thirty-one votes; Steward followers protested; on next vote Mitchell's brother, S. T. Mitchell, was elected. SOURCE: McGinnis, *A History and an Interpretation of Wilberforce University*, 55–56.

‡For last seventeen months minister of Metropolitan African Methodist Episcopal Church, Washington, DC; has reduced debt by $4,000. SOURCE: Cleveland *Gazette*, 3 Dec 1887.

‡Letter from Col. James Biddle, commander, 9th Cavalry, Ft Robinson, NE, to Steward, 31 Jan 1893, says Biddle has never been in action with his regiment but has with colored soldiers, whose casualties wholly equaled whites: "in garrison my soldiers are the peers of any, and I doubt not in action [that they] would prove the same." SOURCE: LS, Ft Robinson.

‡Letter from Lt. Gen. Nelson Miles to Steward, 5 Aug 1893, praises 40th Infantry, which Miles commanded after Civil War. SOURCE: Nankivell, *History of the Twenty-fifth Infantry*, 9.

‡"One of the most scholarly ministers of the A.M.E. Church," recently appointed chaplain. SOURCE: Cleveland *Gazette*, 8 Aug 1891.

‡Mentioned as third Afro-American chaplain. SOURCE: Cleveland *Gazette*, 29 Aug 1891.

Text of letter discussing his relationship with officers of the 25th Infantry, from Ft Missoula, Oct 1891. SOURCE: Schubert, *Voices of the Buffalo Soldier*, 173.

‡Son Benjamin visited him at Ft Missoula, Christmas 1891. SOURCE: *ANJ* 29 (9 Jan 1891): 347.

‡Efficiency Report, Ft Missoula, 16 Feb 1893, notes that Steward knows French, German, Hebrew, and Greek. SOURCE: AGO File 4634 ACP 91, T. G. Steward.

‡Authorized one-month leave from Ft Missoula. SOURCE: *ANJ* 30 (18 Mar 1893): 495.

‡Andrew S. Burt, Efficiency Report, 12 Feb 1894, calls Steward "the most conscientious chaplain in the discharge of his duties I have ever served with. I deem him an ornament to the service." SOURCE: AGO File 4634 ACP 91, T. G. Steward.

‡Author of "Mortality of Negro," *Social Economist* 9 (1895): 204.

‡Expected to leave Ft Missoula this week to go East for Christmas. SOURCE: *ANJ* 34 (14 Nov 1896): 174.

‡Student at University of Montana, 1897–98. SOURCE: Joiner, *A Half Century of Freedom*, 51.

‡Author of "a little publication titled, 'Active Service or Gospel Work among the U.S. Soldiers.'" SOURCE: Indianapolis *Freeman*, 11 Sep 1897.

‡At Chattanooga, TN, with regiment; his wife a practicing physician "and a thorough scholar . . . also a musician." SOURCE: Indianapolis *Freeman*, 30 Apr 1898.

‡Letters from Chickamauga, GA, 28 May 1898, and Manila, Philippines, 19 Jan 1900, in Gatewood, *"Smoked Yankees,"* 25–26, 262–63.

‡At Chickamauga forced with family "to travel to and from the park, with the common herd and not permitted to travel as a United States officer." SOURCE: Indianapolis *Freeman*, 24 Dec 1898.

‡Author of "The New Colored Soldier," *The Independent* 50 (13 Jun 1898): 782–83.

Supported efforts of William McBryar and Edward L. Baker to obtain commissions in regular Army. SOURCE: Schubert, *Black Valor*, 111, 154–55.

‡Speaker at Peace Jubilee, Bridge Street Church, Brooklyn, sponsored by Montauk Soldiers Relief Association, Dr. Susan McKinney Steward, president; praised black troops as "reserved, obedient and . . . good soldiers . . . filled with a stock of good humor and good cheer." SOURCE: Cleveland *Gazette*, 24 Sep 1898.

‡Desiring to preserve for future and state to present generation of Negroes the history of "the valorous conduct of the four black regiments in Cuba" and to further justify policy that keeps blacks in Army, asks for four months on detached service, including one month in Cuba, to gather data, write, publish, especially while Chaplain McCleery is available to replace him, all "for the cause of my race and my country." SOURCE: Steward, Ft Logan, CO, to AG, USA, 19 Dec 1898, AGO File 4634 ACP 91, T. G. Steward.

‡Authorized one-month leave by Special Order 122, Department of Colorado, 22 Dec 1898.

‡Three months of leave approved by memorandum, Adjutant General's Office, 14 Jan 1899.

‡Leave extended two months by Special Order 12, Adjutant General's Office, 16 Jan 1899.

‡Transferred to Ft Apache, AZ, at end of leave in accordance with Special Order 44, Adjutant General's Office, 23 Feb 1899.

‡Ordered to Ft Apache. SOURCE: *ANJ* 36 (4 Mar 1899): 631.

‡Bishop Benjamin Arnett, Wilberforce University, endorsed his plan to write history of colored regiments and asked President McKinley for approval, 23 Feb 1899. SOURCE: AGO File 4634 ACP 91, T. G. Steward.

‡The War Department agreed with Bishop Arnett that Steward was "a very suitable man to write the proposed history and that every facility will be accorded him for the prosecution of this task," in letter from Adjutant General, 1 Mar 1899. SOURCE: AGO File 4634 ACP 91, T. G. Steward.

‡L. J. Coppin, pastor, Bethel African Methodist Episcopal Church, Philadelphia, wrote President McKinley, 7 Mar 1899, expressing regret of Philadelphia African Methodist Episcopal pastors regarding Steward's assignment

to Ft Apache. SOURCE: AGO File 4634 ACP 91, T. G. Steward.

‡General Miles rescinded Steward's transfer to Ft Apache because chaplain should be on duty with his regiment, 8 Mar 1899. SOURCE: AGO File 4634 ACP 91, T. G. Steward.

‡"The well-known author" has undertaken important work of an accurate, complete history of the four black regiments in Cuba; now has a novel in press; "he will bring to the work wide literary experience, a painstaking regard to accuracy, as well as an enthusiastic admiration for the black soldier." SOURCE: Indianapolis *Freeman*, 18 Mar 1899.

‡Ordered on temporary duty to Wilberforce. SOURCE: *ANJ* 36 (25 Mar 1899): 710.

‡To write history of black regular regiments after visit to Cuba to go over battlefield where they distinguished themselves. SOURCE: Cleveland *Gazette*, 15 Apr 1899.

‡His most important theological works are *Death, Hades, and the Resurrection*, *Divine Attributes*, *End of the World*, and *Genesis Re-Read*, which examines latest conclusions of science and their bearing on Old Testament; this last book "extensively read, highly endorsed by press and clergy," and used as reference book at Wilberforce; also wrote *Religious Life in the U.S. Army*. SOURCE: Indianapolis *Freeman*, 20 May 1899.

‡Author of pamphlet on "how the Black St. Domingo Legion saved the patriot army in the siege of Savanna in 1779." SOURCE: Cleveland *Gazette*, 1 Jul 1899.

‡To proceed to the Philippines on U.S. Army Transport *Newport* on or about 23 Oct 1899. SOURCE: *ANJ* 37 (28 Oct 1899): 195.

‡Arrived in Manila from detached service; appointed by Secretary of War to write complete history of colored troops in war with Spain, which he just finished; will preach at Soldiers Institute tomorrow. SOURCE: Manila *Times*, 25 Nov 1899.

‡Arrived in the Philippines, early Dec 1899; "the boys were glad to welcome him as his literary work is a rare treat and his presence is much enjoyed after an extended absence." SOURCE: Private Rienzi Lemus in Richmond *Planet*, 27 Jan 1900.

‡Letter. SOURCE: *The Independent* 52 (1 Feb 1900): 312–14.

‡Letter from Manila, no date, comments on sins of Americans in the Philippines and immorality of open door policy. SOURCE: Cleveland *Gazette*, 29 Dec 1900.

‡Poem "The Aged Patriot's Lament," in Manila *Times*, 6 Feb 1901.

‡Visiting regimental garrisons, Philippines, Dec 1900. SOURCE: Richmond *Planet*, 16 Feb 1901.

‡Author of articles "Holy Week in Manila," *Colored American Magazine* 2 (Apr 1901): 446–48; "Two Years in Luzon," *Colored American Magazine* 4 (Nov 1901): 4–10, 4 (Jan–Feb 1902): 164–70, 5 (Aug 1902): 244–49.

‡Granted three-month furlough, May 1901, "in view of exceptional circumstances." SOURCE: *ANJ* 38 (22 Jun 1901): 1043.

‡Just back from twelve months in the Philippines; delivered lecture at Wilberforce Chapel last Tuesday on "the Philippines," with Mrs. Steward appearing on platform "in full Philippino costume, the dress having been presented to her through the chaplain, by the distinguished sister of the great Philippine scholar, author, and statesman, Don Pedro A. Paterno, late chief of Aguinaldo's cabinet." SOURCE: Indianapolis *Freeman*, 27 Jul 1901.

‡Visited General Hospital, Presidio of San Francisco, CA, then went to Philippines with son on 1 Oct 1901 to resume duty after four-month leave. SOURCE: Cleveland *Gazette*, 26 Oct 1901.

‡25th Infantry band recently gave concert to Mrs. Steward, visiting husband at Ft Niobrara, NE. SOURCE: Indianapolis *Freeman*, 15 Nov 1903.

‡Lt. Gen. Adna R. Chaffee thanks Steward for sending translation of French "Military Education and Instruction" from Ft Niobrara, 3 Feb 1904. SOURCE: AGO File 4634 ACP 91, T. G. Steward.

‡Praise for his just-published *The Colored Regulars in the United States Army*, with editorial against prejudice against blacks in Army; claims Steward seeks to arouse American people to proper sense of gratitude and win open door to promotion for blacks. SOURCE: New York *Age*, 8 Jun 1905.

‡Undated letter from Ft Niobrara advocates military education. SOURCE: Indianapolis *Freeman*, 19 Aug 1905.

‡On recent trip to Mexico observed that Mexican army had no color distinction; in New York City and Philadelphia saw that blacks' hold on labor market for common labor was improving as compared to "Pat and Antonio." SOURCE: Cleveland *Gazette*, 22 Dec 1906.

‡Steward, Bridgeton, NJ, 12 Jan 1907, requests retirement to Wilberforce, OH, as soon as possible. SOURCE: AGO File 4634 ACP 91, T. G. Steward.

‡Retires in Apr to home at Wilberforce on reaching mandatory retirement age; born Apr 1843. SOURCE: Cleveland *Gazette*, 23 Feb 1907.

‡Marriage of son, Dr. Charles G. Steward, to Maude A. Trotter, reported. SOURCE: Washington *Bee*, 2 Mar 1907.

‡African Methodist Episcopal clergyman, retired from service Apr 1907, after twenty-five years. SOURCE: *Colored American Magazine* 12 (May 1907): 391.

‡Elected vice president of Wilberforce University in 1908. SOURCE: Joiner, *A Half Century of Freedom*, 47.

‡B. F. Lee, Secretary, Council of Bishops, African Methodist Episcopal Church, Wilberforce, informs President Taft, 8 Feb 1911, that he has commissioned Steward to represent his church at the Universal Races Conference, London, England, Jul 1911. SOURCE: AGO File 4634 ACP 91, T. G. Steward.

‡Resident of Wilberforce; will preach at St. John's African Methodist Episcopal Church, Cleveland, OH, on 3 May, and give his famous lecture, "Our Civilization," on 4 May. SOURCE: Cleveland *Gazette*, 2 May 1914.

‡Author of *The Haitian Revolution, 1791 to 1804, or, Sidelights on the French Revolution* (New York: Neale Publishing Co., 1914).

‡Advertisement: *The Army and Navy Register* says of his new book, *The Haitian Revolution*, "No more interesting book has ever been written"; Albert Bushnell Hart says, "It cannot fail to be serviceable both for the understanding of the Negro race and the relations of France with the West Indies." SOURCE: Cleveland *Gazette*, 10 Jul 1915.

‡Vice president of Wilberforce University, in charge of "Wilberforce Week" campaign to interest people of Cleveland in the university; will deliver principal address at mass meeting, St. John's African Methodist Episcopal Church, 30 Jul 1916; goal is $50,000; Steward and others will take campaign to Indianapolis, Louisville, and elsewhere. SOURCE: Cleveland *Gazette*, 29 Jul 1916.

‡"A master of controversy." SOURCE: Cromwell, *The Negro in American History*.

‡Dr. S. Maria Steward, wife of Chaplain Steward, born in Brooklyn, NY, 1845, to Sylvanus and Anna Smith; valedictorian, New York Homeopathic College for Women; practiced medicine in New York State for many years; member, King's Co. Homeopathic Society and New York State Medical Society; organist at Bridge Street African Methodist Episcopal Church for twenty-eight years; mother of two and lately resident physician at Wilberforce University; "a woman of rare charm and ability." SOURCE: "Men of the Month," *Crisis* 18 (May 1918): 15.

‡Susan Maria Steward, Resident Physician, College of Arts and Sciences, Wilberforce, 1900–1908. SOURCE: McGinnis, *A History and an Interpretation of Wilberforce University*, 151.

‡Susan Steward was author and publisher of *Woman in Medicine*, 1915.

‡Family history. SOURCE: Steward and Steward, *Gouldtown*; Broadstone, *History of Greene County*, 968–73.

‡Listed with publications. SOURCE: Coyle, *Ohio Authors and Their Books*, 599.

‡Biographical article. SOURCE: Indianapolis *Freeman*, 20 May 1899.

‡Biographical sketch. SOURCE: Logan and Winston, eds., *Dictionary of American Negro Biography*, 570–71.

Life and career discussed, with emphasis on his rapport with enlisted men. SOURCE: Dobak and Phillips, *The Black Regulars*, 117–19, 121–22, 152, 161, 227.

‡Pictures. SOURCE: Cashin, *Under Fire with the Tenth Cavalry*, 141; Nankivell, *History of the Twenty-fifth Infantry*, 55.

‡Biographical sketch of wife Susan McKinney Steward. SOURCE: Hine et al., eds., *Black Women in America*, 1109–12.

‡Mentioned. SOURCE: Acknowledgements to Mary Curtis, *The Black Soldier*.

‡Biography of son Gustavus A. Steward. SOURCE: Boris, ed., *Who's Who in Colored America*, 192.

STEWART, Charles S.; Corporal; 9th Cav. Received Philippine Campaign Badge number 11747 for service as corporal in E/9th Cavalry; in 9th Cavalry at Ft Leavenworth, KS, Mar 1905. SOURCE: Philippine Campaign Badge list, 29 May 1905.

STEWART, Frank; D/38th Inf. Buried 29 Dec 1868 in section A, row G, plot 45, Ft Bayard, NM. SOURCE: Erickson, Burials at Fort Bayard National Cemetery, NM.

STEWART, James; Private; B/10th Cav. Died at Ft Davis, TX, on 9 Mar 1883; buried at San Antonio National Cemetery, Section I, number 1559. SOURCE: San Antonio National Cemetery Locator.

STEWART, John; Private; B/9th Cav. Received Philippine Campaign Badge number 11748 for service as private in E/9th Cavalry; in 9th Cavalry at Ft Leavenworth, KS, Mar 1905. SOURCE: Philippine Campaign Badge list, 29 May 1905.

‡Veteran, private, B/9th Cavalry, of Philippine Insurrection; at Ft D. A. Russell, WY, in 1910. SOURCE: *Illustrated Review: Ninth Cavalry.*

STEWART, John; Sergeant; B/10th Cav. ‡Blacksmith, at Ft Apache, AZ, 1890, subscribed $.50 to testimonial to General Grierson. SOURCE: List of subscriptions, 23 Apr 1890, 10th Cavalry papers, MHI.

‡Served as blacksmith in 10th Cavalry in Cuba, 1898. SOURCE: Cashin, *Under Fire with the Tenth Cavalry*, 338.

‡Retired as sergeant, Apr 1900. SOURCE: *ANJ* 37 (5 May 1900): 851.

Died 14 May 1912; buried at San Antonio National Cemetery, Section B, number 137. SOURCE: San Antonio National Cemetery Locator.

STEWART, Moses; Private; 24th Inf. ‡Died of chronic pulmonary tuberculosis on board U.S. Army Transport *Kilpatrick* bound for San Francisco, 22 Mar 1902. SOURCE: *ANJ* 39 (5 Apr 1902): 786.

Died 22 Mar 1902 on *Kilpatrick* en route from Manila, Philippines, to San Francisco, CA; arrived 30 Mar 1902; buried in plot NEW A806 at San Francisco National Cemetery. SOURCE: San Francisco National Cemetery.

STEWART, Samuel; Private; 38th Inf. At Ft Harker, KS, 1867, confined for six months for desertion. SOURCE: Dobak and Phillips, *The Black Regulars*, 187.

STICKLES, Robert; Private; C/49th Inf. Died in the Philippines on 22 Apr 1900; body received 15 Apr 1902 at San Francisco National Cemetery, buried in plot NEW A1018. SOURCE: San Francisco National Cemetery.

STIRLING, Martin; 9th Cav. Born in Maryland; black complexion; cannot read or write, age 31, Sep 1870, at Ft McKavett, TX. SOURCE: Bierschwale, *Fort McKavett*, 107.

STOKES, Earnest; Private; F/24th Inf. ‡Recommended for certificate of merit for gallantry, Naguilian, Luzon, Philippines, 7 Dec 1899. SOURCE: *ANJ* 39 (15 Feb 1902): 594–95.

Awarded certificate of merit for most distinguished gallantry in action at Naguilian, Luzon, 7 Dec 1899. SOURCE: Gleim, *The Certificate of Merit*, 50.

‡Awarded certificate of merit for distinguished gallantry, Naguilian, Luzon, 7 Dec 1899, on 10 Mar 1902. SOURCE: GO 86, AGO, 24 Jul 1902.

Born and resided in Wartrace, TN; received Distinguished Service Medal in lieu of certificate of merit. SOURCE: *American Decorations*, 844.

STOKES, Henry; Private; D/25th Inf. Died 7 Aug 1904; buried at Ft Leavenworth National Cemetery, plot 3544. SOURCE: Ft Leavenworth National Cemetery.

STOKES, Isaac; Private; 9th Cav. Received Philippine Campaign Badge number 11869 for service as private in C/9th Cavalry; in 9th Cavalry at Ft Leavenworth, KS, Mar 1905. SOURCE: Philippine Campaign Badge list, 29 May 1905.

STONE; Corporal; G/9th Cav. At Ft Robinson, NE, some time between 1894 and 1898; broke three ribs when wagon loaded with timber turned over. SOURCE: Williams, Jessie, interview, 26 Sep 1941.

STONE, Jerry; Private; K/9th Cav. Injured in action against Nana, Carrizo Canyon, NM, Aug 1881, by falling off horse, hospitalized until discharged on surgeon's certificate of disability, Mar 1882. SOURCE: Kenner, *Buffalo Soldiers and Officers of the Ninth Cavalry*, 149.

STONE, Minor; Private; L/9th Cav. Enlisted 21 Aug 1878 at Cincinnati, OH; stationed at Ft Bliss, TX, Nov 1879–Feb 1880; in the field in New Mexico in pursuit of Victorio's band of Apaches 8 Jan–22 Feb 1880, troop left Ojo Caliente 24 Feb and marched via Canada Alamosa and Cuchillo Negro, arriving at Chase's Ranch, 26 Feb 1880, after marching 621 miles in Jan and Feb; troop at Chase's Ranch 29

Feb 1880 awaiting further orders; starting 8 Jul 1880 marched twenty miles to Ft Cummings, NM; left camp on Rio Mimbres, NM, on 8 Jul 1880 and marched twenty miles to Ft Cummings; left 8 Aug, marched to Rio Grande at Leas Ferry, and returned to camp at Rio Mimbres after march of 104 miles; marched 945 miles in the field in New Mexico, Sept–Oct 1880. SOURCE: Muster Rolls, L/9th Cavalry, 31 Oct 1879–29 Feb 1880; 30 June–31 Oct 1880.

‡On detached service in the field, New Mexico, 21 Jan–24 Feb 1881. SOURCE: Regt Returns, 9 Cav, Feb 1881.

STOREY, Charles J.; Private; K/9th Cav. ‡At Ft D. A. Russell, WY, in 1910; resident of Luray, VA. SOURCE: *Illustrated Review: Ninth Cavalry*, with picture.

Also served in D/25th Infantry; died in 21 Feb 1917; buried in plot ESIDE482-A at San Francisco National Cemetery. SOURCE: San Francisco National Cemetery.

STOUT, Albert; Ord Sgt; U.S. Army. ‡Sergeant, M/9th Cavalry, wounded in action in San Mateo Mountains, New Mexico, 17 Jan 1880, along with Privates Bolt and Shaw. SOURCE: Hamilton, "History of the Ninth Cavalry," 54.

‡Appointed ordnance sergeant from sergeant, M/9th Cavalry, 24 Jun 1887. SOURCE: Roster, 9 Cav.

Appointed ordnance sergeant 20 Jun 1887, from sergeant, M/9th Cavalry. SOURCE: Dobak, "Staff Noncommissioned Officers."

STOVEL, Alexander; Private; I/25th Inf. Died at Ft Stockton, TX, on 29 Jul 1872; buried at San Antonio National Cemetery, Section C, number 437. SOURCE: San Antonio National Cemetery Locator.

STOWERS, Elijah; C/25th Inf. Born in Pennsylvania; black complexion; can read and write, age 22, 5 Sep 1870, at Ft McKavett, TX. SOURCE: Bierschwale, *Fort McKavett*, 109.

STRAMBOLD, George; Private; K/25th Inf. Born in St Louis, MO; Ht 5'6", black complexion; occupation carpenter; enlisted in A/39th Infantry for three years on 3 Sep 1867, age 23, at Greenville, LA; transferred to K/25th Infantry at Jackson Bks, LA, 20 Apr 1869. SOURCE: Descriptive Roll of A/39th Inf.

STRATTON, George; Private; A/38th Inf. ‡Arrested for part in soldiers' revolt at Ft Cummings, NM, autumn 1867; acquitted by court martial. SOURCE: Billington, *New Mexico's Buffalo Soldiers*, 40, 42.

One of six 38th Infantrymen acquitted by military court of mutiny, New Mexico, 1868. SOURCE: Dobak and Phillips, *The Black Regulars*, 324.

STRAWBERRY, Gabriel M.; Private; 25th Inf. Born in Christ Church, SC; occupation miner; Ht 5'4 3/4", dark

complexion, black hair and eyes; enlisted, age 23, Charleston, SC, 13 Jun 1881; left recruit depot, David's Island, NY, 17 Aug 1881, and after trip on steamer *Thomas Kirby* to Central Depot, New York City, and train via Chicago to Running Water, Dakota Territory, 22 Aug 1881, marched forty-seven miles to Ft Randall, SD, arrived 24 Aug 1881. SOURCE: Descriptive & Assignment Rolls, 25 Inf.

STRAWS, Thomas; Private; H/10th Cav. Born in Frankfort, KY, 1852; enlisted Cincinnati, OH, 26 Sep 1879; Ht 5'3", black complexion, eyes, hair; occupation laborer; treated in the field 5 July 1880, Eagle Springs, TX; treated intermittently 14 Nov 1880–Apr 1881, Ft Davis, TX; treated in Nov and Dec 1881, Pena Colorado, TX; treated intermittently Mar 1882–June 1883, Ft Davis. SOURCE: Sayre, *Warriors of Color*, 426–27.

STRICKLAND, Joseph; Private; H/48th Inf. ‡Died of variola in the Philippines, 20 Mar 1900. SOURCE: *ANJ* 37 (31 Mar 1900): 731.

Died in Manila, Philippines, 22 Mar 1900; body received 31 Dec 1900 at San Francisco National Cemetery, buried in plot ES 1207. SOURCE: San Francisco National Cemetery.

STRICKMAN, Ernest; Corporal; F/10th Cav. Died at Camp Eagle Pass, TX, on 2 Aug 1878; buried at San Antonio National Cemetery, Section F, number 1141. SOURCE: San Antonio National Cemetery Locator.

STRIDER, George; Private; E/10th Cav. In Troop E/10th Cavalry stationed at Bonita Cañon Camp, AZ, 28 Feb 1886. SOURCE: Tagg, *The Camp at Bonita Cañon*, 232.

STROTHER, Albert; Private; H/25th Inf. Born in Fairfax County, VA; Ht 5'8", black hair and eyes, black complexion; occupation laborer; resided in Fairfax County, VA, when he enlisted at age 22, Washington, DC, 20 Sep 1886; arrived Ft Snelling, MN, 20 Jan 1887. SOURCE: Descriptive & Assignment Rolls of Recruits, 25 Inf.

‡Died in Cuba, 1 Jul 1898. SOURCE: *ANJ* 36 (18 Feb 1899): 590.

‡Killed in action at El Caney, Cuba, 1 Jul 1898; buried one mile south of El Caney; wood headboard, surrounded by stones, has name cut into it; name enclosed in tightly corked bottle buried at head of grave. SOURCE: Scrapbook, 25 Inf, II.

STUART, Thomas; Corporal; G/9th Cav. Appointed corporal 12 Dec 1896; in G/9th Cavalry at Ft Robinson, NE, Jan 1897. SOURCE: Ninth Cavalry, Roster of NCOs, 1897.

STUCKEY, Amos W.; Private; H/24th Inf. Awarded certificate of merit for most distinguished gallantry in action at Naguilian, Luzon, Philippines, 7 Dec 1899. SOURCE: Gleim, *The Certificate of Merit*, 50.

‡Fined $2 by summary court, San Isidro, Philippines, for appearing at inspection with dirty rifle, 8 Feb 1902, fourth conviction. SOURCE: Register of Summary Court, San Isidro.

‡Recommended for certificate of merit for gallantry at Naguilian, Luzon, 7 Dec 1899. SOURCE: *ANJ* 39 (15 Feb 1902): 594–95.

‡Awarded certificate of merit for gallantry in the Philippines, 7 Dec 1899; already discharged when award was made, 10 Mar 1902. SOURCE: GO 86, AGO, 24 Jul 1902.

SULLIVANT, James W.; Comsy Sgt; U.S. Army. Born in Ohio; mulatto complexion; can read and write, age 23, Jul 1870; in D/24th Infantry at Ft McKavett, TX. SOURCE: Bierschwale, *Fort McKavett*, 95.

Sergeant major, 24th Infantry, wrote letter to General William Sherman regarding status of black soldiers in 1877. SOURCE: Dobak and Phillips, *The Black Regulars*, 191.

Appointed commissary sergeant 5 Jun 1879, from regimental sergeant major, 24th Infantry. SOURCE: Dobak, "Staff Noncommissioned Officers."

‡Served 1879. *See* JEFFERS, David B., Commissary Sergeant, U.S. Army

SUMNER, John; Private; K/25th Inf. Private, received Indian Wars Campaign Badge number 1400 on 13 Jul 1909. SOURCE: Carroll, *Indian Wars Campaign Badge*, 40.

SURRY, Calvin A.; Trumpeter; L/9th Cav. Enlisted 10 Aug 1875 in Boston, MA; discharged from L/9th Cavalry at Ft Bliss, TX, 9 Aug 1880, character good. SOURCE: Muster Rolls, L/9th Cavalry, 30 June–31 Aug 1880.

SUTTER, John W.; Private; 10th Cav. Died at Ft Concho, TX, on 11 Aug 1878; buried at San Antonio National Cemetery, Section D, number 704. SOURCE: San Antonio National Cemetery Locator.

SWAN, Abraham; H/25th Inf. Born in North Carolina; black complexion; can read and write, age 22, 5 Sep 1870, at Ft McKavett, TX. SOURCE: Bierschwale, *Fort McKavett*, 107.

SWAN, Edward; Private; L/9th Cav. Enlisted 5 Feb 1879 at Baltimore, MD; stationed at Ft Bliss, TX, Nov 1879–Feb 1880; in the field in New Mexico in pursuit of Victorio's band of Apaches 8 Jan–22 Feb 1880, left Ojo Caliente 24 Feb and marched via Canada Alamosa and Cuchillo Negro, arriving at Chase's Ranch, 26 Feb 1880, after marching 621 miles in Jan and Feb; troop at Chase's Ranch 29 Feb 1880 awaiting further orders; starting 8 Jul 1880 marched twenty miles to Ft Cummings, NM; left camp on Rio Mimbres, NM, on 8 Jul 1880 and marched twenty miles to Ft Cummings; left 8 Aug on march to Rio Grande at

Leas Ferry, and returned to Rio Mimbres camp after march of 104 miles; marched 945 miles in the field in New Mexico, Sept–Oct 1880; left Ft Stanton, NM, 11 Nov 1880, arrived Ft Bliss, TX, 18 Nov 1880. SOURCE: Muster Rolls, L/9th Cavalry, 31 Oct 1879–29 Feb 1880; 30 June–31 Dec 1880.

‡Pvt. E. Swan, L/9th Cavalry, on detached service in the field, New Mexico, 21 Jan–24 Feb 1881. SOURCE: Regt Returns, 9 Cav, Feb 1881.

SWAN, Edward; Private; C/9th Cav. Died 4 Apr 1901; buried at Ft Bayard, NM, in plot N 27. SOURCE: "Fort Bayard National Cemetery, Records of Burials."

Edw'd Swan, G/9th Cavalry, buried at Ft Bayard. SOURCE: "Buffalo Soldiers Buried at Ft Bayard, NM."

Buried 4 Apr 1901, section A, row V, plot 27, at Ft Bayard. SOURCE: Erickson, Burials at Fort Bayard National Cemetery, NM.

SWANN, Thomas E.; Private; C/49th Inf. Died 26 Jun 1900; buried in plot NA 497 at San Francisco National Cemetery. SOURCE: San Francisco National Cemetery.

SWEAT, George; Private; 10th Cav. At Ft Duncan, TX, Dec 1877, put in guardhouse for failure to obey order of sergeant. SOURCE: Kinevan, *Frontier Cavalryman*, 66–67.

At Ft Stockton, TX, 1879, served as orderly to Lt. Louis Orleman. SOURCE: Barnett, *Ungentlemanly Acts*, 142.

‡G. W. Sweat, private, B/10th Cavalry, served as striker (personal servant) to Lt. L. H. Orleans, Ft Stockton, 1879. SOURCE: Stallard, *Glittering Misery*, 119–20.

SWEENEY, Robert; Saddler; F/10th Cav. Died 17 Nov 1890; originally buried at Ft Grant, AZ; reburied at Santa Fe National Cemetery, NM, plot A-1 758. SOURCE: Santa Fe National Cemetery, Records of Burials.

SYKES, Zekiel; Sergeant; E/9th Cav. ‡Enlisted New Orleans, LA, 4 Oct 1866; reenlisted Ft Clark, TX, 4 Oct 1871; discharged 25 Oct 1876, character good; enlisted Ft Union, NM, 24 Nov 1876; discharged 12 Dec 1881, character very good; enlisted in B/9th Cavalry, Ft Hays, KS, 22 Dec 1881; discharged 21 Dec 1886, character excellent; enlisted Ft DuChesne, UT, 22 Dec 1886; discharged 21 Dec 1891, character excellent; enlisted Ft DuChesne, 22 Dec 1891; discharged 21 Dec 1896, character excellent. SOURCE: VA File XC 2650122, Zekiel Sykes.

‡Occupation servant; Ht 5'6", yellow complexion; second enlistment, age 25, Ft Clark, 4 Oct 1871; discharged Ft Wingate, NM, 25 Oct 1876, character good. SOURCE: Register of Enlistments.

‡Sergeant, B/9th Cavalry, authorized six-month furlough from Ft DuChesne. SOURCE: *ANJ* 24 (4 Dec 1886): 370.

‡Born in Corinth, LA; fifth enlistment, as sergeant, B/9th Cavalry, Ft DuChesne, 22 Dec 1886; discharged Ft DuChesne, 21 Dec 1891, character excellent. SOURCE: Register of Enlistments.

‡Corporal, E/9th Cavalry, authorized to reenlist as married soldier, by letter, Adjutant General's Office, 21 Nov 1896.

‡Retires from Ft Robinson, NE, as corporal, E/9th Cavalry, in accordance with Special Order 16, Adjutant General's Office, 29 Jan 1897. SOURCE: *ANJ* 34 (30 Jan 1897): 384.

Enlisted in E/9th Cavalry in 1866; one of three original members of E/9th Cavalry still in it in 1879, with James Williams and William Howard; served on honor guard when body of Col. Edward Hatch was transported from Ft Robinson to Ft Leavenworth, KS, in 1889; retired as 30-year man in late 1890s. SOURCE: Kenner, *Buffalo Soldiers and Officers of the Ninth Cavalry*, 48–49, 326.

At Ft Robinson in E/9th Cavalry Jan 1897; appointed corporal 11 Jun 1896. SOURCE: Ninth Cavalry, Roster of NCOs, 1897.

‡Married Margaret, 14 Apr 1890; divorced Nov 1912 for desertion, Cook Co., IL; married Lucinda Hurd, Crown Point, IN, 12 Dec 1912; resided in Chicago, 1905–26; retired pay $56 per month in 1923; death benefits $335 from Metropolitan Life Insurance Co. SOURCE: VA File XC 2650122, Zekiel Sykes.

‡Died 13 Jul 1926; unremarried widow Lucinda resided at 4213 Champlain, Chicago, in 1933, received $40 per month pension as of 8 Jun 1944, died at age 92 on 7 Mar 1948. SOURCE: VA File XC 2650122, Zekiel Sykes.

SYLVESTER, George; F/9th Cav. Born in Louisiana; black complexion; cannot read or write, age 25, Jul 1870, at Ft McKavett, TX. SOURCE: Bierschwale, *Fort McKavett*, 98.

T

TADLOCK, Patrick; Sergeant; C/9th Cav. Died at Ft Concho, TX, on 19 Jan 1872; buried at San Antonio National Cemetery, Section D, number 634. SOURCE: San Antonio National Cemetery Locator.

TALL, Frank; Private; 25th Inf. Stationed Ft Davis, TX, Nov 1873, shot and killed white stage driver who bullied him. SOURCE: Tate, *Frontier Army*, 63.

TALLEY, John C.; Private; F/24th Inf. Died 10 Mar 1912; buried in plot W.SID365 at San Francisco National Cemetery. SOURCE: San Francisco National Cemetery.

TALLIAFERRO, Daniel; Corporal; 9th Cav *See* TALLIFORO, Daniel, Corporal, I/9th Cavalry

TALLIFERRO, Daniel; Corporal; I/9th Cav. *See* TALLIFORO, Daniel, Corporal, I/9th Cavalry

TALLIFORO, Daniel; Corporal; I/9th Cav. Daniel Talliaferro, corporal, 9th Cavalry, native of Washington, DC; just completed his third year of service when he was shot and killed by wife of Lt. Fred Kendall, Fort Davis, TX, Nov 1872, after he had forced his way into her quarters. SOURCE: Kenner, *Buffalo Soldiers and Officers of the Ninth Cavalry*, 58, 323.

‡At Ft Davis, 1872; shot and killed by wife of Lt. Frederic Kendall after he had broken into her bedroom. SOURCE: Leiker, *Racial Borders*, 86.

‡Daniel Talliforro, corporal, 9th Cavalry, shot and killed by wife of Lt. Frederic Kendall, Ft Davis, 21 Nov 1872, while climbing in her bedroom window. SOURCE: Stallard, *Glittering Misery*, 38; Carroll, *The Black Military Experience*, 262.

Cpl. Daniel Taliaferro, 9th Cavalry, shot and killed by wife of Lt. Frederic Kendall while trying to break into Kendalls' quarters, Ft Davis. SOURCE: Dobak and Phillips, *The Black Regulars*, 197.

Daniel Talliforro, corporal, I/9th Cavalry, died at Ft Davis on 20 Nov 1871 [*sic*]; buried at San Antonio National Cemetery, Section I, number 1548. SOURCE: San Antonio National Cemetery Locator.

TALTON, Jefferson; Private; 25th Inf. At Ft Shaw, MT, 1889, told post surgeon that he got hernia "sky-larking around with women." SOURCE: Dobak and Phillips, *The Black Regulars*, 198.

TAPER, Charles; QM Sgt; F/10th Cav. ‡Farrier, F/10th Cavalry, served in 10th Cavalry in Cuba, 1898. SOURCE: Cashin, *Under Fire with the Tenth Cavalry*, 343.

QM Sgt. Charles Taper, F/10th Cavalry, died 17 Jan 1907; buried at Ft Leavenworth National Cemetery, plot 3512. SOURCE: Ft Leavenworth National Cemetery.

TATUM, King James; Private; G/10th Cav. Born in Plains, GA, in 1864; enlisted 4 Feb 1887 in Baltimore, MD; married with eight children; died 3 Mar 1925 in San Antonio, TX. SOURCE: Fachon A. Walker letter to Frank N. Schubert, May 20, 2002.

‡At Ft Apache, AZ, 1890, subscribed $.50 to testimonial to General Grierson. SOURCE: List of subscriptions, 23 Apr 1890, 10th Cavalry papers, MHI.

Born 6 Dec 1864; died 19 Mar 1925; buried in plot G 0 1413, San Antonio National Cemetery. SOURCE: San Antonio National Cemetery, Records of Burials.

TAYLOR; C/10th Cav. ‡Shot and killed by Walker, K/10th Cavalry, Crawford, NE, 31 May 1904, after rumpus in West Elm Street dive. SOURCE: Crawford *Bulletin*, 3 Jun 1904.

Taylor incorrectly named as victim of shooting 31 May 1904 in Crawford *Bulletin*; Pvt. Harry Walker, K/10th Cavalry was murdered by Private Wilson, C/10th Cavalry, taken by guard to Ft Robinson, NE. SOURCE: Buecker, Fort Robinson Burials.

TAYLOR, Buck; Private; 9th Cav. With Pvt. Leone Baquie, sentenced to twenty years for assault on Lt. Robert Webb and desertion, Ft Quitman, TX, 1869. SOURCE: Leiker, *Racial Borders*, 78.

TAYLOR, Charles; Private; L/9th Cavalry. Enlisted 8 Aug 1878 at Cincinnati, OH; at Ft Bliss, TX. SOURCE: Muster Roll, L/9th Cavalry, 31 Oct 1879–31 Dec 1879.

TAYLOR, Charles; Private; I/10th Cav. ‡Honorable mention for conspicuous bravery against Apaches, Salt River, AZ, 7 Mar 1890. SOURCE: Baker, Roster.

Died 15 Feb 1928; buried at Ft Leavenworth National Cemetery, plot I 35. SOURCE: Ft Leavenworth National Cemetery.

TAYLOR, Charles H.; Private; B/25th Inf. Died at Ft Stockton, TX, on 26 Jun 1880; buried at San Antonio National Cemetery, Section C, number 343. SOURCE: San Antonio National Cemetery Locator.

TAYLOR, Daniel T.; Sergeant; G/9th Cav. Received Philippine Campaign Badge number 11843 for service as private in G/24th Infantry, 23 Jul 1900–18 Mar 1902; private in G/9th Cavalry, Ft Leavenworth, KS, Mar 1905. SOURCE: Philippine Campaign Badge Recipients; Philippine Campaign Badge list, 29 May 1905.

‡Sergeant, G/9th Cavalry, veteran of Philippine Insurrection; at Ft D. A. Russell, WY, in 1910; marksman. SOURCE: *Illustrated Review: Ninth Cavalry*, with picture.

TAYLOR, Frank; Corporal; G/48th Inf. Died 15 Nov 1900; buried in plot NADD 827 at San Francisco National Cemetery. SOURCE: San Francisco National Cemetery.

TAYLOR, Henry; Private; C/9th Cav. Died at Ft Davis, TX, on 28 Jan 1868; buried at San Antonio National Cemetery, Section I, number 1462. SOURCE: San Antonio National Cemetery Locator.

TAYLOR, Henry C.; Private; 24th Inf. Enlisted, Nashville, TN, 1867; reenlisted Ft Griffin, TX, 1870; learned to write name during first enlistment; later served as company clerk and teacher to other soldiers. SOURCE: Dobak and Phillips, *The Black Regulars*, 126.

TAYLOR, Henry C.; 9th Cav. Born in Tennessee; mulatto complexion; can read and write, age 21, Sep 1870, at Ft McKavett, TX. SOURCE: Bierschwale, *Fort McKavett*, 107.

TAYLOR, John; Private; A/25th Inf. Died 21 Jun 1867; buried at Ft Bayard, NM, in plot G 38. SOURCE: "Fort Bayard National Cemetery, Records of Burials."

Buried 21 Jul 1867, section A, row I, plot 40, at Ft Bayard. SOURCE: Erickson, Burials at Fort Bayard National Cemetery, NM.

TAYLOR, John; Private; K/25th Inf. Civil War veteran; reported sick at Fort Stockton, TX, 30 Apr 1873; ultimately confined in guardhouse for malingering; died there 9 Jul 1873; twenty-one soldiers protesting his treatment were court martialed and dishonorably discharged. SOURCE: Kenner, *Buffalo Soldiers and Officers of the Ninth Cavalry*, 85–90.

At Ft Stockton, 1873, died in guardhouse after complaining about being sick and being confined for malingering. SOURCE: Barnett, *Ungentlemanly Acts*, 142.

Died of enlarged spleen, Ft Stockton, 1873, after post surgeon refused to admit him to hospital. SOURCE: Dobak and Phillips, *The Black Regulars*, 188.

Died at Ft Stockton on 10 Jul 1873; buried at San Antonio National Cemetery, Section C, number 441. SOURCE: San Antonio National Cemetery Locator.

TAYLOR, John; Private; 25th Inf. Got into argument with black saloonkeeper Abe Hill, Sturgis, SD, 1885, after which group of armed infantrymen fired fusillade into building. SOURCE: Dobak and Phillips, *The Black Regulars*, 240.

TAYLOR, John T.; Sergeant; H/10th Cav. Born in Scott County, KY; enlisted 15 May 1879, Cincinnati, OH; black complexion, eyes, hair; occupation laborer; served in H/10th Cavalry; injured 12 Jun 1881 in camp near Presidio, TX; discharged Ft Davis, TX, 14 May 1884; enlisted 15 May 1884, Ft Davis; including 1883–87, in campaign against Geronimo; resided in Albuquerque, NM, 1897–99, age 37; wife Mamie E. later married James Hester. SOURCE: Sayre, *Warriors of Color*, 52, 54, 79, 263, 280, 428.

Sergeant in H/10th Cavalry; detached service H/10th Cavalry at Ft Grant, AZ, 28 Oct 1885–28(?) Feb 1886; sergeant in H/10th Cavalry stationed at Bonita Cañon Camp, AZ, 30 Apr 1886. SOURCE: Tagg, *The Camp at Bonita Cañon*, 66, 231.

TAYLOR, Jordan; Private; B/10th Cav. ‡Born in Alabama; served five years; died at Ft Robinson, NE, age 26, 13 May 1906; full military burial. SOURCE: Monthly Report, Chaplain Anderson, 1 Jun 1906; List of Interments, Ft Robinson.

Crawford *Tribune* reported 18 May 1906 that Taylor escaped from Ewing building, Crawford, NE, and was shot by assembled crowd; before he died of wounds, Taylor stated that Sgt. John Reid shot Deputy Marshal Art Moss and could be found in the Ewing house; Taylor was killed by parties unknown 13 May 1906. SOURCE: Buecker, Fort Robinson Burials.

TAYLOR, Joseph; Private; K/9th Cav. Died 9 Jun 1868; buried at San Antonio National Cemetery, Section I, number 1518. SOURCE: San Antonio National Cemetery Locator.

TAYLOR, Lewis; Corporal; K/10th Cav. Died 16 Jun 1877 of disease at Ft Clark, TX. SOURCE: Regimental Returns, 10th Cavalry, 1877.

TAYLOR, Lewis; Corporal; D/9th Cav. ‡Appointed corporal 23 Apr 1891. SOURCE: Roster, 9 Cav.

Appointed corporal 23 Apr 1894; in D/9th Cavalry at Ft Washakie, WY, Jan 1897. SOURCE: Ninth Cavalry, Roster of NCOs, 1897.

‡In Lander, WY, publicizing appearance of minstrels from Ft Washakie. SOURCE: Fremont *Clipper*, 9 Apr 1897.

TAYLOR, Louis; C/25th Inf. Born in Washington, DC; mulatto complexion; can read and write, age 24, 5 Sep 1870, at Ft McKavett, TX. SOURCE: Bierschwale, *Fort McKavett*, 108.

TAYLOR, Richard; Private; C/24th Inf. Born in Virginia; buried at Ft McKavett, TX, before 17 May 1879; body removed to National Cemetery, San Antonio, TX, 23 Nov 1883. SOURCE: Bierschwale, *Fort McKavett*, 123.

Died at Ft McKavett on 1 Jan 1872; buried at San Antonio National Cemetery, Section E, number 877. SOURCE: San Antonio National Cemetery Locator.

TAYLOR, Richard H.; Private; K/25th Inf. Born in King and Queen County, VA; Ht 5'7", dark brown complexion; occupation printer; enlisted in A/39th Infantry for three years on 9 Oct 1866, age 24, at Richmond, VA; transferred to K/25th Infantry at Jackson Bks, LA, 20 Apr 1869. SOURCE: Descriptive Roll of A/39th Inf.

TAYLOR, Samuel; D/24th Inf. Born in Tennessee; mulatto complexion; cannot read or write, age 24, Jul 1870, at Ft McKavett, TX. SOURCE: Bierschwale, *Fort McKavett*, 95.

TAYLOR, Samuel; Sergeant; K/48th Inf. ‡Died of variola in the Philippines, 14 Jul 1900. SOURCE: *ANJ* 37 (28 Jul 1900): 1142.

Died 14 Jan 1900; body received 15 Apr 1902 at San Francisco National Cemetery, buried in plot NEW 822. SOURCE: San Francisco National Cemetery.

TAYLOR, Stephen; Chief Trumpeter; 9th Cav. ‡With band on detached service at headquarters, District of New Mexico, Santa Fe, 1880; played E-flat cornet. SOURCE: Billington, *New Mexico's Buffalo Soldiers*, 226.

‡Authorized four-month furlough from Ft Robinson, NE. SOURCE: *ANJ* 25 (25 Feb 1888): 605.

‡Appointed chief trumpeter 15 Mar 1888. SOURCE: Roster, 9 Cav.

Appointed chief trumpeter 15 Mar 1888; in 9th Cavalry at Ft Robinson, Jan 1897. SOURCE: Ninth Cavalry, Roster of NCOs, 1897.

Served on honor guard when body of Col. Edward Hatch was transported from Ft Robinson to Ft Leavenworth, KS, in 1889. SOURCE: Kenner, *Buffalo Soldiers and Officers of the Ninth Cavalry*, 48–49.

‡With regiment on practice march from Ft Robinson, Aug 1890.

‡Retires from Ft Robinson. SOURCE: *ANJ* 35 (9 Apr 1898): 603.

Wife Ella born in St. Louis, MO, ca. 1866, daughter of Violet Cragg, who later married 9th Cavalry Sgt. Allen Cragg, and white Howard Whitney; resided at Santa Fe, NM, with wife 1906. SOURCE: Schubert, *Voices of the Buffalo Soldier*, 248.

Died 25 Dec 1916; buried at Santa Fe National Cemetery, NM, plot A 1146. SOURCE: Santa Fe National Cemetery, Records of Burials.

TAYLOR, Thomas; Private; B/25th Inf. Enlisted 19 Sep 1899, discharged as private G/48th Infantry 30 Jun 1901, character excellent; reenlisted 16 Jul 1901, discharged as private B/25th Infantry 15 Jul 1904, character very good; reenlisted 18 Jul 1904, discharged without honor 19 Nov 1906. SOURCE: Powell, "Military Record of the Enlisted Men Who Were Discharged Without Honor."

‡Dishonorable discharge, Brownsville, TX. SOURCE: SO 266, AGO, 9 Nov 1906.

TAYLOR, Thomas W.; 24th Inf. ‡Born in Freetown, Sierra Leone, 17 Jan 1870; claimed to be Zulu prince; enlisted 12 Mar 1896; fought at San Juan Hill, Santiago, Cuba, 1898, and accompanied regiment to San Francisco. SOURCE: Clark, "A History of the Twenty-fourth," 79–81.

Prince Jerger Okodudek, son of Jerger, King of the Zulus; attended Cambridge University where he married Rosella Williams, French daughter of university teacher; enlisted in 24th Infantry at Ft Barrancas, FL; six weeks after he enlisted, wife died after brief illness in England; served at Alcatraz Island, CA, 1899. SOURCE: Lee, "Once Zulu Prince."

TAYLOR, Walker; Private; B/10th Cav. ‡Original member of 10th Cavalry; in troop when organized, Ft Leavenworth, KS, 1 Apr 1867. SOURCE: McMiller, "Buffalo Soldiers," 69.

Died 16 Aug 1870 of disease at Ft Sill, OK. SOURCE: Regimental Returns, 10th Cavalry, 1870.

Died 30 Jul 1870; buried at Camp Douglas, UT. SOURCE: Record Book of Interments, Post Cemetery, 252.

TAYLOR, William; Private; F/10th Cav. Killed in action in canyon north of Bowen Springs, Guadalupe Mountains, Texas, 4 Aug 1880. SOURCE: Baker, Roster; Regimental Returns, 10th Cavalry, 1880.

TAYLOR, Zachariah; F/9th Cav. Born in Kentucky; mulatto complexion; cannot read or write, age 23, Jul 1870, at Ft McKavett, TX. SOURCE: Bierschwale, *Fort McKavett*, 98.

TAYLOR, Zachariah; M/9th Cav. Born in Kentucky; mulatto complexion; cannot read or write, age 21, Jul 1870, at Ft McKavett, TX. SOURCE: Bierschwale, *Fort McKavett*, 100.

TELLIES, Robert; Private; Band/25th Inf. Born in Williamson Co., TN; black hair and eyes, black complexion; occupation teamster; enlisted at age 21, Nashville, TN, 23 Mar 1886; arrived Ft Snelling, MN, 31 Jul 1886. SOURCE: Descriptive & Assignment Rolls of Recruits, 25 Inf.

‡Born in Williamson Co., TN; Ht 5'8"; in B and F/25th Infantry, 23 Mar 1886–22 Mar 1891, character good, single; reenlisted Ft Missoula, MT, 23 Mar 1891; six summary courts martial and two general courts martial, both of which sentenced him to two months' confinement; marksman, 1887–89, 1892–94; first class marksman, 1890; participated in expedition against strikers, Idaho, 1892, single, no character, 9 Feb 1895; enlisted in H/25th Infantry, 9 Jul 1896, single, character very good; enlisted Nashville, 19 Apr 1899. SOURCE: Descriptive & Assignment Cards of Recruits, 25 Inf.

‡Private, Band/25th Infantry, authorized four-month furlough from Ft Logan, CO, 24 Mar 1899. SOURCE: AAG, USA, to CG, Department of Colorado, 24 Mar 1899, Misc Records, 25 Inf.

‡Private, Band/25th Infantry, fined $.50 for absence from reveille, Subig, Philippines, Oct 1900. SOURCE: Misc Records, 25 Inf.

TELLISBANNER, John; C/25th Inf. Born in Louisiana; black complexion; cannot read or write, age 26, 5 Sep 1870, at Ft McKavett, TX. SOURCE: Bierschwale, *Fort McKavett*, 109.

TEMPLE, Guy; Farrier; K/9th Cav. Native of Virginia; Ht 5'3", in second enlistment, age 28, when killed in action against Nana, Carrizo Canyon, New Mexico, Aug 1881. SOURCE: Kenner, *Buffalo Soldiers and Officers of the Ninth Cavalry*, 149.

‡Killed in action against Nana, Carrizo Canyon, 12 Aug 1881. SOURCE: Hamilton, "History of the Ninth Cavalry," 61; Leckie, *The Buffalo Soldiers*, 232; Billington, *New Mexico's Buffalo Soldiers*, 105; *Illustrated Review: Ninth Cavalry*.

TERRY, Charles Lincoln; Private; H/10th Cav. ‡Charles K. Terry, private, H/10th Cavalry, born in Delphi, IN; mulatto, Ht 5'6"; assigned to Band/25th Infantry, Ft Missoula, MT, 12 Apr 1897; on fourth enlistment, age 39 in 1897; most recent service in Band/10th Cavalry, discharged 16 Jan 1897, character good. SOURCE: Descriptive & Assignment Cards, 25 Inf.

Charles Lincoln Terry born in Delphi, IN, Jul 1865; father David born in Delphi; mother Mary Adams; enlisted Chicago, IL, 8 Feb 1884; Ht 5'6"; light yellow complexion, hazel eyes, black hair; occupation barber; served H/10th Cavalry; in Geronimo campaign 1885–86; commended in orders by Brig. Gen. Nelson Miles, Commanding, Department of Arizona, for valuable service in capture of Apache chief Mangus and his band, 18 Oct 1886; discharged San Carlos, AZ, 7 Feb 1889; enlisted Ft Marcy, NM, 8 May 1889; served in C/24th Infantry, transferred to H/10th Cavalry 20 Mar 1890; discharged Ft Apache, AZ, 16 May 1891; enlisted Ft Bliss, TX, 17 Jan 1892; served in Band/10th Cavalry; discharged Fort Assiniboine, MT, 16 Jan 1897; enlisted Chicago, 25 Mar 1897; served in Band/25th Infantry and I/25th Infantry; served in Spanish-American War, battle of El Caney, Cuba, 1–2 Jul 1898; discharged Ft Logan, CO, 15 Aug 1899; enlisted Chicago, 18 Apr 1900; served in Band/10th Cavalry; served two years in Philippines with 25th Infantry; injured 5 Jan 1903 when thrown from wagon, Ft Robinson, NE; discharged Ft Robinson, 17 Apr 1903; enlisted Ft Robinson, 18 Apr 1903; served in Band/10th Cavalry, played cornet; discharged Ft Robinson, 17 Apr 1906; enlisted Jefferson Bks, MO, 29 Jan 1908; served in Band/10th Cavalry and 25th Infantry; discharged Ft Lawton, WA, 29 Jan 1911; enlisted Jefferson Bks, 18 Feb 1911; served in Band/25th Infantry and H/10th Cavalry; discharged Recruit Depot, Ft Slocum, NY, 27 Nov 1911, on surgeon's certificate of disability, with emphysema; admitted to U.S. Soldiers Home, Washington, DC, Dec 1911; resided at U.S. Soldiers Home 29 May 1912; married Grace Hemsley Clayton, Smyrna, DE, 15 Dec 1919; no children; received $20 per month pension, Oct 1926, increased to $25 in Jan 1929, $30 in Oct 1930, $35 in Jan 1931, reduced to $15 in Sep 1933, restored to $35 in Sep 1935, $40 in Jun 1937, $60 in Sep 1937, $100 in Mar 1939, $120 in Apr 1950; admitted to U.S. Soldiers Home, Jan 1927; resided at 122 N. Main St., Smyrna, in Mar 1937; resident of State Welfare Home, Smyrna, practically blind and helpless, kept in adult crib, Aug 1951; died 9 Nov 1951; buried in Union Cemetery, Smyrna; widow received $65 per month pension when she died, 27 Nov 1959. SOURCE: Sayre, *Warriors of Color*, 8, 219, 429–55.

Private in H/10th Cavalry stationed at Bonita Cañon Camp, AZ, 30 Apr 1886. SOURCE: Tagg, *The Camp at Bonita Cañon*, 232.

‡Honorable mention for services rendered as private, H/10th Cavalry, in capture of Apache Mangas and his band, Rio Bonito, AZ, 18 Oct 1886. SOURCE: Baker, *Roster*.

‡Jailed for fifteen days for being absent without leave for twenty-six hours, Ft Missoula, MT, 16–17 Mar 1897, and being absent from guard duty, 17 Sep 1897. SOURCE: Descriptive & Assignment Cards, 25 Inf.

‡Wounded in side in Cuba, 1898; arrived at home in Indianapolis. SOURCE: Indianapolis *Freeman*, 20 Aug 1898.

Private, received Indian Wars Campaign Badge number 1565 on 21 Feb 1910. SOURCE: Carroll, *Indian Wars Campaign Badge*, 45.

TEUER, Jackson; Private; Band/25th Inf. Died 2 Nov 1882; buried at Ft Leavenworth National Cemetery, plot G 2996. SOURCE: Ft Leavenworth National Cemetery.

THOMAS, Benedict; Private; B/25th Inf. Member of three-man detachment led by Sgt. Joseph Luckadoe, along with Pvts. Joshua Newby and Henry Williams, 25th Infantry, who defended Eagle Springs, TX, mail station against attack, New Year's Eve, 1873. SOURCE: Dobak and Phillips, *The Black Regulars*, 258–59, 332.

THOMAS, Benjamin; Private; G/9th Cav. Died 2 Jan 1866; buried at San Antonio National Cemetery, Section D, number 797. SOURCE: San Antonio National Cemetery Locator.

THOMAS, Charles; Private; F/10th Cav. ‡Original member of 10th Cavalry; in troop when organized, Ft Leavenworth, KS, 21 Jun 1867. SOURCE: McMiller, "Buffalo Soldiers," 73.

Died 4 Jun 1868, shot accidentally, at Ft Riley, KS. SOURCE: Regimental Returns, 10th Cavalry, 1868.

THOMAS, Charles; Private; H/10th Cav. In Troop H/10th Cavalry stationed at Bonita Cañon Camp, AZ, 30 Apr 1886. SOURCE: Tagg, *The Camp at Bonita Cañon*, 232.

THOMAS, Charles; Private; D/24th Inf. Buried 30 Nov 1895, section A, row M, plot 25, at Ft Bayard, NM. SOURCE: Erickson, Burials at Fort Bayard National Cemetery, NM.

THOMAS, Frank; Private; L/9th Cav. At Ft Duncan, TX, 1870, with Pvt. Humphrey Williams, L/9th Cavalry, stole pig that belonged to Pvt. Henry Fletcher, and ate it; sentenced to dishonorable discharge and imprisonment for remainder of his enlistment, Dec 1870. SOURCE: Kenner, *Buffalo Soldiers and Officers of the Ninth Cavalry*, 177.

THOMAS, Frank; Private; 25th Inf. Born in Queen Anne County, MD; Ht 5'8", black hair and brown eyes, brown complexion; occupation sailor; enlisted at age 23, Baltimore, MD, 9 Apr 1886; arrived Ft Snelling, MN, 19 Aug 1886. SOURCE: Descriptive & Assignment Rolls of Recruits, 25 Inf.

THOMAS, George; Private; D/10th Cav. Shot by deputy sheriff, died 10 Jun 1878 at Ft Concho, TX. SOURCE: Regimental Returns, 10th Cavalry, 1878.

Died at Ft Concho on 10 Jan 1878; buried at San Antonio National Cemetery, Section D, number 637. SOURCE: San Antonio National Cemetery Locator.

THOMAS, George; Private; 9th Cav. Served in all four black regiments, then resided in Leavenworth, KS, where he "just chored around and did whatever he could get to do." SOURCE: Dobak and Phillips, *The Black Regulars*, 272.

THOMAS, Gus; Sergeant; B/24th Inf. Died 3 Jun 1915; buried in plot W S 476 at San Francisco National Cemetery. SOURCE: San Francisco National Cemetery.

THOMAS, Henry; Sergeant; A/24th Inf. ‡Corporal, designated to participate in Department of Arizona rifle meet. SOURCE: Order 119, Ft Huachuca, 10 Aug 1893, Letters & Orders Received, 24 Inf, 1893.

Convicted by general court martial, Ft Huachuca, AZ, of assault with deadly weapon; sentenced to reduction to private and confinement for one month. SOURCE: *ANJ* 32 (22 Dec 1894): 279.

‡Sergeant, died in the Philippines, 27 Apr 1901. SOURCE: *ANJ* 38 (4 May 1901): 876.

Died 27 Apr 1901; buried in plot NEW A411 at San Francisco National Cemetery. SOURCE: San Francisco National Cemetery.

THOMAS, Henry; Musician; B/25th Inf. ‡Died at Palauig, Luzon, Philippines, 2 Aug 1901. SOURCE: *ANJ* 39 (28 Sep 1901): 81.

Musician, B/25th Infantry, died 2 Aug 1905; buried in plot N/A 1027 at San Francisco National Cemetery. SOURCE: San Francisco National Cemetery.

THOMAS, Jacob B.; Sgt Maj; 10th Cav. Served as sergeant major from Oct 1867 until he deserted Apr 1868. SOURCE: Schubert, *Black Valor*, 166.

THOMAS, James E.; Corporal; H/25th Inf. Born in Maryland; mulatto complexion; can read and write, age 24, 5 Sep 1870, in C/25th Infantry at Ft McKavett, TX. SOURCE: Bierschwale, *Fort McKavett*, 108.

‡Sergeant, 25th Infantry; resident of Baltimore; has five honorable discharges; blind in one eye from arrow wound. SOURCE: Guthrie, *Camp-Fires of the Afro-American*, 646.

‡Retires from Ft Missoula, MT, as corporal, H/25th Infantry. SOURCE: *ANJ* 34 (1 May 1897): 545.

THOMAS, James H.; Private; M/25th Inf. Died 10 Sep 1900; buried 27 Jun 1902 in plot NK 1020 at San Francisco National Cemetery. SOURCE: San Francisco National Cemetery.

THOMAS, John; M/9th Cav. Born in Kentucky; black complexion; cannot read or write, age 24, Jul 1870, at Ft McKavett, TX. SOURCE: Bierschwale, *Fort McKavett*, 100.

THOMAS, John; D/24th Inf. Born in Alabama; black complexion; can read and write, age 24, Jul 1870, at Ft McKavett, TX. SOURCE: Bierschwale, *Fort McKavett*, 95.

THOMAS, John; F/9th Cav. Born in Tennessee; black complexion; can read and write, age 23, Jul 1870, at Ft McKavett, TX. SOURCE: Bierschwale, *Fort McKavett*, 97.

THOMAS, John; Private; U.S. Army. Seminole Negro Scout, served 1893–94. SOURCE: Schubert, Consolidated List of Seminole Negro Scouts.
Born in Texas; Ht 5'10", black hair and eyes, black complexion; enlisted 5 Jul 1893 at Camp Carrizo, TX, age 21; discharged 4 Mar 1894 at Ft Ringgold, TX. SOURCE: Swanson, 43.

THOMAS, John; Private; F/24th Inf. Died 4 Dec 1901; buried in plot NA 725 at San Francisco National Cemetery. SOURCE: San Francisco National Cemetery.

THOMAS, John H.; 1st Sgt; 24th Inf. Died of typhoid fever, Ft Elliott, TX, 1887, after nearly twenty-three years' service, more than twenty as sergeant and eighteen as first sergeant. SOURCE: Dobak and Phillips, *The Black Regulars*, 260.

THOMAS, John W.; F/9th Cav. Born in Louisiana; black complexion; cannot read or write, age 23, Jul 1870, at Ft McKavett, TX. SOURCE: Bierschwale, *Fort McKavett*, 98.

THOMAS, Leonard; F/9th Cav. Lenard Thomas born in Kentucky; black complexion; cannot read or write, age 22, Jul 1870, at Ft McKavett, TX. SOURCE: Bierschwale, *Fort McKavett*, 97.
‡Leonard Thomas served in F/9th Cavalry, admitted to Soldiers Home with disability, age 44, after three years' service, 25 Feb 1891. SOURCE: SecWar, *AR 1891*, 752.

THOMAS, Lewis; Private; H/10th Cav. In Troop H/10th Cavalry stationed at Bonita Cañon Camp, AZ, 30 Apr 1886. SOURCE: Tagg, *The Camp at Bonita Cañon*, 232.
Served during first half of 1880s; mailing address Box 848, Helena, MT, in 1929. SOURCE: Sayre, *Warriors of Color*, 219.

THOMAS, Marcus; Private; G/9th Cav. Received Philippine Campaign Badge for service as sergeant in C/24th Infantry, 2 July 1899–19 Jun 1902; private in G/9th Cavalry, Ft Leavenworth, KS, Mar 1905. SOURCE: Philippine Campaign Badge Recipients.

THOMAS, Moses; Private; E/48th Inf. ‡Died of variola in the Philippines 31 Jul 1900. SOURCE: *ANJ* 37 (11 Aug 1900): 1191.
Died 31 Jul 1900; buried in plot NEW A862 at San Francisco National Cemetery. SOURCE: San Francisco National Cemetery.

THOMAS, Napoleon; Saddler; F/9th Cav. Received Philippine Campaign Badge number 11749 for service as cook in L/9th Cavalry; in 9th Cavalry at Ft Leavenworth, KS, Mar 1905. SOURCE: Philippine Campaign Badge list, 29 May 1905.
Saddler, F/9th Cavalry, died 23 Sep 1907; buried in plot ADDN 1205 at San Francisco National Cemetery. SOURCE: San Francisco National Cemetery.

THOMAS, Sharp; Private; G/25th Inf. Born in Nottoway County, VA, 1855; enlisted 3 Jan 1882; Ht 5'4", black complexion, eyes, and hair; occupation laborer; served in H/10th Cavalry at Fort Davis, TX, 1885; discharged Ft Apache, AZ, 2 Jan 1887; enlisted St. Louis, MO, 24 Jan 1887; served in G/25th Infantry; discharged Ft Sisseton, SD, 13 Mar 1888, on surgeon's certificate of disability, loss of sight in right eye due to accidental shotgun wound; received $17 per month pension Feb 1889; resided in Great Falls, MT, May 1897. SOURCE: Sayre, *Warriors of Color*, 10, 12, 66, 456–58.
Private in H/10th Cavalry, sick in hospital at Ft Bowie, AZ, 7 Feb 1886 until after 30 Jun 1886; in H/10th Cavalry stationed at Bonita Cañon Camp, AZ, but absent or on detached service 30 Apr 1886. SOURCE: Tagg, *The Camp at Bonita Cañon*, 68, 232.
Discharged from H/10th Cavalry 2 Jan 1887; second reenlistment in 25th Infantry, age 33, 24 Jan 1887; arrived Ft Snelling, MN, 22 Mar 1887. SOURCE: Descriptive & Assignment Rolls of Recruits, 25 Inf.

THOMAS, Spencer; QM Sgt; H/9th Cav. ‡Ranked number 8 in rifle competition, Departments of the Platte and Dakota, Bellevue, NE, 4–9 Aug 1890. SOURCE: *ANJ* 27 (16 Aug 1890): 943; GO 112, AGO, 2 Oct 1890.
‡Private, A/9th Cavalry, on special duty at Ft Robinson, NE, canteen. SOURCE: Order 74, 10 Apr 1891, Post Orders, Ft Robinson.
‡Relieved from special duty at post canteen, Ft Robinson. SOURCE: Order 103, 18 May 1891, Post Orders, Ft Robinson.
‡Ranked number 4 in carbine competition and number 8 in revolver competition, Departments of the East, the Platte, and California, Bellevue, 17–22 Aug 1891; distinguished marksman, revolver, 1890 and 1891, and carbine, 1891. SOURCE: GO 81, AGO, 6 Oct 1891.
‡Private, at rifle competition, Ft Sheridan, IL, Sep 1891. SOURCE: *ANJ* 29 (5 Sep 1891): 25.

‡Private, A/9th Cavalry; leave extended fifteen days in accordance with letter, Department of the Platte, 23 Sep 1893. SOURCE: Regt Returns, 9 Cav, Sep 1893.

‡Promoted from lance corporal to corporal, H/9th Cavalry, 22 Aug 1894. SOURCE: *ANJ* 32 (1 Sep 1894): 6.

‡Corporal, H/9th Cavalry, ranked number 2 in competition of Army carbine team, 1894. SOURCE: GO 15, AGO, 15 Nov 1894.

Appointed corporal 22 Aug 1894; in H/9th Cavalry at Ft Robinson, Jan 1897. SOURCE: Ninth Cavalry, Roster of NCOs, 1897.

‡At Ft Robinson, 1896–98, deposited $115 with paymaster; promoted to sergeant, 1898.

‡Quartermaster sergeant, H/9th Cavalry, ranked number 8 among expert riflemen, 1904, with 81 percent. SOURCE: GO 79, AGO, 1 Jun 1905.

Received Philippine Campaign Badge number 11854 for service as quartermaster sergeant in H/9th Cavalry; in 9th Cavalry at Ft Leavenworth, KS, Mar 1905. SOURCE: Philippine Campaign Badge list, 29 May 1905.

‡Distinguished marksman, 1905. SOURCE: GO 173, AGO, 20 Oct 1905.

‡Ranked number 410 among expert riflemen, 1905, with 69 percent. SOURCE: GO 101, AGO, 31 May 1906.

THOMAS, Theodore; Private; I/10th Cav. In Troop I/10th Cavalry stationed at Bonita Cañon Camp, AZ, 30 Jun 1886. SOURCE: Tagg, *The Camp at Bonita Cañon*, 232.

THOMAS, William; Private; G/10th Cav. ‡Original member of 10th Cavalry; in troop when organized, Ft Leavenworth, KS, 5 Jul 1867. SOURCE: McMiller, "Buffalo Soldiers," 74.

Died 6 Aug 1867 of cholera at Ft Hays, KS. SOURCE: Regimental Returns, 10th Cavalry, 1867.

THOMAS, William; Private; C/25th Inf. Tried for conduct to prejudice of good order and military discipline in general court martial convened 19 Aug 1881 at Ft Sully, Dakota Territory; charged that he interfered with and forcibly obstructed sergeant of the guard, Sgt. I. Woodow, E/25th Infantry, who was trying to quell disturbance at post trader's store at Ft Hale, Dakota Territory, around 19 May 1881; threatened to kill or injure Sergeant Woodow with loaded rifle; disarmed by Cpl. Squire Williams, E/25th Infantry; found guilty except threatened some person or persons, rather than Sergeant Woodow; sentenced to confinement at hard labor and forfeit of $10 per month for six months. SOURCE: General Court-Martial Orders No. 99, Ft Snelling, MN, 19 Aug 1881.

THOMAS, William; Private; B/25th Inf. Enlisted 14 Feb 1904, discharged without honor 19 Nov 1906. SOURCE: Powell, "Military Record of the Enlisted Men Who Were Discharged Without Honor."

‡Dishonorable discharge, Brownsville, TX. SOURCE: SO 266, AGO, 9 Nov 1906.

THOMAS, William H.; L/10th Cav. Private, 4th USCT; lives at 752 Waesche St., Baltimore, MD. SOURCE: United States Colored Troops Resident in Baltimore, 1890 Census.

‡Original member of 10th Cavalry; in troop when organized, Ft Riley, KS, 21 Sep 1867. SOURCE: McMiller, "Buffalo Soldiers," 78.

THOMAS, William H.; Private; E/24th Inf. Died 8 Mar 1902; buried in plot NA 784 at San Francisco National Cemetery. SOURCE: San Francisco National Cemetery.

THOMAS, William R.; Private; G/9th Cav. Enlisted 1 Mar 1879 at Ft Lyon, CO; in L/9th Cavalry at Ft Bliss, TX, Nov–Dec 1879; starting 8 Jul 1880 marched twenty miles to Ft Cummings, NM; on detached duty as company cook, July–Oct 1880; L/9th Cavalry left Ft Stanton, NM, 11 Nov 1880, arrived Ft Bliss 18 Nov 1880. SOURCE: Muster Rolls, L/9th Cavalry, 31 Oct 1879–29 Feb 1880; 30 June–31 Dec 1880.

‡Private, L/9th Cavalry, on detached service in the field, New Mexico, 21 Jan–24 Feb 1881. SOURCE: Regt Returns, 9 Cav, Feb 1881.

‡Corporal, F/9th Cavalry; reduced to private, fined $120, and confined for one year, Ft Robinson, NE, for drawing pistol on private and menacing him while on guard; "severe but just." SOURCE: *ANJ* 27 (4 Jan 1890): 368.

‡Private, G/9th Cavalry; at Ft Robinson, 1894. SOURCE: Court Martial Records, Plummer.

‡Retired as private, G/9th Cavalry, Jun 1901. SOURCE: *ANJ* 38 (22 Jun 1901): 1043.

THOMPKINS, William H.; Sergeant; D/25th Inf. Pled guilty of involvement in affray at Suggs, WY, 1892, as private, 9th Cavalry, and fined $.50, but spent three months in jail awaiting trial. SOURCE: Dobak and Phillips, *The Black Regulars*, 243, 329.

Private, witness for defense in Sgt. Barney McKay, G/9th Cavalry, court martial, Ft Robinson, NE, 1893. SOURCE: Court Martial Records, McKay.

‡At Ft Robinson, NE, 1893.

‡Born in Paterson, NJ; awarded Medal of Honor on 30 Jun 1899 while on occupation duty at Manzanillo, Cuba. SOURCE: Lee, *Negro Medal of Honor Men*, 92, 98.

‡Private, G/10th Cavalry, promoted to corporal 18 Feb 1898. SOURCE: *ANJ* 35 (5 Mar 1898): 498.

‡Corporal, A/10th Cavalry; commended for distinguished gallantry while private, G/10th Cavalry, Tayabacoa, Cuba, with force that had landed and had been forced to withdraw to boats, leaving their killed and missing ashore; along with Pvt. Fitz Lee, M/10th Cavalry (now out of service), Pvt. Dennis Bell, H/10th Cavalry, and Pvt. George

Wanton, M/10th Cavalry (now out of service), voluntarily returned to shore in face of enemy fire and aided in rescue of wounded comrades who otherwise would have been captured; all four awarded Medal of Honor. SOURCE: GO 15, AGO, 13 Feb 1900.

One of four sergeants accompanying Lt. Carter Johnson on expedition to southern Cuba to deliver arms to insurgents, June 1898; one of four to receive Medal of Honor for rescue at Tayabacoa during expedition; life and career narrated. SOURCE: Schubert, *Black Valor*, 135–38, 141, 143, 166.

‡Medal of Honor mentioned. SOURCE: Steward, *The Colored Regulars*, 205.

‡Corporal, A/10th Cavalry; cited for distinguished service, 30 Jun 1898. SOURCE: *ANJ* 37 (24 Feb 1900): 611.

‡Sergeant, H/25th Infantry; commended for gallantry while private, G/10th Cavalry, saving comrade from drowning at Tayabacoa, 30 Jun 1898. SOURCE: Cleveland *Gazette*, 24 Jun 1906.

Corporal in D/25th Infantry, received Indian Wars Campaign Badge number 1610 on 27 Oct 1910. SOURCE: Carroll, *Indian Wars Campaign Badge*, 46.

Sergeant, D/25th Infantry; died 24 Sep 1916; buried in plot W S 1036-A at San Francisco National Cemetery. SOURCE: San Francisco National Cemetery.

THOMPSON, Alfred; 10th Cav. Resided at 1037 Part St., Nashville, TN, in 1903. SOURCE: Sayre, *Warriors of Color*, 141.

THOMPSON, Clarence; Private; D/9th Cav. With Captain Dodge at battle at Milk River, CO, 2–10 Oct 1879. SOURCE: Miller, *Hollow Victory*, 167, 206–7.

THOMPSON, Clarence; Private; I/25th Inf. Born in Caroline County, VA; Ht 5'11", black hair and eyes, yellow complexion; resided Washington, DC, when enlisted at age 24, Washington, DC, 21 Sep 1885; assigned to I/25th Infantry; arrived Ft Snelling, MN, 5 Feb 1886. SOURCE: Descriptive & Assignment Rolls of Recruits, 25 Inf.

THOMPSON, Garfield; Private; G/24th Inf. ‡Served as private, G/10th Cavalry, 1898; remained in U.S. during war with Spain. SOURCE: Cashin, *Under Fire with the Tenth Cavalry*, 345.

‡Accidentally drowned in the Philippines, 3 Oct 1899. SOURCE: *ANJ* 37 (14 Oct 1899): 155.

Died 3 Oct 1899; buried in plot E S 702 at San Francisco National Cemetery. SOURCE: San Francisco National Cemetery.

THOMPSON, Henry; Private; B/25th Inf. Died 11 May 1878; buried at San Antonio National Cemetery, Section I, number 1664. SOURCE: San Antonio National Cemetery Locator.

THOMPSON, James; Private; D/48th Inf. ‡Died of appendicitis in the Philippines, 10 Mar 1900. SOURCE: *ANJ* 37 (17 Mar 1900): 682.

Died in Manila, PI, 10 Mar 1900; buried in plot ES 808 at San Francisco National Cemetery. SOURCE: San Francisco National Cemetery.

THOMPSON, James A.; Chief Musician; 9th Cav. ‡Private, D/9th Cavalry, in hands of civil authorities, Crawford, NE, 15–20 Feb 1891. SOURCE: Regt Returns, 9 Cav, Feb 1891.

‡Private, Band/9th Cavalry, in hands of civil authorities, Chadron, NE, 5–7 Nov 1896. SOURCE: Regt Returns, 9 Cav, Nov 1896.

Chief musician, 9th Cavalry, received Indian Wars Campaign Badge number 861 on 6 Jan 1909. SOURCE: Carroll, *Indian Wars Campaign Badge*, 25.

THOMPSON, Joe; Private; U.S. Army. Seminole Negro Scout, served in 1875. SOURCE: Schubert, Consolidated List of Seminole Negro Scouts.

Age 25 in 1875, resided at Ft Duncan, TX, with Lida age 25, Emma age 1, Martha age 7, and Jenny age 4. SOURCE: NARA Record Group 393, Special File.

THOMPSON, John; Private; U.S. Army. Seminole Negro Scout, served 1870–83. SOURCE: Schubert, Consolidated List of Seminole Negro Scouts.

John Thomason, born in Mexico; son of Cherokee Negro Indian married to Seminole; enlisted at Ft Duncan, TX, 16 Aug 1870, age 18; discharged 15 Feb 1871, reenlisted next day at Ft Duncan; discharged, reenlisted for six months five times at Ft Duncan, 31 Aug 1871–1 Jan 1874; discharged, reenlisted 1 Jul 1874 at Camp Palafox, TX; discharged 3 Jan 1875, reenlisted 25 Jan 1875 at Ft Clark, TX; one of three Scouts who deserted on field duty at Ft McKavett, TX, when enlistment expired, excused when he reported to duty at Ft Clark, formally discharged 25 Feb 1876; enlisted 25 Jan 1877, discharged 1 Feb 1879 at Ft Clark; enlisted 1 Feb 1879, discharged 1 May 1880 at Ft Clark; enlisted 20 Aug 1880 at Ft Clark, discharged 23 Sep 1881 at Camp Myers, TX; enlisted 26 Sep 1881 at Ft Clark; discharged 23 Sep 1882, reenlisted for one year 31 Sep 1882 at Ft Clark; died of gunshot wounds 7 Sep 1883 at Ft Clark. SOURCE: Swanson, 44.

In original detachment of Scouts enlisted at Ft Duncan, Aug 1870. SOURCE: NARA Record Group 393, Special File.

Private, U.S. Indian Scouts, died 7 Sep 1885, buried at Seminole Indian Scout Cemetery, Kinney County, TX. SOURCE: Indian Scout Cemetery, Kinney County, Texas.

THOMPSON, Joseph; Private; U.S. Army. Seminole Negro Scout, served 1872–85. SOURCE: Schubert, Consolidated List of Seminole Negro Scouts.

Born in Alabama, a Cherokee Negro; also known as Joe; Ht 5'8", black hair and eyes, black complexion; enlisted at Ft Duncan, TX, 2 Aug 1872, age 23; discharged 2 Feb 1873, reenlisted 11 May 1873 at Ft Duncan; discharged 1 Nov 1873 at Camp Comanche, TX; enlisted 23 Feb 1874 at Ft Clark, TX, where he was discharged 23 Aug 1874; enlisted 4 Feb 1875 at Ft Duncan, discharged 24 Sep 1875 at Camp Supply, TX; enlisted for one year and discharged at Ft Clark six times, 1 Feb 1877–18 May 1883; enlisted 27 Dec 1884 at Ft Clark, discharged 25 Dec 1885 at Camp Neville Springs, TX; enlisted 24 Apr 1894 at Ft Clark, discharged 27 Oct 1894 at Ft Ringgold, TX; married to Seminole; died 17 May 1915; buried at Seminole Indian Scout Cemetery, Kinney County, TX. SOURCE: Swanson, 44.

THOMPSON, Maryland; Corporal; I/9th Cav. Appointed corporal 19 Dec 1896; in I/9th Cavalry at Ft Washakie, WY, Jan 1897. SOURCE: Ninth Cavalry, Roster of NCOs, 1897.

‡Served as private in G/10th Cavalry in Cuba, 1898. SOURCE: Cashin, *Under Fire with the Tenth Cavalry*, 345.

‡Died of yellow fever in Cuba, 10 Aug 1898. SOURCE: AG, *Correspondence Regarding the War with Spain*, I:218.

THOMPSON, Mason; F/9th Cav. Born in Missouri; black complexion; can read, cannot write, age 23, Jul 1870, at Ft McKavett, TX. SOURCE: Bierschwale, *Fort McKavett*, 97.

THOMPSON, Merrick; Private; U.S. Army. Seminole Negro Scout, served 1872–74. SOURCE: Schubert, Consolidated List of Seminole Negro Scouts.

Born in Mobile, Al, probably former slave of Cherokee Indian; Ht 5'5", black hair and eyes, black complexion; enlisted at Ft Duncan, TX, 2 Aug 1872, age 49; discharged 2 Feb 1873 at Ft Duncan where he reenlisted 12 May 1873; discharged 12 Nov 1873 at Ft Duncan where he reenlisted 8 Jan 1874; discharged 8 Jul 1874 at Ft Duncan. SOURCE: Swanson, 45.

THOMPSON, Morris; Corporal; E/10th Cav. In Troop E/10th Cavalry stationed at Bonita Cañon Camp, AZ, 28 Feb 1886. SOURCE: Tagg, *The Camp at Bonita Cañon*, 231.

THOMPSON, Philip; Private; L/9th Cav. Enlisted 29 Jul 1878 at New York, NY; at Ft Bliss, TX; starting 8 Jul 1880 marched twenty miles to Ft Cummings, NM; left camp on Rio Mimbres, NM, on 8 Jul 1880 and marched twenty miles to Ft Cummings; left 8 Aug on march to Rio Grande at Leas Ferry and returned to Rio Mimbres camp after march of 104 miles; on detached service at Ft Cummings, Sep–Oct 1880; L/9th Cavalry left Ft Stanton, NM, 11 Nov 1880, arrived at Ft Bliss 18 Nov 1880. SOURCE: Muster Rolls, L/9th Cavalry, 31 Oct–31 Dec 1879; 30 June–31 Oct 1880.

THOMPSON, Prymus; Private; U.S. Army. Seminole Negro Scout, served 1877–85, 1889–1902. SOURCE: Schubert, Consolidated List of Seminole Negro Scouts.

Born in Mexico; Ht 5'4", black hair and eyes, black complexion; enlisted at Ft Clark, TX, 24 Jan 1877, age 18; discharged and reenlisted for one year four times at Ft Clark, 20 Jan 1878–6 Jun 1881; discharged 22 Jun 1882, reenlisted next day at Camp Myers, TX; discharged 22 Jun 1883, reenlisted next day at Ft Clark; discharged 22 Jun 1884 at Camp Myers, enlisted 9 Jul 1884 at Ft Clark where he was discharged 31 Aug 1885; enlisted 23 Feb 1889 at Ft Clark; discharged 5 Mar 1889, reenlisted 19 Mar 1889 at Camp Neville Springs, TX; discharged 18 Sep 1890 at Camp Neville Springs, enlisted 19 Mar 1891 at Camp Neville Springs; discharged 19 Sep 1891 at Camp Palvo, TX, enlisted 8 Apr 1892; discharged 7 Oct 1892, reenlisted next day at Ft Ringgold, TX; discharged 7 Apr 1893, reenlisted next day at Los Angeles, TX; discharged 7 Oct 1893, reenlisted 9 Oct 1893 at Ft Ringgold; discharged 7 Apr 1894 at Ft Ringgold, enlisted 7 Mar 1898 at Ft Clark; discharged 6 Mar 1901, reenlisted next day for three years at Ft Clark; discharged without honor 11 Jun 1902 at Ft Clark; died 13 Mar 1926; buried at Seminole Indian Scout Cemetery, Kinney County, TX. SOURCE: Swanson, 45.

THOMPSON, Robert; Private; A/24th Inf. Died 4 Nov 1906; buried at Ft Bayard, NM, in plot 0 20. SOURCE: "Fort Bayard National Cemetery, Records of Burials."

Buried 4 Nov 1906, section A, row W, plot 20, at Ft Bayard. SOURCE: Erickson, Burials at Fort Bayard National Cemetery, NM.

THOMPSON, Thomas; Private; K/25th Inf. Born in New Orleans, LA; Ht 5'4", brown complexion; occupation barber; enlisted in A/39th Infantry for three years on 11 Sep 1866, age 21, at Shreveport, LA; transferred to K/25th Infantry at Jackson Bks, LA, 20 Apr 1869. SOURCE: Descriptive Roll of A/39th Inf.

Private, A/39th Infantry, acquitted of involvement in New Iberia, LA, mutiny, Jul 1867. SOURCE: Dobak and Phillips, *The Black Regulars*, 222.

THOMPSON, Thomas; C/25th Inf. Born in New York; mulatto complexion; can read and write, age 21, 5 Sep 1870, at Ft McKavett, TX. SOURCE: Bierschwale, *Fort McKavett*, 109.

THORNTON, Beverly F.; Cook; K/10th Cav. ‡Corporal, K/10th Cavalry; served in regiment, 1898; remained in U.S. during war with Spain. SOURCE: Cashin, *Under Fire with the Tenth Cavalry*, 349.

‡Age 43, married Miss Sallie A. Conley of Huntsville, AL, age 42, at Ft Robinson, NE, 21 Apr 1904. SOURCE: Monthly Report, Chaplain Anderson, 1 May 1904; Medical History, Ft Robinson.

‡Guest with wife at K/10th Cavalry Thanksgiving dinner, Ft Robinson. SOURCE: Simmons, "Thanksgiving Day in the Tenth Cavalry," 664.

‡Read paper entitled "Economy" at YMCA, Ft Robinson, 4 Jan 1905, published in *Colored American Magazine* 9 (Mar 1905): 150–51.

After discharge lived with wife at home of daughter Jessie Lee and her husband Zan Marion Scruggs and their seven children at 40 Franklin St., Winooski, VT; died 8 Jan 1922; buried at Lakeview Cemetery, Burlington, VT. SOURCE: Dickerson, Sandy, Letter to Frank Schubert, October 5, 1997.

‡Deposition, 11 Jul 1906, supports pension claim of Caleb Benson. SOURCE: VA File XC 2499129, Caleb Benson.

THORNTON, Jacob; 1st Sgt; F/10th Cav. ‡Adjutant, 10th Cavalry, informed Capt. George F. Armes, F/10th Cavalry, Ft Harker, KS, 18 Jul 1867, that his first sergeant was Jake Thornton, not Thorn, as Armes referred to him. SOURCE: LS, 10 Cav, 1866–67.

Jacob Thornton, first sergeant, F/10th Cavalry, wounded in action, gunshot wound in right leg, near Beaver Creek, KS, 21 Aug 1867. SOURCE: LR, DeptMo, 1867.

First sergeant, had horse shot out from under him in fight against Indians, Saline River, KS, 2 Aug 1867; wounded in action against Indians at Beaver Creek, 21 Aug 1867. SOURCE: Schubert, *Voices of the Buffalo Soldier*, 13, 20.

‡Shot through left leg below knee in engagement with Indians at Camp Price, on Beaver Creek, 21 Aug 1867; broke leg so he could not stand. SOURCE: Armes, *Ups and Downs*, 244, 247.

‡Wounded in knee by arrow, discharged, and returned to home in Dayton, OH. SOURCE: VA File SC 11405, John Taylor.

THORNTON, Luther G.; Sergeant; B/25th Inf. Sgt. Luther T. Thornton, B/25th Infantry, enlisted 14 May 1898, honorably discharged as private L/10th Cavalry 26 Feb 1899, character excellent; reenlisted 5 Apr 1899, discharged as corporal L/10th Cavalry 4 Apr 1902, character very good; reenlisted 21 May 1902, discharged as sergeant B/25th Infantry 20 May 1905, character excellent; reenlisted 21 May 1905, discharged without honor as sergeant 22 Nov 1906, Brownsville, TX. SOURCE: Powell, "Military Record of the Enlisted Men Who Were Discharged Without Honor."

‡Pvt. Luther T. Thornton, L/10th Cavalry, served with regiment in 1898, remained in U.S. during war with Spain. SOURCE: Cashin, *Under Fire with the Tenth Cavalry*, 351.

‡Sgt. Luther G. Thornton, B/25th Infantry, dishonorable discharge, Brownsville. SOURCE: SO 266, AGO, 9 Nov 1906.

THORNTON, William; Comsy Sgt; U.S. Army. ‡Born in Washington Court House, OH; enlisted from residence at Great Falls, MT; awarded Distinguished Service Cross in lieu of certificate of merit for distinguished service, Santiago, Cuba, 1 Jul 1898. SOURCE: *Decorations, U.S. Army. Supplement I*, 30; GO 15, AGO, 13 Feb 1900.

‡Corporal, G/24th Infantry; led detachment of four that was first group of U.S. troops to enter blockhouse on San Juan Hill, Santiago, 1 Jul 1898; awarded certificate of merit. SOURCE: Scipio, *Last of the Black Regulars*, 29, 130; Steward, *The Colored Regulars*, 280.

‡Commissary sergeant, 1900; certificate of merit mentioned. SOURCE: *ANJ* 37 (24 Feb 1900): 611.

Awarded certificate of merit for distinguished service in battle, Santiago, 1 Jul 1898. SOURCE: Gleim, *The Certificate of Merit*, 46.

Born in Washington Court House, OH, resided Great Falls, MT; received Distinguished Service Medal in lieu of certificate of merit. SOURCE: *American Decorations*, 844.

THROWER, Jesse; Sergeant; B/9th Cav. Appointed sergeant 27 Nov 1895; in B/9th Cavalry at Ft DuChesne, UT, Jan 1897. SOURCE: Ninth Cavalry, Roster of NCOs, 1897.

‡Promoted from corporal to sergeant, Ft DuChesne, Nov 1895. SOURCE: *ANJ* 33 (7 Dec 1895): 236.

‡First sergeant, seriously wounded in leg during attack by insurgents, Lupi, Luzon, Philippines, 13 May 1901. SOURCE: *ANJ* 38 (1 Jun 1901): 967; Hamilton, "History of the Ninth Cavalry," 105.

‡Veteran of Philippine Insurrection; sergeant, B/9th Cavalry, at Ft D. A. Russell, WY, in 1910; sharpshooter. SOURCE: *Illustrated Review: Ninth Cavalry*, with picture.

‡Sergeant and Mrs. Thrower of Cleveland, OH, recently had dinner in honor of their niece and nephews from Atlanta. SOURCE: Cleveland *Gazette*, 8 Sep 1917.

TICKLE, Henry; Private; M/10th Cav. Died 8 Oct 1874 of disease at Ft Sill, OK. SOURCE: Regimental Returns, 10th Cavalry, 1874.

TILLARY, Albert; Private; E/38th Inf. Died 11 Sep 1867; originally buried at Ft Hays, KS; reburied at Ft Leavenworth National Cemetery, plot 3294. SOURCE: Ft Leavenworth National Cemetery.

TILLMAN, Lafayette A.; 1st Lt; 49th Inf. ‡Born in Evansville, IN, 15 Mar 1860; educated in Evansville public schools, Wayland Seminary, Washington, DC, and Kansas City School of Law; served as private and quartermaster sergeant, 7th Volunteer Infantry, until discharged 28 Feb 1899 with excellent record; now in F/49th Infantry. SOURCE: *ANJ* 37 (14 Oct 1899): 145.

‡Served in 9th Volunteer Infantry, 5 Jul 1898–28 Feb 1899; commissioned first lieutenant, 49th Infantry, 9 Sep

1899; now with I/49th Infantry. SOURCE: Descriptive Book, I/49 Inf.

‡One of twenty-three officers of 49th Infantry recommended as regular Army second lieutenants. SOURCE: CG, DivPI, Manila, 8 Feb 1901, to AGO, AGO File 355163.

Born in 1859; attended Oberlin College before continuing studies at Wayland Seminary; traveled with New Orleans University singers as bass, later with Don Tennesseans who performed at the White House; opened restaurant in Kansas City, MO; married, worked as barber in Kansas City; opened six-chair barber shop for white patrons in 1889; commissioned as notary public in 1894; enrolled in Kansas City School of Law in 1896; enlisted in 1898; served two years as first lieutenant in Luzon, Philippines; returned permanently to Kansas City, where he was appointed to police force; oldest policeman on force when he died in 1914. SOURCE: Ford, Susan Jezak, "Kansas City Public Library, Special Collections, Lafayette A. Tillman."

TIMMS, James T.; Private; F/9th Cav. ‡Pvt. James T. Timos, F/9th Cavalry, died in the Philippines, 15 Feb 1901. SOURCE: *ANJ* 38 (23 Feb 1901): 631.

Died 15 Feb 1901; buried in plot NA 1386 at San Francisco National Cemetery. SOURCE: San Francisco National Cemetery.

TIMOS, James T.; Private; F/9th Cav. *See* TIMMS, James T., Private, F/9th Cavalry

TINSLEY, George; Corporal; 9th Cav. Received Philippine Campaign Badge number 11793 for service as corporal in F/9th Cavalry; in 9th Cavalry at Ft Leavenworth, KS, Mar 1905. SOURCE: Philippine Campaign Badge list, 29 May 1905.

‡Veteran of Philippine Insurrection; at Ft D. A. Russell, WY, in 1910; resident of Pittsburgh, KY. SOURCE: *Illustrated Review: Ninth Cavalry*, with picture.

TIPTON, Calvin; Private; L/9th Cav. Pvt. Calvin Tipton enlisted 12 Apr 1877 at Santa Fe, NM; stationed at Ft Bliss, TX, Nov 1879–Feb 1880; in the field in New Mexico in pursuit of Victorio's band of hostile Apaches 8 Jan 1880–22 Feb 1880, left Ojo Caliente 24 Feb and marched via Canada Alamosa and Cuchillo Negro, arriving at Chase's Ranch, 26 Feb 1880, after marching 621 miles in Jan and Feb; troop at Chase's Ranch, NM, 29 Feb 1880 awaiting further orders; on detached service July–Aug 1880; marched 945 miles in the field in New Mexico Sep–Oct 1880; L/9th Cavalry left Ft Stanton, NM, 11 Nov 1880, arrived at Ft Bliss 18 Nov 1880. SOURCE: Muster Rolls, L/9th Cavalry, 31 Oct 1879–29 Feb 1880; 30 June–31 Dec 1880.

‡Pvt. C. Tipton, L/9th Cavalry, on detached service in the field, New Mexico, 21 Jan–24 Feb 1881. SOURCE: Regt Returns, 9 Cav, Feb 1881.

TIPTON, Samuel; D/38th Inf. Buried 10 Jul 1868 in section A, row G, plot 38, Ft Bayard, NM. SOURCE: Erickson, Burials at Fort Bayard National Cemetery, NM.

TIPTON, Samuel J.; Sergeant; H/24th Inf. Sergeant, received Indian Wars Campaign Badge number 1186 on 23 Jan 1909. SOURCE: Carroll, *Indian Wars Campaign Badge*, 34.

TITUS, Joseph; Private; B/10th Cav. ‡Drowned in the Rio Grande, Aug 1876. SOURCE: Leckie, *The Buffalo Soldiers*, 151.

Drowned 3 Aug 1876 in Rio Grande River, Texas. SOURCE: Regimental Returns, 10th Cavalry, 1876.

TODD, Lewis; E/9th Cav. *See* RANDOLPH, Adolphus, E/10th Cavalry

TOLBERT, Thomas; Private; K/48th Inf. ‡Died of variola in the Philippines, 19 Jul 1900. SOURCE: *ANJ* 37 (28 Jul 1900): 1142.

Died 19 Jul 1900; buried in plot NA 856 at San Francisco National Cemetery. SOURCE: San Francisco National Cemetery.

TOLER, Miller; Sergeant; D/9th Cav. ‡M. Toler, D/9th Cavalry, appointed corporal 13 Sep 1888. SOURCE: Roster, 9 Cav.

‡Corporal, ranked number 4 in carbine competition, Departments of Dakota and the Platte, Bellevue, NE, 4–9 Aug 1890. SOURCE: GO 112, AGO, 2 Oct 1890.

‡Corporal, D/9th Cavalry, ranked fourth in rifle competition, Departments of the Platte and Dakota, Bellevue. SOURCE: *ANJ* 27 (16 Aug 1890): 943.

‡Corporal, D/9th Cavalry; reenlistment as married soldier authorized by telegram, Adjutant General's Office, 8 Aug 1891.

‡Corporal, ranked number 5 in revolver competition, Departments of the East, the Platte, and California, Bellevue, 17–22 Aug 1891. SOURCE: GO 81, AGO, 6 Oct 1891.

Appointed sergeant 19 Feb 1894; in D/9th Cavalry at Ft Washakie, WY, Jan 1897. SOURCE: Ninth Cavalry, Roster of NCOs, 1897.

‡Sergeant, ranked number 4 in revolver competition and number 6 in carbine competition, Departments of the East, the Platte, and California, Bellevue, 18–25 Aug 1894; distinguished marksman, 1890, 1891, 1894. SOURCE: GO 62, AGO, 15 Nov 1894.

‡Distinguished marksman, 1906. SOURCE: GO 198, AGO, 6 Dec 1906.

TOLIVER, Frederick; Private; H/25th Inf. Private, received Indian Wars Campaign Badge number 1311 on 20

Mar 1909. SOURCE: Carroll, *Indian Wars Campaign Badge,* 38.

TOLIVER, Lewis; Sergeant; H/9th Cav. ‡Cook at post exchange lunch counter, Ft Robinson, NE, with wage of $15 per month, Sep 1894. SOURCE: Reports of Inspections, DP, II.

Late Sgt. Lewis Tollifer, H/9th Cavalry, died 15 Sep 1903; buried at Ft Robinson. SOURCE: Buecker, Fort Robinson Burials.

‡Died at Ft Robinson, 25 Sep 1903. SOURCE: List of Interments, Ft Robinson.

‡No Veterans Administration pension file.

TOLLIFER, Lewis; Sergeant; H/9th Cav. *See* TOLIVER, Lewis, Sergeant, H/9th Cavalry

TOLLOVER, Jackson; Private; E/24th Inf. Died at Ft Griffin, TX, on 23 Jan 1870; buried at San Antonio National Cemetery, Section D, number 740. SOURCE: San Antonio National Cemetery Locator.

TOMPKINS, William; Private; G/9th Cav. *See* THOMPKINS, William H., Sergeant, D/25th Infantry

TOOMBS, Anthony; Private; A/25th Inf. Enlisted Sep 1866; after discharge remained with company as captain's personal servant. SOURCE: Dobak and Phillips, *The Black Regulars,* 272.

TORBERT, Lewis; Private; K/24th Inf. Died 28 Jan 1872; buried at San Antonio National Cemetery, Section F, number 1156. SOURCE: San Antonio National Cemetery Locator.

TORPLY, Green; Private; D/24th Inf. Born in Pulaski County, TN; buried at Ft McKavett, TX, before 17 May 1879; body removed to National Cemetery, San Antonio, TX, 23 Nov 1883. SOURCE: Bierschwale, *Fort McKavett,* 123.

Died at Ft McKavett on 25 Aug 1871; buried at San Antonio National Cemetery, Section E, number 841. SOURCE: San Antonio National Cemetery Locator.

TOWNSEND, Edward; Private; E/10th Cav. ‡Honorable mention of Sergeant Townsend for gallantry against Kiowas and Comanches, Wichita Agency, Indian Territory, 22–23 Aug 1874. SOURCE: Baker, Roster.

Killed Sgt. John Jones, E/10th Cavalry, 15 Sep 1876. SOURCE: Regimental Returns, 10th Cavalry, 1876.

TOWNSEND, Quince; Private; M/24th Inf. Died 22 Mar 1902; buried at Ft Bayard, NM, in plot M 31. SOURCE: "Fort Bayard National Cemetery, Records of Burials."

Buried 22 Mar 1902, section A, row U, plot 31 at Ft Bayard. SOURCE: Erickson, Burials at Fort Bayard National Cemetery, NM.

TRACY, George; 1st Sgt; D/9th Cav. ‡Private, K/9th Cavalry, on detached service in the field, New Mexico, 30 Jan–2 Feb 1881; discharged, end of term, Ft Cummings, NM, 22 Feb 1881. SOURCE: Regt Returns, 9 Cav, Feb 1881.

Replaced Madison Ingoman as first sergeant in 1889 and remained in position until 1898. SOURCE: Kenner, *Buffalo Soldiers and Officers of the Ninth Cavalry,* 279.

Appointed first sergeant 16 Sep 1889; in D/9th Cavalry at Ft Washakie, WY, Jan 1897. SOURCE: Ninth Cavalry, Roster of NCOs, 1897.

‡Appointed first sergeant, D/9th Cavalry, 16 Sep 1889; sergeant since 31 Mar 1886. SOURCE: Roster, 9 Cav.

‡First sergeant, I/9th Cavalry, witness at trial of Joe Jemson, Private, I/9th Cavalry, Ft Robinson, NE, 6 May 1891. SOURCE: Summary Court Record, Ft Robinson, I.

‡Son Clarence Ernest Tracy buried at Ft Robinson, 15 Mar 1893. SOURCE: List of Interments, Ft Robinson.

‡First sergeant, D/9th Cavalry; examined for position of ordnance sergeant, Ft Robinson. SOURCE: *ANJ* 30 (1 Jul 1893): 745.

‡Sergeant, D/9th Cavalry, resides at Ft Robinson with wife and child, Aug 1893. SOURCE: Medical History, Ft Robinson.

‡First sergeant, D/9th Cavalry; conducted military convicts Herman Hector and George Washington, 9th Cavalry, from Ft Robinson to Ft Omaha, with guard, Pvt. Harry Rice, D/9th Cavalry. SOURCE: Order 77, 3 Oct 1894, Post Orders, Ft Robinson.

‡First sergeant, D/9th Cavalry, at Ft Washakie, 1897. *See* OTT, JONES, Lewis, Cook, M/9th Cavalry

TRENT, Nathan; Private; L/9th Cav. Born in Virginia; fined eight times and imprisoned twice before acquittal at age 25 of murder for killing in barroom, Las Animas, CO, Aug 1876, along with Blacksmith James Payne and Pvt. William Jones, L/9th Cavalry. SOURCE: Kenner, *Buffalo Soldiers and Officers of the Ninth Cavalry,* 183.

TRIBLES, Proter; Private; F/25th Inf. Died at Ft Stockton, TX, on 8 Oct 1872; buried at San Antonio National Cemetery, Section C, number 438. SOURCE: San Antonio National Cemetery Locator.

TRIMBLE, Anderson; Private; K/9th Cav. ‡Killed in action against force of 900 Kickapoos, Navahos, Mexicans, and white renegades, Ft Lancaster, TX, along with Pvts. William Sharpe and Edward Bowers, K/9th Cavalry, 26 Dec 1867. SOURCE: Hamilton, "History of the Ninth Cavalry," 7; *Illustrated Review: Ninth Cavalry.*

One of three troopers killed in pre-dawn Indian attack on Fort Lancaster, 26 Dec 1867. SOURCE: Schubert, *Black Valor*, 17.

TRIPPS, George A.; Private; H/10th Cav. Born in Howard County, MD, 1858; enlisted 20 Aug 1879; kicked by horse Jan 1880, Ft Davis, TX; treated for pain in the field 5 July 1880 at Eagle Springs, TX; treated intermittently Jun–Aug 1881, Presidio, TX; treated intermittently Feb 1882–May 1883, Ft Davis; Ht 5'8", black complexion, eyes, and hair; occupation laborer. SOURCE: Sayre, *Warriors of Color*, 459.

TROUT, Henry; Saddler; E/9th Cav. Born in Virginia; mulatto complexion; cannot read or write, age 24, Sep 1870, in 9th Cavalry at Ft McKavett, TX. SOURCE: Bierschwale, *Fort McKavett*, 107.

As private, B/9th Cavalry, involved in fight against Apache Nana, Gavilan Canyon, NM, 19 Aug 1881; served as saddler, E/9th Cavalry at Ft Robinson, NE, in 1894. SOURCE: Schubert, *Black Valor*, 84, 86, 191.

‡Retires from Ft Robinson. SOURCE: *ANJ* 34 (24 Jul 1897): 873.

‡Thirty years in Army; retired to Crawford, NE; died at post hospital, Ft Robinson, 14 Aug 1908. SOURCE: Crawford *Tribune*, 21 Aug 1908.

‡Buried at Ft Robinson, 15 Aug 1908. SOURCE: List of Interments, Ft Robinson.

‡No Veterans Administration pension file.

TROUTMAN, Edward; Sergeant; G/9th Cav. ‡On patrol from Ft Ringgold, TX, with four privates, Jan 1875, when ambushed by civilians; Pvts. Jerry Owsley and Moses Turner killed; Pvts. Charley Blackstone and John Fredericks escaped. SOURCE: Leckie, *The Buffalo Soldiers*, 108.

In G/9th Cavalry, led five-man patrol that was ambushed by ranchers within sixteen miles of Ft Ringgold, early 1875; Pvts. Moses Turner and Jeremiah Owsley, G/9th Cavalry, killed. SOURCE: Kenner, *Buffalo Soldiers and Officers of the Ninth Cavalry*, 60.

With Pvts. Charley Blackstone and John Fredericks, survived attack by Mexicans near Rio Grande, 26 Jan 1875, in which two cavalrymen were killed; later indicted and jailed at Rio Grande City, TX, for killing one of attackers. SOURCE: Leiker, *Racial Borders*, 54.

TRUETT; Private; 25th Inf. At Ft Randall, Dakota Territory, 1880. SOURCE: Barnett, *Ungentlemanly Acts*, 197.

TUCKER, Dred; M/9th Cav. Born in Kentucky; black complexion; can read and write, age 24, Jul 1870, at Ft McKavett, TX. SOURCE: Bierschwale, *Fort McKavett*, 100.

TUCKER, E.; Farrier; K/9th Cav. ‡Served 1872–73. *See* SLAUGHTER, Rufus, Private, K/9th Cavalry

Text of court martial order convicting Capt. J. Lee Humfreville of brutality. SOURCE: Schubert, *Voices of the Buffalo Soldier*, 55–62.

TUCKER, J. A.; Farrier; 9th Cav. Died 27 Apr 1881; buried at Ft Leavenworth National Cemetery, plot 2779. SOURCE: Ft Leavenworth National Cemetery.

TULLEY, William; Private; I/25th Inf. Pvt. William Tulley or Wa Tully died 2 Jul 1904; Wa Tully originally buried at Ft Niobrara, NE; reburied at Ft Leavenworth National Cemetery, plot G 3542. SOURCE: Ft Leavenworth National Cemetery.

TULLY, Wa; Private; I/25th Inf. *See* TULLEY, William, Private, I/25th Infantry

TUNNIA, Edward L.; Private; C/9th Cav. Died 16 Jan 1877; buried at Ft Bayard, NM, in plot F 29. SOURCE: "Fort Bayard National Cemetery, Records of Burials."

E. L. (Edward) Tunia buried 16 Jan 1877, section A, row G, plot 28, at Ft Bayard. SOURCE: Erickson, Burials at Fort Bayard National Cemetery, NM.

TURK, Robert H.; Private; H/10th Cav. Died 14 Nov 1882 of heart disease at Ft Concho, TX. SOURCE: Regimental Returns, 10th Cavalry, 1882.

Died at Ft Concho on 4 Nov 1882; buried at San Antonio National Cemetery, Section E, number 816. SOURCE: San Antonio National Cemetery Locator.

TURNBULL, Reese; Private; D/9th Cav. With Captain Dodge at battle at Milk River, CO, 2–10 Oct 1879. SOURCE: Miller, *Hollow Victory*, 167, 206–7.

Died 9 Jan 1880; buried at Ft Leavenworth National Cemetery, plot E 2648. SOURCE: Ft Leavenworth National Cemetery.

TURNER, Charles B.; Sgt Maj; 2nd Sqdn/10th Cav. ‡Born in Wisconsin; private, E/10th Cavalry, 15 Nov 1875; corporal, 20 Nov 1879; sergeant, 1 Jan 1882; first sergeant, 5 Aug 1890; sergeant, 1 Jan 1891; at Ft Custer, MT, 1897. SOURCE: Baker, Roster.

‡Born in Mineral Point, WI; Ht 5'8", mulatto; promoted from corporal, E/10th Cavalry, to sergeant major, 2nd Squadron/10th Cavalry, 27 Dec 1902; assigned to Ft Mackenzie, WY, 2 Jan 1903; retired to Louisville, 21 Sep 1903; campaigns: Lipans, 1876, Victorio, 1880, disarming Kiowas and Comanches, 1881, Geronimo, 1885–86, Philippines, 1900–1901; character on retirement excellent; married to Clara B. Turner; clothing not drawn $51.99. SOURCE: Descriptive Book, 10 Cav Officers & NCOs.

‡Born 25 Jan 1859; early education in Cincinnati; enlisted Indianapolis, age 16, 15 Nov 1875; delegate to national convention of Regular Army and Navy Union, St. Louis, 1893; on recruiting duty in Kentucky during Cuban campaign, 1898; Odd Fellow and Mason; sergeant major as of 6 Nov 1898. SOURCE: Cashin, *Under Fire with the Tenth Cavalry*, 314–16, with picture, 315.

In Troop E/10th Cavalry stationed at Bonita Cañon Camp, AZ, 28 Feb 1886. SOURCE: Tagg, *The Camp at Bonita Cañon*, 231.

‡Sergeant, E/10th Cavalry, Ft Grant, AZ, to be examined for regimental quartermaster sergeant. SOURCE: *ANJ* 25 (29 Oct 1887): 262.

‡Sergeant, E/10th Cavalry, Ft Grant, to be examined for post quartermaster sergeant. SOURCE: *ANJ* 25 (7 Jan 1888): 462.

‡Sergeant, E/10th Cavalry, Ft Apache, AZ, 1890, subscribed $.50 to testimonial to General Grierson. SOURCE: List of subscriptions, 23 Apr 1890, 10th Cavalry papers, MHI.

‡First sergeant, E/10th Cavalry, authorized six-month furlough from Ft Apache. SOURCE: *ANJ* 28 (8 Nov 1890): 170.

‡Sergeant, E/10th Cavalry, on furlough at New Orleans, to be furnished transportation back to Ft Apache by Quartermaster Department. SOURCE: *ANJ* 28 (6 Jun 1891): 692.

‡Sergeant, E/10th Cavalry, examined for post commissary sergeant, Ft Custer, MT. SOURCE: *ANJ* 29 (6 Aug 1892): 863.

Served as first sergeant, E/10th Cavalry, 1898; remained in U.S. during war with Spain. SOURCE: Cashin, *Under Fire with the Tenth Cavalry*, 343.

‡Commissioned from 10th Cavalry as second lieutenant, 48th Infantry, and ordered to report to New York. SOURCE: *ANJ* 37 (7 Oct 1899): 122.

Second lieutenant, 48th Infantry, as of 9 Sep 1899; to report at Ft Thomas, KY. SOURCE: *ANJ* 37 (14 Oct 1899): 147.

‡Mentioned as second lieutenant, K/48th Infantry. SOURCE: Beasley, *Negro Trailblazers*, 284.

‡Appointed sergeant major, 2nd Squadron/10th Cavalry, from corporal, E/10th Cavalry, 27 Dec 1902; arrived 4 Jan 1903. SOURCE: Muster Roll, Det Field and Staff, 2nd Sqdn, 10 Cav, Dec 1902–Feb 1903.

‡Retires from Ft Mackenzie, 2 Oct 1903; transport furnished to his home, Louisville. SOURCE: Muster Roll, Det Field and Staff, 2nd Sqdn, 10 Cav, Aug–Oct 1903.

Retired squadron sergeant major, received Indian Wars Campaign Badge number 1017 on 23 Nov 1908. SOURCE: Carroll, *Indian Wars Campaign Badge*, 29.

TURNER, Charley; Private; H/10th Cav. Resided at Julious, AR, in 1903. SOURCE: Sayre, *Warriors of Color*, 27.

TURNER, Clemon; Private; K/24th Inf. Awarded certificate of merit for rescuing fellow soldier from drowning at risk of his own life, near Camp McGrath, Batangas, Philippines, 12 Nov 1914. SOURCE: Gleim, *The Certificate of Merit*, 63.

Born in Gainesville, AL; resided Cincinnati, OH; received Distinguished Service Medal in lieu of certificate of merit. SOURCE: *American Decorations*, 844.

TURNER, Daniel; Corporal; K/38th Inf. *See* TURNER, David, Corporal, K/38th Infantry

TURNER, Daniel; Sergeant; 10th Cav. Convicted by general court martial of stealing uniform coat, sentenced to dishonorable discharge and six months; because he had previously been a model soldier, allowed to reenlist. SOURCE: Dobak and Phillips, *The Black Regulars*, 61.

TURNER, David; Corporal; K/38th Inf. ‡Cpl. Daniel Turner, K/38th Infantry, with small detachment at Wilson Creek, KS, repulsed large Indian party and killed five. SOURCE: Rickey, "The Negro Regulars," 5.

Repulsed Indian attack near Wilson's Creek, 26 Jun 1867, in first combat action by black regulars after Civil War. SOURCE: Schubert, *Voices of the Buffalo Soldier*, 8–9.

TURNER, George; Private; K/25th Inf. Born in Jackson, MS; Ht 5'8", black complexion; occupation laborer; enlisted in A/39th Infantry for three years on 13 Sep 1866, age 23, at Shreveport, LA; transferred to K/25th Infantry at Jackson Bks, LA, 20 Apr 1869. SOURCE: Descriptive Roll of A/39th Inf.

TURNER, Henry; Private; A/10th Cav. ‡Original member of 10th Cavalry; in troop when organized, Ft Leavenworth, KS, 18 Feb 1867. SOURCE: McMiller, "Buffalo Soldiers," 68.

Died 21 Jun 1867 of disease at Ft Larned, KS. SOURCE: Regimental Returns, 10th Cavalry, 1867.

TURNER, Joseph H.; 24th Inf. Corporal, 19th USCT; lives at 666 Sarah Ann St., Baltimore, MD. SOURCE: United States Colored Troops Resident in Baltimore at the Time of the 1890 Census, printout in authors' files.

Born in Delaware; black complexion; cannot read or write, age 24, 5 Sep 1870, at Ft McKavett, TX. SOURCE: Bierschwale, *Fort McKavett*, 108.

TURNER, Peter H.; Blacksmith; 9th Cav. ‡$59 gold watch and chain that Turner had pawned to Cpl. William H. Harper, E/9th Cavalry, stolen by Pvt. Herman Hector, Ft Robinson, NE, 1894. SOURCE: Court Martial Records, Hector.

‡Veteran of Spanish-American War and Philippine Insurrection; at Ft D. A. Russell, WY, in 1910. SOURCE: *Illustrated Review: Ninth Cavalry*, with picture.

Received Philippine Campaign Badge number 11713 for service as blacksmith in E/9th Cavalry; in 9th Cavalry at Ft Leavenworth, KS, Mar 1905. SOURCE: Philippine Campaign Badge list, 29 May 1905.

TURNER, Samuel; Private; 9th Cav. Received Philippine Campaign Badge number 11900 for service as private in A/49th Infantry, United States Volunteers, and G/25th Infantry; in 9th Cavalry at Ft Leavenworth, KS, Mar 1905. SOURCE: Philippine Campaign Badge list, 29 May 1905.

TURNER, Simon; Private; B/10th Cav. ‡Enlisted in Baltimore in H/10th Cavalry, 7 May 1873; reenlisted in B/10th Cavalry, 1878; engaged against Kiowas, Apaches, Comanches; member of Col. R. S. Mackenzie Camp No. 13, National Indian War Veterans, Stockton, CA. SOURCE: *Winners of the West* 7 (Nov 1930): 11.

At Ft Stockton, TX, 1879; witness in court martial of Lt. William H. Beck, 10th Cavalry, San Antonio, TX, Feb 1879. SOURCE: Kinevan, *Frontier Cavalryman*, 287.

‡After service, resided in San Antonio; was captain, A/Excelsior Guards, 1886. SOURCE: *Winners of the West* 8 (Jul 1931): 8.

‡Wife, Mrs. Lucy Turner, age 80, died in San Francisco. SOURCE: *Winners of the West* 11 (Aug 1934): 3.

TURNER, Thomas; Private; 9th Cav. Received Philippine Campaign Badge number 11792 for service as private in K/24th Infantry; in 9th Cavalry at Ft Leavenworth, KS, Mar 1905. SOURCE: Philippine Campaign Badge list, 29 May 1905.

TURNER, Wallace; L/9th Cav. Enlisted in Baltimore, MD, 2 Feb 1880; released from 4-month confinement 17 July 1880 as per SO 55, Dept of MO 17 Dec 1879; on detached service in New Mexico July–Aug 1880; on detached service at Ft Cummings, NM, Sep–Oct 1880; L/9th Cavalry left Ft Stanton, NM, 11 Nov 1880, arrived Ft Bliss, TX, 18 Nov 1880; at Ft Bliss, Jan–Feb 1881. SOURCE: Muster Rolls, L/9th Cavalry, 30 June 1880–28 Feb 1881.

Died 27 Apr 1900; buried at Ft Leavenworth National Cemetery, plot 3190. SOURCE: Ft Leavenworth National Cemetery.

‡Private bill passed by Congress, authorizing $12 per month pension for widow Winnie Turner. SOURCE: *Winners of the West* 3 (Apr 1926): 2.

TURNER, William; Corporal; 10th Cav. Commanded detachment in Kansas skirmish with Indians, July 1867. SOURCE: Dobak and Phillips, *The Black Regulars*, 235.

TURNER, William; Private; F/10th Cav. ‡Original member of 10th Cavalry; in troop when organized, Ft Leavenworth, KS, 21 Jun 1867. SOURCE: McMiller, "Buffalo Soldiers," 73.

Wounded in action, gunshot wound in right shoulder, near Beaver Creek, KS, 21 Aug 1867. SOURCE: LR, DeptMo, 1867.

‡Wounded in battle, Kansas, 21 Aug 1867. SOURCE: Armes, *Ups and Downs*, 248.

Wounded in action against Indians at Beaver Creek, 21 Aug 1867. SOURCE: Schubert, *Voices of the Buffalo Soldier*, 20.

TURNER, William; Private; C/10th Cav. Served with Pvt. George Washington, C/10th Cavalry, early 1870s; bunked with him. SOURCE: Schubert, *Voices of the Buffalo Soldier*, 234.

TURNER, William; Private; D/9th Cav. Five-year veteran, at Ringgold Barracks, TX, 1899; beaten and shot by local residents, Rio Grande City, TX, in brawl, October 1899. SOURCE: Leiker, *Racial Borders*, 124.

TURNER, William; Corporal; C/25th Inf. Corporal, received Indian Wars Campaign Badge number 1797 on 20 Jul 1916. SOURCE: Carroll, *Indian Wars Campaign Badge*, 52.

TURPIN, Edward; Private; F/10th Cav. Died 29 Jul 1867 of unknown causes at Ft Hays, KS. SOURCE: Regimental Returns, 10th Cavalry, 1867.

Private, G/38th Infantry, died 29 Jul 1867; buried at Ft Leavenworth National Cemetery, plot 3325. SOURCE: Ft Leavenworth National Cemetery.

TURPIN, George; Sergeant; H/9th Cav. Commanded detachment which took bodies of men killed at Gavilan Canyon, NM, Aug 1881, to Ft Bayard, NM, for burial; after retirement in 1898 lived in Kansas. SOURCE: Kenner, *Buffalo Soldiers and Officers of the Ninth Cavalry*, 230.

TURPIN, John; D/24th Inf. Born in Kentucky; black complexion; can read and write, age 24, Jul 1870, at Ft McKavett, TX. SOURCE: Bierschwale, *Fort McKavett*, 95.

TYLER, Jacob J.; Private; 25th Inf. Born in Orangeburg, SC; Ht 5'6", brown hair and eyes, fair complexion; occupation farmer; enlisted at age 26, Charleston, SC, 16 May 1881; left recruit depot, David's Island, NY, 2 Jul 1881, arrived at Ft Randall, SD, 7 Jul 1881. SOURCE: Descriptive & Assignment Rolls of Recruits, 25 Inf.

TYREE, George; Private; K/25th Inf. Born in Spotsylvania, VA; Ht 5'9", brown complexion; occupation shoemaker; enlisted in A/39th Infantry for three years on 8 Oct 1866, age 23, at Richmond, VA; ten days' confinement; transferred to K/25th Infantry at Jackson Bks, LA, 20 Apr 1869. SOURCE: Descriptive Roll of A/39th Inf.

U

UMBER, Green; F/9th Cav. Born in Kentucky; black complexion; can read, cannot write, age 34, Jul 1870, at Ft McKavett, TX. SOURCE: Bierschwale, *Fort McKavett*, 98.

UNDERWOOD, Clifford; Private; I/24th Inf. Died 17 Mar 1913; buried at Ft Bayard, NM, in plot U 6. SOURCE: "Fort Bayard National Cemetery, Records of Burials."

C. Underwood, B/24th Infantry, buried at Ft Bayard. SOURCE: "Fort Bayard National Cemetery, Records of Burials."

Buried 17 Mar 1913, section B, row F, plot 8, at Ft Bayard. SOURCE: Erickson, Burials at Fort Bayard National Cemetery, NM.

UNDERWOOD, Elisha M.; Private; B/24th Inf. ‡First place, hasty entrenchment contest, military tournament, Albany, NY, autumn 1909. SOURCE: Muller, *The Twenty Fourth Infantry*, 60.

Died 27 Mar 1913; buried at Ft Bayard, NM, in plot U 23. SOURCE: "Fort Bayard National Cemetery, Records of Burials."

Buried 27 Mar 1913, section B, row F, plot 23, at Ft Bayard. SOURCE: Erickson, Burials at Fort Bayard National Cemetery, NM.

V

VADER, Louis E.; Corporal; K/9th Cav. ‡Promoted from lance corporal, Ft Robinson, NE, Mar 1895. SOURCE: *ANJ* 32 (30 Mar 1895): 506.

‡Teacher, Ft Robinson school, 1 Nov–31 Dec 1895, 6 Jan–29 Feb 1896. SOURCE: Report of Schools, Ft Robinson.

Died 14 Dec 1899; originally buried at Ft DuChesne, UT; reburied at Santa Fe National Cemetery, NM, plot A-4 1096. SOURCE: Santa Fe National Cemetery, Records of Burials.

VALENTINE, John; Private; D/48th Inf. Died 23 Nov 1900; reburied in plot E.SID1089 at San Francisco National Cemetery. SOURCE: San Francisco National Cemetery.

VALENTINE, Ranson; M/9th Cav. Born in Kentucky; black complexion; can read and write, age 25, Jul 1870, at Ft McKavett, TX. SOURCE: Bierschwale, *Fort McKavett*, 100.

VAN DYKE, Richard; Private; E/9th Cav. Died 17 Nov 1899; buried 14 Mar 1932 at Santa Fe National Cemetery, NM, plot P 108. SOURCE: Santa Fe National Cemetery, Records of Burials.

VANLEER, Percy L.; Private; E/24th Inf. Died 12 Mar 1915; buried at Ft Bayard, NM, in plot W 46. SOURCE: "Fort Bayard National Cemetery, Records of Burials."

Buried 12 Mar 1915, section B, row H, plot 46 at Ft Bayard, NM. SOURCE: Erickson, Burials at Fort Bayard National Cemetery, NM.

VARNON, William; Private; E/10th Cav. In Troop E/10th Cavalry stationed at Bonita Cañon Camp, AZ, 28 Feb 1886. SOURCE: Tagg, *The Camp at Bonita Cañon*, 232.

VASS, Charley; Private; F/10th Cav. Died 17 Nov 1902; originally buried at Ft Washakie, WY; reburied at Ft Leavenworth National Cemetery, plot 3487. SOURCE: Ft Leavenworth National Cemetery.

VAUGHN, Henry; Private; U.S. Army. Seminole Negro Scout, served 1875–76. SOURCE: Schubert, Consolidated List of Seminole Negro Scouts.

Born in Choctaw Nation, IT; probably a slave or descendant of a slave of Choctaw Indian; Ht 5'4", black hair and eyes, black complexion; enlisted 24 Apr 1875 at Ft Duncan, TX, where he was discharged 1 Jan 1876; reported still alive in Del Rio, TX, 1941. SOURCE: Swanson, 46.

Age 25, resided at Ft Duncan in 1875. SOURCE: NARA Record Group, Special File.

VISITO, Cyle V.; Corporal; G/25th Inf. Corporal, received Indian Wars Campaign Badge number 756 on 21 Oct 1908. SOURCE: Carroll, *Indian Wars Campaign Badge*, 21.

VOLCOME, Eugene; Private; I/10th Cav. In Troop I/10th Cavalry stationed at Bonita Cañon Camp, AZ, absent or on detached service 30 Jun 1886. Tagg questions spelling of Volcome. SOURCE: Tagg, *The Camp at Bonita Cañon*, 232.

VOSKER, Santon; Private; U.S. Army. Seminole Negro Scout, served 1884. SOURCE: Schubert, Consolidated List of Seminole Negro Scouts.

Santon Voskes, born in Mexico; Ht 5'7", black hair and eyes, black complexion; enlisted at Ft Clark, TX, 20 May 1884, age 21; discharged at Ft Clark 31 Aug 1884. SOURCE: Swanson, 46.

VROOMAN, William A.; Regt QM Sgt; 9th Cav. ‡Enlisted at Buffalo, NY, 18 Jun 1886; assigned to I/9th Cavalry, 22 Jan 1887; appointed sergeant, 17 Sep 1888; served in Sioux campaign, including engagement at Drexel Mission, SD, 28 Dec 1890; reenlisted and assigned to G/9th Cavalry, 10 Jul 1887; appointed sergeant, 17 Apr 1892; competitor, Departments of the Platte, the East, and Columbia rifle and pistol competitions, 1892–94, and ranked second, third, and fifth with rifle, seventh with pistol; distinguished marksman, 1894; veteran of Indian wars, Spanish-American War, and Philippine Insurrection; appointed regimental quartermaster sergeant, 1 Jan 1909; at Ft D. A.

Russell, WY, in 1910. SOURCE: *Illustrated Review: Ninth Cavalry*, with picture.

‡Acquitted by general court martial, Jefferson Bks, MO, of attempting to steal raincoat from Recruit James E. Russell, Company D of Instruction, 24 Nov 1886.

‡Corporal, G/9th Cavalry; ranked number 2, carbine competition, Departments of the Platte, the East, and California, Bellevue, NE, 15–20 Aug 1892. SOURCE: GO 75, AGO, 3 Nov 1892.

‡Corporal, G/9th Cavalry; witness for defense. SOURCE: Court Martial Records, McKay.

‡Appointed sergeant, G/9th Cavalry, 28 Jul 1893. SOURCE: Roster, 9 Cav.

‡Sergeant, G/9th Cavalry; ranked number 7 in carbine competition, Departments of the Platte, the East, and California, Bellevue, 14–19 Aug 1893. SOURCE: GO 82, AGO, 24 Oct 1893.

‡Recognized for role in capturing escaping prisoner, Ft Robinson, NE, 24 Jun 1894. SOURCE: CO, Ft Robinson, to Vrooman, 25 Jun 1894, LS, Ft Robinson.

‡Sergeant, G/9th Cavalry; ranked number 3, carbine competition, and number 7, revolver competition, Departments of the Platte, the East, and Columbia, Bellevue, 18–25 Sep 1894; distinguished marksman, revolver, 1892, 1893, and 1894, and carbine, 1894. SOURCE: GO 62, AGO, 15 Nov 1894.

Appointed sergeant 28 Jul 1893; in G/9th Cavalry at Ft Robinson, Jan 1897. SOURCE: Ninth Cavalry, Roster of NCOs, 1897.

‡Lieutenant, Crispus Attucks Lodge No. 3, Knights of Pythias, State of Nebraska, Ft Robinson. SOURCE: Richmond *Planet*, 18 Dec 1897.

Squadron sergeant major, 9th Cavalry, received Indian Wars Campaign Badge number 859 on 6 Jan 1909; regimental quartermaster sergeant reported it lost on 15 Apr 1910, received badge number 1577. SOURCE: Carroll, *Indian Wars Campaign Badge*, 24, 46.

‡Retires as regimental quartermaster sergeant, 9th Cavalry, age 45, with thirty years' service and pension of $67.50 per month. SOURCE: Cleveland *Gazette*, 2 Oct 1915.

W

WADDELL, Fred; Private; I/9th Cav. Died 19 Apr 1900; originally buried at Ft DuChesne, UT; reburied at Santa Fe National Cemetery, NM, plot A-4 1094. SOURCE: Santa Fe National Cemetery, Records of Burials.

WADE, Chester; Private; D/10th Cav. ‡Original member of 10th Cavalry; in troop when organized, Ft Leavenworth, KS, 1 Jun 1867. SOURCE: McMiller, "Buffalo Soldiers," 71.

Died 23 Oct 1870 of fever at Ft Sill, OK. SOURCE: Regimental Returns, 10th Cavalry, 1870.

Buried at Camp Douglas, UT. SOURCE: Record Book of Interments, Post Cemetery, 252.

WADE, Henry; Private; A/10th Cav. ‡Arrived at Ft Leavenworth, KS, from Jefferson Bks, MO, 9 Oct 1866. SOURCE: LS, 10 Cav, 1866–67.

‡Original member of 10th Cavalry; in troop when organized, Ft Leavenworth, KS, 18 Feb 1867. SOURCE: McMiller, "Buffalo Soldiers," 68.

Died 4 May 1870 of disease at Camp Supply, OK. SOURCE: Regimental Returns, 10th Cavalry, 1870.

WADE, Jim; Private; K/9th Cav. ‡Served 1872–73. See SLAUGHTER, Rufus, Private, K/9th Cavalry

Court martial order convicting Capt. J. Lee Humfreville of brutality published. SOURCE: Schubert, *Voices of the Buffalo Soldier*, 55–62.

WADE, John C.; Private; C/24th Inf. Shot and killed by Texas Rangers for allegedly trying to escape arrest after disturbance at brothel near Ft Bliss, TX, 9 Apr 1916. SOURCE: Leiker, *Racial Borders*, 123.

‡Killed at Del Rio, TX, 8 Apr 1916, when Texas Rangers tried to arrest sixteen soldiers for disturbance. SOURCE: Cleveland *Gazette*, 15 Apr 1916.

WAKES, Robert; Private; A/25th Inf. Died 15 Aug 1874; buried at San Antonio National Cemetery, Section F, number 1134. SOURCE: San Antonio National Cemetery Locator.

WALKER; Private; K/10th Cav. *See corrected entry,* WALKER, Harry, Private, K/10th Cavalry

WALKER, Alexander; Private; B/25th Inf. Enlisted 16 Oct 1899, discharged as artificer F/49th Infantry 30 Jun 1901; reenlisted 30 Jul 1901, discharged as cook B/25th Infantry 29 Jul 1904, character very good; reenlisted 30 Jul 1904, discharged without honor 19 Nov 1906. SOURCE: Powell, "Military Record of the Enlisted Men Who Were Discharged Without Honor."

‡Dishonorable discharge, Brownsville, TX. SOURCE: SO 266, AGO, 9 Nov 1906.

WALKER, Harry; Private; K/10th Cav. ‡Involved in rumpus in dive on W. Elm Street, Crawford, NE, early 31 May 1904; shot and killed. SOURCE: Crawford *Bulletin*, 3 Jun 1904.

In southern part of Crawford, shot in neck by Private Wilson, C/10th Cavalry, and killed instantly at 1 A.M. Tues. 31 May 1904; Wilson taken back by guard to Ft Robinson. SOURCE: Buecker, Fort Robinson Burials.

‡Buried at Ft Robinson, NE, 30 May 1904. SOURCE: List of Interments, Ft Robinson.

WALKER, Henry; Blacksmith; H/10th Cav. Born in Shelbyville, KY, 15 Sep 1860; enlisted Louisville, KY, 18 Jan 1881; Ht 5'5", mulatto complexion, brown eyes, black hair; occupation laborer; lost sight of right eye when struck by fragment of steel while working in blacksmith shop, Ft Davis, TX, Nov 1884; discharged Ft Davis, 18 Mar 1885; married Louise Brown, Jeffersonville, IN, 12 Sep 1885; wife died 8 Apr 1947; daughter Octavia born 26 Mar 1887, married name Cain, resided 435 So. 19th St., Louisville; sons Dave born 15 Oct 1891 and Willie born 7 Sep 1893; worked as hostler, resided at 2525 Eddy St., Louisville, in 1892; received $4 per month pension in Aug 1892; admitted to National Military Home, Marion, IN, Sep 1911, where he died 29 Apr 1914; effects forwarded to widow at 1917 Congress St., Louisville; widow received $30 per month pension from Apr 1932, decreased to $27 in Jul 1934; April 1944 pension of $50 per month; moved from 1812 Cedar St., Louisville, 4 Oct 1946 to 24 Keystone Ave.,

Indianapolis, IN; daughter reports 22 Apr 1947 that her mother died. SOURCE: Sayre, *Warriors of Color*, 460–70.

WALKER, James; F/9th Cav. Born in Klein County, KY; enlisted in F/9th Cavalry 6 Oct 1866 at Greenville, LA, age 20, occupation soldier; discharged 6 Oct 1871 at Ft McKavett, TX. SOURCE: Williams 27 Mar 1996 letter to Margaret A. Lewis.

Born in Kentucky; black complexion; cannot read or write, age 26, Jul 1870, at Ft McKavett. SOURCE: Bierschwale, *Fort McKavett*, 97.

WALKER, James; C/25th Inf. Born in Pennsylvania; mulatto complexion; cannot read or write, age 21, 5 Sep 1870, at Ft McKavett, TX. SOURCE: Bierschwale, *Fort McKavett*, 109.

WALKER, Jeff; Sergeant; K/25th Inf. Served during early 1870s, brought charges which resulted in dishonorable discharge of William Watkins, K/25th Infantry. SOURCE: Schubert, *Voices of the Buffalo Soldier*, 53–54.

WALKER, John; Private; 10th Cav. In regiment in 1888; resided in Albuquerque, NM, age 69, in 1914. SOURCE: Sayre, *Warriors of Color*, 111.

WALKER, John; Sergeant; D/10th Cav. ‡Served as corporal, D/10th Cavalry, in Cuba, 1898. SOURCE: Cashin, *Under Fire with the Tenth Cavalry*, 341.

‡Narrates role of 10th Cavalry on San Juan Hill. SOURCE: Cashin, *Under Fire with the Tenth Cavalry*, 267–70.

‡Sergeant, 1900; recommended by Capt. John Bigelow for Medal of Honor; awarded certificate of merit for heroism in Cuba; cut barbed-wire fence before San Juan Hill, 1 Jul 1898, so advance could continue. SOURCE: Steward, *The Colored Regulars*, 280; SecWar, *AR 1898*, 710; GO 15, AGO, 13 Feb 1900; Bigelow, *Reminiscences of Santiago*, 130–33, 163.

Awarded certificate of merit for distinguished service in battle, Santiago, Cuba, 1 Jul 1898. SOURCE: Gleim, *The Certificate of Merit*, 45.

Born in Orange County, VA; resided at Thornhill, VA; received Distinguished Service Medal in lieu of certificate of merit. SOURCE: *American Decorations*, 844.

WALKER, John; Sergeant; G/9th Cav. Received Philippine Campaign Badge number 11816 for service as private in G/9th Cavalry, 16 Sep 1900–16 Sep 1902; cook in G/9th Cavalry, Ft Leavenworth, KS, Mar 1905. SOURCE: Philippine Campaign Badge Recipients; Philippine Campaign Badge list, 29 May 1905.

Sgt. John Walker, G/9th Cavalry; died 20 Jan 1916; buried at Ft Leavenworth National Cemetery, plot H 3374-C. SOURCE: Ft Leavenworth National Cemetery.

WALKER, Samuel; Private; M/25th Inf. Died 2 Nov 1901; buried in plot New Add, 1046 at San Francisco National Cemetery. SOURCE: San Francisco National Cemetery.

WALKER, Silas; F/9th Cav. Born in Clark County, KY; enlisted at Greenville, LA, 6 Oct 1866, age 25, occupation soldier; deserted 1 Apr 1867. SOURCE: Williams 27 Mar 1996 letter to Margaret A. Lewis.

WALKER, Thomas; Private; 9th Cav. Received Philippine Campaign Badge number 11901 for service as private in H/9th Cavalry; in 9th Cavalry at Ft Leavenworth, KS, Mar 1905. SOURCE: Philippine Campaign Badge list, 29 May 1905.

WALKER, William; Private; I/10th Cav. Accidentally shot, died 9 Dec 1872 at Ft Sill, OK. SOURCE: Regimental Returns, 10th Cavalry, 1872.

WALL, Archy; Principal Musician; 24th Inf. ‡Born in Murray Co., TN; brown complexion, Ht 5'5"; first enlistment in Band/24th Infantry completed 17 Feb 1881, age 26; reenlisted, Ft Supply, Indian Territory, 21 Feb 1881; discharged, end of term, Ft Bayard, NM, 20 Feb 1886, character "excellent—reliable and trustworthy. A very good baritone player," married with three children; deposits $535, 1881–86, retained $60, clothing $114.63.

‡Born in Franklin, Williams Co., TN, 1857; enlisted in H/24th Infantry, Nashville, TN, 18 Feb 1876; served in Victorio campaign, in Cuba, on nursing duty at Montauk Point, NY, and in the Philippines as second lieutenant, A/49th Infantry; principal musician, 24th Infantry, 15 Mar 1885; served eighteen years as principal musician with at least twenty-six men under him; charter member of Guy V. Henry Post No. 3, Spanish-American War Veterans; married Miss Fanny McKay of Louisville, KY, 1 Jun 1885; wife "one of the most active workers in the California Federation of Colored Women's Clubs," with seven years as state treasurer, who presided over city and district work of orphanage; active in organization of Spanish-American War auxiliary and now president; president, Art and Industrial Club of Oakland; children: Clifton, Florence Wall-Murry, and Lillian Wall-Williams, all musically inclined and educated in Oakland, CA, public schools; girls attractive "leaders in society of the Bay cities, marrying befitting their station." SOURCE: Beasley, *Negro Trailblazers*, 228, 284, 297–98.

‡In E/24th Infantry, married, at Ft Bayard. SOURCE: *ANJ* 29 (17 Oct 1891): 133.

‡At Ft Douglas, UT. SOURCE: Clark, "A History of the Twenty-fourth," 69.

‡*See* OTT, BRYANT, Ferdinand, 24th Infantry; GOODLOE, Thomas, Sergeant Major, 9th Cavalry

‡Retired from Ft Harrison, MT, 13 Jul 1903; died at age 74 as retired staff sergeant, of arteriosclerosis, Letterman Hospital, Presidio of San Francisco, CA, 7 Apr 1931; application for hospitalization shows his race as white and color as ruddy; wife had pension of $30 per month, resided at 6114 Telegraph, Oakland, CA, with daughter Florence Wall-White until her death 11 May 1944. SOURCE: VA File C 2643745, Archy Wall.

‡Mollie Green, age 72 in 1931, resided at Ft Supply in 1885 when Wall took furlough to Louisville to marry; his wife came to Ft Supply in 1886 and was entertained in Green home for several days before Walls settled in their own house; has been with or near Walls at military posts and in Oakland since. SOURCE: Affidavit, Mollie Green, 962 63rd Street, Oakland, 28 Oct 1931, VA File C 2643745, Archy Wall.

‡Fanny Wall's maiden name Franklin, born Sumner Co., TN; married to George McKay at age 16 in 1878; McKay died in Louisville, 1882. SOURCE: VA File C 2643745, Archy Wall.

‡Fanny Wall motivating spirit behind Fanny Wall Children's Home and Day Nursery, Linden near 8th, Oakland, which is "a colossal monument to the efforts of the [California Federation of Colored Women's Clubs] and to Mrs. Wall." SOURCE: Davis, *Lifting as They Climb*, 280.

Staff sergeant, Band/24th Infantry; died 11 May 1931; buried in plot B 1179 at San Francisco National Cemetery. SOURCE: San Francisco National Cemetery.

WALLACE, Al; Private; K/48th Inf. ‡Died of variola in the Philippines, 16 Jul 1900. SOURCE: *ANJ* 37 (28 Jul 1900): 1142.

Died 16 Jul 1900; buried in plot NEW A872 at San Francisco National Cemetery. SOURCE: San Francisco National Cemetery.

WALLACE, Benjamin F.; Private; H/10th Cav. Born in Doe Run, Chester County, PA, 1 Nov 1842; enlisted in Baltimore, MD, 1 Dec 1880; Ht 5'5", brown complexion, brown eyes, black hair; occupation laborer; received medical treatment 5 Sept 1881 in camp near Presidio, TX; stationed at Ft Davis, TX, 5 May 1882; discharged at Camp Bowie, AZ, 30 Jan 1885; stationed at Ft Davis, 28 Feb 1885; en route to and at Ft Grant, AZ, 30 Apr 1885; en route to and at Pinery Creek, AZ, 31 Aug 1885; at Bonita Cañon, AZ, 31 Oct 1885; married Amanda Wilson; daughter Alice Wallace; employed as street sweeper, city of Philadelphia, PA; received pension of $20 per month from Mar 1917; living with niece Helen Gaillard, Feb 1924, at 326 Norris St., Chester, PA; died 13 Aug 1926; buried at Green Lawn Cemetery, Chester, PA. SOURCE: Sayre, *Warriors of Color* 471–74.

WALLACE, Harry; Private; L/9th Cav. Enlisted 26 Jul 1878 at Cincinnati, OH; also on rolls in Sept–Oct 1879 at Ft Bliss, TX; left camp on Rio Mimbres, NM, on 8 Jul 1880 and marched twenty miles to Ft Cummings, NM; left Ft Cummings 8 Aug on march to Leas Ferry on Rio Grande and returned to Rio Mimbres camp after march of 104 miles; on detached duty as company clerk and post mail carrier Nov 1880–Feb 1881. SOURCE: Muster Rolls, L/9th Cavalry, 31 Oct 1879–31 Dec 1879, 30 June 1880–28 Feb 1881.

WALLACE, Harry; Sergeant; C/9th Cav. ‡Appointed sergeant, C/9th Cavalry, as of 1 Jul 1885. SOURCE: Roster, 9 Cav.

‡Ranked number 8 in revolver competition, Departments of the East, the Platte, and California, Bellevue, NE, 14–19 Aug 1893. SOURCE: GO 82, AGO, 24 Oct 1893.

‡Examined for post quartermaster sergeant at Ft Robinson, NE, Aug 1895. SOURCE: *ANJ* 32 (10 Aug 1895): 823.

Appointed sergeant 1 Jul 1885; in C/9th Cavalry at Ft Robinson, Jan 1897. SOURCE: Ninth Cavalry, Roster of NCOs, 1897.

‡Ordered by post commander, Ft Robinson, to send his son to school, despite Wallace's claim that his son is out because he helps his mother. SOURCE: CO, Ft Robinson, to Superintendent, Post School, 15 Feb 1898, LS, Ft Robinson.

‡Two children, Gertrude, age 4, and Mattie, age 2, burned to death in quarters, Ft Robinson, after their mother locked them in while she went visiting, 22 Mar 1898. SOURCE: Medical History, Ft Robinson; CO, Ft Robinson, to AG, DeptMo, 23 Mar 1898, LS, Ft Robinson.

Son and daughter buried in same grave 22 Mar 1898, Ft Robinson. SOURCE: Buecker, Fort Robinson Burials.

‡Kansas City, MO, *Times* reports that everyone in Army sympathizes with Wallace and his wife for the loss of two little children in recent fire. SOURCE: *ANJ* 35 (2 Apr 1898): 582.

Died 11 Feb 1906; buried at Ft Leavenworth National Cemetery, plot G 3446. SOURCE: Ft Leavenworth National Cemetery.

WALLACE, Henry; C/25th Inf. Born in Tennessee; black complexion; cannot read or write, age 24, 5 Sep 1870, at Ft McKavett, TX. SOURCE: Bierschwale, *Fort McKavett*, 109.

WALLACE, John; Private; L/9th Cav. Enlisted 29 Jul 1878 at Cincinnati, OH; in Nov or Dec 1879 sentenced by general court martial to forfeit $10 pay per month and confinement at hard labor for four months at Ft Bliss, TX;

released from confinement 17 Jul 1880, on detached service at Ft Cummings, NM; L/9th Cavalry left Ft Stanton, NM, 11 Nov 1880, arrived at Ft Bliss 18 Nov 1880; at Ft Bliss Jan–Feb 1881. SOURCE: Muster Roll, L/9th Cavalry, 31 Oct 1879–31 Dec 1879; 31 Aug 1880–28 Feb 1881.

WALLACE, Maxillary; Private; F/24th Inf. Moved from New Mexico to U.S. Soldiers Home, Washington, DC, 1894; former comrades took up collection to pay his wife's fare, but she took the money and moved in with another soldier; company commander forbade her from moving with regiment to Salt Lake City, UT, in 1896. SOURCE: Dobak and Phillips, *The Black Regulars*, 173.

WALLACE, Washington; Private; K/25th Inf. Born in Jackson County, MO; Ht 5'7", black hair and dark eyes, yellow complexion; occupation clerk; enlisted at age 22, Cincinnati, OH, 10 May 1886; from Columbus Bks, OH, arrived at Ft Snelling, MN, 17 Sep 1886. SOURCE: Descriptive & Assignment Rolls of Recruits, 25 Inf.

WALLER, John L.; Captain; 23rd Kans Inf. Issued call 24 Jun 1898 for all who wish to join his Negro regiment to meet at armory in Kansas City, MO; hopes to serve as colonel, but will be satisfied as captain. SOURCE: "Ex-Consul Waller Will Fight, Kansas City Negroes Preparing for the War," Leavenworth *Times*, 25 Jun 1898.

‡Prominent black Republican and former consul in Madagascar; encouraged black emigration to Cuba through his 1899 Afro-American Emigration Society; urged only blacks with capital or particular skills to go. SOURCE: Gatewood, "Kansas Negroes and the Spanish-American War," 312.

‡*See* Allison Blakeley, "The John L. Waller Affair, 1895–1896," *Negro History Bulletin* 37 (Feb–Mar 1974): 216–18.

WALLER, Reuben; Private; H/10th Cav. ‡Born a slave in 1840; servant to Confederate cavalry general in Civil War; enlisted in H/10th Cavalry, 16 Jul 1867; fought at Beecher's Island, KS; served ten years and settled at El Dorado, KS. SOURCE: Carroll, *The Black Military Experience*, 193–99.

‡Original member of 10th Cavalry; in troop when organized, Ft Leavenworth, KS, 21 Jul 1867. SOURCE: McMiller, "Buffalo Soldiers," 75.

‡Enlisted Ft Leavenworth for five years, 16 Jul 1867; drilled and trained for horse riding about two months, marched to Ft Hays, KS, under Capt. Louis H. Carpenter; near Ft Harker, KS, Indians refused to engage in battle; later five enlisted men and white scout captured while hunting; Indians scalped and burned white, stripped and beat blacks and sent them away, saying "black man's scalp no good"; resides in El Dorado. SOURCE: *Winners of the West* 1 (Jul 1924): 1.

Text of his account of the rescue of the men trapped by Indians on Beecher's Island in Republican River. SOURCE: Schubert, *Voices of the Buffalo Soldier*, 24–30.

‡At battle of Beaver Creek, KS, H and I/10th Cavalry protected Gen. E. A. Carr as escort from Ft Wallace, KS: "Our soldiers . . . scalped some of the Indians, but we soon put a stop to that kind of barbarity amongst the Tenth cavalrymen." SOURCE: *Winners of the West* 1 (Oct 1924): 3.

‡Now 89 years old, with $50 per month pension; to attend sixtieth anniversary commemoration of Beecher's Island fight on Republican River, to be held in Colorado, 14–16 Sep 1928: "History shows that Colonel Carpenter and his colored orderly were the first to rescue the men, and the colored orderly was myself." SOURCE: *Winners of the West* 5 (Aug 1928): 2.

‡Delivered opening address at Beecher's Island celebration last year to about two thousand in attendance: "My old buddies of Troop H, 10th U.S. Cavalry, if any of you are still living, do you remember on September 19, 1868, when we charged into the Indians and stampeded them, rescuing 20 men who were living out of the 51 that went into the fight? Let us hear from you." SOURCE: *Winners of the West* 6 (May 1929): 2.

‡Letter. SOURCE: *Winners of the West* 7 (Mar 1930): 2.

‡Age 94, last survivor of Beecher's Island fight. SOURCE: *Winners of the West* 10 (Nov 1933): 2, with picture.

WALLEY, Augustus; Sgt 1st Class; Sanitary Corps. ‡Born in Reisterstown, MD; awarded Medal of Honor for heroism against Apache Nana, Cuchillo Negro Mountains, New Mexico, while private, I/9th Cavalry, 16 Aug 1881. SOURCE: Lee, *Negro Medal of Honor Men*, 71, 74.

Enlisted in Baltimore, MD, Nov 1878; reported to I/9th Cavalry Apr 1879; called as witness to court martial of Johnson Whitaker, a black cadet at West Point, first half of 1881; rejoined troop in mid-June 1881 at Ft Wingate, NM; at Cuchillo Negro, Aug 1881; career as private in I/9th Cavalry and Medal of Honor discussed. SOURCE: Kenner, *Buffalo Soldiers and Officers of the Ninth Cavalry*, 242–49.

Life, career, and valor against Apaches, for which he received Medal of Honor, narrated. SOURCE: Schubert, *Black Valor*, 81–83, 87, 117, 166–67, 170.

Medal of Honor mentioned. SOURCE: Dobak and Phillips, *The Black Regulars*, 261.

Text of letter from former Lt. George Burnett, describing heroism of Walley and 1st Sgt. Moses Washington against Apaches, Aug 1881. SOURCE: Schubert, *Voices of the Buffalo Soldier*, 100–104.

‡Awarded medal for heroism against Nana, Carrizo Canyon, NM, 12 Aug 1881. SOURCE: Carroll, *The Black Military Experience*, 365–69; Billington, *New Mexico's Buffalo Soldiers*, 106.

‡Medal of Honor mentioned. SOURCE: Leckie, *The Buffalo Soldiers*, 232–33; Koger, *The Maryland Negro in Our Wars*, 23.

‡Served as private, E/10th Cavalry in Cuba, 1898. SOURCE: Cashin, *Under Fire with the Tenth Cavalry*, 342.

‡Narrates Spanish-American War experiences. SOURCE: Cashin, *Under Fire with the Tenth Cavalry*, 364–65.

‡Showed "great gallantry" before Santiago, Cuba, 24 Jun 1898; with Capt. C. G. Ayers and Privates Neal, Nelson, and White, dragged wounded Major Bell of 1st Cavalry to safety. SOURCE: SecWar, *AR 1898*, 355.

‡Recently promoted from cook to sergeant; has Medal of Honor; will retire with thirty years' service on 1 Feb 1907. SOURCE: Fremont *Clipper*, 14 Dec 1906.

Sergeant first class, received Indian Wars Campaign Badge number 1845 on 17 Dec 1918. SOURCE: Carroll, *Indian Wars Campaign Badge*, 53.

WALLOW, Samuel; Private; C/10th Cav. Died 12 Nov 1870 of disease at Ft Sill, OK. SOURCE: Regimental Returns, 10th Cavalry, 1870.

WALLS, Buck; Private; E/10th Cav. In Troop E/10th Cavalry stationed at Bonita Cañon Camp, AZ, 28 Feb 1886. SOURCE: Tagg, *The Camp at Bonita Cañon*, 232.

WALLS, Henry F.; 2nd Lt; A/49th Inf. ‡H. F. Walls, private, corporal, sergeant, D/9th Cavalry, 4 Feb 1893–3 Feb 1898; reenlisted in D/9th Cavalry, 4 Feb 1898; sergeant until 24 Nov 1898; wounded in action at San Juan, Cuba, 1 Jul 1898; in hospital, Ft McPherson, GA, 11 Jul–8 Aug 1898; saddler sergeant, 9th Cavalry, 24 Nov 1898; squadron sergeant major, 9th Cavalry, 15 Mar 1899; commissary sergeant, 9th Cavalry, 1 May 1899; second lieutenant, 49th Infantry, 13 Sep 1899. SOURCE: Descriptive Book, A/49 Inf.

‡Promoted from private to corporal, D/9th Cavalry, Ft Robinson, NE, 10 May 1895. SOURCE: *ANJ* 32 (25 May 1895): 642.

Appointed corporal 10 May 1895; in D/9th Cavalry at Ft Washakie, WY, Jan 1897. SOURCE: Ninth Cavalry, Roster of NCOs, 1897.

‡Relieved from special duty as assistant librarian, Ft Robinson. SOURCE: Order 30, 16 May 1895, Post Orders, Ft Robinson.

‡Corporal, D/9th Cavalry; ranked number 5 in carbine competition, Departments of the Platte, Columbia, and Dakota, Ft Robinson, 27–30 Sep 1897. SOURCE: GO 64, AGO, 18 Nov 1897.

‡Former commissary sergeant, 9th Cavalry, commissioned second lieutenant, 49th Infantry. SOURCE: *ANJ* 37 (9 Dec 1899): 345b.

WALLY, Augustus; Sergeant; E/10th Cav. *See* WALLEY, Augustus, Sergeant First Class, Sanitary Corps

WALTERS, Joseph; Private; E/9th Cav. Died 10 Jan 1882; originally buried at Ft Hays, KS; reburied at Ft Leavenworth National Cemetery, plot 3377. SOURCE: Ft Leavenworth National Cemetery.

WALTON, Samuel; Private; D/10th Cav. Died 11 Nov 1870; buried at Camp Douglas, UT. SOURCE: Record Book of Interments, Post Cemetery, 252.

WALZE, Olmstead; Private; F/9th Cav. Born in Kentucky; died and buried at Ft McKavett, TX, before 17 May 1879; body removed to National Cemetery, San Antonio, TX, 23 Nov 1883. SOURCE: Bierschwale, *Fort McKavett*, 122.

WANTON, George H.; Master Sgt; QM Corps. Born 15 May 1866; attended public schools in Paterson, NJ; entered Navy 1884 and served four years; enlisted in 10th Cavalry where he served until 1915; promoted to corporal 1892; promoted to sergeant 1898; awarded Congressional Medal of Honor for gallantry at Tayabacoa, Cuba, 30 Jun 1898 when he was among volunteers who rescued sixteen American prisoners; enlisted in Quartermaster Corps 1915; promoted to master sergeant 1924; retired 1925; member of American Legion, Spanish War Veterans, Retired Service Men's Association; a Republican, member of Methodist Church; first wife Eliza Jackson Wanton; died 24 Nov 1940; survived by three children from first marriage: George H., Jr., of Columbia, SC, Elizabeth McCleary of Port Jarvis, NY, Vivian Dixon of Washington, DC, and second wife, Helen B. Wanton; buried at Arlington National Cemetery. SOURCE: "George Henry Walton," *Negro History Bulletin* 4 (Jan 1941): 87.

‡Born in Paterson, NJ; awarded Medal of Honor for heroism in Cuba; received medal in Paterson 30 Jun 1899. SOURCE: Lee, *Negro Medal of Honor Men*, 92, 98.

Life, career, and valor at Tayabacoa, Jun 1898, for which he received Medal of Honor, narrated. SOURCE: Schubert, *Black Valor*, 137–39, 143–44, 166–67.

‡Served as corporal, M/10th Cavalry, in Cuba, 1898. SOURCE: Cashin, *Under Fire with the Tenth Cavalry*, 352.

‡Left service shortly after service in Cuba, for which he won medal, as private, M/10th Cavalry. SOURCE: Steward, *The Colored Regulars*, 205; *ANJ* 37 (24 Feb 1900): 611.

WARD, Baleford; Private; A/39th Inf. Sentence of death for involvement in New Iberia, LA, mutiny, Jul 1867, reduced to two years. SOURCE: Dobak and Phillips, *The Black Regulars*, 222.

WARD, James; Corporal; F/25th Inf. ‡Killed in action, Cabangan, eight miles north of San Felipe, Luzon, Philippines,

Jul 1900. SOURCE: *ANJ* 37 (28 Jul 1900): 1142; "Richmond *Planet*, 8 Sep 1900; Cleveland *Gazette*, 15 Sep 1900.

Died 15 Jul 1900; buried 8 Jul 1902 in plot NEW 1047 at San Francisco National Cemetery. SOURCE: San Francisco National Cemetery.

WARD, John; Private; 24th Inf. Seminole Negro Scout, served 1870–94; brother of Scouts Scott and Bill Warrior; father of Scout Carolina Warrior; daughter Dolly, born ca. 1870; pension file in National Archives. SOURCE: Schubert, Consolidated List of Seminole Negro Scouts.

Seminole Negro Scout, born John Warrior, ca. 1847, in Arkansas, about 5'7"; one of original group of recruits, Aug 1870, Ft Duncan, TX; received Medal of Honor for valor with Lt. John Bullis on Pecos River, TX, Apr 1875; daughter Dolly married Scout Billy July; claimed that he contracted rheumatism while sergeant of the guard, Ft Duncan, Jan 1878; retired in 1895 because he could no longer mount a horse; stayed in Brackettville area, worked as gardener, received pension until he died in 1911; widow Julia received pension until he died in 1926. SOURCE: Schubert, *Black Valor*, 30, 34, 36, 39.

Born in Mexico (or Arkansas?); brother of Scouts John and Scott Warrior; Ht 5'8", black hair and eyes, black complexion; enlisted at Ft Duncan, 6 Aug 1870, age 25; name changed from Warrior to Ward by enlisting officer; one of eighteen original Scouts selected by Major Bliss; discharged 15 Feb 1871, reenlisted next day at Ft Duncan; discharged 31 Aug 1871, reenlisted next day at Ft Duncan; discharged 29 Feb 1872, reenlisted next day at Ft Duncan; discharged 9 Sep 1872, reenlisted 12 Sep 1872 at Ft Clark, TX; discharged as corporal 10 Sep 1873, reenlisted 12 Sep 1873 at Ft Clark; discharged as corporal 27 Mar 1874 at Ft Clark; enlisted 24 Dec 1874 at Ft Clark where he was discharged as sergeant 24 Jun 1875; with Scouts Pompey Factor and Isaac Payne awarded Medal of Honor for saving life of Lieutenant Bullis Apr 1875; enlisted 4 Oct 1875, discharged as private 4 Feb 1876 at Ft Clark; enlisted 8 Feb 1876 at Ft Clark; discharged as corporal 8 Aug 1876 at Camp Pecos, TX; enlisted 31 Jan 1877, discharged as private 31 Jan 1878 at Ft Clark; enlisted 17 May 1874, discharged as corporal 11 Dec 1874 at Ft Clark; enlisted 1 Feb 1878, discharged as sergeant 1 Feb 1879 at Ft Clark; enlisted 1 Feb 1879 at Ft Clark, discharged as sergeant 21 Mar 1880 at Camp Chinati, TX; enlisted 14 Dec 1881 at Ft Clark, discharged as private at Camp Myers, TX; enlisted 20 Dec 1882 at Ft Clark, discharged as private 23 Dec 1883, reenlisted 29 Dec 1883 at Camp Myers; discharged as private 29 Dec 1884, reenlisted 29 Dec 1884 at Ft Clark; discharged as private 25 Dec 1885 at Camp Pena Colorado, TX; enlisted as private for one year, discharged at Ft Clark four times, 8 Jan 1886–8 Jan 1890; enlisted 9 Jan 1890 at Ft Clark, discharged as private 8 Jul 1890 at Camp Neville Springs, TX; enlisted 9 Jul 1890 at Ft Clark, discharged as private and reenlisted

8 Jan 1891 at Ft Clark; discharged as corporal 8 Jul 1891 at Camp Palvo, TX; enlisted 19 Jul 1891 at Ft Clark; discharged as sergeant 18 Jan 1892, reenlisted next day at Camp Palvo; discharged as sergeant 18 Jul 1892, reenlisted next day at Camp Presidio, TX; discharged as private 18 Jan 1893, reenlisted next day at Ft Ringgold, TX; discharged as sergeant 18 Jul 1893, reenlisted next day at Ft Ringgold; discharged as sergeant 18 Jan 1894 at Camp San Pedro, TX; enlisted 1 Mar 1894 at Ft Clark; discharged as private 4 Oct 1894 at Ft Ringgold; 1880 Census lists wife Juda and children Laura, Dolly, Abby, Nancy, Caroline, Tony; died 24 May 1911; buried at Seminole Indian Scout Cemetery, Kinney County, TX. SOURCE: Swanson, 46.

‡Seminole-Negro Scout; awarded Medal of Honor for heroism, Pecos River, TX, with Lieutenant Bullis, 26 Apr 1875. SOURCE: Carroll, *The Black Military Experience*, 390.

Age 20 in original detachment of Scouts enlisted at Ft Duncan Aug 1870; promoted from private to corporal Mar 1878, appointed sergeant May 1878; daughter Dolly married Scout Billy July; pension file, widow certificate 7289965 and invalid certificate 961935; widow Julia. SOURCE: NARA Record Group 393, Special File; NARA, M 929, Roll 2; Porter, *The Negro on the American Frontier,* 476.

Sergeant, died 24 May 1911, buried at Seminole Indian Scout Cemetery, Kinney County, TX. SOURCE: Indian Scout Cemetery, Kinney County, Texas.

WARD, Joseph; Private; 9th Cav. Received Philippine Campaign Badge number 11794 for service as private in F/9th Cavalry; in 9th Cavalry at Ft Leavenworth, KS, Mar 1905. SOURCE: Philippine Campaign Badge list, 29 May 1905.

WARD, Nathan; Blacksmith; A/9th Cav. ‡At Ft Niobrara, NE, member of committee that drafted resolution of sympathy for William H. Carter, trumpeter, shot and killed in 1889. SOURCE: *ANJ* 26 (29 Jun 1889): 900.

‡Veteran of Indian wars and Philippine Insurrection; at Ft D. A. Russell, WY, in 1910; marksman. SOURCE: *Illustrated Review: Ninth Cavalry*, with picture.

Blacksmith, received Indian Wars Campaign Badge number 670 on 21 Oct 1908. SOURCE: Carroll, *Indian Wars Campaign Badge*, 19.

WARDEN, Clerk; C/25th Inf. Born in Kentucky; mulatto complexion; cannot read or write, age 21, 5 Sep 1870, at Ft McKavett, TX. SOURCE: Bierschwale, *Fort McKavett,* 109.

WARFIELD, Edward; Private; B/25th Inf. Enlisted 26 Jul 1905, discharged without honor 19 Nov 1906; one of fourteen men allowed back into Army by U.S. Senate court of inquiry in 1910. SOURCE: Powell, "Military

Record of the Enlisted Men Who Were Discharged Without Honor."

‡Dishonorable discharge, Brownsville, TX. SOURCE: SO 266, AGO, 9 Nov 1906.

‡One of fourteen cleared of involvement in Brownsville raid by court, 1910, and authorized to reenlist. SOURCE: Weaver, *The Brownsville Raid*, 248.

WARFIELD, Samuel A.; Corporal; F/9th Cav. ‡Private, E/9th Cavalry, arrived Ft Robinson, NE, 28 Feb 1894. SOURCE: Regt Returns, 9 Cav, Feb 1894.

‡Col. James Biddle, commander, 9th Cavalry, will accept William Jenkins, Andrew Murry, and Samuel A. Warfield, all old soldiers deserving to enlist, to keep his regiment from becoming training center for others. SOURCE: CO, 9 Cav, to AG, USA, 24 Feb 1894, Appointment File 3406 PRD 1894, Dillon.

Appointed corporal 16 Jul 1895; in F/9th Cavalry at Ft DuChesne, UT, Jan 1897. SOURCE: Ninth Cavalry, Roster of NCOs, 1897.

WARN, George; Corporal; I/9th Cav. ‡Promoted from lance corporal, Ft DuChesne, UT, Mar 1896. SOURCE: *ANJ* 33 (28 Mar 1896): 540.

‡Stationed at Ft Washakie, WY, late in 1896.

Appointed corporal 19 Mar 1896; in I/9th Cavalry at Ft Washakie, Jan 1897. SOURCE: Ninth Cavalry, Roster of NCOs, 1897.

WARREN, Daniel; Saddler; C/9th Cav. ‡Private, C/9th Cavalry, at Ft McKinney, WY, 1894.

Wounded in action at San Juan, Cuba, 1 Jul 1898. SOURCE: *Illustrated Review: Ninth Cavalry*.

Saddler, C/9th Cavalry, died 19 Jun 1904; buried at Ft Leavenworth National Cemetery, plot 3249. SOURCE: Ft Leavenworth National Cemetery.

WARREN, George; 1st Sgt; E/9th Cav. Received Philippine Campaign Badge number 11696 for service as quartermaster sergeant in E/9th Cavalry; in 9th Cavalry at Ft Leavenworth, KS, Mar 1905. SOURCE: Philippine Campaign Badge list, 29 May 1905.

‡Veteran of Philippine Insurrection; expert rifleman at Ft D. A. Russell, WY, in 1910; resident of Riding, TN. SOURCE: *Illustrated Review: Ninth Cavalry*, with picture.

WARREN, Henry; Private; K/24th Inf. Died at Camp Eagle Pass, TX, on 21 Mar 1893; buried at San Antonio National Cemetery, Section F, number 1131. SOURCE: San Antonio National Cemetery Locator.

WARREN, John; Private; I/25th Inf. Born in Prince Georges County, MD; Ht 5'6", black hair and eyes, black complexion; occupation laborer; enlisted at age 22, Washington, DC, 9 Mar 1885; arrived Ft Snelling, MN, 6 Oct 1886. SOURCE: Descriptive & Assignment Rolls of Recruits, 25 Inf.

WARREN, Samuel; Private; E/38th Inf. Died 17 Jul 1867; originally buried at Ft Hays, KS; reburied at Ft Leavenworth National Cemetery, plot H 3271. SOURCE: Ft Leavenworth National Cemetery.

WARREN, Walter; Private; I/49th Inf. ‡Died in the Philippines, 24 Oct 1900. SOURCE: *ANJ* 38 (10 Nov 1900): 259.

Died 22 Nov 1900; buried 14 Jul 1902 in plot NEW A1059 at San Francisco National Cemetery. SOURCE: San Francisco National Cemetery.

WARRIOR, Bill; Private; U.S. Army. Seminole Negro Scout, brother of Scouts Scott Warrior and John Ward, served 1871–82. SOURCE: Schubert, Consolidated List of Seminole Negro Scouts.

Born in Mexico, son of Tony Warrior, a collaborator of John Horse in departure for Indian Territory and trip to Mexico; Ht 5'5", black hair and eyes, black complexion; enlisted at Ft Duncan, TX, 9 Nov 1871, age 17; discharged 9 May 1872; reenlisted for six months and discharged at Ft Duncan three times, 10 May 1872–12 Nov 1873; enlisted 12 May 1873 at Ft Duncan; discharged at 1 Jun 1874 at Camp San Pedro, TX; enlisted 22 Aug 1874 at Ft Clark, TX; appointed corporal 31 Dec 1874; discharged as corporal and reenlisted 22 Feb 1875 at Ft Clark; discharged as corporal 9 Sep 1875 at Ft Supply, TX; enlisted for four months 4 Oct 1875 at Ft Clark where he was discharged as private 4 Feb 1876; enlisted 3 Oct 1876 at Ft Clark; discharged as private, reenlisted 13 Apr 1877 at Camp Rio Grande, TX; discharged, reenlisted 3 Apr 1877, Camp Howards C; discharged as private, reenlisted 3 Apr 1878 at Camp Howards C; appointed blacksmith 1 Jul 1878; discharged 24 Apr 1879 at Ft Clark; enlisted 3 Jun 1879 at Ft Clark where he was discharged 8 Jun 1890; enlisted 9 Jun 1880 at Ft Clark where he was discharged 8 Jun 1881; enlisted 9 Jun 1881 at Ft Clark; discharged 8 Jun 1882 at Camp Myers, TX; died 10 Apr 1893; buried at Seminole Indian Scout Cemetery, Kinney County, TX. SOURCE: Swanson, 47.

Corporal, U.S. Indian Scouts, born in Mexico about 1853; died 10 Apr 1903; buried at Seminole Indian Scout Cemetery, Kinney County, TX. SOURCE: Indian Scout Cemetery, Kinney County, Texas.

WARRIOR, Carolina; Sergeant; U.S. Army. Seminole Negro Scout, son of Scout John Ward; served 1893–94, 1901–14. SOURCE: Schubert, Consolidated List of Seminole Negro Scouts.

Born in Texas; Ht 5'11", black hair and eyes, copper complexion; enlisted at Ft Clark, TX, 11 Oct 1893, age 21; discharged 10 Apr 1894, reenlisted next day at Ft Ringgold,

TX; discharged 10 Oct 1894 at Ft Ringgold; enlisted 13 Jan 1895 at Ft Clark; discharged 12 Jul 1895 at Ft Ringgold; enlisted 9 Mar 1901 at Ft Clark; discharged 8 Mar 1904, reenlisted next day at Ft Ringgold; discharged 8 Mar 1907, reenlisted next day at Ft Clark; discharged as corporal 8 Mar 1910, reenlisted next day at Ft Clark; discharged as sergeant 8 Mar 1913, reenlisted next day at Ft Clark; transferred to 9th Cav 14 July 1914; William Warrior claimed that his grandfather, Carolina Warrior, died in the Philippines. SOURCE: Swanson, 47.

WARRIOR, Scott; Private; U.S. Army. Seminole Negro Scout, brother of Scouts John Ward and Bill Warrior, served 1871–74, 1876. SOURCE: Schubert, Consolidated List of Seminole Negro Scouts.

Born in Mexico; Ht 5'5", black hair and eyes, black complexion; enlisted at Ft Duncan, TX, 9 Nov 1871, age 15; discharged 9 May 1872, reenlisted next day at Ft Duncan; discharged 10 Nov 1872, reenlisted next day at Ft Duncan; discharged 11 May 1873, reenlisted next day at Ft Duncan; discharged 23 Nov 1873 at Ft Duncan; enlisted 6 Jan 1874 at Ft Duncan where he was discharged 6 Jul 1874; enlisted 8 Feb 1876 at Ft Clark, TX; discharged 8 Aug 1876 at Camp Pecos, TX. SOURCE: Swanson, 47.

WASHINGTON, Abe; Private; F/9th Cav. Back injury caused when beaten by Sgt. Emanuel Stance, sometime before summer of 1883. SOURCE: Kenner, *Buffalo Soldiers and Officers of the Ninth Cavalry*, 167.

Hospitalized with back injury, Ft Reno, OK, 1883, after being struck by 1st Sgt. Emanuel Stance. SOURCE: Schubert, *Voices of the Buffalo Soldier*, 135.

WASHINGTON, Alfred; Private; U.S. Army. Seminole Negro Scout, served 1888–89. SOURCE: Schubert, Consolidated List of Seminole Negro Scouts.

Born in Texas; Ht 5'8", black hair and eyes, black complexion; enlisted at Ft Clark, TX, 1 Jan 1888, age 24; discharged 10 Jan 1889. SOURCE: Swanson, 48.

WASHINGTON, Andrew; Private; U.S. Army. Seminole Negro Scout, served 1872–80; pension file in National Archives. SOURCE: Schubert, Consolidated List of Seminole Negro Scouts.

Born in Florida; accompanied Wild Cat and John Horse on trek to Mexico; Ht 5'11", black hair and eyes, black complexion; enlisted at Ft Duncan, TX, 2 Aug 1872, age 38: discharged Feb 2 1873, reenlisted 1 Mar 1873 at Ft Duncan; discharged 1 Sep 1873, reenlisted 20 Nov 1873 at Ft Duncan; discharged 20 Mar 1874, enlisted 7 May 1874 at Camp Palafox, TX; discharged 7 Dec 1874, reenlisted 1 Jan 1875 at Ft Duncan; discharged 18 Jul 1875 at Ft Concho, TX; enlisted 17 Oct 1876 at Ft Clark, TX; discharged, reenlisted 17 Apr 1877 at Camp Painted Comanche, TX; discharged, reenlisted 17 Apr 1878 at Camp Howards;

discharged 24 Apr 1879, reenlisted 1 Jul 1879 at Ft Clark; discharged 1 Jul 1880 at Ft Clark. SOURCE: Swanson, 48

In 1875 resided at Ft Duncan, age 30, with Clara age 40, Christova age 14, Susie age 4; pension VA file C 2613202. SOURCE: NARA Record Group, Special File; NARA, M 929, Roll 2.

WASHINGTON, Andrew; Private; U.S. Army. Seminole Negro Scout, served 1893–94. SOURCE: Schubert, Consolidated List of Seminole Negro Scouts.

Born in Texas; Ht 5'8", black hair and eyes, black complexion; enlisted at Ft Clark, TX, 14 Jan 1893; discharged 13 Jul 1893, reenlisted next day at Ft Ringgold, TX; discharged 10 Jan 1894 at Ft Ringgold. SOURCE: Swanson, 48.

WASHINGTON, Dan; Private; H/9th Cav. Died at Ft Davis, TX, on 8 Sep 1867; buried at San Antonio National Cemetery, Section I, number 1531. SOURCE: San Antonio National Cemetery Locator.

WASHINGTON, David L.; Cook; H/9th Cav. Received Philippine Campaign Badge number 11902 for service as corporal, K/49th Infantry, United States Volunteers, and G/25th Infantry; in 9th Cavalry at Ft Leavenworth, KS, Mar 1905. SOURCE: Philippine Campaign Badge list, 29 May 1905.

‡Veteran of Philippine Insurrection; at Ft D. A. Russell, WY, in 1910; marksman; resident of Leesburg, VA. SOURCE: *Illustrated Review: Ninth Cavalry*, with picture.

WASHINGTON, Ernest; Private; A/10th Cav. Buried at Ft Bayard, NM, in plot W 24. SOURCE: "Fort Bayard National Cemetery, Records of Burials."

Buried 29 Jun 1915, section B, row H, plot 24 at Ft Bayard. SOURCE: Erickson, Burials at Fort Bayard National Cemetery, NM.

WASHINGTON, Frank; Sergeant; B/9th Cav. Murdered, Ft DuChesne, UT, 7 Oct 1887, apparently by Pvt. Thomas Collins, rival for affections of laundress with whom he lived. SOURCE: Kenner, *Buffalo Soldiers and Officers of the Ninth Cavalry*, 234, 339.

Died 1 Oct 1887; buried at Santa Fe National Cemetery, NM, plot A-4 1108. SOURCE: Santa Fe National Cemetery, Records of Burials.

WASHINGTON, George; 1st Sgt; B/9th Cav. ‡First man to enlist in 9th Cavalry, 5 Aug 1866; assigned to A Troop. SOURCE: Hamilton, "History of the Ninth Cavalry," 1.

‡"Almost as an omen of the fame to be enjoyed by the new Regiment, the first man enlisted upon its rosters was George Washington, who signed for service on August 5, 1866, and who later was assigned to Troop A." SOURCE: Ninth Cavalry, *Historical and Pictorial Review*, 44.

‡Appointed sergeant, B/9th Cavalry, 1 May 1882. SOURCE: Roster, 9 Cav.

Army and Navy Journal erroneously reported 1st Sgt. George Washington as victim of shooting by Pvt. Thomas Collins at Ft DuChesne, UT, 1887; slain sergeant was Frank Washington, B/9th Cavalry. SOURCE: Kenner, *Buffalo Soldiers and Officers of the Ninth Cavalry*, 234, 339.

Appointed first sergeant 23 May 1895; in B/9th Cavalry at Ft DuChesne, Jan 1897. SOURCE: Ninth Cavalry, Roster of NCOs, 1897.

‡Retires as first sergeant, from Ft DuChesne. SOURCE: *ANJ* 34 (19 Jun 1897): 781.

Died 30 Jan 1920; buried in plot NAWS 483-A at San Francisco National Cemetery. SOURCE: San Francisco National Cemetery.

WASHINGTON, George; Private; C/10th Cav. Born in Mexico, about 1852; enlisted 1867, discharged at Ft Supply, OK, 1872; reenlisted in A/10th Cavalry and served at Fts Sill, OK, and Concho, TX, until discharged with disability, 1875; also known as Rafel Hannõn and Wash Robinson; remained in Oklahoma, first lived with Lucinda Marshall Carter, then married Clara Mountain; still alive in Dec 1905; text of documents from his pension file published. SOURCE: Schubert, *Voices of the Buffalo Soldier*, 226–37.

‡Enlisted in C/10th Cavalry at St Louis, MO. SOURCE: LS, 10 Cav, 1866–67.

‡Original member of 10th Cavalry; in C Troop when organized, Ft Leavenworth, KS, 18 Feb 1867. SOURCE: McMiller, "Buffalo Soldiers," 70.

‡On extra duty in C/10th Cavalry at Ft Leavenworth. SOURCE: CO, 10 Cav, to Adj, Ft Leavenworth, 15 May 1867, LS, 10 Cav, 1866–67.

WASHINGTON, George; Sergeant; K/9th Cav. Native of Washington, DC; enlisted for K/9th Cavalry, Oct 1869, with prior infantry experience. SOURCE: Kenner, *Buffalo Soldiers and Officers of the Ninth Cavalry*, 335.

WASHINGTON, George; F/9th Cav. Born in Louisiana; mulatto complexion; can read and write, age 24, Jul 1870, at Ft McKavett, TX. SOURCE: Bierschwale, *Fort McKavett*, 98.

WASHINGTON, George; Private; U.S. Army. Born in Arkansas, nephew of John Horse; Ht 5'9", black hair and eyes, black complexion; enlisted at Ft Duncan, TX, 16 Aug 1870, age 28; discharged, reenlisted same or next day at Ft Duncan, 15 Feb 1871–1 Mar 1872; discharged at Ft Duncan 31 Aug 1872, reenlisted 10 Sept 1872 at Ft Duncan; discharged 10 Mar 1873, reenlisted 10 May 1873 at Ft Duncan; discharged 1 Nov 1873 at Camp Comanche, TX, enlisted 1 Jan 1874 at Ft Duncan; discharged 1 Jul 1874 at Camp Palafox, TX; shot in stomach by gunslinger King Fisher at Blue Saloon, Eagle Pass, TX, Christmas 1874, managed to wound Fisher. SOURCE: Swanson, 49. *See* JOHNSON, Daniel, Private, U.S. Army

Seminole Negro Scout, served 1870–74; father of Scout Sam Washington. SOURCE: Schubert, Consolidated List of Seminole Negro Scouts.

Recuperating from dangerous gunshot wound in 1875, age 40, resided at Ft Duncan with Mamey age 9, Amelia age 21, Millie age 2, Kibbitts age 3, Lizzie age 2, and Rose age 40. SOURCE: NARA Record Group 393, Special File.

Corporal, died of stomach wound received in barroom gun battle with whites near Eagle Pass, 1875. SOURCE: Porter, *The Negro on the American Frontier*, 485.

WASHINGTON, George; Private; K/25th Inf. With Pvt. Robert Gregory, A/9th Cavalry, convicted, Ft Stockton, TX, Dec 1871, of breaking into and looting home of local Mexican women; received dishonorable discharge and sentenced to three years. SOURCE: Leiker, *Racial Borders*, 79, 207.

WASHINGTON, George; 1st Sgt; M/9th Cav. Native of Alabama; trumpeter, on third enlistment when served in M/9th Cavalry, Ft Stanton, NM, Dec 1876, and brawled with Sgt. Emanuel Stance; prevented from killing Stance by Cpl. George McCampbell and Pvt. Louis Horton; consistent "excellent" evaluations; later served as first sergeant for nearly a decade. SOURCE: Kenner, *Buffalo Soldiers and Officers of the Ninth Cavalry*, 165–66.

‡Detached from post, Ft Bayard, NM, and detailed in charge of music, Ft Cummings, NM, late 1880. SOURCE: Billington, *New Mexico's Buffalo Soldiers*, 116.

‡Authorized four-month furlough from Ft Washakie, WY. SOURCE: *ANJ* 24 (5 Feb 1887): 550.

‡Recently shot and killed at Ft DuChesne, UT, by Private Collins of M/9th Cavalry. SOURCE: *ANJ* 25 (10 Dec 1887): 382.

WASHINGTON, George; Private; 10th Cav. At Ft Davis, TX, served as soldier servant or striker for Lt. John Bigelow, Jr., for extra pay; on 14 Jan 1885 successfully requested increase in pay from $5 to $10 per month because he cooks and waits. SOURCE: Bigelow, *Garrison Tangles*, 44, 78–79.

WASHINGTON, George; Private; I/10th Cav. Died 8 Feb 1889; buried at Ft Leavenworth National Cemetery, plot 1839. SOURCE: Ft Leavenworth National Cemetery.

WASHINGTON, George; Private; G/10th Cav. Died 25 Mar 1890; originally buried at Ft Grant, AZ; reburied at Santa Fe National Cemetery, NM, plot A-1 755. SOURCE: Santa Fe National Cemetery, Records of Burials.

WASHINGTON, George; Sergeant; K/9th Cav. ‡Appointed 10 Jul 1892. SOURCE: Roster, 9 Cav.

Appointed sergeant 10 Jul 1892; in K/9th Cavalry at Ft Robinson, NE, Jan 1897. SOURCE: Ninth Cavalry, Roster of NCOs, 1897.

WASHINGTON, Henry; Private; U.S. Army. Seminole Negro Scout, served 1882–95. SOURCE: Schubert, Consolidated List of Seminole Negro Scouts.

Born in Tennessee; Ht 5'10", black hair and eyes, black complexion; enlisted at Ft Clark, TX, 20 Nov 1882, age 30; discharged 21 Nov 1883, reenlisted next day at Camp Myers, TX; discharged 31 Aug 1884 at Ft Clark; enlisted at Ft Clark 27 Dec 1884; discharged 26 Dec 1885 at Camp Neville Springs, TX; enlisted and discharged three times at Ft Clark, 7 Jan 1886–8 Jan 1889; enlisted 8 Jan 1889 at Ft Clark; discharged 8 Jan 1890 at Camp Neville Springs; enlisted 9 Jan 1890 at Ft Clark; discharged 8 Jul 1890, reenlisted next day at Camp Neville Springs; discharged 8 Jan 1891, reenlisted next day at Ft Clark; discharged 8 Jul 1891 at Camp Palvo, TX; enlisted 19 Jul 1891 at Ft Clark; discharged 18 Jul 1892 at Camp Presidio, TX; enlisted 17 Aug 1892 at Ft Clark; discharged 16 Feb 1893 at Agua Nueva, TX; enlisted, reenlisted next day at Ft Ringgold, TX, 17 Feb 1893–15 Feb 1895; enlisted for three years 17 Feb 1895 at Ft Ringgold where he was discharged for disability 25 Sep 1895. SOURCE: Swanson, 50.

WASHINGTON, Henry F.; Private; G/25th Inf. Civil War veteran, served in 5th Massachusetts Cavalry; enlisted for 40th Infantry, Boston, MA, 1867; transferred to 25th Infantry, 1869; enlisted in 9th Cavalry, Ft Davis, TX, 1875, and served with regiment for ten years; hospitalized twice with rheumatism, Ft Reno, OK, 1885, and Ft Sisseton, SD, 1886; went from Indian Territory to Minnesota, 1885, and enlisted in old company of 25th Infantry; served another five years, lived in Missoula, MT, and Minneapolis, MN, then entered Soldiers Home, 1904, where he died 18 Apr 1927. SOURCE: Dobak and Phillips, *The Black Regulars*, 274–77.

‡Sergeant, E/25th Infantry, stationed at Ft Buford, ND, 1891. SOURCE: Cleveland *Gazette*, 19 Sep 1891.

‡Former private, G/25th Infantry; Chaplain Steward attended funeral of his child, Missoula, 26 Dec 1892. SOURCE: Monthly Report, Chaplain Steward, Dec 1892.

WASHINGTON, James; Private; G/25th Inf. Born in Gainsville, AL; Ht 5'10", black hair and eyes, brown complexion; occupation laborer; resided in Loudon County, VA, when enlisted 28 Aug 1886, age 24, at Washington, DC; assigned to G/25th Infantry; arrived Ft Snelling, MN, 14 Dec 1886. SOURCE: Descriptive & Assignment Rolls of Recruits, 25 Inf.

WASHINGTON, James H.; Private; A/24th Inf. ‡Died of dysentery in the Philippines, 24 Feb 1900. SOURCE: *ANJ* 37 (10 Mar 1900): 659.

Died in the Philippines 24 Feb 1900; body received 29 Mar 1901 at San Francisco National Cemetery, buried in plot EAST 1367. SOURCE: San Francisco National Cemetery.

WASHINGTON, John; Private; I/10th Cav. ‡Original member of 10th Cavalry; in troop when organized, Ft Riley, KS, 15 Aug 1867. SOURCE: McMiller, "Buffalo Soldiers," 76.

Died 8 Feb 1869 of gunshot wound at Ft Wallace, KS. SOURCE: Regimental Returns, 10th Cavalry, 1869.

Died 8 Feb 1869; buried at Ft Leavenworth National Cemetery, plot C 1939. SOURCE: Ft Leavenworth National Cemetery.

WASHINGTON, John; Private; G/25th Inf. Died 22 Aug 1903; buried at Ft Bayard, NM, in plot L 39. SOURCE: "Fort Bayard National Cemetery, Records of Burials."

John Washington, C/25th Infantry, buried 22 Aug 1903, section A, row S, plot 45, at Ft Bayard. SOURCE: Erickson, Burials at Fort Bayard National Cemetery, NM.

WASHINGTON, John H.; Sergeant; D/9th Cav. With Captain Dodge at battle at Milk River, CO, 2–10 Oct 1879. SOURCE: Miller, *Hollow Victory*, 167, 206–7.

WASHINGTON, Lincoln; Sqdn Sgt Maj; 9th Cav. ‡Enlisted at Baltimore, MD, 21 Jul 1885; second lieutenant, 48th Infantry, Sep 1899–30 Jun 1901; served in the Philippines Jan 1900–1 May 1901 and 31 May 1907–15 May 1909; squadron sergeant major, 9th Cavalry, and expert rifleman at Ft D. A. Russell, WY, in 1910. SOURCE: *Illustrated Review: Ninth Cavalry*.

‡Appointed corporal, B/9th Cavalry, 28 Dec 1891. SOURCE: Roster, 9 Cav.

‡Promoted from corporal to sergeant, B/9th Cavalry, Ft DuChesne, UT, Jan 1895. SOURCE: *ANJ* 32 (26 Jan 1895): 358.

Appointed sergeant 16 Jan 1895; in B/9th Cavalry at Ft DuChesne, Jan 1897. SOURCE: Ninth Cavalry, Roster of NCOs, 1897.

‡Appointed second lieutenant, 48th Infantry, from squadron sergeant major, 9th Cavalry, Ft DuChesne. SOURCE: *ANJ* 37 (23 Sep 1899): 81; *ANJ* 37 (9 Dec 1899): 284.

‡Mentioned as second lieutenant, A/48th Infantry. SOURCE: Beasley, *Negro Trailblazers*, 284.

‡One of nineteen officers of 48th Infantry recommended as regular Army second lieutenants. SOURCE: CG, DivPI, Manila, 8 Feb 1901, to AGO, AGO File 355163.

‡Commander, 10th Cavalry, has no objection to his enlistment in 10th Cavalry, provided he distinctly understands he will not be entitled to any special privilege by reason of marriage; no vacant quarters on post for enlisted families at Ft Robinson, NE. SOURCE: Endorsement, CO,

Ft Robinson, 22 Jun 1902, to request of Washington to re-enlist as married, LS, 10 Cav.

‡Discharged as farrier, K/10th Cavalry, Jul 1905. SOURCE: Regt Returns, 10 Cav, Jul 1905.

‡Squadron sergeant major, 9th Cavalry; advised to seek information he wants from Adjutant General; chief clerk is not authorized to give it. SOURCE: Chief Clerk, DeptMo, to Washington, 13 Apr 1910, Misc Records, DeptMo.

WASHINGTON, Littleton; Private; K/25th Inf. Born in La Fourche, LA; Ht 5'5", black complexion; occupation soldier; enlisted in A/39th Infantry for three years on 29 Jan 1867, age 24, at Greenville, LA; promoted to corporal 24 Mar 1867; reduced as incompetent 14 Apr 1867; transferred to K/25th Infantry at Jackson Bks, LA, 20 Apr 1869. SOURCE: Descriptive Roll of A/39th Inf.

WASHINGTON, Morgan G.; Corporal; B/25th Inf. Born in Nashville, TN; Ht 5'8", black hair and eyes, yellow complexion; occupation shoemaker; enlisted in 25th Infantry at age 25, Nashville, 27 Apr 1886; arrived Ft Snelling, MN, 30 Aug 1886. SOURCE: Descriptive & Assignment Rolls of Recruits, 25 Inf.

‡Private, C/24th Infantry; on extra duty as saddler, Quartermaster Department, Ft Huachuca, AZ, 3 Jun–20 Jul 1893. SOURCE: Order 80, Ft Huachuca, 3 Jun 1893, and Order 104, Ft Huachuca, 20 Jul 1893, Name File, 24 Inf.

‡Killed in action at Arayat, Philippines, in ambush, 5 Jan 1900; died of stomach wounds; thirteen-year veteran, native of Nashville; served in both 24th and 25th Infantry; "He was respected by all who knew him." SOURCE: Richmond *Planet*, 17 Feb 1900; Nankivell, *History of the Twenty-fifth Infantry*, 90.

Died 5 Jan 1900; buried in plot ES 1217 at San Francisco National Cemetery. SOURCE: San Francisco National Cemetery.

WASHINGTON, Peter; Private; G/10th Cav. ‡Original member of 10th Cavalry; in troop when organized, Ft Leavenworth, KS, 5 Jul 1867. SOURCE: McMiller, "Buffalo Soldiers," 74.

Died 30 Jul 1867 of cholera at Wilson Creek, KS. SOURCE: Regimental Returns, 10th Cavalry, 1867.

WASHINGTON, Philip; Private; B/10th Cav. Tried by court martial, Ft Duncan, TX, Dec 1877. SOURCE: Kinevan, *Frontier Cavalryman*, 79.

WASHINGTON, Richard; Sergeant; B/9th Cav. ‡Appointed sergeant 28 Dec 1891. SOURCE: Roster, 9 Cav.

‡Resigned as sergeant, Ft DuChesne, UT, Jan 1895. SOURCE: *ANJ* 32 (26 Jan 1895): 358.

Private, B/9th Cavalry, died 18 Dec 1896; originally buried at Ft DuChesne; reburied at Santa Fe National Cemetery, NM, plot A-3 1073-C. SOURCE: Santa Fe National Cemetery, Records of Burials.

WASHINGTON, Sam; Private; U.S. Army. Seminole Negro Scout, son of Scout George Washington; served 1893–1913. SOURCE: Schubert, Consolidated List of Seminole Negro Scouts.

Born in Texas, son of Scout George Washington; Ht 5'7", black hair and eyes, black complexion; enlisted at Ft Clark, TX, 13 Jan 1893, age 23; discharged 12 Jul 1893, reenlisted next day at Ft Ringgold, TX; discharged 12 Jan 1894, reenlisted next day at Camp San Pedro, TX; discharged, reenlisted at Ft Ringgold five times, 12 Jul 1894–16 Jan 1904; discharged, reenlisted at Ft Clark three times, 15 Jan 1907–17 Jan 1913; honorably discharged 31 Jul 1914 at Ft Clark. SOURCE: Swanson, 19

Married. SOURCE: NARA, M 929, Roll 2.

Buried at Seminole Indian Scout Cemetery, Kinney County, TX. SOURCE: Indian Scout Cemetery, Kinney County, Texas.

WASHINGTON, William; Sqdn Sgt Maj; 2nd Sqdn/9th Cav. ‡Born in New Orleans; occupation waiter; mulatto; enlisted in M/9th Cavalry, 12 Sep 1883; reenlisted in E/9th Cavalry, 25 Sep 1888 and 21 Oct 1893; transferred to F/9th Cavalry, 17 May 1894; commissioned first lieutenant, 8th Infantry, U.S. Volunteers, 4 Aug 1898; in F/9th Cavalry, 9 Mar 1899; cited for highly courageous conduct against enemy, Camalig, Albay, Philippines, 8 Nov 1900, by Capt. George B. Pritchard, 5th Cavalry; sergeant major, 2nd Squadron, 9th Cavalry, 1 Oct 1901; two children with first wife Marcia, who died at Ft Walla Walla, WA, Aug 1903; married Louise E. Roberts of Baltimore, age 21, single, 6 Jul 1910; kicked in head by mule just before retirement, 1910; died 1 Feb 1920 and buried in national cemetery, Baltimore; widow resided at 758 George Street, Baltimore, and remarried 14 May 1921, becoming Louise E. Johnson, 1514 12th Street, NW, Washington, DC; her claim for pension rejected because his death of cerebral hemorrhage took place nearly ten years after his retirement. SOURCE: VA File WC 894780, William Washington.

‡Appointed first sergeant, E/9th Cavalry, 21 Jun 1893; sergeant since 8 Dec 1888. SOURCE: Roster, 9 Cav.

‡Resides with wife on Laundress Row, Ft Robinson, NE, Aug 1893. SOURCE: Medical History, Ft Robinson.

‡First sergeant, E/9th Cavalry; letter from Adjutant General's Office, 7 Oct 1893, concerns his reenlistment.

‡Ranked number 36 among carbine sharpshooters with 75.14 percent; third qualification. SOURCE: GO 1, AGO, 2 Jan 1894.

‡Transfer from Hospital Corps to G/9th Cavalry disapproved by letter, Department of the Platte, 4 Oct 1895.

Appointed first sergeant 1 May 1895; in F/9th Cavalry at Ft DuChesne, UT, Jan 1897. SOURCE: Ninth Cavalry, Roster of NCOs, 1897.

‡First sergeant, F/9th Cavalry, commissioned first lieutenant, 8th Volunteer Infantry, after Spanish-American War. SOURCE: Cashin, *Under Fire with the Tenth Cavalry*, 359–60.

‡Commissioned for gallantry at Santiago, Cuba, 1–2 Jul 1898. SOURCE: Richmond *Planet*, 13 Aug 1898; Thweatt, *What the Newspapers Say*, 9.

‡Served with 9th Cavalry in the Philippines, 16 Sep 1900–16 Sep 1902 and 31 May 1907–15 May 1909; squadron sergeant major, 9th Cavalry, from 1 Oct 1901; sharpshooter, 1889–96, 1900–1901, 1906–09. SOURCE: *Illustrated Review: Ninth Cavalry*, with picture.

‡Major, Milton T. Dean, former sergeant major, 9th Cavalry, served with William Washington in 9th Cavalry from 1903 at Ft Walla Walla to Washington's retirement, May 1910. SOURCE: VA File WC 894780, William Washington.

‡*See* PENN, William H., First Sergeant, K/9th Cavalry

WASHINGTON, William; Private; C/10th Cav. Private, received Indian Wars Campaign Badge number 1409 on 15 Jul 1909; cancelled 23 Dec 1909. SOURCE: Carroll, *Indian Wars Campaign Badge*, 40.

WASHINGTON, William H.; D/24th Inf. Born in Alabama; black complexion; can read and write, age 30, Jul 1870, at Ft McKavett, TX. SOURCE: Bierschwale, *Fort McKavett*, 96.

WASLEM, James; Corporal; A/39th Inf. Civil War veteran, served in D/117th U.S. Colored Infantry; sentence of five years for involvement in New Iberia, LA, mutiny, Jul 1867, reduced to six months. SOURCE: Dobak and Phillips, *The Black Regulars*, 222.

WATERFORD, George; Blacksmith; F/9th Cav. At Ft Robinson, NE, Nov 1887, fined $10 for disobedience to Sgt. Emanuel Stance. SOURCE: Kenner, *Buffalo Soldiers and Officers of the Ninth Cavalry*, 171.

‡Fined $10 for absence without leave, disturbance in troop dining room, and insubordination to 1st Sgt. Emanuel Stance, all at Ft Robinson, on 22 Nov 1887. SOURCE: Order 238, 2 Dec 1887, Post Orders, Ft Robinson.

WATERS, Benjamin; Private; 9th Cav. Received Philippine Campaign Badge number 11750 for service as private in M/25th Infantry; in 9th Cavalry at Ft Leavenworth, KS, Mar 1905. SOURCE: Philippine Campaign Badge list, 29 May 1905.

WATKINS, Albert; Private; B/10th Cav. At Ft Stockton, TX, 1879; witness in court martial of Lt. William H. Beck, 10th Cavalry, San Antonio, TX, Feb 1879. SOURCE: Kinevan, *Frontier Cavalryman*, 287.

WATKINS, Benjamin; Private; D/9th Cav. Private, D/9th Cavalry, when sexually molested by 1st Sgt. James Dickerson, D/9th Cavalry, Ft Riley, KS, 1883. SOURCE: Kenner, *Buffalo Soldiers and Officers of the Ninth Cavalry*, 273.

WATKINS, Benjamin; Private; 9th Cav. Injured hand sparring with another soldier, "just boxing in fun." SOURCE: Dobak and Phillips, *The Black Regulars*, 150.

WATKINS, George; Private; I/10th Cav. ‡Original member of 10th Cavalry; in troop when organized, Ft Riley, KS, 15 Aug 1867. SOURCE: McMiller, "Buffalo Soldiers," 76.

Shot and killed by trooper, late 1870. SOURCE: Leckie, *The Buffalo Soldiers*, 56.

Died 4 Dec 1870, wounded by A. E. Tracy in self-defense at Camp Supply, OK. SOURCE: Regimental Returns, 10th Cavalry, 1870.

WATKINS, Henry; Private; A/38th Inf. ‡Arrested for part in soldiers' revolt at Ft Cummings, NM, autumn 1867; acquitted by court martial. SOURCE: Billington, *New Mexico's Buffalo Soldiers*, 40, 42.

One of six 38th Infantrymen acquitted by military court of mutiny, New Mexico, 1868. SOURCE: Dobak and Phillips, *The Black Regulars*, 324.

WATKINS, Isaac; Sergeant; 9th Cav. Received Philippine Campaign Badge number 11864 for service as sergeant in H/10th Cavalry; in 9th Cavalry at Ft Leavenworth, KS, Mar 1905. SOURCE: Philippine Campaign Badge list, 29 May 1905.

WATKINS, Jacob; Private; H/10th Cav. Born in Bowling Green, KY, 1855; enlisted Bowling Green, 11 Sep 1876; Ht 5'6", black complexion, eyes, and hair; occupation farmer and laborer; joined B/10th Cavalry 10 Dec 1876 at St. Louis, MO; discharged Ft Stockton, TX, 10 Sep 1881; enlisted St. Louis, 8 Oct 1881; joined H/10th Cavalry 11 Apr 1881 at Jefferson Bks, MO; stationed 1 Jan 1884–1 Apr 1885 at Ft Davis, TX, 2 May 1885–May 1886 at Ft Grant, AZ, May 1886 until discharged at Ft Apache, AZ, 7 Oct 1886; married Frances (Fannie) Washington 28 Nov 1891; employed three to four years by Shockley Transfer Company; died at 813 Brooklyn Ave., Kansas City, MO, 2 Sep 1899; son John Alfred born 24 Feb 1900, Kansas City. SOURCE: Sayre, *Warriors of Color*, 475–92.

‡Private Watkins, H/10th Cavalry, served as Capt. John Bigelow's driver between Ft Grant and Crittenden, AZ, 1885; served in B/10th Cavalry at Ft Duncan, TX, 1877, when Bigelow first joined regiment; also served under Bigelow at Ft Stockton. SOURCE: Bigelow, *On the Bloody Trail of Geronimo*, 91.

Private Iacob [*sic*] Watkins in H/10th Cavalry stationed at Bonita Cañon Camp, AZ, but absent or on detached service 30 Apr 1886. SOURCE: Tagg, *The Camp at Bonita Cañon*, 232.

WATKINS, James M.; QM Sgt; C/10th Cav. ‡Sergeant, at Ft Apache, AZ, 1890, subscribed $.50 to testimonial to General Grierson. SOURCE: List of subscriptions, 23 Apr 1890, 10th Cavalry papers, MHI.

‡Corporal, served in 10th Cavalry in Cuba, 1898. SOURCE: Cashin, *Under Fire with the Tenth Cavalry*, 339.

‡Quartermaster sergeant at Ft Robinson, NE, 1902; detailed to color guard. SOURCE: SO 62, 9 Jul 1902, Special Orders, 10 Cav.

‡Retirement address: 1514 S Street, NW, Washington, DC; knew John C. Proctor in 10th Cavalry. SOURCE: VA File XC 2659372, John C. Proctor.

Sergeant, C/10th Cavalry, received Indian Wars Campaign Badge number 1410 on 15 Jul 1909; cancelled 23 Dec 1909; received badge number 1467 on 10 Feb 1910. SOURCE: Carroll, *Indian Wars Campaign Badge*, 40, 42.

WATKINS, Leroy; Corporal; F/24th Inf. ‡Died of variola in the Philippines. SOURCE: *ANJ* 37 (3 Mar 1900): 635.

Died 23 Feb 1900; buried in plot NA 248 at San Francisco National Cemetery. SOURCE: San Francisco National Cemetery.

WATKINS, Morgan; Private; I/25th Inf. Died at Ft Davis, TX, on 10 Oct 1879; buried at San Antonio National Cemetery, Section I, number 1501. SOURCE: San Antonio National Cemetery Locator.

WATKINS, Wesley; QM Sgt; F/9th Cav. ‡Unassigned recruit at Ft Robinson, NE, awaiting assignment, Jul 1892. SOURCE: Regt Returns, 9 Cav, Jul 1892.

‡Reenlisted; warrant as corporal continuous since 2 Apr 1897. SOURCE: *ANJ* 34 (17 Jun 1897): 854.

Received Philippine Campaign Badge number 11795 for service as corporal in F/10th Cavalry; in 9th Cavalry at Ft Leavenworth, KS, Mar 1905. SOURCE: Philippine Campaign Badge list, 29 May 1905.

Quartermaster Sergeant Wesley, F/10th Cavalry; died 28 Sep 1909; buried at Ft Leavenworth National Cemetery, plot G 3654. SOURCE: Ft Leavenworth National Cemetery.

WATKINS, William; Private; K/25th Inf. Text of Works Progress Administration interview with Watkins, who was born a slave in Virginia in 1850, served during early 1870s, received dishonorable discharge because of animosity of Sgt. Jeff Walker, K/25th Infantry, and resided with William Branch at 322 Utah St., San Antonio, TX, in 1930s. SOURCE: Schubert, *Voices of the Buffalo Soldier*, 53–54.

WATKINS, William; Private; E/10th Cav. ‡Killed in saloon, San Angelo, TX, Jan 1881. SOURCE: Leckie, *The Buffalo Soldiers*, 235.

At Ft Concho, TX, 1881; murdered by local sheep rancher. SOURCE: Leiker, *Racial Borders*, 123.

Died 1 Feb 1881 of pistol shot wounds at San Angelo. SOURCE: Regimental Returns, 10th Cavalry, 1881.

Shot and killed by white civilian, San Angelo, winter 1881. SOURCE: Dobak and Phillips, *The Black Regulars*, 238.

Died at Ft Concho on 1 Feb 1881; buried at San Antonio National Cemetery, Section E, number 819. SOURCE: San Antonio National Cemetery Locator.

WATLINGTON, Wade H.; Corporal; B/25th Inf. Enlisted 12 Dec 1895; discharged corporal C/25th Infantry 11 Dec 1898, character excellent; reenlisted 3 Mar 1899, discharged as corporal 2 Mar 1902, character excellent; reenlisted 5 Mar 1902, discharged as sergeant Mar 1905, character excellent; reenlisted 3 Mar 1905, discharged without honor as corporal of B/25th Infantry 22 Nov 1906, Brownsville, TX. SOURCE: Powell, "Military Record of the Enlisted Men Who Were Discharged Without Honor."

‡Dishonorable discharge, Brownsville. SOURCE: SO 266, AGO, 9 Nov 1906.

WATSON, Adam; Private; B/38th Inf. Adam or Allen Watson died 9 Mar 1867 or 1868; buried at Ft Leavenworth National Cemetery, plot C 1522. SOURCE: Ft Leavenworth National Cemetery.

WATSON, Allen; Private; B/38th Inf. *See* WATSON, Adam, Private, B/38th Infantry

WATSON, Isaac; Private; F/25th Inf. ‡Died of malaria in the Philippines, 20 Dec 1899. SOURCE: *ANJ* 37 (30 Dec 1899): 412.

Died 20 Dec 1899; buried in plot ESIDE639 at San Francisco National Cemetery. SOURCE: San Francisco National Cemetery.

WATSON, John; Corporal; K/25th Inf. Born in Westmoreland, VA; Ht 5'7", black complexion; occupation soldier; enlisted in A/39th Infantry for three years on 3 Sep 1866, age 21, at Ft Pike, LA; transferred to K/25th Infantry at Jackson Bks, LA, 20 Apr 1869. SOURCE: Descriptive Roll of A/39th Inf.

WATSON, Peter; Private; U.S. Army. Comrade of Augustus Walley at Colored Detachment, Columbus Bks, OH, recruit depot before Walley's 1893 discharge. SOURCE: Schubert, *Black Valor*, 47.

WATSON, Samuel; M/9th Cav. ‡Private in C/10th Cavalry, sick in post hospital, Ft Riley, KS, Apr 1868. SOURCE: LR, Det 10 Cav, 1868–69.

Born in Kentucky; black complexion; cannot read or write, age 22, Jul 1870, in M/9th Cavalry at Ft McKavett, TX. SOURCE: Bierschwale, *Fort McKavett*, 100.

WATSON, Walter; Private; F/10th Cav. Died 2 Jun 1877 of disease at Ft Concho, TX. SOURCE: Regimental Returns, 10th Cavalry, 1877.

Died at Ft Concho on 1 Jun 1877; buried at San Antonio National Cemetery, Section E, number 878. SOURCE: San Antonio National Cemetery Locator.

WATSON, William S.; Private; G/10th Cav. ‡Sick at Ft Robinson, NE, hospital, 18 Jun 1906; returned to Ft D. A. Russell, WY, 14 Oct 1906. SOURCE: Regt Returns, 10 Cav.

Died 23 Feb 1928; buried in plot R 5 at San Francisco National Cemetery. SOURCE: San Francisco National Cemetery.

WATTS, David A.; Farrier; I/10th Cav. In Troop I/10th Cavalry stationed at Bonita Cañon Camp, AZ, 30 Jun 1886. SOURCE: Tagg, *The Camp at Bonita Cañon*, 231.

WAYES, Armsted; Private; F/9th Cav. Died at Ft McKavett, TX, on 1 Jun 1870; buried at San Antonio National Cemetery, Section E, number 892. SOURCE: San Antonio National Cemetery Locator.

WEARING, Thomas; Private; 25th Inf. Born in Charleston, SC; Ht 5'7", black hair and eyes, fair complexion; occupation waiter; enlisted at age 21, Charleston, 10 Jun 1881; left recruit depot, David's Island, NY, 2 Jul 1881, arrived Ft Randall, SD, 7 Jul 1881. SOURCE: Descriptive & Assignment Rolls of Recruits, 25 Inf.

WEATHERLY, James; Corporal; F/9th Cav. ‡Private and principal musician, F/9th Cavalry band, Ft DuChesne, UT. SOURCE: *ANJ* 34 (29 May 1897): 733.

Received Philippine Campaign Badge number 11797 for service as trumpeter in F/9th Cavalry; in 9th Cavalry at Ft Leavenworth, KS, Mar 1905. SOURCE: Philippine Campaign Badge list, 29 May 1905.

‡Veteran of Indian wars and Philippine Insurrection; corporal at Ft D. A. Russell, WY, in 1910; marksman; resident of Marshall Co., MS. SOURCE: *Illustrated Review: Ninth Cavalry*, with picture.

WEATHERS, Reuben; Private; L/25th Inf. ‡Died of malaria in the Philippines, 29 Dec 1899. SOURCE: *ANJ* 37 (13 Dec 1900): 463.

‡Died of spinal meningitis at Malabacat, Philippines, last week of December 1899. SOURCE: Richmond *Planet*, 10 Feb 1900.

Rheuben Weathers died in Manila, 29 Dec 1899; buried in plot E.S 1221 at San Francisco National Cemetery. SOURCE: San Francisco National Cemetery.

WEBB, Benjamin; Private; H/24th Inf. ‡At Ft Supply, Indian Territory, 1888; subscriber to Cleveland *Gazette*. SOURCE: Cleveland *Gazette*, 25 Feb 1888.

‡At Ft Grant, AZ, 1890. *See* BERRY, Edward, Sergeant, H/24th Infantry

Died 4 Dec 1908; buried at Santa Fe National Cemetery, NM, plot H 718. SOURCE: Santa Fe National Cemetery, Records of Burials.

WEBB, Charles; Private; D/24th Inf. Born in West Virginia; buried at Ft McKavett, TX, before 17 May 1879; body removed to National Cemetery, San Antonio, TX, 23 Nov 1883. SOURCE: Bierschwale, *Fort McKavett*, 123.

Died at Ft McKavett on 27 Mar 1870; buried at San Antonio National Cemetery, Section E, number 839. SOURCE: San Antonio National Cemetery Locator.

WEBB, John; Private; 25th Inf. Born in Richmond, VA; Ht 5'6", black hair and eyes, dark complexion; occupation hostler; enlisted at age 24, Charleston, SC, 18 May 1881; left recruit depot, David's Island, NY, 2 Jul 1881, arrived Ft Randall, SD, 7 Jul 1881. SOURCE: Descriptive & Assignment Rolls of Recruits, 25 Inf.

WEBB, Moses; Sergeant; E/9th Cav. Received Philippine Campaign Badge number 11751 for service as private in E/9th Cavalry; in 9th Cavalry at Ft Leavenworth, KS, Mar 1905. SOURCE: Philippine Campaign Badge list, 29 May 1905.

‡Veteran of Philippine Insurrection; sergeant in E/9th Cavalry at Ft D. A. Russell, WY, in 1910; resident of Oxford, MS. SOURCE: *Illustrated Review: Ninth Cavalry*, with picture.

WEBB, Will; Private; C/24th Inf. *See* WEBB, William, Private, C/24th Infantry

WEBB, William; Private; C/24th Inf. ‡Killed in action at Manicling, Luzon, Philippines, northeast of San Isidro, 4 Jul 1900. SOURCE: Muller, *The Twenty Fourth Infantry*, 38.

‡Killed at Manicling, 4 Jul 1900. SOURCE: *ANJ* 37 (14 Jul 1900): 1083.

Pvt. William Webb, C/24th Infantry, died 4 Jul 1900; buried in plot N/A 334 at San Francisco National Cemetery. SOURCE: San Francisco National Cemetery.

WEBB, William K.; Sergeant; C/25th Inf. Died 7 Feb 1903; originally buried at Ft Niobrara, NE; reburied at Ft Leavenworth National Cemetery, plot G 3533. SOURCE: Ft Leavenworth National Cemetery.

WEBBER, Perry M.; Private; 25th Inf. Enlisted for 10th Cavalry in 1867; deserted spring 1868; reenlisted under false name in 1869 and assigned to 10th Cavalry, recognized, tried, convicted, and sentenced to three years; after serving sentence, enlisted under his own name at General Recruiting Service Station for 25th Infantry; turned over to civil authorities in Texas, 1877, for forging paymaster's certificates of deposit. SOURCE: Dobak and Philips, *The Black Regulars*, 196.

‡Original member of 10th Cavalry; in B Troop when organized, Ft Leavenworth, KS, 1 Apr 1867. SOURCE: McMiller, "Buffalo Soldiers," 69.

WEEDEN, Jefferson; Private; G/24th Inf. Pvt. Jefferson Weedon rumored to have made advances toward Sgt. Barney McDougal's wife, so McDougal fired three or four pistol shots at him. SOURCE: Dobak and Phillips, *The Black Regulars*, 177.

‡Admitted to Soldiers Home with disability, age 30, after two years and eleven months' service, 21 Mar 1891. SOURCE: SecWar, *AR 1891*, 753.

WEEDON, Jefferson; Private; 24th Inf. *See* WEEDEN, Jefferson, Private, G/24th Infantry

WEIR, Mack; D/24th Inf. Born in Kentucky; mulatto complexion; cannot read or write, age 24, Jul 1870, at Ft McKavett, TX. SOURCE: Bierschwale, *Fort McKavett*, 95.

WELCH, William; H/25th Inf. Born in North Carolina; mulatto complexion; can read and write, age 21, 5 Sep 1870, at Ft McKavett, TX. SOURCE: Bierschwale, *Fort McKavett*, 108.

WELLONS, Andrew; Sergeant; L/10th Cav. Born 27 May 1880; died 23 May 1970; buried at Santa Fe National Cemetery, NM, plot V 1668. SOURCE: Santa Fe National Cemetery, Records of Burials.

WELLS, Allen; Private; D/9th Cav. Private, D/9th Cavalry, when sexually molested by 1st Sgt. James Dickerson, D/9th Cavalry, Ft Riley, KS, Nov 1882. SOURCE: Kenner, *Buffalo Soldiers and Officers of the Ninth Cavalry*, 274.

WESLEY, Augustus; Private; F/10th Cav. Died 2 Aug 1867 of cholera at Ft Hays, KS. SOURCE: Regimental Returns, 10th Cavalry, 1867.

Died 1 Aug 1867; buried at Ft Leavenworth National Cemetery, plot 3284. SOURCE: Ft Leavenworth National Cemetery.

WESLEY, Lane; Private; B/10th Cav. Died at Ft Davis, TX, on 2 Oct 1883; buried at San Antonio National Cemetery, Section I, number 1565. SOURCE: San Antonio National Cemetery Locator.

WESSON, James L.; Private; F/10th Cav. Died 29 Mar 1870 of typhoid at Ft Leavenworth, KS. SOURCE: Regimental Returns, 10th Cavalry, 1870.

WEST, Harrison; Private; L/9th Cav. Enlisted 28 Jan 1879 at Baltimore, MD; stationed at Ft Bliss, TX, Nov 1879–Feb 1880; in the field in New Mexico in pursuit of Victorio's band of hostile Apaches, 8 Jan–22 Feb 1880, left Ojo Caliente 24 Feb and marched via Canada Alamosa and Cuchillo Negro, arriving at Chase's Ranch, 26 Feb 1880, after marching 621 miles in Jan and Feb; troop at Chase's Ranch 29 Feb 1880 awaiting further orders; marched 945 miles in the field in New Mexico, Sep–Oct 1880; L/9th Cavalry left Ft Stanton, NM, 11 Nov 1880, arrived Ft Bliss 18 Nov 1880; at Ft Bliss Jan–Feb 1881. SOURCE: Muster Rolls, L/9th Cavalry, 31 Oct 1879–29 Feb 1880, 31 Aug 1880–28 Feb 1881.

‡Private H. West, L/9th Cavalry, on detached service in the field, New Mexico, 21 Jan–24 Feb 1881. SOURCE: Regt Returns, 9 Cav, Feb 1881.

‡Tracked deserter Pvt. William Richardson, D/9th Cavalry, who broke into his sergeant's locker and stole $550 belonging to three men of company at Ft Craig, NM, in Nov 1881; Private Richardson was found and disarmed by Sergeant Stewart and Private West, who recovered $180 and killed Richardson when he tried to escape. SOURCE: Billington, *New Mexico's Buffalo Soldiers*, 131.

WEST, James; Private; 9th Cav. At Ft Duncan, TX, 1871, acquitted of charges he sold more than 200 pounds of commissary supplies to local Mexicans. SOURCE: Leiker, *Racial Borders*, 83.

WEST, John H.; Private; E/10th Cav. In Troop E/10th Cavalry stationed at Bonita Cañon Camp, AZ, 28 Feb 1886. SOURCE: Tagg, *The Camp at Bonita Cañon*, 232.

WEST, John P.; B/24th Inf. May be J. B. West; died 22 Oct 1893; buried at Ft Huachuca, AZ, cemetery. SOURCE: Ft Huachuca Cemetery, Cochise County, AZ.

WEST, Melvin L.; Private; G/9th Cav. Received Philippine Campaign Badge number 11846 for service as private in G/9th Cavalry, 16 Sep 1900–16 Feb 1901; private in G/9th Cavalry, Ft Leavenworth, KS, Mar 1905. SOURCE: Philippine Campaign Badge Recipients; Philippine Campaign Badge list, 29 May 1905.

WEST, Sampson; Private; M/10th Cav. Born in Lexington, KY, 1857; enlisted Chicago, IL, 27 Dec 1881; Ht 5'4", brown complexion, black eyes and hair; occupation gardener; served in H/10th Cavalry; discharged 26 Dec 1886; enlisted Presidio of San Francisco, CA, 25 Nov 1889; served in M/10th Cavalry. SOURCE: Sayre, *Warriors of Color*, 493.

Private in H/10th Cavalry stationed at Bonita Cañon Camp, AZ, 30 Apr 1886. SOURCE: Tagg, *The Camp at Bonita Cañon*, 232.

WESTLEY, Lawrence; Private; 10th Cav. Died 8 Feb 1908 while on detached duty; buried at Ft Bayard, NM, in plot F 23. SOURCE: "Fort Bayard National Cemetery, Records of Burials."

Buried 8 Feb 1908, section B, row A, plot 23 at Ft Bayard. SOURCE: Erickson, Burials at Fort Bayard National Cemetery, NM.

WETHERLY, Richard; Sergeant; B/10th Cav. ‡Original member of 10th Cavalry; in troop when organized, Ft Leavenworth, KS, 1 Apr 1867. SOURCE: McMiller, "Buffalo Soldiers," 69.

Died 16 Aug 1867 of disease at Camp Hoffman, KS. SOURCE: Regimental Returns, 10th Cavalry, 1867.

WHALEY, Lewis; Private; A/49th Inf. Died 31 Jan 1900; buried in plot 746 at San Francisco National Cemetery. SOURCE: San Francisco National Cemetery.

WHEELER, Charles; Private; Band/25th Inf. Shot and killed by black bartender named Overman at saloon near Missoula, MT, 1888, as a result of horseplay. SOURCE: Dobak and Phillips, *The Black Regulars*, 198.

WHEELER, Henry; Private; L/10th Cav. ‡Original member of 10th Cavalry; in troop when organized, Ft Riley, KS, 21 Sep 1867. SOURCE: McMiller, "Buffalo Soldiers," 78.

Died 21 Apr 1868 of disease at Ft Arbuckle, OK. SOURCE: Regimental Returns, 10th Cavalry, 1868.

WHEELER, James; Private; G/10th Cav. Awarded certificate of merit for gallant and meritorious conduct while member of escort of Maj. Joseph W. Wham, paymaster, who was ambushed by bandits between Ft Grant, AZ, and Ft Thomas, AZ, 11 May 1889. SOURCE: Gleim, *The Certificate of Merit*, 44.

Text of report of Paymaster Wham, describing bravery of escort. SOURCE: Schubert, *Voices of the Buffalo Soldier*, 159–62.

Cited for bravery against robbers near Cedar Springs, AZ, in May 1889 by Maj. Joseph W. Wham, and awarded certificate of merit; wounded during fight; left Army before end of 1890. SOURCE: Schubert, *Black Valor*, 93, 95, 98.

‡Mentioned among men who distinguished themselves in 1889; received certificate of merit for gallant and meritorious conduct while escorting Maj. Joseph W. Wham, paymaster, when he was attacked by robbers between Fts Grant and Thomas; now out of service. SOURCE: GO 18, AGO, 1891.

‡At Ft Apache, AZ, 1890, subscribed $.50 to testimonial to General Grierson. SOURCE: List of subscriptions, 23 Apr 1890, 10th Cavalry papers, MHI.

‡Stationed at Ft Grant, 1890; certificate of merit mentioned. SOURCE: SecWar, *AR 1890*, 289

‡Certificate of merit for gallant conduct, 11 May 1889, mentioned. SOURCE: Baker, Roster.

WHEELER, Pride; Private; 9th Cav. Received Philippine Campaign Badge number 11742 for service as private in D/24th Infantry; in 9th Cavalry at Ft Leavenworth, KS, Mar 1905. SOURCE: Philippine Campaign Badge list, 29 May 1905.

WHITE, Daniel; Private; B/10th Cav. Drowned 12 Jun 1872 in Indian Territory. SOURCE: Regimental Returns, 10th Cavalry, 1872.

WHITE, Dillard; Corporal; K/9th Cav. As corporal received Indian Wars Campaign Badge number 1365 on 28 May 1909. SOURCE: Carroll, *Indian Wars Campaign Badge*, 39.

‡Veteran of Indian wars and Philippine Insurrection; at Ft D. A. Russell, WY, in 1910; marksman; resident of Clay Co., KY. SOURCE: *Illustrated Review: Ninth Cavalry*, with picture.

WHITE, Frazier; Private; Band/25th Inf. Private, received Indian Wars Campaign Badge number 1579 on 28 Apr 1910. SOURCE: Carroll, *Indian Wars Campaign Badge*, 46.

WHITE, George; C/10th Cav. Private, USCT; lives at 546 Oxford, Baltimore, MD. SOURCE: United States Colored Troops Resident in Baltimore at the Time of the 1890 Census, printout in authors' files.

‡Original member of 10th Cavalry; in troop when organized, Ft Leavenworth, KS, 18 Feb 1867. SOURCE: McMiller, "Buffalo Soldiers," 70.

WHITE, George; Private; 9th Cav. Received Philippine Campaign Badge number 11752 for service as private in E/9th Cavalry; in 9th Cavalry at Ft Leavenworth, KS, Mar 1905. SOURCE: Philippine Campaign Badge list, 29 May 1905.

WHITE, Isaac; QM Sgt; F/25th Inf. ‡Ranked number 179 among rifle experts with 68.67 percent in 1904. SOURCE: GO 79, AGO, 1 Jun 1905.

Sergeant, F/25th Infantry, died 21 Nov 1909; buried at Ft Bayard, NM, in plot R 24. SOURCE: "Fort Bayard National Cemetery, Records of Burials."

Buried 21 Nov 1909, section B, row C, plot 24, at Ft Bayard. SOURCE: Erickson, Burials at Fort Bayard National Cemetery, NM.

WHITE, James; Private; A/25th Inf. Stationed at San Antonio, TX, 1873, when flogged by white citizen for writing offensive letters to his daughter; as a result of subsequent tensions, company removed to Ft Clark, TX. SOURCE: Dobak and Phillips, *The Black Regulars*, 237.

WHITE, James H.; Private; Band/9th Cav. ‡With band on detached service at headquarters, District of New Mexico, Santa Fe, 1880; played second tenor. SOURCE: Billington, *New Mexico's Buffalo Soldiers*, 226.

Enlisted 1878; transferred to band 1879; died of illness, Oct 1882. SOURCE: Kenner, *Buffalo Soldiers and Officers of the Ninth Cavalry*, 21–22.

WHITE, John; Private; A/10th Cav. ‡Original member of 10th Cavalry; in troop when organized, Ft Leavenworth, KS, 18 Feb 1867. SOURCE: McMiller, "Buffalo Soldiers," 68.

Died of disease 1 Aug 1867 at Ft Larned, KS. SOURCE: Regimental Returns, 10th Cavalry, 1867.

WHITE, John; Private; H/10th Cav. Died 21 May 1868 of disease at Ft Hays, KS. SOURCE: Regimental Returns, 10th Cavalry, 1868.

WHITE, John D.; Sergeant; K/9th Cav. ‡Corporal, A/9th Cavalry, on special duty instructing recruits since 26 May 1902. SOURCE: SD List, A/9, Nueva Caceres, Philippines, 31 May 1902.

Sergeant, received Indian Wars Campaign Badge number 1366 on 28 May 1909. SOURCE: Carroll, *Indian Wars Campaign Badge*, 39.

‡Veteran of Indian wars, Spanish-American War, and Philippine Insurrection; expert rifleman and sergeant, K/9th Cavalry, at Ft D. A. Russell, WY, in 1910; resident of Powhattan Co., VA. SOURCE: *Illustrated Review: Ninth Cavalry*, with picture.

WHITE, Joseph; Sergeant; B/24th Inf. ‡Born in New Orleans; Ht 6'2", black complexion; enlisted Ft Leavenworth, KS, 28 Feb 1888; transferred from G/24th Infantry to Band/24th Infantry, Ft Bayard, NM, 1 Sep 1892; discharged Ft Bayard, 27 Feb 1893, single, character very good; retained $60, clothing $65. SOURCE: Descriptive Book, 24 Inf NCS & Band.

‡Awarded certificate of merit for distinguished conduct in rescue of comrade from drowning, Rio Grande de la Pampagna, Cabanatuan, Philippines, 8 Nov 1900, while musician, B/24th Infantry. SOURCE: GO 32, AGO, 6 Feb 1904.

Awarded certificate of merit for distinguished conduct in rescuing comrade from drowning, Rio Grande de Pampanga [*sic*], Cabanatuan, 8 Nov 1900. SOURCE: Gleim, *The Certificate of Merit*, 53.

Born in New Orleans; received Distinguished Service Medal in lieu of certificate of merit. SOURCE: *American Decorations*, 844.

‡Retired as sergeant, B/24th Infantry, Jun 1902. SOURCE: *ANJ* 39 (14 Jun 1902): 1037.

‡Commended for rescue of comrade from Rio Grande de la Pampagna, 8 Nov 1900; now retired. SOURCE: Cleveland *Gazette*, 24 Nov 1906.

‡Served thirty years; Portland, OR, camp of Spanish-American War veterans named in his honor; in Nov 1900 fight, held band of insurgents at bay and saved patrol of 13th Infantry from ambush; awarded certificate of merit. SOURCE: Wharfield, *10th Cavalry and Border Fights*, 74.

WHITE, Joseph; Sergeant; M/10th Cav. Born in Georgetown, SC; occupation porter; Ht 5'4", fair complexion, black hair and eyes; enlisted, age 21, Charleston, 6 Jun 1881; assigned 25th Infantry, left recruit depot, David's Island, NY, 17 Aug 1881, and after trip on steamer *Thomas Kirby* to Central Depot, New York City, and train via Chicago to Running Water, Dakota Territory, 22 Aug 1881, marched forty-seven miles to Ft Randall, SD, arrived 24 Aug 1881. SOURCE: Descriptive & Assignment Rolls, 25 Inf.

‡Born in Georgetown; died at Ft Robinson, NE, age 42, with twenty-three years' service, 27 Mar 1904. SOURCE: Monthly Report, Chaplain Anderson, 1 Apr 1904; List of Interments, Ft Robinson.

Died 27 Mar 1904 of disease contracted in line of duty, Ft Robinson; buried at Ft Robinson. SOURCE: Buecker, Fort Robinson Burials.

WHITE, Lewis; Private; C/9th Cav. ‡Wounded in action while with 1st Lt. P. Cusack's expedition east of Ft Davis, TX, against Mescalero Apaches, in which twenty-five Indians were killed, 198 animals captured, Sep 1868; Pvts. S. Collyer, F/9th Cavalry, and John Foster, K/9th Cavalry, also were wounded. SOURCE: SecWar, AR 1868, 716.

Praised for gallantry in action in which he was wounded against Lipan Apaches near Ft Davis, Sep 1868. SOURCE: Kenner, *Buffalo Soldiers and Officers of the Ninth Cavalry*, 53.

WHITE, Lewis; Private; U.S. Army. Seminole Negro Scout; served 1874–84. SOURCE: Schubert, Consolidated List of Seminole Negro Scouts.

Born in North Carolina; also known as Louis; parents born in Texas; Ht 5'4", black hair and eyes, black complexion; enlisted at Ft Duncan, TX, 9 Feb 1874, age 44; discharged 11 Aug 1874 at Ft Duncan where he reenlisted 5 Apr 1875; discharged, reenlisted 5 Oct 1875 at Camp Supply, TX; discharged, reenlisted 5 Apr 1876 at Ft Duncan; discharged 5 Oct 1876, reenlisted 9 Oct 1876 at Ft Duncan; discharged, reenlisted 16 May 1877 at Ft Clark, TX; discharged 16 May 1878 at Camp Devils R.; enlisted 16 May

1879 at Ft Clark; discharged 27 May 1880, reenlisted next day at Ft Clark; discharged 6 Jun 1881, reenlisted 23 Jun 1882 at Ft Clark; discharged 22 Jun 1883, reenlisted, age 52, next day at Ft Clark; discharged 22 Jun 1884 at Ft Clark; 1880 Census lists wife Dolly and child Adelia. SOURCE: Swanson, 50.

In 1875, age 38, resided at Ft Duncan with Dolly age 37 and daughter age 1; widow Dolly filed pension application in 1904. SOURCE: NARA Record Group 393, Special File.

Buried at Seminole Indian Scout Cemetery, Kinney County, TX. SOURCE: Indian Scout Cemetery, Kinney County, Texas.

WHITE, Peter; Private; 25th Inf. Born in Georgetown, SC; Ht 5'6", black hair and eyes, dark complexion; occupation seaman; enlisted at age 23, Charleston, SC, 13 Jun 1881; left recruit depot, David's Island, NY, 2 Jul 1881, arrived Ft Randall, SD, 7 Jul 1881. SOURCE: Descriptive & Assignment Rolls of Recruits, 25 Inf.

WHITE, Robert; 9th Cav. Born in Virginia; mulatto complexion; married July 1870; can read, cannot write, age 22, 5 Sep 1870, at Ft McKavett, TX. SOURCE: Bierschwale, *Fort McKavett,* 107.

WHITE, Theophilus T.; Sergeant; A/9th Cav. In E/9th Cavalry, allowed by Capt. Jarauld Olmsted to marry laundress named Edna, alleged prostitute, in defiance of orders from Maj. James Randlett, 9th Cavalry, Ft DuChesne, UT, 1887. SOURCE: Kenner, *Buffalo Soldiers and Officers of the Ninth Cavalry,* 234.

‡Sergeant in A/9th Cavalry, on special duty as post gardener, Ft Robinson, NE. SOURCE: Order 68, 25 Sep 1895, Post Orders, Ft Robinson.

‡Sergeant, A/9th Cavalry, died at Ft Robinson 11 Sep 1896; buried 13 Sep 1896. SOURCE: Special Order 100, 12 Sep 1896, Post Orders, Ft Robinson; List of Interments, Ft Robinson.

Died 11 Sep 1896 in hospital of pulmonary hemorrhage, Ft Robinson. SOURCE: Buecker, Fort Robinson Burials.

WHITE, Thomas; Sergeant; M/10th Cav. Tried and found guilty at Ft Davis, TX, of absenting himself for several days with "disreputable women," instead of hunting as assigned; reduced to private 10 Jan 1885. SOURCE: Bigelow, *Garrison Tangles,* 78.

WHITE, Washington; M/9th Cav. Born in Kentucky; black complexion; cannot read or write, age 23, Jul 1870, at Ft McKavett, TX. SOURCE: Bierschwale, *Fort McKavett,* 100.

WHITE, William; Sergeant; G/9th Cav. Received Philippine Campaign Badge number 11806 for service as corporal in G/9th Cavalry, 16 Sep 1900–16 Sep 1902; sergeant in G/9th Cavalry, Ft Leavenworth, KS, Mar 1905. SOURCE: Philippine Campaign Badge Recipients; Philippine Campaign Badge list, 29 May 1905.

‡At Ft D. A. Russell, WY, in 1910; sharpshooter. SOURCE: *Illustrated Review: Ninth Cavalry,* with picture.

WHITEHURST, James; Private; 25th Inf. Born in Barbour, AL; Ht 5'7", black hair and eyes, black complexion; occupation fireman; enlisted in 25th Infantry at age 22, Cleveland, OH, 9 Dec 1886; arrived Ft Snelling, MN, 1 Apr 1887. SOURCE: Descriptive & Assignment Rolls of Recruits, 25 Inf.

WHITESIDE, Alexander; Cook; A/49th Inf. ‡Alex Whitesides died of malaria in the Philippines, 18 Sep 1900. SOURCE: *ANJ* 38 (29 Sep 1900): 115.

Alexander Whiteside, buried in plot NA 1132 at San Francisco National Cemetery. SOURCE: San Francisco National Cemetery.

WHITESIDES, Alex; Cook; A/49th Inf. *See* WHITESIDE, Alexander, Cook, A/49th Infantry

WHITESIDES, H.; Private; 25th Inf. Born in Christ Church, SC; occupation farmer; Ht 5'11", fair complexion, black hair and eyes; enlisted, age 23, Charleston, SC, 28 Jun 1881; left recruit depot, David's Island, NY, 17 Aug 1881, and after trip on steamer *Thomas Kirby* to Central Depot, New York City, and train via Chicago to Running Water, Dakota Territory, 22 Aug 1881, marched forty-seven miles to Ft Randall, SD, arrived 24 Aug 1881. SOURCE: Descriptive & Assignment Rolls, 25 Inf.

WHITESIDES, Zachariah; M/9th Cav. Born in Kentucky; black complexion; cannot read or write, age 24, Jul 1870, at Ft McKavett, TX. SOURCE: Bierschwale, *Fort McKavett,* 100.

WHITLEY, Benjamin F.; Sergeant; D/24th Inf. ‡Reenlisted for E/9th Cavalry, Ft Duchesne, UT, because he thought he had been too long in Indian Territory, according to Kansas City, MO, *Times.* SOURCE: *ANJ* 25 (3 Mar 1888): 629.

Applied to reenlist in 9th Cavalry, 1889, because his company had been seven years in Indian Territory, including 2.5 at Fort Supply; reenlistment approved and Whitley assigned to Ft DuChesne. SOURCE: Dobak and Phillips, *The Black Regulars,* 98.

WHITLOW, Samuel A.; H/25th Inf. Born in New York; mulatto complexion; can read and write, age 22, 5 Sep 1870, at Ft McKavett, TX. SOURCE: Bierschwale, *Fort McKavett*, 108.

WICKHAM, Thomas W.; Sergeant; K/25th Inf. Born in Henrico County, VA; Ht 5'6", bright complexion; occupation barber; enlisted in A/39th Infantry for three years on 4 Nov 1867, age 21, at Richmond, VA; appointed corporal 14 May 1868; ; transferred to K/25th Infantry at Jackson Bks, LA, 20 Apr 1869. SOURCE: Descriptive Roll of A/39th Inf.

WIG, Simpson; Private; F/48th Inf. *See* SIMPSON, Wig, Private, F/48th Infantry

WIGGINS, Westley; Private; A/39th Inf. Sentence of fifteen years for involvement in New Iberia, LA, mutiny, Jul 1867, reduced to three years. SOURCE: Dobak and Phillips, *The Black Regulars*, 222.

WILBURN, James; Private; A/39th Inf. Civil War veteran, served in C/10th Heavy Artillery; convicted of involvement in New Iberia, LA, mutiny, Jul 1867, with court deadlocked over death sentence. SOURCE: Dobak and Phillips, *The Black Regulars*, 222.

WILBURN, Thomas G.; Musician; K/25th Inf. ‡Native of Missouri, played trumpet, one-time student at Lincoln Institute, Jefferson City, MO; died of dysentery and appendicitis, age 21, in hospital, Castillejos, Philippines; "one of ablest young men in the service"; funeral conducted by Reverend William M. Wimms, K/25th Infantry. SOURCE: Richmond *Planet*, 8 Sep 1900.

Died 7 Jul 1900; buried in plot NEW A1045 at San Francisco National Cemetery. SOURCE: San Francisco National Cemetery.

WILCOX; Sergeant; 24th Inf. Stationed at Ft Bayard, NM, Jan 1894, attended masquerade ball given by F/24th Infantry, dressed as English dude. SOURCE: Schubert, *Voices of the Buffalo Soldier*, 198.

WILES, George; Private; 24th Inf. Served in 1880s. SOURCE: Dobak and Phillips, *The Black Regulars*, 186.

WILEY, Ambrose; Private; C/10th Cav. Served in 1881 at Eagle Springs, TX; resided at 1127 Morris Ally St., Baltimore, MD, at age 38, in 1891; resided at 509 Jasper St., Baltimore, in 1894. SOURCE: Sayre, *Warriors of Color*, 407, 409.

WILEY, Robert; Private; D/24th Inf. Born in Lebanon, TN; buried at Ft McKavett, TX, before 17 May 1879; body removed to National Cemetery, San Antonio, TX, 23 Nov 1883. SOURCE: Bierschwale, *Fort McKavett*, 123.

Died at Ft McKavett on 19 Jun 1871; buried at San Antonio National Cemetery, Section E, number 842. SOURCE: San Antonio National Cemetery Locator.

WILKERSON, James; Private; H/10th Cav. Born in Toronto, Canada, 1834; enlisted Lockport, NY, 26 Sep 1864; Ht 5'7", black complexion, eyes, and hair; occupation laborer; served in 1879; at Ft Davis, TX, 1882–84. SOURCE: Sayre, *Warriors of Color*, 494.

WILKES, Isaac J.; Private; 24th Inf. While at Ft Sill, OK, hunted small game. SOURCE: Dobak and Phillips, *The Black Regulars*, 150.

WILKES, Jacob; F/9th Cav. *See* WILKS, Jacob W., Sergeant, F/9th Cavalry

WILKES, William; Regt QM Sgt; 24th Inf. ‡Born in Columbia, Maury Co., TN, 29 Jun 1856; enlisted Nashville, TN, 10 Jan 1876; sent to Columbus Bks, OH, and then to Ft Duncan, TX; corporal, 1 Aug 1876; sergeant, 1 Jan 1877; discharged, Cantonment at North Fork, Canadian River, Indian Territory, 9 Jan 1881; enlisted in 9th Cavalry, St Louis, MO, 4 Feb 1881; joined L/9th Cavalry, Ft Bliss, TX, 24 Mar 1881; in the field, New Mexico, May–Nov 1881; transferred to Ft Riley, KS, Dec 1881; served against Utes in Colorado, 1882; corporal, 7 Aug 1883; sergeant, Ft McKinney, WY, 2 Dec 1885; discharged 3 Feb 1886; reenlisted in F/24th Infantry, Ft Leavenworth, KS, 26 Feb 1886; sergeant, 7 May 1886; at Ft Bayard, NM, 7 Jun 1888; discharged and reenlisted, 25 Feb 1891 and 25 Feb 1896; at Ft Douglas, UT, Oct 1896; at Chickamauga, GA, and Cuba, contracted yellow fever 3 Aug 1898; at Ft Douglas, Sep 1898; commissioned first lieutenant, 9th Infantry, U.S. Volunteers, 24 Oct 1898. SOURCE: Coston, *The Spanish-American War Volunteer*, 51–52.

Enlisted 4 Feb 1881 at St Louis; at Ft Bliss, May–June 1881. SOURCE: Muster Roll, L/9th Cavalry, 30 Apr–30 Jun 1881.

‡Sergeant, F/24th Infantry, at Ft Elliott, TX, 1886. *See* SMITH, Jacob Clay, Saddler Sergeant, 10th Cavalry

‡At Ft Bayard, Jul 1888; selected for Department of Arizona rifle competition, Ft Wingate, NM. SOURCE: Billington, *New Mexico's Buffalo Soldiers*, 154.

‡At Ft Bayard; qualified as sharpshooter. SOURCE: *ANJ* 28 (27 Sep 1890): 70.

‡Sergeant, F/24th Infantry, ranked number 5 in competition of Army rifle team, 1892; distinguished marksman, rifle, 1890, 1891, 1892. SOURCE: GO 75, AGO, 3 Nov 1892.

‡Sergeant, F/24th Infantry; commissioned first lieutenant, 9th Volunteer Infantry, after Spanish-American War. SOURCE: Cashin, *Under Fire with the Tenth Cavalry*, 360.

‡Promoted from lance corporal to corporal, 24th Infantry, Apr 1900. SOURCE: *ANJ* 37 (5 May 1900): 851.

Retired regimental quartermaster sergeant, received Indian Wars Campaign Badge number 1098 on 30 Dec 1908. SOURCE: Carroll, *Indian Wars Campaign Badge*, 31.

‡Retired as quartermaster sergeant, 24th Infantry, in 1904; gave talk at sixty-fourth anniversary of 9th Cavalry, Ft Leavenworth, 28 Jul 1930. SOURCE: *Cavalry Journal* 29 (Oct 1930): 616.

WILKINS, Julius; Private; B/25th Inf. Enlisted 29 Dec 1888, discharged as private A/25th Infantry 28 Dec 1893, character good; reenlisted 30 Dec 1893, discharged as private 29 Dec 1898, character good; reenlisted 2 Jan 1899, discharged as sergeant B/25th Infantry 4 Jan 1902, character excellent; reenlisted 3 Apr 1902, discharged as private 2 Apr 1905, character excellent; reenlisted 3 Apr 1905, discharged as private without honor 19 Nov 1906. SOURCE: Powell, "Military Record of the Enlisted Men Who Were Discharged Without Honor."

‡Dishonorable discharge, Brownsville, TX. SOURCE: SO 266, AGO, 9 Nov 1906.

WILKINS, Melvin; Private; E/9th Cav. ‡Reduced to private and fined $20 at Ft DuChesne, UT, for engaging in drunken brawl, for showing disrespect and using insubordinate language to troop commander, and for making false statements. SOURCE: *ANJ* 24 (9 Apr 1887): 734.

‡First sergeant, E/9th Cavalry, authorized four-month furlough from Ft DuChesne. SOURCE: *ANJ* 24 (1 Jan 1887): 450.

Native of Canada; 24-year-old private in fourth year of service when promoted to first sergeant, E/9th Cavalry, "barely able to write his name, given to explosive outbursts of temper, and a heavy drinker"; got into fight with Brent Woods at stables, Ft McKinney, WY, 1886; reduced to ranks and fined $20 for insubordination, drunkenness, absence without leave, Ft DuChesne, Jan 1887; discharged at end of enlistment, Feb 1887. SOURCE: Kenner, *Buffalo Soldiers and Officers of the Ninth Cavalry*, 232–33.

WILKINSON, Thomas H.; H/25th Inf. Born in Washington, DC; black complexion; can read and write, age 25, 5 Sep 1870, at Ft McKavett, TX. SOURCE: Bierschwale, *Fort McKavett*, 108.

WILKS, Cleveland; Private; D/9th Cav. Died 15 Nov 1916; buried in plot 1228-A at San Francisco National Cemetery. SOURCE: San Francisco National Cemetery.

WILKS, Jacob W.; Sergeant; F/9th Cav. Born in slavery about 1840 in Clark County, KY; owned by John P. Wilks; escaped with father John P. Wilks, mother, and sibling; raised in Ohio by Mrs. Waddell after parents died; Civil War veteran, enlisted 16 Sept 1863 in C/116th Regiment

U.S. Army Colored Volunteer Infantry at Camp Nelson, KY; present at Appomattox Courthouse, VA, when General Robert E. Lee surrendered; discharged 25 Oct 1886; reenlisted 25 Oct 1886 at Greenville, LA, in F/9th Cavalry; sergeant at Ft McKavett, TX, fined $5 of monthly pay on 1 Oct 1870 for neglecting to report to hospital with Company Sick Book; fined $10 of monthly pay 3 Oct 1870 for playing cards for money after Taps; fined $15 of monthly pay 19 Jan 1871 at Ft McKavett for neglecting order to repair corral; at Ft McKavett on 25 May 1871, reduced to ranks and confined to hard labor for one day for being absent without authority and intoxication rendering him unfit to attend roll call; fined $5 of monthly pay for neglecting duties while on guard duty at Ft McKavett; discharged 24 Oct 1871, reenlisted same day; Sergeant Wilks on detail in 1873 with twelve others carrying mail to Ft Bliss, TX, when attacked by Apache Indians at Eagle Springs, TX, who were driven off after Private Johnson was killed; at Ft McKavett, 1869–74; participated in Staked Plains Campaign in Texas; while at Ft Sill, OK, contracted chrome disease from exposure in line of duty; discharged 2 Oct 1876 at Ft Seldon, NM; married 20 Oct 1884 part Indian Elizabeth Moore, born 1854 in Jasper County, TX, at Ft McKavett; wife's parents were Bartlett Moore and Fannie Ship or Shipp; owned property in Ft McKavett and San Angelo, TX; family moved to 663 W. Avenue G, San Angelo, from Ft McKavett about 1897; later moved to 314 W. Avenue G, San Angelo; drew pension until he died on 6 Feb 1922; wife died in 1930 and buried at Pleasant View inside Fairmont Cemetery, San Angelo, with daughters Mammie Sue, Olveia, and Bernice; daughter Mary Wils is buried in Dallas, TX; daughter Maggie and Ophelia moved to San Diego, CA, in 1940. SOURCE: Margaret Lewis, "A Soldiers's Story," undated manuscript, in authors' files.

Enlisted 6 Oct 1866, age 22, Ht 5'6", occupation soldier; F/9th Cavalry transferred to Texas Mar 1866; arrived at Ft Davis, TX, July 1867; company detailed to Ft Quitman, TX, Jan 1868; returned to Ft Davis Aug 1868; company ordered to Ft McKavett, Feb 1869, transferred to Ft Concho, TX, Jan 1874, to Ft Clark, TX, Feb 1875, to Ft Seldon, Feb 1876. SOURCE: Williams 27 Mar 1996 letter to Margaret A. Lewis.

‡At his home in San Angelo, 1914, told life story to John W. Hunter: born slave around thirty miles south of Ohio River in Kentucky; escaped with parents to Ohio while still an infant; served forty-five months in 116th U.S. Colored Troops in Civil War, sergeant at Appomattox, VA; enlisted in 9th Cavalry after war; came to Ft Concho from Ft McKavett in 1874. SOURCE: Hunter, "A Negro Trooper of the Ninth Cavalry."

Born in Kentucky; black complexion; cannot read or write, age 25, Jul 1870, in F/9th Cavalry at Ft McKavett. SOURCE: Bierschwale, *Fort McKavett*, 97.

Article based on interview with Wilks, detailing his frontier experience, from *Frontier Times*, Apr 1927, reprinted. SOURCE: Schubert, *Voices of the Buffalo Soldier*, 40–46.

WILLIAMS, Aaron; Private; 25th Inf. Born in Ridgeway, SC; Ht 5'7", black hair and eyes, fair complexion; occupation cotton hand; enlisted at age 21, Charleston, SC, 19 May 1881; left recruit depot, David's Island, NY, 2 Jul 1881, arrived Ft Randall, SD, 7 Jul 1881. SOURCE: Descriptive & Assignment Rolls of Recruits, 25 Inf.

WILLIAMS, Alfred N.; Sergeant; B/25th Inf. Enlisted 9 Feb 1897, discharged as private 8 Feb 1900, character very good; enlisted 12 Dec 1900, discharged as sergeant 11 Dec 1903, character very good; reenlisted 12 Dec 1903, discharged as private without honor 19 Nov 1906. SOURCE: Powell, "Military Record of the Enlisted Men Who Were Discharged Without Honor."

‡Dishonorable discharge, Brownsville, TX. SOURCE: SO 266, AGO, 9 Nov 1906.

WILLIAMS, Ansterd; F/9th Cav. Born in Kentucky; black complexion; cannot read or write, age 29, Jul 1870, at Ft McKavett, TX. SOURCE: Bierschwale, *Fort McKavett*, 98.

WILLIAMS, Arthur; Private; F/10th Cav. Died 20 Apr 1874 of disease at Ft Griffin, TX. SOURCE: Regimental Returns, 10th Cavalry, 1874.

Died at Ft Griffin on 26 Apr 1874; buried at San Antonio National Cemetery, Section D, number 660. SOURCE: San Antonio National Cemetery Locator.

WILLIAMS, Benjamin T.; Private; M/24th Inf. John Williams, a colored civilian, ex-soldier, at Ft Robinson, NE, for a few days; found dead of chronic alcoholism in bed on 19 Jul 1903; Pvt. Benjamin T. Williams, M/24th Infantry buried at Ft Robinson 19 Jul 1903. SOURCE: Buecker, Fort Robinson Burials.

WILLIAMS, Bill; Sergeant; U.S. Army. Seminole Negro Scout, served 1882–1907; brother of Scout Charles Williams; retired. SOURCE: Schubert, Consolidated List of Seminole Negro Scouts.

Born in Texas; Ht 6', dark hair and eyes, yellow complexion; enlisted at Ft Clark, TX, 20 Nov 1882, age 31; discharged 21 Nov 1883, reenlisted next day at Camp Myers, TX; discharged 31 Aug 1884 at Ft Clark; enlisted 9 Jan 1886 at Ft Clark; discharged, reenlisted next day at Ft Clark, 8 Jan 1887–9 Jan 1890; discharged 8 Jul 1890, reenlisted next day at Camp Neville Springs, TX; discharged 8 Jan 1891, reenlisted next day at Ft Clark; discharged, reenlisted next day 15 Jul 1891; discharged as corporal 15 Jan 1892, reenlisted next day at Camp Palvo, TX; discharged as corporal, reenlisted 15 Jan 1892 at Camp Presidio, TX; discharged as corporal 15 Jan 1893, reenlisted next day at Ft Ringgold, TX; discharged as sergeant 15 Jul 1893, reenlisted next day at Ft. Ringgold; discharged as sergeant 14 Jan 1894, reenlisted next day at Camp San Pedro, TX; discharged as sergeant, reenlisted next day at Ft Ringgold, 15 Jul 1894–17 Jan 1907; retired 4 Feb 1907 at Ft Clark. SOURCE: Swanson, 51.

Born in Texas; private, Indian Scouts; died 6 Jul 1914; buried at Seminole Indian Scout Cemetery, Kinney County, TX. SOURCE: Indian Scout Cemetery, Kinney County, Texas.

WILLIAMS, Brister; Private; B/25th Inf. Enlisted 25 Jan 1901, discharged as private E/25th Infantry 24 Jan 1904, character good; reenlisted 5 Feb 1904, discharged without honor 19 Nov 1906. SOURCE: Powell, "Military Record of the Enlisted Men Who Were Discharged Without Honor."

‡Dishonorable discharge, Brownsville, TX. SOURCE: SO 266, AGO, 9 Nov 1906.

WILLIAMS, Cathay; Private; A/38th Inf. Born in Independence, MO; enlisted for three years in St. Louis, MO, as William Cathey, 15 Nov 1866; age 22, occupation cook; illiterate; Ht 5'9", black hair and eyes, black complexion; assigned to 38th Infantry; stationed at Jefferson Bks, MO, until Feb 1867; mustered into A/38th Infantry 13 Feb 1867; hospitalized in Feb 1867 in St Louis; marched to Ft Riley, KS, Apr 1867; hospitalized 10 Apr 1867; ill in quarters 30 Apr 1867 with pay docked $10 per month for three months, returned to duty 14 May 1867; at Ft Harker, KS, Jun 1867; marched 536 miles to arrive at Ft Union, NM, on 20 Jul 1867; marched 7 Sep–1 Oct 1867 to Ft Cummings, NM, to stay eight months; admitted to post hospital 27 Jan 1868 for three days with rheumatism; hospitalized 20 Mar 1868 for three days with rheumatism; marched forty-seven miles to Ft Bayard, NM, 6–7 Jun 1868; hospitalized 13 Jul 1868 for a month with neuralgia; discharged at Ft Bayard 14 Oct 1868 with surgeon's certificate of disability; certificate states Williams was "feeble both physically and mentally, and much of time quite unfit for duty"; only documented black woman to serve in regular Army during 19th century; resumed identity as Cathay Williams; worked as cook for colonel at Ft Union, 1869–70; worked as laundress for Mr. Dunbar at Pueblo, CO, for two years; lived and worked as laundress in Las Animas County, CO, for one year; settled as laundress in Trinidad, CO; hospitalized in Trinidad in late 1889 or early 1890 for over a year; filed for an invalid pension based on military service Jun 1891, age 41; examined 9 Sep 1891 in Trinidad by doctor employed by Pension Bureau who reported Ht of 5'7", 160 pounds, large, stout, age 49, with toes on both feet amputated, necessitating crutches to walk, in good general health with "nil" on disability rating; claim for pension denied Feb 1892 because no disability existed; lawyers Charles and William King of Washington, DC, tried again in Apr 1892 stating she lost her toes because of frostbite during military service, no evidence of response from Pension Bureau or receipt of pension based on military service; 1900 Census for Trinidad, CO, does not list Cathay Williams. SOURCE: Blanton, "Cathay Williams."

Born in Jackson Co., MO, Sep 1844; enlisted as William Cathay, St. Louis, 15 Nov 1866; occupation cook; black eyes, hair, and complexion; discharged with disability 14 Oct 1868; applied for pension as Cathay Williams, 1891, at which time she was described as "a large stout woman in good general health"; pension application denied; resided in Trinidad, CO, 1892; discharge and pension application reproduced. SOURCE: Schubert, *Voices of the Buffalo Soldier*, 33–35.

Mentioned as claiming to have spent two years in 38th Infantry. SOURCE: Dobak and Phillips, *The Black Regulars*, 288.

Biographical account. SOURCE: Philip Thomas Tucker, *Cathy Williams: From Slave to Female Buffalo Soldier* (2002).

WILLIAMS, Charles; Recruit; A/10th Cav. ‡Original member of 10th Cavalry; in troop when organized, Ft Leavenworth, KS, 18 Feb 1867. SOURCE: McMiller, "Buffalo Soldiers," 68.

Died 1 Jun 1867 of disease at Ft Leavenworth. SOURCE: Regimental Returns, 10th Cavalry, 1867.

‡Recruit, 10th Cavalry, died in post hospital, Ft Leavenworth, 31 May 1867. SOURCE: LS, 10 Cav, 1866–67.

WILLIAMS, Charles; Private; A/39th Inf. Sentence of ten years for involvement in New Iberia, LA, mutiny, Jul 1867, overturned. SOURCE: Dobak and Phillips, *The Black Regulars*, 222.

WILLIAMS, Charles; H/25th Inf. Born in Missouri; mulatto complexion; can read and write, age 22, 5 Sep 1870, at Ft McKavett, TX. SOURCE: Bierschwale, *Fort McKavett*, 108.

WILLIAMS, Charles; Private; 25th Inf. Born in Spotsylvania, VA; occupation soldier; Ht 5'4 1/2", brown complexion, brown hair and black eyes; enlisted, age 35, Baltimore, MD, 4 Aug 1881; left recruit depot, David's Island, NY, 17 Aug 1881, and after trip on steamer *Thomas Kirby* to Central Depot, New York City, and train via Chicago to Running Water, Dakota Territory, 22 Aug 1881, marched forty-seven miles to Ft Randall, SD, arrived 24 Aug 1881. SOURCE: Descriptive & Assignment Rolls, 25 Inf.

WILLIAMS, Charles; Private; U.S. Army. Seminole Negro Scout, brother of Scout Bill Williams; served 1882–84. SOURCE: Schubert, Consolidated List of Seminole Negro Scouts.

Born in Texas; Ht 5'8", black hair and eyes, black complexion; enlisted for one year at Ft Clark, TX, 11 Sep 1882, age 24; discharged 21 Aug 1884. SOURCE: Swanson, 51.

WILLIAMS, Charles; Private; F/24th Inf. Private, received Indian Wars Campaign Badge number 1621 on 16 Dec 1910. SOURCE: Carroll, *Indian Wars Campaign Badge*, 47.

WILLIAMS, David; Private; G/9th Cav. Received Philippine Campaign Badge number 11847 for service as private in G/9th Cavalry, 16 Sep 1900–16 Feb 1901; private in G/9th Cavalry, Ft Leavenworth, KS, Mar 1905. SOURCE: Philippine Campaign Badge Recipients; Philippine Campaign Badge list, 29 May 1905.

WILLIAMS, Edward; Corporal; I/38th Inf. Died 5 Dec 1868; buried at Ft Leavenworth National Cemetery, plot C 1934. SOURCE: Ft Leavenworth National Cemetery.

WILLIAMS, Edward; Private; L/9th Cav. Drowned while fording Pecos River, Texas, Jun 1869. SOURCE: Kenner, *Buffalo Soldiers and Officers of the Ninth Cavalry*, 176.

‡Drowned in Pecos River in pursuit of Indians, Jun 1869. SOURCE: Hamilton, "History of the Ninth Cavalry," 11; *Illustrated Review: Ninth Cavalry*.

WILLIAMS, Fielding; H/25th Inf. Born in Mississippi; black complexion; can read and write, age 24, 5 Sep 1870, at Ft McKavett, TX. SOURCE: Bierschwale, *Fort McKavett*, 108.

WILLIAMS, Fletcher; Corporal; K/48th Inf. ‡Died of variola in the Philippines, 17 Jul 1900. SOURCE: *ANJ* 37 (28 Jul 1900): 1142.

Died in the Philippines, 15 Jul 1900; buried in plot 877 at San Francisco National Cemetery. SOURCE: San Francisco National Cemetery.

WILLIAMS, Frank; Private; C/25th Inf. Died 4 May 1902; buried in plot N/A 1204 at San Francisco National Cemetery. SOURCE: San Francisco National Cemetery.

WILLIAMS, George; 9th Cav. Born in Virginia; black complexion; can read and write, age 21, Sep 1870, at Ft McKavett, TX. SOURCE: Bierschwale, *Fort McKavett*, 106.

WILLIAMS, George; F/9th Cav. Born in Kentucky; black complexion; cannot read or write, age 21, Jul 1870, at Ft McKavett, TX. SOURCE: Bierschwale, *Fort McKavett*, 97.

WILLIAMS, George; C/25th Inf. On duty 5 July 1881 at Ft Hale, Dakota Territory, in charge of boat's crew in Quartermaster Department, issued order to Pvt. Henry Mason,

E/25th Infantry, who refused to turn out and help make a trip across the Missouri River; Mason found not guilty but guilty of conduct to the prejudice of good order and military discipline; court was lenient because of hard work of boat's crew on 4 July. SOURCE: General Court-Martial Orders No. 99, Ft Snelling, MN, 19 Aug 1881, photocopy in authors' files.

WILLIAMS, George; Private; E/10th Cav. In Troop E/10th Cavalry stationed at Bonita Cañon Camp, AZ, 28 Feb 1886. SOURCE: Tagg, *The Camp at Bonita Cañon*, 232.

WILLIAMS, George; Private; E/9th Cav. Struck over head with a clawhammer by Pvt. Walter W. Boston at brothel near Ft Meade, SD. SOURCE: Dobak and Phillips, *The Black Regulars*, 176.

WILLIAMS, Gus J.; Sergeant; D/10th Cav. Born in Anniston, AL; resided in Jacksonville, AL; as private in A/24th Infantry at Naguilian, Luzon, Philippines, 7 Dec 1899, volunteered to swim Rio Grande de Cagayan in face of well-entrenched enemy, swam the river, returned with raft for small arms and ammunition, crossed again, took part in attack that drove off superior enemy force; awarded Distinguished Service Cross in 1925. SOURCE: *American Decorations*, 633.
    ‡Commissioned first lieutenant at Camp Des Moines, IA, 15 Oct 1917. SOURCE: Glass, *History of the Tenth Cavalry*, appendix M.
    ‡Retired as sergeant; won Distinguished Service Cross for heroism at Naguilian, Luzon, 1899. SOURCE: *Crisis* 30 (Jun 1925): 78

WILLIAMS, Harrison; Private; G/9th Cav. ‡Died at Ft Robinson, NE, 1 Oct 1897, and buried there. SOURCE: Special Order 119, 3 Oct 1898, Post Orders, Ft Robinson; List of Interments, Ft Robinson.
    Found dead of gunshot wound three miles southwest of Ft Robinson, 2 Oct 1897; George Crousen, colored soldier charged with murder of Williams, requested postponement of preliminary trial until 25 Oct 1897, according to 22 Oct 1897 Harrison, NE, *Northwestern Press*. SOURCE: Buecker, Fort Robinson Burials.
    ‡$30.75 due deceased Private Harrison, killed near Ft Robinson, 1 Oct 1897, forwarded to paymaster. SOURCE: CO, G/9 Cav, to Chief Paymaster, DP, 22 Nov 1897, Misc Records, DP.

WILLIAMS, Harry; Private; I/10th Cav. In Troop I/10th Cavalry stationed at Bonita Cañon Camp, AZ, 30 Jun 1886. SOURCE: Tagg, *The Camp at Bonita Cañon*, 232.

WILLIAMS, Harry J.; Corporal; M/24th Inf. Died 7 Jun 1913; buried in plot WSIDE1151 at San Francisco National Cemetery. SOURCE: San Francisco National Cemetery.

WILLIAMS, Henry; M/9th Cav. Born in Kentucky; mulatto complexion; can read and write, age 23, Jul 1870, at Ft McKavett, TX. SOURCE: Bierschwale, *Fort McKavett*, 100.

WILLIAMS, Henry; Private; B/25th Inf. Member of three-man detachment led by Sgt. Joseph Luckadoe, along with Pvts. Joshua Newby and Benedict Thomas, 25th Infantry, who defended Eagle Springs, TX, mail station against attack, New Year's Eve, 1873. SOURCE: Dobak and Phillips, *The Black Regulars*, 258–59, 332.

WILLIAMS, Henry; Private; I/25th Inf. Born in Jefferson County, NY; Ht 5'6", black hair and dark brown eyes, yellow complexion; occupation farmer; enlisted at age 23, Buffalo, NY, 16 Aug 1882; arrived Ft Snelling, NM, 21 Nov 1882. SOURCE: Descriptive & Assignment Rolls of Recruits, 25 Inf.

WILLIAMS, Henry; Private; U.S Army. Born in North Carolina; Seminole Negro Scout; Ht 5'8", black hair and eyes, black complexion; enlisted at Ft Clark, TX, 21 Sep 1882, age 41; discharged 20 Sep 1883, reenlisted next day at Ft Clark; discharged 31 Aug 1884 at Ft Clark; 1880 Census lists laborer Henry Williams age 38, wife Felipi age 28, Leonides age 7, Louis age 3, Petani, age 1. SOURCE: Swanson, 51.

WILLIAMS, Horace; Private; L/9th Cav. Died on 7 Nov 1901; buried at San Antonio National Cemetery, Section F, number 1080. SOURCE: San Antonio National Cemetery Locator.

WILLIAMS, Humphrey; Private; L/9th Cav. At Ft Duncan, TX, 1870, with Pvt. Frank Thomas, L/9th Cavalry, stole pig that belonged to Pvt. Henry Fletcher and ate it; sentenced to dishonorable discharge and imprisonment for remainder of his enlistment, Dec 1870. SOURCE: Kenner, *Buffalo Soldiers and Officers of the Ninth Cavalry*, 177.

WILLIAMS, Israel; Private; C/9th Cav. Died at Camp Eagle Pass, TX, on 9 Dec 1872; buried at San Antonio National Cemetery, Section F, number 1160. SOURCE: San Antonio National Cemetery Locator.

WILLIAMS, Jack; Private; 25th Inf. Born in Mt Pleasant, SC; occupation laborer; Ht 5'7", dark complexion, black hair and eyes; enlisted, age 22, Charleston, SC, 27 Jun 1881; left recruit depot, David's Island, NY, 17 Aug 1881, and after trip on steamer *Thomas Kirby* to Central Depot, New York City, and train via Chicago to Running Water, Dakota

Territory, 22 Aug 1881, marched forty-seven miles to Ft Randall, SD, arrived 24 Aug 1881. SOURCE: Descriptive & Assignment Rolls, 25 Inf.

WILLIAMS, James; Private; E/24th Inf. Died at Ft Griffin, TX, on 16 Dec 1869; buried at San Antonio National Cemetery, Section D, number 741. SOURCE: San Antonio National Cemetery Locator.

WILLIAMS, James; Private; K/10th Cav. Died 3 Mar 1870 of pneumonia at Camp Supply, OK. SOURCE: Regimental Returns, 10th Cavalry, 1870.

‡Commander of troop transmits inventory of effects and final statement of Private Williams to regimental commander, Apr 1870. SOURCE: ES, 10 Cav, 1866–71.

WILLIAMS, James; C/25th Inf. Born in Louisiana; mulatto complexion; can read, cannot write, age 29, 5 Sep 1870, at Ft McKavett, TX. SOURCE: Bierschwale, *Fort McKavett*, 109.

WILLIAMS, James; Private; H/10th Cav. Born in Louisa Court House, VA, 1848; enlisted Toledo, OH, 8 Dec 1869; Ht 5'8", black complexion, eyes, and hair; occupation laborer; served in H/10th Cavalry; at Ft Wallace, KS, Nov 1868 and Apr 1869; at Camp Supply, OK, Aug–Oct 1869; at Ft Sill, OK, Nov 1870; at Ft Davis, TX, Jul 1881; at camp near Presidio, TX, 31 Aug 1881; at Ft Davis, Apr–Jun 1883; at Ft Davis, 1884. SOURCE: Sayre, *Warriors of Color*, 495.

WILLIAMS, James; 1st Sgt; E/9th Cav. Native of Louisiana; private in E/9th Cavalry in April 1867, at time of San Pedro Springs, TX, mutiny; promoted to first sergeant shortly afterward; first sergeant serving with E/9th Cavalry in New Mexico in 1879, one of three original members still in troop with William Howard and Zekiel Sykes. SOURCE: Kenner, *Buffalo Soldiers and Officers of the Ninth Cavalry*, 75, 109, 326.

‡Company clerk and witness at court martial of soldiers charged with mutiny and desertion for role in mutiny at San Pedro Springs, near San Antonio, TX, April 1867. SOURCE: Dobak and Phillips, *The Black Regulars*, 208.

‡Hunting party under Sgt. James Williams rescued Sgt. Henry Robinson, E/9th Cavalry, and four-man mail escort attacked by Victorio, 28 Sep 1879, near Ojo Caliente, NM. SOURCE: Billington, *New Mexico's Buffalo Soldiers*, 91.

‡Sergeant, with small hunting party that prevented Indians from attacking mail escort near Ojo Caliente, 28 Sep 1879. SOURCE: Hamilton, "History of the Ninth Cavalry," 44; *Illustrated Review: Ninth Cavalry*.

‡Sergeant, on detached service in the field, Columbus, NM, 30 Dec 1880–2 Jan 1881. SOURCE: Regt Returns, 9 Cav, Jan 1881.

WILLIAMS, James; Private; U.S. Army. Seminole Negro Scout, also known as Jim, served 1874–76. SOURCE: Schubert, Consolidated List of Seminole Negro Scouts.

Born in Arkansas; occupation ex-soldier; Ht 5'8", black hair and eyes, black complexion; enlisted Ft Clark, TX, 14 May 1874, age 23; discharged 14 Nov 1874 at Ft Clark where he reenlisted 2 Dec 1874; discharged 2 Jun 1875 at Ft Clark where he reenlisted 13 Jun 1875; discharged 1 Jan 1876 at Ft Duncan, TX. SOURCE: Swanson, 52.

WILLIAMS, James; Private; I/10th Cav. In Troop I/10th Cavalry stationed at Bonita Cañon Camp, AZ, 30 Jun 1886. SOURCE: Tagg, *The Camp at Bonita Cañon*, 232.

WILLIAMS, James; Private; 9th Cav. Received Philippine Campaign Badge number 11903 for service as private, F/9th Cavalry; in 9th Cavalry at Ft Leavenworth, KS, Mar 1905. SOURCE: Philippine Campaign Badge list, 29 May 1905.

WILLIAMS, James W.; Wagoner; A/10th Cav. Died 11 Jan 1868 of accidental discharge of carbine at Ft Larned, KS. SOURCE: Regimental Returns, 10th Cavalry, 1868.

WILLIAMS, Jerry; Private; K/9th Cav. ‡Served 1872–73. *See* SLAUGHTER, Rufus, Private, K/9th Cavalry

‡Struck on head with carbine by Capt. J. Lee Humfreville while held by two noncommissioned officers, then struck with club, then suspended from tree, Ft Richardson, TX, 15 Dec 1872; Pvt. James Imes received same treatment. SOURCE: GCMO 23, AGO, 3 Apr 1874.

Brutal treatment by Capt. J. Lee Humfreville, summer 1872, described. SOURCE: Kenner, *Buffalo Soldiers and Officers of the Ninth Cavalry*, 141–45.

Text of court martial order convicting Capt. J. Lee Humfreville of brutality. SOURCE: Schubert, *Voices of the Buffalo Soldier*, 55–62.

WILLIAMS, Jessie; Private; G/9th Cav. Born in Thomasville, GA, 25 Dec 1862; at age 4, father died; mother worked as domestic and cook in Thomasville and Norfolk, VA, where he learned to read; worked as bootblack, teamster, and shucked and sold oysters in Norfolk; in Newark, NJ, Mar 1888, worked for Lehigh Valley Coal Co.; enlisted in G/9th Cavalry at Newark 2 Jul 1889; sent for training at Jefferson Bks, MO, until Oct 1889; transferred to Ft Robinson, NE, Oct 1889 for two months; in the field at Rosebud Agency Reservation, Pine Ridge, Wounded Knee, SD; in 1894 at Ft Robinson where he was discharged 2 Jul 1894, character excellent; marksmanship Class 1; balance due $254.87 paid in full 13 Jul 1894; reenlisted 13 Jul 1894 as first cook for G/9th Cavalry; married Jennie Burdick of Crawford, NE, 13 Jul 1894; rented house outside of Ft Robinson barracks main entrance gate and established small lunchroom with wife; hospitalized for three days when wagon loaded with timber turned over; troop went to Chickamauga Park, GA, Ft Tampa, FL, and landed in Santiago, Cuba, 22 Jun 1898; selected as color guard for 9th Cavalry; relieved 71st New York Volunteers in battle in Jul 1898; contracted malaria, troop left Cuba 22 Aug 1898, landed at Long Island, NY; treated for malaria at Boston City Hospital 13 Sep 1898–3 Oct 1898; granted one-month furlough to return to Ft Robinson; sent to Ft Apache, AZ, where he was discharged 2 Jul 1899, character excellent, service honest and faithful; went to Lincoln, NE, where wife lived during last years of service; on 25 Jul 1899 settled in Omaha for remainder of life; hired by Swift & Company packinghouse 17 Aug 1899, retired after thirty-two years with pension along with Spanish-American War veteran pension; belonged to Methodist Church, voted Republican all his life; resided at 1145 North 20th Street, Omaha, 16 Sep 1941. SOURCE: Williams, Jessie, interview, Sep 1941.

WILLIAMS, Joe; Private; G/9th Cav. Received Philippine Campaign Badge number 11845 for service as private in G/9th Cavalry, 3 Mar 1902–16 Sep 1902; in G/9th Cavalry, Ft Leavenworth, KS, Mar 1905. SOURCE: Philippine Campaign Badge Recipients; Philippine Campaign Badge list, 29 May 1905.

WILLIAMS, John; Private; A/39th Inf. Civil War veteran, served in D/10th Heavy Artillery; sentence of five years for involvement in New Iberia, LA, mutiny, Jul 1867, reduced to one month. SOURCE: Dobak and Phillips, *The Black Regulars*, 222.

WILLIAMS, John (1st); Private; C/10th Cav. ‡Original member of 10th Cavalry; in troop when organized, Ft Leavenworth, KS, 18 Feb 1867. SOURCE: McMiller, "Buffalo Soldiers," 70.

Died 3 Feb 1868 of disease at Ft Riley, KS. SOURCE: Regimental Returns, 10th Cavalry, 1868.

Note: (1st) refers to (1st) and (2nd) John Williams in OTT.

WILLIAMS, John; Private; K/9th Cav. Died at Ft Davis, TX, on 20 Mar 1871; buried at San Antonio National Cemetery, Section I, number 1511. SOURCE: San Antonio National Cemetery Locator.

WILLIAMS, John; Private; H/9th Cav. In ninth year of service when fined $10 per month for six months by garrison court martial, May 1881; wounded in thigh, Gavilan Canyon, New Mexico, Aug 1881, and leg later amputated. SOURCE: Kenner, *Buffalo Soldiers and Officers of the Ninth Cavalry*, 230.

‡Seriously wounded in action, Gavilan Pass, Mimbres Mountains, NM, 19 Aug 1881, along with Pvt. Wesley Harris. SOURCE: Hamilton, "History of the Ninth Cavalry," 60.

WILLIAMS, John; Corporal; B/25th Inf. Member of bicycle corps that cycled from Fort Missoula, MT, to Yellowstone Park, WY, 1896. SOURCE: Dobak and Phillips, *The Black Regulars*, 182.

WILLIAMS, John; QM Sgt; 25th Inf. At Ft Missoula, MT, 16-year-old daughter Etta eloped with Pvt. Samuel Lundy. SOURCE: Dobak and Phillips, *The Black Regulars*, 142.

‡Retires from Ft Missoula. SOURCE: *ANJ* 34 (20 Mar 1897): 525.

WILLIAMS, John; Private; E/49th Inf. Died 7 Feb 1901; buried in plot E SID 1113 at San Francisco National Cemetery. SOURCE: San Francisco National Cemetery.

WILLIAMS, John; Private; L/25th Inf. ‡Fined $7 by summary court, San Isidro, Philippines, for being off limits, 14 Jun 1902, first conviction. SOURCE: Register of Summary Court, San Isidro.

Died 3 Jul 1903; buried at Ft Leavenworth National Cemetery, plot G 3523. SOURCE: Ft Leavenworth National Cemetery.

WILLIAMS, John. Died 19 Jul 1903 at Ft Robinson, NE. *See* WILLIAMS, Benjamin T., Private, M/24th Infantry

WILLIAMS, John G.; 1st Sgt; F/25th Inf. Corporal, F/25th Infantry, rode in 25th Infantry Bicycle Corps, Ft Missoula, MT, summer 1896. SOURCE: Sorenson, List of Buffalo Soldiers Who Rode in the 25th Infantry Bicycle Corps, in authors' files.

‡Eleven-year veteran, killed by Corporal Nelson, F/25th Infantry, May 1900. SOURCE: Richmond *Planet*, 28 Jul 1900.

‡Died, homicide victim, in the Philippines, 19 May 1900. SOURCE: *ANJ* 37 (2 Jun 1900): 951.

WILLIAMS, John T.; Sergeant; G/24th Inf. ‡Awarded certificate of merit for service in Cuban campaign, 1898. SOURCE: Scipio, *Last of the Black Regulars*, 130.

‡Certificate of merit mentioned. SOURCE: Steward, *The Colored Regulars*, 280.

‡Only Sgt. J. T. Williams, Capt. Robert Gordon Woods, I/49th Infantry, Sgt. W. H. Carroll and Pvt. Samuel Bradshaw, G/24th Infantry, did not get yellow fever while stationed at Siboney, Cuba, yellow fever camp in 1898. SOURCE: Coston, *The Spanish-American War Volunteer*, 79, 82.

Awarded certificate of merit for distinguished service in battle, Santiago, Cuba, 1 Jul 1898. SOURCE: Gleim, *The Certificate of Merit*, 46.

‡Commended for distinguished service, battle of Santiago, 1 Jul 1898; awarded certificate of merit; now out of service. SOURCE: GO 15, AGO, 13 Feb 1900.

WILLIAMS, John W.; Wagoner; A/10th Cav. Died from accidental discharge of carbine 11 Jan 1868 at Ft Larned, KS. SOURCE: Regimental Returns, 10th Cavalry, 1868.

WILLIAMS, Jonas; Trumpeter; E/9th Cav. Died 15 Aug 1903; buried at Ft Bayard, NM, in plot K 1. SOURCE: "Fort Bayard National Cemetery, Records of Burials."

Buried 15 Aug 1903, section A, row Q, plot 2, at Ft Bayard. SOURCE: Erickson, Burials at Fort Bayard National Cemetery, NM.

WILLIAMS, Joseph E.; Private; L/9th Cav. Enlisted 16 Aug 1879 at Ft Bliss, TX; with L/9th Cavalry, left camp on Rio Mimbres, NM, on 8 Jul 1880 and marched twenty miles to Ft Cummings, NM; left Ft Cummings 8 Aug on march to Leas Ferry on Rio Grande and returned to Rio Mimbres camp after march of 104 miles; marched 945 miles in New Mexico Sep–Oct 1880; left Ft Stanton, NM, with L/9th Cavalry 11 Nov 1880, arrived at Ft Bliss 18 Nov 1880; at Ft Bliss Jan–Feb 1881, $5 sentence for General Court Martial Order 4 stopped. SOURCE: Muster Rolls, L/9th Cavalry, 30 June 1880–28 Feb 1881.

WILLIAMS, Kinney; H/25th Inf. Born in New York; black complexion; can read and write, age 24, 5 Sep 1870, at Ft McKavett, TX. SOURCE: Bierschwale, *Fort McKavett*, 108.

WILLIAMS, Larkin; F/9th Cav. Born in Georgia; black complexion; cannot read or write, age 24, Jul 1870, at Ft McKavett, TX. SOURCE: Bierschwale, *Fort McKavett*, 97.

WILLIAMS, Levi; Private; K/24th Inf. ‡Died of variola in the Philippines, 18 Jul 1900. SOURCE: *ANJ* 37 (4 Aug 1900): 1166.

Levie Williams died in the Philippines 18 Jul 1900; buried in plot NEW A311 at San Francisco National Cemetery. SOURCE: San Francisco National Cemetery.

WILLIAMS, Moses; Ord Sgt; U.S. Army. Born in Louisiana; mulatto complexion; can read and write, age 24, Jul 1870, in F/9th Cavalry at Ft McKavett, TX. SOURCE: Bierschwale, *Fort McKavett*, 96

‡Born in Carroll Co., LA; awarded Medal of Honor for heroism against Nana, Carrizo Canyon, NM, 12 Aug 1881. SOURCE: Carroll, *The Black Military Experience*, 279–80, 365–69; Leckie, *The Buffalo Soldiers*, 232–33; Lee, *Negro Medal of Honor Men*, 71.

‡Sergeant, I/9th Cavalry; Medal of Honor for heroism in action against Nana, Cuchillo Negro Mountains, New Mexico, 16 Aug 1881, mentioned. SOURCE: Billington, *New Mexico's Buffalo Soldiers*, 106.

Life, career, and bravery against Apaches, for which he received Medal of Honor, narrated. SOURCE: Schubert, *Black Valor*, 10, 79–83, 87–88.

Bravery against Apaches and application for Medal of Honor described. SOURCE: Dobak and Phillips, *The Black Regulars*, 254–55, 261, 330, 332.

Documents relating to his successful application for Medal of Honor published. SOURCE: Schubert, *Voices of the Buffalo Soldier*, 100–106.

Appointed ordnance sergeant 23 Sep 1886, from first sergeant, I/9th Cavalry. SOURCE: Dobak, "Staff Noncommissioned Officers."

‡First sergeant, I/9th Cavalry, Ft Niobrara, NE, appointed ordnance sergeant, U.S. Army, as of 28 Sep 1886. SOURCE: *ANJ* 24 (2 Oct 1886): 189; Roster, 9 Cav.

Mentioned as recipient of Medal of Honor; spent youth in East Carroll Parish, LA; career discussed; retired 1898 after thirty-two years of service from Ft Stevens, OR; died 23 Aug 1899, Vancouver, WA, at age 52. SOURCE: Kenner, *Buffalo Soldiers and Officers of the Ninth Cavalry*, 159, 240–48.

WILLIAMS, Newton; M/9th Cav. Born in Kentucky; black complexion; can read and write, age 30, Jul 1870, at Ft McKavett, TX. SOURCE: Bierschwale, *Fort McKavett*, 100.

WILLIAMS, Oliver; Private; 25th Inf. Born in Collinsville, PA; Ht 5'8", black hair and eyes, black complexion; occupation cook; recruited as trumpeter, enlisted at age 19, Pittsburgh, PA, 21 Jun 1882; arrived Ft Snelling, MN, 21 Nov 1882. SOURCE: Descriptive & Assignment Rolls of Recruits, 25 Inf.

WILLIAMS, Oliver; Private; M/48th Inf. ‡Died of hydrophobia in the Philippines, 15 Sep 1900. SOURCE: *ANJ* 38 (29 Sep 1900): 115.

Died 15 Sep 1900; buried in plot NEW A1044 at San Francisco National Cemetery. SOURCE: San Francisco National Cemetery.

WILLIAMS, Preston; Private; 24th Inf. Died on detached service 13 May 1907; buried in plot NADD 1158 at San Francisco National Cemetery. SOURCE: San Francisco National Cemetery.

WILLIAMS, Richard; Sergeant; B/24th Inf. ‡"Worthy of especial mention for bravery and fidelity." SOURCE: SecWar, *AR 1898*, 715.

‡Awarded certificate of merit for service as corporal in Cuban campaign, 1 Jul 1898. SOURCE: GO 15, AGO, 13 Feb 1900; Scipio, *Last of the Black Regulars*, 130; *ANJ* 37 (24 Feb 1900): 611; Steward, *The Colored Regulars*, 280.

Awarded certificate of merit for distinguished service in battle, Santiago, Cuba, 1 Jul 1898. SOURCE: Gleim, *The Certificate of Merit*, 46.

Born in Cincinnati, OH; resided in Dayton, OH; received Distinguished Service Medal in lieu of certificate of merit. SOURCE: *American Decorations*, 845.

‡Sergeant, B/24th Infantry; on special duty as provost sergeant, Cabanatuan, Philippines, Jan 1901. SOURCE: Name File, 24 Inf.

WILLIAMS, Robert E.; Private; B/24th Inf. Died 21 Mar 1914; buried in plot W SID146-A at San Francisco National Cemetery. SOURCE: San Francisco National Cemetery.

WILLIAMS, S. W.; Private; Band/10th Cav. Private, received Indian Wars Campaign Badge number 538 on 16 Apr 1909. SOURCE: Carroll, *Indian Wars Campaign Badge*, 15.

WILLIAMS, Samuel F.; Musician; Band/10th Cav. Drowned 15 Aug 1880 at Ft Concho, TX. SOURCE: Regimental Returns, 10th Cavalry, 1880.

Died at Ft Concho on 15 Aug 1880; buried at San Antonio National Cemetery, Section E, number 818. SOURCE: San Antonio National Cemetery Locator.

WILLIAMS, Sidney; Corporal; K/10th Cav. ‡Private, released to duty from treatment for gonorrhea, Ft Robinson, NE, 7 Aug 1903. SOURCE: Post Surgeon to CO, K/10, 7 Aug 1903, LS, Post Surgeon, Ft Robinson.

‡Released to duty from treatment for gonorrhea, Ft Robinson, 24 Aug 1903. SOURCE: Post Surgeon to CO, K/10, 24 Aug 1903, LS, Post Surgeon, Ft Robinson.

‡Member of troop orchestra. SOURCE: Barrow, "Christmas in the United States Army," 96.

Corporal, K/10th Cavalry, died 7 Jun 1937; buried in plot DWEST1085 at San Francisco National Cemetery. SOURCE: San Francisco National Cemetery.

WILLIAMS, Squire; Corporal; D/24th Inf. Corporal in E/25th Infantry, disarmed Pvt. William Thomas, C/25th Infantry, who was accused of threatening Sgt. I. Woodow, E/25th Infantry, with loaded rifle following disturbance at post trader's store at Ft Hale, Dakota Territory, around 19 May 1881. SOURCE: General Court-Martial Orders No. 99, Ft Snelling, MN, 19 Aug 1881, photocopy in authors' files.

‡Pvt. Squire Williams mentioned among men who distinguished themselves in 1889; awarded certificate of merit for gallant and meritorious conduct as escort for Maj. Joseph W. Wham, paymaster, when attacked by robbers between Fts Grant and Thomas, AZ; now in B/24th Infantry. SOURCE: GO 18, AGO, 1891.

Private in K/24th Infantry, eighteen-year veteran, cited for bravery against robbers near Cedar Springs, AZ, in May 1889 by Maj. Joseph W. Wham, and awarded certificate of merit; wounded in leg during fight; still in Army at end of 1890. SOURCE: Schubert, *Black Valor*, 93, 95.

Text of report of Paymaster Wham, describing bravery of escort. SOURCE: Schubert, *Voices of the Buffalo Soldier*, 159–62.

Awarded certificate of merit for gallant and meritorious conduct while member of escort of Maj. Joseph W. Wham, paymaster, who was ambushed by bandits between Fts Grant and Thomas, 11 May 1889. SOURCE: Gleim, *The Certificate of Merit*, 44.

‡Transferred from Reserve Divisional Hospital, Siboney, Cuba, to U.S. on U.S. Army Transport *Santiago* with yellow fever, 25 Jul 1898. SOURCE: Hospital Papers, Spanish-American War.

‡Pvt. William Workman, D/24th Infantry, was fined for insubordination to Cpl. Squire Williams, D/24th Infantry, at Cabanatuan, Philippines, 19 Dec 1900. SOURCE: Name File, 24 Inf.

‡Pvt. Wheeler Pride, D/24th Infantry, fined 16 Jan 1901 for failure to obey lawful order of Cpl. Squire Williams, D/24th Infantry, to go to quarters at Cabanatuan, 1901. SOURCE: Name File, 24 Inf.

‡Retired as corporal D/24th Infantry, Jun 1901. SOURCE: *ANJ* 38 (15 Jun 1901): 1019.

‡Served with Buford Parker; settled in Salt Lake City. SOURCE: Clark, "A History of the Twenty-fourth," 69.

‡Now retired; commended for gallantry, 11 May 1889, while private, K/24th Infantry, on escort duty. SOURCE: Cleveland *Gazette*, 24 Nov 1906.

WILLIAMS, Thomas; Recruit; A/10th Cav. ‡Recruit from Jefferson Barracks, MO; arrived Ft Leavenworth, KS, 9 Oct 1866; died of pneumonia in Ft Leavenworth hospital same day. SOURCE: McMiller, "Buffalo Soldiers," 45.

Died 9 Oct 1866 of pneumonia at Ft Leavenworth. SOURCE: Regimental Returns, 10th Cavalry, 1866.

WILLIAMS, Thomas; Private; K/9th Cav. Born in Galveston, TX, 25 Dec 1863; father Benjamin F. resided near Mt. Sterling, Montgomery County, KY; mother Sarah Ann; sisters Lucinda, Betty, Malinda, Bell, Nan; brothers Bill, Albert, Buford, Sandford; enlisted Cincinnati, OH, 2 Jan 1884; Ht 5'5", brown complexion, black eyes and hair; occupation hostler and laborer; served in H/10th Cavalry, discharged at San Carlos, AZ, 1 Jan 1889; enlisted 2 Aug 1895; served in K/9th Cavalry, discharged at Santiago, Cuba, 1 Aug 1898; first wife Annie S. Crittenden, married 31 May 1893, Cincinnati; second wife Julia Arnold, married ca. 1902, died 6 Aug 1920, Cincinnati; also married Hattie Ringgold, no date; applied for pension based on malaria and rheumatism contracted in Cuba, Jul 1898; received $18 per month from Mar 1925, increased to $40 in Jun 1932, increased to $50 in Jul 1932, reduced to $15 in Jul 1933, restored to $50 in Sep 1935, increased to $60 in Dec 1938; resided at 2049 5th Ave., College Hill, Cincinnati, in 1945; died at Hamilton County Home, Cincinnati, 10 Mar 1948; buried at Union Baptist Cemetery, Cincinnati. SOURCE: Sayre, *Warriors of Color*, 219, 496–510.

In Troop H/10th Cavalry stationed at Bonita Cañon Camp, AZ, but absent or on detached service 30 Apr 1886. SOURCE: Tagg, *The Camp at Bonita Cañon*, 232.

WILLIAMS, Thomas; Private; F/25th Inf. ‡Deserted in Luzon, Philippines, 27 Sep 1900. SOURCE: Regt Returns, 25 Inf, Oct 1899.

‡Died of syphilis in the Philippines, 3 Aug 1901. SOURCE: *ANJ* 39 (28 Sep 1901): 81.

Died in the Philippines, 3 Aug 1901; buried in plot ADD689 at San Francisco National Cemetery. SOURCE: San Francisco National Cemetery.

WILLIAMS, Thomas; Private; H/48th Inf. Died 11 Nov 1900; buried in plot N ADD878 at San Francisco National Cemetery. SOURCE: San Francisco National Cemetery.

WILLIAMS, Thomas; Private; L/24th Inf. Mailing address Station K, College Hill, Cincinnati, OH, in 1924. SOURCE: Sayre, *Warriors of Color*, 501.

WILLIAMS, Walter; Private; B/9th Cav. Died at Calaoango, Philippines, 29 May 1902; buried in plot NA WS600 at San Francisco National Cemetery. SOURCE: San Francisco National Cemetery.

WILLIAMS, Washington; Private; 25th Inf. Born in New Orleans, LA; Ht 5'5", brown hair and eyes, brown complexion; discharged from K/9th Cavalry 31 Jan 1886; third enlistment at age 32, Chicago, IL, 11 May 1886; assigned to D/25th Infantry; arrived Ft Snelling, MN, 25 Apr 1887. SOURCE: Descriptive & Assignment Rolls of Recruits, 25 Inf.

WILLIAMS, William; Private; D/24th Inf. Born in Adair, KY; buried at Ft McKavett, TX, before 17 May 1879; body removed to National Cemetery, San Antonio, TX, 23 Nov 1883. SOURCE: Bierschwale, *Fort McKavett*, 123.

Died at Ft McKavett on 1 Apr 1870; buried at San Antonio National Cemetery, Section E, number 838. SOURCE: San Antonio National Cemetery Locator.

WILLIAMS, William; Private; F/10th Cav. Died Jun 1889; originally buried at Ft Grant, AZ; reburied at Santa Fe National Cemetery, NM, plot A-1 753. SOURCE: Santa Fe National Cemetery, Records of Burials.

WILLIAMS, William; Private; G/23rd Kan Inf. Died 9 Mar 1899; buried at Ft Leavenworth National Cemetery, plot G 3176. SOURCE: Ft Leavenworth National Cemetery.

WILLIAMS, William; Private; E/25th Inf. ‡Died of variola in the Philippines, 21 Sep 1901. SOURCE: *ANJ* 39 (7 Dec 1901): 339.

Died 21 Sep 1901; buried in plot NADD 858 at San Francisco National Cemetery. SOURCE: San Francisco National Cemetery.

WILLIAMS, William; Private; G/25th Inf. ‡Died of heart failure in the Philippines, 10 Apr 1902. SOURCE: *ANJ* 39 (14 Jun 1902): 1046.

Died 10 Apr 1902; buried in plot N ADD383 at San Francisco National Cemetery. SOURCE: San Francisco National Cemetery.

WILLIAMS, William H.; Private; A/9th Cav. Served in H/40th Infantry, 1866–69; in I/25th Infantry, 1869–84; enlisted in H/10th Cavalry, May or June 1885; corporal at Bonita Canon, AZ, in 1885; at Ft Apache, AZ; discharged 1890; enlisted 1890 in A/9th Cavalry, served until Feb 1892, discharged with disability caused by anemia and rheumatism; resided in Anacostia, DC, on Nichols Ave., driver for Government Hospital for the Insane, St. Elizabeth, age 49, in 1902. SOURCE: Sayre, *Warriors of Color*, 362.

‡Served at Ft Sill, Indian Territory, with William Branch; resides at 217 Starr Avenue, San Antonio, TX, age 46. SOURCE: Affidavit, 21 Mar 1899, VA File C 2581520, William Branch.

Private in Troop E/10th Cavalry stationed at Bonita Cañon Camp, AZ, 30 Apr 1886. SOURCE: Tagg, *The Camp at Bonita Cañon*, 232.

‡Junior Vice Commander, Camp 30, National Indian War Veterans, San Antonio. SOURCE: *Winners of the West* 6 (Oct 1929): 7.

‡Picture with comrades of Camp 30, National Indian War Veterans. SOURCE: *Winners of the West* 9 (Mar 1932): 7.

Died on 6 Oct 1936; buried at Fort Sam Houston National Cemetery, Section A, number 41. Also known as William Rideout. SOURCE: Buffalo Soldiers Interred in Fort Sam Houston National Cemetery.

WILLIAMS, William O.; Corporal; G/9th Cav. ‡Corporal, G/9th Cavalry; veteran of Philippine Insurrection; at Ft D. A. Russell, WY, in 1910; sharpshooter; resident of Chattanooga, TN. SOURCE: *Illustrated Review: Ninth Cavalry*, with picture.

Master sergeant, 9th Cavalry; died 19 May 1946; buried at Ft Leavenworth National Cemetery, plot E 3011. SOURCE: Ft Leavenworth National Cemetery.

WILLIAMS, Willie H.; Private; 9th Cav. Received Philippine Campaign Badge for service as private in D/25th Infantry; in 9th Cavalry at Ft Leavenworth, KS, Mar 1905. SOURCE: Philippine Campaign Badge list, 29 May 1905.

WILLIAMS, Wilson; Private; E/25th Inf. ‡Drowned in the Philippines; body recovered. SOURCE: *ANJ* 39 (8 Feb 1902): 577.

Died 30 Nov 1901; buried in plot N/A 1038 at San Francisco National Cemetery. SOURCE: San Francisco National Cemetery.

WILLIAMSON, Alexander; Private; D/10th Cav. ‡Original member of 10th Cavalry; in troop when organized, Ft Leavenworth, KS, 1 Jun 1867. SOURCE: McMiller, "Buffalo Soldiers," 71.

Died 1 Jan 1869 of no listed cause in the field, Indian Territory. SOURCE: Regimental Returns, 10th Cavalry, 1869.

WILLIAMSON, David; Corporal; F/9th Cav. Corporal, received Indian Wars Campaign Badge number 1369 on 1 Jun 1909. SOURCE: Carroll, *Indian Wars Campaign Badge*, 39.

WILLIAMSON, David; Private; G/9th Cav. Received Philippine Campaign Badge number 11848 for service as sergeant in E/9th Cavalry, 16 Sep 1900–16 Sep 1902; private in G/9th Cavalry, Ft Leavenworth, KS, Mar 1905. SOURCE: Philippine Campaign Badge Recipients; Philippine Campaign Badge list, 29 May 1905.

WILLIAMSON, Richard; Private; K/25th Inf. Born in Richmond, VA; Ht 5'4", black complexion; occupation farmer; enlisted in A/39th Infantry for three years on 18 Jul 1867, age 21, at Philadelphia, PA; transferred to K/25th Infantry at Jackson Bks, LA, 20 Apr 1869. SOURCE: Descriptive Roll of A/39th Inf.

WILLIAMSON, Sam; Private; G/25th Inf. One of twenty men who cycled 1,900 miles from Ft Missoula, MT, to St. Louis, MO, 14 Jun–24 Jul 1897, in 25th Infantry Bicycle Corps to test durability and practicality of bicycles as a means of transportation for troops. SOURCE: File 60178, GC, AGO Records.

WILLIAMSON, William; Private; G/25th Inf. One of twenty men who cycled 1,900 miles from Ft Missoula, MT, to St. Louis, MO, 14 Jun–24 Jul 1897, in 25th Infantry Bicycle Corps to test durability and practicality of bicycles as a means of transportation for troops. SOURCE: File 60178, GC, AGO Records.

WILLIAMSON, William; Private; H/25th Inf. Died 10 Aug 1901; buried in plot N ADD1039 at San Francisco National Cemetery. SOURCE: San Francisco National Cemetery.

WILLINGHAM, Ephraine; Private; Band/24th Inf. ‡Born in Tuscaloosa, AL; occupation minister; Ht 5'10", black eyes and hair, mulatto complexion; enlisted Ft Gibson, Indian Territory, age 28, 4 Dec 1888; assigned to F/24th Infantry, 9 Dec 1888; on detached service in Band/24th Infantry, learning music, 7 Feb–22 Mar 1889, then transferred to band; died of consumption in post hospital, Ft Bayard, NM, 7 Sep 1889, character excellent, single, clothing $10.32. SOURCE: Descriptive Book, 24 Inf NCS & Band.

Died 7 Sep 1889; buried at Ft Bayard in plot G 16. SOURCE: "Fort Bayard National Cemetery, Records of Burials."

E. M. (Ephraim) Willingham buried 7 Sep 1889, section A, row I, plot 18, at Ft Bayard. SOURCE: Erickson, Burials at Fort Bayard National Cemetery, NM.

WILLINGHAM, William; Private; M/25th Inf. ‡Drowned, Iba, Luzon, Philippines, 10 Aug 1901; body recovered. SOURCE: *ANJ* 39 (12 Oct 1901): 140.

Pvt. William Willimgham, H/25th Infantry; died 10 Aug 1901; buried in plot N ADD1038 at San Francisco National Cemetery. SOURCE: San Francisco National Cemetery.

WILLIS, Alexander; Private; L/9th Cav. Enlisted 3 Feb 1879 at Baltimore, MD; stationed at Ft Bliss, TX, Nov 1879–Feb 1880; in the field in New Mexico in pursuit of Victorio's band of hostile Apaches 8 Jan 1880–22 Feb 1880, left Ojo Caliente 24 Feb and marched via Canada Alamosa and Cuchillo Negro, arriving at Chase's Ranch, 26 Feb 1880, after marching 621 miles in Jan and Feb; troop at Chase's Ranch, NM, 29 Feb 1880 awaiting further orders; on detached duty as orderly for CO July–Aug 1880; on detached duty at Ft Cummings, NM, as orderly for Lieutenant Colonel Dudly, 9th Cavalry, Sep–Oct 1880; left Ft Stanton, NM, with L/9th Cavalry 11 Nov 1880, arrived Ft Bliss 18 Nov 1880; at Ft Bliss Jan–Feb 1881. SOURCE: Muster Rolls, L/9th Cavalry, 31 Oct 1879–29 Feb 1880, 30 June 1880–28 Feb 1881.

‡Pvt. Alex Willis on detached service in the field, New Mexico, 21 Jan–24 Feb 1881. SOURCE: Regt Returns, 9 Cav, Feb 1881.

WILLIS, Findley; Corporal; L/9th Cav. Retired; died 15 Mar 1917; buried at Ft Leavenworth National Cemetery, plot H 3292-E. SOURCE: Ft Leavenworth National Cemetery.

WILLIS, John; Private; F/9th Cav. Died 3 Feb 1906; buried at Ft Leavenworth National Cemetery, plot G 3444. SOURCE: Ft Leavenworth National Cemetery.

WILLS, William B.; Private; E/10th Cav. In Troop E/10th Cavalry stationed at Bonita Cañon Camp, AZ, 28 Feb 1886. SOURCE: Tagg, *The Camp at Bonita Cañon*, 232.

WILSON, Alexander; H/25th Inf. Born in Virginia; mulatto complexion; can read and write, age 24, 5 Sep 1870, at Ft McKavett, TX. SOURCE: Bierschwale, *Fort McKavett*, 108.

WILSON, Amos; Private; D/9th Cav. ‡Born and resided in North Carolina; prisoner No. 125, U.S. Military Prison, Leavenworth, KS, died 29 Aug 1877 of consumption, age 28, single. SOURCE: Certificates of Disability, DivMo, 1875–87.

Anne [*sic*] Wilson, Private, D/9th Cavalry, died 29 Aug 1877; buried at Ft Leavenworth National Cemetery, plot 1492. SOURCE: Ft Leavenworth National Cemetery.

WILSON, Ariel; Private; U.S. Army. Seminole Negro Scout, served 1874–77. SOURCE: Schubert, Consolidated List of Seminole Negro Scouts.

Born in Mexico; Ht 5'7", black hair and eyes, black complexion; enlisted at Ft Clark, TX, 1 Oct 1874, age 24; discharged 1 Apr 1875 at Ft Clark where he reenlisted 5 Apr 1875; discharged, reenlisted 5 Oct 1875 at Ft Supply, TX; appointed corporal 23 Feb 1876; discharged as corporal, reenlisted 13 Apr 1876 at Ft Clark; discharged as private 12 Oct 1876, reenlisted next day at Ft Clark; discharged 31 Apr 1877 at Camp Painted Comanche, TX. SOURCE: Swanson, 52.

WILSON, Arthur; 25th Inf. ‡Born in Charleston, SC; enlisted in 25th Infantry, Charleston, 1866; discharged from Jackson Bks, LA, 1868; went as part of crew of eighty colored waiters and forty-two colored chambermaids to San Francisco, where Palace Hotel opened; worked there three years; worked five years with Fletchheime & Gooskine wholesale warehouse, five years as porter with Pullman Car Company, twenty-five years as private car porter, Southern Pacific Railroad; retired and lived three years; died of heart trouble; second wife was youngest daughter of Reverend Sanderson; trustee of 15th Street African Methodist Episcopal Church, Oakland, CA. SOURCE: Beasley, *Negro Trailblazers*, 299.

Pvt. Arthur Wilson, B/25th Infantry, died 22 Jun 1918; buried in plot N/A 550-A at San Francisco National Cemetery. SOURCE: San Francisco National Cemetery.

WILSON, Bailey; Artificer; K/25th Inf. Born in Pass Christian, MS; Ht 5'4", black complexion; occupation laborer; enlisted in A/39th Infantry for three years on 7 Sep 1866, age 23, at Ft Pike, LA; daily duty as post quartermaster since 1 Apr 1869; transferred to K/25th Infantry at Jackson Bks, LA, 20 Apr 1869. SOURCE: Descriptive Roll of A/39th Inf.

WILSON, Ben; Private; U.S. Army. Seminole Negro Scout, served 1871–94. SOURCE: Schubert, Consolidated List of Seminole Negro Scouts.

Born in Mexico; Ht 5'7", black hair and eyes, black complexion; enlisted at Ft Duncan, TX, 7 Oct 1871, age 16; discharged 7 Apr 1872, enlisted next day at Ft Duncan; discharged 8 Oct 1872 at Ft Duncan where he reenlisted 14 Oct 1872; discharged 19 Apr 1873, enlisted next day at Ft Clark, TX; discharged, reenlisted 20 Oct 1873 at Ft Clark; discharged 23 Apr 1874 at Ft Clark where he enlisted 22 Jun 1874; discharged 22 Dec 1874 at Ft Clark where he enlisted 26 Jan 1875; discharged 9 Sep 1875 at Camp Supply, TX; enlisted 4 Oct 1875 at Ft Clark; discharged, reenlisted 4 Feb 1876 at Ft Clark; discharged, reenlisted 4 Aug 1876 at Camp Pecos, TX; dropped 1 Mar 1877 while absent, in hands of civil authorities; enlisted for one year, discharged at Ft Clark three times, 4 Mar 1878–12 May 1881; enlisted 13 May 1881 at Ft Clark; discharged 22 May 1882, reenlisted next day at Camp Pecos; discharged as corporal 23 May 1884 at Camp Myers, TX, reenlisted next day at Ft Clark; discharged as private 2 Jun 1885 at Camp Neville Springs, TX, where he reenlisted 4 Jun 1885; discharged as private 3 Jun 1886 at Ft Clark, reenlisted next day at Camp Neville Springs; discharged 3 Jun 1887 at Camp San Carlos, reenlisted next day at Ft Clark; discharged 3 Jun 1888, reenlisted next day at Camp Pena Colorado, TX; discharged, reenlisted for one year next day at Camp Neville Springs twice, 3 Jun 1889–9 Jun 1890; discharged, reenlisted 9 Jun 1891 at Camp Palvo, TX; discharged, reenlisted 9 Dec 1891 at Camp Palvo; discharged 7 Nov 1892 at Ft Ringgold, TX; enlisted for six months, age 35, 27 Feb 1894 at Ft Clark; discharged without honor at Ft Ringgold; 1880 Census lists Ben Wilson age 24, parents born in Arkansas, wife Mintee age 22, born in Alabama, daughter Mary. SOURCE: Swanson, 53.

WILSON, Ben, Jr.; Private; U.S. Army. Seminole Negro Scout, served in 1884. SOURCE: Schubert, Consolidated List of Seminole Negro Scouts.

Promoted from private to corporal Jun 1884. SOURCE: NARA, M 929, Roll 2.

WILSON, Ben, Sr.; Private; U.S. Army. Seminole Negro Scout, served 1871–72, 1874–88. SOURCE: Schubert, Consolidated List of Seminole Negro Scouts.

Born in Arkansas; Ht 5'8", black hair and eyes, black complexion; enlisted at Ft Duncan, TX, 31 Aug 1871, age 32; discharged, reenlisted 29 Feb 1872 at Ft Duncan; discharged 14 Oct 1872 at Ft Clark, TX; enlisted 1 Jan 1874 at Ft Duncan; discharged 1 Jul 1874 at Camp Palafox, TX; enlisted 1 Feb 1875 at Ft Duncan; discharged 1 Aug 1875 at Ft Concho, TX; enlisted 1 Feb 1876 at Ft Duncan; discharged 30 Jul 1876 at Ft Duncan; enlisted 1 Aug 1876 at Camp Supply, TX; discharged 1 Feb 1877 at Ft Duncan, reenlisted for one year and discharged at Ft Clark 1 Mar 1877–12 May 1881; enlisted 13 May 1881 at Ft Clark; discharged 22 May 1882 at Camp Pecos, TX; enlisted 2 Jun 1882 at Camp Myers, TX; discharged 1 Jun 1883, reenlisted next day at Ft Clark; discharged 1 Jun 1884, reenlisted 3 Jun 1884 at Camp Myers; discharged 31 Aug 1884 at Ft Clark where he reenlisted 27 Dec 1884; discharged 26 Dec 1885 at Camp Neville Springs, TX; enlisted 9 Jan 1886, discharged 8 Jan 1887 at Ft Clark; enlisted 8 Jan 1887 at Ft Clark where he was discharged 8 Jan 1888; 1880 Census lists Ben Wilson age 45, Catherine, born in Arkansas, age 30, and Plenty, Crecia, Hannah, Termes, Maggii, Millie; died 16 Sep 1918; buried at Seminole Indian Scout Cemetery, Kinney County, TX. SOURCE: Swanson, 52.

In 1875, age 45, resided at Ft Duncan with Katie age 30, Mollie age 11, Planty age 9, Creasi age 7, Penny age 1; daughter Penny, born 1874, married name Factor. SOURCE: NARA Record Group 393, Special File; Porter, *The Negro on the American Frontier,* 477.

Daughter Penny Factor, born 4 Sep 1874, died 8 Apr 1970, buried at Seminole Indian Scout Cemetery, Kinney County, TX. SOURCE: Indian Scout Cemetery, Kinney County, Texas.

WILSON, Bill; Private; U.S. Army. Seminole Negro Scout, also known as Billy, served 1893–94, 1901–14; wife Rebecca was niece of Chief John Horse and daughter of Scout Sampson July. SOURCE: Schubert, Consolidated List of Seminole Negro Scouts.

Born in Texas; Seminole Negro Scout also known as Billy; Ht 5'6", black hair and eyes, black complexion; enlisted at Ft Clark, TX, 13 Jan 1893, age 21; twice discharged, reenlisted for six months next day at Ft Ringgold, TX, 12 Jul 1893–13 Jan 1894; discharged 12 Jul 1894 at Ft Ringgold; enlisted 17 Aug 1894 at Ft Clark; discharged 30 Nov 1894 at Ft Ringgold; enlisted 8 Mar 1901 at Ft Clark; discharged 8 Mar 1904, reenlisted for three years next day at Ft Ringgold; twice discharged, reenlisted next day at Ft Clark 7 Mar 1907–9 Mar 1910; discharged 8 Mar 1913, reenlisted 10 Mar 1913 for seven years at Ft Clark; honorably discharged 31 Aug 1914 when Seminole Scouts Detachment was decommissioned. SOURCE: Swanson, 53.

Married to daughter of Scout Sampson July. SOURCE: Schubert, *Black Valor,* 30.

Billy Wilson, born 13 Jan 1873; died 22 Jul 1952, buried at Seminole Indian Scout Cemetery, Kinney County, TX. SOURCE: Indian Scout Cemetery, Kinney County, Texas.

Rebecca Wilson, born 9 Aug 1881, died 10 Jun 1960, buried at Seminole Indian Scout Cemetery, Kinney County, TX. SOURCE: Indian Scout Cemetery, Kinney County, Texas.

WILSON, Brisban; Private; U.S. Army. Seminole Negro Scout, also known as Bristow Wilson, served 1877–78, 1883–84. SOURCE: Schubert, Consolidated List of Seminole Negro Scouts.

Born in Mexico; Ht 5'7", black hair and eyes, black complexion; enlisted Ft Clark, TX, 17 Aug 1877, age 22;

discharged 8 Aug 1878; enlisted 1 Mar 1883, age 23, at Ft Clark; discharged 29 Feb 1884, reenlisted next day at Ft Clark; discharged 31 Aug 1884. SOURCE: Swanson, 54.

WILSON, Clay; F/9th Cav. Born in Kentucky; black complexion; cannot read or write, age 22, Jul 1870, at Ft McKavett, TX. SOURCE: Bierschwale, *Fort McKavett,* 97.

WILSON, Coffy; Private; U.S. Army. Seminole Negro Scout, also known as Cuffy, served 1871–74. SOURCE: Schubert, Consolidated List of Seminole Negro Scouts.

Born in Mexico; Ht 5'10", black hair and eyes, mulatto complexion; enlisted at Ft Duncan, TX, 7 Oct 1871, age 18; discharged 7 Apr 1872, reenlisted next day at Ft Duncan; discharged 7 Oct 1872, reenlisted next day at Ft Clark, TX; twice discharged, reenlisted for six months at Ft Clark, 9 Apr 1873–11 Oct 1873; final discharge 11 Apr 1874 at Ft Clark. SOURCE: Swanson, 54.

WILSON, Cuff; Private; U.S. Army. Seminole Negro Scout, served 1882–84. SOURCE: Schubert, Consolidated List of Seminole Negro Scouts.

Born in Mexico; Ht 5'11", black hair and eyes, black complexion; enlisted at Ft Clark, TX, 17 Dec 1882, age 26; discharged 26 Dec 1883, reenlisted next day at Camp Myers, TX; discharged 11 Apr 1884 at Ft Clark. SOURCE: Swanson, 54.

WILSON, Daniel; Private; F/9th Cav. Born in Kentucky; black complexion; cannot read or write, age 23, Jul 1870, at Ft McKavett, TX. SOURCE: Bierschwale, *Fort McKavett,* 98.

Died at Ft McKavett while in F/9th Cavalry on 1 Jun 1870; buried at San Antonio National Cemetery, Section E, number 893. SOURCE: San Antonio National Cemetery Locator.

WILSON, David; Private; F/9th Cav. Born in Kentucky; died and buried at Ft McKavett, TX, before 17 May 1879; body removed to National Cemetery, San Antonio, TX, 23 Nov 1883. SOURCE: Bierschwale, *Fort McKavett,* 122.

WILSON, Felix; Private; E/10th Cav. Enlisted in Washington, DC; in Troop E/10th Cavalry stationed at Bonita Cañon Camp, AZ, 28 Feb 1886. SOURCE: Tagg, *The Camp at Bonita Cañon,* 66, 232.

WILSON, Frank; Sgt Maj; 10th Cav. Served as sergeant major from Apr 1868 until he deserted Sep 1870. SOURCE: Schubert, *Black Valor,* 57.

WILSON, Frederick; Private; E/10th Cav. Pvt. Fred Wilson, E/10th Cavalry, stationed at Bonita Cañon Camp, AZ, 28 Feb 1886. SOURCE: Tagg, *The Camp at Bonita Cañon,* 232.

‡Honorable mention for skill in successful pursuit of raiding parties in Arizona, 1888. SOURCE: Baker, Roster.

‡At Ft Apache, AZ, 1890, subscribed $.50 to testimonial to General Grierson. SOURCE: List of subscriptions, 23 Apr 1890, 10th Cavalry papers, MHI.

WILSON, George; H/25th Inf. Born in Illinois; mulatto complexion; can read and write, age 22, 5 Sep 1870, at Ft McKavett, TX. SOURCE: Bierschwale, *Fort McKavett,* 108.

WILSON, George; Private; K/25th Inf. Born in Bayou La Fourche, LA; Ht 5'11", black complexion; occupation laborer; enlisted in A/39th Infantry for three years on 17 Dec 1866, age 21, at Greenville, LA; transferred to K/25th Infantry at Jackson Bks, LA, 20 Apr 1869. SOURCE: Descriptive Roll of A/39th Inf.

WILSON, George; Private; K/25th Inf. Died at Ft Davis, TX, on 19 Jul 1876; buried at San Antonio National Cemetery, Section I, number 1510. SOURCE: San Antonio National Cemetery Locator.

WILSON, George; Sergeant; I/9th Cav. Served during operations against "boomers" in Indian Territory, 1884. SOURCE: Kenner, *Buffalo Soldiers and Officers of the Ninth Cavalry,* 203.

WILSON, George; Private; L/9th Cav. At Ft Leavenworth, KS, 1890, superb long-distance runner. SOURCE: Kenner, *Buffalo Soldiers and Officers of the Ninth Cavalry,* 19.

WILSON, George; Private; 25th Inf. Died 18 May 1908 while on detached duty; buried at Ft Bayard, NM, in plot Q 19. SOURCE: "Fort Bayard National Cemetery, Records of Burials."

In B/25th Infantry; buried 18 May 1908, section B, row B, plot 19 at Ft Bayard. SOURCE: Erickson, Burials at Fort Bayard National Cemetery, NM.

WILSON, George W.; Private; I/10th Cav. In Troop I/10th Cavalry stationed at Bonita Cañon Camp, AZ, 30 Jun 1886. SOURCE: Tagg, *The Camp at Bonita Cañon,* 232.

WILSON, Harrison; Sergeant; 24th Inf. Complimented for his honesty in Sep 1871 by Secretary of War after sending through chain of command a letter received by Pvt. Benjamin Norman, offering exact facsimiles of U.S. currency. SOURCE: Dobak and Phillips, *The Black Regulars,* 144, 313.

WILSON, Herbert; Private; 9th Cav. Received Philippine Campaign Badge number 11798 for service as private in F/9th Cavalry; in 9th Cavalry at Ft Leavenworth, KS,

Mar 1905. SOURCE: Philippine Campaign Badge list, 29 May 1905.

WILSON, Isaac; Private; U.S. Army. Seminole Negro Scout, served 1907–14. SOURCE: Schubert, Consolidated List of Seminole Negro Scouts.

Born in Eagle Pass, TX; Ht 5'8", black hair, dark eyes, dark complexion; enlisted at Ft Clark, TX, 15 Mar 1907; discharged 14 Mar 1910, reenlisted next day at Ft Clark; discharged 11 Mar 1913, reenlisted next day at Ft Clark; honorably discharged 30 Sep 1914 at Ft Clark. SOURCE: Swanson, 54.

WILSON, Jacob; Private; 10th Cav. At Ft Stockton, TX, 1876, in guardhouse for offenses related to drunkenness, got out by promising to abstain for one year. SOURCE: Dobak and Phillips, *The Black Regulars,* 166.

WILSON, Jacob B.; Private; G/9th Cav. Jacob B. or D. Wilson died 8 Feb 1891; originally buried at Ft Niobrara, NE; reburied at Ft Leavenworth National Cemetery, plot G 3573. SOURCE: Ft Leavenworth National Cemetery.

WILSON, Jacob D.; Private; G/9th Cav. *See* WILSON, Jacob B., Private, G/9th Cavalry

WILSON, James; Private; B/10th Cav. ‡Original member of 10th Cavalry; in troop when organized, Ft Leavenworth, KS, 1 Apr 1867. SOURCE: McMiller, "Buffalo Soldiers," 69.

‡Sick in post hospital, Ft Riley, KS. SOURCE: LR, Det 10 Cav, 1868–69.

Died 3 Apr 1869 of disease at Ft Dodge, KS. SOURCE: Regimental Returns, 10th Cavalry, 1869.

WILSON, James; Private; U.S. Army. Seminole Negro Scout, also known as Jim, served 1871–75. SOURCE: Schubert, Consolidated List of Seminole Negro Scouts.

Born in Mexico; Ht 5'11", black hair and eyes, mulatto complexion; enlisted at Ft Duncan, TX, 7 Oct 1871, age 22; discharged 7 Apr 1872, reenlisted next day at Ft Clark, TX; discharged 23 Oct 1872, reenlisted 25 Oct 1872 at Ft Clark; discharged 24 Sept 1873, reenlisted 27 Sep 1873 at Ft Clark; discharged 29 Mar 1874 at Ft Clark where he enlisted 16 Jul 1874; discharged 27 Jan 1875 at Ft Clark where he enlisted for three months 2 Mar 1875; discharged 9 Jun 1875. SOURCE: Swanson, 55.

In 1875, age 25, resided at Ft Duncan with Hannah age 29, Sam age 9, Cilla age 8, Betsy age 6. SOURCE: NARA Record Group 393, Special File.

WILSON, James; Sergeant; I/9th Cav. Served on honor guard when body of Col. Edward Hatch was transported from Ft Robinson, NE, to Ft Leavenworth, KS, in 1889.

SOURCE: Kenner, *Buffalo Soldiers and Officers of the Ninth Cavalry*, 48–49.

WILSON, James; Private; L/9th Cav. Enlisted at Baltimore, MD, 20 Jan 1881; at Ft Bliss, TX. SOURCE: Muster Roll, L/9th Cavalry. 30 Apr–30 Jun 1881.

WILSON, Jasper; Private; U.S. Army. Seminole Negro Scout, served 1893–94. SOURCE: Schubert, Consolidated List of Seminole Negro Scouts.

Born in Mexico; Ht 5'6", black hair and eyes, black complexion; enlisted at Ft Clark, TX, 13 Jan 1893, age 23; discharged 12 Jul 1893, reenlisted next day at Ft Ringgold, TX; discharged 12 Jan 1894 at Ft Ringgold, reenlisted next day at Camp San Pedro, TX; discharged 12 Jul 1894, reenlisted next day at Ft Ringgold; discharged 30 Nov 1894, Ft Ringgold. SOURCE: Swanson, 57.

WILSON, Jasper; Wagoner; 9th Cav. Received Philippine Campaign Badge number 11799 for service as wagoner in F/9th Cavalry; in 9th Cavalry at Ft Leavenworth, KS, Mar 1905. SOURCE: Philippine Campaign Badge list, 29 May 1905.

WILSON, John; Private; G/10th Cav. Died 31 Jul 1867 of cholera at Wilson Creek, KS. SOURCE: Regimental Returns, 10th Cavalry, 1867.

WILSON, John; F/9th Cav. Born in Louisiana; black complexion; cannot read or write, age 21, Jul 1870, at Ft McKavett, TX. SOURCE: Bierschwale, *Fort McKavett*, 97.

WILSON, John H.; Private; G/25th Inf. One of twenty men who cycled 1,900 miles from Ft Missoula, MT, to St. Louis, MO, 14 Jun–24 Jul 1897, in 25th Infantry Bicycle Corps to test durability and practicality of bicycles as a means of transportation for troops. SOURCE: File 60178, GC, AGO Records.

WILSON, John W.; H/25th Inf. Born in Ohio; mulatto complexion; can read and write, age 21, 5 Sep 1870, at Ft McKavett, TX. SOURCE: Bierschwale, *Fort McKavett*, 107.

WILSON, Joseph L.; Private; B/25th Inf. Enlisted 28 Nov 1904, discharged without honor 19 Nov 1906. SOURCE: Powell, "Military Record of the Enlisted Men Who Were Discharged Without Honor."

‡Dishonorable discharge, Brownsville, TX. SOURCE: SO 266, AGO, 9 Nov 1906.

WILSON, Krling; Private; U.S. Army. Seminole Negro Scout, also known as Kelina Wilson, served 1871–72. SOURCE: Schubert, Consolidated List of Seminole Negro Scouts.

Kelina Wilson born in Arkansas; Ht 5'7", black hair and eyes, black complexion; enlisted at Ft Duncan, TX, 31 Aug 1871, age 35; discharged 29 Feb 1872, reenlisted 11 Mar 1872 at Ft Duncan; discharged 1 Sep 1872 at Ft Duncan; died 7 Sep 1873; buried at Seminole Indian Scout Cemetery, Kinney County, TX. SOURCE: Swanson, 55.

Age 35 at Ft Duncan, Mar 1872. SOURCE: NARA Record Group 393, Special File.

Originally Creek Indian slave; born in Arkansas about 1836; died 7 Sep 1873; buried at Seminole Indian Scout Cemetery, Kinney County, TX. SOURCE: Indian Scout Cemetery, Kinney County, Texas.

WILSON, Lewis; F/9th Cav. Born in Kentucky; black complexion; cannot read or write, age 30, Jul 1870, at Ft McKavett, TX. SOURCE: Bierschwale, *Fort McKavett*, 97.

WILSON, Peter; Private; U.S. Army. Seminole Negro Scout, served 1871–73. SOURCE: Schubert, Consolidated List of Seminole Negro Scouts.

Born in Arkansas; Wilson family were slaves owned by Creek Indians; Ht 5'7", black hair and eyes, black complexion; enlisted at Ft Duncan, TX, 7 Oct 1871, age 45; discharged 7 Apr 1872, enlisted next day at Ft Duncan; twice discharged, reenlisted next day at Ft Clark, TX, 8 Oct 1872–10 Apr 1873; discharged 10 Oct 1873 at Ft Clark. SOURCE: Swanson, 55.

WILSON, Randall; Corporal; K/25th Inf. Born in Cumberland, VA; Ht 5'5", brown complexion; occupation soldier; enlisted in A/39th Infantry for three years on 29 Aug 1866, age 21, at Ft St Philip, LA; promoted to corporal 18 Dec 1867; transferred to K/25th Infantry at Jackson Bks, LA, 20 Apr 1869. SOURCE: Descriptive Roll of A/39th Inf.

WILSON, Richard; Private; C/10th Cav. Private, received Indian Wars Campaign Badge number 1411 on 15 Jul 1909. SOURCE: Carroll, *Indian Wars Campaign Badge*, 41.

WILSON, Roy; Private; L/9th Cav. Enlisted 20 Jan 1879 at Baltimore, MD; stationed at Ft Bliss, TX, Nov 1879–Feb 1880; in the field in New Mexico in pursuit of Victorio's band of hostile Apaches 8 Jan 1880–22 Feb 1880, left Ojo Caliente 24 Feb and marched via Canada Alamosa and Cuchillo Negro, arriving at Chase's Ranch, 26 Feb 1880, after marching 621 miles in Jan and Feb; troop at Chase's Ranch, NM, 29 Feb 1880 awaiting further orders; aide-de-camp to Knight's Ranch, NM, July–Aug 1880; marched 945 miles in the field in New Mexico, Sep–Oct 1880; left Ft Stanton, NM, with L/9th Cavalry 11 Nov 1880, arrived Ft Bliss 18 Nov 1880; $5 sentence from General Court Martial Order 12 stopped, at Ft Bliss Jan–Jun 1881. SOURCE:

Muster Rolls, L/9th Cavalry, 31 Oct 1879–29 Feb 1880, 30 Jun 1880–30 Jun 1881.

‡On detached service in the field, New Mexico, 21 Jan–24 Feb 1881. SOURCE: Regt Returns, 9 Cav, Feb 1881.

WILSON, Royal; Private; E/9th Cav. Served against Apaches in New Mexico, 1879. SOURCE: Dobak and Phillips, *The Black Regulars*, 192.

Died 16 Dec 1902; buried at Santa Fe National Cemetery, NM, plot 649. SOURCE: Santa Fe National Cemetery, Records of Burials.

WILSON, Samuel; Private; C/10th Cav. Died 16 Jun 1868 of disease near Ft Wallace, KS. SOURCE: Regimental Returns, 10th Cavalry, 1868.

WILSON, Thomas; Private; K/25th Inf. Born in Iberville, LA; Ht 5'8", brown complexion; occupation shoemaker; enlisted in A/39th Infantry for three years on 3 Sep 1867, age 21, at Greenville, LA; appointed corporal 15 Apr 1868; reduced as incompetent 14 Apr 1869; transferred to K/25th Infantry at Jackson Bks, LA, 20 Apr 1869. SOURCE: Descriptive Roll of A/39th Inf.

WILSON, Thomas; Private; M/10th Cav. Born near Cecilton, MD, 1855; enlisted Baltimore, MD, 29 Jul 1879; Ht 5'6", black complexion, eyes, and hair; occupation laborer, farmer; present with recruits 29 Oct 1879 with 10th Cavalry which left Jefferson Bks, MO, and arrived at Ft Concho, TX, 25 Nov 1879; 16 Dec 1879–12 Jan 1880 at Ft Davis, TX; 14 Jan 1880–24 Mar 1880 encamped at Chinati Mountains, Texas; 26 Mar 1880–20 May 1880 at Ft Davis; May–2 Jul 1880 encamped at Eagle Springs, TX; 2 July 1880–Nov 1880, en route to and encamped on Rio Grande near Hot Springs, TX; 13 Nov 1880–12 Dec 1880 at Ft Davis; 26 Feb 1881 at Ft Davis; 23 Dec 1881 at Pena Colorado, TX; at Ft Davis, Apr 1882 until discharged 28 Jul 1884; resided 8 Decatur St., Wilmington, DE; unsuccessfully sought pension based on injury incurred when mule fell on him, Ft Davis, Dec 1880; last rejection of pension request 13 Jan 1926. SOURCE: Sayre, *Warriors of Color*, 511–14.

WILSON, Thomas C.; C/25th Inf. Born in Mississippi; mulatto complexion; can read, cannot write, age 21, 5 Sep 1870, at Ft McKavett, TX. SOURCE: Bierschwale, *Fort McKavett*, 109.

WILSON, Tony; Private; U.S. Army. Seminole Negro Scout, served 1871–76, 1879–82. SOURCE: Schubert, Consolidated List of Seminole Negro Scouts.

Born in Arkansas; Wilsons were slaves originally of Creek Indians; Ht 5'6", black hair and eyes, complexion black; enlisted at Ft Duncan, TX, 7 Oct 1871, age 24; dis-

charged 7 Apr 1872, reenlisted next day at Ft Duncan; twice discharged, reenlisted next day at Ft Clark, TX, 8 Oct 1872–10 Apr 1873; discharged 10 Oct 1873 at Ft Clark; enlisted 1 Jan 1874 at Ft Duncan; discharged 1 Jul 1874 at Camp Palafox, TX; enlisted 8 Feb 1875 at Ft Clark; discharged 8 Aug 1876 at Camp Pecos, TX; enlisted 20 Nov 1879 at Camp Pecos; discharged 9 Nov 1880 at Camp Black H.; enlisted 16 Dec 1881 at Ft Clark; discharged 15 Dec 1882 at Camp Myers, TX. SOURCE: Swanson, 55.

Born in Arkansas about 1847; died Apr 1903; buried at Seminole Indian Scout Cemetery, Kinney County, TX. SOURCE: Indian Scout Cemetery, Kinney County, Texas.

WILSON, Tony; Private; U.S. Army. Born in Mexico; Ht 5'7", black hair and eyes, black complexion; enlisted at Ft Clark, TX, 17 Jan 1893, age 26; discharged 16 Jul 1893, reenlisted next day at Ft Ringgold, TX; discharged 16 Jan 1894, reenlisted next day at Camp San Pedro, TX; discharged 16 Jan 1894, reenlisted next day at Camp San Pedro; discharged 17 Jul 1894 at Ft Ringgold; died 1 Apr 1938; buried at Seminole Indian Scout Cemetery, Kinney County, TX. SOURCE: Swanson, 56.

Seminole Negro Scout, served 1893–95. SOURCE: Schubert, Consolidated List of Seminole Negro Scouts.

Served in 1894; married. SOURCE: NARA, M 929, Roll 2.

Born about 1867 in Arkansas; died Apr 1938; buried at Seminole Indian Scout Cemetery, Kinney County, TX. SOURCE: Indian Scout Cemetery, Kinney County, Texas.

WILSON, William; H/25th Inf. Born in Louisiana; mulatto complexion; cannot read or write, age 27, 5 Sep 1870, at Ft McKavett, TX. SOURCE: Bierschwale, *Fort McKavett*, 108.

WILSON, William; Private; U.S. Army. Seminole Negro Scout, served 1872–87. SOURCE: Schubert, Consolidated List of Seminole Negro Scouts.

Born in Louisiana; Ht 5'5", black hair and eyes, black complexion; enlisted Ft Clark, TX, 9 Sep 1872, age 21; discharged 9 Mar 1873, reenlisted next day at Ft Clark; discharged 10 Sep 1873, reenlisted 12 Sep 1873 at Ft Clark; discharged 20 Mar 1874, reenlisted 31 Mar 1874 at Ft Clark; discharged 11 Dec 1874, reenlisted 11 Jan 1875 at Ft Clark; discharged 28 Aug 1875 at Camp Pecos, TX; enlisted 28 Feb 1876 at Ft Clark; discharged, reenlisted 28 Aug 1876 at Camp Pecos; discharged, reenlisted 28 Feb 1877 at Camp Crow C.; five times discharged, reenlisted for one year at Ft Clark, 28 Feb 1878–15 May 1883; discharged 14 May 1884, reenlisted 16 May 1884 at Camp Myers, TX; discharged 31 Aug 1884 at Ft Clark; enlisted 27 Dec 1884, discharged 15 Jun 1885 at Ft Clark; enlisted 9 Jan 1886, discharged 8 Jan 1887 at Ft Clark; 1880 Census lists William Wilson age 40, born in Ohio, parents born in Ohio; wife Elvira age 25, born in Mexico; children Lizzie, Norris,

William, Martha, Cepetha, Kaziah, Jake. SOURCE: Swanson, 56.

WILSON, William; Private; U.S. Army. Seminole Negro Scout, served 1894, 1901–14. SOURCE: Schubert, Consolidated List of Seminole Negro Scouts.

Born in Texas, son of William Wilson; Ht 5'7", black hair and eyes, black complexion; enlisted at Ft Clark, TX, 28 Apr 1894, age 24; discharged 27 Oct 1894 at Ft Ringgold, TX; enlisted 9 Mar 1901 at Ft Clark; discharged 8 Mar 1904, reenlisted next day at Ft Ringgold; twice discharged, reenlisted next day at Ft Clark, 8 Mar 1907–9 Mar 1910; discharged 8 Mar 1913, reenlisted for seven years 19 Mar 1913 at Ft Clark; honorably discharged 31 Sep 1914. SOURCE: Swanson, 56.

WILSON, William; Private; D/25th Inf. Born in Boonsboro, MD; Ht 5'7", black hair and brown eyes, yellow complexion; occupation hostler; resided in Boonsboro when he enlisted 5 Oct 1885, age 21, at Washington, DC; assigned to D/25th Infantry; arrived Ft Snelling, MN, 26 Apr 1886. SOURCE: Descriptive & Assignment Rolls of Recruits, 25 Inf.

WILSON, William; Private; A/10th Cav. ‡Served in 10th Cavalry, 1898; remained in U.S. during war with Spain. SOURCE: Cashin, *Under Fire with the Tenth Cavalry*, 337.

Died of disease contracted in line of duty 8 Jun 1905 at Ft Robinson, NE. SOURCE: Buecker, Fort Robinson Burials.

‡Died at Ft Robinson, 8 Jun 1905. SOURCE: List of Interments, Ft Robinson.

WILSON, William O.; Corporal; I/9th Cav. ‡Born in Hagerstown, MD; received Medal of Honor at Ft Robinson, NE, 17 Sep 1891. SOURCE: Lee, *Negro Medal of Honor Men*; Leckie, *The Buffalo Soldiers*, 258.

‡Cited among men who distinguished themselves in 1890; carried message for help through country occupied by enemy when wagon train under escort of Capt. John Loud was attacked by Sioux near Pine Ridge Agency, SD; awarded Medal of Honor. SOURCE: GO 100, AGO, 17 Dec 1898.

‡Wagon train attacked by hostile Indians on morning of 31 Dec 1890; Corporal Wilson volunteered to ride for help; chased by Indians but succeeded; "such an example of soldier-like conduct is worthy of imitation, and reflects credit not only upon Corpl Wilson but also upon the 9th Cavalry." SOURCE: Order 13, Battalion of 9 Cav, Pine Ridge, 1 Jan 1891, quoted in *ANJ* 28 (17 Jan 1891): 355.

Text of documents relating to award of Medal of Honor and subsequent desertion. SOURCE: Schubert, *Voices of the Buffalo Soldier*, 163–69.

‡Commissary Department clerk, Ft Robinson; forged checks for $350 drawn on Lt. James Bettens, commissary

officer, and deserted with horse and equipment; captured at Chadron, NE, and returned to post. SOURCE: *ANJ* 28 (25 Apr 1891): 593.

‡Reduced to private for absence without leave, forgery, and borrowing and failing to return Winchester rifle; department commander not satisfied that forgery was proved and remitted dishonorable discharge and hard labor portion of sentence. SOURCE: *ANJ* 28 (18 Jul 1891): 800.

Mentioned as last buffalo soldier to receive Medal of Honor for valor during Indian wars. SOURCE: Kenner, *Buffalo Soldiers and Officers of the Ninth Cavalry*, 127.

Private, H/9th Cavalry; life, service, and valor on Pine Ridge, SD, against Sioux in Dec 1890, as well as desertion, narrated. SOURCE: Schubert, *Black Valor*, 117, 123–32, 165–66, 168, 170.

WINCHESTER, Sandy; Sergeant; F/10th Cav. ‡With F/10th Cavalry from 1867 until accidentally shot and killed in Santa Rosa, Mexico, early 1877; "a sore loss." SOURCE: Leckie, *The Buffalo Soldiers*, 152.

Died 15 Jan 1877 of gunshot wounds at Santa Rosa Mountains, Mexico. SOURCE: Regimental Returns, 10th Cavalry, 1877.

WINFIELD, Alexander; D/24th Inf. Born in South Carolina; black complexion; cannot read or write, age 24, Jul 1870, at Ft McKavett, TX. SOURCE: Bierschwale, *Fort McKavett*, 96.

WINFIELD, Augustus P.; Private; G/9th Cav. ‡Sergeant, A/10th Cavalry, at Ft Apache, AZ, 1890, subscribed $.50 to testimonial to General Grierson. SOURCE: List of subscriptions, 23 Apr 1890, 10th Cavalry papers, MHI.

‡Private, D/9th Cavalry, transferred to Hospital Corps by letter, Adjutant General's Office, 11 Mar 1892.

‡First sergeant, I/9th Cavalry, stationed at Ft Washakie, WY; sick in post hospital, Ft Robinson, NE, 12 Jul–29 Aug 1896. SOURCE: Regt Returns, 9 Cav, 1896.

Appointed first sergeant 1 Dec 1895; in I/9th Cavalry at Ft Washakie, Jan 1897. SOURCE: Ninth Cavalry, Roster of NCOs, 1897.

‡Reenlistment as private, G/9th Cavalry, authorized by telegram, Adjutant General's Office, 26 Nov 1897.

WINN, Reese; Corporal; 9th Cav. Refused to perform guard duty, threatened officers, Aug 1869; sentence of death reduced to five years by Judge Advocate General. SOURCE: Kenner, *Buffalo Soldiers and Officers of the Ninth Cavalry*, 58.

WINTERS, Alvin B.; Private; H/48th Inf. ‡Died of variola in the Philippines, 25 May 1900. SOURCE: *ANJ* 37 (2 Jun 1900): 951.

Died in Manila, Philippines, 1 May 1900; body received at San Francisco National Cemetery 15 Apr 1902, buried in plot NA 876. SOURCE: San Francisco National Cemetery.

WINTERS, Eli; Private; A/39th Inf. Civil War veteran, served in D/81st U.S. Colored Infantry; sentence of death for involvement in New Iberia, LA, mutiny, Jul 1867, reduced to term of service. SOURCE: Dobak and Phillips, *The Black Regulars*, 222.

WINTHROP, Robert; Private; E/9th Cav. Private in E/9th Cavalry in April 1867, at time of San Pedro Springs, TX, mutiny; slashed and beaten with saber by Lt. Edward Heyl. SOURCE: Kenner, *Buffalo Soldiers and Officers of the Ninth Cavalry*, 76.

WISE, James; Private; E/10th Cav. In Troop E/10th Cavalry stationed at Bonita Cañon Camp, AZ, but absent or on detached service 28 Feb 1886. SOURCE: Tagg, *The Camp at Bonita Cañon*, 232.

WISMAN, Robert; Private; I/10th Cav. Died 19 Nov 1867 of typhoid at Ft Hays, KS. SOURCE: Regimental Returns, 10th Cavalry, 1867.

WOOD, John; Private; U.S. Army. Seminole Negro Scout, also known as Picayune John, served in 1870. SOURCE: Schubert, Consolidated List of Seminole Negro Scouts.

Born in Florida, reportedly John Horse's brother-in-law; called Picayune John due to diminutive stature; noted for his piety; one of eighteen first chosen by Major Bliss to form Seminole Scouts; Ht 5', grey hair, black eyes; enlisted for six months 16 Aug 1870, age 60, at Ft Duncan, TX; deserted Ft Duncan 28 Nov 1870. SOURCE: Swanson, 57.

In original detachment of scouts enlisted at Ft Duncan Aug 1870. SOURCE: NARA Record Group 393, Special File.

WOODARD, Major; Private; L/9th Cav. *See* WOODWARD, Major, Private, L/9th Cavalry

WOODARD, Major; Corporal; Band/25th Inf. Died 4 Feb 1909; buried at Ft Leavenworth National Cemetery, plot 3652. SOURCE: Ft Leavenworth National Cemetery.

WOODED, Abner; Private; E/10th Cav. Died 23 Dec 1880 of wounds inflicted by Private Ray of E/10th Cavalry at Grierson Springs, TX. SOURCE: Regimental Returns, 10th Cavalry, 1880.

WOODEN, Henry; Private; L/10th Cav. ‡Original member of 10th Cavalry; in troop when organized, Ft Riley, KS, 21 Sep 1867. SOURCE: McMiller, "Buffalo Soldiers," 78.

Served with Pvt. George Washington, C/10th Cavalry, early 1870s; later employed at post trader store, Ft Sill, OK. SOURCE: Schubert, *Voices of the Buffalo Soldier*, 228, 230.

WOODLAND, William; Private; L/9th Cav. Enlisted 1 Jul 1879 at Baltimore, MD; stationed at Ft Bliss, TX, Nov 1879–Feb 1880; in the field in New Mexico in pursuit of Victorio's band of hostile Apaches 8 Jan 1880–22 Feb 1880, left Ojo Caliente 24 Feb and marched via Canada Alamosa and Cuchillo Negro, arriving at Chase's Ranch, 26 Feb 1880, after marching 621 miles in Jan and Feb; troop at Chase's Ranch, NM, 29 Feb 1880 awaiting further orders; left camp on Rio Mimbres, NM, on 8 Jul 1880 and marched twenty miles to Ft Cummings, NM; left Ft Cummings 8 Aug on march to Leas Ferry on Rio Grande and returned to Rio Mimbres camp after march of 104 miles; on detached service at Ft Bliss, Sep–Oct 1880; left Ft Stanton, NM, with L/9th Cavalry 11 Nov 1880, arrived Ft Bliss 18 Nov 1880; at Ft Bliss Jan–Jun 1881. SOURCE: Muster Rolls, L/9th Cavalry, 31 Oct 1879–29 Feb 1880, 30 June 1880–30 Jun 1881.

‡Pvt. W. Woodland, L/9th Cavalry, on detached service in the field, New Mexico, 21 Jan–24 Feb 1881. SOURCE: Regt Returns, 9 Cav, Feb 1881.

WOODOW, I.; Sergeant; E/25th Inf. Tried to quell disturbance at post trader's store at Ft Hale, Dakota Territory, around 19 May 1881; Pvt. William Thomas, C/25th Infantry, charged with threatening to kill or injure Sergeant Woodow with loaded rifle during disturbance; Private Thomas found guilty but not of threatening Sergeant Woodow. SOURCE: General Court-Martial Orders No. 99, Ft Snelling, MN, 19 Aug 1881, photocopy in authors' files.

WOODS, Brent; Sergeant; H/9th Cav. ‡Born in Pulaski, KY; enlisted Jan 1879; awarded Medal of Honor as sergeant, B/9th Cavalry, rescuing white cowboys ambushed by Nana in Gavilan Canyon, around fifteen miles from McEver's Ranch, NM, 19 Aug 1881. SOURCE: Carroll, *The Black Military Experience*, 401; Leckie, *The Buffalo Soldiers*, 233; Lee, *Negro Medal of Honor Men*, 76.

‡Private, B/9th Cavalry, wounded in action in Mimbres Mountains, New Mexico, along with Private Garnett, B/9th Cavalry, 3 Feb 1880. SOURCE: Hamilton, "History of the Ninth Cavalry," 50.

Career and award of Medal of Honor discussed; reprimanded for threatening at gunpoint Pvt. Allen Dale, B/9th Cavalry, new recruit, Apr 1880. SOURCE: Kenner, *Buffalo Soldiers and Officers of the Ninth Cavalry*, 228–36.

‡Sergeant, B/9th Cavalry, took charge after commander was killed in Apache ambush, Gavilan Canyon, Aug 1881; awarded Medal of Honor. SOURCE: Billington, *New Mexico's Buffalo Soldiers*, 106–7.

Valor against Apaches described. SOURCE: Dobak and Phillips, *The Black Regulars*, 262.

Pvt. Herman Hector, E/9th Cavalry, confined for one month for insubordination to Sgt. Brent Woods, at Ft DuChesne, UT, 1887. SOURCE: Kenner, *Buffalo Soldiers and Officers of the Ninth Cavalry*, 235.

‡First sergeant, E/9th Cavalry, reduced to ranks at own request and transferred to B/9th Cavalry, Ft DuChesne. SOURCE: Order 22, 9 Cav, 1 May 1888, Regimental Orders.

‡Private, C/9th Cavalry, presented Medal of Honor in front of Ft McKinney, WY, garrison by Maj. E. G. Fechet, 9th Cavalry; Fechet said, "All who know you say that this medal has been worthily bestowed." SOURCE: *ANJ* 31 (11 Aug 1894): 874–75.

‡Promoted from lance corporal to corporal, C/9th Cavalry, Ft Robinson, NE. SOURCE: *ANJ* 33 (12 Oct 1895): 87.

‡Appointed regimental color guard, Ft Robinson, Mar 1896. SOURCE: *ANJ* 33 (28 Mar 1896): 540.

Appointed corporal 1 Oct 1895; in C/9th Cavalry at Ft Robinson, Jan 1897. SOURCE: Ninth Cavalry, Roster of NCOs, 1897.

‡Authorized to wear knot in lieu of Medal of Honor by letter, Adjutant General's Office, 8 Oct 1897.

Life, career, and valor against Apaches, for which he received Medal of Honor, narrated. SOURCE: Schubert, *Black Valor*, 84–88, 170.

WOODS, Charles; Corporal; E/9th Cav. One of ten soldiers charged with mutiny and desertion for role in mutiny at San Pedro Springs, near San Antonio, TX, April 1867; pled guilty to desertion but not mutiny; mutiny charge dropped; convicted of desertion, sentenced to death, sentence remitted, charges dropped, and soldier restored to duty. SOURCE: Dobak and Phillips, *The Black Regulars*, 208–10.

WOODS, Charles; Private; E/9th Cav. Died 16 Jun 1881; buried at San Antonio National Cemetery, Section D, number 764. SOURCE: San Antonio National Cemetery Locator.

WOODS, Eugene; Corporal; G/9th Cav. Died 30 Dec 1889; originally buried at Ft Niobrara, NE; reburied at Ft Leavenworth National Cemetery, plot G 3567. SOURCE: Ft Leavenworth National Cemetery.

WOODS, George F.; Private; B/10th Cav. Born 2 Feb 1876; died 19 Apr 1950; reburied at Ft Leavenworth National Cemetery, plot B 588 A. SOURCE: Ft Leavenworth National Cemetery.

WOODS, Henry; Private; L/9th Cav. Enlisted at Baltimore, MD, 18 Jan 1881; at Ft Bliss, TX, May–June 1881. SOURCE: Muster Roll, L/9th Cavalry, 30 Apr–30 Jun 1881.

WOODS, Marion; Private; 25th Inf. Born in Williamsburg, SC; occupation miner; Ht 5'8 1/4", dark complexion, black hair and eyes; enlisted, age 26, Charleston, SC, 20 Jun 1881; left recruit depot, David's Island, NY, 17 Aug 1881, and after trip on steamer *Thomas Kirby* to Central Depot, New York City, and train via Chicago to Running Water, Dakota Territory, 22 Aug 1881, marched forty-seven miles to Ft Randall, SD, arrived 24 Aug 1881. SOURCE: Descriptive & Assignment Rolls, 25 Inf.

WOODS, Solomon; M/9th Cav. Born in Kentucky; black complexion; cannot read or write, age 21, Jul 1870, at Ft McKavett, TX. SOURCE: Bierschwale, *Fort McKavett*, 100.

WOODS, William; Private; L/9th Cav. Enlisted at Louisville, KY, 16 Nov 1880; recruit from depot, en route to join company; at Ft Bliss, TX, Jan–Feb 1881. SOURCE: Muster Rolls, L/9th Cavalry, 31 Oct 1880–28 Feb 1881.

WOODWARD, Major; Private; L/9th Cav. Born in Virginia; in mid-30s when killed 30 Sep 1879 in action with Pvt. John Johnson, L/9th Cavalry, Cuchillo Negro Canyon, NM, where he was buried. SOURCE: Kenner, *Buffalo Soldiers and Officers of the Ninth Cavalry*, 188.

Born in Virginia; black complexion; cannot read or write, age 28, Jul 1870, in M/9th Cavalry at Ft McKavett, TX. SOURCE: Bierschwale, *Fort McKavett*, 100.

‡Private Woodward, L/9th Cavalry, killed in action, Mimbres Mountains, New Mexico, along with Private Johnson, 30 Sep 1879. SOURCE: Hamilton, "History of the Ninth Cavalry," 47; *Illustrated Review: Ninth Cavalry*.

One of two troopers killed in action against Apaches, Mimbres Mountains, 30 Sep 1879. SOURCE: Schubert, *Black Valor*, 57.

While in L/9th Cavalry, died 30 Sep 1879; buried 14 Oct 1891 at Ft Bayard, NM, in plot I 37. SOURCE: "Fort Bayard National Cemetery, Records of Burials."

Died 30 Sep 1879; buried 14 Oct 1891, section A, row F, plot 44 at Ft Bayard. SOURCE: Erickson, Burials at Fort Bayard National Cemetery, NM.

WOODWARD, Major; 1st Sgt; 9th Cav. Received Philippine Campaign Badge number 11796 for service as first sergeant in D/9th Cavalry; in 9th Cavalry at Ft Leavenworth, KS, Mar 1905. SOURCE: Philippine Campaign Badge list, 29 May 1905.

WOODY, Clayborn; Private; A/9th Cav. ‡In K/9th Cavalry, convicted by garrison court martial, Ft Robinson, NE, of abusive language to employee of post trader and insubordination to 1st Sgt. George Jordan, K/9th Cavalry; sentenced to ten days. SOURCE: Order 238, 2 Dec 1887, Post Orders, Ft Robinson.

Died of sarcoma of right lung in Ft Robinson post hospital 9 Aug 1891; final statement and inventory of effects forwarded to AGO 9 Aug 1891; character "very good"; buried at Ft Robinson. SOURCE: Buecker, Fort Robinson Burials.

‡Funeral at Ft Robinson, 9 Aug 1891. SOURCE: Order 161, 8 Aug 1891, Post Orders, Ft Robinson.

WORD, Peter; Private; K/25th Inf. Born in Franklin, MS; Ht 5'3", black complexion; occupation farmer; enlisted in A/39th Infantry for three years on 16 Sep 1866, age 22, at Shreveport, LA; on detached service as orderly since 13 Mar 1869; transferred to K/25th Infantry at Jackson Bks, LA, 20 Apr 1869. SOURCE: Descriptive Roll of A/39th Inf.

Private, A/39th Infantry, acquitted of involvement in New Iberia, LA, mutiny, Jul 1867. SOURCE: Dobak and Phillips, *The Black Regulars*, 222.

WORKMAN, Charles; Private; C/9th Cav. Died at Ft Davis, TX, on 9 May 1868; buried at San Antonio National Cemetery, Section I, number 1570. SOURCE: San Antonio National Cemetery Locator.

WORLD, William; Sergeant; B/9th Cav. Appointed sergeant 27 Jan 1886; in B/9th Cavalry at Ft DuChesne, UT, Jan 1897. SOURCE: Ninth Cavalry, Roster of NCOs, 1897.

‡Appointed sergeant as of 27 Jan 1886. SOURCE: Roster, 9 Cav.

WORMLEY, George; Sergeant; I/10th Cav. Died 24 Aug 1884 at Ft Hancock, TX; buried at San Antonio National Cemetery, Section I, number 1628. SOURCE: San Antonio National Cemetery Locator.

WORRELL, William; Saddler; F/9th Cav. Died 4 Jan 1903; buried at Ft Bayard, NM, in plot L 9. SOURCE: "Fort Bayard National Cemetery, Records of Burials."

Buried 4 Jan 1903, section A, row S, plot 11, at Ft Bayard. SOURCE: Erickson, Burials at Fort Bayard National Cemetery, NM.

WORYER, Henry; Private; U.S. Army. Seminole Negro Scout, served 1882–84. SOURCE: Schubert, Consolidated List of Seminole Negro Scouts.

Born in Mexico; Ht 5'11", black hair and eyes, black complexion; enlisted at Ft Clark, TX, 27 Dec 1882, age 22; discharged 26 Dec 1883, reenlisted next day at Camp Myers, TX; discharged 26 Dec 1884 at Ft Clark. SOURCE: Swanson, 57.

Born about 1860 in Mexico; died 12 Sep 1931; buried at Seminole Indian Scout Cemetery, Kinney County, TX. SOURCE: Indian Scout Cemetery, Kinney County, Texas.

WRIGHT, Boyer; Corporal; G/9th Cav. Received Philippine Campaign Badge number 11809 for service as private in F/9th Cavalry, 12 Apr 1902–16 Sep 1902; corporal in G/9th Cavalry, Ft Leavenworth, KS, Mar 1905. SOURCE: Philippine Campaign Badge Recipients; Philippine Campaign Badge list, 29 May 1905.

WRIGHT, Clark; Private; H/10th Cav. Born in Gloversville, NY, 1 May 1863 or 1864; enlisted Rochester, NY, 18 Apr 1884; Ht 5'3", Negro complexion, black eyes and hair; occupation laborer and carriage washer; served in H/10th Cavalry; at Ft Apache, AZ, Jul 1886; on detached service 31 Aug 1886 at Ft Wingate, NM; hospitalized for fractured femur 31 Dec 1886–28 Feb 1887 and 30 Apr 1887–30 Jun 1887 at Ft Apache; at San Carlos, AZ, 30 Jun 1888–31 Dec 1888; at Ft Apache, 31 Dec 1888 until discharged 17 Apr 1889; applied for pension based on broken leg incurred while playing baseball on parade ground, Aug 1886; unmarried; could not write his name in 1889; received $8 per month pension, Jan 1890; admitted to U.S. Soldiers Home, Washington, DC, Jul 1919; patient at Fitzsimmons Hospital, Denver, CO, 1921; died 4 Sep 1922. SOURCE: Sayre, *Warriors of Color*, 515–19.

Private in H/10th Cavalry stationed at Bonita Cañon Camp, AZ, but absent or on detached service 30 Apr 1886. SOURCE: Tagg, *The Camp at Bonita Cañon*, 232.

WRIGHT, J. W.; Sergeant; C/25th Inf. Born in Virginia; mulatto complexion; can read and write, age 21, 5 Sep 1870, at Ft McKavett, TX. SOURCE: Bierschwale, *Fort McKavett*, 109.

Led detachment of eight from station at Ft Stockton, TX, in search of overdue mail stage in vicinity of Pecos Station, TX, Oct 1877. SOURCE: Nankivell, *History of the Twenty-fifth Infantry*, 28.

WRIGHT, James; Sergeant; M/9th Cav. Died 12 Dec 1900; buried at Ft Bayard, NM, in plot N 14. SOURCE: "Fort Bayard National Cemetery, Records of Burials."

Buried 12 Dec 1900, section A, row V, plot 14 at Ft Bayard. SOURCE: Erickson, Burials at Fort Bayard National Cemetery, NM.

WRIGHT, Samuel; Corporal; D/9th Cav. ‡Killed in action near Ft Lancaster, TX, by Kickapoos, 11 Oct 1867, while escorting Camp Hudson-Ft Stockton, TX, mail along with Pvt. Eldridge T. Jones, D/9th Cavalry. SOURCE: Leckie, *The Buffalo Soldiers*, 84–85; Hamilton, "History of the Ninth Cavalry," 7; Ninth Cavalry, *Historical and Pictorial Review*, 45; *Illustrated Review: Ninth Cavalry*; Schubert, *Black Valor*, 17.

WRIGHT, Thomas; Private; B/9th Cav. Died 8 Feb 1906; Private 167546, buried at Ft Bayard, NM, in plot H 34. SOURCE: "Fort Bayard National Cemetery, Records of Burials."

Buried 8 Feb 1906, section A, row K, plot 41, at Ft Bayard. SOURCE: Erickson, Burials at Fort Bayard National Cemetery, NM.

WRIGHT, W. H.; Private; E/25th Inf. Died at Ft Clark, TX; buried at Fort Sam Houston National Cemetery, Section PE, number 54. SOURCE: Buffalo Soldiers Interred in Fort Sam Houston National Cemetery.

WYATT, Washington; Private; E/9th Cav. Private in E/9th Cavalry, April 1867, at time of San Pedro Springs, TX, mutiny; became separated from troop during hunt for deserters after shooting; a week later he was found dead and stripped of his equipment and arms. SOURCE: Kenner, *Buffalo Soldiers and Officers of the Ninth Cavalry*, 78.

WYLIE, Daniel; Sergeant; K/9th Cav. ‡Sergeant as of 26 Feb 1883. SOURCE: Roster, 9 Cav.

‡Vice president of K Troop's Diamond Club, Ft Robinson, NE, 1891. SOURCE: *ANJ* 28 (2 May 1891): 620.

‡At Ft Robinson, 1895; sergeant since 6 [*sic*] Feb 1883. SOURCE: *ANJ* 33 (7 Dec 1895): 236.

‡Reenlistment as married soldier authorized by letter, Adjutant General's Office, 6 Nov 1895.

Appointed sergeant 6 Feb 1883; in K/9th Cavalry at Ft Robinson, Jan 1897. SOURCE: Ninth Cavalry, Roster of NCOs, 1897.

Y

YATES, Wyatt; Corporal; B/9th Cav. Died on 1 Jul 1866; buried at San Antonio National Cemetery, Section D, number 800. SOURCE: San Antonio National Cemetery Locator.

YEARGOOD, Evert; Private; H/9th Cav. ‡Died of cholera in the Philippines, 10 Jun 1902. SOURCE: *ANJ* 39 (9 Aug 1902): 1248.

Pvt. Evert Yearwood, H/9th Cavalry; died in the Philippines 10 Jun 1902; buried in plot NEW A798 at San Francisco National Cemetery 18 May 1905. SOURCE: San Francisco National Cemetery.

YEARWOOD, Evert; Private; H/9th Cav. *See* YEARGOOD, Evert, Private, H/9th Cavalry

YEATMAN, William; 1st Sgt; 38th Inf. ‡At Ft Cummings, NM, autumn 1867. SOURCE: Billington, *New Mexico's Buffalo Soldiers*, 39–40, 42.

Witness for the prosecution in New Mexico mutiny trial of seven soldiers of 38th Infantry, 1868. SOURCE: Dobak and Phillips, *The Black Regulars*, 324.

At Ft Selden, NM, Jan 1868 trial of Cpl. Robert Davis, C/38th Infantry, defense counsel Thomas B. Catron challenged witness Yeatman's intelligence and competency to stand as witness, "being a Colored Man"; deemed competent by the Court, and Judge Advocate (prosecutor) would examine witness Yeatman as he thought proper. SOURCE: Dobak, "Trial of Corporal Robert Davis."

YEBBY, Oscar; H/25th Inf. Born in Virginia; black complexion; can read and write, age 24, 5 Sep 1870, at Ft McKavett, TX. SOURCE: Bierschwale, *Fort McKavett*, 108.

YEIZER, Charles C.; Private; D/24th Inf. ‡Pvt. Charles G. Yerzer, 24th Infantry, drowned at Cabanatuan, Philippines, 27 Nov 1900, while unassigned. SOURCE: Name File, 24 Inf; *ANJ* 38 (12 Jan 1901): 479.

Pvt. Charles C. Yeizer, D/24th Infantry died 27 Nov 1900; buried 14 Jun 1901 in plot NADD 337 at San Francisco National Cemetery. SOURCE: San Francisco National Cemetery.

YEIZER, Mordecai; Private; L/9th Cav. Born ca. 1860; nickname Mode; paternal grandfather Harry, father Edward, and mother Eugenia all born free; parents married in 1850; enlisted in Cincinnati, OH, 7 July 1879, age 21, complexion mulatto; marriage to Margaret Redwood did not last; daughter Florence raised by maternal grandmother; last of Yeizer family still in Kentucky in 1881 moved to Chicago, IL; Mordecai worked as barber, lived with brothers Austin, Robert, Edward, Jr., and Alonzo in Chicago; daughter Florence's children include Jackie Ridley and Margaret Morrison; grandniece Sarah Jackson one of first thirty-nine black women officers in Army. SOURCE: Lang, "Mordecai Yeizer."

Attended school 1870; literate, as are parents; living with seven siblings in Frankfort, KY, 8 Jun 1870. SOURCE: 1870 United States Federal Census, photocopy of printout from Ancestry.com in authors' files.

In L/9th Cavalry, left Ft Bliss, TX, 12 Sep 1879 on march to old Ft Cummings, NM; proceeded through Mimbres Mountains on trail of Victorio's Indians to Ft Bayard, NM; arrived old Ft Cummings 16 Oct 1879 after marching 412 miles; on duty at Ft Bliss while troop is in the field, 31 Dec 1879–29 Feb 1880; at Ft Bliss 31 Oct 1879–19 Feb 1880; stationed at Ft Cummings, in the field in New Mexico, 30 Jun–31 Aug 1880; on duty as company cook, 31 Aug–31 Oct 1880; marched 240 miles from Tularosa, NM, via Ft Stanton, NM, to Ft Bliss; at Ft Bliss, 31 Dec 1880–28 Feb 1881; discharge at Ft Bliss not honorable 21 May 1881. SOURCE: Muster Rolls for L/9th Cavalry, 31 Aug 1879–29 Feb 1880, 30 Jun 1880–28 Feb 1881, 30 Apr–30 Jun 1881.

Listed as age 19 in Frankfort, KY, 1880 Census; listed as age 21 on 11 June 1880 by census taker in El Paso, TX. SOURCE: 1880 United States Census, photocopies in authors' files.

Order for discharge, having enlisted under false pretences; not entitled to pay or allowances. SOURCE: SO 95, AGO, 26 Apr 1881.

Born in Frankfort, KY, occupation barber; age 21, Ht 5'5", complexion mulatto; discharged from L/9th Cavalry 21 May 1881 per SO 94, at Ft Bliss, character none. SOURCE: Register of Enlistments, L/9th Cavalry, photocopy in authors' files.

Resided in Pine Bluff, AR; married Margaret Redwood, age 18, of Pine Bluff on 14 Jan 1884. SOURCE: State of Arkansas Marriage License, Certificate of Marriage, photocopy in authors' files.

Occupation barber, at 6501 S. Halstead, Chicago; resided at 6329 S. Carpenter with Edward, Edward J., Matthew, and Robert. SOURCE: Chicago Directory, 1904, photocopy in authors' files.

Owned barbershop; listed as nephew living with Mr. McCleod and daughter Mary E. McCleod in St. Louis, MO, in 1910 directory. SOURCE: 24 Jan 1903 e-mail message from Judith B. Lang, printout in authors' files.

YERZER, Charles G.; Private; 24th Inf. *See* YEIZER, Charles C., Private, D/24th Infantry

YOUNG, Alfred; Private; K/9th Cav. Born in Cambridge, MD; enlisted at Baltimore, MD, on 2 Jul 1879, age 21; occupation farmer; Ht 5'5", black hair and eyes, black complexion; died at Ojo Caliente, NM, in 1880 of pneumonia. SOURCE: Register of enlistments, photocopy in authors' files.

YOUNG, Charles; Lt Col; U.S. Army. ‡Born in Kentucky, 1868; U.S. Military Academy graduate. SOURCE: *Leslie's Weekly* 87 (25 Aug 1898): 143.

‡On graduation from Military Academy, assigned to A/25th Infantry, Ft Custer, MT. SOURCE: *ANJ* 27 (12 Oct 1889): 122.

‡Second lieutenant, 9th Cavalry; mentioned as 1889 graduate of U.S. Military Academy. SOURCE: Billington, *New Mexico's Buffalo Soldiers*, 190.

‡"A colored man, graduate of West Point, joined the post [Ft Robinson, NE] for duty." SOURCE: Corliss, Diary, II, 28 Nov 1889.

‡Arrived at Ft Robinson after graduation leave; assigned to B/9th Cavalry; transferred to Ft DuChesne, UT, with unit. SOURCE: Post Returns, Ft Robinson, Nov 1889–Sep 1890.

‡Mentioned. SOURCE: *ANJ* 27 (16 Nov 1889) and 27 (18 Jan 1890).

‡Commander, Ft Robinson, to Young, 5 Apr 1890, complains of his "tactical errors" as officer of the guard. SOURCE: LS, Ft Robinson.

‡Commander, Ft Robinson, to Young, 28 Apr 1890, reprimands him for neglect of stable duty. SOURCE: LS, Ft Robinson.

‡Young has had more consideration than any white officer; commander hopes he will improve. SOURCE: CO, Ft Robinson, through AAG, DP, to AG, USA, 7 May 1890, LS, Ft Robinson.

‡Young required to vacate his quarters; Major Randlett's quarters to be considered two sets when he vacates and Young will be allowed to choose one of them. SOURCE:

CO, Ft Robinson, to Post QM, 24 Jun 1890, LS, Ft Robinson.

‡Granted forty-five days' leave from Ft DuChesne. SOURCE: *ANJ* 28 (20 Jun 1891): 732.

‡Officer-in-charge and teacher, post school, Ft DuChesne, 1 Nov 1892–30 Apr 1893. SOURCE: Reports of Post School, Ft DuChesne.

‡At Ft DuChesne with 9th Cavalry, then transferred to Wilberforce University as professor of military science, then to L/9th Cavalry. SOURCE: Clark, "A History of the Twenty-fourth," 11–12.

‡To succeed Lieutenant Alexander as military instructor, Wilberforce University. SOURCE: Cleveland *Gazette*, 26 May 1894.

‡On detached service from Ft Robinson at Wilberforce University from 1 Sep 1894. SOURCE: Post Returns, Ft Robinson, Sep 1894.

‡Directed to appear before examination board, Ft Leavenworth, KS, by Special Order 208, Adjutant General's Office, 3 Sep 1896.

‡In Leavenworth for promotion examination, could not get accommodations in town and had to stay in Kansas City, MO. SOURCE: *ANJ* 34 (19 Sep 1896): 40.

‡Military instructor at Wilberforce, passed examination at Leavenworth for promotion to first lieutenant; now paid $1,800 per year, "has a handsomely furnished home free, and is only 32 years old." SOURCE: Cleveland *Gazette*, 12 Dec 1896.

‡Relieved from duty at Wilberforce to command battalion of Ohio colored volunteers; said to be first instance in which colored officer has commanded battalion in Army. SOURCE: Richmond *Planet*, 21 May 1898.

‡Commander, I/9th Cavalry, Ft DuChesne, as of 31 Dec 1900. SOURCE: Hamilton, "History of the Ninth Cavalry," 102.

‡Captain, I/9th Cavalry, Nov 1901. SOURCE: *ANJ* 39 (9 Nov 1901): 234.

‡"The colored officer of the Ninth Cavalry, who will in future be stationed at the Presidio, was a great favorite on the *Sheridan* coming from Manila to San Francisco, and was in great demand. His skin is of the darkest hue of the race, but he is exceedingly clever, a West Point graduate, and a pianist of rare ability." SOURCE: Indianapolis *Freeman*, 27 Dec 1902.

‡At the Presidio of San Francisco, CA, 1902. *See* FEARINGTON, George W., Sergeant, F/25th Infantry

‡Lt. B. R. Tillman, son of Benjamin R. Tillman, "the South Carolina Negro hater," gave banquet to number of Army officers, including Captain Young; when asked if he had made a mistake in inviting Young, he said, "No, he is a gentleman and a friend of mine." SOURCE: Indianapolis *Freeman*, 31 Jan 1903.

‡Biographical article. SOURCE: *Colored American Magazine* 4 (Jan–Feb 1904): 249–50.

‡Selected for duty as military attaché to Haiti and Santo Domingo. SOURCE: Indianapolis *Freeman*, 4 Jun 1904.

‡Young's letter from Wilberforce, OH, 29 Jun 1907, solicits funds to build monument to Paul Lawrence Dunbar; $500 collected so far, mostly from whites. SOURCE: Cleveland *Gazette*, 3 Aug 1907.

Mentoring of Benjamin O. Davis, Ft DuChesne, described; text of appeal for funds to build monument to poet Paul Lawrence Dunbar in Cleveland *Gazette*, Aug 1907, published. SOURCE: Schubert, *Voices of the Buffalo Soldier*, 220, 247.

‡Captain and commander, I/9th Cavalry, at Ft D. A. Russell, WY, in 1910; veteran of Philippine Insurrection. SOURCE: *Illustrated Review: Ninth Cavalry*, with picture.

‡On three-officer board investigating vandalism at Ft D. A. Russell. SOURCE: Wyoming *Tribune*, 5 Aug 1911.

‡To be promoted to major in the autumn; will command third squadron, 9th Cavalry, and have achieved highest rank except for chaplains. SOURCE: Cleveland *Gazette*, 12 Aug 1911.

‡Went to Liberia with three young men of his choosing to organize and equip the Liberian army, his group including Wilson Ballard, Major, Liberian Defense Forces, who stayed five years; Young replaced in 1916 by John Green, who continued to help government settle its many border disputes. SOURCE: Fletcher, "The Negro Soldier," 172, 178.

‡Assigned to military attaché duty in Liberia; soon to be major. SOURCE: Cleveland *Gazette*, 6 Jan 1912.

‡Accompanied to Liberia by three bright young Afro-American college men to organize Liberian constabulary; they have military titles conferred by Liberian government and include Dr. (Capt.) Arthur M. Brown, at $1,600 per year and quarters. SOURCE: Cleveland *Gazette*, 10 Feb 1912.

‡Just promoted, on duty as military attaché in Liberia; holds highest rank of any Negro in regular Army; graduate of U.S. Military Academy, "quiet, unassuming and very popular." SOURCE: Wyoming *Tribune*, 14 Sep 1912.

‡Mentioned. SOURCE: Work, *The Negro Year Book, 1912*, 77.

‡Led successful Liberian effort to suppress revolt of coastal Croo tribe. SOURCE: Cleveland *Gazette*, 15 Feb 1913.

‡Slightly wounded in action in recent conflict with Liberian natives. SOURCE: Cleveland *Gazette*, 5 Apr 1913.

‡"An army officer in Washington, D.C., is authority for the following 'tribute' to Young's discretion: 'Army etiquette requires that all officers at a post make a call on a newcomer, an officer, at the earliest possible moment after his arrival. Major Charles Young, who was stationed at a post where I was, waited as long as possible, and then having ascertained beyond a doubt that the new officer was not at home, called and left his card. It goes to show Major Young's appreciation of his position.' Rats!" SOURCE: Cleveland *Gazette*, 11 Apr 1914.

‡To command Haitian constabulary although he wants to resume command of his battalion of the 10th Cavalry on the Mexican border in Arizona. SOURCE: Cleveland *Gazette*, 12 Feb 1916.

‡Awarded Spingarn Medal by Governor S. W. McCall of Massachusetts at meeting of the National Association for the Advancement of Colored People; medal for "the Afro-American male or female, who has made the highest achievement during the preceding year in any field of elevated or honorable human endeavor." SOURCE: Cleveland *Gazette*, 26 Feb 1916.

‡Received Spingarn Medal for work in organizing and training Liberian constabulary. SOURCE: Cleveland *Gazette*, 4 Mar 1916.

‡Promoted to lieutenant colonel. SOURCE: Cleveland *Gazette*, 15 Jul 1916.

‡Led in fight against Pancho Villa at Aguas Calientes, Chihuahua, Mexico; charged on horseback and routed enemy without fire; led 10th Cavalry to rescue of 13th Cavalry at Santa Cruz de Villegas, Chihuahua, 1916; Maj. Frank Tompkins of 13th said, "By God, Young, I could kiss every black face out there"; Young, unsmiling, responded, "Well, Tompkins, if you want to, you may start with me." SOURCE: Clendenen, *Blood on the Border*, 257, 259.

‡Camp No. 24, National Indian War Veterans, Washington, DC, first all-black camp and also bears his name, meets at U.S. Soldiers Home but membership drawn from city as well as the Home. SOURCE: *Winners of the West* 6 (May 1929): 1.

‡Biographical sketch. SOURCE: Logan and Winston, eds., *Dictionary of American Negro Biography*, 677–79.

Life and career narrated. SOURCE: Kenner, *Buffalo Soldiers and Officers of the Ninth Cavalry*, 299–309.

YOUNG, Charles H.; Private; H/9th Cav. Served at Ft Sill, OK, 1883. SOURCE: Kenner, *Buffalo Soldiers and Officers of the Ninth Cavalry*, 257, 353.

YOUNG, Clark; Private; M/10th Cav. ‡Killed in action at Cheyenne Agency, Indian Territory, 6 Apr 1875. SOURCE: Leckie, *The Buffalo Soldiers*, 139.

‡Died of wounds received in action at Cheyenne Agency. SOURCE: CO, 10 Cav, to AG, USA, 18 Jun 1875, ES, 10 Cav, 1873–83.

Died 12 Apr 1875, killed in action at Cheyenne Agency. SOURCE: Regimental Returns, 10th Cavalry, 1875.

YOUNG, David; Private; L/10th Cav. ‡Original member of 10th Cavalry; in troop when organized, Ft Riley, KS, 1 Sep 1867. SOURCE: McMiller, "Buffalo Soldiers," 77.

‡Detailed teamster in K/10th Cavalry. SOURCE: SO 54, HQ, Det 10 Cav, Camp Supply, Indian Territory, 31 Jul 1869, Orders, Det 10 Cav.

In L/10th Cavalry; died 30 Sep 1869 of disease at Canadian River, OK. SOURCE: Regimental Returns, 10th Cavalry, 1869.

‡Commander, 10th Cavalry, forwards final statement of late Private Young to Adjutant General, 18 Jan 1870. SOURCE: LS, 10 Cav, 1866–67.

YOUNG, David; D/24th Inf. Born in Kentucky; mulatto complexion; cannot read or write, age 27, Jul 1870, at Ft McKavett, TX. SOURCE: Bierschwale, *Fort McKavett*, 96.

YOUNG, Douglas; Sergeant; M/9th Cav. Buried 22 Feb 1911, section B, row E, plot 23 at Ft Bayard, NM. SOURCE: Erickson, Burials at Fort Bayard National Cemetery, NM.

YOUNG, Douglass; 1st Sgt; G/9th Cav. Received Cuban Campaign Badge for service as saddler in G/9th Cavalry, 22 Jun 1898–13 Aug 1898. SOURCE: Cuban Campaign Badge Recipients.

Received Philippine Campaign Badge number 11803 for service as corporal in G/9th Cavalry, 16 Sep 1900–16 Sep 1902; first sergeant in G/9th Cavalry, Ft Leavenworth, KS, Mar 1905. SOURCE: Philippine Campaign Badge Recipients; Philippine Campaign Badge list, 29 May 1905.

YOUNG, George; Private; L/9th Cav. Enlisted 14 Nov 1876 at Santa Fe, NM; sick in post hospital at Ft Bliss, TX; with L/9th Cavalry, left camp on Rio Mimbres, NM, 8 Jul 1880 and marched twenty miles to Ft Cummings, NM; left Ft Cummings 8 Aug on march to Leas Ferry on Rio Grande and returned to Rio Mimbres camp after march of 104 miles; on detached service at Ft Cummings, Sep–Oct 1880; in confinement at Ft Bliss awaiting trial by general court martial, Dec 1880–Feb 1881; at Ft Bliss May–June 1881. SOURCE: Muster Rolls, L/9th Cavalry, 31 Oct 1879–29 Feb 1880, 30 June 1880–30 Jun 1881.

YOUNG, George E.; Private; B/10th Cav. Convicted of abusing a woman in Eagle Pass, TX, Dec 1877, and fined $40; in guardhouse at Ft Duncan, TX, Jan 1878, when he assaulted another prisoner, escaped, was recaptured; at Ft Stockton, TX, 1879; witness in court martial of Lt. William H. Beck, 10th Cavalry, San Antonio, TX, Feb 1879; in post hospital, Ft Stockton, Jun 1879, after fight with white soldier in which Young's finger was bitten and later amputated, awaiting discharge for disability; considering returning to Georgia and being waiter, Jul 1879. SOURCE: Kinevan, *Frontier Cavalryman*, 66, 80–81, 181, 287.

YOUNG, George W.; Private; H/9th Cav. Died 31 Mar 1908; buried at San Antonio National Cemetery, Section D, number 565. SOURCE: San Antonio National Cemetery Locator.

YOUNG, Jacob; 1st Sgt; B/10th Cav. ‡Adjutant, 10th Cavalry, Ft Sill, Indian Territory, returns Private Young's complaint of unjust treatment and request for trial, 16 Dec 1870; Young is former first sergeant, H/10th Cavalry, reduced in accordance with law and transferred for sufficient reason; should be thankful he was not tried as he would have gotten heavier punishment. SOURCE: ES, 10 Cav, 1866–71.

‡Request of Sergeant Young, B/10th Cavalry, for transfer disapproved; no reason shown. SOURCE: CO, 10 Cav, to Young, 18 Dec 1875, ES, 10 Cav, 1873–83.

According to Lt. John Bigelow, Ft Duncan, TX, Dec 1877, Young is "an intelligent darkey who has been in the regiment ever since its organization." SOURCE: Kinevan, *Frontier Cavalryman*, 57.

At Ft Stockton, TX, 1879; witness in court martial of Lt. William H. Beck, 10th Cavalry, San Antonio, TX, Feb 1879; granted 60-day furlough Sep 1879. SOURCE: Kinevan, *Frontier Cavalryman*, 209, 287.

YOUNG, James; Private; E/10th Cav. ‡Original member of 10th Cavalry; in troop when organized, Ft Leavenworth, KS, 15 Jun 1867. SOURCE: McMiller, "Buffalo Soldiers," 72.

Died 24 Jun 1870 of typhoid at Ft Sill, OK. SOURCE: Regimental Returns, 10th Cavalry, 1870.

‡Commander, 10th Cavalry, forwards duplicate final statement and inventory of effects of late Private Young to Adjutant General, 30 Jun 1870. SOURCE: ES, 10 Cav, 1866–71.

Died 23 Jun 1870; buried at Camp Douglas, UT. SOURCE: Record Book of Interments, Post Cemetery, 252.

YOUNG, James; Private; K/24th Inf. ‡Mentioned among men who distinguished themselves in 1889; awarded certificate of merit for gallant and meritorious service while escort for Maj. Joseph W. Wham, paymaster, when he was attacked by band of robbers between Fts Grant and Thomas, AZ; now out of service. SOURCE: GO 18, AGO, 1891.

Cited for bravery against robbers near Cedar Springs, AZ, in May 1889 by Maj. Joseph W. Wham, and awarded certificate of merit; not wounded in fight but hospitalized with venereal ailment; left Army before end of 1890. SOURCE: Schubert, *Black Valor*, 93, 95, 98.

Text of report of Paymaster Wham, describing bravery of escort, published. SOURCE: Schubert, *Voices of the Buffalo Soldier*, 159–62.

Awarded certificate of merit for gallant and meritorious conduct while member of escort of Maj. Joseph W. Wham, paymaster, who was ambushed by bandits between Fts Grant and Thomas, 11 May 1889. SOURCE: Gleim, *The Certificate of Merit*, 44.

YOUNG, James; Private; K/10th Cav. Died 20 Oct 1898; buried at San Antonio National Cemetery, Section I, number 1671. SOURCE: San Antonio National Cemetery Locator.

YOUNG, Jerry; Sergeant; L/10th Cav. ‡Original member of 10th Cavalry; in troop when organized, Ft Riley, KS, 21 Sep 1867. SOURCE: McMiller, "Buffalo Soldiers," 78.

Drowned 21 Oct 1870 at Ft Sill, OK. SOURCE: Regimental Returns, 10th Cavalry, 1870.

‡Commander, L/10th Cavalry, forwards final statement of late Sergeant Young to Commander, 10th Cavalry, Dec 1870. SOURCE: ES, 10 Cav, 1866–71.

Sergeant, L/10th Cavalry, died 20 Oct 1870; buried at Camp Douglas, UT. SOURCE: Record Book of Interments, Post Cemetery, 252.

YOUNG, John W.; Sergeant; 9th Cav. Received Philippine Campaign Badge for service as sergeant in C/9th Cavalry; in 9th Cavalry at Ft Leavenworth, KS, Mar 1905. SOURCE: Philippine Campaign Badge list, 29 May 1905.

YOUNG, Joseph; Private; C/9th Cav. Died 20 Nov 1891; reburied at Ft Leavenworth National Cemetery, plot E 2358. SOURCE: Ft Leavenworth National Cemetery.

YOUNG, Roman; Private; 9th Cav. Received Philippine Campaign Badge number 11753 for service as private in G/49th Infantry, United States Volunteers; in 9th Cavalry at Ft Leavenworth, KS, Mar 1905. SOURCE: Philippine Campaign Badge list, 29 May 1905.

‡At Ft D. A. Russell, WY, in 1910. SOURCE: *Illustrated Review: Ninth Cavalry*, with picture.

YOUNG, Thornton; Ord Sgt; U.S. Army. Appointed ordnance sergeant 27 Jul 1887, from first sergeant, G/24th Infantry. SOURCE: Dobak, "Staff Noncommissioned Officers."

YOUNG, William; Private; F/9th Cav. Joined F/9th Cavalry at end of 1884; by Nov 1886 had seven court-martial convictions and had spent five months in confinement; injured Pvt. C. E. Woods with stones shot from slingshot, Ft Robinson, NE, Apr 1887; sentence of dishonorable discharge overturned because no prison term was ordered, so he returned to duty; involved in fight with Sgt. Emanuel Stance in barracks, Aug 1887; dishonorably discharged and sentenced to six months at hard labor. SOURCE: Kenner, *Buffalo Soldiers and Officers of the Ninth Cavalry*, 169, 171.

YOUNG, William; Corporal; C/10th Cav. Received Indian Wars Campaign Badge number 1412 on 15 Jul 1909. SOURCE: Carroll, *Indian Wars Campaign Badge*, 41.

YOURS, Robert; Sergeant; I/25th Inf. ‡At San Isidro, Philippines, 1902. *See* OTT, WILLIAMS, John, Private, I/25th Infantry

‡At Ft Niobrara, NE, 1903. *See* OTT, LINAIRE, Private, I/25th Infantry

Died 17 Apr 1903; buried at Ft Niobrara Post Cemetery. SOURCE: Ft Niobrara Post Cemetery, Complete Listing.

YOUSTING, John; Private; 25th Inf. Sentenced to fifteen-day punishment of standing on barrel from reveille to noon and carrying forty-pound log from noon to night, Ft Duncan, TX, 1870, for allowing prisoners to play cards while he conversed with Mexican women. SOURCE: Leiker, *Racial Borders*, 78.

Bibliography

This bibliography of works cited in this volume follows the format of the bibliography in *On the Trail of the Buffalo Soldier* (1995). However, the works cited here fall into six, rather than nine, main categories. Reflecting the ongoing interest in the history of African American military service, a number of books and articles have been completed since *On the Trail of the Buffalo Soldier* appeared nearly a decade ago. "Unpublished Manuscripts and Documents" contains materials provided to the authors in the intervening years by descendants of soldiers and by other people interested in specific soldiers' lives. A new category, "Electronic Sources," includes lists of interments in national cemeteries where many of these men were buried. Because data available on the World Wide Web are highly changeable and impermanent, citations to these collections include the dates on which they were accessed. In addition, we have indicated when we printed copies of lists that we obtained on the Internet and filed with the rest of our research materials for this book. Some works cited in the bibliography to the original volume have been repeated here (marked with an asterisk) in cases where information had been overlooked or incorrectly used. Please consult the 1995 volume as well as this *Supplement* for the complete list of sources.

Books

*Armes, George A. *Ups and Downs of an Army Officer*. Washington, DC, 1900.

Ball, Larry D. *Ambush at Bloody Run: The Wham Paymaster Robbery of 1889*. Tucson: Arizona Historical Society, 2000.

Barnett, Louise. *Ungentlemanly Acts: The Army's Notorious Incest Trial*. New York: Hill & Wang, 2000.

Bierschwale, Margaret. *Fort McKavett, Texas, Post of the San Saba*. Salado, TX: Anson Jones Press, 1966.

Bigelow, John, Jr. *Garrison Tangles in the Friendless Tenth: The Journal of First Lieutenant John Bigelow, Jr., Fort Davis, Texas*. Edited with an Introduction by Douglas C. McChristian. Mattituck, NY: J. M. Carroll, 1985.

Carroll, John M., editor. *The Indian Wars Campaign Medal: Its History and Its Recipients*. Mattituck, NY: J. M. Carroll & Company, 1992.

Dobak, William A., and Thomas D. Phillips. *The Black Regulars, 1866–1898*. Norman: University of Oklahoma Press, 2001.

Gleim, Albert F. *The Certificate of Merit: U.S. Army Distinguished Service Award, 1847–1918*. Arlington, VA: Albert F. Glein, 1979.

Greene, Robert Ewell. *Swamp Angels, a Biographical Study of the 54th Massachusetts Regiment; True Facts about the Black Defenders of the Civil War*. N.p. BoMark/Greene Publishing Group, 1990.

Haley, J. Evetts. *Fort Concho and the Texas Frontier*. San Angelo, TX: San Angelo Standard-Times, 1952.

Kenner, Charles L. *Buffalo Soldiers and Officers of the Ninth Cavalry, 1867–1898: Black and White Together*. Norman: University of Oklahoma Press, 1999.

Kinevan, Marcos. *Frontier Cavalryman: Lieutenant John Bigelow with the Buffalo Soldiers in Texas*. El Paso: Texas Western Press, 1998

*Leckie, William H. *The Buffalo Soldiers: A Narrative of the Negro Cavalry in the West*. Norman: University of Oklahoma Press, 1967.

Leiker, James N. *Racial Borders: Black Soldiers along the Rio Grande*. College Station: Texas A&M University Press, 2002.

Miller, Mark E. *Hollow Victory: The White River Expedition of 1879 and the Battle of Milk Creek.* Niwot, CO: University Press of Colorado, 1997.

Mulroy, Kevin. *Freedom on the Border: The Seminole Maroons in Florida, the Indian Territory, Coahuila, and Texas.* Lubbock: Texas Tech University Press, 1993.

Porter, Kenneth Wiggins. *The Negro on the American Frontier.* New York: Arno Press, 1971.

Sayre, Harold R. *Warriors of Color.* Fort Davis, TX: Harold R. Sayre, 1995.

Schubert, Frank N. *Black Valor: Buffalo Soldiers and the Medal of Honor, 1870–1898.* Wilmington, DE: Scholarly Resources, 1997.

_____. *Voices of the Buffalo Soldier: Records, Reports, and Recollections of Military Life and Service in the West.* Albuquerque: University of New Mexico Press, 2003.

Smith, Thomas T. *The U.S. Army and the Texas Frontier Economy, 1845–1900.* College Station: Texas A&M University Press, 1999.

Tate, Michael L. *The Frontier Army in the Settlement of the West.* Norman: University of Oklahoma Press, 1999.

Tucker, Philip Thomas. *Cathy Williams: From Slave to Female Buffalo Soldier.* Mechanicsburg, PA: Stackpole Books, 2002

Wooster, Robert. *Soldiers, Sutlers, and Settlers: Garrison Life on the Texas Frontier.* College Station: Texas A&M University Press, 1987.

Articles

Blanton, De Anne. "Catla Williams: Black Woman Soldier, 1866–1868." *Minerva: Quarterly Report on Women and the Military* 10 (Fall/Winter 1992): 1–12.

"Colored Troops, They Who Fought So Nobly, The Sable Heroes Arrive in Cheyenne—How they were Received by our citizens—the Band Serenade." *Cheyenne Daily Leader*, 22 Oct 1879.

Pollard, Ken, and Vicki J. Hagen. "Edward 'Sancho' Mozique," 85–91, in *Black Cowboys of Texas*, edited by Sara R. Massey. College Station: Texas A&M University Press, 2000.

Romeyn, Charles A. "The First Sergeant." *Cavalry Journal* (July 1925). Reprinted in *Cavalry Journal* (June 2001): 5–7.

Seraile, William. "Saving Souls on the Frontier, A Chaplain's Labor." *Montana, The Magazine of Western History* 42 (Winter 1992).

U.S. Government Publications and Documents

Adjutant General, U.S. Army. *American Decorations: A List of Awards of the Congressional Medal of Honor, the Distinguished Service Cross, and the Distinguished Service Medal, Awarded under Authority of the Congress of the United States, 1862–1926.* Washington, DC: Government Printing Office, 1927.

_____. *Secretary of War. Annual Report*, 1904.

U.S. Department of the Interior. Tagg, Martyn D. *The Camp at Bonita Cañon, A Buffalo Soldier Camp in Chiricahua National Monument, Arizona.* Publications in Anthropology, No. 42. Tucson, AZ: Western Archeological and Conservation Center, National Park Service, January 1987.

Unpublished Manuscripts and Documents

Buecker, Thomas R. Fort Robinson Burials. Unpublished compilation, Fort Robinson Museum, Crawford, Nebraska.

Buffalo Soldiers Interred in Fort Sam Houston National Cemetery. 1 p. Photocopy in authors' files.

Cunningham, Roger. E-mail message, 28 Jan 2000, in authors' files.

Dobak, William A. "Staff Noncommissioned Officers from Black Regiments." Typescript in authors' files.

_____. "Trial of Corporal Robert Davis, Company C, 38th Infantry, Fort Selden, New Mexico, January 1868." Typescript in authors' files.

Erickson, Patricia. Burials at Fort Bayard National Cemetery, Fort Bayard, New Mexico; Survey March 11–13, 2003. Typescript in authors' files.

"Pikes Peak Region Black History, (part 2): Charles Banks (1880–1976)." 26 Dec 1996 printout in authors' files.

Post Cemetery at Presidio of Monterey. "Record Book of Interments." 2 pp. Photocopy in authors' files.

"Roster of the Non-Commissioned Officers of the Ninth U.S. Cavalry." Headquarters, Ninth U.S. Cavalry, Fort Robinson, Nebraska, January 1897.

San Antonio National Cemetery, Locator of Buffalo Soldiers, 1886–1900. 9 pp. Photocopy in authors' files.

Schubert, Frank N., compiler. "Consolidated List of all Seminole Negro Scouts known to author," 1996. Manuscript in authors' files.

_____, compiler. "Seminole-Negro Scouts." Manuscript in authors' files.

Sorenson, George. "List of Buffalo Soldiers Who Rode in the 25th Infantry Bicycle Corps, Ft Missoula, Montana 1896 and 1897," with 12 Mar 1996 letter in authors' files.

Swanson, Donald A. Enlistment Record of Indian Scouts Who Served in One of the Detachments at Fort Clark, Texas, researched by Donald A. Swanson. Bronte, TX: Ames-American Printing Co., n.d. Photocopy in authors' files.

Walker, Fachon A. Letter to Frank N. Schubert about King James Tatum, 20 May 2002. In authors' files.

Williams, Jessie. Interview conducted by John H. Hinrichs, Omaha, Nebraska, Sep 1941. Photocopy of Ft Robinson Museum copy in authors' files.

Williams, Mary L., Park Ranger, Ft Davis National Historic Site, Ft Davis, Texas. Letter to Margaret A. Lewis, 27 Mar 1996. Photocopy in authors' files.

Military Records

Documents Relating to the Military and Naval Service of Blacks Awarded the Congressional Medal of Honor from the Civil War to the Spanish-American War. Microcopy M-929, 3 reels, National Archives
> Cuban Campaign Badge Recipients, with cover memorandum dated 23 March 1905. Frame 785, Reel 2.
> Philippine Campaign Badge Recipients, with cover memorandum dated 23 March 1905. Frames 783-4, Reel 2.
> Philippine Campaign Badge list, 29 May 1905. Frames 785-800, Reel 2.

General Court-Martial Orders No. 99, Ft Snelling, MN, 19 Aug 1881. Photocopy in authors' files.

Organization Index to Pension Files of Veterans Who Served between 1861 and 1900. Microfilm T-289, National Archives.

*Records of the Adjutant General's Office, 1780–1917, Record Group 94, National Archives
> General Correspondence, 1890–1917.
> Muster Rolls, L/9th Cavalry, 31 Aug 1879–29 Feb 1880, 30 Jun 1880–28 Feb 1881, 30 Apr–30 Jun 1881.
> Regimental Returns, 10th Cavalry, 1866–Nov 1882.
> *Register of Enlistments in the U.S. Army, 1798–1914. Microfilm M-233.

*Records of the Office of the Judge Advocate General (Army). Record Group 153, National Archives
> Proceedings of General Court Martial, Barney McKay.

*Records of United States Regular Army Mobile Units, 1821–1942. Record Group 391, National Archives
> *Descriptive and Assignment Rolls, 25th Infantry
> Descriptive Roll of A/39th Infantry Transferred 20 Apr 1869 to K/25th Infantry, Jackson Barracks, LA.

Records of United States Army Continental Commands, 1821–1920. Record Group 393, National Archives
> *Letters Received, Department of the Missouri, 1867.

Electronic Sources

"The Buffalo Sailor," American Forces Information Service News Articles, April 4, 2000. http://www.defenselink. mil/news/Apr2000/n04042000_20004044.html. 10 Jan 2003 printout in authors' files.

"Buffalo Soldiers & Indian Wars," Part 1, Personal Profile. http://www.buffalosoldier.net. 15 Sep 2002 printout in authors' files.

"Buffalo Soldiers Buried at Ft. Bayard, NM," compiled by C.A. Savage, sent to afrigeneas list June 1997. http://www.msstate.edu/listarchives/afrigeneas/199706/msg00067.html. 29 Oct 2002 printout in authors' files.

Ford, Susan Jezak. "Kansas City Public Library, Special Collections, Lafayette A. Tillman." http://www.kclibrary. org/sc/bio/tillman.htm. 3 Mar 2003 printout in authors' files.

"Fort Bayard National Cemetery, Fort Bayard, Grant County, New Mexico, Records of Burials." U.S. Department of Veterans Affairs. Database at http://www.interment.net/data/us/nm/grant/ftbaynat/index.htm. 28 Oct 2002.

Fort Leavenworth National Cemetery, Fort Leavenworth, Leavenworth County, Kansas, Records of Burials. U.S. Department of Veterans Affairs Database at http://www.interment.net/data/us/ks/leavenworth/fortleavnat/ 7 Jan 2004.

Fort McPherson National Cemetery, Maxwell, Lincoln County, Nebraska. Record of burials provided by U.S. Department of Veterans Affairs on July 2, 2000. Database at http://www.interment.net/data/us/ne/lincoln/ ftmcphnat/ 22 Jun 2003.

Fort Meade National Cemetery, Sturgis, Meade County, South Dakota, Records of Burials. U.S. Department of Veterans Affairs Database. http://www.interment.net/data/us/sd/meade/ftmeanat/index.htm. 3 Mar 2003 printout in authors' files.

Ft Niobrara Post Cemetery, Complete Listing. http://www.rootsweb.com/~necherry/Ftniob.htm. 2 Mar 2003 printout in authors' files.

Gordon, Asa. "Alexandria National Cemetery, Pineville, Louisiana; Resting Place of Seminole Negro Indian Scouts." http://www.bjmjt.com/sisca/july_paine.htm. 25 Feb 2003 printout in authors' files.

Indian Scout Cemetery, Kinney County, Texas. http://www.rootsweb.com/~txkinney/is_cemetery.html. 26 Feb 2003 printout in authors' files.

Lee, Annabel. "Once Zulu Prince, Now Private for Uncle Sam," San Francisco Call, 2 Jul 1899. Transcribed text with picture of Thomas W. Taylor at http://www.sfmuseum.org/hist10/buffalo.html. 18 May 2002 printout in authors' files.

Powell, Anthony, compiler. "Military Record of the Enlisted Men Who Were Discharged Without Honor, By Direction of President Theodore Roosevelt. Pursuant to Special Orders, No. 266, War Department, November 9, 1906." Undated. http://www.coax.net/people/lwf/ap_mrb.htm. 20 Sep 2002 printout in authors' files.

Record Book of Interments in Post Cemetery at Camp Douglas, Utah, 252. http://www.rootsweb.com/~usgenweb/ special/military/vitals/images/burialreg/v1-252.jpg. 11 Feb 2003 printout in authors' files.

Sage, Vynette. Ft. Huachuca Cemetery, Cochise County, Arizona. USGenWeb Archives, March 2, 2001. http:// ftp.rootsweb.com/pub/usgenweb/az/cochise/cemetery/ft_huachuca.txt?sourceid=00388786186972681241

San Antonio National Cemetery, Records of burials provided by U.S. Department of Veterans Affairs, on July 2, 2000. Http://ww.interment.net/data/us/tx/bexar/sananat/ 22 Jun 2003.

San Franciso National Cemetery, San Francisco, San Francisco County, California. U.S. Department of Veterans Affairs Records of Burials. Database at http://www.interment.net/data/us/nm/grant/ftbaynat/index.htm. 19 June 2003.

Santa Fe National Cemetery, Santa Fe, Santa Fe County, New Mexico, Records of Burials. U.S. Department of Veterans Affairs. Database at http://www.interment.net/data/us/nm/grant/ftbaynat/index.htm. 29 October 2002.

U.S. Army Intelligence Center and Fort Huachuca, History Program. "Mourning Hearts." http://usaic.hua.army. mil/history/PDFS/cemetery.pdf. 3 Mar 2003 printout in authors' files.

United States Colored Troops Resident in Baltimore at the Time of the 1890 Census. Maryland State Archives, Revised 5/30/95. http://www.mdarchives.state.md.us/msa/speccol/3096/html/000_10001.html. 18 November 2003 printout in authors' files.

Appendix

Battles Involving Buffalo Soldiers and Western Indians, 1867–1890

Information for this table of engagements in which buffalo soldiers participated during the Indian war period, 1867–1890, was extracted from three sources:

Adjutant General's Office. *Chronological List of Actions & c., With Indians, from January 1, 1866, to January 1891.*

Heitman, Francis B. *Historical Register and Dictionary of the United States Army, from its organization, September 29, 1789, to March 2, 1903.* Vol. 2. Washington, DC: Government Printing Office, 1903.

Webb, George W. *Chronological List of Engagements between the Regular Army of the United States and Various Tribes of Hostile Indians Which Occurred during the Years 1790 to 1898, Inclusive.* St. Joseph, MO: Wing Printing & Publishing Company, 1939.

These three compilations overlap to a very large extent, but there are small discrepancies. Together they list a total of 1,296 combat encounters involving U.S. troops and western Indians. Of these, 168 actions involved black soldiers, sometimes serving alone and at other times alongside white units. The Webb compilation is the most comprehensive of the three, with 1,282 total encounters and 163 involving black soldiers. The 168 actions found here amount to 13.8 percent of the 1,296 engagements overall. During the period in question, black soldiers made up about 12 percent of the Army.

Battles Involving Buffalo Soldiers and Western Indians, 1867–1890

Date	Location	Units	Commander
26 Jun 67	Wilson's Creek, KS	Det, K/38 Inf	CPL D. Turner
29 Jul 67	nr Ft Hays, KS	Det, G/38 Inf	
2 Aug 67	Saline River, KS	F/10 Cav	CPT G. A. Armes
21-22 Aug 67	Prairie Dog Creek, KS	F/10 Cav	CPT G. A. Armes
16 Sep 67	Saline River, KS	Det, G/10 Cav	SGT C. H. Davis
1 Oct 67	Howard's Well, TX	Det, D/9 Cav	CPL S. Wright
5 Dec 67	Eagle Springs, TX	Det, F/9 Cav	NCO
26 Dec 67	nr Ft Lancaster, TX	Det, K/9 Cav	CPT W. T. Frohock
Jan 68	Ft Quitman, TX	Det, E/9 Cav	
6 Aug 68	Ft Quitman, TX	H/9 Cav	
27 Aug 68	Hatchet Mountains, NM	F/38 Inf	CPT Alex. Moore
14 Sep 68	Horse Head Hills, TX	Dets, C, F, K/9 Cav	LT Patrick Cusick
15 Sep 68	Big Sandy Creek, CO	I/10 Cav	CPT G. W. Graham
17-25 Sep 68	Arickaree Fork, Republican R, KS	H/10 Cav	CPT L. H. Carpenter
18 Oct 68	Beaver Creek, KS	H, I, M/10 Cav	CPT L. H. Carpenter
19 Nov 68	nr Ft Dodge, KS	Det, A/10 Cav	SGT John Wilson
29 Jan 69	Mulberry Creek, KS	Dets, C, G, H, K/9 Cav	CPT Edward Byrne
26 Mar 69	San Francisco Mountains, NM	Det, C/38 Inf	
7 Jun 69	Johnson's R & Pecos R, TX	Dets, G, L, M/9 Cav	COL R. S. Mackenzie
16 Sep 69	Salt Fork, Brazos R, TX	B, C, F, M/9 Cav; Det, 41 Inf	CPT Henry Carroll
20-21 Sep 69	Brazos R, TX	Dets, B, E/9 Cav	CPT Henry Carroll
29 Sep-6 Oct 69	Mimbres Mountains, NM	A, C/38 Inf	
28-29 Oct 69	Headwaters, Brazos R, TX	B, C, F, G, L, M/9 Cav; Det, 24 Inf	CPT J. M. Bacon
24 Nov 69	Headwaters, Llano R, TX	Dets, F, M/9 Cav	CPT E. M. Heyl
25 Dec 69	Johnson's Mail Station, TX	Det, E/9 Cav	NCO
3 Jan-6 Feb 70	Rio Grande & Pecos R, TX	G & Det, L/9 Cav; Dets, L, K/24 Inf	CPT J. M. Bacon
6 Jan 70	Guadalupe Mountains, TX	H/9 Cav	
11 Jan 70	Lower Pecos R, TX	L/9 Cav	LT Charles Parker
16 Jan 70	Indian Village, TX	G & Det, L/9 Cav	
20 Jan 70	Delaware Creek, Guadalupe Mtns, TX	Dets, C, D, I, K/9 Cav	CPT F. S. Dodge
3 Apr 70	San Martine Springs, TX	Det, H/9 Cav	NCO
6 Apr 70	nr Clear Creek, TX	Det, M/10 Cav	LT W. R. Harmon
25 Apr 70	Crow Springs, TX	Dets, C, K/9 Cav	MAJ A. P. Morrow
19-20 May 70	Kickapoo Springs, TX	Det, F/9 Cav	SGT E. Stance
29 May 70	Bass Canyon, TX	K/9 Cav	LT I. W. Trask
2 Jun 70	nr Copper Canyon, AZ	Dets, 24 Inf	
8 Jun 70	btwn Ft Dodge, KS & Camp Supply, IT	F, H/10 Cav	LT J. A. Bodamer

10 Jun 70	Snake Creek, IT	H/10 Cav	CPT L. H. Carpenter
11 Jun 70	Camp Supply, IT	A, F, G, I, K/9 Cav	LTC A. D. Nelson
27 Apr 71	Ft Sill, IT	Det, E/10 Cav	LT S. L. Woodward
12 May 71	nr Red R, TX	Det, L/10 Cav	
17 May 71	Ft Sill, IT	B, D, E, H/10 Cav	
21 May 71	Camp Melvin Station, TX	Det, K/25 Inf	SGT J. Walker
30 Jun 71	Staked Plains, TX	Det, I/9 Cav; Det, 24 Inf	LTC W. R. Shafter
22 Jul 71	Headwaters, Concho R, TX	Det, F/9 Cav	
31 Jul 71	nr Ft McKavett, TX	Det, M/9 Cav; Det, A/24 Inf	CPT F. M. Crandal
1 Sep 71	nr Ft McKavett, TX	Det, M/9 Cav; Det. E/24 Inf	CPT J. W. Clous
19 Sep 71	Foster Springs, IT	Det, B/10 Cav	CPT J. B. Van de Weile
20 Apr 72	nr Howard's Well, TX	A, H/9Cav	CPT Michael Cooney
20 May 72	La Pendencia, TX	Dets, C/9 Cav, K/24 Inf	LT Gustavus Valois
12 Jul 72	Deep River, IT	A, L/10 Cav	CPT Nicholas Nolan
22 Jul 72	Otter Creek, IT	A, L/10 Cav	CPT Nicholas Nolan
28 Jul 72	Central Station, TX	Det, K/25 Inf	SGT J. Walker
6 Dec 72	nr Rio Grande, TX	Det, 9 Cav	SGT Bruce
27 Apr 73	Eagle Springs, TX	Det, B/25 Inf	CPL E. Parker
30 Apr 73	nr Ft Sill, IT	Det, 10 Cav	LT Wm. R Harmon
May 73	Barrilla Springs, TX	Det, D/25 Inf	SGT W. Smith
19 Aug 73	Barrilla Springs, TX	Det, E/25 inf	CPL G. Collins
31 Aug 73	nr Pease R, TX	E, I/10 Cav	CPT T. A. Baldwin
30 Sep 73	Mesquite Flats, TX	E, I/10 Cav	CPT T. A. Baldwin
1 Oct 73	Central Station, TX	Det, K/25 Inf	SGT B. Mew
5 Dec 73	Elm Creek, TX	Det, D/10 Cav	LT E. Turner
27 Dec 73	Deep Red Creek, IT	Det, 25 Inf	CPL Wright
31 Dec 73	Eagle Springs, TX	Det, B/25 Inf	NCO
2 Feb 74	Home Creek, TX	Det, A/10 Cav	SGT T. Allsup
5 Feb 74	Double Mtn Fork, Brazos R, TX	G , Det, D/10 Cav	LTC G. P. Buell
Apr 74	China Tree Creek, TX	K/10 Cav; Det, C/25 Inf	CPT W. C. Beach
2 May 74	btwn Red and Big Wishita R, TX	Det, K/10 Cav	LT Q. O'M. Gilmore
18 May 74	Carrizo Mtns, TX	Det, B/25 Inf	CPT Charles Bentzoni
22-23Aug 74	Wichita Agency, IT	E, H, L/10 Cav, I/25 Inf	LTC J. W. Davidson
Oct 74	nr Canadian R, TX	E, K/9 Cav	CPT A. E. Hooker
4-31 Oct 74	nr Ft Sill, IT	K/9 Cav	CPT Charles Parker
1 Oct-8 Nov 74	Exped from Ft Sill, IT	B, C, F, H, L, M/10 Cav	LTC J. W. Davidson
24 Oct 74	Elk Creek, IT	3 troops/10 Cav	MAJ G. W. Schofield
8 Nov 74	nr McClellan, TX	B, D, F, H/10 Cav	CPT Charles D. Viele
7 Dec 74	Kingfisher Creek, IT	D, Det, M/10 Cav	CPT A. S. B. Keyes
20 Dec 74	Kingfisher Creek, IT	D, Det, M/10 Cav	CPT A. S. B. Keyes
28 Dec 74	North Fork, Canadian R, IT	I, M/10 Cav	CPT A. S. B. Keyes
26 Jan 75	Solis Ranch, nr Ringgold Bks, TX	Det, G/9 Cav	COL Edward Hatch
27 Jan 75	nr Ringgold Bks, TX	Dets, B, G/9 Cav	COL Edward Hatch
23 Feb 75	Salt Fork, Red R, TX	10 Cav	LTC J. W. Davidson
6 Apr 75	nr Cheyenne Agency, IT	D, M/10 Cav	LTC T. H. Neill
25 Apr 75	Eagle Nest Crossing, Pecos R,TX	24 Inf	LT J. L. Bullis
5 May 75	Battle Point, TX	Dets, A, F, G, I, L/10 Cav	SGT John Marshall
2 Nov 75	nr Pecos R, TX	G, L/10 Cav	LT Andrew Geddes
18 Feb 76	Carrizo Mtns, TX	Det, B/25 Inf	CPT Charles Bentzoni
Apr 76	Central Station, TX	Det, D/25 Inf	SGT W. Smith
30 Jul 76	nr Saragossa, Mexico	Det, B/10 Cav	LT J. L. Bullis
15 Sep 76	Florida Mtns, NM	F/9 Cav	CPT Henry Carroll
23 Jan 77	Florida Mtns, NM	Det, C/9 Cav	LT H. H. Wright
28 Jan 77	Siena Boca Grande, Mexico	Det. C/9 Cav	CPT C. D. Beyer
1 Apr 77	Rio Grande, nr Devils R, TX	Seminole Negro Scouts	LT J. L. Bullis

4 May 77	Lake Quemado, TX	G/10 Cav	CPT P. L. Lee
6 May 77	Canon Resecata,TX	G/10 Cav	CPT P. L. Lee
26 Sep 77	Saragossa, Mexico	Det, C/10 Cav	LT J. L. Bullis
1 Nov 77	Big Bend, Rio Grande,TX	Seminole Negro Scouts	LT J. L. Bullis
29-30 Nov 77	Sierra Carmel Ranch, Mexico	C/10 Cav	CPT S. B. M. Young
16 Jan 78	Russell's Ranch, Rio Grande, TX	H/10 Cav; A, H/25 Inf	CPT M. L. Courtney
15 Apr 78	Carrizo Mtns, TX	Det, K/10 Cav	LT Andrew Geddes
15 Apr 78	nr Escondido Station, TX	Det, B/10 Cav	LT John Bigelow
30 Jun 78	on South Concho R,TX	Det, D/10 Cav	LT C. R. Ward
2 Aug 78	Guadalupe Mtns,TX	Det, H/10 Cav	SGT Claggett
5 Aug 78	Dog Canyon, NM	F, H/9 Cav	CPT Henry Carroll
15 Jan 79	Cormedos Mtns, NM	A/9 Cav	LT M. W. Day
8 Mar 79	Ojo Caliente, NM	I/9 Cav	LT C. W. Merritt
29 May 79	Black Range, Mimbres Mtns, NM	Dets, C, I/9 Cav	CPT C. D. Beyer
25 Jul 79	nr Salt Lake or Sulphur Springs, TX	Det, H/10 Cav; Det, H/25 Inf	CPT M. L. Courtney
27 Jul 79	nr Carrizo Mtns, TX	Det, H/10 Cav	CPT M. L. Courtney
4 Sep 79	Ojo Caliente, NM	Det, E/9 Cav	SGT S. Chapman
16 Sep 79	Van Horn Mtns,TX	Det, H/10 Cav; H/25 Inf	CPT M. L. Courtney
18 Sep 79	Las Animas R, NM	A, B, C, G/9 Cav	CPT C. D. Beyer
26-30 Sep 79	nr Ojo Caliente, Black Range, NM	Dets, 9 Cav	MAJ A. P. Morrow
29-30 Sep 79	Cuchillo Negro R, Mimbres Mtns, NM	B. C, G, L/9 Cav	MAJ A. P. Morrow
30 Sep 79	nr Canada de Alamosa, NM	Det, E/9Cav	
2-4 Oct 79	Milk Creek, CO	D/9 Cav	CPT F. S.Dodge
5 Oct 79	Milk Creek, CO	D/9 Cav	COL Wesley Merritt
10 Oct 79	White R, CO	D/9 Cav	COL Wesley Merritt
27 Oct 79	Guzman Mtns, nr Corralitos R, Mexico	Dets, B, C, G, H/9 Cav	MAJ A. P. Morrow
12 Jan 80	Rio Puerco, NM	B, C, F, G, H, M/9 Cav	MAJ A. P. Morrow
17 Jan 80	San Mateo Mtns, NM	B, C, F, H, M/9 Cav	MAJ A. P. Morrow
30 Jan 80	Cabello Mtns, NM	Dets, B, M/9Cav	CPT L. H. Rucker
3 Feb 80	San Andreas Mtns, NM	B, C, F, H, M/9 Cav	MAJ A. P. Morrow
28 Feb 80	Sacramento Mtns, NM	A/9 Cav	LT John Conline
3 Apr 80	nr Pecos Falls, TX	F, L/10 Cav	LT Calvin Esterly
5 Apr 80	Miembrillo Canyon, San Andreas Mtns, NM	A/9 Cav	LT John Conline
6-9 Apr 80	Miembrillo Canyon, San Andreas Mtns, NM	A, D. F, G/9 Cav	CPT Henry Carroll
9 Apr 80	Shakehand Springs, TX	K/10 Cav	CPT Thomas C. Lebo
16 Apr 80	camp nr South Fork, NM	Det, G/9Cav	CPT Charles Steelhammer
16 Apr 80	Mescalero Agency, NM	Dets, H, L/9Cav; D, E, F, K, L/10 Cav; Dets, 25 Inf	COL Edward Hatch
17 Apr 80	nr Dog Canyon, NM	D, L/9 Cav	MAJ A. P. Morrow
20 Apr 80	Sacramento Mtns, NM	Det, L/10 Cav	LT M. M. Maxon
14 May 80	Old Ft Tularosa, NM	Dets, E, I, K/9 Cav	SGT George Jordan
5 Jun 80	Cook's Canyon, NM	A, D, K, L/9 Cav	MAJ A. P. Morrow
30 Jul 80	Rocky Ridge or Eagle's Pass, TX	Dets, A, C, D, G/10 Cav	COL Benjamin Grierson
3 Aug 80	Sierra Diablo, TX	K/10 Cav	CPT Thomas C. Lebo
3 Aug 80	Alamo Springs, TX	Dets, B, C, G, H/10 Cav	CPL Asa Weaver
4 Aug 80	Camp Safford, Guadalupe Mtns,TX	Det, F/10 Cav	SGT Wm Richardson

6 Aug 80	Guadalupe Mtns, TX	F/10 Cav	CPT W. B. Kennedy
6 Aug 80	nr Rattlesnake Springs, TX	Det, H/10 Cav; H/24 Inf	CPT J. C. Gilmore
6 Aug 80	Rattlesnake Springs, TX	Dets, B, C, G, H/10 Cav	CPT L. H. Carpenter
11 Aug 80	nr old Ft Quitman, TX	A/10 Cav	CPT Nicholas Nolan
1 Sep 80	Agua Chiquita, Sacramento Mtns, NM	G/9 Cav	SGT J. Robinson
28 Oct 80	Ojo Caliente, TX	Dets, B, I, K/10 Cav	SGT C. Perry
24 Jan 81	nr Canada de Alamosa, NM	Det, D/9 Cav	SGT M. Ingoman
5 Feb 81	Candelaria Mtns, NM	Det, K/9 Cav	LT J. A. Maney
29 Apr 81	nr Mexican border, Ft Cummings, NM	Det, K/9 Cav	LT J. A. Maney
3 May 81	Sierra del Burro, Mexico	Seminole Negro Scouts	LT J. L. Bullis
17 Jul 81	Alamo Canyon, NM	Det, L/9 Cav	LT J. F. Guilfoyle
19 Jul 81	Arena Blanca, NM	Det, L/9 Cav	LT J. F. Guilfoyle
25 Jul 81	San Andreas Mtns, NM	Det, L/9 Cav	LT J. F. Guilfoyle
25 Jul 81	White Sands, NM	Det, L/9 Cav	LT J. F. Guilfoyle
26 Jul 81	San Andreas Mtns, NM	Det, L/9 Cav	LT J. F. Guilfoyle
3 Aug 81	Monica Springs, NM	Det, L/9 Cav	LT J. F. Guilfoyle
12 Aug 81	Carrizo Canyon, NM	Det, K/9 Cav	CPT Charles Parker
15 Aug 81	Rio Cuchillo Negro, NM	I/9 Cav	LT Gustavus Valois
16 Aug 81	nr San Mateo Mtns, Black Range, NM	Dets, B, H/9 Cav	CPT Charles W. Taylor
19 Aug 81	McEvers' Ranch, Guerillo Canyon, NM	Dets, B, F/9 Cav	LT G. W. Smith
4 Oct 81	South Pass, Dragoon Mtns, AZ	F, H, D/9 Cav	COL O. B. Wilcox
3 May 86	nr Penito Mtns, Sonora, Mexico	K/10 Cav	CPT Thomas C. Lebo
18 Oct 86	Black River Mtns, AZ	H/10 Cav	CPT C. L. Cooper
10 Mar 87	San Carlos Agency, AZ	10 Cav	LT Seward Mott
11 Jun 87	Rincon Mtns, AZ	Dets, E, L/10 Cav	LT Carter P. Johnson
5 Nov 87	Crow Agency, MT	H/9 Cav	BG T. H. Ruger
11 May 89	Cedar Springs, AZ	Dets, 10 Cav, 24 Inf	MAJ J. W. Wham
11 Mar 90	Salt R, nr mouth of Cherry Creek, AZ	Det, K/10 Cav	LT J. W. Watson
30 Dec 90	nr Pine Ridge Agency, SD	D/9 Cav	CPT John S. Loud
30 Dec 90	nr Pine Ridge Agency, SD	E, I, K/9 Cav	MAJ Guy Henry
30 Dec 90	White Clay Creek, SD	D, E, I, K/9 Cav	COL J. W. Forsyth

Buffalo Soldier Recipients of the Certificate of Merit, 1881–1914

During the period between the Civil War and World War I, the Army recognized the bravery and valor of its soldiers with two awards, the Medal of Honor and the Certificate of Merit. By the twentieth century, it was clear that the Medal of Honor took precedence. Frequently, the certificate was awarded in recognition of bravery or exceptional service in situations that did not involve armed conflict with an enemy, but this was not always the case. By the end of the 1920s, surviving holders of the Certificate of Merit received either the Distinguished Service Cross or the Distinguished Service Medal in lieu of the certificate. In this table, ranks with units are those held by the buffalo soldiers when they were granted the awards.

Buffalo Soldier Recipients of the Certificate of Merit, 1881–1914

Name	Rank/Unit	Citation	Place	Date
ANDERSON, Levi	Pvt, D/10th Cav.	Rescue drowning comrade	Ft Ethan Allen, VT	6 Jul 1911
ARRINGTON, George	Pvt, C/24th Inf.	Defend military payroll	Cedar Springs, AZ	11 May 1889
ASH, John M.	Sgt, E/24th Inf.	Gallantry in action	Tabon-Tabon, PI	24 Jul 1906
ASKEW, Preston	Cpl, E/24th Inf.	Gallantry in action	Tabon-Tabon, PI	24 Jul 1906
BATES, James	Pvt, H/9th Cav.	Distinguished service in battle	Santiago, Cuba	1 Jul 1898
BROADUS, Lewis	1st Sgt, M/25th Inf.	Prevent murder of comrade	Ft Niobrara, NE	3 Jul 1906
BURGE, Benjamin	Pvt, E/24th Inf.	Defend military payroll	Cedar Springs, AZ	11 May 1889
CLARK, Lig J.	Pvt, H/24th Inf.	Gallantry in action	Naguilian, PI	7 Dec 1899
CRANSHAW, Tennie	Sgt, K/24th Inf.	Bravery in action	Santa Ana, PI	6 Oct 1899
CROSBY, Scott	Pvt, A/24th Inf.	Distinguished service in battle	Santiago, Cuba	1 Jul 1898
DAVIS, Edward	Pvt, H/9th Cav.	Distinguished service in battle	Santiago, Cuba	1 Jul 1898
ELLIOTT, James	Sgt, D/10th Cav.	Distinguished service in battle	Santiago, Cuba	1 Jul 1898
FASIT, Benjamin	Sgt, E/10th Cav.	Distinguished service in battle	Santiago, Cuba	1 Jul 1898
FEARINGTON, George	Pvt, I/9th Cav.	Fighting barracks fire	Ft DuChesne, UT	13 Dec 1899
GATHER, Ozrow	Sgt, E/10th Cav.	Distinguished service in battle	Santiago, Cuba	1 Jul 1898
GOFF, George W.	Sgt, K/9th Cav.	Distinguished service in battle	Santiago, Cuba	1 Jul 1898
GOODE, Benjamin H.	Pvt, H/24th Inf.	Gallantry in action	Naguilian, PI	7 Dec 1899
GRAHAM, John	Sgt, E/10th Cav.	Distinguished service in battle	Santiago, Cuba	1 Jul 1898
HAGEN, Abram	Cpl, G/24th Inf.	Distinguished service in battle	Santiago, Cuba	1 Jul 1898
HAMS, Thornton	Pvt, C/10th Cav.	Defend military payroll	Cedar Springs, AZ	11 May 1889
HARRISON, Julius	Pvt, B/24th Inf.	Defend military payroll	Cedar Springs, AZ	11 May 1889

Name	Rank/Unit	Citation	Location	Date
HERBERT, Thomas H.	Cpl, E/10th Cav.	Distinguished service in battle	Santiago, Cuba	1 Jul 1898
HOUSTON, Adam	1st Sgt, C/10th Cav.	Distinguished service in battle	Santiago, Cuba	1 Jul 1898
HUMPHREY, John A.	Pvt, I/10th Cav.	Gallantry under fire	Las Guasimas, Cuba	24 Jun 1898
JACKSON, Elisha	Sgt, H/9th Cav.	Distinguished service in battle	Santiago, Cuba	1 Jul 1898
JACKSON, John J.	1st Sgt, C/9th Cav.	Distinguished service in battle	Santiago, Cuba	1 Jul 1898
JACKSON, Julius	Pvt, E/25th Inf.	Rescue drowning comrade	Malabang, PI	16 Dec 1907
JACKSON, Peter	Cpl, G/24th Inf.	Distinguished service in battle	Santiago, Cuba	1 Jul 1898
JEFFERSON, Chas W.	1st Sgt, B/9th Cav.	Distinguished service in battle	Santiago, Cuba	1 Jul 1898
JOHNSON, John H.	Cpl, H/24th Inf.	Distinguished gallantry in battle	Naguilian, PI	7 Dec 1899
JOHNSON, Thomas	1st Sgt, I/24th Inf.	Prevent murder of comrade	Camp McGrath, PI	22 Aug 1912
JORDAN, George	Sgt, K/9th Cav.	Gallantry in action	Carrizo Canyon, NM	12 Aug 1881
LEWIS, Hamilton	Pvt, B/24th Inf.	Defend military payroll	Cedar Springs, AZ	11 May 1889
LIGHTFOOT, James R.	Sgt, K/25th Inf.	Distinguished gallantry in action	Camansi, PI	5 Jan 1900
LYONS, John R.	Pvt, D/10th Cav.	Rescue drowning comrade	Ft Ethan Allen, VT	6 Jul 1911
McCOWN, Peter	1st Sgt, E/10th Cav.	Distinguished service in battle	Santiago, Cuba	1 Jul 1898
MADISON, Ingoman	Sgt, D/9th Cav.	Gallantry in action	Ojo Caliente, NM	23 Jan 1881
MILLER, Richard	Sgt, F/9th Cav.	Distinguished conduct in action	Tagbac, PI	17 Dec 1900
MOORE, Loney	Pvt, A/24th Inf.	Distinguished service in battle.	Santiago, Cuba	1 Jul 1898
NEWHOUSE, Robert	Pvt, K/24th Inf.	Rescue drowning comrade	Camp McGrath, PI	12 Nov 1914
ODEN, Oscar N.	Trmptr, E/10th Cav.	Distinguished service in battle	Santiago, Cuba	1 Jul 1898
PARKER, Jesse E.	Artfcr, D/24th Inf.	Rescue officer under heavy fire	Santiago, Cuba	1 Jul 1898
PAYNE, William	Sgt, E/10th Cav.	Distinguished service in battle	Santiago, Cuba	1 Jul 1898
PUMPHREY, George W.	Cpl, H/9th Cav.	Distinguished service in battle	Santiago, Cuba	1 Jul 1898

Name	Rank, Unit	Citation	Place	Date
ROGERS, John	Trmptr, I/9th Cav.	Distinguished gallantry under fire	Cuchillo Negro, NM	16 Aug 1881
SATCHELL, James	Sgt, A/24th Inf.	Distinguished service in battle	Santiago, Cuba	1 Jul 1898
SETTLERS, James	Pvt, E/9th Cav.	Rescue drowning officer	Wind River, WY	19 Jul 1889
SMITH, John	Pvt, E/24th Inf.	Rescue drowning comrade	Rio Grande, PI	22 Nov 1899
SMITH, Luscious	Pvt, D/10 Cav.	Distinguished service in battle	Santiago, Cuba	1 Jul 1898
STEVENS, Jacob W.	1st Sgt, K/24th Inf.	Coolness and good judgment in action	Santa Ana, PI	6 Oct 1899
STOKES, Earnest	Pvt, F/24th Inf.	Distinguished gallantry in action	Naguilian, PI	7 Dec 1899
STUCKEY, Amos W.	Pvt, H/24th Inf.	Distinguished gallantry in action	Naguilian, PI	7 Dec 1899
THORNTON, William	Cpl, G/24th Inf.	Distinguished service in battle	Santiago, Cuba	1 Jul 1898
TURNER, Clemon	Pvt, K/24th Inf.	Rescue drowning soldier	Camp McGrath, PI	2 Nov 1914
WALKER, John	Cpl, D/10 Cav.	Distinguished service in battle	Santiago, Cuba	1 Jul 1898
WHEELER, James	Pvt, G/10th Cav.	Defend military payroll	Cedar Springs, AZ	11 May 1889
WHITE, Joseph	Mus, B/24th Inf.	Rescue drowning comrade	Rio Grande de Pampanga, PI	8 Nov 1900
WILLIAMS, John T.	Sgt, G/24th Inf.	Distinguished service in battle	Santiago, Cuba	1 Jul 1898
WILLIAMS, Richard	Cpl, B/24th Inf.	Distinguished service in battle	Santiago, Cuba	1 Jul 1898
WILLIAMS, Squire	Pvt, K/24th Inf.	Defend military payroll	Cedar Springs, AZ	11 May 1889
YOUNG, James	Pvt, K/24th Inf.	Defend military payroll	Cedar Springs, AZ	11 May 1889

Index

This index combines biographical entries in the original *On the Trail of the Buffalo Soldier* (1995) and in this *Supplement.*

- References are to buffalo soldiers' names rather than to page numbers.
- References to soldiers' names in the original *On the Trail* (1995) are in **BOLD CAPITALS**.
- Soldiers' names in PLAIN CAPITALS refer to biographical entries in the *Supplement.*

Indexed terms include Indian tribes and other proper names such as officers, wives, organizations, schools, and ships as well as all people for whom there are no biographical entries in either volume. Officers are indexed by full name when they are recorded in Francis B. Hietman, *Historical Register and Dictionary of the United States Army, from its organization, September 29, 1789, to March 2, 1903* (Washington, DC: Government Printing Office, 1903).

To verify place names, the following authorities were consulted:

- *Webster's New Geographical Dictionary* (Springfield, MA: Merriam-Webster, 1988).
- "North American Fortifications, A Catalogue and Gazetteer of Forts and Fortresses, Frontier Posts and Camps, Blockhouses and Seacoast Batteries in the United States and Canada," http://www.geocities.com/naforts/forts.html
- U.S. place names: U.S. Geological Survey, Geographic Names Information System (GNIS), http://geonames.usgs.gov/
- Foreign place names: National Imagery and Mapping Agency Web Site, http://www.nima.mil/gns/html/

Cities and towns, counties, forts, and geographic features such as creeks are listed under names of current states. Place names not listed first by state include Indian agencies and reservations, some geographic features that cross state lines, and cemeteries. The latter are found at "Cemeteries," which is subdivided by state. Because locations of some place names, such as temporary camps, could not be verified, they are not listed in the index.

Adair, Dr.
  McKAY, Barney
Adair, Henry R.
  BLOODGOOD (Sergeant; 10th Cav)
Adams, Mamie Nellie
  BROWN, Arthur M.
Adams, Mary
  TERRY, Charles Lincoln
Addison, John T.
  JOHNSON, Joseph S.
Africa. *See also names of*
  individual countries
    GLADDEN, Washington W. E.
    QUEEN, Howard D.
The African Abroad
  COSTON, W. Hilary
African Methodist Episcopal
  Church. *See also names of*
  individual churches
    ALLENSWORTH, Allen
    ANDERSON, William T.
    BLEW, Joseph
    CHENAULT, Walter
    CLEMENS, Benjamin
    COSTON, W. Hilary
    GOINS, Joshua Van Buren
    GREGG, John A.
    HANKINS, W. A.
    HARTWELL, Benjamin
    JAMESON, Henry W.
    PLUMMER, Henry Vinton
    PRIOLEAU, George W.
    RICKS, William Nauns
    SADDLER, Louis
    SCOTT, Oscar J. W.
    SMITH, Arthur R. D.
    STEWARD, Theophilus G
    WIGGINS, S. T.
    WILLIAMS, Noah W.
    WILSON, Arthur
Afro-American Council
  BATIE, Henry
Afro-American Emigration
  Society
    WALLER, John L.
Afro-American Press, Worcester,
  MA
    JACKSON, William Hubert
Aguinaldo, Tomas
  CAMPBELL, Thomas C.
Aguirre, Marcebia
  AGUIRRE, Martiriano
Alabama
  ALEXANDER, James H.
  Anniston
    CAMPLE, Sandy
    DOCKEY, Stanton
    FLEMING, Faust
    SMITH, Jacob C.
    WILLIAMS, Gus J.

Barbour County
  WHITEHURST, James
Bessemer
  BROWN, Arthur M.
  NORMAN, Almer
Bibb County
  MILLER, Alexander
Birmingham
  BROWN, Arthur M.
  BUTLER, Garland
  CARTER, Thomas
  DAVIS, Horace G.
  DIAL, Samuel
  HALL, Arthur
  MURRAY, George
  WILLIAMS, Arthur
BRADDEN, Alfred
BRUNER, Joseph
CAMPBELL, John W.
Camp Forse
  BOYLE, Frank
  BRANCH, James
  BROOKS, John R.
  BROWN, William
  BUNN, William N.
  CALLOWAY, H. T.
  DICKERSON, Frank K.
  DRANE, Lucilius
  EATON, James
  FORD, James W.
  GAINES, Henry P.
  GARRETT, Daniel
  HARRIS, Mack
  HENRY, Edward
  HENRY, Frank
  LEWIS, John E.
  MURPHY, Marion W.
  NORRIS, James
  RATCLIFFE, George R.
  ROBINSON, Forrest
  SCHWATZ, Charles
  SHROPSHIRE, Shelvin
  WALLACE, John
  WESTFALL, John E. N.
  WHEELER, Arthur G.
  WHITE, John
  WILLIAMS, James Clifford
Camp Shipp
  BAKER, W. A.
CHATMON, Anderson
Colbert County
  ARRINGTON, John H.
  COLTON, WILLIE
Courtland
  MALONE, John
CRAWFORD, Lexis
Cusseta
  ASKEW, Blunt
Dadeville
  CHAMBLISS, Arthur
Etowah County
  SMITH, Luscious

Eufaula
  BROWN, Samuel
  GAMBLE, John
Fort Payne
  BEASON, Roy
Gainesville
  TURNER, Clemon
  WASHINGTON, James
Gaston
  MYRICKS, John
  HAYNES, Oscar
  HEAGOOD, George
Huntsville
  BOOKER, James F.
  CONLEY, Paschall
  HOLT, Lindsey P.
  JONES, Alex
  JONES, Archie
  LANGFORD, Hayes
  LOWRY, Richard T.
  McCALLEY, Charles
  POPE, Thomas
  REED, George
  THORNTON, Beverly F.
  TONEY, Hart
  WILLIAMS, James Clifford
  WILSON, George
Iron City
  JOHNSON, Robert J.
Jacksonville
  WILLIAMS, Gus J.
  JAMES, Morris
  JENKINS, Adam
  JOHNSON, George S.
  KANE, Simon
  LANE, Pope
Larkinsville
  PARKER, Henry
Lee County
  MOORE, Henry
  LUCKY, Frank
  McCALLIP, Pleasants
Madison
  TAYLOR, Alex
Madison County
  DRAKE, Ellie
  JAMAR, Hessiekiah
  MARTIN, Adkins
Maysville
  WHITE, William
Mobile
  BATTISE, Joseph
  BIZZELLE, John
  BROOM, Swain P.
  CARTER, Joe
  CHATMOUN, Littleton
  CLAY, Henry
  CLEMMAN, Edward
  DAYES, Joseph
  DRAPER, Thomas M.
  FRANKLIN, George
  GILLIARD, William

PLAIN CAPS indicate names from this volume • **BOLD CAPS** indicate names from *On the Trail* (1995)

GOODMAN, **Paul**
HOBBS, Louis
LUCKY, Joseph D.
MINOR, Dennis
SHERRELL, Moses
THOMPSON, Joseph
THOMPSON, Merrick
THORTON, Moses
WILLIAMS, Richard
Pineville
   MONTGOMERY, Henry
Randolph
   SMELLY, Dock
SCOTT, Praley
Scottsboro
   PARKER, Henry
Selma
   GOLDSBY, George
   HARPER, James
   HURT, Burnett J.
   RICHARDSON, Will H.
Sheffield
   SADDLER, Middeton W.
SHROPSHIRE, Shelvin
Talladega
   MILLIMAN, Jerry
   STONE, George
TAYLOR, Jordon
THOMAS, John
THOMPSON, Joseph
Tuscaloosa
   CUNNINGHAM, Eugene
   WILLINGHAM, Ephraine
Tuscumbia
   MALONE, John
   SMITH, James
Tuskegee
   BROOKS, William P.
   BROWN, Arthur M.
   JOHNSTON, Brooks
WASHINGTON, George
WASHINGTON, William H.
WILLIAMS, Elbert
Alabama State Penitentiary,
  Wetumpka
   THOMPSON, Albert
Alaska
  Ft Wrangel
   BARNETT, Peter W.
  Haines Mission Post
   ROBINSON, Henry
  Skagway
   BATIE, Henry
   BORDINGHAMMER, Edward D.
   CASSELLE, Nelson A.
   COLLINS, Edward J.
   GREEN, Benjamin
   O'CONNOR (Sergeant)
   WILLIAMS, Edward
   WILLIAMS, George H.
   TURNER, John M.

Alexander, John Hanks
   LEWIS, Frank
Alexander, W. W.
   SCOTT, Winfield
Allen, Frederick D.
   ANDERSON, William T.
Allen, Leona M. Howard
   ALLEN, David M.
Allensworth, Eva
   ALLENSWORTH, Allen
Allensworth, Josephine Leavell
   ALLENSWORTH, Allen
Allensworth, Nella
   ALLENSWORTH, Allen
Allensworth, William
   ALLENSWORTH, Allen
Allsup, Bertha Louise
   ALLSUP, Thomas H.
Allsup, George A.
   ALLSUP, Thomas H.
Allsup, James A.
   ALLSUP, Thomas H.
Allsup, Margaret
   ALLSUP, Thomas H.
Allsup, Sadie H. Johnson
   ALLSUP, Thomas H.
   MILLER, Cooper
Allsup, Thomas, Jr.
   ALLSUP, Thomas H.
Alvord, Henry Elijah
   FLETCHER, Isaiah
A.M.E. Church, *see* African
  Methodist Episcopal Church
American Baptist Association
   ALLENSWORTH, Allen
American Baptist Publication
  Society
   ALLENSWORTH, Allen
American Legion
   ANDERSON, William T.
   WANTON, George H.
American Pilot, Bloomington, IN
Amick, Myron J.
   BAILEY, Willis
Anderson, Carter
   ANDERSON, Henry
Anderson, Cay
   ANDERSON, John B.
Anderson, Clifton C.
   ANDERSON, John B.
Anderson, Ellen
   BATTLE, William P.
Anderson, Lillie
   ANDERSON, Henry
Anderson, Lizzie
   CAMPBELL, Thomas C.
Anderson, Lotta
   ANDERSON, Henry

Anderson, Minicha
   ANDERSON, Henry
Anderson, Minnie
   ANDERSON, Henry
Anderson, Richard
   ANDERSON, Henry
Anderson, Sada J.
   ANDERSON, William T.
Anderson, Wister Homer
   ANDERSON, Henry
Annin, W. E.
   ALEXANDER, John Hanks
Apaches. *See also* Lipan
  Apaches; Mescalero Apaches;
  names of Apaches: Costillito
  (Lipan Apache Chief);
  Geronimo; Kid (Apache);
  Mangus (Apache leader); Nana
  (Apache leader); Victorio
  (Apache leader)
   ADAMS, John Q.
   ARMSTEAD (Private)
   ARMSTRONG, Walter
   BADIE, David
   BAILEY, Isaac
   BLUNT, Randall
   BOYER (Blacksmith)
   BOYNE, Thomas
   BROWN, J. F.
   BROWN, Washington
   BROWN, William H.
   CAMMEL, Joseph
   CASEY, John F.
   CHAPMAN, Silas
   CHATMOUN, Webb
   COLE, Pollard
   CRAVEN, Luther
   DENNY, John
   DILLARD, James H.
   DRAKE, Alonzo
   EPPS, Richard
   FOSTER, George
   GAINES, Norman E.
   GIBSON, James
   GRADDON, Silas
   GRAY, Charles
   GREAVES, Clinton
   GREEN, Charles A
   HANCE, George W.
   HARPER, Henry
   HARRISON, John
   HAWKINS, William
   HOKE, Lafayette E.
   HOLLINS, William A.
   INGOMAN, Madison
   JACKSON, Isaac
   JAMESON, Henry W.
   JOHNSON, John
   JOHNSON, Monroe
   JONES, Henry C.

JONES, Silas
JONES, William
JORDAN, George
KELLY, William H.
LOVELACE, Scott
LYMAN, George
MACKADOO, Richard
McKIBBIN, Care
MILLER, Colonel E.
MILLER, Richard
MILLER, William
MURPHY, William
OSBORN, Stanley
OVERSTREET, Monroe
PERCIVAL, Abram
ROGERS, John
ROUSEY, Joseph
SCOTT, Edward
SCOTT, Frank
SHAW, Thomas
SMITH, Robert
STANTON, Daniel
STONE, Minor
SWAN, Edward
TERRY, Charles Lincoln
TIPTON, Calvin
TROUT, Henry
TURNER, Simon
TURNER, William
WALLEY, Augustus
WEST, Harrison
WHITE, Lewis
WILKS, Jacob W.
WILLIAMS, Moses
WILLIS, Alexander
WILSON, Roy
WILSON, Royal
WOODLAND, William
WOODS, Brent
WOODWARD, Major
Arapahoes
TURNER, Tom
Arce, Ruperto A.
BROWN, Charles S.
Archer, Barteen
ARCHER, Sylvester
Archer, Gertrude
ARCHER, Sylvester
Archer, Henrietta
ARCHER, Sylvester
Archer, Ida Jackson
ARCHER, Sylvester
Archer, Martha
ARCHER, Sylvester
Archer, Zephyr
ARCHER, Sylvester
Arizona. *See also* **Cemeteries;**
San Carlos Reservation
Apache County
ALLSUP, Thomas H.

Apache Junction
THOMPSON, George S.
Arivaca
WILLIAMS, Alexander
Atasco Cañon
ALEXANDER, Samuel H.
Bonita Cañon
ANDERSON, William
ARMSTRONG, Walter
AUSTIN, Frank
BANKS, Robert
BATTLE, William P.
BENNET, John
BISMUKES, Samuel
BLACK, Top
BLUNT, Randall
BOLAND, John
BOLLER, Solomon
BRADDOCK, Thomas
BRADLEY, Levi
BROWN, Daniel
BROWN, Frank B.
BROWN, James
BRUFF, Thomas
BUCHANAN, Charles
BUTLER, Henry
BUTLER, William
CAMMEL, Joseph
CARTER, Lewis
CASEY, John F.
CEPHAS, Joseph E.
CHATMOUN, Webb
CHEATHAM, Alexander
CHESTNUTT, Henry
CLAGGETT, Joseph
CLAYBORNE, Peter
COLE, Pollard
COLEMAN, Archie
COTTMAN, Thomas
DAMMOND, John W.
DAVIS, John
DAVIS, Nelson E.
DAWSON, William
DAY, Louis
DeGROAT, Curtis
DEHONEY, Peter
DILLARD, James H.
DIXON, Joseph
DOMSON, James
DOUGLASS, Primas
DREW, Albert
EMERY, Andrew J.
FACCETT, William
FAULKNER, Charles S. C.
FIELDS, John
FINNEGAN, Michael
FLETCHER, James Robert
FRANKLIN, Isaac
FRINK, George
GAINES, George W.
GIBSON, Henry

GIBSON, James
GIBSON, Murry
GILLET, John W.
GRAFTON, William
GRAY, Charles (Private; D/24th Inf)
GRAY, Charles (Sergeant; A/9th Cav)
GREEN, Charles A.
GRIFFIN, Charles
GUYSON, Edward
HALL, Allen
HALL, Frank W.
HARRIS, George
HARRIS, George G.
HARRIS, Hyder
HARRIS, Lewis
HARRIS, Sherman
HARRISON, William H.
HAWKINS, William
HIBBITT, John
HOLT, Richard
HORTON, George
HUGHES, David
HUMPHRIES, Samuel
HUTCHENS, George H.
ISAM, Frank J.
JACKSON, Isaac
JAMES, Richard
JOHNSON, Alfred
JOHNSON, Mack
JOHNSON, Richard
JOHNSON, William
JOHNSON, William H.
JONES, Clayton
JONES, David
JONES, Henry C.
JONES, Silas
KEENE, Howard
KENDRICK, Lindsay
KEY, Charles
KIMBER, John
LEE, Charles
LEWIS, John
LEWIS, Minor
LLOYD, Jerry
LOGAN, James
LOVE, Charles H.
LUMKINS, Ananias
LYNCH, William
McCLATCHIE, Henry
McDANIELS, Nathaniel
McKIBBIN, Care
MADISON, John
MASSEY, James
MATHEWS, Jessie
MEILLBROWN, Robert
MILLER, Colonel E.
MILLER, Girard
MILLER, John W.
MOCFIELD, Doc
NEWMAN, George H.

PLAIN CAPS indicate names from this volume • **BOLD CAPS** indicate names from *On the Trail* (1995)

NEWMAN, Henry
NEWSOM, James H.
NOBLE, John
OUTLEND, Jerry R.
OWENS, Charles H.
PARKER, George
PICKENS, Edward
PIPKINS, Charles H.
PLEASANT, Hardaway
PLEASANTS, Thomas
PORTER, Samuel H.
POTTS, Benjamin F.
PRESTON, Lloyd
PROCTOR, William
REDMAN, William
REED, Charles
REED, George
RICHARDS, Solomen
ROBERTS, Philip
ROBINSON, John
ROUSEY, Joseph
SMALLWOOD, Lee
SMITH, John
SMITH, Lewis M.
SORRELL, Frank
SPARKS, Augustus
SPEAR, James
STEWARD, Edward
STRICKMAN, Ernest
TAYLOR, John T.
TERRY, Charles Lincoln
THOMAS, Charles
THOMAS, Lewis
THOMAS, Sharp
THOMAS, Theodore
THOMPSON, Morris
TURNER, Charles B.
VARNON, William
VOLCOME, Eugene
WALLACE, Benjamin F.
WALLS, Buck
WATKINS, Jacob
WATTS, David A.
WEST, John H.
WEST, Sampson
WILLIAMS, George
WILLIAMS, Harry
WILLIAMS, James
WILLIAMS, Thomas
WILLIAMS, William H.
WILLS, William B.
WILSON, Felix
WILSON, Frederick
WILSON, George W.
WISE, James
WRIGHT, Clark
Bowie Station
   BATTLE, William P.
   BLUNT, Randall
   BRANSFORD, Wesley
   CAMMEL, Joseph

HAWKINS, William
Cedar Springs
   ARRINGTON, George
   BROWN, Benjamin
   BROWN, David
   BURGE, Benjamin
   FOX, Oscar
   HAMS, Thornton
   HARRISON, Julius
   LEWIS, Hamilton
   MAYS, Isaiah
   SHORT, George
   WHEELER, James
   WILLIAMS, Squire
   YOUNG, James
Clifton
   FITZGERALD (Private; K/10th Cav)
   MAYS, Isaiah
   YOUNG, Curley
Crittenden
   WATKINS, Jacob
Douglas
   CARTER, Louis A.
   NORMAN, Willie
   SMITH, Hezekiah K.
Florence
   BIRD, Matthew
Ft Apache
   ADAMS, Joseph
   ADAMS, Nimrod
   ADAMS, William
   ALBERT, Stewart
   ALEXANDER (Private; A/10th Cav)
   ALEXANDER (Private; B/10th Cav)
   ALEXANDER, James H.
   ALEXANDER, Wesley
   ALLEN, William H.
   ALLSUP, Thomas H.
   ANCRUM, William
   ANDERSON, Benjamin A.
   ANDERSON, John
   ANDERSON, Robert
   ANDERSON, Walker
   ANDERSON, William
   ANDREWS (Private)
   ARMFIELD, John
   ATKINSON, Russell
   AUSTIN (Private)
   BAGBY (Private)
   BAILEY, Isaac
   BAKER, Charles W.
   BAKER, Edward L., Jr.
   BANKS (Private; B/10th Cav)
   BANKS (Private; E/10th Cav)
   BANKS, Robert
   BANKS, Robert B.
   BARNES, William
   BARR, Edward

BATSON (Private)
BATTLE, Arthur
BATTLE, William P.
BECKETT, William C.
BELL (Private; A/10th Cav)
BELL (Private; B/10th Cav)
BELL, William
BENNETT (Private; E/10th Cav)
BENSON, Caleb
BERRY, George
BEST (Private; E/10th Cav)
BIRD (Private; A/10th Cav)
BIRD (Private; K/10th Cav)
BIVINS, Horace W.
BLACKWELL (Private; B/10th Cav)
BLOOM (Private; A/10th Cav)
BLUNT, Randall
BOLAND (Private; A/10th Cav)
BOLDEN (Private; E/10th Cav)
BOLLER, Solomon
BOWMAN (Private; B/20th Cav)
BOYD (Private; A/10th Cav)
BRADLEY, Levi
BRICE, Walter H.
BRIGS, Tazwell
BRISCOE, Edward
BROOKS, William C.
BROWN (Private; A/10th Cav)
BROWN, James
BROWN, Washington
BROWN, William
BUCK, John
BUCKNER, Benjamin
BUNDY, Arthur S.
BURNS, Calvin C.
BUSH (Private; C/10th Cav)
BUTCHER, Joseph
CAMMEL, Joseph
CANTY, Henry
CARRICO (Private)
CARTER, Robert
CASEY, John F.
CASTER, John W.
CEE, William
CEPHAS, Joseph E.
CHATMOUN, Webb
CHEATHAM, Alexander
CHESTER (Private)
CLAGGETT, Joseph
CLAYBORNE, Peter
CLEMENS, James
COLE, Pollard
COLEMAN (Private; C/10th Cav)
COLLINS, Thomas
COMBS, Richard
COOK (Private)
CORDIN, C. W.
CROUCH (Private; D/10th Cav)

DALRYMPLE, John
DAVIS, David L.
DAY, Louis
DeGROAT, Curtis
DEHONEY, Peter
DICKERSON, Jefferson
DILLARD, James H.
DISBERRY (Private)
DOLBY (Private)
DOLBY, Eli R.
EATON (Private)
EDMUNDS (Private)
ELLISTON, Amos
EMERY, Andrew J.
ENNIS (Private)
EWELL, William C.
FACIT (Private)
FAULKNER, Charles S. C.
FIELDS, John W.
FINNEGAN, Michael
FISHER (Private)
FITZGERALD (Private)
FLETCHER, James Robert
FORD (Private; D/10th Cav)
FORD (Private; G/10th Cav)
FORD, James A.
FORD, John W.
FORD, S. S.
FORREST, Samuel H.
FOSTER (Private)
FOSTER, George
FOSTER, Saint
FRANKLIN, William
FRANKLIN, William H.
FRY, Frank
FULLER, Jefferson
GAGE (Private)
GANAWAY (Private)
GARNETT, George R.
GARRETT (Private)
GIBBS (Private)
GIBSON, Murry
GILLISPIE, James R.
GIVENS, William H.
GLASS (Private)
GOLDSBURY (Chief Musician)
GORDON, Bryant
GRAHAM (Private)
GRANT (Private)
GRAVES, Johnson
GRAY, Charles (Private; D/24th Inf)
GRAY, Charles (Sergeant; A/9th Cav)
GREEN, John R.
GRIFFIN, Thomas
GUYWN, Edward
HADDOX, Press
HAGER (Private)
HALL (Private; A/10th Cav)
HALL, Frank W.

HALL, George C.
HARPER, Henry
HARRIS (Private; A/10th Cav)
HARRIS (Private; C/10th Cav)
HARRIS (Private; F/10th Cav)
HARRIS, Charles G.
HARRIS, Jeff
HARRIS, John
HARRIS, Mack
HARRISON, Richard
HARTWOOD, Andrew
HASKINS, David
HATCHER (Private)
HAWKINS, William
HIBBITT, John
HOLLOWAY (Private)
HOLMES (Private)
HOPKINS, Val
HOPPER, James
HORTON, George
ISAM, Frank J.
JACKSON (Private; A/10th Cav)
JACKSON (Private; B/10th Cav)
JACKSON (Private; D/10th Cav)
JACKSON, John H.
JAMES (Private; E/10th Cav)
JENIFER, Theopolous E.
JENKINS (Private)
JENKINS, Blunt
JENKINS, Joseph
JOHNSON (Private)
JOHNSON, Israel
JOHNSON, John W.
JOHNSON, Smith
JOHNSON, Walker
JOHNSON, William H.
JONES, A.
JONES, A. J.
JONES, G.
JONES, Philip
JONES, Silas
KANE (Private)
KEARNEY, Robert
KELLIS, John
KENDRICK, Lindsay
KERR, Moses
LAMPKIN, William M.
LANE, Thomas
LARTER (Private)
LEE (Private)
LEE, Nathaniel
LEE, Richard
LEWIS (Private; B/10th Cav)
LILLY (Private)
LOVE, Charles H.
LYLES (Private)
McBRYAR, William
McCLAIN, Henry
McCORMACK, Henry
McDANIELS, Nathaniel
McDONALD, Robert

McFARLAND (Private)
McGRAW (Private)
MARSHALL (Private)
MATTHEWS, Courtney
MEADE (Private)
MEARS, George W.
MILLBROWN, Robert
MILLER (Private; B/10th Cav)
MILLER (Private; D/10th Cav)
MILLER, Colonel E.
MILLER, Girard
MILLER, Richard
MINAR, James L.
MOORE (Private; E/10th Cav)
MORRIS (Private)
MORROW, Alexander
MOTLEY, Solomon
MOULTRIE (Private)
MURRAY (Private)
MURRAY, Charles E.
MURRELL (Private)
NEELY (Private)
NELSON (Private)
NEWKIRK (Private)
NOAL, Robert J.
NOEL (Private)
OLE, Henry R.
PARKER, Amos A.
PARKER, Charles E.
PARNELL, Edward
PAYNTER (Private)
PENDERGRASS, John C.
PERRY, Charles
PETERS, Michael
PICKETT (Private)
PINKSTON (Private)
PITTER, Charles
PITTER, Richard
PLEASANT, Harry R.
POTTS, Benjamin F.
POTTS, Samuel
POWER (Private)
PRICE (Private)
PRINCE (Private)
PRIOR (Private)
PULPRESS, Walter T.
PUMPHREY, James H.
READ (Private)
REED (Private)
RICE (Private; B/10th Cav)
RICHARDS (Private)
ROBB (Private)
ROBERTS (Private)
ROBERTS, Less
ROBINSON (Private; A/10th Cav)
ROBINSON, Henry
RODGERS, A. N.
ROLLINS, Horace
ROPER, Neil

PLAIN CAPS indicate names from this volume • **BOLD CAPS** indicate names from *On the Trail* (1995)

ROSS, John
ROUSEY, Joseph
SALTER (Private)
SHAW, Perry
SIMMONS (Private)
SIMS, Sprague
SMALLS (Private)
SMITH (Private; C/10th Cav)
SMITH (Private; E/10th Cav)
SMITH, Albert
SMITH, G. R. S.
SMITH, Lewis M.
SMITH, Thomas
SPARKS, Augustus
SPEAR, James
SPENCER (Private)
SPURLOCK, Charles
STANLEY, William
STEWARD (Private)
STEWARD, Theophilus G.
STEWART, John
STITH (Private)
STOKES, Harry D.
STROUP, Henry
SWANN (Private)
SWEENEY (Private)
TATUM, King James
TERRY, Charles Lincoln
THACKER, William
THOMAS, Colvin C.
THOMAS, James H.
THOMAS, John
THOMAS, John W.
THOMAS, Joseph
THOMAS, Sharp
THOMPSON, George S.
THOMPSON, James
THOMPSON, William
THOMPSON, William W.
THRASHER, George
TRUMAN (Private)
TURNER (Private; H/10th Cav)
TURNER (Private; I/10th Cav)
TURNER, Charles B.
VANDERHOST (Private)
VIELE, Madison
VOORHEIS (Private)
WALKER (Private)
WARFIELD (Private)
WASHINGTON (Private; K/10th Cav)
WATKINS, Jacob
WATKINS, James M.
WETTENTON, William
WHEELER, James
WHITE (Private; E/10th Cav)
WHITE (Private; M/10th Cav)
WHITNEY, William S.
WIGGINS, John
WILLIAMS (Private)
WILLIAMS, George J.
WILLIAMS, Jessie

WILLIAMS, Roy
WILLIAMS, William
WILLIAMS, William H.
WILLIS, James H.
WILLMORE (Private)
WILSON, Frederick
WILSON, James E.
WINFIELD (Private)
WINFIELD, Augustus P.
WRIGHT, Clark
WRIGHT, John W.
YOUNG (Private)
Ft Bowie
  HALL, Frank W.
Ft Grant
  ADAMS, King
  ALLEN, William
  ALLEN, William H.
  ALLENSWORTH, Allen
  ARRINGTON, George
  BAILEY, A.
  BAKER, B.
  BAKER, Bird
  BATTLE, William P.
  BEASLEY, Cole
  BELL, William
  BERRY, Edward
  BIVINS, Horace W.
  BLUNT, Randall
  BOLLER, Solomon
  BOOKER, William H.
  BRANSFORD, Wesley
  BROWN, Frank B.
  BROWN, Oscar S.
  BROWN, William H.
  BUDERIS, W.
  BURGE, Benjamin
  CAMMEL, Joseph
  CAMPBELL, Robert
  CEPHAS, Joseph E.
  CLAY, William
  COLE, W.
  COX, James
  DAVIS, David L.
  DAVIS, John
  DEHONEY, Peter
  EARLES, Armstead
  ELLIS, James
  EWELL, Levi
  FOREMAN, William A.
  FRANKLIN, Simon P.
  GARDNER, William George
  GILLISPIE, James R.
  GIVENS, William H.
  GOENS, Henry
  GRANT, William
  GRAY, Charles
  HAMS, Thornton
  HARRIS, James H.
  HARRISON, Julius
  HASKINS, David
  HAWKINS, William

HENDERSON, Reuben W.
HENSON, William
HIBBITT, John
HILL, J. H.
HUMBLES, John C.
JENKINS, Joseph
JENNINGS, Irving
JOHNSON, Horace
JOHNSON, John H.
JOHNSON, William
JONES, Henry C.
KELLY, William H.
KNOX, Marion
LANGFORD, Edward
LEE, Arthur
LEWIS, Hamilton
LEWIS, John
LEWIS, John
LOGAN, James
MAYS, Isaiah
McBRYAR, William
McCLAIN, Henry
MILLER, William
MYERS, William H.
NEWMAN, William T.
PAYNE, Charles
PAYNE, Hayes B.
PEARCALL, W.
PITTER, Charles
PORTER, James
POWELL, G. D.
POWELL, George D.
PRIOLEAU, George W.
PROCTOR, Ernest
PULPRESS, Walter T.
REED, William C.
ROBINSON, David
ROBINSON, Houston
ROUNDS (Musician; H/24th Inf)
SHIPLEY, John
SMITH, Arthur
SMITH, Augustus
SMITH, Jacob C.
SWEAT, George
TAYLOR, John T.
TURNER, Charles B.
VARNES, L.
WALKER, Otis
WALLACE, Benjamin F.
WASHINGTON, George
WATKINS, Jacob
WEBB, Benjamin
WETTENTON, William
WHEELER, James
WHITE, Thomas
WHITNEY, William S.
WILLIAMS, Squire
WILLIAMS, W.
WILLIAMS, William
WRIGHT, John W.
YOUNG (Sergeant)

PLAIN CAPS indicate names from this volume • **BOLD CAPS** indicate names from *On the Trail* (1995)

YOUNG, Curley
YOUNG, James
YOUNG, Thomas
Ft Huachuca. *See also* Cemeteries
ALEXANDER, Fred
ALLEN, Loyd D.
BACKERS, William
BANKS, Frank
BEASLEY, David E.
BLANEY, William F.
BOGGS, Carter
BOOKER, William H.
BRENT (Private; A/24th Inf)
BRENT, William
BRIDGEWATER, Samuel
BROWN, Alfred
BROWN, Benjamin
BROWN, Thomas
BURNS, Carter
BUTLER, Charles
CAMPBELL, James
CAMPBELL, John B.
CARTER, Louis A.
CHEATHAM, Boyd
CHRISTOPHER, Andrew
COX, Thomas
CURD, R.
CYRUS (Articifer; A/24th Inf)
DAMUS, Manie
DAVIS, James
DAVIS, Martin
DODSON, John H.
DORSEY, William H.
ESTILL, Allen P.
EVANS, Robert
EWING, George W.
FOX, William
FREEMAN, Charles L.
FRIERSON, Eugene
GARDNER, Sandy
GILES (Sergeant)
GOODWIN, Theophilus
GRANT, John
GRANT, Thomas
GREEN, John R.
HAM, James
HAMBRIGHT (Private)
HAMMOND, Wade H.
HARDEE, James A.
HARRIS, Louis
HATCHER, Alex
HEMPHILL, Lank
HINES, Will
HODGE, William J.
HOLDEN, David
HOLSEN, Bailey
HUDSON, Gus
HUGHES, Sam
HUMPHREY, John A.
JACKSON, Thornton
JOHNSON, Charles
JOHNSON, W. S.

JOHNSON, William F.
JONES, Archie
JONES, Jeremiah
JONES, Maurice
JONES, Robert
KENNEDY, Samuel
LUCAS (Corporal)
McDOWELL, John
MARCHBANKS, Vance H.
MAYES, Hilliard
MOSELEY, William
MURPHY, Samuel
PAYNE, Godfrey J.
PAYNE, William
PHILLIPS, James
PRESTON, William
RANDOLPH, John
RANDOLPH, Ruford
ROBERTSON, Tom
RODGERS, William
RUGER, William
SANDS (Private)
SCOTT, Solomon
SEALS, Benjamin
SMITH (Private)
SMITH, George
SNODGRASS, Carlos
SPRIGGS, John H.
STAFF, William R.
STEED, Albert
TAYLOR, Robert
TAYLOR, William
TEAGLE, James
THOMAS, Henry
THOMPSON, William W.
TUCKER, Joseph H.
VARNES, L.
WARNZER, Alonzo
WASHINGTON, Ernest S.
WASHINGTON, Morgan G.
WHEDBEE, Samuel
WILLIAMS, Albert
WILLIAMS, James H.
WILLIAMS, Washington
Ft McDowell
BIVINS, Horace
BRIGHT, Spencer
CLIFFORD, Charles
FOSTER, Saint
JONES, A. J.
LEE, Joel
MOSLEY, Zechoriah
SHAW, Perry
Ft Thomas
ANTONIO, Joseph
ARRINGTON, George
BURGE, Benjamin
CALDWELL (Private)
CAMPBELL, Robert
FINNEGAN, Michael
FLETCHER, James Robert
GIVENS, William H.

HAMS, Thornton
HARRISON, Julius
JENNINGS, Irving
LEWIS, Hamilton
McBRYAR, William
McCLAIN, Henry
McDONALD, Robert
MAYS, Isaiah
MONTGOMERY, Morgan
SPEAR, James
WHEELER, James
WILLIAMS, Squire
YOUNG, James
Galeyville
EVANS, Robert
Globe
BRANSFORD, Wesley
Graham County
JOHNSON, W. S.
GREEN, John E.
GREEN, Nathan
LAWSON (Private)
Mesa
LIVINGSTON, James
Naco
BOYD, George
BRADFORD, Caesar
BROWN, Charles W.
CAIN, Allen
CLAY, C. C.
EVERHART, Harry
HENSON, George J.
JONES, Archie
LUMPKIN, J. H.
McALLISTER, Noah
McCARVER, P. N.
MILLER, J. W.
PATTERSON, Walter
SEMLER, James
SMART, G. H.
STITH, Nathan
WAKEFIELD, Daniel
WATSON, R. B.
WILSON, Howard
Nogales
CHAMBLISS, Arthur
HARRIS, Louis
HORNER, Reuben
JOHNSON, William D.
JORDAN, Thomas
KING, Leslie
PENNY, James T.
TAYLOR, John J. L.
Phoenix
BRANSFORD, Wesley
CAMPBELL, John B.
DICKSON, Ben
GRAY, Charles
MAYS, Isaiah
PROCTOR, Clarence L.
Pinery Creek
BLUNT, Randall

PLAIN CAPS indicate names from this volume • **BOLD CAPS** indicate names from *On the Trail* (1995)

CAMMEL, Joseph
WALLACE, Benjamin F.
Prescott
JONES, Nathan
RICHARDS, James A.
Rio Bonito
ARMSTRONG, Walter
BATTLE, William P.
BOLLER, Solomon
BRUFF, Thomas
CAMMEL, Joseph
CASEY, John F.
COLE, Pollard
DILLARD, James H.
FOSTER, George
GIBSON, James
GREEN, Charles A.
HAWKINS, William
JACKSON, Isaac
JONES, Silas
McKIBBIN, Care
MILLER, Colonel E.
NEWMAN, George W.
ROUSEY, Joseph
ROSS, Milton
Salt River
CHEATHAM, Alexander
McBRYAR, William
TAYLOR, Charles
TURNER, William
San Carlos
ABBOTT, James W.
ALLEN, William H.
ALLSUP, Thomas H.
BAILEY, Isaac
BARKLEY, William H.
BATIE, Henry
BATTLE, William P.
BORDINGHAMMER, Edward D.
BOUNCLER, Willis S.
BROWN, David
BROWN, Washington
BUFORD, James J.
BURGESS, Lewis
BURTON, John
BUTCHER, A. F.
CHATMOUN, Webb
CHEATHAM, Alexander
COVINGTON, James C.
CURTIS, Alexander
EARLES, Armstead
EDWARDS, James
EWING, Calvin
FAULKNER, George
FLEMING, William M.
FLEMMING, Will
FRANKLIN, William H.
GIBSON, Edward
GILBERT, I. W.
GILES, Henry
GIVENS, William H.
HARDEE, James A.

HENRY, Charley
HENSON, William
JACKSON, Isaac
JACKSON, John H.
JONES, Jack
JONES, Patrick J.
JONES, Philip
KYLE, D. A.
LARKINS, James
LOGAN, James
McCLAIN, Henry
MAXWELL, George
MILLER, Richard
MOULTON, Prince A.
MYERS, William H.
ODOM, R. M.
PATTERSON, T. H.
PORTER, R. A.
POWELL, George D.
RHODES, Dorsey
RICHARDSON, Henry
SCOTT, Richard
SQUIRES, Albert H.
STEWARD, George
SULLIVEN, George
TAYLOR, James
TERRY, Charles Lincoln
THOMAS, James
THOMPSON, W. M.
WILLIAMS, Harry
WILLIAMS, Henry
WILLIAMS, Thomas
WOODS, Robert Gordon
WRIGHT, Clark
San Carlos Reservation, *see* San
Carlos Reservation, AZ
Santa Cruz
Mowry Mine
CROPPER, Samuel
GILES, Isaiah P. H.
HADDOX, Press
HAYNE (Trumpeter)
Somerton
BROWN, George
SUTPHIN, William
Tanner Canyon
JOHNSON, Charles
Tombstone
BROWN, Alfred
BROWN, Benjamin
GRANT, Thomas
Tucson
BENTLEY, James B.
JONES, Archie
LEE, Harvey M.
SMITH, Sidney
Turkey Creek
DEHONEY, Peter
WARREN, William
Whipple Barracks
BRISCOE, Edward
DIXON, Joseph

JONES, Jeremiah
WHITMAN, Charles
YOUNG, Charles
Yuma
McDONALD (Private)
Arizona State Hospital Cemetery,
Phoenix, AZ, *see* Cemeteries,
Arizona
Arkansas
BLANTON, Joseph
BRUNER, Monday
BRUNER, Peter
Conway
BIRDSONG, Eugene
COOK, Joe
COON, Joe
DANIELS, Elijah
FACTOR, Dindie
FACTOR, Pompey
Ft Smith
BROOKS, George
BROWN, Alfred
GOLDSBY, George
HAYMAN, Perry A.
GOSS, Isaac
Helena
ALEXANDER, John Hanks
STARR, Stephen G.
THOMPSON, Samuel
WILSON, Morgan
Hot Springs
ANDERSON, William T.
BROWN, Washington
CARTER, John T.
DAVIS, David L.
EDWARDS, William D.
GIVENS, William H.
GREEN, Bailey
HALL, Frank W.
KIBBETTS, Robert
SCROGGINS, William H.
Julius
TURNER, Charley
KIBBETTS, Robert
Lafayette County
THARP, Lafayette
Little Rock
ANDERSON, Fred
DIXON, Jerry
DIXON, John
DRYE, Frank L.
JOHNSON, Henry
ROBINSON, David
SMITH, James
SMITH, William
THOMAS, Willis
WEST, Henry
WEST, James
WOODS, Robert Gordon
Newport
HUBBARD, Walter
PERRYMAN, Isaac

PLAIN CAPS indicate names from this volume • **BOLD CAPS** indicate names from *On the Trail* (1995)

PLAIN CAPS indicate names from this volume • **BOLD CAPS** indicate names from *On the Trail* (1995)

Battle, Ellen Anderson
  BATTLE, William P.
Battle, Joseph
  BATTLE, William P.
Battle, Mary Ellen
  BATTLE, William P.
Beck, Ellen
  GOLDSBY, George
  LYNCH, William
Beck, Nicholas
  HARRIS, Louis
Beck, William Henry
  FORD, Samuel
  FULSOME, Albert
  GIVENS, William H.
  MACK, Clayborn
  TURNER, Simon
  WATKINS, Albert
  YOUNG, George E.
  YOUNG, Jacob
Belarmino, Vito
  DuBOSE, Edmond
  SHORES, Garth
  VICTOR, William
Bell, James Montgomery
  NEAL, Burr
  NELSON, William R.
  WALLEY, Augustus
Benardo, Leandro
  GIBSON, James
  HAMMOND, George
Benham, Robert Bruce
  WRACKS, Charles
Benjamin, Clara
  BENJAMIN, Robert
Benjamin, Isaac Alfred Augustus
  BENJAMIN, Robert
Benjamin, Mary G. Young
  BENJAMIN, Robert
Benjamin, Syrene E.
  BENJAMIN, Robert
Bennett, Eugenia
  DRAPER, Frank
Benson, Percilla Smith
  BENSON, Caleb
Bentley, George, Jr.
  BENTLEY, George
Bernard, Reuben Frank
  JONES, Jeremiah
Berry, Julia
  JACKSON, Isaac
Berryman, Emma Christopher
  BERRYMAN, Henry
Bethel African Methodist Episcopal Church, Hagerstown, MD
  COSTON, W. Hilary
Bettens, Philip Augustus, Jr.
  WILSON, William O.
Beyer, Charles D.
  COLE (Private)

JONES, Alexander
LYMAN, George
MABRY, Isam
PAYNE, Thomas
PENN, Delemar
ROSS, Alfred
Bicycle Corps, 25th Infantry
  BRIDGES, Travis
  BROWN, William W.
  BUTTON, Francis
  COOK, John
  DINGMAN, Hiram L. B.
  FINDLEY, John
  FORMAN, Elwood A.
  GREEN, Dalbert P.
  HAYNES, William
  JOHNSON, Elias
  JOHNSON, Frank L.
  JOHNSON, Sam
  JONES, Eugene
  MARTIN, Abram
  PROCTOR, William
  REID, Samuel
  ROUT, Richard
  SANDERS, Mingo
  SCOTT, George
  WILLIAMS, John G.
  WILLIAMSON, Sam
  WILLIAMSON, William
  WILSON, John H.
Biddle, James
  DENNY, John
  DILLON, David R.
  HICKS, William B.
  STEWARD, Theophilus G.
  WARFIELD, Samuel A.
Bigelow, John, Jr.
  BAIMER, John
  BOARMAN, Lewis
  CROPPER, Samuel
  DILWOOD, Thomas J.
  DIXON, Charles
  FITZGERALD (Private; K/10th Cav)
  FORD, Steven
  GIVENS, William H.
  HAYNE (Trumpeter)
  HAZZARD (Private)
  LIGGINS, Edward C.
  McDONALD, Robert
  PRIDE, Alfred
  RAY, Albert
  REINHART, Robert
  SMITH, Archie
  SMITH, C. O.
  STRATTON, John H.
  WALKER, John
  WASHINGTON, George
  WATKINS, Jacob
  YOUNG, Curley
  YOUNG, Jacob
Bivins, Charles W.
  BIVINS, Horace

Bivins, Claudia
  BIVINS, Horace
Bizzelle, Addie
  BIZZELLE, John
Black, Emily Drake
  BLACK, Solomon
Black, Virginia
  BLACK, Solomon
Blackburn, Grace Ella
  BLACKBURN, Joseph A.
Blackburn, Lizzie A.
  BLACKBURN, Joseph A.
Black Kettle (Cheyenne chief)
  CLAYBORNE, Peter
The Black Soldier, by Mary Curtis
  FRIERSON, Eugene
Bletson, Herbert
  HARTWELL, Benjamin
Blew, Celia
  BLEW, Joseph
Blew, Dave
  BLEW, Joseph
Blew, Dora Hammet Green
  BLEW, Joseph
Blew, George
  BLEW, Joseph
Blew, Malinda
  BLEW, Joseph
Blew, Viola
  BLEW, Joseph
Bliss, Zenas Randall
  DIXIE, Joe
  FACTOR, Hardy
  WARD, John
  WOOD, John
Blodgett, L. M.
  ALLENSWORTH, Allen
Blodgett, Nella Allensworth
  ALLENSWORTH, Allen
Blunt, Dr.
  BLUNT, Randall
Blunt, Randall K.
  BLUNT, Randall
Blunt, Thema K.
  BLUNT, Randall
Boller, Henry
  BOLLER, Solomon
Booker, Venia
  BOOKER, James F.
Bosley, Frank H.
  ANDERSON, John H.
Boston & Albany Railroad
  LEMUS, Rienzi Brock
Boston & Maine Railroad
  LEMUS, Rienzi Brock
Boston *Chronicle*
  LEMUS, Rienzi Brock
Boston University
  JACKSON, William Hubert

PLAIN CAPS indicate names from this volume • **BOLD CAPS** indicate names from *On the Trail* (1995)

Bowen, Evelyn A. Fletcher
  FLETCHER, James Robert
Bowersock, Justin De Witt
  FORD, George W.
Bowlegs (Bowlik) (Seminole
  chief)
  BOWLEGS, Friday
  BOWLEGS, Zack
Bowlegs, Annia
  BOWLEGS, Friday
Bowlegs, Annie
  BOWLEGS, David
Bowlegs, Camilia
  BOWLEGS, David
Bowlegs, David
  BOWLEGS, David
Bowlegs, Davis
  BOWLEGS, David
Bowlegs, Hagar
  BOWLEGS, Cyrus
Bowlegs, Hannah
  BOWLEGS, Friday
Bowlegs, Leah
  BOWLEGS, David
Bowlegs, Mary
  BOWLEGS, Friday
Bowlegs, Nancy
  BOWLEGS, David
Bowlegs, Nanny
  BOWLEGS, David
Bowlegs, Noble
  BOWLEGS, David
Bowlegs, Pancho
  BOWLEGS, Friday
Bowlegs, Pompey
  BOWLEGS, David
Bowlegs, Priscilla
  BOWLEGS, David
Bowlegs, Sandy
  BOWLEGS, David
Bowlegs, William J.
  BOWLEGS, George
Bowman, W. S.
  BOWMAN, Ashton J.
Bows, Cecilia
  LYMAN, George
Boxing (sport)
  NASH, Robert N.
  WOOLEY, William
Boy Scouts
  JAMESON, Henry W.
Boycotts
  HAMMOND, Wade H.
  LOGAN, John A.
Boyd, Charles Trumbull
  BIGSTAFF, Peter
  JETER, John
Bradden, Laura
  BRADDEN, Alfred

Brady, Mary Ann
  CUNNINGHAM, Charles
Branch, Ada Livingston
  BRANCH, William
Branch, Ella Scott
  BRANCH, William
Branch, Julia Nelson
  BRANCH, William
Branch, Rebecca Bryan
  BRANCH, William
Bransford, Archie
  BRANSFORD, Wesley
Bransford, Margaret
  BRANSFORD, Wesley
Bransford, Martha
  BRANSFORD, Wesley
Brinsmead, William
  ANDERSON, Benjamin A.
Brisbin, James Sanks
  LEWIS, George
Briscoe, Alex
  BRISCOE, Henry
Briscoe, Callie
  BRISCOE, Henry
Briscoe, Ellen
  BRISCOE, Henry
Briscoe, George
  BRISCOE, Henry
Briscoe, Jane
  BRISCOE, Henry
Briscoe, Jennie
  BRISCOE, Thomas
Briscoe, Mary
  BRISCOE, Henry
Briscoe, N. B.
  FORD, George W.
Britain. *See also* England
  FINNEGAN, Michael
Britton, John
  HOWERTON, John C
Brock, Mamie L.
  LEMUS, Rienzi Brock
Brook, Beatriz Valdez
  VALDEZ, Julian
Brooke, John Rutter
  SUTER, George
Brooks, Anna Griffin
  BROOKS, Preston
Brooks, Catherine Beatrice Hall
  HALL, Frank W.
Brooks, Harriet
  BROOKS, Preston
Brooks, Mary Anna
  BROOKS, Preston
Brooks, Preston, Jr.
  BROOKS, Preston
Broom, Susan
  BROOM, Swain P.

Brotherhood of Dining Car
  Employees
  LEMUS, Rienzi Brock
Brown, Alice A.
  BROWN, William W.
Brown, Annie L.
  JONES, Jeremiah
Brown, Anthony
  HAWKINS, William
Brown, Arthur
  BROWN, Arthur M.
Brown, Catherine Rebecca Hill
  BROWN, Caesar B.
Brown, Elizabeth Holliday
  HOLLIDAY, Presley
Brown, Herald
  BROWN, Arthur M.
Brown, Jane M.
  BROWN, Arthur M.
Brown, Laura V.
  BROWN, John
Brown, Lillian
  BROWN, Caesar B.
Brown, Louise
  WALKER, Henry
Brown, Lydia
  CLAYTON, Andy
Brown, Mamie Lou Coleman
  BROWN, Arthur M.
Brown, Mamie Nellie Adams
  BROWN, Arthur M.
Brown, Marjorie
  BROWN, Arthur M.
Brown, Mollie
  FAULKNER, Charles S. C.
Brown, Sarah
  HAWKINS, William
Brown, Vertie
  HAWKINS, William
Brown, Walter
  BROWN, Arthur M.
Brown, Winfield Scott
  BROWN, Arthur M.
Bruce, Blanche K.
  DERBIGNY, Benjamin
Bruce, Henrietta
  FORD, George W.
Bruce, William B.
  HOWERTON, John C
Bruner, Adelia
  BRUNER, Peter
Bruner, Alvina
  BRUNER, Peter
Bruner, Didia
  BRUNER, James
Bruner, James
  BRUNER, James
Bruner, Jennie
  BRUNER, Zack

Bruner, Juno
  BRUNER, Zack
Bruner, Lucy
  BRUNER, James
Bruner, Matilda
  BRUNER, James
Bruner, Susie
  BRUNER, Zack
Bruner, William
  BRUNER, James
Bryan, Rebecca
  BRANCH, William
Bryan, William Jennings
  BLUNT, Hamilton H.
Bryant, Ira T.
  HAMMOND, Thomas C.
Buey, Emily
  BIVENS, George E.
Buford, James J.
  BUFORD, Parker
Buford, Parker
  BUFORD, James J.
Bullis, John Lapham
  FACTOR, Pompey
  HICKMAN, French
  JOHNSON, Daniel
  MILLER, William
  PAYNE, Isaac
  PERRYMAN, James
  WARD, John
Bunch, Clifford
  BUNCH, Richard
Bunch, Eliza
  BUNCH, Richard
Bunch, Herbert
  BUNCH, Richard
Bunch, John
  BUNCH, Richard
Bunch, Joseph
  BUNCH, Richard
Bunch, Margaret
  BUNCH, Richard
Bunch, Richard
  BUNCH, Richard
Bunch, Rose
  BUNCH, Richard
Bunch, Virginia
  BUNCH, Richard
Bundy, Leroy N.
  ANDERSON, William T.
Burdett, Sadie
  CUMMERS, William
Burdick, Jennie
  WILLIAMS, Jessie
Burnett, George Ritter
  BURTON, James
  MARTIN, David G.
  ROGERS, John
  WALLEY, Augustus

Burney, David G.
  McKNIGHT, A. H.
Burt, Andrew Sheridan
  BASKERVILLE, E. S.
  BROWN, Charles S.
  BROWN, Elmer
  BUTLER, Thomas C.
  COLEMAN, Frank
  DALES, John
  FULSOME, A.
  GREEN, Dalbert P.
  JOHNSON, C. W.
  JOHNSON, James
  SANDERS, Mingo
  STEWARD, Theophilus G.
  TRUMAN, John
Bush, Alice Curtis
  BUSH, James W.
Bush, Gertrude Henrietta Smith
  BUSH, William Henry
Bush, Mary Curtis
  BUSH, James W.
Butler, Alexander
  PROCTOR, John C.
Butler, Fannie
  JONES, Seth
Butler, Frank
  LONG, Robert
Butler, Martha
  PROCTOR, John C.
Butler-Slater Drug Co., Atlanta, GA
  CRUMBLY, Floyd H.
Butler University, Indianapolis, IN
  CHENAULT, Walter
Byers, Sarah Bell Richardson
  BYERS, George
Byrne, Edward
  CASTILLO, Pedro
Bythewood, Harriett E.
  FORD, George W.
Cain, Octavia Walker
  WALKER, Henry
Caldwell, Vernon Avondale
  BUTLER, Thomas C.
California. *See also* Cemeteries
  Alcatraz Island, *see below* Ft Alcatraz;
    U.S. Military Prison, Alcatraz
  Allensworth
    ALLENSWORTH, Allen
    BYRD, Anderson
    GRIMES, James
    HICKS, George
    OVERR, Oscar
  Angel Island, *see below* Post at Angel Island
  Bakersfield
    ALLENSWORTH, Allen
  Benicia Barracks

  BELL, William
  BETHEL, Elijah
  BIZZELLE, John
  BOOZE, Richard
  SMITH, Frank
Berkeley
  GOODLOE, Thomas
  COLE, Pollard
  DALRYMPLE, John
Ft Alcatraz
  TAYLOR, Thomas W.
Ft McDowell
  BAKER, Edward L., Jr
Ft Mason
  SCRUGGS, Gilbert
Los Angeles
  ALLENSWORTH, Allen
  ALLSUP, Thomas H.
  BATIE, Henry
  BOLLER, Solomon
  BRABHAM, Jeremiah
  BROWN, John
  BROWN, William W.
  CRAGG, Allen
  CRUMBLY, Floyd H.
  DENNY, Elbiron
  GILLUM, William
  LOVING, Walter H.
  MASON, George F.
  MURPHY, Israel B.
  PRIOLEAU, George W.
  REYNOLDS, William
  RICKS, William Nauns
  SNOTEN, Peter
  TAYLOR, Belford
  TAYLOR, John J. L.
  WHEATON, Horace F.
  WILLIAMS, George A.
  LOVELACE, Scott
  McDONALD, James M.
  McDOUGAL, John
Monterey, Presidio of. *See also* Cemeteries
  PRAYER, James J.
  ROBINSON, John
  SMITH, John H.
  WHITE, Andrew J.
Oakland
  ALLENSWORTH, Allen
  BIVINS, Horace W.
  BLEW, Joseph
  BRYANT, Ferdinand
  ELLIS, Arthur
  FIELDS, William
  FIRMES, Thomas A.
  HANCOCK, George W.
  JOHNSON, Robert T.
  RICHARD, Raymond
  RICKS, William Nauns
  WALL, Archy
  WILSON, Arthur

PLAIN CAPS indicate names from this volume • **BOLD CAPS** indicate names from *On the Trail* (1995)

Ord Barracks
  GOLDEN, John
  JACKSON, Jason J.
  JONES, Nathan
  KELLEY, George B.
  LITTLEJOHN, James C.
  LOGAN, James E.
  MOORE, Joseph
  PETTIE, Samuel
  SMALLWOOD (Sergeant)
Pacific Grove
  JACKSON, Jason J.
  KELLEY, George B.
  SMALLWOOD (Sergeant)
  SMITH, G. W.
Pasadena
  BUFORD, Parker
  REYNOLDS, William
  WILLIAMS, Walter B.
PORTER, Issac
Post at Angel Island
  BIRCH, William A.
  CARTER, Henry
  HARRIS, Louis
  JEFFERS, David B.
Presidio of San Francisco
  ALLENSWORTH, Allen
  BAKER, Hiram, Jr.
  BIVENS, George E.
  BIVINS, Horace
  BROOKS, Robert H.
  CLARK, Gordon
  CORDIN, C. W.
  CRUMBLY, Floyd H.
  FAGEN, David
  FEARINGTON, George W.
  GALLOWAY, Alonzo
  GRANT, John
  GREEN, William W.
  HALL, James
  HANSTON, Charles H.
  HAWKINS, Emmett
  JACKSON, Andrew
  JOHNSON, Edward
  JOHNSON, Henry
  JOHNSON, William H.
  KIRBY, Wesley
  LOCKETT, Walter
  MANN, Frank T.
  MYERS, Rath
  NORRIS, Thomas H.
  PAYNE, James
  ROBINSON, Henry
  ROSS, William
  SMITH, Eugene
  SMITH, Henry
  SMITH, John
  SPEAKS, Perry E.
  STARLING, Eli
  STEWARD, Theophilus G.
  TURNER, Samuel
  WALL, Archy

  WALLACE, Elias
  WEST, Sampson
  WILSON, Thomas P.
  YOUNG, Charles
  YOUNG, Lee
Sacramento
  CRAGG, Allen
San Bernardino
  ALLSUP, Thomas H.
San Diego
  BATIE, Henry
  GIBSON, William H.
  REAVES, Transum
  WILKS, Jacob W.
San Diego Barracks
  GARDNER, Sandy
  GARDNER, William
San Francisco. *See also above*
  Presidio of San Francisco; *see also*
  Cemeteries
    ANDERSON, William T.
    BALSER, Linsey
    BLACK, Schuyler C.
    BLUNT, Randall
    BROYLES, William
    DAGGETT, Samuel
    DUNDEE, James P.
    FRANKLIN, W. W.
    GOOCH, John H.
    HUBBARD, George
    JACKSON, Daniel
    JAMES, William H.
    JEFFERSON, John
    LEWIS, Joseph
    NEWLANDS, Goodson M.
    NICHOLSON, Edward
    ODEN, Oscar N.
    POLK, Edward
    PRICE, Charles
    PURNELL, William Whipple
    RICKS, William Nauns
    ROBINSON, Charles
    ROSE, Charles P.
    SHEPPARD, King W.
    TAYLOR, Maston
    TURNER, Simon
    TYNES, Edward
    WILLIAMS, Edward A.
    WILSON, Arthur
    WOOD, John
Santa Ana
  JOHNSON, John A.
Sawtelle
  SNOTEN, Peter
Stockton
  TURNER, Simon
Three Rivers
  BAKER, Hiram, Jr.
  BIVENS, George E.
  BROOKS, Robert H.
  FAGEN, David
  FOSTER, Leslie J.

  GALLOWAY, Alonzo
  GILLIARD, William
  HALL, James
  HAWKINS, Emmett
  HUBBARD, George
  JOHNSON, William H.
  MANN, Frank T.
  MYERS, Rath
  SMITH, Eugene
  SPEAKS, Perry E.
  WILSON, Thomas P.
Vallejo
  JETER, John
Yosemite National Park
  JONES, Nathan
California Colony and Home
  Promotion Association
  ALLENSWORTH, Allen
California Federation of Colored
  Women's Clubs
  WALL, Archy
California Packing Company
  RICKS, William Nauns
California State Republican
  Committee
  RICKS, William Nauns
Calvert, Edward
  BENSON, Caleb
Calvert, Robert Bernard
  TAYLOR, William
Camacho, Sabastiana
  VICTOR, William
Cambridge University
  TAYLOR, Thomas W.
Campbell, Frankie
  CAMPBELL, Robert
Campbell family
  BOLLER, Solomon
Canada
  Amherstburg (Ontario)
    BUSH, William Henry
  Manitoba
    McCAULEY, William
  MARTIN, James
  Montreal
    REDMOND, Francis
    SMITH, William H.
  Ontario
    COSTON, W. Hilary
    BUSH, William Henry
  Prince Edward Island
    HARVEY, Anthony
  SWAN, Edward
  Toronto
    ALLENSWORTH, Allen
    POPE, David F.
    WILKERSON, James
    WILKINS, Melvin
    WILLIAMS, William J.
Canido, Anastacia
  DANDRIDGE, George

Carig, Leon
  STANFORD, John G.
Caron, Henry
  JORDAN, Thomas
Carpenter, Louis Henry
  BARD, Benjamin
  RATCLIFF, Toney
  WALLER, Reuben
Carr, Eugene Asa
  WALLER, E.
  WALLER, Reuben
Carr, Lizzie
  WATKINS, William
Carroll, Henry
  BAKER, William
  DAYES, Joseph
Carter (Lieutenant)
  HENRY, Frank
  PORTER, William
  SMITH, Lewis M.
Carter, Alice
  WYLIE, Milton
Carter, Helen
  CARTER, Charles McD.
Carter, Ida M.
  BUTLER, Thomas C.
Carter, Lucinda Marshall
  CARTER, Henry
  WASHINGTON, George
Carter, Myrtle B.
  CRUMBLY, Floyd H.
Casey, Eliza Turner
  CASEY, John F.
Casey, Ellen
  CASEY, John F.
Casey, Emma Louise Thomas
  CASEY, John F.
Casey, Frank
  CASEY, John F.
Casey, Mary
  CASEY, John F.
Casey, Mary Narra
  CASEY, John F.
Casey, Pabla Nalla
  FAIR, Robert
Casselle's Poetical Works, see
  Consular of Light, or Casselle's
  Poetical Works
Castro, John
  MENDENHAL, William
Catron, Thomas B.
  DAVIS, Robert
  YEATMAN, William
Cavallo, John
  COON, Joe
Cemeteries
  Arizona
    Ajo Cemetery, Ajo
      GRAY, Charles

Arizona State Hospital Cemetery
  [Asylum Cemetery], Phoenix
  MAYS, Isaiah
Ft Huachuca cemetery
  BOWEN, Major
  CAMPBELL, John B.
  CARTER, Louis A.
  FRIERSON, Watts
  WEST, John P.
California
  Lincoln Cemetery (Los Angeles)
    BOLLER, Solomon
  Presidio of Monterey, Post Cemetery
    FRAZIER, Petrum R.
    JOHNSON, George S.
    POLK, Thomas
  San Francisco National Cemetery
    CANNTE, Fred
    CARTER, George
    CHASE, William H.
    CHATMAN, John
    CLARK, Edward
    CLAY, William
    COFFEE, Nathan
    CONTEE, William
    COOK, Ermine
    COOMBS, Isaac
    COOPER, Archie
    COUNTEE, Thomas W.
    CUNNINGHAM, Henry
    DANCE, William
    DAVIS, Edward
    DAVIS, Henry
    DAVIS, James A.
    DAVIS, Thomas J.
    DAVIS, Will
    DEAN, John
    DENIS, John H.
    DENT, Robert I.
    DIRKS, Harrison
    DOBLER, Fred
    DORSEY, William H.
    EVANS, John
    EVANS, Robert
    FEARINGTON, George W.
    FINLEY, Louis G.
    FOSTER, Perrent
    FRANKLIN, William M.
    FRANKS, Benjamin
    FRY, Frank
    FRY, Henry
    FULLER, Cornelius
    FURMAN, John
    GASKINS, John
    GOODLOE, Thomas
    GORDON, Edward
    GRASHEN, Rudolph
    HENRY, Charles
    HILL, Thomas
    HOBBS, John H.
    HOLLAND, Elijah
    HOLLAND, Robert C.

HORTON, Lewis
HOSKINS, Isaac M.
HOWELL, James
HUNTER, Isaac
HURLEY, Bartholomew A.
HYMES, Pompy
IRWIN, Samuel
JACKSON, Charles
JACKSON, Frank
JACKSON, Lawrence M.
JACKSON, Romeo
JACKSON, William
JACKSON, William C.
JAMES, Robert
JAMES, William H.
JEFFERSON, John D.
JINKINS, Joseph
JOHNSON, Dennis
JOHNSON, James G.
JOHNSON, John A.
JOHNSON, John J.
JOHNSON, Luke J.
JOHNSON, Richard
JOHNSON, Robert D.
JOHNSON, William (Private;
  G/49th Inf)
JOHNSON, William (Corporal;
  F/25th Inf)
JOHNSON, William D.
JOHNSON, William J.
JOHNSON, Willie
JONES, Edward (Private; F/24th
  Inf)
JONES, Edward (Private; D/24th
  Inf)
JONES, Ira
JONES, Leroy C.
KELLY, Vernon
KENDALL, Hampton
KILER, Samuel H., Jr.
KING, Jason C.
KITCHEN, George
KLINE, Louis
KNIGHT, Daniel
KURTZ, Arthur
LATIMER, Grant
LAWRENCE, Thomas A.
LEE, James
LEE, Joseph
LEE, Robert E.
LEVERETT, Hark
LEWIS, James J.
LEWIS, Richard D.
LOGAN, John A.
LYONS, Daniel
McDANIELS, Henry
McDOUGALE, John H.
McINTOSH, Robert
McKINEY, Claud W.
McMILLAN, Emmett
MARSHALL, Hoyle
MARTIN, William J.

PLAIN CAPS indicate names from this volume • **BOLD CAPS** indicate names from *On the Trail* (1995)

MASON, John H.
MIMS, John
MINGO, Arthur
MITCHELL, James
MITCHELL, Thomas C.
MOORE, William T.
MORRIS, Reuben B.
MOSBY, James A.
MOTLEY, George
MURRAY, Henry
MYERS, William H.
NELSON, Samuel A.
NICHOLS, Leroy
NICHOLSON, Edward
NOYED, James
OLIVER, William H.
OWENS, Richard
OWENS, William
PARNELL, Edward
PAYNE, Harry
PAYNE, James L.
PEARSON, Frank
PLEASANT, John
PORTER, Augustus
PORTER, John L.
POSEY, John
POWELL, Robert
PRICE, George
PROFFETT, Shannon
PRYOR, James
PUGH, Alvin
PURNELL, George
PURNELL, William Whipple
QUARLES, John
RANDALL, Wesley
RANDOLPH, William
REED, Charles
REESE, Cicero
RICE, Ernest
RICHARD, Raymond
RIDDLE, Alfred
RIDEOUT, Albert
RILE, Augustus M.
ROBERTSON, Robert
ROBINSON, Andrew
ROBINSON, Harry
ROBINSON, James
ROCHE, Michael F.
RODGERS, Henry R.
ROPER, Charles H.
RUSSELL, Charles A.
RUSSELL, Thomas
SALLY, John M.
SAMMONS, William H.
SANDERS, George S.
SCOTT, Nelson
SHELTON, Thomas D.
SHEPARDSON, George
SIMPSON, Wig
SMITH, James
SMITH, William
SPENCE, William

STAFFORD, James N.
STANSON, John J.
STEAD, Eugene
STEWARD, James
STEWART, Moses
STICKLES, Robert
STOREY, Charles J.
STRICKLAND, Joseph
SWANN, Thomas E.
TALLEY, John C.
TAYLOR, Frank
TAYLOR, Samuel
Thomas, Gus
THOMAS, Henry (Sergeant;
  A/24th Inf)
THOMAS, Henry (Musician;
  B/25th Inf)
THOMAS, James H.
THOMAS, John
THOMAS, Moses
THOMAS, Napoleon
THOMAS, William H.
THOMPKINS, William H.
THOMPSON, Garfield
THOMPSON, James
TIMMS, James T.
TOLBERT, Thomas
VALENTINE, John
WALKER, Samuel
WALL, Archy
WALLACE, Al
WARD, James
WARREN, Walter
WASHINGTON, George
WASHINGTON, James H.
WASHINGTON, Morgan G.
WATKINS, Leroy
WATSON, Isaac
WATSON, William S.
WEATHERS, Reuben
WEBB, Moses
WHALEY, Lewis
WHITESIDE, Alexander
WILBURN, Thomas G.
WILKS, Cleveland
WILLIAMS, Fletcher
WILLIAMS, Frank
WILLIAMS, Harry J.
WILLIAMS, John
WILLIAMS, Levi
WILLIAMS, Oliver
WILLIAMS, Preston
WILLIAMS, Robert E.
WILLIAMS, Sidney
WILLIAMS, Thomas (F/25th Inf)
WILLIAMS, Thomas (Private;
  H/48th Inf)
WILLIAMS, Walter
WILLIAMS, William (Private;
  E/25th Inf)
WILLIAMS, William (Private;
  G/25th Inf)

WILLIAMS, Wilson
WILLIAMSON, William
  (Private; E/25th Inf)
WILLINGHAM, William
  (G/25th Inf)
WILSON, Arthur
WINTERS, Alvin B.
YEARGOOD, Evert
YEIZER, Charles C.
Delaware
  Union Cemetery, Smyrna
    TERRY, Charles Lincoln
Illinois
  Camp Butler National Cemetery,
    Springfield
      FORD, George W.
      FORD, George W.
        (Superintendent)
  Lincoln Cemetery, Chicago
    LANIER, Frank
Kansas
  Ft Leavenworth National Cemetery
    CARTER, Henry
    CARTER, William H.
    CHELF, John
    CHESTNUT, Grundy
    CLARIDY, Henry
    CLARKE, John H.
    COLBERT, John A.
    COLEMAN, Jordan
    COMBS, H.
    CUSTARD, Elijah
    GAINES, Henry
    GAINES, Levin S.
    GAMBLE, John E.
    GAREY, Charles
    GILBERT, Charles
    GOHEINS, Samuel
    GROSS, Thomas
    GUINN, Floyd
    HALL, Thomas
    HAMMONS, Isaiah
    HANAON, James S.
    HARRIS, David
    HARRIS, Foster
    HATCHET, John R.
    HENRY, William
    HOBSON, John
    HUNTINGDON, Sylvester
    HUTCHINSON, Robert
    INGOMAN, Madison
    INGRAHAM, Roden
    JACKSON, James
    JACKSON, Thornton
    JENKINS, Daniel
    JENKINS, Filmen
    JOHNSON, Edward
    JOHNSON, John W.
    JOHNSON, Monroe
    JONES, Charles
    JORDAN, Albert E.
    KELSEY, Edward

PLAIN CAPS indicate names from this volume • **BOLD CAPS** indicate names from *On the Trail* (1995)

KEMP, Charlie
KINNEY, Isaac
LANE, Edward
McFERRIN, Jesse L.
McKEE, Henry
McMAHON, Andrew
MAJORS, Harry
MAXWELL, Albert E.
MILESTON, Fillmore
MILLER, Lounie
MORTON, Alexander
MOSBY, Thomas
MURRAY, John A.
NANCE, William H.
NEAL, Burr
NEIL, Jeff J.
NICHOLAS, William
NICHOLS, Richard
NOLAND, Howard
NUNN, Moses J.
OLIVER, Floyd
OWENS, James
PAGE, Edwin
PARKER, Henry
PAULEY, Charles J.
PICKENS, Peter
PORTER, Charles W.
PORTER, Clark C.
PRUETT, Hugh
REED, Samuel C.
RICHARDSON, Arthur
RICHARDSON, William
ROGERS, Nathan
ROLLINS, John
ROSS, Revo
ST. CLAIR, Jean
SANDERS, James C.
SCOTT, Beverly
SCOTT, Sterling
SCOTT, Thomas J.
SCOTT, Wesley
SIMPSON, William
SINGLETON, Charles
SLOAN, Miles
SMITH, Ewing
SMITH, John
SMITH, Joseph
SMITH, Thompson W.
STAFF, Edward
STANLEY, William
STOKES, Henry
TAPER, Charles
TAYLOR, Charles
TEUER, Jackson
TILLARY, Albert
TUCKER, J. A.
TULLEY, William
TURNBULL, Reese
TURNER, Wallace
TURPIN, Edward
VASS, Charley
WALKER, John

WALLACE, Harry
WALTERS, Joseph
WARREN, Daniel
WARREN, Samuel
WASHINGTON, George
WASHINGTON, James H.
WATKINS, Wesley
WATSON, Adam
WEBB, William K.
WESLEY, Augustus
WILLIAMS, David
WILLIAMS, John
WILLIAMS, William
WILLIAMS, William O.
WILLIS, Findley
WILLIS, John
WILSON, Amos
WILSON, Jacob B.
WOODARD, Major
WOODS, Eugene
WOODS, George F.
YOUNG, Joseph
Ft Scott National Cemetery
   FORD, George W. (supervisor)
Highland Cemetery, Geary County
   BENJAMIN, Robert
Kentucky
  Eastern Kentucky Asylum,
    Lexington
     ALLEN, William
  Zachary Taylor National Cemetery,
    Louisville
     BALLARD, Wilson C.
Louisiana
  Alexandria National Cemetery,
    Pineville
     JULY, John
     PAYNE, Robert
  Port Hudson National Cemetery,
    Zachary
     FORD, George W. (employee)
Maryland
  Baltimore National Cemetery
    BIVINS, Horace
    GARDNER, William George
    WASHINGTON, William
  Loudon Park National Cemetery,
    Baltimore City
    MOLOCK, Andrew M.
Minnesota
  Ft Snelling National Cemetery
    DEHONEY, Peter
Nebraska
  Ft Crook cemetery, Offutt Air Force
    Base, Omaha
     COMBS, Richard
  Ft McPherson National Cemetery,
    Maxwell
     BROOKS, Preston
  Ft Niobrara Post Cemetery
    DAVIS, William J.
    YOURS, Robert

  Prospect Hill, Omaha
    McCLARE, Allen
New Jersey
  Bayview-New York Bay Cemetery,
    Hudson County
     McDANIELS, Nathaniel
New Mexico
  Fairview Cemetery,
    Albuquerque
    JACKSON, Isaac
  Ft Bayard National Cemetery
    ALEXANDER, James H.
    BAILEY, Charles
    BAKER, Bird
    BALDWIN, Buster B.
    BALLENTINE, Cyrus
    BARDISON, George
    BARTLETT, Squires
    BETTIS, James
    BOYD, Hampton
    BOYD, Thomas W.
    BOYER, George W.
    BROWN, Creed
    BUNCH, Thomas
    BUNDY, Paul
    BUTLER, Hiram
    CANNON, Thomas
    CARROLL, Robert T.
    CARTER, Frank
    CAY, McKinley
    CHASE, Levi
    CHESTER, Stanley
    CLARK, Cornelius
    CLAY, Matthew G.
    CLEMENTS, Charles F.
    CROOM, Mills B.
    CROSS, J. C.
    CUNNINGHAM, George
    DAVIS, Richard
    DAWSON, John W.
    DERCHILD, Joseph
    DERRICK, Samuel
    DRAKE, Luther
    EADS, Norman
    EDWARDS, Charles
    EDWARDS, John
    ELLIS, Robert
    EVANS, Elijah
    FINNEY, Will
    FORMAN, Andrew
    FOSTER, Leon D.
    FOWLER, Arthur
    FOX, Lafayette
    FRAZIER, Lewis
    FRISBY, John T.
    GANT, John
    GASKINS, William E.
    GAY, McKinley
    GIVENS, John C.
    GRAN, George
    GRANT, Henry C.
    GRAY, Gilbert

PLAIN CAPS indicate names from this volume • **BOLD CAPS** indicate names from *On the Trail* (1995)

GRAY, Robert
GREAR, Charles O.
GREEN, George
GRICE, Perry
GRIFFIN, George
GROSS, James J.
HAMPTON, George W.
HARPER, Henry
HARRIS, John
HARRISON, Julius
HARRISON, Richard
HAWKINS, William H.
HENDRICKS, Louie
HENRY, Oscar D.
HOOD, John
HORSLER, Waddy
HORTON, Walter
HUDDLESTON, William
JOHNSON, Charles
JOHNSON, E.
JOHNSON, Freeman
JOHNSON, John
JOHNSON, Thomas
JONES, Edmund
JONES, William
JUNIOR, Joe
KELLY, Joseph, Jr.
LANKFORD, Henry
LAWRENCE, James O.
LEONARD, Thomas
LONG, Gid
LYONS, David
McCALLEY, Wiley
MACK, William
MAJOR, Alfred
MARTIN, John
MARTS, Harry
MASON, Charles
MASON, Henry
MATHIGLEY, Henry
MAYFIELD, Walter
MILES, James
MILLER, Sylvester
MOORE, Arthur L.
MOSES, Paul S.
MUNROE, Daniel
NEWLANDS, Goodson M.
NICHOLS, Richard
NORMAN, Charley
NORRIS, Jefferson
RAINS, Henry R.
REED, Charles
RHODES, Roy
ROBINSON, James
ROSS, Leon
ROSS, William H.
RUCK, Samuel E.
RUDDLE, John
RUSSEL, Solomon
SHAW, Perry
SIEGLER, Fred
STEARNS, George W.

STEWART, Frank
SWAN, Edward
TAYLOR, Henry C.
THOMAS, Charles
THOMPSON, Robert
TIPTON, Samuel
TOWNSEND, Quince
TUNNIA, Edward L.
UNDERWOOD, Clifford
UNDERWOOD, Elisha M.
VANLEER, Percy L.
WASHINGTON, John
WESTLEY, Lawrence
WHITE, Isaac
WILLIAMS, Jonas
WILLINGHAM, Ephraine
WILSON, George
WOODWARD, Major
WORRELL, William
WRIGHT, James
WRIGHT, Thomas
YOUNG, Douglas
Santa Fe National Cemetery
BAILY, Richard
BANKS, Robert
BEASLEY, Cole
BELL, William
BERRY, Edward
BRANCH, Haywood
BRAUN, Hanson T.
BROWN, John
CHAFFIN, John H.
CHANDLER, Richard
COX, James
CURTIS, John H.
DAVIS, John
DOUGLAS, Lewis
DOUGLAS, Will
DRATON, Charles
EARLES, Armstead
EDWARDS, James
EWELL, Levi
FORSTER, George W.
FREMAN, Andrew P.
GARCIA, Ignacio
GLASS, John T.
Glynn, George
GRANT, William
GRIM, James
Holland, Ernest
HOPKINS, Val
HUNTER, Robert
JAMES, Isaac H.
JARIMO, Juan
JOHNSON, Charles
JOHNSON, Henry
JOHNSON, Horace
JOHNSON, William (Private;
  C/9th Cav)
JOHNSON, William (Private;
  F/10th Cav)

JOHNSON, William (Private;
  M/9th Cav)
JONES, Douglas
KNOX, Marion
MILLER, George
MILLER, William
MOTIN, Harry
MYERS, John E.
NEWMAN, William T.
OGDEN, Harvey
OPPERMAN, Henry
PEARSON, Oliver
PENN, Will
PHILLIPS, Shardon
POLK, James K.
PORTER, James
POWELL, G. D.
POWERS, William A.
PROCTOR, Ernest
REED, William C.
ROSE, David
SAUNDERS, William H.
SIMMONS, William
SLAMP, Demer
SMITH, John
SMITH, Richard
SMITH, Robert
SOLOMON, Robert
STANTON, Daniel
STEELE, James T.
SWEAT, George
TAYLOR, Stephen
VADER, Louis E.
VAN DYKE, Richard
WADDELL, Fred
WASHINGTON, Frank
WASHINGTON, George
WASHINGTON, Richard
WEBB, Benjamin
WELLONS, Andrew
WILLIAMS, William
WILSON, Royal
New York
  Cypress Hills National Cemetery,
  Brooklyn
    BROKER, Powell H.
    DURANT, Will
    GOOCH, Philip
    NERO, Ambrose
    RANKIN, Frank
    ROPER, Neil
    WRIGHT, Nealy
  Forest Lawn Cemetery, Buffalo
    MILLER, Girard
North Carolina
  Plummer Cemetery, Warrenton
    HALL, Frank W.
Ohio
  Union Baptist Cemetery, Cincinnati
    WILLIAMS, Thomas
Oklahoma
  Citizen Cemetery, Ft Gibson

PLAIN CAPS indicate names from this volume • **BOLD CAPS** indicate names from *On the Trail* (1995)

LYNCH, William
Rosedale Cemetery
ANDERSON, Henry
Pennsylvania
Green Lawn Cemetery, Chester
WALLACE, Benjamin F.
Menon Cemetery, Philadelphia
CEPHAS, Joseph E.
South Carolina
Beaufort National Cemetery
FORD, George W. (employee)
South Dakota
Ft Meade National Cemetery,
Sturgis
COPELAND, Benjamine
DINNIWIDDLE, Daniel
GIBSON, James
GUIDINE, Olive
HALLON, Ross
HINES, Clinton
ROBERTS, John
SMITH, George
STANTON, R. W.
Tennessee
Chattanooga National Cemetery
FORD, George W.
(superintendent)
Nashville National Cemetery
HATCHER, Alex
Texas
Cemeterio Viejo Loma de la Cruz,
Del Rio
FRAUSTO, Gregario
FRAUSTO, Quirino
FRAUSTO, Thomas
FRAUSTO, Vector
Fairmont Cemetery, San Angelo
WILKS, Jacob W.
Ft Bliss National Cemetery
HULL, James
Ft Sam Houston National Cemetery
ADAMS, Walter
ANDREWS, Archie
BENNETT, Thomas
BRANCH, William
BROWN, Thomas
BUSTER, Jacob
COMBS, Henry
DORSEY, A. J.
DUDLEY, Joseph P.
FLANBEAU, Adam
GRIFFIN, Isaac
HAGGER, William
JACKSON, Harvey
KELLY, Joseph W.
KELLY, William H.
McNARY, Presley
PARKER, William
PRIEST, I. A.
SCRUGGINS, Marshal
SHEPPARD, Horace
SMITH, John

WILLIAMS, William H.
WRIGHT, W. H.
Indian Scout Cemetery (Kinney
County)
BOWLEGS, John
BOWLEGS, John H.
DANIELS, Caesar
DANIELS, Charles
DANIELS, Elijah
DANIELS, Jerry
DANIELS, John
DANIELS, Thomas
DIXIE, Joe
FACTOR, Dembo
FACTOR, Pompey
GERRY, William
GORDON, Sam
GRAYSON, Renty
GRINIER, Dallas
HALL, Morell
JEFFERSON, Charles W.
JEFFERSON, John
JEFFERSON, Sam
JULY, Benjamin
JULY, Billy
JULY, Carolina
JULY, Charles
JULY, Fay
JULY, Sampson
KIBBETTS, George
KIBBETTS, John
KIBBETTS, Robert
KIBBITS, "L" H.
McCLAIN, Adam
PAYNE, Aaron
PAYNE, Adam
PAYNE, David
PAYNE, Isaac
PERRYMAN, Ignacio
PERRYMAN, Isaac
PERRYMAN, James
PERRYMAN, Pompey
PHILIPS, John
PHILIPS, Joseph
REMO, John F.
SHIELDS, Archibald
SHIELDS, John
THOMPSON, John
THOMPSON, Joseph
THOMPSON, Prymus
WARD, John
WARRIOR, Bill
WASHINGTON, Sam
WHITE, Lewis
WILLIAMS, Bill
WILSON, Ben, Sr.
WILSON, Bill
WILSON, Krling
WILSON, Tony (born in
Arkansas)
WILSON, Tony (born in Mexico)
WORYER, Henry

San Antonio National Cemetery
ANDERSON, Sandy
ARMFIELD, John
ASHBERRY, William
AUSTIN, Charles
BACON, Martin
BAKER, Thomas
BALL, W. S.
BANCROFT, George
BANKS, Benjamin
BAPTISTE, Andrew J.
BARKER, Alexander
BARROW, Blaize
BAYNES, Joseph
BENEFIELD, Edward
BENT, John
BENTON, Mark
BERRYMAN, James
BETHEL, Charles
BIDLEY, Robert
BLACKWELL, Isaac
BLAIR, Henry
BOOKER, Andreson
BOYD, Daniel
BRADY, Isaac
BRANCH, James
BRITTEN, Reuben
BROWN, Champ
BROWN, George
BROWN, James S.
BROWN, John
BROWN, John L.
BROWN, Samuel B.
BUCHANAN, Andrew J.
BUNTON, Mark
BURNET, John
BURNETT, John
BUSH, Adam
BUTCHER, Henry
BUTLER, Edward
CALLOWAY, Charles
CAMPBELL, Henry (Corporal;
L/10th Cav)
CAMPBELL, Henry (Private;
A/10th Cav)
CAMPBELL, Isaac
CAMPBELL, Murphy
CARPENTER, Hess
CARROLL, George
CASE, Charles L.
CASS, Austin
CHESTNUT, Grundy
CHRISTOPHER, Albert
CLARK, Alexander
CLARK, Allen
CLAY, Samuel
COLEMAN, Mitchell
COLEMAN, Reuben
COOK, French
COSY, Levi
CROWDER, Daniel
CUMMINGS, Robert

PLAIN CAPS indicate names from this volume • **BOLD CAPS** indicate names from *On the Trail* (1995)

DALLAS, George M.
DANIELS, Jerremiah
DAVIS, Isom
DAVIS, Jacob P.
DAVIS, John
DAWSON, Joseph
DEMPSEY, Patrick
DONOHOE, John
DORSEY, Caleb
DOWTHA, Washington
DUOTTE, Edward
DYSON, John
EBSTEIN, Oscar
EDMORE, James
EDMUNDSON, George
EGLI, Edward
EMORY, Robert
EVERETT, Frank
FIELDS, Wallace
FORD, Albert
FORD, John
FOSTER, George
FOSTER, Henry
FRANK, Jacob
FREDERICKS, John
FREEMAN, Jerry R.
FRY, James
FRY, John
GADDESS, John
GADDIS, John
GALLAGHAN, W. E.
GARNER, James
GEE, Marion
GEORGE, William
GIBSON, Thomas
GLENN, Frank
GLOVER, William
GRAVES, John
GRAVES, John J.
GREEN, Ezekiel
GREEN, M. J.
HAINES, Andrew J.
HALL, Charles
HALL, Grooms
HALL, Joseph
HANLEY, Edward
HAPER (Sergeant)
HARPER, John W.
HARRIS, Albert
HARRIS, Anderson
HARRIS, George W.
HARRIS, Lafayette
HARRISON, Milford
HAWKINS, Jordon
HELM, Benjamin
HENRY, William
HENSON, Mahlon S.
HILL, Charles
HILL, Colony
HITE, Leonard P.
HONESTY, Gustavus
HOPKINS, Julius

HOWARD, James
HUGHES, John
HUNLEY, Edward
HUSTON, Charles
JACKSON, Abram
JACKSON, Anthony
JACKSON, Smith
JACOBS, George
JOHNSON, Alfred
JOHNSON, Carter
JOHNSON, David
JOHNSON, Dorsey
JOHNSON, Harry
JOHNSON, James
JOHNSON, James O.
JOHNSON, John W.
JOHNSON, Joseph
JOHNSON, Oliver
JOHNSON, Randall
JOHNSON, Sidney
JONES, Edward
JONES, William
JORDON, John
KARRICK, James
KINNEY, Sanford
LANCASTER, Henry
LANGSTON, John
LAWS, Alfred
LEAUMONT, Henry
LEEK, Allen
LETT, William
LISBY, John
LIVINGSTON, George W.
LOGAN, Robert D.
LOOKERS, William
LOOMIS, Richard
LUSK, Green
LUSK, James
McCOLUM, Virgil
McGINTY, Joseph
MADDOX, Thomas
MAHO, Thomas
MAPP, Solomon
MARSHALL, Albert
MARTIN, Daniel
MARTIN, John
MARTIN, Shadrach
MASON, Alexander
MASON, John H.
MASSIE, Adam
MEHAMITT, Jeremiah
MERRYWEATHER, A.
MEYERS, William
MITCHELL, J. S.
MOBLEY, David
MODE, Henry
MORGAN, John M.
MORGAN, Paul
MORTON, Henry
MURRAY, Charles
MURRAY, Enos
NANCE, David

NEFF, William
NELSON, John
NEW, Benjamin
OSBORNE, James
PARKER, Charles E.
PARKER, John
PATRICK, George
PINKARD, James
PITTS, Anthony
PLANT, James W.
PORTER, Sanford
POWELL, Toby
PRESTER, Daniel
PRICE, Moses
PRIESTLY, Joseph A.
RANKINS, Marcus
REEDE, Aleck
RICHARDSON, Jacob
RILEY, William
ROACH, Frank
ROBERTSON, Daniel
ROBINSON, Berry
ROBINSON, James
ROBINSON, John H.
ROWERSON, Prince
ROY, Johnson
SAUTER, Marcus
SCOTT, Frank
SEWELL, Isaiah
SEWELL, James
SHARP, G. W.
SHELTON, Leonard
SHOOP, Thomas
SIMMONS, Joseph
SIMMONS, William
SMALLEY, Benjamin
SMALLWOOD, Eli
SMITH, Aaron
SMITH, Adam T.
SMITH, Admerson
SMITH, Edward
SMITH, John
SMITH, John H.
SMITH, Robert
SOLOMAN, Henry
SPINNER, John
STARKS, Daniel
STARKS, Solomon
STEVENSON, Samuel
STEWART, James
STEWART, John
STOVEL, Alexander
STRICKMAN, Ernest
SUTTER, John W.
TADLOCK, Patrick
TALLIFORO, Daniel
TATUM, King James
TAYLOR, Charles H.
TAYLOR, Henry
TAYLOR, John
TAYLOR, Joseph
TAYLOR, Richard

PLAIN CAPS indicate names from this volume • **BOLD CAPS** indicate names from *On the Trail* (1995)

THOMAS, Benjamin
THOMAS, George
THOMPSON, Henry
TOLLOVER, Jackson
TORBERT, Lewis
TORPLY, Green
TRIBLES, Proter
TURK, Robert H.
WAKES, Robert
WALZE, Olmstead
WARREN, Henry
WASHINGTON, Dan
WATKINS, Morgan
WATKINS, William
WATSON, Walter
WAYES, Armsted
WEBB, Charles
WESLEY, Lane
WILEY, Robert
WILLIAMS, Ansterd
WILLIAMS, Horace
WILLIAMS, Israel
WILLIAMS, James
WILLIAMS, John
WILLIAMS, Samuel F.
WILLIAMS, William
WILSON, Daniel
WILSON, David
WILSON, George
WOODS, Charles
WORKMAN, Charles
WORMLEY, George
YATES, Wyatt
YOUNG, George W.
YOUNG, James
St. Mary's Cemetery, Brackettville
LONGORIO, Manuel
Utah
Camp Douglas
ANDERSON, James
BAKER, Richard
BICHERENS, Jesse
BOYD, Daniel
BROWN, Alfred
CLARK, Charles
CLARK, William
COLLINS, Dudley
CRAIG, George
CROPPER, John S.
FIELDS, Henry
JACKSON, Samuel
JOHNSON, James E.
JONES, Joseph
JONES, Nelson
KENNEDY, Henry
MARSHALL, Joseph
MILES, Julius
MOORE, John
OWINGS, Alfred
PARKER, James
PAYNE, Jesse
PIPES, Nelson

RIDDLE, George
ROACH, George W.
ROWLAND, Samuel
SPENCER, Jeremiah
TAYLOR, Thomas W.
WADE, Chester
WALTON, Samuel
YOUNG, James
YOUNG, Jerry
Ft Douglas
BUFORD, Parker
CARTER, William H.
COMPTON, Elisha
FRANCIS, Dongel
GRANT, John
HARLAN, William
HUNTER, Jerry
HUTCHINSON, Charles
JACKSON, John J.
JAM, James
LEE, Edward
MANWELL, George
PERRY, John W.
SHIPLEY, Lee
THOMAS, Samuel
WILLIAMS, Alexander
Vermont
Lakeview Cemetery, Burlington
THORNTON, Beverly F.
Virginia
Arlington National Cemetery
ANDERSON, John B.
BUTLER, Thomas C.
CRUMP, Edward W.
DAY, James E.
FLETCHER, James Robert
FORD, George W. (employee)
HIBBITT, John
HINES, Will
JOHNSON, Henry
MATHEWS, Charlie
PRIDE, Alfred
SANDERS, Mingo
SIMS, John
WANTON, George H.
Washington, DC
Harmony Cemetery
McKAY, Barney
Mt. Olivet Cemetery
HAWKINS, William
U.S. Soldiers' and Airmen's Home
BROWN, Benjamin
DAVIS, Benjamin F.
Central Law School, Louisville, KY
JAMESON, Henry W.
Cephas, Sarah L. Jackson
CEPHAS, Joseph E.
Chaffee, Adna Romanza
CALLOWAY, John W.
DuBOSE, Edmond
STEWARD, Theophilus G.

Chambers, Louisa Proctor
CHAMBERS, Henry
SMITH, Jacob C.
Charis, Miss A.
PEOPLES, R.
Charleston & Savannah Railroad
BUSH, James W.
Chatmoun, Juanita
CHATMOUN, Littleton
Chatmoun, Minerva West
CHATMOUN, Webb
Chatmoun, Priscilla Davis
CHATMOUN, Webb
Chenault, Charles
CHENAULT, Walter
Chenault, Evelyn
CHENAULT, Walter
Chenault, Harriet
CHENAULT, Walter
Chenault, Juanita
CHENAULT, Walter
Chenault, Melvin
CHENAULT, Walter
Chenault, Wade
CHENAULT, Walter
Chenault, William
CHENAULT, Walter
Cherokee Bill
GOLDSBY, George
Cherokees
GOLDSBY, George
THOMPSON, John
THOMPSON, Joseph
THOMPSON, Merrick
Cheyenne Agency, OK
GREEN, John
HAYMAN, Perry A.
LEWIS, Richard
LOGAN, Robert
SADDLER, David
SLIMP, Jacob
SMITH, Benjamin
SMITH, Ephriam
VINCENT, Sammy
YOUNG, Clark
Cheyennes. *See also* Black Kettle (Cheyenne chief)
BARD, Benjamin
BERRYMAN, Henry
BRANCH, William
BROWN, James
CHRISTOPHER, Andrew
CRUMBLY, Floyd H.
DAVIS, Charles H.
FARRELL, Charles H.
RANDALL, John
SHROPSHIRE, Shelvin
SMITH, John
TURNER, Tom

PLAIN CAPS indicate names from this volume • **BOLD CAPS** indicate names from *On the Trail* (1995)

Chicago & Northwestern Railroad
  BOND, Howard H.
Chilocco Creek
  BROOKS, Preston
China
  ANDERSON, William T.
Chinn, Mary
  WILLIAMS, James Clifford
Choctaws
  HAMPTON, Wade
  VAUGHN, Henry
Christian Endeavor Society
  ALLENSWORTH, Allen
  DICKERSON (Corporal; 24th Inf)
  DICKERSON, James M.
Christian Endeavor Union
  FRANKLIN, Henry O.
Christian Recorder (Philadelphia, PA)
  CHENAULT, Walter
Christopher, Emma
  BERRYMAN, Henry
Church, James Robb
  BENTON, Willie
Church of Jesus Christ of Latter-Day Saints, *see* Mormons
Cincinnati Hamilton & Dayton Railroad
  LANIER, Frank
Citizens' Bank of New Orleans
  FRANKLIN, Henry O.
City College of New York
  GREENE, Hallett
  GREENE, William H.
City of Washington (steamship), *see* U.S. Army Transport *City of Washington*
Civil War veterans
  ALLEN, Henry
  ALLENSWORTH, Allen
  ANDERSON, Richard
  ARCHER, Sylvester
  ASHPORT, Lemuel
  BAILEY, Battier
  BAILEY, John H
  BAMBRICK, Joseph
  BAQUI, Rodolphe
  BENTFORD, David
  BERRY, Edward
  BIAS, Samuel
  BISHOP, James
  BLACK, Solomon
  BOWLEGS, Cyrus
  BOWLEGS, George
  BOYNE, Thomas
  BRADDEN, Alfred
  BRADFORD, Harrison
  BROOKS, Henry
  BROOKS, Preston
  BRUCE, George

CHINN, Charles
COLE, Pollard
COLLINS, Frederick
CRAGG, Allen
CUNNINGHAM, Charles
DAVIS, Benjamin F.
DERBIGNY, Benjamin
DOUGLAS, Joseph
DOWNS, Allen
DUPREE, Luzienne
FAIR, Robert
GAMBLE, John E.
GOINGS, Alfred
GOLDSBY, George
GRANT, Thomas
GREEN, William H.
HARASHAW, James
HARE, Solomon
HARRIS, George W.
HELM, Benjamin
HOWARD, Silas
JACKSON, Isaac
JEFFERDS, Wesley
JOHNSON, Joseph S.
JOHNSON, Joshua
JOHNSON, Monroe
JONES, John R.
JOSEPH, Leon
LINCOLN, Daniel
LOGAN, James
LUCKADOE, Joseph
MACKEY, Robert
MILLIMAN, Jerry
MITCHELL, Paul
MONTGOMERY, Seaborn
MOORE, Miles
MOZIQUE, Edward
MUNDY, LaFayette
MURPHY, Israel B.
MURPHY, Samuel
NEWSOME, Felix
OILDS, James
ONLY, John
PAGE, Bassett
PARKER, Henry
PEAKER, Stephen P.
PERKINS, Frank
PLUMMER, Henry Vinton
RANDOLPH, Adolphus
ROBINSON, William
SAMPLE, John
SCOTT, John H.
SCOTT, Praley
SHIPLEY, Lee
SHROPSHIRE, Shelvin
SPEAKES, James
STARR, Stephen G.
STEVENSON, James
TAYLOR, John
TAYLOR, John
THOMAS, William H.
TURNER, Joseph H.

WALLER, Reuben
WASHINGTON, Henry F.
WASLEM, James
WHITE, George
WILBURN, James
WILKS, Jacob W.
WILLIAMS, John
WINTERS, Eli
Claflin College, Orangeburg, SC
  BENJAMIN, Robert
  PRIOLEAU, George W.
Clark, Powhatan Henry, *see* Clarke, Powhatan Henry
Clark College, Atlanta, GA
  TAYLOR, Charles I.
Clarke, Powhatan Henry
  CHEATHAM, Alexander
  SCOTT, Edward
Clayton, Grace Hemsley
  TERRY, Charles Lincoln
Cleveland Homeopathic Medical College, *see* Homeopathic Medical College, Cleveland
Clouds, Fannie
  ALLEN, William
Colbert, Agnes Malinda Sheppard
  COLBERT, Frederick
Colbert, Frederick
  COLBERT, Frederick
Cole, Estephana Gonzales
  COLE, Pollard
Cole, Joseph
  COLE, Pollard
Coleman, Mamie Lou
  BROWN, Arthur M.
Coles, Nannie T.
  FARRIS, Eugene
Collins, Nannie China
  LANIER, Frank
Collins, S. T.
  COLLINS, Griffin
Colorado
  BAKER, Edward L.
  BENSON, Caleb
  Big Sandy Creek
    WIGGINS, John
  Colorado Springs
    BANKS, Charles
    GLADDEN, Washington W. E.
    McADAMS, Clifford
    MASON, George F.
    MATHEWS, Edward
  Denver
    ANDERSON, William T.
    BANKS, Jordon
    DOWNS, Allen
    GLADDEN, Washington W. E.
    JOHNSON, Henry
    KNOX, George
    MORRIS, William

PLAIN CAPS indicate names from this volume • **BOLD CAPS** indicate names from *On the Trail* (1995)

ONLEY, John
PORTER, Issac
ROSS, Patrick
SCOTT, Oscar J. W.
SMITH, James W.
WRIGHT, Clark
DOOLEY, William
Ft Garland
BLEW, Joseph
BROADUS, Joseph
CARTER, Henry H. B.
DENT, Henry
JOHNSON, Charles
JOHNSON, Charles
JOHNSON, Robert
KIRKLEY, Samuel
Ft Lewis
ALEXANDER (Corporal)
CUNNINGHAM, Charles
DENT, Henry
FERGUSON (Sergeant)
PRESTON, W.
WESLEY, James
WEST, F. A.
Ft Logan
BADGETT, Green
CLAY (Private)
CRAIG, James
FAIRFAX, Jesse J. A.
HOLLAND, Robert
JOHNSON, John H.
JONES, Jeremiah
LEACH, Samuel
LEWIS, Jackson
McBRYAR, William
PORTER, Issac
QUARLES, Ennis
SMITH, William
STEWARD, Theophilus G.
TELLIES, Robert
TERRY, Charles Lincoln
Ft Lyon
ANDERSON, William
CARTER, James
CRUMIEL, Christopher P.
FOSTER, John
FRISBY, Isaac
GOLDSBY, George
HARRISON, William
HAWKINS, Charles
HENRY, Thomas
HICKS, Charles H.
JOHNSON, William
KELL, John
LOWE, Hampton
MADDISON, Charles
MASON, George
MILES, Thomas
MILLER, James
NEELY, George
NORRIS, Benjamin
NORTHROP, Clark H.

PARKER, John
PORTER, Samuel H.
REED, James T.
STEVENSON, James
SWEENEY, Robert
THOMAS, William R.
TURNER, Tom
WASHINGTON, George
WASHINGTON, William
YOUNG, Robert
Las Animas
CUNNINGHAM, Charles
JONES, William
MILLER, James
SMITH, Benjamin
TRENT, Nathan
Las Animas County
WILLIAMS, Cathay
Milk Creek (River)
ADAMS, John D.
BALL, George
BENSON, Caleb
BOHN, Robert
BOWMAN, Jeremiah
BRATCHET, Joseph
COOK, Alexander
CRAWFORD, John
DENT, Henry
EMANUEL, George H.
EWEN, Peter
FORT, Lewis
FOWLER, Albert
GOODMAN, George W.
GRANT, Henry C.
GUDDY, Lusk
HASKINS, James
HATCHET, John R.
HOLLIDAY, William F.
HOPE, Jasper Pickens
INGOMAN, Madison
JACOBS, Innocent
JAMES, William
JOHNS, Joseph
JOHNSON, Henry
JOHNSON, John W.
JOHNSTON, Perry
JOINER, Gabriel
JONES, Thomas (2)
KELLEY, Richard
KELSEY, Edward
LANGSTON, John
MORRIS, Emanuel
ONLEY, John
PICKETT, Sonny
PREWIT, David
REDDICK, David F.
REED, William
SCOTT, Edward
SHIPLEY, John
THOMPSON, Clarence
TURNBULL, Reese
WASHINGTON, John H.

Pueblo
DOWNS, Allen
HASKINS, James
WILLIAMS, Cathay
Rock Creek
CUNNINGHAM, Charles
San Francisco Creek
JENNINGS, Oliver
Trinidad
ABBOTT, James W.
BURKS, Henry
WILLIAMS, Cathay
Uncompahgre River
HAYDEN (Private)
JOHNSON, Robert T.
WALLER, Reuben
WILKES, William
Colored American Magazine
(Washington, DC)
BARROW, Stephen B.
CLARKE, Thomas H. R.
CLEMENS, Benjamin
FRIERSON, Eugene
LEMUS, Rienzi Brock
LOWE, Albert S.
The Colored Regulars in the
United States Army
STEWARD, Frank R.
STEWARD, Theophilus G.
SIMPSON, James Thomas
Colored Women's Clubs of
Montana
BIVINS, Horace
Colson family
BRADLEY, Levi
CROSS, William
LOGAN, James
MILLER, Chris
Comanches
ALEXANDER, Joseph
ANDERSON, John
ANDERSON, Robert
BACKERS, William
BAKER, Charles
BARD, Benjamin
BERRYMAN, Henry
BRANCH, William
BULGER, William
BURNS, Carter
BUTLER, Charles
COLE, Pollard
CORK, Adam
DAVIS, Dudley
DUVALL, William H.
ELLINGTON, Jack
FARRELL, Charles H.
FERRER, Jackson
FRANKLIN, Walter
GARNETT, George R.
HELM, Sherred
KELLEY, John

PLAIN CAPS indicate names from this volume • **BOLD CAPS** indicate names from *On the Trail* (1995)

BECKETT, William C.
BELL, James
BENSON, Abram
BERRY, Thomas
BIGGS, John
BIRD, Joseph
BLACKBURNE, Leonard R.
BLUE, Daniel
BLUFORD, Clarence L.
BLUFORD, Emmitt L.
BOARD, Walter W.
BOLLING, Willie
BOUNCLER, Pearl
BOURROUGHS, Ossie O.
BOWENS, Alonzo
BOYD, Charles
BOYD, Frederick D.
BOYD, Thomas
BRANCH, Norwood
BRANTLY, James
BRAXTON, George E.
BRIGS, Tazwell
BRINKLEY, Frank
BROADEN, William
BROADUS, Lewis
BROOKS, Benjamin
BROOKS, Harry
BROWN, David T.
BROWN, Garfield
BROWN, George A.
BROWN, John
BROWN, Tracy F.
BROWN, William (Private; D/10th Cav)
BROWN, William (1) (Private;
   G/10th Cav)
BROWN, William H.
BRUFF, Thomas
BRYANT, Benjamin F.
BUCHANAN, James
BULLOCK, Nathaniel
BURNS, Calvin C.
BURRUS, Grant
BUSH, Robert
BUTCHER, Joseph
BUTLER, Harry
BYERS, George
CAGER, John T.
CALLOWAY, John W.
CAMPBELL, William
CAMPER, James H.
CANNON, William
CARNEY, Lewis G.
CARROLL, Charles H.
CARTER, Robert
CARTY, James
CATLETT, James H.
Cauto
   ROBERTS, Robert
CHAMBERS, William
CHAMP, Abraham
CHELF, Edward C.
CHENAULT, Walter

CHESTER, William L.
CHEVIN, John F., Jr.
CHISHOLM, Frank R.
CICEL, Richard
CLARK, Lig J.
CLARK, William
CLAY, Charles F.
CLIFFORD, Charles
CLINTON, Princeton A.
COATS, William H.
COBB, Edward F.
COLE, Felix J.
COLE, James T.
COLE, John H.
COLEMAN, Richard M.
COLLINS, William
COLLINS, William H.
COMBS, Richard
COOK, Joshua
COOK, William H.
COOPER, Andrew
COOPER, James H.
COPELLE, Charles
COVINGTON, Samuel
CRAWFORD, Lexis
CREIGHTON, John R.
Cristo
   BLUNT, Hamilton H.
CRITTENDEN, Paul
CROLLY, James
CROWER, Eugene
CURTIS, Grant
CURTIS, Richard
CUTHBERT, John F.
DADE, Charles
Daiquiri
   COBB, Edward F.
   ENGLISH, George
DANIELS, Edward L.
DANIELS, William H.
DARROW, Washington
DAUGLASH, J. W. B., Jr.
DAVIS, Abraham
DAVIS, Albert
DAVIS, James
DAVIS, James A.
DAVIS, John
DAVIS, Thomas
DAVIS, Ulysses
DAVIS, William J.
DEAN, William
DELANEY, George
DEMORE, George
DENNY, Elbiron
DIGGS, Charles H.
DIXON, William
DODSON, John H.
DOLBY, Eli R.
DOOMS, Thomas
DORSEY, Charles A.
DOUGLASS, Samuel W.
DOYLE, Richard F.

DRAKE, Robert I.
DREW, Albert
DREW, John B.
DUFF, John
DUNTON, John
EARLY, Herbert
EASLY, Reuben
EDWARDS, Amos K.
EDWARDS, Joseph S.
EIGHMIE, Isaac G.
El Caney
   BEVILL, James
   BOYD, John
   BRIGHTWELL, Henry
   BROOKS, William P.
   BROWN, Tom
   BROWNE, Stephen A.
   BUCKNER, David
   BUTLER, Thomas C.
   COLEMAN, Frank
   COOPER, George B.
   COUSINS, Benjamin
   DANIELS, Alvin
   DOUGLAS, Boney
   FOX, Oscar
   GAMBLE, John E.
   GILBERT, Henry
   GILLAM, David C.
   GOODWIN, Robert
   GRAY, Conny
   HARLEY, Samuel W.
   HOWARD, James
   HOWE, Tom
   HUFFMAN, Wyatt
   HUNTER, James O.
   JEFFERSON, Charles W.
   JOHNSON, Joseph L.
   JONES, Eugene
   JONES, J. H.
   LEFTWICH, Aaron
   McBRYAR, William
   PAYNE, Charles
   PHELPS, John B.
   RICHARDS, Hayden
   RUSSELL, Macon
   SADDLER, John
   SADDLER, Louis
   SANDERS, Mingo
   SINCLAIR, Thomas
   SMITH, Andrew J.
   STATON, Governor
   STEELE, John W.
   STROTHER, Albert
   SWANN, Hugh
   TALIAFERRO, Spottswood W.
   TERRY, Charles Lincoln
   THOMAS, John
   ELLIOTT, Rufus
   ELLIS, Merriman H.
   EUBANKS, John
   EVANS, Harry V.
   FALL, William H.

PLAIN CAPS indicate names from this volume • **BOLD CAPS** indicate names from *On the Trail* (1995)

FEARINGTON, George W.
FEASON, Henry
FENNELL, Eugene S.
FIELDS, John W.
FINNEY, Richard
FISHER, Fred
FLYNT, Robert
FORD, George W.
FORD, James W.
FRANKLIN, Benjamin
FRIERSON, Eugene
FRISLEY, John L.
FULBRIGHT, William R.
FULTZ, George
GARDNER, Seymour
GARDNER, William George
GASKINS, Albert
GASTON, Albert
GATES, Joseph
Gibara
   ANDERSON, William T.
   HOLLIDAY, Presley
GIBSON, Edward
GIBSON, Murry
GIVENS, Gilmore
GLOVER, Robert
GOFF, George W.
GOLDWAITE, Silas
GOUGH, Robert
GOULD, Luther D.
GRAHAM, John
GRAY, Edward
GREEN, Dalbert P.
GREEN, Hamilton
GREEN, McCallin
GREEN, Morris
GRICE, Theodore
GRIFFIN, Alfred E.
GRIGGS, William H.
GRIMES, James
GROVER, John
GROVES, Wills
GULLION, George W.
GULLION, John
GUY, John R.
HALL, Clarence
HALL, John W.
HALL, Lafayette
HAMBRIGHT, Peter
HAMILTON, Arthur
HAMILTON, William
HAMILTON, William H.
HAMMOND, Pleasant H.
HAMMOND, Thomas C.
HANKS, Frank
HARDAWAY, Henry
HARDMAN, Benjamin H.
HARRINGTON, William
HARRIS, Charles
HARRIS, Douglas
HARRIS, John
HARRIS, Rand

HARRIS, William
HARVEY, Robert F.
HATCHER, Willis
Havana
   GILLISPIE, James R.
   McDONALD, Robert
HAWKINS, Emmett
HAWKINS, William
HELLEMS, Frank
HENDERSON, John (Sergeant;
   G/10th Cav)
HENDERSON, John (Private;
   G/10th Cav)
HENDERSON, John H.
HENDERSON, Lewis
HENDERSON, Richard
HENDERSON, William N.
HENRY, John
HENRY, Vodrey
HENSON, Barry
HENSON, George J.
HICKS, Absom
HICKS, Charles
HILL, H. W.
HILL, William H.
HILTON, George T.
HINES, Joseph J.
HIPSHIRE, Riley
HOCKINS, Major
HOLDEN, David
Holguín
   ANDERSON, William T.
   BROOKS, Harry
   CONLEY, Paschall
   FARRALL, William H.
   OBANION, Otis
   ODEN, Oscar N.
   SMITH, Tom
   WILSON, George
HOLLIDAY, Presley
HOLLOWAY, Lewis W.
HOLMES, Conley
HOLT, Lindsey P.
HOPKINS, John
HOPKINS, Richard
HOUSTON, William A.
HOWARD, Charles
HOWARD, William
HUGHES, Grant
HUGHES, John
HUGHES, Sam
JACKSON, Bernard A.
JACKSON, George
JACKSON, Turner
JACKSON, William
JACKSON, William H.
JACKSON, William M.
JAMES, Isaac
JAMES, Jesse
JAMES, John
JAMES, Richard
JANES, Edward

JELKES, James B.
JEWELL, Bradey
JOHNSON, B. F.
JOHNSON, James
JOHNSON, Robert J.
JOHNSON, Silas
JOHNSON, William (Private; D/10th
   Cav)
JOHNSON, William F.
JOHNSON, William H. (1)
JOHNSON, Willie
JONES, Allen
JONES, Elsie
JONES, G. M.
JONES, Henry C.
JONES, Jefferson
JONES, Paul
JONES, Samuel M.
JORDAN, Thomas
KELLEY, William
KELLUM, D. F.
KINSLOW, Thomas
KIRTLEY, Sidney
LANE, John M.
Las Guásimas
   BAKER, Edward L., Jr
   BELL, William
   BOLAND, John
   BUCK, John
   BUNN, William N.
   FORD, James W.
   FOSTER, Saint
   GIVENS, William H.
   HARRIS, Sherman
   HOLLIDAY, Presley
   HUMPHREY, John A.
   JONES, Elsie
   JONES, Wesley
   PENNISTON, James W.
   WHEELER, Arthur G.
LAWS, John H.
LAWSON, James H.
LAWSON, William
LEE, James K.
LEE, Robert E.
LEE, William
LESTER, Isaac A.
LEWERS, Carey
LEWIS, George
LEWIS, Isaac
LIDELL, Thomas
LIGHTFOOT, James R.
LOVING, Lelwood
LOWE, Albert S.
LOWE, Charles H.
LUMKINS, Ananias
LYMAN, George
MABERRY, Kelley
McCURDY, Walter
McDONALD, Robert
MADEN, Ebbert
MANLEY, Edward W.

PLAIN CAPS indicate names from this volume • **BOLD CAPS** indicate names from *On the Trail* (1995)

Manzanillo
  ANDERSON, William T.
  BLENKINSHIP, William
  FAULKNER, Charles S.
  HOLLIDAY, Presley
  LEWIS, John E.
  PENDERGRASS, John **C.**
  PENNISTON, James W.
  THOMPKINS, William H.
  WATKINS, Edward
  WILLOUGHBY, S. J.
  YANCEY, Thomas
MARSHALL, Louis
MARSHELL, Victor L.
MARTIN, Cornelius
MARTIN, William C.
MASON, George F.
MASON, Thomas (Private; B/10th Cav)
MASON, Thomas (Private; D/10th Cav)
Mayari
  DELAND, Johnson
  JAMESON, Henry W.
MAYBERRY, Kelly
MAYO, George
MILLER, John R.
MILLER, Richard
MILLS, D. M.
MINAR, James L.
MITCHELL, Edward
MITCHELL, Joseph G.
MITCHELL, William H.
MITCHEM, Thomas
MITCHEM, William H.
MONTGOMERY, Humphrey
MOORE, Loney
MORRIS, John
MORROW, Alexander
MOSS, James
MOSS, Jesse S.
MOTLEY, Solomon
MURPHY, Marion W.
MURRELL, James
MURRY, Frank
NEWMAN, John D.
NICHOLSON, Edward
NOAL, Robert J.
NOBLE, John
NORRIS, Jerry
OBANION, Otis
OFFUTT, Benjamin F.
OLE, Henry R.
OWENS, Fred
PADGETT, Andrew
PAGE, Edward W.
PARKER, Charles E.
PARKER, George
PATTERSON, Stephen
PATTERSON, William
PAYNE, John H.
PAYNE, Robert A.

PENDER, Freeman E.
PENDLETON, Ross
PENN, William H.
PENNISTON, James W.
PETER, Major H.
PETERS, James
PHILLIPS, Willie
PIERSAUL, Leonidas
PLEASANT, Harry R.
PORTER, Harrison
PORTER, Issac
PORTER, William
POTTS, Benjamin F.
POWELL, George D.
PRESTON, Emmet
PRESTON, Lloyd
PRICE, James
PRIM, John
PRIOLEAU, George W.
PROCTOR, Clarence L.
PRYOR, Lee
PULLEN, Frank W., Jr.
QUEEN, William
QUEENER, William
QUICKLEY, William H.
RACKS, George H.
RACKS, Washington H.
RAMSAY, Robert
RANSOM, Robert
RAY, Albert
RAY, John I.
REDDIE, Charles
REED, Amos B.
REED, Kirby
REED, Miller
REEVES, Walter
REYNOLDS, William
RICHARDS, James A.
RICHARDS, John
RICHARDSON, William
Río San Juan
  BLACK, Aaron
  BONNSELOR, Pearl
  BRIDGEWATER, Samuel
  MARSHALL, Louis
  PARKER, Charles
ROBERTS, Robert W. (Private; M/10th Cav)
ROBERTS, Robert W. (Corporal; B/24th Inf)
ROBERTSON, Henry
ROBERTSON, Tom
ROBINSON, Benjamin
ROBINSON, Forrest
ROBINSON, John
ROLLINS, Walker S.
ROSS, James R.
ROWLETT, Virgil
RUCKER, Julius B.
RUSSELL, James
SALTER, Emory
SANDERS, James C.

San Juan Hill
  ANCRUM, William
  BAILEY, Isaac
  BAKER, Edward L., Jr
  BALDWIN (Private)
  BELL, William
  BERRY, George
  BIVINS, Horace W.
  BOWMAN, Lewis
  BROWN (Corporal; 10th Cav)
  BROWN, Alfred
  BROWN, William H.
  BULLOCK (Private; C/9th Cav)
  CALLOWAY, John W.
  CAMPBELL, John W.
  CANDY (Private)
  CLAY, James
  COATS, William H.
  CONWAY, Henry
  CRAIG, Thomas B.
  CRIPPEN, Elijah A.
  DAVIS, Edward
  DODSON, John H.
  DUDLEY, John H.
  ERVINE, James W.
  FINNEY, Corbin B.
  FORD, James W.
  FORT, Lewis
  FRAZIER, Benjamin T.
  GARDNER, William H.
  GIVENS, William H.
  GOUGH, Robert
  GRIFFIN, Thomas
  HARRIS, Sherman
  HAZZARD, George H.
  HENDERSON, J. W.
  HENDRICKS, William
  HOLLIDAY, Presley
  HOYLE (Private)
  HUDSON, Gus
  HUTTON, George R.
  JACKSON, Andrew
  JENIFER, Theopolous E.
  JOHNSON, James
  JOHNSON, John J.
  JOHNSON, Joseph
  JOHNSON, William F.
  KELLEY, George B.
  LEE, James
  LOCKMAN, George H.
  LOMAX, John
  McCAULEY, William
  McNABB, Lewis W.
  MASON, John
  MOORE, Adam
  MOSELEY, William
  NELSON, Edward D.
  OLE, Henry R.
  PARKER, Charles
  PEREA, Beverly
  PRINCE, Noah
  RAINEY, William

PLAIN CAPS indicate names from this volume • **BOLD CAPS** indicate names from *On the Trail* (1995)

RICHARDSON, Alexander V.
RIDDLE, Alfred
SAYRE, Benjamin F.
SHEPPARD, Marshall
SMITH, Jacob C.
SMITH, Luscious
SMITH, Walter E.
SNODGRASS, Carlos
SPURLOCK, Charles
STAFF, William R.
STAFFORD, James N.
STARR, Stephen G.
STROTHER, Edward
TAYLOR, Elijah
TAYLOR, Thomas W.
TAYLOR, William
THORNTON, William
TUCKER, Joseph H.
TULL, Joseph
TURNER (Private)
TURNER, Samuel
WAGNER, Robert S.
WALKER, John
WALKER, Phillip E.
WALLS, Henry F.
WARREN, Daniel
WILSON, Alfred
WILSON, George
WOODS, Robert Gordon
San Juan River, *see above* Rio San
 Juan
San Luis
BEARD, George J.
BROWN, John W.
BROWN, Simon
BURNS, Frank
CROCKETT, W. W.
ROBERTS, W. B.
ROSS, Harry H.
WALKER, C. T.
WORMSLEY, William C.
Santiago
ANDERSON, Lewis S.
ANDERSON, William T.
APPLEBY, Frayer
ARNOLD, John
ARTHUR, Charles
BAFFIT, E. J.
BATES, James
BAYLOR, George
BENNETT, Frank D.
BISSELL, Richard H.
BLEDSOE, Wade
BOARMAN, Lewis
BROOKS, John
BROOKS, William P.
BROWN, Hillery
BROWN, John
BROWN, William H.
BUCK, John
BURKLEY, Thornton
CAMPBELL, J. H.

CHINN, John
COOPER, William
CROSBY, Scott
DANIELS, William H.
DAVIS, Edward
DODSON, John H.
ELLIOTT, James
ELLIS, Merriman H.
ELLISTON, Amos
FASIT, Benjamin
FEARN, Henry
FINNEY, Corbin B.
FRANKLIN, Benjamin
FRANKLIN, James Edward
FRANKLIN, William H.
GAINES, Mosely
GAITHER, Ozrow
GASKINS, Benjamin F.
GIVENS, Gilmore
GIVENS, William H.
GOUGH, Robert
GOULD, Luther D.
GRAHAM, John
GREGORY, John T.
GREGORY, William
GUNTER, Ulysses G.
HAGEN, Abram
HARDY, Thomas S.
HATCHER, Willis
HENDERSON, J. W.
HERBERT, Thomas H.
HILL, Frank
HILL, J. H.
HIPSHER, Wiley
HOLLIDAY, Presley
HOPKINS, Charles
HOUSTON, Adam
HUFFMAN, Wyatt
INGOMAN, Madison
JACKSON, Elisha
JACKSON, John J.
JACKSON, Peter
JAMESON, Henry W.
JEFFERSON, Charles W.
JENKINS, John
JOHNSON, Smith
JOHNSON, Walker
JOHNSON, William (Private;
 D/24th Inf)
JOHNSON, William F.
JOHNSON, William H.
JONES, Allen
KELLEY, George B.
KEYS, Pat
LANE, Edward
LEE, James
LEWIS, C. J.
LEWIS, Sprague
LOVE (Corporal)
MABERRY, Kelley
McBRYAR, William
McCORMACK, Henry

McCOWN, Peter
McNABB, Lewis W.
MARSHALL, John R.
MARSHALL, Louis
MARTIN, Henry L.
MARTIN, James W.
MASON, John
MATTHEWS, William
MILLBROWN, Robert
MILLER, Frank A.
MILLER, Henry
MILLER, James H.
MINOR, Samuel T.
MOORE, Adam
MOORE, Harry
MOORE, Loney
NEAL, Burr
NELSON, Edward D.
NELSON, William R.
ODEN, Oscar N.
OLE, Henry R.
PARKER, James E.
PARKER, Jesse C.
PAYNE, William
PENDERGRASS, John C.
POPE, Charles F.
PRINCE, Noah
PROCTOR, John C.
PUMPHREY, George W.
RANKIN, Frank
REDD, Samuel
RIDDELL, Houston
RIDGELY, Frank
ROBERTSON, Charles
ROBINSON, Mason
RUSSELL, James
RUSSELL, Macon
SADDLER, Louis
SANDERS, Mingo
SATCHELL, James
SAUNDERS, Peter
SAYRE, Benjamin F.
SHEPPARD, Marshall
SHOCKLEY, Fred
SLAUGHTER, William H.
SMITH, Andrew J.
SMITH, Luscious
SMITH, Walter E.
SMOOT, John H.
SPURLOCK, Charles
STAFF, William R.
STAFFORD, James N.
STARR, Stephen G.
STOVALL, George
STROTHER, Edward
STURGIS, Harry
TALIAFERRO, Charles L.
TATE, William
TAYLOR, Isom
TAYLOR, James F.
TAYLOR, John J. L.
TAYLOR, Thomas W.

PLAIN CAPS indicate names from this volume • **BOLD CAPS** indicate names from *On the Trail* (1995)

TAYLOR, William
THORNTON, William
TURNER, Samuel
TYLER, Benjamin F.
WALKER, John
WALLEY, Augustus
WASHINGTON, Ernest S.
WASHINGTON, William
WATSON, John
WEST, Benjamin
WHEELER, Arthur G.
WHITE, Allen C.
WHITE, William L.
WILLIAMS, Jessie
WILLIAMS, John T.
WILLIAMS, Joseph
WILLIAMS, Richard
WILLIAMS, Thomas
WRIGHT, Marcellous
WYATT, Nathan
SAWYER, Henry
SCHOCKLEY, Alexander
SCOTT, Charles
SCOTT, Oscar
SEDDEN, James R.
SENTERS, Charles C.
SHAW, Harry A.
SHEFFIELD, Frederick
SHOCKLEY, Fred
SHOECRAFT, William H.
Siboney
ANDERSON, Robert
APPLEBY, Frayer
ARCH, William
BAYLESS, John M.
BOGGS, Carter
BOOKER, Robert
BOSSLEY, Robert
BOUNCLER, Willis S.
BRADSHAW, Samuel
BRATTON, James
BRENT, William
BROWN, Robert
BURTON, Dock
CALLOWAY, John W.
CARNEY, Lewis G.
CARROLL, W. H.
CLARK, Andrew
COATS, William H.
CONN, John
COOK, Jesse A.
COOK, William L.
COX, Thomas
CRAIGWELL, Ernest
CRAWFORD, Lexis
DAVIS, James A.
DEMORE, George
DIGGS, Charles H.
EAGLIN, Thomas
ERVINE, James W.
ESTILL, Allen P.
FAGEN, David

FLEMING, Richard
FRANKLIN, William H.
FULLER, John
GOUGH, Robert
GREEN, Warren
GREGORY, Nathanial
GRIGGS, William H.
HARRIS, Robert
HARTNETT, Allen J.
HILL, Herbert
HIPSHIRE, Riley
HOLLOMON, Solomon
ISAACS, Will
JACKSON, Albert
JACKSON, Levorsiear
JOHNSON, Ernest
JOHNSON, Louis
JOHNSON, William
JONES, Frank H.
JONES, Jack
KELLEY, George B.
KINEAD, Caspar
LAWSON, James
LEWIS, John A.
McGEE, Allen
MARRIS, Eugene
MARTIN, Walker
MILLER, Harry
MILLER, Jesse C.
MILLINGTON, Samuel
MITCHELL, Harry
MOSELEY, William
NUNN, Duffy
PENDLETON, Ross
PHILLIPS, Jacob P.
PHILLIPS, James
PLEDGER, William A., Jr.
POTTER, Bradford
POWELL, Thomas R.
PRESTON, Charles R.
PRINCE, Noah
QUEEN, Emanuel
QUEEN, Howard D
RAY, Edward M.
REESE, Manning H.
RICHARDS, Hayden
RICHARDSON, Robert
RIVERS, Robert
RODGERS, Henry R.
RUSSELL, John
RUSSELL, Macon
SAMMONS, William H.
SCOTT, Robert
SCOTT, Solomon
SMALLS, Cyrus
SMITH, Dennis A.
SMITH, Sandy
SMITH, Solomon
SMITH, William
SPANKLER, Robert
SPENCER, Mortimer E.
STAFF, William R.

STARLING, Eli
STATON, Samuel
SULLIVAN, George
TAYLOR, William
THOMPSON, George S.
TUCKER, Joseph H.
TURNER, Matthew
WALKER, Arthur
WALKER, Jesse W.
WASHINGTON, Louis W.
WASHINGTON, Walter L.
WEBSTER, Francis
WHITE, Henry
WILLIAMS, H. A.
WILLIAMS, Henry
WILLIAMS, John G.
WILLIAMS, John T.
WILLIAMS, Squire
WILLIAMS, Walter B.
WILLIAMS, Willie
WOODS, Robert Gordon
WRIGHT, Jerry
WRIGHT, R. L.
SIMMS, Elsie
SIMMS, John W.
SIMPSON, James S.
SIMS, Sprague
SINGLETON, Isaac
SMITH, Benjamin
SMITH, Daniel
SMITH, George (Private; G/10th Cav)
SMITH, George (Corporal; I/10th Cav)
SMITH, George (Color Sgt; 10th Cav)
SMITH, John E. (Private; A/10th Cav)
SMITH, John E. (1) (Private; E/10th Cav)
SMITH, John E. (2) (Private; E/10th Cav)
SMITH, Joseph M.
SMITH, Lewis M.
SMITH, Roy
SMITH, Thomas
SNOWDEN, William E.
Songo
PINCHBACK, Walter A.
SPRIDDLES, Hamilton O.
SQUIRES, Albert H.
STANFIELD, Mack
STANLEY, William
STARKEY, George
STEELE, John W.
STEWARD, James
STEWARD, Zachariah
STEWART, John
STEWART, Johnie
STRANGE, Edward R.
STRATTON, John H.
STREET, William

PLAIN CAPS indicate names from this volume • **BOLD CAPS** indicate names from *On the Trail* (1995)

SULDER, Alexander
SUTTON, Edward
SUTTON, James
SWAN, Harry
SWAN, John R.
SWIFT, Thomas
TAPER, Charles
Tayabacoa
   BELL, Dennis
   HENRY, Frank
   LEE, Fitz
   PORTER, William
   THOMPKINS, William H.
   WANTON, George H.
TAYLOR, George R.
TAYLOR, Henry
TAYLOR, Isom
TAYLOR, Julius
TEMPLE, Abraham
TERRY, Charles Lincoln
THACKER, William
THOMAS, Eston
THOMAS, Frank
THOMAS, Wilson M.
THOMPSON, James
THOMPSON, Joseph
THOMPSON, Maryland
THOMPSON, Murry
THORNTON, Cliff
THRASHER, George
TOLBERT, Walter
TRAVILLION, Thomas
TUTTLE, Aleck
TWISBY, James P.
TYLER, William
TYNES, James E.
VANDEBURG, Burt
VENABLE, Henry
VINE, Frank A.
WADE, Silas N.
WALKER, John
WALL, Archy
WALLER, John L.
WALLEY, Augustus
WANGLE, Charles
WARE, Burges
WASHINGTON, Israel
WASHINGTON, Louis W.
WASHINGTON, William (Private; A/10th Cav)
WASHINGTON, Winter
WATERS, John
WATKINS, James M.
WATSON, Arthur C.
WATSON, John
WATTS, Thomas
WELBER, John
WELCH, Alfred
WELLS, John
WELLS, Robert
WELLS, William T.
WEST, Benjamin

WHITE, Charles
WHITE, Henry
WHITE, Joseph
WHITE, William
WHITE, William H.
WHITE, William L.
WHITING, John
WHITLOCK, William
WHITSON, Edward N.
WHITSON, Irvin
WIGGINS, John
WILEY, Purcell
WILKES, William
WILLIAMS, Edward (Private; M/10th Cav)
WILLIAMS, Edward (1st Sgt; L/24th Inf)
WILLIAMS, Fred
WILLIAMS, Harry
WILLIAMS, James H.
WILLIAMS, John P.
WILLIAMS, Noah W.
WILLIAMS, Seth
WILLIAMS, Solomon
WILLIAMS, Tony
WILLIS, Cupid
WILLIS, James H.
WILSON, Charley
WILSON, John
WILSON, Percy T.
WILSON, Willie
WIMBERLY, William
WOODS, Thomas
WOODWARD, Otho J.
WORMLEY, James
YOUNG, Charles
YOUNG, Douglass
YOUNG, John W. H.
YOUNG, William
ZELLARS, John C.
Cuevas, Ymiela
  PRIDE, Wheeler
Cuff, Fanny
  GOULD, Luther D.
Cunningham, Charlotte
  CUNNINGHAM, Charles
Cunningham, Frances Smith
  CUNNINGHAM, Charles
Cunningham, Jennie V.
  CUNNINGHAM, Charles
Cunningham, Mary Ray
  CUNNINGHAM, Charles
Cunningham, Sarah
  CUNNINGHAM, Charles
Cusack, Patrick
  COLLYER, S.
JOHNSON, Bushrod
REEDER, James A.
WHITE, Lewis

Custer's defeat, 50th anniversary commemoration
  DARE, Lewis
Daggett, Aaron Simon
  HUFFMAN, Wyatt
  RUSSELL, Macon
  SMITH, Andrew J.
Daniels, Bill
  DANIELS, Elijah
  DANIELS, John
Daniels, Jam
  DANIELS, Jerry
Daniels, Judia
  DANIELS, Jerry
Davidson, Francis Snelling
  SCOTT (Private)
  SMITH, Robert
Davis, Henry T.
  ALLEN, Henry
  EVANS, Henry
  JACKSON, Orange
Davis, John P.
  LEMUS, Rienzi Brock
Davis, Priscilla
  CHATMOUN, Webb
Day, Matthias Walter
  FORD, Thomas
  GOODLOE, Thomas
De Los Ris, Volentina
  MOORE, Simon
Deane, William G.
  DEAN, Milton T.
Death, Hades, and the Resurrection
  STEWARD, Theophilus G.
Deaver, Mary R.
  DEAVER, Alphonse W.
Decker, Theodore
  ROLLINS, John
DeGress, Charles Smith
  KIBBETTS, John
Dehoney, Abraham L.
  DEHONEY, Peter
Dehoney, Clark
  DEHONEY, Peter
Dehoney, Elisa White
  DEHONEY, Peter
Dehoney, George A.
  DEHONEY, Peter
Dehoney, James L.
  DEHONEY, Peter
Dehoney, John
  DEHONEY, Peter
Dehoney, Reason
  DEHONEY, Peter
Delaware. *See also* Cemeteries
  BAILEY, Isaac W.
  BROWN, Richard
  CALDWELL, Charles

PLAIN CAPS indicate names from this volume • **BOLD CAPS** indicate names from *On the Trail* (1995)

CARPENTER, Robert
DUDLEY, John H.
Middletown
   TURNER, Walter
Smyrna. *See also* Cemeteries
   JOHNSON, Benjamin
   TERRY, Charles Lincoln
   STEWARD, Theophilus G.
   TURNER, Joseph H.
Wilmington
   DORSEY, Henry
   DORSEY, Wesley
   DUDLEY, John H.
   EMPSON, Theodore
   HARRIS, Alexander
   JOHNSON, Henry
   STEWARD, Frank R.
   WATSON, James T.
   WATSON, William H.
   WILSON, Thomas
Delhi Institute, Delhi, LA
   GOINS, Joshua Van Buren
Deming decision, *see* U.S.
  Supreme Court
Dent, Henry L.
   DENT, Henry
Dent, Rosa B. Ross
   DENT, Henry
DePauw University, Greencastle,
  IN
   WILLIAMS, Noah W.
Diamond Club
   GOFF, George W.
   JORDAN, George
   MOORE, Henry
   SHAW, Thomas
   WYLIE, Daniel
Dick, Charles
   ANDERSON, William T.
Dickinson, Joseph
   SMITH, Thomas
Dickinson, Suzie Hunter
   SMITH, Thomas
Dickson, Mary
   ALLENSWORTH, Allen
Dillon, Mary J.
   DILLON, Robert
Dimmick, Eugene Dumont
   CRUMBLE, Richard
Dining Car Cooks and Waiters
  Association
   LEMUS, Rienzi Brock
District of Columbia, *see* Wash-
  ington, DC
Divine Attributes
   STEWARD, Theophilus G.
Dixie, Rose
   DIXIE, Joe
   FAY, Adam

Dixon, Vivian Wanton
   WANTON, George H.
Dockey, Jinnie
   DOCKEY, Stanton
Dodge, Francis Safford
   ADAMS, John D.
   BALL, George
   BENSON, Caleb
   BOHN, Robert
   BOWMAN, Jeremiah
   BRATCHET, Joseph
   COOK, Alexander
   CRAWFORD, John
   DENT, Henry
   EMANUEL, George H.
   EWEN, Peter
   FORT, Lewis
   FOWLER, Albert
   GOODMAN, George W.
   GRANT, Henry C.
   GUDDY, Lusk
   HASKINS, James
   HATCHET, John R.
   HOLLIDAY, William F.
   INGOMAN, Madison
   JACOBS, Innocent
   JAMES, William
   JOHNS, Joseph
   JOHNSON, Henry
   JOHNSON, John W.
   JOHNSTON, Perry
   JOINER, Gabriel
   JONES, Thomas (2)
   KELLEY, Richard
   KELSEY, Edward
   LANGSTON, John
   MORRIS, Emanuel
   ONLEY, John
   PICKETT, Sonny
   PREWIT, David
   REDDICK, David F.
   REED, William
   SCOTT, Edward
   SHIPLEY, John
   THOMPSON, Clarence
   TURNBULL, Reese
   WASHINGTON, John H.
Dolan, John
   GANTZ, Frank
Dolby, Eli Ross, Jr.
   DOLBY, Eli R.
Dolby, Maria Angela Elias
   DOLBY, Eli R.
Donnan, A. S.
   ANDERSON, Benjamin A.
Dorsey, George
   DORSEY (9th Cav)
Dorsey, Julia
   DENT, Henry
Dorsey, Viola Rucker
   DORSEY (9th Cav)

Dotson, Frida Moore
   MOORE, Fredrick Thomas
Douglass, Jessie L. Evans
   EVANS, Frank, Sr.
Downingtown (PA) Industrial and
  Agricultural School
   QUEEN, Howard D
Drake, Emily
   BLACK, Solomon
Draper, Eugenia Bennett
   DRAPER, Frank
Drew Theological Seminary,
  Madison, NJ
   SCOTT, Oscar J. W.
Drexel Mission, *see* Pine Ridge
  Reservation
Earlham College, Richmond, IN
   WILLIAMS, Noah W.
Eastern Star. *See also* Masons
   REYNOLDS, William
   SANDERS, Mingo
Edmonds, Henry
   EDMONDS, John
Edmonds, Mary Hancock
   EDMONDS, John
Edward Waters College, Jack-
  sonville, FL
   GREGG, John A.
Egypt
   ANDERSON, William T.
Elias, Maria Angela
   DOLBY, Eli R.
Eliot National Bank, Boston, MA
   HARRIS, Israel
Elks, Benevolent and Protective
  Order of
   LEMUS, Rienzi Brock
   PURNELL, William Whipple
Emery, Arthur J.
   EMERY, Andrew J.
Emery, Charles Clifford
   EMERY, Andrew J.
Emery, Dolly
   EMERY, Andrew J.
Emery, Dora M. Packard
   EMERY, Andrew J.
Emery, Grant D.
   EMERY, Andrew J.
Emery, Hazel May
   EMERY, Andrew J.
Emmet, Robert Temple
   HICKS, William B.
End of the World
   STEWARD, Theophilus G.
England
   BENJAMIN, Robert
   DAVIS, Edward
  London
    STEWARD, Theophilus G.

PLAIN CAPS indicate names from this volume • **BOLD CAPS** indicate names from *On the Trail* (1995)

PERKINS, Levi
RICHARDS, James A.
RICKS, William Nauns
TAYLOR, Thomas W.
Episcopal Church
BASKERVILLE, E. S.
FORD, George W.
PURNELL, William Whipple
Estrada, Refugia
ROLLINS, John
Eubanks, Della
ANDERSON, William T.
Evans, Frank
EVANS, Frank, Sr.
Evans, Jessie L.
EVANS, Frank, Sr.
Evans, Lillard
EVANS, Frank, Sr.
Evans, Mollie Steward
EVANS, Frank, Sr.
Evans, Willie
EVANS, Frank, Sr.
Ewing, Annie
MADEN, Ebbert
Expatriates in Cuba
FEASON, Henry
HARRIS, Sherman
WILSON, George
Expatriates in the Philippines
BLAKENY, William F.
CARTER, Pat
CHATMOUN, Littleton
COLEMAN, James
CORDIN, C. W.
CUMMERS, William
GREEN, F. E.
GRILLS, Eugene H.
HENRY, John
JOHNSON, Henry
LLOYD, Isaac H.
McCREMENS, David
MERRITT, Julius
ROBINSON, Wiley
SEWELL, George
SIMONDS (A/24th Inf)
SIMS, Albert
SPENCE, William
THOMAS, James
VALDEZ, Julian
WALLER, John L.
WHITE, Thomas
WILSON, John
WOODS, Robert Gordon
Factor, Dindie
FACTOR, Pompey
Factor, Esther
FACTOR, Hardy
Factor, Frederic
FACTOR, Hardy
Factor, Hardy
FACTOR, Hardy

Factor, Hester
FACTOR, Hardy
Factor, Josephine
FACTOR, Dindie
Factor, Nelly
FACTOR, Dembo
FACTOR, Dindie
FACTOR, Hardy
Factor, Penny Wilson
WILSON, Ben, Sr.
Factor, Silvia
FACTOR, Allen
Factor, Suzie
FACTOR, Allen
Farrell, Ella
McKAY, Barney
Farris, Nannie T. Coles
FARRIS, Eugene
Faulkner, Julia
FAULKNER, Charles S. C.
Faulkner, Mollie Brown
FAULKNER, Charles S. C.
Fay, Rose Dixie
FAY, Adam
Fechét, Edmond Gustave
WOODS, Brent
Federated Women's Clubs
REYNOLDS, William
Fernandez, Pablo
BURNETT, John
Fillmore, Winslow
ALLEN, David M.
Finkbone, Charlotte Cunningham
CUNNINGHAM, Charles
Finley, Walter Lowry
BYRON, Thomas H.
FINLEY, Augustus
Firmes, Mary I.
FIRMES, Thomas A.
Fisher, King
WASHINGTON, George
Fleming, Edward
MOZIQUE, Edward
Fletcher, Charles
FLETCHER, James Robert
Fletcher, Earnestine C.
FLETCHER, James Robert
Fletcher, Edmonia
FLETCHER, James Robert
Fletcher, Evelyn A.
FLETCHER, James Robert
Fletcher, Fannie
FLETCHER, Nathan
Fletcher, George
FLETCHER, James Robert
Fletcher, Lavinia B.
FLETCHER, James Robert
Fletcher, Lee James
FLETCHER, James Robert

Fletcher, Lucy Beatrice Williams
FLETCHER, James Robert
Fletcher, Luvinia
FLETCHER, James Robert
Fletcher, Norman E.
FLETCHER, James Robert
Fletcher, Roland S.
FLETCHER, James Robert
Fletchheime & Gooskine
(wholesale warehouse), San
Francisco, CA
WILSON, Arthur
Florida
BOWLEGS, David
BOWLEGS, Friday
BOWLEGS, Zack
BYERS, George
Daytona
HARRIS, Joe
FACTOR, Allen
FACTOR, Dembo
FACTOR, Dindie
FACTOR, Hardy (Enlisted 1870)
FACTOR, Hardy (Enlisted 1874)
Ft Barrancas
TAYLOR, Thomas W.
Ft Jefferson
BAQUI, Rodolphe
GOINS, Joshua Van Buren
GORDON, Isaac
HAYWOOD, Joseph
Jacksonville
BENSON, Caleb
BROWN, Henry
GREGG, John A.
JELKES, James B.
LOVELACE, Scott
JOHNSON, Dan
KIBBETTS, John
Lakeland
LEWIS, John E.
WILLIAMS, James Clifford
Madison County
FINNEGAN, Michael
Micanopy
JULY, Sampson
PAYNE, Adam
PAYNE, Caesar
PAYNE, Titus
Pensacola
CARTER, William
GREENE, William H.
SHEPHARD, Henry
PHILIPS, John
PHILIPS, Ned
POLK, Thomas Elzey
St Francis Barracks
ROBINSON, William
WILLIAMS, Elbert
Tampa
ALEXANDER, Fred

PLAIN CAPS indicate names from this volume • **BOLD CAPS** indicate names from *On the Trail* (1995)

BLANEY, William
BURNETT, Ripling
CALLOWAY, John W.
CLARK, Andrew
CLARK, Lig J.
CONN, John
COOK, William L.
COX, Charles
DRY, Will
DUDLEY, John H.
FAGEN, David
GARDNER, William George
HUTTON, George R.
HUTTON, James T.
JACKSON, Levorsiear
JENKINS, Randolph
JOHNSON, John H.
JOHNSON, Louis
MARROW, Anthony A.
MITCHELL, Loyd
PLEDGER, William A., Jr.
POPE, Zachariah
POWELL, George D.
PRESTON, Charles R.
PRIOLEAU, George W.
RICHARDS, James A.
SETPHEIN, Benjamin
SMALLS, Cyrus
SMITH, Arthur
SMITH, Walter E.
STEED, Albert
STRATTON, John H.
TALIAFERRO, Spottswood W.
WALLIS, Ingraham
WILLIAMS, Jessie
WILLIAMS, John G.
WILSON, Thomas P.
WASHINGTON, Andrew
WOOD, John
Flowers, Lucy A.
PRIOLEAU, George W.
Football
BIRD, Savage
CLEMENS, Benjamin
JOSEPH, Leon E.
Foraker, Joseph B.
SANDERS, Mingo
Forbes, Minnie
ALEXANDER, Fred
Forbush, William Curtis
SHORES, Garth
Ford, Cecil B.
FORD, George W.
Ford, Darby
QUEEN, William
Ford, Donald G.
FORD, George W.
Ford, Elise
FORD, George W.
Ford, George, Jr.
FORD, George W.

Ford, Harriet C.
FORD, George W.
Ford, Harriett E. Bythewood
FORD, George W.
Ford, Henrietta Bruce
FORD, George W.
Ford, Henry
BROOKS, Preston
Ford, Rev. J.
ALLENSWORTH, Allen
Ford, James I.
FORD, George W.
Ford, Lucy B.
FLETCHER, James Robert
Ford, Noel B.
FORD, George W.
Ford, Vera
FORD, George W.
Ford, West
FORD, George W.
Foreign Wars, Military Order of
ANDERSON, William T.
Foresters, Independent Order of
PURNELL, William Whipple
Forniss, Cesaria Perazo
FORNISS, George
Forniss, Josephine
FORNISS, George
Forniss, Severiana Tijeria
FORNISS, George
Fort, Bertie G.
FORT, Lewis
Forts, *see states in which located*
Fortune, Timothy Thomas
WOODS, Robert Gordon
Forum Club, Los Angeles, CA
CRUMBLY, Floyd H.
Foster, Theodora Sanches
FOSTER, William
Foushee, Annie W.
HAMLIN, James E.
France. *See also* Meuse-Argonne
Corsica
QUEEN, Howard D.
Metz
QUEEN, Howard D.
Saumur
BAKER, Edward L., Jr
Vosges Mountains
QUEEN, Howard D.
Franklin, Annie B. Walker
FRANKLIN, Alfred J.
Franklin, Fanny
WALL, Archy
Fraternal Printing & Publishing
Company, Chicago, IL
JACKSON, Robert R.
Frazier, Grace Ella Blackburn
BLACKBURN, Joseph A.

Frazier, Hattie
FRAZIER, Jacob
Freedmen's Bank, Macon, GA
STEWARD, Theophilus G
Freedmen's Bureau
ALLENSWORTH, Allen
A Freeman Yet a Slave
(Burlington [IA]: Wohlwend
Bros., printers [1888])
COSTON, W. Hilary
French, James Hansell
CRUMBLE, Richard
Frierson, Julia E.
FRIERSON, Eugene
Gadsden, Elizabeth
STEWARD, Theophilus G.
Gaillard, Helen
WALLACE, Benjamin F.
Galloway, James
GALLOWAY, Alonzo
Gambel, Suzie
GARDNER, William George
Gamble, Heistand
GAMBLE, John E.
Gardner, Emma
GARDNER, William George
Gardner, Mattie Hughes
GARDNER, William H.
Gardner, Rose Mason
MASON, George F.
Gardner, Suzie Gambel
GARDNER, William George
Gate City Drug Co., Atlanta, GA
CRUMBLY, Floyd H.
Geddes, Andrew
BUCKNEY, Wilson
CRAIGE, Richard
PHELPS, William
General Harrison Gray Otis
Marching Club
BATIE, Henry
Genesis Re-Read
STEWARD, Theophilus G.
Georgia
Acworth
MASON, William
Aikenton
HUNTER, Fred
Albany
CLARK, Gordon
Athens
WILLIAMS, Arthur
Atlanta
ANDERSON, John B.
BROWN, Arthur M.
BROWN, David T.
BROWN, Sterling Price
CRUMBLY, Floyd H.
EDWARDS, E. W.
GRANT, Thomas

PLAIN CAPS indicate names from this volume • **BOLD CAPS** indicate names from *On the Trail* (1995)

GREER, Pierce
GUNTER, James
HAWK, Luther M.
JONES, William B.
LOCKHART, Fred
LOVELACE, Scott
LOWE, Albert S.
NORWOOD, West
ROBINSON, Charles
SHORTER, Charles
TAYLOR, Charles I.
WILSON, Arthur
WOODEN, Robert
Augusta
   BRIGGS, Albert J.
   GALLOWAY, Lawrence
   LOCKETT, George
   SIMMONS, Harry
BLANEY, William F.
Brunswick
   CRUMBLY, Floyd H.
Camp G. H. Thomas
   (Chickamauga)
     SMITH, Solomon
     WALKER, Arthur
Canton
   GRISHON, David
Cartersville
   FULLER, Cornelius
Cave Springs
   ALLEN, George
Chickamauga. *See also above*
   Camp G. H. Thomas
     BARNETT, Peter W.
     BURGESS, Ed P.
     CLARKE, Thomas H. R.
     DAVIS, Benjamin O.
     PROCTOR, John C.
     RAY, Albert
     STEWARD, Theophilus G.
     THOMAS, James H.
     WILKES, William
     WILLIAMS, Jessie
COLLIER, Gilbert
Columbus
   KING, Charles
   O'NEAL, Arthur
   SPANKLER, Robert
CORDIN, C. W.
CRUMBLY, Floyd H.
Culloden
   JACKSON, William H.
Dallas
   LYNCH, Luther
Dalton
   BLACK, Solomon
   McCOMBS, Henry
Doraville
   REVERE, Robert
DOUGLASS, Samuel W.
Eatonton
   REID, Augustus

ELLIOTT, James
Forsyth
   SHANNON, George
Ft Benning
   McCAULEY, William
   SPEARMAN, Edward W.
Ft McPherson
   BURBE, Lester
   CHINN, Charles
   FAGEN, David
   GOODE, Benjamin H.
   GREGORY, John T.
   HUNTER, Fred
   MITCHELL, Joseph
   MITCHELL, Loyd
   POOLE, John E.
   PRICE, Charles E.
   SCOTT, John
   SPENCER, Mortimer E.
   STARLING, Eli
   STEED, Albert
   WALLS, Henry F.
FRANGE, Taseo
GOLDEN, Thomas
Griffin
   MYRICK, Sam
GRIFFIN, Isaac
HALL, Thomas
Hampton
   NEALY, James
   HARDAY, Wesley
Hartwell
   RUCKER, DeWitt
HARVEY, Howard
HERD, Ira
JONES, Alexander
Jones County
   GORDON, Henry
LaFayette
   GOODSON, Isaac
La Grange
   COX, George
   CRUMBLY, Floyd H
   JOHNSTON, Charles
   LESLIE, Robert
   WALKER, Henry D.
   WRIGHT, James
Lytle
   BARNETT, Charles
McIntosh
   ARMS, Benjamin
Macon
   ADAMS, Howard
   BROWN, Andrew J.
   BROWN, George W.
   BUCKNER, Earnest
   DANNELS, Milton
   GRANT, Thomas
   HARRIS, Silas
   HILLIARD, Mack
   HOLMES, Thomas
   JONES, John P.

   JONES, Nathan
   McCARTHY, Elijah
   MAYS, Peter
   MIMS, Lewis
   RODGERS, William
   SHELLY, James W.
   STEWARD, Theophilus G
   WILLIAMS, James H.
   WYLIE, Milton
Marietta
   GREEN, William H.
   SADDLER, Louis
   WARING, Robert
   WILLIAMS, Gardner
Milledgeville
   BATES, Henry
   PHILLIPS, Joseph
   SANFORD, Sol
Monroe
   CONYERS, Boyd
Monroe County
   HOMES, Marcus
MONTGOMERY, Everett
MORRIS, Henry
Moss Lake
   ANDERSON, Louis
Newton County
   ANDERSON, John B.
Plains
   TATUM, King James
Quitman
   CLARK, Andrew
RICHARD, Raymond
Roberta
   WEBB, Robert
Rome
   BLACK, Solomon
   CRUMBLY, Floyd H.
   MADDEN, David
SAMPSON, Marshall
Sandersville
   REID, Arthur
Savannah
   GARNEY, John D.
   HOUSTON, Lewis
   JOHNSON, Scott
   LUCAS, Willie
   MILLER, Charles
   SAPP, Wiliam B.
   TURNER, James
SCANDRICH, Jerry
SCOTT, Praley
Spalding County
   EVANS, Frank, Sr.
SPENCER, George
Stewart County
   STEWARD, Theophilus G
Thomasville
   WILLIAMS, Jessie
Thompson, *see below* Thomson
Thomson
   SCOTT, George W.

PLAIN CAPS indicate names from this volume • **BOLD CAPS** indicate names from *On the Trail* (1995)

PLAIN CAPS indicate names from this volume • **BOLD CAPS** indicate names from *On the Trail* (1995)

Hall, Rachel
CASEY, John F.
Hall, Rachel Ann Norman
HALL, Frank W.
RIVERS, Richard
Hall & Haddox, Mowry Mine, AZ, store
HALL, John
Halley, Polley
BERRYMAN, Henry
Hamilton, Rosa Arnold
HAMILTON, William H.
Hamilton, Woodrow Henry
HAMILTON, William H.
Hamlin, Annie Ethel
HAMLIN, James E.
Hamlin, Annie W. Foushee
HAMLIN, James E.
Hamlin, V. C.
HAMLIN, James E.
Hammet, Dora
BLEW, Joseph
Hammond, Dora
ANDERSON, John B.
Hampton Institute, VA
BIVINS, Horace W.
CLEMENS, Benjamin
Hancock, Benjamin
EDMONDS, John
Hancock, Darah
EDMONDS, John
Hancock, Mary
EDMONDS, John
Hancock (ship), *see* U.S. Army Transport *Hancock*
Hanley, Mary
HANLEY, Edward
Hanley, Sarah J.
HANLEY, Edward
Hannay, John Robert Rigby
BENJAMIN, James H.
BROWN, Thomas C.
Hannibal & St. Joseph Railroad
HOWERTON, John C
Hardeman, Letcher
JOHNSON, William
Harding, William Gamaliel
RUCKER, Alfred
Harlan, John M.
ALLENSWORTH, Allen
Harmon, Mrs.
ANDERSON, William T.
Harmon, William R.
JONES, Philip
Harper, Fannie
HARPER, John W.
Harris, Fenton
HENDERSON (D/10th Cav)

Harris, Clara
SMITH, Charles H.
Harris, Estella
CHENAULT, Walter
Harris, Frances Jones
HARRIS, Theodore
Harris, Jane Holland
HARRIS, Hyder
Hart, Suzie
MILLER, Cooper
Hartwell, J. H.
JORDAN, George
Harvard College
STEWARD, Frank R.
Harvard Law School
WILLIAMS, William J.
Hatch, Edward
BADIE, David
BOOTH, Adam
BURLEY, Robert
CARTER, Norman F.
FLETCHER, Nathan
GOODPASTURE, Logan
McKENZIE, Edward
SHAW, Thomas
SYKES, Zekiel
TAYLOR, Stephen
WILSON, James
Hathaway, Fannie
WHITE, Randolph F.
Hawaii
SCOTT, Oscar J. W.
WILLIAMS, Walter B.
Ft Shafter
FIRMES, Thomas A.
Honolulu
BOYD, James
BROWN, William W.
BUTLER, Thomas C.
CHAMBERS, William
HATCHER, Willie
MAHAN, Foster
MAHI, Joe
PRIOLEAU, George W.
Maui
KAHOLOKULA, John
Schofield Barracks
GREEN, Dalbert P.
LAMPLEY, Wellington H.
Hawkins, Charles
HAWKINS, William
Hawkins, Charles B.
HAWKINS, William
Hawkins, Charles L.
HAWKINS, William
Hawkins, Ethel Teresa
HAWKINS, William
Hawkins, Fielder

HAWKINS, William
Hawkins, Ivy Elizabeth
HAWKINS, William
Hawkins, Ivy Lee Johnson
HAWKINS, William
Hawkins, James H.
HAWKINS, William
Hawkins, Joseph Edward
HAWKINS, William
Hawkins, Matilda
PRIDE, Alfred
Hawkins, Mildred Elizabeth
HAWKINS, William
Hawkins, Sarah Brown
HAWKINS, William
Hawkins, Sarah Catherine
HAWKINS, William
Hawkins, William Anthony
HAWKINS, William
Hawley, Heber
BAKER, Edward L., Jr.
Hawley, Mary Elizabeth
BAKER, Edward L., Jr.
Hay, William Henry
BIRD, Robert
BIVINS, Horace
Hayes, Rutherford B.
ALLENSWORTH, Allen
Hazen, William Babcock
GREENE, Hallett
Heard, William H.
BIVINS, Horace W.
Heistand, Henry Olcot Sheldon
PEAL, Allen S.
Helm, Charles
PRIDE, Alfred
Helm, Marcella Pride
PRIDE, Alfred
Henderson, Agnes
HENDERSON (Sergeant)
Henderson, Mary Theodosia Ardella Suaya
HENDERSON, Elmer
Henry, Guy Vernor
BROWN, John
Henry, Julia
BROWN, John
Henson, Jonah Edward
HENSON, John
Hester, James
TAYLOR, John T.
Hester, Mamie E. Taylor
TAYLOR, John T.
Heyl, Edward Miles
BAILEY, Albert
BRADFORD, Harrison
CHARLES, Irving
GOODMAN, Alphonse

HALL, Fayette
HANDY, Frank
HILL, John
WINTHROP, Robert
Heyle, E. M., *see* Heyl, Edward
   Miles
Hibbitt, Harry
   HIBBITT, John
Hibbitt, John, Jr.
   HIBBITT, John
Hibbitt, Mary
   HIBBITT, John
Hibbitt, Savada
   HIBBITT, John
Hibbitt, Willie
   HIBBITT, John
Hicks, Mary E.
   BALLARD, Wilson C.
Higgins, James A.
   DADE, Charles
Hill, Abe
   TAYLOR, John
Hill, Catherine Rebecca
   BROWN, Caesar B.
Hill, Estelle M.
   HOLLIDAY, Presley
Hill, J. T. V.
   BARNETT, Peter W.
Hill, Mrs. Missouri
   HILL, William H.
Holcomb, John
   BANKS, Benjamin
Holcomb, Mary Jane
   BANKS, Benjamin
Holland, Jane
   HARRIS, Hyder
Holliday, Elizabeth
   HOLLIDAY, Presley
Holliday, Estelle M. Hill
   HOLLIDAY, Presley
Holliday, Hope Louise
   HOLLIDAY, Presley
Holliday, Presley, Jr.
   HOLLIDAY, Presley
Hollinger, Camilla
   CLEMMAN, Edward
Holloman, Ida Rebecca
   HOLLOMON, Solomon
Homeopathic Medical College,
   Cleveland
   ANDERSON, William T.
Hood, Fannie Rice
   HOOD, Perry
Hood, Lorraine
   HOOD, Perry
Hood, Millie Wilson
   HOOD, Perry
Hooker, Ambrose Eugene
   BOOTH, Adam

FOSTER, Allen
JACKSON, Thornton
PETERS, David
Horse, John (Seminole chief)
   COON, Joe
   JEFFERSON, John
   JULY, Sampson
   KIBBETTS, John
   PAYNE, Titus
   WASHINGTON, Andrew
   WASHINGTON, George
   WILSON, Bill
   WOOD, John
Hospital Ship *Missouri*
   HIPSHIRE, Riley
How the Black St. Domingo
   Legion Saved the Patriot Army
   in the Siege of Savannah
   STEWARD, Theophilus G.
Howard, Charles
   OWENS, Wesley
Howard, Emma
   HOWARD, William
Howard, Leona M.
   ALLEN, David M.
Howard University
   ANDERSON, William T.
   CAMPBELL, Thomas C.
   JONES, Moses H.
   PURNELL, William Whipple
   QUEEN, Howard D.
   WHITE, Randolph F.
Howe, Jerome H.
   HOUSTON, Henry C.
Howerton, Dewey
   HOWERTON, John C
Howerton, Henry
   HOWERTON, John C
Howerton, Joseph
   HOWERTON, John C
Howerton, Mary Eliza Pollard
   HOWERTON, John C
Howerton, Robert
   HOWERTON, John C
Howerton, Ursula
   HOWERTON, John C
Hubert, Edgar
   BARTON (I/9th Cav)
Hudson, Charles L.
   GRAYSON, Renty
Hudson, Polly Ann
   BROOKS, Preston
Hudson, Robert
   BROOOKS, Preston
Hudson, Zella M. Williams
   WILLIAMS, James Clifford
Hughes, Martin Briggs
   FOWLER, Albert
Hughes, Mattie
   GARDNER, William H.

Hughes' Attitude towards the
   Negro
   McKAY, Barney
Hulme & Kelly flour mills, Great
   Bend, KS
   GLADDEN, Washington
   W. E.
Humfreville, Jacob Lee
   BUCHANAN, William
   COMER, Levi
   DUVAL, George
   IMES, James
   JORDAN, George
   POPE, Malachi
   ROBINSON, Henry
   SLAUGHTER, Rufus
   TUCKER, E.
   WADE, Jim
   WILLIAMS, Jerry
Humphrey, Ballard Smith
   TURNER, Daniel
Humphreys, B. S., *see*
   Humphrey, Ballard Smith
Hungerford, Joseph D.
   PENNY, James T.
Hunt, Celeste F.
   HUMPHREY, Cornelius
Hunt, Clayton
   HUNT (Private)
Hunt, Parthenia
   McDANIELS, Nathaniel
Hunter, Edith
   HUNTER, James O.
Hunter, Suzie
   SMITH, Thomas
Huntt, George Gibson
   ARTHUR, Joseph
Hurd, Lucinda
   SYKES, Zekiel
Hutcheson, Grote
   ALEXANDER, John Hanks
Hysten, Zephyr Archer
   ARCHER, Sylvester
Idaho
   Avery
      JAMES, John
   Bitterroot Mountains
      BUCK, John
   Coeur d'Alene
      HAYDEN, David F.
      HAYES, West
      SMITH, G. W.
      SMITH, Lewis M.
      TELLIES, Robert
Illinois. *See also* Cemeteries
   Alton
      SIMPSON, John
      WASHINGTON, Scott
      ANDERSON, William T.
      ASH, John M.

BATES, William
BAYLESS, John M.
BLACKBURN, John
Bloomington
    JAMESON, Henry W.
BOOKER, Robert
Braidwood
    HOWERTON, John C
BUTLER, Thomas C.
Cairo
    PARKER, Nathan
Champaign
    JAMESON, Henry W.
Chicago. *See also* Cemeteries
    ASHBY, Leo
    BOYER, Carl D.
    BROWN, Arthur M.
    BROWN, Thomas Hatcher
    CALDWELL, Henry
    CALLOWAY, John W.
    CAMPHOR, George
    COLWELL, Lawrence
    COVINGTON, James C.
    DALLANGER, George
    DAVIS, James A.
    DeALEXANDER, Alexis
    FINNEGAN, Michael
    FORD, George W.
    GARRETT, Clarence
    GREEN, Walter
    HODGES, George
    HOLLAND, Irvin W.
    HOLLOMON, Solomon
    HOWERTON, John C
    HURD, William
    JACKSON, Robert R.
    JOHNSON, George
    JONES, William B.
    LANIER, Frank
    LEE, William
    LINDSEY, Henry
    MARSHALL, John R.
    MURPHY, George
    NELSON, Foster L.
    NEWHOUSE, Robert
    ONLY, John
    PARISH, Willie
    PAYNE, Matthew
    PEAL, Allen S.
    POWELL, Samuel
    PURNELL, William Whipple
    RATLIFFE, Benjamin
    RUSH, Wash
    SALTON, Armp
    SMITH, William E.
    STAFFORD, James N.
    STOKES, Marshal
    SYKES, Zekiel
    TANNER, Charles D.
    TERRY, Charles Lincoln
    THOMAS, Benjamin F.
    THOMPSON, John R.

TURNER, Ernest E.
TURNER, Tom
WADE, Lawrence
WALKER, George P.
WALLACE, Lewis W.
WARRICK, Robert
WEST, Sampson
WILLIAMS, John
WILLIAMS, Washington
WILSON, John
WILSON, Will
YEIZER, Mordecai
Cook County
    SYKES, Zekiel
Coulterville
    REES, Ed
Danville
    RATLIFFE, Benjamin
    SMITH, Arthur
Du Quoin
    HOLMES, Robert
East Carondelet
    POPE, Zachariah
East St. Louis
    ANDERSON, William T.
    ATKINS, Jackson
    SINGLETON, George A.
    WOODS, Harry
    YOUNG, Tom
Ft Sheridan
    BAILEY, Isaac
    BARNER, George
    BETTIS, Benjamin
    BIVINS, Horace W.
    DAVIS, Charles
    FLOYD, John
    FOX, Oscar
    GRIFFIN, John
    HAMILTON, William H.
    HAWKINS, Emmett
    HILL, Abraham
    JACKSON, George
    JACKSON, James F.
    JACKSON, John
    JEFFERSON, Horace
    LOGAN, James E.
    MATHEWS, Charles
    NANCE, Fred
    PINKSTON, Irvin
    POWELL, George D.
    PROCTOR, John C.
    REESE, Manning H.
    ROBINSON, Oscar G.
    SANDERS, Chester
    SCARSCE, Henry
    SMITH, Joseph C.
    STILL, Revere N.
    TATE, William
    TAYLOR, William
    THOMAS, Spencer
    WILLIAMS, John
    WILLIAMS, Walter B.

Galena
    JAMESON, Henry W.
Galesburg
    JAMESON, Henry W.
Grand Chain
    YOUNG, Clem
    YOUNG, Seth
Jacksonville
    RAYMOND, Ira Curtis
Malta
    JACKSON, Robert R.
Oak Forest
    WILLIAMS, James Clifford
PENDERGRASS, John C.
Peoria
    FORD, George W.
Riverton
    FORD, George
SMITH, Henry C.
Springfield
    BEARD, George J.
    BLAKEMAN, Robert
    FORD, George W.
    LOGAN, Addie L.
    PENDERGRASS, John C.
    WILLIAMS, Noah W.
Tuscola
    WILLIAMS, Noah W.
WILSON, George
India
    ANDERSON, William T.
    GORDON, Charles
Indian reservations, *see* Pine
    Ridge Reservation, SD; Rose-
    bud Reservation, SD; San
    Carlos Reservation, AZ; Wind
    River Reservation, WY
Indian Territory, *see* Oklahoma
Indian war veterans. *See also*
    National Indian War Veterans
    (organization)
    ALLEN, Frank
    ALLSUP, Thomas H.
    ANDERSON, James
    ANDERSON, William
    BADIE, David
    BAILEY, Isaac
    BAKER, Edward L., Jr.
    BANKS, Plum
    BARD, Benjamin
    BENJAMIN, Robert
    BENSON, Caleb
    BERRY, George
    BISMUKES, Samuel
    BLACKBURN, Joseph A.
    BLAKE, Henry E.
    BLEW, Joseph
    BLUNT, Randall
BOWEN, Major
BOWERS, Edward
BOWLEGS, David

PLAIN CAPS indicate names from this volume • **BOLD CAPS** indicate names from *On the Trail* (1995)

BRADDEN, Alfred
BRANSFORD, Wesley
BRISCOE, Edward
BROADEN, William
BROWN, Benjamin
BROWN, George
BROWN, James
BUCK, John
BURTON, Francis
BURTON, John
BUTLER (Corporal)
CARPENTER, Allen
CARROLL, George
CASEY, John F.
CHAMBERS, Henry
CHAPMAN, Silas
CHRISTOPHER, Andrew
CLARK, Oscar
CLARK, Robert
CLAYBORNE, Peter
CLIFFORD, Charles
COLLYER, S.
COMBS, Richard
COOPER, Frank
COOPER, John
COSBY, Nick
CREEK, Charles
CROPPER, Samuel
CROSBY, T.
CRUMMEL, C. A.
DAVIS, Benjamin F.
DAVIS, Dudley
DAVIS, Edward
DAVIS, Lewis
DAVIS, S.
DAY, John
DEARING, Ruben
DILWOOD, Thomas J.
DOOLEY, William
DUDLEY, John H.
DUKE, Thomas
DUNLAP (Corporal)
EARLY, Anthony
ELLIS, George W.
EVANS, Frank, Sr.
FARRELL, Charles H.
FLINT, Robert T.
FORD, George W.
FOSTER, George
FREELAND, A.
FRY, John
GADSDEN, Peter
GANT, Stephen
GANT, Thomas
GARTRILL, Charles
GIBSON, Edward
GLASBY (Private)
GODFIELD, G.
GOULD, Luther D.
GRAY, Charles
GRAYSON, Renty

GREEN, Ezekiel
GREEN, Lewis T.
GWYNN, Edward
HADDOX, Press
HALL, Christian
HARRIS, George
HARRIS, John
HASKINS, David
HENDERSON, James W.
HILL, Jacob
HILL, William H.
HOLLOMON, Solomon
HOUSTON, Adam
HOWARD, William
INGOMAN, Madison
JEFFERDS, Wesley
JEFFERS, David B.
JEFFERSON, Charles W.
JENKINS, Frank
JENKINS, William
JOHNSON, Henry
JOHNSON, James M.
JOHNSON, Robert J.
JOHNSON, Silas
JOHNSON, Thomas
JOHNSON, William
JONES, Henry C.
JONES, Horatio F. M.
JONES, Lewis
JONES, Lewis
JONES, Philip
KIRTLEY, Preston
KURNEY, Robert
LANE, Edward
LETCHER, Philip
LEWIS, William
LOVE, Charles H.
LOVELACE, Scott
LUMKINS, Ananias
LUST, Houston
LUSTER, Charles
LYMAN, George
McCAULEY, William
McCOMBS, Henry
McCOWN, Peter
MACKADOO, Richard
MADEN, Ebbert
MANN, Simpson
MARSHALL, Hoyle
MARSHALL, Isaac
MARSHALL, John
MATHEWS, Abraham
MILLER, John D.
MILLER, Toler
MORRIS, William S.
MORTON, George
MOSS, John
MURPHY, Israel B.
MURRAY, Charles
NEWMAN, George H.
NOAL, Robert J.

PARKER, John
PATTERSON, Andrew
PATTERSON, Andrew J.
PAYNE, Adam
PENDERGRASS, John C.
PENN, William H.
PERRY, Charles
PHILIPS, James
PHILLIPS, Thomas
POLK, Thomas
POOL, Henry Green
POPE, Zachariah
POSY (Private)
PRICE, Joseph
PUMPHREY, James H.
QUEEN, Edgar
RAY, Albert
REID, John
RICE, Henry
RICH, Frederick
RICHARDSON, Alexander V.
RINGO, Walter
ROBERTS, Dennis
ROBINSON, Henry
ROBINSON, James
ROBINSON, John W.
ROSS, Milton
SCOTT, John
SHELTON, Thomas D.
SHEPARD, Thomas
SHIPLEY, John (Private; D/9th Cav)
SHIPLEY, John (Sergeant; A/9th Cav)
SHROPSHIRE, Shelvin
SIMS, Lewis
SMITH, Arthur
SMITH, Edward
SMITH, George
SMITH, Lewis M.
SMITH, Robert
SMITH, William H.
SNODGRASS, Carlos
SNOTEN, Peter
SPRIGGS, Eliord
STANCE, Emanuel
STROUP, Henry
SUMNER, John
SUTPHIN, William
TERRY, Charles Lincoln
THOMPKINS, William H.
THOMPSON, James A.
THORNTON, Jacob
TIPTON, Samuel J.
TOLIVER, Frederick
TUCKER, George C.
TURNER, Charles B.
TURNER, David
TURNER, William (Corporal; 10th Cav)
TURNER, William (Private; F/10th Cav)
VISITO, Cyle V.

PLAIN CAPS indicate names from this volume • **BOLD CAPS** indicate names from *On the Trail* (1995)

VROOMAN, William A.
WALLACE, Lewis H.
WALLER, Reuben
WARD, Nathan
WAREFIELD, Harry
WASHINGTON, William
WATKINS, James M.
WEATHERLY, James
WEBB, William J.
WHITE, Dillard
WHITE, Frazier
WHITE, John D.
WHITE, Lewis
WIGGINS, John
WILKS, Jacob W.
WILLIAMS, Charles
WILLIAMS, Charley W.
WILLIAMS, James
WILLIAMS, S. W.
WILLIAMSON, David
WILSON, Augustus
WILSON, Edward
WILSON, Richard
WILSON, William O.
YEIZER, Mordecai
YOUNG, William
Indians, *see names of Indians:*
  Black Kettle (Cheyenne chief);
  Costillitto (Lipan Apache chief);
  Geronimo; Horse, John (Semi-
  nole chief); Kid (Apache); Kub-
  bit-che (Seminole chief);
  Mangus (Apache leader);
  Micanopy (Seminole chief);
  Nana (Apache leader); Payne,
  King (Seminole chief); Satank
  (Kiowa chief); Silver Moon
  (Kiowa chief); Sitting Bull,
  Stanta (Kiowa chief); Victorio
  (Apache leader); *see names of
  tribes:* Apaches; Arapahoes;
  Cherokees; Cheyennes
  Comanches; Crees; Kickapoos;
  Kiowas; Sioux; Utes; *see* Trail
  of Tears
Indiana
  Bedford
    HARTSELL, Clarence L.
  Bluffton
    MOSLEY, Benedict
  Brightwood
    HUNTER, James O.
  Connersville
    LEWIS, Edward F.
  Crown Point
    SYKES, Zekiel
  Delphi
    TERRY, Charles Lincoln

Elkhart
  LYONS, James
Evansville
  CLAY, Matthew G.
  DANIELS, Blane J.
  DUNCAN, Lee
  HARRIS, Charles, Jr.
  HARTWOOD, Andrew
  HATCHER, Alex
  McCLAIN, Henry
  PHELPS, Mack
  THOMAS, James H.
  TILLMAN, Lafayette A.
  WILLIAMS, George A.
  GORDON, Isaac
Greencastle
  WILLIAMS, Noah W.
HARRIS, Charles L.
HUNTER, John G.
Indianapolis
  BARNETT, Peter W.
  BELL, Robert
  BIRCH, William A.
  BRANSFORD, Wesley
  CHENAULT, Walter
  DEHONEY, Peter
  EVANS, Samuel T.
  FIELDS, Alfred H.
  GIBSON, James W.
  GREGORY, John T.
  HAMPTON, Jesse
  HEAGAN, Joel
  HIBBITT, John
  HOWERTON, John C.
  JACKSON, Isaac
  McKAY, Barney
  MILLER, Frank A.
  SMITH, John
  THOMAS, James H.
  THOMAS, Millard
  WALKER, Henry
  WATTS, Thomas
JEFFERS, David B.
Jefferson County
  LIVAS, Harry
Jeffersonville
  WALKER, Henry
Lafayette
  WILSON, Alonzo
LaFORCE, David
Lyles
  GREER, Willis
  HARDIMAN, Henry
Madison
  JONES, George
  PHILLIPS, Henry
  TURNER, George C.
Marion
  CHENAULT, Walter
  WALKER, Henry
Mellon, *see below* Mellott

Mellott
  TUMPKIN, Hezekiah
Muncie
  CHENAULT, Walter
New Albany
  HUDNELL, George
New Castle
  POINDEXTER, Horace
Nobleville
  SCOTT, Levi
POWELL, James F.
Richmond
  WILLIAMS, Noah W.
Rushville
  SMITH, Jacob C.
Shirley
  FRANKLIN, James A.
South Bend
  WALLACE, Charles E.
Terre Haute
  BARNETT, Peter W.
  MILLER, Robert
  WILLIAMS, Noah W.
Vincennes
  THOMAS, Samuel
  WIMBERLY, William
Indiana State Normal School,
  Terre Haute
  BARNETT, Peter W.
  WILLIAMS, Noah W.
Indianapolis ABCs
  TAYLOR, Charles I.
Indianapolis *Freeman*
  BARNETT, Peter W.
  GILMER, David J.
  WILLIAMS, Walter B.
Indianapolis *Recorder*
  BARNETT, Peter W.
  CHENAULT, Walter
Infania, Juan
  CRUMBLY, Floyd H.
Ingersoll, Robert Green
  FULBRIGHT, William R.
Ingraham, Mrs. Isaac
  BIVINS, Horace W.
International Boundary
  Commission
  WILLIAMS, Alexander
Interstate Oil, Gas, Mining, &
  Refining Company
  WIGGINS, S. T.
Iowa
  Buxton
    RHODES, Addison G.
  Camp Des Moines
    BARROW, Stephen B.
    BEARD, James E.
    BETTIS, Benjamin
    BOOKER, James W.

PLAIN CAPS indicate names from this volume • **BOLD CAPS** indicate names from *On the Trail* (1995)

BROADUS, Lewis
BROWN, Rosen T.
BROWN, William H., Jr.
BURNES, William T.
COLLIER, William
COMBS, John
CRANSON, James
DEAN, Milton T.
DEHAVEN, John W.
DOUGLAS, Vest
ECTON, Charles
EDWARDS, George F.
ELLIS, Roscoe
EVERETT, James
FIRMES, Thomas A.
GILLUM, William
GILMER, Floyd
GOODNER, Frank M.
GREEN, Miles M.
GREEN, Thomas E.
GREEN, Walter
HALL, George C.
HENDERSON, Almando
HENRY, Vodrey
HOLLAND, George A.
HORNER, Reuben
HOUSTON, Henry C.
JACKSON, London
JOHNSON, Hansom
JOHNSON, William T.
LEWIS, William H.
LINDSEY, John Q.
LYONS, Walter
McLANE, Carey P.
MALONE, Edgar
MARCHBANKS, Vance H.
MARTIN, Cuby
MORRIS, Richard M.
MORROW, Cleveland
PECK, Henry
QUEEN, Howard D.
RAINE, Hazel L.
ROBERTS, Clyde
SANDERS, Chester
SANDERS, Walter P.
SANDRIDGE, Clifford A.
SCOTT, William F.
SEWELL, Fletcher
SHOBE, Robert T.
SMITH, Daniel
SMITH, Russell
SPEARMAN, Edward W.
STAFFORD, Lloyd A.
STEELE, Waddell C.
STITH, William A.
THOMPSON, William W.
TURNER, Samuel
WALKER, John P.
WALLACE, Lewis W.
WASHINGTON, Genoa S.
WATSON, Baxter W.
WILLIAMS, Gus J.

WILLIAMS, Walter B.
WILLIAMS, William H.
WINSTON, George W.
Camp Dodge
   DEAN, Milton T.
Clinton
   RICHARDSON, William
   THOMPSON, George S.
COSTON, W. Hilary
Council Bluffs
   SALTON, Armp
Des Moines
   BLANEY, William F.
   McDOWELL, John H.
   PEAL, Allen S.
   WILLIAMS, James Clifford
Iowa City
   BRUMMSICK, George
Knoxville
   GAMBLE, John E.
Sioux City
   BRUMMSICK, George
   WATKINS, Murray

Italy
   Sardinia
      QUEEN, Howard D.
   Sicily
      QUEEN, Howard D.
Ivins, O. K.
   BENTON, Willie
Jackson, Agnes Marshall
   JACKSON, Emmett J.
Jackson, Alberta Broyles
   BLEW, Joseph
Jackson, Annie B. Thompson
   JACKSON, James F.
Jackson, Annie Green
   JACKSON, Robert R.
Jackson, Eliza
   WANTON, George H.
Jackson, Elizabeth Miller
   JAMESON, Henry W.
Jackson, George
   JACKSON, Robert R.
Jackson, John
   MARSHALL, Albert
   MURRAY, Charles
Jackson, Julia Berry
   JACKSON, Isaac
Jackson, Mrs. L.
   HARRIS, Theodore
Jackson, Naomi
   JACKSON, Robert R.
Jackson, Oliver H.
   JACKSON, Emmett J.
Jackson, Rosa Ann
   MILLIMAN, Jerry
Jackson, Sarah
   YEIZER, Mordecai

Jackson, Sarah L.
   CEPHAS, Joseph E.
Jamaica
   BENJAMIN, Robert
   FISHER, William J.
   PALMER, Joseph
   RICHARDS, James A.
   Kingston
      BENJAMIN, Robert
      HENDERSON, Elmer
      SMITH, George
Jameson, Henry W., Jr.
   JAMESON, Henry W.
Jameson, Lilliam E. Jenkins
   JAMESON, Henry W.
Jameson, Nannie L. Crabb
   JAMESON, Henry W.
Jameson, William
   JAMESON, Henry W.
Japan
   ANDERSON, William T.
   Nagasaki
      CLAY, William
      STREET, William
Jenkins, Elise Ford
   FORD, George W.
Jenkins, Lilliam E.
   JAMESON, Henry W.
Jerger, King of the Zulus
   TAYLOR, Thomas W.
Jersey *Tribune*
   McKAY, Barney
Johns, Carter Page
   MINAR, James L.
Johns, Missouri
   PEREA, Beverly
Johnson, Absalom
   ALLSUP, Thomas H.
Johnson, Alice
   MOZIQUE, Edward
Johnson, Belva
   MOZIQUE, Edward
Johnson, Ben
   JOHNSON, Isaac M.
Johnson, Benjamin
   WILLIAMS, Noah W.
Johnson, Carter Page
   BROWN, David T.
   BROWN, William H.
   NOAL, Robert J.
   SMITH, Lewis M.
   THOMPKINS, William H.
Johnson, Ciley
   McDANIELS, Nathaniel
Johnson, Ella
   WATERS, Charles
Johnson, Elnora Allsup
   ALLSUP, Thomas H.
Johnson, Hannah

McDANIELS, Nathaniel
Johnson, Hattie C.
WILLIAMS, Noah W.
Johnson, Ivy Lee
HAWKINS, William
Johnson, Lewis
FLEMMING, Will
SMITH, John
Johnson, Louise E. Roberts
Washington
WASHINGTON, William
Johnson, Lucilla C.
DEHONEY, Peter
Johnson, Robert
ALLSUP, Thomas H.
Johnson, Roberta
BATIE, Henry
Johson, Sadie H.
ALLSUP, Thomas H.
Johnson, Sallie
WILLIAMS, Noah W.
Johnson, Silas
ALLSUP, Thomas H.
Johnson, William
McDANIELS, Nathaniel
Jones, Annie L. Brown
JONES, Jeremiah
Jones, Fannie Butler
JONES, Seth
Jones, Flora Crumbly
CRUMBLY, Floyd H.
Jones, Frances
HARRIS, Theodore
Jones, Helen
JONES, John A.
Jones, Josie Lee
JONES, Edward
Jones, Mrs. Henry
GAMBLE, John E.
Jones, Nellie
JONES, Silas
Jones, William
JONES, Edward
Jones, Willis N.
CRUMBLY, Floyd H.
Juana, Laures
MOSS, James
July, Carolina
JULY, Sampson
July, Cato
JULY, Sampson
July, Dolly Ward
JULY, Billy
WARD, John
July, Jhonar Laslie
JULY, Carolina
July, Jim
JULY, Charles
July, Martha

JULY, Benjamin
July, Mary
JULY, Sampson
July, Rebecca
JULY, Sampson
WILSON, Bill
July, Sampson
JULY, Carolina
Justices of the Peace
ALEXANDER, John Hanks
OVERR, Oscar
Kansas. *See also* Cemeteries;
Wadsworth Veterans Adminis-
tration Hospital, KS
Atchison
TAYLOR, John P.
BAKER, Edward L., Jr
BATTER (Corporal)
Baxter Springs
COLE, Samuel
Beaver Creek
ANDERSON, James
BROWN, James (1st Sgt; I/10th Cav)
BROWN, James (Private; F/10th
Cav)
BUTLER (Corporal)
COSBY, Nick
CROSBY, T.
CRUMMEL, C. A.
DANIELS, John
GARTRILL, Charles
JOHNSON, William
MARSHALL, Isaac
MURRAY, Charles
ROBINSON, John W.
SHEPARD, Thomas
SMITH, Thomas
THORNTON, Jacob
TURNER, William
WALLER, E.
WALLER, Reuben
Beecher's Island, Arickaree River
THOMAS, James H.
WALLER, Reuben
Big Creek
HARPER, Henry
BROWN, J.
Buffalo Creek
SALLEY, Coleman
Caldwell
BOYNE, Thomas
GOLDSBOROUGH, William H.
Camp Cary Sanger
GOOSLEY, Samuel
Camp Hoffman
WETHERLY, Richard
CARROLL, George
Cimarron Crossing
MILLER, Thomas
Claridy, Henry

Coffeyville
WIGGINS, S. T.
Concordia
BUSH, James W.
CRUMBLE, C. A.
DAVIS, Ed
Dodge City
BRABHAM, Jeremiah
COOK, Charles
Doniphan County
HOWERTON, John C.
DOOLEY, William
El Dorado
WALLER, Reuben
Elk City
TAYLOR, John
Emporia
GREGG, John A.
Eureka
GREGG, John A.
FORD, George W.
Ft Arbuckle
AIKIN, John P.
FORD, George W.
Ft Dodge
BALDOCK, Thomas
BUTLER, Patrick
CARSON, Hiram
CLAYBORNE, Peter
CRAWFORD, Preston
CROWDY, George W.
GARTRILL, Christopher
GORDON, Isaac
HAWKINS, Charles
HOWARD, James
JASON, William
JOHNSON, John H.
JOHNSON, Joseph
MILLER, George A.
MORTON, Thomas
OLIVER, William
POSEY, Abner
RICHARDSON, William
ROSS, William
SMITH, Benjamin
STEVENS, John
SWEENEY, Robert
WILSON, James
Ft Harker
BOROLER, William
CULLINS, John
DORSETT, Edward
HOWARD (Corporal)
JOHNSON, Richard
MARTIN, Charles
NELIS (QM Sgt)
PHILLIPS, Andrew
ROBINSON, Bill
STEWART, Moses
TAYLOR (Sergeant)
THORNTON, Jacob
TURNER, Tom

WALLER, Reuben
WILLIAMS, Cathay
Ft Hays
ARMSTRONG, William
BALDOCK, Thomas
BATTIES, Edward
BOWERS, Charles
BRISCOE, Henry
BURKS, Dock
BURTON, Hardy
CHRISTOPHER, Andrew
DANDRIDGE, Richard
DAVIS, Frank
DUNCAN, Austin
FORD, George W.
GAINES, Henry
GAINES, Levin S.
GREEN, George
HUMPHREY, John
JACKSON, Thornton
JOHNSON, Edward
LOGAN, John
McMAHON, Andrew
MILES, Sandy
MILESTON, Fillmore
MILLSTONE, Tillmon
NICHOLS, Richard
PARKER, Henry
PICKENS, Peter
PITTMAN (Sergeant)
RANDALL, John
ROGERS, Nathan
SCOTT, Frank
SCOTT, Sterling
SIMPSON, William
SYKES, Zekiel
THOMAS, William
TILLARY, Albert
TURNER, Tom
TURPIN, Edward
WALLER, Reuben
WALTERS, Joseph
WARREN, Samuel
WESLEY, Augustus
WHITE, John
WISMAN, Robert
Ft Larned
BAKER, George
BENNIN, Thomas
HAROLD, Aleck
MASON, Willie
TURNER, Henry
WHITE, John
WILLIAMS, James W.
WILLIAMS, John W.
WILSON, Augustus
Ft Leavenworth. *See also* Cemeteries
ACKFORTH, William
ACRE, Henry
ADAMS, Alexander
ADAMS, Henry
ADAMS, Howard

ADAMS, John
ADAMS, John
AIKEN, Flex
ALBERT, John
ALDNGE, George
ALDRIDGE, George
ALEXANDER, Andrew
ALEXANDER, Cook
ALEXANDER, John Hanks
ALEXANDER, Joseph
ALEXANDER, Thomas
ALLEN, Henry
ALLEN, Hubert F
ALLEN, Willie
ALLEY, John
ANDERSON, Charles
ANDERSON, George
ANDERSON, George W.
ANDERSON, Isaac
ANDERSON, James (Private; F/10th Cav)
ANDERSON, James (Corporal; M/10th Cav)
ANDERSON, Jenon
ANDERSON, Robert
ANDERSON, William
ANDERSON, William H.
ANSIL, Jeramiah
ARMSTRONG, Allen
ARMSTRONG, William
ARNOLD, Joseph
ASH, Joseph
ASH, Ruben
AVERY, Stephen
BACON, Martin
BADIE, David
BADY, Robert
BAILEY, Willis
BAILY, William
BAINES, Arthur
BAKER, Franklin M.
BAKER, George
BAKER, John
BAKER, William (Private; A/10th Cav)
BAKER, William (Recruit; B/10th Cav)
BALDOCK, Thomas
BALDWIN, Andrew
BALLANGER, George
BALMAN, John
BANKS, Robert
BANKS, Robert B.
BARNETT, George E.
BARNSWELL, John
BARTON, Hardy
BARTON, Henry
BATES, Anchor
BATTIAS, Edward
BEAMON, William Henry
BEARD, George
BEARD, Oatis

BEASLEY, Arnie
BELL, James
BELL, John
BELL, Matthew
BENNETT, Aleck
BENNETT, William
BENNIN, Thomas
BERNHARD, Robert
BEVERLY, William
BIGGER, William
BILLINGS, John
BINNS, Robert
BIRT, Cape
BISHOP, Alexander
BIVENS, George E.
BLACK, Allen
BLACK, Charles
BLACK, William
BLACKBURN (D/10th Cav)
BLANCH, John
BLAND, William
BLASTON, Francis M.
BOADLEY, Levi
BOLLING, Willie
BOMEN, Austin
BOMEN, Samuel
BOND, James Oliver
BOODSON, Frank
BOOKES, Albert
BOOKS, Robert
BOON, Andrew
BOROLER, William
BORZOTIE, James
BOUDOW, John
BOWEN, Austin
BOWEN, Major
BOWERS, Charles
BOYD, John
BOZIER, Charles
BRABHAM, Jeremiah
BRADSHAW, William
BRAIN, Norman
BRIDGES, Randell
BRIGGS, Moses
BRIGHT, Perry
BRIGHTWELL, Henry
BROOKINGS, George W.
BROOKS, Clifford
BROOKS, Henry
BROOKS, Robert H.
BROOKS, Thomas
BROOMFIELD, George
BROWN, Benjamin
BROWN, Charles R.
BROWN, Edward
BROWN, George L.
BROWN, Griggs
BROWN, James
BROWN, James E.
BROWN, John (Private; A/10th Cav)
BROWN, John (Private; E/10th Cav)

PLAIN CAPS indicate names from this volume • **BOLD CAPS** indicate names from *On the Trail* (1995)

BROWN, John (Private; H/10th
Cav)
BROWN, John H.
BROWN, Thomas
BROWN, William
BRYSON, Walter
BULLARD, William H.
BUMSIDE, Robert
BURGESS, Lewis
BURLEY, Robert
BURNHAM, William
BURNS, Charles
BUSH, Robert
BUTLER, Lewis
BUTLER, Nathaniel
CAGER, John T.
CAGLE, Walter W.
CAIN, Adam
CALDWELL, Arthur
CALDWELL, Frank
CALDWELL, William
CALHOUN, James N.
CAMIL, William
CAMPBELL, James (Private;
B/10th Cav)
CAMPBELL, James (Private;
D/10th Cav)
CAMPBELL, William
CANIE, Alexander
CARPENTAR, Kenny
CARPENTER, John
CARR, John M.
CARROLL, Charles H.
CARSON, Earley
CARSON, Hiram
CARTER, Charles McD.
CARTER, Frederick
CARTER, James
CARTER, Lewis
CARTER, William
CARTY, James
CARVIN, John
CASTILLO, Pedro
CATHEY, Joseph
CAULDER, Charles
CHANDLER, Alphonzo
CHAPMAN, Wilson
CHOLIKELY, Alonzo
CHRISTOPHER (Private)
CIRCY, James
CLAGGETT, John H.
CLAGGETT, Joseph
CLAPTON, Alexander
CLARK, Charles
CLARK, Cornelius
CLARK, James
CLARK, Richard
CLARKE, John W.
CLARKE, Ollie
CLARY, Henry
CLAY, William
CLAYBORN, John

CLAYBORNE, Peter
CLAYTON, James
CLINTON, Francis
CLOMPTON, Jethro
CLYBURN, Peter
CODY, Nick
COLBERT, Boyd
COLE, Pollard
COLEMAN, Fortino
COLLANO, John
COLWELL, Aaron
CONE, William
CONTEE, James S.
COOPER, John
CORBITT, George
CORINGTON, Wiley
CORK, Adam
COSTLY, John
COUTTS, Frank
COXMIRE, Amos
CRADDOCK, Calvin
CRAIG, Thomas B.
CRAPPER, John
CRIFF, Samuel
CRISTY, William
CROSS, Harvey
CROSS, William
CROWDER, Julius
CROWDER, Rufus
CROWDER, William
CROWDER, William A.
CRUDER, William
CRUMP, Edward W.
CUMMERS, William
CURRY, Perry
CUTHBERT, John F.
DAILY, Daniel T.
DANDRIDGE, Richard
DANIEL, Thomas
DANIELS, Hayes
DANIELS, Jordan
DANIELS, Thomas
DARCOTT, Thomas
DAVID, James
DAVIS, Benjamin O.
DAVIS, Charles
DAVIS, Charles D.
DAVIS, Charles H.
DAVIS, Cornelius
DAVIS, Edward (Private; K/9th
Cav)
DAVIS, Edward (Private; K/9th Cav,
born in Nashville, TN)
DAVIS, Henry
DAVIS, Sam
DAVIS, Silas
DENNIS, Clark
DICEY, Dennis
DICKERSON, William
DICKSON, Solomon
DIXON, Alfred
DIXON, Carrol

DIXON, Charles
DIXON, David
DIXON, John
DOBBS, George
DOBBS, Scipin
DODD, Charles
DODGE, Cleveland
DOOLEY, William
DORSETT, Edward
DORSEY, George
DORSEY, John
DOUGHERTY, Charles
DOUGLAS, Daniel
DOUGLAS, Turner
DRAIN, Simeon
DRUMMAN, Hamilton
DUMAS, Washington W.
DUNCAN, Austin
DUNN, David
EDMONDS, Robert
EDMONDS, Thomas
EDWARDS, Julius
EDWARDS, Robert
EGLIN, Ellis Moss
ELLINGTON, Jacob
ELMORE, Thomas
ENOICE, William
EVANS, Aaron
EVANS, Charles
EVANS, Edward
EVANS, Elleck
EVANS, Henry
EVANS, John
EWING, Jacob
FARLEY, Beauford
FARRELL, Louis
FEDER, Mathew
FERGUSON, James
FIELDS, Frank
FIELDS, George
FILL, Haron
FISHER, Henry
FISHER, Robert
FISHER, Samuel
FITCH, Thomas N.
FITTISWATER, John
FLETCHER, Edward
FLETCHER, Nathan
FLETCHER, Stephen
FLOWERS, Benjamin
FORD, George W.
FORD, Jefferson
FORD, Thomas
FOSTER, George
FOSTER, Larkin
FOSTER, Lorenzo
FOSTER, Peter
FOSTER, Samuel
FREDERICK, John
FREELAIN, William
FREEMAN, Augustus C.
FREEMAN, Jerry B.

PLAIN CAPS indicate names from this volume • **BOLD CAPS** indicate names from *On the Trail* (1995)

FRISBY, Isaac
FRY, Edward
FULLER, Cornelius
FUQUA, Eulous
GABBOND, Moses
GADMIN, Willis
GAINS, Henry
GALLOWAY, William
GARDNER, William
GARDNER, William A.
GARDNER, William H.
GAREY, Charles
GARFIELD, James
GARNETT, George R.
GARRISON, Richard
GARTRILL, Christopher
GIBBS, Franklin
GIBBS, John
GIBBS, Senior
GIBSON, George
GIBSON, Robert
GIBSON, Thomas
GIBSON, William
GILBERT, Charles
GILBERT, Wilson S.
GILMORE, Frank
GIVENS, Edward
GLADDEN, Washington W. E.
GOLDEN, John
GOODRUM, Jack
GOODWINE, Nathan
GRAHAM, William
GRANT, Frank
GRANT, William D.
GRANVILLE, John A.
GRAY, Lewis
GRAYER, Frank
GREEN, Bailey
GREEN, Edward
GREEN, Frank E.
GREEN, George (Private; E/10th Cav)
GREEN, George (Private; F/10th Cav)
GREEN, Wesley
GREENE, William
GRESON, William
GRIDER, Henry
GRIFFIN, Henry
GRIGSBY, Jeff
GRISSEN, Daniel
HACKET, Robert
HAILSTALK, James
HALE, Lewis
HALE, William
HAMILTON, Charles
HAMILTON, Ernest
HAMILTON, Nelson
HAMILTON, Thomas
HAMMIN, Wyle
HAMON, Charles
HAMPTON, Thornton

HANES, George
HANNOVER, John
HARDEN, William J.
HARMON, Charles
HARPER, Clay
HARPER, Henry
HARRILLA, Lews
HARRIS, Aleck
HARRIS, Gene
HARRIS, George
HARRIS, Henry (1)
HARRIS, Henry (2)
HARRIS, James
HARRIS, Jerry
HARRIS, Jesse
HARRIS, Silas
HARRIS, William
HARRISON, George
HARRISON, Henry
HARWARD, Lewis
HAWKINS, Henry
HAYDEN, Thomas
HAYE, Henry
HAYS, Jackson
HAYS, James
HAYS, John
HEGWOOD, Samuel
HENDERSON, Charles
HENDERSON, Edward
HENDERSON, George
HENRY, James
HENRY, Thomas (A/10th Cav)
HENRY, Thomas (F/10th Cav)
HENSLEY, John
HENSON, John
HICKS, Charles H.
HICKS, Stephen
HIGGINS, Ansas
HILDRETH, Sandy
HILL, Bolton H.
HILL, H. W.
HILL, Rubin
HINES, Sylvester
HIPSHER, Wiley
HOCKADAY, William
HODSDEN, Euclid T.
HOGEKINS, John
HOGINS, Jerry
HOLLIDAY, Henry
HOLLIER, William
HOLLINS, Robert
HOLLSMEER, George
HOLMES, Walter S.
HOOD, John
HORNOLD, Aleck
HOUSTON, Andrew
HOWARD, James
HUBBARD, David W.
HUCKSTEP, Henderson
HUGHES, Isaac
HUKA, Stephen
HULEY, James

HULL, Thornton
HUMKINS, Andrew
HUMPHERY, John H.
HUNT, Eugene
HUNT, Simon
HUNTER, Samuel
INGRAM, Roy
ISAIAH, Basil
IVANS, Lewis
JACKSON, Alexander
JACKSON, Andrew
JACKSON, Brown
JACKSON, Charles
JACKSON, Harvey
JACKSON, James
JACKSON, Jerry
JACKSON, Jesse
JACKSON, John
JACKSON, Samuel (B/10th Cav)
JACKSON, Samuel (H/10th Cav)
JACKSON, William
JACOBS, Henry
JAMES, Henry
JAMES, John
JAMES, William
JENKINS, Andrew
JENKINS, Tillman
JOHNSON, Edward
JOHNSON, Ernie
JOHNSON, Frank
JOHNSON, Green
JOHNSON, Henry (F/10th Cav)
JOHNSON, Henry (A/10th Cav)
JOHNSON, Henry (G/10th Cav)
JOHNSON, Henry W.
JOHNSON, Isaiah
JOHNSON, Isiak E.
JOHNSON, James
JOHNSON, James E.
JOHNSON, Jim
JOHNSON, Joseph
JOHNSON, Lewis
JOHNSON, Mack
JOHNSON, Richard
JOHNSON, Robert
JOHNSON, Samuel (A/10th Cav)
JOHNSON, Samuel (Band/24th Inf)
JOHNSON, Simon
JOHNSON, William
JOHNSON, William
JOHNSON, Wyatt
JOHNSON, York
JOHNSTON, William B.
JONES, Alfred
JONES, B.
JONES, Charles S.
JONES, Edward
JONES, Emanuel
JONES, Henry
JONES, Jesse
JONES, John

PLAIN CAPS indicate names from this volume • **BOLD CAPS** indicate names from *On the Trail* (1995)

JONES, Manuel
JONES, Mitchell
JONES, Robert
JONES, Silas
JONES, Wallace
JONES, William (A/10th Cav)
JONES, William (C/10th Cav)
JONES, William H.
JORDON, Robert
KANE, George
KEATES, Charles
KELLAM, Alfred
KELLEY, George B.
KELLEY, George W.
KENDALL, Jackson
KENEDY, Washington
KEWCONDA, Benjamin
KEY, Charles
KIDD, Henry
KIMBLE, Richmond
KING, Randall
KING, William
KING, Willie
KURNEY, Robert
LACY, George
LAND, Robert
LANDIES, George
LAOOS, Lewis
LATONE, Foichoill
LATTY, John
LAWERANCE, Frank E.
LAWRENCE, Earnest
LAWSON, Davis
LAWSON, Frank
LEAKE, Lawrence M.
LEE, Henry (A/10th Cav)
LEE, Henry (B/10th Cav)
LEE, Herman
LEE, Jordan
LEE, Robert E.
LEE, Samuel
LEE, Warren
LEELY, Robert
LENIOUS, Alfred
LEONARD, John E.
LETCHER, Philip
LEVENBERRY, Arthur
LEWIS, Charles
LEWIS, George
LEWIS, James
LIGGINS, Robert
LIGGINS, William
LIGHER, James
LIMISON, Frank
LITTLE, William
LIVINGSTON, James
LOGAN, Isam
LOGAN, John
LOGERN, Thomas
LOKEMAN, Alferdo
LONE, Milton
LONG, Charles

LOOMIS, Amos
LOVE, Frank W.
LOWE, Hampton
LUCAS, Aron
LUSK, John H.
LYNCH, Washington
LYONS, John
LYONS, Lewis
LYONS, Wilson
LYTLE, John
McBRYAR, William
McCAW, Melvin
MacCRARY, Andrew
McEWING, Duke
McKENZIE, Edward
McKINSEY, Meack
McLAUGHLIN, Ephraim
McLEARY, James
McMICKEN, William
McNEAR, Elijah
MACON, Joseph
McPHERSON, Alfred
MAIN, Mark
MALONE, James E.
MARIN, Benjamin
MARSHALL, Isaac
MARSHALL, John
MARTIN, George
MARTIN, John
MARTIN, Lloyd D.
MASON, George
MASON, Samuel
MASON, Thomas
MATES, Barlett
MATHEWS, Charles E.
MATHEWS, William
MATTHEWS, Daniel
MAXWELL, George
MAXWELL, William
MEAD, David H.
MEINE, James
MILERTON, Filevions
MILES, James
MILES, Joseph
MILES, Silas
MILES, Williams
MILLER, Alexander
MILLER, Edwin
MILLER, George A.
MILLER, Homer
MILLER, John R.
MILLER, Samuel
MIMS, Charles
MIMS, Lewis
MINER, William
MINOR, Francis
MITCHELL, George
MODELIN, Alexander
MONROE, James
MONTGOMERY, Seaborn
MOORE, Columbus
MOORE, Ellis E.

MOORE, Henry
MOORE, John
MOORE, Richard
MOORE, Russell
MOORE, Sam B.
MORATIER, Charles
MORGAN, John
MORROW, William
MORSE, James
MOTT, William
MURPHY, Joseph
MURRAY, Charles
MURRAY, Clinton
MURRAY, James H.
MURRAY, John A.
MUSON, Thomas
NEVITT, John W.
NICHOLSON, George H.
NILES, John R.
NORRIS, Benjamin
NORTHROP, Clark H.
NORTON, West
OLIVER, William
OWENS, Stephan
PARKER, Hiram C.
PARKER, John
PATTERSON, Albert
PATTERSON, William (Private;
    C/10th Cav)
PATTERSON, William (QM Sgt;
    G/9th Cav)
PATTON, John
PECK, Henry
PERKINS, Frank
PERKINS, Thomas
PERRY, Charles E.
PERRY, Jerry
PETER, Simon
PETERS, Richard W.
PETINO, William
PETTIGREW, William M.
PETTIS, Charles M.
PHILLIPS, Andrew
PHILLIPS, Thomas
PICKENS, Peter
PICKINGPACK, Thomas J.
PIERCE, James
PIERCE, William
PIERCE, William P.
PINKLE, Scott
PIPES, Nelson
PITTS, Hoppie
POLK, Thomas Elzey
POPE, Zachariah
POPER, William
PORTEE, Wade H.
PORTER, Issac
PORTER, Johnson
POSEY, Moure
POTTER, Ewing
POWELL, Toby
PRATER, Lonie

PLAIN CAPS indicate names from this volume • **BOLD CAPS** indicate names from *On the Trail* (1995)

PRICE, Brady D.
PRICE, John D.
PROCTOR, Charles R.
PULLIAMS, Alfred
PUMPHREY, George W.
RAMSEY, Henry
RANDALL, John
RANSOM, James
RATCLIFF, Toney
RATCLIFF, Tony
REDMAN, Jesse I.
REED, George
REED, James
REED, James T.
REED, Richard
REESE, Cicero
REID, Edward C.
RICHARDSON, Jefferson
RICHARDSON, William
RICKERT, Eugene
RIVERS, William
ROBESIN, Peter
ROBINSON, Bill
ROBINSON, David
ROBINSON, Henry
ROBINSON, John
ROBINSON, John
ROBINSON, John W.
ROBINSON, William H.
ROE, John W.
ROGERS, Edward
ROGERS, Samuel
ROLAND, Samuel
ROLLINS, Green
ROSE, Amos
ROSE, John W.
ROSS, Hercules
ROWLETT, John C.
ROYSTER, George
ROYSTON, Jim
RUFFING, William
RUSSELL, Clarence
RUSSELL, Moses
SALLEY, Coleman
SAMPSON, Charles
SANDERS, Braxton
SANDERS, Sidney
SANFORD, Sol
SASSDESS, Bass
SATCHELL, J.
SAWYER, Joseph
SAXTON, Sam
SCHLOSS, Columbus
SCOTT, Edward
SCOTT, Hugh C.
SCOTT, Isaac
SCOTT, Joseph
SCOTT, Robert
SCOTT, William
SCOTT, William
SCRUGGS, Gilbert
SEAWRIGHT, Albert

SEBASTON, Lewis (A/10th Cav)
SHAW, Thomas
SHAWN, Edward
SHEPARD, Thomas
SHEPPARD, Bernhard
SHEPPARD, William
SHERWOOD, Edward
SHIELDS, Frank H.
SIMMINS, George
SIMMONS, Anderson
SIMMONS, Frank
SIMMONS, William
SIMMONS, William H.
SIMON, John J.
SIMPSON, Williams
SKINIER, James T.
SMALLS, George W.
SMART, Robert
SMISH, John
SMITH, Albert
SMITH, Alexander
SMITH, Anis
SMITH, Augustus
SMITH, Benjamin
SMITH, Charles
SMITH, Ewing
SMITH, Frederick (1)
SMITH, Frederick (2)
SMITH, Henry W.
SMITH, Jacob C.
SMITH, James (1)
SMITH, James (2)
SMITH, John (D/10th Cav)
SMITH, John (G/10th Cav)
SMITH, Keith H.
SMITH, Lewis
SMITH, Mathew
SMITH, Robert A.
SMITH, Stanley
SMITH, Thomas
SMITH, William
SNOTEN, Peter
SOLOMON, Abraham
SOLOMON[?], Miles
SOYSERN, Shelson
SPEAKES, James
SPRIGGS, Eliord
ST. CLAIR, Aron
STAFF, Edward
STEEL, Elder
STEPHENSON, Henry
STEVENS, John
STEVENSON, William
STEVESON, James W.
STEWART, Charles S.
STEWART, John
STEWART, William
STOKES, Isaac
STONE, Arthur
STRONG, Christopher
SUMMERS, Matthew
SUMMERS, Michael

SWEENEY, Robert
SYKES, Zekiel
TAYLOR, Benjamin
TAYLOR, Daniel T.
TAYLOR, James
TAYLOR, John
TAYLOR, Lewis
TAYLOR, Stephen
TAYLOR, Thomas W.
TAYLOR, William (A/10th Cav)
TAYLOR, William (D/10th Cav)
TAYLOR, Willie
TEDDER, John
TERRY, George
THISTLE, James T.
THOMAS, Charles
THOMAS, Hardin
THOMAS, James H.
THOMAS, John (Sergeant; C/10th Cav)
THOMAS, John (G/10th Cav)
THOMAS, Lankin
THOMAS, Marcus
THOMAS, Napoleon
THOMAS, Spencer
THOMAS, William
THOMAS, William
THOMAS, Willis
THOMPSON, Aleck
THOMPSON, Harvey A.
THOMPSON, John (E/10th Cav)
THOMPSON, John (H/10th Cav)
THORNTON, Cliff
THRASH, Robert
THURSTON, Jacob
TILLIMON, Britton
TINSLEY, George
TORTE, John
TRICKLER, Joyner
TUCKER, Daniel
TURKIN, Edward
TURNER, Henry
TURNER, Peter H.
TURNER, Samuel
TURNER, Thomas
TURNER, William
TURNER, William
UICEY, Samuel
VIELE, Madison
WADE, Chester
WADE, Henry
WAIN, William
WALEY, Thomas
WALKER, James
WALKER, John
WALKER, Thomas
WALLER, John L.
WALLER, Reuben
WALSH, William
WAMAN, Aleck
WARD, Joseph
WARREN, George

PLAIN CAPS indicate names from this volume • **BOLD CAPS** indicate names from *On the Trail* (1995)

WASHINGTON, David L.
WASHINGTON, George
WASHINGTON, Grand G.
WASHINGTON, John H.
WASHINGTON, Peter
WASHINGTON, William
WATERS, Benjamin
WATKINS, Calib
WATKINS, Isaac
WATKINS, Major
WATKINS, Wesley
WEATHERLY, James
WEBB, Moses
WEBBER, Perry M.
WESSON, James L.
WEST, Henry
WEST, Melvin L.
WETHERLY, Richard
WHEELER, Pride
WHINE, Minton
WHITE, Fitan
WHITE, George (C/10th Cav)
WHITE, George (Private; 9th Cav)
WHITE, Harry
WHITE, Janas
WHITE, John
WHITE, Joseph
WHITE, Tony
WHITE, William
WHITEHEAD, William
WHITWORTH, Judge
WHYTHE, Johnson
WILKES, William
WILKESON, Peter
WILKO, Abraham
WILLIAMS, Arlan
WILLIAMS, Charles
WILLIAMS, Charles
WILLIAMS, Daniel
WILLIAMS, Darryl
WILLIAMS, David
WILLIAMS, Henry
WILLIAMS, James
WILLIAMS, James (D/10th Cav)
WILLIAMS, James (G/10th Cav)
WILLIAMS, Jerry
WILLIAMS, Joe
WILLIAMS, John (B/10th Cav)
WILLIAMS, John (C/10th Cav)
WILLIAMS, John (1st)
WILLIAMS, John (2nd)
WILLIAMS, Joliet W.
WILLIAMS, Norman
WILLIAMS, Robert
WILLIAMS, Rodney
WILLIAMS, Samuel
WILLIAMS, Thomas
WILLIAMS, Van
WILLIAMS, Walter B.
WILLIAMS, Willie H.
WILLIAMSON, Alexander
WILLIAMSON, David

WILSON, Broslon
WILSON, George
WILSON, George
WILSON, Henry
WILSON, Herbert
WILSON, James (Sergeant; C/10th Cav)
WILSON, James (Private; B/10th Cav)
WILSON, Jasper
WILSON, John
WILSON, Julius
WILSON, Tede
WINSLOW, Oliver
WIRLEY, Augustus
WOODS, Noah
WOODS, Woodson
WOODWARD, Major
WORLEY, George
WORTHINGTON, Moses
WRIGHT, Boyer
WRIGHT, James
WRIGHT, Thomas (A/10th Cav)
WRIGHT, Thomas (B/10th Cav)
YOUNG, Charles
YOUNG, Douglass
YOUNG, James
YOUNG, John W.
YOUNG, Roman
YOUNGS, Arthur B.

Ft Riley
ADAMS, John
AIKEN, John H.
ALEXANDER, William C.
ALLEN, George
ALLEN, Thomas F.
ANDERSON, Andrew
ANDERSON, Benjamin A.
ANDERSON, Cornelius
ANDERSON, Henry
ANDERSON, William T.
ANKIN, Edward
ASH, Alexander
BADY, George
BAKER, Edward L., Jr
BAKER, Jesse
BALDRIDGE, John
BANKS, Isaac
BARNES, Andrew
BARNES, Henry S.
BARNES, James H.
BATES, Richard
BAUSBRY, Arthur
BECHERES, Isaac
BELL, Andrew (M/10th Cav)
BELL, Andrew (I/10th Cav)
BELL, Benjamin
BELL, Ernie
BELL, John
BENNETT, Frank D.
BERRY, George
BIDDLE, George

BLACKBURN, Joseph A.
BOLLEN, William H.
BOWMAN, John
BOYD, Daniel
BRACKETT, Joseph
BRADFORD, Caesar
BRADLEY, William
BRAHAM, Josiah
BREWSTER, William
BRICE, Walter H.
BRIDGEWATER, Scott
BROCK, William H.
BROOKS, Isaiah
BROOKS, Preston
BROWN, Charles W.
BROWN, Daniel
BROWN, Darrell
BROWN, George H.
BROWN, James (Private; K/10th Cav)
BROWN, James (1st Sgt; I/10th Cav)
BROWN, John
BROWN, Robert
BRYANT, George
BRYANT, Jessey H.
BURDETTE, Nelson
BURKS, Dock
BURNS, Doc
BURTON, John
BUTLER, Benjamin G. W.
BUTLER, John H.
BUTLER, Patrick
CALDWELL, Henry
CALDWELL, Lewis A.
CALLEY, Elmwood
CAMPBELL, Henry
CARR, James
CARTER, Isaac
CARTER, James
CEIGHTON, Franklin
CHAPMAN, Henry
CHEATHAM, Alexander
CIRINTEE, Charles
CLARY, Heiney
CLAUGHS, Frank
COLEMAN, James
COLLINS, Francis
CONONDY, Noah
CONYERS, Alexander
COOK, Cyrus
COOTS, Robert
CORNISH, Isaac S.
COTTON, Stephen W.
COX, James
CRAICE, George
CRAWFORD, Henry
CROOK, Anthony
CROWDY, George W.
CROWN, George
CRUMP, Horace
CUNNINGHAM, Samuel

PLAIN CAPS indicate names from this volume • **BOLD CAPS** indicate names from *On the Trail* (1995)

CURTIS, Felix
DAGGS, William H.
DANIELS, John
DAPSON, Augustus
DARRACE, John
DAVIS, Benjamin F.
DAVIS, James
DAVIS, William (1)
DAVIS, William (2)
DENMARK, Hamilton
DENNIS, Alfred
DENNIS, Janius
DENT, Henry
DICKERSON, Richard T.
DIXON, Frank
DIXON, Henry
DOLMAN, Norman
DORILY, John
DORSEY, Henry
DORSEY, James
DORSEY, Trace
DOUGLAS, William
DUESCAIR, Ortise
DULTON, John
EDDY, William
EDMONDS, Ralph
ELLISON, James
ELSBERRY, Isaiah C.
EMPOIRE, Theodore
EVANS, Isaac
FACE, Bucker
FAIRHOLDS, Charles
FARRELL, Charles H.
FISHER, Ruben
FLETCHER, Isaiah
FLOWERS, Robert
FLOYD, William
FOLLIERAU, Frank
FORD, George W.
FORD, William H.
FOX, George
FREEMAN, George M.
FRIERSON, Eugene
FROST, John
FULLER, Peter
GABBARD, Monroe
GADDEN, Parris
GAINES, Joseph
GALAGER, Samuel
GARNETT, Robert
GARRETT, James
GARROD, James
GIBBS, James
GIBINS, William
GIBSON, James W.
GLOVER, Robert
GOLDSMITH, Jefferson
GOODMAN, Alfred
GORMER, Richard
GRATES, Lawson
GRAVES, Thomas R.
GREEN, Archer

GREEN, John
GRIFFIN, Samuel
GUDDY, P.
HAINES, Levi
HALE, Harvey
HAMILTON, William H.
HAMPTON, Moat
HANSON, George W.
HARKINS, Charles
HARKINS, John
HARPER, Jordan
HARRIS, George W.
HARRIS, Sylvestor
HARRIS, Willie
HASKINS, David
HAZZARD, Miller
HENRY, John (K/10th Cav)
HENRY, John (L/10th Cav)
HIBBARD, George
HIGH, John H.
HILL, Abraham
HINES, Peter
HIRBERT, John
HOLEMAN, Edmond
HOLLAND, James T.
HOPE, Henry
HOPKINS, James
HOPKINS, Robert
HORTON, Louis
HOWARD, John A.
HUBBERT, Lewellen
HURNS, Thomas H.
JACKSON, Henry
JACKSON, Orange
JACKSON, Preston
JACKSON, Willie H.
JAMES, Augustus
JAMES, Robert
JEFFERSON, William
JENKINS, Albert
JENKINS, Joseph
JENNINGS, Oliver
JENNISON, Perry
JIMISON, Charles D.
JOHNSON, Albert
JOHNSON, George
JOHNSON, Henry
JOHNSON, James
JOHNSON, John
JOHNSON, John C.
JOHNSON, John H.
JOHNSON, Marshall H.
JOHNSON, Peter
JOHNSON, Robert M.
JOHNSON, Rubin
JOHNSON, Thomas
JOHNSON, William H.
JONES, Douglas
JONES, George
JONES, Henry
JONES, John
JONES, John S.

JONES, Philip
JONES, Robert H.
JONES, Samuel
JORDAN, Henry
JUNIFER, Samuel
KAPPS, Isaac
KELLY, James
KENNEDY, Henry
KENNEDY, John
KERRY, Issac
KING, Taylor
KIRK, James
KIRTLEY, Sidney
LAIRE, James
LARUE, Bernhard
LAWSON, Isa
LEE, David
LEGRAND, John
LEWIS, Edward
LEWIS, George W.
LEWIS, Peter
LOGAN, James E.
LOVERY, Crawford
LOWE, James
LYMAN, George
MABREY, York
McCALL, Henry
McCLOUD, Washington
McHUE, Martin
MACKENS, Wallace
MADDERSON, Charles J.
MAILEY, Thomas
MALONE, Henry
MANNY, George
MATHEWS, Gene H.
MATHEWS, Gletcheri
MATHEWS, Pleas
MATTHEWS, Courtney
MILES, Candy
MILES, Julius
MILLER, Daniel
MILLER, Edward
MILLER, John
MILLER, Thomas
MILLER, William F.
MISTY, John
MITCHELL, Basil
MITCHELL, William
MONTGOMERY, Jesse
MOORE, Bazil B.
MOORE, Daniel
MORRISON, Henry J.
MORRISON, James
MOSLEY, Zechoriah
MYERS, Alfred
NELSON, Calab
NELSON, Henry
NELSON, Moses
NORTON, Thomas
OBEY, Thomas
OVERALL, Nathaniel
OVERTON, George

PLAIN CAPS indicate names from this volume • **BOLD CAPS** indicate names from *On the Trail* (1995)

OWENS, Frederick
PARKER, James E.
PARNETT, John H.
PERSINGER, Mason
PETTIE, Samuel
PHELPS, Allen
PINN, Nathan
PINN, Newton
PLUMER, Darrel
PLUMER, Joseph P.
PLUMER, William
PRETTY, Augustus
RECTOR, William L.
REED, William
REILLY, John
REYNOLDS, Henry
RICE, Robert
RICHARDS, Alfred
RIVERS, Richard
ROBERTS, Filmore
ROBINSON, David
ROBINSON, Jeremiah
ROBINSON, Oscar G.
RUSSELL, Anthony
ST. JOHN, Henry R.
SANDERS, Braxton
SANDERS, George
SCEAR, William
SCOTT, Alexander
SCOTT, Jacob
SCOTT, John
SCOTT, John H.
SELTRY, Jerry
SHANNON, James
SHARPS, Joseph
SHIELDS, James
SIMMONS, Robert
SIMONS, Benjamin
SISUES, Henry L.
SKIDAISK, Fredrick
SMALL, Thomas
SMITH, Calton
SMITH, Franklin
SMITH, Frederick
SMITH, George (I/10th Cav)
SMITH, George (K/10th Cav)
SMITH, Gus
SMITH, Henry
SMITH, Jacob
SMITH, John
SMITH, Samuel
SMITH, William (K/10th Cav)
SMITH, William (Corporal; M/10th Cav)
SOROSORI, Robert
SORRIE, Morris A.
STANDEMIRE, Taylor
STEINTON, Elijah
STEWARD, Isaiah
STITH, Nathan
STOKES, Elwood
SULLIVAN, Jermiah

TASKER, Lyman
TAYLOR, Albert
TAYLOR, Anderson
TEMPER, James
TERRER, Jackson
THOMAS, Charles
THOMAS, Henry
THOMAS, John
THOMAS, Littleton
THOMAS, William
THOMAS, William H.
THOMPSON, Lorenzo
TURNER, Daniel
TURNER, John
TURNER, Simon
VERNON, Joseph
WADKINS, Henry
WALKER, George
WALKER, Neely
WALLACE, Joseph
WALTERS, Alfred
WARFIELD, Kearry
WASHINGTON, Claude
WASHINGTON, Ernest S.
WASHINGTON, James
WASHINGTON, James H.
WASHINGTON, John
WATKINS, Benjamin
WATKINS, George
WATSON, Frank
WATSON, George
WATSON, Samuel
WEAVER, Henry
WEISMAN, Robert
WEISS, Joseph
WELKEY, Stock
WELLS, Allen
WENSLOW, Nelson
WHEELER, Henry
WHITE, John
WHITE, Thomas (Private; G/10th Cav)
WHITE, William
WHITING, James
WIGGINS, John
WILKES, William
WILLIAMS, Alexander
WILLIAMS, Berg
WILLIAMS, Cathay
WILLIAMS, George W.
WILLIAMS, John (Private; C/9th Cav)
WILLIAMS, John (Corporal; L/10th Cav)
WILLIAMS, John (1st)
WILLIAMS, John W.
WILLIAMS, Joseph
WILLIAMS, Underhill
WILLS, Frank
WILLS, James
WILSON, James

WILSON, James (Private; I/10th Cav)
WILSON, James (Private; M/10th Cav)
WOLFE, Abraham
WOODEN, Henry
WOODWARD, Otho J.
WRIGHT, Aaron
WRIGHT, John
WRIGHT, Jonas
WRIGHT, Thomas H.
YOUNG, David
YOUNG, Jerry
YOUNG, Joseph
YOUNG, Robert
Ft Scott
  FORD, George W.
Ft Wallace
  ADAMS, Alexander
  BANKS, Robert B.
  GREEN, John
  HARRISON, William
  KENNY, Isaac
  MILES, Sandy
  PRICE, John D.
  SMITH, Ewing
  TURNER, Tom
  WALLER, Reuben
  WASHINGTON, James H.
  WILLIAMS, James
  WILLIAMS, Osborne
  WILSON, Samuel
  GRAFTON, William
Great Bend
  GLADDEN, Washington W. E.
  SHROPSHIRE, Shelvin
GREEN, William H.
Hays
  BURKS, Dock
  JOHNSON, John H.
  REED, James
  WILSON, Frank
Henshaw's Station
  MICHAEL (Private)
Hill City
  MOORE, Fredrick Thomas
Hutchinson
  BROOKS, Henry
  JOHNSON, Moses
  PLUMMER, Henry Vinton
INGRAM, W. H.
Iola
  ALLEN, John
JOHNSTON (Sergeant)
Junction City
  BENJAMIN, Robert
  BRABHAM, Jeremiah
  BROOKS, Preston
  COLEMAN, Moses
  CRAGG, Allen
  DAVIS, Benjamin F.
  HUNTER, Bedford B.

PLAIN CAPS indicate names from this volume • **BOLD CAPS** indicate names from *On the Trail* (1995)

MASON, George F.
MURPHY, Israel B.
RANDOLPH, F. B.
Kansas City
PLUMMER, Henry Vinton
PRIOLEAU, George W.
ROGAN, Wilbur
Lawrence
GREGG, John A.
THURSTON, William T.
Leavenworth. *See also* National
Military Home, Leavenworth, KS;
U.S. Military Prison, Ft
Leavenworth, KS
ALEXANDER, Fred
BACKMAN, Harrison
BLAKE, Isaac
BRENT, John
CLAYBORN, John
EDWARDS, William
GAREY, Charles
GREGG, John A.
HALL, Frank W.
LEE, Fitz
LYONS, Edward
PRICE, James
STAFF, William R.
THOMAS, George
LOVE, Frank W.
Manhattan
PRINCE, Noah
Meriden
ARCHER, Sylvester
Mound City
SIMONS, Frank
Newton
ANDERSON, Henry
Parsons
BROOKS, Norman H.
GRIMES, Woody W.
Pawnee Creek
ROSS, Hercules
Quindaro
HAMMOND, Wade H.
Republican River
CLAYBORNE, Peter
COOK, Cyrus
WALLER, Reuben
Rice County
CARVIN, John
FISHER, Samuel
GATE, John
HALL, Thornton
LOVE, Milton
RUSSELL, Jeremiah
SCHLOSS, Columbus
STEPHENS, Avery
Saline River
CHRISTOPHER, Andrew
DAVIS, Charles H.
JOHNSON, William

POSY (Private)
SPRIGGS, Eliord
THORNTON, Jacob
TURNER, Tom
WIGGINS, John
Salt Creek
CLAYBORNE, Peter
SMITH, F.
Strong City
ARCHER, Sylvester
Topeka
ALLSUP, Thomas H.
ARCHER, Sylvester
BROWN, William
CRITH, Frank
FORD, George W.
HALE, Wesley
JOHNS, Edward C.
REYNOLDS, William
TURNER, William
TURPIN, George
WALLER, John L.
WHITE, Jerry M.
White Rock Station, Trego
County
REID, John
Wichita
BRYANT, M. C.
EVANS, Frank, Sr.
McDOUGAL, John
MURRY, Mat
PLUMMER, Henry Vinton
ROLAND, Samuel
WHITTED, Eugene R.
WILLIAMS, John S.
Wilson Creek
DAVIS, Benjamin F.
FERGUSON, James
HARMON, Charles
JACKSON, James
KELLY, George C.
LANDERS, Bass
TURNER, David
WASHINGTON, Peter
WILSON, John
Kansas City Monarchs
ROGAN, Wilbur
Kansas City School of Law
TILLMAN, Lafayette A.
Kansas State University
GREGG, John A.
Kelley, Joseph M.
ANDERSON, William T.
Kelley, Rena B.
KELLEY, George B.
Kendall, Frederic Augustus
PERRY, Denbar
TALLIFORO, Daniel
Kennedy, Joseph
ANDERSON, William T.

Kentucky. *See also*
Cemeteries
ABBOTT, James W.
Adair County
DEHONEY, Peter
SPERLIN, George
WILLIAMS, William
ALLENSWORTH, Allen
ANDERSON, Henry
BAKER, Peter
BANHAM, Jerry
Bardstown
McCLAIN, Henry
BARNER, George
BARNES, Samuel
BATES, David
BATES, Milton F.
Berkeville, *see below* Burkesville
BERKLEY, Scott
BIRCH, Philip
Bourbon County
DOOMS, Thomas
McCABBIN, Care
BOWIE, James
Bowling Green
COOK, French
COVINGTON, John
DAWSON, Eb
WATKINS, Jacob
BOWMAN, Bartley
BRADFORD, Harrison
BRISCOE, Henry
BROMBACK, William
BROOKINS, Richard
BUNDY, George W.
BUNTON, Mark
Burkesville
ALEXANDER, Henry E.
BURNET, John
BURNS, George
Camp Nelson
WILKS, Jacob W.
Camp Sanger
BARNES, Samuel G.
JERMON, W. S.
CARPENTER, Allen
Carter County
BARNES, William
Catlettsburg
JACKSON, Isaac
CHINN, Charles
CHRISTOPHER, Andrew
CLARK, James T.
CLARK, Louis
Clark County
SHELTON, Leonard
WALKER, Silas
WILKS, Jacob W.
Clay County
WHITE, Dillard

CLEMENS, Benjamin
COLEMAN, Robert
COLLINS, Robert
Columbia
  DEHONEY, Peter
Columbus
  WILLIAMS, Doc
COMFREY, Charles
CONNOR (M/9th Cav)
COOK, George
COOPER, William H.
Covington
  HISLE, Charles
  JACKSON, Edward
  MOORE, William
  SHAW, Thomas
CRAGG, Allen
CRAIG, John
CROW, James
CROWDIS, David
CRUSE, Peter
Cynthiana
  CALDWELL, William
Danville
  BENTLEY, George
Davidson County, *see below* Daviess
  County
Daviess County
  JAMES, Edward
DAVIS, Charles
DAVIS, George
DAVIS, Matt
DAVIS, William
DeGRAFFEURILL, John
DOOMS, Thomas
DOWTHA, Washington
DUNCAN, Austin
DUNIHY, Smith
Edmonton
  PULLIAM, Fealex B.
EDWARDS, Samuel
ELDERBERRY, Hiram
FANTROY, Basil
FAULKNER, Charles S. C.
Fayette County
  BERRYMAN, Henry
  GERRY, William
  HENRY, Jesse
  IRVIN, Allen
FIELDS, Harvey
FINLEY, Rae
Flat Lick
  FITTS, Ned
Flemingsburg
  ROBINSON, Alvin H.
  THOMAS, George
Flemmingburg, *see above*
  Flemingsburg
Ft Thomas
  BELL, John A.
  BUCK, John

CLARKE, Thomas H. R.
DAVIS, Benjamin O.
JEFFERS, David B.
RUSSELL, Macon
SMITH, Lewis M.
STARR, Stephen G.
TURNER, Charles B.
WEBBER, George
WIGGINS, S. T.
Frankfort
  CARROLL, Joseph H.
  STRAWS, Thomas
  YEIZER, Mordecai
FREEMAN, James
GARNETT, William
Georgetown
  BRISCOE, Henry
  BURNS, Lee
  COLE, Pollard
  JACKSON, Benjamin
  WARREN, William
  WILLIAMS, James Clifford
GILL, Spencer
GIVENS, Adam
GIVENS, William H.
GOOD, Talton
GOVER, John W.
Grant County
  SALTON, Armp
GREY, James
GRIFFIN, Thomas
GRIMDER, Henry
GRIMDY, Edward
Hardin County
  SEWARD, William
HARRIS, John
Harrodsburg
  JOHNSON, Charles
Haskingsville
  BLAKEMAN, Robert
Haskinsville, *see above*
  Haskingsville
Henderson
  ASH, John M.
  BRYANT, James A.
  MARTIN, Albert
HILL, Conway
HOCKINS, Benjamin
Hopkinsville
  ALLENSWORTH, Allen
  SMITH, Lawson
  TUCKER, Turner
HOWARD, Joseph
HUFF, John
HUGHES, Charles
HUMPHREY, Cornelius
HUNTER, Lewis
HUTCHISON, George
INGOMAN, Madison
Jackson
  COLEMAN, Andrew

JACKSON, Henry C.
JACKSON, Thomas (age 24)
JACKSON, Thomas (age 25)
Jefferson County
  SMITH, Theodore H.
Jericho
  REED, John
JOHNSON, Beverly
JOHNSON, Merrit
JOHNSON, Robert M.
JOHNSON, Smith
JOHNSON, William
JOHNSTON, Albert
JONES, John
JONES, William
KNOWLES, Columbus
Knox County
  WESTERFIELD, George
Lancaster
  DOTY, Timothy
LANGSTER, John
LANGSTON, John
Lawrenceburg
  HARRIS, John
Lebanon
  HILL, Colony
  PENNICK, Lloyd
LETCHER, Philip
LEWIS, Edward
Lexington. *See also* Cemeteries
  BERRYMAN, Henry
  BURNS, Lee
  BUSH, James W.
  CAMPBELL, Murphy
  CAULDER, Nathan
  CHENAULT, Walter
  DAVIS, Charles
  DRAKE, Robert I.
  FITCH, Thomas N.
  GRAVES, John
  LYMAN, George
  McINTYRE, Burnett A.
  SCROGGINS, William H.
  SHIPLEY, Lee
  SLANTER, William
  STREETS, Deleware
  WASHINGTON, George
  WEST, Sampson
  WHITE, Randolph F.
  WILLIAMS, James Clifford
LIVINGSTON, George W.
Livingston County
  BARNETT, Peter W.
LONG, David
Louisville. *See also* Cemeteries
  ALEXANDER, Wesley
  ALLENSWORTH, Allen
  BACON, Henry
  BALLARD, Wilson C.
  BEARD, Allen
  BELL, William

PLAIN CAPS indicate names from this volume • **BOLD CAPS** indicate names from *On the Trail* (1995)

BLEW, Joseph
BOOKER, Edward
BOOM, William
BRANNER, George
BROWN, Robert
BUCHANAN, Lawrence
BURKS, Lewis
CAIN, Scott
CLARK, Alexander
COLE, Pollard
COVINGTON, James C.
CRAYCROFT, Richard
CUSHINGBERRY, Porter
DEAN, Charles H.
DRY, Will
FOREMAN, William A.
GRAHAM, William
GREEN, John E.
GUILLORY, Jerome
HEISER, Richard
HELM, Benjamin
HENDERSON, Joseph
HINSON, Walter
HUTSON, Charles G.
ISAACS, Thomas
ITSON, Albert
JACKSON, Isaac
JACKSON, James F.
JOHNSON, Benjamin
JOHNSON, Thomas
KIMBER, John
McCLAIN, Henry
McDOWELL, Martin
McDUFFIN, Ennis
McELROY, Marshall
MARATTA, William H.
MILES, Grabt A.
MILLER, Richard
MILLER, William
MONTGOMERY, Morgan
PARKER, John H.
PINKNEY, John C.
PORTER, Wesley
REDD, Kid
REED, Charles
ROGERS, Edward
ROSS, William
SCOTT, John
SEARS, Richard
SHARP, G. W.
SIMS, Henry W.
SLAUGHTER, Clarence
SMART, Hugh M.
SMITH, Elijah
TAYLOR, Thomas W.
TEWELL, Frank
THOMAS, Littleton
THOMPSON, Charles N.
THURMAN, John A.
TURNER, Charles B.
WALKER, Henry

WALL, Archy
WATTS, William W.
WEEKS, Henry C.
WHITE, Randolph F.
WIGFALL, Frank
WILLIAMS, Henry
WOODFORK, Joseph
WOODS, William
MACK, William
McKAY, Barney
Madison County
    CAMMEL, Joseph
    JONES, Sherman
    MILLER, Richard
    MORRELL, Benjamin
Madisonville
    LEWIS, Glendee
    LITTLEPAGE, Junius
    SPRINGFIELD, Herman
Manchester
    ALLEN, William
    GILBERT, Saint
    GRIFFIN, Stephen
    WALKER, John
MASON, George
MASON, Lewis
Maysville
    LOCHLIN, William
Meade County
    CRAYCROFT, Richard
Mercer County
    LEE, Robert E.
    MILLER, Charles
    MILLER, Richard
    MILLER, Stephen
    MILLIMAN, Jerry
    MITCHELL, John H.
    MONROE, James
Montgomery County
    WILLIAMS, Thomas
MOORE, Robert
MORRELL, Benjamin
MOSEBY, Houry
Mt. Olivet
    CLEMENS, James
Mt. Sterling
    BUSH, Emanuel
    JONES, William
MOZIQUE, Edward
Newport Barracks
    DAVIS, Amos
    DELONG, George
    McCOWAN, James G.
Nicholasville
    COTTON, J. H.
NUNN, Bess
Oak Grove
    QUARLES, William M.
OLFORD, Isaac
OVERSTREET, Monroe
Owensboro

WHITE, Randolph F.
Paducah
    ANDERSON, George G.
    DUNLAP, Shurley
    STOW, Benjamin
Paris
    HALL, Brice
    JACKSON, Samuel
PARKER, Henry
Peneville, see below Pineville
Perryville
    CARRICK, James
Pineville
    DAVIS, Elijah
PITMAN, Samuel
Pittsburg
    TINSLEY, George
Plano
    SAPP, Wiliam B.
Pulaski
    WOODS, Brent
Pulaski County
    BLEW, Joseph
RALPY, Andrew
RAY, Joseph
REDDON, Shelton
RHODES, Charles
Richmond
    BALLEW, John
    EMERY, Andrew J.
ROBINSON, Henry
ROCHESTER, Nicholas
Rock Springs
    SUMMERS, Charles A.
Rockcastle County
    CRUSE, Peter
ROSS, Lewis
ROUT, Richard
SADDLER, Louis
SAUNDERS, Stephen
SCOTT, Henry
SCOTT, James
Scott County
    BERRYMAN, Henry
    BRADFORD, Harrison
    TAYLOR, John T.
Sharpsburg
    RENFRO, Golden E.
Shelbyville
    MADISON, John
    OGLESBY, Charles, Sr.
    WALKER, Henry
    WILLIAMS, Noah W.
SIMMONS, Charles
SMALL, George
SMITH, Benjamin
SMITH, Gilbert
SMITH, Henry
SMITH, Herbert
SMITH, Jesse B.
SMITH, Sidney

PLAIN CAPS indicate names from this volume • **BOLD CAPS** indicate names from *On the Trail* (1995)

SMITH, William
Spencer County
  BENTON, Mark
Springfield
  WATTS, Thomas
TAYLOR, Charles
TAYLOR, Zachariah (F/9th Cav)
TAYLOR, Zachariah (M/9th Cav)
Taylorsville
  SMITH, Jacob C.
THACKER, William
THOMAS, John
THOMAS, Leonard
TILLEY, James D.
Todd County
  DILLARD, James H.
TUCKER, Dred
TURNER, Charles B.
TURPIN, John
UMBER, Green
VALENTINE, Ranson
Versailles
  BROWN, Thomas
WALKER, John
WALZE, Olmstead
WARDEN, Clerk
Warren County
  MASON, George F.
WATSON, Samuel
WEIR, Mack
WHITE, Washington
White Hall
  CARR, David
WHITESIDES, Zachariah
WILLIAMS, Ansterd
WILLIAMS, George
WILLIAMS, Henry
WILLIAMS, Newton
WILSON, Clay
WILSON, Daniel
WILSON, David
WILSON, Lewis
Winchester
  HOOD, Perry
  MORGAN, Richard
  WHEELER, Samuel
Woodford County
  DRAKE, Robert I.
  JOHNSON, Thomas
WOODS, Solomon
YEIZER, Mordecai
YOUNG, Charles
YOUNG, David
Kerwin, Arthur Raphael
  CALLOWAY, John W.
Keyes, Alexander Scammel
  Brooks
  LIVINGSTON, James
Kibbetts, George
  KIBBETTS, Robert

Kibbetts, Missouri
  KIBBETTS, John
Kibbetts, Nancy
  KIBBETTS, John
Kibbetts, Phyllis
  KIBBETTS, Robert
Kickapoos
  BOWERS, Edward
  CLAYBORNE, Peter
  JONES, Eldridge T.
  MOZIQUE, Edward
  TRIMBLE, Anderson
  WIGGINS, John
  WRIGHT, Samuel
Kid (Apache)
  BRISCOE, Edward
  BROWN, William H.
  McBRYAR, William
Kilpatrick (ship), *see* U.S. Army
  Transport *Kilpatrick*
King, Alice
  POLK, Thomas Elzey
Kiowas
  ANDERSON, Robert
  BARD, Benjamin
  BERRYMAN, Henry
  BRANCH, William
  COLE, Pollard
  CORK, Adam
  FARRELL, Charles H.
  FERRER, Jackson
  FORD, George W.
  FRANKLIN, Walter
  GARNETT, George R.
  GIVENS, Edward
  KELLEY, John
  KEY, Charles
  LOGAN, James
  MACK, Louis
  MEIKS, William
  PINKSTON, Alfred
  ROBINSON, Henry
  SHROPSHIRE, Shelvin
  SMITH, Andrew J.
  SMITH, John
  STEVENS, Milton
  TOWNSEND, Edward
  TURNER, Charles B.
  TURNER, Simon
  WALKER, Lorenzo
Knights of Pythias
  BADIE, M. V.
  BATTLE, William P.
  CLINTON, F. R.
  GOFF, George W.
  JACOBS, Camp
  JOHNSON, J.
  MASON, George F.
  PRIOLEAU, George W.

PURNELL, William Whipple
VROOMAN, William A.
Knights Templar
  REYNOLDS, William
Knox College, Galesburg, IL
  JAMESON, Henry W.
Kub-bit-che (Seminole chief)
  KIBBETTS, John
Kyte, Virginia
  BUNCH, Richard
Lambert and Baker, Washington,
DC
  McKAY, Barney
Lanier, Nannie China Collins
  LANIER, Frank
Larkins, William H.
  LUCKY, Joseph D.
Latter-Day Saints, *see* Mormons
Laverty, James Coriston
  ALLENSWORTH, Allen
Lawrason, George C.
  SANDERS, Mingo
Lawson, Gaines
  DERBIGNY, Benjamin
Lawson, Millie
  LAWSON, Walter
Leavell, Josephine
  ALLENSWORTH, Allen
Ledyard (U.S. marshal)
  FINLEY, Augustus
Lee, Fitzhugh (Confederate
general)
  McCAULEY, William
Lee, Josie
  JONES, Edward
Lee, R. Rainey
  LEE, Robert E.
Lee, Theodora
  PURNELL, William Whipple
Lehigh Valley Coal Co., Newark,
NJ
  WILLIAMS, Jessie
Lemus, Charles H.
  LEMUS, Rienzi Brock
Lemus, Mamaie L. Brock
  LEMUS, Rienzi Brock
Lesaca, Poteaciano
  ROBINSON, Michael H., Jr.
LeSage, Julius
  STOKES, Henry A.
Lewis, Minnie
  HALLON, Ross
Liberia
  BALLARD, Wilson C.
  BROWN, Arthur M.
  DAVIS, Benjamin O.
  GILLISPIE, James R.
  GREEN, John E.

NEWTON, Richard H.
YOUNG, Charles
Liggins, Elta A.
LIGGINS, Edward C.
Lincoln, Robert Todd
GREENE, Hallett
Lincoln Institute, Jefferson City, MO
WILBURN, Thomas G.
Lincoln State Normal, Jefferson City, MO
JORDAN, Leon H.
Lincoln University, PA
BROWN, Arthur M.
Lipan Apaches. *See also* Costillitto (Lipan Apache chief)
ALSIE, Ross
CLAYBORNE, Peter
GRAYSON, Renty
HARRISON, John
PERRYMAN, James
TURNER, Charles B.
WHITE, Lewis
WIGGINS, John
Literary clubs
ALLENSWORTH, Allen
CAMPBELL, James
CRAWFORD, E. L.
HAMILTON, J. H.
KELLEY, George B.
MINER, James S.
SMALLWOOD (Sergeant)
Livingston, Ada
BRANCH, William
Livingston, Bertha
JACKSON, Jason K.
Lloyd, Cecilio
LLOYD, Isaac H.
Lloyd, Ynez Rocha
LLOYD, Isaac H.
Locker, Georgianna
PROCTOR, John C.
Lodge, Henry Cabot
SANDERS, Mingo
Logan, Hessie
CRUMBLY, Floyd H.
Logan, Randolph
CRUMBLY, Floyd H.
Logan (ship), *see* U.S. Army Transport *Logan*
Lomax, Julia
PLUMMER, Henry Vinton
Longorio, Arthur
LONGORIO, Julian
Longorio, Matildia
LONGORIO, Julian
Longorio, Refugio
LONGORIO, Julian

Los Angeles Forum Club
RICKS, William Nauns
Loud, John Sylvanus
FORT, Lewis
HAYWOOD, Charles
JONES, Lewis
WILSON, William O.
Louisiana. *See also* Cemeteries
ALEXANDER, Lewis
Alexandria
JOHNSON, Henry
SHORTER, Lloyd
Attakapas
HENRY, Lewis
BALLARD, Wilson C.
BASEY, Henry
Baton Rouge
ANDERSON, Richard
GRIGSBY, Jeff
Bayou Lafourche
MANOLT, Joseph
MASON, Surrie
Bayou Sara
CRUMP, Edward W.
DAY, Charles N.
GOINGS, Alfred
ROBINSON, George
BLUNT, Hamilton H.
BRADDOCK, Granderson
BRADY, Jewel
Carroll Parish
STANCE, Emanuel
COLE, James T.
Columbus
WATKINS, Isaac
Concordia Parish
BALLARD, Wilson C.
Corinth
SYKES, Zekiel
DAVIS, George
Donaldsonville
CARMOUCHE, Pierre L.
Donaldsville, *see above* Donaldsonville
DUNLAP, George
East Carroll Parish
WILLIAMS, Moses
Ft Jackson
ALEXANDER, Willis
Ft Pike
DERBIGNY, Benjamin
WATSON, John
WILSON, Bailey
Ft St. Philip
GOSS, Isaac
MAGEE, Alfred
MANOLT, Joseph
MOISE, Augustine
ROBINSON, George
WILSON, Randall
Franklin
GANAWAY, Joseph

Glenwood
MITCHELL, Luke
GOINS, Joshua Van Buren
Greenville
GANAWAY, Joseph
HENRY, Jesse
HOMES, Marcus
IRVIN, Allen
MASON, Surrie
RICE, John
SANDERS, Joseph
SMITH, Robert
STRAMBOLD, George
WALKER, James
WALKER, Silas
WASHINGTON, Littleton
WILKS, Jacob W.
WILSON, George
WILSON, Thomas
GRIFFIN, George
HAINES, John
HICKMAN, John H.
Iberville
MOISE, Augustine
WILSON, Thomas
Jackson
RICE, John
Jackson Barracks
ABBOTT, Winney
ALLMOND, Howard
AUSTIN, Edward S.
BORELAND, Peter
BRETT, James
COLUMBUS, Robert H.
COTTRELL, Robert H.
EVANS, James
GANAWAY, Joseph
GOINGS, Alfred
GOSS, Isaac
GOULD, Peter
GRAHAM, Charles
GRAY, James
GREGOIRE, Gabriel
GREGORY, Andrew
HARRIS, Alexander
HENRY, Jesse
HENRY, Lewis
HOGAN, James
HOLLOMON, Solomon
HOMES, Marcus
IRVIN, Allen
JACKSON, William L.
JOHNSON, James
LEWIS, Robert
MAGEE, Alfred
MANOLT, Joseph
MASON, Surrie
MOISE, Augustine
MORSE, William
RICE, John
RINGO, Walter
ROBERTS, John

ROBINSON, George
SANDERS, Joseph
SCOTT, Praley
SMALLGOOD, Eli
SMITH, Robert
STRAMBOLD, George
TAYLOR, Richard H.
THOMPSON, Thomas
TURNER, George
TYREE, George
WASHINGTON, Littleton
WATSON, John
WICKHAM, Thomas W.
WILLIAMSON, Richard
WILSON, Arthur
WILSON, Bailey
WILSON, George
WILSON, Randall
WILSON, Thomas
WORD, Peter
JOHNSON, Horace
Lafourche
WASHINGTON, Littleton
WILSON, George
MARSHALL, Joseph
MASON, Samuel
Monroe
HILL, H. W.
Morgan City
MURRAY, Jordan
NECO, Isidro
New Iberia
BAMBRICK, Joseph
BISHOP, James
COLLINS, Frederick
GOINGS, Alfred
JOSEPH, Leon
MACKEY, Robert
MITCHELL, Paul
NEWSOME, Felix
ROBINSON, William
SCOTT, Praley
THOMPSON, Thomas
WARD, Baleford
WASLEM, James
WIGGINS, Westley
WILBURN, James
WILLIAMS, Charles
WILLIAMS, John
WINTERS, Eli
WORD, Peter
New Orleans
ABBOTT, Winney
AUGUSTIN, Frank E.
BROWN, Sterling Price
DERBIGNY, Benjamin
EVANS, James
FOBUS, Perry J.
FRANKLIN, Henry O.
GAMBLE, John E.
GARNEY, John D.
GOINGS, Alfred

GREGOIRE, Gabriel
GREGORY, Andrew
HATCHER, Willie
HENRY, Lewis
JACKSON, William L.
JOHNSON, Monroe
McDUFFIN, Ennis
McKENNON, John
MOORE, Miles
MOZIQUE, Edward
MURPHY, George
MYERS, Thomas C.
PINCHBACK, Walter A.
PORTER, Issac
PRIOLEAU, George W.
ROBINSON, W. H.
SCOTT, Praley
STEWARD, Lewis
SYKES, Zekiel
THARP, Lafayette
THOMPSON, Thomas
TURNER, Charles B.
WASHINGTON, William
WHITE, Joseph
WILLIAMS, Washington
NUGENT, William
Port Hudson
STARR, Stephen G.
ROBERTS, George W.
ROBERTSON, Victor
St. Francisville
CRUMP, Edward W.
Shreveport
DEAN, Milton T.
SMITH, James
THOMPSON, Thomas
TURNER, George
WORD, Peter
SMITH, Alfred
STEVENSON, Peter
SYLVESTER, George
TELLISBANNER, John
Thibodaux
FRANKLIN, Henry O.
THOMAS, John W.
Washington
WALLACE, Lewis H.
WASHINGTON, George
WILLIAMS, James (1st Sgt; E/9th Cav)
WILLIAMS, James (C/25th Inf)
WILSON, John
WILSON, William (H/25th Inf)
WILSON, William (Private; U.S. Army)
Lovett, Lulu
POTTER, Thomas
Lundy, Etta Williams
LUNDY, Samuel
WILLIAMS, John
Lynch, Ellen Beck
LYNCH, William

Lynch, H. P.
HALLON, Ross
Lyons, Laura
FLIPPINS, Benjamin
McAnaney, William David
PUMPHREY, James H.
SMITH, Lamb
McBee, Bert
McDONALD (Private)
McBlain, John
ARMSTEAD (Private)
WHITE, Thomas
McBlaine, John Ferral
SMITH, Myles Y.
McCarthy, Lizzy
JONES, Robert
McClain, Louisa M. Massey
McCLAIN, Henry
McCleary, Elizabeth Wanton
WANTON, George H.
McCleod, Mary E.
YEIZER, Mordecai
McConkey, Mary
McCONKEY, Nathan
McCormack, Sallie
SMITH, Arthur
McCremens, Thomas
McCREMENS, David
McDaniel, James
McDANIELS, Nathaniel
McDaniel, Parthenia Hunt
McDANIELS, Nathaniel
McDaniels, Catherine Cooley
McDANIELS, Nathaniel
McDaniels, Hannah Johnson
McDANIELS, Nathaniel
McDaniels, Sarah Scott
McDANIELS, Nathaniel
McDougal, Mary
McKAY, Barney
McKay, Barney
McKAY, Barney
McKay, Fanny
WALL, Archy
McKay, George
WALL, Archy
McKay, Julia Moore
McKAY, Barney
McKay, Mary McDougal
McKAY, Barney
McKellop, James
McCALLIP, Pleasants
Mackenzie, Ranald Slidell
GRAYSON, Renty
LONGORIO, Julian
PAYNE, Adam
PERRYMAN, James
McKenzie, Thomas
DILLARD, C. D.

PLAIN CAPS indicate names from this volume • **BOLD CAPS** indicate names from *On the Trail* (1995)

McKenzie, V. C.
  BROOKS, Preston
McKinley, Pres. William
  ALEXANDER, William
  BLUNT, Hamilton H.
  FEASTER, Thomas
  HOLT, Lindsey P.
  JOHNSON, Silas
  MURPHY, George
  NELSON, Samuel A.
  PEAL, Allen S.
  STANLEY, Benjamin
  WILSON, Willie
McKinney, Frank
  ALLSUP, Thomas H.
McKinney, Susan
  STEWARD, Theophilus G.
McKinney, William
  STEWARD, Theophilus G.
McMartin, John
  LIEUSS, George
  SMITH, G. W.
Madagascar
  WALLER, John L.
Maden, Annie Ewing
  MADEN, Ebbert
Mangas, *see* Mangus
Mangus (Apache leader)
  BATTLE, William P.
  BOLLER, Solomon
  BOYER (Blacksmith)
  BRUFF, Thomas
  CAMMEL, Joseph
  CASEY, John F.
  COLE, Pollard
  DILLARD, James H.
  FOSTER, George
  GIBSON, James
  GREEN, Charles A.
  HAWKINS, William
  JACKSON, Isaac
  JONES, Silas
  McKIBBIN, Care
  MILLER, Colonel E.
  NEWMAN, George W.
  ROUSEY, Joseph
  SPARKS, Augustus
  TERRY, Charles Lincoln
Mann, Wella
  MANN, Frank T.
Maraschal, Amanda
  MARASCHAL, Trinida
Maraschal, Molly
  MARASCHAL, Trinida
Marcalina, Don Antucaio
  REDDING, Willie
Marcalina, Senung
  REDDING, Willie
Maroney, Lizzie
  JONES, Ira
Marrow, Anthony

MARROW, Anthony A.
Marshall, Agnes
  JACKSON, Emmett J.
Marshall, Lucinda
  CARTER, Henry
Martin, Carl Anson
  WILMORE, Leonard
Maryatt, The Misses
  ALLENSWORTH, Allen
Maryland. *See also*
  Cemeteries
  ABBOTT, Winney
  Allen
    POLK, Thomas Elzey
  ALLSUP, Thomas H.
  ANDERSON, William H.
  Annapolis
    CALDWELL, Henry
    CREEK, Charles
  Anne Arundel County
    GREEN, Charles A.
    HENSON, John
    PUMPHREY, George W.
  Aquasco
    ANDERSON, John B.
  Baltimore. *See also* Cemeteries
    BANKS, Benjamin
    BETHEL, Elijah
    BIVENS, George E.
    BIVINS, Horace
    BLAKE, Isaac
    BLAKE, William H.
    BLUNT, Randall
    BOOZE, Richard
    BRANCH, William
    BRISCOE, Edward
    BROOKS, Robert H.
    BROWN, John W.
    BROWN, Morris
    BUTLER, Thomas C.
    CAINE, George
    CAMPHOR, George
    CHAMBERS, Robert
    CLAVON, Merritt
    COATS, William H.
    COLBERT, Frederick
    COLBERT, John A.
    COLLINS, William Thomas
    CORNISH, Harry
    CORNISH, Samuel
    COTTMAN, Charles W.
    CRUMP, Edward W.
    DEMBY, Sheridan
    DENIS, John H.
    DENT, Henry
    EAGLIN, Thomas
    EVANS, Frank
    FINNEGAN, Michael
    GAINES, Norman E.
    GALVIN, Orpheus
    GARDNER, William George

GRAHAM, John W.
GRAY, Charles
GREEN, Charles A.
GROOMS, George A.
HALL, Frank W.
HALL, James
HARRIS, George W.
HARRIS, Hyder
HARRIS, James H.
HAWKINS, James H.
HAWKINS, William
HILL, Jacob
JACKSON, Hilary
JACKSON, Robert
JAMES, Charles
JOHNSON, Henry
JOHNSON, Henry
JOHNSON, William H.
JONES, Charles
JONES, George
JONES, John A.
KELLY, Walter
KENNEDY, Richard
LEE, William
McCONKEY, Nathan
McINTOSH, Robert
MATHEWS, Levi
MERRIWEATHER, Henry
MILLER, Colonel E.
MILLER, Frank
MILLIMAN, Jerry
MINOR, Abraham L.
MINUS, Washington
MOORE, Fredrick Thomas
MORE, Samuel
NEWMAN, George H.
NEWTON, Richard H.
NICHOLSON, George H.
NORRIS, Thomas H.
OLLY, W. C.
PATTERSON, James E.
PENN, William H.
POLK, Thomas Elzey
POSEY, Frank
PRATT, Richard
PRESTON, William
PUMPHREY, George W.
ROBESIN, Peter
ROBINSON, Stephen V.
ROUSEY, Joseph
SATTERTHWAITE, Romeo
SAVAGE, Jesse
SCHLADE, James W.
SCOTT, John H.
SHIELDS, James
SMITH, Frank
SMITH, Robert
SMITH, William J.
SNEED, John
SNOWDEN, Joseph
SPRIGGS, John
SPRIGGS, Stephen

PLAIN CAPS indicate names from this volume • **BOLD CAPS** indicate names from *On the Trail* (1995)

STEVENS, Jacob W.
STEVENSON, James
STEWARD, Lewis
STEWART, John
SWAN, Edward
TATUM, King James
THOMAS, Frank
THOMAS, George
THOMAS, James E.
THOMAS, William H.
TILLISON, Samuel
TRIPP, William
TURNER, Goodricks
TURNER, John C.
TURNER, Joseph H.
TURNER, Simon
TURNER, Wallace
TURNER, Walter
WALLACE, Benjamin F.
WALLEY, Augustus
WASHINGTON, William
WATERS, Joseph W.
WATKINS, Walter
WEST, Harrison
WHITE, George
WHITE, John W.
WILEY, Ambrose
WILLIAMS, Charles
WILLIAMS, John
WILLIS, Alexander
WILSON, James
WILSON, Roy
WILSON, Thomas
WOODLAND, William
WOODS, Henry
YOUNG, Alfred
Berlin
    VICTOR, William
Bethesda
    REED, Samuel
BIRD, Savage
Boonsboro
    WILSON, William
Brookville
    WASHINGTON, William
BROWN, Daniel
BROWN, Washington
BROWN, William
CAMPBELL, John
Cambridge
    YOUNG, Alfred
Caroline County
    CAINE, George
Carroll County
    JONES, George
    POSEY, Frank
Catonsville
    COSTON, W. Hilary
Cecil County
    MOORE, Fredrick Thomas
Cecilton
    WILSON, Thomas

Charles County
    BAXTER, William C.
    COLE, Gonza
    JONES, Jeremiah
Chesapeake Beach
    COLBERT, Frederick
Chesapeake City
    WARRICK, Robert
Chestertown
    BLAKE, William H.
    CLAGGETT, Joseph
    COLBERT, Frederick
    COLLINS, Melvin R.
Cumberland
    EDWARDS, Richard C.
    DENT, Allen
    DENT, Henry
    DICKERSON, James M.
    DORSEY, Horace A.
Easton
    GARDNER, William H.
    MILLER, Henry
Eden
    POLK, Thomas Elzey
Elkridge
    HARRIS, Hyder
Elkton
    MILLER, Colonel E.
    ENNIS, Joseph
Fairmount Heights
    KELLAM, Alfred
Frederick
    JONES, Emanuel
    SMALLGOOD, Eli
    SPEAKES, William
GANT, Joseph
Hagerstown
    COSTON, W. Hilary
    WILSON, William O.
HANSON, John
HARRIS, George
Havre de Grace
    PRESTON, William
HENSON, Barry
HOOPER, George
HOWARD, Lewis
Howard County
    TRIPPS, George A.
Hyattsville
    PLUMMER, Henry Vinton
JACOBS, George
JONES, Beverly
Kent County
    JAMES, Charles
Knoxville
    BATTLE, William P.
MILLBROWN, Robert
Montgomery County
    COLE, Gonza
    HERBERT, Thomas H.
    POSEY, Frank
    SCOTT, Edward

NOAL, Robert J.
Oxon Hill
    PROCTOR, John C.
PORTER, John H.
PORTER, Joseph H.
PRATT, Richard
Prince Georges County
    BOYNE, Thomas
    CLAGGETT, Joseph
    COLBERT, Frederick
    GREAVES, Clinton
    MEEKS, Joseph
    SIMMS, Squire
    SIMONS, Henry
    TUTTLE, Aleck
    WARREN, John
PUMPHREY, James H.
Queen Anne's County
    THOMAS, Frank
Queenstown
    RINGGOLD, Henry
Reisterstown
    WALLEY, Augustus
ROBERTS, Henry
ROBERTS, Philip
St. Mary's City
    BRISCOE, Edward
St. Mary's County
    DENT, Henry
    STEVENS, John F.
Sandy Spring
    DAVIS, John W.
SCHOENOCKER, John
STIRLING, Martin
Suitland
    MINOR, Samuel T.
Talbot County
    ALLSUP, Thomas H.
THOMAS, James E.
THOMPSON, James
Towson
    GRAY, Charles
TUBEMAN, Josiah G.
TURNER, William
Upper Marlboro
    HAWKINS, William
WILLIAMS, James H.
Mason, Ada White
    MASON, George F.
Mason, Rose
    MASON, George F.
Masons (Freemasons)
    ANDERSON, William T.
    BROOKS, Preston
    BRUMMSICK, George
    CRUMBLY, Floyd H.
    LEMUS, Rienzi Brock
    PRIOLEAU, George W.
    PURNELL, William Whipple
    SANDERS, Mingo
    TURNER, Charles B.
    WIGGINS, S. T.

PLAIN CAPS indicate names from this volume • **BOLD CAPS** indicate names from *On the Trail* (1995)

Massachusetts
  Andover
    PINCHBACK, Walter A.
  Belmont
    WILLIAMS, Harry J.
  Boston
    AUSTIN, Edward S.
    BROWN, Frank B.
    CHISHOLM, Frank R.
    CLARK, Henry
    CORNELIUS, George W.
    DOUGLAS, William
    FRANKLIN, Henry O.
    HARRIS, Israel
    HOWARD, Julius
    HURBERT, David
    HUTTON, James T.
    JACKSON, William Hubert
    JOHNSON, Edward B.
    JONES, Philip
    KELLY, George H.
    LEONARD, John E.
    MINTUS, Aurelius
    PEREA, Beverly
    QUARLES, James T.
    SCOTT, John
    SMITH, William H.
    SURRY, Calvin A.
    TAYLOR, John
    THOMPSON, Albert
    WASHINGTON, George
    WASHINGTON, Henry F.
    WHEATON, Horace F.
    WILLIAMS, Jessie
  Brockton
    ASHPORT, Lemuel
  Cambridge
    PEREA, Beverly
    SHEAFF, Joseph E.
  Chelsea
    WILLIAMS, William J.
    CURTIS, William H.
  Great Barrington
    SMITH, William H.
    LATIMER, George A.
  Lowell
    TAYLOR, John
  Readville
    BUSH, James W.
    MILLIMAN, Jerry
    MOORE, Miles
  Roxbury
    SANDERS, Walter P.
  Springfield
    HUTTON, George R.
    HUTTON, James T.
  Taunton
    ASHPORT, Lemuel
  West Bridgewater
    ASHPORT, Lemuel
  Worcester
    BELDEN, James H.

    JACKSON, William Hubert
Massey, George
    McCLAIN, Henry
Massey, Louisa M.
    McCLAIN, Henry
Mathews, Annie
    ELIXANDER, Charles
Matney, Ray
    SMITH, Arthur
Maus, Marion Perry
    THOMAS, James H.
Maxon, Mason Marion
    EVANS, John
Maxwell, Emmett
    BRECKENRIDGE, William
Maxwell, William
    BRECKENRIDGE, William
Mayers, Frank
    STOKES, Henry A.
Meadows, Hiram
    MEADOWS, Edward
    MEADOWS, John
Meadows, Wilson
    BRANSFORD, Wesley
Mechanics Savings Bank,
  Richmond, VA
    HANKINS, W. A.
Meharry Medical College
    BROWN, Sterling Price
Meilley's Commercial Night
  School, New Orleans
    FRANKLIN, Henry O.
Merritt, Jesus
    MERRITT, Julius
Merritt, Wesley
    ROGERS, John
Mertz, M. L.
    MOZIQUE, Edward
Mescalero Apaches
    COLLYER, S.
    WHITE, Lewis
Mescalero Reservation, NM
    Mescalero Indian Agency
    KENNEDY, Richard
Meserve, C. F.
    YOUNG, James H.
Messenger (U.S. marshal)
    GOULD, Charley
Methodist Church
    COATES, Robert F.
    CRUMBLY, Floyd H.
    ELLISON, Lewis A.
    WANTON, George H.
    WHELDON, Samuel
    WILLIAMS, Jessie
    YELVERTON, Aaron
Metropolitan African Methodist
  Episcopal Church, Washington,
  DC
    STEWARD, Theophilus G.

Meuse-Argonne battle
    CAMPBELL, John B.
    QUEEN, Howard D.
Mew, Martha
    MEW, Benjamin
Mexico. *See also* Pershing, John
  Joseph; Villa, Pancho
    ADAIR, Clifford J.
  Aguascalientes
    MOORE, Richard
    YOUNG, Charles
    AGUIRRE, Martiriano
    BARRA, Juan
    BARRERA, Espetacion
    BOWLEGS, Harkless
    BOWLEGS, John H.
    BRUNER, Cipio
    BRUNER, James
    BRUNER, Zack
  Buena Vista
    STARR, Stephen G.
    BUSH, James W.
    BUSH, William Henry
  Carrizal
    BIGSTAFF, Peter
    BLOODGOOD (Sergeant; 10th
      Cav)
    DAY, James E.
    HARRIS, Sam H.
    HENDERSON, Monola
    HINES, Will
    HOUSTON, Henry C.
    JETER, John
    JONES, Archie
    LEE, Harvey M.
    LYONS (Sergeant)
    MATHEWS, Charlie
    MOSES, Thomas
    OLIVER, Joe
    PAGE, Felix
    QUEEN, Howard D.
    RUCKER, DeWitt
    TALBOTT, Lee
    TURNER, George
    WINROW, William
    CASSAS, Luce
    CLAYBORNE, Peter
    DANIELS, Charles
    DANIELS, Jerry
    DINNY, Henry
    DIXIE, Joe
    DIXON, Joe
    DIXON, Joseph
    DOOLEY, William
    FACTOR, Pompey
    FACTOR, Tobe
    FAY, Adam
    FAY, Sandy
    FRAUSTO, Gregario
    FRAUSTO, Quirino
    FRAUSTO, Thomas
    FRAUSTO, Vector

PLAIN CAPS indicate names from this volume • **BOLD CAPS** indicate names from *On the Trail* (1995)

GOODWIN, **Albert**
GORDON, Sam
GRAYSON, Renty
HARASHAW, James
HATCHER, Alex
HUDNELL, George
JAMESON, Henry W.
JEFFERSON, Sam
JOHNSON, Daniel
JULY, Benjamin
JULY, Billy
JULY, Carolina
JULY, Charles
JULY, Fay
JULY, John
KIBBETTS, John
Laguna de Parras
   KIBBETTS, John
LONGORIO, Julian
LONGORIO, Manuel
McBRYAR, William
MARASCHAL, Natividad
MARASCHAL, Trinida
Matamoros
   FOSTER, William
MILLER, William
MORTON, Willis
Naciemientos, *see below*
   Nacimiento
Nacimiento
   KIBBETTS, John
   KIBBETTS, Robert
   PAYNE, Isaac
Parral
   WILLINGHAM, Walter E.
PAYNE, Aaron
PAYNE, Adam (2)
PAYNE, Billy
PAYNE, Daniel
PAYNE, David
PAYNE, Isaac
PAYNE, Plantz
PAYNE, Robert
PERRYMAN, Ignacio
PERRYMAN, James
PHILIPS, Joe
PHILIPS, Joseph
Piedra Negras
   LONGORIO, Julian
Pineto Mountains, *see below* Sierra
   de Pinitos
Presidio del Norte
   JOHNSTON, Charles
Remolino
   GRAYSON, Renty
   PERRYMAN, James
SANCHEZ, Antonio
Santa Cruz de Villegas
   YOUNG, Charles
Santa Rosa
   WINCHESTER, Sandy
SCOTT, EDWARD

SHIELDS, William
Sierra de Pinitos
   FOLLIS (Private)
STEWARD, Theophilus G.
THOMPSON, John
THOMPSON, Prymus
VOSKER, Santon
WARD, John
WARRIOR, Bill
WARRIOR, Scott
WASHINGTON, Andrew
WASHINGTON, George
WIGGINS, John
WILSON, Ariel
WILSON, Ben
WILSON, Brisban
WILSON, Coffy
WILSON, Cuff
WILSON, James
WILSON, Jasper
WILSON, Tony
WILSON, William
WORYER, Henry
Micanopy (Seminole chief)
   JULY, Sampson
Michigan
   Alamando
      STAFFORD, Haywood M.
   Aleman, *see above* Alamando
   Ann Arbor
      WILLIAMS, George A.
   Cassopolis
      ROBINSON, Ira
   Detroit
      CHEEK, Frank W.
      COOK, William
      FINNEGAN, Michael
      McCOWN, Peter
   Eaton County
      ODEN, Oscar N.
   Saginaw
      DUNCAN, William
Miles, Nelson Appleton
   BUTLER, Thomas C.
   STEWARD, Theophilus G.
   TERRY, Charles Lincoln
Military Order of Foreign Wars
   ANDERSON, William T.
Miller, Alonzo
   ANDERSON, Louis
   PORTER, John H.
Miller, Carrall
   MILLER, Girard
Miller, Elizabell
   MILLER, John D.
Miller, Elizabeth
   JAMESON, Henry W.
   MILLER, Girard
Miller, Gerrard, Jr.
   MILLER, Girard
Miller, Henrietta
   MILLER, William F.

Miller, Martha A. Parrish
   MILLER, Girard
Miller, Nola Montgomery
   MILLER, Jesse C.
Miller, Sarah Anne
   BENJAMIN, Robert
Miller, William L.
   MILLER, Girard
Milliman, Elizabeth Van
   MILLIMAN, Jerry
Milliman, Rosa Ann Jackson
   MILLIMAN, Jerry
Mills, Anson
   CALDWELL (Private)
Miner, John B.
   BROWN, John W.
Miner, Julia
   BROWN, John W.
Minnesota. *See also* Cemeteries
   BURRELL, James H.
   CRINER, Walter
   DURANT, Empire Adam
   EDDINGS, James
   EMBREE, Benjamin
   Ft Snelling. *See also* Cemeteries
      ARNEL, William
      BALDWIN, Stephen
      BALL, John F.
      BARNER, Moses
      BARNETT, John
      BARTON, George
      BAXTER, William C.
      BEALE, Willington
      BELL, William
      BIRCH, Philip
      BOYNE, Thomas
      BRANSON, James
      BROWN, Henry
      BROWN, John
      BROWN, Joseph
      BUTLER, James H.
      CAINE, George
      CALDWELL, Henry
      CANSBY, John H.
      CARMICHAEL, John
      CARTER, Lewis
      CLARK, Henry
      CLAVON, Merritt
      COLE, Gonza
      CONNELL, Jim
      CONWAY, Johnson
      COOPER, James D.
      CORNELIUS, George W.
      COVINGTON, James C.
      COWAN, James D.
      CROCHERON, Luther
      CROCKET, George H.
      CROSS, Joseph
      CRUMP, Edward W.
      DAVIS, John W.
      DeALEXANDER, Alexis
      DEMBY, Sheridan

PLAIN CAPS indicate names from this volume • **BOLD CAPS** indicate names from *On the Trail* (1995)

DENNIS, Herman
DOTY, Timothy
DOUGLAS, William
DRAIN, Peter
DUNN, Nathan
FISHER, Henry
FISHER, William J.
FITZGERALD, James
FORD, Wiley
FRAGER, Robert
GAMBLE, John
GOODE, Benjamin H.
GRAHAM, John W.
GRAVES, William
GRIFFIN, George
GUY, John
HALL, Edward M.
HAMILTON, Charles
HANCE, George W.
HARE, Solomon
HARRIS, Henry
HAYWOOD, James
HENDERSON, William
HOWARD, Julius
HURBERT, David
JAMES, Charles
JAMES, Edward
JOHNSON, Benjamin
JOHNSON, James
JOHNSON, James
JOHNSON, William
JONES, Bular
JONES, John S.
JONES, William
JONES, William B.
JONES, William T.
KELLY, Walter
KIRK, William
LARK, Aaron
LAWS, James
LAWSON, Walter
LEE, Ulysses G.
LEE, William
LEE, William H.
LEWIS, Charles
LOCHLIN, William
LOCKADOO, Nathan
McCLATCHIE, Henry
MARTIN, George
MEADE, William
MEBANE, Samuel
MEEKS, Joseph
MERRIWEATHER, Henry
MIDDLETON, Richard
MILLER, Alexander
MILLER, David A.
MILLER, Frank
MILLER, John
MILLIMAN, Jerry
MORE, Samuel
MORRELL, Benjamin
MOSLEY, Robert

NEWMAN, Henry
NEWSOME, Felix
OGLESBY, Walter
OILDS, James
OLLY, W. C.
PATTERSON, Stephen
PENDLETON, Joseph
POKE, Samuel
POSEY, Frank
PRATT, Richard
PRESTON, William
RAY, Albert
REDDICK, Charles
RINGGOLD, Henry
RIVERS, Samuel
ROADS, Charles A. E.
ROBBS, William
ROBINSON, Charles (Private; H/25th Inf)
ROBINSON, Charles (Private; K/25th Inf)
ROBINSON, Henry C.
ROBINSON, John
ROBINSON, Lewis
ROUT, Richard
SAVAGE, Jesse
SCOTT, John
SIMMONS, Charles
SIMONS, Henry
SMALLWOOD, Lee
SMART, Ransom
SMITH, Andrew J.
SMITH, George H.
SMITH, Richard
SMITH, William H.
SMITH, William H.
SNEED, John
SPEAKES, William
SPERLIN, George
SPRIGGS, John
STEWARD, David
STROTHER, Albert
TELLIES, Robert
THOMAS, Frank
THOMAS, Sharp
THOMPSON, Clarence
WALLACE, Washington
WARREN, John
WASHINGTON, James
WASHINGTON, Morgan G.
WHITEHURST, James
WILLIAMS, Oliver
WILLIAMS, Squire
WILLIAMS, Washington
WILSON, William
GASTON, William H.
HAYNES, Oscar
HENDERSON, William
JAMES, Louis M.
JAMES, Morris
JONES, Thomas P.
KELLEY, George B.

LEE, Allen H.
LYTLE, Claude
McCARTHY, Archie
McFADDEN, William C.
McKINNEY, James
MEADE, Robert
MILLER, Thomas
Minneapolis
    COBLE, Andrew J.
    DEHONEY, Peter
    WASHINGTON, Henry F.
    WILLIS, Dorsie W.
Minnetonka Beach
    EMERY, Andrew J.
MITCHELL, James A.
Moorhead
    DEHONEY, Peter
MUNDIN, George A.
NEAL, Thomas
NEWTON, George
PARKER, Calvin
RAYMOND, Ira Curtis
ROGERS, David L.
St Paul
    ALLENSWORTH, Allen
    CONWAY, Henry
    HALL, Frank W.
    JOHNSON, William
    KNOX, Durward B.
    LOVING, Walter H.
    POSEY, Frank
SHELVIN, Robert
SMITH, Henry C.
SMITH, Lawson
STEPP, Thaddeus W.
STRATTON, John H.
TAYLOR, Oliver
THURSTON, William T.
TODD, Arthur J.
TURNER, James E.
WASHINGTON, Henry F.
WASHINGTON, George
WIGGINGTON, Frank B.
WILKERSON, Alphonse G.
WILLIAMS, James
WILLIAMS, Robert
WIMBERLY, William
Minstrels
    HOOD, Perry
    POTTER (Private)
    SMITH, Jacob C.
    TAYLOR, Lewis
Miss Purdy's Kindergarten, Cleveland, OH
    PEAL, Allen S.
Mississippi
    ALEXANDER, John Hanks
    ALLSUP, Thomas H.
    Bolivar County
        BENNETT, John
    Brookhaven
        CAIN, Scott

PLAIN CAPS indicate names from this volume • **BOLD CAPS** indicate names from *On the Trail* (1995)

BROWN, Joseph
Clarksdale
 GORDON, John
Columbus
 WOODS, Robert Gordon
Franklin
 WORD, Peter
Gulfport
 BENTLEY, James B.
HALL, Morell
Harrison County
 EVANS, James
Holly Springs
 McCLATCHIE, Henry
 WOODS, Robert Gordon
Jackson
 ADAMS, King
 JOHNSON, James
 SANFORD, Pelm
 TURNER, George
KAY, Alexander
Lee County
 BEACHEM, Will
Liberty
 MAGEE, Alfred
Marshall County
 WEATHERLY, James
Natchez
 KNOX, Durward B.
Oxford
 WEBB, Moses
Pass Christian
 WILSON, Bailey
Pike County
 BRETT, James
Port Gibson
 TRAVILLION, Thomas
Prentiss County
 POLK, Edward
SCOTT, Nelson
Ship Island
 BORELAND, Peter
 BRETT, James
 BUSHWAR, John
 HANDY, Frank
 JOHNSON, Henry
 LOCK, James
 STAPLETON, Charles
Ship's Island, *see above* Ship Island
SIMMONS, George
Starkville
 WOODS, Robert Gordon
Tate County
 ANDERSON, Henry
 TRAVILLION, Thomas
Tunica County
 WITHERS, George
Vicksburg
 MYERS, Thomas C.
Waynesboro
 JACKSON, James F.

West Point
 WILLIAMS, Washington
 WHITE, William
 WILLIAMS, Fielding
 WILSON, Thomas C.
Woodville
 ADAMS, Alexander H.
Missouri
ANDERSON, Richard
Bevier
 CHATMOUN, Webb
 BOWEN (Corporal; H/25th Inf)
 BROWN, John
Brunswick
 HOPKINS, Clarence
 HOWERTON, John C
Caldwell County
 CASEY, John F.
Callaway County
 CANSBY, John H.
Calloway County, *see above* Callaway County
Carondelet
 MILLER, Charles
Cassville
 GRAMMER, Edward L.
Coal County, *see below* Cole County
Cole County
 WILLIAMS, Joseph E.
Columbia
 EPPERSON, Stephen O.
 GREEN, Wallace W.
DeSoto
 NAPIER, Henry F.
Farmington
 HOLLIDAY, Presley
 SMITH, Charles
Green County, *see below* Greene County
Greene County
 ANDERSON, Roudie
Hamilton
 THOMPSON, Fred F.
Hannibal
 BOHON, Robert O.
 WILLIAMS, Noah W.
 HARVEY, John W.
Independence
 WILLIAMS, Cathay
Jackson
 FRANKLIN, Walter
 WILLIAMS, Cathay
Jackson County
 WALLACE, Washington
Jefferson Barracks
 ADAMS, Alexander
 ALDRIDGE, George
 ALLEN, Lee
 ANDERSON, Charles N.
 ANDERSON, William
 BAKER, Benjamin O.
 BAKER, George

BEAMON, William Henry
BEAUMAN, William N.
BENNETT, John
BIVINS, Horace W.
BOGGS, Jesse
BOLIN, Robert
BOWEN, Austin
BRISCOE, Henry
BRONTZ, Elijah
BROOKS, William W.
BROWN, John
BURRELL, Cornelius
CAMMEL, Joseph
CAMPBELL, John M.
CARTY, James
CASH, Richard
CHASE, Levi
CHESTER, Stanley
CLAY, Abraham L. J.
COLEMAN, Theodore
COLLINS, Francis
COLWELL, Aaron
COOKSEY, Kirk
CRAIG, Daniel
CRUDER, William
CRUTCHFIELD, Daniel
DAVIS, Henry
DEAGONS, Joseph E.
DOUGHERTY, Charles
DUFFRE, Charles
ELLIS, Arthur
EUSTON, Henry
EVANS, Elleck
EVANS, Henry
GEORGE, Lorenzo
GREEN, Frank E.
GREEN, Warren
GREEN, William
GROSS, Thomas
GUNTER, William H.
GUY, Frank
HALL, William
HAMILTON, William H.
HARRIS, Jerry
HAWKINS, George
HAYS, James
HAZZARD, Frank
HENDERSON, Charles
HENSON, Clem
HIBBITT, John
HILLIARD, Peter
HINSLEY, Joseph
HUFF, Albert
HUNTER, Ellis
JACKSON, Brown
JACKSON, Thomas
JAMES, Henry
JENKINS, Tillman
JOHNSON, Henry
JOHNSON, James
JOHNSON, Jim
JOHNSON, Leoid

PLAIN CAPS indicate names from this volume • **BOLD CAPS** indicate names from *On the Trail* (1995)

JONES, Edward
JONES, Henry
JONES, James
JONES, Jeremiah
JONES, Stephen
KANE, George
KENNEDY, Richard
LAWSON, William A.
LEE, Asberry
LEE, Charles
LEE, Joseph
LOVING, John
MACK, James L.
MASON, Thomas
McBRIDE, George
McCLAIN, Henry
McCLAIN, John H.
McCOY, Charles
McNABB, Lewis W.
MERRYFIELD, William
MILES, Silas
MILLER, Charles
MILLION, Perry
MOORE, Joseph
MORE, Charles
MOULTON, Edward
MOZIQUE, Edward
PARKER, Amos A.
PARKER, Archie
PAYNE, George E.
PERKINS, Thomas
PERRY, Charles
PERRY, Henry
PLEDGER, William A., Jr.
PORTERFIELD, Henry
PRANN, Charles W.
PROCTOR, John C.
RAY, Albert
REED, James T.
REED, William
ROMONS, Isaac W.
ROUSEY, Joseph
RUSSELL, Edward
RUSSUM, Louis H.
SANDERS, Braxton
SAXTON, Sam
SAYERS, Willie
SEALS, Dock
SHERIDAN, David
SHERWOOD, James H.
SIMMONS, Frank
SMITH, Jeff
SMITH, Thomas
SPENCER, Jeremiah
STEWARD, Frank R.
SUMMERS, Matthew
TAYLOR, Alonzo
TAYLOR, Herbert
TAYLOR, John
TERRY, Charles Lincoln
THOMAS, James H.
THOMAS, William

THOMPSON, Samuel
TILLMAN, Charles W.
TOLER, George
TRENT, Leonidas B.
VROOMAN, William A.
WADE, Henry
WATKINS, Jacob
WAXWOOD, Harvy
WHEATON, Horace F.
WHITE, Andrew
WHITE, George F.
WILLIAMS, Arthur
WILLIAMS, Cathay
WILLIAMS, Edward
WILLIAMS, Henry
WILLIAMS, James
WILLIAMS, Jessie
WILLIAMS, Minor
WILLIAMS, Thomas
WILLIAMS, Walter
WILLIS, John R.
WILSON, Henry
WILSON, John
WILSON, Thomas
WITCH, Henry
WRIGHT, Benjamin
Jefferson City
DAVIS, Robert
JOHNSON, Henry
JORDAN, Leon H.
WILBURN, Thomas G.
Joplin
WATTS, Willie
Kansas City
BRANSFORD, Wesley
BRISCOE, Henry
CASEY, John F.
DRANE, Lucilius
FOSTER, Leslie J.
HATCHER, Alex
HENDERSON (Sergeant)
INGRAM, W. H.
JACKSON, Henry
LOWE, Charles H.
MILLER, Colonel E.
SCOTT, Oscar J. W.
SHAW, Thomas
TILLMAN, Lafayette A.
TOLSON, Marion
WALKER, George
WALLACE, Harry
WALLER, John L.
WATKINS, Jacob
WHITLEY (Sergeant)
WILSON, William
YOUNG, Charles
LaClede
HOWERTON, John C
Lexington
COLLEY, William E.
JOHNSON, William L.
McCORMACK, Henry

Macon
JAMESON, Henry W.
Macon County
BLEW, Joseph
Madison
BURTON, Hayes
Morgan County
HENDERSON, Edward
PERRY, Charles
Platte City
BROWN, Benjamin
Rolla
BOWENS, Marcellus
St. Charles
GIBSON, James W.
St. Francis County, *see below*
St. Francois County
St. Francois County
HILL, William H.
St. Joseph
ADAMS, Singleton
BANKS, Gabriel H.
BARNETT, Grant
BENTLEY, James B.
BUNION, Thomas
BUSH, William Henry
CARTER, Alfred
CASEY, John F.
CHATMOUN, Webb
COKER, Abram
COLBERT, Frederick
DENT, Henry
EVANS, Frank, Sr.
GREGG, John A.
HAMPTON, Wade
HENDERSON, William A.
HOWERTON, John C
HURBURT, J. D. C.
JOHNSON, Moses
JONES, Eugene
St. Louis
ALEXANDER, Nicholas
ALLENSWORTH, Allen
ANDERSON, Louis
ANDERSON, Richard
ANDREWS, Clyde C.
AUSTIN, John T.
BARD, Benjamin
BENJAMIN, Robert
BIRCH, Philip
BRIDGES, Travis
BROWN, John
BUTTON, Francis
CAMPBELL, Thomas C.
CANSBY, John H.
CHAMBERS, Clifford
CHANDLER, Ed D.
CHILDRESS, William
CONAC, Washington C.
COOK, John
COOPER, Barney
CRAGG, Allen

DADE, Allen
DeALEXANDER, Alexis
DILLON, Robert
DINGMAN, Hiram L. B.
DIXON, Charley
DRAIN, Peter
EDWARDS, Robert
ELLIS, Arthur
ELZY, Robert
EVANS, Robert
FAULKNER, Charles S. C.
FINDLEY, John
FITZGERALD, James
FORMAN, Elwood A.
GOODE, Benjamin H.
GREEN, Richard
HAMILTON, Thomas
HARRIS, James H.
HAYNES, William
HENDERSON, Edward
HENDERSON, William
JOHNSON, Elias
JOHNSON, Frank L.
JOHNSON, Leoid
JOHNSON, Robert
JOHNSON, Sam
JONES, Eugene
JONES, Jefferson
JONES, William S.
LANE, William
LEE, Joseph
LEWIS, Fred
McCLATCHIE, Henry
MARSHALL, Frank W.
MARTIN, Abram
MIDDLETON, Richard
MILES, James
POKE, Samuel
PORTER, Harrison
PORTER, Samuel H.
PROCTOR, William
REID, Samuel
ROBINSON, Robert W.
ROUT, Richard
SANDERS, Mingo
SCOTT, George
SENOR, Mack
SIMMONS, Charles
SLANTER, William
STEWART, Leon
STRAMBOLD, George
TAYLOR, Stephen
THOMAS, Jessie
THOMAS, Sharp
WAKEFIELD, Samuel
WASHINGTON, George
WASHINGTON, John H.
WASHINGTON, Samuel
WATKINS, Jacob
WHITE, Burrel
WILKES, William
WILLIAMS, Cathay

WILLIAMS, John
WILLIAMSON, Sam
WILLIAMSON, William
WILSON, John H.
WOODS, Harry
WOODS, Robert Gordon
WOODSIDE, Lee
YEIZER, Mordecai
St. Louis Barracks
  BRITTON, William H.
  GARDNER, Jacob N.
  HARRISON, William H.
  MITCHELL, James
  ST. CLAIR, Charles H.
  SMITH, Thomas
  SMITH, Thompson W.
  WHITE, Henry
Saline County
  JONES, Silas
  WILLIAMS, Lilburn
Sedalia
  COUNCE, Joseph F. M.
Smithton
  JACKSON, John H.
Springfield
  McBROOM, James
  NEESE, Kern
Thomasville
  OLE, Henry R.
  THOMPSON, Mason
  TURNER (Private)
  WILLIAMS, Charles
Missouri (hospital ship)
  HIPSHIRE, Riley
Missouri River
  MASON, Henry
Missouri State Penitentiary, Jefferson City
  DAVIS, Robert
  JOHNSON, Henry
  JONES, Samuel
Mitchell, Mason
  DREW, James L.
Montana. *See also* Tongue River Reservation, MT
  BELL, Dennis
  Big Horn Mountains
    BROWNING, Andrew
    FRIERSON, Eugene
    JENKINS, Blunt
    JUDSON, John
  Billings
    BIVINS, Horace W.
    BIVINS, Horace W.
  Butte
    ANDERSON, John B.
    BROWN, William H.
    JONES, Jeremiah
    CHAMBERS, William
    CROUCH, Edward
  Ft Assiniboine

ALEXANDER, James H.
ALLEN, Henry
ALLSUP, Thomas H.
ANCRUM, William
ANDERSON, William T.
BAKER, Edward L., Jr.
BAKER, Jesse
BATTLE, Arthur
BIVINS, Horace W.
BROWN, Benjamin
BROWN, Daniel
BROWN, David T.
BROWN, James
BROWN, William
BUCKNER, Benjamin
CHEATHAM, Alexander
CLAGGETT, Joseph
CLAYBORNE, Peter
CONLEY, Paschall
DEHONEY, Peter
DENNY, Elbiron
DOOMS, Thomas
DORSEY, Charles A.
DOWLING, Jefferson
DRANE, Lucilius
DUNTON, John
DYALS, George
ELLIOTT, James
ELLISTON, Amos
EWELL, William C.
FAULKNER, Charles S. C.
FOSTER, Saint
GANTZ, Frank
GASKINS, Albert
GEE, William
GIVENS, William H.
GRIFFIN, Thomas
GUNTER, Ulysses G.
HAMILTON, William H.
HASKINS, David
HENRY, Vodrey
HENSON, Barry
HICKS, Charles H.
HOUSTON, Adam
JOHNSTON, William
JONES, James
JONES, Philip
JONES, Silas
KEITH, Howard
KINSLOW, Thomas
KURNEY, Robert
LANE, Edward
LUMKINS, Ananias
MILLBROWN, Robert
MINAR, James L.
MINGUS, Charles
MORI, Philip
PAYNE, James H.
PROCTOR, Clarence L.
PULLEN, Frank W., Jr.
RAY, Albert
REED, Miller

PLAIN CAPS indicate names from this volume • **BOLD CAPS** indicate names from *On the Trail* (1995)

ROBERTS, Philip
ROBINSON (Private)
ROLLINS, Walker S.
SCOTT, Winfield
SHROPSHIRE, Shelvin
SMITH, George
SMITH, Jacob C.
SMITH, T. Clay
STRATTON, John H.
TAYLOR, Charles
TERRY, Charles Lincoln
THACKER, William
THOMAS, James H.
THOMPSON, George S.
WALTERS, Smith
WESTACOTT, Charles
WHITE, J. E.
WILCOX, Mitchell
WILLIAMS, Tony
WIMBERLY, William
Ft Benton
ALLSUP, Thomas H.
Ft Custer
ANDERSON, Robert (Saddler
    Sgt; 10th Cav)
ANDERSON, Robert (Sergeant;
    B/10th Cav)
BRADLEY, Levi
BUCK, John
BAILEY, Isaac
BAILEY, Isaac W.
BAILEY, John H.
BAKER, Charles W.
BALDWIN, Lewis
BARNES, Francis I.
BARNES, Samuel
BECKETT, William C.
BOOKER, James F.
BROWN, Washington
CRUISE, John H.
DAVIS, Matt
DORSEY, Solomon T.
DOUGLASS, Samuel W.
FORD, James W.
FRANKLIN, John
FRIERSON, Eugene
GOENS, Henry
GRAHAM, John
GREEN, Walter
HOLLIDAY, Presley
HUMPHREY, Cornelius
IRVING, Lee
JEFFERS, David B.
JOHNSON, Daniel
JOHNSON, Robert M.
JOHNSON, Smith
JOHNSON, Walker
KIMBLERN, Calvin
LETCHER, Philip
McCLAIN, Henry
McCORMACK, Henry
McCOWN, Peter

MARSHALL, Hoyle
OWENS, Charles H.
PIERSON, David
ROWENS, Chester R.
SMITH, Jacob C.
SMITH, Lewis M.
SNOTEN, Peter
SPURLOCK, Charles
STANLEY, William
TAYLOR, John J. L.
THOMPSON, James
TILLEY, James D.
TRAVILLION, Thomas
TUBEMAN, Josiah G.
TURNER, Charles B.
TURNER, William
UPSHUR, George C.
WILLIAMS, George
YOUNG, Charles
YOUNG, Thomas
Ft Harrison
ALLENSWORTH, Allen
CARTER, Amos A.
DAVIS, John B.
DICKERSON
MALONE, John
ROBERTS (Color Sgt)
TATE, William
WALL, Archy
WILLIAMS, Walter B.
Ft Keogh
ANDERSON, Benjamin A.
BAILEY, Isaac W.
BIVINS, Horace W.
BROOKS, James
BUCK, John
FINNEGAN, Michael
HAYES, James C.
JACKSON, John H.
JOHNSON, Robert M.
JONES, Philip
MATTHEWS, Courtney
MILLER, Cooper
MITCHELL, Joseph G.
PAYNE, William
SMITH, Lewis M.
TAYLOR, Addison
TAYLOR, George R.
THOMAS, Charles
WILEY, Frederick
Ft Missoula
BIVINS, Horace
BOYNE, Thomas
BRIDGES, Travis
BROWN, Walker
BROWN, William W.
BUCK, John
BURDEN, Henry
BUTLER, Thomas C.
BUTTON, Francis
CALLOWAY, John W.
CAMPBELL, Robert

CANSBY, John H.
CASSELLE, Nelson A.
CHAMBERS, William
CHAPMAN, Joseph
CHATMAN, William
COOK, John
COTHRAN, Nesbert
COX, Jonas W.
CROSSWAY, Turner
DANIEL, J. R.
DEARING, Edward
DINGMAN, Hiram L. B.
ELLIOTT, James
FIELDS, Harvey
FINDLEY, John
FORMAN, Elwood A.
FREEMAN, Samuel
GARNEY, John D.
GILLISPIE, James R.
GRAY, Robert
GRAYSON, A. L.
GREEN, Dalbert P.
HALL, Frank W.
HARE, Solomon
HARWOOD, Thomas
HAWKINS, Emmett
HAYNES, William
HAYNES, William J.
HOWARD, John D.
JACKSON, F.
JOHNSON, Elias
JOHNSON, Isaiah
JOHNSON, James
JOHNSON, Sam
JOHNSON, Thomas
JONES, Eugene
JONES, Henry C.
LIPPS, O. H.
LUNDY, Samuel
MARTIN, Abram
OTEY, James
PAYNE, Charles
PENDLETON, Joseph
PHILLIPS, Albert
PILLOW, Alexander
POLK, Edward
POWELL, George D.
PROCTOR, William
PULLEN, Frank W., Jr.
REDDICK, Charles
REID, Samuel
ROSE, Alexander
ROUT, Richard
SANDERS, Mingo
SCARSCE, Henry
SCOTT, George
SCOTT, Richard
STEWARD, Theophilus G..
TELLIES, Robert
TERRY, Charles Lincoln
THOMAS, James E.
WEIGHT, John

PLAIN CAPS indicate names from this volume • **BOLD CAPS** indicate names from *On the Trail* (1995)

WHINE, Minton
WILCOX, Mitchell
WILKINSON, Thomas H.
WILLIAMS, Elbert
WILLIAMS, John (Corporal; B/25th Inf)
WILLIAMS, John (QM Sgt; 25th Inf)
WILLIAMS, John G.
WILLIAMS, Maxwell A.
WILLIAMSON, Sam
WILLIAMSON, William
WILSON, John H.
YOUNG, Hartwell
Ft Shaw
  COTHRAN, Nesbert
  GORDON, J.
  HORTON, George
  HUNT, John
  POSEY, Frank
  RAY, Albert
  ROBINSON, Robert
  TALTON, Jefferson
Great Falls
  THOMAS, Sharp
  THORNTON, William
Havre
  ALLSUP, Thomas H.
  BROWN, James
  CONLEY, Paschall
  JOHNSON, William
  JONES, Philip
  JONES, Silas
  WHITE, J. E.
Helena
  ALLEN, Henry
  ALLENSWORTH, Allen
  CLAGGETT, Joseph
  CONN, John
  THOMAS, Lewis
Kalispell
  WHITE, John
  LIGHTFOOT, James R.
  McCAULEY, William
Miles City
  SMITH, Thomas
Missoula
  GRISSEN, Daniel
  JOHNSON, Frank L.
  JONES, Ira
  WASHINGTON, Henry F.
  WHEELER, Charles
Sun River
  ROBINSON, Robert
Sweet Grass
  MALONE, John
Warm Springs
  BIVINS, Horace
Montgomery, Nola
  MILLER, Jesse C.
Montgomery, Queeny
  ROBINSON, Robert

Moore, Ardelle Rosemary
  MOORE, Miles
Moore, Arthur
  MOORE, Miles
Moore, Bartlett
  WILKS, Jacob W.
Moore, Benjamin
  MOORE, Fredrick Thomas
Moore, Coleman
  SNOTEN, Peter
Moore, David
  MOORE, Miles
Moore, Elizabeth
  MOORE, Miles
  WILKS, Jacob W.
Moore, Frida
  MOORE, Fredrick Thomas
Moore, George
  MOORE, Miles
Moore, Julia
  McKAY, Barney
Moore, Mary
  McKAY, Barney
Moore, Richard
  MOORE, Miles
Moore, Samuel
  McKAY, Barney
Moran, Mary Watts
  TAYLOR, John
Morey, Lewis Sidney
  HENDERSON, Monola
Mormons
  ALLENSWORTH, Allen
Moros (Philippine insurgents)
  FLINT, Robert T.
Morrell, Freddie
  MORRELL, Benjamin
Morris Brown College, Atlanta
  JAMESON, Henry W.
Morrow, Albert Payson
  BADIE, David
  FREDERICKS, Thomas
  HOLBROOK, Isaac
  JONES, William
  PARKER, Charles L.
Morton, Eugene
  PRIDE, Alfred
Morton, Mary Ann Pride
  PRIDE, Alfred
Morton, Samuel
  MORTON, Willis
Moss, Art
  REID, John
  TAYLOR, Jordan
Moss, James Alfred
  GREEN, Dalbert P.
  JONES, Eugene
Moss, Laures Juana
  MOSS, James

Mound Street Church, Cincinnati, OH
  ALLENSWORTH, Allen
Mount Vernon, VA
  FORD, George W.
Mountain, Clara
  WASHINGTON, George
Mountauk Soldiers Relief Association
  STEWARD, Theophilus G.
  TALIAFERRO, Spottswood W.
Mozique, Alice Johnson
  MOZIQUE, Edward
Mozique, Edward
  MOZIQUE, Edward
Mure, Nannie L.
  MURE, John
Murphy, John W.
  MILLER, Charles
Murphy, William
  FRANKLIN, James Edward
Murray, Angeline Pierce
  MURRAY, Othniel, III
Murray, Lightning
  PITTS, Ephriam R.
Murray, Othniel, II
  MURRAY, Othniel, III
Murry, Florence Wall
  WALL, Archy
Music, instrumental groups
  EWING, Calvin
  FOREMAN, William A.
  GREEN, Elder
  HARTWELL, O. B.
  HUBBRET, Edward
  MORGAN, Charles P.
  STEWART, Frank
  WILLIAMS, Lonnie
  WILLIAMS, Sidney
Music, singing and dancing groups
  Don Tennesseans (singers)
    TILLMAN, Lafayette A.
  High School Minstrels, Salt Lake City
    LOVING, Walter H.
  Imperial Quartet
    CRAWFORD, William
    ROBINSON, George
    TOAST, Sam
    WISEMAN, Turner H.
  Magnolia Four
    CASSELLE, Nelson A.
    COLLINS, Edward J.
    GREEN, Benjamin
    WILLIAMS, George H.
  Oak and Ivy Dancing Club, Ft Robinson, NE
    BAYLOR, George
  24th Infantry sextet
    WILLIAMS, Walter B.

Myers, George
  ANDERSON, William T.
Myers, John
  WASHINGTON, George
Myers, Mallisee
  MYERS, Rath
Nalla, Pabla
  FAIR, Robert
Nalls, Edmonia Roy
  BARD, Benjamin
Nalls, John
  BARD, Benjamin
Nana (Apache leader)
  ANDERSON, Richard
  BAKER, William
  BURTON, James
  BUSH, James W.
  HARRIS, Wesley
  MARTIN, David G.
  PENN, William H.
  PERRY, Charles
  PHILLIPS, James D.
  ROGERS, John
  SHAW, Thomas
  SHIDELL, John S.
  STONE, Jerry
  TEMPLE, Guy
  TROUT, Henry
  WALLEY, Augustus
  WILLIAMS, Moses
  WOODS, Brent
Narra, Pabla
  CASEY, John F.
National Association for the
  Advancement of Colored
  People
    BANKS, Charles
    CHENAULT, Walter
    DAVIS, Benjamin F.
    PRIOLEAU, George W.
    RICKS, William Nauns
    YOUNG, Charles
National Bank of Commerce,
  Cleveland, OH
    CARROLL, Joseph H.
National Cemeteries, *see*
  Cemeteries
National Education Association
  ALLENSWORTH, Allen
National Indian War Veterans
  (organization)
    ALLEN, Joseph
    AMS, Singleton
    BANKS, Gabriel H.
    BARNETT, Grant
    BENTLEY, James B.
    BRANCH, William
    BUNION, Thomas
    BURNSIDE, Richard

BUSH, William Henry
CARTER, Alfred
COKER, Abram
COLBERT, Frederick
CRITH, Frank
DANDRIDGE, Turner
DENT, Henry
DILWOOD, Thomas J.
EVANS, Frank, Sr.
FIELDING, Frank
FLETCHER, James
FLETCHER, Samuel
GROSS, Robert G.
HAMPTON, Wade
HARRIS, Maston
HENDERSON, William A.
HILLIARD, Peter
HOLLY, Henry J.
HOWERTON, John C
HURBURT, J. D. C.
JACKSON, Stephen
JOHNSON, Moses
JOHNSON, William
KELLY, William H.
LEE, Alexander
LEE, Joseph H.
LEWIS, Edward
LEWIS, Morgan
McALLISTER, James
McCOMBS, Henry
McDOWELL, John H.
McKEEN, Robert
MARTIN, Thomas P.
MATHEWS, Abraham
MOLOCK, Andrew M.
POLK, Thomas Elzey
POWELL, Samuel
POWELL, William
RATLIFFE, Benjamin
RAYSON, Benjamin
REED, John
REED, Samuel
SCOTT, Levi
SMITH, William
SULLIVAN, R. E.
TURNER, Simon
WAREFIELD, Harry
WILLIAMS, William H.
YOUNG, Charles
National Medical Association
  BROWN, Arthur M.
National Military Home, Dayton,
  OH
    FOSTER, George
    JONES, Emanuel
National Military Home,
  Leavenworth, KS
    BACKMAN, Harrison
    CASEY, John F.
National Military Home, Marion, IN

WALKER, Henry
National Military Home, Santa
  Monica, CA
    CORDIN, C. W.
    SNOTEN, Peter
National Parks, *see* California,
  Yosemite National Park;
  Wyoming, Yellowstone National
  Park
Navahos
  BOWERS, Edward
  TRIMBLE, Anderson
Nebraska. *See also* Cemeteries
  Alliance
    LEWIS, George
    SLAUGHTER, Rufus
  BAKER, Edward L., Jr.
  Bellevue
    EDWARDS, William D.
    JACKSON, James F.
    KINCAID, M. L.
    MADEN, Ebbert
    MASON, William
    MURPHY, Israel B.
    PRICE, John D.
    PROCTOR, John C.
    SHEPERD, Frank
    SIMONS (Sergeant)
    STROTHER, Alonzo W.
    THOMAS, Spencer
    TOLER, Miller
    VROOMAN, William A.
    WALLACE, Harry
    WARNER, F.
  Chadron
    DENE, William
    GRAVELY, G. S.
    McCLAIN, Henry
    MACE, Alfred
    MADEN, Ebbert
    MILDS, Miller
    SMITH, Myles Y.
    THOMPSON, James A.
    TILTON, William
    WALKER, Robert H.
    WILSON, William O.
  Crawford
    ALLEN, Luther
    ANDERSON, William T.
    BECKETT, William C.
    BELL, William
    BENSON, Caleb
    BENTON, Willie
    BOONE, Adrick
    BRADDEN, Alfred
    BRIGGS, Allen
    BROOKS, Preston
    CHASE, Henry
    COLLIER, Stephen J.
    COLLINS, Robert

COLSTON, Daniel
COOPER, Andrew
COOPER, John
CROSBY (Private)
DAVIS, Edward
DORSEY, Robert
ELIXANDER, Charles
FLIPPINS, Benjamin
FLYNT, Robert
FORT, Lewis
FUQUA, William R.
GOULD, Charley
GREEN, William E.
HAMMOND, Thomas C.
HARRIS, Fenton H.
HARRIS, Theodore
HARTWELL, Benjamin
HENDERSON (D/10th Cav)
HENDERSON, John
HENSON, George J.
HOLLIDAY, Presley
HOWARD, William
IRVING, Lee
JOHNSON, Y.
JONES, George F.
JONES, John A.
JONES, Wesley
JORDAN, George
LANE, Edward
LEE (Trumpeter)
LETCHERE (C/9th Cav)
LEWIS, Ezekiel
LEWIS, William H.
McCLAIN, Henry
MACK, Dolpheus
McKAY, Barney
McKENZIE, Frank
MANNING, James E.
MASON, George
MOODY, Alex
MORRIS, Reuben B.
NELSON, Edward D.
PAGE, Edward W.
PENN, William H.
PRICE, Charles E.
PRIOLEAU, George W.
PROCTOR, John C.
PUMPHREY, James H.
PURDY (Private)
REID, John
SAMPSON, J.
SAUNDERS, Henry B.
SCOTT, David
SIMMONS, James
SLAUGHTER, Rufus
SMITH, Luscious
SMITH, W. E.
SNOTEN, Peter
SOUTHALL, James
SPAIN, Fred
STANCE, Emanuel
TAYLOR (C/10th Cav)

TAYLOR, Jordan
TAYLOR, Morris
THOMPSON, James A.
TOURNAGE, Sandy
TROUT, Henry
TRUE, Otto
VAUGHN, Louis L.
WALKER, Harry
WASHINGTON, William
WATKINS, William
WILLIAMS, B. W.
WILLIAMS, James
WILLIAMS, Jessie
WILSON, George
WINFIELD, Arthur
YOUNG, Charles H.
YOUNG, William
Dawes County
  BENSON, Caleb
Elkhorn
  HOWERTON, John C
Ft Crook. *See also* Cemeteries
  GREEN (Private)
  SMITH, John
  STRAWDER, M.
  TUCKER, Joseph H.
  TYLER, Thomas S.
  WALKER, Samuel W.
Ft Niobrara. *See also* Cemeteries
  ALEXANDER, John Hanks
  ANDERSON, George G.
  ANDREWS, William
  BAUSBRY, Arthur
  BILL, John B.
  BLAND, Robert C.
  BLEW, Joseph
  BLUE, Joseph
  BOND, Rhoden
  BOOKER, Andrew J.
  BOOKER, Powhattan E.
  BREGES, John
  BRIGHT, Spencer
  BROADUS, Lewis
  BROWN, Daniel
  BROWN, George
  BROWN, Henry R.
  BROWN, William
  CARTER, Nelson
  CARTER, William H.
  CLANTON, Elbert B.
  CLARK, Spencer
  COKER, Henry
  COTTON, James T.
  CRAIG, Richard
  CUSTARD, Elijah
  DAIS, William
  DAUGHERTY, Harvey
  DAVIS, Benjamin F.
  FERGUSON, John H.
  FIRMES, Thomas A.
  FOX, William
  GAMBLE, John

GANT, Elias
GARROTT, Clarence
GREEN, Henry
GREENWOOD, George
HAMLIN, Thomas
HAMPTON, George W.
HANCOCK, George W.
HARRILL, Doc L.
HARRIS, David
HARRIS, Lee
HARRISON, Samuel A.
HAUGER, William
HENDERSON, John, Jr.
HENRY, Horace T.
HOLLOMON, Solomon
HOOVER, Alfred C.
HOPKINS, Richard
HUNT, George W.
JACKSON, Emmett J.
JACKSON, James F.
JACKSON, London
JEFFERDS, Wesley
JENKINS, Daniel
JOHNSON, William D.
LATIMER, James C.
LEWIS, Stephen
LINAIRE (Private)
LITTLE, Frank
LONG, Frank
McGEE, Henry
McKEE, Henry
MAXWELL, Albert E.
MAYFIELD, John
MORRIS, Edward
MORSE, H. C.
MOSBY, Thomas
MOSS, Parker
NAYES, John
OULDO, James
PARKS, Frank H.
POOL, Robert L.
POWELL, William
RANDOLPH, Walter
RAY, Albert E.
ROBINSON, George R.
ROBINSON, John H.
SADDLER, Louis
SCOTT, Edward
SIMS, Lewis
STEPHENS, William
STEWARD, Theophilus G.
SWENTON, Norman E.
TATE, William
TAYLOR, Alexander
THOMAS, Joseph
THOMPSON, George S.
TOAST, Sam
TRICE, Green
TULLEY, William
TURNER, Samuel
WARD, Nathan
WASHINGTON, Lewis

PLAIN CAPS indicate names from this volume • **BOLD CAPS** indicate names from *On the Trail* (1995)

WATSON, Baxter W.
WEBB, William K.
WELLS, Morgan
WHITTINGTON, Len
WILLIAMS, Moses
WILLIAMS, Odia
WILSON, Jacob B.
WISEMAN, Turner H.
WOODS, Eugene
WRIGHT, George
YOUNG, George
YOURS, Robert

Ft Omaha
CAYSON, Frank
DICKSON, Leonard E.
JACKSON, John H.
MILDS, Miller
RICE, Harry
TRACY, George
WILLIAMS, George A.
WILLIAMS, Joseph E.

Ft Robinson
ADAMS, Alexander H.
ALEXANDER, John Hanks
ALEXANDER, Julius
ALEXANDER, Samuel H.
ALLEN, David M.
ALLEN, Kendrick
ALLENSWORTH, Allen
ANDERSON, Benjamin A.
ANDERSON, George
ANDERSON, Isaac
ANDERSON, John H.
ANDERSON, Robert
ANDERSON, William T.
ANTHONY (Wagoner)
ARCHER (Private)
ARMSTRONG, Wilson H.
ARNETT, Budd
ATUS, George
BADIE, David
BADIE, M. V.
BAILEY, George
BAILEY, Guss
BAILEY, Isaac
BAIRD, J. H.
BALDWIN, James R.
BARKS, William
BARNS, Benjamin R.
BARROW, Stephen B.
BARTON (I/9th Cav)
BATTER, Henry
BAYLOR, George
BECKETT, William C.
BELL, Mark
BELL, Thomas
BELL, Wade
BELL, William
BENJAMIN, Robert
BENSON, Caleb
BENTON, Willie
BERKLEY, Alex B.

BIRD, Matthew
BIRD, Robert
BIRD, Savage
BLACKBURN, Charles
BLACKBURN, George W.
BLAIR, Jacob
BLAKE, Isaac
BLAKE, William H.
BLEW, Joseph
BOLDEN, I. G.
BOND, Howard H.
BOOKER, O. H.
BOONE, Adrick
BOONE, William
BORDEN, Frank F.
BOWENS, Alonzo
BOWSER, Frank T.
BOYD, John
BOYLE, Frank
BRADDEN, Alfred
BRADFORD, Rudolph
BRADLEY, Taylor
BRANDT (Private; B/10th Cav)
BRIGGS, Allen
BRINSON, Theodore M.
BRON, William
BROOKS, Charles H.
BROOKS, Preston
BROWN, Albert
BROWN, Caesar B.
BROWN, George W.
BROWN, Isaac
BROWN, John
BROWN, John H.
BROWN, John W.
BROWN, Joseph
BROWN, Smith
BROWN, William (Private; E/9th Cav)
BROWN, William (Sergeant; H/10th Cav)
BROWN, William (Private; I/10th Cav)
BROWN, William (Private; D/9th Cav)
BROWN, William H.
BROWNING, Andrew
BRYAN, William
BUCHANAN, Clarence
BUCHANAN, James
BUCK, John
BUDELL (Private; K/9th Cav)
BUFORD, John
BULLOCK, B. H.
BURGESS, Ed P.
BURLES, Charles
BURLEY, Robert
BURNS, Lee
BURTON, William E.
BUTCHER, George N.
BUTLER, Abram
BUTLER, Henry

BUTLER, James H.
BUTLER, Thomas C.
BUTTON, Francis
BYERS, George
BYRON, Thomas H.
CAINE, George
CAMPBELL, William
CANNON, Henry
CAPITE, Charles
CARSON, Willie
CARTER, Amos A.
CARTER, Charles McD.
CARTER, John T.
CARTER, Neander N.
CARTER, Richard
CAYSON, Frank
CHAMBERS, John
CHAMBERS, Robert
CHAPMAN, James
CHASE, Henry
CHASE, Levi
CHEATHAM, Eugene B.
CHENAULT, Robert
CHILDS, Jacob
CLARK, Oscar
CLAY, William
CLEMENS, Benjamin
CLINTON, F. R.
CLOTTER, Dennis
COATES, Benjamin
COLE, Gonza
COLEMAN, Jesse
COLLIER, Stephen J.
COMAGER, Charles W.
CONLEY, Paschall
CONRAD, Barton
CONTEE, Clarence
COOK, James H.
COOPER, Horace
COVINGTON, Samuel
CRAGG, Allen
CRAIG, James
CRAWFORD, Henry
CREGG, John L.
CRUSE, Peter
CUNNINGHAM, George
CURRY, George
DAILY, Daniel T.
DANIELS, Charles
DAVIS, Benjamin
DAVIS, Benjamin F.
DAVIS, Benjamin O.
DAVIS, Clifford H.
DAVIS, Henry
DAVIS, Henry R.
DAVIS, James
DAVIS, Jerry A.
DAVIS, Martin
DAVIS, William (Private; B/9th Cav)
DAVIS, William (Private; M/10th Cav)

PLAIN CAPS indicate names from this volume • **BOLD CAPS** indicate names from *On the Trail* (1995)

DAVIS, William J.
DAVIS, William N.
DENNY, John
DICKSON, Leonard E.
DIGGS, James
DILLARD, C. D.
DILLON, David R.
DILLON, Thomas
DIXON (Private)
DIXON, Dennis
DOBSON, Theophilus
DODSON, Lucious
DOLBY, Eli R.
DOOLEY, William J.
DOOMS, Thomas
DORSEY, Harry
DORSEY, Robert
DOUGLAS, Barney
DOUGLASS, John
DOVER, Philip H.
DREW, Albert
EDWARDS, George F.
EDWARDS, Joe
EDWARDS, William D.
ENNIS, Evan
ERVIN, William A.
ERVINE, James W.
ERWIN, George
ESTILL, Robert L.
EVANS, Tommie
FAGG, John
FAIN, Frank
FAIRFAX, Jesse J. A.
FALL, William H.
FARR, John H.
FERGUSON, Arthur J.
FIELDS, Henry
FINLEY, Augustus
FISHBURN, William G.
FISHER, Leonard
FISHER, Walter R.
FLETCHER, Edward
FLETCHER, Nathan
FLIPPINS, Benjamin
FLORENCE, Alexander
FORD, James W.
FORT, Lewis
FORTUNE, John T.
FOX (Sergeant)
FOX, Robert J.
FRANKLIN, Simon P.
FREDERICKS, George
FRIEDMAN, Arthur
FRIERSON, Eugene
FRYE, William G.
FUQUA, William R.
GAINES, George W.
GARDNER, William H.
GARROTT, Langston E.
GASKINS, Alfred
GATES, George
GEASON, James

GIBBS, William
GIBSON, Philip
GILFRED, Alfred
GILL, Wesley
GILLENWATER, Walter
GILMORE (Sergeant)
GLENN, Louis
GOFF, George W.
GOINS, Charles M.
GOODLOE, Thomas
GOULD, Charley
GOULD, Samuel
GRAMMER, Edward L.
GRASS, Harry
GRAVELY, G. S.
GRAYSON (Corporal)
GREEN, Elder
GREEN, Ernest
GREEN, James
GREEN, John C.
GREEN, Lewis T.
GREEN, Moses
GREEN, Walter
GREEN, William E.
GREGG (Private)
GREY, John R.
GRIFFIN, George
GRIFFITH, William B.
GROSS, Harry
GUILFORD, Alfred
HAGUE, Lucius J.
HAIRSTON, William
HALE, U.
HAMILTON, Albert
HAMILTON, Edward
HAMILTON, William H.
HAMILTON, William M.
HAMMOND, Thomas C.
HAMPTON, Nathan
HARPER, Charles
HARPER, Michael
HARPER, William H.
HARRIS (Private)
HARRIS, Fenton H.
HARRIS, George
HARRIS, John
HARRIS, John W.
HARRIS, Moses
HARRIS, Robert
HARRIS, Simon P.
HARRIS, William
HARRISTON (C/10th Cav)
HARTWELL, Benjamin
HARTWELL, O. B.
HARVEY, William
HAWKINS (Corporal)
HAYDEN, James
HAYGOOD, Claude
HAYWOOD, Charles
HAYWOOD, Larry
HENDERSON, Albert J.
HENDERSON, Elmer

HENDERSON, Harrison
HENRY, Edward
HENRY, Vodrey
HENSON (Private)
HERBERT, Thomas H.
HICKMAN, Charles
HICKS, William B.
HILL, H. W.
HILL, John
HILL, William H.
HILLIARD, Henry
HINKLE, Jonee
HIPSHER, Wiley
HOCKINS, Benjamin
HOLDEN, James
HOLLIDAY, Presley
HOLLOMON, Solomon
HOLMES, Conley
HOLMES, Robert H.
HOLSEN, Bailey
HOPKINS, Peter
HORN, George W.
HOUSTON, John
HOWARD, William
HUBBRET, Edward
HUCKSTEP, Henderson
HUFF, Willis
HUMPHREY, Cornelius
HUNT (Trumpeter)
HUNT (Private)
HUNT, William S.
HUNTER, Charles
HURLEY, Otto
HURT, John L.
INGOMAN, Madison
INMAN, William F.
IRVING, Lee
JACKSON (Private)
JACKSON, Elisha
JACKSON, Frank
JACKSON, Garfield
JACKSON, George H.
JACKSON, James
JACKSON, James F.
JACKSON, John
JACKSON, John H.
JACKSON, John J.
JACKSON, Robert
JACKSON, William (Private; G/9th Cav)
JACKSON, William (Private; H/9th Cav)
JACKSON, William M.
JACOBS, Camp
JAMES (Private)
JAMES, Frank
JAMES, John
JEFFERDS, Wesley
JEFFERSON, Charles W.
JEFFERSON, John
JEMSON, Joe
JENKINS, Blunt

PLAIN CAPS indicate names from this volume • **BOLD CAPS** indicate names from *On the Trail* (1995)

JENKINS, William
JENSON, Joseph
JOHNSON, Alexander
JOHNSON, Andrew
JOHNSON, Benjamin
JOHNSON, C. J.
JOHNSON, George
JOHNSON, George H.
JOHNSON, Henry
JOHNSON, Isaiah
JOHNSON, J.
JOHNSON, Jacob
JOHNSON, John (Sergeant; K/9th Cav)
JOHNSON, John (Private; L/25th Inf)
JOHNSON, John A.
JOHNSON, John W. L.
JOHNSON, K. A.
JOHNSON, Robert J.
JOHNSON, Robert M.
JOHNSON, Silas
JOHNSON, William
JOHNSON, William M.
JOHNSTON, Charles
JONES, Alexander
JONES, Andrew
JONES, Edward
JONES, Frank
JONES, George F.
JONES, Jasper
JONES, Jeremiah
JONES, John A.
JONES, Lewis
JONES, Richard
JONES, Samuel E.
JONES, Samuel G.
JONES, Wesley
JONES, William
JONES, William S.
JORDAN, Charles
JORDAN, George
JORDAN, Henry
JORDAN, Moses
JOSEPH, Leon E.
KAHOLOKULA, John
KANE, George
KELLAM, Alfred
KELLY, George H.
KELLY, William
KENDRICK, David
KILLEAN, Thomas P.
KIRTLEY, Sidney
LANAM, George
LAST, H.
LAWS, A.
LEACH, Samuel
LEE, Edward
LEE, George
LEE, Henry
LEE, James
LEE, James

LEONARD, John H.
LETCHER, Philip
LEWIS, C. J.
LEWIS, Clarence
LEWIS, Ezekiel
LEWIS, Frank
LEWIS, George
LEWIS, George P.
LEWIS, Jackson
LEWIS, William H.
LINDSAY, Gus
LOCKMAN, George H.
LOCKSLEY, Thomas I.
LOGAN, Fred
LOGAN, John A.
LONG, Isaiah
LOVING, Charles K.
LOWE, Albert S.
LUST, Houston
LYMAN, George
LYNCH, William
LYONS, Edward
LYTTLE, Peter
McCABE, William
McCARTHY (Private)
McCLAIN, Allen
McCLAIN, Henry
McCLARE, Allen
McCOY, Emmett
McDONALD, John
McDOWELL, William A.
MACE, Alfred
MACK (Private)
McKAY, Barney
McKEEN, Robert
McKENZIE, Edward
McLANE, Carey P.
MADEN, Ebbert
MANAGAULT, William
MANN, Louis
MANN, Simpson
MARCHBANKS, Vance H.
MARRS, Charles
MARSHALL, E.
MARTIN, Jerry
MARTIN, Richard
MASON, George
MASON, George H.
MASON, John
MATHEWS, William
MATTHEWS, H.
MEARS, George W.
MELTON, William
MENLOW, Thomas
MERRIWEATHER, Henry C.
MIDDLETON, Charles N.
MILDS, Miller
MILES, Charles
MILES, Chester
MILLER, John D.
MILLER, John E.
MILLER, Walter

MILLS, Archie
MITCHELL, Woody
MOFFETT, Drayton H.
MONROE, George
MOODY, Alex
MOORE, Adam
MOORE, Henry
MOORE, Joseph
MOORE, Samuel
MORGAN, Charles P.
MORRIS, William S.
MORTON, George
MOSS, James
MOTLEY, Solomon
MUKES, Matthew
MURRY, Andrew
MYERS, James C.
NASH, Robert N.
NELSON, Edward D.
OGLESBY, John E.
OLIVER, William
ONLY, John
PAPPY, John H.
PARHAM, Julius
PARIS, Joseph A.
PARKER, Hiram C.
PARKER, Richard
PARKS, Frank H.
PASCHALL, Lincoln
PATON, Jerome
PAYNE, Charles
PECK, Henry
PEMBERTON, Harce
PENDERGRASS, John C.
PENN, William H.
PENNISTON, James W.
PERNELL, Eleven
PERRIN, William H.
PERRY, Charles
PETERS, Albert
PETERSON, Allen
PETERSON, Willie A.
PETTES, Charles M.
PHILLIPS, Thomas
PINKSTON, Samuel
PITTS, Ephriam R.
PITTS, Lonnie
PLEASANTS, Thomas
PLEDGER, William A., Jr.
PLUMMER, Henry Vinton
PLUMMER, Solomon
POLK, Thomas Elzey
PORTER, William K.
PORTER, Willie
PRANN, Charles W.
PRATER, Jacob P.
PRATHER, John (Private; H/9th Cav)
PRATHER, John (Private; B/10th Cav)
PRICE, Charles E.
PRICE, John M.

PLAIN CAPS indicate names from this volume • **BOLD CAPS** indicate names from *On the Trail* (1995)

PRICE, Joseph
PRIDE, Alfred
PRINCE, Noah
PRIOLEAU, George W.
PROCTOR, Alexander
PROCTOR, John C.
PULPRESS, Walter T.
PUMPHREY, George W.
PUMPHREY, James H.
PURDY (Private)
PURKINS, Louis
QUEEN, Edgar
RAMSEY, Horace W.
RAND, Carlton F.
RANSOM, Arthur E.
RASH, William
RATCLIFFE, Eddie
REDMOND, Francis
REED, William
REESE, Thomas
REYNOLDS, Eleazer N.
RHEA, Samuel
RICHARDSON (Private)
RICHARDSON, Artie
RICHARDSON, Thomas
RIVERS, John A.
RIVERS, Samuel
ROBERTS, George
ROBERTS, Henry
ROBERTS, William
ROBINSON, Charles
ROBINSON, Charles C.
ROBINSON, Daniel C.
ROBINSON, John
ROBINSON, Lee
ROBINSON, William
ROCK, Pierre
ROGERS (Corporal)
ROGERS, John
ROSE, John W.
ROSS, Edward
ROUSE, Curtis
ROYSTER, Charles
ROYSTER, Henry
RUCKER, Henry
RUSSELL, Edward
RUSSELL, James
SCARSCE, Henry
SCOTT, David
SCOTT, Nelson
SCOTT, Oliver
SCOTT, Washington
SCRUGGS, Gilbert
SETTLERS, James
SHARP, Charles E.
SHAW, Thomas
SHAWES, Dick
SHELTON, Thomas D.
SHIDELL, John S.
SHINEHOUSE, James
SHIPLEY, John
SHOECRAFT, Charles

SILBERT, William
SILVERS, George
SIMMONS, Charles
SIMON, John J.
SIMPSON, James T.
SINGLETON, William
SKELTON, Newton J.
SKINNER, James
SLAUGHTER, Rufus
SLAUTER, William
SMITH, Arthur
SMITH, Charles P.
SMITH, Emile
SMITH, Fred
SMITH, George
SMITH, George A.
SMITH, Gloster
SMITH, James W.
SMITH, Lamb
SMITH, Levi
SMITH, Lewis M.
SMITH, Luscious
SMITH, Myles Y.
SMITH, Thomas
SMITH, Walter
SMITH, William
SMITH, William (Farrier; C/9th Cav)
SMITH, William (Private; F/9th Cav)
SMITH, William (Lance Cpl; I/9th Cav)
SNYDER, George
SOLLY, Ross
SPAIN, Fred
STANCE, Emanuel
STAPLES, Hamilton
STEWARD, Theophilus G.
STEWART, Frank
STEWART, Frank H.
STEWART, William
STILL, Revere N.
STOKES, Henry A.
STONE (Corporal)
STREETER, William
STRUTTER, Joshua
STUART, Thomas
SULLIVAN, Allen
SURDY, Allen
SYKES, Zekiel
TALBERT, Willie P.
TARY, Saint
TATE, John
TATE, Rufus
TAYLOR (C/10th Cav)
TAYLOR, Alexander
TAYLOR, George
TAYLOR, Jordan
TAYLOR, Lewis N.
TAYLOR, Stephen
TERRY, Charles Lincoln
THOMAS, Alfred J.

THOMAS, Charles
THOMAS, H. R.
THOMAS, John (Private; F/9th Cav)
THOMAS, John (Private; G/25th Inf)
THOMAS, Spencer
THOMAS, William H.
THOMAS, William R.
THOMPKINS, William H.
THOMPSON, Joseph
THORNTON, Beverly F.
THRASHER, George
TILTON, William
TOLIVER, Lewis
TOLSON (Blacksmith)
TOLSON, Charles
TOURNAGE, Sandy
TRACY, George
TRAVILLION, Thomas
TROUT, Henry
TRUE, Otto
TRUMAN, Isaac W.
TUCKER, Charles
TULL, Joseph
TURLEY (Private)
TURNER (Private)
TURNER, Daniel
TURNER, John
TURNER, Peter H.
TURNER, Robert
VADER, Louis E.
VALENTINE, Israel
VAUGHN, Louis L.
VENABLE, Henry
VICTOR, William
VROOMAN, William A.
WALKER (Blacksmith)
WALKER, Harry
WALKER, Harry
WALKER, Ralph
WALLACE, Harry
WALLS, Henry F.
WARE, John
WARFIELD, Samuel A.
WARREN, William
WASHINGTON, George
WASHINGTON, George (Private; C/9th Cav)
WASHINGTON, George (Private; B/9th Cav)
WASHINGTON, George (Private; 9th Cav)
WASHINGTON, George W.
WASHINGTON, Lincoln
WASHINGTON, William
WATERFORD, George
WATERS, George
WATKINS, Isaac
WATKINS, James M.
WATKINS, Murray
WATKINS, Wesley

PLAIN CAPS indicate names from this volume • **BOLD CAPS** indicate names from *On the Trail* (1995)

WATSON, John
WATSON, William S.
WATTS, Fred
WATTS, Willis
WEAKLEY, Richard
WEBSTER, F.
WELSH, George
WEST, Willie
WHEAT (Private)
WHEELER, Thomas
WHEELOCK, Joseph M.
WHITE, George W.
WHITE, Joseph
WHITE, Theophilus T.
WHITEN, Walter J.
WHITING, John
WHITMIRE, Joe
WILEY, Daniel
WILEY, Frederick
WILLIAMS, Arthur
WILLIAMS, Benjamin T.
WILLIAMS, Charley W.
WILLIAMS, Edward
WILLIAMS, Elbert
WILLIAMS, George
WILLIAMS, George A.
WILLIAMS, Hamilton
WILLIAMS, Harrison
WILLIAMS, Harry
WILLIAMS, Herbert
WILLIAMS, James Clifford
WILLIAMS, Jeremiah
WILLIAMS, Jessie
WILLIAMS, John
WILLIAMS, Joseph
WILLIAMS, Joseph E.
WILLIAMS, Lonnie
WILLIAMS, Moses
WILLIAMS, Sidney
WILLIAMS, Thomas
WILLIAMS, Walter
WILLIS, Cupid
WILLIS, James H.
WILSON, Alfred
WILSON, George (1st Sgt; M/9th
  Cav)
WILSON, George (Private; C/9th
  Cav)
WILSON, William
WILSON, William O.
WINFIELD, Arthur
WINFIELD, Augustus P.
WINROW, William
WINTERS, Willie
WITHERS, William H.
WOOD, Manlus
WOODFIN, Richard
WOODS, Brent
WOODY, Clayborn
WORMSLEY, William C.
WYATT, Mathew
WYLIE, Daniel

WYNN, Alexander
YOUNG, Charles
YOUNG, Charles H.
YOUNG, Lewellen
YOUNG, William
Hastings
  WEBSTER, Joseph
Hemingford
  ANDERSON, John H.
Hyannis
  FITTS, Charles
Kearney
  MABREY, Alfred
  WEBSTER, Joseph
Lincoln
  BUSH, James W.
  CASH, Richard
  CONRAD, L.
  WILLIAMS, Charley W.
  WILLIAMS, Jessie
Niobrara. *See also above* Ft Niobrara
  GAMBLE, John E.
Norfolk
  BOONE, Adrick
  GAMBLE, John E.
Omaha. *See also* Cemeteries
  BAILEY, Isaac
  BELL, Wade
  BIRD, Matthew
  BLAKE, Isaac
  BLEW, Joseph
  BOCK, Henry
  BURLES, Charles
  CLARK, Sherman H.
  FINLEY, Augustus
  GAMBLE, John E.
  HAND, William
  HARVEY, William
  HOOVER, Alfred C.
  JACKSON, John
  JOHNSON, Alexander
  JOHNSON, Robert T.
  LETCHER, Philip
  MILDS, Miller
  MORRIS, Edward
  PATON, Jerome
  PROCTOR, John C.
  PURNELL, William Whipple
  QUEEN, Edgar
  REID, John
  SMITH, Arthur
  WATTS, Willis
  WILLIAMS, Charley W.
  WILLIAMS, George
  WILLIAMS, Jessie
Pine Ridge, *see* Pine Ridge
  Reservation
Running Water Station
  BARNETT, John
  EDWARDS, Lewis
  DILLARD, C. D.
  FLADGER, John J.

FRASER, Carlos
GILLIAM, Chauncey
GRAHAM, Joseph
GREEN, Alfred
HUGGINS, Cumsey
IRVING, Lee
LINCOLN, Robert
LUNNEY, Mack
McCANTS, William
McINTOSH, Henry
MARCHBANKS, Vance H.
MIDDLETON, Robert
MOSBY, Thomas
MYERS, William H.
ROBINSON, Henry
SIMMONS, Marcus
SIMMONS, Peter
SMALLS, Henry
STRAWBERRY, Gabriel M.
WHITE, Joseph
WHITESIDES, H.
WILLIAMS, Charles
WILLIAMS, Jack
WOODS, Marion
South Omaha
  TAYLOR, Alexander
  TUCKER, George C.
Valentine
  BROOKS, Edward
  CONRAD, L.
  JACKSON, Emmett J.
Negro League baseball
  CHARLESTON, Oscar
  ROGAN, Wilbur
Negro State Fair, North
  Carolina
  HAMLIN, James E.
Nelson, Anderson D.
  EDMONDSON, John
Nelson, Annie Ray
  NELSON, Edward D.
Nelson, Benjamin
  McCLAIN, Henry
Nelson, Celia Ann
  GREGG, John A.
Nelson, Julia
  BRANCH, William
Nelson, Louisa M.
  McCLAIN, Henry
Nelson, Mary E.
  McCLAIN, Henry
Nevada
  Las Vegas
    DOWNS, Allen
  Winnemucca
    SMITH (Sergeant)
Nevares, Josephine
  CROCKETT, George D.

New England
JACKSON, Thornton
New Hampshire
Manchester
HENDERSON, John H.
New Jersey. *See also* Cemeteries
Atlantic City
HENSON, John
BORELAND, Peter
Bridgeton
STEWARD, Theophilus G.
Burlington
BENSON, Abram
Camden
McKAY, Barney
Camp Dix
BIVINS, Horace W.
Cape May
KEY, Charles
CROCHERON, Luther
Hillsdale
McKAY, Barney
JACKSON, Andrew
Jersey City
McDANIELS, Nathaniel
Madison
SCOTT, Oscar J. W.
Montclair
WILLIAMS, James Clifford
New Brunswick
MARTIN, George
Newark
DONOHOE , John
GREEN, Charles A.
MARROW, Anthony A.
MULFORD, Charles
POWELL, William
WILLIAMS, Jessie
Paterson
THOMPKINS, William H.
WALLEY, Augustus
Rahway
GOULD, Peter
Sea Girt
FOX, Oscar
HAMILTON, William H.
HAWKINS, Emmett
JOHNSON, Robert M.
LOGAN, James E.
TATE, William
VROOMAN, William A.
New Mexico. *See also*
Cemeteries; Mescalero Reservation, NM
Agua Chiquita Canyon
DRAKE, Alonzo
ROBINSON, James
SMITH, Robert
STANTON, Daniel
Alamosa Canyon
INGOMAN, Madison
STONE, Minor

SWAN, Edward
TIPTON, Calvin
WEST, Harrison
WILLIS, Alexander
WILSON, Roy
WOODLAND, William
Albuquerque. *See also* Cemeteries
BRABHAM, Jeremiah
CAMMEL, Joseph
HUTCHINSON, George
JACKSON, Isaac
TAYLOR, John T.
WALKER, John
Animas River
CAUMP (Private)
DENNY, John
FREELAND, A.
HAINES, Peter
ARMISTEAD (Private)
ASHBRIDGE, George
BAKER, Edward L., Jr
BAKER, J.
BIRDSON, D.
Black Range
BETTERS, James
DORSEY, Frank
LYMAN, George
BOOTH, Adam
BORBON, J. H.
BOWSER, Frank T.
BOYCE, Alex
BROWN, W. A.
CAMPBELL, Thomas
Canada
JONES, William
Carrizo Canyon
JORDAN, George
PENN, William H.
PERRY, Charles
SHAW, Thomas
SHIDELL, John S.
STONE, Jerry
TEMPLE, Guy
WALLEY, Augustus
WILLIAMS, Moses
Central City
ALLSUP, Thomas H.
CHESTER, Stanley
LIVINGSTON, James
Cimarron
BRECKENRIDGE, William
HANSON, John
HARVEY, Anthony
SMALL, George
SMALLOW, George
COLEMAN, J.
Columbus
WILLIAMS, James
CONNLEY, F.
CONNOR, F.
CRAVEN, Luther
Cuchillo Negro Creek

BOYNE, Thomas
BURTON, James
GAINES, Nathan
GLASBY (Private)
JOHNSON, John
JOHNSON, Monroe
MARTIN, David G.
PHILLIPS, James D.
ROGERS, John
STONE, Minor
SWAN, Edward
TIPTON, Calvin
WALLEY, Augustus
WEST, Harrison
WILLIS, Alexander
WILSON, Roy
WOODLAND, William
WOODWARD, Major
DAYES, Joseph
Deming
ABBOTT, James W.
ALLSUP, Thomas H.
CROUCH, Albert S.
DENNY, John
McCOWN, Peter
DOOLEY, William
DORSEY, G.
DOWNING, D.
DRAIN, S.
DUTTON, W. V.
Eagle Creek
BUSH, James W.
EDDINGS, W.
EDWARDS, L.
Farmington
JORDAN, George
FAY, Sandy
FIELDS, J. M.
Florida Mountains
ADAMS, John Q.
BEAND, Harrison
EPPS, Richard
GREAVES, Clinton
MACKADOO, Richard
PARKER, Richard
FORD, Thomas
Ft Bascom
MOORE, Henry
PIPES, Nelson
ROSE, John W.
SMITH, Henry W.
Ft Bayard. *See also* Cemeteries
ABBOTT, James W.
ALEXANDER, Cook
ALEXANDER, James H.
ALEXANDER, Wesley
ALLENSWORTH, Allen
ALLSUP, Thomas H.
ANDERSON, Charles L.
ANDERSON, R.
ARMS, Benjamin
BAILEY, Charles

PLAIN CAPS indicate names from this volume • **BOLD CAPS** indicate names from *On the Trail* (1995)

BAILEY, Willis
BALLENTINE, Cyrus
BAYLOR, George
BELL, Henry
BELL, Matthew
BENSON, Abram
BETHEL, James
BETTERS, James
BETTIS, James
BILLIONS, James
BINNER, L.
BLACK, Solomon
BONDS, George
BOOKRUM, Edward
BOYD, Hampton
BOYD, Thomas W.
BOYER, George W.
BRABHAM, Jeremiah
BRISCOE, Henry
BROWN, Alfred
BROWN, Benjamin
BROWN, Creed
BROWN, J. F.
BROWN, James E.
BROWN, Oscar S.
BROWN, Thomas Hatcher
BUFORD (Sergeant)
BUNCH, Thomas
BUNDY, Paul
BUSH, James W.
BUTLER, Hiram
CAINE, W. H.
CARROLL, Robert T.
CARTER, Frank
CARTER, H.
CARTER, Henry
CARTER, Henry H. B.
CAY, McKinley
CHATMAN, Calvin
CHESTER, Stanley
CHRISHOLM, Lee
CLARK, Cornelius
CLAY, William
COLBERT, Frederick
COLBURN, Jessie
COTTON, J. H.
COVINGTON, James C.
COX, Richard
CRAIG, Thomas
CROSBY, Scott
CROUCH, Albert S.
CUNNINGHAM, Charles
CUNNINGHAM, George
CURTIS, Edward O.
DABNEY, G.
DADE, Allen
DANIELS, Henry
DAVIS, Ben
DAVIS, John
DENNY, John
DICKERSON, James
DUDLEY, G. W.

DUDLEY, John H.
DUNCAN, R.
EASLEY, James
ELLIS, Merriman H.
ERNEST, Thomas A.
EVANS, Frank
FIELDS, A.
FINNEGAN, Michael
FINNEY (Sergeant)
FITCH, Thomas N.
FOX, William
FULLER, Cornelius
FURGESON, DeWitt
GOENS, Robert
GRAYSON, Charles H.
GREAVES, Clinton
GREEN, John E.
GREEN, John R.
HAINES, Jack
HARLAN, William
HARRIS, A.
HARRIS, Maston
HARRISON, Richard
HARTWOOD, Andrew
HAYS, J. H.
HAYS, John R.
HENDRICKS, Lewis
HENRY, H.
HILL, Ezekiel H.
HOLDEN, David
HOLLINGSWORTH, Isaac M.
HUCKSTEP, Henderson
JACKSON, Samuel
JAMES, Henry
JASPER, James
JENKINS, William
JOHNSON, Henry
JOHNSON, James M.
JOHNSON, John A.
JOHNSON, John H.
JOHNSON, Luther
JOHNSON, Samuel
JOHNSON, William
JONES, Adrian
JONES, George
JONES, Jack
JONES, Robert
JULIUS, Lawrence J.
LAMBERT, H.
LAWSON, L. W.
LEE, Robert E.
LEE, W.
LIVINGSTON, James
LOVING, Walter H.
LUCAS, M.
LUST, Houston
McCOWN, Peter
McEWING, Duke
McNABB, Lewis W.
MAYS, Isaiah
MORRIS, T.
MURRAY, William

NEWLANDS, Goodson M.
NICHOLSON, George H.
OWENS, Charles H.
PAGE, Bassett
PAGE, William
PARKER, Edward
PARNELL, Edward
PEARCE, Thomas
PEARM, John
PEREA, Beverly
POLK, Marshall
POTTER (Private)
PRICE, A. W.
RAFEN, Robert
RAMBER, E.
RICHARDS, H.
RICHARDS, James A.
RICHARDSON, Dick
RICHTER, William J.
RIDLEY, Charles
ROBINSON, J. A.
ROSE, D.
ROSE, David
ROSE, William B.
ROSS, Milton
ROWLAND, Ernest
RUSSELL, William H.
SCOTT, John
SCOTT, Raleigh A.
SCOTT, W. C.
SCRUGGS, Gilbert
SHAW, Thomas
SHROPSHIRE, Shelvin
SIEGLER, Fred
SIMMS, A.
SIMMS, J. D.
SMITH, O.
SMITH, Richard
SNEED, John
SNYDER, James W.
SOUTHERNER, Charles
SPURLING, John D.
STEED, Albert
STEPHEN, H.
THOMAS, Samuel
THOMAS, William H.
THOMPSON, George S.
THOMPSON, William
TILMAN, George
TUBEMAN, Josiah G.
TURNER, Robert
TURPIN, George
TURPIN, P. B.
WALL, Archy
WARREN, W.
WASHINGTON, Ernest
WASHINGTON, George
WATERS, Charles
WATKINS, Isom
WATSON, T. J.
WHITE, James M.
WHITE, Joseph

PLAIN CAPS indicate names from this volume • **BOLD CAPS** indicate names from *On the Trail* (1995)

WILCOX (Sergeant)
WILKES, William
WILLIAMS, B.
WILLIAMS, Cathay
WILLIAMS, Charles
WILLIAMS, Edward
WILLIAMS, Elbert
WILLIAMS, James
WILLINGHAM, Ephraine
WOLLEY, Elbert
WOODS, Robert Gordon
WOOLEY, William
YEIZER, Mordecai
YOUNG, Oscar
Ft Craig
BELL, Riley
BROADUS, Joseph
CANADA, A.
DENT, Henry
DICKERSON (Sergeant)
GOLDEN, Thomas
GREEN, T. W.
HAWKINS, G. S.
KELSEY, Edward
MATCHETT, John R.
MINOTT, Joseph
NEWTON, John R.
PICKETT, W. E.
RICHARDSON, William
SMITH, F.
STEWART (Sergeant)
WEST, Harrison
WISHER, J. W.
Ft Cummings
ALLEN, Samuel
BAKER, William
BELL, James
BERRY, Robert
BILLS, Thomas
BOOKER, James
BRADLEY (Private; 9th Cav)
BROWN, George
BROWN, J. F.
BROWN, W. H.
BROWN, William
CAMPBELL, Thomas
CARTER, Isaac
CHESNEY, Thomas
COLE, Charles
CRAWFORD, W. A.
DAVIS, Robert
DENNY, John
DUNCAN, William
FRANCIS, Richard
GRANT (Corporal)
GREAVES, Clinton
HAMILTON, Paul
HARRIS, Milton
HEISER, Richard
HENRY, Philip
HERRON, William
HOCKINS, Benjamin

HOLLOWAY, William H.
HOLT, John
HUGHES, John
JOHNSON, G.
JONES, B.
JONES, John
KING, James
LOGAN, Isam
LUCAS, M.
LUCAS, William
LYMAN, George
LYONS, Edward
MAYOR, J. H.
MEADOWS, Benjamin
NEWTON, George
PERKINS, Henry
PETERS, Isaac
REEVES, Thornton
RICHARDS, John
ROSS, Milton
SHAW, Thomas
SHEPHERD, S. J.
SMITH, John
SPRIGGS, Stephen
STONE, Minor
STRATTON, George
SURGEON, Forester
SWAN, Edward
THOMAS, William R.
THOMPSON, Philip
TOWNSEND, Allen
TRACY, George
TURNER, Wallace
TYLER, Jacob N.
WALLACE, Harry
WALLACE, John
WASHINGTON, George
WATKINS, Henry
WHITE, Henry
WHITE, Thomas
WHITFIELD, James
WILLIAMS, Cathay
WILLIAMS, Joseph E.
WILLIS, Alexander
WORMLEY, Fredrick
YEATMAN, William
YEIZER, Mordecai
YOUNG, Douglas
Ft Marcy
BURKS, Henry
TERRY, Charles Lincoln
Ft Selden
DAVIS, Robert
DENT, Henry
GIBSON, James
GILL, Robert
HAMMOND, George
LOGAN, Isam
READ, Job
WILKS, Jacob W.
WILLIAMS, J. W.
YEATMAN, William

Ft Stanton
AHREN, Irwin
ALDRIDGE, J. E.
ALLEN, J.
BAILY, Richard
BILL, I.
BOYER, A.
BRISCOE, Henry
BROOKS, W.
BROWN, Randall
BROWN, Wilson
BURLEY, Robert
BUSH, James W.
CARROLL, F.
CARTER, Samuel
COOMBS, S. J.
COOMBS, T.
CUNNINGHAM, Charles
CURTIS, John H.
DANIELL, Robert
DAVIS, Elijah
DUNCAN, D.
DUNLAP (Corporal)
EDDINGS, W.
EDWARDS, James
EDWARDS, L. J.
EVANS, F.
FORD, F.
FORD, William
FREEMAN, F. P.
FRELAND, G.
GARLAND, G.
GREEN, T. W.
GUNN, J.
HAMILTON, Paul
HAWKINS, D. C.
HAWKINS, G. S.
HOLME, C. E.
HORTON, Louis
HUNTER, F. C.
IRWIN, J. W.
JACKSON, J. T.
JACKSON, W. A.
JAMES, Isaac H.
JOHNSON, G.
JOHNSON, H.
JOHNSON, Isaac
JOHNSON, J.
JOHNSON, L.
JOHNSON, T. A.
JONES, Douglas
JONES, James
KENNEDY, Richard
LYLE, George
McBAIN, Edward
McCAMPBELL, George
MILLIMAN, Jerry
MONDAY, Israel
MYERS, Rath
NELSON, Robert
PARKER, Charles L.
PETERSON, George

PLAIN CAPS indicate names from this volume • **BOLD CAPS** indicate names from *On the Trail* (1995)

PHILLIPS, J. H.
POLK, Thomas
REED, James
ROBINSON, A.
ROBINSON, James
RUSSELL, J.
SAUNDERS, William H.
SIDNEY, S.
SMALLWOOD, T. L.
SMITH, Robert
STANTON, Daniel
SWAN, Edward
THOMAS, J.
THOMAS, William R.
THOMPSON, Philip
TIPTON, Calvin
TURNER, P.
TURNER, Wallace
WALLACE, John
WARREN, S.
WASHINGTON, George
WEST, Harrison
WHEAT, John
WICKERSON, W.
WILLIAMS, Frank
WILLIAMS, Joseph E.
WILLIS, Alexander
WILSON, Roy
WOODLAND, William
YEIZER, Mordecai
Ft Tularosa
JORDAN, George
Ft Union
BRUINS, Robert B.
BUSH, James W.
FOWLER, Albert
HANSON, John
HARVEY, Anthony
MASON, George
MILLER, James
SMALL, George
SYKES, Zekiel
WILLIAMS, Cathay
Ft Wingate
BONDS, George
BURTON, James
CHANDLER, Richard
CHATMAN, Calvin
COLEMAN, William M.
CUNNINGHAM, Charles
DANIELS, Henry
DICKSON, Leonard E.
FINNEGAN, Michael
FLAKE, Stephen
FORD, S. S.
FRASER, Carlos
GRIGSBY, Jeff
HARRISON, Richard
HUNTER, Fred
JACKSON, Thornton
JARIMO, Juan

JONES, A. J.
JONES, Adrian
JONES, Seth
McNABB, Lewis W.
PHILLIPS, James D.
PHILLIPS, Marshall
PHILLIPS, Shardon
ROGERS, John
SMITH, Lewis M.
SPARKS, Augustus
SYKES, Zekiel
THOMPSON, Richard
WALLEY, Augustus
WATKINS, Isaac
WHEELER, Samuel
WHEELER, Thomas
WILKES, William
WILSON, George
WRIGHT, Clark
FOSTER, Allen
FRANCIS, James
Gabaldon Canyon
BROWN, J. F.
GALBREATH, J. F.
Galestee, *see below* Galisteo
Galisteo
JOHNSON, York
SHROPSHIRE, Shelvin
SMITH, Charles
Gallup
BOLLER, Solomon
Gavilan Canyon
ANDERSON, Richard
BAKER, William
BROWN, James
GOLDEN, Thomas
HARRIS, Wesley
HOLLINS, William A.
OVERSTREET, Monroe
TROUT, Henry
TURPIN, George
WILLIAMS, John
WOODS, Brent
Gavillon Pass, *see above* Gavilan
Canyon
GILES, W.
GILLEM, T.
GROSS, W.
Guadaloupe, *see below* Guadalupe
Guadalupe
BUSH, James W.
HARRIS, A.
HARRIS, D.
HARVEY, J. W.
Hillsboro
DENNY, John
Hillsborough, *see above* Hillsboro
HUNTER, Charles
JACKSON, G. A.
JACKSON, Hilary
JEFFERDS, Wesley

JENKINS, L. H.
JOHNSON, A.
JOHNSON, B. J.
JOHNSON, Bushrod
JOHNSON, J.
JONES, B.
JONES, J. H.
Las Animas Creek
FREELAND, A.
JACKSON, James
LAWSON, T. J.
LEE, Alexander
LEWIS, C.
LEWIS, T.
Lincoln
ROBINSON, Berry
Lincoln County
DALE, Thomas
LYONS, J.
McTRAMMICK, Charles
Magdalena Mountains
DENNY, John
Mimbres Mountains
BOYNE, Thomas
DORSEY, Frank
GARNETT (Private)
GOLDEN, Thomas
JOHNSON, John
MOORE, George W.
OSBORN, Stanley
PENN, Delemar
WILLIAMS, John
WOODS, Brent
WOODWARD, Major
YEIZER, Mordecai
Mimbres River
HEISER, Richard
STONE, Minor
SWAN, Edward
THOMPSON, Philip
WALLACE, Harry
WILLIAMS, Joseph E.
WOODLAND, William
YOUNG, Douglas
MINOR, William
Mogollon Mountains
BETHEL, James
BETTERS, James
NICHOLSON, George H.
Nogal Canyon
BADIE, David
Ojo Caliente
CHAPMAN, Silas
COLLINS, McHenry
GRADDON, Silas
GREEN, Isom
HOKE, Lafayette E.
HOWARD, John
HUMPHREY, William
INGOMAN, Madison
JONES, William

PLAIN CAPS indicate names from this volume • **BOLD CAPS** indicate names from *On the Trail* (1995)

MURPHY, William
PERCIVAL, Abram
ROBINSON, Henry
STONE, Minor
SWAN, Edward
TIPTON, Calvin
WEST, Harrison
WILLIAMS, James
WILLIS, Alexander
WILSON, Roy
YOUNG, Alfred
ONLY, John
Perchas, Rito de las
 GROSS, Daniel
PETERS, Isaac
PHELPS, W. H.
QUINN, Floyd
REDDICK, P. A.
RICHARDSON, N.
Rio Perchas, *see above* Perchas,
 Rito de las
ROLLY, J.
ROSS, W. C.
Roswell
 BUSH, James W.
San Francisco Mountains
 MINOTT, Joseph
San Mateo Mountains
 STOUT, Albert
Santa Fe. *See also* Cemeteries
 ASBURRY, Samuel H.
 BAKER, Edward L., Jr.
 BRAUN, Hanson T.
 BROWN, W.
 BUTLER, John
 CAMPHOR, George
 CEE, William
 CHAFFIN, John H.
 COLBURN, Jessie
 COLEMAN, William N.
 CRAGG, Allen
 DILLON, David
 DOUGLAS, Will
 DRATON, Charles
 DUNLAP, Nicholas
 HAMILTON, Paul
 HAMMONS, Isaiah
 HARRIS, S.
 HILL, J. H.
 JACKSON, Squire
 JONES, Fielding
 LEE, Edward
 LEE, William T.
 LYONS, Edward
 MARSHALL, Joseph
 MASON, Elijah
 NEWMAN, William T.
 OGDEN, Harvey
 REDMOND, Francis
 REED, Richard
 ROBINSON, Alexander

ROBINSON, Benjamin
ROBINSON, Charley
ROBISON, George
SEALS, Benjamin
SMITH, John
SMITH, P.
STRAW, Patrick
TAYLOR, Stephen
TIPTON, Calvin
WHITE, James H.
YOUNG, Douglas
SCOTT, H.
SOWELL, Berry
Silver City
 FITCH, Thomas N.
 GARRETT, William
 GRANT, Matthew
 HOLDEN, David
 POTTER (Private)
SMITH, E.
SMITH, W. E.
SULLIVAN, Melvin
TERRELL, S. C.
THOMPSON, Charles A.
THOMPSON, O.
TIPTON, Calvin
TRAVILLION, Thomas
Tularosa
 YEIZER, Mordecai
WALLACE, Maxillary
WALLUS, J.
WASHINGTON, C. S.
WEST, Harrison
WILKES, William
WILLIAMS, J. E.
WILSON, L.
WILSON, Royal
WOODLAND, William
New Orleans University
 TILLMAN, Lafayette A.
New York. *See also* **Cemeteries**
 Albany
 DAVES, John E.
 EMERSON, William
 LAWSON, Samuel
 MARTIN, Cuby
 MORROW, Cleveland
 PARILLA, Juan G.
 UNDERWOOD, Elisha M.
 BENJAMIN, Robert
 Big Flats
 DENNY, John
 Binghamton
 ARCHER, Sylvester
 BAKER, Benjamin O.
 Brooklyn. *See also* Cemeteries
 FORD, George W.
 RIDDLE, Alfred
 STEWARD, Theophilus G.
 TALIAFERRO, Spottswood W.

WATSON, Arthur C.
WILLIAMS, Elbert
WILSON, George
Broome County
 ARCHER, Sylvester
Brunswick
 GRAMMAR, Nelson
Buffalo. *See also* Cemeteries
 BROWN, John
 BROWN, Joseph
 JOHNSON, Mose
 McKAY, Barney
 PETERSON, John
 VROOMAN, William A.
 WILLIAMS, Henry
Camp Wikoff
 ANDERSON, John R.
 BELL, Hezerial
 BROWN, Alfred
 BROWN, R. H.
 CRAWFORD, John H.
 DIXON, Dennis
 GARDNER, William George
 GARRET, John
 GOOCH, Philip
 GRIGGS, William H.
 GRIGSBY, Jeff
 HOLT, Lindsey P.
 JOHNSON, Louis
 RANKIN, Frank
 SAWYER, Henry
 SIMPSON, Anthony
 WILLIAMS, James Clifford
 WILLIAMS, Joseph E.
CURTIS, Edward O.
David's Island
 ALLEN, William
 ASKEW, Blunt
 BARNETT, John
 BLY, Caesar
 BOYKIN, Charles
 BROOM, Dargan
 BROWN, Jacob
 BROWN, John
 BROWN, Sterling Price
 BYTHEWOOD, James
 CARROLL, Rufus
 CHANDLER, Noah
 EDWARDS, Lewis
 FLADGER, John J.
 FRAGER, Robert
 FRASER, Carlos
 GIBBS, Thomas (born in Charleston,
  SC)
 GIBBS, Thomas (born in Columbia,
  SC)
 GILLIAM, Chauncey
 GORDON, Thomas
 GRAHAM, Joseph
 GREEN, Alfred
 GREEN, Moses

GREER, Pierce
GUIRDIN, Eugene
HAMILTON, Thomas
HARRIS, Abram
HAYWOOD, Joseph
HENDERSON, William
HOPKINS, Julius
HUGGINS, Cumsey
JOHNSON, Peter
JONES, Ira
JONES, John
LINCOLN, Robert
LUNNEY, Mack
McCANTS, William
McINTOSH, Henry
MACKI, Edward
MARCHBANKS, Vance H.
MARTIN, Abram
MIDDLETON, Charles
MIDDLETON, Robert
MITCHELL, Andrew
MORAN, Charles
MORANEY, Elihu
MOSBY, Thomas
MYERS, William H.
NOBLE, John
ROBINSON, Henry
ROBINSON, Scott
SANDERS, Mingo
SIMMONS, Marcus
SIMMONS, Peter
SMALLS, Henry
SMART, Ransom
SMITH, Frank
STRAWBERRY, Gabriel M.
TAYLOR, Levi J.
TYLER, Jacob J.
WASHINGTON, Andrew
WEARING, Thomas
WEBB, John
WHITE, Joseph
WHITE, Peter
WHITESIDES, H.
WILLIAMS, Aaron
WILLIAMS, Charles
WILLIAMS, Jack
WOODS, Marion
Elmira
  MOORE, Miles
Flushing
  FOX, Oscar
Ft Columbus
  JOHNSON, Reuben
  MOORE, Miles
  TROTT, Robert D.
Ft Niagara
  BOND, Rhoden
  HAWKINS, Emmett
Ft Ontario
  ASKEW, Preston
  BIVINS, Horace
  WHITE, George W.

Ft Slocum
  TERRY, Charles Lincoln
Ft Terry
  ANDERSON, Benjamin A.
Ft Wadsworth
  SPANKLER, Robert
FOX, Oscar
  Glen Falls
  MILLIMAN, Jerry
Gloversville
  WRIGHT, Clark
Ithaca
  MOORE, Miles
Jefferson County
  WILLIAMS, Henry
Lockport
  WILKERSON, James
Long Island
  WILLIAMS, Jessie
Long Island City
  ALEXANDER, William
  JOHNSON, Silas
Madison Barracks
  COLEMAN, Louis D.
  GLADDEN, Washington W. E.
  HAYS (Corporal)
  HOWARD, Rodney
  JENNINGS, Julius
  MILLER, John G.
  THREAT (Private)
  WHITE, George W.
Mamaroneck
  CROCHERON, Luther
MANSFIELD, Harry
Marlborough
  BROWN, Joseph
MERMIER, Joseph
Montauk
  ALEXANDER, Fred
  BROKER, Powell H.
  ELLIOTT, James
  HOLT, Lindsey P.
  JORDAN, Thomas W.
  MITCHELL, Joseph G.
  NELSON, William R.
  PRIOLEAU, George W.
  TAYLOR, George R.
  WILLIAMS, James H.
  WILSON, George
  WIMBERLY, William
Montauk Point
  COLE, James F.
  DORSEY, Wesley
  DURANT, Will
  HOLT, Lindsey P.
  MURRAY, William
  RANKIN, Frank
  SAWYER, Henry
  TWISBY, James P.
  WALL, Archy
  WRIGHT, Nealy

Mount Vernon
  FISHER, William J.
New Rochelle
  JOHNSON, William
New York City
  ALEXANDER, William
  BARNETT, John
  BROWN, Garfield
  BROWN, Henry
  BUTLER, Thomas C.
  COOK, James R.
  DORSEY, Ephraim
  DUNCAN, William
  DYER, John
  EDWARDS, Lewis
  EDWARDS, William D.
  FORD, George W.
  GREENE, William H.
  HEDGEMAN, John H.
  HOLLIDAY, Presley
  JACKSON, Peter
  JACKSON, William Hubert
  JAMES, Edward
  JOHNSON, Daniel
  JOHNSON, Hansom
  JOHNSON, James
  JOHNSON, Joseph S.
  JOHNSON, Louis
  JOHNSON, Silas
  JOHNSON, William
  JONES, Jehu
  JONES, William
  JONES, William T.
  LEMUS, Rienzi Brock
  McBRYAR, William
  MARTIN, George
  PERRY, Charles
  POLSON, Dillon
  RHODES, Dorsey
  RIDDLE, Alfred
  ROBINSON, Henry
  SADDLER, Louis
  SMITH, Frank
  SMITH, Leonard
  SOMERS, Charles
  STANDLEY, Charles
  STANLEY, James
  STEWARD, Theophilus G.
  THOMPSON, Philip
  TOWNSEND, William J.
  WALLER, John L.
  WESTFALL, John E. N.
  WHEELER, Arthur G.
  WILLIAMS, Elbert
  WILSON, Charles
  WOODS, Herbert
PLANT, James W.
Plattsburg Barracks
  CHEATHAM, Boyd
Port Jarvis, *see below* Port Jervis
Port Jervis
  WANTON, George H.

PLAIN CAPS indicate names from this volume • **BOLD CAPS** indicate names from *On the Trail* (1995)

Rochester
  GREENE, William H.
  WRIGHT, Clark
Rome
  PETERSON, John
Saratoga Springs
  MOORE, Miles
  SMITH, Augustus
  STEPHENS, Isaac
Syracuse
  JOHNSON, David Albert
  THOMPSON, Thomas
  TURNER, Charles B.
  WHITLOW, Samuel A.
  WILLIAMS, Kinney
New York *Age*
  LEMUS, Rienzi Brock
New York Central Railroad
  LEMUS, Rienzi Brock
New York Institute of Musical Art
  POLSON, Dillon
  RHODES, Dorsey
  THOMAS, Alfred J.
New York, New Haven, & Hartford Railroad
  LEMUS, Rienzi Brock
Newland, Nora E. Spurling
  NEWLANDS, Goodson M.
Newport (ship), *see* U.S. Army Transport *Newport*
Nixon, John Benson
  GRAYSON, Charles H.
  LANE, John
Nolan, Nicholas
  ALLSUP, Thomas H.
  UMBLES, William S.
Nordstrom, Charles Eben
  PARKER, James E.
Normal College, Muncie, IN
  CHENAULT, Walter
Norman, Rachel Ann
  HALL, Frank W.
  RIVERS, Richard
North Carolina. *See also* Cemeteries
  Alamance
  HAYWOOD, James
  Asheville
    NEWLANDS, Goodson M.
    SEABRON, Emerson
    WHITMIRE, Henry
  BATTLE, Arthur
  Beaufort
    DAVIS, William H.
  Benfort, *see above* Beaufort
  Bertie County
    SMALLWOOD, Lee
  Black Creek
    WOODARD, Larry H.
  BRIGGS, Allen

Bullock
  MANLEY, Edward W.
BUNCH, Richard
Burke County
  DICKERSON, Lamar M.
Camden County
  AUSTIN, Edward S.
Cape Hatteras
  BUTLER, Thomas C.
Charlotte
  BLAKE, Henry E.
  DAULUPHUS, Jean
  DOUGLAS, Vest
  PORTER, William K.
  STEPHENSON, Frank J.
  WHEELER, William L.
COOK, Edward
Dunn
  SMITH, John
Durham
  FEARINGTON, George W.
DYALS, George
Edenton
  GREGORY, Andrew
  JOHNSON, Henry
Elizabethtown
  McBRYAR, William
Enfield
  HUNTER, Isaac
  PULLEN, Frank W., Jr.
GLASBY, Edward
Goldsboro
  CARR, Hayes
  SMITH, William
GORAM, Richard
GREEN, Walter
GREEN, William L.
Greensboro
  GILLUM, William
  WILSON, John
Greenville
  BLUNT, Randall
HAGINS, William H.
HAIRSTON, William
Halifax
  ARRINGTON, George
HAYES, Leander W.
Henderson County
  YOUNG, James H.
HENRY, Vodrey
HOKE, Lafayette E.
JOHNSTON, William
JOINER, Oliver
Kernersville
  CHAVIES, Lewis C.
KINDRED, Jacob
Lincoln County
  DUPREE, John
LLOYD, Isaac H.
Lowell
  WRIGHT, John C.

McDowell County
  TATE, Willie L.
  MINGUS, Charles
Morganton
  FLEMING, Faust
Mount Airy
  GILBERT, William M.
New Bern
  SMITH, Levi
  WILLIAMS, Alexander
New Berne, *see above* New Bern
PAGE, Bassett
PAYNE, John
PERRY, Alfred
PICKENS, Peter
Pitt County
  SATTERTHWAITE, Romeo
Plymouth
  WRIGHT, James H.
Raleigh
  ALEXANDER, John Hanks
  BROWN, Arthur M.
  BURNS, Willie
  DAWSON, John W.
  DUNN, Nathan
  HAMLIN, James E.
  O'KELLY, John A.
  WATSON, John
  YOUNG, James H.
  RAND, Carlton F.
Rockingham County
  MEBANE, Samuel
SANDERS, Joseph
SMITH, Andrew J.
SOMMERVILLE, Edward
Statesville
  WOODSIDE, John
Sugar Creek
  RUSSELL, Macon
SWAN, Abraham
TAYLOR, Charles I.
TAYLOR, John J. L.
Vance County
  MOSS, John
WALKER, Andrew
Warrenton. *See also* Cemeteries
  HALL, Frank W.
Washington County
  GRAY, James
WELCH, William
Wentworth
  MEBANE, Samuel
WHITE, Lewis
Whiteville
  MOSBY, Thomas
WILLIAMS, Henry
Wilmington
  DURANT, Empire Adam
  LUCKADOE, Joseph
  SPILLER, Noah
WILSON, Amos

PLAIN CAPS indicate names from this volume • **BOLD CAPS** indicate names from *On the Trail* (1995)

Winston
  MEYER, Robert S.
North Carolina Mutual Industrial
Association
  HAMLIN, James E.
North Dakota
  Bismarck
    DEHONEY, Peter
    MURRAY, Freeman
  Fargo
    DEHONEY, Peter
  Ft Buford
    BAILEY, William
    CLAGGETT, Joseph
    COLE, Pollard
    DALES, John
    FAULKNER, Charles S. C.
    FLINT, Robert T.
    JONES, Silas
    MARTIN, William
    MILLER, Colonel E.
    MOORE, John T.
    SMITH, Andrew J.
    SMITH, Joseph C.
    SNEED, John
    THORNTON, William
    TOLER, George
    WASHINGTON, Henry F.
    WESTACOTT, Charles
    WILLIAMS, Maxwell A.
    WOODS (Corporal)
  SMITH, Thomas
Norvell, Stevens Thomson
  HAZZARD, Miller
O'Loughlin, Frank C.
  GILMER, David J.
Oakland (CA) Chamber of
Commerce
  PURNELL, William Whipple
Oberlin College
  ALEXANDER, John Hanks
  JORDAN, Leon H.
  TILLMAN, Lafayette A.
Odd Fellows, Grand Union of
  ABBOTT, James W.
  HENDRICKS, Lewis
  PRIOLEAU, George W.
  RICKS, William Nauns
  THOMPSON, Harvey A.
  TURNER, Charles B.
Odd Fellows, Grand United Order of
  ALLENSWORTH, Allen
Ohio. *See also* Cemeteries
  Bethel
    ANDERSON, Benjamin A.
    BUTCHER, Henry
  Cadiz
    ANDERSON, William T.
    WHITE, George W.
  Camp Dennison
    WALTON, Harold F.

Camp Perry
  FOX, Oscar
Cincinnati. *See also* Cemeteries
  ALLEN, William
  ALLENSWORTH, Allen
  BAKER, Edward L., Jr
  BRISCOE, Henry
  BUNCH, Richard
  BUSH, William Henry
  CAMMEL, Joseph
  CHATMOUN, Webb
  CHESTNUTT, Henry
  COLEMAN, Henry
  CROCKETT, George D.
  CROSS, Joseph
  DAY, Charles N.
  DICKERSON, Richard T.
  DILLARD, James H.
  DOTY, Timothy
  EMERY, Andrew J.
  FAULKNER, Charles S. C.
  FLEETWOOD, Miles E.
  FORD, Wiley
  FRANKLIN, Walter
  FREDERICKS, Harry
  GAMBLE, John
  GAMBLE, John E.
  GIBSON, Thomas
  GRAFTON, William
  GRAMMER, Edward L.
  GREEN, Charles
  HOUSTON, John
  JACKSON, Benjamin
  JACOBS, Camp
  JEFFERS, David B.
  JOHNSON, Charles
  JONES, Edward
  LANIER, Frank
  LOCHLIN, William
  LYNCH, William
  McCABBIN, Care
  McCOWN, Peter
  McINTYRE, Calvin
  MERRITT, Julius
  MILLER, Alexander
  MILLER, John
  OGLESBY, Walter
  PAYNE, Charles
  ROUT, Richard
  SCROGGINS, William H.
  SMALLWOOD, Lee
  SMITH, Richard
  SMITH, Richard
  SMITH, Sidney
  SPERLIN, George
  STONE, Minor
  STRAWS, Thomas
  TAYLOR, Charles
  TAYLOR, John T.
  TOWSEY, Arthur J.
  TURNER, Charles B.
  TURNER, Clemon

WALLACE, Harry
WALLACE, John
WALLACE, Washington
WILLIAMS, Richard
WILLIAMS, Thomas
YEIZER, Mordecai
CLARK, James A.
Cleveland
  ALEXANDER, John Hanks
  ANDERSON, William T.
  BERRY, Edward
  BOLLER, Solomon
  BOOKER, William
  BROWN, Arthur M.
  BURKE, William A.
  CARROLL, Joseph H.
  CLARK, Sherman H.
  CORDIN, C. W.
  COTTON, J. H.
  CROCKETT, George D.
  DEHONEY, Peter
  MANN, Frank T.
  PEACE, Bradford
  POSEY, Frank
  RUSSELL, James
  SCHUMAN, James
  STEWARD, Theophilus G.
  THOMPSON, Charles A.
  THROWER, Jesse
  WALLACE, Lewis W.
  WHEATON, Horace F.
  WHITEHURST, James
Columbus
  ANDERSON, William T.
  BALLARD, Wilson C.
  BARROW, Stephen B.
  BROWN, John
  CARROLL, Joseph H.
  DRAKE, Grover C.
  GREAVES, Clinton
  HENSON, John
  LYLE, Julius R.
  MARION, G. F.
  PEACE, Bradford
  SCOTT, Oscar J. W.
  WATSON, Peter
  WIGGINS, S. T.
  WILLIAMS, Henry
Columbus Barracks
  ABBOTT, John W.
  BARNETT, John
  BROWN, Richard
  BURSE, Jet
  CARMICHAEL, John
  DENNEY, Labian
  DERBIGNY, Benjamin
  FISHBACK, Moses
  GAMBLE, John
  GREAVES, Clinton
  HALE, Joseph
  HANCE, George W.
  HARMAN, James R.

PLAIN CAPS indicate names from this volume • **BOLD CAPS** indicate names from *On the Trail* (1995)

PLAIN CAPS indicate names from this volume • **BOLD CAPS** indicate names from *On the Trail* (1995)

BOYNE, Thomas
BROWN, George
Byars
   ANDERSON, Henry
Cache Creek
   MURRALL, George
Camp Russell
   REDMOND, Francis
Camp Supply
   ARCHER, Sylvester
   BAINES, Arthur
   BANKS, Robert B.
   BOOKER, William
   BRIDGEWATER, Scott
   BROWN, Edmond
   BROWN, William
   BURLEY, William
   BUTLER, Louis
   CLARK, John
   DOUGLASS, John H.
   EDMONDSON, John
   EVANS, Isaac
   EVANS, John
   FAY, Adam
   FAY, Sandy
   GRAYSON, Renty
   HARRIS, Joseph
   JAMES, Augustus
   JOHNSON, John S.
   JONES, John
   JORDAN, George
   LEWIS, George
   McCUTCHIN, Ephriam
   MATHEWS, Stephen
   RICHARDSON, William
   SCOTT, Beverly
   SHEARS, William H.
   SIMMONS, William
   SIMMS, Henry
   SKIDRICK, Frank
   SMALL, Thomas
   SMITH, Albert
   STEPHENSON, James
   TAYLOR, John
   THOMAS, Henry
   WADE, Henry
   WATKINS, George
   WIGGINS, John
   WILLIAMS, James (Private; K/10th Cav)
   WILLIAMS, James (Private; H/10th Cav)
   YOUNG, David
Canadian River
   JEFFERSON, William
   WILKES, William
   YOUNG, David
Chandler
   EVANS, Frank, Sr.
Cherokee
   ROSS, John H.

Chicaskia River, *see below* Chikaskia River
Chikaskia River
   BROOKS, Preston
Cimarron River
   REDMOND, Francis
DARE, Lewis
DONNELLY, Thomas
Fallis
   EVANS, Frank, Sr.
Ft Arbuckle
   AIKEN, John H.
   BELL, Lewis
   BLACK, Allen
   BREWSTER, William
   BROWN, Albert
   CLARK, John W.
   CONE, Willis
   DAVIS, James
   DORSEY, James
   GALLAGHER, Samuel
   HIGH, John H.
   JENNISON, Perry
   LEELY, Robert
   MAHUE, Martin
   ROBERTS, Filmore
   WHEELER, Henry
Ft Gibson. *See also* Cemeteries
   BRIGHT, William
   BROWN, George H.
   CASEY, John F.
   CLINTON, Francis
   DAVIS, George
   FORD, George W.
   GREEN, George
   HAMILTON, Edward
   HAMPTON, Wade
   JOHNSON, George
   LYNCH, William
   MILLER, Henry C.
   MOORE, Jack
   PARKER, John
   POWELL, Toby
   REDMOND, Washington
   ROBERTS, Filmore
   SHEAR, Robert
   SMITH, James
   SMITH, Robert A.
   SMITH, William
   THOMAS, Willis
   TURNER, William
   WEST, Henry
   WHITE, Joseph
   WILLIAMS, Doc
   WILLINGHAM, Ephraine
Ft Reno
   ARMS, Benjamin
   BELL, Henry
   BOWEN (Corporal; H/25th Inf)
   CAMPBELL, James
   COOK, Alexander

COOPER, Barney
COOPER, Robert A.
CRAWFORD, E. L.
CRUMBLY, Floyd H.
DADE, Charles
DAVIS, William
DUDLEY, John H.
FOREMAN, William A.
GILES, Henry
GREEN, Moses
GREEN, William
HAMILTON, J. H.
HAYMAN, Perry A.
HOPE, Jasper Pickens
KING, L. S.
LEE, William
MATHEWS, C. C.
MINER, James S.
MOULTON, Prince A.
MURRAY, Othniel, III
REYNOLDS, M. E.
ROUSE, Curtis
SANDERS, Mingo
SIMONS, David
SMITH, Joseph C.
THOMPSON, George S.
WASHINGTON, Abe
WASHINGTON, Henry F.
WEBSTER, Porter
WRIGHT, Daniel
Ft Sill
   ABBOTT, James W.
   ADAMS, Alexander H.
   ANDERSON, George
   ANDERSON, Henry
   ANDERSON, James
   AUSTIN, Edward S.
   BAKER, Richard
   BAKER, William
   BANKS, Robert B.
   BARBER, William
   BERRY, George
   BERRYMAN, Henry
   BIDDLE, George
   BLACKBURN, Joseph A.
   BLEW, Joseph
   BOYD, Daniel
   BRABHAM, Jeremiah
   BRADLEY, Taylor
   BRANCH, William
   BROWN, Alfred
   BROWN, Benjamin
   BROWN, James E.
   BROWN, John (Sergeant; C/9th Cav)
   BROWN, John (9th Cav)
   BUSH, Paton
   BYERS, George
   CASEY, John F.
   CHESTER, Rubus
   CLAGGETT, Joseph
   CLARK, Charles

PLAIN CAPS indicate names from this volume • **BOLD CAPS** indicate names from *On the Trail* (1995)

CLAY (Private)
COLE (Private)
COLE, Pollard
COLLINS, Dudley
CORK, Adam
CRAIG, George
CROPPER, John S.
CRUMBLY, Floyd H.
DAILY (Private)
ELLIOTT, _all
EUSTILL, Clayborne
EVANS, Frank, Sr.
FIELDS, Henry
FLIPPER, Henry O.
FORD, George W.
GARDNER, Jacob N.
GIBSON, George
GIVENS, Edward
GOLDSMITH, Jefferson
GRAVES, Thomas R.
GRUNKE, Washington
HAINES, Levi
HAMILTON, Edward
HAMPTON, Wade
HARRIS, Jeremiah
HARRISON, Richard
HAZZARD, Charles
HENDERSON, William
HOLDEN, Charles
HUBBARD, George
HULL, Moses
HUNTER, George
JACKSON, Jason K.
JACKSON, Samuel
JACOBS, Camp
JOHNSON, Bushrod
JOHNSON, George
JOHNSON, Henry
JOHNSON, James E.
JOHNSON, Joshua
JOHNSON, Levi
JOHNSON, Thomas
JONES, Alexander
JONES, Emanuel
JONES, Jack
JONES, Joseph
JONES, Nelson
JONES, Philip
JONES, Silas
KENNEDY, Henry
KENNEDY, John
KEWCONDA, Benjamin
KURNEY, Robert
LEE, William
LEWIS (Private)
LOVELACE, Scott
LOWE, Charles H.
LYMAN, George
McCALLEY, Charles
MACK, Louis
McKAY, Barney

McKAY, George
MASON, William
MILES, Julius
MILLIMAN, Jerry
MOORE, John
MOSLEY, Zechoriah
NICHOLSON, George H.
OWINGS, Alfred
PARKER, Henry
PARKER, John
PAYNE, Jesse
PEREA, Beverly
PERRYMAN, Isaac
PIPES, Nelson
POLK, Thomas Elzey
POWELL, George D.
PRIDE, Alfred
READ, Scott
REDDICK, Charles
REED, John W.
REED, Richard
ROE, John W.
ROSS, Alfred
SCOTT, Praley
SHEPERD, Frank
SIMMS, Squire
SMITH, Albert
SMITH, J. P.
SMITH, William
SPENCER, Jeremiah
TAYLOR, Thomas W.
THOMPSON, George S.
TICKLE, Henry
TURNER (Private)
WADE, Chester
WALKER, William
WALLOW, Samuel
WASHINGTON, George
WHITE, John
WILKES, Isaac J.
WILKS, Jacob W.
WILLIAMS, James
WILLIAMS, William H.
WOODEN, Henry
YOUNG, Charles H.
YOUNG, Jacob
YOUNG, James
YOUNG, Jerry
Ft Supply
ALEXANDER, Cook
ALLENSWORTH, Allen
ARMS, Benjamin
BELL, Matthew
BRABHAM, Jeremiah
BRADDEN, Alfred
BROWN, Albert
BROWN, Benjamin
BURLES, Charles
CONLEY, Paschall
COOK, Charles
CRABB (Private)

CRAYCROFT, Richard
CURTIS, Edward O.
DAY, Charles N.
DUDLEY, John H.
ELLIS, Merriman H.
FITZGERALD, John
FRANKLIN, Simon P.
FRAZER, Solomon
FULLER, Cornelius
GOLDSBOROUGH, William H.
HOLDEN, James
JOHNSON, Henry
JOHNSON, Luther
JORDAN, George
LEWIS, George
MANSON, William D.
McEWING, Duke
MILES, John B.
OAKELY, Bud
REED, Richard
SAMPLE, John
SCROGGINS, William H.
SLAUGHTER, Rufus
STARR, Stephen G.
THOMAS, George
WALL, Archy
WASHINGTON, George
WEBB, Benjamin
WHITLEY, Benjamin F.
WILLIAMS, Alexander
WOLLEY, Elbert
ZANEY, John
FOSTER, Larkin
Geary. *See also* Cemeteries
HAWKINS, Henry
HUGHES, Isaac
GOINS, Joshua Van Buren
GRINIER, Dallas
GUDDY, P.
Hackberry Creek
FRISBY, Isaac
HILL, Issam
LEWIS, Richard
Lincoln County
HIBBITT, John
Little River
ROBERTS, Filmore
LOGAN, James
LOGAN, Robert
McAlester
WIGGINS, S. T.
McClain County
ANDERSON, Henry
HOWARD, Andrew
Medicine Bluff Creek
BECHERES, Isaac
Muskogee
BENNARD, Bert
CAMPBELL, Thomas C.
DIXON, David
HARRIS, Ben

PLAIN CAPS indicate names from this volume • **BOLD CAPS** indicate names from *On the Trail* (1995)

Doe Run
  WALLACE, Benjamin F.
  DORSEY, Solomon T.
Downingtown
  QUEEN, Howard D.
DYER, Joshua
Frankford
  STEWARD, Theophilus G
Franklin County
  CUNNINGHAM, Charles
Gettysburg
  JONES, William T.
GIBBS, Algernon
GOLDSBY, George
GREEN, John S.
Halifax
  BANKS, Robert B.
Harrisburg
  BANKS, Robert B.
  BRANSON, James
  BYERS, George
  DUNN, Nathan
  GIBSON, George
  GRAVES, William
  GUY, John
  HALL, Edward M.
  JONES, Bular
  JONES, Emanuel
  KELLEY, George S.
  KIRK, William
  LEE, Ulysses G.
  McDANIELS, Nathaniel
  RHODES, Harry A.
  RINGGOLD, Henry
  ROADS, Charles A. E.
  SPEAKES, William
  WILLIS, William
Hookstown
  JACKSON, Samuel
JOHNSON, Charles
Lansdowne
  WILLIAMS, Richard A.
Lebanon
  BYERS, George
Lewiston, *see below* Lewistown
Lewistown
  MOORE, Bazil B.
Marietta
  BATTLE, William P.
MARTIN, George
Media
  RICHTER, William J.
Middleton
  TAYLOR, Charles E.
Middletown (Dauphin County)
  CUNNINGHAM, Charles
Montgomery County
  HOGAN, James
Montrose
  BAKER, Benjamin O.
Moore Station

BAILEY, Isaac W.
Mount Pleasant
  JOHNSON, Clarence W.
MURDOCK, Richard
Newville
  BYERS, George
  GOFF, Henry A.
Norristown
  FISHER, Henry
Philadelphia. *See also* Cemeteries
  ALLMOND, Howard
  BARD, Benjamin
  BENJAMIN, Robert
  BENSON, Abram
  BLAKE, Isaac
  CEPHAS, Joseph E.
  CHAMBERS, Clifford
  CHAPMAN, Silas
  CLARK, Henry
  COLUMBUS, Robert H.
  CONN, John
  COWAN, James D.
  CROCKET, George H.
  DAVENGER, Jacob B.
  DEMBY, Sheridan
  DORSEY, Ephraim
  EDMONDS, John
  FIELDS, Eddie
  FINNEGAN, Michael
  FISHER, Henry
  FITZGERALD, John
  FLETCHER, James Robert
  GALLOWAY, Alonzo
  GOULD, Peter
  GREEN, Joseph
  HARRIS, Alexander
  HAYMAN, Perry A.
  HAZZARD, George H.
  HENRY, Robert A.
  HOGAN, James
  JACKSON, Emmett J.
  JACKSON, George W.
  JACKSON, William L.
  JOHNSON, Benjamin
  JOHNSON, Jacob
  JOHNSON, William
  JONES, James
  JONES, Stephen
  KEY, Charles
  LEE, William H.
  LEVENBERRY, Arthur
  LEWIS, Robert
  LOGAN, James
  MATHIGLEY, Henry
  McCOWN, Peter
  MILLER, Girard
  MILLER, James
  MITCHELL, Andrew
  MONROE, Edward M.
  MOSLEY, Robert
  OWENS, Charles H.

  PARKER, Edward
  PURNELL, William Whipple
  RICE, Levi
  RINGO, Walter
  ROBBS, William
  SADDLER, Louis
  SMITH, James
  SMITH, John H.
  SMITH, Walter E.
  SPEAKES, James
  SPEAKES, William
  STEWARD, Theophilus G
  TURNER, James B.
  WALLACE, Benjamin F.
  WATSON, William H.
  WEEKS, Henry
  WILLIAMS, Richard A.
  WILLIAMSON, Richard
Pittsburgh
  BAKER, Benjamin O.
  BANKS, Benjamin
  BATTLE, William P.
  BLANEY, William
  BROWN, William H.
  BUNCH, Richard
  CAMPBELL, Robert
  COSTON, W. Hilary
  DEARING, Edward
  GAINES, Mosely
  GAYTION, William
  HAMMOND, Noah
  HAMMOND, Thomas C.
  HARRIS, Thomas M.
  HENRY, Charles
  HOWARD, Nathaniel
  LAWS, James
  LAWSON, Walter
  LEWIS, Charles
  MORRISON, James N.
  PLEASANTS, Thomas
  SMITH, Eugene
  SMITH, James
  SMITH, Luscious
  STEWARD, David
  STEWARD, Frank R.
  STRANGE, Edward R.
  SUTPHIN, William
  THOMAS, Wilber
  TIGLES, John J.
  WILLIAMS, Oliver
Reading
  HALL, Edward M.
  ROBERTS, Louis
  ROBINSON, Daniel
Rochester
  EDMONDS, John
  SCOTT, Winfield
Scranton
  BROWN, David
Sharon Hill
  HAYMAN, Perry A.

PLAIN CAPS indicate names from this volume • **BOLD CAPS** indicate names from *On the Trail* (1995)

SMITH, Wesley P.
South Bethlehem
    TAYLOR, Levi J.
Steelton
    HOLLIDAY, Presley
    KIRK, William
    WILLIAMS, Robert E.
STOWERS, Elijah
STRATTON, John H.
WALKER, James
West Chester
    HAZZARD, George H.
York
    BROWN, James E.
    GUY, John
    HALL, Edward M.
    ROADS, Charles A. E.
    SMITH, Lewis M.
Pennsylvania (ship), *see* U.S.
Army Transport *Pennsylvania*
Pennsylvania Railroad
    BARD, Benjamin
    JONES, Stephen
    LEMUS, Rienzi Brock
Pennsylvania State Revenue
Department
    QUEEN, Howard D
Penrose, George Wilkinson
    SANDERS, Mingo
Penski (8th Cav boxer)
    BAILEY, Isaac
People's Drug Store, Louisville, KY
    WHITE, Randolph F.
Peoples, A. Charis
    PEOPLES, R.
Perazo, Cesaria
    FORNISS, George
Perea, Margaret M.
    PEREA, Beverly
Perea, Missouri Johns
    PEREA, Beverly
Perryman, Deacon Warren Juan
    PERRYMAN, James
Perryman, Lea
    PERRYMAN, Isaac
Perryman, Nelia
    PERRYMAN, Isaac
    PERRYMAN, James
Perryman, Teresita
    GRAYSON, Renty
    PERRYMAN, James
Pershing, John Joseph
    ANDERSON, William T.
    GILLESPIE, Archibald Honduras
    GLADDEN, Washington W. E.
    GOODWIN, Albert
    HUDNELL, George
    JETER, John
    LYNN, Albert
    McCAULEY, William

Peters, Lemmie
    SMITH, Arthur
Philip, King
    PHILIPS, Ned
Philippine Constabulary Band
    LOVING, Walter H.
Philippine Insurrection, *see* Philippines
Philippine question
    CALLOWAY, John W.
Philippines. See also Expatriates
in the Philippines *[N.B. In several
biographical entries such as
"FURMAN, John," the Philippines is not mentioned but the
soldier's service in the 48th
Infantry and burial at San
Francisco indicate his duty
there.]*
ABERNATHY, Wooten R.
ACKFORTH, William
ADAMS, Howard
ADAMS, John
Alaminos
    BASS, Emanuel D.
    PERRY, Charles
    STEWARD, Frank R.
Albay
    DALRYMPLE, John
    GILMER, David J.
    HUNTER, Fred
    MILLER, Richard
    SHORES, Garth
    THOMPSON, George S.
Albuera
    TAYLOR, William
Alcala
    EVANS, John
ALEXANDER, Henry
ALEXANDER, Henry E.
ALLEN, Frank
ALLISON, Walter
ALSTON, Douglas
AMMONS, William
ANDERSON, Abby
ANDERSON, George G.
ANDERSON, Isaac
ANDERSON, Jenon
ANDERSON, Louis
ANDERSON, William
ANDREWS, Joseph C.
Angeles
    CRAWFORD, William
Anibongan
    BATES (Corporal)
Aparri
    BLAKEMAN, Robert
    BROWN, Louis
    CHAMBERS, Clifford
    CLAY, Henry

    GILMER, David J.
    KELLEY, George B.
    ROBINSON, James
APPLEWHITE, Richard
Ararat, *see below* Arayat
Arayat
    ANDERSON, Anthony
    BURNS, Willie
    CAMPLE, Sandy
    CLARK, Lig J.
    CUSHINGBERRY, Porter
    DEAVER, Alphonse W.
    FOSTER, Leslie J.
    HARVEY, John W.
    McCONKEY, Nathan
    McCURDY, Walter
    McINTOSH, Robert
    QUARLES, James T.
    SADDLER, Louis
    SCHLADE, James W.
    SKINNER, Edward
    TURNER, Charles B.
    TURNER, James B.
    WASHINGTON, Morgan G.
ARMSTRONG, Fred
ARNOLD, Julius
ASH, Robert H.
ATKISON, Willis
AUSTIN, John
AUSTIN, John T.
BACON, Henry
BACON, Martin
BADGETT, Green
BADIE, William E.
BAILEY, Isaac W.
BAILEY, John
BAILEY, Mack
BAILEY, Matthew
BAKER, Edward L., Jr
BAKER, Franklin M.
BAKER, Lewis J.
BALLANGER, George
BALLARD, Wilson C.
BALLENGER, George
BALLEW, John
BALTINGER, Henry
Bam Bam, *see below* Bamban
Bamban
    MARROW, Anthony A.
    POGUE, Peter C.
    SANDERS, Mingo
Bancal
    ROBINSON, Michael H., Jr.
Bangued
    SHELTON, Joseph
Bani
    GREENBERRY, Grant
BANKS, Plum
BANKS, Robert
BANKS, William
Bantonan

RUSHINGBO, William B.
BARNER, George
BARNETT, George E.
BARTON, Ignatius
BASKERVILLE, E. S.
BASS, Walter
Batangas. *See also below* Camp
  McGrath
    JOHNSON, Thomas
BATES, Milton F.
BATTON, Henry
Bautista
  MORSE, Abraham
  ROBINSON, Wiley
  SIMONDS (A/24th Inf)
BEARD, George
BEARD, Oatis
BELL, James
BELL, John
BELL, John
BELL, Thomas (Corporal; A/9th Cav)
BELL, Thomas (Private; A/24th Inf)
BENNETT, Aleck
BENSON, Caleb
BENTON, Willie
BERRY, George
BERRY, Henry
Bicol River
  WALKER, Samuel
BIGGER, William
Bilibid Prison
  BOOTHE, Virgil
  PRIDE, Wheeler
  VICTOR, William
BIRCH, William A.
BIRT, Cape
BISMUKES, Samuel
BIVENS, George E.
BIVINS, Horace W.
BLACKBURN, John
BLACKMAN, Andrew M.
BLAKE, Henry E.
BLANCH, John
BLEADSOE, Robert
BLUNT, Hamilton H.
BOARD, Walter W.
BOLLING, Willie
Bololo
  OLIVER, Philip
Bonga River
  FIELDS, Henry
Bongabon
  FOWLISS, Kirk
  THOMAS, George H.
  THOMAS, James H.
BOOKER, Andrew J.
BOOKER, James
BOONE (Private; L/25th Inf)
BOOZE, Richard
BOSWELL, John T.
Botolan
  DUNN, James

ELLISON, Lewis A.
GOODMAN, John
GRANT, Tony
HENRY, John
ROBINSON, Michael H., Jr.
SMITH, John
WHELDON, Samuel
YELVERTON, Aaron
BOWEN, Major
BOWMAN, Willie
BRENSTON, Tevis
BRIGGS, Albert J.
BRIGGS, James
BRIGHT, Aaron D.
BROADNAX, Van
BROADUS, Lewis
BROOKS, Clifford
BROOKS, Isaiah
BROOKS, Robert H.
BROOKS, Thomas
BROOM, Swain P.
BROWN, Andrew J.
BROWN, Charles R.
BROWN, Daniel
BROWN, Edward
BROWN, George L.
BROWN, George W.
BROWN, John
BROWN, John H.
BROWN, John W.
BROWN, Milton M.
BROWN, Morris
BROWN, Thomas
BROWN, William
BROWN, William M.
BROWNIE, George
BROYLES, William
BRUXTON, Isaiah
BRYANT, Lounie
BRYANT, M. C.
BRYSON, Walter
BUCHANAN, Lawrence
BUCK, John
BUCKHALTER, James
BUCKNER, Dock
BULLARD, William H.
BURDES, William
BURGESS, Lewis
BURNELL, George
BURTON, John
BUSH, Robert
BUTLER, Arthur B.
BUTLER, William H.
BYRD, Anderson
BYRD, J. C.
Cabanatuan
  ALLEN, Charles
  BAKER, Hiram, Jr.
  BANKS (Private)
  BERRY, William H.
  BERTS, Willie
  BLACK, Henry

BRICE, William H.
BROOKS, Robert F.
BROWN, Philip
BUFORD, James J.
CAMIL, William
CASHY, George S.
CHESTNUT, Philip
CHRISTON (Private)
COLLINS, William
COOK, Isaiah
COOK, Julius
COOK, Samuel
CORTER (Private)
COSBY, George S.
DANDRIDGE, George
DAVIS, J. D.
DAVIS, Rufus A.
DAVIS, William
DAWSON (Sergeant)
DEAVER, Alphonse W.
DOCKEY, Stanton
DRISCOLL, George
DUVALL, Robert L.
ELLIOT, George J.
ELLIS, Merriman H.
FAGGINS, John H.
FORTNER, Hugh
GIBSON (Private)
GREEN (Sergeant)
GRIFFIE, William
HALE, Moses
HALL, John W.
HAMPTON, Wade
HARGRAVES, John C.
HARRIS, Thomas M.
HAYDEN, William
HENRY, Samuel T.
HIPSHIRE, Riley
HOLLAND, George A.
INGMAN, James
ITSON, Albert
JACKSON (Corporal)
JACKSON, Emmett J.
JACKSON, Frank
JACKSON, Walter B.
JAMES, Frank
JOHNSON, George
JOHNSON, James
JOHNSON, Jason
JOHNSON, Otto
JOHNSON, Thomas
JOHNSON, William
KEYS, Pat
KIBBY (Private)
KIRK, William
LACY, George
LARRIMORE, Herman F.
LEAVELL, William
LEE, George
LEE, William
McHENRY, Joseph
McINTYRE, Burnett A.

PLAIN CAPS indicate names from this volume • **BOLD CAPS** indicate names from *On the Trail* (1995)

MASON, Patrick
MEAD, James P.
MILLER, Charles
MITCHELL, Charles F.
MONROE, F. J.
MOORE, Cato
MOORE, Simon
MORANDERS, Joseph
MORGAN, David
MORRIS, Thomas
MORROW, Alston
MYERS, Frank
NEIL (Private)
NEWELL, Frank
NICKLE, Elijah
POPE, Henry
POWELL, Thomas R.
PRAYER, James J.
PRIDE, Wheeler
RANSOM, Henry
REYNOLDS, Moses
RIDGELY, Edward A.
RIZ, Charles
ROBINSON (Private)
ROBINSON, Mason
ROGERS, Lemuel J.
ROSS, William
SALES, Clarence
SAUNDERS, George I.
SHAVER, Lee
SHERRELL, Moses
SHORT, David
SIMES, James W.
SIMPSON, James A.
SMITH, Byrd
SMITH, Horace J.
SMITH, John
SMITH, John
STEVENS, Jacob W.
STEVENS, Samuel
STONE, John H.
STORGEN, Albert
STREETER, Wallace
TAGGART, Henry
TATES, Rollins
TAYLOR, Albert B.
TAYLOR, Eugene
TAYLOR, George N.
THOMPSON, Joseph
THOMPSON, Montague
THURMAN, Harry
TURNER, Goodricks
VALENTINE, Thomas P.
WALKER, Samuel W.
WASHINGTON (Private)
WASHINGTON, Claude
WATSON, William H.
WHITE, Joseph
WHITE, Leonard
WILLIAMS, Anderson
WILLIAMS, Richard
WILLIAMS, Richard

WILLIAMS, Squire
WILLIS (Private)
WORKMAN, William
WYLIE, Milton
YEIZER, Charles C.
YOUNG, Frank
YOUNG, James H.
Cabangan
  FLEMING, John
  LIGHTFOOT, James R.
  POGUE, Peter C.
  SANDERS, Mingo
  WARD, James
Cabayan
  BUTLER, Thomas C.
Cagayan
  COOPER, William
  COPELAND, Samuel
  EVANS, John
  FORMAN, Madison W.
  MONROE, Edward M.
  WHEATON, Horace F.
  WILLIAMS, Gus J.
CAGLE, Walter W.
CAIN, Adam
Calamba
  ROBINSON, Harry
Calaoango
  WILLIAMS, Walter
  CALDWELL, Charles C.
  CALDWELL, William
  CALDWELL, William
  CALHOUN, James N.
Camalig
  BACON, Martin
  BROOKS, William P.
  DALRYMPLE, John
  DuBOSE, Edmond
  HARRISON, Lee
  McKINZIE, Job
  RUSHINGBO, William B.
  WASHINGTON, William
Camansi
  LIGHTFOOT, James R.
  QUARLES, James T.
Camp Downes
  TAYLOR, William
Camp McGrath (Batangas)
  JOHNSON, Thomas
  NEWHOUSE, Robert
  PRIOLEAU, George W.
  TURNER, Clemon
Camp Overton (Mindanao)
  BIVINS, Horace
Camp Stotsenburg
  CARTER, Louis A.
  GLADDEN, Washington W. E.
  CAMPBELL, Thomas C.
  CANNON, Horace
  CARROLL, Charles H.
  CARSON, Earley
  CARTER, Amos A.

CARTER, Henry
CARTER, Louis A.
CARY, Wilson
CASSAWAY, Charles
Castillegos, *see below* Castillejos
Castillejos
  BATES, Milton F.
  BLAKENY, William F.
  BROWN, Charles S.
  EDWARDS, Benjamin
  FULBRIGHT, William R.
  GRAHAM (Private)
  GREENWOOD, George
  HENRY, Horace T.
  JOHNSON, Henry E.
  JONES, Palmer
  JONES, Thomas
  LEMUS, Rienzi Brock
  McCABE, Lorenzo
  MASON, Calvin
  PRYOR, Frank M.
  REDDING, Willie
  SMITH, Jesse B.
  THOMPSON (Sergeant)
  WILBURN, Thomas G.
  WIMBERLY, William
  WISEMAN, Turner H.
  WOODFOLK, Joseph
Catbalogan
  STEVENSON, Guy
CATHEY, Joseph
CAULDER, Charles
CAULDER, Nathan
CAVILLE, Charles W.
Cebu, *see below* Warwick Barracks,
  Cebu
CHAMBERS, William
CHAPMAN, Silas
CHASE, William H.
CHATMAN, John
CHATMAN, William
CHEEK, Frank W.
CHISHOLM, Frank R.
CHOLIKELY, Alonzo
CLARK, Cornelius
CLARK, Edward
CLARKE, Edward
CLARKE, Ollie
Claveria
  ROBINSON, James
CLAY, William
CLAY, William
CLAYBORN, John
CLINTON, Frank
COFFEE, Nathan
COLE, Samuel
COLEMAN, James
COLEMAN, John
COMMONS, John
CONWAY, Louis
COOK, Ermine
COOPER, Archie

PLAIN CAPS indicate names from this volume • **BOLD CAPS** indicate names from *On the Trail* (1995)

COOPER, Charles E.
COOPER, George P.
COOPER, William
COPELAND, Charles L.
COPES, Samuel
CORBITT, George
Cordin
   SHEPARDSON, George
Corregidor
   MASON, Patrick
COVINGTON, John
CRAIG, Thomas B.
CROWDER, Julius
CROWDER, Rufus
CROWDER, William A.
CRUSE, Peter
CUMBY, George
CUMMERS, William
CUSTER, Levi
CUTHBERT, John F.
DAKEY, Wesley
DALRYMPLE, John
DANCE, William
DANIELS, E. C.
DANIELS, Hayes
DARLING, James A.
DAVENPORT, Leonard
DAVIS, Charles
DAVIS, Charles D.
DAVIS, Edward (Private; K/9th Cav)
DAVIS, Edward (Corporal; 9th Cav)
DAVIS, J. D.
DAVIS, Rufus A.
DAVIS, Thomas J.
DAVIS, Walter R.
DAVIS, William
DAWSON (Sergeant)
DAWSON, Eb
DAWSON, George W.
DELLUM, Wesley
DENISON, Leon W.
Deposito
   BRANNER, George
   CECIL, John
   HOWE, Willis
   MURPHY, George
   PRICE, L. B.
   RUCKER, Clarence
   SAMPSON, John W.
   WEBSTER, Samuel
DERRY, Lewis
DICKERSON, William
DILLARD, Charlie
DILLON, Robert
DIRKS, Harrison
DIXON, Carrol
DOBLER, Fred
Dolores
   BLANEY, William F.
Donsol
   FIELDS, Henry
DORSEY, George

DORSEY, William H.
DOUGLAS, Vest
DUNCAN, Samuel
DUNKERSON, Pomp
EASTMAN, Frank
EDWARDS, Benjamin
EDWARDS, Robert
EDWARDS, William D.
El Deposito, *see above* Deposito
ELLETT, Luther M.
ELLIS, James
ELLIS, Merriman H.
ELLIS, Thomas
ELLISON, Lewis A.
EPHRAIM, Randall
EVANS, EDWARD
EVANS, Joseph B.
FARLEY, Beauford
FARMAN, John
FARRELL, Louis
FAULKIN (Private)
FEARINGTON, George W.
FENWICK, William J.
FERRICK, Silas E.
FIELDS, Eddie
FINNEGAN, John
FISHBACK, Benjamin
FLEMING, Clarence T.
FLETCHER, Edward
FLINT, Robert T.
FLOYD, John
FLYNT, Robert
FOLSOM, William
FORMAN, Elwood A.
Ft William McKinley
   ANDERSON, William T.
   BOND, Rhoden
   HENRY, Vodrey
   JENNINGS, Julius
   STILL, Revere N.
   WILLIAMS, Walter B.
FOSTER, Perrent
FOSTER, Samuel
FRANKLIN, George
FRANKLIN, James A.
FRANKLIN, William M.
FRANKS, Benjamin
FREAR, Wilson
FREDERICKS, Harry
FREELAIN, William
FULLER, John
FUQUA, Eulous
GAGE, Henry
GAINES, Underwood
GAMBLE, John E.
Gamu
   BUTLER, Thomas C.
Gapan
   JOHNSON, Edward
GARDNER, William
GARDNER, William H.
GARFIELD, James

GARR, Henry B.
GASKINS, John
GASKINS, William E.
GATCHELL, Walter G.
GATEWOOD, George
GIBSON, Peter G.
GILBERT, Charles
GILBERT, Saint
GILES, Henry
GILLESPIE, Archibald Honduras
GILLISPIE, James R.
GIVENS, George
Goa
   TURNER, William
   WASHINGTON, George
GOLDEN, John
GOODWINE, Nathan
GOUGH, Robert
GOULDEN, Ruck
GRAHAM, William
GRAHAM, William H.
GRANDON, John
GRANT, Thomas
GRANT, William B.
GRANT, William D.
GRAW, George R.
GRAY, Charles
GRAYER, Frank
GREEN, Charles
GREEN, Dalbert P.
GREEN, James
GREEN, James H.
GREEN, Joseph
GREEN, William H.
GREENLEAF, Edward
GREGGS, Austin
GREY, Lawrence T.
GRIFFIN, Stephen
GRIFFITH, William B.
GRUBE, Howard A.
Guinobatan
   DuBOSE, Edmond
   GRIGSBY, Jeff
   HUNTER, Fred
   MILLER, Richard
   NELSON, Louis
   OLIVER, Philip
   OWENS, William
   SHORES, Garth
   VICTOR, William
GUNTER, James
HAGUE, Lucius J.
HAILEY, Benjamin
HALEY, Frank
HALEY, James
HAMILTON, Ernest
HAMILTON, George
HAMILTON, Nelson
HAMILTON, William H.
HAMLIN, James E.
HAMMOCK, Charles E.
HAMMOND, Pleasant H.